> *"Now, Charley is a mind-reading dog. There have been many trips in his lifetime, and often he has to be left at home. He knows we are going long before the suitcases come out, and he paces and worries and whines and goes into a state of mild hysteria, old as he is."*

from John Steinbeck's *Travels With Charley*, (©1962, page 11)

Like Charley and his famous owner, you too can embark on your own adventures across America (Canada & Mexico, too) and create your own creature chronicles ... without having to sleep in a truck.

In fact, you can:

- Frolic with your four legged friends at such fine establishments as the Four Seasons, enjoying their VIP (Very Important Pets) program in selected hotels

- Get the presidential treatment at the San Ysidro Ranch near scenic Santa Barbara, where many a president has catnapped

- Star Gaze at Aspen's The Little Nell, the cool, hot spot for Hollywood stars and their hounds

- Luxuriate at over 100 posh pet-friendly accommodations

THE "MUST HAVE" RESOURCE FOR *EVERY* PET OWNER

Whether you "take 'em" or "leave 'em". Since 1990, it's the longest running pet travel resource of its kind. You get the answers you need to prepare for, and feel good about, whatever type of petcare you choose. It includes advice from pet experts:

- Avoid faux paws with "Pet-Etiquette" tips from Mathew Margolis NBC Today Show pet expert

- Make tracks with travel training tips from Hollywood animal behaviorist Maureen Hall

- Dr. Carin Smith, DVM & Petcare Author "de-tails" health considerations, feeding, and first-aid preparedness

- Avoid lodging industry Pet Peeves with the 10 Commandments of good guest & pet behavior

- Learn the Plane Truth about taking your pet along on airplanes - Crucial DOs & DON'Ts

- Point yourself and your pet in the right direction with pointers for smooth moves

- Pack for pet travel and first-aid needs using our comprehensive, time-tested checklists

2

EVERY PET OWNER NEEDS THIS BOOK!
because
Every day *ANY* pet owner may need to decide what to do with pets when travel (planned or *EMERGENCY*) disrupts normal routines.

This is the only sourcebook with ALL the answers: from pet sitting, to taking them with you, to day-kenneling along the way, to extended kennel stays, to pet motels, veterinarians and more!

THE ONLY COMPREHENSIVE SOURCEBOOK OF TRAVELTIME PETCARE OPTIONS

Over 25,000 Resources for Pets and their Owners:

- Tens of thousands of accommodations from posh to primitive where PETS-R-PERMITTED

- Kenneling and petcare information for theme parks and tourist attractions

- ABKA kennels for day-boarding along the way or extended kennel stays

- Arrange in-home care with a listed petsitter or through a listed referral service

- Find a veterinarian in a new city or on-the-road through listings or AAHA referral

This book is dedicated to Dorothy who danced across the rainbow bridge on January 19, 1997 and to Tennyson who has just embarked on his adventures on this side of the rainbow bridge.

You are both cherished and loved far beyond mere words.

--Lisa

Rainbow Bridge

There is a bridge connecting Heaven and Earth. It is called the Rainbow Bridge because of its many colors. Just this side of the Rainbow Bridge there is a land of meadows, hills and valleys with lush green grass.

When a beloved pet dies, the pet goes to this place. There is always food and water and warm spring weather. The old and frail animals are young again. Those who are maimed are made whole again. They play all day with each other.

There is only one thing missing. They are not with their special person who loved them on Earth. So each day they run and play until the day comes when one suddenly stops playing and looks up! The nose twitches! The ears are up! The eyes are staring! And this one suddenly runs from the group!

You have been seen, and when you and your special friend meet, you take him or her in your arms and embrace. Your face is kissed again and again, and you look once more into the eyes of your trusting pet.

Then you cross Rainbow Bridge together, never again to be separated.

--Anonymous

!!!!WARNING!!!!

THIS BOOK IS
SELF DESTRUCTING!!!

According to studies by the American Hotel & Motel Association, as many as 1 in 3 accommodations will be sold, change names, phone numbers or replace management. When management changes, so can PET POLICIES! To receive information on updates you must complete and send in the registration form on the back of this page.

YOU MUST SEND IN THIS FORM TO REGISTER TO KEEP UPDATED

FREE $200 VALUE PET SAVINGS PACK
WHILE QUANTITY LASTS

We have arranged with a number of pet products and services to provide special offers for our readers. There's only a limited quantity of Pet Savings Packs available, so act soon!

The free $200 value PET SAVINGS PACK is available by sending a business size SASE "self addressed stamped envelope" with 2oz. postage (currently $0.55)

I WANT TO REGISTER FOR UPDATES

Name_____

Address_____

City_____ State_____ Zip_____

Type of pet(s), breed(s) & name(s)_____

_____

where purchased_____

Mail to: ACI, Purchase Registration, PO Box 11374, Torrance, CA 90510-1374

****FREE $200 VALUE PET SAVINGS PACK****
WHILE QUANTITY LASTS

I am enclosing a business sized SASE "self addressed stamped envelope" with 2oz. postage (currently $0.55)

Name_____

Address_____

City_____ State_____ Zip_____

Mail to: ACI, Pet Savings Pack, PO Box 11374, Torrance, CA 90510-1374

25,000 PETS-R-PERMITTED
Accommodations, Petsitters, Kennels & More!
8th Edition

Copyright © 1990, 1991, 1992, 1993, 1994, 1995, 1997, 1998
ACI ALL RIGHTS RESERVED

The Annenberg Communications Institute
Lisa Loeffler, Publisher
P.O. Box 3930
Torrance, CA 90510-3930
310-374-6246
fax 310.374.4806

PetExpert@RocketMail.Com
http://www.flash.net/~menelson/pets-r-permitted.html

Original Cover Photo by Marie Stadden

Graphic Design by Tamara Harmsen

♟ PETS-R-PERMITTED ™ Travel Series ♟

TRAVEL WITH
OR WITHOUT
PETS

25,000 PETS-R-PERMITTED
Accommodations, Petsitters, Kennels & More!
8th Edition

COPYRIGHT AND LICENSING WARNING!!

ALL RIGHTS RESERVED. NO PART OF THIS BOOK MAY BE REPRODUCED, STORED OR TRANSMITTED IN ANY FORM OR BY ANY MEANS, ELECTRONIC OR MECHANICAL, INCLUDING PHOTOCOPYING, RECORDING, OR BY ANY INFORMATION STORAGE AND RETRIEVAL SYSTEM WITHOUT THE EXPRESS WRITTEN CONSENT OF THE ANNENBERG COMMUNICATIONS INSTITUTE, EXCEPT FOR THE INCLUSION OF BRIEF QUOTATIONS IN A REVIEW. PERMISSION IS GRANTED ONLY FOR PRIVATE, NONCOMMERCIAL USE. ANY OTHER USE OF THIS PUBLICATION, INCLUDING LIST COMPILATION PURPOSES, IS A VIOLATION OF LAW AND MAY RESULT IN PROSECUTION.

While we have strived to provide you with accurate information, we cannot be responsible for any errors or omissions. Listing in this directory does not imply any endorsement or recommendation.

©Copyright 1990-1998 ACI ALL RIGHTS RESERVED

Library of Congress Cataloging in Publication Data
Annenberg Communications Institute, The
TRAVEL WITH OR WITHOUT PETS: 25,000 PETS-R-PERMITTED
Accommodations, Petsitters, Kennels & More!
M. E. Nelson, Editor
1. Pets and Travel
2. Dogs--Transportation
3. Cats--Transportation
4. Pets--Handbooks, Manuals, etc.
5. Travel--Handbooks, Manuals, etc.
I. Title

ISBN 1-56471-797-6: Softcover

TABLE OF CONTENTS

Introduction   11

Preparing for Travel   14
Pet Packing List   14
Keeping Fido &Fluffy Happy on a Trip   15
Help for Pets Who Hate Riding in Cars   16
Creatures of Habit   18
Calm, Cool and Collected   18
Your Creature's Comfort   19
Unconditional Love   19
Home Sweet "Crate"   19

The Plane Truth   20
Get Some Help   22

Loss Prevention & Proper Behavior   23
Prior Planning Prevents Poor Performance   23
Proper Hotel & Motel Pet-Etiquette   24
Paying the Price   24
Identification   25
If Your Pet Gets Lost   25

10 Commandments for Pets & Guests   28

Health Considerations   30
Medical First Aid Kit   30
Emergencies: Finding a Veterinarian   30
Health Certificate and Vaccination   31
Feeding on the Road   31
Tranquilizers   32
Car Sickness   33

Regional Health Concerns   34
Heat Stroke & Heat Exhaustion   34
Heartworm   35
Fleas & Ticks   36

Relocating with Pets   **37**
Pointers for Smooth Moves   37
Find a New Veterinarian   38
Register Your Pet   38
Learn Your New Pet Laws   38

Posh Places PETS-R-PERMITTED   **39**
Posh Pet-friendly Accommodations   42

How To Use This Directory   **45**

US Accommodations   **48**

Zip Index   **398**

Canada Accommodations   **408**
Rules for Successful Pet Travel   408

Mexico Accommodations   **429**
Rules for Successful Pet Travel   429

Theme Parks   **431**

Boarding Kennels   **436**
Tips for Boarding S.U.C.C.E.S.S.   436
Boarding Kennel Directory   439

Petsitters   **453**
Choosing a Petsitter   453
Petsitter Directory   456

Veterinarians   **472**
Finding a Veterinarian   472
Veterinarian Directory   473

Toll Free Directory   **503**
Accommodations   503
Tourist Bureaus   504

Reorder Form   **505**
Recommend New Listings   **506**

INTRODUCTION

Since nearly every other home in America has a pet, everyday many of us face the question of what to do with our pets when travel (planned or emergency) disrupts our normal routine. This directory has the answers ... *from boarding to pet sitting to taking them with you*.

And this directory does much more than list hotels, motels, kennels and petsitters. It gives you the answers you need to prepare for, and feel good about, whatever type of petcare you choose.

It includes advice from pet experts:

Maureen Hall, frequent TV & radio guest and professional Hollywood animal behaviorist provides down-to-earth information on preparing your pet (and yourself) for *Happy Trails full of Happy Tails*.

Matthew Margolis, pet expert on NBC's TODAY SHOW provides pointers in the areas of pet safety, pet loss prevention and proper "Pet Etiquette" in hotels & motels.

Dr. Carin Smith, DVM and petcare author, provides the detailed information you need on health considerations, feeding and first-aid preparedness.

Because pet lovers come in all price ranges, we've included a special section detailing posh places Pets-R-Permitted. Especially for "haute dogs" and "classy cats" who've got no bones about paying big bucks for a place to catnap.

We also profile the kennels at or near major tourist attractions and give you tips for boarding S.U.C.C.E.S.S. We've included tips for picking a petsitter and checklists for filling your pet's travelpack and first-aid kit. To assure proper "Pet Etiquette" when at a hotel or motel, you must follow the 10 commandments of appropriate pet behavior.

We've also included plane, train and bus information. We've even included a toll-free nationwide veterinary location service and nationwide petsitter location services as well. To help you save money, you can send for our FREE "PET SAVINGS PACK" that includes over $200 in coupons, discounts, and offers on pet products, services, and accommodations (while supplies last).

Why did we go to all the trouble to put so much information, into this directory? A scene we witnessed in a nearby restaurant will explain.

An extended family is seated at a large table happily discussing their plans for an upcoming family vacation. The table falls silent after grandpa announces he won't be going this year. Stunned, a family member asks why. Grandpa says, "Because I'm not going to leave Mike." The table grows noisy again as family members scoffingly retort. "Just leave him at a kennel," "Get a petsitter." "Have your neighbor look in on him."

Grandpa answers each, "I don't want to leave him in a kennel, and besides Mike has trouble getting up and he'd have to get up and down every time they came in to spray the concrete. And, I don't know any petsitters and my neighbor won't be available to look in on him. So, I'm not leaving Mike!"

The table gets louder, tempers rise. The family cannot believe that Grandpa is going to forego their family vacation in preference to the company of Mike.

As pet lovers, we DO believe it. But with our directory, Grandpa wouldn't have to forego the vacation. Ideally, the family could agree upon a destination where there would be a hotel or motel that would welcome Mike. Or Grandpa could use the directory to find a reliable petsitter or kennel more to his and Mike's liking.

We understand Grandpa's attachment to Mike. This is why we endeavored to include so much information. So people like Grandpa and Mike and you would know your petcare options when you travel, and have some happy choices.

WE HOPE THIS DIRECTORY WILL HELP YOU TO FIND MANY HAPPY TRAILS FULL OF HAPPY TAILS AND EVEN HAPPIER TALES!

BONE VOYAGE!

PET PACKING LIST

❏ Pet first aid kit   ❏ Flea & tick spray

❏ Emergency care book   ❏ Bed & bedding

❏ Regular pet food   ❏ Sturdy collar

❏ Water from home   ❏ Leash/harness

❏ Treats & toys   ❏ ID & rabies tags

❏ Food and water bowls   ❏ Flashlight

❏ Soap to clean bowls   ❏ Crate/carrier

❏ Mat to place under bowls   ❏ Pooper scooper/bags

❏ Paper towels   ❏ Litter/litter box

❏ Hair remover if pet sheds

❏ Veterinarian-issued health and rabies certificates

❏ Grooming/shampoo supplies

❏ Can opener and spoon for food

❏ Photo, written description, and flyer in case of loss

❏ You local vet's emergency number for referral

❏ Copy of medical records and prescriptions if needed

PREPARING FOR TRAVEL

The following advice on preparing your pet for travel is from Maureen Hall, frequent TV & radio guest and professional Hollywood animal trainer with over 40 Years experience. Having traveled extensively in the company of animals (sometimes for months with a mobile menagerie of up to a dozen different species), Maureen Hall is an expert at putting animals at ease on the road.

1.   KEEPING FIDO & FLUFFY HAPPY ON A TRIP

Whether your traveling companion has two legs or four, it is no fun to take a trip with someone who is scared of just plain grouchy. If your grouch is the two legged type, you are on your own. However, a little pre-trip work can definitely change the attitude of your four footed friends.

I can already hear some of you saying: "But, you don't know MY dog/cat. They climb the wall at the mere mention of a ride." You're right, I don't know your animal. However, having traveled over 30 years (many trips lasting months) with anywhere from 1 to 12 animals including dogs, cats, birds, horses, a pet fox, a pet raccoon, goat ... well you get the picture. I believe my experience may help your trip be a delightful, hassle-free adventure.

2. HELP FOR PETS WHO HATE RIDING IN CARS

Due to my work with animals and my cross country tours, all my animals must enjoy travel. No matter how hard I try, I cannot pick up my keys quietly enough to sneak out of the house alone. There are always at least 10 animals jumping and begging for a ride. From cats to horses, they all want to go.

The most insistent pleading comes from my small black and white dog. Some would find this hard to believe because at one time she was absolutely terrified of getting into a car. You see, she was thrown out of a car when just a puppy and nearly died as a result. Her training took just two weeks. However, if you have an animal that is this terrified, I suggest you start training a month to 6 weeks in advance of your trip.

CAR - PET TRAINING

Training a cat to ride in the car also takes a little longer and requires a little more patience. Cats usually travel better in a carrier. Give them a month or more to become comfortable in the carrier at home by making it extra inviting and cozy. (See the tips for acclimating pets to carriers in the section below.) Eventually you can fasten them in the carrier for an hour or so with their favorite treat or toy. Once they are used to their carrier, you can begin training them on car rides.

A. Start by taking the animal on short rides. Perhaps just a couple of trips around the block. It helps if you can take another person with you on these first few runs. Instruct your helper to sit the animal down calmly, yet firmly.

B.   Keeping one hand on the animal, speak in a low reassuring voice and WITH AUTHORITY! Resist the temptation to cuddle and use baby-talk. Over cuddling only serves to reward the trembling, scared action. In a sense cuddling tells the animal that it is doing right by shaking and feeling terrified.

        What we want instead is to instill confidence in the animal. This is accomplished by being there for it and encouraging it to be strong and brave. You will be surprised at just how quickly the animal will forget the fear and really enjoy the trip. If your dog is small it may need to see out; in which case it may sit on the helper's lap. But this must be handled in a calm manner. No baby talk.

C.   After a few trips around the block, you will need to go in somewhere, leaving your pet in the car with the windows cracked. Only leave pets if the temperature is comfortable. Never leave a pet when it is hot or cold.

D.   Always pet them or give them a treat when you get back as a reward for waiting for you. This part of the training is important. You don't want to go cross country with an animal and never be able to leave it alone while you go inside a roadstop or restaurant.

My sister's dog was such a basket case in a car because it was never taken anywhere except to the vet for shots. This only made it worse for her dog because it thought - you go in the car and then you get punished. Suddenly the dog's attitude did a complete turnaround. The solution? My sister started going straight from the vet's office to the drive-thru hamburger stand!

E. Your pet can also learn to enjoy rides, especially if they get to go to places other than the vet. Your pet wants to be by your side wherever you go. With a little thought on your part, your dog or cat will be first in the car every time you reach for your keys.

3. CREATURES OF HABIT

Habits, both good and bad, are easily formed. If you routinely take your pet with you in the car, it quickly becomes a habit. If you set up a workable travel routine for: walks, playtime, food, etc., your pet will quickly fall into the pattern.

4. CALM, COOL AND COLLECTED

If you allow yourself to be overly nervous and apprehensive, your pet will pick up those feelings and become fearful of the car and the trip. For your good and theirs, remain calm and in control. Your best friend will also be much more cooperative if they know their importance to you. Even with the rushing that comes with travel, take a second to give a few extra pats on the head. This will do wonders for your pet's frame of mind, and keep them from feeling like just so much extra baggage.

5. YOUR CREATURE'S COMFORT

You are responsible for your animal's needs. See that they eat and drink on time and receive adequate exercise. A 15 minute romp in the park (on leash, please!) a couple times a day is good for everyone. And while traveling pets may need to relieve themselves more often than when they are at home, a ten minute pit stop every few hours is usually adequate. Also offer your pet water at each pit stop. And always leash or harness your pet BEFORE opening the car.

6. UNCONDITIONAL LOVE

Never yell at your pet. Punishment is never needed. Focus on communication, instructing and guiding in a manner they can understand, and they will do everything they can to please you.

7. HOME SWEET "CRATE"

For safety always keep your pet in a carrier or crate while driving. This will keep your pet from interfering with your driving and increases your pet's comfort & security. Their crate becomes their "home away from home,"a familiar bed in a strange hotel.

Conditioning your pet to their crate is a gradual process you need to begin at home. Set the crate by your pet's food and let them explore it. Put treats in it to make it more appealing. Feed your pet in it and make it into a bed. At travel time you'll be glad you took the time to make them comfortable with their crate.

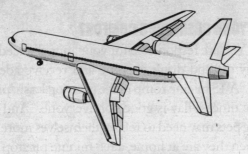

THE PLANE TRUTH

Pets are not allowed on most trains and buses, but most airlines transport them. If you plan to transport your pet on an airline, do your homework and make travel plans well in advance. Air travel for pets is a serious undertaking and some pets should not fly. Air travel can be very unsafe for older, nervous, sickly, or pregnant animals. Pets must be over 8 weeks of age to fly.

Small pets can go as carry-on baggage but must fit in a carrier under the seat and must not disturb others. Make reservations early since only a few animals are allowed in the cabin and the rules vary by airline. Bring your pet's travel health certificates. Most airlines require a veterinarian exam within 30 days before flight. Be sure to allow time for a vet appointment before you travel.

**THERE ARE MANY DETAILS AND MANY RISKS FOR
PETS THAT MUST FLY AS BAGGAGE!
YOU MUST DO YOUR OWN HOMEWORK!**

If at all possible, schedule direct, nonstop flights to avoid your pet missing a plane or enduring delays and time outside in the cold or heat. Avoid holiday, weekend or busy times so airline personnel have extra time to give your pet special handling.

Ascertain the airline's **"heat & cold policy."**
Airlines won't take pets if departure or destination
temperatures are over 80 degrees. Avoid flights through
hot states and fly early morning or late evening. Pets
may also be turned away if temperatures are too low. If
this is the case, you'd want to schedule daytime routes
through warm states.

Get the airline's **SPECIFIC** pet carrier requirements
since type and size are **STRICTLY** controlled. Be sure
your regulation pet carrier is big enough for your pet to
stand, lie and turn around in. Bigger however, is not
better. Too much space inside the carrier can increase
your pet's chances of being tossed about. A cozy carrier
is best. Also reduce stress by introducing your pet to
the carrier well before the trip. Allowing your pet to
become acclimated
to the kennel will
greatly reduce stress
and increase your
pet's comfort.
Carriers must be
marked **LIVE
ANIMAL** in letters

at least one inch high on both the top and sides and
marked with arrows or **This End Up**.
Your pet's food and watering schedule should be
attached to the outside of the carrier along with a bag
of food if the trip is over 12 hours. Also attach a
permanent waterproof label with the following
information: pet name, your name, address & phone;
the name, address, & phone of the person picking up

your pet; and your veterinarian's information. And make sure your pet is wearing a tag with this information in case your pet becomes separated from the carrier (as did a noted feline who took several trips around the world in the belly of a Boeing 747!).

Feed, water and exercise your pet within 4-6 hours of the trip. Feed lightly the morning of travel. A full stomach can make the trip uncomfortable. Determine how much time the airline requires for check in so you can limit the amount of time your pet spends in the baggage area. Exercise your pet again right before travel. Cover the bottom of the carrier with towels and shredded paper to absorb both accidents and bumps.

2.   GET SOME HELP

The American Dog Owners Association advocates safe pet travel. Website is http://www.global2000.net/adoa/ Of special interest are their Travel Tips and Airline Update. They offer a free brochure, Canine Travel Tips Membership is $10/year. Write ADOA, 1654 Columbia Turnpike, Castleton, NY 12033 or call (518) 477-8469.

The Independent Pet and Animal Transportation Association can also help with shipping pets. Contact them at 903.769.2267 or at RR1, Box 747, Big Sandy, TX 75755

The American Society for the Prevention of Cruelty to Animals Website is http://www.aspca.org/petcare/travel.htm. 212.876.7700 Address: ASPCA, 424 E. 92nd St., NY NY 10128-6804.

EXPERT ADVICE ON PET LOSS PREVENTION & PROPER BEHAVIOR

The following advice is from Matthew Margolis, pet expert on NBC's "TODAY SHOW," accomplished dog trainer with over 30 years experience and founder of the National Institute of Dog Training.

1. PRIOR PLANNING PREVENTS POOR PERFORMANCE & LOST PETS

Obedience training is very important because only dogs that have been trained in at least "basic commands" should travel. Having your dog obey your commands, especially from a distance or when there are distractions is very important and could ultimately save your dog's life. If your dog were to get loose and wind up across a busy street, being able to call "DOWN" from a distance might save your pet's life and keep it from straying out of your sight.

To avoid losing your pet in unfamiliar areas, ALWAYS maintain direct control of your pet ... AT ALL TIMES! By using a leash, crate or carrier you can help to assure that your pet will not break away from your care. Even when carrying your pet, it is wise to have a leash attached so you have something to grab in case your pet does manage to break lose.

Attach your dog's leash or cat's harness while your pet is in a secured, controlled environment. New environments can be frightening and distracting. Your pet may be prompted to run off before you have the chance to secure their leash or harness. For example, when making, "pit stops," unfamiliar surroundings can

 distract and disorient your pet. To avoid the danger of having your pet dash across a street, ALWAYS secure your pet's leash before opening the car door. The same thing goes when leaving your room. To avoid knocking over other guests in the hallway, ALWAYS make sure your pet is securely leashed or crated before opening the door to your room.

2.   PROPER HOTEL & MOTEL PET-ETIQUETTE

Margolis offers these pointers on proper "Pet Etiquette" in hotels and motels. Hotel and motel owners will ONLY continue to Permit Pets if pet owners keep their pets from becoming pests. If you keep your pet from disturbing other guests and from doing damage, management will be more likely to continue to permit pets. If you allow your pet to be a pest, chances are you'll be asked to leave and you will ruin it for other pet owners who come looking for lodging. Strive to be a good example, or you'll be a dog-GONE example.

3.   PAYING THE PRICE

You must remember that you will have to take the time to help your pet adjust to the strange new surroundings it will encounter as you travel. Giving words of reassurance, petting and comforting will help your pet adjust. Keeping your pet calm and under control is the best way to insure no person or no thing gets damaged ... a small price to pay to avoid damage to persons and property.

Minimizing your pet's exposure to other people is the best way to keep your pet from becoming overexcited or aggressive. And since not every guest is a pet lover, it will also minimize complaints to management. If you must encounter other people, always have your pet leashed or crated. Even if your pet is normally friendly and outgoing, strange new surroundings may cause a change in temperament and tolerance. Lessening your pet's interaction with other people will lessen the chance for unfriendly altercations and lessen complaints from other guests.

If you keep your pet calm and under direct control, your travels should go off without a hitch. However, if your pet does get out of line, always report and volunteer to pay for any damages. Before traveling consider obedience training, in at least basic commands to help make your travels go more smoothly.

Matthew Margolis is the coauthor of 9 books on dog training including "WOOF," "When Good Dogs Do Bad Things," and "Good Dog, Bad Dog." He can be reached at the National Institute of Dog Training by calling (800) 334-DOGS

PET IDENTIFICATION AND RECOVERY

1.   IDENTIFICATION

Traveling pets must wear a sturdy collar with firmly secured identification tags. Keeping a leash attached at all times can also help to keep your pet from breaking away. Be sure to accustom your cat to wearing a collar before your trip. There are cat "safety collars" that attach with elastic or velcro to keep cats from getting caught.

Your pet's tag should include: your pet's name, your name, address, phone & PHONE NUMBERS OF A FRIEND OR YOUR VET so they can be contacted since you won't be home to receive calls.

Collars can fall off, so there is permanent identification like microchips & tattooing now available. The success of these methods depends on finders knowing to look.

2.   IF YOUR PET GETS LOST

If your pet gets lost, there are a number of things you must do. The first things should be done before you even leave on your trip. You should write a complete specific description of your pet. Include: breed, height, weight, color, length & texture of coat, sex, age, type of tail, eye color, markings, description of collar & tags.

Take close-up photos of your pet and make photocopies along with the description. Take the photocopies on your trip so you can post them in case your pet gets lost. Be sure to leave room to write the address & phone number where you are staying locally.

It is best to do this at home when you are calm. Making the effort to do this before your trip might also help to reinforce how important it is to keep your pet under your direct control AT ALL TIMES.

If you should lose your pet, remain calm and systematically search the immediate area in progressively wider circles. Enlist the aid of others and offer a reward to motivate them. After an hour, take the photocopies of your pet's description and give them to the local animal control agencies, police, mail carriers, shop keepers and post them in a widening circle from the area where your pet was lost. Contact vets and emergency animal clinics in case your pet has been injured and is receiving care. Place ads offering rewards.

Continue your search in the area as long as you can. If you must go, leave phone numbers with the local animal control agencies and the place you were staying and with anyone else whose help you've enlisted. Check back often and leave instructions for them to call you by phoning collect at any time.

10 COMMANDMENTS FOR PETS & GUESTS

what your host, the hotel or motel management assumes...

1. ALWAYS CALL AHEAD - Since many places only have a few "pet rooms" you'll need to call ahead for reservations & to confirm that your SPECIFIC pet will be welcomed. There may be size or breed restrictions. Since pet policies can change, calling ahead will help you to avoid being turned away.

2. ALWAYS DECLARE YOUR PET AT CHECK-IN - To keep pets in "pet rooms" & to allow management to warn maids, always declare your pet. Also make sure your pet is well groomed, presentable, flea-free, HOUSEBROKEN, and well-behaved to avoid being turned away.

3. THERE'S A PLACE FOR EVERYTHING - Ask the management where they prefer you to walk your pet. You should stay away from public areas where other guests congregate such as the pool, lounge, children's playground or dining areas. And ALWAYS take a bag or pooper scooper to pick up what your pet leaves behind.

4. DO NOT DISTURB - Your pet should NOT be seen and it should NOT be heard by other guests. Remember not all guests are pet lovers. And the last thing some guests want is to hear or see a pet in the place they are vacationing, To avoid complaints, keep pets "out of sight and out of mind" of people who might complain.

5. BEST BEHAVIOR NOT PEST BEHAVIOR - You must not let your pet disturb other guests or do damage. BE FOREWARNED, If you allow your pet to misbehave, it is likely you'll be asked to leave. And, you'll ruin it for other traveling pet owners.

6. DO NOT LEAVE YOUR PET IN YOUR ROOM UNATTENDED. Accommodations make this rule for very good reasons. For example, if a maid opens the door and is not aware of your pet, you risk having your pet escape or having your startled pet attack the maid.

Since the room will be a strange new place, your pet is likely to scratch, bark and cry at every sound. This will disturb other guests! And scratching can result in costly nail marks on the door. To avoid costly damage and disturbing other guests, NEVER LEAVE YOUR PET ALONE IN THE ROOM.

Traveling with a pet requires advance planning. If while you are traveling you plan to go somewhere that won't allow pets, you will need to make pet care arrangements. Check the kennel & pet sitter listings in this directory to find people to help you with temporary petcare while you're traveling. Also check the local yellow pages. Additionally, many tourist attractions have kennels, or use nearby kennels. Simply call them for information or check the section in this directory that details kennel information at major tourist attractions. You will also need to call the attraction directly to reserve kennel space and take your pet's health certificate and documentation of vaccination.

7. BRING BEDDING - Plan in advance where your pet will sleep. If your pet sleeps on a rug or a blanket or in a basket be sure to bring this along. If your pet MUST sleep on the bed with you, you MUST bring a bed covering. This minimizes pet odor and pet hairs being left on beds and carpeting.

8. KEEP CLEAN INSIDE & OUTSIDE- Since hotels and motels are mainly for human guests, always make the extra effort to remove all pet traces from your room ... and the grounds if your pet uses them for a rest room. Before checking out, give your room a good once-over. Be sure to remove any empty food cans and clean up any spills, accidents and shed hair. AND ALWAYS REPORT & PAY FOR ANY DAMAGES!!

9. CHOW TIME CONSIDERATIONS - Planning ahead for your pet's meals is a must. You need to bring your pet's food and water dishes and a mat on which to set them. Set the mat and dishes in the bathroom on the tile. Don't feed your pet on the carpet. Also set your cat's litter box on the tile.

10. MANAGEMENT'S WORD IS GOSPEL - At the very least, Management assumes your pet will be quiet, well-behaved, kept from view of other guests, flea-free, HOUSEBROKEN, and never left alone in the room. These are the basics. Additionally, they may require that your pet be kept in a carrier or they may only allow pets in smoking rooms, or any other number of restrictions. And restrictions may change from visit to visit.

You must find out what is allowed prior to checking in and abide by the rules. If you are not willing to do that or if your pet is not well-behaved enough to travel, you should consider kenneling or hiring a pet sitter. Only by obeying the word of management, will pets continue to be permitted.

HEALTH CONSIDERATIONS

The following information is from Dr. Carin A. Smith, practicing Doctor of Veterinary Medicine and nationally known petcare author.

1. MEDICAL FIRST AID KIT

o First aid book
o Tweezers
o Ice pack
o Blunt-tip scissors
o Antibacterial ointment
o Heartworm preventive (if indicated)
o Antiseptic solution (iodine solution not iodine tincture)
o Antiseptic soap (iodine soap)
o Slip-on muzzle (injured dogs in pain will bite)
o Copy of medical records if health problem
o Copy of prescriptions, if any

o Bandage tape
o Roll gauze
o Rectal thermometer
o Pet's medications
o Towels

2. EMERGENCIES: FINDING A VETERINARIAN

If your pet becomes ill during travel, go to a vet at once. Find a vet in the area where you're traveling in the local yellow pages or call the American Animal Hospital Association (AAHA) at (800) 252-2242. They can give you the location of a nearby AAHA veterinarian clinic 9 - 5 Mountain Time, Monday through Friday.

If your pet is sick at other times, don't wait for weekday hours. Take your pet to a close-by emergency clinic.

3. HEALTH CERTIFICATE & VACCINATION REQUIREMENTS

Careful planning can help your pet stay healthy during trips. If your pet is on regular medication or has an ongoing health problem, take copies of your pet's health record with you. This will avoid unnecessary delays if complications arise or if medication runs out.

If you are traveling to another state, your pet needs a health certificate and proof of your pet's inoculations including rabies and kennel cough. This documentation is required at some state lines. The health certificate is filled out by a veterinarian and shows that your pet is free of any infectious disease. Your pet must be examined and the certificate filled out within a week of departure. A health certificate is not the same as the rabies certificate. You must carry both. Additionally, you must have written evidence that other vaccinations have been given within the past year.

Consult your veterinarian about any special health concerns in the areas you plan to travel and about any additional vaccines that may be necessary. Also, if you plan to kennel your pet consult your veterinarian about preventing kennel cough.

4. FEEDING ON THE ROAD

Changing your pet's diet can cause digestive upset, so feed consistently while traveling. Since your brand of food may not always be available, take plenty with you. Take note of the time of day you usually feed your pet, and the amount of time after a meal that passes before the pet needs to urinate or defecate. Try to keep a travel schedule that allows your pet to eat and eliminate at the same times as at home.

If your schedule on the road will be different than what you keep at home, change to that schedule gradually during the week before your trip. For instance, pets travel best when fed lightly in the morning, with their main meal at the end of the day. Begin feeding this way before you leave,

Cats won't usually eat or use their litter box while you're driving. They will wait until you have set out their litter box and food bowls in a quiet place. Some dogs also don't eat or drink when nervous or excited. Plan stops to let your pet relax enough to do so.

5. TRANQUILIZERS

Tranquillizing should be reserved for the occasional stressful trip with a pet unaccustomed to travel. Pets should not be brought on optional trips unless they enjoy travel without tranquilizing. Yet you may be moving and your pet must come along. Some cats will meow constantly. Certain dogs become anxious and whine all the time. You can prevent some problems by training your pet to tolerate driving ahead of time. Catnip works to calm some cats.

If all else fails, your veterinarian can prescribe a mild tranquilizer or anti-nausea medication. Every pet reacts differently to tranquilizers. You want your pet to be relaxed but not totally asleep. Consider giving half the dose, then waiting to see how your pet responds before giving the rest.

Most pets need only one dose of a tranquilizer for a full day of travel. Although the drug wears off before day's end, the pet has become accustomed to the drive and remains calm. Be cautious in extreme temperatures since tranquilized pets are less able to regulate their body heat. Some airlines do not allow animals to be tranquilized while they are airborne. If your pet will be traveling by air, call the airline ahead of time to ask.

6. CAR SICKNESS

Car sickness occurs in kittens and puppies but they usually outgrow it. Vets can prescribe medication for adult pets. You can condition your pet by taking them on short practice drives when their stomach is empty. Drive and make turns slowly and your pet will become accustomed to the motion.

Withhold food or feed less than normal on the morning of the car ride. Feed the bulk of the day's meal at night. A pet that has never before been carsick, but suddenly becomes so during your trip, is likely to be sick for another reason and should be examined by a vet.

HEALTH CONSIDERATIONS
Regional Concerns

1. HEAT STROKE & HEAT EXHAUSTION

Problems with heat aren't limited to extremely hot days. Heat Stroke can occur if your pet doesn't drink enough water and can't get out of the sun. High humidity increases the chance of heat exhaustion as does being confined in a small area with poor ventilation, like a car.

With an outside daytime temperature of 85 degrees, inside a car can reach 102 degrees in 10 minutes, 120 degrees in thirty minutes — even with the windows cracked. NEVER leave your pet alone in a car.

Dogs and cats release only a little body heat by sweating. Unlike people, they do not sweat through their skin, so they release body heat by panting. Breeds with pug noses, elderly and overweight pets have a higher risk of heat stroke. Any pet on medication could be prone to trouble. For instance, some tranquilizers can disrupt the pet's natural heat regulation.

To determine how your pet is tolerating the heat, lift its lips to look at the color of the gums. Normal mucous membranes are light pink. Press your finger into the gum and note the white spot that refills with pink color within a second or two. With heat stroke, the gums are dark red and refill time is prolonged.

Panting, plus weakness, vomiting, and diarrhea are other signs. Pets may go into convulsions or a coma and the brain, heart, and kidneys may receive permanent damage. Using a rectal thermometer, your pet's normal temperature should be around 101 to 102 degrees Fahrenheit. It can rise to over 106 with heat stroke. A pet with heat stroke must be cooled immediately by dousing it with lots of water, then taken to a veterinarian without delay.

Prevent heat problems by driving with the air conditioner on or the window slightly open. Stop frequently during long drives to allow your pet to drink. Consider driving at night and sleeping during the day if you plan a long drive during hot weather. If you must drive in the heat without air conditioning, wrap an ice pack in a towel and place that in your pet's carrier. If it is extremely hot, wet down your pet occasionally.

2. HEARTWORM

Heartworms can be transmitted anywhere there is an infected dog and a mosquito. The treatment is costly and dangerous. Prevention is far preferable and easily accomplished using a daily or monthly medication. Cats are rarely infested by heartworms.

If you live in a heartworm area, it's likely your dog is receiving heartworm medication already. Dogs that will be traveling through heartworm areas should be put on the preventative. Heartworm medication is available only from veterinarians. The vet may require that your dog be tested before prescribing the preventive, since its use can be dangerous to a dog already infected.

3. FLEAS AND TICKS

Fleas and ticks are other regional problems. If you are just passing through an affected region, bring a bottle of flea and tick spray and apply it as directed. To Prevent ticks from attaching, spray your dog before it runs in brushy or wooded areas. Use a cloth to apply the spray to the ears and face. Always check your pet for ticks and fleas during daily brushing.

Use tweezers to extract any ticks you may find. Gently grasp the tick and pull it straight out. If the head of the tick remains, watch the area for a few days. Usually the head will fester out. If the area becomes red or swollen, see a veterinarian. If your stay in a region with fleas or ticks will be of longer duration or if you live in an area plagued by these pests, you should educate yourself on how to protect your pet.

"The Flea and Tick Book" is available for $7.95 from Smith Veterinary, Box 695, Leavenworth, WA 98826.

RELOCATING WITH PETS
POINTERS FOR SMOOTH MOVES

Moving can be a busy time. Though there are many tasks to juggle and normal routines can be upset, do your best to keep your pet on its regular feeding and exercising routine. Also take time to rub and comfort your pet to help it cope with the change. If you are moving across town, your biggest challenge will be to make your pet comfortable in its new home. If you have a dog, you can begin walking him around your new neighborhood before you move. And, before introducing your pet to its new home, be sure to put out its food and water dishes, familiar toys, bedding, litter box and so forth. These familiar objects will help ease the transition.

If you are moving a greater distance, there are many details to consider. All of the details in the previous sections that apply to preparing your pet for travel will apply to preparing your pet for relocating.

These include: regional and seasonal health concerns, the proper way to transport and feed pets, advice on tranquilizers and carsickness, a checklist of what to pack, a first-aid kit checklist, finding a veterinarian in case your pet becomes ill during the trip, and finding lodging that accepts pets.

In addition to those details, you must attend to the following:

1.   FIND A NEW VETERINARIAN

You will need to find a new veterinarian. You can ask your current veterinarian for recommendations and you can call the American Animal Hospital Association at (800) 252-2242 for recommendations on veterinarians in your new locale. Before you move, be sure to obtain a copy of your pet's medical records. It will help your new veterinarian to have your pet's medical history.

2.   REGISTER YOUR PET

You will need to contact the city offices in the community where you are relocating to determine the animal registration procedures and any associated fees. Often proof of rabies vaccination will be required. Additionally, proof of spaying or neutering will sometimes allow you to pay a reduced registration fee.

3.   LEARN YOUR NEW PET LAWS

When contacting the city offices you will also want to inquire about city pets laws. For example, does the community have leash laws? Do they have "poop scooping" ordinances or barking ordinances? Are there a limit to the number of pets a person may own?

Though moving can be a busy time, following the above tips will help you and your pet have a "smooth move."

POSH PLACES PETS-R-PERMITTED

*Frolic at the Four Seasons
with your Four-Pawed Friend*

*Star gaze at Aspen's The Little Nell, a Hollywood
Hangout for Hound Lovers*

*Pets get Presidential treatment with San Ysidro
Ranch's "Pampered Pets Program" A place
many a president has cat-napped.*

When room service is delivered on a silver tray and includes a personal note from the manager you know you are traveling in style - especially when all the fuss is for your "four-legged" traveling companion. For pets traveling in the lap of luxury, there are upscale hotels and resorts that cater to canines and felines for a fancier fee than middle of the road establishments.

Many of the posh Four Seasons Hotels give pets as much pampering as their owners receive. Staff learn the pet's name and write personal notes to accompany the Evian water, fresh ground sirloin and other treats that  are served on a silver tray. Millie, Barbara Bush's dog and Bubbles, Michael Jackson's chimp have stayed at the Four Seasons. As has Spuds MacKenzie who was served steak and dog biscuits on a silver tray.

Four Seasons Hotels that participate in the "PAMPERED PETS PROGRAMS" include such things as crystal water bowls, designer pet beds with turn-down service featuring special pet treats, grooming and walking services, and gourmet food served on silver trays, of course. Often you'll find grilled chicken and fresh corn, poached salmon with steamed rice, sponge cakes with fresh whipped cream for desert and other gourmet dished on the menu which is "strictly for pets."

Loews L'enfant Plaza in D.C. and the Loews Annapolis Hotel both have V.I.P. (Very important Pets) Programs. Upon arrival, all top dogs and fat cats receive dog bones or cat treats delivered by room service on a silver tray. These hotels also donate 5% of the room rate to their local S.P.C.A.

Both coasts also boast posh hotels with long histories of pet-friendliness. On the East coast on New York's fashionable 5th Avenue, you'll find the posh Hotel Pierre complete with all pet amenities at the front desk. On the West coast "haute dogs" and "classy cats" catnap at L.A.'s high class Hotel Bel-Air. The stay will take an

extra bite out of your budget since you'll have to scratch up a $250 non-refundable fee to cover the extra cleaning costs.

The west coast also boasts the elegant San Ysidro Ranch in Santa Barbara. This country resort is not only pet-friendly; it is also President friendly. President Nixon stayed here. And John F. Kennedy and his bride Jacqueline spent their honeymoon here. The management hopes to purr-suade President Clinton and Boots to come for a cat-nap too. Even non-presidential cats and dogs are pampered by the ranch's privileged pet program which includes an extra comfy bed., personalized bowls, toys and more. Privileged pets even have their own registration at the front desk.

Our Posh Accommodations section contains over 100 pet-friendly premium hotels in most of the larger markets of the United States. You and your precious will never need to move from the lap of luxury again. In our thousands of other pet-friendly listings, you can find over 500 hotels, motels, inns, and lodges in the $$$$ range (over $100/nightly) to round out luxurious places to stay all across the country.

ARIZONA

Marriott Resort
5641 E Lincoln Dr
Paradise Valley Az 85253
602.948.7111
Small

Biltmore
24th St & Missouri
Phoenix Az 85016
602.955.6600

Radisson Inn
3333 E University Dr
Phoenix Az 85034
602.437.8400
Small Pets Allowed

The Phoenician Resort
6000 E Camelback Rd
Scottsdale Az 85251
602.941.8200
Small Dogs Allowed In
Casita Area

Sheraton Inn
10000 N Oracle Rd
Tucson Az 85737
520.544.5000

CALIFORNIA

The Beverly Hilton Hotel
9876 Wilshire Blvd
Beverly Hills Ca 90210
800.922.5432

The Pennisula
9882 Little Santa Monica
Blvd
Beverly Hills Ca 90212
310.551.2888

The Regent Beverly Wilshire
9500 Wilshire Blvd
Beverly Hills Ca 90212
310.275.5200

Highlands Inn
Highway 1
Carmel Ca 93921
408.624.3801

Quail Lodge Resort
8205 Valley Greens Dr
Carmel Ca 93923
408.324.1581

Loews Hotel
4000 Coronado Bay Rd
Coronado Ca 92118
619.424.4000
Small Below The Knee Size

Dana Point Resort
25135 Park Lantern
Dana Point Ca 92629
714.661.5000

La Quinta Resort
49499 Eisenhower Dr
La Quinta Ca 92253
619.564.4111
Call For Fees & Size Limits

Century Plaza Hotel
2025 Ave Of The Stars
Los Angeles Ca 90067
310.277.2000

Chateau Marmont Hotel
8221 W Sunset Blvd
Los Angeles Ca 90046
213.656.1010

Hotel Bel Air
701 Stone Canyon Rd
Los Angeles Ca 90077
800.648.4097

Hotel Nikko
465 S La Cienega Blvd
Los Angeles Ca 90048
310.247.0400

Hotel Sofitel Ma Maison
8555 Beverly Blvd
Los Angeles Ca 90048
310.278.5444
Bellman Can Walk, Notify
Staff Of Pet

The Four Seasons
300 S Doheny Dr
Los Angeles Ca 90048
310.273.2222
Small Pets Allowed

Radisson Inn
1400 Park View Ave
Manhattan Beach Ca 90266
800.333.3333

The Four Seasons
690 Newport Center Dr
Newport Beach Ca 92660
714.759.0808
Small Pets Allowed

The Lodge At Pebble Beach
1700 17-Mile Dr
Pebble Beach Ca 93953
408.624.3811

Westin Resort
71333 Dinah Shore Dr
Rancho Mirage Ca 92270
619.328.5955
Small

Red Lion Inn
2001 Point West Way
Sacramento Ca 95815
916.929.8855
Call For Fees & Restrictions

Marriott Hotel
701 A St
San Diego Ca 92101
619.696.9800
With Approval

Red Lion Inn
7450 Hazard Center Dr
San Diego Ca 92108
619.297.5466
Call For Fees & Restrictions

The Clift Hotel
495 Geary St
San Francisco Ca 94102
415.775.4700
Small Pets Allowed

Hotel Nikko
222 Mason St
San Francisco Ca 94102
415.394.1111

The Pan Pacific Hotel
500 Post St
San Francisco Ca 94102
415.771.8600

Westin Hotel
335 Powell St
San Francisco Ca 94102
415.397.7000
Small Dogs Accepted

Red Lion Inn
2050 Gateway Pl
San Jose Ca 95110
408.453.4000
Call For Fees & Restrictions

Fess Parkers Red Lion
Resort
633 E Cabrillo Blvd
Santa Barbara Ca 93103
805.564.4333

San Ysidro Ranch
900 San Ysidro Ln
Santa Barbara Ca 93108
805.969.5046

The Four Seasons
1260 Channel Dr
Santa Barbara Ca 93108
805.969.2261

Loews Hotel
1700 Ocean Ave
Santa Monica Ca 90401
310.458.6700
Small Dogs Under 30 Lb
Ground Level Only

Tahoe Keys Resort
599 Tahoe Keys Blvd
South Lake Tahoe Ca 96150
916.544.5397

COLORADO

Hotel Jerome
330 E Main St
Aspen Co 81611
970.920.1000

The Little Nell
675 E Durant Ave
Aspen Co 81611
970.920.4600

Red Lion Inn
1775 E Cheyenne Mountain
Blvd
Colorado Springs Co 80906
719.576.8900
Call For Fees & Restrictions

Loews Hotel
41501 E Mississippi Ave
Denver Co 80222
303.782.9300

Red Lion Inn
3203 Quebec St
Denver Co 80207
800.547.8010
Call For Fees & Restrictions

COLORADO

POSH ACCOMMODATIONS

NEW YORK

Red Lion Inn
501 Camino Del Rio
Durango Co 81301
970.259.6580
Call For Fees & Restrictions

Doral Telluride Resort
145 Country Club Dr
Telluride Co 81435
800.443.6725

DISTRICT OF COLUMBIA

Loews Hotel
480 L'Enfant Plaza SW
Washington Dc 20024
202.484.1000
Vip Pet Program

The Four Seasons
2800 Pennsylvania Ave NW
Washington Dc 20007
202.342.0444
Small Pets Allowed

The Watergate Hotel
2650 Virginia Ave NW
Washington Dc 20037
202.965.2300
Small Dogs

FLORIDA

Sheraton Inn
9701 Collins Ave
Bal Harbour Fl 33154
305.865.7511

Admirals Court Resort Motel
21 Hendricks Is
Fort Lauderdale Fl 33301
954.462.5072

Mirador Resort Motel
901 S Ocean Dr
Hollywood Fl 33019
305.922.7581

Sofitel Hotel
5800 Blue Lagoon Dr
Miami Fl 33126
305.264.4888

Fontainbleau Hilton Resort
4441 Collins Ave
Miami Beach Fl 33140
305.538.2000

Delta Orlando Resort
5715 Major Blvd
Orlando Fl 32819
407.351.3340

The Four Seasons
2800 S Ocean Blvd
Palm Beach Fl 33480
407.582.2800

GEORGIA

Westin Hotel
2101 Nw Peachtree St
Atlanta Ga 30303
404.659.1400

IDAHO

Red Lion Inn
1800 Fairview Ave
Boise Id 83702
208.344.7691
Call For Fees & Restrictions

ILLINOIS

The Four Seasons
120 E Delaware Pl
Chicago Il 60611
312.280.8800
Small Pets Allowed

The Ritz Carlton
160 E Pearson St
Chicago Il 60611
312.266.1000
Small Pets Allowed

Hotel Sofitel
5550 N River Rd
Rosemont Il 60018
847.678.4488

KENTUCKY

Seelbach Hotel
200 S 4th Ave
Louisville Ky 40202
800.333.3399

LOUISIANA

Windsor Court Hotel
300 Gravier St
New Orleans La 70130
504.523.6000

MARYLAND

Loews Hotel
126 West St
Annapolis Md 21401
410.263.7777
Vip Pet Program

The Columbia Inn
10207 Wincopin Cir
Columbia Md 21044
800.638.2817

MASSACHU-SETTS

Boston Harbor Hotel
70 Rowes Wharf
Boston Ma 02110
617.439.7000

Swissotel
1 Avenue De Lafayette
Boston Ma 02111
617.451.2600

The Four Seasons
200 Boylston St
Boston Ma 02116
617.338.4400

The Ritz Carlton
15 Arlington St
Boston Ma 02117
617.536.5700

Harvard Square
1 Bennett St
Cambridge Ma 02138
617.864.1200

MICHIGAN

Westin Hotel
Renaissance Center
Detroit Mi 48243
313.568.8000
Small Pets Accepted

MINNESOTA

Crown Sterling Suites
7901 34Th Ave S
Minneapolis Mn 55425
612.854.1000

MISSOURI

Westin Hotel
1 E Pershing Rd
Kansas City Mo 64108
816.474.4400
Small Pets Accepted

NEW JERSEY

Radisson Inn
601 From Rd
Paramus Nj 07652
201.262.6900

NEW MEXICO

Hotel Santa Fe
1501 Paseo De Peralta
Santa Fe Nm 87501
800.825.9876

NEW YORK

The Garden City Hotel
45 7Th St
Garden City Ny 11530
516.747.3000

Hotel Pierre
2 E 61st St
New York Ny 10021
212.838.8000
Pet Friendly Special Treatment

Loews Hotel
569 Lexington Ave
New York Ny 10022
212.752.7000
Small

Marriott Hotel
1535 Broadway
New York Ny 10036
212.393.1900

Mayfair Hotel
610 Park Ave
New York Ny 10021
212.288.0800
Small Pets Only, $30/Night Charge

Novotel New York
226 W 52nd St
New York Ny 10019
212.315.0100

The Carlyle
35 E 76Th St
New York Ny 10021
212.744.1600
$10 Per Day

The Four Seasons
57 E 57Th St
New York Ny 10022
212.758.5700
Small

The Lowell
28 E 63rd St
New York Ny 10021
212.838.1400

The Peninsula
700 5Th Ave
New York Ny 10019
212.247.2200
$20 Nightly Charge, Pet
Waiver Required

The Plaza Hotel
5Th Ave At 59Th St
New York Ny 10019
212.759.3000
Small Pets Accepted

The Regency Hotel
540 Park Ave
New York Ny 10021
212.759.4100
Sign Agreement

The Waldorf Astoria
301 Park Ave
New York Ny 10022
212.355.3000

OHIO

Westin Hotel
At Fountain Square
Cincinnati Oh 45202
513.621.7700
Small Pets Accepted

OKLAHOMA

Marriott Hotel
3233 Nw Expwy
Oklahoma City Ok 73112
405.842.6633

OREGON

Red Lion Inn
1401 N Hayden Island Dr
Portland Or 97217
503.283.2111
Call For Fees & Restrictions

River Place Hotel
1510 Sw Harbor Way
Portland Or 97201
503.228.3233
$10 Fee

PENNSYLVA-NIA

The Four Seasons
1 Logan Sq
Philadelphia Pa 19103
215.963.1500
Small Pets Allowed

Westin Hotel
530 William Penn Pl
Pittsburgh Pa 15219
412.281.7100
Small Pets Accepted

RHODE ISLAND

Providence Biltmore
Kennedy Plaza
Providence Ri 02903
401.421.0700

TEXAS

The Four Seasons
98 San Jacinto Bl
Austin Tx 78701
512.478.4500

Worthington Hotel
200 Main St
Fort Worth Tx 76102
817.870.1000

Doubletree Hotels
5353 Westheimer Rd
Houston Tx 77056
713.961.9000

The Four Seasons
1300 Lamar St
Houston Tx 77010
713.650.1300
Small Pets Allowed

Westin Oaks
5011 Westheimer Rd
Houston Tx 77056
713.960.8100
Small Pets Accepted

The Four Seasons
4150 N Macarthur Blvd
Irving Tx 75038
214.717.0700
Small Pets Allowed

La Mansion Del Rio Hotel
112 College St
San Antonio Tx 78205
210.225.2581

Plaza San Antonio Hotel
555 S Alamo St
San Antonio Tx 78205
210.229.1000
Small

UTAH

Blue Church Lodge
424 Park Ave
Park City Ut 84060
801.649.8009
Small Pets $10 Per Day

VERMONT

Topnotch At Stowe Resort
4000 Mountain Rd
Stowe Vt 05672
802.253.8585
Under 30 Lbs

VIRGINIA

The Ritz Carlton
1700 Tysons Blvd
Mc Lean Va 22102
703.506.4300
Small

WASHINGTON

Red Lion Inn
18740 Pacific Hwy S
Seatac Wa 98188
206.433.1881
Call For Fees & Restrictions

The Alexis Hotel
1007 1st Ave
Seattle Wa 98104
206.624.4844

The Four Seasons
411 University St
Seattle Wa 98101
206.621.1700
Small Pets Allowed

HOW TO USE THIS DIRECTORY

To help you find accommodations easily, we have arranged the listings alphabetically by geography. First, states are listed alphabetically. Then, within each state, towns are listed alphabetically. We've also included dictionary-like page headings to provide you with quick reference points as you flip through the directory.

If you cannot find an accommodation in a certain town, be sure to check nearby areas. To do this, refer to the **ZipIndex** that follows the listings. Look for zip codes that are sequentially similar to the area you wish to stay. This method works because towns with similar zip codes are usually located near each other.

When possible, we gathered information regarding each accommodation's **SPECIFIC** pet policy. Be reminded however that management and their policies change quite frequently. Notes regarding sizes allowed, deposits, fees and so forth are subject to change. And just because  an accommodation doesn't have any notes, it doesn't mean there aren't any restrictions. To get the current policy, **ALWAYS CALL AHEAD!**

Policies Subject to Change

We have tried to be as accurate as humanly possible while compiling this directory. While we did our best to verify each listing, it is still just a snapshot at publication date. Management changes, places get bought and sold, and state and local laws change. Thus, we can take no responsibility for information listed in this directory, nor do we endorse any organization, business, or facility. **YOU MUST ALWAYS CALL AHEAD!**

SPECIAL RESTRICTIONS AND POLICIES MAY APPLY

Some accommodations may have special restrictions not listed here. Examples of special restrictions include: pets stay in their crate/kennel while in the room, designated special sections of rooms where pets are permitted, or smoking rooms only. You may not be able to get that suite with your pet in tow. And, many properties limit the number of pet rooms available. ALWAYS CALL AHEAD!

Some accommodations may have policies such as dogs allowed, but no cats. Also, some places may ask you to keep your pet out of the sight of other guests and ask you to use a back entrance. *We must obey the rules management has set or we will have to travel without our pets!*

HELPFUL INFORMATION FOR TRAVEL WITH PETS

Throughout the directory, we provide reminders for safe and responsible pet travel. Please observe these few simple hints and you and your pet will be better travelers.

 Pet policies, space availability, and fees can change. You should always call to reserve a room and declare your pet.

  Your pet should be on leash or in crate and under control at all times. Don't let your pet harass other guests.

  Out of sight, out of mind. Keep your pet quiet and away from other guests. Don't parade through the lobby with your pet.

  Train your pet well. This will keep your pet from harming itself, other pets, or travelers.

 You don't want your pet to have fleas, nor do other guests or pet owners. Keep your pet flea-free.

 Pet policies, regulations, space availability, fees change. Be sure to ask when you call to reserve a room and when you arrive.

Alabama

• Andalusia •
Days Inn
1604 E Bypass
(36420) 334.427.0050
$6

• Anniston •
Days Inn ($$)
1 Recreational Dr
(36203) 205.835.0300

Econo Lodge ($$)
25 Elm St
(36203) 205.831.9480
owners enjoy pets

Holiday Inn
US 78 & 21
(36203) 205.831.3410

Ramada Inn
900 Hwy 21
(36203) 205.237.9777

• Athens •
Days Inn
Hwy 72
(35611) 205.233.7500
$10/pet dep

• Attalla •
Holiday Inn
801 Cleveland Ave
(35954) 205.538.7861

• Bessemer •
Days Inn
1121 - 9th Ave
(35023) 205.424.6078
$6

• Birmingham •
Best Western ($$)
2230 Civic Center Blvd
(35203) 205.328.6320

Bugetel Inn ($$)
513 Cahaba Park Cir
(35242) 205.995.9990

Crown Sterling
2300 Woodcrest Pl
(35209) 205.879.7400

Days Inn ($$)
1535 Montgomery Hwy
(35216) 205.822.6030
mgr preapproval reqd

Econo Lodge ($$)
103 Green Springs Hwy
(35209) 800.424.4777

Hampton Inn ($$$)
2731 Uw Hwy 280
(35223) 205.870.7822

Hampton Inn ($$)
1466 Montgomery Hwy
(35216) 205.822.2224

Howard Johnson ($)
275 Oxmoor Rd
(35209) 205.942.0919

Howard Johnson ($$)
1485 Montgomery Hwy
(35216) 205.823.4300
small pets only

La Quinta Inn ($$)
905 11th Ct
(35204) 205.324.4510
call re: fees

Microtel ($)
251 Summit Pkwy
(35209) 205.945.5550

Motel Birmingham ($)
7905 Crestwood Blvd
(35210) 205.956.4440

Mountain Brook Inn ($$$)
2800 Hwy 280
(35223) 205.870.3100

Parliament House ($$)
420 20th St
(35233) 205.322.7020

Red Roof Inn ($$)
151 Vulcan Rd
(35209) 205.942.9414
fees/limits may apply

Residence Inn ($$$)
3 Greenhill Pkwy
(35242) 205.991.8686
fee from $125 - $165

The Tutwiler ($$$$)
2021 Park Place
(35205) 205.322.2100

• Boaz •
Best Western ($$)
751 US 431
(35957) 205.593.8410
under 5 lbs

Boaz IMotel ($)
Box# 218 Hwy 431
(35957) 205.593.2874

Key West Inn ($$)
10535 Alabama Hwy
(35957) 205.593.0800

• Camden •
Bassmaster Motel
125 Broad St
(36726) 334.682.4254
$5/day

Days Inn ($$)
39 Camdel Bypass
(36726) 334.682.4555

• Cedar Bluff •

Jrs Marina
Country Rd 102
(35959) 205.779.6461

Riverside Motel ($)
RR 1 Box# 83H
(35959) 205.779.6117

• Childersburg •
Days Inn ($$)
33669 US Hwy 280
(35044) 205.378.6007

• Clanton •
Best Western ($$)
109 Bradberry Ln
(35045) 800.528.1234

Holiday Inn ($$)
2000 Holiday Inn Dr
(35045) 205.755.0510
mgr preapproval reqd

Key West Inn ($$)
2045 7th St
(35045) 205.755.8500

Rodeway Inn ($)
2301 7th St
(35046) 205.755.4049

Shoneys Inn ($$)
946 Lake Mitchell Rd
(35045) 205.280.0306
$10 deposit

• Collinsville •
Hojo Inn ($$)
Hwy 68
(35961) 205.524.2114

• Cullman •
Anderson Motel ($)
1834 2nd Ave NW
(35055) 205.734.0122

Best Western ($$)
1917 Commerce Ave NW
(35055) 205.737.5009

Days Inn ($)
1841 4th St SW
(35055) 205.739.3800
$3/pets

Friendly Village Motel
607 2nd Ave NW
(35055) 205.734.2770

Holiday Inn
I-65 Ex 304
(35055) 205.734.2691

Howard Johnson ($$)
I-65 & US 278
(35056) 205.739.4603

Ramada Inn ($$)
I-65 & Hwy 69
(35056) 205.737.7275

Super 8 ($$)
Hwy 157 & I-65 Ex 310
(35057) 205.734.8854
call re: fees

• Daleville •
Econo Lodge ($$)
444 N Daleville Ave
(36322) 334.598.6304

Greenhouse Inn ($)
501 Daleville Ave
(36322) 334.598.1475
$4/day

$=under $35 $$=$35-60 $$$=$60-100 $$$$=over $100

The Greenhouse ($)
761 S Daleville Ave
(36322) 334.598.1475

● Daphne ●
Eastern Shore Motel ($)
29070 Hwy 98
(36526) 334.626.6601
$6/day

Legacy Inn ($$)
70 Hwy 90
(36526) 334.626.3500

● Decatur ●
Days Inn ($$)
810- 6th Ave NE
(35601) 205.355.3520
$5/ under 10 lbs

Decatur Motel ($$)
3429 Hwy 31
(35603) 205.355.0190

Holiday Inn ($$)
1101 6th Ave NE
(35601) 205.355.3150
mgr preapproval reqd

Ramada Ltd ($$)
1317 Hwy 67
(35601) 205.353.0333

● Demopolis ●
Heritage Motel ($)
1324 Hwy 80
(36732) 334.289.1175

Riverview Inn ($)
Hwy 45
(36732) 334.289.0690

● Dothan ●
Comfort Inn ($$)
3595 Ross Clark Cir
(36303) 334.793.9090
mgr preapproval reqd

Days Inn ($$)
2841 Ross Clark Cir
(36301) 334.793.2550

Eastgate Inn ($)
1885 E Main St
(36301) 334.794.6643

Hampton Inn ($$)
3071 Ross Clark Cir
(36301) 334.671.3700

Holiday Inn ($$)
3053 Ross Clark Cir
(36301) 334.794.6601
mgr preapproval reqd

Holiday Inn ($$)
2195 Ross Clark Cir
(36301) 334.794.8711
mgr preapproval reqd

Motel 6 ($)
2907 Ross Clark Cir
(36301) 334.793.6013
1 small pet/room

Olympia Resort ($$)
Box# 6108
(36302) 334.677.3321

Ramada Inn ($$)
3011 Ross Clark Cir
(36301) 334.692.0031

Town Terrace Motel ($)
251 N Oates St
(36303) 334.792.1135

● Elba ●
Riviera Motel ($)
154 Yelverton Ave
(36323) 334.897.2204

● Enterprise ●
Comfort Inn ($$)
615 Hwy 84 Bypass
(36330) 334.395.2304
mgr preapproval reqd

Ramada Inn ($$)
630 Glover Ave
(36330) 334.347.6262

● Eufaula ●
Best Western ($)
1337 Hwy 431 S
(36027) 334.687.3900
small pets only

Days Inn ($$)
1521 Eufaula Ave
(36027) 334.687.1000

Holiday Inn ($$)
631 E Barbour St
(36027) 334.687.2021
mgr preapproval reqd

● Evergreen ●
Days Inn ($)
901 Liberty Hill Dr
(36401) 334.578.2100

● Fairhope ●
Barons Motel ($)
701 S Mobile St
(36532) 334.929.8000
$5 pets

Oakhaven Cottages ($$)
355 S Mobile St
(36532) 334.928.5431

● Fayette ●
Journeys End ($$)
2502 Temple Ave
(35555) 205.932.6727
small

● Florence ●
Best Western ($$)
504 S Court St
(35630) 205.766.2331

Ho Jo Inn
1241 Florence Blvd
(35630) 205.764.5421

Super 8
Hwy 72
(35631) 205.757.2167
$5

● Foley ●
Holiday Inn
2682 S McKenzie St
(36535) 334.943.9100

● Fort Payne ●
Adams Outdoors ($)
6102 Mitchell Rd NE
(35967) 205.845.2988
keep on deck or out

● Fultondale ●
Days Inn
616 Decatur Hwy
(35068) 205.849.0111
$5

Super 8 ($$)
624 Decatur Hwy
(35068) 205.841.2200
mgr preapproval reqd

● Gadsden ●
Broadway Inn ($)
2704 W Meighan Blvd
(35904) 205.543.3790

Days Inn ($$)
1600 Rainbow Dr
(35901) 205.543.1105
$10 fee

Friendly Village Inn ($)
2110 Rainbow Dr
(35901) 205.547.3041

Rodeway Inn ($)
2110 Rainbow Dr
(35901) 205.547.9053

Travel 8 Motel ($)
3909 W Meighan Blvd
(35904) 205.543.7261

● Gaylesville ●
The Lighthouse
Hwy 68 Box# 167
(35973) 205.779.8400

● Greenville ●
Best Western ($$)
106 Cahaba Rd
(36037) 334.382.9200

Econo Lodge ($$)
946 Fort Dale Rd
(36037) 334.382.3118
$2 per day

● Gulf Shores ●
Bon Secour Lodge
16730 Oyster Bay Pl
(36542) 334.968.7814
$6 pets

Gulf Pines Motel
245 E 22nd Ave
(36542) 334.968.7911
$6 pets

Ramada Ltd ($)
310 W Beach Blvd
(36542) 334.948.8141

Ward Rentals
1709 Gulf Shores Pkwy
(36542) 334.968.8423

Youngs ($)
401 E Beach Blvd
(36542) 334.948.4181

Well
Behaved

ALABAMA, Guntersville

● Guntersville ●
Days Inn ($$)
14040 Hwy 431
(35976) 205.582.3200
$10/pet deposit

Macs Motel ($$)
7001 Val Monte Dr
(35976) 205.582.1000

Overlook Mtn Lodge ($)
13045 Hwy 431
(35976) 205.582.3256

● Haleyville ●
Haleyville Motel ($)
RR 6 Box# 449
(35565) 205.486.2263
$2 pets

● Hamilton ●
Best Western ($$)
2031 Military St
(35570) 205.921.7831
under 30 lbs

Hamilton Motel ($)
Bexar Ave Hwy 78
(35570) 205.921.2171

● Hanceville ●
Motel I 65 ($)
14466 Hwy 91
(35077) 205.287.1114

● Heflin ●
Hojo Inn ($)
RR 2
(36264) 205.463.2900

● Hope Hull ●
Days Inn ($)
7725 Mobile Hwy
(36043) 800.329.7466
mgr preapproval reqd

● Huntsville ●
Budgetel ($$)
4890 University Dr NW
(35816) 205.830.8999

Carriage Inn ($)
3911 University Dr NW
(35816) 205.722.0880

Econo Lodge ($)
1304 N Memorial Pkwy
(35801) 800.424.4777

Hilton ($$$)
401 Williams Ave SW
(35801) 205.533.1400

Holiday Inn ($$)
3808 University Dr NW
(35806) 205.721.1000

Holiday Inn ($$)
3810 University Dr NW
(35816) 205.837.7171
mgr preapproval reqd

Howard Johnson ($)
4404 University Dr NW
(35816) 205.837.3250

La Quinta Inn ($$)
3141 University Dr NW
(35816) 205.533.0756
call re: fees

Motel 6 ($)
3200 University Dr NW
(35816) 205.539.8448
1 small pet/room

Radisson Inn ($$$)
6000 Memorial Pkwy SW
(35802) 205.882.9400
small pets allowed

Ramada Inn ($$)
3502 Memorial Pkwy SW
(35801) 205.881.6120
mgr preapproval reqd

Residence Inn ($$$)
4020 Independence Dr NW
(35816) 205.837.8907
$50 fee

Villager Lodge ($)
3100 University Dr NW
(35816) 205.533.0610

● Jasper ●
Travel Rite Inn ($)
200 Mallway Dr
(35501) 205.221.1161

● Linden ●
Country Inn
705 S Main St
(36748) 334.295.8704

Policies Subject to Change

● Loxley ●
Wind Chaser($$)
13156 N Hickory St
(36551) 334.964.4444
$6 pets

● Madison ●
Days Inn ($$)
102 Arlington Dr
(35758) 205.772.9550
$5 per day

Federal Motel ($$)
8781 Hwy 20
(35758) 205.772.8470

Motel 6 ($)
8995 Hwy 20
(35758) 205.772.7479
1 small pet/room

● Mobile ●
Adams Mark ($$$)
64 Water St
(36602) 334.43>.8400

Best Inns ($$)
156 S Beltline Hwy
(36608) 334.343.4911

Best Suites ($$$)
150 S Beltline Hwy
(36608) 334.343.4949

Best Western ($$)
2701 Battleship Pkwy
(36601) 334.432.2703
small or caged pets

Days Inn ($$)
5480 Inn Dr
(36619) 334.661.8181

Days Inn ($$)
3650 Airport Blvd
(36608) 334.344.3410
$10 per stay

Drury Inn ($$)
824 S Beltline Hwy
(36609) 334.344.7700

Econo Lodge ($$) 1 S
Beltline Hwy
(36606) 334.479.5333

Economy Inn ($)
1119 Government St
(36604) 334.433.8800

Fiesta Plaza Hotel ($$$)
4101 Airport Blvd
(36608) 334.476.6400

Holiday Inn ($$)
I-10 Tillmans Corner
(36619) 334.666.5600
mgr preapproval reqd

Holiday Inn ($$)
301 Government St
(36602) 334.694.0100
mgr preapproval reqd

Holiday Inn ($$)
850 S Beltline Hwy
(36609) 334.342.3220
mgr preapproval reqd

Howard Johnson ($$)
3132 Government Blvd
(36606) 334.471.2402

La Quinta Inn ($$)
816 S Beltline Hwy
(36609) 334.343.4051
call re: fees

Motel 6 ($)
5488 Inn Dr
(36619) 334.660.1483
1 small pet/room

Motel 6 ($$)
400 S Beltline Hwy
(36608) 334.343.8448
1 small pet/room

Motel 6 ($)
1520 Matzenger Dr
(36605) 334.473.1603
1 small pet/room

Motel 6 ($)
5470 Tillmans Corner Pkwy
(36619) 334.600.1483
1 small pet/room

Oak Tree Inn
255 Church St
(36602) 334.433.6923

Olssons Motel ($)
4137 Government Blvd
(36693) 334.661.5331

Ramada Inn ($$)
1525 Battleship Pkwy
(36630) 334.626.7200

$=under $35 $$=$35-60   **50** $$$=$60-100 $$$$=over $100

Red Roof Inn ($$)
5450 Coca Cola Rd
(36619) 334.666.1044
fees/limits may apply

Shoneys Inn ($$)
5472 Tilmans Cnr Pkwy
(36619) 334.660.1520

The Clarion Hotel ($$)
3101 Airport Blvd
(36606) 334.476.6400

● Monroeville ●
Holiday Inn
Hwy 21
(36460) (800)HOLIDAY

Knights Inn ($)
RR 3 Box# 227
(36460) 334.743.3154

● Montgomery ●
Best Suites ($$$)
5155 Carmichael Rd
(36106) 334.270.3223

Best Western ($$)
977 W South Blvd
(36105) 334.288.5740
small pets only

Best Western ($$)
5835 Monticello Dr
(36117) 334.288.0876
small pets only

Budgetel ($)
5225 Carmichael Rd
(36106) 334.277.6000

Capitol Inn ($)
205 N Goldthwaite St
(36104) 334.265.3844

Coliseum Inn ($)
1550 Federal Dr
(36107) 334.265.0586

Days Inn ($$)
2625 Zelda Rd
(36107) 334.269.9611
$8 fee

Days Inn
4180 Tryo Hwy
(36116) 334.284.9944
$5

Days Inn ($)
1150 W South Blvd
(36105) 334.281.8000
$2/small dogs only

Econo Lodge ($$)
4135 Troy Hwy
(36116) 334.284.3400

Embassy Suites ($$$)
300 Tallapoosa St
(36104) 334.269.5055

Holiday Inn ($$)
1100 W South Blvd
(36105) 334.281.1660
mgr preapproval reqd

Holiday Inn ($$$)
1185 Eastern Blvd
(36117) 334.272.0370
mgr preapproval reqd

Inn South Hotel ($)
4243 Inn South Ave
(36105) 334.288.7999

La Quinta Inn ($$)
1280 East Blvd
(36117) 334.271.1620
call re: fees

Motel 6 ($$)
1051 Eastern Blvd
(36117) 334.277.6748
1 small pet/room

Regency Inn ($$)
1771 Congressman
(36109) 334.260.0444

Residence Inn ($$$)
1200 Hilmar Ct
(36117) 334.270.3300

Statehouse Inn ($$)
924 Madison Ave
(36104) 334.265.0741

Villager Inn ($)
2750 Chestnut St
(36107) 334.834.4055

● Muscle Shoals ●
Days Inn
2700 Woodward
(35661) 205.383.3000

● Opelika ●
Best Western ($)
1002 Columbus Pkwy
(36801) 334.749.1461
pets 1 night

Days Inn ($$)
1014 Anand Ave
(36801) 334.749.5080
$5/pets

Motel 6 ($)
1015 Columbus Pkwy
(36804) 334.745.0988
1 small pet/room

● Orange Beach ●
Island Resort
Box# 9
(36561) 334.981.4255
small must reserve ahead

● Ozark ●
Best Western ($$)
Hwy 231
(36361) 334.774.5166
1 pet under 15 lb

Candlelight Motel ($)
2015 Hwy 231
(36360) 334.774.4947

Holiday Inn ($$)
151 US 231
(36360) 334.774.7300
mgr preapproval reqd

● Phenix City ●
Best Western ($$)
1600 Hwy E 280 Byp
(36867) 334.298.8000
small pets only

● Prattville ●
Days Inn ($$)
I-65 & Hwy 31
(36067) 334.365.3311

● Scottsboro ●
Days Inn ($$)
1106 John T Reid
(35768) 205.574.1212

Rainbow Inn ($)
1401 E Willow St
(35768) 205.574.1115

● Selma ●
Best Western ($$)
1915 W Highland Ave
(36701) 334.872.1900
small dogs only

Holiday Inn ($$)
1806 US 80W
(36701) 334.872.0461
mgr preapproval reqd

Passport Inn ($)
601 Highland Ave
(36701) 334.872.3451

Travelers Inn ($)
2006 W Highland Ave
(36701) 334.875.1200

● Sheffield ●
Holiday Inn
4900 Hatch Bl
(35660) 205.381.4710

Ramada Inn ($$)
4205 Hatch Blvd
(35660) 205.381.3743
mgr preapproval reqd

● Shorter ●
Days Inn ($$)
327 Shorter Depot Rd
(36075) 334.727.6034
small under 10 lbs

● Troy ●
Days Inn
1260 Hwy 231
(36081) 334.566.1630
$5

Econo Lodge ($$)
1013 Hwy 231
(36081) 334.566.4960

Econo Lodge ($)
1105 Columbus
(36081) 334.745.0988

Holiday Inn ($$)
Hwy 231
(36081) 334.670.0012

Scottish Inn ($)
186 Hwy 231
(36081) 334.566.4090

$=under $35 $$=$35-60 $$$=$60-100 $$$$=over $100

ALABAMA, Tuscaloosa

● Tuscaloosa ●
La Quinta Inn ($$)
4122 McFarland Blvd
(35405) 205.349.3270
call re: fees

Masters Economy Inn ($)
3600 McFarland Blvd
(35405) 205.556.2010

Motel 6 ($)
4700 McFarland Blvd
(35405) 205.759.4942
1 small pet/room

Ramada Inn ($$)
631 Skyland Blvd
(35405) 205.759.4431

● Wetumpka ●
Westumpka Inn ($)
8534 Hwy 231
(36092) 334.567.9316

● York ●
Days Inn ($$)
17700 Hwy 17
(36925) 205.392.9675

Alaska

● Anchorage ●
8th Avenue Hotel ($$$)
630 8th Ave
(99520) 907.274.6213

Anchorage Eagle Nest ($$)
4110 Spenard Rd
(99517) 907.243.3433

Arctic Inn Motel
842 W Intl Airport Rd
(99518) 907.561.1328

Best Western ($$$)
4616 Spenard Rd
(99517) 907.243.3131
pets mngrs discretion/$50
deposit

Big Timber Motel
2037 E 5th Ave
(99501) 907.272.2541

Black Angus Inn
1430 Gambell St
(99501) 907.272.7503

Bonanza Lodge
4455 Juneau St
(99503) 907.563.3590

Chelsea Inn ($$)
3836 Spenard Rd
(99517) 907.276.5002

Comfort Inn ($$$)
111 Ship Creek Ave
(99501) 907.277.6887
mgr preapproval reqd

Days Inn ($$)
321 E 5th Ave
(99501) 907.276.7226

Executive Suite ($$$)
4360 Spenard Rd
(99517) 907.243.6366

Hillside On Gambell ($$)
2150 Gambell St
(99503) 907.258.6006

Kenai Magic Lodge ($$$)
2440 E Tudor Rd # 205
(99507) 888.262.6644

Kenai Lodge ($$)
3074 Commercial Dr
(99501) 907.262.4390

Merrill Field Motel ($$)
420 Sitka St
(99501) 907.276.4547

Mush Inn Motel
333 Concrete St
(99501) 907.277.4554

Puffin Inn ($$)
4400 Spenard Rd
(99517) 907.243.4044

Regal Alaskan Hotel ($$$)
4800 Spenard Rd
(99517) 907.243.2300
$50 deposit

Sourdough Lodge ($$$)
801 E Erickson St
(99520) 907.279.4148

Spenard Motel
3960 Spenard Rd
(99517) 907.243.6917

Super 8 ($$$)
3501 Minnesota Dr
(99503) 907.276.8884
pets with deposit

● Cantwell ●
Reindeer Mtn Lodge
Mp 210 Park Hwy
(99729) 907.768.2420

● Cooper Landing ●
Sunrise Inn Motel ($$)
Sterling Hwy
(99572) 907.595.1222

● Delta Junction ●
Alaska 7 Motel
3548 Richardson Hwy
(99737) 907.895.4848

Black Spruce Lodge
2740 Old Richardson Hwy
(99737) 907.895.4668

Delta Int'L Hostel
Main St USA North
(99737) 907.895.5074

Summit Lake Lodge
Richardson Hwy
(99737) 907.822.3969

● Denali National Park ●
Denali Grizzly Bear Cabins
($$)
Box# 7
(99755) 907.683.2696

McKinley Denali Cabins
($$$)
Box# 90
(99755) 907.683.2733

Mt McKinley Motel ($$$)
Box# 118
(99755) 907.683.1240

Sourdough Cabins ($$$)
Box# 118
(99755) 907.683.2773

● Fairbanks ●
Alaska Motel ($$)
1546 S Cushman St
(99701) 907.456.6393
no pit bulls

Captain Bartlett Inn ($$$$)
1411 Airport Way
(99701) 907.452.1888

Chena Hot Springs Resort
($$$)
Box# 73440
(99707) 907.452.7867
$100 deposit

Gold Camp
5550 Old Steese Hwy
(99712) 907.389.2414

Regency Fairbanks ($$$)
95 10th Ave
(99701) 907.452.3200

Super 8 ($$$)
1909 Airport Way
(99701) 907.451.8888
pets with deposit

● Gakona ●
Gokona Junction Vlge ($$)
Box# 222
(99586) 800.962.1933

● Gustavus ●
Bear Track Inn
255 Rink Creek Rd
(99826) 907.697.3017

● Haines ●
Captains Choice Motel ($$)
Box# 250
(99827) 907.766.2891

Fort Seward Lodge ($$)
Box# 307
(99827) 907.766.2009

Mountain View Motel ($$)
Box# 62
(99827) 907.766.2900

Thunderbird Motel ($$)
242 Dalton St
(99827) 800.327.2556
small pets only

● Healy ●
Earthsong Lodge ($$$)
Box# 89
(99743) 907.683.2863

Be
Discreet

• Homer •
Best Western ($$$)
575 Sterling Hwy
(99603) 907.235.8148
mgr preapproval reqd

Driftwood Inn ($$)
135 W Bunnell Ave
(99603) 907.235.8019

Heritage Hotel Lodge ($$)
147 E Pioneer Ave
(99603) 907.235.7787

Lakewood Inn
984 Ocean Dr # 1
(99603) 907.235.6144

Lands End Resort ($$)
4786 Homer Spit Rd
(99603) 907.235.2500

Ocean Shores Motel ($$)
3500 Crittenden Dr
(99603) 800.770.7775
$5 fee

• Juneau •
Prospector Hotel ($$$)
375 Whittier St
(99801) 907.586.3737

Super 8 ($$$)
2295 Trout St
(99801) 907.789.4858
pets with deposit

The Driftwood Lodge ($$$)
435 Willoughby Ave
(99801) 907.586.2280

• Kenai •
Kenai Kings Inn ($$$)
Box# 1080
(99611) 907.283.6060

• Ketchikan •
Best Western ($$$)
3434 Tongass Ave
(99901) 907.225.5166
limited to pet rooms

Ingersoll Hotel ($$)
303 Mission St
(99901) 907.225.2124
$20 deposit

Super 8 ($$$)
2151 Sea Level Dr
(99901) 907.225.9058
call re: fees

The Gilmore Hotel ($$)
Box# 6814
(99901) 907.225.9423

• Kodiak •
Buskin River Inn ($$$)
1395 Airport Way
(99615) 907.487.2700

Kalsin Bay Inn
Box# 1696
(99615) 907.486.2659

• Petersburg •
Narrows Inn ($$$)
Box# 1048
(99833) 907.772.4284

Scandia House
110 Nordic Dr
(99833) 907.772.4281

• Seward •
Aroka Inn ($$)
Box# 2448
(99664) 907.224.8975

• Sitka •
Baranof Wilderness Lodge
($$$$)
Box# 2187
(99835) 916.582.8132

Super 8 ($$$)
404 Sawmill Creek Rd
(99835) 907.747.8804
pets with deposit

• Skagway •
Golden North Hotel ($$)
Box# 431
(99840) 907.983.2294

Wind Valley Lodge ($$$)
Box# 354
(99840) 907.983.2236

• Soldotna •
Best Western ($$$)
33546 Kenai Spur Hwy
(99669) 907.262.5857
pets @ mgrs discretion

Capt Blighs Lodge
Box# 4300
(99669) 907.262.7919

Kenai River Lodge ($$)
393 Riverside Dr
(99669) 907.262.4292
small pets only

Soaring Eagle Lodge ($$)
HC 1 Box# 1203
(99669) 907.337.1223

• Sterling •
Anglers Lodge ($$)
Box# 508
(99672) 907.262.1747

Morgans Landing Cabins
($$)
Box# 422
(99672) 907.262.8343

• Talkeetna •
Latitude 62 Lodge
Box# 478
(99676) 907.733.2262

• Tok •
Snowshoe Motel ($$)
Box# 559
(99780) 907.883.4511

Tok Lodge ($$$)
Box# 135
(99780) 907.883.2851

Youngs Motel ($$$)
Mile 1313 Alaska Hwy
(99780) 907.883.4411

Youngs Motel ($$)
Mile 1313 Alaska Hwy
(99780) 907.883.4411

• Valdez •
Tiekel River Lodge ($$)
Richardson Hwy Mile 56
(99686) 907.822.3259

Totem Inn ($$)
Box# 648
(99686) 907.835.4443

Arizona

• Ajo •
Siesta Motel ($)
2561 N Ajo Gila Bend Hwy
(85321) 520.387.6569

Marine Motel ($)
1966 N 2nd Ave
(85321) 520.387.7626

• Alpine •
Coronado Cabins ($$)
25302 Hwy 191
(85920) 520.339.4772

Talwi Lodge ($$)
40 County Rd 2220
(85920) 520.467.2511

• Benson •
Best Western ($$)
699 N Ocotillo Rd
(85602) 520.586.3646
mgr preapproval reqd

• Bisbee •
Travel Lodge ($)
901 Tombstone Cyn
(85603) 520.432.4636

Main Street Inn ($$)
26 Main St
(85603) 520.432.5237

San Jose Lodge ($)
1002 Naco Hwy
(85603) 520.432.5761

• Bullhead City •
Arizona Bluffs
2220 Karis Dr
(86442) 520.763.3839

Colorado River Resort ($)
434 River Glen Dr
(86429) 520.754.4101

Days Inn ($$)
2200 Karis Dr
(86442) 520.758.1711

Desert Rancho Motel ($)
1041 Hwy 95
(86430) 520.754.2578

La Plaza Inn ($)
1978 S Hwy 95
(86442) 520.763.8080

ARIZONA, Bullhead City

Lake Mohave Resort ($$)
At Katherine Landing
(86430) 520.754.3245

Motel 6 ($)
1616 S Hwy 95
(86442) 520.763.1002
1 small pet/room

River Queen Resort ($)
125 Long Ave
(86429) 520.754.3214

Sunridge Hotel ($$)
839 Landon Dr
(86429) 520.754.4700

Travelodge ($$)
2360 4th St
(86429) 520.754.3000

● Camp Verde ●
Best Western ($$)
Box# 3430 Middle Verde Rd
(86322) 520.567.6611
mgr preapproval reqd

Fort Verde Motel ($)
628 S Main St
(86322) 520.567.3486

● Casa Grande ●
Best Western ($$)
665 N Via Del Cielo Rd
(85222) 520.836.1600
mgr preapproval reqd

Francisco Grande ($$)
26000 W Gila Bend Hwy
(85222) 520.836.6444

Holiday Inn
777 N Pinal Ave
(85222) 520.426.3500

Motel 6 ($)
4965 N Sunland Gin Rd
(85222) 520.836.3323
1 small pet/room

Setay Motel ($)
901 N Pinal Ave
(85222) 520.836.7489

Sunland Inn ($)
7190 S Sunland Gin Rd
(85222) 520.836.5000

● Chandler ●
Aloha Motel ($$$)
445 N Arizona Ave
(85224) 602.963.3403

Super 8 ($$)
7171 W Chandler Blvd
(85226) 602.961.3888
pets w/permission

Wyndham Hotel ($$$)
7475 W Chandler Blvd
(85226) 602.961.4444

● Chinle ●
Holiday Inn
Indian Rt 7
(86503) 520.674.5000

● Cottonwood ●
Best Western ($$)
993 S Main St
(86326) 520.634.5576

Daisy Motel ($$)
34 S Main St
(86326) 520.634.7865

The View Motel ($)
818 S Main St
(86326) 520.634.7581

● Douglas ●
Motel 6 ($)
111 E 16th St
(85607) 520.364.2457
1 small pet/room

Price Canyon Ranch ($$$)
Box# 1065
(85608) 520.558.2383

Thriftlodge ($)
1030 E 19th St
(85607) 520.364.8434

● Eagar ●
Best Western ($$)
128 N Main
(85925) 520.333.2540
mgr preapproval reqd

● Flagstaff ●
Arizon Mt Inn ($$$)
685 Lake Mary Rd
(86001) 520.774.8959

Best Western ($$)
1560 Santa Fe
(86001) 520.774.7186
small pets welcome!

Comfort Inn ($$)
914 S Milton Rd
(86001) 520.774.7326
mgr preapproval reqd

Days Inn ($$)
1000 W Route 66
(86001) 520.774.5221

Days Inn ($$)
2735 Woodland Vlg Blvd
(86001) 520.779.1575
mgr preapproval reqd

Flagstaff Inn ($)
2285 E Butler Ave
(86004) 520.774.1821

Frontier Motel ($)
1700 E Route 66
(86004) 520.774.8993

Highland Country Inn ($$)
223 S Milton Rd
(86001) 520.774.5041

Holiday Inn ($$$)
2320 Lucky Ln
(86004) 520.526.1150
mgr preapproval reqd

Howard Johnson ($$)
2200 E Butler Ave
(86004) 520.779.6944

Innsuites ($)
1108 E Route 66
(86001) 520.774.7356

Knights Inn ($)
602 W Route 66
(86001) 520.774.4581

Master Host ($$)
2610 E Route 66
(86004) 520.526.1399

Motel 6 ($)
2440 E Lucky Ln
(86001) 520.774.8756
1 small pet/room

Motel 6 ($)
2745 Woodland Vlg Blvd
(86001) 520.779.3757
1 small pet/room

Motel 6 ($)
2010 E Butler Ave
(86004) 520.774.1801
1 small pet/room

Motel 6 ($)
2500 Lucky Ln
(86004) 520.779.6164
1 small pet/room

Pinecrest Motel ($)
2818 E Route 66
(86004) 520.526.1950

Ramada Ltd ($$)
2755 Woodland Vlg Blvd
(86001) 520.773.1111
mgr preapproval reqd

Relax Inn Motel ($)
1416 E Santa Fe
(86001) 520.774.5123

Residence Inn ($$$)
3440 N Country Club Dr
(86004) 520.526.5555
$10 per day

Rodeway Inn ($)
2650 E SHwy 66
(86004) 520.526.2200

Rodeway Inn ($)
2350 Lucky Ln
(86004) 520.779.3614

Royal Inn ($$)
2140 E Route 66
(86004) 520.774.7308

Ski Lift Lodge ($)
6355 Hwy 180
(86001) 520.774.0729

Super 8 ($$)
3725 N Kasper Ave
(86004) 520.526.0818
pets w/permission

Town House Motel ($)
122 W Route 66
(86001) 520.774.5081

Travelodge ($)
801 W Route 66
(86001) 520.774.3381

Travelodge ($$$)
2520 Lucky Ln
(86004) 520.779.5121

Western Hills Motel ($)
1580 E Route 66
(86001) 520.774.6633

● Gila Bend ●
Best Western ($$)
401 E Pima St
(85337) 520.683.2273

Yucca Motel ($)
836 E Pima St
(85337) 520.683.2211

● Glendale ●
Holiday Inn
7885 Arrowhead Townctr
(85308) 602.412.2000

● Globe ●
Cloud Motel ($$)
1649 E Ash St
(85501) 520.425.5741

Rey Motel ($)
1201 E Ash St
(85501) 520.425.4427

Holiday Inn
Hwy 60 & 70
(85502) 520.425.7008

● Goodyear ●
Best Western ($$)
1100 N Litchfield Rd
(85338) 602.932.3210
mgr preapproval reqd

Holiday Inn
1313 Litchfield Rd
(85338) 602.535.1313

Super 8 ($$)
1710 N Dysart Rd
(85338) 602.932.9622
w/permission

● Grand Canyon ●
Bright Angel Lodge ($$)
Box# 699
(86023) 520.638.6284

El Tovar Hotel ($$$$)
Box# 699
(86023) 520.638.6384

Kachina Lodge ($$$)
Box# 699
(86023) 520.628.4

Maswik Lodge ($$$)
Box# 699
(86023) 520.638.6784

Red Feather Lodge ($$)
Box# 1460
(86023) 520.638.2414

Thunderbird Lodge ($$$)
Box# 699
(86023) 520.638.2631
onsite kennels $5-8 must
reserve

Yavapai Lodge ($$$)
Box# 699
(86023) 520.638.7584

● Green Valley ●
Holiday Inn
19200 S I-19 Frontage
(85614) 520.625.0900

● Holbrook ●
Best Western ($$)
2508 Navajo Blvd
(86025) 520.524.2611
small dogs

Best Western ($$)
615 W Hopi Dr
(86025) 520.524.3948
small pets only

Budget Host ($)
235 W Hopi Dr
(86025) 520.524.3809
mgr preapproval reqd

Comfort Inn ($$)
2602 Navajo Blvd
(86025) 520.524.6131
mgr preapproval reqd

Econo Lodge ($$)
2596 Navajo Blvd
(86025) 520.524.1448

Holiday Inn ($$)
1308 Navajo Blvd
(86025) 520.524.1466
mgr preapproval reqd

Motel 6 ($)
2514 Navajo Blvd
(86025) 800.440.6000
1 small pet/room

Rainbow Inn ($)
2211 Navajo Blvd
(86025) 520.524.2654

Ramada Inn ($$)
2608 Navajo Blvd
(86025) 520.524.2566

Travelodge ($)
2418 Navajo Blvd
(86025) 520.524.6815

● Kingman ●
Best Western ($$)
2930 E Andy Devine Ave
(86401) 520.753.6101
mgrs discretion

Best Western ($$)
2815 E Andy Devine Ave
(86401) 520.753.6271
1 night & dep

Days Inn ($$)
3023 E Andy Devine Ave
(86401) 520.753.7500
$10 fee

High Desert Inn ($)
2803 E Andy Devine Ave
(86401) 520.753.2935

Hill Top Motel ($)
1901 E Andy Devine Ave
(86401) 520.753.2198

Holiday Inn ($$)
3100 E Andy Devine Ave
(86401) 520.753.6262
mgr preapproval reqd

Motel 6 ($$)
424 W Beale St
(86401) 520.753.9222
1 small pet/room

Motel 6 ($)
3270 E Andy Devine Ave
(86401) 520.757.7121
1 small pet/room

Motel 6 ($)
3351 W Andy Devine
(86401) 520.757.7151
1 small pet/room

Quality Inn ($$)
1400 E Andy Devine Ave
(86401) 520.753.4747
mgr preapproval reqd

Rodeway Inn ($)
411 W Beale St
(86401) 520.753.5521

Silver Queen Motel ($)
3285 E Andy Devine Ave
(86401) 520.757.4315

Super 8 ($)
3401 E Andy Devine Ave
(86401) 520.757.4808
small dogs w/permission

● Lake Havasu City ●
Best Western ($$)
31 Wings Loop
(86403) 520.855.2146
$5 - prior arrangement

Bridgeview Motel ($)
101 London Bridge Rd
(86403) 520.855.5559

Easy Eight Motel ($)
41 Acoma Blvd
(86403) 520.855.4023

Havasu All Suites ($)
2035 Acoma Blvd
(86403) 520.855.2311

Holiday Inn ($$)
245 London Bridge Rd
(86403) 520.855.4071
mgr preapproval reqd

Island Inn Hotel ($$$)
1300 W McCulloch Blvd
(86403) 520.680.0606
small lap pets

Lakeview Motel ($)
440 London Bridge Rd
(86403) 520.855.3605

CALL
AHEAD!

$=under $35 $$=$35-60 $$$=$60-100 $$$$=over $100

London Bridge ($$$)
1477 Queens Bay
(86403) 520.855.0888
small on 1st floor only

Pecos Condos ($$)
451 Lake Havasu
(86403) 520.855.1111

Sandman Inn ($)
1700 McCulloch Blvd
(86403) 520.855.7841

Super 8 ($$)
305 London Bridge Rd
(86403) 520.855.8844
mgr preapproval reqd

Windsor Inn ($)
451 London Bridge Rd
(86403) 520.855.4135

● Lakeside ●
Lake Of The Woods ($$)
2244 W White Mtn
(85929) 520.368.5353

Lazy Oaks Cottages ($$)
RR 2 Box# 1215
(85929) 520.368.6203

Moonridge Lodge ($)
Box# 1058
(85929) 520.367.1906

The Place Resort Cabins
($$$)
RR 3 Box# 2675
(85929) 520.368.6777

● Marble Canyon ●
Lees Ferry Lodge ($$)
HC 67 Box# 1
(86036) 520.355.2231

Marble Canyon Lodge ($$)
Box# 1 Hwy 89A
(86036) 520.355.2225

● Mesa ●
Arizona Golf Resort ($$$)
425 S Power Rd
(85206) 602.832.3202

Best Western ($)
1625 E Main St
(85203) 520.964.8000
1 small pet/$10 deposit

Best Western ($$)
1342 S Power Rd
(85206) 602.641.1164
mgr preapproval reqd

Hampton Inn ($$)
1563 S Gilbert Rd
(85204) 602.926.3600

Holiday Inn ($$)
1600 S Country Club Dr
(85210) 602.964.7000
mgr preapproval reqd

Maricopa Inn ($)
3 E Main St
(85201) 602.834.6060

Motel 6 ($)
630 W Main St
(85201) 602.969.8111
1 small pet/room

Motel 6 ($)
1511 S Country Club Dr
(85210) 602.834.0066
1 small pet/room

Motel 6 ($)
336 W Hampton Ave
(85210) 602.844.8899
1 small pet/room

Ramada Inn ($)
1410 S Country Club Dr
(85210) 602.964.2897

Red Rock Motel
2 Mi E On US 26
(85213) 307.455.2337

Rodeway Inn ($$)
5700 E Main St
(85205) 602.985.3600

Sandy Motel ($$)
6649 E Main St
(85205) 602.985.1912

Travelodge ($)
22 S Country Club Dr
(85210) 602.964.5694

● Miami ●
Best Western ($$)
RR 1 Box# 506
(85539) 520.425.7151
small pets/$5 charge

● Mount Lemmon ●
Summerhaven Suites ($$$$)
Box# 757
(85619) 520.576.1542

● Munds Park ●
Motel In The Pines ($)
Box# 18171
(86017) 520.286.9699

● Nogales ●
Americana Hotel ($$)
639 N Grand Ave
(85621) 520.287.7211

Best Western ($)
921 N Grand Ave
(85621) 520.287.4627
small pets only

Best Western ($$)
673 N Grand Ave
(85621) 520.287.4671
one small pet per room

Motel 6 ($)
141 W Mariposa Rd
(85621) 520.281.2951
1 small pet/room

● Page ●
Best Western ($)
207 N Lake Powell Blvd
(86040) 520.645.2451
deposit required

Econo Lodge ($)
121 S Lake Powell Blvd
(86040) 520.645.2488

Empire House ($$)
100 S Lake Powell Blvd
(86040) 520.645.2406

Holiday Inn ($$)
287 N Lake Powell Blvd
(86040) 520.645.8851
mgr preapproval reqd

Inn At Lake Powell ($)
716 Rim View Dr
(86040) 520.645.2466

Lake Powell Motel ($$)
Hwy 89
(86040) 520.645.2477

Wahweap Lodge ($$$)
100 Lake Shore Dr
(86040) 520.645.2433

● Paradise Valley ●
Marriotts Resort ($$$$)
5641 E Lincoln Dr
(85253) 602.948.7111
small pets only

Marriott Hotel ($$$$)
5402 E Lincoln Dr
(85253) 602.948.1700

Red Lion Inn ($$$)
4949 E Lincoln Dr
(85253) 602.952.0420
call re: fees

Residence Inn ($$$$)
6040 N Scottsdale Rd
(85253) 602.948.8666
$50 fee

Stouffer Renaissance ($$$$)
6160 N Scottsdale Rd
(85253) 602.991.1414
under 10 lbs

● Parker ●
Budget Inn ($)
912 Agency Rd
(85344) 520.669.2566

El Rancho Motel ($)
709 S California Ave
(85344) 520.669.2231

Havasu Springs Resort ($$$)
RR 2 Box# 624
(85344) 520.667.3361

Holiday Kasbah ($$)
604 S California Ave
(85344) 520.669.2133

Stardust Motel ($)
700 S California Ave
(85344) 520.669.2278

● Patagonia ●
Stage Stop Inn ($$)
Box# 777
(85624) 520.394.2211

● Payson ●
Christopher Creek Motel ($$)
Star Rt Box# 119
(85541) 520.478.4300

$=under $35 $$=$35-60   Well Behaved $$$=$60-100 $$$$=over $100

Grey Lodge ($$)
Star Rt Box# 145
(85541) 520.478.4392

Holiday Inn
206 S Beeline Hwy
(85547) 520.472.7484

Guest Ranch ($$)
E Hwy 260
(85541) 520.478.4211

Majestic Mt Inn ($$)
602 E Hwy 260
(85541) 520.474.0185

Pueblo Inn ($)
809 E Hwy 260
(85541) 520.474.5241

Swiss Village Lodge ($$)
801 N Beeline H Wy
(85541) 520.474.3241

Travelodge ($$)
101 W Phoenix St
(85541) 520.474.4526

● Phoenix ●
Best Western ($$)
17211 N Black Canyon Hwy
(85023) 602.993.8300
1 small dog w/ $10 fee

Best Western ($$)
2425 S 24th St
(85034) 602.273.7251
mgr preapproval reqd

Biltmore ($$$$)
24th St & Missouri
(85016) 602.955.6600

Days Inn ($$)
2420 W Thomas Rd
(85015) 602.257.0801

Days Inn ($$$)
3333 E Van Buren St
(85008) 602.244.8240

Easy Eight Motel ($)
1820 S 7th St
(85034) 602.254.9787

Econo Lodge ($)
3541 E Van Buren St
(85008) 602.273.7121

Embassy Suites ($$)
2333 E Thomas Rd
(85016) 602.957.1910
$3 fee

Embassy Suites ($$$)
3210 Grand Ave
(85017) 602.279.3211
$25 fee

Fountains Suite ($$$)
2577 W Greenway Rd
(85023) 602.375.1777

Hampton Inn ($$)
8101 N Black Canyon Hwy
(85021) 602.258.6271

Holiday Inn
4321 N Central Ave
(85012) 602.200.8888

Holiday Inn
2531 W Peoria
(85029) 602.943.2341

Holiday Inn
4300 E Washington
(85034) 602.273.7778

La Quinta Inn ($$)
2510 W Greenway Rd
(85023) 602.993.0800
call re: fees

Lexington Hotel ($$$)
100 W Clarendon Ave
(85013) 602.279.811

Olivos Hotel ($$)
202 E McDowell Rd
(85004) 602.258.6911

Motel 6 ($)
2323 E Van Buren St
(85006) 602.267.7511
1 small pet/room

Motel 6 ($)
5315 E Van Buren St
(85008) 602.267.8555
1 small pet/room

Motel 6 ($$)
2548 W Indian School Rd
(85017) 602.248.8881
1 small pet/room

Motel 6 ($)
4130 N Black Canyon Hwy
(85017) 602.277.5501
1 small pet/room

Motel 6 ($)
2330 W Bell Rd
(85023) 602.993.2353
1 small pet/room

Motel 6 ($)
2735 W Sweetwater Ave
(85029) 602.942.5030
1 small pet/room

Motel 6 ($$)
214 S 24th St
(85034) 602.244.1155
1 small pet/room

Motel 6 ($)
1530 N 52nd Dr
(85043) 602.272.0220
1 small pet/room

Motel 6 ($$)
8152 N Black Canyon Hwy
(85051) 602.995.7592
1 small pet/room

Phoenix Motel ($)
3644 E Van Buren St
(85008) 602.275.7661

Premier Inn ($$)
10402 N Black Canyon Hwy
(85051) 602.943.2371

Quality Hotel ($$)
3600 N 2nd Ave
(85013) 602.248.0222
mgr preapproval reqd

Quality Inn ($$)
5121 E La Puente Ave
(85044) 602.893.3900
mgr preapproval reqd

Radisson Inn ($$$$)
3333 E University Dr
(85034) 602.437.8400
small pets allowed

Ramada Inn ($$)
12027 N 28th Dr
(85029) 602.866.7000
mgr preapproval reqd

Residence Inn ($$$$)
8242 N Black Canyon Hwy
(85051) 602.864.1900
$75 fee

Ritz Carlton ($$$)
2401 E Camelback Rd
(85016) 602.468.0700

Royal Palms Inn ($$)
5200 E Camelback Rd
(85018) 602.840.3610

Sheraton Inn ($$$$)
2620 W Dunlap Ave
(85021) 602.943.8200

Travelodge ($$)
8617 N Black Canyon Hwy
(85021) 602.995.9500

Travelodge ($$)
3101 N 32nd St
(85018) 602.956.4900

Wyndham Hotel ($$)
10220 N Metro Pkwy
(85051) 602.997.5900

Wyndham Hotel ($$$)
2641 W Union Hills Dr
(85027) 602.978.2222

Phoenix Metro

● Casa Grande ●
Best Western ($$)
665 N Via Del Cielo Rd
(85222) 520.836.1600
mgr preapproval reqd

Francisco Grande ($$)
26000 W Gila Bend Hwy
(85222) 520.836.6444

Holiday Inn
777 N Pinal Ave
(85222) 520.426.3500

Motel 6 ($)
4965 N Sunland Gin Rd
(85222) 520.836.3323
1 small pet/room

Setay Motel ($)
901 N Pinal Ave
(85222) 520.836.7489

Policies Subject to Change

57

Sunland Inn ($)
7190 S Sunland Gin Rd
(85222) 520.836.5000

● Chandler ●
Aloha Motel ($$$)
445 N Arizona Ave
(85224) 602.963.3403

Super 8 ($$)
7171 W Chandler Blvd
(85226) 602.961.3888
pets with permission

Wyndham Hotel ($$$)
7475 W Chandler Blvd
(85226) 602.961.4444

● Goodyear ●
Best Western ($$)
1100 N Litchfield Rd
(85338) 602.932.3210
mgr preapproval reqd

Holiday Inn
1313 Litchfield Rd
(85338) 602.535.1313

Super 8 ($$)
1710 N Dysart Rd
(85338) 602.932.9622
w/permission

● Mesa ●
Arizona Golf Resort ($$$)
425 S Power Rd
(85206) 602.832.3202

Best Western ($)
1625 E Main St
(85203) 520.964.8000
1 small pet/$10 deposit

Best Western ($$)
1342 S Power Rd
(85206) 602.641.1164
mgr preapproval reqd

Hampton Inn ($$)
1563 S Gilbert Rd
(85204) 602.926.3600

Holiday Inn ($$)
1600 S Country Club Dr
(85210) 602.964.7000
mgr preapproval reqd

Maricopa Inn ($)
3 E Main St
(85201) 602.834.6060

Motel 6 ($)
630 W Main St
(85201) 602.969.8111
1 small pet/room

Motel 6 ($)
1511 S Country Club Dr
(85210) 602.834.0066
1 small pet/room

Motel 6 ($)
336 W Hampton Ave
(85210) 602.844.8899
1 small pet/room

Ramada Inn ($)
1410 S Country Club Dr
(85210) 602.964.2897

Red Rock Motel
2 Mi E On US 26
(85213) 307.455.2337

Rodeway Inn ($$)
5700 E Main St
(85205) 602.985.3600

Sandy Motel ($$)
6649 E Main St
(85205) 602.985.1912

Travelodge ($)
22 S Country Club Dr
(85210) 602.964.5694

● Paradise Valley ●
Marriott Hotel ($$$$)
5402 E Lincoln Dr
(85253) 602.948.1700

● Paradise Valley ●
Marriotts Resort ($$$$)
5641 E Lincoln Dr
(85253) 602.948.7111
small pets only

Red Lion Inn ($$$)
4949 E Lincoln Dr
(85253) 602.952.0420
call re: fees

Residence Inn ($$$$)
6040 N Scottsdale Rd
(85253) 602.948.8666
$50 fee

Stouffer Renaissance ($$$$)
6160 N Scottsdale Rd
(85253) 602.991.1414
under 10 lbs

● Phoenix ●
Best Western ($$)
17211 N Black Canyon Hwy
(85023) 602.993.8300
1 small dog w/ $10 fee

Best Western ($$)
2425 S 24th St
(85034) 602.273.7251
mgr preapproval reqd

Biltmore ($$$$)
24th St & Missouri
(85016) 602.955.6600

Days Inn ($$)
2420 W Thomas Rd
(85015) 602.257.0801

Days Inn ($$$)
3333 E Van Buren St
(85008) 602.244.8240

E Z 8 Motel ($)
1820 S 7th St
(85034) 602.254.9787

Econo Lodge ($)
3541 E Van Buren St
(85008) 602.273.7121

Embassy Suites ($$)
2333 E Thomas Rd
(85016) 602.957.1910
$3 fee

Embassy Suites ($$$)
3210 Grand Ave
(85017) 602.279.3211
$25 fee

Fountains Suite ($$$)
2577 W Greenway Rd
(85023) 602.375.1777

Hampton Inn ($$)
8101 N Black Canyon Hwy
(85021) 602.258.6271

Holiday Inn
4321 N Central Ave
(85012) 602.200.8888

Holiday Inn
2531 W Peoria
(85029) 602.943.2341

Holiday Inn
4300 E Washington
(85034) 602.273.7778

La Quinta Inn ($$)
2510 W Greenway Rd
(85023) 602.993.0800
call re: fees

Lexington Hotel ($$$)
100 W Clarendon Ave
(85013) 602.279.811

Los Olivos Exec Hotel ($$)
202 E McDowell Rd
(85004) 602.258.6911

Motel 6 ($)
2323 E Van Buren St
(85006) 602.267.7511
1 small pet/room

Motel 6 ($)
5315 E Van Buren St
(85008) 602.267.8555
1 small pet/room

Motel 6 ($$)
2548 W Indian School Rd
(85017) 602.248.8881
1 small pet/room

Motel 6 ($)
4130 N Black Canyon Hwy
(85017) 602.277.5501
1 small pet/room

Motel 6 ($$)
2330 W Bell Rd
(85023) 602.993.2353
1 small pet/room

Motel 6 ($$)
2735 W Sweetwater Ave
(85029) 602.942.5030
1 small pet/room

Motel 6 ($$)
214 S 24th St
(85034) 602.244.1155
1 small pet/room

Be
Discreet

Motel 6 ($$)
1530 N 52Nd Dr
(85043) 602.272.0220
1 small pet/room

Motel 6 ($$)
8152 N Black Canyon Hwy
(85051) 602.995.7592
1 small pet/room

Phoenix Sunrise Motel ($)
3644 E Van Buren St
(85008) 602.275.7661

Premier Inn ($$)
10402 N Black Canyon Hwy
(85051) 602.943.2371

Quality Hotel ($$)
3600 N 2Nd Ave
(85013) 602.248.0222
mgr preapproval reqd

Quality Inn ($$)
5121 E La Puente Ave
(85044) 602.893.3900
mgr preapproval reqd

Radisson Inn ($$$$)
3333 E University Dr
(85034) 602.437.8400
small pets allowed

Ramada Inn ($$)
12027 N 28th Dr
(85029) 602.866.7000
mgr preapproval reqd

Residence Inn ($$$$)
8242 N Black Canyon Hwy
(85051) 602.864.1900
$75 fee

Ritz Carlton ($$$)
2401 E Camelback Rd
(85016) 602.468.0700

Royal Palms Inn ($$)
5200 E Camelback Rd
(85018) 602.840.3610

Sheraton Inn ($$$$)
2620 W Dunlap Ave
(85021) 602.943.8200

Travelodge ($$)
8617 N Black Canyon Hwy
(85021) 602.995.9500

Travelodge ($$)
3101 N 32Nd St
(85018) 602.956.4900

Wyndham Hotel ($$)
10220 N Metro Pkwy
(85051) 602.997.5900

Wyndham Hotel ($$$)
2641 W Union Hills Dr
(85027) 602.978.2222

● Scottsdale ●
Adobe Hotel ($$)
3635 N 68th St
(85251) 602.945.3544
$100 dep

Days Inn ($$)
4710 N Scottsdale Rd
(85251) 602.947.5411
$10/pets

Embassy Suites ($$$$)
5001 N Scottsdale Rd
(85250) 602.948.2100

Holiday Inn ($$$)
7353 E Indian School Rd
(85251) 602.994.9203
mgr preapproval reqd

Hospitality Suites ($$)
409 N Scottsdale Rd
(85257) 602.949.5115

Howard Johnson ($$)
5101 N Scottsdale Rd
(85250) 602.945.4392
under 24 lbs

The Citadel Inn ($$$)
8700 E Pinnacle Peak Rd
(85255) 602.585.6133

Inn Suites ($$$)
7707 E McDowell Rd
(85257) 602.941.1202

Motel 6 ($$)
6848 E Camelback Rd
(85251) 602.946.2280
1 small pet/room

Park Inn Intl ($)
2934 N Scottsdale Rd
(85251) 602.947.5885

Ramada Inn ($$)
6850 E Main St
(85251) 602.945.6321
under 20 lbs

Safari Resort ($$)
4611 N Scottsdale Rd
(85251) 602.945.0721

Scottsdale Motel ($$)
7330 N Pima Rd
(85258) 602.948.3800

The Phoenician Resort
($$$$)
6000 E Camelback Rd
(85251) 602.941.8200
small dogs casita area

● Sun City ●
Best Western ($$)
11201 Grand Ave
(85373) 602.933.8211
designated pet rooms

● Surprise ●
Windmill Inn ($$)
12545 W Bell Rd
(85374) 602.583.0133

● Tempe ●
Country Suites ($$)
1660 W Elliot Rd
(85284) 602.345.8585

Embassy Suites ($$$)
4400 S Rural Rd
(85282) 602.897.7444

Fiesta Inn ($$)
2100 S Priest Dr
(85282) 602.967.1441

Holiday Inn
5300 S Priest
(85283) 602.820.7500

Holiday Inn ($$)
915 E Apache Blvd
(85281) 602.968.3451
mgr preapproval reqd

Innsuites ($$)
1651 W Baseline Rd
(85283) 602.897.7900

La Quinta Inn ($$)
911 S 48th St
(85281) 602.967.4465
call re: fees

Motel 6 ($$)
1612 N Scottsdale Rd
(85281) 602.945.9506
1 small pet/room

Motel 6 ($)
1720 S Priest Dr
(85281) 602.968.4401
1 small pet/room

Motel 6 ($)
513 W Broadway Rd
(85282) 602.967.8696
1 small pet/room

Paramount Hotel ($$)
225 E Apache Blvd
(85281) 602.967.9431

Ramada Inn ($$)
1635 N Scottsdale Rd
(85281) 602.947.3711
mgr preapproval reqd

Residence Inn ($$$$)
5075 S Priest Dr
(85282) 602.756.2122
$50fee & $6/day under 30 lbs

Rodeway Inn ($$)
1550 S 52nd St
(85281) 602.967.3000

Super 8 ($$$)
1020 E Apache Blvd
(85281) 602.967.8891
small pets with permission

Tempe Mission ($$$$)
60 E 5th St
(85281) 602.894.1400

The Buttes ($$$)
2000 W Westcourt Way
(85282) 602.225.9000

● Tolleson ●
Econo Lodge ($$)
1520 N 84th Dr
(85353) 602.936.4667

**End of Phoenix
Metro**

$=under $35 $$=$35-60 $$$=$60-100 $$$$=over $100

● Pinetop ●
Best Western ($$)
404 S White Mountain Blvd
(85935) 520.367.6667
mgr preapproval reqd

Buck Springs Resort ($$)
Box# 130
(85935) 520.369.3554

Double B Lodge ($)
Box# 747
(85935) 520. 36.7274

Econo Lodge ($$)
458 E White Mountain Blvd
(85935) 520.367.3636

Meadow View Lodge ($$)
Box# 325
(85935) 520.367.4642

Mountain Hacienda ($)
Box# 713
(85935) 520.367.4146

Northwoods Resort ($$$)
165 E White Mountain Blvd
(85935) 520.367.2966

● Prescott ●
Antelope Suites ($$)
6000 Willow Creek Rd
(86301) 520.778.6000

Antelope Resort
6200 N Hwy 89
(86301) 520.776.2600

Apache Motel ($$)
1130 E Gurley St
(86301) 520.445.1422

Best Western ($$)
1317 E Gurley St
(86301) 520.445.3096
mgr preapproval reqd

Cascade Motel ($)
805 White Spar Rd
(86303) 520.445.1232

Forest Hotel ($$$)
3645 Lee Cir
(86301) 520.445.9091

Heritage House ($$)
819 E Gurley St
(86301) 520.717.1200

High Resort ($)
1001 White Spar Rd
(86303) 520.445.0588

Lynn Creek Farm ($$$)
Box# 4301 S Hwy 69
(86302) 520.778.9573

Motel 6 ($$)
1111 E Sheldon St
(86301) 520.776.0160
1 small pet/room

Nine Pines Cottage ($$)
Box# 2099
(86302) 520.778.3620

Pine View Motel ($)
500 Copper Basin Rd
(86303) 520.445.4660

Prescott Sierra Inn ($)
809 White Spar Rd
(86303) 520.445.1250

Senator Inn ($)
117 E Gurley St
(86301) 520.445.1440

Skyline Motel ($)
523 E Gurley St
(86301) 520.445.9963

Super 8 ($$)
1105 E Sheldon St
(86301) 520.776.1282
call re: fees

● Prescott Valley ●
Days Inn ($$)
7875 E Hwy 69
(86314) 520.772.8600

Prescott Vly Motel ($)
8350 East Hwy 69
(86314) 520.772.9412

● Rio Rico ●
Rio Rico Resort ($$$)
1069 Camino Caralampi
(85648) 520.281.1901

● Safford ●
Best Western ($$)
1391 W Thatcher Blvd
(85546) 520.428.0521
1 small trained pet

Comfort Inn ($$)
1578 W Thatcher Blvd
(85546) 520.428.5851
mgr preapproval reqd

Ramada Inn ($$)
420 E Hwy 70
(85546) 800.272.6232

Sandia Motel ($$)
520 E Hwy 70
(85546) 520.428.5000

● Saint Johns ●
Days Inn ($)
185 E Commercial St
(85936) 520.337.4422

Super 8 ($)
75 E Commercial St
(85936) 520.337.2990
call re: fees

● Scottsdale ●
Adobe Hotel ($$)
3635 N 68th St
(85251) 602.945.3544
$100 dep

Days Inn ($$)
4710 N Scottsdale Rd
(85251) 602.947.5411
$10/pets

Embassy Suites ($$$$)
5001 N Scottsdale Rd
(85250) 602.948.2100

Holiday Inn ($$$)
7353 E Indian School Rd
(85251) 602.994.9203
mgr preapproval reqd

Hospitality Suites ($$)
409 N Scottsdale Rd
(85257) 602.949.5115

Howard Johnson ($$)
5101 N Scottsdale Rd
(85250) 602.945.4392
under 24 lbs

Inn At The Citadel ($$$)
8700 E Pinnacle Peak Rd
(85255) 602.585.6133

Inn Suites ($$$)
7707 E McDowell Rd
(85257) 602.941.1202

Motel 6 ($$)
6848 E Camelback Rd
(85251) 602.946.2280
1 small pet/room

Park Inn Intl ($)
2934 N Scottsdale Rd
(85251) 602.947.5885

Ramada Inn ($$)
6850 E Main St
(85251) 602.945.6321
under 20 lbs

Safari Resort ($$)
4611 N Scottsdale Rd
(85251) 602.945.0721

Scottsdale Motel ($$)
7330 N Pima Rd
(85258) 602.948.3800

The Phoenician Resort
($$$$)
6000 E Camelback Rd
(85251) 602.941.8200
small dogs casita area

● Sedona ●
Best Western ($$$)
1200 W Hwy 89A
(86336) 520.282.3072
under 25 lbs & $10 fee

Canyon Mesa Ctry Club
($$$$)
500 Jacks Canyon Rd
(86351) 520.284.2176

Desert Inn ($$)
666 Hwy 179
(86336) 520.284.1433

Forest Resort ($$$)
HC 30 Box# 250
(86336) 520.282.2999

Holiday Inn
6175 Hwy 179
(86351) 520.284.0711

Lo Lo Mai Springs ($$)
Page Springs Rd
(86340) 520.634.4700

Matterhorn Motel ($$)
230 Apple Ave
(86336) 520.282.7176

Well
Behaved

New Earth Lodge ($$$)
665 S Sunset Dr
(86336) 520.282.2644

Oak Creek Resort ($$$)
Star Rt 3 Box# 110
(86336) 520.282.3562

Quail Ridge Resort ($$$)
120 Canyon Circle Dr
(86351) 520.284.9327

Quality Inn ($$$)
771 S Hwy 179
(86336) 520.282.7151
mgr preapproval reqd

Railroad Inn ($$)
2545 W Hwy 89A
(86336) 520.282.1533
under 30 lbs

Sky Ranch Motel ($$)
Hwy 89A (Airport Rd)
(86336) 520.282.6400

Sugar Loaf Lodge ($$)
1870 W Hwy 89A
(86336) 520.282.9451

White House Inn ($)
2986 W Hwy 89A
(86336) 520.282.6680

● Seligman ●
Cyn Shadows Motel ($)
114 E Chino
(86337) 520.422.3255

Supai Motel ($)
134 W Chino
(86337) 520.422.3663

● Show Low ●
Days Inn ($$)
480 W Deuce Of Clubs
(85901) 520.537.4356

Kiwa Motel ($)
261 E Deuce Of Clubs
(85901) 520.537.4542

Snowy River Motel ($)
13640 Deuce Of Clubs
(85901) 520.537.2926

Super 8 ($$)
19410 Deuce Of Clubs
(85901) 520.537.7694
mgr preapproval reqd

● Sierra Vista ●
Motel 6 ($)
1551 E Fry Blvd
(85635) 520.457.5035
1 small pet/room

Sierra Suites ($$)
391 E Fry Blvd
(85635) 520.459.4221

Sun Canyon Inn ($$)
260 N Garden Ave
(85635) 520.459.0610

Super 8 ($$)
100 Fab Ave
(85635) 520.459.5380
call re: fees

Thunder Mt Inn ($$)
1631 S Hwy 92
(85635) 520.458.7900

Vista Inn ($)
201 W Fry Blvd
(85635) 520.458.6711

Wyndmere Hotel ($$$)
2047 S Hwy 92
(85635) 520.459.5900

● Springerville ●
El Jo Motor Inn ($)
425 E Main St
(85938) 520.333.4314

Reeds Motor Lodge ($)
514 E Main St
(85938) 520.333.4323

● Strawberry ●
The Strawberry Lodge ($$)
HC 1 Box# 331
(85544) 520.476.3333

● Sun City ●
Best Western ($$)
11201 Grand Ave
(85373) 602.933.8211
designated pet rooms

● Surprise ●
Windmill Inn ($$)
12545 W Bell Rd
(85374) 602.583.0133

● Taylor ●
Whiting Motor Inn ($$)
825 North Hwy 77
(85939) 520.536.2600

● Tempe ●
Country Suites ($$)
1660 W Elliot Rd
(85284) 602.345.8585

Embassy Suites ($$$)
4400 S Rural Rd
(85282) 602.897.7444

Fiesta Inn ($$)
2100 S Priest Dr
(85282) 602.967.1441

Holiday Inn
5300 S Priest
(85283) 602.820.7500

Holiday Inn ($$)
915 E Apache Blvd
(85281) 602.968.3451
mgr preapproval reqd

Innsuites ($$)
1651 W Baseline Rd
(85283) 602.897.7900

La Quinta Inn ($$)
911 S 48th St
(85281) 602.967.4465
call re: fees

Motel 6 ($$)
1612 N Scottsdale Rd
(85281) 602.945.9506
1 small pet/room

Motel 6 ($)
1720 S Priest Dr
(85281) 602.968.4401
1 small pet/room

Motel 6 ($)
513 W Broadway Rd
(85282) 602.967.8696
1 small pet/room

Paramount Hotel ($$)
225 E Apache Blvd
(85281) 602.967.9431

Ramada Inn ($$)
1635 N Scottsdale Rd
(85281) 602.947.3711
mgr preapproval reqd

Residence Inn ($$$$)
5075 S Priest Dr
(85282) 602.756.2122
$50 fee & $6/day under 30 lbs

Rodeway Inn ($$)
1550 S 52nd St
(85281) 602.967.3000

Super 8 ($$$)
1020 E Apache Blvd
(85281) 602.967.8891
small pets w/permission

Tempe Mission Palms ($$$$)
60 E 5th St
(85281) 602.894.1400

The Buttes ($$$)
2000 W Westcourt Way
(85282) 602.225.9000

● Tolleson ●
Econo Lodge ($$)
1520 N 84th Dr
(85353) 602.936.4667

● Tombstone ●
Best Western ($$)
Hwy 8
(85638) 520.457.2223
2 pet rooms $5 & $100 dep

● Tuba City ●
Tuba City Motel ($$$)
Box# 247
(86045) 520.283.4545

● Tubac ●
Tubac Golf Resort ($$$)
1 Otero Rd
(85646) 520.398.2211

● Tucson ●
Best Western ($$)
6201 N Oracle Rd
(85704) 520.297.8111
mgr preapproval reqd

Best Western ($$)
333 W Drachman St
(85705) 520.791.7551
mgr preapproval reqd

Be Discreet

$=under $35 $$=$35-60   **61** $$$=$60-100 $$$$=over $100

ARIZONA, Tucson

Best Western ($$)
801 W Miracle Mile
(85705) 520.791.7565

Best Western ($$)
7007 E Tanque Verde Rd
(85715) 520.298.2300
mgr preapproval reqd

Candlelights Suites ($$)
1440 S Craycroft Rd
(85711) 520.747.1440

Chateau Sonata ($$)
550 S Camino Seco
(85710) 520.886.2468

Clarion Hotel ($$)
6801 S Tucson Blvd
(85706) 520.746.3932
mgr preapproval reqd

Country Suites ($$)
7411 N Oracle Rd
(85704) 520.575.9255

Doubletree ($$$)
445 S Alvernon Way
(85711) 520.881.4200

Econo Lodge ($)
3020 S 6th Ave
(85713) 520.623.5881

Embassy Suites ($$$)
7051 S Tucson Blvd
(85706) 520.573.0700

Embassy Suites ($$$)
5335 E Broadway Blvd
(85711) 520.745.2700

Flying V Ranch ($$)
6800 N Flying V Ranch Rd
(85750) 520.299.4372

Franciscan Inn ($)
1165 N Stone Ave
(85705) 520.622.7763

Hampton Inn ($$)
1365 W Grant Rd
(85745) 800.426.7866

Hampton Inn ($$)
6971 S Tucson Blvd
(85706) 520.889.5789
small pets only

Holiday Inn ($$)
181 W Broadway Blvd
(85701) 520.624.8711
mgr preapproval reqd

La Quinta Inn ($$)
6404 E Broadway Blvd
(85710) 520.747.1414
call re: fees

La Quinta Inn ($$)
665 N Freeway Rd
(85745) 520.622.6491
call re: fees

Motel 6 ($)
4950 S Outlet Center Dr
(85706) 520.746.0030
1 small pet/room

Motel 6 ($)
755 E Benson Hwy
(85713) 520.622.4614
1 small pet/room

Motel 6 ($)
1222 S Freeway St
(85713) 520.624.2516
1 small pet/room

Motel 6 ($)
1031 E Benson Hwy
(85713) 520.628.1264
1 small pet/room

Motel 6 ($$)
4630 W Ina Rd
(85741) 520.744.9300
1 small pet/room

Motel 6 ($)
960 S Freeway Rd
(85745) 520.628.1339
1 small pet/room

Pueblo Inn ($$$)
350 S Freeway Rd
(85745) 520.622.6611

Radisson Inn ($$)
6555 E Speedway Blvd
(85710) 520.721.7100
smalls pets allowed

Ramada Inn ($$)
6944 E Tanque Verde Rd
(85715) 520.886.9595

Ramada Inn ($$$)
5251 S Julian Dr
(85706) 520.294.5250
mgr preapproval reqd

Red Roof Inn ($$$)
3700 E Irvington Rd
(85714) 520.571.1400
only 1 pet room $5 fee

Residence Inn ($$$)
6477 E Speedway Blvd
(85710) 520.721.0991
call for fee & availability

Rodeway Inn ($$)
810 E Benson Hwy
(85713) 520.884.5800

Rodeway Inn ($$)
1365 W Grant Rd
(85745) 520.622.7791

Sheraton Inn ($$$$)
10000 N Oracle Rd
(85737) 520.544.5000

Smugglers Inn Hotel ($$)
6350 E Speedway Blvd
(85710) 520.296.3293

The Lodge On The Desert
($$)
306 N Alvernon Way
(85711) 520.325.3366

Travelodge ($$)
401 W Lavery Ln
(85704) 520.797.1710

Travelodge ($$)
1300 N Stone Ave
(85705) 520.770.1910

Hilton ($$)
7600 E Broadway Blvd
(85710) 520.721.5600

University Inn ($)
950 N Stone Ave
(85705) 520.791.7503

Wayward Winds Lodge ($$)
707 W Miracle Mile
(85705) 520.791.7526

Westward Look Resort ($$$)
245 E Ina Rd
(85704) 520.297.1151

Windmill Inn ($$)
4250 N Campbell Ave
(85718) 520.577.0007

● Wickenburg ●
Best Western ($$)
293 E Wickenburg Way
(85390) 520.684.5445

Super 8
1021 Tegner
(85390) 800.800.8000

Westerner Motel ($)
680 W Wickenburg Way
(85390) 520.684.2493

● Willcox ●
Best Western ($$)
1100 W Rex Allen Dr
(85643) 520.384.3556
small pets only

Days Inn ($)
724 N Bisbee Ave
(85643) 520.384.4222
smoking room only

Motel 6 ($)
921 N Bisbee Ave
(85643) 520.384.2201
1 small pet/room

Royal Western Lodge ($)
590 S Haskell Ave
(85643) 520.384.2266

● Williams ●
Arizona Motel
831 W Route 66
(86046) 520.635.4552

Big Six Motel ($)
134 E Route 66
(86046) 520.635.4591

Budget Host ($)
620 W Route 66
(86046) 520.635.4415
small pets only

Canyon Motel ($)
Old E Hwy 66
(86046) 520.635.9371

Family Inn ($)
200 E Route 66
(86046) 520.635.2562

Policies Subject to Change

$=under $35 $$=$35-60 $$$=$60-100 $$$$=over $100

Gateway Motel ($)
219 E Route 66
(86046) 520.635.4601

Grand Motel ($)
234 E Route 66
(86046) 520.635.4601

Highlander Motel ($)
533 W Route 66
(86046) 520.635.2541

Holiday Inn
950 N Grand Canyon Blvd
(86046) 520.635.4114

Howard Johnson ($$)
511 Grand Canyon Rd
(86046) 520.635.9561

Park Inn Intl ($)
710 W Route 66
(86046) 520.635.4464

Quality Inn ($$$)
RR 1 Box# 35
(86046) 520.635.2693
mgr preapproval reqd

Ramada Inn ($$)
642 E Route 66
(86046) 520.635.4431
limited number of rooms

Super 8
2001 B Williams Ave
(86046) 520.635.4700
with permission

Travelodge ($)
430 E Route 66
(86046) 520.635.2651
very small w/permission&$20
dep

Westerner Motel ($$$)
530 W Route 66
(86046) 520.635.4312

● Window Rock ●
Navajo Nation Inn ($$)
48 W Hwy 264
(86515) 520.871.4108

● Winslow ●
Best Western ($$)
1914 W 3rd St
(86047) 520.289.4611

Best Western ($$)
1701 N Park Dr
(86047) 520.289.4638
1 pet room

Comfort Inn ($$)
520 W Desmond St
(86047) 520.289.9581
mgr preapproval reqd

Econo Lodge ($$)
1706 N Park Dr
(86047) 520.289.4687

Super 8 ($$)
1916 W 3rd St
(86047) 520.289.4606
pets w/permission

● Youngtown ●
Motel 6 ($$)
11133 Grand Ave
(85363) 602.977.1318
1 small pet/room

● Yuma ●
Best Western ($$)
300 E 32nd St
(85364) 520.344.1050
pets @ mgrs discretion

Best Western ($)
233 S 4th Ave
(85364) 520.783.4453
mgr preapproval reqd

Best Western ($$)
1450 S Castle Dome Ave
(85365) 520.783.8341

Caravan Motel ($)
10574 S Fortuna Rd
(85367) 520.342.1292

Holiday Inn ($$)
3181 S 4th Ave
(85364) 520.344.1402
mgr preapproval reqd

Interstate 8 Inn ($)
2730 S 4th Ave
(85364) 520.726.6110

Motel 6 ($)
1640 S Arizona Ave
(85364) 520.782.6561
1 small pet/room

Motel 6 ($)
1445 E 16th St
(85365) 520.782.9521
1 small pet/room

Park Inn Intl ($$$)
2600 S 4th Ave
(85364) 520.726.4830

Royal Motor Inn ($$)
2941 S 4th Ave
(85364) 520.344.0550

Shilo Inn ($$$)
1550 S Castle Dome Ave
(85365) 520.782.9511
call re: fees

Travelodge ($$)
711 E 32nd St
(85365) 520.726.4721

Yuma Cabana Motel ($)
2151 S 4th Ave
(85364) 520.783.8311

Arkansas

● Alma ●
Days Inn
250 Hwy 71
(72921) 501.632.4595
$5

● Arkadelphia ●
Best Western ($$)
I-30 Ex 78
(71923) 501.246.5592
mgr preapproval reqd

College Inn
1015 Pine St
(71923) 501.246.2404

Days Inn ($$)
137 Valley St
(71923) 501.246.3031

Econo Lodge ($$)
106 Crystal Palace Dr
(71923) 501.246.8026

Holiday Inn ($$$)
150 Valley
(71923) (800)HOLIDAY

Quality Inn ($$)
I-30 & Hwy 7
(71923) 501.246.5855
mgr preapproval reqd

● Ashdown ●
Budget Inn
Hwy 71
(71822) 501.898.3357

● Batesville ●
Economy Inn
Hwy 233
(72501) 501.793.3871

Ramada Inn ($$)
1325 N Saint Louis St
(72501) 501.698.1800

● Beebe ●
Adams Motel
2110 Devil Hive
(72012) 501.882.6473

● Benton ●
Best Western ($)
17036 I-30
(72015) 501.778.9695
small pets only

Capri Motel
15631 I-30
(72015) 501.778.8216

Days Inn ($$)
17701 I-30
(72015) 501.776.3200

Econo Lodge ($)
1221 Hot Springs Hwy
(72015) 501.776.1515

Troutt Motel ($)
15348 I-30
(72015) 501.778.3633

● Bentonville ●
Best Western ($$)
2307 SE Walton Blvd
(72712) 501.273.9727
mgr preapproval reqd

Hartland Motel
1002 S Walton Blvd
(72712) 501.273.3444

$=under $35 $$=$35-60 $$$=$60-100 $$$$=over $100

ARKANSAS, Bismarck

● Bismarck ●
Lakeview Cottages
RR 3 Box# 450
(71929) 501.865.3389

Morris Cottages
RR 3
(71929) 501.865.4872

● Blytheville ●
Best Budget Inn
357 S Division St
(72315) 501.763.4588

Comfort Inn ($$)
1520 E Main
(72316) 501.763.7081
mgr preapproval reqd

Days Inn
Hwy 18 E
(72315) 501.763.1241
$4

Days Inn ($$)
I-55
(72316) 501.763.1241
$4

Delta K Motel ($)
Box# 1472
(72316) 501.763.1410

Drury Inn ($$)
201 N I-55
(72315) 501.763.2300

Holiday Inn ($$)
Hwy 18
(72316) 501.763.5800
mgr preapproval reqd

● Boles ●
Mountain Inn
HC 69 Box# 199
(72926) 501.577.2211

● Brinkley ●
Best Western ($$)
1306 Hwy 17
(72021) 501.734.1650
small pets only

Brinkley Inn
1124 S Main St
(72021) 501.734.3141

Days Inn
I-40 & SHwy 49
(72021) 501.734.1052

Econo Lodge ($$)
I-40 & Hwy 49 NE
(72021) 501.734.2035

Heritage Inn ($)
1507 Hwy 17
(72021) 501.734.2121

Super 8 ($$)
I-40 & Hwy 49
(72021) 501.734.4680
w/permission

● Bull Shoals ●
Dogwood Lodge
Shorecrest Dr
(72619) 501.445.4311

Driftwood Resort
Box# 75
(72619) 501.445.4455

Mar Mar Resort
Shorecrest Dr & Hwy 178
(72619) 501.445.4444

White River Landng
Box# 748
(72619) 501.445.4166

● Cabot ●
Days Inn ($$)
1114 W Main St
(72023) 501.843.0145
$10/pets

● Caddo Gap ●
Arrowhead Cabins
HC 65 Box# 2
(71935) 501.356.2944

● Calico Rock ●
Forest Lodge
HC 61 Box# 72
(72519) 501.297.8211

Jenkins Motel
605 Hwy 56
(72519) 501.297.8987

Wiseman Motel
Box# 546
(72519) 501.297.3733

● Camden ●
Airport Inn
2115 Hwy 79
(71701) 501.574.0400

American Family Inn
Hwy 7 S & Goodgame
(71701) 501.231.6661

● Carlisle ●
Best Western ($$)
I-40 & Hwy 13
(72024) 501.552.7566
small pets

● Clarkridge ●
Treasure Cove Resort
902 County Road 470
(72623) 501.425.4325

● Clarksville ●
Best Western ($$)
I-40
(72830) 501.754.7900
small attended pets

Comfort Inn
1167 S Rogers Ave
(72830) 501.754.3000
mgr preapproval reqd

Days Inn ($)
2600 W Main St
(72830) 501.754.8555

Taylor Motel
Hwy 64
(72830) 501.754.2106

● Clinton ●
Best Western ($)
Hwy 65
(72031) 501.745.4700
mgr preapproval reqd

Super 8 ($$)
Hwy 65
(72031) 501.754.8800
$5

● Conway ●
Best Western ($)
I-40
(72033) 501.329.9855
mgr preapproval reqd

Comfort Inn ($$)
150 Hwy 65
(72032) 501.329.0300
mgr preapproval reqd

Continental Motel
134 Harkrider St
(72032) 501.327.7736

Days Inn
1002 E Oaks St
(72032) 501.450.7575
mgr preapproval reqd

Economy Inn ($)
Box# 606
(72033) 501.327.4800

Holiday Inn
Hwy 65 & I 40
(72033) 501.329.2961

Motel 6 ($)
1105 Hwy 65
(72032) 501.327.6623
1 small pet/room

Ramada Inn ($$)
815 E Oak St
(72032) 501.329.8392

● Cotter ●
Chamberlains
Denton Ferry Rd # 620
(72626) 501.435.6535

Rainbow Resort
Rt 1 Box# 1185
(72626) 501.430.5217

White Sands Motel
Box# 216
(72626) 501.435.2244

● Crossett ●
The Ashley Inn
Hwy 72
(71635) 501.364.4911

● De Queen ●
Scottish Inn ($)
1314 US Hwy 71
(71832) 501.642.2721

● De Witt ●
Sahara Motel
Box# 309
(72042) 501.946.3581

Well
Behaved

64

• Deer •
The Piney Inn
Box# 10
(72628) 501.428.5878

• Dermott •
Economy Inn
Rt 1 Box# 60 Hwy 65
(71638) 501.222.4017

• Dogpatch •
Erbys Lodge ($$$)
HC 73 Box# 145
(72648) 501.446.5851

• Dover •
Pines
22816 SHwy 7
(72837) 501.331.3261

• Drasco •
Tannebaum Resort
1329 Tannebaum
(72530) 501.362.3075

• Dumas •
Executive Inn
310 Hwy 65
(71639) 501.382.5115

Pendleton Inn
Rt 1
(71639) 501.382.4215

Ramada Ltd ($)
722 Hwy 65
(71639) 501.382.2707

• El Dorado •
Best Western ($$)
1920 Junction City Rd
(71730) 501.862.5191
mgr preapproval reqd

Comfort Inn ($$)
2303 Junction City Rd
(71730) 501.863.6677
mgr preapproval reqd

El Dorado Inn Motel
3019 N West Ave
(71730) 501.862.6676

Flamingo Motel
420 S West Ave
(71730) 501.862.4201

Whitehall Motel
840 W Hillsboro St
(71730) 501.863.4136

• Elizabeth •
Holiday Hills Resort
RR 1 Box# 22
(72531) 501.488.5303

Kellers Kove Resort
RR 1 Box# 45
(72531) 501.488.5360

• Eureka Springs •
1876 Inn ($)
RR 6 Box# 247
(72632) 501.253.7183

Alpine Motel ($$)
RR 4 Box# 580
(72632) 501.253.9475

Basin Park Hotel
12 Spring St
(72632) 501.253.7837

Best Western ($)
Hwy 62
(72632) 501.253.9768
small attended

Best Western ($)
Hwy 62, Box 430
(72632) 501.253.9501
pets must be attended

Brackenridge Lodge
Rt 4 Box# 60
(72632) 501.253.6803

Carriage House
75 Lookout Cir
(72632) 501.253.5259

Chalet Inn ($)
RR 6 Box# 156
(72632) 501.253.9687

Days Inn ($$)
102 Kingshighway
(72632) 501.253.8863
$10 per day

Dogwood Cottages
RR 1 Box# 168
(72632) 501.253.8897

Dogwood Inn ($)
RR 6 Box# 20
(72632) 501.253.7200

Eureka Sunset Ctges
10 Dogwood Rdg
(72632) 501.253.9565

Four Runners Inn
RR 4 Box# 306
(72632) 501.253.6000

Hidden Valley Ranch
777 Hidden Valley Ranch
(72632) 501.253.9777

Indian Mountain Lodge
RR 4 Box# 570
(72632) 501.253.5221

Willow Cottages
RR 6 Box# 354
(72632) 501.253.8199

Kings Inn
92 Kingshighway
(72632) 501.253.7311

Lake Leatherwood Park
Hwy 62
(72632) 501.253.8624

Lake Lucerne Resort
Box# 441
(72632) 501.253.8085

Lazy Days Log Cabin
RR 1 Box# 196
(72632) 501.253.7026

Log Cabin Inn
42 Kingshighway
(72632) 501.253.9400

Mariposa Inn
3 Echols St
(72632) 501.253.9169

Oak Crest Cottages ($)
RR 6 Box# 126
(72632) 501.253.9493

Old Homestead
82 Armstrong St
(72632) 501.253.7501

Pine Lodge
Rt 2 Box# 18
(72632) 501.253.8065

Pine Top Lodge ($)
RR 6 Box# 265
(72632) 501.253.7331

Pointe West Resort
RR 2 Box# 87
(72631) 501.253.9050

Potters Motel
Passion Play Rd
(72632) 501.253.7398

Purple Inn
RR 6 Box# 339
(72632) 800.831.4747

Red Carpet Inn ($)
RR 4 Box# 309A
(72632) 501.253.6665
$5 pet fee

Regency 7
62E Passion Play Rd
(72632) 800.470.5959

Roadrunner Inn ($$)
RR 2 Box# 158
(72631) 501.253.8166

Rogues Manor
124 Spring St
(72632) 501.253.4911

Sherwood Court
27 Glen Ave
(72632) 501.253.8920

Southern Country Inn
RR 1 Box# 460
(72632) 501.253.5600

Statue Motel
RR 1 Box# 965
(72632) 501.253.9163

Studio Guest House
120 N Main St
(72632) 501.253.8773

Swiss Village Inn ($$)
RR 6 Box# 5
(72632) 501.253.9541

Tradewinds Motel ($)
77 Kingshighway
(72632) 501.253.9774

ARKANSAS, Eureka Springs

Travelers Inn ($)
RR.1 Box# 269
(72632) 501.253.8386

Whispering Oaks Motel
RR 6 Box# 338
(72632) 501.253.9459

Wildflower Cottages
22 Hale St
(72632) 501.253.9173

● Fayetteville ●
Chief Motel
1818 N College Ave
(72703) 501.442.7326

Days Inn ($$)
2402 N College Ave
(72703) 501.443.4323
$50/pet deposit (refundable)

Hilton ($$)
70 N East Ave
(72701) 501.442.5555

Holiday Inn ($$)
1251 N Shiloh Dr
(72704) 501.444.6006
mgr preapproval reqd

Motel 6 ($)
2980 N College Ave
(72703) 501.443.4351
1 small pet/room

Ramada Inn ($$)
3901 N College Ave
(72703) 501.443.3431

The Inn Of Fayetteville ($$)
1000 Hwy 71 Byp
(72701) 501.442.3041

Twin Arch Motel
521 N College Ave
(72701) 501.521.9452

● Flippin ●
Seawrights Motel
1st & Sunset Sts
(72634) 501.453.2555

Shady Oaks Cottages ($$)
HC 62 Box# 128
(72634) 501.626.5474

Sportsmans Resort
HC 62 Box# 96
(72634) 501.453.2424

White Hole Resort
HC 62 Box# 100
(72634) 501.453.2913

Wildcat Shoals Resort
Box# 1032
(72634) 501.453.2321

● Fordyce ●
Ok Motel
2403 N Hwy 167 # &79
(71742) 501.352.3197

Antlers Motel
2400 Bypass
(71742) 501.352.5174

● Forrest City ●
Best Western ($$)
2333 N Washington St
(72335) 501.633.0870
mgr preapproval reqd

Econo Lodge ($)
204 Holiday Dr
(72335) 800.424.4777

Holiday Inn ($$)
Hwy 1 N & I-40
(72335) 501.633.6300
mgr preapproval reqd

Luxury Inn ($)
315 Barrow Wheel Rd
(72335) 501.633.8990

Regency Inn
907 E Broadway St
(72335) 501.633.4433

Save Inn
105 NW St Hwy 70
(72335) 501.633.3214

● Fort Smith ●
Best Western ($$)
101 N 11th St
(72901) 501.785.4121
small pets only

Best Western ($$)
5801 Rogers Ave
(72903) 501.452.4200
mgr preapproval reqd

Budgetel ($$)
2123 Burnham Rd
(72903) 501.484.5770

Days Inn ($)
1021 Garrison Ave
(72901) 501.783.0548

Dennis Motel
5100 Midland Blvd
(72904) 501.782.4064

Econo Lodge ($$)
301 N 11th St
(72901) 800.424.4777

Fifth Season Motel ($$)
2219 S Waldron Rd
(72903) 501.452.4880

Holiday Inn ($$$)
700 Rogers Ave
(72901) 501.783.1000
mgr preapproval reqd

Motel 6 ($)
6001 Rogers Ave
(72903) 501.484.0576
1 small pet/room

Sheraton Inn ($$)
5711 Rogers Ave
(72903) 501.452.4110

● Gamaliel ●
Bayou Resort
HC 66 Box# 390
(72537) 501.467.5277

Castaways Resort
Hwy 101
(72537) 501.467.5348

Driftwood Resort
HC 66 Box# 6000
(72537) 501.467.5330

Lakeside Resort
Koeller Rd Cr 801
(72537) 501.467.5196

Lucky 7 Resort
HC 66 Box# 1345
(72537) 501.467.5451

Shady Valley Resort
HC 66 Box# 220
(72537) 501.467.5350

Twin Gables Resort
HC 66 Box# 1385
(72537) 501.467.5686

● Gassville ●
Red Dock Motel
RR 2 Box# 541
(72635) 501.435.6303

● Gateway ●
Holiday Hill Motel
Hwy 62 E Gateway
(72733) 501.656.3395

● Gentry ●
Gentry Motel
Box# 177
(72734) 501.736.8006

● Gilbert ●
Buffalo Camping
Box# 504
(72636) 501.439.2888

General Store Cabins
1 Frost St
(72636) 501.439.2386

● Gillett ●
Rice Motel
Box# 536
(72055) 501.548.2223

● Glenwood ●
Caddo River Motel
RR 2 Box# 786
(71943) 501.356.4117

Mt Inn
Box# 32
(71943) 501.356.3737

● Hampton ●
Smiths Motel
Box# 823
(71744) 501.798.2755

● Hardy ●
Frontier Motel
RR 1 Box# 62
(72542) 501.966.3377

Hideaway Inn
RR 1 Box# 199
(72542) 501.966.4770

$=under $35 $$=$35-60 $$$=$60-100 $$$$=over $100

Motor Center Motel
RR 1 Box# 57-A
(72542) 501.856.3282

Razorback Motel
RR 1 Box# 234
(72542) 501.856.2465

Weaver Motel
RR 1 Box# 2
(72542) 501.856.3224

● Harrison ●
Airport Motel
1605 Hwy 62-65
(72601) 501.741.5900

Cresthaven Inn
825 N Main St
(72601) 501.741.9522

Holiday Inn ($$)
816 N Main St
(72601) 501.741.2391
mgr preapproval reqd

Little Switzerland
Jasper Star Rt Hwy 7
(72601) 501.446.2693

Ramada Inn ($)
1222 N Main St
(72601) 501.741.7611

Rock Candy Mt
Hwy 7 South
(72601) 501.743.1531

Scenic 7 Motel
RR 1 Box# 16
(72601) 501.741.9648

Super 8 ($$)
1330 Hwy 62/65
(72601) 501.741.1741
w/permission

● Heber Springs ●
Arkansas Inn
2233 Hwy 25 Nb
(72543) 501.362.2500

Barnett Motel ($$)
616 W Main St
(72543) 501.362.8111

Lake River Inn ($)
2322 Hwy 25B
(72543) 501.362.3161

Lakeshore Motel ($$)
801 Case Ford Rd
(72543) 501.362.2315

Ozark Trail Motel
1631 Hwy 25B
(72543) 501.362.3102

Pines Motel
1819 25 B
(72543) 501.362.3176

● Helena ●
Riverbluff Hotel ($$)
Box# 730
(72342) 501.338.6431

● Henderson ●
Crystal Cove Resort
HC 66 Box# 845
(72544) 501.488.5373

Rodeway Inn ($)
US 62
(72544) 501.488.5144

● Heth ●
Best Western ($$)
Hwy 149
(72346) 501.657.2101
small under 30 lbs

● Higden ●
Ozark Motel
7650 Edgemont Rd
(72067) 501.825.6607

Narrows Inn
7910 Edgemont Rd
(72067) 501.825.6246

Red Bird Inn
9174 Edgemont Rd
(72067) 501.825.6256

● Hindsville ●
Forxfire Camp
RR 1 Box# 198
(72738) 501.789.2122

● Hope ●
Best Western ($$)
Jct I-30 & SHwy 4 Ex 30
(71801) 501.777.9222

Days Inn ($)
1500 N Hervey St
(71801) 501.722.1904

Friendly Inn
Box# 930
(71802) 501.777.4665

Holiday Inn ($)
2600 Hervey
(71801) 800.465.4329

Quality Inn ($)
I-30 & Hwy 29
(71801) 501.777.0777
mgr preapproval reqd

● Horseshoe Bend ●
Boxhound Resort
1313 Tri-Lake Dr
(72512) 501.670.4496

● Hot Springs Nati'l Park ●
Appletree Inn
805 E Grand Ave
(71901) 501.624.4672

Avanelle Motel ($$)
1204 Central Ave
(71901) 501.321.1332

Buena Vista Resort ($$)
201 Aberina St
(71913) 800.255.9030

Days Inn
1506 SHwy 95
(71913) 501.354.5101

El Rancho Motel
1611 Central Ave
(71901) 501.624.1273

Fountain Motel
1622 Central Ave
(71901) 501.624.1262

Hamilton Inn ($$)
106 Lookout Pt
(71913) 501.525.5666

Hill Wheatley Inn ($)
400 W Grand Ave
(71901) 800.999.4441

Hot Springs Resort
1871 E Grand Ave
(71901) 501.623.8824

Kings Inn Motel
2101 Central Ave
(71901) 501.623.8824

Lake Hamilton Resort ($$$)
2803 Albert Pike Rd
(71913) 501.767.5511

Majestic Hotel ($$)
Park & Central Ave
(71901) 501.623.5511

Mar gate Motel ($)
217 Fountain St
(71901) 501.623.1192

Mt Springs Inn
1127 Central Ave
(71901) 501.624.7131

Park Hotel
211 Fountain St
(71901) 501.624.5323

Pattons Lake Resort
100 San Carlos Pt
(71913) 501.525.1678

Quality Inn ($$)
1125 E Grand Ave
(71901) 501.624.3321

Royale Vista Inn
2204 Central Ave
(71901) 501.624.5551

Shamrock Motel
508 Albert Pike Rd
(71913) 501.624.3833

Shorecrest Resort ($$)
360 Lakeland Dr
(71913) 800.447.9914

Taylor Motel
316 Park Ave
(71901) 501.624.1255

Town House Motel
100 Cove St
(71901) 501.624.9271

Travelier Motel ($)
1045 E Grand Ave
(71901) 501.624.4681

Vagabond Motel
4708 Central Ave
(71913) 501.525.2769

Willow Beach Resort
260 Lake Hamilton Dr
(71913) 501.525.1362

$=under $35 $$=$35-60 $$$=$60-100 $$$$=over $100

ARKANSAS, Huttig

• Huttig •
Tracks Inn Motel
1141 K Ave
(71747) 501.943.2943

• Jacksonville •
Days Inn ($$)
1414 John Harden Dr
(72076) 501.982.1543

Oxford Inn
920 S Hwy 161
(72076) 501.982.1976

Ramada Inn ($$)
200 Hwy 67
(72076) 501.982.2183
mgr preapproval reqd

Sands Motel
1008 S Hwy 161
(72076) 501.985.0266

• Jasper •
Lookout Mt Cabins
HC 31 Box# 90
(72641) 501.446.6224

Mockingbird Motel
HC 31 Box# 64-B
(72641) 501.446.2643

• Jessieville •
Ochita Motel
6127 N Hwy 7
(71949) 501.984.5363

• Jonesboro •
Autumn Inn Motel ($)
2406 Phillips Dr
(72401) 501.932.9339

Best Western ($$)
2901 Phillips Dr
(72401) 501.932.6600
small pets only

Holiday Inn ($$)
3006 S Caraway Rd
(72401) 501.935.2030
mgr preapproval reqd

Holiday Inn
2407 Phillips Dr
(72401) 501.932.5554

Jami Motel
3423 E Nettleton Ave
(72401) 501.932.1611

Jonesboro Motel
403 S Gee St
(72401) 501.932.6615

Motel 6 ($)
2300 S Caraway Rd
(72401) 501.932.1050
1 small pet/room

Park Place Inn
1421 S Caraway Rd
(72401) 501.935.8400

Ramada Inn ($$)
3000 Apache Dr
(72401) 501.932.5757

Scottish Inn ($)
3116 Mead Dr
(72404) 501.972.8300

Super 8 ($)
2500 S Caraway Rd
(72401) 501.972.1849
call re: fees

Wilson Inn ($)
2911 Gilmore Dr
(72401) 501.972.9000

• Kirby •
Daisy Motel
HC 71 Box# 255
(71950) 501.398.5173

Lakeside Motel
HC 71 Box# 67
(71950) 501.398.5304

• Lake Village •
La Villa Motel
Hwys 65 & 82
(71653) 501.265.2277

Lake Shore Motel
Box# 231
(71653) 501.265.2238

Plaza Motel
Hwys 65 & 82
(71653) 501.265.5341

• Lakeview •
Bay Breeze Resort
Box# 185
(72642) 501.431.5261

Cedar Oaks Resort ($$)
RR 1 Box# 694
(72642) 501.431.5351

Gastons White River ($$)
1 River Rd
(72642) 501.431.5202

Last Resort
Box# 144
(72642) 501.431.5681

Newland Lodge
Rt 1 River Rd
(72642) 501.431.8620

Twin Fin Resort
Box# 218
(72642) 501.431.5377

• Lead Hill •
Bon Terre Inn
Hwy 281
(72644) 501.436.7318

Hill Top Cottages
RR 1 Box# 280
(72644) 501.436.5365

• Little Rock •
Budget Inn
9351 I-30
(72209) 501.565.0111

Budgetel ($$)
1010 Breckenridge Dr
(72205) 501.225.7007

Cimarron Inn
10200 I-30
(72209) 501.565.1181

Comfort Inn ($$)
3200 Bankhead Dr
(72206) 501.490.2010
mgr preapproval reqd

Courtyard By Marriott
10900 Financial Ctr
(72211) 501.227.6000

Days Inn ($)
2600 W 65th St
(72209) 501.562.1122

Doubletree
424 W Markham St
(72201) 501.372.4371

Heritage House Inn
7500 S University Ave
(72209) 501.565.2055

Holiday Inn
3201 Bankhead Dr
(72295) 501.490.1000

Holiday Inn ($$)
617 S Broadway St
(72201) 501.376.4000
mgr preapproval reqd

Holiday Inn ($$)
3121 Bankhead Dr
(72206) 501.490.4000
mgr preapproval reqd

Holiday Inn ($$$)
201 S Shackleford Rd
(72211) 501.223.3000
mgr preapproval reqd

Jacks Motel
9515 Hwy 365
(72206) 501.897.4951

La Quinta Inn ($$)
901 Fair Park Blvd
(72204) 501.664.7000
call re: fees

La Quinta Inn ($$)
11701 I-30/I-430
(72209) 501.455.2300
call re: fees

La Quinta Inn ($$)
2401 W 65th St
(72209) 501.568.1030
call re: fees

La Quinta Inn ($$)
200 Shackelford Rd
(72211) 501.224.0900
call re: fees

Legacy Hotel
625 W Capitol Ave
(72201) 501.374.0100

Markham Inn
5120 W Markham St
(72205) 501.666.0161

$=under $35 $$=$35-60 $$$=$60-100 $$$$=over $100

Motel 6 ($)
7501 I-30
(72209) 501.568.8888
1 small pet/room

Motel 6 ($)
9525 I-30
(72209) 501.565.1388
1 small pet/room

Motel 6 ($)
10524 W Markham St
(72205) 501.225.7366
1 small pet/room

Ramada Ltd
9709 Hwy I-30
(72209) 501.568.6800

Red Roof Inn ($)
7900 Scott Hamilton Dr
(72209) 501.562.2694
fees/limits may apply

Wilson Inn ($)
4301 E Roosevelt Rd
(72206) 501.376.2466

● Lonoke ●
Economy Inn
Hwy 31 N & I-40
(72086) 501.676.3116

Perrys Motel
200 Nathan Dr
(72086) 501.676.3181

● Magnolia ●
Best Western ($$)
420 E Main St
(71753) 501.234.6122
small pets

Castle Inn Motel
912 E Main St
(71753) 501.234.2262

Flamingo Motel
100 N Vine St
(71753) 501.234.4752

Kings Inn Motel
411 E Main St
(71753) 501.234.3612

Be
Discreet

● Malvern ●
Super 8
RR 8 Box# 719-6
(72104) 501.332.5755
mgr preapproval reqd

Town House Motel
304 E Page Ave
(72104) 501.332.5437

● Mammoth Spring ●
Riverview Motel
Box# 281
(72554) 501.625.3218

● Marion ●
Best Western ($$)
RR 2 Box# 398C
(72364) 501.739.3278
small pets only

● Marked Tree ●
Days Inn ($$)
201 Hwy 63
(72365) 501.358.2700
$5 fee

● Marshall ●
Rose Motel
Box# 913
(72650) 501.448.2596

Sunset Motel
Box# 205
(72650) 501.448.3348

● Mc Gehee ●
Senator Motel
222 Hwy 65
(71654) 501.222.5511

● Mena ●
Best Western ($$)
804 Hwy 71
(71953) 501.394.6350
small housebroken pets only

Holiday Motel
1162 US 71
(71953) 501.394.2611

Country Inn
203 US 71
(71953) 501.394.6433

Ozark Inn
Box# 1071
(71953) 501.394.1100

● Midway ●
Holiday Shores Resort
RR 1 Box# 283
(72651) 501.431.5370

Howard Creek Resort
RR 1 Box# 282
(72651) 501.431.5371

Red Arrow Resort
RR 1 Box# 281
(72651) 501.431.5375

Sunset Point Resort
RR 1 Box# 290
(72651) 501.431.5372

● Monticello ●
Best Western ($$)
365 Hwy 425
(71655) 501.354.0181
mgr preapproval reqd

Highway Inn
617 W Gaines St
(71655) 501.367.8555

● Morrilton ●
Econo Lodge ($$)
1506 Hwy 95
(72110) 501.354.5101

● Mount Ida ●
Colonial Motel
HC 63 Box# 306
(71957) 501.867.2431

Denby Lodge ($)
Box# 241
(71957) 501.867.3651

Mount Ida Motel
HC 67 Box# 67X
(71957) 501.867.3456

● Mountain Home ●
Best Western ($)
963 US 62
(72653) 501.425.6001
small pets only

Blackburns Resort
RR 6 Box# 280
(72653) 501.492.5115

Paradise Resort ($)
RR 6 Box# 379-Cc
(72653) 501.492.5113

Bungalow Resort
RR 4 Box# 439
(72653) 501.492.5105

Chit Chat Resort
RR 1 Box# 157
(72653) 501.431.5584

Durbons Creek Resort
RR 1 Box# 128
(72653) 501.431.5574

Edgewater Resort
RR 1 Box# 150
(72653) 501.431.5222

Fishfiddle Resort
RR 10 Box# 430
(72653) 501.491.5161

Genes Fishing Resort
RR 3 Box# 348
(72653) 501.499.5381

Holiday Inn ($$)
1350 Hwy 62 SW
(72653) 501.425.5101
mgr preapproval reqd

Lasalle Resort
RR 4 Box# 485-C
(72653) 501.492.5133

Mockingbird Resort
Rt 3 Box# 183-Mh
(72653) 501.491.5112

Mt Home Motel
411 S Main St
(72653) 501.425.2171

Ozarks Motel
147 S Main St
(72653) 501.425.4881

Peals Resort
RR 3 Box# 252
(72653) 501.499.5215

Promise Land Resort
RR 1 Box# 140
(72653) 501.431.5576

Rim Shoals Resort
RR 2 Box# 594
(72653) 501.435.6695

ARKANSAS, Mountain Home

Rocking Chair Ranch ($$)
RR 6 Box# 445
(72653) 501.492.5157

Rocky Ridge Resort
RR 10 Box# 610
(72653) 501.491.5665

Royal Motel Resort ($)
RR 6 Box# 500
(72653) 501.492.5288

Scott Valley Ranch ($$$)
Box# 1447
(72653) 501.425.5136

Silver Leaf Lodge ($)
RR 9 Box# 544
(72653) 501.492.5187

Silver Saddle Motel
128 N College St
(72653) 501.425.9998

Sister Creek Resort
RR 1 Box# 147
(72653) 501.531.5587

Spring Valley Motel
548 Hwy 62 NE
(72653) 501.425.3717

Sunrise Pt Resort
RR 10 Box# 620-Cc
(72653) 501.491.5188

Teal Point Resort ($$)
RR 6 Box# 369
(72653) 501.492.5145

Watertree Inn
RR 4 Box# 495
(72653) 501.492.6477

Wimpys Resort
RR 1 Box# 141
(72653) 501.431.5325

Y Cabins
Hwy 5 S & Hwy 177
(72653) 501.499.5294

● Mountain View ●
Days Inn
Hwys 5 9 & 14
(72560) 501.269.3287
mgr preapproval reqd

Hidden Valley Cabins
Box# 740
(72560) 501.269.2655

Jacks Fishing Resort
Hwy 5
(72560) 501.585.2211

Sycamore Lodges
Box# 1378
(72560) 501.585.2221

● Murfreesboro ●
American Heritage Inn
705 N Washington St
(71958) 501.285.2131

Shamrock Motel
919 N Washington St
(71958) 501.285.2342

Riverside Motel
Rfd 1
(71958) 501.285.2255

● Nashville ●
Holiday Motor Lodge
Hwy 27-B
(71852) 501.845.2953

● Newport ●
Days Inn ($$)
101 Olivia Dr
(72112) 501.523.6411

Lakeside Inn
203 Malcolm Ave
(72112) 501.523.2787

Newport Motel
1504 Hwy 67
(72112) 501.523.2768

Park Inn Intl ($$)
901 Hwy 67
(72112) 501.523.5851

● North Little Rock ●
Budgetel ($$)
4311 Warden Rd
(72116) 501.758.8888

Days Inn
5800 Pritchard
(72117) 501.945.4100
$10

Days Inn
7200 Bicentennial
(72118) 501.851.3297
$8

Hampton Inn ($$)
500 W 29th St
(72114) 501.771.2090

Holiday Inn ($$)
111 W Pershing Blvd
(72114) 501.758.1440
mgr preapproval reqd

La Quinta Inn ($$)
4100 E McCain Blvd
(72117) 501.945.0808
call re: fees

Masters Economy Inn ($)
2508 Jacksonville Hwy
(72117) 501.945.4167

Motel 6 ($)
400 W 29th St
(72114) 501.758.5100
1 small pet/room

● Oakland ●
Black Oak Resort
Box# 100
(72661) 501.431.8363

Fin N Feather Resort
RR 1 Box# 14
(72661) 501.431.5621

Henrys Resort
RR 1 Box# 16
(72661) 501.431.5626

Hidden Bay Resort
RR 1 Box# 320
(72661) 501.431.8121

Persimmon Point
RR 1 Box# 169
(72661) 501.431.8877

Southern Comfort Res
RR 1 Box# 40
(72661) 501.431.8470

● Ola ●
Mimas Motel
Box# 157
(72853) 501.489.5611

● Omaha ●
Aunt Shirleys Loft
RR 1 Box# 84D
(72662) 501.426.5408

● Osceola ●
Best Western ($$)
Off 1-55
(72370) 501.563.3222
small pets only

● Ozark ●
Budget Host ($)
1711 W Commercial St
(72949) 501.667.2166

● Paragould ●
Linwood Motel
1611 Linwood Dr
(72450) 501.236.7671

● Paris ●
Blakely Inn
2010 E Walnut St
(72855) 501.963.2400

● Parthenon ●
Cabin In The Woods
HC 72 Box# 134
(72666) 501.446.2293

● Pea Ridge ●
Battlefield Inn Motel
14753 Hwy 62
(72751) 501.451.1188

● Perryville ●
Coffee Creek Motel
Harrisbrake
(72126) 501.889.2745

● Piggott ●
Open Roads Motel
148 Independence St
(72454) 501.598.5941

● Pine Bluff ●
Best Western ($$)
2700 E Harding Ave
(71601) 501.535.8640
small & $25

Classic Inn
4125 Rhinehart Rd
(71601) 501.535.1200

Policies Subject to Change

$=under $35 $$=$35-60 $$$=$60-100 $$$$=over $100

Days Inn ($$)
8006 Sheridan Rd
(71602) 501.247.1339

Econo Lodge ($$)
321 W 5th Ave
(71601) 800.424.4777

Holiday Inn ($$$)
2 Convention Center Plz
(71601) 501.535.3111
mgr preapproval reqd

● Pocahontas ●
Scottish Inn ($)
1501 Hwy 67
(72455) 501.892.4527
$5 per day

● Ponca ●
Lost Valley Lodging
Hwy 43
(72670) 501.861.5522

● Prescott ●
Broadway Hotel
123 W 1st
(71857) 501.887.5446

● Rogers ●
Beaver Lake Lodge ($$)
14733 Dutchmans Dr
(72756) 501.925.2313

Days Inn ($$)
2102 S 8th St
(72758) 501.636.3820

Hartland Lodge
2931 W Walnut St
(72756) 501.631.6000

Highway Host Inn
915 S 8th St
(72756) 501.636.9400

Jan Motel
1601 71-B
(72756) 501.636.1733

Park Inn Intl
3714 W Walnut St
(72756) 501.631.7000

Ramada Inn ($$)
1919 Hwy 71-B
(72756) 501.636.5850

Second Home
100 W Locust St
(72756) 501.530.1773

Super 8 ($$)
915 S 8th St
(72756) 501.636.9600
mgr preapproval reqd

Tanglewood Lodge
RR 6
(72756) 501.925.2100

● Russellville ●
Best Western ($$)
Hwy 7
(72811) 501.967.1000
one dog under 12 lbs

Budget Inn ($)
2200 N Arkansas Ave
(72801) 501.968.4400
$10 deposit

Holiday Inn ($$)
2407 Arkansas
(72801) 501.958.4300

Holly Motel
1206 E Main St
(72801) 501.968.4959

Lakeside Resort Motel
3320 N Arkansas Ave
(72801) 501.968.9715

Merrick Motel
1320 E Main St
(72801) 501.968.6332

Motel 6 ($)
215 W Birch St
(72801) 501.968.3666
1 small pet/room

Park Motel ($)
2615 W Main St
(72801) 501.968.4862

Southern Inn Motel ($)
704 Dyke Rd
(72801) 501.968.5511

Sunrise Inn
154 E Aspen Ln
(72801) 501.968.7200

Woodys Classic Inn
1522 E Main St
(72801) 501.968.7774

● Saint Joe ●
Maplewood Motel
Box# 1
(72675) 501.439.2525

● Searcy ●
Hampton Inn ($$)
3204 E Race Ave
(72143) 501.268.0654

Kings Inn ($)
3109 E Race Ave
(72143) 501.268.6171

● Siloam Springs ●
Eastgate Motel
1951 Hwy 412
(72761) 501.524.5157

Hartland Lodge ($$)
1801 Hwy 412
(72761) 501.524.2025

● Springdale ●
Budgetel
1300 S 48th St
(72762) 501.451.2626

Econo Lodge ($)
2001 S Thompson St
(72764) 800.424.4777

Executive Inn ($$)
2005 Hwy 71-B
(72764) 501.756.6101

Hampton Inn ($$$)
1700 S 48th St
(72762) 501.756.3500

Holiday Inn ($$$)
1500 S 48th St
(72762) 501.751.8300
mgr preapproval reqd

● Stamps ●
Lafayette Motel
Hwy 72
(71860) 501.533.4333

● Story ●
Aqua Motel
HC 64 Box# 105
(71970) 501.867.2123

● Stuttgart ●
Best Western ($$)
704 W Michigan St
(72160) 501.673.2575
small pets only

Town House Motel ($)
701 W Michigan St
(72160) 501.673.2611

Walker Motor Inn
405 E Michigan St
(72160) 501.673.2671

● Trumann ●
Weems Motel
404 Hwy 63
(72472) 501.483.6331

● Van Buren ●
Motel 6 ($)
1716 Fayetteville Rd
(72956) 501.474.8001
1 small pet/room

Super 8 ($$)
106 N Plaza Ct
(72956) 501.471.8888
pets w/permission

● Walnut Ridge ●
Alamo Court Motel ($)
Hwy 67
(72476) 501.886.2441

Phillips Motel
501 Hwy 67
(72476) 501.886.6767

● Warren ●
Economy Inn
108 E Church St
(71671) 501.226.5881

Town House Motel
201 E Church St
(71671) 501.226.5822

● West Helena ●
Harbor Inn Motel
Hwy 49-B
(72390) 501.572.2597

Sands Motel
Hwy 49-B
(72390) 501.572.6774

ARKANSAS, West Memphis

● West Memphis ●
Econo Lodge ($)
2315 S Service Rd
(72301) 800.424.4777

Econo Lodge ($)
2315 S Service Rd
(72301) 501.732.2830

Express Inn
3700 Service Road Loop
(72301) 501.732.5688

Motel 6 ($)
2501 S Frontage Rd
(72301) 501.735.0100
1 small pet/room

Super 8 ($$)
901 N Club Rd
(72301) 501.735.8818
mgr preapproval reqd

● Wynne ●
Nation Wide 9 Motel
706 Hwy 64
(72396) 501.238.9399

● Yellville ●
Silver Run Cabins
HC 66 Box# 364A
(72687) 501.449.6355

Wild Bills Cabins
HC 66 Box# 380
(72687) 501.449.6235

California

● Adelanto ●
Days Inn ($$)
11628 Bartlett Ave
(92301) 619.246.8777

● Agoura Hills ●
Radisson Inn ($$)
30100 Agoura Rd
(91301) 818.707.1220
under 30 lbs

● Ahwahnee ●
Deer Valley Inn ($$)
45013 Hwy 49 Nipinnawasee
(93601) 800.676.5647

● Alameda ●
Islander Lodge Motel ($$)
2428 Central Ave
(94501) 510.865.2121

● Altaville ●
Angels Inn Motel ($$)
600 N Main St
(95221) 209. .

● Alturas ●
Best Western ($$)
343 N Main St
(96101) 916.233.4111
small pets only

Drifters Inn ($$)
395 Lake View Rd
(96101) 916.233.2428

Essex Motel ($$)
1216 N Main St
(96101) 916.233.2821

Frontier Motel ($)
1033 N Main St
(96101) 916.233.3383

Hacienda Motel ($)
201 E 12th St
(96101) 916.233.3459
not unattended

● Anaheim ●
Anaheim Angel Inn ($)
1800 E Katella Ave
(92805) 714.634.9121

Anaheim Harbor Inn ($$)
2171 S Harbor Blvd
(92802) 714.750.3100

Anaheim Inn ($)
1855 S Harbor Blvd
(92802) 714.750.1811

Anaheim Plaza Hotel ($$$)
1700 S Harbor Blvd
(92802) 800.228.1357

Best Western ($$)
2040 S Harbor Blvd
(92802) 714.750.6100
$10 fee $100 dep

Cavalier Inn ($$)
11811 Harbor Blvd
(92802) 714.750.1000

Crown Sterling ($$$$)
3100 E Frontera St
(92806) 714.632.1221

Desert Palm Inn ($$)
631 W Katella Ave
(92802) 714.535.1133

Econo Lodge ($$)
871 S Harbor Blvd
(92805) 714.535.7878

Friendship Inn ($)
705 S Beach Blvd
(92804) 800.424.4777

Grand Hotel ($$$)
7 Greedman Way
(92802) 800.421.6662

Hampton Inn ($$)
300 E Katella Way
(92802) 714.772.8713
small pets only

Hilton ($$$$)
777 W Convention Way
(92802) 800.233.6904

Holiday Inn ($$$)
1221 S Harbor Blvd
(92805) 714.758.0900
mgr preapproval reqd

Marriott Hotel ($$$$)
700 W Convention Way
(92802) 714.750.8000

Motel 6 ($)
921 S Beach Blvd
(92804) 714.220.2866
1 small pet/room

Motel 6 ($$)
100 W Freedman Way
(92802) 714.520.9696
1 small pet/room

Raffles Inn ($$)
2040 S Harbor Blvd
(92802) 800.654.0196

Red Roof Inn ($)
1251 N Harbor Blvd
(92801) 714.635.6461

Residence Inn ($$$)
1700 S Clementine St
(92802) 714.533.3555

Rodeway Inn ($$)
800 S Beach Blvd
(92804) 800.424.4777

Station Inn ($)
989 W Ball Rd
(92802) 800.874.6265

The Pan Pacific ($$$$)
1717 S West St
(92802) 714.999.0990

Travelodge ($$)
5710 E La Palma Ave
(92807) 714.779.0252

Travelodge ($)
1166 W Katella Ave
(92802) 714.774.7817

● Anderson ●
Anderson Valley Inn ($$)
2661 McMurry Dr
(96007) 916.365.2566

Best Western ($$)
2688 Gateway Dr
(96007) 916.365.2753
small pets

● Angels Camp ●
Gold Country Inn ($$)
720 S Main St
(95222) 209.736.4611

● Antioch ●
Ramada Inn ($$$)
2436 Mahogany Way
(94509) 510.754.6600

● Applegate ●
Firehouse Motel ($)
17855 Lake Arthur Rd
(95703) 916.878.7770

● Arcadia ●
Embassy Suites ($$$$)
211 E Huntington Dr
(91006) 818.445.8525
small lap dogs

Hampton Inn ($$$)
311 E Huntington Dr
(91006) 818.574.5600

Motel 6 ($$)
225 Colorado Pl
(91007) 818.446.2660
1 small pet/room

Residence Inn ($$$$)
321 E Huntington Dr
(91006) 818.446.6500
call for fee & availability

● Arcata ●
Best Western ($$)
4827 Valley West Blvd
(95521) 707.826.0313
small/ pet rooms

Hotel Arcata ($$)
708 9th St
(95521) 707.826.0217

Motel 6 ($)
4755 Valley West Blvd
(95521) 707.822.7061
1 small pet/room

Quality Inn ($$)
3535 Janes Rd
(95521) 707.822.0409
mgr preapproval reqd

Super 8 ($)
4887 Valley West Blvd
(95521) 800.800.8000
call re: fees

● Arnold ●
Ebbetts Pass Lodge ($$)
Box# 2591
(95223) 209.795.1563

Sierra Rentals ($$$$)
Box# 1080
(95223) 800.995.2422

Meadowmont ($$)
2011 Hwy 4
(95223) 209.795.1394

● Arroyo Grande ●
Best Western ($$)
850 Oak Park Blvd
(93420) 805.481.7398
mgr preapproval reqd

Econo Lodge ($$)
611 E Camino Real
(93420) 805.489.9300

● Atascadero ●
Best Western ($$)
3600 El Camino Real
(93422) 805.466.4449
mgr preapproval reqd

Motel 6 ($)
9400 El Camino Real
(93422) 805.466.6701
1 small pet/room

Rancho Motel ($$)
6895 El Camino Real
(93422) 805.466.2231

Super 8 ($$)
6505 Morro Rd
(93422) 805.466.0794
some small pets

● Atwater ●
Super 8
1501 Sycamore Ave
(95301) 209.357.0202
call re: fees

● Auburn ●
Best Western ($$)
13450 Lincoln Way
(95603) 916.885.8611
small pet w/$10 refundable
deposit

Country Squire Inn ($$)
13480 Lincoln Way
(95603) 916.885.7025

Holiday Inn
120 Grass Valley Hwy
(95603) 916.887.8787

Holiday Inn ($$$)
Hwy 49
(95603) 800.814.8787
mgr preapproval reqd

● Avalon ●
Hotel Monterey ($$$)
108 Sumner Ave
(90704) 310.510.0264

● Baker ●
Hawaiian Motel ($$)
200 W Baker Blvd
(92309) 619.733.4326

● Bakersfield ●
Best Western ($$)
700 Truxtun Ave
(93301) 805.327.4064
pets limited

Best Western ($$)
889 Oak St
(93304) 805.324.9686
limited avail

Best Western ($$$$)
2620 Pierce Rd
(93308) 805.327.9651
$10 under 50 lbs

Comfort Inn ($$)
830 Wible Rd
(93304) 805.831.1922
mgr preapproval reqd

Econo Lodge ($$)
200 Trask St
(93312) 805.764.5221

Economy Inn ($)
6501 Colony Rd
(93307) 800.826.0778

Economy Inn ($)
6100 Knudsen Dr
(93308) 800.826.0778

La Quinta Inn ($$)
3232 Riverside Dr
(93308) 805.325.7400
call re: fees

Oak Inn ($$)
10614 Rosedale Hwy
(93312) 805.589.6600

Motel 6 ($)
2727 White Ln
(93304) 805.834.2828
1 small pet/room

Motel 6 ($)
5241 Olive Tree Ct
(93308) 805.392.9700
1 small pet/room

Motel 6 ($)
1350 Easton Dr
(93309) 805.372.1686
1 small pet/room

Quality Inn ($$)
1011 Oak St
(93304) 805.325.0772
mgr preapproval reqd

Quality Inn ($$)
4500 Pierce Rd
(93308) 805.324.5555

Red Lion Inn ($$$$)
3100 Camino Del Rio Ct
(93308) 805.323.7111
call re: fees

Regency Inn ($$)
818 Real Rd
(93309) 805.324.6666

Residence Inn ($$$)
4241 Chester Ln
(93309) 800.331.3131

Rio Bravo Resort ($$$$)
11200 Lake Ming Rd
(93306) 805.872.5000

Sheraton Inn ($$$$)
5101 California Ave
(93309) 805.325.9700
in 1 bldg

● Baldwin Park ●
Motel 6 ($)
14510 Garvey Ave
(91706) 818.960.5011
1 small pet/room

● Banning ●
Super 8 ($)
1690 W Ramsey St
(92220) 800.800.8000
call re: fees

Travelodge ($$$)
1700 W Ramsey St
(92220) 909.849.1000

● Barstow ●
Astro Budget Motel ($)
1271 E Main St
(92311) 760.256.2204

Barstow Inn ($)
1261 E Main St
(92311) 760.256.7581

Best Motel ($)
1281 E Main St
(92311) 760.256.6836

Days Inn
1590 Coolwater Lane
(92311) 760.256.1737
$10

Desert Inn Motel ($)
1100 E Main St
(92311) 760.256.2146

$=under $35 $$=$35-60 $$$=$60-100 $$$$=over $100

CALIFORNIA, Barstow

Econo Lodge ($)
1230 E Main St
(92311) 760.256.2133

Economy Inn ($)
1590 Coolwater Ln
(92311) 800.826.0778

El Rancho Motel ($)
112 E Main St
(92311) 760.256.2401

Gateway Motel ($)
1630 E Main St
(92311) 760.256.8931

Good Nite Inn ($$)
2551 Commerce Pkwy
(92311) 760.253.2121

Hillcrest Motel ($)
1111 E Main St
(92311) 760.256.1063

Howard Johnson ($$)
1431 E Main St
(92311) 800.446.4656

Motel 6 ($)
150 Yucca Ave
(92311) 760.246.1752
1 small pet/room

Motel 6 ($)
3195 E Main St
(92311) 760.256.0653
1 small pet/room

Quality Inn ($$)
1520 E Main St
(92311) 760.256.6891
mgr preapproval reqd

Stardust Inn ($)
901 E Main St
(92311) 760.256.7116

Sunset Inn ($)
1350 W Main St
(92311) 760.256.8921

Super 8 ($$)
170 Coolwater Ln
(92311) 760.256.8443
call re: fees

Vagabond Inn ($$)
1243 E Main St
(92311) 760.234.9607

● Bass Lake ●
Forks Resort ($$$)
39150 Road 222
(93604) 209.642.3737

● Beaumont ●
Budget Host ($$)
625 E 5th St
(92223) 714.845.2185

Golden West Motel ($)
625 E 5th St
(92223) 909.845.2185

Windsor Motel ($)
1265 E 6th St
(92223) 909.845.1436

● Bellflower ●
Motel 6 ($$)
17220 Downey Ave
(90706) 310.531.3933
1 small pet/room

● Belmont ●
Motel 6 ($$)
1101 Shoreway Rd
(94002) 415.591.1471
1 small pet/room

● Benicia ●
Best Western ($$)
1955 E 2nd St
(94510) 707.746.0401
small pets only

● Berkeley ●
Blue Sky Hotel ($$)
2520 Durant Ave
(94704) 510.540.7688

Golden Bear Motel ($$)
1620 San Pablo Ave
(94702) 510.525.6770

Ramada Inn ($$)
920 University Ave
(94710) 510.849.1121

● Beverly Hills ●

The Beverly Hilton Hotel
($$$$)
9876 Wilshire Blvd
(90210) 800.922.5432

The Pennisula ($$$$)
9882 Santa Monica Blvd
(90212) 310.551.2888

The Regent Beverly Wilshire
($$$$)
9500 Wilshire Blvd
(90212) 310.275.5200

● Big Bear Lake ●
Bear Claw Cabins ($$)
586 Main St
(92315) 909.866.2666

Big Cabins Cabins ($$)
39774 Big Bear Blvd
(92315) 909.866.2723

Big Pine Motel ($)
370 S Main
(92315) 619.938.2282

Black Forest Lodge ($$)
Box# 156
(92315) 909.866.2166

Boulder Creek Resort ($$)
Box# 92
(92315) 909.866.2665

Cal Pine Chalets ($$)
41545 Big Bear Blvd
(92315) 909.866.2574

Cozy Hollow Lodge ($$$)
40409 Big Bear Blvd
(92315) 909.866.9694

Creek Runners Lodge ($$)
374 Georgia St
(92315) 909.866.7473

Edgewater Inn ($$$)
40570 Simonds Dr
(92315) 909.866.4161

Frontier Lodge ($$)
40472 Big Bear Blvd
(92315) 909.866.5888
$10 charge

Bear Cottages ($$$)
39367 Big Bear Blvd
(92315) 909.866.2010

Squirrel Resort ($$$)
39372 Big Bear Blvd
(92315) 909.866.4335
$5 night

Grizzly Inn ($$)
39756 Big Bear Blvd
(92315) 800.423.2742

Bear Village ($$)
40154 Big Bear Blvd
(92315) 909.866.2350

Honey Bear Lodge ($)
40994 Pennsylvania
(92315) 909.866.7825

Motel 6 ($$)
42899 Big Bear Blvd
(92315) 909.585.6666
1 small pet/room

Quail Lodge ($$$)
39117 N Shore Dr
(92315) 909.866.5957

Robinhood Inn ($$$)
Box# 3706
(92315) 909.866.4643

Shore Acres Lodge ($$)
40090 Lakeview Dr
(92315) 909.866.8200

Smoketree Resort ($$)
40210 Big Bear Blvd
(92315) 909.866.2415

Snuggle Creek Lodge ($$$)
40440 Big Bear Blvd
(92315) 909.866.2555

Timber Haven Lodge ($$$)
877 Tulip Ln
(92315) 909.866.7207

Timberline Lodge ($$)
Box# 2801
(92315) 800.352.8581

Wishing Well Motel ($$)
540 Pine Knot
(92315) 909.866.3505

● Bishop ●
Best Western ($$)
1025 N Main St
(93514) 760.873.3543
mgr preapproval reqd

Comfort Inn ($$$)
805 N Main St
(93514) 760.873.4284
mgr preapproval reqd

Paradise Lodge ($$)
Lower Rock Creek Rd
(93514) 760.387.2370

Rodeway Inn ($$)
150 E Elm St
(93514) 800.424.4777

Sierra Motel ($)
535 S Main St
(93514) 760.872.1386

Sportsmans Lodge ($)
636 N Main St
(93514) 760.872.2423

Sunrise Motel ($)
262 Grove St
(93514) 760.873.3656

Thunderbird Motel ($)
190 W Pine St
(93514) 760.873.4215

Vagabond Inn ($$)
1030 N Main St
(93514) 760.873.6351
small only with fee

Village Motel ($)
286 W Elm St
(93514) 760.873.3545

● Blairsden ●
Feather River Park ($$$)
Box# 37
(96103) 916.836.2328

Gray Eagle Lodge ($$$$)
Box# 38
(96103) 916.836.2511

Layman Resort ($$)
Box# 8
(96103) 916.836.2356

River Pines Resort ($$)
Box# 117
(96103) 916.836.2552

● Blythe ●
Astro Motel ($)
801 E Hohsonway
(92225) 760.922.3101

Best Western ($$)
9274 E Hobson Way
(92225) 760.922.5101
small pets ok

Best Western ($$)
825 W Hobson Way
(92225) 760.922.7105
small pets

Econo Lodge ($$)
1020 W Hobson Way
(92225) 760.922.3161

Hampton Inn ($$)
900 W Hobson Way
(92225) 800.426.7866

Holiday Inn ($$$)
600 W Donlon St
(92225) 760.921.2300
mgr preapproval reqd

Motel 6 ($)
500 W Donlon St
(92225) 760.922.6666
1 small pet/room

Super 8 ($$)
550 W Donlon St
(92225) 800.800.8000
call re: fees

Travelodge ($$)
850 W Hobson Way
(92225) 800.367.2250

● Bolinas ●

Beach House ($$$)
59 Brighton Ave
(94924) 800.982.2545

● Boulder Creek ●
Merrybrook Lodge ($$$)
123420 Big Basin Way
(95006) 408.338.6813

● Brawley ●
Town House Lodge ($$)
135 Main St
(92227) 619.344.5120

● Brea ●
Hyland Motel ($$)
727 S Brea Blvd
(92821) 714.990.6867

Woodfin Suite Hotel ($$$)
3100 E Imperial Hwy
(92821) 714.579.3200

● Bridgeport ●
Best Western ($$)
333 Main St
(93517) 619.932.7241
small pets only

Silver Maple Inn ($$)
310 Main St
(93517) 619.932.7383

Walker River Lodge ($$$)
Box# 695
(93517) 619.932.7021

● Brookdale ●
Brookdale Lodge ($$)
11570 Hwy 9
(95007) 408.338.6433

● Buellton ●
Econo Lodge ($$)
630 Ave Of Flags
(93427) 805.688.0022

Motel 6 ($)
333 McCurray Rd
(93427) 805.688.7797
1 small pet/room

● Buena Park ●
Covered Wagon Motel ($)
7830 Crescent Ave
(90620) 714.995.0033

Embassy Suites ($$$)
7762 Beach Blvd
(90620) 711.739.5600

Motel 6 ($)
7051 Valley View St
(90620) 714.522.1200
1 small pet/room

Travelodge ($)
7640 Beach Blvd
(90620) 714.522.8460

● Burbank ●
Hilton ($$$$)
2500 N Hollywood Way
(91505) 800.468.3576

Holiday Inn ($$$)
150 E Angeleno Ave
(91502) 800.465.4329
mgr preapproval reqd

Ramada Inn ($$$)
2900 N San Fernando Blvd
(91504) 800.272.6232
mgr preapproval reqd

● Burlingame ●
Doubletree ($$$)
835 Airport Blvd
(94010) 415.344.5500

Marriott Hotel ($$$$)
1800 Old Bayshore Hwy
(94010) 415.692.9100

Radisson Inn ($$$$)
1177 Airport Blvd
(94010) 415.342.9200
small dogs

Red Roof Inn ($$$)
777 Airport Blvd
(94010) 415.342.7772
if the pet room is available
$10 charge

Vagabond Inn ($$)
1640 Old Bayshore Hwy
(94010) 415.692.4040
small only with fee

● Burney ●
Charm Motel ($$)
37363 Main St
(96013) 916.335.2254

Green Gables Motel ($$)
37385 Main St
(96013) 916.335.2264

Shasta Pines Motel ($)
37386 Main St
(96013) 916.335.2201

Sleepy Hollow Lodge ($)
Box# 1105
(96013) 916.335.2285

● Buttonwillow ●
Good Nite Inn ($)
20645 Tracy Ave
(93206) 805.764.5121

Motel 6 ($)
3810 Tracy Ave
(93206) 805.764.5207
1 small pet/room

CALL AHEAD!

CALIFORNIA, Button Willow

Super 8 ($)
20681 Tracy Ave
(93206) 805.764.5117
call re: fees

● Calimesa ●
Calimesa Inn Motel ($)
1205 Calimesa Blvd
(92320) 909.795.2536

Downtown Motel ($)
101 N Redington St
(92320) 209.582.9036

● Calipatria ●
Calipatria Inn ($$)
Box# 30
(92233) 619.348.7348

● Calistoga ●
Meadowlark House ($$$$)
601 Petrified Forest Rd
(94515) 707.942.5651

Pink Mansion ($$$)
1415 Foothill Blvd
(94515) 707.942.0558

Triple Ranch ($$)
4600 Mtn Home Ranch
(94515) 707.942.6730

Washington Lodging ($$$)
1605 Washington St
(94515) 707.942.6968

● Calpine ●
Sierra Valley Lodge ($$)
Box# 115
(96124) 916.994.3367

● Camarillo ●
Country Inn ($$$)
1405 Del Norte Rd
(93010) 805.983.7171

Motel 6 ($)
1641 E Daily Dr
(93010) 805.388.3467
1 small pet/room

● Cambria ●
Cambria Pines ($$$)
2905 Burton Dr
(93428) 800.445.6868

Cambria Lodge
2905 Burton Dr
(93428) 805.972.4200
owner rfd

Cambria Shores Inn ($$)
6276 Moonstone Beach Dr
(93428) 805.927.8644

Fogcatcher Inn ($$$)
6400 Moonstone Beach Dr
(93428) 800.425.4121

● Cameron Park ●
Best Western ($$)
3361 Coach Ln
(95682) 916.677.2203
under 20 lbs

● Campbell ●
Campbell Inn ($$$)
675 E Campbell Ave
(95008) 408.374.4300
$10 per night

Executive Inn ($$$)
1300 Camden Ave
(95008) 800.888.3611

Motel 6 ($$)
1240 Camden Ave
(95008) 408.371.8870
1 small pet/room

Residence Inn ($$$)
2761 S Bascom Ave
(95008) 800.331.3131

● Canoga Park ●
Super 8 ($$)
7631 Topanga Canyon Blvd
(91304) 818.883.8888
mgr preapproval reqd

Warner Center Motel ($$)
7132 Desoto Ave
(91303) 818.346.5400
$8 night

● Capitola ●
Capitola Inn ($$)
822 Bay Ave
(95010) 408.462.3004

● Carlsbad ●
E Z 8 Motel ($)
2484 Hotel Circle Pl
(92018) 619.291.8252

Economy Inn ($)
751 Raintree Dr
(92009) 619.931.1185

Motel 6 ($)
1006 Carlsbad Village Dr
(92008) 619.434.7135
1 small pet/room

Motel 6 ($)
750 Raintree Dr
(92009) 619.431.0745
1 small pet/room

Motel 6 ($)
6117 Paseo Del Norte
(92009) 619.438.1242
1 small pet/room

Ramada Inn ($$$)
751 Macadamia Dr
(92009) 619.438.2285
mgr preapproval reqd

Travelodge ($)
760 Macadamia Dr
(92009) 800.367.2250

● Carmel ●
Best Western ($$$)
3665 Rio Rd
(93923) 408.624.1841
sall/ $25 fee

Carmel Tradewinds ($$$)
Box# 3403
(93921) 408.624.2776

Coachmans Inn ($$$)
San Carlos & 7th St
(93921) 408.624.6421

Cypress Inn ($$$)
Lincoln & 7 th St
(93921) 408.624.3671
up to 3 pets/ $15/day

Dolores Lodge ($$$)
Box# 3756
(93921) 408.625.3263

Highlands Inn ($$$$)
Highway 1
(93921) 408.624.3801

Quail Lodge Resort ($$$$)
8205 Valley Greens Dr
(93923) 408.324.1581

Vagabond House Inn ($$$)
2747 Dolores&4th
(93921) 408.624.7738
$10 per night

Wayside Inn ($$$)
Mission & 7th
(93921) 408.624.5336

● Carmel Valley ●
Blue Sky Lodge ($$$)
Flight Rd
(93924) 408.659.2935

Carmel Valley Inn ($$)
Box# 115 Carmel Valley Rd
(93924) 800.541.3113

Valley Lodge ($$$)
8 Ford Rd
(93924) 408.659.2261

● Carnelian Bay ●
Lakesidwe Chalets ($$$)
5240 N Lake Blvd
(96140) 916.546.5857

● Carpinteria ●
Best Western ($$$)
4558 Carpinteria Ave
(93013) 800.528.1234
mgrs discretion

Motel 6 ($)
4200 Via Real
(93013) 805.684.6921
1 small pet/room

Motel 6 ($)
5550 Carpinteria Ave
(93013) 808.684.8602
1 small pet/room

● Castaic ●
Castac Inn ($)
31411 Ridge Rd
(91384) 805.257.0229

Comfort Inn ($$)
31558 Castaic Rd
(91384) 805.295.1100

● Castroville ●
Castroville Motel ($$)
11656 Merritt St
(95012) 408.633.2502

● Cathedral City ●
Charleene Apts Motel ($$)
37112 Palo Verde Dr
(92234) 619.328.5427

Days Inn ($$$)
69151 E Palm Canyon Dr
(92234) 619.324.5939

Doubletree ($$)
67967 Vista Chino
(92234) 619.322.7000

Drury Inn ($$)
602 N Bluff Rd
(92234) 618.345.7700

Emerald Court Hotel ($)
69375 Ramon Rd
(92234) 619.324.4521

● Cayucos ●
Cypress Tree Motel ($$)
125 S Ocean Ave
(93430) 805.995.3917

Dolphin Inn ($$)
399 S Ocean Ave
(93430) 805.995.3810

Estero Bay Motel ($)
25 S Ocean Ave
(93430) 805.995.3614

● Cazadero ●
Cazadero Lodge ($$$)
100 Kid Creek Rd
(95421) 707.632.5255

● Cedarville ●
Sunrise Motel ($)
Highway 29
(96104) 916.279.2161

● Cerritos ●
Sheraton Inn ($$)
12725 Center Court Dr
(90703) 310.809.1500

● Chatsworth ●
Summerfield Suites ($$$)
21902 Lassen St
(91311) 818.773.0707
$6/pet $250 dep

● Chester ●
Cedar Lodge Motel ($)
Box# 677
(96020) 916.258.2904

Drakesbad Gst Ranch ($$$$)
Cr Chester Warner Valley
(96020) 916.529.1512

Seneca Motel ($)
Box# 504
(96020) 916.258.2815

Timber House Lodge ($)
First & Main Sts
(96020) 916.258.2729

● Chico ●
Deluxe Inn ($$)
2507 Esplanade
(95926) 916.342.8386

Holiday Inn ($$$)
685 Manzanita Ct
(95926) 916.345.2491
mgr preapproval reqd

Matador Motel ($)
1934 Esplanade
(95926) 916.342.7543

Motel 6 ($)
665 Manzanita Ct
(95926) 916.345.5500
1 small pet/room

Oxford Suites ($$)
2035 Business Ln
(95928) 916.899.9090

Safari Motel ($)
2352 Esplanade
(95926) 916.343.3201
$25 deposit

Town House Motel ($)
2231 Esplanade
(95926) 916.343.1621
small pets only

Vagabond Inn ($$)
630 Main St
(95928) 916.895.1323

● Chino ●
Motel 6 ($)
12266 Central Ave
(91710) 909.591.3877
1 small pet/room

● Chowchilla ●
Days Inn ($$)
220 E Robertson Blvd
(93610) 209.665.4821

● Chula Vista ●
Good Nite Inn ($$)
225 Bay Blvd
(91910) 619.425.8200

La Quinta Inn ($$)
150 Bonita Rd
(91910) 619.691.1211
call re: fees

Motel 6 ($)
745 E St
(91910) 619.422.4200
1 small pet/room

Rodeway Inn ($)
778 Broadway
(91910) 800.424.4777

Traveler Motel ($)
2325 Woodlawn Ave
(91910) 619.427.9170

Travelodge ($$)
394 Broadway
(91910) 619.420.6600

Vagabond Inn ($$)
2300 Broadway
(91910) 619.422.8305
small only with fee

● Claremont ●
Claremont Inn ($$)
555 W Foothill Blvd
(91711) 800.854.5733

Howard Johnson ($$)
721 S Indian Hill Blvd
(91711) 609.626.2431
small cats & dogs $10/day

Ramada Inn ($$)
840 S Indian Hillb Blvd
(91711) 800.228.2828
mgr preapproval reqd

● Clearlake ●
Sunset Lodge ($$)
13961 Lakeshore Dr
(95422) 707.994.6642

Travelodge ($)
4775 Old Hwy 53
(95422) 707.994.1499

● Clearlake Oaks ●
Lake Haven Motel ($$)
100B Short St
(95423) 707.998.3908

Lake Point Lodge ($$)
13440 E Hwy 20
(95423) 707.998.4350

Twenty Oaks Court ($$)
10503 E Hwy 20
(95423) 707.998.3012

● Coalinga ●
Big Country Inn ($$)
25020 W Dorris St
(93210) 209.935.0866

Motel 6 ($)
25008 W Dorris St
(93210) 209.935.1536
1 small pet/room

Motel 6 ($)
25278 W Dorris St
(93210) 209.935.2063
1 small pet/room

The Inn At Harris Ranch
($$$)
24505 W Dorris St
(93210) 209.935.0717

● Coleville ●
Andruss Motel ($$)
Box# 64
(96107) 916.495.2216

Meadowcliff Motel ($)
Rte 1 Box# 126
(96107) 916.495.2255

● Colton ●
Days Inn ($$)
2830 Iowa St
(92324) 909.788.9900

Thriftlodge ($)
225 E Valley Blvd
(92324) 909.824.1520

**Policies
Subject
to Change**

CALIFORNIA, Columbia

● Columbia ●
Columbia Gem Motel ($)
22131 Parrotts Ferry Rd
(95310) 209.532.4508

Columbia Inn Motel ($)
22646 Broadway St
(95310) 209.533.0446

● Compton ●
Ramada Inn ($$)
1919 W Artesia Blvd
(90220) 800.272.6232

● Concord ●
El Monte Motor Inn ($$)
3555 Clayton Rd
(94519) 510.682.1601

Holiday Inn ($$)
1050 Burnett Ave
(94520) 510.687.5500
mgr preapproval reqd

Sheraton Inn ($$)
45 John Glenn Dr
(94520) 510.825.7700

● Corcoran ●
Budget Inn ($$)
1224 Whitley Ave
(93212) 209.992.3171

●-Corning ●
Corning Olive Inn ($)
2165 Solano St
(96021) 916.824.2468

Days Inn ($)
3475 Hwy 99
(96021) 916.824.2000
$25 deposit/pets

Shilo Inn ($$)
3350 Sunrise Way
(96021) 916.824.2940

● Corona ●
Motel 6 ($)
200 N Lincoln Ave
(91720) 909.735.6408
1 small pet/room

Travelodge ($)
1701 W 6th St
(91720) 909.735.5500
$2 night

● Coronado ●
El Cordova Motel ($$$)
1351 Orange Ave
(92118) 619.465.4131

Loews Hotel ($$$$)
4000 Coronado Bay Rd
(92118) 619.424.4000
small below the knee size

● Costa Mesa ●
Ana Mesa Suites ($$)
3597 Harbor Blvd
(92626) 714.662.3500

Best Western ($$)
2642 Newport Blvd
(92627) 714.650.3020
small pets only

La Quinta Inn ($$)
1515 S Coast Dr
(92626) 714.957.5841
call re: fees

Marriott Hotel ($$)
500 Anton Blvd
(92626) 714.957.1100

Motel 6 ($)
1441 Gisler Ave
(92626) 714.957.3063
1 small pet/room

Newport Bay Inn ($)
2070 Newport Blvd
(92627) 714.631.6000

Ramada Ltd ($$)
16870 Superior Ave
(92627) 714.645.2221

Red Lion Inn ($$$$)
3050 Bishop St
(92626) 714.540.7000
call re: fees

Residence Inn ($$$)
881 Baker St
(92626) 714.241.8800
call for fee & availability

Vagabond Inn ($$)
3205 Harbor Blvd
(92626) 714.557.8360
small only with fee

Westin ($$$$)
686 Anton Blvd
(92626) 714.540.2500

● Covelo ●
Wagon Wheel Motel ($)
75860 Covelo Rd
(95428) 707.983.6717

● Covina ●
Embassy Suites ($$$)
1211 E Garvey St
(91724) 818.915.3441

● Crescent City ●
Days Inn
220 "M" St
(95531) 707.464.9553
$5 pet room available

Econo Lodge ($)
119 L St
(95531) 707.464.2181

Patio Budget Motel ($)
725 Hwy 101
(95531) 707.464.6106

Holiday Inn
100 Walton St
(95531) 707.646.3885

Pacific Motor Hotel ($$)
440 Hwy 101
(95531) 70P.464.4141

Royal Inn ($)
102 L St
(95531) 707.464.4113

Super 8 ($$)
685 Hwy 101
(95531) 707.464.4111
small dogs & fee

● Crestline ●
Crest Lodge Resort ($$)
23508 Lake Dr
(92325) 909.338.2418

● Culver City ●
Ramada Inn ($$$)
6333 Bristol Pkwy
(90230) 310.670.3200
mgr preapproval reqd

Red Lion Inn ($$$)
6161 W Centinela Ave
(90230) 310.649.1776
call re: fees

Sunburst Motel ($$)
3900 Sepulveda Blvd
(90230) 310.398.7523

● Cupertino ●
Cupertino Inn ($$$)
10889 N De Anza Blvd
(95014) 408.996.7700

● Cypress ●
Ramada Inn ($$$)
5865 Katella Ave
(90630) 714.827.1010
mgr preapproval reqd

Woodfin Suite Hotel ($$$$)
5905 Coporate Ave
(90630) 714.828.4000

● Dana Point ●
Dana Point Resort ($$$$)
25135 Park Lantern
(92629) 714.661.5000

● Danville ●
Danville Inn ($$$)
803 Camino Ramon
(94526) 510.838.8080

● Dardanelle ●
Dardanelle Resort ($$)
Highway 108
(95314) 209.965.4355

● Davis ●
Best Western ($$$)
123 B St
(95616) 916.756.7890
small pets

Davis Inn ($$)
4100 Chiles Rd
(95616) 916.757.7378

Econo Lodge ($$)
221 D St
(95616) 916.756.1040
$5 per day

Motel 6 ($)
4835 Chiles Rd
(95616) 916.753.3777
1 small pet/room

Well
Behaved

$=under $35 $$=$35-60 $$$=$60-100 $$$$=over $100

● Death Valley ●
Stove Pipe Village ($$)
Hwy 190
(92328) 619.786.2387

● Del Mar ●
Del Mar Hilton ($$$)
15575 Jimmy Durante Blvd
(92014) 619.792.5200

● Delano ●
Comfort Inn ($$)
2211 Girard St
(93215) 800.221.2222
mgr preapproval reqd

Shilo Inn ($$)
2231 Girard St
(93215) 805.725.7551
call re: fees

● Desert Hot Springs ●
Atlas Lodge ($)
18336 Avenida Hermosa
(92240) 760.329.5446

Broadview Lodge ($)
12672 Eliseo Rd
(92240) 760.329.8006

Caravan Spa ($$)
66-810 E 4th St
(92240) 760.329.7124

Desert Hot Spgs Hotel ($$)
10805 Palm Dr
(92240) 760.329.6495

El Reoso Motel ($)
66-334 W 5th St
(92240) 760.329.6632

Kismet Lodge ($$)
13340 Mountain View Rd
(92240) 760.329.6451

Las Primaveras Resort ($$)
66659 6th St
(92240) 760.251.1677

Mineral Springs ($)
11000 Palm Dr
(92240) 760.329.6484

Miracle Manor ($$)
12589 Reposo Way
(92240) 760.329.6641

Royal Palms Inn ($$)
12885 Eliseo Rd
(92240) 760.329.7975

San Marcus Inn ($)
66-540 Marcus Rd
(92240) 760.329.5304

Stardust ($$)
66634 - 5th
(92240) 760.329.5443

Stardust Spa Motel ($$)
66634 5th St
(92240) 760.329.5443

Sunset Inn ($$)
67585 Hacienda Ave
(92240) 760.329.4488

Swiss Health Resort ($$)
66729 8th St
(92240) 760.329.6912

Tamara Motel ($)
66185 Acoma Ave
(92240) 760.329.6615

● Diamond Bar ●
Radisson Inn ($$)
21725 E Gateway Dr
(91765) 800.333.3333

● Dinuba ●
Best Western ($$)
Alta Ave & Kamm Rd
(93618) 209.595.8401
small pets only

● Dixon ●
Best Western ($$)
1345 Commercial Way
(95620) 916.678.1400
under 20 lbs

● Douglas City ●
Indian Creek Lodge ($)
Hwy 299
(96024) 916.623.6294

● Downey ●
Embassy Suites ($$$$)
8425 Firestone Blvd
(90241) 562.861.1900
$15

● Downieville ●
Dyers Resort ($$)
Box# 406
(95936) 916.289.3308

● Doyle ●
Seven Motel ($)
434-455 Doyle Loop
(96109) 916.827.3331

Midway Motel ($)
Doyle Loop
(96109) 916.827.2208

● Duarte ●
Travelodge ($$)
1200 Huntington Dr
(91010) 626.357.0907

● Dunnigan ●
Best Western ($$)
3930 Rd 89
(95937) 916.724.3471
pets at managers discretion

Value Lodge ($$)
Rd 89
(95937) 916.724.3333

● Dunsmuir ●
Caboose Motel ($$)
100 Railroad Park Rd
(96025) 916.235.4440

Cave Springs Resort ($$)
4727 Dunsmuir Ave
(96025) 916.235.2721

Cedar Lodge ($)
4201 Dunsmuir Ave
(96025) 916.235.4331

Alpine Inn ($)
4221 Siskiyou Ave
(96025) 916.235.0930

Shasta Alpine Inn ($)
4221 Dunsmuir Ave
(96025) 916.235.0930

Travelodge ($$)
5400 Dunsmuir Ave
(96025) 916.235.4395

● El Cajon ●
Best Western ($$)
1355 E Main St
(92021) 619.440.7378

Days Inn ($)
1250 El Cajon Blvd
(92020) 619.588.8808
mgr preapproval reqd

Motel 6 ($)
550 Montrose Ct
(92020) 619.588.6100
1 small pet/room

Thriftlodge ($)
1220 W Main St
(92020) 619.442.2576

Villa Embasadora ($)
1556 E Main St
(92021) 619.442.9617

● El Centro ●
Best Western ($$)
2352 S 4th St
(92243) 760.337.8677
small pets only

Brunners Motel ($$)
215 N Imperial Ave
(92243) 760.352.6431

Carnation Inn ($$)
2000 Cottonwood Cir
(92243) 760.352.9523

Del Coronado Motel ($$)
330 N Imperial Ave
(92243) 760.353.0030
$6 fee

Executive Inn ($)
7025 State St
(92243) 760.352.8500

Laguna Inn ($$)
2030 Cottonwood Cir
(92243) 760.353.7750

Motel 6 ($)
395 Smoketree Dr
(92243) 760.353.6766
1 small pet/room

Sands Motel ($)
611 N Imperial Ave
(92243) 760.352.0715

Travelodge ($$)
1464 Adams Ave
(92243) 760.352.7333

● El Cerrito ●
Frewway Motel ($$)
11645 San Pablo Ave
(94530) 510.234.5581

● El Monte ●
Motel 6 ($)
3429 Peck Rd
(91731) 818.448.6660
1 small pet/room

● El Portal ●
Yosemite View Lodge ($$$)
Box# D
(95318) 209.379.2681

● El Segundo ●
Crown Sterling ($$$$)
1440 E Imperial Ave
(90245) 310.640.3300

Summerfield Suites ($$$$)
810 S Douglas St
(90245) 310.725.0100

Travelodge ($$)
1804 E Sycamore Ave
(90245) 310.615.1073

● Elk ●
The Greenwood Pier Inn
($$$)
Box# 36
(95432) 707.877.9997

● Emigrant Gap ●
Rancho Sierras ($$)
43440B Laing Rd
(95715) 916.389.8572

● Encinitas ●
Budget Motel ($)
133 Encinitas Blvd
(92024) 619.944.0260

Friendship Inn ($)
410 N Hwy 101
(92024) 619.436.4999

● Escondido ●
Best Western ($$)
1700 Seven Oaks Rd
(92026) 760.740.1700
mgr preapproval reqd

Castle Creek Inn ($$$)
29850 Circle R Way
(92026) 619.751.8800

Econo Lodge ($$)
1250 W Valley Pkwy
(92029) 800.424.4777

Lawrence Welk Resort ($$$)
8860 Lawrence Welk Dr
(92026) 619.749.3000

Motel 6 ($)
509 W Washington Ave
(92025) 619.743.6669
1 small pet/room

Motel 6 ($)
900 N Quince St
(92025) 619.745.9252
1 small pet/room

Motel Mediteranian ($)
2336 S Escondido Blvd
(92025) 619.743.1061

Pine Tree Lodge ($$)
425 W Mission Ave
(92025) 619.740.7613

Sunshine Motel ($)
1107 S Escondido Blvd
(92025) 619.743.3111

Super 7 Motel ($)
515 W Washington Ave
(92025) 619.743.7979

Super 8 ($)
528 W Washington Ave
(92025) 619.747.3711
call re: fees

The Sheridan Inn ($$)
1341 N Escondido Blvd
(92026) 619.743.8338

● Eureka ●
Bayview Motel ($$)
Hwy 101
(95501) 707.442.1673

Budget Host ($)
933 4th St
(95501) 800.445.6888
some pets

Carson House Inn ($$$)
1209 4th St
(95501) 707.443.1601

Eureka Inn ($$$)
518 7th St
(95501) 707.442.6441

Fireside Inn ($)
5th & R Sts
(95501) 707.443.6312

Matador Motel ($)
129 4th St
(95501) 707.443.9751

Motel 6 ($)
1934 Broadway St
(95501) 707.445.9631
1 small pet/room

Nendels Valu Inn ($$)
2223 4th St
(95501) 707.442.3261

Red Lion Inn ($$$)
1929 4th St
(95501) 707.445.0844
call re: fees

Safari Budget 6 ($)
801 Broadway St
(95501) 707.443.4891

Sandpiper Motel ($)
4055 Broadway St
(95503) 707.443.7394

Town House Motel ($)
933 4th St
(95501) 707.443.4536

Travelodge ($)
4 4th St
(95501) 707.443.6345
small to medium

Vagabond Inn ($)
1630 4th St
(95501) 707.443.8041

● Fairfax ●
Arbor Inn ($$$)
1058 Munras Ave
(94930) 408.372.3381

● Fairfield ●
Motel 6 ($)
1473 Holiday Ln
(94533) 707.425.4565
1 small pet/room

Motel 6 ($)
2353 Magellan Rd
(94533) 707.427.0800
1 small pet/room

● Fall River Mills ●
High Mnt Motel ($$)
43021B Hwy 299
(96028) 916.336.5541

● Fallbrook ●
Best Western ($$$)
1635N S Mission Rd
(92028) 619.728.6174
small pets

Lastancia Inn ($$)
3135 Old Hwy 395
(92028) 619.723.2888

● Ferndale ●
Ferndale Motel ($$)
632 Main St
(95536) 707.786.9471

● Firebaugh ●
Apricot Inn ($$)
46290 W Panoche Rd
(93622) 209.659.1444

● Fish Camp ●
Marriott Hotel ($$$$)
1122 Hwy 41
(93623) 209.683.6555

● Folsom ●
Radisson Inn ($$$)
720 Gold Lake Dr
(95630) 916.351.1500
small pets allowed

● Fontana ●
Motel 6 ($)
10195 Sierra Ave
(92335) 909.823.8686
1 small pet/room

● Fort Bidwell ●
Fort Bidwell Hotel ($)
Box# 100
(96112) 916.279.2050

● Fort Bragg ●
Beachcomber Motel ($$)
1111 N Main St
(95437) 707.664.2402

$=under $35 $$=$35-60 $$$=$60-100 $$$$=over $100

Cleone Lodge Inn ($$$)
24600 N Hwy 1
(95437) 707.964.2788

Coast Motel ($$)
18661 N Hwy 1
(95437) 707.964.2852

Ebb Ridge Lodge ($$)
250 S Main St
(95437) 707.964.5321

The Rendezvous Inn ($$)
647 N Main St
(95437) 800.491.8142

Wishing Well Cottages ($$)
Hwy 20
(95437) 800.362.9305

● Fortuna ●
Best Western ($$)
1528 Kenmar Rd
(95540) 707.725.6822
small dogs no cats

Econo Lodge ($$)
275 12th St
(95540) 707.725.6993

Holiday Inn ($)
1859 Alamar Way
(95540) 707.725.5500
mgr preapproval reqd

National 9 ($)
819 Main St
(95540) 707.725.5136

Super 8 ($$)
1805 Alamar Way
(95540) 707.725.2888
desposit

● Fountain Valley ●
Ramada Inn ($$)
9125 Recreation Cir Dr
(92708) 714.847.3388
mgr preapproval reqd

Residence Inn ($$$$)
9930 Slater Ave
(92708) 714.965.8000
call for fee & availability

● Fremont ●
BestWestern ($$$)
5400 Mowry Ave
(94538) 510.792.4300
mgr preapproval reqd

Good Nite Inn ($$)
4135 Cushing Pkwy
(94538) 510.656.9307

Islander Motel ($)
4101 Mowry Ave
(94538) 510.796.8200

Bradleys Inn ($$$)
43344 Mission Blvd
(94539) 510.490.0520

Mission Peak Lodge ($)
43643 Mission Blvd
(94539) 510.656.2366

Motel 6 ($)
46101 Research Ave
(94539) 510.490.4528
1 small pet/room

Motel 6 ($)
34047 Fremont Blvd
(94555) 510.793.4848
1 small pet/room

Residence Inn ($$$)
5400 Farwell Pl
(94536) 510.794.5900
$75 fee

● Fresno ●
Best Western ($$)
2141 N Parkway Dr
(93705) 209.237.1881
small $5

Blackstone Inn ($$)
4061 N Blackstone Ave
(93726) 209.222.5641

Brooks Ranch Inn ($)
4278 W Ashian Ave
(93722) 209.275.2727

Days Inn ($$)
1101 N Parkway Dr
(93728) 209.268.6211
small only with fee

Economy Inn ($)
2570 S East Ave
(93706) 800.826.0778

Economy Inn ($)
5021 N Barcus Ave
(93722) 800.826.0778

Executive Suites ($$$$)
Box# 42
(93707) 209.237.7444

Hilton ($$$)
1055 Van Ness Ave
(93721) 209.485.9000

Holiday Inn ($$$)
2233 Ventura St
(93721) 209.268.1000
mgr preapproval reqd

Howard Johnson ($$)
4071 N Blackstone Ave
(93726) 800.654.2000

La Quinta Inn ($$)
2926 Tulare St
(93721) 209.442.1110
call re: fees

Motel 6 ($)
445 N Parkway Dr
(93706) 209.485.5011
1 small pet/room

Motel 6 ($)
4245 N Blackstone Ave
(93726) 209.221.0800
1 small pet/room

Motel 6 ($)
4080 N Blackstone Ave
(93726) 209.222.2431
1 small pet/room

Motel 6 ($)
933 N Parkway Dr
(93728) 209.233.3913
1 small pet/room

Motel 6 ($)
1240 N Crystal Ave
(93728) 209.237.0855
1 small pet/room

Residence Inn
5322 N Diana Ave
(93710) 209.222.8900

Rodeway Inn ($)
949 N Parkway Dr
(93728) 209.268.0363

Super 8 ($$)
1087 N Parkway Dr
(93728) 209.268.0741
call re: fees

Travelodge ($$)
2345 N Parkway Dr
(93705) 209.268.0711

● Fullerton ●
Fullerton Inn ($)
2601 W Orangethorpe Ave
(92833) 714.773.4900

Marriott Hotel ($$$)
2701 E Nutwood Ave
(92631) 714.738.7800
1st floor smoking rooms

Motel 6 ($)
1440 N State College
(92631) 714.956.9690
1 small pet/room

Motel 6 ($)
1415 S Euclid St
(92832) 714.992.0660
1 small pet/room

● Garberville ●
Best Western ($$)
701 Redwood Dr
(95542) 707.923.2771
small pets

Garberville Motel ($$)
948 Redwood Dr
(95542) 707.923.2422

Redwoods ($$)
900 Hwy 101
(95542) 707.247.3305

Sherwood Forest ($$)
814 Redwood Dr
(95542) 707.923.2721

● Gardena ●
Carson Plaza Hotel ($)
111 W Albertoni St
(90248) 310.329.0651

● Gilroy ●
Leavesley Inn ($$)
8430 Murray Ave
(95020) 408.847.5500

$=under $35 $$=$35-60 $$$=$60-100 $$$$=over $100

CALIFORNIA, Gilroy

Motel 6 ($)
6110 Monterey Hwy
(95020) 408.842.6061
1 small pet/room

Sunrest Inn ($$)
8292 Murray Ave
(95020) 408.848.3500

Super 8 ($)
8435 San Ysidro Ave
(95020) 408.848.4108
pets w/permission

● Glendale ●
Days Inn ($$$)
600 N Pacific Ave
(91203) 818.956.0202
smoking rooms only

Red Lion Inn ($$$$)
100 W Glenoaks Blvd
(91202) 818.956.5468
call re: fees

Vagabond Inn ($$)
120 W Colorado St
(91204) 818.240.1700
small only with fee

● Glenhaven ●
Indian Beach Resort ($)
Box# 648
(95443) 707.998.3760

● Goleta ●
Holiday Inn
5650 Calle Real
(93117) 805.964.6241

Motel 6 ($$)
5897 Calle Real
(93117) 805.964.3596
1 small pet/room

● Grass Valley ●
Alta Sierra Motel ($$)
135 N Tammy Way
(95949) 916.273.9102

Best Western ($$$)
11972 Sutton Way
(95945) 916.273.1393
mgr preapproval reqd

Holiday Lodge ($$)
1221 E Main St
(95945) 916.273.4406

Swan House ($$$)
328 S Church St
(95945) 916.273.1873

● Green Valley Lake ●
Green Valley Lodge ($$$)
33655 Green Vly Lake
(92341) 909.867.4281

● Greenville ●
Hideaway Resort Motel ($$)
101 Hideaway Rd
(95947) 916.284.7915

Oak Grove Motel ($$)
Box# 827
(95947) 916.284.6671

Sierra Lodge ($)
Box# 578
(95947) 916.284.6565

Spring Meadow Motel ($$)
18964 Hwy 89
(95947) 916.284.6768

● Groveland ●
Buckmeadows Lodge ($$)
7647 Hwy 120
(95321) 209.962.5281

Groveland Hotel ($$$)
18767 Main St
(95321) 209.962.4000

Mountain River Motel ($$)
12655 Jacksonville Rd
(95321) 209.984.5071

Sugar Pine Ranch ($$$)
Box# 784
(95321) 209.962.7823

Yosemite Inn ($)
31191 Hardin Flat Rd
(95321) 209.962.0103

Yosemite Westgate ($$)
7366 Hwy 120
(95321) 209.962.5281

● Grover Beach ●
Oak Park Inn ($$)
775 N Oak Park Blvd
(93433) 805.481.4448

● Gualala ●
Gualala Country Inn ($$$)
Hwy 1
(95445) 707.884.4343

Surf Motel Gualala ($$$)
39170 Hwy
(95445) 707.884.3571

● Guerneville ●
Avalon Inn ($$)
16484 4th St
(95446) 707.869.9566

Creekside Inn ($$)
16180 Neeley Rd
(95446) 707.869.3623

The Highlands ($$)
14000 Woodland Dr
(95446) 707.869.0333

● Gustine ●
Holiday Inn
28976 W Plaza Dr
(95322) 209.826.8282

Motel 6 ($)
12733 S Hwy 33
(95322) 209.826.6644
1 small pet/room

Super 8
28821 Gonzaga Rd
(95322) 209.827.8700
call re: fees

● Hacienda Heights ●
Motel 6 ($)
1154 7th Ave
(91745) 818.968.9462
1 small pet/room

● Half Moon Bay ●
Holiday Inn ($$$)
230 Cabrillo Hwy
(94019) 415.726.3400
mgr preapproval reqd

Ramada Ltd ($$$)
3020 Hwy 1
(94019) 415.726.9700

● Hanford ●
Irwin Street Inn ($$$)
522 N Irwin St
(93230) 209.583.8791

● Happy Camp ●
Forest Lodge Motel ($$)
63712 Hwy 96
(96039) 916.493.5424

● Harbor City ●
Motel 6 ($$)
820 Sepulveda Blvd
(90710) 800.440.6000
1 small pet/room

Travelodge ($$)
1665 Pacific Coast Hwy
(90710) 310.326.9026

● Hayfork ●
Big Creek Lodge ($)
Big Creek Rd
(96041) 916.628.5521

● Hayward ●
Executive Inn ($$$)
20777 Hesperian Blvd
(94541) 510.732.6300
under 20 lbs

Hayward Islander ($)
29083 Mission Blvd
(94544) 510.538.8700

Motel 6 ($)
30155 Industrial Pkwy SW
(94544) 510.489.8333
1 small pet/room

Phoenix Motor Lodge ($$)
500 W A St
(94541) 510.786.0417

Phoenix Lodge ($$)
2286 Industrial Pkwy
(94545) 510.786.2844

Super 8
2460 Whipple Rd
(94544) 510.489.3888
call re: fees

Vagabond Inn ($$)
20455 Hesperia Blvd
(94541) 510.785.5480
small only with fee

● Healdsburg ●
Best Western ($$)
198 Dry Creek Rd
(95448) 707.433.0300
$10 mgrs discretion

Policies Subject to Change

82

$=under $35 $$=$35-60 $$$=$60-100 $$$$=over $100

Fairview Motel ($$)
74 Healdsburg Ave
(95448) 707.433.5548

Madrona Manor ($$$$)
1001 Westside Rd
(95448) 707.433.4231

● Hemet ●
Best Western ($$)
2625 W Florida Ave
(92545) 909.925.6605
$10 mgrs discretion

Coachlight Motel ($)
1640 W Florida Ave
(92543) 909.658.3237

Super 8 ($$)
3510 W Florida Ave
(92545) 909.658.2281
call re: fees

Travelodge ($$)
1201 W Florida Ave
(92543) 909.766.1902

● Hesperia ●
Days Inn ($$)
14865 Bear Valley Rd
(92345) 619.948.0600
small pets allowed

● Hollister ●
Cinderella Motel ($$)
110 San Felipe Rd
(95023) 408.637.5761

Ridgemark Cottages ($$$)
3800 Airline Hwy
(95023) 408.637.8151

● Homewood ●
Homeside Motel ($$$$)
5205 W Lake Blvd
(96141) 800.824.6348

● Huntington Beach ●
Beach Comfort Motel ($$)
11 11th St
(92647) 714.536.4170

Best Western ($$$)
19360 Beach Blvd
(92648) 800.528.1234
sunder 25 lbs

Motel Europa ($$)
7561 Center Ave 46
(92647) 714.892.7336

● Hyampom ●
Zieglers Trails End ($$)
1 Main St
(96046) 916.628.4929

● Idyllwild ●
Fireside Inn ($$)
54540 N Circle Dr
(92549) 909.659.2966

Idyllwild Inn ($$)
Box# 515
(92549) 909.659.2552

Knotty Pine Cabins ($$)
54340 Pine Crest Dr
(92549) 909.659.2933

Mile High Lodge ($$$)
54635 N Circle Dr
(92549) 909.659.2931

● Imperial Beach ●
Hawaiian Gardens ($$)
1031 Imperial Beach Blvd
(91932) 619.429.5303

● Indian Wells ●
Easy Eight Motel ($)
3325 Midway Dr
(92210) 619.223.9500

Garden Resort ($$)
76-477 Hwy 111
(92210) 619.346.8021

Stouffer ($$$$)
44400 Indian Wells Ln
(92210) 619.773.4444

● Indio ●
Best Western ($$)
81909 Indio Blvd
(92201) 760.347.3421

Comfort Inn ($$)
43505 Monroe St
(92201) 760.347.4044
mgr preapproval reqd

Holiday Inn
84096 Indio Springs Dr
(92201) 760.342.6344

Indio Holiday Motel ($$)
44301 Sun Gold St
(92201) 760.347.6105

Motel 6 ($)
82195 Indio Blvd
(92201) 760.342.6311
1 small pet/room

Motel 6 ($)
78100 Varner Rd
(92203) 760.345.0550
1 small pet/room

Palm Inn ($$)
80761 Hwy 111
(92201) 760.347.3476

Penta Inn ($)
84115 Indio Blvd
(92201) 760.342.4747

Rodeway Inn ($$)
84096 Indio Springs Dr
(92201) 800.424.4777

Royal Plaza Inn ($$)
82347 Hwy 111
(92201) 760.347.0911

Super 8 ($$)
81753 Hwy 111
(92201) 760.342.0264
pets w/permission

● Inglewood ●
Best Western ($$)
1730 Centinela Ave
(90302) 310.568.0071
mgr preapproval reqd

Econo Lodge ($)
4123 W Century Blvd
(90304) 310.672.7285

Econo Lodge ($$)
439 W Manchester Blvd
(90301) 800.424.4777

Hampton Inn ($$$)
10300 S La Cienega Blvd
(90304) 310.337.1000
under 25 lbs

Motel 6 ($$)
5101 W Century Blvd
(90304) 310.419.1234
1 small pet/room

● Inverness ●
Inverness ($$$)
Box# 1110
(94937) 415.669.1034

Motel Inverness ($$)
12718 Francis Drake
(94937) 415.669.1081

Rosemary Cottage ($$$$)
75 Balboa Ave
(94937) 415.663.9338

● Inyokern ●
Three Flags Inn ($)
1233 Brown Rd
(93527) 619.377.3300

● Irvine ●
Atrium Marquis Hotel ($$$)
18700 Macarthur Blvd
(92612) 714.833.2770

Holiday Inn ($$$)
17941 Von Karman Ave
(92614) 714.863.1999
mgr preapproval reqd

La Quinta Inn ($$)
14972 Sand Canyon Ave
(92618) 714.551.0909
call re: fees

Marriott Hotel ($$$)
18000 Von Karman Ave
(92612) 714.553.0100

Residence Inn ($$$)
10 Morgan
(92618) 714.380.3000

● Jackson ●
Amador Motel ($)
12408 Kennedy Flat Rd
(95642) 209.223.0970

Campo Casa Motel ($)
12548 Kennedy Flat Rd
(95642) 209.223.0100

Jackson Holiday Lodge ($$)
850 N Hwy 49
(95642) 209.223.0486

Linda Vista Motel ($)
10708 N Hwy 49
(95642) 209.223.1096

● Jamestown ●
Sonora Country Inn ($$)
18755 Charbroullian Ln
(95327) 800.847.2211

● Jenner ●
Stillwater Cove Ranch ($$)
22555 Coast Hwy 1
(95450) 707.847.3227

Timber Cove Inn ($$$)
21780 Coasy Hwy 1
(95450) 707.847.3231

● Joshua Tree ●
Joshua Tree Inn ($$$)
61259 29 Palms Hwy
(92252) 619.366.1188

● Julian ●
Eden Creek Orchard ($$)
1052 Julian Orchards Dr
(92036) 619.765.2102

Pine Hills Lodge ($$)
Box# 2260
(92036) 619.765.1100

● Junction City ●
Bigfoot Campground ($$$)
Hwy 299
(96048) 916.623.6088

Steelhead Cottages ($$)
Hwy 299
(96048) 916.623.6325

● June Lake ●
Gull Lake Lodge ($$$)
Box# 25
(93529) 619.648.7516

June Lake Motel ($$)
Box# 98
(93529) 619.648.7547

Reverse Creek Lodge ($$)
4479 Hwy 158
(93529) 619.648.7535

● Kelseyville ●
Creekside Lodge ($)
79901 Hwy 29
(95451) 707.279.9258

Jims Soda Bay Resort ($$)
6380 Soda Bay Rd
(95451) 707.279.4837

● Kenwood ●
The Little House ($$$$)
255 Adobe Canyon Rd
(95452) 707.833.2536

● Kernville ●
Hi Ho Resort Lodge ($$)
11901 Sierra Way
(93238) 619.376.2671

Kern Lodge Motel ($$)
67 Valley View Dr
(93238) 619.376.2223

Lazy River Lodge ($$)
15729 Sierra Way
(93238) 619.376.2242

River View Lodge ($$$)
2 Sirretta St
(93238) 619.476.6019

● Kettleman City ●
Best Western ($$)
33410 Powers Dr
(93239) 800.528.1234
under 25 lbs

● King City ●
Best Western ($$)
1190 Broadway St
(93930) 408.385.6733
small dogs under 20lbs

Courtesy Inn ($$)
4 Broadway Cir
(93930) 408.385.4646

Motel 6 ($)
3 Broadway Cir
(93930) 408.385.5000
1 small pet/room

Palm Motel ($)
640 Broadway St
(93930) 408.385.3248

Sage Motel ($)
630 Broadway St
(93930) 408.385.3274

● Kings Beach ●
Falcon Lodge ($$$)
8258 N Lake Blvd
(96143) 916.546.2583

North Lake Lodge ($$)
8716 North Lake Blvd
(96143) 800.824.6348

Stevenson Inn ($$)
8742 N Lake Blvd
(96143) 916.546.2269

● Kings Canyon National Pk ●

Grant Grove Lodge ($)
Hwy 180
(93633) 209.561.3314

● Kingsburg ●
Swedish Inn ($$)
401 Conejo St
(93631) 209.897.1022

● Klamath ●
Camp Marigold Motel ($)
16101 Hwy 101
(95548) 707.482.3585

● La Habra ●
La Habra Inn ($$)
700 N Beach Blvd
(90631) 562.694.1991

Motel 6 ($)
870 N Beach Blvd
(90631) 562.694.2158
1 small pet/room

● La Jolla ●
Colonial Inn ($$$$)
910B Prospect St
(92037) 619.454.2181

Holiday Inn
6705 La Jolla Bl
(92037) 619.454.7101

La Jolla Shores Inn ($$)
5390 La Jolla Blvd
(92037) 619.454.0715

Marriott Hotel ($$$$)
4240 La Jolla Village Dr
(92037) 619.587.1414

Residence Inn ($$$)
8901 Gilman Dr
(92037) 619.587.1770
call for fee & availability

Scripps Inn ($$$)
555 Coast Blvd S # 5
(92037) 619.454.3391

The Inn At La Jolla ($$)
5440 La Jolla Blvd
(92037) 800.525.6552

U S Suites Of San Diego
($$$$)
3262 Holiday Ct Ste 205
(92037) 800.877.8483

● La Mesa ●
Comfort Inn ($$)
8000 Parkway Dr
(91942) 619.698.7747
mgr preapproval reqd

La Mesa Springs Hotel ($)
4210 Spring St
(91941) 619.589.7288

Travelodge ($)
9550 Murray Dr
(91942) 619.466.0200

● La Mirada ●
Residence Inn ($$$)
14419 Firestone Blvd
(90638) 714.523.2800

● La Palma ●
La Quinta Inn ($$)
3 Centerpointe Dr
(90623) 714.670.1400
call re: fees

● La Puente ●
Sheraton Resort ($$$$)
1 Indurtry Hills Pkwy
(91744) 818.965.0861

● La Quinta ●
La Quinta Inn ($$$$)
49499 Eisenhower Dr
(92253) 619.564.4111
call re: fees

● Laguna Beach ●
Trade Winds Motel ($)
2020 S Coasy Hwy
(92651) 714.494.5450

Vacation Village ($$$)
647 S Coast Hwy
(92651) 714.494.8566

Well
Behaved

$=under $35 $$=$35-60 $$$=$60-100 $$$$=over $100

● Laguna Hills ●
Laguna Hills Lodge ($$)
23932 Paseo Dr Valencia
(92653) 714.830.2550

● Lake Arrowhead ●
Arrowhead Tree Top ($$)
Box# 186
(92352) 909.337.2311

Lake Arrowhead Resort
($$$)
27984 Hwy 189
(92352) 909.336.1511
small in lakeshore villa units

● Lake Elsinore ●
Lakeview Inn ($$)
31808 Casino Dr
(92530) 909.674.6749

● Lake Tahoe ●
see South Lake Tahoe
see Tahoe City
see Tahoe Vista

● Lakehead ●
Antlers Resort ($$$)
Box# 140
(96051) 800.238.3924

Obanions Cottages ($$)
19667 Lakeshore Dr
(96051) 916.238.2448

Sandy Resort ($$)
19990 Lakeshore Dr
(96051) 916.238.2575

● Lakeport ●
Chalet Motel ($)
2802 Lakeshore Blvd
(95453) 707.263.5040

Cove Resort ($$)
2812 Lakeshore Blvd
(95453) 707.263.6833

Rainbow Motel ($)
23569 Lakeshore Blvd
(95453) 707.263.4309

● Lakeshore ●
Lakeview Cottages ($$)
58374 Huntington Lodge Rd
(93634) 310.697.6556

● Lakewood ●
Crazy 8 Motel ($)
11535 Carson St
(90715) 562.860.0546

● Lancaster ●
Best Western ($$)
44055 Sierra Hwy
(93534) 805.948.4651
$25 non-refundable cleaning
charge

Motel 6 ($)
43540 17th St
(93534) 805.948.0435
1 small pet/room

● Laytonville ●
Gentle Valley Ranch ($$$)
Box# 1535
(95454) 707.984.8456

The Ranch Motel ($)
Box# 1535
(95454) 707.984.8456

● Lebec ●
Flying J Inn ($$)
42810 Frazier Mtn Park Rd
(93243) 805.248.2700

● Lee Vining ●
Murpheys Motel ($$)
Box# 57
(93541) 619.647.6316

● Leggett ●
Redwood Retreat ($)
75000 Hwy 101
(95585) 707.925.6249

● Lemoore ●
Best Western ($$)
877 E D St
(93245) 209.924.1261
mgr preapproval reqd

● Lewiston ●
Lakeview Resort ($$)
Star Rt Box# 250
(96052) 916.778.3803

Lewiston Motel ($)
Trinity Dam Bl
(96052) 916.778.3942

● Lindsay ●
Olive Tree Inn ($$)
390 N Hwy 65
(93247) 209.562.5188

● Littleriver ●
Seafoam Lodge ($$$)
6751 N Hwy 1
(95456) 707.937.1827

● Livermore ●
Motel 6 ($)
4673 Lassen Rd
(94550) 510.443.5300
1 small pet/room

Residence Inn ($$$)
1000 Airway Blvd
(94550) 510.373.1800
$50 fee & $6 per day

Springtown Motel ($$)
933 Bluebell Dr
(94550) 510.449.2211

● Lodi ●
Best Western ($$)
710 S Cherokee Ln
(95240) 209.369.8484
small pets

Comfort Inn ($$$)
118 N Cherokee Ln
(95240) 209.367.4848
mgr preapproval reqd

Lodi Motor Inn ($$$)
1140 S Cherokee Ln
(95240) 209.334.6322

● Lomita ●
Eldorado Coast Hotel ($$)
2037 Pch
(90717) 310.534.0700

● Lompoc ●
Best Western ($$)
940 E Ocean Ave
(93436) 805.735.7731
$10 day

Holiday Inn
1417 H St
(93436) (800)HOLIDAY

Inn Of Lompoc ($$)
1122 H St
(93436) 800.548.8231

Motel 6 ($)
1521 H St
(93436) 805.735.7631
1 small pet/room

Quality Inn ($$)
1621 H St
(93436) 805.735.8555

Redwood Inn ($$)
1200 H St
(93436) 805.735.3737

Tally Ho Motor Inn ($)
1020 E Ocean Ave
(93436) 805.735.6444

● Lone Pine ●
Alabama Inn ($$)
1920 S Main St
(93545) 619.876.8700

Best Western ($$)
1008 S Main St
(93545) 760.876.5571
1 pet per room

Dow Villa Motel ($$)
310 S Main St
(93545) 619.876.5521

National 9 ($)
633 S Main St
(93545) 619.876.5555

● Long Beach ●
Best Western ($$)
1725 N Long Beach Blvd
(90813) 562.599.5555

Days Inn ($$)
1500 E Pacific Coast Hwy
(90806) 562.591.0088
$5

Hilton ($$$$)
2 World Trade Ctr
(90831) 562.983.3400
sign waiver

Holiday Inn ($$)
2640 N Lakewood Blvd
(90815) 562.597.4400

Howard Johnson ($$$)
1133 Atlantic Ave
(90813) 800.654.2000

CALIFORNIA, Long Beach

Marriott Hotel ($$$)
4700 Airport Plaza Dr
(90815) 562.425.5210

Motel 6 ($$)
5665 E 7th St
(90804) 562.597.1311
1 small pet/room

Ramada Inn ($$$)
5325 E Pacific Coast Hwy
(90804) 562.597.1341
mgr preapproval reqd

Residence Inn ($$$)
4111 E Willow St
(90815) 800.331.3131

Sheraton Inn ($$$$)
333 E Ocean Blvd
(90802) 562.436.3000

Travelodge ($$)
700 Queensway Dr
(90802) 562.435.7676

Travelodge ($$)
80 Atlantic Ave
(90802) 562.435.2471

Vagabond Inn ($$)
185 Atlantic Ave
(90802) 562.435.7621

● Los Alamos ●
Skyview Motel ($$$)
9150 Hwy 101
(93440) 805.344.3770

● Los Angeles ●
Best Western ($$)
818 N Hill St
(90012) 213.617.3077
mgr preapproval reqd

Best Western ($$)
6141 Franklin Ave
(90028) 213.464.5181
$10 fee

Beverly Hills Plaza ($$$$)
10300 Wilshire Blvd
(90024) 310.275.5575

Beverly Laurel Hotel ($$)
8018 Beverly Blvd
(90048) 213.651.2441

Brentwood Motel ($$)
12200 W Sunset Blvd
(90049) 310.476.9981

Brentwood Suites ($$$)
199 N Church Ln
(90049) 310.476.6255

Century Plaza Hotel ($$$$)
2025 Ave Of The Stars
(90067) 310.277.2000

Century Wilshire Hotel ($$$)
10776 Wilshire Blvd
(90024) 800.421.7223

Chateau Marmont Hotel
($$$$)
8221 W Sunset Blvd
(90046) 213.656.1010

Continental Plaza ($$$)
9750 Airport Blvd
(90045) 310.645.4600

Doubletree ($$$)
5400 W Century Blvd
(90045) 800.528.0444

Econo Lodge ($$)
3400 W 3rd St
(90020) 213.385.0061

Embassy Suites ($$$)
9801 Airport Blvd
(90045) 800.362.2779

Hallmark Hotel ($$)
7023 W Sunset Blvd
(90028) 213.464.8344

Holiday Inn
1520 N La Brea Ave
(90028) (800)HOLIDAY

Holiday Inn ($$$)
170 N Church Ln
(90049) 310.476.6411
mgr preapproval reqd

Holiday Inn ($$$)
1020 S Figueroa St
(90015) 213.748.1291
mgr preapproval reqd

Holiday Inn ($$$)
750 Garland Ave
(90017) 800.465.4329
mgr preapproval reqd

Holiday Select Inn ($$$)
1150 S Beverly Dr
(90035) 310.553.6561

Hollywood Celebrity Hotel
($$$)
1775 Orchid Ave
(90028) 800.222.7090

Hotel Bel Air ($$$$)
701 Stone Canyon Rd
(90077) 800.648.4097

Hotel Del Capri ($$$)
10587 Wilshire Blvd
(90024) 800.444.6835

Intercontinental ($$$$)
251 S Olive St
(90012) 213.617.3300

Hotel Nikko ($$$$)
465 S La Cienega Blvd
(90048) 310.247.0400

Hotel Ma Maison ($$$$)
8555 Beverly Blvd
(90048) 310.278.5444
bellman can walk

Howard Johnson ($$)
8620 Airport Blvd
(90045) 310.645.7700

Kawada Hotel ($$$)
200 S Hill St
(90012) 800.752.9232

Marriott Hotel ($$$$)
5855 W Century Blvd
(90045) 800.228.9290

Oban Hotel ($)
6364 Yucca St
(90028) 213.466.0524

Omni Hotel ($$$$)
930 Wilshire Blvd
(90017) 800.445.8667

Quality Hotel ($$)
5249 W Century Blvd
(90045) 800.266.2200

Radisson Inn ($$)
6300 Telegraph Rd
(90040) 800.333.3333

Radisson Inn ($$$$)
3515 Wilshire Blvd
(90010) 213.381.7411

Ramada Inn ($$)
7272 E Gage Ave
(90040) 310.806.4777
mgr preapproval reqd

Skyway Inn ($$)
9250 Airport Blvd
(90045) 800.336.0025

The Four Seasons ($$$$)
300 S Doheny Dr
(90048) 310.273.2222
small pets allowed

Travelodge ($$)
5547 W Century Blvd
(90045) 310.649.4000

Vagabond Inn ($$)
1904 W Olympic Blvd
(90006) 213.380.9393
small only with fee

Vagabond Inn ($$$$)
3101 S Figueroa St
(90007) 213.746.1531
small only with fee

Westin Hotel ($$$$)
404 S Figueroa St
(90071) 213.624.1000
small pets accepted

Westwood Marquis ($$$$)
930 Hilgard Ave
(90024) 310.208.8765

Wilshire Motel ($$)
12023 Wilshire Blvd
(90025) 310.478.3545

Wyndham Hotel ($$$)
535 S Grand Ave
(90071) 213.624.0000

Wyndham Hotel ($$$$)
5757 Telegraph Rd
(90040) 213.887.8100

LA/Central Metro

● Arcadia ●
Embassy Suites ($$$$)
211 E Huntington Dr
(91006) 818.445.8525
small lap dogs

Hampton Inn ($$$)
311 E Huntington Dr
(91006) 818.574.5600

Motel 6 ($$)
225 Colorado Pl
(91007) 818.446.2660
1 small pet/room

Residence Inn ($$$$)
321 E Huntington Dr
(91006) 818.446.6500
call for fee & availability

● Bellflower ●
Motel 6 ($$)
17220 Downey Ave
(90706) 562.531.3933
1 small pet/room

● Beverly Hills ●
Lowell Hotel ($$$$)
929 Burton Way
(90210) 800.800.2113

The Beverly Hilton Hotel
($$$$)
9876 Wilshire Blvd
(90210) 800.922.5432

The Pennisula ($$$$)
9882 Santa Monica Blvd
(90212) 310.551.2888

The Regent Beverly Wilshire
($$$$)
9500 Wilshire Blvd
(90212) 310.275.5200

● Burbank ●
Hilton ($$$$)
2500 N Hollywood Way
(91505) 800.468.3576

Holiday Inn ($$$)
150 E Angeleno Ave
(91502) 800.465.4329
mgr preapproval reqd

Ramada Inn ($$$)
2900 N San Fernando Blvd
(91504) 800.272.6232
mgr preapproval reqd

● Canoga Park ●
Super 8 ($$)
7631 Topanga Canyon Blvd
(91304) 818.883.8888
mgr preapproval reqd

Warner Center Motel ($$)
7132 Desoto Ave
(91303) 818.346.5400
$8 night

● Culver City ●
Ramada Inn ($$$)
6333 Bristol Pkwy
(90230) 310.670.3200
mgr preapproval reqd

Red Lion Inn ($$$)
6161 W Centinela Ave
(90230) 310.649.1776
call re: fees

Sunburst Motel ($$)
3900 Sepulveda Blvd
(90230) 310.398.7523

● Downey ●
Embassy Suites ($$$$)
8425 Firestone Blvd
(90241) 562.861.1900
$15

● Duarte ●
Travelodge ($$)
1200 Huntington Dr
(91010) 626.357.0907

● El Monte ●
Motel 6 ($)
3429 Peck Rd
(91731) 818.448.6660
1 small pet/room

● El Segundo ●
Crown Sterling ($$$$)
1440 E Imperial Ave
(90245) 310.640.3300

Summerfield Suites ($$$$)
810 S Douglas St
(90245) 310.725.0100

Travelodge ($$)
1804 E Sycamore Ave
(90245) 310.615.1073

● Gardena ●
Carson Plaza Hotel ($)
111 W Albertoni St
(90248) 310.329.0651

● Glendale ●
Days Inn ($$$)
600 N Pacific Ave
(91203) 818.956.0202
smoking rooms only

Red Lion Inn ($$$$)
100 W Glenoaks Blvd
(91202) 818.956.5468
call re: fees

Vagabond Inn ($$)
120 W Colorado St
(91204) 818.240.1700
small only with fee

● Inglewood ●
Best Western ($$)
1730 Centinela Ave
(90302) 310.568.0071
mgr preapproval reqd

Econo Lodge ($)
4123 W Century Blvd
(90304) 310.672.7285

Econo Lodge ($$)
439 W Manchester Blvd
(90301) 800.424.4777

Hampton Inn ($$$)
10300 S La Cienega Bl
(90304) 310.337.1000
under 25 lbs

Motel 6 ($$)
5101 W Century Blvd
(90304) 310.419.1234
1 small pet/room

● Los Angeles ●
Best Western ($$)
818 N Hill St
(90012) 213.617.3077
mgr preapproval reqd

Best Western ($$)
6141 Franklin Ave
(90028) 213.464.5181
$10 fee

Beverly Hills Plaza ($$$$)
10300 Wilshire Blvd
(90024) 310.275.5575

Beverly Laurel Hotel ($$)
8018 Beverly Blvd
(90048) 213.651.2441

Brentwood Motel ($$)
12200 W Sunset Blvd
(90049) 310.476.9981

Brentwood Suites ($$$)
199 N Church Ln
(90049) 310.476.6255

Century Plaza Hotel ($$$$)
2025 Ave Of The Stars
(90067) 310.277.2000

Century Wilshire Hotel ($$$)
10776 Wilshire Blvd
(90024) 800.421.7223

Chateau Marmont Hotel
($$$$)
8221 W Sunset Blvd
(90046) 213.656.1010

Continental Plaza ($$$)
9750 Airport Blvd
(90045) 310.645.4600

Doubletree ($$$)
5400 W Century Blvd
(90045) 800.528.0444

Econo Lodge ($$)
3400 W 3Rd St
(90020) 213.385.0061

Embassy Suites ($$$)
9801 Airport Blvd
(90045) 800.362.2779

Hallmark Hotel ($$)
7023 W Sunset Blvd
(90028) 213.464.8344

Holiday Inn
1520 N La Brea Ave
(90028) (800)holiday

Holiday Inn ($$$)
170 N Church Ln
(90049) 310.476.6411
mgr preapproval reqd

Policies Subject to Change

$=under $35 $$=$35-60 $$$=$60-100 $$$$=over $100

CALIFORNIA, Los Angeles

Holiday Inn ($$$)
1020 S Figueroa St
(90015) 213.748.1291
mgr preapproval reqd

Holiday Inn ($$$)
750 Garland Ave
(90017) 800.465.4329
mgr preapproval reqd

Holiday Select Inn ($$$)
1150 S Beverly Dr
(90035) 310.553.6561

Hollywood Celebrity Hotel
($$$)
1775 Orchid Ave
(90028) 800.222.7090

Hotel Bel Air ($$$$)
701 Stone Canyon Rd
(90077) 800.648.4097

Hotel Del Capri ($$$)
10587 Wilshire Blvd
(90024) 800.444.6835

Hotel Ma Maison ($$$$)
8555 Beverly Blvd
(90048) 310.278.5444
bellman can walk

Hotel Nikko ($$$$)
465 S La Cienega Blvd
(90048) 310.247.0400

Howard Johnson ($$)
8620 Airport Blvd
(90045) 310.645.7700

Intercontinental ($$$$)
251 S Olive St
(90012) 213.617.3300

Kawada Hotel ($$$)
200 S Hill St
(90012) 800.752.9232

Marriott Hotel ($$$$)
5855 W Century Blvd
(90045) 800.228.9290

Oban Hotel ($)
6364 Yucca St
(90028) 213.466.0524

Omni Hotel ($$$$)
930 Wilshire Blvd
(90017) 800.445.8667

Quality Hotel ($$)
5249 W Century Blvd
(90045) 800.266.2200

Radisson Inn ($$)
6300 Telegraph Rd
(90040) 800.333.3333

Radisson Inn ($$$$)
3515 Wilshire Blvd
(90010) 213.381.7411

Ramada Inn ($$)
7272 E Gage Ave
(90040) 310.806.4777
mgr preapproval reqd

Skyway Inn ($$)
9250 Airport Blvd
(90045) 800.336.0025

The Four Seasons ($$$$)
300 S Doheny Dr
(90048) 310.273.2222
small pets allowed

Travelodge ($$)
5547 W Century Blvd
(90045) 310.649.4000

Vagabond Inn ($$)
1904 W Olympic Blvd
(90006) 213.380.9393
small only with fee

Vagabond Inn ($$$$)
3101 S Figueroa St
(90007) 213.746.1531
small only with fee

Westin Hotel ($$$$)
404 S Figueroa St
(90071) 213.624.1000
small pets accepted

Westwood Marquis ($$$$)
930 Hilgard Ave
(90024) 310.208.8765

Wilshire Motel ($$)
12023 Wilshire Blvd
(90025) 310.478.3545

Wyndham Hotel ($$$)
535 S Grand Ave
(90071) 213.624.0000

Wyndham Hotel ($$$$)
5757 Telegraph Rd
(90040) 213.887.8100

● Lynwood ●
Marina Del Rey Hotel ($$$)
13534 Bali Way
(90262) 310.301.1000

● Manhattan Beach ●
Radisson Inn ($$$$)
1400 Park View Ave
(90266) 800.333.3333

Residence Inn ($$$)
1700 N Sepulveda Blvd
(90266) 310.546.7627
under 20 lbs

● Marina Del Rey ●
Foghorn Inn ($$)
4140 Via Marina
(90292) 310.823.4626

Marina Motel ($$)
3130 Washington Blvd
(90292) 310.821.5086

Marriott Hotel ($$$$)
13480 Maxella Ave
(90292) 800.228.9290

● Monrovia ●
Holiday Inn ($$)
924 W Huntington Dr
(91016) 818.357.1900
mgr preapproval reqd

Oak Tree Inn ($$)
788 W Huntington Dr
(91016) 818.358.8981

Wyndham Hotel ($$)
700 W Huntington Dr
(91016) 818.357.5211

● Montebello ●
Howard Johnson ($$)
7709 Telegraph Rd
(90640) 213.721.4410

● Pasadena ●
Holiday Inn ($$$)
303 Cordova St
(91101) 626.449.4000
mgr preapproval reqd

Pasadena Inn ($$)
400 S Arroyo Pkwy
(91105) 626.795.8401

Ramada Inn ($$)
3500 E Colorado Blvd
(91107) 626.792.1363
mgr preapproval reqd

Vagabond Inn ($$)
1203 E Colorado Blvd
(91106) 626.449.3170

Vagabond Inn ($$)
2863 E Colorado Blvd
(91107) 626.449.3020
small only with fee

Westway Inn ($$)
1599 E Colorado Blvd
(91106) 626.304.9678

● Reseda ●
Howard Johnson ($$)
7432 Reseda Blvd
(91335) 818.344.0324

● Rosemead ●
Motel 6 ($)
1001 San Gabriel Blvd
(91770) 626.572.6076
1 small pet/room

Vagabond Inn ($$)
3633 Rosemead Blvd
(91770) 626.288.6661
small only with fee

● Rowland Heights ●
Motel 6 ($)
18970 Labin Ct
(91748) 818.964.5333
1 small pet/room

● San Pedro ●
Sheraton Inn ($$$)
601 S Palos Verdes St
(90731) 310.519.8200

Vagabond Inn ($$)
215 Gaffey St
(90731) 310.831.8911
small only with fee

$=under $35 $$=$35-60 $$$=$60-100 $$$$=over $100

● Santa Monica ●
Days Inn ($$$)
3007 Santa Monica Blvd
(90404) 310.829.6333
mgr preapproval reqd

Holiday Inn ($$$)
120 Colorado Ave
(90401) 310.451.0676
mgr preapproval reqd

Loews Hotel ($$$$)
1700 Ocean Ave
(90401) 310.458.6700
dogs under 30 lb ground floor

The Georgian ($$$$)
1415 Ocean Ave
(90401) 310.395.9945

● Torrance ●
Days Inn ($$)
4111 Pacific Coast Hwy
(90505) 800.329.7466
mgr preapproval reqd

Howard Johnson ($$$)
2880 Pacific Coast Hwy
(90505) 310.325.0660

Residence Inn ($$$$)
3701 Torrance Blvd
(90503) 310.543.4566
$40 fee & $6 per day

Summerfield Suites ($$$)
19901 Prairie Ave
(90503) 310.371.8525

● Venice ●
Lincoln Inn ($$$)
2447 Lincoln Blvd
(90291) 310.822.0686

● Whittier ●
Best Whittier Inn ($)
14226 Whittier Blvd
(90605) 562.698.0323

Motel 6 ($)
8221 Pioneer Blvd
(90606) 562.692.9101
1 small pet/room

Vagabond Inn ($)
14125 Whittier Blvd
(90605) 562.698.9701
$3 charge

● Woodland Hills ●
Vagabond Inn ($$)
20157 Ventura Blvd
(91364) 818.347.8080
small only with fee

End of LA/Central Metro

LA/East Metro
● Colton ●
Days Inn ($$)
2830 Iowa St
(92324) 909.788.9900

Thriftlodge ($)
225 E Valley Blvd
(92324) 909.824.1520

● Fontana ●
Motel 6 ($)
10195 Sierra Ave
(92335) 909.823.8686
1 small pet/room

● Hesperia ●
Days Inn ($$)
14865 Bear Valley Rd
(92345) 619.948.0600
small pets allowed

● Idyllwild ●
Fireside Inn ($$)
54540 N Circle Dr
(92549) 909.659.2966

Idyllwild Inn ($$)
Box# 515
(92549) 909.659.2552

Knotty Pine Cabins ($$)
54340 Pine Crest Dr
(92549) 909.659.2933

Mile High Lodge ($$$)
54635 N Circle Dr
(92549) 909.659.2931

● Ontario ●
Country Inn ($$)
2359 S Grove Ave
(91761) 800.770.1887

Country Suties By Carlson ($$$)
231 N Vineyard Ave
(91764) 909.983.8484
$25 fee

Doubletree ($$$)
429 N Vineyard Ave
(91764) 800.582.2946

Good Nite Inn ($$$)
1801 E G St
(91764) 909.983.3604

Holiday Inn ($$$)
3400 Shelby St
(91764) 909.406.9600
mgr preapproval reqd

Howard Johnson ($$)
2425 S Archibald Ave
(91761) 909.923.2728
small pets only

Marriott Hotel ($$)
2200 E Holt Blvd
(91761) 800.284.8811

Motel 6 ($)
1560 E 4th St
(91764) 909.984.2424
1 small pet/room

Motel 6 ($)
1515 N Mountain Ave
(91762) 909.956.6632
1 small pet/room

Ramada Inn ($)
1120 E Holt Blvd
(91761) 909.984.9655
$25 dep

Red Lion Inn ($$$)
222 N Vineyard Ave
(91764) 909.983.0909
call re: fees

Red Roof Inn ($$)
1818 E Holt Blvd
(91761) 909.988.8466

Residence Inn ($$$)
2025 E D St
(91764) 909.983.6788
call re pets & cleaning fee

Travelodge ($)
755 N Euclid Ave
(91762) 909.984.1775

● Pomona ●
Sheraton Suites ($$$)
600 W McKinley Ave
(91768) 909.622.2220

Shilo Inn ($$$)
3200 W Temple Ave
(91768) 909.598.0073

● Riverside ●
Circle Inn Motel
9220 Granite Hill Dr
(92509) 714.360.1132

Courtyard By Marriott ($$)
1510 University Ave
(92507) 909.276.1200

Dynasty Suites ($$)
3735 Iowa Ave
(92507) 909.369.8200

Econo Lodge ($$)
1971 University Ave
(92507) 909.684.6363

Hampton Inn ($)
1590 University Ave
(92507) 909.686.6666

Motel 6 ($)
1260 University Ave
(92507) 909.784.2131
1 small pet/room

Motel 6 ($)
3663 La Sierra Ave
(92505) 909.351.0764
1 small pet/room

Quality Hotel ($$)
616 Convention Way
(92502) 714.750.3131

Super 8 ($)
1199 University Ave
(92507) 909.682.9011
call re: fees

Travelodge ($$)
11043 Magnolia Ave
(92505) 909.688.5000

● San Bernardino ●
Hilton ($$$)
285 E Hospitality Ln
(92408) 909.889.0133

La Quinta Inn ($$)
205 E Hospitality Ln
(92408) 909.888.7571
call re: fees

$=under $35 $$=$35-60 $$$=$60-100 $$$$=over $100

Motel 6 ($)
1960 Ostems Way
(92407) 909.887.8191
1 small pet/room

Motel 6 ($)
111 Redlands Bl
(92408) 909.825.6666
1 small pet/room

● Victorville ●
Budget Inn ($)
14153 Kentwood Blvd
(92392) 619.241.8010

Holiday Inn ($$)
15494 Palmdale Rd
(92392) 619.245.6565
mgr preapproval reqd

Red Roof Inn
13409 Mariposa Rd
(92392) 619.241.1577

End of LA/East Metro

LA/San Fernando Valley Metro

● Agoura Hills ●
Radisson Inn ($$)
30100 Agoura Rd
(91301) 818.707.1220
under 30 lbs

● Burbank ●
Hilton ($$$$)
2500 N Hollywood Way
(91505) 800.468.3576

Holiday Inn ($$$)
150 E Angeleno Ave
(91502) 800.465.4329
mgr preapproval reqd

Ramada Inn ($$$)
2900 N San Fernando Blvd
(91504) 800.272.6232
mgr preapproval reqd

● Canoga Park ●
Super 8 ($$$)
7631 Topanga Canyn Bl
(91304) 818.883.8888
mgr preapproval reqd

Warner Center Motel ($$)
7132 Desoto Ave
(91303) 818.346.5400
$8 night

● Castaic ●
Castac Inn ($)
31411 Ridge Rd
(91384) 805.257.0229

Comfort Inn ($$)
31558 Castaic Rd
(91384) 805.295.1100

● Chatsworth ●
Summerfield Suites ($$$)
21902 Lassen St
(91311) 818.773.0707
$6/pet $250 dep

● Glendale ●
Days Inn ($$$)
600 N Pacific Ave
(91203) 818.956.0202
smoking rooms only

Red Lion Inn ($$$$)
100 W Glenoaks Blvd
(91202) 818.956.5468
call re: fees

Vagabond Inn ($$)
120 W Colorado St
(91204) 818.240.1700
small only with fee

● Mission Hills ●
Best Western ($$$)
10621 Sepulveda Blvd
(91345) 818.891.1771
mgrs discretion

● Newbury Park ●
Easy 8 Motel ($)
2434 W Hillcrest Dr
(91320) 805.499.0755

Motel 6 ($)
1516 Newbury Rd
(91320) 805.499.0711
1 small pet/room

● Newhall ●
Hampton Inn ($$$)
25259 The Old Rd
(91381) 805.253.2400
$8 pet fee

Residence Inn
25320 The Old Rd
(91381) 805.290.2800

● Reseda ●
Howard Johnson ($$)
7432 Reseda Blvd
(91335) 818.344.0324

● Sun Valley ●
Scottish Inn
8365 Lehigh
(91352) 818.504.2671

● Sylmar ●
Motel 6 ($)
12775 Encinitas Ave
(91342) 818.362.9491
1 small pet/room

● Thousand Oaks ●
Best Western ($$)
12 Conejo Blvd
(91360) 805.495.7011
$5/pet

Thousand Oaks Inn ($$)
75 W Thousand Oaks Blvd
(91360) 805.497.3701

● Valencia ●
Best Western ($$$)
27143 Tourney Rd
(91355) 805.255.0555
mgr preapproval reqd

Hilton ($$$)
27710 The Old Rd
(91355) 805.254.8800
sign waiver

● Winnetka ●
Best Western ($$)
20122 Vanowen St
(91306) 818.883.1200
under 20 lbs

● Woodland ●
Cinderella Motel ($)
99 W Main St
(95695) 916.662.1091

Motel 6 ($)
1564 E Main St
(95776) 916.666.6777
1 small pet/room

● Woodland Hills ●
Vagabond Inn ($$)
20157 Ventura Blvd
(91364) 818.347.8080
small only with fee

End of LA/San Fernando Valley Metro

LA/South Bay Metro

● Compton ●
Ramada Inn ($$)
1919 W Artesia Blvd
(90220) 800.272.6232

● Downey ●
Embassy Suites ($$$$)
8425 Firestone Blvd
(90241) 562.861.1900
$15

● El Segundo ●
Crown Sterling ($$$$)
1440 E Imperial Ave
(90245) 310.640.3300

Summerfield Suites ($$$$)
810 S Douglas St
(90245) 310.725.0100

Travelodge ($$)
1804 E Sycamore Ave
(90245) 310.615.1073

● Gardena ●
Carson Plaza Hotel ($)
111 W Albertoni St
(90248) 310.329.0651

● Inglewood ●
Best Western ($$)
1730 Centinela Ave
(90302) 310.568.0071
mgr preapproval reqd

Econo Lodge ($)
4123 W Century Blvd
(90304) 310.672.7285

Econo Lodge ($$)
439 W Manchester Blvd
(90301) 800.424.4777

Well Behaved

$=under $35 $$=$35-60 $$$=$60-100 $$$$=over $100

Hampton Inn ($$$)
10300 S La Cienega Blvd
(90304) 310.337.1000
under 25 lbs

Motel 6 ($$)
5101 W Century Blvd
(90304) 310.419.1234
1 small pet/room

● Manhattan Beach ●
Radisson Inn ($$$$)
1400 Park View Ave
(90266) 800.333.3333

Residence Inn ($$$)
1700 N Sepulveda Blvd
(90266) 310.546.7627
under 20 lbs

● Redondo Beach ●
The Portofino Hotel ($$$$)
260 Portofino Way
(90277) 310.379.8481
w/permission from mgr

Travelodge ($$$)
206 S Pacific Coast Hwy
(90277) 310.318.1811

Vagabond Inn ($$)
2226 S Pacific Coast Hwy
(90277) 310.378.8555

● San Pedro ●
Sheraton Inn ($$$)
601 S Palos Verdes St
(90731) 310.519.8200

Vagabond Inn ($$)
215 Gaffey St
(90731) 310.831.8911
small only with fee

● Santa Monica ●
Days Inn ($$$)
3007 Santa Monica Blvd
(90404) 310.829.6333
mgr preapproval reqd

Holiday Inn ($$$)
120 Colorado Ave
(90401) 310.451.0676
mgr preapproval reqd

Loews Hotel ($$$$)
1700 Ocean Ave
(90401) 310.458.6700
dogs under 30 lb ground floor

The Georgian ($$$$)
1415 Ocean Ave
(90401) 310.395.9945

● Torrance ●
Days Inn ($$)
4111 Pacific Coast Hwy
(90505) 800.329.7466
mgr preapproval reqd

Howard Johnson ($$$)
2880 Pacific Coast Hwy
(90505) 310.325.0660

Residence Inn ($$$$)
3701 Torrance Blvd
(90503) 310.543.4566
$40 fee & $6 per day

Summerfield Suites ($$$)
19901 Prairie Ave
(90503) 310.371.8525

● Venice ●
Lincoln Inn ($$$)
2447 Lincoln Blvd
(90291) 310.822.0686

End of LA/South Bay Metro

● Los Banos ●
Best Western ($$)
301 W Pacheco Blvd
(93635) 209.827.0954
pets mgrs discretion

Regency Inn ($)
349 W Pacheco Blvd
(93635) 209.826.3871

● Los Gatos ●
Beverly Heritage Hotel ($$$)
1820 Barber Ln
(95033) 408.943.9080

Los Gatos Motor Inn ($$)
55 Los Gatos Saratoga Rd
(95032) 408.356.9191

Toll House Motel ($$$)
140 S Santa Cruz Ave
(95030) 408.395.7070

● Los Osos ●
Back Bay Inn ($$)
1391 2nd St
(93402) 805.528.1233

● Lost Hills ●
Economy Inn ($)
14684 Aloma St
(93249) 800.826.0778

Motel 6 ($)
14685 Warren St
(93249) 805.797.2346
1 small pet/room

● Lucerne ●
Beachcomber Resort ($$)
Box# 358
(95458) 707.274.6639

Lake Sands Resort ($$)
6335 E Hwy 20 # 48
(95458) 707.274.7732

Starlite Motel ($$)
Box# 467
(95458) 707.274.5515

● Lynwood ●
Marina Del Rey Hotel ($$$)
13534 Bali Way
(90262) 310.301.1000

● Madera ●
Best Western ($$)
317 G St
(93637) 209.673.5164
mgrs discretion

Economy Inn ($)
1855 W Cleveland Ave
(93637) 800.826.0778

Gateway Inn ($$)
25327 Avenue 16
(93637) 209.674.8817

● Malibu ●
Malbiu Cntry Inn ($$$)
6506 Westward Beach Rd
(90265) 310.457.9622

Malibu Rivera Motel ($$)
28920 Pacific Coast Hwy
(90265) 310.457.9503

● Mammoth Lakes ●
Austria Hof Lodge ($$)
Box# 607
(93546) 619.934.2764

Convict Lake Resort ($$$)
Rt 1 Box# 204
(93546) 619.934.3800

Crystal Lodge ($$)
307 Crystal Crag Dr
(93546) 619.934.2436

Econo Lodge ($$$)
3625 Main St
(93546) 619.934.6855

Englehof Lodge ($)
6156 Minaret Rd
(93546) 619.934.2416

Executive Inn ($$)
54 Sierra Blvd
(93546) 619.934.8892

Holiday Inn
3262 Main St
(93546) (800)HOLIDAY

International Inn ($$)
3554 Main St
(93546) 619.934.2542

Motel 6 ($$)
3372 Main St
(93546) 619.934.6660
1 small pet/room

North Village Inn ($$$)
103 Lake Mary Rd
(93546) 619.934.2925

Royal Resort ($$)
Box# 348
(93546) 619.934.2306
$5 charge some rooms only

Shilo Inn ($$$)
2963 Main St
(93546) 619.934.4500
call re: fees

Thriftlodge ($$)
6209 Minaret Rd
(93546) 619.934.8576

Zwart Lodge ($$)
Box# 174
(93546) 619.934.2217

● Manhattan Beach ●
Radisson Inn ($$$$)
1400 Park View Ave
(90266) 800.333.3333

$=under $35 $$=$35-60 $$$=$60-100 $$$$=over $100

CALIFORNIA, Manhattan Beach

Residence Inn ($$$)
1700 N Sepulveda Blvd
(90266) 310.546.7627
under 20 lbs

● Manteca ●
Best Western ($$)
1415 E Yosemite Ave
(95336) 209.825.1415
small pets only

● Marina ●
Motel 6 ($)
100 Reservation Rd
(93933) 408.384.1000
1 small pet/room

Travelodge ($$)
3290 Dunes Rd
(93933) 408.883.0300

● Marina Del Rey ●
Foghorn Inn ($$)
4140 Via Marina
(90292) 310.823.4626

Marina Motel ($$)
3130 Washington Blvd
(90292) 310.821.5086

Marriott Hotel ($$$$)
13480 Maxella Ave
(90292) 800.228.9290

● Mariposa ●
Best Western ($$)
499 Hwy 140
(95338) 209.966.7545
small pets only

Mariposa Lodge ($)
Box# 733
(95338) 209.966.3607

Miners Inn ($$$)
Box# 1989
(95338) 209.742.7777

Mothers Lodge ($)
Box# 986
(95338) 209.966.2521

Mountain House ($$)
5070 Allred Rd
(95338) 209.966.6033

The Clubbs ($$)
5060 Charles St
(95338) 209.966.5085

The Guest House Inn ($$$)
4962 Triangle Rd
(95338) 209.742.6869

Twelve Oaks House ($$$)
4877 Wildwood Dr
(95338) 209.966.3231

● Markleeville ●
J Marklee Hotel ($$)
Box# 395
(96120) 916.694.2507

Sorensens Resort ($$)
14255 N Hwy 88
(96120) 916.694.2203

● Marysville ●
Holiday Lodge
530 10th St
(95901) 916.742.7147

Marysville Motel ($)
904 E St
(95901) 916.743.1531

● McKinleyville ●
Sea View Motel ($)
1186 Central Ave
(95519) 707.839.1321

● Mendocino ●
Blackberry Inn ($$$)
4495 Larkin Rd
(95460) 707.937.5281

Main Street Inn ($$$$)
44781 Main St
(95460) 707.937.5150

Mendocino Cottages ($$)
46320 Little Lake St
(95460) 707.937.0866

Sears House ($$)
44840 Main
(95460) 707.937.4076

● Merced ●
Best Western ($$)
1213 V St
(95340) 209.723.3711
$10 fee

Days Inn ($$)
1199 Motel Dr
(95340) 209.722.2726
deposit reqd

Motel 6 ($)
1983 E Childs Ave
(95340) 209.384.3702
1 small pet/room

Motel 6 ($)
1215 R St
(95340) 209.722.2737
1 small pet/room

Motel 6 ($)
1410 V St
(95340) 209.384.2181
1 small pet/room

Sandpiper Lodge ($$)
1001 Motel Dr
(95340) 209.723.1034

Super 8
1983 Childs Ave
(95340) 209.384.1303
call re: fees

● Mi Wuk Village ●
Mi Wuk ($$)
Motor Lodge
(95346) 209.586.3031

● Millbrae ●
Clarion Hotel ($$$)
401 E Millbrae Ave
(94030) 415.692.6363
mgr preapproval reqd

Comfort Inn ($$$)
1390 El Camino Real
(94030) 415.952.3200
mgr preapproval reqd

Homestead Guest Ranch
($$$)
1100 El Camino Real
(94030) 415.588.8500

Westin Hotel ($$$$)
1 Old Bayshore Hwy
(94030) 415.692.3500
small pets

● Milpitas ●
Economy Inn ($$)
270 S Abbott Ave
(95035) 408.946.8889

● Miranda ●
Miranda Resort ($$)
6766 Ave Of The Giants
(95553) 707.943.3011

Whispering Pines ($$)
Avenue Of Giants
(95553) 707.943.3182

● Mission Hills ●
Best Western ($$$)
10621 Sepulveda Blvd
(91345) 818.891.1771
mgrs discretion

● Mission Viejo ●
Fairfield Inn ($$)
26238 Oso Pkwy
(92691) 714.582.7100

● Modesto ●
Best Western ($$)
909 16th St
(95354) 209.524.7261
small pets only

Chalet Motel ($$)
115 Downey Ave
(95354) 209.529.4370

Motel 6 ($)
722 Kansas Ave
(95351) 209.524.3000
1 small pet/room

Motel 6 ($)
1920 W Orangebury Ave
(95350) 209.522.2721
1 small pet/room

Red Lion Inn ($$$)
1150 9th St
(95354) 209.526.6000
call re: fees

Tropics Hotel ($)
936 McHenry Ave
(95350) 209.523.7701

Vagabond Inn ($$)
1525 McHenry Ave
(95350) 209.521.6340
small only with fee

● Mojave ●
Motel 6 ($)
16958 Hwy 58
(93501) 805.824.4571
1 small pet/room

Scottish Inn ($)
16352 Sierra Hwy
(93501) 805.824.9317
$5 fee

Vagabond Inn ($)
2145 Hwy 58
(93501) 805.824.2463

Western Inn ($)
16200 Sierra Hwy
(93501) 805.824.3601

● Monrovia ●
Holiday Inn ($$)
924 W Huntington Dr
(91016) 818.357.1900
mgr preapproval reqd

Oak Tree Inn ($$)
788 W Huntington Dr
(91016) 818.358.8981

Wyndham Hotel ($$)
700 W Huntington Dr
(91016) 818.357.5211

● Montclair ●
Ontario Inn ($)
5361 W Holt Ave
(91763) 909.625.3806

● Monte Rio ●
Angelos Resort ($$)
20285 River Blvd
(95462) 707.865.9080

● Montebello ●
Howard Johnson ($$)
7709 Telegraph Rd
(90640) 213.721.4410

● Monterey ●
Bay Park Hotel ($$$)
1425 Munras Ave
(93940) 408.649.1020

Bayside Inn ($)
2055 Fremont St
(93940) 408.372.8071

Best Western ($$$)
487 Foam St
(93940) 408.373.8000
$100 deposit/$75 ref

Best Western ($$$)
2600 Sand Dunes Dr
(93940) 408.394.3321
under 30 lbs

Cannery Row Inn ($$$)
200 Foam St
(93940) 408.649.8580

Colton Inn ($$$)
707 Pacifi Cst
(93940) 408.649.6500

Cypress Gardens Inn ($$$)
1150 Munras Ave
(93940) 408.373.2761
not unattended

Cypress Tree Inn ($$)
2227 Fremont St
(93940) 408.372.7586

Driftwood Motel ($$)
2362 Fremont St
(93940) 408.372.5059

El Adobe Inn ($$)
936 Munras Ave
(93940) 408.372.5409

Holiday Inn ($$$)
1000 Aguajito Rd
(93940) 408.373.6141

Marriott Hotel ($$$$)
350 Calle Principal
(93940) 408.649.4232

Monterey Bay Lodge ($$)
55 Camino Aguajito
(93940) 408.372.8057

Monterey Fireside ($$)
1131 10th St
(93940) 408.373.4172
$10 per day

Motel 6 ($$)
2124 Fremont St
(93940) 408.646.8585
1 small pet/room

Munras Lodge ($$$)
1010 Munras Ave
(93940) 408.646.9696

Westerner Motel ($)
2041 Fremont St
(93940) 408.373.2911

● Monterey Park ●
Days Inn ($$$)
434 Potero Grande Dr
(91755) 213.728.8444
mgr preapproval reqd

● Moreno Valley ●
Motel 6 ($)
23581 Alessandro Blvd
(92553) 909.656.4451
1 small pet/room

Motel 6 ($)
24630 Sunnymead Blvd
(92553) 909.243.0075
1 small pet/room

● Morgan Hill ●
Best Western ($$)
16525 Condit Rd
(95037) 408.779.0447
attended small pets

Budget Inn ($)
19240 Monterey St
(95037) 408.778.3341

Executive Inn ($$$)
16505 Condit Rd
(95037) 408.778.0404

Inn At Morgan Hill ($$$)
16115 Condit Rd
(95037) 408.779.7666

Morgan Hill Inn ($$)
16250 Monterey St
(95037) 408.779.1900

● Morro Bay ●
Adventure Inn ($$)
1148 Front St
(93442) 805.772.5607

Best Value Inn ($)
220 Beach St
(93442) 805.772.3333

Best Western ($$)
2460 Main St
(93442) 805.772.2212
small pets

Best Western ($$)
225 Beach St
(93442) 805.772.7376
small pets

Breakers Motel ($$)
780 Market Ave
(93442) 805.772.7317

Econo Lodge ($$)
1100 Main St
(93442) 800.424.4777

Gold Coast Motel ($)
670 Main St
(93442) 805.772.7740

Golden Pelican Inn ($$)
3270 Main St
(93442) 805.772.7135

Morro Hilltop House ($$)
1200 Morro Ave
(93442) 805.772.1890

Motel 6 ($)
298 Atascadero Rd
(93442) 805.772.5641
1 small pet/room

Sundown Motel ($)
640 Main St
(93442) 805.772.7381

Sunset Travelodge ($$)
1080 Market Ave
(93442) 805.772.1259

● Mount Shasta ●
Alpine Lodge Motel ($)
908 S Mount Shasta Blvd
(96067) 916.926.3145

Best Western ($$$)
I-5 & Lake St
(96067) 916.926.3101
small pets only

Cedar Pond Chalet ($$$)
1701 N Old Stage Rd
(96067) 916.926.3200

Evergreen Lodge ($)
1312 S Mount Shasta Blvd
(96067) 916.926.2143

Mountain Air Lodge ($)
1121 S Mount Shasta Blvd
(96067) 916.926.3446

Travel Inn ($)
504 S Mount Shasta Blvd
(96067) 916.926.4617

CALL AHEAD!

$=under $35 $$=$35-60 $$$=$60-100 $$$$=over $100

Villas Cabins ($)
Box# 344
(96067) 916.926.3313

● Mountain View ●
Best Western ($$$)
1720 W El Camino Real
(94040) 415.961.0220

Residence Inn ($$$)
1854 El Camino Readl
(94040) 415.940.1300
$50 fee & $6 per day

● Napa ●
Budget Inn ($$)
3380 Solano Ave
(94558) 707.257.6111
1 small pet per room

Sheraton Inn ($$$)
3425 Solano Ave
(94558) 800.325.3335

● National City ●
Holiday Inn ($$)
700 National City Blvd
(91950) 619.474.2800

Radisson Inn ($$)
810 National City Blvd
(91950) 619.336.1100

● Needles ●
Best Motel
1900 W Broadway
(92363) 760.326.3824

Best Western ($$)
2371 W Broadway
(92363) 760.326.4552
small pets

Imperial 400 ($)
644 Broadway
(92363) 760.326.2145

Motel 6 ($)
1420 J St
(92363) 760.326.3399
1 small pet/room

Motel 6 ($)
1215 Hospitality Ln
(92363) 760.326.5131
1 small pet/room

River Valley Motel ($)
1707 W Broadway
(92363) 760.326.3839

Super 8 ($)
1102 E Broadway St
(92363) 760.326.4501
call re: fees

● Nevada City ●
Nevada St Cottages ($$)
690 Nevada Street Ext
(95959) 916.265.8071

● Newark ●
Motel 6 ($)
5600 Cedar Ct
(94560) 510.791.5900
1 small pet/room

Woodfin Suites ($$$)
39150 Cedar Blvd
(94560) 510.795.1200

● Newbury Park ●
E Z 8 Motel ($)
2434 W Hillcrest Dr
(91320) 805.499.0755

Motel 6 ($)
1516 Newbury Rd
(91320) 805.499.0711
1 small pet/room

● Newhall ●
Hampton Inn ($$$)
25259 The Old Rd
(91381) 805.253.2400
$8 pet fee

Residence Inn
25320 The Old Rd
(91381) 805.290.2800

● Newport Beach ●
Aladdin Lodge ($)
73-793 Shadow Mtn Dr
(92660) 619.346.6816

Marriott Hotel ($$$$)
900 Newport Center Dr
(92660) 714.640.4000

Marriott Suites ($$$$)
500 Bayview Cir
(92660) 714.854.4500

Palm Desert Ldoge ($$)
74-527 Hwy 111
(92660) 619.346.3875

The Four Seasons ($$$$)
690 Newport Center Dr
(92660) 714.759.0808
small pets allowed

● Nice ●
Talleys ($$)
3827 E Hwy 20
(95464) 707.274.1177

● North Highlands ●
Days Inn
3425 Orange Grove
(95660) 916.488.4100
$25/pets

Motel 6 ($$)
4600 Watt Ave
(95660) 916.973.8637
1 small pet/room

Rodeway Inn ($$)
3425 Orange Grove Ave
(95660) 800.424.4777

● North Hills ●
Motel 6 ($)
15711 Roscoe Blvd
(91343) 818.894.9341
1 small pet/room

● North Palm Springs ●
Motel 6 ($)
63-920 20th Ave
(92258) 619.251.1425
1 small pet/room

● Norwalk ●
Econo Lodge ($$)
1225 E Firestone Blvd
(90650) 310.868.0791

Motel 6 ($)
10646 Rosecrans Ave
(90650) 310.864.2567
1 small pet/room

● Novato ●
Days Inn ($$)
8141 Redwood Blvd
(94945) 415.897.7111

Golden Resort ($)
13363 SHwy 49
(94949) 916.273.7279

Travelodge ($$)
7600 Redwood Blvd
(94945) 415.892.7500

● Oak View ●
Oakridge Inn ($$)
780 Ventura Ave
(93022) 805.649.4018
credit card&liable for damage

● Oakdale ●
Knights Inn ($$$)
17525 Sonora Rd
(95361) 209.881.3349

● Oakhurst ●
Best Western ($$)
40530 Hwy 41
(93644) 209.683.2378
small pets

Comfort Inn ($$$)
40489 Hwy 41
(93644) 209.683.8282
mgr preapproval reqd

Ramada Ltd ($$)
48800 Royal Oaks Dr
(93644) 209.658.5500

● Oakland ●
Clarion Hotel ($$$)
1800 Madison St
(94612) 510.832.2300
mgr preapproval reqd

Days Inn ($$)
8350 Edes Ave
(94621) 510.568.1880
mgr preapproval reqd

Hampton Inn ($$$)
8485 Enterprise Way
(94621) 800.426.7866

Holiday Inn ($$$)
500 Hegenberger Rd
(94621) 510.562.5311

Motel 6 ($$)
1801 Embarcadero
(94606) 510.436.0103
1 small pet/room

Be Discreet

94

$=under $35 $$=$35-60 $$$=$60-100 $$$$=over $100

Motel 6 ($$)
8480 Edes Ave
(94621) 510.638.1180
1 small pet/room

Parc Hotel ($$$$)
1001 Broadway
(94607) 800.338.1338

Travelodge ($$)
423 7th St
(94607) 800.578.7878

Oakland Metro

● Fremont ●
Lord Bradleys Inn ($$$)
43344 Mission Blvd
(94539) 510.490.0520

Mission Peak Lodge ($)
43643 Mission Blvd
(94539) 510.656.2366

Motel 6 ($)
46101 Research Ave
(94539) 510.490.4528
1 small pet/room

Residence Inn ($$$)
5400 Farwell Pl
(94536) 510.794.5900
$75 fee

● Hayward ●
Executive Inn ($$$)
20777 Hesperian Blvd
(94541) 510.732.6300
under 20 lbs

Phoenix Lodge ($$)
500 W A St
(94541) 510.786.0417

Vagabond Inn ($$)
20455 Hesperia Blvd
(94541) 510.785.5480
small only with fee

● Livermore ●
Motel 6 ($)
4673 Lassen Rd
(94550) 510.443.5300
1 small pet/room

Residence Inn ($$$)
1000 Airway Blvd
(94550) 510.373.1800
$50 fee & $6 per day

Springtown Motel ($$)
933 Bluebell Dr
(94550) 510.449.2211

● Oakland ●
Browns Cabin ($$)
7187 Yosemite Pkwy
(94605) 510.430.8466

Clarion Hotel ($$$)
1800 Madison St
(94612) 510.832.2300
mgr preapproval reqd

Days Inn ($$)
8350 Edes Ave
(94621) 510.568.1880
mgr preapproval reqd

Hampton Inn ($$$)
8485 Enterprise Way
(94621) 800.426.7866

Holiday Inn ($$$)
500 Hegenberger Rd
(94621) 510.562.5311

Motel 6 ($$)
1801 Embarcadero
(94606) 510.436.0103
1 small pet/room

Motel 6 ($$)
8480 Edes Ave
(94621) 510.638.1180
1 small pet/room

Parc Hotel ($$$$)
1001 Broadway
(94607) 800.338.1338

Travelodge ($$)
423 7th St
(94607) 800.578.7878

● Pleasanton ●
Doubletree ($$$)
5990 Stoneridge Mall Rd
(94588) 510.463.3330
$15 charge

Hilton ($$$)
7050 Johnson Dr
(94588) 510.463.8000
$15 per day

Holiday Inn ($$$)
11950 Dublin Canyon Rd
(94588) 510.847.6000
mgr preapproval reqd

Motel 6 ($$)
5102 Hopyard Rd
(94588) 510.463.2626
1 small pet/room

● Walnut Creek ●
Embassy Suites ($$$$)
1345 Treat Blvd
(94596) 415.934.2500

Motel 6 ($$)
2389 N Main St
(94596) 415.935.4010
1 small pet/room

Walnut Creek Motel ($$$)
1960 N Main St
(94596) 415.932.2811

End of Oakland Metro

● Occidental ●
Negrin Lodge ($$)
3610 Bohemian Hwy
(95465) 707.874.3623

Union Hotel ($)
3731 Main St
(95465) 707.874.3555

● Oceanside ●
Motel 6 ($)
3708 Plaza Dr
(92056) 619.941.1011
1 small pet/room

Motel 6 ($)
1403 Mission Ave
(92054) 619.721.6662
1 small pet/room

Sandman Motel ($$)
1501 Carmelo Dr
(92054) 619.722.7661

● Ojai ●
Los Padres Inn ($$)
1208 E Ojai Ave
(93023) 805.646.4365

Ojai Manor Hotel ($$)
210 E Matilija St
(93023) 805.646.0961

Ojai Valley Inn ($$$)
SHwy 150
(93023) 805.646.5511
in pet rooms only

● Olema ●
Ridgetop Inn ($$$)
9865 Francis Drake
(94950) 415.663.1500

● Ontario ●
Country Inn ($$)
2359 S Grove Ave
(91761) 800.770.1887

Country Suites ($$$)
231 N Vineyard Ave
(91764) 909.983.8484
$25 fee

Doubletree ($$$)
429 N Vineyard Ave
(91764) 800.582.2946

Good Nite Inn ($$$)
1801 E G St
(91764) 909.983.3604

Holiday Inn ($$$)
3400 Shelby St
(91764) 909.406.9600
mgr preapproval reqd

Howard Johnson ($$)
2425 S Archibald Ave
(91761) 909.923.2728
small pets only

Marriott Hotel ($$)
2200 E Holt Blvd
(91761) 800.284.8811

Motel 6 ($)
1560 E 4th St
(91764) 909.984.2424
1 small pet/room

Motel 6 ($)
1515 N Mountain Ave
(91762) 909.956.6632
1 small pet/room

Ramada Inn ($)
1120 E Holt Blvd
(91761) 909.984.9655
$25 dep

Well Behaved

$=under $35 $$=$35-60 $$$=$60-100 $$$$=over $100

CALIFORNIA, Ontario

Red Lion Inn ($$$)
222 N Vineyard Ave
(91764) 909.983.0909
call re: fees

Red Roof Inn ($$)
1818 E Holt Blvd
(91761) 909.988.8466

Residence Inn ($$$)
2025 E D St
(91764) 909.983.6788
call re pets & fee

Travelodge ($)
755 N Euclid Ave
(91762) 909.984.1775

● Orange ●
Doubletree ($$$$)
100 The City Dr
(92868) 714.634.4500

Good Nite Inn ($)
101 N State College Blvd
(92868) 714.634.9500

Hilton ($)
400 N State College
(92668) 714.634.9500

Residence Inn ($$$)
201 N State College Blvd
(92868) 714.978.7700

Orange County Metro

● Anaheim ●
Anaheim Angel Inn ($)
1800 E Katella Ave
(92805) 714.634.9121

Anaheim Harbor Inn ($$)
2171 S Harbor Blvd
(92802) 714.750.3100

Anaheim Inn ($)
1855 S Harbor Blvd
(92802) 714.750.1811

Anaheim Plaza Hotel ($$$)
1700 S Harbor Blvd
(92802) 800.228.1357

Best Western ($$)
2040 S Harbor Blvd
(92802) 714.750.6100
$10 fee $100 dep

Cavalier Inn ($$)
11811 Harbor Blvd
(92802) 714.750.1000

Crown Sterling ($$$$)
3100 E Frontera St
(92806) 714.632.1221

Desert Palm Inn ($$)
631 W Katella Ave
(92802) 714.535.1133

Econo Lodge ($$)
871 S Harbor Blvd
(92805) 714.535.7878

Friendship Inn ($)
705 S Beach Blvd
(92804) 800.424.4777

Grand Hotel ($$$)
7 Greedman Way
(92802) 800.421.6662

Hampton Inn ($$)
300 E Katella Way
(92802) 714.772.8713
small pets only

Hilton ($$$$)
777 W Convention Way
(92802) 800.233.6904

Holiday Inn ($$$)
1221 S Harbor Blvd
(92805) 714.758.0900
mgr preapproval reqd

Marriott Hotel ($$$$)
700 W Convention Way
(92802) 714.750.8000

Motel 6 ($)
921 S Beach Blvd
(92804) 714.220.2866
1 small pet/room

Motel 6 ($$)
100 W Freedman Way
(92802) 714.520.9696
1 small pet/room

Raffles Inn ($$)
2040 S Harbor Blvd
(92802) 800.654.0196

Red Roof Inn ($)
1251 N Harbor Blvd
(92801) 714.635.6461

Residence Inn ($$$)
1700 S Clementine St
(92802) 714.533.3555

Rodeway Inn ($$)
800 S Beach Blvd
(92804) 800.424.4777

Station Inn ($)
989 W Ball Rd
(92802) 800.874.6265

The Pan Pacific ($$$$)
1717 S West St
(92802) 714.999.0990

Travelodge ($$)
5710 E La Palma Ave
(92807) 714.779.0252

Travelodge ($)
1166 W Katella Ave
(92802) 714.774.7817

● Brea ●
Hyland Motel ($$)
727 S Brea Blvd
(92821) 714.990.6867

Woodfin Suite Hotel ($$$)
3100 E Imperial Hwy
(92821) 714.579.3200

● Costa Mesa ●
Ana Mesa Suites ($$)
3597 Harbor Blvd
(92626) 714.662.3500

Best Western ($$)
2642 Newport Blvd
(92627) 714.650.3020
small pets only

La Quinta Inn ($$)
1515 S Coast Dr
(92626) 714.957.5841
call re: fees

Marriott Hotel ($$)
500 Anton Blvd
(92626) 714.957.1100

Motel 6 ($)
1441 Gisler Ave
(92626) 714.957.3063
1 small pet/room

Newport Bay Inn ($)
2070 Newport Blvd
(92627) 714.631.6000

Ramada Ltd ($$)
16870 Superior Ave
(92627) 714.645.2221

Red Lion Inn ($$$$)
3050 Bishop St
(92626) 714.540.7000
call re: fees

Residence Inn ($$$)
881 Baker St
(92626) 714.241.8800
call for fee & availability

Vagabond Inn ($$)
3205 Harbor Blvd
(92626) 714.557.8360
small only with fee

Westin ($$$$)
686 Anton Blvd
(92626) 714.540.2500

● Fountain Valley ●
Ramada Inn ($$)
9125 Recreation Cir Dr
(92708) 714.847.3388
mgr preapproval reqd

Residence Inn ($$$$)
9930 Slater Ave
(92708) 714.965.8000
call for fee & availability

● Fullerton ●
Fullerton Inn ($)
2601 W Orangethorpe Ave
(92833) 714.773.4900

Marriott Hotel ($$$)
2701 E Nutwood Ave
(92631) 714.738.7800
1st floor smoking rooms

Motel 6 ($)
1440 N State College
(92631) 714.956.9690
1 small pet/room

Motel 6 ($)
1415 S Euclid St
(92832) 714.992.0660
1 small pet/room

● Huntington Beach ●
Best Western ($$$)
19360 Beach Blvd
(92648) 800.528.1234
sunder 25 lbs

● Irvine ●
Atrium Marquis Hotel ($$$)
18700 Macarthur Blvd
(92612) 714.833.2770

Holiday Inn ($$$)
17941 Von Karman Ave
(92614) 714.863.1999
mgr preapproval reqd

La Quinta Inn ($$)
14972 Sand Canyon Ave
(92618) 714.551.0909
call re: fees

Marriott Hotel ($$$)
18000 Von Karman Ave
(92612) 714.553.0100

Residence Inn ($$$)
10 Morgan
(92618) 714.380.3000

● La Mirada ●
Residence Inn ($$$)
14419 Firestone Blvd
(90638) 714.523.2800

● Laguna Beach ●
Trade Winds Motel ($)
2020 S Coasy Hwy
(92651) 714.494.5450

Vacation Village ($$$)
647 S Coast Hwy
(92651) 714.494.8566

● Laguna Hills ●
Laguna Hills Lodge ($$)
23932 Paseo Dr Valencia
(92653) 714.830.2550

● Long Beach ●
Hilton ($$$$)
2 World Trade Ctr
(90831) 310.983.3400
sign waiver

Holiday Inn ($$)
2640 N Lakewood Blvd
(90815) 310.597.4400

Marriott Hotel ($$$)
4700 Airport Plaza Dr
(90815) 510.425.5210

Motel 6 ($$)
5665 E 7th St
(90804) 310.597.1311
1 small pet/room

Ramada Inn ($$$)
5325 E Pacific Coast Hwy
(90804) 310.597.1341
mgr preapproval reqd

Residence Inn ($$$)
4111 E Willow St
(90815) 800.331.3131

Long Beach Metro

● Bellflower ●
Motel 6 ($$)
17220 Downey Ave
(90706) 562.531.3933
1 small pet/room

● Cerritos ●
Sheraton Inn ($$)
12725 Center Court Dr S
(90703) 310.809.1500

● Downey ●
Embassy Suites ($$$$)
8425 Firestone Blvd
(90241) 562.861.1900
$15

● Harbor City ●
Motel 6 ($$)
820 Sepulveda Blvd
(90710) 800.440.6000
1 small pet/room

Travelodge ($$)
1665 Pacific Coast Hwy
(90710) 310.326.9026

● Huntington Beach ●
Best Western ($$$)
19360 Beach Blvd
(92648) 800.528.1234
sunder 25 lbs

● La Mirada ●
Residence Inn ($$$)
14419 Firestone Blvd
(90638) 714.523.2800

● Lakewood ●
Crazy 8 Motel ($)
11535 Carson St
(90715) 562.860.0546

● Lomita ●
Eldorado Coast Hotel ($$)
2037 Pch
(90717) 310.534.0700

● Long Beach ●
Best Western ($$)
1725 N Long Beach Blvd
(90813) 562.599.5555

Days Inn ($$)
1500 E Pac Coast Hwy
(90806) 562.591.0088
$5

Hilton ($$$$)
2 World Trade Ctr
(90831) 562.983.3400
sign waiver

Holiday Inn ($$)
2640 N Lakewood Blvd
(90815) 562.597.4400

Howard Johnson ($$$)
1133 Atlantic Ave
(90813) 800.654.2000

Marriott Hotel ($$$)
4700 Airport Plaza Dr
(90815) 562.425.5210

Motel 6 ($$)
5665 E 7th St
(90804) 562.597.1311
1 small pet/room

Ramada Inn ($$$)
5325 E Pacific Coast Hwy
(90804) 562.597.1341
mgr preapproval reqd

Residence Inn ($$$)
4111 E Willow St
(90815) 800.331.3131

Sheraton Inn ($$$$)
333 E Ocean Blvd
(90802) 562.436.3000

Travelodge ($$)
700 Queensway Dr
(90802) 562.435.7676

Travelodge ($$)
80 Atlantic Ave
(90802) 562.435.2471

Vagabond Inn ($$)
185 Atlantic Ave
(90802) 562.435.7621

● San Pedro ●
Sheraton Inn ($$$)
601 S Palos Verdes St
(90731) 310.519.8200

Vagabond Inn ($$)
215 Gaffey St
(90731) 310.831.8911
small only with fee

● Seal Beach ●
Radisson Inn ($$$)
600 Marina Dr
(90740) 310.493.7501

● Westminster ●
Motel 6 ($)
6266 Westminster Blvd
(92683) 714.891.5366
1 small pet/room

Motel 6 ($)
13100 Goldenwest St
(92683) 714.895.0042
1 small pet/room

End of Long Beach Metro

● Newport Beach ●
Aladdin Lodge ($)
73-793 Shadow Mtn Dr
(92660) 619.346.6816

Marriott Hotel ($$$$)
900 Newport Centere Dr
(92660) 714.640.4000

Marriott Suites ($$$$)
500 Bayview Cir
(92660) 714.854.4500

Palm Desert Ldoge ($$)
74-527 Hwy 111
(92660) 619.346.3875

The Four Seasons ($$$$)
690 Newport Center Dr
(92660) 714.759.0808
small pets allowed

$=under $35 $$=$35-60 $$$=$60-100 $$$$=over $100

CALIFORNIA, Ontario

● Ontario ●
Country Inn ($$)
2359 S Grove Ave
(91761) 800.770.1887

Country Suties By Carlson
($$$)
231 N Vineyard Ave
(91764) 909.983.8484
$25 fee

Doubletree ($$$)
429 N Vineyard Ave
(91764) 800.582.2946

Good Nite Inn ($$$)
1801 E G St
(91764) 909.983.3604

Holiday Inn ($$$)
3400 Shelby St
(91764) 909.406.9600
mgr preapproval reqd

Howard Johnson ($$)
2425 S Archibald Ave
(91761) 909.923.2728
small pets only

Marriott Hotel ($$)
2200 E Holt Blvd
(91761) 800.284.8811

Motel 6 ($)
1560 E 4th St
(91764) 909.984.2424
1 small pet/room

Motel 6 ($)
1515 N Mountain Ave
(91762) 909.956.6632
1 small pet/room

Ramada Inn ($)
1120 E Holt Blvd
(91761) 909.984.9655
$25 dep

Red Lion Inn ($$$)
222 N Vineyard Ave
(91764) 909.983.0909
call re: fees

Red Roof Inn ($$)
1818 E Holt Blvd
(91761) 909.988.8466

Residence Inn ($$$)
2025 E D St
(91764) 909.983.6788
call re pets & cleaning fee

Travelodge ($)
755 N Euclid Ave
(91762) 909.984.1775

● Orange ●
Doubletree ($$$$)
100 The City Dr S
(92868) 714.634.4500

Good Nite Inn ($)
101 N State College Blvd
(92868) 714.634.9500

Hilton ($)
400 N State College
(92668) 714.634.9500

Residence Inn ($$$)
201 N State College Blvd
(92868) 714.978.7700

● San Clemente ●
Holiday Inn ($$$)
111 S Avenida De Estrella
(92672) 714.361.3000
mgr preapproval reqd

● San Juan Capistrano ●
Best Western ($$$)
27174 Ortega Hwy
(92675) 714.493.5661
small pets

● San Pedro ●
Sheraton Inn ($$$)
601 S Palos Verdes St
(90731) 310.519.8200

Vagabond Inn ($$)
215 Gaffey St
(90731) 310.831.8911
small only with fee

● Santa Ana ●
Crown Sterling ($$$)
1325 E Dyer Rd
(92705) 800.433.4600

Howard Johnson ($$)
939 E 17th St
(92701) 714.558.3700

Motel 6 ($)
1623 E 1st St
(92701) 714.558.0500
1 small pet/room

Motel 6 ($$)
1717 E Dyer Rd
(92705) 714.261.1515
1 small pet/room

Radisson Inn ($$$)
2720 Hotel Terrace Dr
(92705) 714.556.3838

Red Roof Inn
2600 N Main St
(92705) 714.542.0311

Travelodge ($$)
1400 SE Bristol St
(92707) 714.557.8700

● Seal Beach ●
Radisson Inn ($$$)
600 Marina Dr
(90740) 310.493.7501

● Temecula ●
Comfort Inn ($$)
27338 Jefferson Ave
(92590) 909.699.5888
mgr preapproval reqd

Motel 6 ($)
41900 Moreno Rd
(92590) 909.676.7199
1 small pet/room

Ramada Inn ($$)
28980 Front St
(92590) 909.676.8770

● Westminster ●
Motel 6 ($)
6266 Westminster Blvd
(92683) 714.891.5366
1 small pet/room

Motel 6 ($)
13100 Goldenwest St
(92683) 714.895.0042
1 small pet/room

**End of Orange
County Metro**

● Orick ●
Park Inn ($)
Davidson Rd
(95555) 707.488.3841

● Orland ●
Amber Light Inn ($)
828 Newville Rd
(95963) 916.865.7655

Orland Inn ($)
1052 South St
(95963) 916.865.7632

Orlanda Motel ($)
827 Newville Rd
(95963) 916.865.4162

● Oroville ●
Best Western ($$)
1470 Feather River Blvd
(95965) 916.553.9673
mgr preapproval reqd

Days Inn ($$)
1745 Feather River Blvd
(95965) 916.533.3297
$25/pet deposit

Econo Lodge ($$)
1835 Feather River Blvd
(95965) 916.533.8201

Jeans Riverside Inn ($$)
45 Cabana Dr
(95965) 916.533.1413

Motel 6 ($)
505 Montgomery St
(95965) 916.532.9400
1 small pet/room

Travelodge ($$)
580 Oro Dan Blvd
(95965) 916.533.7070

● Oxnard ●
Ambassador Motel ($$)
1631 S Oxnard Blvd
(93030) 805.486.8404

Best Western ($$)
1156 S Oxnard Blvd
(93030) 805.483.9581
mgr preapproval reqd

City Motel ($$)
550 S Oxnard Blvd
(93030) 805.486.2522

Hilton ($$$)
600 E Esplanade Dr
(93030) 805.485.9666

Radisson Inn ($$$)
2101 W River Ridge
(93030) 805.988.0130

Vagabond Inn ($$)
1245 N Oxnard Blvd
(93030) 805.983.0251
small only with fee

Villa Motel ($$)
1715 S Oxnard Blvd
(93030) 805.487.1370

● Pacific Grove ●
Andril Cottages ($$$)
569 Asilomar Blvd
(93950) 408.375.0994

Best Western ($$$)
1150 Lighthouse Ave
(93950) 408.655.2111
under 25 lbs

Bidawee Motel ($$)
221 Asilomar Blvd
(93950) 408.372.2330

Old Inn ($$$)
321 Central Ave
(93950) 408.372.3246

Olympia Motor Lodge ($$)
1140 Lighthouse Ave
(93950) 408.373.2777

● Pacifica ●
Days Inn ($$$)
200 Rockaway Beach Ave
(94044) 415.359.7700
mgr preapproval reqd

Holiday Inn
519 Nick Ciust Way
(94044) (800)HOLIDAY

Lighthouse Hotel ($$)
105 Rockaway Beach Ave
(94044) 415.355.6300

● Palm Desert ●
Casa Resort ($$)
73811 Larrea St
(92260) 760.568.0311

Desert Inn ($$)
73758 Shadow Mountain Dr
(92260) 760.346.9161

Embassy Suites ($$$)
74700 Hwy 111
(92260) 760.340.6600

Inn At Deep Canyon ($)
74470 Abronia Trl
(92260) 760.346.8061

Motel 6 ($)
78100 Varner Rd
(92211) 760.345.0550
1 small pet/room

● Palm Springs ●
A Bella Hotel ($$)
650 E San Lorenzo Rd
(92264) 760.325.1487

A Sunbeam Inn ($)
291 E Camino Monte Vis
(92262) 760.323.3812

American Hotel ($)
1200 S Palm Canyon Dr
(92264) 760.320.4399

Bahama Hotel ($)
2323 N Palm Canyon Dr
(92262) 760.325.8190

Bermuda Resort ($$)
650 E Palm Canyon Dr
(92264) 760.323.1839

Best Western ($$)
1633 S Palm Canyon Dr
(92264) 760.325.9177
mgr preapproval reqd

Biltmore Hotel ($$)
1000 E Palm Canyon Dr
(92264) 760.323.1811

Cabana Resort ($$)
970 E Parocela Pl
(92264) 760.323.8842

Casa Cody ($$)
175 S Cahuilla Rd
(92262) 760.320.9346

Case De Camero Hotel ($$)
1480 N Indian Canyon Dr
(92262) 760.320.1678

Desert Rivera Hotel ($)
610 E Palm Canyon Dr
(92264) 760.327.5314

Duesenberg Motel ($$)
269 E Chuckwalla Rd
(92262) 760.326.2567

Estrella Inn ($$$)
415 S Belardo Rd
(92262) 760.320.4117

Hilton ($$$)
400 E Tahquitz Canyon Way
(92262) 760.320.6868

Holiday Oasis ($)
117 W Tahquitz Canyon Way
(92264) 760.320.7205

Howard Johnson ($$)
701 E Palm Canyon Dr
(92264) 760.320.2700

Hyatt Hotel ($$$)
285 N Palm Canyon Dr
(92262) 760.322.9000
under 15 lbs

Ingleside Inn ($$$)
200 W Ramon Rd
(92264) 760.325.0046

Inn At Racquet Club ($$$)
2743 N Indian Canyon Dr
(92262) 760.325.1281

Ironside Hotel ($)
310 E Palm Canyon Dr
(92264) 760.325.1995

Korakia Inn$$)
257 S Patencio Rd
(92262) 760.864.6411

La Serna Villas ($$)
339 S Belardo Rd
(92262) 760.325.3216

Los Dolores Hotel ($$)
312 E Camino Monte Vis
(92262) 760.327.4000

Motel 6 ($)
660 S Palm Canyon Dr
(92264) 760.327.4200
1 small pet/room

Motel 6 ($)
595 E Palm Canyon Dr
(92264) 760.325.6129
1 small pet/room

Musicland Hotel ($)
1342 S Palm Caynon Dr
(92264) 760.325.1326

Pepper Tree Inn ($)
645 N Indian Canyon Dr
(92262) 760.325.9505

Place In The Sun ($$)
754 E San Lorenzo Rd
(92264) 760.325.0254

Quality Inn ($$)
1269 E Palm Canyon Dr
(92264) 760.323.2775
mgr preapproval reqd

Ramada Inn ($$$)
1800 E Palm Canyon Dr
(92264) 760.323.1711
mgr preapproval reqd

Rivera Resort ($$)
1600 N Indian Canyon Dr
(92262) 760.327.8311

Rodeway Inn ($)
390 S Indian Canyon Dr
(92262) 760.322.8789

Royal Sun ($)
1700 S Palm Canyon Dr
(92264) 760.327.1564

Smoke Tree Villa ($$$)
1586 E Palm Canyon Dr
(92264) 760.323.2231

Super 8 ($$)
1900 N Palm Canyon Dr
(92262) 760.322.3757
call re: fees

The Dunes Hotel ($)
390 S Indian Canyon Dr
(92262) 760.322.8789

Tuscany Garden Resort ($$)
350 W Chino Canyon Rd
(92262) 760.325.2349

CALL AHEAD!

$=under $35 $$=$35-60 $$$=$60-100 $$$$=over $100

CALIFORNIA, Palmdale

● Palmdale ●
Motel 6 ($)
407 W Palmdale Blvd
(93551) 805.272.0660
1 small pet/room

● Palo Alto ●
Cardinal Hotel ($$)
235 Hamilton Ave
(94301) 415.323.5101

Coronet Motel ($$)
2455 El Camino Real
(94306) 415.326.1081

Days Inn ($$)
4238 El Camino Real
(94306) 415.493.4222
mgr preapproval reqd

Hyatt Hotel ($$$)
4219 El Camino Real
(94306) 415.493.8000

Motel 6 ($$)
4301 El Camino Real
(94306) 415.949.0833
1 small pet/room

● Paradise ●
Lantern Motel ($$)
5799 Wildwood Ln
(95969) 916.877.5553

Lime Saddle Marina ($$$$)
3428 Pentz Rd
(95969) 916.877.2414

Palos Verdes Motel ($)
5423 Skyway
(95969) 916.877.2127

Ponderosa Gdns Motel ($$)
7010 Skyway
(95969) 916.872.9094
$4 charge

● Pasadena ●
Holiday Inn ($$$)
303 Cordova St
(91101) 626.449.4000
mgr preapproval reqd

Pasadena Inn ($$)
400 S Arroyo Pkwy
(91105) 626.795.8401

Ramada Inn ($$)
3500 E Colorado Blvd
(91107) 626.792.1363
mgr preapproval reqd

Vagabond Inn ($$)
1203 E Colorado Blvd
(91106) 626.449.3170

Vagabond Inn ($$)
2863 E Colorado Blvd
(91107) 626.449.3020
small only with fee

Westway Inn ($$)
1599 E Colorado Blvd
(91106) 626.304.9678

● Paso Robles ●
Budget Inn ($$)
2745 Spring St
(93446) 805.238.2770

Farmhouse Motel ($)
425 Spring St
(93446) 805.238.1720

Motel 6 ($)
1134 Black Oak Dr
(93446) 805.239.9090
1 small pet/room

Travelodge ($)
2701 Spring St
(93446) 805.238.0078
$4 night

● Pebble Beach ●
The Lodge ($$$$)
1700 17-Mile Dr
(93953) 408.624.3811

● Petaluma ●
Motel 6 ($)
5135 Montero Way
(94954) 707.664.9090
1 small pet/room

Motel 6 ($)
1368 N McDowell Blvd
(94954) 707.765.0033
1 small pet/room

Quality Inn ($$)
5100 Montero Way
(94954) 707.664.1155
mgr preapproval reqd

● Petrolia ●
Mattole River Resort ($$)
42354 Mattole Rd
(95558) 707.629.3445

● Phelan ●
Economy Inn ($$)
8317 Hwy 138 Cajon Pass
(92371) 619.249.6777

● Piercy ●
Hartsook Inn ($$)
900 N Hwy 101
(95587) 707.247.3305

● Pinecrest ●
Pinecrest Chalet ($)
500 Dodge Ridge Rd
(95364) 209.965.3276

● Pinole ●
Motel 6 ($$)
1501 Fitzgerald Dr
(94564) 510.222.8174
1 small pet/room

● Pismo Beach ●
Knights Rest Motel ($$)
2351 Price St
(93449) 805.773.4617

Motel 6 ($)
860 4th St
(93449) 805.773.2665
1 small pet/room

Ocean Palms Motel ($)
390 Ocean View Ave
(93449) 805.773.4669

Quality Suites ($$$)
651 Five Cities Dr
(93449) 805.773.3773
$6 per day

Sandcastle Inn ($$$$)
100 Stimson Ave
(93449) 805.773.2422

Spyglass Inn ($$$)
2705 Spyglass Dr
(93449) 805.773.4855
$10/night

The Cliffs ($$$)
2757 Shell Beach Rd
(93449) 805.773.5000

● Pittsburg ●
Motel 6 ($)
2101 Loveridge Rd
(94565) 510.427.1600
1 small pet/room

● Placentia ●
Residence Inn ($$$)
700 W Kimberly Ave
(92870) 714.996.0555

● Placerville ●
Best Western ($$)
6850 Green Leaf Dr
(95667) 916.622.9100
$10/pet

Gold Trail Motel ($$)
1970 Broadway
(95667) 916.622.2906

Moter Lode Motel ($)
1940 Broadway
(95667) 916.622.0895
small pets only

● Pleasant Hill ●
Residence Inn ($$$)
700 Ellinwood Way
(94523) 510.689.1010
$50 fee & $6 per day

● Pleasanton ●
Doubletree ($$$)
5990 Stoneridge Mall Rd
(94588) 510.463.3330
$15 charge

Hilton ($$$)
7050 Johnson Dr
(94588) 510.463.8000
$15 per day

Holiday Inn ($$$)
11950 Dublin Canyon Rd
(94588) 510.847.6000
mgr preapproval reqd

Motel 6 ($$)
5102 Hopyard Rd
(94588) 510.463.2626
1 small pet/room

● Plymouth ●
Shenandoah Inn ($$)
17674 Village Dr
(95669) 209.245.4991

$=under $35 $$=$35-60 $$$=$60-100 $$$$=over $100

• Point Reyes Station •
Grays Retreat ($$$$)
Box# 547
(94956) 415.663.2000

Jasmine Cottage ($$$$)
Box# 547
(94956) 415.663.2000

Knob Hill Cottage ($$)
Box# 1108
(94956) 415.663.1784

• Pollock Pines •
Stagecoach Motel ($$)
5940 Pony Express Trl
(95726) 916.644.2029

• Pomona •
Motel 6 ($)
2470 S Garey Ave
(91766) 909.591.1871
1 small pet/room

Shilo Inn ($$$)
3200 W Temple Ave
(91768) 909.598.0073

Sheraton Suites ($$$)
600 W McKinley Ave
(91768) 909.622.2220

• Port Hueneme •
Country Inn ($$$)
350 E Hueneme Rd
(93041) 805.986.5353

Surfside Motel ($$)
615 E Hueneme Rd
(93041) 805.488.3686

• Porterville •
Motel 6 ($)
935 W Morton Ave
(93257) 209.781.7600
1 small pet/room

• Poway •
Poway Country Inn ($$)
13845 Poway Rd
(92064) 619.748.6320

• Quincy •
Gold Motel ($$)
200 Crescent St
(95971) 916.283.3686

• Ramona •
Ramon Valley Inn ($$)
416 Main St
(92065) 619.789.6433

• Rancho Cordova •
Best Western ($$)
11269 Point East Dr
(95742) 916.635.4040
mgr preapproval reqd

Comfort Inn ($$)
3240 Mather Field Rd
(95670) 916.363.3344
mgr preapproval reqd

Days Inn ($$)
11131 Folsom Blvd
(95670) 800.329.7466
mgr preapproval reqd

Economy Inn ($)
12249 Folsom Blvd
(95742) 916.351.1213

Motel 6 ($)
10694 Olson Dr
(95670) 916.635.8784
1 small pet/room

Motel 6 ($)
10271 Folsom Blvd
(95670) 916.362.5800
1 small pet/room

• Rancho Mirage •
Marriott Hotel ($$$)
41000 Bob Hope Dr
(92270) 619.568.2727

Motel 6 ($)
69-570 Hwy 111
(92270) 619.324.8475
1 small pet/room

Westin Resort ($$$$)
71333 Dinah Shore Dr
(92270) 619.328.5955
small pets only

• Rancho Santa Fe •
Rancho Santa Fe Inn ($$$)
5951 Linea Del Cielo
(92067) 619.756.1131

Morgan Resort ($$$$)
5690 Cancha De Golf
(92091) 619.756.2471

• Ravendale •
Ravendale Lodge ($)
Hwy 395
(96123) 916.728.0028

• Red Bluff •
Cindrella Inn ($)
600 Rio St
(96080) 916.527.5490

Flamingo Hotel ($)
250 Main
(96080) 916.527.3454

Value Lodge ($$)
30 Gilmore Rd
(96080) 916.529.2028

Kings Lodge ($)
38 Antelope Blvd
(96080) 916.527.6020

Motel 6 ($)
20 Williams Ave
(96080) 916.527.9200
1 small pet/room

Super 8 ($$)
203 Antelope Blvd
(96080) 916.527.8882
pets w/permission

• Redding •
Americana Lodge ($)
1250 Pine St
(96001) 916.241.7020

Bel Air Motel ($)
540 N Market St
(96003) 916.243.5291

Best Western ($$)
2220 Pine St
(96001) 916.241.6300
mgr discretion

Bridge Resort ($$)
10300 Bridge Bay Rd
(96003) 916.241.6464
small pets $25 deposit

Capri Motel ($)
4620 Hwy 90
(96001) 916.241.1156

Cedar Lodge
513 N Market St
(96003) 916.244.3251

Comfort Inn ($$)
2059 Hilltop Dr
(96002) 916.221.6530
mgr preapproval reqd

Economy Inn ($)
525 N Market St
(96003) 916.246.9803

Fawndale Lodge ($)
15215 Fawndale Rd
(96003) 916.275.8000

Holiday Inn
1080 Twin View Bl
(96003) 916.241.5500

River Inn ($$)
1835 Park Marina Dr
(96001) 916.241.9500

La Quinta Inn ($$)
2180 Hilltop Dr
(96002) 916.221.8200
call re: fees

Motel 6 ($$)
1640 Hilltop Dr
(96002) 916.221.1800
1 small pet/room

Motel 6 ($)
1250 Twin View Blvd
(96003) 916.246.4470
1 small pet/room

Motel 6 ($)
2385 Bechelli Ln
(96002) 916.221.0562
1 small pet/room

Motel 99 ($)
533 N Market St
(96003) 916.241.4942

North Gate Lodge ($)
1040 Market St
(96001) 916.243.4900

Oxford Suites ($$$)
1967 Hilltop Dr
(96002) 916.221.0100

Park Terrace Inn ($$$)
1900 Hilltop Dr
(96002) 916.221.7500

Red Lion Inn ($$$)
1830 Hilltop Dr
(96002) 916.221.8700
call re: fees

Redding Lodge ($)
1135 Market St
(96001) 916.243.5141

Saratoga Motel ($)
3025 S Market St
(96001) 916.243.8586

Shasta Lodge ($)
1245 Pine St
(96001) 916.243.6133

Star Dust Motel ($)
1200 Pine St
(96001) 916.241.6121

Thriftlodge ($)
413 N Market St
(96003) 916.241.3010

Vagabond Inn ($)
2010 Pine St
(96001) 916.243.3336

Vagabond Inn ($$)
536 E Cypress Ave
(96002) 916.223.1600
small only with fee

● Redlands ●
Best Western ($$)
1120 W Colton Ave
(92374) 909.793.2001
mgr discretion

Good Nite Inn ($$)
1675 Industrial Park Ave
(92374) 909.793.3723

Redlands Inn ($)
1235 W Colton Ave
(92374) 909.793.6648

● Redondo Beach ●
The Portofino Hotel ($$$$)
260 Portofino Way
(90277) 310.379.8481
w/permission from mgr

Travelodge ($$$)
206 S Pacific Coast Hwy
(90277) 310.318.1811

Vagabond Inn ($$)
2226 S Pacific Coast Hwy
(90277) 310.378.8555

● Redway ●
Budget West ($$)
3223 Redwood Dr
(95560) 707.923.2660

● Redwood City ●
Good Nite Inn ($$)
485 Veterans Blvd
(94063) 415.365.5500

Super 8 ($$)
2526 Camino Real
(94061) 415.366.0880
call re: fees

● Reedley ●
Edgewater Inn ($$)
1977 W Manning Ave
(93654) 209.637.7777

● Reseda ●
Howard Johnson ($$)
7432 Reseda Blvd
(91335) 818.344.0324

● Rialto ●
Best Western ($$)
475 W Valley Blvd
(92376) 909.877.0690

● Ridgecrest ●
El Dorado Motel ($)
400 S China Lake Blvd
(93555) 619.375.1354

El Rancho ($$)
507 S China Lake Blvd
(93555) 619.375.9731

Hacienda Court ($$)
150 Miguel St
(93555) 619.375.5066

Heritage Inn ($$$)
1050 N Norma St
(93555) 619.446.6543

Heritage Suites ($$$)
919 N Heritage Dr
(93555) 619.446.7951

Motel 6 ($)
535 S China Lake Blvd
(93555) 619.375.6866
1 small pet/room

Pan Mint Springs ($$)
Hwy 190
(93555) 619.764.2010

Ridgecrest Motel ($)
329 E Ridgecrest Blvd
(93555) 619.371.1695

● Rio Dell ●
Humbolt Gables Motel ($)
40 W Davis St # T
(95562) 707.764.5609

● Rio Nido ●
Rio Nido Lodge ($)
1458 River Rd
(95471) 707.869.0821

● Riverside ●
Circle Motel
9220 Granite Hill Dr
(92509) 714.360.1132

Courtyard By Marriott ($$)
1510 University Ave
(92507) 909.276.1200

Dynasty Suites ($$)
3735 Iowa Ave
(92507) 909.369.8200

Econo Lodge ($$)
1971 University Ave
(92507) 909.684.6363

Hampton Inn ($)
1590 University Ave
(92507) 909.686.6666

Motel 6 ($)
1260 University Ave
(92507) 909.784.2131
1 small pet/room

Motel 6 ($)
3663 La Sierra Ave
(92505) 909.351.0764
1 small pet/room

Quality Hotel ($$)
616 Convention Way
(92502) 714.750.3131

Super 8 ($)
1199 University Ave
(92507) 909.682.9011
call re: fees

Travelodge ($$)
11043 Magnolia Ave
(92505) 909.688.5000

● Rocklin ●
First Inns ($$$)
4420 Rocklin Rd
(95677) 916.624.4500

● Rohnert Park ●
Best Western ($$)
6500 Redwood Dr
(94928) 707.584.7435
small pets

Motel 6 ($)
6145 Commerce Blvd
(94928) 707.585.8888
1 small pet/room

Red Lion Inn ($$$$)
1 Red Lion Dr
(94928) 707.584.5466
call re: fees

Rohnert Park Inn ($)
6288 Redwood Dr
(94928) 707.584.1005

● Rosamond ●
Devonshire Inn Motel ($$)
Box# 2080
(93560) 805.256.3454

● Rosemead ●
Motel 6 ($)
1001 San Gabriel Blvd
(91770) 626.572.6076
1 small pet/room

Vagabond Inn ($$)
3633 Rosemead Blvd
(91770) 626.288.6661
small only with fee

● Roseville ●
Best Western ($$)
220 Harding Blvd
(95678) 916.782.4434
small pets only

● Rowland Heights ●
Motel 6 ($)
18970 Labin Ct
(91748) 818.964.5333
1 small pet/room

Well
Behaved

● Running Springs ●
Giant Oaks Motel ($$)
32180 Hilltop Bl
(92382) 800.786.1689

● Sacramento ●
Residence Inn ($$)
3721 Watt Ave
(95821) 916.485.7125

Americana Lodge ($)
818 15th St
(95814) 916.444.8085

Best Western ($$)
15 Massie Ct
(95823) 916.689.4425
small pets only

Beverly Hotel ($$$)
1780 Tribute Rd
(95815) 916.929.7900

Canterbury Inn ($$)
1900 Canterbury Rd
(95815) 916.927.3492

Clarion Hotel ($$$)
700 16th St
(95814) 916.444.8000
mgr preapproval reqd

Coral Lodge ($$)
2700 Fulton Ave
(95821) 916.483.6461

Crossroads Inn ($$)
221 Jibboom St
(95814) 916.442.7777

Days Inn ($$)
350 Bercut Dr
(95814) 916.442.6971
mgr preapproval reqd

Econo Lodge ($$)
711 16th St
(95814) 916.443.6631

Expo Inn ($$$)
1413 Howe Ave
(95825) 916.922.9833

Golden Tee Inn ($)
3215 Auburn Blvd
(95821) 916.482.7440

Guest Suites ($$)
2806 Grasslands Dr
(95833) 916.641.2617

Hilton ($$$)
2200 Harvard St
(95815) 916.922.4700
$25 fee

Holiday Inn ($$)
5321 Date Ave
(95841) 916.338.5800

Howard Johnson ($$)
3343 Bradshaw Rd
(95827) 916.366.1266

Inns Of America ($)
25 Howe Ave
(95826) 916.386.8408

La Quinta Inn ($$)
200 Jibboom St
(95814) 916.448.8100
call re: fees

La Quinta Inn ($$)
4604 Madison Ave
(95841) 916.348.0900
call re: fees

Masion View Lodge ($$)
771 16th St
(95814) 916.443.6631

Motel 6 ($)
7407 Elsie Ave
(95828) 916.689.6555
1 small pet/room

Motel 6 ($$)
1415 30th St
(95816) 916.457.0777
1 small pet/room

Motel 6 ($)
7850 College Town Dr
(95826) 916.383.8110
1 small pet/room

Motel 6 ($)
5110 Interstate Ave
(95842) 916.331.8100
1 small pet/room

Motel 6 ($)
227 Jibboom St
(95814) 916.441.0733
1 small pet/room

Motel 6 ($)
7780 Stockton Blvd
(95823) 916.689.9141
1 small pet/room

Motel Orleans ($$)
228 Jibboom St
(95814) 916.443.4811

Point West ($$$)
1761 Heritage Ln
(95815) 916.922.5882

Radisson Inn ($$$)
500 Leisure Ln
(95815) 916.922.2020
deposit

Ramada Inn ($$)
2600 Auburn Blvd
(95821) 916.487.7600
mgr preapproval reqd

Red Lion Inn ($$$)
2001 Point West Way
(95815) 916.929.8855
call re: fees

Red Lion Inn ($$$)
1401 Arden Way
(95815) 916.922.8041
call re: fees

Residence Inn ($$)
2410 W El Camino Ave
(95833) 916.649.1300

Sierra Inn ($$)
2600 Auburn Blvd
(95821) 916.482.4470

Sky Riders Motel ($$)
6100 Freeport Blvd
(95822) 916.421.5700

Super 8 ($$)
7216 55th St
(95823) 916.427.7925
pets w/permission

Travelodge ($$)
1111 H St
(95814) 916.444.8880

Vagabond Inn ($$)
1319 30th St
(95816) 916.454.4400
small pets only

● Saint Helena ●
El Bonita Motel ($$)
195 Main St
(94574) 707.963.3216

Harvest Inn ($$$)
1 Main St
(94574) 707.963.9463

Hyphen Inn ($$$$)
Box# 190
(94574) 707.942.0434

● Salinas ●
Best Western ($$)
175 Kern St
(93905) 800.528.1234
small pets only

Days Inn ($)
1226 De La Torre St
(93905) 408.759.9900
mgr preapproval reqd

El Dorado Motel ($)
1351 N Main St
(93906) 408.449.2442

Motel 6 ($)
1010 Fairview Ave
(93905) 408.758.2122
1 small pet/room

Motel 6 ($)
140 Kern St
(93905) 408.753.1711
1 small pet/room

Motel 6 ($)
1275 De La Torre St
(93905) 408.757.3077
1 small pet/room

Travelodge ($$)
555 Airport Blvd
(93905) 408.424.1741

Vagabond Inn ($$)
131 Kern St
(93905) 408.758.4693
small only with fee

● San Andreas ●
Black Inn ($$)
35 Main St
(95249) 209.754.3808

CALIFORNIA, San Bernardino

● San Bernardino ●
Hilton ($$$)
285 E Hospitality Ln
(92408) 909.889.0133

La Quinta Inn ($$)
205 E Hospitality Ln
(92408) 909.888.7571
call re: fees

Motel 6 ($)
1960 Ostems Way
(92407) 909.887.8191
1 small pet/room

Motel 6 ($)
111 Redlands Bl
(92408) 909.825.6666
1 small pet/room

● San Bruno ●
Summerfield Suites ($$$$)
1350 Huntington Ave
(94066) 800.833.4353

● San Clemente ●
Holiday Inn ($$$)
111 S Avenida De Estrella
(92672) 714.361.3000
mgr preapproval reqd

● San Diego ●
Arena Inn ($$)
3330 Rosecrans St
(92110) 619.224.8266

Best Western ($$$)
2270 Hotel Circle ln
(92108) 619.297.1101
mgr preapproval reqd

Days Inn ($$)
9350 Kearny Mesa Rd
(92126) 619.578.4350

Doubletree ($$$)
14455 Penasquitos Dr
(92129) 619.672.9100

Doubletree ($$$$)
11915 El Camino Real
(92130) 619.481.5900

E Z 8 Motel ($)
4747 Pacific Hwy
(92110) 619.294.2512

Econo Lodge ($)
445 Hotel Cir
(92108) 619.692.1288

Embassy Suites ($$$$)
601 Pacific Hwy
(92101) 619.239.2400

Good Nite Inn ($)
4545 Waring Rd
(92120) 619.286.7000

Good Nite Inn ($$)
3880 Greenwood St
(92110) 619.543.9944

Grosvenor Inn ($$)
810 Ash St
(92101) 619.233.8826

Holiday Inn ($$$)
1355 N Harbor Dr
(92101) 619.232.3861
mgr preapproval reqd

Hotel Circle Inn ($$)
2201 Hotel Cir
(92108) 619.291.2711

Howard Johnson ($$)
1430 17th Ave
(92101) 619.696.0911

La Quinta Inn ($$)
10185 Paseo Montril
(92129) 619.484.8800
call re: fees

Lamplighter Inn ($$)
6474 El Cajon Blvd
(92115) 619.582.3088

Marriott Hotel ($$$$)
333 W Harbor Dr
(92101) 619.234.1500

Marriott Hotel ($$$$)
701 A St
(92101) 619.696.9800
w/approval

Motel 6 ($$)
2424 Hotel Cir
(92108) 619.296.1612
1 small pet/room

Motel 6 ($$)
5592 Clairemont Mesa Blvd
(92117) 619.268.9758
1 small pet/room

Old Town Inn ($)
444 Pacific Hwy
(92110) 619.260.8024

Outrigger Motel ($)
1370 Scott St
(92106) 619.223.7105

Pacific Sands Motel ($$)
4449 Ocean Blvd
(92109) 619.483.7555

Pacific Shores Inn ($$)
4802 Mission Blvd
(92109) 619.483.6300

Park Manor Suites ($$$)
525 Spruce St
(92103) 619.291.0999

Pickwick Hotel ($)
132 W Broadway
(92101) 619.234.0141

Radisson Inn ($$$)
1433 Camino Del Rio
(92108) 619.260.0111

Radisson Inn ($$$)
11520 W Bernardo Ct
(92127) 619.451.6600
small pets allowed

Rancho Bernardo Inn ($$$)
17550 Bernardo Oaks Dr
(92128) 619.487.1611

Red Lion Inn ($$$$)
7450 Hazard Center Dr
(92108) 619.297.5466
call re: fees

Residence Inn
11002 Rancho Carmel Dr
(92128) 619.673.1900
$50 fee & $6 per day

Residence Inn ($$$)
5400 Kearny Mesa Rd
(92111) 619.278.2100
$50 fee & $6 per day

Hilton Club ($$$$)
1775 E Mission Bay Dr
(92109) 619.276.4010
small pets only

Marriott ($$$)
8757 Rio San Diego Dr
(92108) 619.692.3800

Hilton ($$$$)
901 Camino Del Rio
(92108) 619.543.9000
small with $25 fee

San Diego Princess ($$$$)
1404 Vacation Rd
(92109) 619.274.4630
in some smoking rooms

Sheraton Inn ($$$)
8110 Aero Dr
(92123) 619.277.8888

South Bay Lodge ($)
1101 Hollister St
(92154) 619.428.7600

Super 8
3275 Rosecrans
(92110) 619.224.2411
call re: fees

Super 8 ($$)
4540 Mission Bay Dr
(92109) 619.274.7888
$20 fee

The Horton Grand Hotel
($$$)
311 Island Ave
(92101) 619.544.1886

Travelodge ($$)
16929 W Bernardo Dr
(92127) 619.487.0445

U S Grant Hotel ($$$$)
326 Broadway
(92101) 619.232.3121

Vagabond Inn ($$)
1655 Pacific Hwy
(92101) 619.232.6391

Vagabond Inn ($$)
625 Hotel Cir
(92108) 619.297.1691
small only with fee

Vagabond Inn ($$)
6440 El Cajon Blvd
(92115) 619.286.2040
small only with fee

$=under $35 $$=$35-60 $$$=$60-100 $$$$=over $100

Vagabond Inn ($$)
1325 Scott St
(92106) 619.224.3371
small only with fee

Wayfarers Inn ($)
3275 Rosecrans St
(92110) 619.224.2411

San Diego Metro

● Carlsbad ●
Economy Inn ($)
751 Raintree Dr
(92009) 619.931.1185

Motel 6 ($)
1006 Carlsbad Village Dr
(92008) 619.434.7135
1 small pet/room

Motel 6 ($)
750 Raintree Dr
(92009) 619.431.0745
1 small pet/room

Motel 6 ($)
6117 Paseo Del Norte
(92009) 619.438.1242
1 small pet/room

Ramada Inn ($$$)
751 Macadamia Dr
(92009) 619.438.2285
mgr preapproval reqd

Travelodge ($)
760 Macadamia Dr
(92009) 800.367.2250

● Chula Vista ●
Good Nite Inn ($$)
225 Bay Blvd
(91910) 619.425.8200

La Quinta Inn ($$)
150 Bonita Rd
(91910) 619.691.1211
call re: fees

Motel 6 ($)
745 E St
(91910) 619.422.4200
1 small pet/room

Rodeway Inn ($)
778 Broadway
(91910) 800.424.4777

Traveler Motel ($)
2325 Woodlawn Ave
(91910) 619.427.9170

Travelodge ($$)
394 Broadway
(91910) 619.420.6600

Vagabond Inn ($$)
2300 Broadway
(91910) 619.422.8305
small only with fee

● Coronado ●
El Cordova Motel ($$$)
1351 Orange Ave
(92118) 619.465.4131

Loews Hotel ($$$$)
4000 Coronado Bay Rd
(92118) 619.424.4000
small below the knee size

● Del Mar ●
Del Mar Hilton ($$$)
15575 Jimmy Durante Blvd
(92014) 619.792.5200

● El Cajon ●
Best Western ($$)
1355 E Main St
(92021) 619.440.7378

Days Inn ($)
1250 El Cajon Blvd
(92020) 619.588.8808
mgr preapproval reqd

Motel 6 ($)
550 Montrose Ct
(92020) 619.588.6100
1 small pet/room

Thriftlodge ($)
1220 W Main St
(92020) 619.442.2576

Villa Embasadora ($)
1556 E Main St
(92021) 619.442.9617

● Escondido ●
Motel 6 ($)
509 W Washington Ave
(92025) 619.743.6669
1 small pet/room

Motel 6 ($)
900 N Quince St
(92025) 619.745.9252
1 small pet/room

Motel Mediteranian ($)
2336 S Escondido Blvd
(92025) 619.743.1061

Pine Tree Lodge ($$)
425 W Mission Ave
(92025) 619.740.7613

Sunshine Motel ($)
1107 S Escondido Blvd
(92025) 619.743.3111

Super 7 Motel ($)
515 W Washington Ave
(92025) 619.743.7979

Super 8 ($)
528 W Washington Ave
(92025) 619.747.3711
call re: fees

● Fallbrook ●
Best Western ($$$)
1635N S Mission Rd
(92028) 619.728.6174
small pets

La Estancia Inn ($$)
3135 Old Hwy 395
(92028) 619.723.2888

● Indio ●
Best Western ($$)
81909 Indio Blvd
(92201) 619.347.3421

Comfort Inn ($$)
43505 Monroe St
(92201) 619.347.4044
mgr preapproval reqd

Holiday Inn
84096 Indio Springs Dr
(92201) 619.342.6344

Indio Motel ($$)
44301 Sun Gold St
(92201) 619.347.6105

Motel 6 ($)
82195 Indio Blvd
(92201) 619.342.6311
1 small pet/room

Palm Shadow Inn ($$)
80-761 Hwy 111
(92201) 619.347.3476

Penta Inn ($)
84115 Indio Blvd
(92201) 619.342.4747

Rodeway Inn ($$)
84096 Indio Springs Dr
(92201) 800.424.4777

Royal Plaza Inn ($$)
82347 Hwy 111
(92201) 619.347.0911

Super 8 ($$)
81753 Hwy 111
(92201) 619.342.0264
pets with permission

● La Jolla ●
Colonial Inn ($$$$)
910B Prospect St
(92037) 619.454.2181

Holiday Inn
6705 La Jolla Bl
(92037) 619.454.7101

La Jolla Shores Inn ($$)
5390 La Jolla Blvd
(92037) 619.454.0715

Marriott Hotel ($$$$)
4240 La Jolla Village Dr
(92037) 619.587.1414

Residence Inn ($$$)
8901 Gilman Dr
(92037) 619.587.1770
call for fee & availability

Scripps Inn ($$$)
555 Coast Blvd S # 5
(92037) 619.454.3391

The Inn At La Jolla ($$)
5440 La Jolla Blvd
(92037) 800.525.6552

U S Suites Of San Diego
($$$)
3262 Holiday Ct Ste 205
(92037) 800.877.8483

CALIFORNIA, San Diego Metro

• La Mesa •
Comfort Inn ($$)
8000 Parkway Dr
(91942) 619.698.7747
mgr preapproval reqd

La Mesa Springs Hotel ($)
4210 Spring St
(91941) 619.589.7288

Travelodge ($)
9550 Murray Dr
(91942) 619.466.0200

• National City •
Holiday Inn ($$)
700 National City Blvd
(91950) 619.474.2800

Radisson Inn ($$)
810 National City Blvd
(91950) 619.336.1100

• Oceanside •
Motel 6 ($)
3708 Plaza Dr
(92056) 619.941.1011
1 small pet/room

Motel 6 ($)
1403 Mission Ave
(92054) 619.721.6662
1 small pet/room

Sandman Motel ($$)
1501 Carmelo Dr
(92054) 619.722.7661

• Poway •
Poway Country Inn ($$)
13845 Poway Rd
(92064) 619.748.6320

• San Diego •
Arena Inn ($$)
3330 Rosecrans St
(92110) 619.224.8266

Best Western ($$$)
2270 Hotel Circle In
(92108) 619.297.1101
mgr preapproval reqd

Days Inn ($$)
9350 Kearny Mesa Rd
(92126) 619.578.4350

Doubletree ($$$)
14455 Penasquitos Dr
(92129) 619.672.9100

Doubletree ($$$$)
11915 El Camino Real
(92130) 619.481.5900

Easy 8 Motel ($)
4747 Pacific Hwy
(92110) 619.294.2512

Econo Lodge ($)
445 Hotel Cir S
(92108) 619.692.1288

Embassy Suites ($$$$)
601 Pacific Hwy
(92101) 619.239.2400

Good Nite Inn ($)
4545 Waring Rd
(92120) 619.286.7000

Good Nite Inn ($$)
3880 Greenwood St
(92110) 619.543.9944

Grosvenor Inn Downtown
($$)
810 Ash St
(92101) 619.233.8826

Hilton ($$$$)
901 Camino Del Rio S
(92108) 619.543.9000
small with $25 fee

Hilton Club ($$$$)
1775 E Mission Bay Dr
(92109) 619.276.4010
small pets only

Holiday Inn ($$$)
1355 N Harbor Dr
(92101) 619.232.3861
mgr preapproval reqd

Hotel Circle Inn ($$)
2201 Hotel Cir S
(92108) 619.291.2711

Howard Johnson ($$)
1430 17th Ave
(92101) 619.696.0911

La Quinta Inn ($$)
10185 Paseo Montril
(92129) 619.484.8800
call re: fees

Lamplighter Inn ($$)
6474 El Cajon Blvd
(92115) 619.582.3088

Marriott ($$$)
8757 Rio San Diego Dr
(92108) 619.692.3800

Marriott Hotel ($$$$)
333 W Harbor Dr
(92101) 619.234.1500

Marriott Hotel ($$$$)
701 A St
(92101) 619.696.9800
w/approval

Motel 6 ($$)
2424 Hotel Cir
(92108) 619.296.1612
1 small pet/room

Motel 6 ($$)
5592 Clairemont Mesa Blvd
(92117) 619.268.9758
1 small pet/room

Old Town Inn ($)
444 Pacific Hwy
(92110) 619.260.8024

Outrigger Motel ($)
1370 Scott St
(92106) 619.223.7105

Pacific Sands Motel ($$)
4449 Ocean Blvd
(92109) 619.483.7555

Pacific Shores Inn ($$)
4802 Mission Blvd
(92109) 619.483.6300

Park Manor Suites ($$$)
525 Spruce St
(92103) 619.291.0999

Pickwick Hotel ($)
132 W Broadway
(92101) 619.234.0141

Radisson Inn ($$$)
1433 Camino Del Rio S
(92108) 619.260.0111

Radisson Inn ($$$)
11520 W Bernardo Ct
(92127) 619.451.6600
small pets allowed

Rancho Bernardo Inn ($$$)
17550 Bernardo Oaks Dr
(92128) 619.487.1611

Red Lion Inn ($$$$)
7450 Hazard Center Dr
(92108) 619.297.5466
call re: fees

Residence Inn
11002 Rancho Carmel Dr
(92128) 619.673.1900
$50 fee & $6 per day

Residence Inn ($$$)
5400 Kearny Mesa Rd
(92111) 619.278.2100
$50 fee & $6 per day

San Diego Princess ($$$$)
1404 Vacation Rd
(92109) 619.274.4630
in some smoking rooms

Sheraton Inn ($$$)
8110 Aero Dr
(92123) 619.277.8888

South Bay Lodge ($)
1101 Hollister St
(92154) 619.428.7600

Super 8
3275 Rosecrans
(92110) 619.224.2411
call re: fees

Super 8 ($$)
4540 Mission Bay Dr
(92109) 619.274.7888
$20 fee

The Horton Grand Hotel
($$$)
311 Island Ave
(92101) 619.544.1886

Travelodge ($$)
16929 W Bernardo Dr
(92127) 619.487.0445

U S Grant Hotel ($$$$)
326 Broadway
(92101) 619.232.3121

Vagabond Inn ($$)
1655 Pacific Hwy
(92101) 619.232.6391

Vagabond Inn ($$)
625 Hotel Cir S
(92108) 619.297.1691
small only with fee

Vagabond Inn ($$)
6440 El Cajon Blvd
(92115) 619.286.2040
small only with fee

Vagabond Inn ($$)
1325 Scott St
(92106) 619.224.3371
small only with fee

Wayfarers Inn ($)
3275 Rosecrans St
(92110) 619.224.2411

● Santee ●
Carlton Oaks Ctry Club ($$)
9200 Inwood Dr
(92071) 619.448.4242

● Vista ●
Hilltop Motor Lodge ($$)
330 Mar Vista Dr
(92083) 619.726.7010

La Quinta Inn ($$)
630 Sycamore Ave
(92083) 619.727.8180
call re: fees

End of San Diego Metro

● San Dimas ●
Motel 6 ($)
502 W Arrow Hwy
(91773) 909.592.5631
1 small pet/room

Red Roof Inn ($$$)
204 N Vilale Ct
(91773) 909.599.2362

● San Francisco ●
Alexander Inn ($$)
415 O'Farrell St
(94102) 415.928.6800

Beresford Arms ($$$)
701 Post St
(94109) 415.673.2600
small pets only

Beresford Hotel ($$$)
635 Sutter St
(94102) 415.673.9900
small pets only

BestWestern ($$$)
364 9th St
(94103) 415.621.2826
small

Chancellor Hotel ($$$)
433 Powell St
(94102) 415.362.2004

Compton Place Hotel ($$$$)
340 Stockton St
(94108) 800.235.4300

Executive Inn ($$$)
3930 Monterey Rd
(94111) 408.281.8700

Executive Suites ($$$$)
1 Saint Francis Pl
(94107) 415.495.5151

Grand Heritage Hotel ($$$$)
495 Ceary St
(94102) 415.775.4700
small pets allowed

Grosvenor House ($$$)
899 Pine St
(94108) 415.421.1899

Holiday Lodge ($$$)
1901 Van Ness Ave
(94109) 800.738.7477

Hotel Beresford ($$)
860 Sutter St
(94109) 415.673.3330
small pets only

Hotel Nikko ($$$$)
222 Mason St
(94102) 415.394.1111

Laurel Motor Inn ($$$)
444 Presidio Ave
(94115) 415.567.8467

Marriott Hotel ($$$$)
55 4th St
(94103) 415.896.1600

Marriott Hotel ($$$$)
1250 Columbus Ave
(94133) 415.775.7555

Ocean Park Motel ($$)
2690 46th Ave
(94116) 415.566.7020

Pacific Heights Inn ($$$)
1555 Union St
(94123) 415.776.3310

Renaissance ($$$$)
905 California St
(94108) 800.227.4736

Sheehan Hotel ($$)
620 Sutter St
(94102) 415.775.6500

Sir Francis Drake ($$$)
450 Powell St
(94102) 415.392.7755

The Juliana Hotel ($$$$)
590 Bush St
(94108) 415.392.2540

The Mansions Hotel ($$$$)
2220 Sacramento St
(94115) 415.929.9444

The Pan Pacific Hotel ($$$$)
500 Post St
(94102) 415.771.8600

The Phillips Hotel ($)
205 9th St
(94103) 415.863.7652

The Phoenix Inn ($$$)
601 Eddy St
(94109) 415.776.1380

The Steinhart ($$$)
952 Sutter St
(94109) 415.928.3855

Travelodge ($$)
2755 Lombard St
(94123) 415.931.8581

Westin Hotel ($$$$)
335 Powell St
(94102) 415.397.7000
small dogs accepted

**Policies
Subject
to Change**

San Francisco Metro

● Alameda ●
Islander Lodge Motel ($$)
2428 Central Ave
(94501) 510.865.2121

● Belmont ●
Motel 6 ($$)
1101 Shoreway Rd
(94002) 415.591.1471
1 small pet/room

● Burlingame ●
Doubletree ($$$)
835 Airport Blvd
(94010) 415.344.5500

Marriott Hotel ($$$$)
1800 Old Bayshore Hwy
(94010) 415.692.9100

Radisson Inn ($$$$)
1177 Airportb Blvd
(94010) 415.342.9200
small dogs

Red Roof Inn ($$$)
777 Airport Blvd
(94010) 415.342.7772
if the pet room is available
$10 charge

Vagabond Inn ($$)
1640 Old Bayshore Hwy
(94010) 415.692.4040
small only with fee

● Fremont ●
Best Western ($$$)
5400 Mowry Ave
(94538) 510.792.4300
mgr preapproval reqd

Good Nite Inn ($$)
4135 Cushing Pkwy
(94538) 510.656.9307

Islander Motel ($)
4101 Mowry Ave
(94538) 510.796.8200

Lord Bradleys Inn ($$$)
43344 Mission Blvd
(94539) 510.490.0520

CALIFORNIA, San Francisco Metro

Mission Peak Lodge ($)
43643 Mission Blvd
(94539) 510.656.2366

Motel 6 ($)
46101 Research Ave
(94539) 510.490.4528
1 small pet/room

Motel 6 ($)
34047 Fremont Blvd
(94555) 510.793.4848
1 small pet/room

Residence Inn ($$$)
5400 Farwell Pl
(94536) 510.794.5900
$75 fee

● Half Moon Bay ●
Holiday Inn ($$$)
230 Cabrillo Hwy
(94019) 415.726.3400
mgr preapproval reqd

Ramada Ltd ($$$)
3020 Hwy 1
(94019) 415.726.9700

● Hayward ●
Executive Inn ($$$)
20777 Hesperian Blvd
(94541) 510.732.6300
under 20 lbs

Hayward Islander ($)
29083 Mission Blvd
(94544) 510.538.8700

Motel 6 ($)
30155 Industrial Pkwy SW
(94544) 510.489.8333
1 small pet/room

Phoenix Lodge ($$)
500 A St
(94541) 510.786.0417

Phoenix Lodge ($$)
2286 Industrial Pkwy
(94545) 510.786.2844

Super 8
2460 Whipple Rd
(94544) 510.489.3888
call re: fees

Vegabond Inn ($$)
20455 Hesperia Blvd
(94541) 510.785.5480
small only with fee

● Livermore ●
Motel 6 ($)
4673 Lassen Rd
(94550) 510.443.5300
1 small pet/room

Residence Inn ($$$)
1000 Airway Blvd
(94550) 510.373.1800
$50 fee & $6 per day

Springtown Motel ($$)
933 Bluebell Dr
(94550) 510.449.2211

● Millbrae ●
Clarion Hotel ($$$)
401 E Millbrae Ave
(94030) 415.692.6363
mgr preapproval reqd

Comfort Inn ($$$)
1390 El Camino Real
(94030) 415.952.3200
mgr preapproval reqd

Homestead Guest Ranch
($$$)
1100 El Camino Real
(94030) 415.588.8500

Westin Hotel ($$$$)
1 Old Bayshore Hwy
(94030) 415.692.3500
small pets

● Mountain View ●
Best Western ($$$)
1720 W El Camino Real
(94040) 415.961.0220

Residence Inn ($$$)
1854 El Camino Readl
(94040) 415.940.1300
$50 fee & $6 per day

● Newark ●
Motel 6 ($)
5600 Cedar Ct
(94560) 510.791.5900
1 small pet/room

Woodfin Suites ($$$$)
39150 Cedar Blvd
(94560) 510.795.1200

● Novato ●
Days Inn ($$)
8141 Redwood Blvd
(94945) 415.897.7111

Golden Chain Resort ($)
13363 Sr 49
(94949) 916.273.7279

Travelodge ($$)
7600 Redwood Blvd
(94945) 415.892.7500

● Oakland ●
Browns Yosemite Cabin ($$)
7187 Yosemite Pkwy
(94605) 510.430.8466

Clarion Hotel ($$$)
1800 Madison St
(94612) 510.832.2300
mgr preapproval reqd

Days Inn ($$)
8350 Edes Ave
(94621) 510.568.1880
mgr preapproval reqd

Hampton Inn ($$$)
8485 Enterprise Way
(94621) 800.426.7866

Holiday Inn ($$$)
500 Hegenberger Rd
(94621) 510.562.5311

Motel 6 ($$)
1801 Embarcadero
(94606) 510.436.0103
1 small pet/room

Motel 6 ($$)
8480 Edes Ave
(94621) 510.638.1180
1 small pet/room

Parc Lane Hotel ($$$$)
1001 Broadway
(94607) 800.338.1338

Travelodge ($$)
423 7th St
(94607) 800.578.7878

● Redwood City ●
Good Nite Inn ($$)
485 Veterans Blvd
(94063) 415.365.5500

Super 8 ($$)
2526 Camino Real
(94061) 415.366.0880
call re: fees

● San Bruno ●
Summerfield Suites ($$$$)
1350 Huntington Ave
(94066) 800.833.4353

● San Francisco ●
Alexander Inn ($$)
415 O'Farrell St
(94102) 415.928.6800

Beresford Arms ($$$)
701 Post St
(94109) 415.673.2600
small pets only

Beresford Hotel ($$$)
635 Sutter St
(94102) 415.673.9900
small pets only

Best Western ($$$)
364 9th St
(94103) 415.621.2826
small

Chancellor Hotel ($$$)
433 Powell St
(94102) 415.362.2004

Compton Place Hotel ($$$$)
340 Stockton St
(94108) 800.235.4300

Executive Inn ($$$)
3930 Monterey Rd
(94111) 408.281.8700

Executive Suites ($$$$)
1 Saint Francis Pl
(94107) 415.495.5151

Grand Heritage Hotel ($$$$)
495 Ceary St
(94102) 415.775.4700
small pets allowed

Well
Behaved

$=under $35 $$=$35-60 $$$=$60-100 $$$$=over $100

Grosvenor House ($$$)
899 Pine St
(94108) 415.421.1899

Holiday Lodge ($$$)
1901 Van Ness Ave
(94109) 800.738.7477

Hotel Beresford ($$)
860 Sutter St
(94109) 415.673.3330
small pets only

Hotel Nikko ($$$$)
222 Mason St
(94102) 415.394.1111

Laurel Motor Inn ($$$)
444 Presidio Ave
(94115) 415.567.8467

Marriott Hotel ($$$$)
55 4th St
(94103) 415.896.1600

Marriott Hotel ($$$$)
1250 Columbus Ave
(94133) 415.775.7555

Ocean Park Motel ($$)
2690 46th Ave
(94116) 415.566.7020

Pacific Heights Inn ($$$)
1555 Union St
(94123) 415.776.3310

Renaissance ($$$$)
905 California St
(94108) 800.227.4736

Sheehan Hotel ($$)
620 Sutter St
(94102) 415.775.6500

Sir Francis Drake ($$$)
450 Powell St
(94102) 415.392.7755

The Juliana Hotel ($$$$)
590 Bush St
(94108) 415.392.2540

The Mansions Hotel ($$$$)
2220 Sacramento St
(94115) 415.929.9444

The Pan Pacific Hotel ($$$$)
500 Post St
(94102) 415.771.8600

The Phillips Hotel ($)
205 9th St
(94103) 415.863.7652

The Phoenix Inn ($$$)
601 Eddy St
(94109) 415.776.1380

The Steinhart ($$$)
952 Sutter St
(94109) 415.928.3855

Travelodge ($$)
2755 Lombard St
(94123) 415.931.8581

Westin Hotel ($$$$)
335 Powell St
(94102) 415.397.7000
small dogs accepted

● San Mateo ●
Best Western ($$$)
2940 S Norfolk St
(94403) 415.341.3300
small pets only

Dunfey Hotel ($$)
1770 S Amphlett Blvd
(94402) 415.573.7661
$50dep

Howard Johnson ($$$)
2110 S El Camino Real
(94403) 415.341.9231

Residence Inn ($$$$)
2000 Winward Way
(94404) 800.331.3131

Villa Hotel Airport ($$)
4000 S El Camino Real
(94403) 415.341.0966
deposit

● San Rafael ●
Casa Soldavini
531 C St
(94901) 415.454.3140
doggy daycare&petsitting

Villa Inn ($$$)
1600 Lincoln Ave
(94901) 415.456.4975

Wyndham Hotel ($$$)
1010 Northgate Dr
(94903) 415.479.8800

● South San Francisco ●
Holiday Inn
275 S Airport Blvd
(94080) 415.873.3550

La Quinta Inn ($$$)
20 Airport Blvd
(94080) 415.583.2223
call re: fees

Radisson Inn ($$$)
275 S Airport Blvd
(94080) 800.333.3333

Ramada Inn ($$$)
245 S Airport Blvd
(94080) 415.589.7200
mgr preapproval reqd

Travelodge ($$)
326 S Airport Blvd
(94080) 415.583.9600

● Sunnyvale ●
Best Western ($$$)
940 W Weddell Dr
(94089) 408.734.3742
ltd rms

Captains Cove Motel ($$)
600 N Mathilda Ave
(94086) 800.322.2683

Motel 6 ($$)
806 Ahwanee Ave
(94086) 408.720.1222
1 small pet/room

Motel 6 ($$)
775 N Mathilda Ave
(94086) 408.736.4595
1 small pet/room

Residence Inn ($$$)
750 Lakeway Dr
(94086) 408.720.1000
$10 fee

Residence Inn ($$$)
1080 Stewart Ave
(94086) 408.720.8893

Summerfield Suites ($$$)
900 Hamlin Ct
(94089) 800.833.4353

Vagabond Inn ($$)
816 Ahwanee Ave
(94086) 408.734.4607

End of San Francisco Metro

● San Jacinto ●
Crown Motel ($$)
138 S Ramona Blvd
(92583) 909.654.7133

● San Jose ●
Airport Inn Int'L ($$)
1355 N 4th St
(95112) 408.453.5340

Best Western ($$)
1440 N 1st St
(95112) 408.453.7750
mgr preapproval reqd

Friendship Inn ($)
2188 The Alameda
(95126) 408.248.8300

Homewood Suites ($$$$)
10 W Trimble Rd
(95131) 408.428.9900
$75 fee & $200 deposit

Howard Johnson ($$)
1755 N 1st St
(95112) 800.446.4656

Le Baron Hotel ($$)
1350 N 1st St
(95112) 408.453.6200

Motel 6 ($$)
2081 N 1st St
(95131) 408.436.8180
1 small pet/room

Motel 6 ($$)
2560 Fontaine Rd
(95121) 408.270.3131
1 small pet/room

Red Lion Inn ($$$$)
2050 Gateway Pl
(95110) 408.453.4000
call re: fees

San Jose Hilton ($$$)
300 Almaden Blvd
(95110) 408.287.2100

$=under $35 $$=$35-60 $$$=$60-100 $$$$=over $100

CALIFORNIA, San Jose

Summerfield Suites ($$$$)
1602 Crane Ct
(95112) 408.436.1600

Vagabond Inn ($$)
1488 N 1st St
(95112) 408.453.8822
small only with fee

● San Juan Bautista ●
San Juan Inn ($$)
410 The Alameda
(95045) 408.623.4380

● San Juan Capistrano ●
Best Western ($$$)
27174 Ortega Hwy
(92675) 714.493.5661
small pets

● San Leandro ●
Islander Lodge Motel ($)
2398 E 14th St
(94577) 510.352.5010

● San Luis Obispo ●
Avila Hot Springs Spa ($)
250 Avila Beach Dr
(93405) 805.595.2359

Best Western ($$)
1000 Olive St
(93405) 805.544.2800
mgr preapproval reqd

Best Western ($$)
214 Madonna Rd
(93405) 805.544.4410
supervised

Campus Motel ($$)
404 Santa Rosa St
(93405) 805.544.0881

Days Inn ($$)
2050 Garfield St
(93401) 805.549.9911
$10

Howard Johnson ($$$)
1585 Calle Joaquin
(93405) 805.544.5300
$10 charge

Motel 6 ($)
1433 Calle Joaquin
(93405) 805.549.9595
1 small pet/room

Motel 6 ($)
1625 Calle Joaquin
(93405) 805.541.6992
1 small pet/room

Sands Motel ($$)
1930 Monterey St
(93401) 805.544.0500

Travelodge ($$)
1825 Monterey St
(93401) 805.543.5110

Travelodge ($$)
950 Olive St
(93405) 805.544.8886

Vagabond Inn ($$)
210 Madonna Rd
(93405) 805.544.4710

● San Marcos ●
Quails Inn Resort ($$$)
1025 La Bonita Dr
(92069) 619.744.0120

● San Mateo ●
Best Western ($$$)
2940 S Norfolk St
(94403) 415.341.3300
small pets only

Dunfey Hotel ($$)
1770 S Amphlett Blvd
(94402) 415.573.7661
$50dep

Howard Johnson ($$$)
2110 S El Camino Real
(94403) 415.341.9231

Residence Inn ($$$$)
2000 Winward Way
(94404) 800.331.3131

Villa Hotel Airport ($$)
4000 S El Camino Real
(94403) 415.341.0966
deposit

● San Miguel ●
Parkfield Inn ($$)
First & Oak Sts
(93451) 805.463.2323

San Miguel Mission ($)
Box# 58
(93451) 805.467.3674

● San Pedro ●
Sheraton Inn ($$$)
601 S Palos Verdes St
(90731) 310.519.8200

Vagabond Inn ($$)
215 Gaffey St
(90731) 310.831.8911
small only with fee

● San Rafael ●
Casa Soldavini
531 C St
(94901) 415.454.3140
doggy daycare&petsitting

Villa Inn ($$$)
1600 Lincoln Ave
(94901) 415.456.4975

Wyndham Hotel ($$$)
1010 Northgate Dr
(94903) 415.479.8800

● San Ramon ●
Residence Inn ($$$)
1071 Market Pl
(94583) 510.277.9292
$75 fee & $5 per day

Marriott ($$$)
2600 Bishop Dr
(94583) 800.228.9290

● San Simeon ●
Best Western ($$$)
9415 Hearst Dr
(93452) 805.927.4688
1 only

Best Western ($$)
9450 Castillo Dr
(93452) 805.927.4691
$10/pet

Motel 6 ($$)
9070 Castillo Dr
(93452) 805.927.8691
1 small pet/room

Ragged Point Inn ($$)
Hwy 1
(93452) 805.927.4502

Silver Surf Motel ($$)
9390 Castillo Dr
(93452) 805.927.4661

● San Ysidro ●
Economy Inn ($)
230 Via De San Ysidro
(92173) 800.826.0778

International Motel ($$)
190 E Calle Primera
(92173) 619.428.4486

Motel 6 ($)
160 E Calle Primera
(92173) 619.690.6663
1 small pet/room

● Santa Ana ●
Crown Sterling ($$$)
1325 E Dyer Rd
(92705) 800.433.4600

Howard Johnson ($$)
939 E 17th St
(92701) 714.558.3700

Motel 6 ($)
1623 E 1st St
(92701) 714.558.0500
1 small pet/room

Motel 6 ($$)
1717 E Dyer Rd
(92705) 714.261.1515
1 small pet/room

Radisson Inn ($$$)
2720 Hotel Terrace Dr
(92705) 714.556.3838

Red Roof Inn
2600 N Main St
(92705) 714.542.0311

Travelodge ($$)
1400 SE Bristol St
(92707) 714.557.8700

● Santa Barbara ●
Alpine Motel ($$$)
2824 State St
(93105) 805.687.2821

Beach House Inn ($$$)
320 W Yanonali St
(93101) 805.966.1126

Blue Sands Motel ($$$)
421 Milpas
(93103) 805.965.1624

$=under $35 $$=$35-60 $$$=$60-100 $$$$=over $100

Santa Paula, CALIFORNIA

Casa Del Mar Inn ($$)
18 Bath St
(93101) 805.963.4418

East Beach Lodge ($$$)
1029 Orilla Del Mar
(93103) 805.965.0546

Fess Parkers Red Lion
($$$$)
633 E Cabrillo Blvd
(93103) 805.564.4333

Hotel State Street ($$$)
121 State St
(93101) 805.966.6586

La Playa Inn ($$)
212 W Cabrillo Blvd
(93101) 805.962.6436

Motel 6 ($$)
443 Corona Del Mar
(93103) 805.564.1392
1 small pet/room

Motel 6 ($$)
3505 State St
(93105) 805.687.5400
1 small pet/room

Ocean Palms Hotel ($$$)
232 W Cabrillo Blvd
(93101) 805.966.9133

Pacifica Suites ($$$$)
5490 Hollister Ave
(93111) 805.683.6722

Plaza Inn ($$$)
3885 State St
(93105) 805.687.3217

Sahara Motel ($$$)
2800 State St
(93105) 805.687.2500

San Ysidro Ranch ($$$$)
900 San Ysidro Ln
(93108) 805.969.5046

Sandy Beach Inn ($$)
122 W Cabrillo Blvd
(93101) 805.963.0405

The Four Seasons ($$$$)
1260 Channel Dr
(93108) 805.969.2261

Travelers Motel ($$$)
3222 State St
(93105) 805.687.6009

● Santa Clara ●
Budget Inn ($$)
2499 El Camino Real
(95051) 408.244.9610

Days Inn ($$)
4200 Great America Pkwy
(95054) 408.980.1525
mgr preapproval reqd

Days Inn ($$)
859 El Caminio Real
(95050) 408.255.2840
mgr preapproval reqd

Econo Lodge ($$$)
2930 El Camino Real
(95051) 408.241.3010

Holiday Inn
2455 El Camino Real
(95051) (800)HOLIDAY

Howard Johnson ($$$)
5405 Stevens Creek Blvd
(95051) 408.257.8600

Marriott Hotel ($$$)
2700 Mission College Blvd
(95054) 408.988.1500
1st floor only

Motel 6 ($$)
3208 El Camino Real
(95051) 408.241.0200
1 small pet/room

Vagabond Inn ($$)
3580 El Camino Real
(95051) 408.241.0771
small only with fee

Westin Hotel ($$$$)
5101 Great America Pkwy
(95054) 408.986.0700
small pets only

● Santa Cruz ●
Candlelite Inn ($)
1101 Ocean St
(95060) 408.423.0440

Edgewater Beach Motel ($$)
525 2nd St
(95060) 408.427.1616

Mission Inn ($$$$)
2250 Mission St
(95060) 408.425.5455

Motel Continental ($$)
414 Ocean St
(95060) 408.429.1221

Ocean Front House ($$$$)
1600 W Cliff Dr
(95060) 408.266.4453

Ocean Pacific Lodge ($$)
120 Washington St
(95060) 408.457.1234
$10 fee

Pacific Inn ($$)
330 Ocean St
(95060) 408.425.3722

Santa Cruz Inn ($)
2950 Soquel Ave
(95062) 408.475.6322

Sunny Cove Motel ($$)
21610 E Cliff Dr
(95062) 408.475.1741

Sunset Inn ($$)
2424 Mission St
(95060) 408.423.3471

Terrace Court Motel ($$$)
125 Beach St
(95060) 408.423.3031

The Inn At Pasatiempo ($$$)
555 Hwy 17
(95060) 408.423.5000

Travelodge ($)
619 Riverside Ave
(95060) 408.423.9515

● Santa Fe Springs ●
Dynasty Suites ($)
13530 Firestone Blvd
(90670) 310.921.8571

Motel 6 ($)
13412 Excelsior Dr
(90670) 310.921.0596
1 small pet/room

Be Discreet

● Santa Maria ●
Best Western ($$)
1725 N Broadway
(93454) 805.922.5200
mgr preapproval reqd

Howard Johnson ($$)
210 Nicholson Ave
(93454) 805.922.5891

Hunters Inn ($$)
1514 S Bway
(93454) 805.922.2123

Motel 6 ($)
2040 Preisker Ln
(93454) 805.928.8111
1 small pet/room

Motel 6 ($)
839 E Main St
(93454) 805.925.2551
1 small pet/room

Ramada Inn ($$)
2050 Preisker Ln
(93454) 805.928.6000
$15 fee

Rose Garden Inn ($$)
1007 E Main St
(93454) 805.922.4505

● Santa Monica ●
Days Inn ($$$)
3007 Santa Monica Blvd
(90404) 310.829.6333
mgr preapproval reqd

Holiday Inn ($$$)
120 Colorado Ave
(90401) 310.451.0676
mgr preapproval reqd

Loews Hotel ($$$$)
1700 Ocean Ave
(90401) 310.458.6700
dogs under 30 lb ground floor

The Georgian ($$$$)
1415 Ocean Ave
(90401) 310.395.9945

● Santa Paula ●
Travelodge ($$)
350 S Peck Rd
(93060) 805.525.1561

$=under $35 $$=$35-60   **111** $$$=$60-100 $$$$=over $100

CALIFORNIA, Santa Rosa

● Santa Rosa ●
Best Western ($$)
1500 Santa Rosa Ave
(95404) 707.546.4031
$10/night

Coopers Grove Ranch ($$$)
5763 Sonoma Mountain Rd
(95404) 707.571.1928

Econo Lodge ($$)
1800 Santa Rosa Ave
(95407) 800.424.4777

Holiday Inn
870 Hopper Ave
(95403) 707.545.9000

Los Robles Lodge ($)
1985 Cleveland Ave
(95401) 707.525.9010

Motel 6 ($)
3145 Cleveland Ave
(95403) 707.525.9010
1 small pet/room

Motel 6 ($)
2760 Cleveland Ave
(95403) 707.546.1500
1 small pet/room

Ramada Ltd ($$)
866 Hopper Ave
(95403) 707.575.0945
mgr preapproval reqd

Travelodge ($$)
1815 Santa Rosa Ave
(95407) 707.542.3472
small only

Travelodge ($$)
635 Healdsburg Ave
(95401) 707.544.4141
small pets only

● Santa Ynez ●
Santa Cota Motel ($$$)
3099 Mission Dr
(93460) 805.688.5525
$5 day

● Santa Ysabel ●
Appletree Inn ($$)
4360 Hwy 78
(92070) 619.765.0222

● Santee ●
Carlton Oaks Ctry Club ($$)
9200 Inwood Dr
(92071) 619.448.4242

● Scotts Valley ●
Best Western ($$$)
6020 Scotts Valley Dr
(95066) 408.438.6666
small dogs

● Seal Beach ●
Radisson Inn ($$$)
600 Marina Dr
(90740) 310.493.7501

● Seaside ●
Bay Breeze Inn ($)
2049 Fremont Blvd
(93955) 408.899.7111

Days Inn ($$$)
1400 Del Monte Blvd
(93955) 408.394.5335
mgr preapproval reqd

Seaside Motel ($$)
81131 Fremont Blvd
(93955) 408.394.8881

Thunderbird Motel ($)
1933 Fremont Blvd
(93955) 408.394.6797

● Sebastopol ●
Green Apple Inn ($$$)
520 Bohemian Hwy
(95472) 707.874.2526

● Selma ●
Best Western ($$)
2799 Floral Ave
(93662) 209.891.0300
1 small/rm

Super 8 ($$)
3142 Highland Ave
(93662) 800.800.8000
call re: fees

● Shasta Lake ●
Shasta Dam Motel ($)
1529 Cascade Blvd
(96079) 916.275.1065

● Sierra City ●
Herringtons Pines ($$)
S Hwy 49
(96125) 916.862.1151

● Simi Valley ●
Motel 6 ($$)
2566 Erringer Rd
(93065) 805.526.3533
1 small pet/room

Radisson Inn ($$$)
999 Enchanted Way
(93065) 805.583.2000
$35 fee

● Smith River ●
Casa Rubio Bch House ($$$)
17285 Crissey Rd
(95567) 800.357.6199

Sea Escape Motel ($$)
15370 Hwy 101
(95567) 707.487.7333

● Soledad ●
Motel 8 Soledad ($$)
1013 Front St
(93960) 408.678.3814

Paraiso Hot Springs ($$$$)
Paraiso Springs Rd
(93960) 408.678.2882

● Solvang ●
Best Western ($$$)
1440 Mission Dr
(93463) 805.688.2383
small pets

Hamlet Motel ($)
1532 Mission Dr
(93463) 805.688.4413

Meadowlark Motel ($$)
2644 Mission Dr
(93463) 805.688.4631
$5 night

Viking Motel ($)
1506 Mission Dr
(93463) 805.688.1337

● Somes Bar ●
Marble Mountain ($)
92520 Hwy 96
(95568) 800.552.6284

● Sonoma ●
Best Western ($$$)
550 2nd St
(95476) 707.938.9200
$10/night

● Sonora ●
Aladdin Motor Inn ($$)
14260 Mono Way
(95370) 209.533.4971

Best Western ($$)
19551 Hess Ave
(95370) 209.553.4400
mgr preapproval reqd

Days Inn
160 Washinton St
(95370) 209.532.2400
$20/pets

Kennedy Cabins ($$)
Box# 4010
(95370) 209.965.3900

Miners Motel ($$)
18740 Hwy 108
(95370) 209.532.7850

Rail Fence Motel ($)
19950 Hwy 108
(95370) 209.532.9191

Sonora Inn Hotel ($$)
160 S Washington St
(95370) 209.532.7468

● South El Monte ●
Ramada Inn ($$$)
1089 Santa Anita Ave
(91733) 818.350.9588
mgr preapproval reqd

● South Lake Tahoe ●
Alder Inn ($$)
1072 Ski Run Blvd
(96150) 916.544.4485

Beachside Inn ($)
930 Park Ave
(96150) 916.544.2400
$5 fee

Best Western ($$$)
4110 Lake Tahoe Blvd
(96150) 916.541.2010

Policies
Subject
to Change

$=under $35 $$=$35-60 $$$=$60-100 $$$$=over $100

Blue Lodge ($$)
4133 Cedar Ave
(96150) 800.258.3529

Blue Jay Lodge ($$)
4133 Cedar Ave
(96150) 916.544.5232

Blue Lake Motel ($$)
1055 Ski Run Blvd
(96150) 916.541.2399

Carneys Cabins ($$$)
Box# 601748
(96153) 916.542.3361

Days Inn ($$)
968 Park Ave
(96150) 916.541.4800
$5

Echo Creek Ranch ($$$$)
(96151) 916.544.5397

Em-Sea Suites ($$$$)
4130 Lake Tahoe Blvd
(96150) 800.362.2779

Embassy Suites ($$$$)
4130 Lake Tahoe Blvd
(96150) 916.544.5400

Heavenly Valley Motel ($$$$)
1261 Ski Run Blvd
(96150) 916.544.4244

High Country Lodge ($)
1227 Emerald Bay Rd
(96150) 916.541.0508

La Bear Inn ($$)
4133 Lake Tahoe Blvd
(96150) 916.544.2139

Lakepark Lodge ($$)
4081 Cedar Ave
(96150) 916.541.5004

Lampliter Motel ($$)
4143 Cedar Ave
(96150) 916.544.2936

Matterhorn Motel ($$)
2187 Lake Tahoe Blvd
(96150) 916.541.0367

Motel 6 ($)
2375 Lake Tahoe Blvd
(96150) 916.542.1400
1 small pet/room

Park Ave Lodge ($$$)
904 Park Ave
(96150) 916.544.3503

Raven Wood Hotel ($$)
4075 Manzanita Ave
(96150) 800.659.4185

Riviera Inn ($$)
890 Stateline Ave
(96150) 916.544.3448

Rodeway Inn ($$)
4082 Lake Tahoe Blvd
(96150) 916.541.7900

Safari Motel ($$$)
966 La Salle St
(96150) 916.544.2912

Sierra Cal Lodge ($$$)
3838 Lake Tahoe Blvd
(96150) 916.541.5400

Super 8 ($$)
3600 Lake Tahoe Blvd
(96150) 916.544.3476
call re: fees

Tahoe Colony Inn ($$)
3794 Montreal Rd
(96150) 916.655.6481

Tahoe Keys Resort ($$$$)
599 Tahoe Keys Blvd
(96150) 916.544.5397

Tahoe Marina Inn ($$)
930 Balbijou Rd
(96150) 916.541.2180

Tahoe Queen Motel ($$)
932 Poplar St
(96150) 916.544.2291

Tahoe Tropicana Lodge ($$)
4132 Cedar Ave
(96150) 916.541.3911

Tahoe Valley Motel ($$$)
2241 Lake Tahoe Blvd
(96150) 916.541.0353

The Montgomery Inn ($$)
966 Modesto Ave
(96150) 916.544.3871

Torchlite Inn ($$)
965 Park Ave
(96150) 916.541.2363

Trade Winds Motel ($)
944 Friday Ave
(96150) 916.544.6459

● South San Francisco ●
Holiday Inn
275 S Airport Blvd
(94080) 415.873.3550

La Quinta Inn ($$$)
20 Airport Blvd
(94080) 415.583.2223
call re: fees

Radisson Inn ($$$)
275 S Airport Blvd
(94080) 800.333.3333

Ramada Inn ($$$)
245 S Airport Blvd
(94080) 415.589.7200
mgr preapproval reqd

Travelodge ($$)
326 S Airport Blvd
(94080) 415.583.9600

● Spring Valley ●
Super 8 ($$)
9603 Campo Rd
(91977) 619.589.1111
call re: fees

● Stanton ●
Motel 6 ($)
7450 Katella Ave
(90680) 714.891.0717
1 small pet/room

● Stockton ●
Best Western ($$)
550 W Charter Way
(95206) 209.948.0321

Days Inn ($$)
33 N Center St
(95202) 209.931.3131
$5

Econo Lodge ($$)
2210 Manthey Rd
(95206) 209.466.5741

Holiday Inn ($$$)
111 E March Ln
(95207) 209.474.3301
mgr preapproval reqd

La Quinta Inn ($$)
2710 W March Ln
(95219) 209.952.7800
call re: fees

Motel 6 ($)
1625 French Camp Tpke
(95206) 209.467.3600
1 small pet/room

Motel 6 ($)
817 Navy Dr
(95206) 209.946.0923
1 small pet/room

Motel 6 ($)
6717 Plymouth Rd
(95207) 209.951.8120
1 small pet/room

Motel 6 ($)
4100 E Waterloo Rd
(95215) 209.931.9511
1 small pet/room

Sunshine Inn ($)
8009 N Hwy 99
(95212) 209.956.5200

● Strawberry ●
Three Rivers Resort ($$$)
Box# 81
(95375) 209.965.3278

● Suisun City ●
Economy Inn ($)
4376 Central Way
(94585) 707.864.1728

● Sun City ●
Travelodge ($)
27955 Encanto Dr
(92586) 909.679.1133

● Sun Valley ●
Scottish Inn
8365 Lehigh
(91352) 818.504.2671

● Sunnyvale ●
Best Western ($$$)
940 W Weddell Dr
(94089) 408.734.3742
ltd rms

Captains Cove Motel ($$)
600 N Mathilda Ave
(94086) 800.322.2683

CALIFORNIA, Sunnyvale

Maple Tree Inn ($$$)
711 E El Camino Real
(94087) 408.720.9700

Motel 6 ($$)
806 Ahwanee Ave
(94086) 408.720.1222
1 small pet/room

Motel 6 ($$)
775 N Mathilda Ave
(94086) 408.736.4595
1 small pet/room

Residence Inn ($$$)
750 Lakeway Dr
(94086) 408.720.1000
$10 fee

Residence Inn ($$$)
1080 Stewart Ave
(94086) 408.720.8893

Summerfield Suites ($$$)
900 Hamlin Ct
(94089) 800.833.4353

Vagabond Inn ($$)
816 Ahwanee Ave
(94086) 408.734.4607

Woodfin Suites Hotel ($$$)
635 E El Camino Real
(94087) 408.738.1700

● Susanville ●
Cozy Motel ($)
2829 Main St
(96130) 916.257.2319

Diamond View Motel ($)
1529 Main St
(96130) 916.257.4585

Frontier Inn Motel ($)
2685 Main St
(96130) 916.257.4141

Knights Inn ($$)
1705 Main St
(96130) 916.257.2168

Mt Lassen Hotel ($$)
27 S Lassen St
(96130) 916.257.6609

River Inn Motel ($)
1710 Main St
(96130) 916.257.6051

Sierra Vista Motel ($)
1067 Main St
(96130) 916.257.6721

Super Budget Motel ($$)
2975 Johnstonville Rd
(96130) 916.257.2782

● Sylmar ●
Motel 6 ($)
12775 Encinitas Ave
(91342) 818.362.9491
1 small pet/room

● Tahoe Vista ●
Beesleys Cottages ($$$)
6674 N Lake Blvd
(96148) 916.546.2448

Holiday House ($$$)
7276 N Lake Blvd
(96148) 916.546.2369

Woodvista Lodge ($)
7699 N Lake Blvd
(96148) 916.546.3839

● Tahoma ●
Captains Alpenhaus ($$$)
6941 W Lake Blvd
(96142) 916.525.5000

Tahoe Lake Cottages ($$$$)
7030 W Lake Blvd
(96142) 800.824.6348

Tahoma Lodge ($$)
7018 W Lake Blvd
(96142) 800.824.6348

● Tehachapi ●
Best Western ($$)
416 W Tehachapi Blvd
(93561) 805.822.5591

Golden Hills Motel ($)
22561 Woodford-Tehachapi
(93561) 805.822.4488

Travelodge ($$)
500 E Steuber Rd
(93561) 805.823.8000

● Temecula ●
Comfort Inn ($$)
27338 Jefferson Ave
(92590) 909.699.5888
mgr preapproval reqd

Motel 6 ($)
41900 Moreno Rd
(92590) 909.676.7199
1 small pet/room

Ramada Inn ($$)
28980 Front St
(92590) 909.676.8770

Temecula Creek ($$$$)
44501 Rainbow Canyon Rd
(92592) 909.694.1000

● Thousand Oaks ●
Best Western ($$)
12 Conejo Blvd
(91360) 805.495.7011
$5/pet

Thousand Oaks Inn ($$)
75 W Thousand Oaks Blvd
(91360) 805.497.3701

● Three Rivers ●
Best Western ($$$)
40105 Sierra Dr
(93271) 209.561.4119

Buckeye Tree Lodge ($$)
46000 Sierra Dr
(93271) 209.561.5900

Lazy J Ranch Motel ($$)
39625 Sierra Dr
(93271) 209.561.4449

Sequoia Village Inn ($)
45971 Sierra Dr
(93271) 209.561.3652

Sierra Lodge ($)
43175 Sierra Dr
(93271) 209.561.3681

The River Inn ($)
45176 Sierra Dr
(93271) 209.561.4367
small pets only

● Torrance ●
Days Inn ($$)
4111 Pacific Coast Hwy
(90505) 800.329.7466
mgr preapproval reqd

Howard Johnson ($$$)
2880 Pacific Coast Hwy
(90505) 310.325.0660

Residence Inn ($$$$)
3701 Torrance Blvd
(90503) 310.543.4566
$40 fee & $6 per day

Summerfield Suites ($$$)
19901 Prairie Ave
(90503) 310.371.8525

● Tracy ●
Best Western ($$)
811 W Clover Rd
(95376) 209.832.0271
small pets only

Motel 6 ($)
3810 Tracy Blvd
(95376) 209.836.4900
1 small pet/room

Phoenix Lodge ($$)
3511 Tracy Blvd
(95376) 209.835.1335

● Trinidad ●
Bishop Pine Lodge ($$)
1481 Patricks Point Dr
(95570) 707.677.3314

Shadow Lodge ($$)
687 Patricks Point Dr
(95570) 707.677.0532

Trinidad Inn ($$)
1170 Patricks Point Dr
(95570) 707.677.3349

View Crest Lodge ($$)
3415 Patricks Point Dr
(95570) 707.677.3393

● Trinity Center ●
Bonanza Resort ($$$)
Rt 2 Box# 4790
(96091) 916.266.3305

Bounty Lodge ($$$$)
Hcr 3 Box# 4659
(96091) 916.266.3277

Cedar Stock Resort ($$$$)
45810 Hwy 3
(96091) 916.286.2225

Coffee Creek Ranch ($$$$)
Coffee Creek Rd
(96091) 916.266.3343

$=under $35 $$=$35-60 $$$=$60-100 $$$$=over $100

Enright Cabins ($)
Box# 244
(96091) 916.266.3600

Ripple Creek Cabins ($$)
Rt 2 Box# 4020
(96091) 916.266.3505

Wyntoon Resort ($)
Box# 70
(96091) 916.266.3337

● Trona ●
Desert Motel ($)
84368 Trona Rd
(93562) 619.372.4572

● Truckee ●
Alpine Village Motel ($$)
12660 Deerfield Dr
(96161) 916.587.3801

Richards Motel ($$)
15758 Donner Pass Rd
(96161) 916.587.3662

Super 8 ($$)
11506 Deerfield Dr
(96161) 916.587.8888
call re: fees

● Tulare ●
Best Western ($$)
1051 N Blackstone St
(93274) 209.688.7537
mgr preapproval reqd

Friendship Inn ($)
26442 S Hwy 99
(93274) 800.424.4777

Green Gable Inn ($$)
1010 E Prosperity Ave
(93274) 209.686.3432

Inns Of America ($)
1183 N Blackstone St
(93274) 209.686.0985
1 small pet per room

Motel 6 ($)
1111 N Blackstone St
(93274) 209.686.1611
1 small pet/room

Tulare Inn Motel ($)
1301 E Paige Ave
(93274) 800.333.8571

● Turlock ●
Best Western ($$)
5025 N Goldlen State Blvd
(95380) 209.667.2827
small pets only

Best Western ($$)
1119 Pedras Rd
(95382) 209.634.9351
mgr preapproval reqd

Comfort Inn ($$)
200 W Glenwood Ave
(95380) 209.668.3400
mgr preapproval reqd

Motel 6 ($)
250 S Walnut Rd
(95380) 209.667.4100
1 small pet/room

● Twain Harte ●
Eldorado Motel ($$)
Box# 368
(95383) 209.586.4479

● Twentynine Palms ●
Circle C Motel ($$$)
6340 El Rey Ave
(92277) 760.367.7615

Motel 6 ($)
72562 - 29Palms Hwy
(92277) 760.367.2833
1 small pet/room

● Twin Peaks ●
Arrowhead Pine Rose ($$)
Hwy 189 At Grand View
(92391) 909.337.2341

● Ukiah ●
Days Inn ($$)
950 N State St
(95482) 707.462.7584
$5

Holiday Lodge ($)
1050 S State St
(95482) 707.462.2906

Motel 6 ($)
1208 S State St
(95482) 707.468.5404
1 small pet/room

Travelodge ($$)
406 S State St
(95482) 707.462.8611

Western Traveler ($)
693 S Orchard Ave
(95482) 707.468.9167

● Upper Lake ●
Narrows Lodge Resort ($$)
5690 Blue Lakes Rd
(95485) 707.275.2718

Pine Acres Resort ($$$)
5328 Blue Lakes Rd
(95485) 707.275.2811

● Vacaville ●
Best Western ($$)
1420 E Monte Vista Ave
(95688) 707.448.8453
small pets

Motel 6 ($)
107 Lawrence Dr
(95687) 707.447.5550
1 small pet/room

● Valencia ●
Best Western ($$$)
27143 Tourney Rd
(91355) 805.255.0555
mgr preapproval reqd

Hilton ($$$)
27710 The Old Rd
(91355) 805.254.8800
sign waiver

● Vallejo ●
Days Inn ($$)
300 Fairgrounds Dr
(94589) 707.554.8000
mgr preapproval reqd

E Z 8 Motel ($)
4 Mariposa St
(94590) 800.326.6835

Holiday Inn ($$)
1000 Fairfrounds Dr
(94590) 707.644.1200
mgr preapproval reqd

Motel 6 ($)
458 Fairgrounds Dr
(94589) 707.642.7781
1 small pet/room

Motel 6 ($)
1455 Marine World Pkwy
(94589) 707.643.7611
1 small pet/room

Motel 6 ($)
597 Sandy Beach Rd
(94590) 707.552.2912
1 small pet/room

Ramada Inn ($$$)
1000 Admiral Callaghan Ln
(94591) 707.643.2700
mgr preapproval reqd

Thriftlodge ($$)
160 Lincoln Rd
(94591) 800.255.3050

Valu Inn ($)
300 Fairgrounds Dr
(94589) 707.554.8000

Windmill Inn ($$)
1596 Fairgrounds Dr
(94589) 707.554.9655

● Venice ●
Lincoln Inn ($$$)
2447 Lincoln Blvd
(90291) 310.822.0686

● Ventura ●
Country Inn ($$$)
298 S Chestnut St
(93001) 805.653.1434

La Quinta Inn ($$)
5818 Valentine Rd
(93003) 805.658.6200
call re: fees

Motel 6 ($)
2145 Harbor Blvd
(93001) 805.643.5100
1 small pet/room

Motel 6 ($$)
3075 Johnson Dr
(93003) 805.650.0080
1 small pet/room

Motel 6 ($)
8223 E Brundage Ln
(93007) 805.366.7231
1 small pet/room

Pacific Inn ($)
350 E Thompson Blvd
(93001) 805.653.0879

Pierpont Inn ($$$)
550 San Jon Rd
(93001) 805.658.6200

Ramada Inn ($$$)
181 E Santa Clara St
(93001) 805.652.0141
mgr preapproval reqd

Vagabond Inn ($$)
756 E Thompson Blvd
(93001) 805.648.5371
small only with fee

Victoria Motel ($)
2350 S Victoria Ave
(93003) 805.642.2173

● Victorville ●
Budget Inn ($)
14153 Kentwood Blvd
(92392) 760.241.8010

Holiday Inn ($$)
15494 Palmdale Rd
(92392) 760.245.6565
mgr preapproval reqd

Motel 6 ($)
16901 Stoddard Wells Rd
(92394) 760.243.0666
1 small pet/room

Red Roof Inn
13409 Mariposa Rd
(92392) 760.241.1577

Sunset Inn ($)
15765 Mojave Dr
(92394) 760.243.2342

Travelodge ($)
16868 Stoddard Wells Rd
(92394) 760.243.7700

● Visalia ●
Best Western ($$)
623 W Main St
(93291) 209.732.4561
mgr dis

Holiday Inn ($$$)
9000 W Airport Dr
(93277) 209.651.5000
mgr preapproval reqd

Oak Tree Inn ($)
401 Woodland Dr
(93277) 209.732.8861

Thriftlodge ($)
4645 W Mineral King Ave
(93277) 209.732.5611

● Vista ●
Hilltop Motor Lodge ($$)
330 Mar Vista Dr
(92083) 619.726.7010

La Quinta Inn ($$)
630 Sycamore Ave
(92083) 619.727.8180
call re: fees

● Walnut Creek ●
Embassy Suites ($$$$)
1345 Treat Blvd
(94596) 415.934.2500

Motel 6 ($$)
2389 N Main St
(94596) 415.935.4010
1 small pet/room

Walnut Creek Motel ($$$)
1960 N Main St
(94596) 415.932.2811

● Watsonville ●
Best Western ($$)
740 Freedom Blvd
(95076) 408.724.3367
dogs only

El Rancho Motel ($)
976 Salinas Rd
(95076) 408.722.2766
extra charge

Monterey Bay Resort ($)
1186 San Andreas Rd
(95076) 408.722.0551

Motel 6 ($)
125 Silver Leaf Dr
(95076) 408.728.4144
1 small pet/room

National 9 ($$)
1 Western Dr
(95076) 408.724.1116

● Weaverville ●
49Er Motel ($)
718 Main St
(96093) 916.623.4937

Motel Trinity ($)
1112 Main St
(96093) 916.623.2129

Victorian Inn ($$)
1709 Main St
(96093) 916.623.4432

● Weed ●
Grand Manor Inn ($$$)
1844 Shastina Dr
(96094) 916.938.1982

Motel 6 ($)
466 N Weed Blvd
(96094) 916.938.4101
1 small pet/room

Sisinn Motel ($)
1825 Shastina Dr
(96094) 916.938.4194

Stewart Springs Cabins ($)
4617 Stewart Springs Rd
(96094) 916.938.2222

Town House Motel ($$)
157 S Weed Blvd
(96094) 916.938.4431

Y Motel ($)
90 N Weed Blvd
(96094) 916.938.4481

● West Hollywood ●
Le Montrose Hotel ($$$$)
900 Hammond St
(90069) 310.855.1115

Le Parc Hotel ($$$$)
733 N West Knoll Dr
(90069) 310.855.8888

Mondrian Hotel ($$$$)
8440 W Sunset Blvd
(90069) 213.650.8999

Ramada Inn ($$$)
8585 Santa Monica Blvd
(90069) 310.652.6400
mgr preapproval reqd

Summerfield Suites ($$$$)
1000 Westmount Dr
(90069) 310.657.7400

Wyndham Hotel ($$$$)
1020 N San Vicente Blvd
(90069) 310.854.1111

● West Sacramento ●
Best Western ($$)
1413 Howe
(95691) 916.922.9833
mgr preapproval reqd

Motel 6 ($)
1254 Halyard Dr
(95691) 916.372.3624
1 small pet/room

● Westley ●
Days Inn ($$)
7144 McCracken Rd
(95387) 209.894.5500
small pets allowed

● Westminster ●
Motel 6 ($)
6266 Westminster Blvd
(92683) 714.891.5366
1 small pet/room

Motel 6 ($)
13100 Goldenwest St
(92683) 714.895.0042
1 small pet/room

● Westport ●
Blue Victorian Inn ($$$)
38921 N Hwy 1
(95488) 707.964.6310

● Westwood ●
Almanor Lakeside Lodge
($$$)
3747 Eastshore Hwy
(96137) 916.284.7376

Clear Creek Motel ($)
667-150 Hwy 147
(96137) 916.256.3166

Lake Almanor Resort ($$)
2706 Big Springs Rd
(96137) 916.596.3337

Lassen View Resort ($$)
7457 Eastshore Hwy
(96137) 916.596.3437

Little Norway Resort ($$)
432 Peninsula Dr
(96137) 916.596.3225

● Whitethorn ●
Marina Motel ($$)
533 Machi Rd
(95589) 707.986.7595

Well
Behaved

$=under $35 $$=$35-60 $$$=$60-100 $$$$=over $100

Shelter Cove Motel ($$$)
205 Wave Dr
(95589) 707.986.7521

● Whittier ●
Best Whittier Inn ($)
14226 Whittier Blvd
(90605) 310.698.0323

Motel 6 ($)
8221 Pioneer Blvd
(90606) 310.692.9101
1 small pet/room

Vagabond Inn ($)
14125 Whittier Blvd
(90605) 310.698.9701
$3 charge

● Williams ●
Motel 6 ($)
455 4th St
(95987) 916.473.5337
1 small pet/room

Stage Stop Motel ($)
330 7th St
(95987) 916.473.2281

Woodcrest Inn ($$)
400 C St
(95987) 916.473.2381
$5 night

● Willits ●
Baechtel Creek Inn ($$$)
101 Gregory Ln
(95490) 707.459.9063

Holiday Lodge ($$)
1540 S Main St
(95490) 707.459.5361

Lark Motel ($)
1411 S Main St
(95490) 707.459.2421

Pepperwood Motel ($)
452 S Main St
(95490) 707.459.2231

Pine Cone Motel ($)
1350 S Main St
(95490) 707.459.5044

Skunk Trail Motel ($$)
500 S Main St
(95490) 707.459.2302

Western Village Inn ($)
1440 S Main St
(95490) 707.459.4011

● Willows ●
Best Western ($$)
249 Humboldt Ave
(95988) 916.934.4603
$10

Blue Gum Inn ($)
Rt 2 Hwy 99
(95988) 916.934.5401

Cross Roads Inn ($)
452 Humboldt Ave
(95988) 916.934.7026

Days Inn ($$)
475 Humboldt Ave
(95988) 916.934.4444
$5

Economy Inn ($)
435 N Tehama St
(95988) 916.934.4224

Grove Motel ($)
Rt 2 Hwy 99
(95988) 916.934.5067

Super 8 ($$)
457 Humboldt Ave
(95988) 916.934.2871
pets w/permission

Western Motel ($)
601 N Tehama St
(95988) 916.934.3856

● Winnetka ●
Best Western ($$)
20122 Vanowen St
(91306) 818.883.1200
under 20 lbs

● Wishon ●
Millers Landing ($$)
37976 Road 222
(93669) 209.642.3633

● Woodland ●
Cinderella Motel ($)
99 W Main St
(95695) 916.662.1091

Motel 6 ($)
1564 E Main St
(95776) 916.666.6777
1 small pet/room

● Woodland Hills ●
Vagabond Inn ($$)
20157 Ventura Blvd
(91364) 818.347.8080
small only with fee

● Yosemite National Park ●
The Redwoods Guest
Cottages ($$$)
Box# 2085 Wawona Station
(95389) 209.375.6666

● Yountville ●
Vintage Inn ($$$$)
6541 Washington St
(94599) 707.944.1112

● Yreka ●
Best Western ($$)
122 E Miner St
(96097) 916.842.4355
under 60 lb

Motel 6 ($)
1785 S Main St
(96097) 916.842.4111
1 small pet/room

Motel Orleans ($)
1804-B Fort Jones Rd
(96097) 916.842.1612

Super 8 ($$)
136 Montague Rd
(96097) 916.842.5781
call re: fees

Thunderbird Lodge ($)
526 S Main St
(96097) 916.842.4404

Wayside Inn ($)
1235 S Main St
(96097) 916.842.4412
$3 fee

● Yuba City ●
Garden Court Inn ($)
4228 S Hwy 99
(95991) 916.674.0210

Motel 6 ($)
700 N Palora Ave
(95991) 916.674.1710
1 small pet/room

Motel Orleans ($)
730 N Palora Ave
(95991) 916.674.1592

● Yucca Valley ●
Oasis Of Eden Inn ($$)
56377- 29 Palms Hwy
(92284) 619.365.6321

Super 8 ($$)
57096- 29 Palms Hwy
(92284) 619.228.1773
pets w/permission

Yucca Inn ($$)
7500 Camino Del Cielo Trl
(92284) 619.365.3311

Colorado
● Alamosa ●
Best Western ($$)
1919 Main St
(81101) 719.589.2567

Holiday Inn
333 Sante Fe Ave
(81101) 719.589.5833

Lamplighter Motel
425 Main St
(81101) 800.359.2138

● Arvada ●
On Golden Pond
7831 Eldridge St
(80005) 303.424.2296

● Aspen ●
Crestahaus Lodge ($$$)
1301 E Cooper St
(81611) 970.925.7081

Hotel Jerome ($$$$)
330 E Main St
(81611) 970.920.1000

Limelite Lodge ($$)
228 E Cooper St
(81611) 970.925.3025

The Little Nell ($$$$)
675 E Durant Ave
(81611) 970.920.4600

Policies
Subject
to Change

$=under $35 $$=$35-60 $$$=$60-100 $$$$=over $100

COLORADO, Aurora

● Aurora ●
Holiday Inn ($$$)
3200 S Parker Rd
(80014) 303.695.1700

La Quinta Inn ($$)
1011 S Abilene St
(80012) 800.531.5900
call re: fees

● Avon ●
Comfort Inn ($$$)
161 Beaver Crk Blvd
(81620) 970.949.5511
$15 fee

● Boulder ●
Best Western ($$$)
770 28th St
(80303) 303.449.3800
under 20 lbs

Boulder Broker Inn ($$$)
555 30th St
(80303) 303.444.3330

Boulder Mtn Lodge ($$)
91 Four Mile Canyon Rd
(80302) 303.444.0882
$50 deposit required

Days Inn ($$)
5397 S Boulder Rd
(80303) 303.499.4422

Foot Of The Mountain Motel
($$)
200 Arapahoe Ave
(80302) 303.442.5688

Highlander Inn Motel ($$)
970 28th St
(80303) 303.443.7800

Holiday Inn ($$$)
800 28th St
(80303) 303.443.3322
mgr preapproval reqd

Homewood Suites ($$$$)
4950 Baseline Rd
(80303) 303.499.9922
sign waiver

Pearl Street Inn ($$$)
1820 Pearl St
(80302) 800.232.5949

Residence Inn ($$$$)
3030 Center Green Dr
(80301) 303.449.5545
$50 fee & $5 per day up to
$250 max

● Brush ●
Best Western ($$)
1208 N Colorado Ave
(80723) 970.842.5146
mgrs approval

Budget Host ($$)
1408 Edison
(80723) 970.842.2876
$2

● Buena Vista ●
Cottonwood Inn
18999 County Road 306
(81211) 719.395.6434

Topaz Lodge Motel ($$)
115 N US 24
(81211) 719.395.2427

● Burlington ●
Budget Host ($)
405 S Lincoln
(80807) 719.346.5361
limited availability

Econo Lodge ($)
450 S Lincoln St
(80807) 719.346.5555

Sloans Motel ($)
1901 Rose Ave
(80807) 719.346.5333

● Byers ●
Longhorn Motel ($)
457 N Main
(80103) 303.822.5205

● Canon City ●
Best Western ($$)
1925 Fremont Dr
(81212) 719.275.3377
mgr preapproval reqd

Canon Inn ($$)
3075 E Hwy 50
(81212) 719.275.8676
$20 deposit

Holiday Motel ($)
1502 Main St
(81212) 719.275.3317

Park Lane Motel ($$)
1401 Main St
(81212) 719.275.7240

Travelodge ($)
2990 E Main St
(81212) 719.275.0461

● Carbondale ●
Cleveholm Manor ($$$)
58 Redstone Blvd
(81623) 970.963.3463

Thunder River Lodge ($$)
Hwy 133
(81623) 970.963.2543

● Castle Rock ●
Super 8 ($$)
1020 Park St
(80104) 303.688.0880
pets with deposit

● Colorado City ●
Greenhorn Mountain ($$)
I-25 Ex 74
(81019) 719.676.3315

● Colorado Springs ●
Doubletree ($$$)
4 S Cascade Ave
(80903) 719.473.5600

Apollo Park Suites ($$)
805 S Circle Dr 2-B
(80910) 800.666.1955

Best Western ($$)
3010 N Chestnut St
(80907) 719.636.5201
mgr preapproval reqd

Chief Motel ($)
1625 S Nevada Ave
(80906) 719.473.5228

Days Inn ($$)
2850 S Circle Dr
(80906) 719.527.0800
dep

Drury Inn ($$)
8155 N Academy Blvd
(80920) 719.598.2500

Economy Inn ($)
1231 S Nevada Ave
(80903) 719.634.1545

Embassy Suites ($$$)
7290 Commerce Center Dr
(80919) 719.599.9100

Hampton Inn ($$)
7245 Commerce Center Dr
(80919) 719.593.9700

Holiday Inn
505 Popes Bluff Trail
(80907) 719.598.7656

Holiday Inn ($)
8th & Cimarron Sts
(80905) 719.473.5530
mgr preapproval reqd

La Quinta Inn ($$)
4385 Sinton Rd
(80907) 719.528.5060
call re: fees

Motel 6 ($)
3228 N Chestnut St
(80907) 719.520.5400
1 small pet/room

Radisson Inn ($$)
1645 Newport Dr
(80916) 800.333.3333

Radisson Inn ($$$)
8110 N Academy Blvd
(80920) 719.598.5770
small pets allowed

Raintree Inn West ($)
2625 Ore Mill Dr
(80904) 719.632.4600

Ramada Inn ($$)
3125 Sinton Rd
(80907) 719.633.5540

Ramada Inn ($$)
520 N Murray Blvd
(80915) 719.596.7660

Red Lion Inn ($$$$)
1775 Cheyenne Mtn Blvd
(80906) 719.576.8900
call re: fees

Residence Inn ($$$)
3880 N Academy Blvd
(80917) 719.574.0370
call for fee & availability

Rodeway Inn ($$)
2409 E Pikes Peak Ave
(80909) 719.471.0990

Sheraton Inn ($$$)
2886 S Circle Dr
(80906) 800.635.3304

Sky Motel ($$$$)
1710 Boulder Hwy
(80901) 702.564.1534

Stagecoach Motel ($)
1647 S Nevada Ave
(80906) 719.633.3894

Swiss Chalet ($)
3410-3420 W Colorado Ave
(80904) 719.471.2260

Travelers Motel ($)
220 E Cimarron St
(80903) 719.473.2774

● Como ●
Herber Valley Park ($$)
7000 N Old Hwy 40
(80432) 801.654.4049

● Cortez ●
Anasazi Motor Inn ($$)
640 S Broadway
(81321) 970.565.3773

Aneth Lodge Budget 6 ($)
645 E Main St
(81321) 970.565.3453

National 9 ($)
440 S Broadway
(81321) 970.565.7778

Bel Lodge ($)
2040 E Main St
(81321) 970.565.3738

Best Western ($$)
535 E Main St
(81321) 970.565.3778
small pets supervised

Comfort Inn ($$)
2308 E Main St
(81321) 970.565.3400
mgr preapproval reqd

Days Inn ($$)
Jet US 160 & 145
(81321) 970.565.8577

Holiday Inn ($$)
2121 E Main St
(81321) 970.565.6000
mgr preapproval reqd

North Broadway Motel ($)
510 N Broadway
(81321) 970.565.2481

Ramada Ltd ($)
2020 E Main St
(81321) 970.565.3474

Sand Canyon Inn ($$)
301 W Main St
(81321) 800.258.3699

Tomahawk Lodge ($)
728 S Broadway
(81321) 970.565.8521

Ute Mountain Motel ($)
531 S Broadway
(81321) 970.565.8507

● Craig ●
A Bar Z Motel ($)
2690 W Hwy 40
(81625) 800.458.7228

Best Western ($)
755 E Victory Way
(81625) 970.824.8101
tended behaved pets

Black Nugget Motel ($)
2855 W Victory Way
(81625) 970.824.8161

Craig Motel ($)
894 Yampa Ave
(81625) 970.824.4491

Holiday Inn ($$)
300 S Hwy 13
(81625) 970.824.4000
mgr preapproval reqd

Ramada Inn ($$)
262 Commerce St
(81625) 800.272.6232

Super 8 ($)
200 S Hwy 13
(81625) 970.824.3471
pets w/permission

● Creede ●
Broadacres Ranch
Box# 39
(81130) 719.658.2291

● Del Norte ●
Del Norte Motel
1050 Grand Ave
(81132) 719.657.3581

● Delta ●
Best Western ($$)
903 Main St
(81416) 970.874.9781
small pets

Southgate Inn ($)
2124 S Main St
(81416) 970.874.9726

● Denver ●
Best Budget ($)
5001 W Colfax Ave
(80204) 303.534.7191

Best Western ($$)
455 S Colorado Blvd
(80222) 303.388.5561
small pets

Best Western ($$$)
4411 Peoria St
(80239) 303.373.5730
mgr preapproval reqd

Burnsley Hotel ($$$)
1000 Grant St
(80203) 303.830.1000

Cameron Motel ($)
4500 E Evans Ave
(80222) 303.757.2100

Comfort Inn ($$)
7201 E 36th Ave
(80207) 303.393.7666
mgr preapproval reqd

Comfort Inn ($$)
3440 S Vance St
(80227) 800.221.2222
mgr preapproval reqd

Concorde Airport Hotel
6090 Smith Rd
(80216) 303.388.4051

Days Hotel ($$)
4590 Quebec St
(80216) 303.320.0260

Days Inn ($$)
36 E 120th Ave
(80233) 303.457.0688
$6/pets

Drury Inn ($$)
4400 Peoria St
(80239) 303.373.1983

Embassy Suites ($$$)
4444 Havana St
(80239) 303.375.0400

Executive Tower Inn ($$$$)
1405 Curtis St
(80202) 303.571.0300

Hampton Inn ($$)
3605 S Wadsworth Blvd
(80235) 800.426.7886

Holiday Chalet ($$)
1820 E Colfax Ave
(80218) 303.321.9975

Holiday Inn ($$$)
10 E 120th Ave
(80233) 800.465.4329
mgr preapproval reqd

Holiday Inn ($$$)
15500 E 40th Ave
(80239) 800.465.4329
mgr preapproval reqd

Holiday Inn ($$$)
1450 Glenarm Pl
(80202) 303.573.1450
mgr preapproval reqd

Holiday Inn ($$$)
4040 Quebec St
(80220) 303.321.6666

Howard Johnson ($$)
6300 E Hampden Ave
(80222) 800.446.4656

CALL AHEAD!

119

COLORADO, Denver

La Quinta Inn ($$)
3975 Peoria Way
(80239) 800.531.5900
call re: fees

La Quinta Inn ($$)
3500 Fox St
(80216) 800.531.5900
call re: fees

La Quinta Inn ($$)
345 W 120th Ave
(80234) 800.531.5900
call re: fees

La Quinta Inn ($$)
1975 S Colorado Blvd
(80222) 800.531.5900
call re: fees

Loews Hotel ($$$$)
41501 E Mississippi Ave
(80222) 303.782.9300

Marriott Hotel ($$$)
1701 California St
(80202) 303.297.1300

Marriott Hotel ($$)
6363 E Hampden Ave
(80222) 303.758.7000

Motel 6 ($)
3050 W 49th Ave
(80221) 303.455.8888
1 small pet/room

Motel 6 ($$)
12020 E 39th Ave
(80239) 303.371.1980
1 small pet/room

Penn House ($$$$)
901 Pennsylvania St
(80203) 303.831.8060

Quality Inn ($$$)
6300 E Hampden Ave
(80222) 303.758.2211
mgr preapproval reqd

Radisson Inn ($$)
1550 Court Pl
(80202) 303.893.3333
deposit required

Ramada Inn ($$$)
110 W 104th Ave
(80234) 303.451.1234

Ramada Inn ($$$)
3737 Quebec St
(80207) 303.388.6161

Ramada Inn ($$$)
1150 E Colfax Ave
(80218) 303.831.7700

Red Lion Inn ($$$$)
3203 Quebec St
(80207) 800.547.8010
call re: fees

Regency Inn ($$)
3900 Elati St
(80216) 303.458.0808

Residence Inn ($$$)
2777 Zuni St
(80211) 303.458.5318
call for fee & availability

Rockies Lodge ($)
4760 E Evans Ave
(80222) 303.757.7601

Sheraton Inn ($$$)
4900 Dtc Pkwy
(80237) 303.779.1100

Sheraton Inn ($$$)
3535 Quebec St
(80207) 303.333.7711

Sheraton Inn ($$$)
3535 Quebec St
(80207) 303.333.7711

Super 8 ($)
2601 Zuni St
(80211) 303.433.6677
call re: fees

Super 8 ($$)
5888 Broadway
(80216) 303.296.3100
w/permission

Super 8 ($$)
12055 Melody Dr
(80234) 303.451.7200
w/permission

The Cambridge Inn ($$$)
1560 Sherman St
(80203) 303.831.1252

Victoria Oaks Inn ($$)
1575 Race St
(80206) 303.355.1818

Warwick Hotel ($$$)
1776 Grant St
(80203) 303.861.2000

Westin Hotel ($$$$)
1672 Lawrence St
(80202) 303.572.9100
small pets accepted

Denver Metro

● Aurora ●
Holiday Inn ($$$)
3200 S Parker Rd
(80014) 303.695.1700

La Quinta Inn ($$)
1011 S Abilene St
(80012) 800.531.5900
call re: fees

● Castle Rock ●
Super 8 ($$)
1020 Park St
(80104) 303.688.0880
pets with deposit

● Denver ●
Best Budget ($)
5001 W Colfax Ave
(80204) 303.534.7191

Best Western ($$)
455 S Colorado Blvd
(80222) 303.388.5561
small pets

Best Western ($$$)
4411 Peoria St
(80239) 303.373.5730
mgr preapproval reqd

Burnsley Hotel ($$$)
1000 Grant St
(80203) 303.830.1000

Cameron Motel ($)
4500 E Evans Ave
(80222) 303.757.2100

Comfort Inn ($$)
7201 E 36th Ave
(80207) 303.393.7666
mgr preapproval reqd

Comfort Inn ($$)
3440 S Vance St
(80227) 800.221.2222
mgr preapproval reqd

Concorde Airport Hotel
6090 Smith Rd
(80216) 303.388.4051

Days Hotel ($$)
4590 Quebec St
(80216) 303.320.0260

Days Inn ($$)
36 E 120th Ave
(80233) 303.457.0688
$6/pets

Drury Inn ($$)
4400 Peoria St
(80239) 303.373.1983

Embassy Suites ($$$)
4444 Havana St
(80239) 303.375.0400

Executive Tower Inn ($$$$)
1405 Curtis St
(80202) 303.571.0300

Hampton Inn ($$)
3605 S Wadsworth Blvd
(80235) 800.426.7886

Holiday Chalet ($$)
1820 E Colfax Ave
(80218) 303.321.9975

Holiday Inn ($$$)
10 E 120th Ave
(80233) 800.465.4329
mgr preapproval reqd

Holiday Inn ($$$)
15500 E 40th Ave
(80239) 800.465.4329
mgr preapproval reqd

Holiday Inn ($$$)
1450 Glenarm Pl
(80202) 303.573.1450
mgr preapproval reqd

Holiday Inn ($$$)
4040 Quebec St
(80220) 303.321.6666

Howard Johnson ($$)
6300 E Hampden Ave
(80222) 800.446.4656

Be
Discreet

La Quinta Inn ($$)
3975 Peoria Way
(80239) 800.531.5900
call re: fees

La Quinta Inn ($$)
3500 Fox St
(80216) 800.531.5900
call re: fees

La Quinta Inn ($$)
345 W 120th Ave
(80234) 800.531.5900
call re: fees

La Quinta Inn ($$)
1975 S Colorado Blvd
(80222) 800.531.5900
call re: fees

Loews Hotel ($$$$)
41501 E Mississippi Ave
(80222) 303.782.9300

Marriott Hotel ($$$)
1701 California St
(80202) 303.297.1300

Marriott Hotel ($$)
6363 E Hampden Ave
(80222) 303.758.7000

Motel 6 ($)
3050 W 49th Ave
(80221) 303.455.8888
1 small pet/room

Motel 6 ($$)
12020 E 39th Ave
(80239) 303.371.1980
1 small pet/room

Penn House ($$$$)
901 Pennsylvania St
(80203) 303.831.8060

Quality Inn ($$$)
6300 E Hampden Ave
(80222) 303.758.2211
mgr preapproval reqd

Radisson Inn ($$)
1550 Court Pl
(80202) 303.893.3333
deposit required

Ramada Inn ($$$)
110 W 104th Ave
(80234) 303.451.1234

Ramada Inn ($$$)
3737 Quebec St
(80207) 303.388.6161

Ramada Inn ($$$)
1150 E Colfax Ave
(80218) 303.831.7700

Red Lion Inn ($$$$)
3203 Quebec St
(80207) 800.547.8010
call re: fees

Regency Inn ($$)
3900 Elati St
(80216) 303.458.0808

Residence Inn ($$$)
2777 Zuni St
(80211) 303.458.5318
call for fee & availability

Rockies Lodge ($)
4760 E Evans Ave
(80222) 303.757.7601

Sheraton Inn ($$$)
4900 Dtc Pkwy
(80237) 303.779.1100

Sheraton Inn ($$$)
3535 Quebec St
(80207) 303.333.7711

Sheraton Inn ($$$)
3535 Quebec St
(80207) 303.333.7711

Super 8 ($)
2601 Zuni St
(80211) 303.433.6677
call re: fees

Super 8 ($$)
5888 Broadway
(80216) 303.296.3100
w/permission

Super 8 ($$)
12055 Melody Dr
(80234) 303.451.7200
w/permission

The Cambridge Inn ($$$)
1560 Sherman St
(80203) 303.831.1252

Victoria Oaks Inn ($$)
1575 Race St
(80206) 303.355.1818

Warwick Hotel ($$$)
1776 Grant St
(80203) 303.861.2000

Westin Hotel ($$$$)
1672 Lawrence St
(80202) 303.572.9100
small pets accepted

● Englewood ●
Days Inn
5150 Quebec St
(80111) 303.721.1144

Embassy Suites ($$$)
10250 E Costilla Ave
(80112) 303.792.0433
$5 fee

Hampton Inn ($$)
9231 E Arapahoe Rd
(80112) 800.426.7886

Motel 6 ($$)
9201 E Arapahoe Rd
(80112) 303.790.8220
1 small pet/room

Residence Inn ($$)
I-25
(80111) 800.331.3131

Residence Inn ($$)
6565 S Yosemite St
(80111) 303.740.7177
$10 per day

Super 8 ($$)
5150 S Quebec St
(80111) 303.771.8000
call re: fees

● Golden ●
Days Inn ($$)
15059 W Colfax Ave
(80401) 303.277.0200
mgr preapproval reqd

Golden Motel
510 24th St
(80401) 303.279.5581

Holiday Inn ($$)
14707 W Colfax Ave
(80401) 800.465.4329
mgr preapproval reqd

La Quinta Inn ($$)
3301 Youngfield Svc
(80401) 800.531.5900
call re: fees

Marriott Hotel ($$$)
1717 Denver West Blvd
(80401) 303.279.9100

● Lakewood ●
Chalet Motel ($)
6051 W Alameda Ave
(80226) 303.237.7775

Foothills Executive Lodging
($$)
7150 W Colfax Ave
(80215) 303.232.2932

Lakewood Inn ($)
7150 W Colfax Ave
(80215) 303.238.1251

Motel 6 ($)
480 Wadsworth Blvd
(80226) 303.232.4924
1 small pet/room

Rodeway Inn ($$)
7150 W Colfax Ave
(80215) 303.238.1251

Sheraton Inn ($$$)
360 Union Blvd
(80228) 303.987.2000
$50 deposit

● Westminster ●
La Quinta Inn ($$$)
8701 Turnpike Dr
(80030) 303.425.9099
call re: fees

● Wheat Ridge ●
Holiday Inn
4700 Kipling
(80033) 303.423.4000

Motel 6 ($)
9920 W 49th Ave
(80033) 303.424.0658
1 small pet/room

Motel 6 ($)
10300 S I-70 Frontage Rd
(80033) 303.467.3172
1 small pet/room

COLORADO, Denver Metro

Quality Inn ($)
12100 W 44th Ave
(80033) 303.476.2400

End of Denver Metro

● Dillon ●
Best Western ($$)
652 Lake Dillon Dr
(80435) 970.468.2341
ltd $15 fee & $50 deposit

Days Inn ($$$)
580 Silvershorne Ln
(80435) 970.468.8661
$10

● Dolores ●
Dolores Mountain Inn ($)
701 Railroad Ave
(81323) 970.882.7203

Far View Lodge ($$$)
Box# 277
(81323) 970.529.4421

Lost Lake Lodge ($$$)
Box# 1289
(81323) 970.882.4913

Outpost Motel ($)
1800 Central Ave
(81323) 970.882.7271

Priest Gulch Ranch ($$)
2670 Hwy 145
(81323) 970.562.3810

Rag Ranch ($$$)
26030 Hwy 145
(81323) 970.562.3803

● Durango ●
Adobe Inn ($$)
2178 Main Ave
(81301) 970.247.2743

Alpine Motel ($)
3515 Main Ave
(81301) 970.247.4042

Best Western ($$$)
49617 US 550
(81301) 970.247.9669
small pets $6 per nite

Budget Inn ($$)
3077 Main Ave
(81301) 970.247.5222

Caboose Motel ($)
3363 Main Ave
(81301) 970.247.1191

Edelweiss Inn ($$)
689 Animas View Dr
(81301) 970.247.5685

Holiday Inn ($$)
800 Camino Del Rio
(81301) 970.247.5393
mgr preapproval reqd

Iron Horse Inn ($$$)
5800 Main Ave
(81301) 970.259.1010

Jarvis Suite Hotel ($$$)
125 W 10th St
(81301) 970.259.6190

National 9 ($)
2855 Main Ave
(81301) 970.247.2653

Red Lion Inn ($$$)
501 Camino Del Rio
(81301) 970.259.6580
call re: fees

Rodeway Inn ($$)
2701 Main Ave
(81301) 970.259.2540

Siesta Motel ($$)
3475 Main Ave
(81301) 970.247.0741

Travelodge ($$)
2970 Main Ave
(81301) 970.247.1741

Western Star Motel ($)
33140 N Main Ave
(81301) 970.247.4895

● Eads ●
Country Manor Motel ($)
609 East 15th St
(81036) 719.438.5451

● Eagle ●
Best Western ($$)
200 Loren Lake
(81631) 970.328.6316
mgr preapproval reqd

● Englewood ●
Days Inn
5150 Quebec St
(80111) 303.721.1144

Embassy Suites ($$$)
10250 E Costilla Ave
(80112) 303.792.0433
$5 fee

Hampton Inn ($$)
9231 E Arapahoe Rd
(80112) 800.426.7886

Motel 6 ($$)
9201 E Arapahoe Rd
(80112) 303.790.8220
1 small pet/room

Residence Inn ($$)
6565 S Yosemite St
(80111) 800.331.3131

Residence Inn ($$)
6565 S Yosemite St
(80111) 303.740.7177
$10 per day

Super 8 ($$)
5150 S Quebec St
(80111) 303.771.8000
call re: fees

● Estes Park ●
American Wilderness Lodge
($$)
481 W Elkhorn Ave
(80517) 970.586.4402

Castle Mtn Lodge ($$)
1520 Fall River Rd
(80517) 970.586.3664

Four Winds Motel ($)
1120 Big Thompson Ave
(80517) 970.586.3313

Machins Cottages ($$$)
Box# 2867
(80517) 970.586.4276

Olympus Lodge ($)
Box# 547
(80517) 970.586.8141

Triple R Cottages ($$)
1000 E Riverside Dr
(80517) 970.586.5552

● Evans ●
Motel 6 ($)
3015 8th Ave
(80620) 970.351.6481
1 small pet/room

Winterset Inn ($)
800 31st St
(80620) 970.339.2493

Winterset Inn ($)
800 31st St
(80620) 970.339.2492

● Fairplay ●
The Western Inn ($$)
Box# 187
(80440) 719.836.2026

● Fort Collins ●
Days Inn ($$)
3625 E Mulberry St
(80524) 970.221.5490
$5 ltd pet rooms

Hampton Inn ($$)
1620 Oakridge Dr
(80525) 970.229.5927

Holiday Inn
425 W Prospect Rd
(80526) 970.482.2626

Holiday Inn ($$$)
3836 E Mulberry St
(80524) 800.465.4329
mgr preapproval reqd

Montclair Motel ($)
1405 N College Ave
(80524) 970.482.5452

Motel 6 ($)
3900 E Mulberry St
(80524) 970.482.6466
1 small pet/room

Mulberry Inn ($$)
4333 E Mulberry St
(80524) 970.493.9000

Super 8 ($$)
409 Centro Way
(80524) 970.493.7701
call re: fees

Well Behaved

LaJunta, Colorado

• Fort Garland •
The Lodge Motel ($)
Box# 160
(81133) 719.379.3434

• Fort Morgan •
Best Western ($$)
725 Main St
(80701) 970.867.8256
smoking rms

Central Motel ($$)
201 W Platte Ave
(80701) 970.867.2401

Econo Lodge ($$)
1409 Barlow Rd
(80701) 970.867.9481

Madison Hotel ($$)
14378 Hwy 34
(80701) 970.867.8208

• Frisco •
Best Western ($$$$)
1202 Summit Blvd
(80443) 970.668.5094
mgr preapproval reqd

Luxury Inn ($)
1205 N Summit Blvd
(80443) 970.668.3220

• Georgetown •
Georgetown Motor Inn ($$)
1100 Rose St
(80444) 970.569.3201

• Glenwood Springs •
Affordable Inns ($)
51823 Hwys 6 & 24
(81601) 970.945.8888

Best Western ($$)
1826 Grand Ave
(81601) 970.945.7451
$5/pet

Budget Host ($$)
51429 Hwy 6 & 24
(81601) 970.945.5682
limited availability

Homestead Inn ($)
52039 Hwys 6 & 24
(81601) 800.456.6685

Ramada Inn ($$)
124 W 6th St
(81601) 970.945.2500
$50 deposit

Silver Spruce Motel ($$)
162 W 6th St
(81601) 970.945.5458

• Golden •
Days Inn ($$)
15059 W Colfax Ave
(80401) 303.277.0200
mgr preapproval reqd

Golden Motel
510 24th St
(80401) 303.279.5581

Holiday Inn ($$)
14707 W Colfax Ave
(80401) 800.465.4329
mgr preapproval reqd

La Quinta Inn ($$)
3301 Youngfield Svc
(80401) 800.531.5900
call re: fees

Marriott Hotel ($$$)
1717 Denver West Blvd
(80401) 303.279.9100

• Granby •
Broken Arrow Motel ($)
Box# 143
(80446) 970.887.3532

Littletree Inn ($$$)
Box# 800
(80446) 970.887.2551

The Inn At Silver Creek ($$)
Box# 4222
(80446) 800.926.4386

• Grand Junction •
Best Western ($$)
708 Horizon Dr
(81506) 970.243.4150
1 small

Days Inn ($$)
733 Horizon Dr
(81506) 970.245.7200

Friendship Inn ($$)
733 Horizon Dr
(81506) 800.424.4777

Hilton ($$$)
743 Horizon Dr
(81506) 970.241.8888

Holiday Inn
755 Horizon Dr
(81506) 970.243.6790

Holiday Inn ($$)
77 Horizon Dr
(81502) 800.465.4329

Horizon Inn
754 Horizon Dr
(81506) 303.245.1410
guest rfd

Howard Johnson ($$)
752 Horizon Dr
(81506) 970.243.5150

Motel 6 ($)
776 Horizon Dr
(81506) 970.243.2628
1 small pet/room

Peachtree Inn ($)
1600 North Ave
(81501) 970.245.5770

Super 8 ($)
728 Horizon Dr
(81506) 970.248.8080
pets w/permission

Value Lodge ($)
104 White Ave
(81501) 970.242.0651

West Gate Inn ($)
2210 Hwys 6 & 50
(81505) 970.241.3020

• Grand Lake •
Riverside Guesthouses
Box# 1469
(80447) 970.627.3619

• Greeley •
Best Western ($$)
701 8th St
(80631) 970.353.8444
small

Holiday Inn
2563 W 29th
(80631) 970.330.7495

• Gunnison •
Days Inn ($)
701 Hwy 50W
(81230) 970.641.0608
$3/pets

Harmels Guest Ranch ($$$$)
Box# 955M
(81230) 970.641.1740

Hylander Inn ($)
412 E Tomichi Ave
(81230) 970.641.0700

• Hesperus •
Canyon Motel
Hwy 160 & Cr 124
(81326) 303.259.6277

• Hotchkiss •
Hotchkiss Inn ($$)
406 Hwy 133
(81419) 970.872.2200

• Idaho Springs •
National 9 ($)
2920 Colorado Blvd
(80452) 303.567.2691

Piana Motel ($)
2901 Colorado Blvd
(80452) 303.567.2021

• Julesburg •
Platte Valley Inn ($)
I-76 And US 385
(80737) 970.474.3336

• Kit Carson •
Stage Stop Motel ($)
Box# 207
(80825) 719.962.3277

• La Junta •
Holiday Inn
27994 Hwy 50
(81050) 719.384.2900

Quality Inn ($$)
1325 E 3rd St
(81050) 719.384.2571
mgr preapproval reqd

Stagecoach Inn ($)
905 W 3rd St
(81050) 719.384.5476

$=under $35 $$=$35-60   **123** $$$=$60-100 $$$$=over $100

COLORADO, Lake City

● Lake City ●
Cinnamon Inn ($$)
426 Gunnison Ave
(81235) 303.944.2641

Western Belle Lodge
1221 Hwy 149
(81235) 303.944.2415

● Lakewood ●
Chalet Motel ($)
6051 W Alameda Ave
(80226) 303.237.7775

Foothills Lodging ($$)
7150 W Colfax Ave
(80215) 303.232.2932

Lakewood Inn ($)
7150 W Colfax Ave
(80215) 303.238.1251

Motel 6 ($)
480 Wadsworth Blvd
(80226) 303.232.4924
1 small pet/room

Rodeway Inn ($$)
7150 W Colfax Ave
(80215) 303.238.1251

Sheraton Inn ($$$$)
360 Union Blvd
(80228) 303.987.2000
$50 deposit

● Lamar ●
Economy Inn ($)
1201 N Main St
(81052) 719.336.7471

● Las Animas ●
Best Western ($$)
Hwy 194
(81054) 719.456.0011
small pets only

● Leadville ●
Alps Motel
Hwy 24 S At Elm
(80461) 719.486.1223

Bel Air Motel
Hwy 24 S At Elm
(80461) 719.486.0881

Club Lead
500 E 7th St
(80461) 719.486.2202

Leadville Inn ($$)
25 Jacktown Rd
(80461) 719.486.3637

Mountain Peaks Motel
1 Harrison Ave
(80461) 719.486.3178

Silver King Motel ($$)
2020 N Poplar St
(80461) 719.486.2610

Timberline Motel
216 Harrison Ave
(80461) 719.486.1876

● Limon ●
Best Western ($)
I-70 & US34
(80828) 719.775.0277
w/permission only

Econo Lodge ($$)
985 Hwy 24
(80828) 719.775.2867

Limon Inn ($$)
250 E Main St
(80828) 719.775.2821

Safari Motel ($)
637 Main St
(80828) 719.775.2363

Super 8
Hwy 24
(80828) 719.775.2889
call re: fees

● Longmont ●
Budget Host ($)
3815 Hwy 119
(80504) 303.776.8700
some pets

First Interstate Inn
3940 Hwy 119
(80504) 303.772.6000

Raintree Plaza Hotel ($$$)
1900 Ken Pratt Blvd
(80501) 303.776.2000

Super 8 ($$)
10850 Turner Blvd
(80504) 303.772.0888
pets w/permission

Super 8 ($$)
2446 N Main St
(80501) 303.772.8106
w/permission

● Loveland ●
Best Western ($$)
5542 Hwy 34E
(80537) 970.667.7810
small dogs ok

● Mancos ●
Blue Spruce Motel ($)
40700 Hwy 160
(81328) 970.533.7073

Ponderosa Cabins ($$)
Cty Road 37 & Hwy 184
(81328) 970.882.7396

● Mesa ●
Wagon Wheel Motel ($$)
1090 Hwy 65
(81643) 970.268.5224

● Monarch ●
Monarch Mtn Lodge ($$)
#1 Power Pl
(81227) 719.539.2581

● Monte Vista ●
Comfort Inn ($$)
1519 Grande Ave
(81144) 719.852.0612

● Montrose ●
Black Canyon Mote ($)
1605 E Main St
(81401) 970.249.3495

Super 8 ($)
1705 E Main St
(81401) 970.249.9294
pets with deposit

● Naturita ●
Ray Motel ($)
123 Main St
(81422) 970.865.2235

● Nederland ●
Nederhaus Motel ($$)
686 Hwy 119 South
(80466) 303.444.4705

● Ouray ●
Ouray Cottage Motel ($$)
4th & Main Sts
(81427) 970.325.4370

Ouray Victorian Inn ($$)
50 3rd Ave
(81427) 970.325.7222

Timber Ridge Motel
1515 N Main St
(81427) 970.325.4523

● Pagosa Springs ●
Super 8 ($$)
34 Piedra Rd
(81147) 970.731.4005
$5 pets w/permission

● Parachute ●
Super Motel ($$)
252 Green Motel
(81635) 970.285.7936
pets allowed

● Pueblo ●
Holiday Inn
4001 N Elizabeth
(81008) 719.543.8050

Motel 6 ($)
4103 N Elizabeth St
(81008) 719.543.6221
1 small pet/room

Motel 6 ($)
960 Hwy 50
(81008) 719.543.8900
1 small pet/room

National 9 ($)
4400 N Elizabeth St
(81008) 719.543.4173

Pueblo Inn ($)
800 Hwy 50
(81008) 719.543.6820

Ramada Inn ($$)
2001 N Hudson Ave
(81001) 719.542.3750

● Ridgway ●
Super 8
373 Palamino Tr
(81432) 970.626.5444
dep

Policies Subject to Change

$=under $35 $$=$35-60 $$$=$60-100 $$$$=over $100

● Rifle ●
Red River Inn ($)
718 Taughenbaugh Blvd
(81650) 970.625.3050

Rusty Cannon Motel ($)
701 Taughenbaugh Blvd
(81650) 970.625.4004

● Rocky Ford ●
Melon Valley Inn ($)
1319 Elm Ave
(81067) 719.254.3306

● Salida ●
Aspen Leaf Lodge ($)
7350 Hwy 50W
(81201) 719.539.6733

Budget Lodge ($)
1146 E Hwy 50
(81201) 719.539.6695

Circle R Motel ($)
304 E Rainbow Blvd
(81201) 719.539.6296

Rainbow Inn ($)
105 Hwy 50E
(81201) 719.539.4444

Salida Motel ($)
1310 E Hwy 50
(81201) 719.539.2895

Western H-day Motel ($)
545 W Rainbow Blvd
(81201) 719.539.2553

Woodland Motel ($)
903 W 1st St
(81201) 719.539.4980

● Silverthorne ●
I 70 Inn
361 Blue River Pkwy
(80498) 970.468.5170

● Silverton ●
Alma House Inn ($$)
220 E 10th St
(81433) 970.387.5336

Wyman Hotel ($$)
1370 Greene St
(81433) 970.387.5372

● Snowmass Village ●
Silvertree Hotel ($$$$)
Box# 5009
(81615) 303.923.3520

● South Fork ●
The Inn Motel
30362 West Hwy 160
(81154) 719.873.5514

Wolf Creek Ski Lodge ($$)
31042 Hwy W 160
(81154) 719.873.5547

● Steamboat Springs ●
Harbor Hotel ($$)
Box# 774109
(80477) 970.879.1522

Holiday Inn ($$)
3190 S Lincoln Ave
(80477) 800.465.4329
mgr preapproval reqd

Rabbit Motel ($$)
201 Lincoln Ave
(80477) 970.879.1150

Sky Valley Lodge ($$)
Box# 773132
(80477) 970.879.7749

Super 8 ($$)
US Hwy 40
(80477) 970.879.5230
pets w/permission

The Alpiner ($$)
424 Lincoln Ave
(80487) 970.879.1430

● Sterling ●
Best Western ($$$)
Overland Trail St
(80751) 970.522.6265
mgr appr

Colonial Motel ($)
915 S Division Ave
(80751) 970.522.3382

Days Inn ($)
12881 Hwy 61
(80751) 970.522.1234
mgr preapproval reqd

First Interstate Inn ($)
20930 Hwy 6
(80751) 970.522.7274

Ramada Inn ($$$)
I-76 & Hwy 6
(80751) 970.522.2625
mgr preapproval reqd

Super 8 ($$)
12883 Hwy 61
(80751) 970.522.0300
call re: fees

● Stratton ●
Best Western ($$)
700 Colorado Ave
(80836) 719.348.5311
mgrs discretion

● Telluride ●
Doral Resort ($$$$)
145 Country Club Dr
(81435) 800.443.6725

The Peaks ($$$$)
136 Country Club Dr
(81435) 970.728.6800

● Trinidad ●
Best Western ($$)
900 W Adams St
(81082) 719.846.2215
under 20 lbs

Budget Host ($)
10301 Santa Fe Trail Dr
(81082) 800.283.4678
$3

Budget Summit Inn
I-25 Ex 11
(81082) 719.846.2251

Days Inn ($$)
702 W Main St
(81082) 719.846.2271
$20 chg deposit

Holiday Inn ($$)
9995 Cr 69
(81082) 719.846.4491

Super 8 ($$)
1924 Freedom Rd
(81082) 719.846.8280
call re: fees

● Vail ●
Antlers At Vail ($$$$)
680 W Lionshead Pl
(81657) 970.476.2471

Lostello ($$)
704 W Lionshead Cir
(81657) 970.476.2050

● Victor ●
Victor Hotel ($$$)
4th & Victor Ave
(80860) 970.689.3553

● Walden ●
North Park Motel ($)
625 Main St
(80480) 970.723.4271

● Walsenburg ●
Anchor Motel ($)
1001 Main St # T
(81089) 719.738.2800

Best Western ($$)
I-25
(81089) 719.738.1121
must declare when booking

Budget Host ($$)
553 US 85
(81089) 719.738.3800
w/permission

● Westcliffe ●
Westcliffe Inn ($)
S Hwy 69 & Hermit Rd
(81252) 719.783.9275

● Westminster ●
La Quinta Inn ($$$)
8701 Turnpike Dr
(80030) 303.425.9099
call re: fees

● Wheat Ridge ●
Holiday Inn
4700 Kipling
(80033) 303.423.4000

Motel 6 ($)
9920 W 49th Ave
(80033) 303.424.0658
1 small pet/room

Motel 6 ($)
10300 S I-70 Frontage Rd
(80033) 303.467.3172
1 small pet/room

Quality Inn ($)
12100 W 44th Ave
(80033) 303.476.2400

Well Behaved

Connecticut

● Avon ●
Avon Farms ($$$)
Box# 1295
(06001) 203.677.1651

● Branford ●
Days Inn ($$$)
375 E Main St
(06405) 203.488.8314
mgr preapproval reqd

Motel 6 ($$)
320 E Main St
(06405) 203.483.5828
1 small pet/room

Motor Inn of Branford ($$)
Box# 449
(06405) 203.488.8314

● Bridgeport ●
Holiday Inn ($$$)
1070 Main St
(06604) 800.465.4329

Holiday Inn
1070 Main St
(06604) 203.334.1234

● Chaplin ●
Pleasant View Motel ($)
Rt 6
(06235) 860.455.9588

● Chester ●
Chester Inn ($$$)
318 Main St
(06412) 203.526.9541

● Clinton ●
Clinton Motel ($$)
163 E Main St
(06413) 860.669.8850

● Cornwall Bridge ●
Cornwall Inn ($$)
Rural Rt 7
(06754) 800.786.6884

● Cromwell ●
Comfort Inn ($$)
111 Berlin Rd
(06416) 800.221.2222
mgr preapproval reqd

Radisson Inn ($$$)
100 Berlin Rd
(06416) 203.635.2000
small pets allowed

Super 8 ($$)
1 Industrial Park Rd
(06416) 860.632.8888
w/permission

● Danbury ●
Ethan Allen Inn ($$$)
21 Lake Ave Extension
(06811) 203.744.1776

Hilton ($$$)
18 Old Ridgebury Rd
(06810) 203.794.0600

Holiday Inn ($$)
80 Newtown Rd
(06810) 203.792.4000

Ramada Inn ($$)
I-84 At Ex 8
(06810) 203.792.3800

● East Hartford ●
Econo Lodge ($)
927 Main St
(06108) 800.424.4777

Holiday Inn
363 Roberts St
(06108) 860.528.9611

Wellesley Inn ($$)
333 Roberts St
(06108) 203.289.4950

● East Lyme ●
Howard Johnson ($$$)
265 Flanders Rd
(06333) 203.739.6921
small pets only

● East Windsor ●
Best Western ($$)
161 Bridge St
(06088) 860.623.9411
$25 fee

● Enfield ●
Motel 6 ($)
11 Hazard Ave
(06082) 860.741.3685
1 small pet/room

Red Roof Inn ($$)
5 Hazard Ave
(06082) 860.741.2571
small pets only

● Fairfield ●
Fairfield Motor Inn ($$$)
417 Post Rd
(06430) 800.257.0496

● Farmington ●
Centennial Suites ($$$)
5 Spring Ln
(06032) 860.677.4647

Farmington Inn ($$$)
827 Farmington Ave
(06032) 860.677.2821

Marriott Hotel ($$$)
15 Farm Springs Rd
(06032) 860.678.1000

● Goshen ●
Goshen Motel ($)
Rt 4
(06756) 860.491.9989

● Groton ●
Gold Star Inn ($$$)
156 Kings Hwy
(06340) 860.446.0660

Trails Corner Motel
580 Poquonnock Rd
(06340) 860.445.0220

● Hartford ●
Days Inn ($$)
207 Brainard Rd
(06114) 860.247.3297

Econo Lodge ($$)
7 Weston St
(06120) 800.424.4777

Holiday Inn ($$$)
50 Morgan St
(06120) 860.549.2400

Ramada Inn ($$)
440 Asylum St
(06103) 860.246.6591

Red Roof Inn ($$)
100 Weston St
(06120) 860.724.0222

Super 8 ($$)
57 W Service Rd
(06120) 860.246.8888
pets w/permission

Hartford Metro

● Avon ●
Avon Olds Farms ($$$)
Box# 1295
(06001) 203.677.1651

● Cromwell ●
Comfort Inn ($$)
111 Berlin Rd
(06416) 800.221.2222
mgr preapproval reqd

Radisson Inn ($$$)
100 Berlin Rd
(06416) 203.635.2000
small pets allowed

Super 8 ($$)
1 Industrial Park Rd
(06416) 860.632.8888
w/permission

● East Hartford ●
Econo Lodge ($)
927 Main St
(06108) 800.424.4777

Holiday Inn
363 Roberts St
(06108) 860.528.9611

Wellesley Inn ($$)
333 Roberts St
(06108) 203.289.4950

● East Windsor ●
Best Western ($$)
161 Bridge St
(06088) 860.623.9411
$25 fee

● Enfield ●
Motel 6 ($)
11 Hazard Ave
(06082) 860.741.3685
1 small pet/room

Red Roof Inn ($$)
5 Hazard Ave
(06082) 860.741.2571
small pets only

CALL AHEAD!

● Farmington ●
Centennial Suites ($$$)
5 Spring Ln
(06032) 860.677.4647

Farmington Inn ($$$)
827 Farmington Ave
(06032) 860.677.2821

Marriott Hotel ($$$)
15 Farm Springs Rd
(06032) 860.678.1000

● Hartford ●
Days Inn ($$)
207 Brainard Rd
(06114) 860.247.3297

Econo Lodge ($$)
7 Weston St
(06120) 800.424.4777

Holiday Inn ($$$)
50 Morgan St
(06120) 860.549.2400

Ramada Inn ($$)
440 Asylum St
(06103) 860.246.6591

Red Roof Inn ($$)
100 Weston St
(06120) 860.724.0222

Super 8 ($$)
57 W Service Rd
(06120) 860.246.8888
pets with permission

● Manchester ●
Clarion Hotel ($$$)
191 Spencer St
(06040) 860.646.5700

Manchester Motel ($$)
100 E Center St
(06040) 860.646.2300

● Wethersfield ●
Motel 6 ($)
1341 Silas Deane Hwy
(06109) 860.563.5900
1 small pet/room

Ramada Inn ($$)
1330 Silas Deane Hwy
(06109) 860.563.2311

● Windsor ●
Residence Inn ($$$)
100 Dunfey Ln
(06095) 860.688.7474
call for fee & availability

● Windsor Locks ●
Budgetel ($)
64 Ella Grasso Blvd
(06096) 860.623.3336

Homewood Suites ($$$)
65 Ella Grasso Blvd
(06096) 860.627.8463
$10 per day

Motel 6 ($)
3 National Dr
(06096) 860.292.6200
1 small pet/room

Sheraton Inn ($$$$)
1 Bradley Intl Airport
(06096) 860.627.5311

The Windsor Court Hotel ($$)
383 S Center St
(06096) 860.623.9811
$2 per day

End of Hartford Metro

● Kensington ●
Hawthorne Inn ($$)
2387 Wilbur Cross Hwy
(06037) 860.828.4181

● Lakeville ●
Interlaken Inn ($$$)
74 Interlaken Est
(06039) 860.435.9878

Iron Masters Motel ($$)
229 Main St
(06039) 860.435.9844

● Ledyard ●
Applewood Farms Inn
528 Col Ledyard Hwy
(06339) 203.536.2022

● Litchfield ●
Tollgate Hill Inn ($$$)
Box# 1339
(06759) 860.567.4545

● Manchester ●
Clarion Hotel ($$$)
191 Spencer St
(06040) 860.646.5700

Manchester Motel ($$)
100 E Center St
(06040) 860.646.2300

● Meriden ●
Hampton Inn ($$)
10 Bee St
(06450) 203.235.5154
small pets only

Ramada Inn ($$$)
275 Research Pkwy
(06450) 203.238.2380
small & controlled

Residence Inn ($$$)
390 Bee St
(06450) 203.634.7770
call for fee & availability

● Milford ●
Hampton Inn ($$)
129 Plains Rd
(06460) 800.426.7866

Howard Johnson ($$)
1052 Boston Post Rd
(06460) 203.878.4611

Red Roof Inn ($$)
10 Rowe Ave
(06460) 203.877.6060
small pets only

● Moosup ●
Plainfield Motel ($$)
RR 2 Box# 101
(06354) 203.564.2791

● Mystic ●
Charleys Harbor Inne ($$$)
15 Edgemont St
(06355) 860.572.9253
owner referred

● New Britain ●
Ramada Inn ($$)
65 Columbus Blvd
(06051) 860.224.9161

● New Haven ●
Motel 6 ($$)
270 Foxon Blvd
(06513) 203.469.0343
1 small pet/room

Quality Inn ($$)
100 Pond Lily Ave
(06515) 203.387.6651

● New London ●
Red Roof Inn ($)
707 Colman St
(06320) 860.444.0001
small pets only

● New Milford ●
Heritage Inn ($$)
34 Bridge St
(06776) 860.354.8883

● New Preston Marble Dale ●
Atha House Cottage ($$$)
Wheaton Rd Off Rt 202
(06777) 203.355.7387

● Niantic ●
Howard Johnson ($)
265 Flanders Rd
(06357) 800.446.4656

Motel 6 ($)
265 Flanders Rd
(06357) 860.739.6991
1 small pet/room

Yankee Motel ($$)
Box# 479
(06357) 800.942.8466

● North Haven ●
Holiday Inn ($$$)
201 Washington Ave
(06473) 203.239.4225

● North Stonington ●
State Line Motel ($)
593 Providence Tpke
(06359) 203.535.0680

● Norwalk ●
Garden Park Motel ($$)
351 Westport Ave
(06851) 203.847.7303

CONNECTICUT, Norwalk

Ramada Inn ($$$)
789 ConnecticutAve
(06854) 203.853.3477

● Oakdale ●
Chesterfield Lodge ($)
1596 Route 85
(06370) 860.442.0039

● Old Lyme ●
Old Lyme Inn ($$$)
85 Lyme St
(06371) 203.434.2600

● Old Saybrook ●
Comfort Inn ($)
100 Essex Rd
(06475) 800.221.2222

Sandpiper Motel ($$)
1750 Boston Post Rd
(06475) 860.399.7973

● Plainville ●
Howard Johnson ($$)
400 New Britain Ave
(06062) 860.747.6876

● Putnam ●
Kings Inn ($$$)
5 Heritage Rd
(06260) 860.928.7961

● Riverside ●
Howard Johnson ($$)
1114 Boston Post Rd
(06878) 203.637.3691

● Rocky Hill ●
Howard Johnson ($$)
1499 Silas Deane Hwy
(06067) 800.446.4656

● Shelton ●
Residence Inn ($$$)
1001 BridgeportAve
(06484) 203.926.9000
call for pet rooms

● Simsbury ●
The Executive Inn ($$)
969 Hopmeadow St
(06070) 860.658.2216

Simsbury House ($$$)
731 Hopmeadow St
(06070) 860.658.7658

● Southington ●
Howard Johnson ($$)
30 Laning St
(06489) 800.446.4656

Motel 6 ($)
625 Queen St
(06489) 860.621.7351
1 small pet/room

Red Carpet Inn
30 Lansing
(06489) 203.628.0921

● Stratford ●
Hojo Inn ($)
360 Honeyspot Rd
(06497) 800.446.4656

● Trumbull ●
Marriott
180 Hawley Ln
(06611) 203.378.1400

● Vernon Rockville ●
Howard Johnson ($$)
451 Hartford Tpke
(06066) 203.875.0781
$15 per pet per night

● Voluntown ●
Tamarack Lodge ($$)
10 Rod Rd
(06384) 860.376.0640

● Waterbury ●
Howard Johnson ($$)
2636 S Main St
(06706) 203.756.7961

Ramada Inn ($$)
Schrafft'S Dr
(06705) 800.272.6232

● Waterford ●
Lamplighter Motel ($$$)
211 Parkway
(06385) 860.442.7227

Oakdell Motel
983 Hartford Tpke
(06385) 860.442.9446

● West Haven ●
Days Hotel ($$$)
490 Saw Mill Rd
(06516) 203.933.0344

Econo Lodge ($$)
370 Highland St
(06516) 203.934.6611

Super 8 ($$)
7 Kimberly Ave
(06516) 203.932.8338
call re: fees

● Westbrook ●
Maples Motel ($$)
1935 Boston Post Rd
(06498) 860.399.9345

● Wethersfield ●
Motel 6 ($)
1341 Silas Deane Hwy
(06109) 860.563.5900
1 small pet/room

Ramada Inn ($$)
1330 Silas Deane Hwy
(06109) 860.563.2311

● Windsor ●
Residence Inn ($$$)
100 Dunfey Ln
(06095) 860.688.7474
call for fee & availability

● Windsor Locks ●
Budgetel ($)
64 Ella Grasso Blvd
(06096) 860.623.3336

Homewood Suites ($$$)
65 Ella Grasso Blvd
(06096) 860.627.8463
$10 per day

Motel 6 ($)
3 National Dr
(06096) 860.292.6200
1 small pet/room

Sheraton Inn ($$$$)
1 Bradley Intl Airport
(06096) 860.627.5311

The Windsor Court Hotel ($$)
383 S Center St
(06096) 860.623.9811
$2 per day

Well
Behaved

Delaware

● Bethany Beach ●
Westward Pines Motel ($$$)
10 Kent Ave
(19930) 302.539.7426

● Claymont ●
Hilton ($$$$)
630 Naamans Rd
(19703) 302.792.2700

● Dover ●
Budget Inn ($$)
1426 N Dupont Hwy
(19901) 302.734.4433

Days Inn ($$)
272 N Dupont Hwy
(19901) 302.674.8002
mgr preapproval reqd

Haynies Motel ($)
1760 N Dupont Hwy
(19901) 302.734.4042

Sheraton Inn ($$$)
1570 N Dupont Hwy
(19901) 302.678.8500
only on the first floor

● Fenwick Island ●
Budget Inn ($$$)
Ocean Hwy & Rt 54
(19944) 302.539.7673

Sands Motel ($$$)
Rt 1 & James St
(19944) 302.539.7745

● Lewes ●
First Port Of Call ($$)
28 Cape Henlopen Dr
(19958) 302.945.1586

Vesuvio Motel ($$$)
105 Savannah Rd
(19958) 302.645.2224

● Millsboro ●
Budget Inn ($$)
210 W Dupont Hwy
(19966) 302.934.6711

● New Castle ●
Days Inn ($$)
3 Memorial Dr
(19720) 302.654.5400
mgr preapproval reqd

Econo Lodge ($)
232 S Dupont Hwy
(19720) 800.424.4777

Howard Johnson ($$)
2162 New Castle Ave
(19720) 800.446.4656

Motel 6 ($$)
1200 West Ave
(19720) 302.571.1200
1 small pet/room

New Castle Motel ($)
196 S Dupont Hwy
(19720) 302.328.1836

Quality Inn ($$)
147 N Dupont Hwy
(19720) 302.328.6666
mgr preapproval reqd

Ramada Inn ($$$)
Rt 13 & I-295
(19720) 302.658.8511

Rodeway Inn ($$)
111 S Dupont Hwy
(19720) 302.328.6246

Travelodge ($$)
1213 West Ave
(19720) 302.654.5544

● Newark ●
Best Western ($$)
260 Chapman Rd
(19702) 302.738.3400
fee

Comfort Inn ($$)
1120 S College Ave
(19713) 302.368.8715
mgr preapproval reqd

Hampton Inn ($$$)
3 Concord Ln
(19713) 302.737.3900
small pets only

Howard Johnson ($$)
1119 S College Ave
(19713) 302.368.8521

Red Roof Inn ($$)
415 Tanto Christiana Rd
(19713) 302.292.2870
small pets only

Residence Inn ($$$)
240 Chapman Rd
(19702) 302.453.9200
call for fee & availability

Travelodge ($$)
268 E Main St
(19711) 302.737.5050

● Rehoboth Beach ●
Airport Motel ($$)
Rt 14
(19971) 302.227.6737

Budget Inn ($$$)
154 Rehoboth Ave
(19971) 302.227.9446

Atlantic Oceanside ($)
1700 Hwy One
(19971) 302.227.8811

Sands Hotel ($$$$)
101 N Boardwalk
(19971) 302.227.2511

Bellbuoy Motel ($$)
21 Vandyke St
(19971) 302.227.6000

Best Western ($$$$)
1400 Hwy One
(19971) 302.226.1100
mgr preapproval reqd

Cape Suites ($$$$)
47 Baltimore Ave
(19971) 302.226.3342

Lord Baltimore Lodge ($)
16 Baltimore Ave
(19971) 302.227.2855

Love Creek Motel ($$)
Rt 24
(19971) 302.945.8909

Renegade Motel ($$$)
Hwy 1
(19971) 302.227.1222

SeaEsta Motel 1 ($$)
2306 Hwy One
(19971) 800.436.6591

SeaEsta Motel 2 ($$$)
140 Rehoboth Ave
(19971) 800.436.6591

SeaEsta Motel 3 ($$$)
1409 Hwy One
(19971) 800.436.6591

The Cupboard Inn ($$$$)
50 Park Afve
(19971) 302.227.8553

● Seaford ●
Comfort Inn ($$)
225 N Dual Hwy
(19973) 302.629.8385
mgr preapproval reqd

● Selbyville ●
Island Inn ($$$)
RR 1
(19975) 302.537.1900

● Wilmington ●
Best Western ($$$)
1807 Concord Pike
(19803) 302.656.9436

Guest Quarters Suites ($$$)
707 N King St
(19801) 302.656.9300

Holiday Inn ($$$)
700 N King St
(19801) 302.655.0400
mgr preapproval reqd

Radisson Inn ($$)
4727 Concord Pike Rt 202
(19803) 302.478.6000

Sheraton Inn ($$$$)
422 Delaware Ave
(19801) 302.654.8300

Tally Ho Motel ($$)
5209 Concord Pike
(19803) 302.478.0300

Washington DC Metro

● Washington ●
Ana Hotel ($$$$)
2401 M St NW
(20037) 202.429.2400
small pets only

Best Western ($$$$)
1121 New Hampshr Ave NW
(20037) 202.457.0565

Carlyle Suites ($$)
1731 New Hampshire Ave
NW
(20009) 202.234.3200

Days Inn ($$)
2700 New York Ave NE
(20002) 202.832.5800
small pets allowed

Econo Lodge ($$)
1600 New York Ave NE
(20002) 800.424.4777

Embassy Suites ($$$$)
4300 Military Rd NW
(20015) 202.362.9300
$10 per day

Georgetown Dutch Inn
1075 Jefferson NW
(20007) 202.337.0900

Georgetown Mews
1111 20th St NW
(20007) 202.298.7731

Guest Quarters Suites ($$$$)
801 New Hampshire Ave NW
(20037) 202.785.2000

Guest Quarters Suites ($$$)
2500 Pennsylvania Ave NW
(20037) 800.424.2900

Hilton ($$$)
1919 Connecticut Ave NW
(20009) 202.483.3000

Hojo Inn ($$)
600 New York Ave NE
(20002) 800.446.4656

Holiday Inn ($$)
1501 Rhode Island Ave NW
(20005) 202.483.2000

Holiday Inn ($$$)
1155 14th St NW
(20005) 202.737.1200

Hotel Washington ($$$$)
15th & Pennsylvania NW
(20004) 202.638.5900

Loews Hotel ($$$$)
480 L'Enfant Plaza SW
(20024) 202.484.1000
VIP Pet Program

Marriott Hotel ($$$$)
1221 22nd St
(20037) 202.872.1500

Master Host ($$)
1917 Bladensburg Rd NE
(20002) 202.832.8600
small pets only

Master Host
6711 Georgia Ave NW
(20012) 202.722.1600

Omni Hotel ($$$$)
2500 Calvert St NW
(20008) 202.234.0700

One Washington Cir ($$$)
1 Washington Cir NW
(20037) 202.872.1680

Park Hyatt ($$$$)
1201 124th St NW
(20037) 202.789.1234

Pullman Highland Hotel
($$$$)
1914 Connecticut NW
(20009) 202.332.9300

Radisson Inn ($$$)
1515 Rhode Island Ave NW
(20005) 800.333.3333

Sheraton Inn ($$$$)
2660 Woodley Rd NW
(20008) 202.328.2000

Stouffer Hotel ($$$$)
1127 Connecticut Ave NW
(20036) 202.347.2000

Swiss Inn Hotel
1204 Massachusetts Ave
NW
(20005) 202.371.1816

The Carlton ($$$$)
923 16th St
(20006) 202.638.2626
under 20 lbs

The Four Seasons ($$$$)
2800 Pennsylvania Ave NW
(20007) 202.342.0444
small pets allowed

The Grand Hotel ($$$$)
2350 M St NW
(20037) 202.429.0100

The Hay Adams Hotel ($$$$)
1 Lafayette Sq NW
(20006) 202.638.6600

The Jefferson Hotel ($$$$)
1200 16th St NW
(20036) 202.347.2200

The Madison Hotel ($$$$)
1177 15th St NW
(20005) 202.862.1600

The Savoy Suites Hotel ($$$)
2505 Wisconsin Ave NW
(20007) 202.337.9700

The Watergate Hotel ($$$$)
2650 Virginia Ave NW
(20037) 202.965.2300
small dogs

The Willard Inter Continental
($$$$)
1401 Pennsylvania Ave NW
(20004) 202.628.9100
under 40 lbs

Travelodge ($$$)
1201 13th St NW
(20005) 202.682.5300

Washington Cap Hill
525 New Jersey Ave NW
(20001) 202.628.2100

Washington Hotel ($$$$)
515 15th St NW
(20004) 800.424.9540

Washington Plaza
10 Thomas Cir NW
(20005) 202.842.1300

Washington Renaissance
($$$$)
999 9th St NW
(20001) 202.898.9000

Westin Hotel ($$$$)
24th & M St NW
(20037) 202.429.2400
small pets only

Wyndham Hotel ($$$$)
2430 Pennsylvania Ave NW
(20037) 202.955.6400

DC/Maryland Metro

● Beltsville ●
Holiday Inn ($$$)
4050 Powder Mill Rd
(20705) 301.937.4422
small pets only

Ramada Inn ($$)
4050 Powder Mill Rd
(20705) 301.572.7100

● Bethesda ●
Holiday Inn ($$$$)
8120 Wisconsin Ave
(20814) 301.652.2000

Marriott Hotel ($$$)
6711 Democracy Blvd
(20817) 301.897.5600
must call ahead

Ramada Inn ($$$)
8400 Wisconsin Ave
(20814) 301.654.1000

Residence Inn ($$$$)
7335 Wisconsin Ave
(20814) 301.718.0200
extra daily fee

● Bowie ●
Econo Lodge ($$)
4502 NW Crain Hwy
(20718) 301.464.2200

● Capitol Heights ●
Days Inn ($$)
55 Hampton Park Blvd
(20743) 800.329.7466
mgr preapproval reqd

Econo Lodge ($)
100 Hampton Park Blvd
(20743) 800.424.4777

Motel 6 ($$)
75 Hampton Park Blvd
(20743) 301.499.0800
1 small pet/room

● Clinton ●
Econo Lodge ($$)
7851 Malcolm Rd
(20735) 301.856.2800

● College Park ●
Park View Inn ($$)
9020 Baltimore Ave
(20740) 301.441.8110

● Gaithersburg ●
Comfort Inn ($$)
16216 S Frederick Ave
(20877) 301.330.0023

Comfort Inn ($$)
16216 Frederick Rd
(20877) 800.221.2222

Econo Lodge ($$)
1875 N Frederick Ave
(20879) 301.963.3840

Hilton ($$$)
620 Perry Pkwy
(20877) 301.977.8900

Holiday Inn ($$$)
2 Montgomery Village Ave
(20879) 301.948.8900

Red Roof Inn ($$)
497 Quince Orchard Rd
(20878) 301.977.3311
fees/limits may apply

● Greenbelt ●
Holiday Inn
7200 Hanover
(20770) 301.982.7000

Marriott Hotel ($$$)
6400 Ivy Ln
(20770) 301.441.3700
$25 fee

● Hyattsville ●
Howard Johnson ($$)
5811 Annapolis Rd
(20784) 301.779.7700

● Jessup ●
Red Roof Inn
8000 Washington Blvd
(20794) 410.796.0380
fees/limits may apply

Metro Virginia, D.C.

• Lanham •
Best Western ($$)
5910 Princess Garden Pkwy
(20706) 800.528.1234

Days Inn
9023 Annapolis Rd
(20706) 301.459.6600

Red Roof Inn ($$)
9050 Lanham Severn Rd
(20706) 301.731.8830
fees/limits may apply

• Laurel •
Motel 6 ($$)
3510 Old Annapolis Rd
(20724) 301.497.1544
1 small pet/room

Red Roof Inn
12525 Laurel Bowie Rd
(20708) 301.498.8811
fees/limits may apply

• New Carrollton •
Sheraton Inn ($$$)
8500 Annapolis Rd
(20784) 301.459.6700

• Oxon Hill •
Red Roof Inn ($)
6170 Oxon Hill Rd
(20745) 301.567.8030
fees/limits may apply

• Rockville •
Days Inn ($$)
16001 Shady Grove Rd
(20850) 301.948.4300
small pets only

Woodfin Suites Hotel ($$$)
1380 Piccard Dr
(20850) 301.590.9880

• Silver Spring •
Econo Lodge ($$)
7990 Georgia Ave
(20910) 301.565.3444

• Suitland •
Motel 6 ($$)
5701 Allentown Rd
(20746) 301.702.1061
1 small pet/room

• Waldorf •
Econo Lodge ($$)
4 Business Park Dr
(20601) 301.645.0022
$15 fee

DC/Virginia Metro

• Alexandria •
Alexandria Hotel
801 N Fairfax St
(22314) 703.549.1000

Comfort Inn ($$)
5716 S Van Dorn St
(22310) 703.922.9200
mgr preapproval reqd

Comfort Inn ($$)
7212 Richmond Hwy
(22306) 703.765.9000
mgr preapproval reqd

Days Inn ($$)
6100 Richmond Hwy
(22303) 703.329.0500
small pets allowed

Days Inn ($$)
110 S Bragg St
(22312) 703.354.4950
$5/pets

Doubletree ($$$)
100 S Reynolds St
(22304) 703.370.9600
$10 per day

Econo Lodge ($$)
8849 Richmond Hwy
(22309) 703.780.0300
$50 deposit

Econo Lodge ($$)
700 N Washington St
(22314) 703.836.5100

Holiday Inn ($$$)
2460 Eisenhower Ave
(22314) 800.465.4329
mgr preapproval reqd

Holiday Inn ($$$)
480 King St
(22314) 703.549.6080
mgr preapproval reqd

Howard Johnson ($$)
5821 Richmond Hwy
(22303) 703.329.1400
small with mgrs approval

Ramada Inn ($$$$)
901 N Fairfax St
(22314) 703.683.6

Ramada Inn ($$$)
4641 Kenmore Ave
(22304) 703.751.4510

Ramada Inn ($$$)
901 N Fairfax St
(22314) 703.683.6000
small pets only

Red Roof Inn ($$)
5975 Richmond Hwy
(22303) 703.960.5200
fees/limits may apply

Sheraton Inn ($$$)
801 N St Asaph St
(22314) 703.836.4700
w/permission from mgr

• Arlington •
Best Western ($$)
2480 S Glebe Rd
(22206) 703.979.4400

Best Western ($$$)
1850 Fort Myer Dr
(22209) 703.522.0400
small pets only

Doubletree ($$$)
300 Army Navy Dr
(22202) 800.222.8733

Econo Lodge ($)
3335 Lee Hwy
(22207) 800.424.4777

Holiday Inn
1489 Jefferson Davis Hwy
(22202) 800.465.4329
mgr preapproval reqd

Holiday Inn
1900 N Ft Meyer
(22209) 703.807.2000

Howard Johnson ($$$)
2650 Jefferson Davis Hwy
(22202) 703.684.7200

Hyatt Hotel ($$$)
1325 Wilson Blvd
(22209) 703.525.1234

Marriott Hotel ($$$$)
1700 Jefferson Davis Hwy
(22202) 703.920.3230

Marriott Hotel ($$$$)
1401 Lee Hwy
(22209) 703.524.6400

Ramada Inn ($$$$)
950 N Stafford St
(22203) 703.528.6000

Stouffer ($$$)
2399 Jefferson Davis Hwy
(22202) 703.418.6800
if small enough to carry

• Chantilly •
Washington Dulles ($$)
333 W Service Rd
(22021) 703.471.9500

• Dumfries •
Holiday Inn ($$)
17133 Dumfries Rd
(22026) 703.221.1141
mgr preapproval reqd

• Fairfax •
Holiday Inn ($$$)
11787 Lee Jackson Hwy
(22033) 703.352.2525
mgr preapproval reqd

Holiday Inn ($$$)
3535 Chain Bridge Rd
(22030) 703.591.5500
mgr preapproval reqd

Hyatt Hotel ($$)
12777 Fair Lakes Cir
(22033) 703.818.1234
small on lower level

Wellesley Inn ($$)
10327 Lee Hwy
(22030) 703.359.2888
$3 charge

Metro Virginia D.C.

● Falls Church ●
Econo Lodge ($$)
5666 Columbia Pike
(22041) 703.820.5600

Marriott Hotel ($$$$)
3111 Fairview Park Dr
(22042) 703.849.9400
small pets only

Quality Inn ($$)
6111 Arlington Blvd
(22044) 703.534.9100
mgr preapproval reqd

Ramada Inn ($$$)
7801 Leesburg Pike
(22043) 703.893.1340
small pets only

Ramada Inn ($$$)
7801 Leeburg Pike
(22043) 703.675.3693

● Herndon ●
Hilton ($$$)
13869 Park Center Rd
(20171) 703.478.2900

Residence Inn ($$)
315 Elden St
(20170) 703.435.0044

Summerfield Suites
13700 Coppermine Rd
(20171) 703.713.6800

● Manassas ●
Red Roof Inn ($$)
10610 Automotive Dr
(20109) 703.335.9333

● Mc Lean ●
The Ritz Carlton ($$$$)
1700 Tysons Blvd
(22102) 703.506.4300
small pets only

Tysons Westpark Hotel ($$)
8401 Westpark Dr
(22102) 703.734.2800
waiver

● Springfield ●
Econo Lodge ($$)
6868 Springfield Blvd
(22150) 703.491.5196

Ramada Inn ($$)
6868 Springfield Blvd
(22150) 703.644.5311

● Vienna ●
Marriott Hotel ($$)
8028 Leesburg Pike
(22182) 703.734.3200

● ● Vienna ● ●
Residence Inn ($$$$)
8616 Westwood Center Dr
(22182) 800.331.3131

● Woodbridge ●
Days Inn ($$)
14619 Potomac Mills Rd
(22192) 703.494.4433
small pets allowed

Econo Lodge ($$)
13317 Gordon Blvd
(22191) 703.491.5196

Friendship Inn ($$)
13964 Jefferson Davis Hwy
(22191) 703.494.4144

Scottish Inn ($$)
951 Annapolis Way
(22191) 703.490.3400

End of Washington DC Metro

Florida
● Alachua ●
Days Inn ($$)
16301 Mlk Blvd
(32615) 904.462.3251
small pets allowed

Ramada Inn ($$)
16305 NW 163rd Ln
(32615) 904.462.4200

Travelodge ($$)
RR 1 Box# 229A
(32615) 904.462.2244

● Altamonte Springs ●
Days Inn ($$$)
235 S Wymore Rd
(32714) 407.862.2800

Embassy Suites ($$$)
225 E Altamonte Dr
(32701) 407.834.2400

La Quinta Inn ($$)
150 S Westmonte Dr
(32714) 800.531.5900
call re: fees

Residence Inn ($$$)
270 Douglas Ave
(32714) 407.788.7991
$150 fee plus $5 per night

● Apalachicola ●
Rainbow Inn
123 Water St
(32320) 904.653.8139

Rancho Inn ($)
240 Hwy 98
(32320) 904.653.9435

● Apopka ●
Crosbys Motor Inn ($$)
1440 W Orange Blossom Trl
(32712) 800.821.6685

● Arcadia ●
Best Western ($$)
504 S Brevard Ave
(34266) 941.494.4884
$10/night

● Bal Harbour ●
Sheraton Inn ($$$$)
9701 Collins Ave
(33154) 305.865.7511

● Bartow ●
Davis Bros Motel ($$)
1035 N Broadway Ave
(33830) 941.533.0711

El Jon Motel ($$)
1460 E Main St
(33830) 941.533.8191

● Bay Harbor Islands ●
Bay Harbor Inn ($$$)
9660 E Bay Harbor Dr
(33154) 305.868.4141

● Boca Raton ●
Radisson Inn ($$$)
7920 Glades Rd
(33434) 407.483.3600
small pets allowed

Ramada Inn ($)
2901 N Federal Hwy
(33431) 407.395.6850

Residence Inn ($$$)
525 NW 77th St
(33487) 407.994.3222
call for pet room availability

● Bonifay ●
Best Western ($$)
2004 S Waukesha St
(32425) 904.547.4251
$3

Econo Lodge ($$)
2210 S Waukesha St
(32425) 904.547.9345

● Bradenton ●
Days Inn ($$)
3506 1st St
(34208) 941.746.1141

Econo Lodge ($)
9727 14th St
(34207) 941.758.7199
$5 fee

Hojo Inn ($)
6511 14th St
(34207) 941.756.8399

Motel 6 ($)
660 67th Street Cir
(34208) 941.747.6005
1 small pet/room

Park Inn Intl ($$)
4450 47th St
(34210) 941.795.4633
$25 pet deposit

● Brooksville ●
Holiday Inn
30307 Cortez Blvd
(34602) 352.796.9481

● Bushnell ●
Best Western ($$)
2224 W-Cr 48
(33513) 352.793.5010
under 15 lbs

• Callahan •
Friendship Inn ($)
US I-301 & 23 North
(32011) 904.879.3451

• Cape Coral •
Del Prado Inn ($$)
1502 Miramar St
(33904) 941.542.3151

• Captiva •
Tween Waters Inn
15951 Capitva Rd
(33924) 941.472.5161

• Carrabelle •
The Moorings At Carrabelle
($$)
1000 US 98
(32322) 904.697.2800

• Cedar Key •
Dockside Motel ($$)
11 Dock St
(32625) 352.543.5432

Park Place Motel ($$$)
Box# 613
(32625) 352.543.5737

• Chattahoochee •
Morgan Motel ($)
E US 90
(32324) 904.663.4336

• Chipley •
Days Inn ($$)
1593 Main St
(32428) 904.638.7335
$5/pets

• Clearwater •
Agean Sands Motel ($$)
421 S Gulfview Blvd
(34630) 800.942.3432

Best Western ($$$)
691 S Gulfview Blvd
(34630) 813.443.7652

Clearwater Beach Hotel
500 Mandalay Ave
(34630) 813.441.2425

Policies
Subject
to Change

Holiday Inn ($$$)
13625 Icot Blvd
(34620) 813.536.7275
mgr preapproval reqd

Howard Johnson ($$)
21030 US Hwy 19
(34625) 813.797.8173

La Quinta Inn ($$)
3301 Ulmerton Rd
(34622) 800.531.5900
call re: fees

Residence Inn ($$$$)
5050 Ulmerton Rd
(34620) 813.573.4444
$125 fee

• Cocoa •
Best Western ($$)
4225 W King St
(32926) 407.632.1065
small pets

Days Inn ($$)
5600 Hwy 524
(32926) 407.636.6500
$5 daily

Econo Lodge ($$)
3220 N Cocoa Blvd
(32926) 407.632.4561
small pets only

Ramada Inn ($$)
900 Friday Rd
(32926) 407.631.1210

• Cocoa Beach •
Econo Lodge ($$)
1275 N Atlantic Ave
(32931) 407.783.2252

Motel 6 ($$)
3701 N Atlantic Ave
(32931) 407.783.3103
1 small pet/room

Surf Studio Resort ($$)
1801 S Atlantic Ave
(32931) 407.783.7100

• Coral Gables •
Howard Johnson ($$)
1430 S Dixie Hwy
(33146) 305.665.7501

• Coral Springs •
Wellesley Inns ($$)
3100 N University Dr
(33065) 954.344.2200

• Crestview •
Days Inn ($$)
4255 Ferdon Blvd
(32536) 904.682.8842
$5/pets

Holiday Inn ($$)
I-10
(32536) 904.682.6111

Super 8 ($)
3925 Ferdon Blvd
(32536) 904.682.9649
$5 charge

• Cross City •
Carriage Inn ($$)
280 E Main
(32628) 352.498.3910

• Crystal River •
Days Inn
2380 Hwy 19
(34428) 352.795.2111
$7 fee

Plantation Inn ($$$)
9301 W Fort Island Trl
(34429) 352.795.4211

• Dania •
Hilton ($$$)
1870 Griffin Rd
(33004) 800.445.8667

Motel 6 ($$)
825 E Dania Beach Blvd
(33004) 954.921.5505
1 small pet/room

Sheraton Inn ($$$)
1825 Griffin Rd
(33004) 954.920.3500
$50 fee

• Davenport •
Days Inn ($)
I-4 & US 27
(33837) 941.424.2596

Motel 6 ($$)
5620 US Hwy 27
(33837) 941.424.2521
1 small pet/room

• Daytona Beach •
Aruba Inn ($)
1254 N Atlantic Ave
(32118) 904.253.5643

Budget Host ($)
1305 S Ridgewood Ave
(32114) 800.283.4678
$5

Casa Marina Motel
828 N Atlantic Ave
(32118) 800.225.3691

Days Inn ($)
1909 S Atlantic Ave
(32118) 904.255.4492
$15

Days Inn ($$)
2900 W Intl Speedway Blvd
(32124) 904.255.0541
$10/pets

Holiday Inn
600 N Atlantic
(32118) 904.255.4471

Howard Johnson ($$)
701 S Atlantic Ave
(32118) 904.258.8522

International Motel ($)
313 S Atlantic Ave
(32118) 904.255.7491

La Quinta Inn ($$)
2725 Intl Speedway Blvd
(32114) 800.221.4731
call re: fees

Paradise Inn ($$$)
333 S Atlantic Ave
(32118) 904.255.8827

Ramada Inn ($$$)
1798 W Intl Speedway Blvd
(32114) 904.255.2422
small pets only

Red Carpet Inn ($)
1855 S Ridgewood Ave
(32119) 904.767.6681
$3 fee

FLORIDA, Daytona Beach

Sand Castle Motel ($)
3619 S Atlantic Ave
(32127) 800.967.4757

Scottish Inn ($)
1515 S Ridgewood Ave
(32114) 904.258.5742
$5 fee

Sea Oats Beach Motel ($$)
2539 S Atlantic Ave
(32118) 904.767.5684

Super 8 ($$)
2992 W Int Speedway Blvd
(32124) 904.253.0643
call re: fees

Travelers Rest Inn ($$)
749 Ridgewood Ave
(32117) 904.255.6511

● De Funiak Springs ●
Best Western ($$)
2343 Freeport Rd
(32433) 904.892.5111
small pets in designated
rooms

Days Inn ($)
472 Hugh Adams Rd
(32433) 904.892.6115
$10

Econo Lodge ($)
1325 S Freeport Rd
(32433) 800.424.4777

● Deerfield Beach ●
Comfort Suites ($$)
1040 E Newport Center Dr
(33442) 954.570.8887
mgr preapproval reqd

Howard Johnson ($$$)
2096 NE 2nd St
(33441) 954.428.2850

La Quinta Inn ($$)
351 W Hillsboro Blvd
(33441) 954.421.1004
call re: fees

Ramada Inn ($$$)
1401 S Fed Hwy US 1
(33441) 954.421.5000

Wellesley Inn ($$)
100 SW 12th Ave
(33442) 954.428.0661

● Deland ●
Holiday Inn ($$$)
350 Int'L Spdwy
(32724) 904.738.5200
mgr preapproval reqd

Quality Inn ($)
2801 E New York Ave
(32724) 904.736.3440

● Delray Beach ●
Colony Hotel ($$)
525 E Atlantic Ave
(33483) 561.276.4123

● Destin ●
Days Inn ($$)
1029 Hwy 98
(32541) 904.837.2599
$10/pets

Frangista Beach Inn ($$)
1860 Old Way 98
(32541) 904.654.5501

Howard Johnson ($$)
713 Hwy 98
(32541) 904.837.5455

● Dundee ●
Holiday Inn
339 Hwy 27
(33838) 941.439.1591

● Dunedin ●
Econo Lodge ($$$)
1414 Bayshore Blvd
(34698) 813.734.8851

● East Palatka ●
The Oaks Motel
RR 3 Box# 50 Hwy17
(32131) 904.328.1545

● Eastpoint ●
Sportsmans Lodge ($)
99 N Bayshore Dr
(32328) 904.670.8423

● Elkton ●
Comfort Inn ($$)
2625 Hwy 207
(32033) 800.221.2222

● Ellenton ●
Best Western ($$)
5218 17th St
(34222) 941.729.8505
under 35 lbs

● Englewood ●
Days Inn ($$)
2540 S McCall Rd
(34224) 941.474.5544
$4/pets

Veranda Inn ($$$)
2073 S McCall Rd
(34224) 941.475.6533

● Fernandina Beach ●
Shoneys Inn ($$$)
2707 Sadler Rd
(32034) 800.222.2222

● Flagler Beach ●
Topaz Motel ($$)
1224 S Oceanshore Blvd
(32136) 904.439.3301

● Fort Lauderdale ●
Admirals Court Motel ($$$$)
21 Hendricks Is
(33301) 954.462.5072

Budgetel ($$)
3800 W Commercial Blvd
(33309) 954.485.7900

Days Inn ($$$)
1700 W Broward Blvd
(33312) 954.463.2500
mgr preapproval reqd

Fort Lauderdale Inn ($$)
57 27 N Federal Hwy
(33308) 954.491.2500

Fort Lauderdale Yacht ($$)
341 N Birch Rd
(33304) 954.463.2821

Guest Quarters Suites ($$$$)
2670 E Sunrise Blvd
(33304) 954.565.3800
$10 per pet per night on 3rd
floor

Holiday Inn
1711 N University
(33322) 954.472.5600

Howard Johnson ($$)
700 N Atlantic Blvd
(33304) 954.563.2451

Howard Johnson ($$)
501 SE 17th St
(33316) 954.525.5194

Mark 2103 Hotel ($$)
2100 N Atlantic Blvd
(33305) 954.566.8383

Motel 6 ($$)
1801 Hwy 84
(33315) 954.760.7999
1 small pet/room

Ramada Inn ($$$)
2275 Hwy 84
(33312) 954.584.4000

Red Carpet Inn
2440 Hwy 84
(33312) 954.792.8181

Riviera Suites ($)
501 Breakers Ave
(33304) 954.564.2525

Three Suns Motel ($)
3016 Windamar Hwy
(33304) 954.563.7926

Trevers At Beach ($$)
552 N N Birch Rd
(33304) 954.564.4341

Wellesley Inns ($$)
5070 N Hwy 7
(33319) 954.484.6909

Westin Hotel ($$$$)
400 Corporate Dr
(33334) 954.772.1331
pets accepted

Wish You Were Here ($)
7 N Birch Rd
(33304) 954.462.0531

● Fort Myers ●
Budgetel ($$)
2717 Colonial Blvd
(33907) 941.275.3500

Comfort Suites ($$$)
13651 Indian Paint Ln
(33912) 941.768.0005
mgr preapproval reqd

Homosassa, FLORIDA

Days Inn
13353 Cleveland Ave
(33903) 941.995.0535
$10

Days Inn ($)
11435 N Cleveland Ave
(33903) 941.936.1311
$6

Econo Lodge ($)
1330U N Cleveland Ave
(33903) 800.424.4777

Golf View Motel ($$)
3523 Cleveland Ave
(33901) 941.936.1858

La Quinta Inn ($$)
4850 S Cleveland Ave
(33907) 941.275.3300
call re: fees

Motel 6 ($)
3350 Marinatown Ln
(33903) 941.656.5544
1 small pet/room

Radisson Inn ($$)
20091 Summerlin Rd
(33908) 941.466.1200

Rock Lake Motel
2930 Palm Beach Blvd
(33916) 941.334.3242

Travelodge ($)
2038 W 1st St
(33901) 941.334.2284

● Fort Myers Beach ●
Anchor Inn Cottages ($$$$)
285 Virginia Ave
(33931) 941.463.2630

Best Western ($$$$)
684 Estero Blvd
(33931) 941.463.6000
small pets

● Fort Pierce ●
Days Inn ($$)
6651 Darter Ct
(34945) 407.466.4066
$10/pets

Holiday Inn ($$)
7151 Okeechobee Rd
(34945) 561.464.5000

Howard Johnson ($$)
7150 Okeechobee Rd
(34945) 407.464.4500

Motel 6 ($)
2500N Peters Rd
(34945) 407.461.9937
1 small pet/room

● Fort Walton Beach ●
Days Inn
135 Miracle Strip Pkwy
(32548) 904.244.6184
$10

Marina Motel ($)
1345 US 98 E Okaloosa Isl
(32548) 904.244.1129

Park Inn Intl ($$)
100 Miracle Strip Pkwy
(32548) 904.244.0121
$10 fee

● Gainesville ●
Apartment Inn Motel ($$$$)
4401 SW 13th St
(32608) 352.371.3811

Days Inn ($$)
7516 W Newberry Rd
(32606) 352.332.3033
$5

Econo Lodge ($$)
2649 SW 13th St
(32608) 352.373.7816
small pets only one pet room

Fairfield Inn ($$)
6901 NW 4th Blvd
(32607) 800.348.6000

Hojo Inn ($)
1900 SW 13th St
(32608) 800.228.2800

La Quinta Inn ($$)
920 NW 69th Ter
(32605) 352.332.6466
call re: fees

Motel 6 ($)
4000 SW 40th Blvd
(32608) 352.373.1604
1 small pet/room

Ramada Inn ($$)
4021 SW 40th Blvd
(32608) 352.373.0392

Residence Inn ($$$)
4001 SW 13th St
(32608) 352.371.2101
call for fee & availability

Super 8 ($$)
4202 SW 40th Blvd
(32608) 352.378.3888
pets w/permission

Travelodge ($$)
3103 NW 13th St
(32609) 352.372.4319

● Haines City ●
Best Western ($$)
605 B Moore Rd
(33844) 941.421.6929
small attended

Econo Lodge ($$)
1504 US 27
(33844) 941.422.8621

● Hallandale ●
Ramada Inn ($$$)
2080 S Ocean Dr
(33009) 800.272.6232

● Hobe Sound ●
Red Carpet Inn
8605 SE Federal Hwy
(33455) 407.546.3600

● Holiday ●
Best Western ($$)
2337 US 19
(34691) 813.937.4121

● Hollywood ●
Comfort Inn ($$)
2520B Stirling Rd
(33020) 954.922.1600
mgr preapproval reqd

Days Inn ($$)
2601 N 29th Ave
(33020) 954.923.7300
$10/day

Green Seas Motel ($$)
1419 S Federal Hwy
(33020) 954.923.6564

Hojo Inn ($$)
2900 Polk Hwy
(33020) 954.923.1516

Mirador Motel ($$$$)
901 S Ocean Dr
(33019) 305.922.7581

Montreal Inn ($)
324-336 Balboa St
(33019) 954.925.4443

Three Palm Motel
930 N 17th Ct
(33020) 954.923.7683

● Holmes Beach ●
The Inn Between ($$$$)
105 66th St
(34217) 941.778.0751

● Homestead ●
Days Inn ($$)
51 S Homestead Blvd
(33030) 305.245.1260

Everglades Motel ($$)
605 S Krome Ave
(33030) 305.247.4117

Flamingo Lodge ($$)
1 Flamingo Lodge Hwy
(33034) 305.253.2241

Hampton Inn ($$)
124 E Palm Dr
(33034) 305.247.8833

Holiday Inn
990 N Homestead
(33030) 305.247.7020

Howard Johnson ($$)
1020 N Homestead Blvd
(33030) 305.248.2121

● Homosassa ●
Ramada Inn ($$$)
4076 S Suncoast Blvd
(34446) 352.628.4311

FLORIDA, Homosassa

Riverside Inn ($$)
Box# 258
(34487) 800.442.2040

● Homosassa Springs ●
Homosassa Lodge ($$)
Box# 8
(34447) 352.628.4311

● Indialantic ●
Quality Suites ($$$)
1665 N Hwy A1A
(32903) 800.221.2222

● Indian Rocks Beach ●
Edgewater Beach Resort
($$)
19130 Gulf Blvd
(33785) 813.595.4028

Holiday Villas
19610 Gulf Blvd
(33785) 813.596.4852

● Inverness ●
The Crown Hotel ($$)
109 N Seminole Ave
(34450) 352.344.5555

● Islamorada ●
Coconut Cove Resort ($)
84801 Old Hwy
(33036) 305.664.0123

Game Fish Resort ($$)
Rt 1 Box# 70
(33036) 305.664.5568

Lookout Lodge
87770 Overseas Hwy
(33036) 305.852.9915

Ocean Dawn Lodge ($$$)
82885 Old Youngerman
(33036) 305.664.4844

Sands Islamorada ($$)
80051 Overseas Hwy
(33036) 305.664.2791

● Jacksonville ●
Best Inns ($)
8220 Dix Ellis Trl
(32256) 904.739.3323
small pets only

Budgetel ($)
3199 Hartley Rd
(32257) 904.268.9999

Comfort Suites ($$)
8333 Dix Ellis Trl
(32256) 904.739.1155
mgr preapproval reqd

Days Inn
460 Lane Ave
(32254) 904.786.7550

Econo Lodge ($)
5221 University Blvd
(32216) 800.424.4777

Economy Inn ($)
4300B Salisbury Rd
(32216) 904.281.0198

Economy Inn ($)
5959 Youngerman Cir
(32244) 904.777.0160

Hampton Inn ($$)
1170 Airport Entrance Rd
(32218) 904.741.4980

Holiday Inn
I-95 & Airport
(32229) 904.741.4404

Homewood Suites ($$$$)
8737 Baymeadows Rd
(32256) 904.733.9299
$95 fee

La Quinta Inn ($)
8555 Blanding Blvd
(32244) 800.531.5900
call re: fees

La Quinta Inn ($$)
8255 Dix Ellis Trl
(32256) 904.731.9940
call re: fees

La Quinta Inn ($$)
812 Dunn Ave
(32218) 800.531.5900
call re: fees

Motel 6 ($)
8286 Dix Ellis Trl
(32256) 904.731.8400
1 small pet/room

Motel 6 ($)
6107 Youngerman Cir
(32244) 904.777.6100
1 small pet/room

Ramada Inn ($$)
3130B Hartley Rd
(32257) 800.272.6232

Ramada Inn ($$)
5624 Cagle Rd
(32216) 904.737.8000
$5 fee

Red Roof Inn ($)
6099 Youngerman Cir
(32244) 904.777.1000
fees/limits may apply

Red Roof Inn ($)
14701 Airport Entrance Rd
(32218) 904.711.4488

Residence Inn ($$$)
8365 Dix Ellis Trl
(32256) 904.733.8088
call for fee & availability

Super 8
5929 Ramona Blvd
(32205) 904.781.3878
call re: fees

Super 8 ($$)
10901 Harts Rd
(32218) 904.751.3888
w/permission

● Jacksonville Beach ●
Days Inn ($$)
1031 1st St
(32250) 904.249.7231
mgr preapproval reqd

● Jasper ●
Days Inn ($)
RR 3 Box# 133
(32052) 904.792.1987
$5

Scottish Inn ($)
RR 3 Box# 136
(32052) 904.792.1234
$5 fee

● Jennings ●
Jennings House Inn ($)
Box# 179
(32053) 904.938.3305

Quality Inn ($$)
I-75 & Hwy 143
(32053) 904.938.3501

● Juno Beach ●
Howard Johnson ($$)
13930B US Hwy 1
(33408) 407.626.1531

● Key Largo ●
Howard Johnson ($$$)
Box# 1024
(33037) 305.451.1400

Kellys Motel ($$)
104220 Overseas Hwy
(33037) 305.451.1622

Sea Trail Motel ($)
Box# 91
(33037) 305.852.8001

● Key West ●
Alexander Palms Ct ($$$)
715 South St
(33040) 305.296.6413

Andrews Inn ($$$)
Whalton Ln
(33040) 305.294.7730

Caribbean House ($$)
226 Petronia St
(33040) 305.296.1600

Casablanca At Bogarts ($$$)
916 Center St
(33040) 305.296.0637

Courtneys Place ($$)
720 Whitmarsh Ln
(33040) 305.294.3480

Cuban Club Suites ($$$)
1102 Duval St Ste A
(33040) 305.296.0465

Days Inn ($$$)
3852 N Roosevelt Blvd
(33040) 305.294.3742
$15 pet chg. comm

Douglas Guest House ($$$)
419 Amelia St
(33040) 305.294.5269

Eden House ($$)
1015 N Fleming St
(33040) 305.296.6868
only in low season up to 20
lbs

Fleming Street Inn ($$$)
618 Fleming St
(33040) 305.294.5181

Halfred Motel ($$$)
51 Truman Ave
(33040) 305.296.5565

Hampton Inn ($$$$)
2801 N Roosevelt Blvd
(33040) 305.294.2917
$10 deposit up to 15 lbs

Incentra Inn ($$)
729 Whitehead St
(33040) 305.296.5565

Key Lodge Motel ($$$)
1004 Duval St
(33040) 305.296.9915

La Casa De Luces ($$)
422 Amelia St
(33040) 305.296.0582

Mahogany House ($$)
812 Simongton St
(33040) 305.293.9464

Merlin Guest House ($$$)
811 Simonton St
(33040) 305.296.3336

Nassau House ($$)
1016 Fleming St
(33040) 305.296.8513

Old Customs House Inn ($$)
124 Duval St #
(33040) 305.294.8507

Ramada Inn ($$$)
3420 N Roosevelt Blvd
(33040) 305.294.5541
$5/pets - $25 deposit

Sea Isle Resort ($$$)
915 Windsor Ln
(33040) 305.294.5188

Sea Shell Motel ($$)
718 South St
(33040) 305.296.5719

Southern Cross Motel ($$$)
326 Duval St
(33040) 305.294.3200

Speak Easy Inn ($$$)
1117 Duval St
(33040) 305.296.2680

Travelers Cottages
815 Catherine St
(33040) 305.294.9560

Wicker Guest House ($$)
913 Duval St
(33040) 305.296.4275

William House ($$$)
1317 Duval St
(33040) 305.294.8233

● Kissimmee ●
Best Western ($$)
5565 Bronson Mem Hwy
(34746) 407.396.0707
under 25 lbs

Comfort Inn ($)
7571 Bronson Mem Hwy
(34747) 800.221.2222
mgr preapproval reqd

Days Inn ($$)
5820 W Irlo Bronson Hwy
(34746) 407.396.7900

Days Inn ($)
7980 Bronson Mem Hwy
(34747) 407.396.7969

Fantasy World ($$$$)
2935 Hart Ave
(34746) 800.874.8047

Fortune Place Resort ($$$$$)
1475 Astro Lake Dr
(34744) 407.348.0330

Holiday Inn
2009 W Vine
(34741) 407.846.2713

Holiday Inn ($$$)
5678 Bronson Mem Hwy
(34746) 407.396.4488
mgr preapproval reqd

Homewood Suites ($$$)
3100 Parkway Blvd
(34746) 407.396.2229

Howard Johnson ($)
2323 N E Hwy 192
(34744) 407.846.4900
$5 charge

Inns Of America ($)
2945 Entry Point Blvd
(34747) 407.396.7743

Larsons Lodge Main Gate
($$)
6075 US W Hwy 192
(34747) 407.396.6100

Motel 6 ($)
5731 W Bronson Hwy
(34746) 407.396.6333
1 small pet/room

Motel 6 ($)
7455 W Bronson Hwy
(34747) 407.396.6422
1 small pet/room

Ramada Inn ($)
4559 W Hwy 192
(34746) 407.396.1212

Ramada Ltd ($)
5055 W Hwy 192
(34746) 407.396.2212
$6fee & $25deposit

Red Roof Inn ($)
4970 Kyng'S Health Rd
(34746) 407.396.0065

Travelodge ($)
2050 Bronson Mem Hwy
(34744) 407.846.4545

● Labelle ●
The Rivers Edge Motel ($$)
285 N River Rd
(33935) 941.675.6062

Be
Discreet

● Lake Buena Vista ●
Days Inn ($$$)
12799 Apopka-Vineland Rd
(32836) 407.239.4441
$10/day

Days Inn ($$)
12490 Apopla-Vineland Rd
(32836) 407.239.4646
$10/day

● Lake City ●
Best Western ($)
RR 13 Box# 1077
(32055) 904.752.3801
mgr preapproval reqd

Comfort Inn ($$)
4515 US 90
(32056) 904.755.1344
mgr preapproval reqd

Cypress Inn ($)
RR 13 Box# 180A
(32055) 904.752.9369

Days Inn ($)
RR 13 Box# 1140
(32055) 904.752.9350
mgr preapproval reqd

Econo Lodge ($)
I-75 & US 90
(32055) 904.752.7891

Econo Lodge ($)
RR 3 Box# 173
(32025) 800.424.4777

Howard Johnson ($)
RR 13 Box# 1082
(32055) 904.752.6262

Motel 6 ($)
1 Hall Of Fame Dr
(32055) 904.755.4664
1 small pet/room

Piney Woods Lodge ($)
RR 13 Box# 1224
(32055) 904.752.8334

Ramada Inn ($)
Ex 82 On I-75
(32055) 904.752.7550
$3/pet

Red Carpet Inn
I-75
(32055) 904.752.7582
$3 fee

Rodeway Inn ($)
RR 18 Box# 35
(32025) 904.755.5203

Scottish Inn ($)
RR 13 Box# 1150
(32055) 904.755.0230
$4 fee

Travelodge ($)
I-75 & US 90
(32055) 904.755.9306

● Lake Placid ●
Best Western ($$)
2165 US 27
(33852) 941.465.3133

● Lake Wales ●
Chalet Suzanne ($$$$)
3800 Chalet Suzanne Dr
(33853) 941.676.6011

Emerald Motel ($)
530 Scenic Hwy
(33853) 941.676.3310

Knights Inn ($)
541 W Central Ave
(33853) 941.676.7925
size limits & fees

Lantern Motel
3949 Hwy 27 North
(33853) 941.676.4821

● Lake Worth ●
Lago Motor Inn ($)
714 S Dixie Hwy
(33460) 561.585.5246

Martinique Motel ($)
801 S Dixie Hwy
(33460) 407.585.2502

White Manor Motel ($)
1618 S Federal Hwy
(33460) 407.582.7437
some allowed under 20 lbs

● Lakeland ●
Comfort Inn ($)
1817 E Memorial Blvd
(33801) 800.221.2222
mgr preapproval reqd

Days Inn ($)
508 E Memorial Blvd
(33801) 941.682.0303
$10

Motel 6 ($)
3120 US Hwy 98
(33805) 941.682.0643
1 small pet/room

Travelodge ($)
3223 Hwy 98
(33805) 941.688.6031
$4/pets

Wellesley Inn
3420 US Hwy 98
(33809) 813.859.3399

● Lantana ●
Motel 6 ($)
1310 W Lantana Rd
(33462) 407.585.5833
1 small pet/room

Super 8 ($$)
1255 Hypoluxo Rd
(33462) 407.585.3970
size limits & fees

● Leesburg ●
Scottish Inn ($)
1321 N 14th St
(34748) 904.787.3343

Shoneys Inn ($$)
1308 N 14th St
(34748) 904.787.1210
$5/pet

Super 8 ($$)
1392 North Blvd
(34748) 352.787.6363
small pets w/permission

● Live Oak ●
Econo Lodge ($$)
US 129 & I-10
(32060) 904.362.7459

● Longboat Key ●
Holiday Inn ($$$$)
4949 Gulf Of Mexico Dr
(34228) 941.383.3771
mgr preapproval reqd

Riviera Beach Motel ($$$$)
5451 Gulf Of Mexico Dr
(34228) 941.383.2552

● Longwood ●
Ramada Inn ($$)
2025 W Hwy 434
(32750) 407.862.4000

● Macclenny ●
Econo Lodge ($)
I-10 & Hwy 121
(32063) 904.259.3000

● Madeira Beach ●
Sandy Shores ($$$)
12924 Gulf Blvd
(33708) 813.392.1281

Sea Dawn Motel ($)
13733 Gulf Blvd
(33708) 813.391.7500

● Madison ●
Days Inn
Rt 1
(32340) 904.973.3330

● Marathon ●
Bonefish Resort ($)
RR 1 Box# 343
(33050) 305.743.7107

Capt Pips Suites
1410 Overseas Hwy
(33050) 305.743.4403

Coral Lagoon Resort ($$$)
12399 US Hwy
(33050) 305.289.0121

Faro Blanco Resort ($$)
1996 Overseas Hwy
(33050) 305.743.2918

Grassy Key Motel ($$)
RR 1 Box# 357
(33050) 305.743.0533

Holiday Inn
13201 Overseas Hwy
(33050) 305.289.0222

Howard Johnson ($$$)
1335U Overseas Hwy
(33050) 305.743.8550

Lagoon Resort ($$)
7200 Aviation Blvd
(33050) 305.743.5463

Peace Inn ($)
7931 US1 Hwy
(33050) 305.743.5124

Pelican Motel ($)
RR 1 Box# 528
(33050) 305.289.0011

Rainbow Bend Resort ($$$$)
RR 1 Box# 159
(33050) 305.289.1505

Sea Cove Motel ($)
12685 Overseas Hwy
(33050) 305.289.0800

Seashell Resort ($$)
RR 1 Box# 154
(33050) 305.289.0265

Seaward Resort Motel ($)
8700 US1 Hwy
(33050) 305.743.5711

Tellowtail Inn ($$)
RR 1 Box# 355B
(33050) 305.743.8400

Yardarm Motel ($$)
6200 Overseas Hwy
(33050) 305.743.2541

● Marianna ●
Best Western ($$)
2086 Hwy 71
(32448) 904.526.5666
mgr choice

Days Inn ($)
4132 Lafayette Inn
(32446) 904.526.4311
$5

Ramada Ltd ($$)
4655 Hwy 90
(32446) 800.272.6232

● Melbourne ●
Hilton ($$$$)
200 Rialto Pl
(32901) 407.768.0200

Well
Behaved

Holiday Inn ($$$)
4500 W New Haven Ave
(32904) 407.724.2050

Rio Vista Motel
1046 S Harbor City Blvd
(32901) 407.727.2818

Travelodge ($)
4505 W New Haven Ave
(32904) 407.724.5450

● Mexico Beach ●
The Surfside Motel ($$)
Hwy 98 & 38th St
(32410) 904.648.5771

● Miami ●
Budgetel ($$)
3501 NW Le Jeune Rd
(33142) 305.871.1777

Crowne Plaza ($$$$)
16701 Collins Ave
(33160) 305.949.1300

Days Inn ($$$)
100-21st
(33139) 305.538.6631

Days Inn
4767 NW 36th St
(33166) 305.888.3661

Hampton Inn ($$$)
2500 Brickell Ave
(33129) 305.854.2070

Holiday Inn
200 SE 2nd Ave
(33131) 305.374.3000

Holiday Inn
148 NW 167th
(33169) 305.949.1441

Holiday Inn ($$$)
1101 NW 57th Ave
(33126) 800.465.4329
small extra fee

Howard Johnson ($$)
1850 NW Lejuene Rd
(33126) 305.871.4350

Howard Johnson ($$$)
10201 S Dixie Hwy
(33156) 305.666.2531

Howard Johnson ($$)
16500 NW 2ndAve
(33169) 305.945.2621

Howard Johnson ($$$)
7330 NW 36th St
(33166) 305.592.5440

La Quinta Inn ($$)
7401 NW 36th St
(33166) 305.599.9902
call re: fees

Hilton ($$$$)
5101 Blue Lagoon Dr
(33126) 305.262.1000

Marriott ($$$$)
1201 NW Le Jeune Rd
(33126) 305.649.5000

Quality Inn ($$$)
14501 S Dixie Hwy
(33176) 305.251.2000

Ramada Ltd ($$)
7600 N Kendall Dr
(33156) 305.595.6000
under 20 lbs

Residence Inn ($$$$)
1212 NW 82ndAve
(33126) 305.591.2211
$60 deposit required

Sofitel Hotel ($$$$)
5800 Blue Lagoon Dr
(33126) 305.264.4888

Super 8
3400 Biscayne Blvd
(33137) 305.573.7700
call re: fees

Wellesley Inn ($$)
11750 Mills Dr
(33183) 305.270.0359
welcome!

● Miami Beach ●
Best Western ($$$)
4333 Collins Ave
(33140) 305.532.3311
under 20 lbs

Days Inn ($$$)
4299 Collins Ave
(33140) 305.673.1513

Fountainbleu Resort ($$$$)
4441 Collins Ave
(33140) 305.538.2000

Howard Johnson ($$$)
4000 Alton Rd
(33140) 305.532.4411

Howard Johnson ($$$)
6261 Collins Ave
(33140) 305.868.1200

Ocean Front Hotel ($$$$)
1230 Ocean Dr
(33139) 305.672.2579

Seacoast Suite Hotel ($$$$)
5151 Collins Ave
(33140) 305.865.5152

● Naples ●
Howard Johnson ($$)
221 9th St
(34102) 941.262.6181

Knights Inn ($$)
6600 Dudley Dr
(34105) 800.843.5644

Red Roof Inn ($$)
1925 Davis Blvd
(34104) 941.774.3117

Wellesley Inn ($$)
1555 5th Ave
(34102) 941.793.4646

World Resort ($$$$)
4800 Airport Rd
(33942) 800.292.6663

● Neptune Beach ●
Days Inn ($$)
1401 Atlantic Blvd
(32266) 904.249.3852
mgr preapproval reqd

● New Smyrna Beach ●
Buena Vista Motel ($)
500 N Causeway
(32169) 904.428.5565

Smyrna Motel ($)
1050 N Dixie Fwy
(32168) 904.428.2495

● Niceville ●
Comfort Inn ($$)
101 Hwy 85
(32578) 904.678.8077
mgr preapproval reqd

● North Palm Beach ●
Holiday Inn
13950 Hwy 1
(33408) 561.622.4366

● Ocala ●
Budget Host ($)
4013 NW Blitchton Rd
(34482) 800.283.4678

Days Inn
3620 Silver Springs Blvd
(34475) 352.629.0091
$10

Days Inn
3811 NW Blichton Rd
(34482) 352.629.7041
$3

Holiday Inn ($$)
3621 Silver Springs
(34475) 352.629.0381
mgr preapproval reqd

Quality Inn ($)
3767 NW Blitchton Rd
(34475) 352.732.2300

Ramada Inn ($$)
3810 NW Blitchton Rd
(34482) 352.732.3131

Scottish Inn ($)
3520 Silver Springs
(34475) 352.629.7961

Southland Motel ($)
1260 Silver Springs
(34470) 352.351.0113

Super 8 ($)
3924 Silver Springs
(34482) 352.629.8794
call re: fees

Western Motel
4013 NW Blichton Rd
(34482) 352.732.6940

FLORIDA, Okeechobee

● Okeechobee ●
Budget Inn ($)
201 S Parrott Ave
(34974) 941.763.3185

Days Inn
2200 Hwy 441
(34974) 941.763.8003

● Old Town ●
Suwannee Gables ($$)
Rt 3 Box# 208
(32680) 352.542.7752

● Orange City ●
Comfort Inn ($$)
445 S Volusia Ave
(32763) 800.221.2222
mgr preapproval reqd

● Orange Park ●
Best Western ($$)
300 Park Ave
(32073) 904.264.1211
under 35 lbs

Holiday Inn ($$)
150 Park Ave
(32073) 904.264.9513
mgr preapproval reqd

● Orlando ●
Best Western ($$)
2014 W Colonial Dr
(32804) 407.841.8600
small pets $5.day + $25/
deposit

Budgetel ($$)
2051 Consulate Dr
(32837) 407.240.0500

Casa Adobe
9107 South Rt 535
(32819) 407.876.5432

Comfort Inn ($)
8442 Palm Pkwy
(32836) 800.221.2222
mgr preapproval reqd

Contemporary Resort
Box# 10000
(32830) 407.824.1000

Days Inn ($$)
3300 S Orange Blossom Trl
(32839) 407.442.4521
mgr preapproval reqd

Days Inn
9990 Int'l Dr
(32819) 407.352.8700

Days Inn
3300 Orange Blossom Tr
(32839) 407.422.4521
$6

Days Inn ($$)
5827 Caravan Ct
(32819) 407.351.3800
$10 small

Days Inn ($$)
7200 International Dr
(32819) 407.351.1200
$5/pets

Days Inn ($)
1851 W Landstreet Rd
(32809) 407.859.7700

Days Inn ($)
2500 33rd St
(32839) 407.841.3731
$6

Days Inn ($)
2323 McCoy Rd
(32809) 407.859.6100
$6/pets

Delta Orlando Resort ($$$$)
5715 Major Blvd
(32819) 407.351.3340

Econo Lodge ($$)
3300 W Colonial Dr
(32808) 407.293.7221

Gateway Inn ($$)
7050 S Kirkman Rd
(32819) 407.351.2000

Holiday Inn
5750 TG Lee Blvd
(32822) 407.851.6400

Holiday Inn
13351 Hwy 355
(32830) 407.239.4500

Howard Johnson ($$)
5905 International Dr
(32819) 407.351.2100

Howard Johnson ($$)
6603 International Dr
(32819) 407.351.2900

Howard Johnson ($$$)
9956 Hawaiian Ct
(32819) 407.351.5100

Howard Johnson ($$)
8501 Palm Pkwy
(32836) 407.239.6900

Howard Johnson ($)
8700 S Orange Blossom Trl
(32809) 407.851.2330

Inns Of America ($)
8222 Jamaican Ct
(32819) 407.345.1172
under 20 lbs

Knights Inn ($$)
221 E Colonial Dr
(32801) 800.843.5644

La Quinta Inn ($$)
8300 Jamaican Ct
(32819) 800.531.5900
call re: fees

La Quinta Inn ($$)
7931 Daetwyler Dr
(32812) 800.531.5900
call re: fees

Motel 6 ($)
5300 Adanson St
(32810) 407.647.1444
1 small pet/room

Motel 6 ($)
5909 American Way
(32819) 407.351.6500
1 small pet/room

Ramada Inn ($$)
736 Lee Rd
(32810) 407.647.1112

Red Roof Inn ($)
9922 Hawaiian Ct
(32819) 407.352.1507
fees/limits may apply

Rodeway Inn ($$)
6327 International Dr
(32819) 407.351.4444

Thriftlodge ($)
6119 S Orange Blossom Trl
(32809) 407.855.1356

Travelodge ($)
7101 S Orange Blossom Trl
(32809) 407.851.4300

Wellesley Inn ($$$)
5635 Windhover Dr
(32819) 407.345.0026

Orlando Metro
● Altamonte Springs ●
Days Inn ($$$)
235 S Wymore Rd
(32714) 407.862.2800

Embassy Suites ($$$)
225 E Altamonte Dr
(32701) 407.834.2400

La Quinta Inn ($$)
150 S Westmonte Dr
(32714) 800.531.5900
call re: fees

Residence Inn ($$$)
270 Douglas Ave
(32714) 407.788.7991
$150 fee plus $5 per night

● Apopka ●
Crosbys Motor Inn ($$)
1440 W Orange Blossom Trl
(32712) 800.821.6685

● Davenport ●
Days Inn ($)
I-4 & US 27
(33837) 941.424.2596

Motel 6 ($$)
5620 U Hwy 27
(33837) 941.424.2521
1 small pet/room

● Kissimmee ●
Best Western ($$)
5565 Bronson Mem Hwy
(34746) 407.396.0707
under 25 lbs

Comfort Inn ($)
7571 Bronson Mem Hwy
(34747) 800.221.2222
mgr preapproval reqd

Days Inn ($$)
5820 W Irlo Bronson Hwy
(34746) 407.396.7900

Days Inn ($)
7980 Bronson Mem Hwy
(34747) 407.396.7969

Fantasy World ($$$$)
2935 Hart Ave
(34746) 800.874.8047

Fortune Place Resort ($$$$)
1475 Astro Lake Dr
(34744) 407.348.0330

Holiday Inn
2009 W Vine
(34741) 407.846.2713

Holiday Inn ($$$)
5678 Bronson Mem Hwy
(34746) 407.396.4488
mgr preapproval reqd

Homewood Suites
3100 Parkway Blvd
(34747) 407.396.2229

Homewood Suites ($$$)
3100 Parkway Blvd
(34746) 407.396.2229

Howard Johnson ($)
2323N E Hwy 192
(34744) 407.846.4900
$5 charge

Inns Of America ($)
2945 Entry Point Blvd
(34747) 407.396.7743

Larsons Lodge Main Gate
($$)
6075US W Hwy 192
(34747) 407.396.6100

Motel 6 ($)
5731 W Bronson Hwy
(34746) 407.396.6333
1 small pet/room

Motel 6 ($)
7455 W Bronson Hwy
(34747) 407.396.6422
1 small pet/room

Ramada Inn ($)
4559 W Hwy 192
(34746) 407.396.1212

Ramada Ltd ($)
5055 W Hwy 192
(34746) 407.396.2212
$6fee & $25deposit

Red Roof Inn ($)
4970 Kyng'S Health Rd
(34746) 407.396.0065

Travelodge ($)
2050 Bronson Mem Hwy
(34744) 407.846.4545

● Lake Buena Vista ●
Days Inn ($$$)
12799Apopka-Vineland Rd
(32836) 407.239.4441
$10/day

Days Inn ($$)
12490 Apopla-Vineland
(32836) 407.239.4646
$10/day

● Leesburg ●
Scottish Inn ($)
1321 N 14th St
(34748) 904.787.3343

Shoneys Inn ($$)
1308 N 14th St
(34748) 904.787.1210
$5/pet

Super 8 ($$)
1392 North Blvd
(34748) 352.787.6363
small pets with permission

● Longwood ●
Ramada Inn ($$)
2025 W Sr 434
(32750) 407.862.4000

● Orlando ●
Best Western ($$)
2014 W Colonial Dr
(32804) 407.841.8600
small pets $5.day + $25/
deposit

Budgetel ($$)
2051 Consulate Dr
(32837) 407.240.0500

CasaAdobe
9107 South Rt 535
(32819) 407.876.5432

Comfort Inn ($)
8442 Palm Pkwy
(32836) 800.221.2222
mgr preapproval reqd

Contemporary Resort
Box# 10000
(32830) 407.824.1000

Days Inn ($$)
3300 S Orange Blossom Trl
(32839) 407.442.4521
mgr preapproval reqd

Days Inn
9990 Int'L Dr
(32819) 407.352.8700

Days Inn ($$)
5827 Caravan Ct
(32819) 407.351.3800
$10 small

Days Inn ($$)
7200 International Dr
(32819) 407.351.1200
$5/pets

Days Inn ($)
1851 W Landstreet Rd
(32809) 407.859.7700

Days Inn ($)
2500 33Rd St
(32839) 407.841.3731
$6

Days Inn ($)
2323 McCoy Rd
(32809) 407.859.6100
$6/pets

Delta Orlando Resort ($$$$)
5715 Major Blvd
(32819) 407.351.3340

Econo Lodge ($$)
3300 W Colonial Dr
(32808) 407.293.7221

CALL
AHEAD!

Gateway Inn ($$)
7050 S Kirkman Rd
(32819) 407.351.2000

Holiday Inn
5750 Tg Lee Blvd
(32822) 407.851.6400

Holiday Inn
13351 Sr 355
(32830) 407.239.4500

Howard Johnson ($$)
5905 International Dr
(32819) 407.351.2100

Howard Johnson ($$)
6603 International Dr
(32819) 407.351.2900

Howard Johnson ($$$)
9956 Hawaiian Ct
(32819) 407.351.5100

Howard Johnson ($$)
8501 Palm Pkwy
(32836) 407.239.6900

Howard Johnson ($)
8700 S Orange Blossom Trl
(32809) 407.851.2330

Inns Of America ($)
8222 Jamaican Ct
(32819) 407.345.1172
under 20 lbs

Knights Inn ($$)
221 E Colonial Dr
(32801) 800.843.5644

La Quinta Inn ($$)
8300Jamaican Ct
(32819) 800.531.5900
call re: fees

La Quinta Inn ($$)
7931 Daetwyler Dr
(32812) 800.531.5900
call re: fees

Motel 6 ($)
5300Adanson St
(32810) 407.647.1444
1 small pet/room

$=under $35 $$=$35-60 $$$=$60-100 $$$$=over $100

FLORIDA, Orlando

Motel 6 ($)
5909 American Way
(32819) 407.351.6500
1 small pet/room

Ramada Inn ($$)
736 Lee Rd
(32810) 407.647.1112

Red Roof Inn ($)
9922 Hawaiian Ct
(32819) 407.352.1507
fees/limits may apply

Rodeway Inn ($$)
6327 International Dr
(32819) 407.351.4444

Thriftlodge ($)
6119 S Orange Blossom Trl
(32809) 407.855.1356

Travelodge ($)
7101 S Orange Blossom Trl
(32809) 407.851.4300

Wellesley Inn ($$$)
5635 Windhover Dr
(32819) 407.345.0026

● Sanford ●
Days Inn ($)
4650 Sr 46
(32771) 407.323.6500
$5/pets

Super 8 ($$)
4750 W State Road 46
(32771) 407.323.3445
w/permission

● Tavares ●
Inn Of The Green ($$)
700 E Burleigh Blvd
(32778) 904.343.6373
End of Orlando Metro

● Ormond Beach ●
Budget Host ($)
1633 US1
(32174) 904.677.7310
$5

Comfort Inn ($)
1567 N US 1
(32174) 800.221.2222
mgr preapproval reqd

Days Inn ($)
1608 N US Hwy 1
(32174) 904.672.7341
small pets allowed $5 extra

Days Inn
839 Atlantic Ave
(32176) 904.677.0438
$10

Driftwood Beach ($)
657 S Atlantic Ave
(32176) 904.677.1331

Howard Johnson ($)
1633 N US 1
(32174) 800.446.4656

Jamaican Beach Motel ($)
505 S Atlantic Ave
(32176) 904.677.3353

Makai Motel
707 S Atlantic Ave
(32176) 904.677.8060

Scottish Inn
1608 Us-1
(32174) 904.677.8860

● Osprey ●
Ramada Inn ($$$)
1660 S Tamiami Trl
(34229) 941.966.2121

● Palm Bay ●
Knights Inn ($)
1170 Malabar Rd
(32905) 407.951.8222

● Palm Beach ●
Heart Of Palm Beach ($$$)
160 Royal Palm Way
(33480) 407.655.5600

Howard Johnson ($$)
2870 S Ocean Blvd
(33480) 407.582.2581

Plaza Inn ($$$)
215 Brazilian Ave
(33480) 407.832.8666

The Four Seasons ($$$$)
2800 S Ocean Blvd
(33480) 407.582.2800

● Palm Harbor ●
Knights Inn ($)
34106 US 19
(34684) 813.789.2002

Travelodge ($)
32000 US 19
(34684) 813.786.2529
$5 per day

● Panacea ●
Oaks Motel
US 98
(32346) 904.984.5370

● Panama City ●
Admiral Imperial Inn
16819 Front Beach Rd
(32413) 904.234.2142

Best Western ($$)
711 W Beach Dr
(32401) 904.763.4622
small

Days Inn ($)
4111 W Hey 98
(32401) 904.784.1777
$2/small pets only

Days Inn ($)
301 W 23rd St
(32405) 904.785.0001
mgr preapproval reqd

Howard Johnson ($$)
4601US W Hwy 98
(32401) 904.785.0222

Passport
5003 Hwy 98
(32401) 904.769.2101

Scottish Inn ($)
4907 W Hwy 98
(32401) 904.769.2432
small pets; $2 fee

Super 8 ($$)
207 N Hwy 231
(32405) 904.784.1988
w/permission

Surf Inn Of The Gulf ($)
10611B Front Beach Rd
(32407) 904.234.2129

● Pensacola ●
Comfort Inn ($)
6919 Pensacola Blvd
(32505) 800.221.2222
mgr preapproval reqd

Comfort Inn ($$)
3 N New Warrington Rd
(32506) 800.221.2222
mgr preapproval reqd

Days Inn ($$)
7051 Pensacola Blvd
(32505) 904.476.9090
$5 per day

Howard Johnson ($$)
6911 Pensacola Blvd
(32505) 904.479.3800

Howard Johnson ($)
4126 Mobile Hwy
(32506) 904.456.5731

La Quinta Inn ($$)
7750 N Davis Hwy
(32514) 800.531.5900
call re: fees

Motel 6 ($)
7226 Plantation Rd
(32504) 904.474.1060
1 small pet/room

Motel 6 ($$)
7827 N Davis Hwy
(32514) 904.476.5386
1 small pet/room

Motel 6 ($)
5829 Pensacola Blvd
(32505) 904.477.7522
1 small pet/room

Pensacola Grand ($$$)
200 E Gregory St
(32501) 904.433.3336

Ramada Inn ($$)
8060 Lavelle Way
(32526) 904.944.0333

Red Carpet Inn
4448 Mobile Hwy
(32506) 904.456.7411

Red Roof Inn ($)
7340 Plantation Rd
(32504) 904.476.7960

Rodeway Inn ($$)
8500 Pine Forest Rd
(32534) 904.477.9150

Shoneys Inn ($$$)
8080 N Davis Hwy
(32514) 904.484.8070

Super 8 ($$)
7220 Plantation Rd
(32504) 904.476.8038
small

● Perry ●
Best Budget Inn ($)
2220 S Byron Butler Pkwy
(32347) 907.584.6231

Southern Inn Motel ($)
2238 S Byron Butler Pkwy
(32347) 904.584.4221

● Pinellas Park ●
La Mark Charles Motel ($$)
6200 34th St
(34665) 813.527.7334

La Quinta Inn ($$)
7500 US 19N
(34665) 800.531.5900
call re: fees

● Plant City ●
Days Inn ($$)
301 S Frontage Rd
(33566) 813.752.3422

Ramada Inn ($$)
2011 N Wheeler St
(33566) 813.752.3141
deposit

● Pompano Beach ●
Days Inn ($)
1411 NW 31st Ave
(33069) 954.972.3700
$5 $50 dep

Howard Johnson ($$$)
9 Pompano Beach Blvd
(33062) 954.781.1300

Sea Castle Motel ($)
730 N Ocean Blvd
(33062) 305.941.2570

● Ponte Vedra Beach ●
Marriott Hotel ($$$$)
1000 Tpc Blvd
(32082) 904.285.7777
user referral

● Port Charlotte ●
Days Inn ($$)
1941 Tamiami Trl
(33948) 941.627.8900
mgr preapproval reqd

Quality Inn ($$)
3400 Tamiami Trl
(33952) 941.625.4181

● Port Richey ●
Days Inn ($$)
11736 US 19
(34668) 813.863.1502
$4/pets

● Port Salerno ●
Pirates Cove Resort ($$)
4307 SE Bayview St
(34992) 407.287.2500

● Punta Gorda ●
Days Inn ($)
26560 Jones Loop Rd
(33950) 941.637.7200

Holiday Inn ($$)
300 W Retta Esplanade
(33950) 941.639.1165

Howard Johnson ($$)
33 Tamiami Trl
(33950) 941.639.2167
$12 fee

Motel 6 ($)
9300 Knights Dr
(33950) 941.639.9585
1 small pet/room

● Quincy ●
Holiday Inn
Rt 3
(32351) 904.875.2500

Quincy Motor Lodge
368 E Jefferson St
(32351) 904.627.8929

● Rockledge ●
Spitzers Swiss Motel ($$)
3220 Fiske Blvd
(32955) 407.631.9445

● Ruskin ●
Ramada Inn ($$)
6414 Surfside Blvd
(33572) 813.645.3271
$25 fee

● Safety Harbor ●
Safety Harbor Resort ($$$$)
105 Bayshore Blvd
(34695) 813.726.1161

● St. Augustine ●
Anchorage Motor Inn
1 Dolphin Dr
(32084) 904.829.9041

Best Western ($$)
3955 Hwy A1A
(32084) 904.471.8010
small

Best Western ($$)
2445 Hwy 16
(32092) 904.829.1999
dogs under 10 lbs

Days Inn ($)
2560 Dr 16
(32092) 904.824.4341
$4 per day

Days Inn ($)
2800 N Ponce De Leon Blvd
(32084) 904.829.6581
$10/small pets

Econo Lodge ($$)
2535 Hwy 16
(32092) 904.828.5643

Holiday Inn
860 A1A Beach Blvd
(32084) 904.471.2555

Howard Johnson ($$)
300 A1A Beach Blvd
(32084) 904.471.2575

Howard Johnson ($)
2550 Hwy 16
(32092) 904.829.5686

Ponce De Leon Resort ($$$)
4000 US Hwy 1
(32095) 904.824.2821

Ramada Inn ($$)
116 San Marco Ave
(32084) 804.824.4352

Scottish Inn ($)
110 San Marco Ave
(32084) 904.824.2871
$5 fee

Seabreeze Motel ($$)
208 Anastasia Blvd
(32084) 904.829.8122

● St. Pete Beach ●
Colonial Gateway Inn ($$$)
6300 Gulf Blvd
(33706) 813.367.2711

● St. Petersburg ●
Howard Johnson ($$)
3600 34th St
(33711) 813.867.6591

La Quinta Inn ($$)
4999 34th St
(33714) 800.531.5900
call re: fees

Sea Horse Cottages ($)
11780 Guld Blvd
(33706) 813.367.2291

Shifting Sands
Treasure Island
(33706) 813.160.7777
referred

Valley Forge Motel ($)
6825 Central Ave
(33710) 813.345.0135

● Sanford ●
Days Inn ($)
4650 Hwy 46
(32771) 407.323.6500
$5/pets

Super 8 ($$)
4750 W State Road 46
(32771) 407.323.3445
w/permission

FLORIDA, Sarasota

● Sarasota ●
Comfort Inn ($$)
4800 N Tamiami Tr
(34234) 941.355.7091

Coquina On The Beach ($$$)
1008 Ben Franklin Dr
(34236) 941.388.2141

Days Inn ($$)
4900 N Tamiami Trl
(34234) 941.955.9721
$6

Days Inn ($$)
6600 S Tamiami Trl
(34231) 941.493.4558
$15 per day

Holiday Inn
7150 N Tamiami Tr
(34243) 941.355.2781

Hyatt Hotel ($$$$)
1000 Blvd Of The Arts
(34236) 941.366.9000

Ramada Inn ($$$)
5774 Clark Rd
(34233) 941.921.7812

Red Carpet Inn
8110 Tamiami Trail
(34243) 813.355.8861

Surfrider Beach ($$$)
6400 Midnight Pass Rd
(34242) 941.349.2121

Tropical Breeze Inn ($$$)
140 Columbus Blvd
(34242) 941.349.1125

Turtle Beach Resort ($$$)
9049 Midnight Pass Rd
(34242) 941.349.4554

Wellesley Inns ($$)
1803 N Tamiami Trl
(34234) 941.366.5128

● Satellite Beach ●
Days Inn ($$)
180 Hwy A1A
(32937) 407.777.3552
rates vary

● Sebring ●
Inn Of The Lakes ($$)
3100 Golfview Re
(33870) 813.471.9400

● Seffner ●
Masters Economy Inn ($)
6010 Hwy 579
(33584) 813.621.4681

● Silver Springs ●
Days Inn
5001 Silver Springs Blvd
(34488) 352.236.2891
$5

Holiday Inn ($$)
5751 Silver Springs
(34488) 352.236.2575

Holiday Inn
5751 W Hwy 40
(34489) 352.236.2575

Howard Johnson ($)
5565 Silver Springs
(34488) 352.236.2616

● South Bay ●
Okeechobee Inn ($$)
265 US Hwy 27
(33493) 407.996.7617

● Spring Hill ●
Holiday Inn
6172 Commercial Way
(34606) 352.596.2007

● Starke ●
Best Western ($$)
1290 N Temple Ave
(32091) 904.964.6744
small pets

Days Inn ($$)
1101 N Temple Ave
(32091) 904.964.7600
$10/pets

Red Carpet Inn
744 N Temple Ave
(32091) 904.964.5590

● Steinhatchee ●
Steinhatchee Landing ($$$)
Hwy 51
(32359) 352.498.3513

● Stuart ●
Howard Johnson ($$)
950 S Federal Hwy
(34994) 407.287.3171

● Sugarloaf Shores ●
Sugar Loaf Lodge ($$$)
Box# 148
(33044) 305.745.3211

● Sun City Center ●
Sun City Cntr Hotel ($$)
1335 Rickenbacker Dr
(33573) 813.634.3331

● Tallahassee ●
American Inn ($)
2726 N Monroe St
(32303) 800.307.5001

Best Inns ($$)
2738 Graves Rd
(32303) 904.562.2378

Collegeiate Inn ($$)
2121 W Tennessee St
(32304) 904.576.6121

Days Inn ($)
3100 Apalachee Pkwy
(32311) 904.877.6121
mgr preapproval reqd

Econo Lodge ($)
2681 N Monroe St
(32303) 904.385.6155

Holiday Inn
316 W Tennessee
(32301) 904.222.8000

Killearn Country Club ($$)
100 Tyron Cir
(32308) 904.893.2186

La Quinta Inn ($$)
2905 N Monroe St
(32303) 800.531.5900
call re: fees

La Quinta Inn ($$)
2850 Apalachee Pkwy
(32301) 800.531.5900
call re: fees

Motel 6 ($)
1027 Apalachee Pkwy
(32301) 904.877.6171
1 small pet/room

Motel 6 ($)
1481 Timberlane Rd
(32312) 904.668.2600
1 small pet/room

Motel 6 ($)
2738 N Monroe St
(32303) 904.386.7878
1 small pet/room

Red Roof Inn ($)
2930B Hospitality St
(32303) 904.385.7884
fees/limits may apply

Seminole Inn ($$)
6737 Mahan Dr
(32308) 904.656.2938

● Tampa ●
Amerisuites ($$$)
4811 W Main St
(33607) 813.282.1037

Budgetel ($)
4811 N US Hwy 301
(33610) 813.626.0885

Budgetel ($$)
602 N Falkenburg Rd
(33619) 813.684.4007

Days Inn ($$)
2520 N 50th St
(33619) 813.247.3300
$10/pets

Days Inn ($$)
701 E Fletcher Ave
(33612) 813.977.1550
$5/pets

Econo Lodge ($)
1701 E Busch Blvd
(33612) 813.933.7681

Holiday Inn
2701 E Fowler
(33612) 813.971.4710

Holiday Inn ($$)
2708 N 50th St
(33619) 813.621.2081

Howard Johnson ($)
4139 E Busch Blvd
(33617) 813.988.9193

Be Discreet

Winter Park, FLORIDA

Howard Johnson ($$)
2055 N Dale Mabry Hwy
(33607) 813.875.8818
$10 per night

La Quinta Inn ($$)
4730 W Spruce St
(33607) 800.531.5900
call re: fees

La Quinta Inn ($)
2904 Melbourne Blvd
(33605) 800.531.5900
call re: fees

Motel 6 ($)
333 E Fowler Ave
(33612) 813.932.4948
1 small pet/room

Motel 6 ($)
6510 N Hwy 301
(33610) 813.628.0888
1 small pet/room

Ramada Inn ($$)
4732 N Dale Mabry Hwy
(33614) 800.272.6232

Ramada Inn ($$)
400 E Bears Ave
(33613) 813.961.1000

Red Roof Inn ($)
10121B Horace Ave
(33619) 813.681.8484
fees/limits may apply

Red Roof Inn ($)
2307 E Busch Blvd
(33612) 813.932.0093

Red Roof Inn ($)
5001 N US 301
(33610) 813.623.5245
fees/limits may apply

Residence Inn ($$$)
3075 N Rocky Point Dr
(33607) 813.281.5677
$100 fee +$6/day must resv

Scottish Inn ($)
11414 N Central Ave
(33612) 813.933.7831

Sheraton Inn ($$$$)
7401 E Hillsborough Ave
(33610) 813.626.0999
small pets only $25 fee

Tahitian Inn ($$)
601 S Dale Mabry Hwy
(33609) 813.877.6721

● Tarpon Springs ●
Days Inn ($)
40050 US Hwy 19
(34689) 813.934.0859
$5/pet charge

Scottish Inn ($)
110 W Tarpon Ave
(34689) 813.937.6121
$5 fee

● Tavares ●
Inn Of The Green ($$)
700 E Burleigh Blvd
(32778) 904.343.6373

● Tavernier ●
Lookout Lodge ($$$)
87770 Overseas Hwy
(33070) 305.852.9915

Tropic Vista Motel ($$)
90701 Overseas Hwy
(33070) 305.852.8799

● Titusville ●
Best Western ($$)
3455 Cheney Hwy
(32780) 407.269.9100
under 10 lbs

Days Inn ($$)
3755 Cheney Hwy
(32780) 407.269.4480
$10

Holiday Inn
4951 S Washington
(32780) 407.269.2121

Howard Johnson ($$)
1829 Riverside Dr
(32780) 407.267.7900

● Treasure Island ●
Lorelei Resort ($$)
10273 Gulf Blvd
(33706) 813.360.4351

● Venice ●
Inn At The Beach ($$)
101 The Esplanade
(34285) 800.255.8471

Motel 6 ($)
281 US Hwy 41 Byp
(34292) 941.485.8255
1 small pet/room

● Vero Beach ●
Days Inn ($$)
8800 20th St
(32966) 407.562.9991
$5 per day

Hojo Inn ($)
1985 90th Ave
(32966) 407.778.1985

Holiday Inn
8797 20th
(32966) 561.567.8321

Super 8 ($$)
8800 20th St
(32966) 407.562.9996
call re: fees

● West Palm Beach ●
Best Western
123 S Ocean Ave
(33404) 407.844.0233
pets $15

Comfort Inn ($$$)
1901 Palm Bch Lakes
(33409) 561.689.6100
mgr preapproval reqd

Days Inn ($$)
2700 N Ocean Dr
(33404) 407.848.8661
$10 per pet per night

Days Inn ($$)
2300 45th St
(33407) 407.689.0450
$10/pet charge

Days Inn ($$)
6255 Okeechobee Blvd
(33417) 561.686.6000
$10 daily charge only 1 pet
allowed

Embassy Suites ($$$$)
4350 PGA Blvd
(33410) 407.622.1000

Knights Inn ($$)
2200 45th St
(33407) 800.843.5644

Macarthurs Inn ($$)
4431 PGA Blvd
(33410) 800.465.4329

Motel 6 ($)
3651 W Blue Heron Blvd
(33404) 407.863.1011
1 small pet/room

Wellesley Inn ($$)
1910 Palm Bch Lakes
(33409) 407.689.8540

● Wildwood ●
Days Inn ($)
551 E Hwy 44
(34785) 352.748.7766
$5

Red Carpet Inn
US 30
(34785) 904.748.4488

● Williston ●
Williston Motor Inn ($)
606 W Noble Ave
(32696) 352.528.4801

● Winter Haven ●
Budget Host ($)
970 Cypress Gardens
(33880) 800.283.4678
small pets only

Cypress Motel ($)
5651 Cypress Gardens Rd
(33884) 941.324.5867

Holiday Inn
1150 3rd St SW
(33880) 941.294.4451

Howard Johnson ($$)
1300 US 17 SW
(33880) 800.446.4656

● Winter Park ●
Days Inn ($$)
901 N Orlando Ave
(32789) 407.644.8000

FLORIDA, Winter Park

Langford Hotel ($$)
300 E New England Ave
(32789) 407.647.1072

● Yulee ●
Days Inn ($$)
3250 N US Hwy 17
(32097) 904.225.2011

Holiday Inn
3276 US Hwy 17
(32097) 904.225.5114

● Zephyrhills ●
Crystal Springs Inn
6736 Gall Blvd
(33541) 813.782.1214

Georgia

● Acworth ●
Days Inn ($)
5035 Cowan Rd
(30101) 770.974.1700
mgr preapproval reqd

Super 8 ($)
Cowan Rd
(30101) 770.966.9700
call re: fees

● Adel ●
Days Inn ($)
1200 W 4th St
(31620) 912.896.4574
$5

Hojo Inn ($)
1103 W 4th St
(31620) 912.896.2244

Scottish Inn ($)
911 W 4th St
(31620) 912.896.2259
$3 fee

Super 8 ($)
1102 W 4th St
(31620) 800.424.4777
mgr preapproval reqd

● Albany ●
Holiday Inn ($$$)
2701 Dawson Rd
(31707) 912.883.8100
mgr preapproval reqd

Knights Inn ($)
1201 Schley Ave
(31707) 912.888.9600

Motel 6 ($)
301 Thornton Dr
(31705) 912.439.0078
1 small pet/room

Ramada Inn ($$)
2505 N Slappey Blvd
(31701) 912.883.3211
$10 fee

Econo Lodge ($$)
1806 E Oglethorpe Blvd
(31705) 912.883.5544

Super 8 ($$)
2444 N Slappey Blvd
(31701) 912.888.8388
pets w/permission

● Alpharetta ●
Days Inn
3000 Mansell Rd
(30202) 772.645.6060
$7

Residence Inn ($$$$)
5465 Windward Pkwy
(30201) 770.664.0664
$100-$200 cleaning fee

● Ashburn ●
Comfort Inn ($$)
803 Shoneys Dr
(31714) 912.567.0080

Days Inn ($)
823 E Washington Ave
(31714) 912.567.3346
$5

● Athens ●
Best Western ($$)
170 N Milledge Ave
(30601) 706.546.7311

Days Inn ($$)
2741 Atlanta Hwy
(30606) 706.353.9750
mgr preapproval reqd

Downtowner Inns ($)
1198 S Milledge Ave
(30605) 706.549.2626
$3 fee

Howard Johnson ($$)
2465 W Broad St
(30606) 706.548.1111

Ramada Inn ($$)
513 W Broad St
(30601) 706.546.8122
small pets only

Scottish Inn ($)
410 Macon Hwys
(30606) 706.546.8161

Super 8 ($)
3425 Atlanta Hwy
(30606) 706.549.0251
call re: fees

Travelodge ($)
898 W Broad St
(30601) 706.549.5400

● Atlanta ●
Beverly Hills Inn ($$$)
65 Sheridan Dr NE
(30305) 404.233.8520

Budgetel ($$)
2480 Old National Pkwy
(30349) 404.766.0000

Budgetel ($$)
2535 Chantilly Dr NE
(30324) 404.321.0999

Days Inn ($$)
1701 Northside Dr NW
(30318) 404.351.6500

Days Inn
720 Lewis St
(30349) 912.685.2700
$10

Doubletree ($$$$)
7 Councourse Parkway
(30328) 770.395.3900

Granada Suite Hotel ($$)
1302 W Peachtree St NW
(30309) 800.548.5631

Granite City Motel ($)
925 Elbert Extension
(30365) 706.283.4221

Hawthorn Suites ($$$)
1500 Parkwood Cir SE
(30339) 770.952.9592

Holiday Inn ($$$)
5010 Old National Hwy
(30349) 404.761.4000

Holiday Inn ($$)
418 Armour Dr NE
(30324) 404.873.8222

Holiday Inn ($$$)
4386 Chamblee-Dunwoody
Rd
(30341) 770.936.9592

Homewood Suites ($$$)
3200 Cobb Pkwy
(30339) 770.988.9449

La Quinta Inn ($$)
4874 Old National Hwy
(30337) 404.768.1241
call re: fees

Marriott Hotel ($$$$)
4711 Best Rd
(30337) 404.766.7900

Motel 6 ($)
3585 Chamblee-Tucker Rd
(30341) 770.455.8000
1 small pet/room

Occidental Hotel ($$$$)
75 14th St
(30309) 800.952.0702

Red Roof Inn ($$)
1960 N Druid Hills Rd
(30329) 404.321.1653
fees/limits may apply

Red Roof Inn ($)
4265N Shirley Dr SW
(30336) 770.696.4391
fees/limits may apply

Residence Inn ($$$$)
2960 Piedmont Rd NE
(30305) 404.239.0677
call for fee & availability

Residence Inn ($$)
1901 Savoy Dr
(30341) 770.455.4446
call for fee & availability

Residence Inn ($$$)
3401 International Blvd
(30354) 404.761.0511
$100-$200 cleaning fee

Summerfield Suites ($$$)
505 Pharr Rd NE
(30305) 404.262.7880

Summit Inn ($)
3900 Fulton Ind Blvd
(30336) 404.691.2444

Super 8 ($$)
111 Cone St NW
(30303) 404.524.7000
call re: fees

Super 8 ($$)
2867 Northeast Expy NE
(30345) 404.633.8451
call re: fees

Westin Hotel ($$$$)
2101 NW Peachtree St
(30303) 404.659.1400

Westin Hotel ($$$$)
4736 Best Rd
(30337) 404.762.7676
under 10 lbs

Atlanta Metro
● Acworth ●
Days Inn ($)
5035 Cowan Rd
(30101) 770.974.1700
mgr preapproval reqd

Super 8 ($)
Cowan Rd
(30101) 770.966.9700
call re: fees

● Alpharetta ●
Days Inn
3000 Mansell Rd
(30202) 772.645.6060
$7

Residence Inn ($$$$)
5465 Windward Pkwy
(30201) 770.664.0664
$100-$200 cleaning fee

● Atlanta ●
Beverly Hills Inn ($$$)
65 Sheridan Dr NE
(30305) 404.233.8520

Budgetel ($$)
2480 Old National Pkwy
(30349) 404.766.0000

Budgetel ($$)
2535 Chantilly Dr NE
(30324) 404.321.0999

Days Inn ($$)
1701 Northside Dr NW
(30318) 404.351.6500

Days Inn
720 Lewis St
(30349) 912.685.2700
$10

Doubletree ($$$$)
7 Councourse Parkway
(30328) 770.395.3900

Granada Suite Hotel ($$)
1302 W Peachtree St NW
(30309) 800.548.5631

Granite City Motel ($)
925 Elbert Extension
(30365) 706.283.4221

Hawthorn Suites ($$$)
1500 Parkwood Cir SE
(30339) 770.952.9592

Holiday Inn ($$$)
5010 Old National Hwy
(30349) 404.761.4000

Holiday Inn ($$)
418 Armour Dr NE
(30324) 404.873.8222

Holiday Inn ($$$)
4386 Chamblee-Dunwoody Rd
(30341) 770.936.9592

Homewood Suites ($$$)
3200 Cobb Pkwy
(30339) 770.988.9449

La Quinta Inn ($$)
4874 Old National Hwy
(30337) 404.768.1241
call re: fees

Marriott Hotel ($$$$)
4711 Best Rd
(30337) 404.766.7900

Motel 6 ($)
3585 Chamblee-Tucker Rd
(30341) 770.455.8000
1 small pet/room

Occidental Hotel ($$$$)
75 14th St
(30309) 800.952.0702

Red Roof Inn ($$)
1960 N Druid Hills Rd N
(30329) 404.321.1653
fees/limits may apply

Red Roof Inn ($)
4265N Shirley Dr SW
(30336) 770.696.4391
fees/limits may apply

Residence Inn ($$$$)
2960 Piedmont Rd NE
(30305) 404.239.0677
call for fee & availability

Residence Inn ($$)
1901 Savoy Dr
(30341) 770.455.4446
call for fee & availability

Residence Inn ($$$)
3401 International Blvd
(30354) 404.761.0511
$100-$200 cleaning fee

Summerfield Suites ($$$)
505 Pharr Rd NE
(30305) 404.262.7880

Summit Inn ($)
3900 Fulton Ind Blvd
(30336) 404.691.2444

Super 8 ($$)
111 Cone St NW
(30303) 404.524.7000
call re: fees

Super 8 ($$)
2867 Northeast Expy NE
(30345) 404.633.8451
call re: fees

Westin Hotel ($$$$)
2101 NW Peachtree St
(30303) 404.659.1400

Westin Hotel ($$$$)
4736 Best Rd
(30337) 404.762.7676
under 10 lbs

● Austell ●
Knights Inn ($$)
1595 Blair Bridge Rd
(30001) 770.944.0824
size limits & fees

La Quinta Inn ($$)
7377 Six Flags Dr
(30001) 800.531.5900
call re: fees

● Conyers ●
Comfort Inn ($$)
1363 Klondike Rd SW
(30207) 770.760.0300

● Decatur ●
Econo Lodge ($$)
2574 Candler Rd
(30032) 404.243.4422

● Duluth ●
Amerisuties ($$$)
3390 Venture Pkwy
(30136) 770.623.6800

Days Inn ($$)
1948 Day Dr
(30136) 770.476.1211

Holiday Inn
3670 Shackelford Rd
(30136) 770.935.7171

Marriott ($$$)
1775 Pleasant Hill Rd
(30136) 970.923.1775

● Forest Park ●
Super 8
410 Old Dixie Way
(30050) 404.363.8811
call re: fees

● Jonesboro ●
Holiday Inn ($$)
6288 Old Dixie Hwy
(30236) 770.968.4300

● Kennesaw ●
Days Inn ($$)
760 Cobb Place Blvd
(30144) 770.419.1576
$5

Red Roof Inn ($)
520 Roberts Ct
(30144) 800.843.7663

Rodeway Inn ($$)
1460 Busbee Pkwy
(30144) 770.590.0519

● Lithonia ●
La Quinta Inn ($$)
2859 Panola Rd
(30058) 800.531.5900
call re: fees

● Marietta ●
Best Inns ($$)
1255 Franklin Rd SE
(30067) 404.955.0004
small pets only

Holiday Inn
2265 Kingston Ct
(30067) 770.952.7581

Howard Johnson ($$)
I-75 & Delk Rd
(30067) 770.951.1144

La Quinta Inn ($$$)
2170 Delk Rd SE
(30067) 770.951.0026
call re: fees

Motel 6 ($$)
2360 Delk Rd SE
(30067) 770.952.8161
1 small pet/room

Ramada Inn ($$)
610 Franklin Rd SE
(30067) 770.919.7878

Super 8 ($$)
2500 Delk Rd SE
(30067) 770.984.1570
$15 & dep

University Inn ($$$)
1767 N Decatur Rd
(30007) 404.634.7327

● Norcross ●
Budgetel ($)
5395 Peachtree Ind Blvd
(30092) 770.446.2882

Days Inn ($$)
5385 Peachtree Ind Blvd
(30092) 800.329.7466

La Quinta Inn ($$)
6187 Dawson Blvd
(30093) 800.531.5900
call re: fees

La Quinta Inn ($$)
5375 Peachtree Ind Blvd
(30092) 800.531.5900
call re: fees

Motel 6 ($$)
6015 Oakbrook Pkwy
(30093) 770.446.2311
1 small pet/room

Shoneys Inn ($$)
2050 Willow Trail Pkwy
(30093) 770.564.0492

Travel Lodge ($$)
6045 Oakbrook Pkwy
(30093) 770.449.7322

● Roswell ●
Best Western ($$)
907 Holcomb Bridge Rd
(30076) 770.961.6300
under 10 lbs

Budgetel ($$)
575 Holcomb Bridge
(30076) 770.552.0200

Hampton Inn ($$$)
9995 Old Dogwood Rd
(30076) 770.587.5161

● Smyrna ●
Residence Inn
2771 Hargrove Rd SE
(30080) 770.433.8877
$100 - $200 cleaning fee

● Stockbridge ●
Best Western ($$)
3509 Hwy 138
(30281) 770.474.8771
small pets

Motel 6 ($)
7233 Davidson Pkwy
(30281) 770.389.1142
1 small pet/room

● Tucker ●
La Quinta Inn ($$)
1819 Mountain Ind Blvd
(30084) 800.531.5900
call re: fees

Motel 6 ($$)
2565 Wesley Chapel
(30085) 404.288.6911
1 small pet/room

Ramada Inn ($$)
2180 Northlake Pkwy
(30084) 770.939.1000

● Villa Rica ●
Super 8 ($$)
195 Hwy 61
(30180) 404.459.8888
pets allowed

End of Atlanta Metro

● Augusta ●
Days Inn ($)
444 Broad St
(30901) 706.724.8100
$5 per day

Holiday Inn
1075 Stevens Creek
(30907) 706.738.8811

Holiday Inn ($$)
2155 Gordon Hwy
(30909) 706.737.0418

Howard Johnson ($)
1238 Gordon Hwy
(30901) 706.724.9613

Howard Johnson ($)
601 Bobby Jones Expwy
(30907) 706.863.2882

La Quinta Inn ($)
3020 Washington Rd
(30907) 800.531.5900
call re: fees

Masters Economy Inn ($)
3027 Washington Rd
(30907) 706.863.5566

Medical Center Inn
1455 Walton Way
(30901) 706.722.2224
referred

Motel 6 ($)
2560 Center West Pkwy
(30909) 404.736.1934
1 small pet/room

Radisson Inn ($$$)
2 10th St
(30901) 800.333.3333

Radisson Inn ($$)
3038 Washington Rd
(30907) 706.868.1800

Ramada Inn ($$$)
640 Broad St
(30901) 706.722.5541

Scottish Inn
1455 Walton Way
(30901) 770.952.3365

Sheraton Inn ($$)
2651 Perimeter Pkwy
(30909) 706.855.8100

Super 8 ($)
954 5th St
(30901) 706.724.0757
$3 & dep

Telfair Inn ($$$)
326 Greene St
(30901) 706.724.3315

● Austell ●
Knights Inn ($$)
1595 Blair Bridge Rd
(30001) 770.944.0824
size limits & fees

La Quinta Inn ($$)
7377 Six Flags Dr
(30001) 800.531.5900
call re: fees

● Baxley ●
Pine Lodge Motel ($)
500 S Main St
(31513) 912.367.3622

● Blackshear ●
Pond View Country Inn
4200 Grady St
(31516) 912.449.3697
working farm

Pond View Inn ($$)
4200B Grady St
(31516) 912.449.3697

● Blairsville ●
7 Creeks Cabins ($$)
5109 Horseshoe Cove Rd
(30512) 706.745.4753

Well
Behaved

● Blue Ridge ●
Blue Ridge Mtn Cabins ($$$)
Box# 1182
(30513) 706.632.7891

Days Inn ($$)
4970 Appalachian Hwy
(30513) 706.632.2100
$4/pets

● Bremen ●
Best Western ($$)
35 Price Creek Rd
(30110) 770.537.4646
under 10 lbs

● Brunswick ●
Best Western ($$)
5323 New Jesup Hwy
(31523) 912.264.0144

Budgetel ($)
105 Tourist Dr
(31520) 912.265.7725

Days Inn ($)
2307 Gloucester St
(31520) 912.265.8830
pets free

Holiday Inn ($$)
5252 New Jesupb Hwy
(31525) 912.264.4033

Motel 6 ($)
403 Butler Dr
(31523) 912.264.8582
1 small pet/room

Ramada Ltd ($$)
3241 Glynn Ave
(31520) 912.264.8611

Ramada Ltd ($$)
3040 Scarlett St
(31520) 912.264.3621

Shoneys Inn ($$)
3030 Scarlett St
(31520) 912.264.3626

Sleep Inn ($$)
5272 New Jesup Hwy
(31523) 912.261.0670

Super 8 ($$)
5280 New Jesup Hwy
(31523) 912.264.8800
call re: fees

● Byron ●
Econo Lodge ($)
106 Old Macon Rd
(31008) 912.956.5600

Masters Economy Inn ($)
RR 3 Box# 1540
(31008) 912.956.5300

Passport Inn ($)
I-75 At Ex 46
(31008) 912.956.5200

● Cairo ●
Days Inn ($$)
35 US Hwy 84
(31728) 912.377.4400
$5

● Calhoun ●
Best Western ($)
2261 Hwy 41 NE
(30701) 706.629.4521

Budget Host ($)
Hwy 53 Ex 129
(30703) 706.629.8644

Days Inn
742 Hwy 53
(30701) 706.629.8271
$4

Econo Lodge ($)
1438 US 41
(30701) 706.625.5421

Quality Inn ($)
915 Hwy 53 East SE
(30701) 706.629.9501

Scottish Inn ($)
1510 Red Bud Rd NE
(30701) 706.629.8261
$4/pets

Super 8 ($)
1446 Hwy 41
(30701) 706.602.1400
w/permission

● Camilla ●
Best Western ($$)
600 U S Hwy 19
(31730) 912.336.0731
small pets only

Days Inn
300 Hwy 19
(31730) 912.336.0330
$5

● Canton ●
Days Inn ($$)
291 Ball Ground Hwy
(30114) 770.479.0301

● Carrollton ●
Days Inn ($$)
180 Centennial Rd
(30116) 770.830.1000

Ramada Inn ($$)
1202 S Park St
(30117) 770.834.7700

● Cartersville ●
Budget Host ($)
851 Class White Rd
(30120) 800.283.4678
$2

Days Inn ($)
5618 Hwy 20 SE
(30121) 706.382.1824
$5

Econo Lodge ($)
25 Carson Loop NW
(30121) 404.386.0700

Holiday Inn ($$)
2336 Hwy 411 NE
(30121) 770.386.0830
mgr preapproval reqd

Howard Johnson ($)
5657 Hwy 20 NE
(30121) 770.386.1449

Knights Inn ($)
420 E Church St
(30121) 770.386.7263

Red Carpet Inn ($)
851 Class White Rd
(30120) 770.382.8000
$2 fee

Super 8 ($$)
41 Hwy 20 Spur SE
(30120) 770.382.8881
small pets only

● Chatsworth ●
Key West Inn ($$)
501 Maddox Pkwy
(30705) 706.517.1155

● Chula ●
Red Carpet Inn ($)
I-75
(31733) 912.382.2686
small $4 per day

● Clayton ●
English Manor Inn
Box# 1605
(30525) 706.782.5789

● Columbus ●
Budgetel ($$)
2919 Warm Springs Rd
(31909) 706.323.4344

Comfort Inn ($$)
3443 Macon Rd
(31907) 706.568.3300

Days Inn ($$)
3452 Macon Rd
(31907) 706.561.4400

Econo Lodge ($$)
4483 Victory Dr
(31903) 706.682.3803

La Quinta Inn ($$)
3201 Macon Rd
(31906) 706.568.1740
call re: fees

Motel 6 ($)
3050 Victory Dr
(31903) 706.687.7214
1 small pet/room

Super 8 ($$)
2935 Warm Springs Rd
(31909) 706.322.6580
$25 deposit

● Commerce ●
Guest House Inn ($)
30934 US 441
(30529) 706.335.5147

Hojo Inn ($$)
RR 1 Box# 163-D
(30529) 706.335.5581

Holiday Inn ($$)
30747 US 441
(30529) 706.335.5183

Ramada Inn ($$)
US Hwy 441 & I85
(30529) 706.335.5191

● Conyers ●
Comfort Inn ($$)
1363 Klondike Rd SW
(30207) 770.760.0300

● Cordele ●
Colonial Inn ($)
2016 16th Ave
(31015) 912.273.5420

Days Inn ($$)
215 7th St
(31015) 912.273.1123
small & quiet

Econo Lodge ($$)
1618 16th Ave
(31015) 800.465.4329

Holiday Inn ($$)
1711 16th Ave
(31015) 912.273.4117

Passport Inn ($)
1602 16th Ave
(31015) 912.273.4088

Ramada Inn ($$)
2016 16th Ave
(31015) 912.273.5000

Rodeway Inn ($)
1609 16th Ave
(31015) 912.273.3390

● Covington ●
Holiday Inn
10111 Alcovy Rd
(30209) 770.787.4900

● Dalton ●
Best Inns ($$)
1529 W Walnut Ave
(30720) 706.226.1100

Best Western ($$)
2106 Chattanooga Rd
(30720) 706.226.5022
under 10 lbs

Days Inn ($$)
1518 W Walnut Ave
(30720) 706.278.0850
$4/pets

Holiday Inn ($$)
515 Holiday Ave
(30720) 706.226.0279

Motel 6 ($)
2200 Chattanooga Rd
(30720) 706.278.5522
1 small pet/room

Super 8 ($$)
236 Connector 3 SW
(30720) 706.277.9323
w/permission

● Darien ●
Holiday Inn
I-95 & Ga 251
(31305) 912.437.5373

Super 8 ($)
Hwy 251 & 195
(31305) 912.437.6660
$10

● Decatur ●
Econo Lodge ($$)
2574 Candler Rd
(30032) 404.243.4422

● Dillard ●
Best Western ($$)
US 23 & 441
(30537) 706.746.5321
under 15 lbs

The Dillard House ($$)
Box# 10
(30537) 706.746.5348

● Donalsonville ●
Days Inn
Hwy 84
(31745) 912.524.6055
$5

● Douglas ●
Days Inn ($)
907 N Peterson Ave
(31533) 912.384.5190

Holiday Inn
1750 S Peterson Av
(31533) 912.384.9100

● Dublin ●
Holiday Inn ($$)
Hwy 441 & 116
(31040) 912.272.7862

● Duluth ●
Amerisuties ($$$)
3390 Venture Pkwy
(30136) 770.623.6800

Marriott ($$$)
1775 Pleasant Hill Rd
(30136) 970.923.1775

Days Inn ($$)
1948 Day Dr
(30136) 770.476.1211

Holiday Inn
3670 Shackelford Rd
(30136) 770.935.7171

● Ellijay ●
Budget Host ($$)
10 Jeff Dr
(30540) 706.635.5311
trained

● Enigma ●
Holiday Inn
I-75 & US 82
(31749) 912.382.6687

● Folkston ●
Days Inn ($)
1201 S 2nd St
(31537) 912.496.2514

● Forest Park ●
Super 8
410 Old Dixie Way
(30050) 404.363.8811
call re: fees

● Forsyth ●
Best Western ($$)
Hwy 42 & I75
(31029) 912.994.9260
small

Days Inn ($$)
I75 & Lee St
(31029) 912.994.2900

Econo Lodge ($)
I-75 & US 83
(31029) 912.994.5603
$4 fee

Hampton Inn ($$)
520 Holiday Cir
(31029) 912.994.9697

Holiday Inn
480 Holiday Cir
(31029) 912.994.5691

Passport Inn ($)
I-75 & Hwy 83
(31029) 912.994.2643
$2 fee

Super 8
900 Hwy 42
(31029) 912.994.9333
call re: fees

● Gainesville ●
Holiday Inn
726 Jesse Jewell Pkwy
(30501) 770.536.4451

Masters Inn Motel ($)
Hwy 129 & Monroe Dr
(30507) 770.532.7531

● Griffin ●
Scottish Inn
1709 North Exp
(30223) 770.228.6000

● Hahira ●
Ramada Inn ($)
I-75 Ex 7
(31632) 912.794.3000

● Hazlehurst ●
The Village Inn ($$)
312 Coffee St
(31539) 912.375.4527

● Helen ●
River Inn ($)
33 Munich Strasse
(30545) 706.878.2271

● Hinesville ●
Shoneys Inn ($$)
786 E Oglethorpe Hwy
(31313) 912.368.5858

● Jeffersonville ●
Days Inn
Hwy 96
(31044) 912.945.3785

● Jekyll Island ●
Clarion Hotel ($$$)
85 S Beachview Dr
(31527) 912.635.2211
mgr preapproval reqd

Comfort Inn ($$$)
711 N Beachview Dr
(31527) 912.635.2211
mgr preapproval reqd

Days Inn ($$)
60 S Beachview Dr
(31527) 912.635.3319
$5

Holiday Inn ($$)
200 S Beachview Dr
(31527) 912.635.3311
mgr preapproval reqd

Villas By The Sea ($$$)
1175 N Beachview Dr
(31527) 800.841.6262

● Jesup ●
Days Inn ($$)
384 S US Hwy 301
(31546) 912.427.3751
$5/day

● Jonesboro ●
Holiday Inn ($$)
6288 Old Dixie Hwy
(30236) 770.968.4300

● Kennesaw ●
Days Inn ($$)
760 Cobb Place Blvd
(30144) 770.419.1576
$5

Red Roof Inn ($)
520 Roberts Ct
(30144) 800.843.7663

Rodeway Inn ($$)
1460 Busbee Pkwy
(30144) 770.590.0519

● Kingsland ●
Comfort Inn ($$)
I-95
(31548) 912.729.6979

Days Inn
1050 KingAve
(31548) 912.729.5454
$5

Holiday Inn
I-95 & Ga 40
(31548) 912.729.3000

● Lagrange ●
Days Inn ($$)
2606 Whitesville Rd
(30240) 706.882.8881
$4/pets

● Lake Park ●
Days Inn
I-75
(31636) 912.559.0229
$2

Holiday Inn ($$)
1198 Lakes Blvd
(31636) 912.559.5181
mgr preapproval reqd

Shoneys Inn ($$)
1075 Lakes Blvd
(31636) 912.559.5660

Travelodge ($)
4912 Timber Dr
(31636) 912.559.0110

● Lakemont ●
Forest Lodges ($$$)
Lake Rabun Rd
(30552) 706.782.6250

● Lavonia ●
Shoneys Inn ($$)
14227 Jones St
(30553) 706.356.8848

● Lawrenceville ●
Days Inn ($$)
731 W Pike St
(30245) 770.995.7782

● Lithonia ●
La Quinta Inn ($$)
2859 Panola Rd
(30058) 800.531.5900
call re: fees

● Locust Grove ●
Red Carpet Inn ($)
4829 Hampton Rd
(30248) 404.957.2601
$4 fee

Scottish Inn
4679 Hampton Rd
(30248) 404.957.9001

Super 8 ($$)
4605 Hampton Rd
(30248) 770.957.2936
w/permission

● Louisville ●
Louisville Motel ($)
308 Hwy 1 Byp
(30434) 912.625.7168

● Macon ●
Comfort Inn ($$)
2690 Riverside Dr
(31204) 912.746.8855
mgr preapproval reqd

Crowne Plaza ($$$)
108 1st St
(31201) 912.746.1461

Days Inn ($$)
2737 Sheraton Dr
(31204) 912.745.8521
$10 per day

Econo Lodge ($)
4951 Rosmeiser Rd
(31206) 912.474.1661

Hampton Inn ($$)
3680 Riverside Dr
(31210) 800.426.7866

Holiday Inn
3590 Riverside Dr
(31210) 912.474.2610

Holiday Inn ($$)
2720 Riverside Dr
(31204) 912.743.1482

Howard Johnson ($)
4709 Chambers Rd
(31206) 912.781.6680

Howard Johnson ($$)
2566 Riverside Dr
(31204) 912.746.7671

Knights Inn ($)
4952 Romeiser Dr
(31206) 912.471.1230
size limits & fees

Masters Economy Inn ($)
4295 Pio Nono Ave
(31206) 912.474.2870
1 small pet per room

Motel 6 ($)
4991 Harrison Rd
(31206) 912.474.2870
1 small pet/room

Passport Inn ($)
5022 Romeiser Dr
(31206) 912.474.2665

Quality Inn ($)
4630 Chambers Rd
(31206) 912.781.7000

Rodeway Inn ($$)
4999 Eisenhower Pkwy
(31206) 912.781.4343

● Madison ●
Burnett Place ($$$)
317 Old Post Rd
(30650) 706.342.4034

Days Inn ($$)
2001 Eatonton Rd
(30650) 706.342.1839

Ramada Inn ($$)
US 441 & I-20
(30650) 706.342.2121

● Marietta ●
Best Inns ($$)
1255 Franklin Rd SE
(30067) 404.955.0004
small pets only

Holiday Inn
2265 Kingston Ct
(30067) 770.952.7581

Howard Johnson ($$)
I-75 & Delk Rd
(30067) 770.951.1144

La Quinta Inn ($$$)
2170 Delk Rd SE
(30067) 770.951.0026
call re: fees

Motel 6 ($$)
2360 Delk Rd SE
(30067) 770.952.8161
1 small pet/room

Ramada Inn ($$)
610 Franklin Rd SE
(30067) 770.919.7878

Super 8 ($$)
2500 Delk Rd SE
(30067) 770.984.1570
$15 & dep

University Inn ($$$)
1767 N Decatur Rd
(30007) 404.634.7327

● Mc Donough ●
Days Inn ($$)
744 Ga 155
(30253) 770.957.5261
$4

Holiday Inn ($$)
930 Hwy 155
(30253) 770.957.2651
mgr preapproval reqd

Red Carpet Inn ($)
1170 Hampton Rd
(30253) 404.957.2458

● Milledgeville ●
Days Inn ($)
3001 Heritage Rd NE
(31061) 912.453.3551
$4/pets

Scottish Inn ($)
2474 N Columbia St
(31061) 912.453.9491
small pets only

● Monroe ●
Days Inn ($$)
Rt 6
(30655) 770.267.3666
$5

● Newnan ●
Days Inn
1344 South Hwy
(30263) 770.253.8550
$5

Days Inn ($$)
1344 S Hwy
(30264) 770.253.8550
$5

● Norcross ●
Budgetel ($)
5395 Peachtree Ind Blvd
(30092) 770.446.2882

Days Inn ($$)
5385 Peachtree Ind Blvd
(30092) 800.329.7466

La Quinta Inn ($$)
6187 Dawson Blvd
(30093) 800.531.5900
call re: fees

La Quinta Inn ($$)
5375 Peachtree Ind Blvd
(30092) 800.531.5900
call re: fees

Motel 6 ($$)
6015 Oakbrook Pkwy
(30093) 770.446.2311
1 small pet/room

Shoneys Inn ($$)
2050 Willow Trail Pkwy
(30093) 770.564.0492

Travel Lodge ($$)
6045 Oakbrook Pkwy
(30093) 770.449.7322

● Perry ●
Hampton Inn ($$)
102 Hampton Ct
(31069) 912.987.7681

New Perry Hotel ($)
800 Main St
(31069) 912.987.1000

Passport Inn
1519 Sam Nunn Blvd
(31069) 912.987.9709

Quality Inn ($)
1504 Sam Nunn Blvd
(31069) 912.987.1345
mgr preapproval reqd

Ramada Inn ($$)
100 Market Place Dr
(31069) 912.987.8400

Red Carpet Inn ($)
105 Carroll Aly
(31069) 912.987.2200

Rodeway Inn ($$)
103 Marshallville Rd
(31069) 912.987.3200

Scottish Inn
106 GC Hodges Blvd
(31069) 912.987.3622

Super 8 ($)
1410 Sam Nunn Blvd
(31069) 800.800.8000
call re: fees

● Pine Mountain ●
White Column Motel ($)
19727 S US 27
(31822) 706.663.2312

● Pooler ●
Ramada Inn ($$)
301 Governor Treutlen Dr
(31322) 912.748.6464

● Richmond Hill ●
Days Inn ($$)
I-95
(31324) 912.756.3371
$5/pets

Holiday Inn
I-95 & US 17
(31324) 912.756.3351

Motel 6 ($)
I-95 & Hwy 17
(31324) 912.756.3543
1 small pet/room

● Ringgold ●
Days Inn ($$$)
5435 Alabama Hwy
(30736) 706.965.5730
$2/pet charge

Friendship Inn ($$)
Box# 405
(30736) 706.965.3428

Super 8 ($$)
401 S Hwy 151
(30736) 706.965.7080
pets w/permission

● Rome ●
Best Western ($$)
Hwy 411
(30161) 800.528.1234
$5/night

Holiday Inn ($$)
20 Hwy 411
(30161) 706.295.1100

Super 8 ($$)
1590 Dodd Blvd
(30161) 706.234.8182
w/permission

● Roswell ●
Best Western ($$)
907 Holcomb Bridge Rd
(30076) 770.961.6300
under 10 lbs

Budgetel ($$)
575 Holcomb Bridge
(30076) 770.552.0200

Hampton Inn ($$$)
9995 Old Dogwood Rd
(30076) 770.587.5161

● St. Simons Island ●
Island Inn ($$)
301 Main St
(31522) 800.673.6323

Seafarer Inn ($$)
700 Beachview Dr
(31522) 912.635.2202

● Savannah ●
Budget Inn ($)
3702 Ogeechee Rd
(31405) 800.949.7666

Budgetel ($$)
8484 Abercorn St
(31406) 912.927.7660

East Bay Inn ($$$)
225 E Bay St
(31401) 800.500.1225

Econo Lodge ($$)
7 W Gateway Blvd
(31419) 912.925.2280

Holiday Inn
I-95 & Ga 204
(31419) 912.925.2770

Homewood Suites ($$$)
5820 White Bluff Rd
(31405) 912.353.8500

La Quinta Inn ($$)
6805 Abercorn St
(31405) 912.355.3004
call re: fees

Marriott Hotel ($$$$)
100 General McIntosh Blvd
(31401) 912.233.7722

Red Carpet Inn ($)
1 Fort Argyle Rd
(31419) 912.925.2640
$5 fee

River Street Inn ($$$)
115 E River St
(31401) 912.234.6400

Scottish Inn
4005 Ogeechee Rd
(31405) 912.236.8236

Shoneys Inn ($$)
17003 Albercorn St
(31419) 912.925.7050

Super 8 ($$)
15 Fort Argyle Rd
(31419) 912.927.8550
$50 dep on 2nd floor

The Ballastone Inn ($$$)
4 E Oglethorpe Ave
(31401) 912.236.1484

• Smyrna •
Residence Inn
2771 Hargrove Rd SE
(30080) 770.433.8877
$100 - $200 cleaning fee

• Sparks •
Red Carpet Inn ($)
RR 1 Box# 212
(31647) 800.251.1962

• Statesboro •
Days Inn ($)
461 Main St
(30458) 912.764.5666
small pets only

Holiday Inn ($$)
425 Main St
(30458) 800.465.4329

Statesboro Inn ($$$)
106 S Main St
(30458) 912.489.8628

• Stockbridge •
Best Western ($$)
3509 Hwy 138
(30281) 770.474.8771
small pets

Motel 6 ($)
7233 Davidson Pkwy
(30281) 770.389.1142
1 small pet/room

• Swainsboro •
Days Inn ($)
654 S Main St
(30401) 912.237.9333

• Sylvester •
Days Inn ($$)
909 Franklin St
(31791) 912.776.9700
$5

• Thomasville •
Days Inn ($$)
15375 US 195
(31792) 912.226.6025
$4/pets

Holiday Inn ($$)
15138 US 195
(31792) 912.226.7111

Shoneys Inn
14866 US Hwy 19
(31792) 912.228.5555

• Thomson •
Days Inn ($)
2658 Cobbham Rd
(30824) 706.595.2262
$10

• Tifton •
Best Western ($$)
1103 King Rd
(31794) 800.528.1234
mgr preapproval reqd

Comfort Inn ($$)
1104 King Rd
(31794) 912.382.4410

Days Inn ($$)
1008 8th St
(31794) 912.382.7210

Hampton Inn ($$)
720 Hwy 319S
(31794) 912.382.8800

Masters Economy Inn ($)
US 82 & 319
(31793) 912.382.8100

Passport Inn ($)
902 W 7th St
(31794) 912.382.1221

Red Carpet Inn ($)
1025 W 2nd St
(31794) 912.382.0280
$2

Scottish Inn
1409 Hwy 82
(31794) 912.386.2350
$3 fee

Super 8
I-75 & W 2nd St
(31793) 912.382.9500
$5

• Toccoa •
Days Inn ($)
Hwy17
(30577) 706.886.9641
$10/pet

• Townsend •
Days Inn
I-95
(31331) 912.832.4365
$5

Days Inn ($)
I-95
(31331) 912.832.4411
$5/pet

Ramada Inn ($)
Hwy 57 & I-95
(31331) 912.832.4444

• Tucker •
La Quinta Inn ($$)
1819 Mountain Ind Blvd
(30084) 800.531.5900
call re: fees

Motel 6 ($$)
2565 Wesley Chapel
(30085) 404.288.6911
1 small pet/room

Ramada Inn ($$)
2180 Northlake Pkwy
(30084) 770.939.1000

• Tybee Island •
Howard Johnson ($)
1501 Butler Ave
(31328) 912.786.0700

Ocean Plaza Inn ($$)
Tybee Island
(31328) 912.786.7664
guest rfd

• Unadilla •
Days Inn ($)
I-75 & US 41
(31091) 912.627.3211
$2/pets

Passport
Rt 1
(31091) 912.627.3258

Red Carpet Inn ($)
101 Robert St
(31091) 912.627.3261

Scottish Inn ($)
RR 2 Box# 82
(31091) 912.627.3228
$2

• Valdosta •
Best Western ($)
1403 N St. Augustine Rd
(31602) 912.244.7600
mgr preapproval reqd

Comfort Inn ($)
I-75
(31602) 912.242.1212

Policies
Subject
to Change

Days Inn ($)
1821 W Hill Ave
(31601) 912.249.8800
$5

Days Inn ($)
4598 N Valdosta Rd
(31602) 912.244.4460
$5

Holiday Inn ($$)
1309 St Augustine Rd
(31601) 912.242.3881

Motel 6 ($)
2003 W Hill Ave
(31601) 912.333.0047
1 small pet/room

Quality Inn ($$)
1209 N St. Augustine Rd
(31601) 912.244.8510

Quality Inn ($)
1902 W Hill Ave
(31601) 912.244.4520

Ramada Inn ($$)
2008 W Hill Ave
(31601) 912.242.1225

Scottish Inn
1114 N St. Augustine Rd
(31601) 912.244.7900

Shoneys Inn ($$)
1828 W Hill Ave
(31601) 912.244.7711

● Vidalia ●
Days Inn ($)
1503 Hwy 280
(30474) 912.537.9251
$10

Holiday Inn ($$)
2619 E 1st St
(30474) 912.537.9000
mgr preapproval reqd

Shoneys Inn
2505 Lyons Hwy
(30474) 912.537.1282

● Villa Rica ●
Super 8 ($$)
195 Hwy 61
(30180) 404.459.8888
pets allowed

● Warner Robins ●
Super 8 ($$)
105 Woodcrest Blvd
(31093) 912.923.8600
$25 fee

● Waycross ●
Days Inn ($)
2016 Memorial Dr
(31501) 912.285.4700
mgr preapproval reqd

Holiday Inn
1725 Memorial Dr
(31501) 912.283.4490

Pine Crest Motel ($)
Box# 1357
(31502) 912.283.3580

Idaho

● American Falls ●
Hillview Motel ($)
2799 Lakeview Rd
(83211) 208.226.5151

Ronnez Motel ($)
411 Lincoln St
(83211) 208.226.9658

● Arco ●
Arco Inn ($)
540 W Grand
(83213) 208.527.3100

D K Motel ($)
316 S Front
(83213) 208.527.8282

Lazy A Motel ($)
Box# 12
(83213) 208.527.8263

Lost River Motel ($)
405 Hwy Dr
(83213) 208.527.3600

Riverside Motel ($)
Box# 22
(83213) 208.527.8954

● Ashton ●
The Four Seasons ($)
Box# 848
(83420) 208.652.7769

● Athol ●
Athol Motel ($)
Box# 275
(83801) 208.683.3476

● Banks ●
The Ponderosa ($)
HC 76 Box# 1010
(83602) 208.793.2700

Trails End Motel ($)
HC 76 Box# 1010
(83602) 208.793.2700

● Bayview ●
Bayview Scenic Motel ($$)
6th & Main St
(83803) 208.683.2215

Macdonalds Resort ($$$)
Box# 38
(83803) 208.683.2211

● Bellevue ●
High Country Motel ($)
Box# 598
(83313) 208.788.2050

● Blackfoot ●
Best Western ($$)
750 Jensen Grove Dr
(83221) 208.785.4144

Riverside Inn ($$)
1229 Park Way Dr
(83221) 208.785.5000

● Boise ●
Boulevard Motel ($)
1121 S Capitol Blvd
(83706) 208.342.4629

Budget Inn ($)
2600 Fairview Ave
(83702) 208.344.8617

Cabana Inn ($)
1600 Main St
(83702) 208.343.6000

Econo Lodge ($$)
2155 N Garden St
(83706) 208.344.4030

Fairfield Inn ($$)
3300 Shoshone St
(83705) 208.331.5656

Fall Creek Resort ($$)
6633 Overland Rd
(83709) 208.653.2242

Flying J Inn ($)
8002 Overland Rd
(83709) 208.322.4404

Hampton Inn ($$)
3270 Shoshone St
(83705) 208.331.5600

Holiday Inn ($$$)
3300 Vista Ave
(83705) 208.344.8375
mgr preapproval reqd

Holiday Motel ($)
5416 Fairview Ave
(83706) 208.376.4631

Middle Fork Lodge
Box# 16278
(83715) 208.342.7888

Motel 6 ($)
2323 Airport Way
(83705) 208.344.3506
1 small pet/room

Nendels Inn ($)
2155 N Garden St
(83706) 208.344.4030

Owyhee Plaza Hotel ($$)
1109 Main St
(83702) 208.343.4611

Quality Inn ($$)
2717 Vista Ave
(83705) 208.343.7505
mgr preapproval reqd

Ramada Inn ($$)
1025 S Capitol Blvd
(83706) 208.344.7971

Red Lion Inn ($$$)
1800 Fairview Ave
(83702) 208.344.7691
call re: fees

Red Lion Inn ($$$)
2900 Chinden Blvd
(83714) 208.343.1871
call re: fees

Residence Inn ($$$$)
1401 S Lusk Pl
(83706) 208.344.1200
call re pets $5 per pet

Rodeway Inn ($$$)
1115 N Curtis Rd
(83706) 208.376.2700

Sawtooth Lodge
1403 E Bannock St
(83712) 208.344.6685

Seven K Motel ($)
3633 Chinden Blvd
(83714) 208.343.7723

Shilo Inn ($$$)
4111 Broadway Ave
(83705) 208.343.7662
call re: fees

Shilo Inn ($$)
3031 Main St
(83702) 208.344.3521
call re: fees

Super 8 ($$)
2773 Elder St
(83705) 208.344.8871
pets w/permission

West River Inn ($)
3525 Chinden Blvd
(83714) 208.338.1155

● Bonners Ferry ●
Best Western ($$)
Kootenai River Plaza
(83805) 208.267.8511
mgr preapproval reqd

Bonners Ferry Resort ($)
RR 4 Box# 4700
(83805) 208.267.2422

Deep Creek Resort ($$)
RR 4 Box# 628
(83805) 208.267.2729

Kootenai Valley Motel ($$)
Hwy 955
(83805) 208.267.7567

Town & Country Motel ($)
RR 4 Box# 4664
(83805) 208.267.7915

● Buhl ●
Siesta Motel
629 Broadway Ave
(83316) 208.543.6427

● Burley ●
Best Western ($$)
800 N. Overland Ave
(83318) 208.678.3501
under 20 lb attended

Budget Motel ($)
900 N Overland Ave
(83318) 208.678.2200

Greenwell Motel ($)
904 E Main St
(83318) 208.678.5576

Lampliter Motel ($)
721 E Main St
(83318) 208.678.0031

Parish Motel ($)
721 E Main St
(83318) 208.678.5505

Starlite Motel ($)
510 Overland Ave
(83318) 208.678.7766

● Calder ●
St Jose Lodge ($$)
Rt 3 Box# 350
(83808) 208.245.3462

● Caldwell ●
Comfort Inn ($$)
901 Specht Ave
(83605) 208.454.2222
mgr preapproval reqd

Holiday Motel ($)
512 E Frontage Rd
(83605) 208.454.3888

● Cambridge ●
Frontier Motel ($)
Box# 178
(83610) 208.257.3851

Hunters Inn ($)
Box# 313
(83610) 208.257.3325

● Cascade ●
Arrowhead Cabins ($)
Box# 337
(83611) 208.382.4534

Aurora Motel ($)
Box# 799
(83611) 208.382.4948

High Country Inn ($)
Box# 548
(83611) 208.382.3315

Mountain View Motel ($)
Box# 1053
(83611) 208.382.4238

North Shore Lodge ($$)
175 N Shorelind Dr
(83611) 208.257.2219

Silver Pines Motel ($)
Box# 70
(83611) 208.382.4370

● Challis ●
Challis Hot Springs ($$)
HC 63 Box# 1779
(83226) 208.879.4442

Challis Motor Lodge ($)
Box# 6
(83226) 208.879.2251

Northgate Inn ($)
HC 63 Box# 1665
(83226) 208.879.2490

The Village Inn ($)
Box# 6 Hwy 93
(83226) 208.879.2239

● Clark Fork ●
River Delta Resort ($$)
Box# 128
(83811) 208.266.1335

● Coeur D Alene ●
Bates Motel ($)
2018 E Sherman Ave
(83814) 208.667.1411

Bennett Bay Inn ($)
E 5144 I-90
(83814) 208.664.6168

Boulevard Motel ($)
2400 Seltice Way
(83814) 208.664.4978

Cedar Motel ($)
319 Coeur D Alene Lake Dr
(83814) 208.664.2278

Coeur D Alene Inn ($$)
414 W Appleway Ave
(83814) 208.765.3200

Coeur D Alene ($$)
906 E Foster Ave
(83814) 208.667.7527

Comfort Inn ($$)
280 W Appleway Ave
(83814) 208.765.5500
mgr preapproval reqd

Days Inn ($$)
2200 Northwest Blvd
(83814) 208.667.8668

El Rancho Motel ($)
1915 E Sherman Ave
(83814) 208.664.8794

Flamingo Motel ($$$)
718 E Sherman Ave
(83814) 208.664.2159

Holiday Inn ($$$)
2209 E Sherman Ave
(83814) 208.667.6777

Monte Vista Motel ($$)
320 Coeur D Alene Lake Dr
(83814) 208.664.8201

Motel 6 ($$)
416 W Appleway Ave
(83814) 208.664.6600
1 small pet/room

Rodeway Inn ($$)
1422 Northwest Blvd
(83814) 208.664.8244

Scenic Bay Motel ($$)
Box# 36
(83816) 208.683.2243

Shilo Inn ($$$)
702 W Appleway Ave
(83814) 208.664.2300
call re: fees

Summer House ($$$$)
1535 Silver Beach Rd
(83814) 208.667.9395

IDAHO, Couer D' Alene

Super 8 ($$)
505 W Appleway Ave
(83814) 208.765.8880
w/ permission $20 deposit

● Coolin ●
Bishops Marina ($$)
Box# 91
(83821) 208.443.2191

The Inn At Priest Lake ($$)
Box# 189
(83821) 800.443.6240

● Donnelly ●
Long Valley Motel ($)
161 S Main St
(83615) 208.325.8545

● Downey ●
Downata Hot Springs ($$)
25900 S Downata Rd
(83234) 208.897.5736

Flags West Motel ($)
Ex 31 I-15
(83234) 208.897.5238

● Driggs ●
Best Western ($$)
476 N Main St
(83422) 208.354.2363
pets at managers discretion

Pines Motel ($)
105 S Main
(83422) 208.354.2774

● Dubois ●
Cross Roads Motel ($)
391 S Reynolds
(83423) 208.374.5258

● Elk City ●
Elk City Hotel ($)
Box# 356
(83525) 208.842.2452

Elk City Motel ($)
Box# 140
(83525) 208.842.2250

Lodgepole Pine Inn
Box# 71
(83525) 208.842.2343

Prospector Lodge ($)
Box# 270
(83525) 208.842.2557

Red River Hot Springs ($$)
Elk City
(83525) 208.842.2587

Sable Trail Ranch ($)
Box# 21
(83525) 208.983.1418

Village Inn Motel ($)
50 South 300
(83525) 208.766.4761

● Elk River ●
Huckleberry Lodge ($$)
Box# 165
(83827) 208.826.3405

● Emmett ●
Holiday Motel ($)
1111 S Washington Ave
(83617) 208.365.4479

L & H Motel ($)
720 S Johns Ave
(83617) 208.365.2482

● Fairfield ●
Country Inn ($)
Box# 393
(83327) 208.764.2247

Motel 6 ($)
Box# 285
(83327) 208.764.2211
1 small pet/room

● Garden Valley ●
Silver Creek Motel ($)
HC 76 Box# 2377
(83622) 208.344.8688

● Gibbonsville ●
Broken Arrow Cabins ($)
Hwy 93
(83463) 208.865.2241

● Glenns Ferry ●
Redford Motel
612 Main St
(83623) 208.366.2421

● Grangeville ●
Elkhorn Lodge ($)
822 SW 1st St
(83530) 208.983.1500

Junction Lodge ($)
HC 67 Box# 98
(83530) 208.842.2459

Montys Motel ($)
700 W Main St
(83530) 208.983.2500

● Hagerman ●
Hagerman Valley Inn ($$)
Box# 480
(83332) 208.837.6196

Rock Lodge Resort ($$)
Box# 449
(83332) 208.837.4822

● Hailey ●
Airport Inn ($$)
820 4th Ave
(83333) 208.788.2477

Hitchrack Motel ($$)
619 S Main
(83333) 208.788.2409

● Hammett ●
Oasis Ranch Motel ($)
HC 63 Box# 6
(83627) 208.366.2025

● Harrison ●
Lakeview Lodge ($$)
Box# 54
(83833) 208.689.3318

Pegs Place ($$$)
202 Garfield Ave
(83833) 208.689.3525

Squaw Bay Resort ($$$)
Rt 2 Box# 130
(83833) 208.664.6450

● Heyburn ●
Tops Motel ($)
RR 1 Box# 1038
(83336) 208.436.4724

● Homedale ●
Sunnydale Motel ($)
Box# 935
(83628) 208.337.3302

● Hope ●
Idaho Country Resort ($$$)
140 Idaho Country Rd
(83836) 208.264.5505

Red Fir Resort ($$$)
450 Red Fir Rd
(83836) 208.264.5287

● Idaho City ●
Idaho City Hotel ($)
215 Montgomery St
(83631) 208.392.4290

● Idaho Falls ●
Best Western ($$)
700 Lindsay Blvd
(83402) 208.522.2910
mgr preapproval reqd

Best Western ($$)
575 River Pkwy
(83402) 208.523.2242
small pets only

Bonneville Motel ($)
200 S Yellowstone Hwy
(83402) 208.522.7847

Comfort Inn ($$)
195 E Colorado Ave
(83402) 208.528.2804
mgr preapproval reqd

Littletree Inn ($$)
888 N Holmes Ave
(83401) 208.523.5993

Motel 6 ($)
1448 W Broadway St
(83402) 208.522.0112
1 small pet/room

Motel West ($)
1540 W Broadway St
(83402) 208.522.1112

Quality Inn ($$)
850 Lindsay Blvd
(83402) 208.523.6260
mgr preapproval reqd

Shilo Inn ($$$)
780 Lindsay Blvd
(83402) 208.523.0088
call re: fees

• Island Park •
A Bar Motel ($$)
H 66 Box# 452
(83429) 208.558.7358

Aspen Lodge ($$)
H 66 Box# 269
(83429) 208.558.7406

Elk Creek Ranch ($$$)
Box# 2
(83429) 208.558.7404
Ponds Lodge ($$)
Box# 258
(83429) 208.558.7221

Staley Sprgs Lodge ($$)
H 66 Box# 102
(83429) 208.558.7471

Wild Rose Ranch
340 W 7th St
(83429) 208.558.7201

• Jerome •
Crest Motel ($)
2983 S Lincoln Ave
(83338) 208.324.2670

Holiday Motel ($)
401 W Main St
(83338) 208.324.2361

• Kamiah •
Clearwater 12 Motel ($$)
Hwy 12 & Cedar St
(83536) 208.935.2671

Lewis Clark Resort ($$)
RR 1 Box# 17X
(83536) 208.935.2556

Sundown Motel ($)
RR 2 Box# 100
(83536) 208.935.2568

Whitewater Outfitters ($$$)
Box# 642
(83536) 208.935.0631

• Kellogg •
Motel 51 ($)
206 E Cameron Ave
(83837) 208.786.9441

Sunshine Inn ($)
301 W Cameron Ave
(83837) 208.784.1186

Silverhorn Motor Inn ($$)
699 W Cameron Ave
(83837) 208.783.1151

Super 8 ($$)
601 Bunker Ave
(83837) 208.783.1234
call re: fees

The Inn At Silver Mountain
($)
305 S Division St
(83837) 208.786.2311

Trail Motel ($)
206 W Cameron Ave
(83837) 208.784.1161

• Ketchum •
Bald Mountain Lodge ($$)
151 S Main
(83340) 208.726.9963

Best Western ($$)
651 Sun Valley Rd
(83340) 208.726.3351
mgr dis

Best Western ($$$)
260 Cottonwood
(83340) 208.726.5336
1st floor only

Sawtooth Hotel ($)
Box# 52
(83340) 208.774.9947

Ski View Lodge
409 S Hwy 75
(83340) 208.726.3441

• Kooskia •
Ida Lee Motel ($)
Box# 592
(83539) 208.926.7146

Mt Stuart Inn Motel ($)
Box# 592
(83539) 208.926.0166

Ryans Wilderness Inn ($)
HC 75 Box# 60A2
(83539) 208.926.4706

Three Rivers Resort ($$)
HC 75 Box# 61
(83539) 208.926.4430

• Lava Hot Springs •
Dempsey Creek Lodge ($)
Box# 600
(83246) 208.776.5000

Lava Hot Springs Inn ($$)
5 Portneuf Ave
(83246) 208.776.5830

Lava Ranch Inn Motel ($)
9611 E Hwy 30
(83246) 208.776.9917

Oregon Trail Lodge
119 E Main
(83246) 208.776.5000

Riverside Inn ($)
255 Portneuf
(83246) 208.776.5504

Tumbling Water Motel ($$)
359 E Main St
(83246) 208.776.5589

• Leadore •
Leadore Inn ($)
Box# 68
(83464) 208.768.2647

• Lewiston •
Bel Air Motel ($)
2018 N And South Hwy
(83501) 208.743.5946

Churchill Inns ($)
1021 Main St
(83501) 208.743.4501

El Rancho Motel ($)
2240 3rd Ave
(83501) 208.743.8517

Hillary Motel ($)
2030 N And South Hwy
(83501) 208.743.8514

Hollywood Inn ($$)
3001 N And South Hwy
(83501) 208.743.9424

Pony Soldier Motel ($$)
1716 Main St
(83501) 208.743.9526

Ramada Inn ($$)
621 21st St
(83501) 208.799.1000

Riverview Inn ($$)
1325 Main St
(83501) 208.746.3311

Sacajawea Motel ($$)
1824 Main St
(83501) 208.746.1393

Sheep Creek Ranch ($$$$)
227 Snake River Ave
(83501) 208.746.6276

Snake River Adventures
($$$)
227 Snake River Ave
(83501) 208.746.6276

Super 8 ($$)
3120 N South Hwy
(83501) 208.743.8808
w/permission

• Lowman •
New Haven Lodge ($$)
HC 77 Box# 3608
(83637) 208.259.3344

Sourdough Lodge ($)
HC 77 Box# 3109
(83637) 208.259.3326

• Mackay •
Wagon Wheel Motel ($$)
809 W Custer
(83251) 208.588.3331

White Knob Motel ($$)
Box# 180
(83251) 208.588.3331

• Macks Inn •
Macks Inn Resort ($)
Box# 10
(83433) 208.558.7272

Sawtell Mtn Resort ($$)
Box# 250
(83433) 208.558.9366

• Mc Call •
Best Western ($$)
415 3rd St
(83638) 208.634.6300
mgr preapproval reqd

Brundage Bungalows ($$)
308 W Lake St
(83638) 208.634.8573

IDAHO, McCall

Forest Condominiums ($$)
Box# 1978
(83638) 208.634.4528

Lakefork Lodge ($$$$)
Box# 4336
(83638) 208.634.3713

Riverside Motel ($$)
400 W Lake St
(83638) 208.634.5610

Super 8 ($$)
303 S 3rd St
(83638) 208.634.4637
call re: fees

Village Inn Motel ($$)
Box# 734
(83638) 208.634.2344

Woodsman ($)
Box# 884
(83638) 208.634.7671

● Montpelier ●
Best Western ($$)
243 N 4th St
(83254) 208.847.1782
small pets only

Budget Motel ($)
240 N 4th St
(83254) 208.847.1273

Michelle Motel ($)
401 Boise St
(83254) 208.847.1772

The Park Motel ($)
745 Washington St
(83254) 208.847.1911

● Moscow ●
Best Western ($$$)
1516 W Pullman Rd
(83843) 208.882.0550

Hillcrest Motel ($)
706 N Main St
(83843) 208.882.7579

Mark IV Motor Inn ($)
414 N Main St
(83843) 208.882.7557

Royal Motor Inn ($)
120 W 6th St
(83843) 208.882.2581

● Mountain Home ●
Best Western ($$)
1080 Hwy 20
(83647) 208.587.8477
$50 dep

Hilander Motel ($)
615 S 3rd
(83647) 208.587.3311

Motel Thunderbird ($)
910 Sunset Strip
(83647) 208.587.7927

Rosestone Inn ($$)
495 N 3rd
(83647) 208.587.8866

Sleep Inn ($)
1180 Hwy 20
(83647) 208.587.9743
mgr preapproval reqd

Towne Center Motel ($)
410 N 2nd
(83647) 208.587.3373

● Nampa ●
Desert Inn Motel ($)
115 9th Ave
(83651) 208.467.1161

Five Crowns Inn ($)
908 3rd St
(83651) 208.466.3594

Shilo Inn ($$$)
617 Nampa Blvd
(83687) 208.465.3250
call re: fees

Starlite Motel ($)
320 11th Ave
(83687) 208.466.9244

Super 8 ($$)
624 Nampa Blvd
(83687) 208.467.2888
call re: fees

● New Meadows ●
Half Way Inn ($)
HC 75 Box# 3760
(83654) 208.628.3259

Pinehurst Resort ($)
5604 Hwy 95
(83654) 208.628.3323

● Nordman ●
Elkins Cabins ($$$)
HCo 1 Box# 40
(83848) 208.443.2432

Kaniksu Resort
HCO1 Box# 152
(83848) 208.443.2609

● North Fork ●
Indian Creek Ranch ($$$)
HC 64 Box# 105A
(83466) 208.394.2126

North Fork Motel ($)
Box# 100
(83466) 208.865.2412

Rivers Fork Inn ($$)
Hwy 93
(83466) 208.865.2301

● Orofino ●
Helgeson Place Hotel ($)
Box# 463
(83544) 208.476.5729

Konkolville Motel ($)
2000 Konkolville Rd
(83544) 208.476.5584

Riverside Motel ($)
10560 Hwy 12
(83544) 208.476.5711

White Pine Motel ($)
222 Brown St
(83544) 208.476.7093

● Pierce ●
Cedar Inn ($)
412 S Main
(83546) 208.464.2704

Key Bar Hotel ($)
Box# 494
(83546) 208.464.2704

Pierce Motel ($)
509 Main St
(83546) 208.464.2324

● Pinehurst ●
Kellogg Vacation Homes ($$)
Box# 944
(83850) 208.786.4261

Pinehurst Cabins ($)
Box# 949
(83850) 208.682.3612

● Plummer ●
Hiway Motel ($)
301 10th St
(83851) 208.686.1310

● Pocatello ●
Best Western ($$)
745 S 5th Ave
(83201) 208.233.5530
small pets only

Best Western ($$$)
1415 Bench Rd
(83201) 208.237.7650
managers discretion

Comfort Inn ($$)
1333 Bench Rd
(83201) 208.237.8155
mgr preapproval reqd

Motel 6 ($)
291 W Burnside Ave
(83202) 208.237.7880
1 small pet/room

Nendels Inn ($)
4333 Yellowstone Ave
(83202) 208.237.3100
$25 deposit + $5 fee

Quality Inn ($$$)
1555 Pocatello Creek Rd
(83201) 208.233.2200
mgr preapproval reqd

Super 8 ($$)
1330 Bench Rd
(83201) 208.234.0888
$2 fee

Thunderbird Motel ($)
1415 S 5th Ave
(83201) 208.232.6330

● Post Falls ●
Best Western ($$)
414 E 1st Ave
(83854) 208.773.1611

Suntree Inn ($$)
W 3705 5th Ave
(83854) 208.773.4541

● Preston ●
Deer Cliff Inn ($)
2106 N Deercliff Rd
(83263) 208.852.0643

● Priest River ●
Hills Resort ($$$)
HC 5 Box# 162A
(83856) 208.443.2551

Selkirk Motel ($)
RR 3 Box# 441
(83856) 208.448.1112

● Rexburg ●
Best Western ($$)
450 W 4th
(83440) 208.356.4646
mgrs discretion

Calaway Motel ($)
361 S 2nd
(83440) 208.356.3217

Days Inn ($$)
271 S 2nd
(83440) 208.356.9222

Rex Motel ($)
357 W 400
(83440) 208.356.5477

● Riggins ●
Bruce Motel ($)
Box# 208
(83549) 208.628.3005

Riggins Motel ($)
Box# 1157
(83549) 208.628.3001

Taylor Motel ($)
206 S Main St
(83549) 208.628.3914

● Rogerson ●
Desert Hot Spgs Motel ($)
General Delivery
(83302) 208.857.2233

● Rupert ●
Flamingo Lodge
RR 1 Box# 227
(83350) 208.436.4321

Uptown Motel ($)
Hwy 24
(83350) 208.546.4036

● Sagle ●
Country Inn ($)
7360 Hwy 95
(83860) 208.263.3333

● St. Maries ●
Benewah Resort ($)
Rt 1 Box# 50
(83861) 208.245.3288

● Salmon ●
Motel De Luxe ($)
112 S Church St
(83467) 208.756.2231

Suncrest Motel ($)
705 S Challis St
(83467) 208.756.2294

Syringa Lodge ($$)
2000 Syringa Dr
(83467) 208.756.4424

Williams Lake Resort ($)
Box# 1150
(83467) 208.756.2007

● Sandpoint ●
Best Spa Motel ($)
521 N 3rd Ave
(83864) 208.263.3532

Bottle Bay Resort ($$)
1360 Bottle Bay Rd
(83864) 208.263.5916

Idaho Country Resort ($$$)
141 Idaho Country
(83864) 208.264.5505

K2 Motel ($)
501 N 4th Ave
(83864) 208.263.3441

Lakeside Inn ($$)
106 Bridge St
(83864) 208.263.3717
$10 per day

Monarch West Inn ($$)
Hwy 95N
(83864) 208.263.1222

Motel 16 ($)
317 S Marion Ave
(83864) 208.263.5323

Quality Inn ($$)
807 N 5th Ave
(83864) 208.263.2111

Super 8 ($)
3245 Hwy 95
(83864) 208.263.2210
pets w/permission

● Shoshone ●
Governors Mansion ($)
315 S Greenwood
(83352) 208.886.2858

● Silverton ●
Molly B Damm Motel ($)
Box# 481
(83867) 208.556.4391

Silver Leaf Motel ($)
Box# 151
(83867) 208.752.0222

● Soda Springs ●
Caribou Lodge Motel ($)
110 W 2nd
(83276) 208.547.3377

Lakeview Motel ($)
341 W 2nd
(83276) 208.547.4351

● Spirit Lake ●
Silver Beach Resort
8350 W Spirit Lake Rd
(83869) 208.632.4842

● Stanley ●
Creek Side Lodge ($$$)
Box# 110
(83278) 208.774.2213

Danners Log Cabin ($$)
Box# 196
(83278) 208.774.3539

Elk Mountain ($$)
Box# 115
(83278) 208.774.2202

Jerry Country Store ($$)
HC 67 Box# 300
(83278) 208.774.3566

Mountain Village ($$)
Box# 150
(83278) 208.774.3661

Redfish Lake Lodge ($$)
Box# 9
(83278) 208.774.3536

Stanley Outpost ($$)
P O Bx 131 Hwy 21
(83278) 208.774.3646

Triangle C Ranch ($$)
Box# 69
(83278) 208.774.2266

● Sun Valley ●
Clarion Hotel ($$)
600 N Main St
(83353) 208.726.5900
mgr preapproval reqd

Heidelberg Inn ($$)
Box# 5704
(83353) 208.724.5361

River Street Inn ($$$$)
Box# 182
(83353) 208.726.3611

● Swan Valley ●
South Fork Lodge ($$)
Box# 22
(83449) 208.483.2112

● Terreton ●
Bks Motel ($)
1073 E 1500
(83450) 208.663.4578

Haven Motel ($)
1079 E 1500
(83450) 208.663.4821

● Twin Falls ●
Comfort Inn ($$)
1893 Canyon Springs Rd
(83301) 208.734.7494
mgr preapproval reqd

Econo Lodge ($)
320 Main Ave
(83301) 208.733.8770

Flat Creek Motel ($$$)
1935 N US 89
(83301) 307.733.5276

Motel 3 ($)
248 2nd Ave
(83301) 208.733.5630

IDAHO, Twin Falls

Motel 6 ($)
1472 Blue Lakes Blvd
(83301) 208.734.3993
1 small pet/room

Prospector Motel ($)
155 Jackson St
(83301) 307.733.4858

Sassy Moose Inn
HC 362 Teton Village Rd
(83301) 307.733.1277

Shilo Inn ($$$)
1586 Blue Lakes Blvd
(83301) 208.733.7545

Western Motel
225 S Glenwood Box# 1569
(83301) 307.733.3291

Weston Inn ($)
906 Blue Lakes Blvd
(83301) 208.733.6095

● Wallace ●
Best Western ($$$)
100 Front St
(83873) 208.752.1252
$25 dep

Myles Motel ($)
Box# 1348
(83873) 208.556.4391

Stardust Motel ($$)
410 Pine St
(83873) 208.752.1213

● Weiser ●
Colonial Motel ($)
251 E Main St
(83672) 208.549.0150

Indianhead Motel ($)
747US Hwy 95
(83672) 208.549.0331

State Street Motel ($)
1279 State St
(83672) 208.549.1390

Illinois
● Altamont ●
Best Western ($)
I-70 Hwy 128
(62411) 618.483.6101
2 pet/smoking room

Super 8
RR 2
(62411) 618.483.6300
call re: fees

● Alton ●
Days Inn
1900 Hm Adams Pkwy
(62002) 618.463.0800
$10

Holiday Inn ($$$)
3800 Homer Adams Pkwy
(62002) 618.462.1220

Super 8
1800 Homer Adams Pkwy
(62002) 618.465.8888
call re: fees

● Anna ●
Anna Plaza Motel
150 E Vienna St
(62906) 618.883.5215

● Antioch ●
Best Western ($$)
350 Hwy 173
(60002) 847.395.3606
under 10 lbs

● Arcola ●
Best Western ($)
610 E Springfield Rd
(61910) 217.268.4000

Budget Host ($)
236 S Jacques St
(61910) 217.268.4971

● Arlington Heights ●
Best Western ($$)
948 E Northwest Hwy
(60004) 847.255.2900
mgr preapproval reqd

La Quinta Inn ($$)
1415 W Dundee Rd
(60004) 847.253.8777
call re: fees

Motel 6 ($$)
441 W Algonquin Rd
(60005) 847.253.8777
1 small pet/room

Motel 6 ($$)
441 W Algonquin Rd
(60005) 847.806.1230
1 small pet/room

Radisson Inn ($$)
75 W Algonquin Rd
(60005) 847.364.7600
small pets allowed

Red Roof Inn ($$)
22 W Algonquin Rd
(60005) 847.228.6650
fees/limits may apply

● Atlanta ●
Route 66 Motel
103 Empire St
(61723) 217.648.2322

● Aurora ●
Motel 6 ($)
2380 N Farnsworth Ave
(60504) 708.851.3600
1 small pet/room

Riverwalk Inn
77 S Stolp Ave
(60506) 708.892.0001

● Barrington ●
Barrington Motor Lodge ($$)
405 W Northwest Hwy
(60010) 847.381.2640

Days Inn ($$)
405 W Northwest Hwy 14
(60010) 847.381.2640
$5

● Beardstown ●
Super 8
Hwy 67 & 100
(62618) 217.323.5858
call re: fees

● Belleville ●
Cinderalla Motel
1438 Centreville Ave
(62220) 618.233.7410

Days Inn ($$)
2120 W Main St
(62226) 618.234.9400

Executive Inn
1234 Centreville Ave
(62220) 618.233.1234

Scott Lodge
1651 Old Hwy 158
(62221) 618.744.1244

● Benton ●
Benton Gray Plaza
706 W Main St
(62812) 618.439.3113

Days Inn ($$)
711 W Main St
(62812) 618.439.3183

● Bloomington ●
Best Inns ($)
1905 W Market St
(61701) 309.827.5333

Days Inn ($$)
1803 E Empire St
(61704) 309.663.1361
pet fee

Days Inn ($$)
1707 W Market St
(61701) 309.829.6292

Howard Johnson ($)
401 Brock Dr
(61701) 309.829.3100

Jumers Chateau ($$$)
1601 Jumer Dr
(61704) 309.662.2020

Ramada Inn ($$)
1219 Holiday Ln
(61704) 309.662.5311

Ramada Inn ($)
403 Brock Dr
(61701) 309.829.7602
$5 fee

Rodway Inn ($$)
2419 Springfield Rd
(61701) 309.828.1505

Super 8 ($$)
818 La A Dr
(61701) 309.663.2388
w/permission

● Bourbonnais ●
Lees Inn
1500 N Rt 50
(60914) 815.932.8080

Chicago, ILLINOIS

Motel 6 ($)
Illinois Rt 50
(60914) 815.933.2300
1 small pet/room

Northgate Motel
Rt 50
(60914) 815.933.8261

● Bradley ●
Ramada Inn ($$)
800 N Kinzie Ave
(60915) 815.939.3501

● Braidwood ●
Sands Motel
1179 W Kennedy Rd
(60408) 815.458.3401

● Breese ●
Knotty Pine Hotel
Old Rt 50
(62230) 618.526.4556

● Bridgeview ●
Exel Inn ($$)
9625 S 76th Ave
(60455) 708.430.1818
under 65 lbs

● Bureau ●
Ranch House Lodge
Rt 26 & 29
(61315) 815.659.3361

● Bushnell ●
Bushnell Inn
Rt 41
(61422) 309.772.3172

● Cairo ●
Days Inn ($)
RR 1 Box# 10
(62914) 618.734.0215
$5

Meltons Fishing Camp ($)
Rural Route
(62914) 618.776.5504

Plaza Motel
3705 Sycamore St
(62914) 618.734.2102

● Canton ●
Siesta Motel
Rt 9
(61520) 309.647.1915

● Carbondale ●
Best Inns ($)
1345 E Main St
(62901) 618.529.4801
small pets only

Holiday Inn ($$)
800 E Main St
(62901) 618.529.1100
mgr preapproval reqd

Knights Inn ($)
3000 W Main St
(62901) 618.529.2424
size limits & fees

Relax Inn
700 E Main St
(62901) 618.549.0889

Super 8 ($$)
1180 E Main St
(62901) 618.457.8822
pets w/permission & sign
agreement

● Carlinville ●
Bel Aire Motel
915 E 1st South St
(62626) 217.854.3287

Carlis Villa Motel ($)
Hwy 4 South
(62626) 217.854.3201

Holiday Inn ($$)
I-55 & Rt 108
(62626) 217.324.2100
mgr preapproval reqd

● Carthage ●
Prairie Winds Motel
Hwy 136 West
(62321) 217.357.3101

● Casey ●
Comfort Inn ($$)
I-70 & Rt 49
(62420) 217.932.2212
mgr preapproval reqd

● Caseyville ●
Best Inns ($$)
2423 Old Country Inn Dr
(62232) 618.397.3300

● Centralia ●
Bell Tower Inn ($$)
200 E Noleman St
(62801) 618.533.1300

● Champaign ●
Budgetel ($$)
302 W Anthony Dr
(61821) 217.356.8900

Campus Inn ($)
1701 S State St
(61820) 217.359.8888

Chancellor Hotel ($$)
1501 S Neil St
(61820) 217.352.7891

Comfort Inn ($$)
305 W Marketview Dr
(61821) 217.352.4055
mgr preapproval reqd

Fairfield Inn ($$)
1807 Moreland Blvd
(61821) 217.355.0604

Howard Johnson ($)
1505 N Neil St
(61820) 217.359.1601

La Quinta Inn ($$)
1 900 Center Dr
(61820) 217.356.4000
call re: fees

Red Roof Inn ($)
212 W Anthony Dr
(61821) 217.352.0101

Super 8 ($$)
202 W Marketview Dr
(61820) 217.359.2388
w/permission

● Chester ●
Hi 3 Motel
Rt 3
(62233) 618.826.4415

● Chicago ●
Blackstone Hotel ($$$)
636 S Michigan Ave
(60605) 312.427.4300

Claridge Hotel ($$$)
1244 N Dearborn St
(60610) 312.787.4980

Essex Inn ($$$)
800 S Michigan Ave
(60605) 312.939.2800

Howard Johnson ($$$)
720 N Lasalle St
(60610) 312.664.8100

Marriott Hotel ($$$)
8535 W Higgins Rd
(60631) 312.693.4444
not too large

Motel 6 ($$$)
162 E Ontario St
(60611) 312.787.3580
1 small pet/room

Palmer House Hilton ($$$$)
17 E Monroe St
(60603) 312.726.7500
sign waiver & not use
elevator

Radisson Inn ($$$$$)
1300 N State Pkwy
(60610) 800.333.3333

Residence Inn ($$$$)
201 E Walton St
(60611) 312.943.9800
$50 fee & $5/day

Spa Motel
5414 N Lincoln Ave
(60625) 312.561.0313

Stutton Place Hotel ($$$$$)
21 E Vellevue Pl
(60611) 312.266.2100

Surf Hotel Neighborhood
Inns ($$$)
555 W Surf St
(60657) 312.528.8400

The Four Seasons ($$$$)
120 E Delaware Pl
(60611) 312.280.8800
small pets allowed

ILLINOIS, Chicago

The Raphael Hotel ($$$$)
201 E E Delaware Pl
(60611) 312.943.5000

The Ritz Carlton ($$$$)
160 E Pearson St
(60611) 312.266.1000
small pets allowed

Treamont Hotel ($$$$)
100 E Chestnut St
(60611) 312.751.1900

Westin Hotel ($$$$)
909 N Michigan Ave
(60611) 312.943.7200
small pets accepted

Chicago Metro
● Arlington Heights ●
Best Western ($$)
948 E Northwest Hwy
(60004) 847.255.2900
mgr preapproval reqd

La Quinta Inn ($$)
1415 W Dundee Rd
(60004) 847.253.8777
call re: fees

Motel 6 ($$)
441 W Algonquin Rd
(60005) 847.253.8777
1 small pet/room

Motel 6 ($$)
441 W Algonquin Rd
(60005) 847.806.1230
1 small pet/room

Radisson Inn ($$)
75 W Algonquin Rd
(60005) 847.364.7600
small pets allowed

Red Roof Inn ($$)
22 W Algonquin Rd
(60005) 847.228.6650
fees/limits may apply

● Bridgeview ●
Exel Inn ($$)
9625 S 76th Ave
(60455) 708.430.1818
under 65 lbs

● Chicago ●
Blackstone Hotel ($$$)
636 S Michigan Ave
(60605) 312.427.4300

Claridge Hotel ($$$)
1244 N Dearborn St
(60610) 312.787.4980

Essex Inn ($$$)
800 S Michigan Ave
(60605) 312.939.2800

Howard Johnson ($$$)
720 N Lasalle St
(60610) 312.664.8100

Marriott Hotel ($$$)
8535 W Higgins Rd
(60631) 312.693.4444
not too large

Motel 6 ($$$)
162 E Ontario St
(60611) 312.787.3580
1 small pet/room

Palmer House Hilton ($$$$)
17 E Monroe St
(60603) 312.726.7500
sign waiver & not use
elevator

Radisson Inn ($$$$)
1300 N State Pkwy
(60610) 800.333.3333

Residence Inn ($$$$)
201 E Walton St
(60611) 312.943.9800
$50 fee & $5/day

Spa Motel
5414 N Lincoln Ave
(60625) 312.561.0313

Stutton Place Hotel ($$$$)
21 E Vellevue Pl
(60611) 312.266.2100

Surf Hotel Neighborhood
Inns ($$$)
555 W Surf St
(60657) 312.528.8400

The Four Seasons ($$$$)
120 E Delaware Pl
(60611) 312.280.8800
small pets allowed

The Raphael Hotel ($$$$)
201 E E Delaware Pl
(60611) 312.943.5000

The Ritz Carlton ($$$$)
160 E Pearson St
(60611) 312.266.1000
small pets allowed

Treamont Hotel ($$$$)
100 E Chestnut St
(60611) 312.751.1900

Westin Hotel ($$$$)
909 N Michigan Ave
(60611) 312.943.7200
small pets accepted

● Crystal Lake ●
Super 8 ($$)
577 Crystal Point Dr
(60014) 815.455.2388
w/permission

● De Kalb ●
Motel 6 ($)
1116 W Lincoln Hwy
(60115) 815.756.3398
1 small pet/room

Unviersity Inn
1212 W Lincon Hwy
(60115) 815.758.8861

● Deerfield ●
Embassy Suites ($$$$)
1445 Lake Cook Rd
(60015) 847.945.4500

Marriott Hotel ($$$$)
2 Parkway
(60015) 847.405.9666

Residence Inn ($$$$)
530 Lake Cook Rd
(60015) 847.940.4644
$25 fee plus $6 per day

● Des Plaines ●
Holiday Inn
5440 N River Rd
(60018) 847.671.6350

● Downers Grove ●
Marriott Hotel ($$$)
1500 Opus Pl
(60515) 708.852.1500

Radison Suite Hotel ($$$)
2111 Butterfield Rd
(60515) 708.971.2000
small pets allowed

Red Roof Inn ($$)
1113 Butterfield Rd
(60515) 708.963.4205
fees/limits may apply

● Elk Grove Village ●
Days Inn ($$)
1920 E Higgins Rd
(60007) 708.437.1650

Exel Inn ($$)
1000 W Devon Ave
(60007) 847.894.2085
small pets only on first floor

Exel Inn ($$)
2881 Touhy Ave
(60007) 847.803.9400
small pets only

Holiday Inn ($$$)
1000 Busse Rd
(60007) 847.437.6010
mgr preapproval reqd

La Quinta Inn ($$$)
1900 Oakton
(60007) 847.439.6767
call re: fees

Motel 6 ($)
1601 Oakton St
(60007) 847.981.9766
1 small pet/room

Sheraton Inn ($$$)
121 NW Point Blvd
(60007) 847.290.1600
$25 fee

● Elmhurst ●
Holiday Inn ($$$)
624 N York Rd
(60126) 708.279.1100
mgr preapproval reqd

● Evanston ●
Homestead Hotel
1625 Hinman Ave
(60201) 847.475.3300

• Glen Ellyn •
Holiday Inn ($$)
1250 Roosevelt Rd
(60137) 708.629.6000
mgr preapproval reqd

• Glenview •
Budgetel ($$)
1625 Milwaukee Ave
(60025) 847.635.8300

Motel 6 ($)
1535 Milwaukee Ave
(60025) 847.390.7200
1 small pet/room

• Hazel Crest •
Days Inn ($$)
17220 Halsted St
(60429) 708.957.5900
mgr preapproval reqd

Motel 6 ($)
17214 Halsted St
(60429) 708.957.9233
1 small pet/room

• Highland •
Cardinal Inn
101 Walnut St
(62249) 618.654.4433

• Hillside •
Holiday Inn
4400 Frontage Rd
(60162) 708.544.9300

• Hinsdale •
Budgetel ($$)
855 79th St
(60521) 708.654.0077

Holiday Inn ($$$)
7800 Kingery Hwy
(60521) 630.325.6400
1st floor only

Red Roof Inn ($$)
7535 Kingery Hwy
(60521) 708.323.8811
fees/limits may apply

• Hoffman Estates •
Budgetel ($$)
2075 Barrington Rd
(60195) 847.882.8848
call for fees & size
restrictions

La Quinta Inn ($$)
2280 Barrington Rd
(60195) 847.882.3312
call re: fees

Red Roof Inn ($)
2500 Hassell Rd
(60195) 847.885.7877
fees/limits may apply

• Itasca •
Holiday Inn
860 W Irving Park Rd
(60143) 630.773.2340

• Joliet •
Days Inn ($$)
19747 Frontage Rd
(60435) 815.725.2180

Fairfield Inn ($$)
3239 Norman Ave
(60431) 800.348.6000

Manor Motel
32926 E Eames
(60436) 815.467.5385

Motel 6 ($)
1850 McDonough St
(60436) 815.729.2800
1 small pet/room

Red Roof Inn ($$)
1750 McDonough St
(60436) 815.741.2304
$3 charge

• La Grange Highlands •
J C Countryside Motel
6401 Joliet Rd
(60525) 708.352.3113

• Lake Forest •
The Deer Path Inn
255 E Illinois Rd
(60045) 847.234.2280

• Lansing •
Holiday Inn
17356 Torrence Ave
(60438) 708.474.6300
mgr preapproval reqd

Red Roof Inn ($)
2450 173Rd St
(60438) 708.895.9570
fees/limits may apply

• Lincolnshire •
Hawthorn Suites ($$$)
10 Westminster Way
(60069) 847.945.9300

Marriott Resort ($$$$)
10 Marriott Dr
(60069) 857.634.0100
small on 1st floor in carrier

• Lisle •
Hilton ($$$)
3003 Corporate West Dr
(60532) 708.505.0900

• Lombard •
Residence Inn ($$$$)
2001 S Highland Ave
(60148) 708.629.7800
call for fee & availability

• Midlothian •
Hampton Inn
13330 Cicero Ave
(60445) 708.597.3330

• Morris •
Comfort Inn ($$)
70 Gore Rd
(60450) 815.942.1433

Holiday Inn ($$)
I-80
(60450) 815.942.6600

• Mundelein •
Super 8 ($$)
1950 S Lake St
(60060) 847.949.8842
show pets allowed

• Naperville •
Days Inn ($$)
1350 E Ogden Ave
(60563) 708.369.3600
mgr preapproval reqd

Exel Inn ($$)
1585 Naperville Wheaton
(60563) 708.357.0022
small pets only

Red Roof Inn ($)
1698 W Diehl Rd
(60563) 708.369.2500
fees/limits may apply

• North Aurora •
Howard Johnson ($$)
306 S Lincolnway St
(60542) 708.892.6481

• Northbrook •
Red Roof Inn ($$)
340 Waukegan Rd
(60062) 847.205.1755
fees/limits may apply

• Palatine •
Motel 6 ($)
1450 E Dundee Rd
(60067) 708.359.0046
1 small pet/room

Ramada Inn ($$)
920 E Northwest Hwy
(60067) 847.359.6900
minature & leashed at all
times

Red Gables Motel
875 W Northwest Hwy
(60067) 847.358.3443

• Prospect Heights •
Exel Inn ($)
540 N Milwaukee Ave
(60070) 847.459.0545
small pets only

Forest Lodge ($)
1246 River Rd
(60070) 847.537.2000

• Rosemont •
Clarion Hotel ($$$)
6810 Mannheim Rd
(60018) 847.297.1234
mgr preapproval reqd

Hotel Sofitel ($$$$)
5550 N River Rd
(60018) 847.678.4488

Marriott Hotel ($$$)
6155 N River Rd
(60018) 847.696.4400

• Schaumburg •
Corporate Suites
1813 Hemlock Pl
(60173) 847.397.8021

ILLINOIS, Chicago Metro

Drury Inn ($$$)
600 N Martingale Rd
(60173) 847.517.7737

Homewood Suites ($$$)
815 American Ln
(60173) 847.605.0400

La Quinta Inn ($$)
1730 E Higgins Rd
(60173) 847.517.8484
call re: fees

Marriott Hotel ($$$)
50 N Martingale Rd
(60173) 847.240.0100

Summerfield Suites
901 E Woodfield Office Ct
(60173) 847.619.6677

● Schiller Park ●
Howard Johnson ($$$)
10249 Irving Park Rd
(60176) 708.671.6000

Motel 6 ($$)
9408 Lawrence Ave
(60176) 847.671.4282
1 small pet/room

Residence Inn ($$$$)
9450 Lawrence Ave
(60176) 847.678.2210
$100 fee

● Skokie ●
Hilton ($$$$)
9599 Skokie Blvd
(60077) 847.679.7000
$450 cash deposit

Holiday Inn ($$$)
5300 Touhy Ave
(60077) 847.679.8900
mgr preapproval reqd

Howard Johnson ($$$)
9333 Skokie Blvd
(60077) 847.679.4200

● South Holland ●
Budgetel ($$)
17225 Halsted St
(60473) 708.596.8700

Red Roof Inn ($$)
17301 Halsted St
(60473) 708.331.1621
fees/limits may apply

● Waukegan ●
Airport Inn
3651 N Lewis Ave
(60087) 708.249.7777

Best Inns ($$)
31 N Green Bay Rd
(60085) 847.336.9000

Best Western ($$)
411 S Green Bay Rd
(60085) 847.244.6100

Slumberland Motel
3030 Belvidere Rd
(60085) 847.623.6830

Travelodge ($$)
222 Grand Ave
(60085) 847.244.8950

● Woodstock ●
Bundling Board Inn
220 E South St
(60098) 815.338.7054

Concord Country Inn
1122 Cass St
(60098) 815.338.1100

End of Chicago Metro

● Cicero ●
Budgetel ($$)
1208 S Cicero Ave
(60804) 708.597.3900

● Clarendon Hills ●
Mayflower Motel
407 Ogden Ave
(60514) 708.325.2500

● Clinton ●
Days Inn ($$)
US 51 Bypass
(61727) 217.935.4140

Town & Country Motel ($)
1151 Rt 54W
(61727) 217.935.2121

Wye Motel ($)
Rt 54 & 10
(61727) 217.935.3373

● Cobden ●
Black Diamond Ranch
RR 3
(62920) 618.833.7629

● Collinsville ●
Best Western ($)
Rt 159
(62234) 618.345.5720
small pets

Days Inn ($$)
1803 Ramada Blvd
(62234) 618.345.8100

Howard Johnson ($)
301 N Bluff Rd
(62234) 618.345.1530

Innkeeper Motel
I-55-Rt 140
(62234) 618.633.2111

Motel 6 ($)
295A N Bluff Rd
(62234) 618.345.2100
1 small pet/room

Pear Tree Inn ($$)
552 Ramada Blvd
(62234) 618.345.9500

Super 8 ($$)
2 Gateway Dr
(62234) 618.345.8008
attended & in carrier

● Crystal Lake ●
Super 8 ($$)
577 Crystal Point Dr
(60014) 815.455.2388
w/permission

● Danville ●
Best Western ($$)
57 S Gilbert St
(61832) 217.431.0200
small pets only

Best Western ($$)
360 Eastgate Dr
(61834) 217.446.2111
mgr discretion

Comfort Inn ($$)
383 Lynch Dr
(61834) 217.443.8004
mgr preapproval reqd

Fairfield Inn ($$)
389 Lunch Rd
(61832) 217.443.3388

Glo Motel ($)
3617 N Vermilion St
(61832) 217.442.2086

Ramada Inn ($$)
338 Eastgate Dr
(61834) 217.446.2400

Redwood Motor Inn ($)
411 Lynch Dr
(61834) 217.443.3690

Super 8 ($$)
377 Lynch Dr
(61834) 217.443.4499
call re: fees

● De Kalb ●
Motel 6 ($)
1116 W Lincoln Hwy
(60115) 815.756.3398
1 small pet/room

Unviersity Inn
1212 W Lincon Hwy
(60115) 815.758.8861

● Decatur ●
Best Western ($$)
450 E Pershing Rd
(62526) 217.877.7255
$25 dep

Budgetel ($)
5100 Hickory Point
(62526) 217.875.5800

Days Inn ($$)
333 N Wyckles Rd
(62522) 217.422.5900

Fairfield Inn ($$)
1417 Hickory Point Dr
(62526) 217.875.3337

Green Valley Motel
145 W Pershing Rd
(62526) 217.877.3123

Be Discreet

Hampton Inn ($$)
1429 Hickory Point Dr
(62526) 217.877.5577

Holiday Inn ($$$)
US 36W & Wyckles Rd
(62522) 217.422.8800
mgr preapproval reqd

Intown Motel
1013 E Eldorado St
(62521) 217.422.9080

Red Carpet Inn ($)
3035 N Water St
(62526) 217.877.3380

Super 8 ($$)
3141 Water St
(62526) 217.877.8888
w/permission

● Deerfield ●
Embassy Suites ($$$$)
1445 Lake Cook Rd
(60015) 847.945.4500

Marriott Hotel ($$$$)
2 Parkway
(60015) 847.405.9666

Residence Inn ($$$$)
530 Lake Cook Rd
(60015) 847.940.4644
$25 fee plus $6 per day

● Des Plaines ●
Holiday Inn
5440 N River Rd
(60018) 847.671.6350

● Dix ●
Scottish Inn
I-57
(62830) 618.266.7254

● Dixon ●
Best Western ($$)
443 State Route 2
(61021) 815.284.1890
$25 pet dep

● Downers Grove ●
Marriott Hotel ($$$)
1500 Opus Pl
(60515) 708.852.1500

Radison Suite Hotel ($$$)
2111 Butterfield Rd
(60515) 708.971.2000
small pets allowed

Red Roof Inn ($$)
1113 Butterfield Rd
(60515) 708.963.4205
fees/limits may apply

● Dwight ●
Super 8 ($$)
14 E Northbrook Dr
(60420) 815.584.1888
$25 dep

● East Dubuque ●
L & L Motel
20170 Rt 20
(61025) 815.747.3931

● East Moline ●
Super 8 ($$)
2201 John Deere Rd
(61244) 309.796.1999
call re: fees

● East Peoria ●
Budget Host ($)
300 N Main St
(61611) 609.694.4261
ltd pets

Motel 6 ($)
104 W Camp St
(61611) 309.699.7281
1 small pet/room

Super 8 ($$)
725 Taylor St
(61611) 309.698.8889
w/permission

● East St. Louis ●
Lakeside Motel
4300 Missouri Ave
(62207) 618.874.4700

● Effingham ●
Abe Lincoln Motel
Jct 32 33 34
(62401) 217.342.4717

Anthony Acres Resort
RR 2
(62401) 217.868.2950

Best Inns ($)
1209 N Keller Dr
(62401) 217.347.5141

Best Western ($$)
I-57 & I-70
(62401) 217.342.4121
smoking rooms

Budget Host ($)
N Rt 45 At I-57 & 70
(62401) 217.342.4133

Budgetel ($)
1103 Ave Of Mid-America
(62401) 217.342.2525

Days Inn ($)
1412 W Fayette Ave
(62401) 217.342.9271

Econo Lodge ($$)
1205 N Keller Dr
(62401) 217.347.7131

Effingham Motel
702 E Fayette Ave
(62401) 217.342.3991

Hampton Inn ($$)
1509 Hampton Dr
(62401) 217.342.4499

Holiday Inn
1600 W Fayette Ave
(62401) 217.342.4161

Howard Johnson ($)
1606 W Fayette Ave
(62401) 217.342.4667

Knights Inn ($)
1000 W Fayette Ave
(62401) 217.342.2165

Ramada Inn ($$)
I-57 & I-70 Rt 32/33
(62401) 217.342.2131

Super 8 ($$)
1400 Thelma Keller Ave
(62401) 217.342.6888
pets allowed

● El Paso ●
Super 8 ($$)
880 S Main
(61738) 309.527.4949
call re: fees

● Elizabeth ●
Zeals Country Motel
2 Rt 20
(61028) 815.858.2205

● Elk Grove Village ●
Days Inn ($$)
1920 E Higgins Rd
(60007) 708.437.1650

Exel Inn ($$)
1000 W Devon Ave
(60007) 847.894.2085
small pets only on first floor

Exel Inn ($$)
2881 Touhy Ave
(60007) 847.803.9400
small pets only

Holiday Inn ($$$)
1000 Busse Rd
(60007) 847.437.6010
mgr preapproval reqd

La Quinta Inn ($$$)
1900 Oakton
(60007) 847.439.6767
call re: fees

Motel 6 ($)
1601 Oakton St
(60007) 847.981.9766
1 small pet/room

Sheraton Inn ($$$)
121 NW Point Blvd
(60007) 847.290.1600
$25 fee

● Elmhurst ●
Holiday Inn ($$$)
624 N York Rd
(60126) 708.279.1100
mgr preapproval reqd

● Evanston ●
Homestead Hotel
1625 Hinman Ave
(60201) 847.475.3300

● Fairview Heights ●
Best Western ($$)
311 Salem Pl
(62208) 618.624.3636
under 20 lbs

ILLINOIS, Fairview Heights

Drury Inn ($$)
12 Ludwig Dr
(62208) 618.398.8530

Fairfield Inn ($$)
140 Ludwig Dr
(62208) 618.398.7124

Hampton Inn ($$)
150 Ludwig Dr
(62208) 618.397.9705

Ramada Inn ($$)
6900 N Illinois St
(62208) 618.632.4747

Super 8 ($$)
45 Ludwig Dr
(62208) 618.398.8338
sign waiver

Trailway Motel
10039 Lincoln Trl
(62208) 618.397.5757

● Farmer City ●
Budget Motel
Rt 54
(61842) 309.928.2157

Days Inn ($$)
I-7J & Rt 54
(61842) 309.928.9434
w/permission $5/day

● Forsyth ●
Comfort Inn ($$)
134 Barnett Ave
(62535) 217.875.1166

● Freeburg ●
Gabriel Motel
600 N State St
(62243) 618.539.5588

● Freeport ●
Best Western ($$)
109 S Galena Ave
(61032) 815.233.0300
mgr preapproval reqd

Countryside Motel ($)
1535 W Galena Ave
(61032) 815.232.6148

Town House Motel
1156 W Galena Ave
(61032) 815.232.2191

West Motel
2084 W Galena Ave
(61032) 815.232.4188

● Galena ●
Country Gardens
1000 3rd St
(61036) 815.777.3062

Exec Inn
305 N Main St
(61036) 815.777.9125

Traingle Motel
Rt 20 West
(61036) 815.777.2897

● Galesburg ●
Aarons Thrifty Motel
1777 Grand Ave
(61401) 309.343.2812

Comfort Inn ($$)
907 W Carl Sandburg Dr
(61401) 309.344.5445
mgr preapproval reqd

Jumers Inn ($$$)
260 S Soangetaha Rd
(61401) 309.343.7151

Motel 6 ($)
1475 N Henderson St
(61401) 309.344.2401
1 small pet/room

Ramada Inn ($$)
29 Public Sq
(61401) 309.343.9161

Regency Hotel
3282 N Henderson St
(61401) 309.344.1111

● Geneseo ●
Deck Plaza Motel ($)
2181 S Oakwood Ave
(61254) 309.944.4651

The Oakwood Motel ($)
225 US Hwy 6
(61254) 309.944.3696

● Gilman ●
Budget Host ($$)
723 S Crescent
(60938) 815.265.7261
limited availability

Days Inn ($$)
834 Hwy 24
(60938) 815.265.7283

Super 8 ($$)
1301 S Crescent St
(60938) 815.265.7000
call re: fees

● Glen Ellyn ●
Holiday Inn ($$)
1250 Roosevelt Rd
(60137) 708.629.6000
mgr preapproval reqd

● Glenview ●
Budgetel ($$)
1625 Milwaukee Ave
(60025) 847.635.8300

Motel 6 ($)
1535 Milwaukee Ave
(60025) 847.390.7200
1 small pet/room

● Golconda ●
San Damiano Retreat
Rt 1 Box# 106
(62938) 618.285.3507

● Granite City ●
Best Western ($$)
1240 Old Chain Rock
(62040) 618.931.2262
small pets only w/$10 deposit

Chain Of Rocks Motel
3228 W Chain Of Rocks Rd
(62040) 618.931.6660

Granite City Lodge
1200 19th St
(62040) 618.876.2600

Illni Motel
1100 Miedringhuas Ave
(62040) 618.877.7100

● Greenup ●
Five Star Motel
US Rt 40 & Rt 130
(62428) 217.923.5512

Gateway Inn Motel
716 E Elizabeth St
(62428) 217.923.3176

● Greenville ●
2 Acres Motel
I-70 & Rt 127
(62246) 618.664.3131

Budget Host ($)
I-70 & Rt 127
(62246) 618.664.1950
extra chg

Prairie House Inn
RR 4 Box# 47Aa
(62246) 618.664.3003

Uptown Motel
323 S 3rd St
(62246) 618.664.3121

● Gurnee ●
Adventure Inns
3732 Grand Ave
(60031) 847.623.7777

Hamtpon Inn ($$$)
5550 Grand Ave
(60031) 847.662.1100

● Harrisburg ●
Plaza Motel
411 E Popar St
(62946) 618.253.7651

Super 8 ($$)
100 Seright St
(62946) 800.800.8000
call re: fees

● Havana ●
Red Lion Inn
136 Use
(62644) 309.543.4407
call re: fees

● Hazel Crest ●
Days Inn ($$)
17220 Halsted St
(60429) 708.957.5900
mgr preapproval reqd

Motel 6 ($)
17214 Halsted St
(60429) 708.957.9233
1 small pet/room

● Hecker ●
River Park Motel
RR 5
(62248) 618.783.2327

● Henry ●
Henry Harbor Inn
208 Cromwell Dr
(61537) 309.364.2365

● Herrin ●
Park Avenue Motel
900 N Park Ave
(62948) 618.942.3159

● Highland ●
Cardinal Inn
101 Walnut St
(62249) 618.654.4433

● Hillsboro ●
Manor Motel
1447 Vandalia Rd
(62049) 217.532.6144

● Hillside ●
Holiday Inn
4400 Frontage Rd
(60162) 708.544.9300

● Hinsdale ●
Budgetel ($$)
855 79th St
(60521) 708.654.0077

Holiday Inn ($$$)
7800 Kingery Hwy
(60521) 630.325.6400
1st floor only

Red Roof Inn ($$)
7535 Kingery Hwy
(60521) 708.323.8811
fees/limits may apply

● Hoffman Estates ●
Budgetel ($$)
2075 Barrington Rd
(60195) 847.882.8848
call for fees & size
restrictions

La Quinta Inn ($$)
2280 Barrington Rd
(60195) 847.882.3312
call re: fees

Red Roof Inn ($)
2500 Hassell Rd
(60195) 847.885.7877
fees/limits may apply

● Hoopeston ●
Downtown Motel
200 E Main St
(60942) 217.283.6605

● Itasca ●
Holiday Inn
860 W Irving Park Rd
(60143) 630.773.2340

● Jacksonville ●
Holiday Inn ($$)
1717 W Morton Ave
(62650) 217.245.9571
mgr preapproval reqd

Motel 6 ($)
1716 W Morton Ave
(62650) 217.243.7157
1 small pet/room

Star Lite Motel ($)
1910 W Morton Ave
(62650) 217.245.7184

● Johnston City ●
Farris Motel
Rt 37 Sout Box# 6
(62951) 618.983.8086

● Joliet ●
Days Inn ($$)
19747 Frontage Rd
(60435) 815.725.2180

Fairfield Inn ($$)
3239 Norman Ave
(60431) 800.348.6000

Manor Motel
32926 E Eames
(60436) 815.467.5385

Motel 6 ($)
1850 McDonough St
(60436) 815.729.2800
1 small pet/room

Red Roof Inn ($$)
1750 McDonough St
(60436) 815.741.2304
$3 charge

● Jonesboro ●
Trail Of Tears Res
RR 1 Old Cape Rd
(62952) 618.833.8697
call for limited availability

● Kankakee ●
Days Inn ($$)
1975 E Court St
(60901) 815.939.7171
mgr preapproval reqd

Fairfiew Courts
2745 S Rt 45-52
(60901) 815.933.7708

Model Motel
1245 S Washington Ave
(60901) 815.932.5013

● Keithsburg ●
The Keithsburg Motel
2nd & Main Sts
(61442) 309.374.2659

● Kewanee ●
Kewanee Motor Lodge ($$)
400 S Main St
(61443) 309.853.4000

● La Grange Highlands ●
J C Countryside Motel
6401 Joliet Rd
(60525) 708.352.3113

● La Salle ●
Howard Johnson ($$)
I-80 & IL251
(61301) 815.224.2500

● Lake Forest ●
The Deer Path Inn
255 E Illinois Rd
(60045) 847.234.2280

● Lansing ●
Holiday Inn
17356 Torrence Ave
(60438) 708.474.6300
mgr preapproval reqd

Red Roof Inn ($)
2450 173rd St
(60438) 708.895.9570
fees/limits may apply

● Le Roy ●
Super 8 ($$)
1 Demma Dr
(61752) 309.962.4700
$50 dep in smoking room

● Libertyville ●
Best Inns ($$)
1809 W Milwaukee Ave
(60048) 847.816.8006

● Lincoln ●
Crossroads Motel
1305 Woodlawn Rd
(62656) 217.735.5571

Days Inn ($)
I-55 Business City Rt
(62656) 217.735.1202

Holiday Inn
130 Olson Rd
(62656) 217.735.5800

Super 8 ($$)
2809 Woodlawn Rd
(62656) 217.732.8886
call re: fees

● Lincolnshire ●
Hawthorn Suites ($$$)
10 Westminster Way
(60069) 847.945.9300

Marriott Resort ($$$$)
10 Marriott Dr
(60069) 857.634.0100
small on 1st floor in carrier

● Lisle ●
Hilton ($$$)
3003 Corporate West Dr
(60532) 708.505.0900

● Litchfield ●
Best Western ($$)
413 Columbian Blvd
(62056) 217.324.2181
small pets only

Super 8 ($$)
I-55
(62056) 217.324.7788
pets w/permission

● Lombard ●
Residence Inn ($$$$)
2001 S Highland Ave
(60148) 708.629.7800
call for fee & availability

● Macomb ●
Macomb Inn ($$)
1400 N Lafayette St
(61455) 309.883.5511

● Mahomet ●
Heritage Inn Motel
I-74 & Rt 47
(61853) 217.586.4975

● Marion ●
Best Inns ($)
RR 8 Box# 70
(62959) 618.997.9421

Best Western ($$)
130 Express Dr
(62959) 618.993.3222

Courts Inn
110 S Court St
(62959) 618.993.8131

Gray Plaza Motel
New Rt 13
(62959) 618.993.2174

Holiday Inn
I-57 & Hwy 13
(62959) 618.997.2326

Motel 6 ($)
1008 Halfway Rd
(62959) 618.993.2631
1 small pet/room

Motel Marion
2100 W Main St
(62959) 618.993.2101

Olds Suqat Inn
RR 7 Box# 246
(62959) 618.982.2916

Shoneys Inn
I-57 & Rt 13
(62959) 618.997.7900

Super 8 ($$)
2601 W De Young St
(62959) 618.993.5577
pets w/permission

● Marshall ●
Lincoln Motel
US Rt 40
(62441) 217.826.2941

Peaks Motor Inn
I-70 Ex 147
(62441) 217.826.3031

● Mason City ●
Mason City Motel
701 W Chestnut St
(62664) 217.482.3003

● Matteson ●
Budgetel ($$)
5210 Southwick Dr
(60443) 708.503.0999

● Mattoon ●
Budget Inn
I-57 & Hwy 45 Ex 184
(61938) 217.235.4011

Howard Johnson ($$)
I-57 & Ex 184
(61938) 217.235.4161

Ramada Inn ($$)
300 Broadway Ave
(61938) 217.235.0313

US Grant Motel
Hwy 45
(61938) 217.235.5695

● Mc Lean ●
Super 8 ($$)
South St & Elm St
(61754) 309.874.2366
$50 depsoit & $3 per day

● Mendota ●
Super 8 ($$)
508 Hwy 34
(61342) 815.539.7429
pets w/permission

● Metropolis ●
Best Inns ($$)
2055 E 5th St
(62960) 618.524.8200

Metropolis Motel
Rts 45 & 24 Ex 37
(62960) 618.524.3723

● Midlothian ●
Hampton Inn
13330 Cicero Ave
(60445) 708.597.3330

● Moline ●
Comfort Inn ($)
2600 52nd Ave
(61264) 309.762.7000

Comfort Inn ($$)
2600 52nd Ave Moline
(61265) 309.762.7000
$5 night

Exel Inn ($)
2501 52nd Ave
(61265) 309.797.5580
small pets only

Fairfield Inn ($$)
2705 48th Ave
(61265) 309.762.9083
smoking rooms

Hampton Inn ($$)
6920 27th St
(61265) 309.762.1711

Holiday Inn
6902 27th St
(61265) 309.762.8811

Holiday Inn
6910 27th
(61265) 309.762.8300

La Quinta Inn ($$)
5450 27th St
(61265) 309.762.9008
call re: fees

Motel 6 ($)
Airport Road
(61265) 309.764.8711
1 small pet/room

● Monmouth ●
Melings Motel ($)
1129 N Main St
(61462) 309.734.2196

● Montrose ●
Motel Montarosa
I-70 Ex 105
(62445) 217.924.4117

● Morris ●
Comfort Inn ($$)
70 Gore Rd
(60450) 815.942.1433

Holiday Inn ($$)
I-80
(60450) 815.942.6600

● Morrison ●
Parkview Motel
15424 Lincoln Rd
(61270) 815.772.2163

● Morton ●
Holiday Inn
115 E Ashland
(61550) 309.266.8310

Howard Johnson ($)
128 Queenswood Rd
(61550) 309.263.2511

● Mount Prospect ●
Ramada Inn ($$$)
200 E Rand Rd
(60056) 847.255.8800

● Mount Sterling ●
Land Of Lincoln Motel
403 E Main St
(62353) 217.773.3311

● Mount Vernon ●
Best Inns ($)
222 S 44th St
(62864) 618.244.4343

Days Inn
750 - 10th
(62864) 618.244.3224
$3

Drury Inn ($$)
145 N 44th St
(62864) 618.244.4550

Holiday Inn ($$)
222 Potomac
(62864) 618.244.3670

Well
Behaved

Motel 6 ($)
333 S 44th St
(62864) 618.244.2383
1 small pet/room

Ramada Inn ($$)
222 Potomac Bld
(62864) 618.244.7100
$10/pets

Super 8 ($$)
401 S 44th St
(62864) 618.242.8800
pets w/permission

Thirfty Inn ($$)
100 N 44th St
(62864) 618.244.7750

● Muddy ●
Days Inn ($)
Rt 45 Box# 3
(62965) 618.252.6354

● Mundelein ●
Super 8 ($$)
1950 S Lake St
(60060) 847.949.8842
show pets allowed

● Murphysboro ●
Appletree Inn ($)
100 N 2nd St
(62966) 618.687.2345

● Naperville ●
Days Inn ($$)
1350 E Ogden Ave
(60563) 708.369.3600
mgr preapproval reqd

Exel Inn ($$)
1585 Naperville/Wheaton
(60563) 708.357.0022
small pets only

Red Roof Inn ($)
1698 W Diehl Rd
(60563) 708.369.2500
fees/limits may apply

● Nashville ●
Mill Creek Inn
560 N Mill St
(62263) 618.327.8424

U S Inn ($)
11640 Hwy 2M
(62263) 618.478.5341

● Nauvoo ●
Nauvoo Family Motel ($$)
150 N Warsaw
(62354) 217.453.6527

Nauvoo Village Inn ($)
1350 Farley St
(62354) 217.453.6634

● Niles ●
Days Inn ($$)
6450 W Touhy Ave
(60714) 847.647.7700

Travelodge ($$)
7247 N Waukegan Rd
(60714) 847.647.9444

● Normal ●
Best Western ($$)
6 Traders Cir
(61761) 309.454.4070
pets must be attended

Comfort Suites ($$$)
310-B Greenbriar Dr
(61761) 309.452.8588
mgr preapproval reqd

Holiday Inn ($$$)
8 Traders Cir
(61761) 309.452.8300
mgr preapproval reqd

Motel 6 ($)
1600 N Main St
(61761) 309.452.0422
1 small pet/room

● North Aurora ●
Howard Johnson ($$)
306 S Lincolnway St
(60542) 708.892.6481

● Northbrook ●
Red Roof Inn ($$)
340 Waukegan Rd
(60062) 847.205.1755
fees/limits may apply

● O Fallon ●
Comfort Inn ($$)
1100 Eastgate Dr
(62269) 618.624.6060
mgr preapproval reqd

Ramada Inn ($$)
1313 Central Park Dr
(62269) 800.272.6232

● Oak Forest ●
The Terrace Motel
15353 Cicero Ave
(60452) 708.687.7500

● Oakbrook Terrace ●
Hilton ($$$)
10 Drury Ln
(60181) 708.941.0100

● Oglesby ●
Holiday Inn
900 Holiday St
(61348) 815.883.3535

● Okawville ●
Original Min Sprgs
506 S Hanover St
(62271) 618.243.5458

Super 8 ($$)
I-64 & Rt 177
(62271) 618.243.6525
$20 dep w/permission

● Olney ●
Super 8 ($$)
Rt 130 & North Ave
(62450) 618.392.7888
call re: fees

● Oregon ●
Vip Motel ($)
1326 Il 2N
(61061) 815.732.6195

● Ottawa ●
Holiday Inn
120 W Stevenson
(61350) 815.433.0029

● Palatine ●
Motel 6 ($)
1450 E Dundee Rd
(60067) 708.359.0046
1 small pet/room

Ramada Inn ($$)
920 E Northwest Hwy
(60067) 847.359.6900
minature & leashed at all
times

Red Gables Motel
875 W Northwest Hwy
(60067) 847.358.3443

● Pana ●
Rose Bud Motel
RR 2 Jct 16 & 51
(62557) 217.562.3929

● Paris ●
Scottish Inn ($)
Hwy Rt 1 & 150
(61944) 217.465.6441

Super 8 ($$)
Hwy 150
(61944) 217.463.8888
call re: fees

● Pekin ●
Comfort Inn ($$)
2340 Vandever Ave
(61554) 309.353.4047
mgr preapproval reqd

Pekin Inn ($$)
2801 Court St
(61554) 309.347.5533

● Peoria ●
Comfort Suites ($$)
4021 N War Memorial Dr
(61614) 309.688.3800
mgr preapproval reqd

Days Inn ($$)
2726 W Lake Ave
(61615) 309.688.7000
mgr preapproval reqd

Holiday Inn ($$$)
500 Hamilton Blvd
(61602) 309.674.2500
mgr preapproval reqd

Holiday Inn ($$$)
4400 N Brandywine Dr
(61614) 309.686.8000
mgr preapproval reqd

Jumers Castle Lodge ($$$)
117 N Western Ave
(61604) 309.673.8040

Marquette Hotel ($$$)
501 Main St
(61602) 800.447.1676

Red Roof Inn ($$)
4031 N War Memorial Dr
(61614) 309.684.3911

Super 8 ($$)
4025 W War Memorial Dr
(61614) 309.688.8074
pets w/permission & sign
release

● Peru ●
Days Inn
I-80
(61354) 815.224.1060

Super 8 ($$)
1851 May Rd
(61354) 815.223.1848
w/permission

● Pinckneyville ●
Fountain Motel ($)
112 S Main St
(62274) 618.357.2128

● Pocahontas ●
Tahoe Motel
Rt 40 & I-70 Ex 36
(62275) 618.669.2404

Wikiup Motel
Plant & Johnson Sts
(62275) 618.669.2293

● Polo ●
Village Inn Motel
1007 S Division Ave
(61064) 815.946.2229

● Pontiac ●
Comfort Inn ($$)
1821 W Reynolds St
(61764) 815.842.2777
mgr preapproval reqd

Fiesta Motel
Rt 66 & 116
(61764) 815.844.7103

Palamar Motel
213 S Ladd St
(61764) 815.744.5191

Super 8 ($$)
601 Deerfield Rd
(61764) 815.844.6888
pets w/permission

● Princeton ●
Days Inn ($$)
2238 N Main St
(61356) 815.875.3371
$6

Princeton Motel ($)
I-80 & Rt 26
(61356) 815.875.1121

● Prophetstown ●
Prophet Motel
201 Washington St
(61277) 815.537.5333

● Prospect Heights ●
Exel Inn ($)
540 N Milwaukee Ave
(60070) 847.459.0545
small pets only

Forest Lodge ($)
1246 River Rd
(60070) 847.537.2000

● Quincy ●
Bel Aire Motel
2314 N 12th St
(62301) 217.223.1356

Comfort Inn ($$)
4100 Broadway
(62301) 217.228.2700
mgr preapproval reqd

Days Inn ($)
200 Maine St
(62301) 217.223.6610

Diamond Motel
4703 N 12th St
(62301) 217.223.1436

Fairfield Inn ($$)
4315 Broadway
(62301) 217.223.5922

Holiday Inn ($$)
201 S 3rd St
(62301) 217.222.2666
mgr preapproval reqd

Super 8 ($$)
224 N 36th St
(62301) 217.228.8808
w/permission

Travelodge ($$)
200 S 3rd St
(62301) 217.222.5620
small pets only

● Rantoul ●
Best Western ($$)
420 S Murray Rd
(61866) 217.892.9292
small pets only

Days Inn ($$)
801 W Champaign
(61866) 217.893.0700

● Red Bud ●
Red Bud Motel
1103 S Main St
(62278) 618.282.2123

● Richmond ●
Days Inn ($$)
11200 N Rt 12
(60071) 815.678.4711
mgr preapproval reqd

Drake Motel
8613 S Rt 12
(60071) 815.678.3501

● Robinson ●
Days Inn ($$)
1500 W Main St
(62454) 618.544.8448
$5 per day

● Rock Falls ●
Holiday Inn ($$)
2105 1st Ave
(61071) 815.626.5500
mgr preapproval reqd

Super 8
2100 1st Ave
(61071) 815.626.8800
call re: fees

● Rock Island ●
Plaza One Hotel ($$$)
17th At 3rd Ave
(61201) 309.794.1212

● Rockford ●
Airport Inn
4419 S 11th St
(61108) 815.397.4000

Apline Inn ($)
4404 E State St
(61108) 815.399.1890

Best Western ($$$)
4850 E State St
(61108) 815.398.5050
attended pets only

Exel Inn ($)
220 S Lyford Rd
(61108) 815.332.4915
small pets only

Motel 6 ($)
3851 11th St
(61109) 815.398.6080
1 small pet/room

Red Roof Inn ($)
7434 E State St
(61108) 815.398.9750
fees/limits may apply

Sixpence Inn ($)
4205 11th St
(61109) 815.398.0066
1 small pet per room

Super 8 ($$)
7646 Colosseum Dr
(61107) 815.229.5522
w/permission

Sweden House Lodge ($$)
4605 E State St
(61108) 815.398.4130

● Rolling Meadows ●
Motel 6 ($)
1800 Winnetka Cir
(60008) 847.818.8088
1 small pet/room

● Rosemont ●
Clarion Hotel ($$$)
6810 Mannheim Rd
(60018) 847.297.1234
mgr preapproval reqd

Hotel Sofitel ($$$$)
5550 N River Rd
(60018) 847.678.4488

Marriott Hotel ($$$)
6155 N River Rd
(60018) 847.696.4400

● Salem ●
Continental Motel ($)
Rt 50
(62881) 618.548.3090

Holiday Inn ($$)
1812 W Main St
(62881) 618.548.4212
mgr preapproval reqd

Motel Lakewood ($)
1500 E Main St
(62881) 618.548.2785

Restwell Motel
700 W Main St
(62881) 618.548.2040

Super 8 ($$)
118 Paragon Rd
(62881) 618.548.5882
pets w/permission

● Savanna ●
Indian Head Motel
3523 Rt 84
(61074) 815.273.2154

Motel 11
Rts 52 & 64
(61074) 815.273.7728

Pine Lodge Motel
2017 Chicago Ave
(61074) 815.273.2291

Radkey Hotel
422 Main St
(61074) 815.273.3713
limited rooms

● Savoy ●
Best Western ($$)
1001 N Dunlap St
(61874) 217.356.1824
restrictions apply

● Schaumburg ●
Corporate Suites
1813 Hemlock Pl
(60173) 847.397.8021

Drury Inn ($$$)
600 N Martingale Rd
(60173) 847.517.7737

Homewood Suites ($$$)
815 American Ln
(60173) 847.605.0400

La Quinta Inn ($$)
1730 E Higgins Rd
(60173) 847.517.8484
call re: fees

Marriott Hotel ($$$)
50 N Martingale Rd
(60173) 847.240.0100

Summerfield Suites
901 E Woodfield Office Ct
(60173) 847.619.6677

● Schiller Park ●
Howard Johnson ($$$)
10249 Irving Park Rd
(60176) 708.671.6000

Motel 6 ($$)
9408 Lawrence Ave
(60176) 847.671.4282
1 small pet/room

Residence Inn ($$$$)
9450 Lawrence Ave
(60176) 847.678.2210
$100 fee

● Sheffield ●
Days Inn ($)
I-80 & Rt 40 Ex 45
(61361) 815.454.2361
$5

Hidden Lake Club
Buda On Rt 40
(61361) 815.454.2603

● Shelbyville ●
Lithia Resort ($$)
RR 4 Box# 105
(62565) 217.774.2882

Spillway Motel
Hwy 16
(62565) 217.774.9591

● Skokie ●
Hilton ($$$$)
9599 Skokie Blvd
(60077) 847.679.7000
$450 cash deposit

Holiday Inn ($$$)
5300 Touhy Ave
(60077) 847.679.8900
mgr preapproval reqd

Howard Johnson ($$$)
9333 Skokie Blvd
(60077) 847.679.4200

● South Holland ●
Budgetel ($$)
17225 Halsted St
(60473) 708.596.8700

Red Roof Inn ($$)
17301 Halsted St
(60473) 708.331.1621
fees/limits may apply

● South Wilmington ●
Hampton Inn ($$)
18501 North Creek Rd
(60474) 708.633.0602

● Sparta ●
Poolside Motel
402 E Broadway St
(62286) 618.443.3187

Sparta Motel
700 S St. Louis St
(62286) 618.443.3614

● Spring Valley ●
Rivera Motel
I-80 & Rt 89
(61362) 815.894.2225

● Springfield ●
Best Inns ($$)
500 N 1st St
(62702) 217.522.1100

Best Western ($$)
101 E Adams St
(62701) 217.523.5661
$10/night

Capitol Plaza Hotel
418 E Jefferson St
(62701) 217.525.1700

Comfort Inn ($$)
3442 Freedom Dr
(62704) 217.787.2250
mgr preapproval reqd

Days Inn ($$)
3000 Stevenson Dr
(62703) 217.529.0171

Drury Inn ($$)
3180 S Dirksen Pkwy
(62703) 217.529.3900

Fairfield Inn ($$)
3446 Freedom Dr
(62704) 217.793.9277

Hilton ($$$)
700 E Adams St
(62701) 217.789.1530

Holiday Inn ($$$)
3100 S Dirksen Pkwy
(62703) 217.529.7171
mgr preapproval reqd

Mansion View Motel ($$)
529 S 4th St
(62701) 217.544.7411

Motel 6 ($)
3125 Wide Track Dr
(62703) 217.789.1063
1 small pet/room

Motel 6 ($)
6010 S 6th Street Rd
(62707) 217.529.1633
1 small pet/room

Park Inn Intl
3751 S Sixth St
(62703) 217.529.5511

Pear Tree Inn ($$)
3190 S Dirksen Pkwy
(62703) 217.529.9100

Ramada Inn ($$)
625 E St. Joseph St
(62703) 217.529.7131

Red Roof Inn ($)
3200 Singer Ave
(62703) 217.753.4302
fees/limits may apply

Super 8 ($$)
1330 S Dirksen Pkwy
(62703) 217.528.8889
pets w/permission & $20
deposit

Super 8 ($$)
3675 S 6th Street Rd
(62703) 217.529.8898
pets w/permission & deposit

CALL AHEAD!

171

ILLINOIS, Springfield

Travelodge ($)
1701 Jones Pkwy
(62702) 217.753.3446

● Staunton ●
Super 8 ($$)
832 E Main St
(62088) 618.635.5353
call re: fees

● Sullivan ●
Gateway Inn
S Hamilton
(61951) 217.728.4314

● Taylorville ●
29 West Motel ($)
709 W Springfield Rd
(62568) 217.824.2216

Ryans Inn
Rt 29 & 48 Bypass
(62568) 217.287.7211

● Tinley Park ●
Budgetel
7255 183rd St
(60477) 800.428.3438

● Troy ●
Scottish Inn ($)
909 Edwardsville Rd
(62294) 618.667.9969

● Tuscola ●
Super 8 ($$)
Rt 36 Box# 202
(61953) 217.253.5488
pets w/permission

● Ullin ●
Best Western ($)
I-57 Ex 18
(62992) 618.845.3773
small pets with approval of
mgr

● Urbana ●
Best Western ($$)
1907 N Cunningham Ave
(61802) 217.367.8331

Jumers Castle Lodge ($$$)
209 S Broadway Ave
(61801) 217.384.8800

Motel 6 ($)
1906 N Cunningham Ave
(61802) 217.344.1082
1 small pet/room

Park Inn Intl
2408 N Cunningham Ave
(61802) 217.344.8000

Ramada Inn ($$)
902 W Killarney St
(61801) 217.328.4400

● Vandalia ●
Days Inn ($)
Hwy 51
(62471) 618.283.4400
deposit reqd

Jays Motel ($)
I-70 P Rt 51
(62471) 618.283.1200

Ramada Ltd ($$)
Rt 40
(62471) 618.283.1400
$10 deposit

Travelodge ($$)
1500 N 6th St
(62471) 618.283.2363

● Villa Park ●
La Quinta Inn ($$)
1 S 666 Medwest Rd
(60181) 800.221.4731
call re: fees

Motel 6 ($$)
10 W Roosevelt Rd
(60181) 708.941.9100
1 small pet/room

● Washington ●
Crestview Motel
1216 Peoria St
(61571) 309.444.4421

Super 8 ($$)
1884 Washington Rd
(61571) 309.444.8881
$20 deposit

● Watseka ●
Carousel Inn Motel ($)
1120 E Walnut St
(60970) 815.432.4966

Super 8 ($$)
710 W Walnut St
(60970) 815.432.6000
w/permission

Watseka Motel
814 E Walnut St
(60970) 815.432.2426

● Waukegan ●
Airport Inn
3651 N Lewis Ave
(60087) 708.249.7777

Best Inns ($$)
31 N Green Bay Rd
(60085) 847.336.9000

Best Western ($$)
411 S Green Bay Rd
(60085) 847.244.6100

Slumberland Motel
3030 Belvidere Rd
(60085) 847.623.6830

Travelodge ($$)
222 Grand Ave
(60085) 847.244.8950

● Wenona ●
Super 8 ($$)
I-39 & Il 17 Ex 35
(61377) 815.853.4371
small w/ dep

● West Frankfort ●
Gray Plaza Motel
1010 W Main St
(62896) 618.932.3116

● Winthrop Harbor ●
Sandpiper Inn ($)
301 Sheridan Rd
(60096) 847.746.7380

● Wood River ●
Bel Air Motel
542 W Ferguson Ave
(62095) 618.254.0683

● Woodstock ●
Bundling Board & Breakfast
220 E South St
(60098) 815.338.7054

Concord Country Inn
1122 Cass St
(60098) 815.338.1100

Indiana

● Alexandria ●
Country Gazebo Inn
RR 1 Box# 323
(46001) 317.754.8783

● Anderson ●
Best Inns ($$)
5706 S Scatterfield Rd
(46013) 317.644.2000

Comfort Inn ($$)
2205 E 59th St
(46013) 765.644.4422

Holiday Inn ($$)
5920 S Scatterfield Rd
(46013) 765.644.2581

Lees Inn ($$)
2114 E 59th St
(46013) 317.649.2500

Ramada Inn ($$$)
5901 S Scatterfield Rd
(46013) 317.649.0451

● Auburn ●
Auburn Inn ($$)
225 Touring Dr
(46706) 800.255.2541

Holiday Inn
404 Touring Dr
(46706) 219.925.1900

● Bedford ●
Rosemount Motel ($)
1923 M St
(47421) 812.275.5953

● Bloomington ●
Best Western ($$)
4501 E 3rd St
(47401) 812.332.2141
under 20 lbs

Courtyard Inn ($)
4501 E 3rd St
(47401) 800.331.3131

Days Inn ($$)
200 E Matlock Rd
(47408) 812.336.0905

Hampton Inn ($$)
2100 N Walnut St
(47404) 800.426.7866

Motel 6 ($)
1800 N Walnut St
(47404) 812.332.0820
1 small pet/room

Ramada Ltd ($)
2601 N Walnut St
(47404) 812.332.9453

Super 8 ($$)
1000 W State Rd
(47401) 800.800.8000
mgr preapproval reqd

● Brazil ●
Howard Johnson ($)
935 W State Road 42
(47834) 812.446.2345

● Brookville ●
Sulina Farm
10052 US 52
(47012) 317.647.2955

● Carlisle ●
Super 8 ($)
Hwy 41
(47838) 812.398.2500
call re: fees

● Centerville ●
Super 8 ($$)
2407 N Centerville Rd
(47330) 317.855.5461
call re: fees

● Clarksville ●
Best Western ($$)
1425 Broadway St
(47129) 812.288.9281
mgr preapproval reqd

Best Western ($$)
1425 Broadway St
(47129) 800.528.1234
mgr preapproval reqd

Howard Johnson ($$)
342 Eastern Blvd
(47129) 812.282.7511

Motel 6 ($)
2016 Old Hwy 31
(47129) 612.283.7703
1 small pet/room

● Clinton ●
Renatto Inn ($)
Hwy 63 & 163
(47842) 317.832.3557

● Columbia City ●
Columbia City Motel ($)
500 Old US 30W
(46725) 219.244.5103

Lees Inn ($$)
235 Frontage Rd
(46725) 219.244.5300

● Corydon ●
Best Western ($$)
Hwy 135
(47112) 800.528.1234
mgr preapproval reqd

● Crawfordsville ●
General Lew Wallace Inn
($$)
309 W Pike St
(47933) 317.362.8400

Holiday Inn ($$)
2500 Lafayette Rd
(47933) 765.362.8700

Super 8 ($$)
1025 Corey Blvd
(47933) 317.364.9999
mgr preapproval reqd

● Dale ●
Scottish Inn ($)
I-64 & US 231
(47523) 812.937.2816
$5 fee

● Daleville ●
Super 8
I-69
(47334) 317.378.0888
call re: fees

● Decatur ●
Days Inn ($$)
1033 N 13th St
(46733) 219.728.2196
$3

● Elkhart ●
Diplomat Motel ($)
52162 Hwy 19N
(46514) 219.264.4118

Econo Lodge ($)
3440 Cassopolis St
(46514) 219.262.0540

Knights Inn ($)
52188 Hwy 19
(46514) 800.843.5644

Quality Hotel ($$)
300 S Main St
(46516) 219.295.0280
mgr preapproval reqd

Red Roof Inn ($)
2902 Cassopolis St
(46514) 800.843.7663

Super 8 ($)
345 E Windsor Ave
(46514) 800.800.8000
call re: fees

● Evansville ●
Comfort Inn ($$)
5006 E Morgan Ave
(47715) 812.477.2211

Days Inn ($$)
4819 Tecumsen Ln
(47715) 812.473.7944

Drury Inn ($$)
3901 US 41N
(47711) 800.325.8300

Lees Inn ($$)
5538 E Indiana St
(47715) 812.477.6663

Super 8 ($$)
4600 E Morgan Ave
(47715) 800.800.8000
call re: fees

● Fishers ●
Holiday Inn ($$)
9790 N By NE Blvd
(46038) 317.578.2000

Ramada Inn ($$$)
9780 N By NE Bird
(46038) 317.578.9000

● Fort Wayne ●
Best Inns ($)
3017 W Coliseum Blvd
(46808) 219.483.0091

Budgetel ($$)
1005 Washington Ctr
(46825) 219.489.2220

Comfort Inn ($$)
2908 Goshen Rd
(46808) 219.484.6262

Days Inn ($)
I-69 Ex 111A
(46825) 219.484.9681

Days Inn ($)
3730 E Washington Blvd
(46803) 219.424.1980
$4 per day

Economy Inn ($)
1401 Washington Ctr
(46825) 219.489.3588

Marriott ($$$)
305 Washington Ctr
(46825) 219.484.0411
small pets only

Hampton Inn ($$$)
5702 Challenger Pkwy
(46818) 219.489.0908

Hometown Inn ($)
6910 Use 30E
(46803) 219.749.5058

Knights Inn ($$)
2901 Goshen Rd
(46808) 800.843.5644

Lees Inn ($$)
5707 Challenger Pkwy
(46818) 219.489.8888

Policies
Subject
to Change

Red Roof Inn ($)
2920 Goshen Rd
(46808) 800.843.7663

Residence Inn ($$$)
4919 Lima Rd
(46808) 800.331,3131

● Franklin ●
Days Inn
2180 King
(46131) 317.736.8000
$7

● Fremont ●
E & L Motel ($)
35 W Hwy 120
(46737) 219.495.3300

● French Lick ●
Lane Motel ($)
Box# 224
(47432) 812.936.9919

The Pines At Patoka Lake
Villa ($$)
RR 2 Box# 255E
(47432) 812.936.9854

● Goshen ●
Best Western ($$)
900 Lincolnway
(46526) 219.533.0408
small pets only

● Greencastle ●
College Inn ($)
315 S Bloomington St
(46135) 317.653.4167

● Greenfield ●
Howard Hughes Motel ($)
1310 W Main St
(46140) 317.462.4493

Lees Inn ($$)
2270 N State St
(46140) 317.462.7112

● Greensburg ●
Lees Inn ($$)
2211 N State Road 3
(47240) 812.663.9998

● Greenwood ●
Comfort Inn ($$)
110 Sheek Rd
(46142) 800.221.2222

● Howe ●
Super 8 ($$)
7333 N Hwy 9
(46746) 800.800.8000
call re: fees

● Indianapolis ●
Budgetel ($$)
2650 Executive Dr
(46241) 317.244.8100

Comfort Inn ($$)
3880 W 92nd St
(46268) 317.872.3100

Courtyard By Marriott ($$)
501 W Washington St
(46204) 800.331.3131

Days Inn ($$)
8275 Craig St
(46250) 317.841.9700
$25 fee

Days Inn
I-465 & 38th
(46224) 317.293.6550

Days Inn ($$)
7314 E 21st St
(46219) 317.359.5500
$10/day small pets only

Days Inn ($$)
450 Bixler Rd
(46227) 317.788.0811
$5/pets

Drury Inn ($$)
9320 N Michigan Rd
(46268) 800.325.8300

Hampton Inn ($$)
2311 N Shadeland Ave
(46219) 800.426.7866

Hampton Inn ($$)
7220 Woodland Dr
(46278) 800.426.7866

Hojo Inn ($)
2602 N High School Rd
(46224) 800.446.4656

Holiday Inn
5120 Victory Dr
(46203) 317.783.7751

Holiday Inn ($$$)
6990 E 21st St
(46219) 317.359.5341

Homewood Suites ($$$)
2501 E 86th St
(46240) 317.253.1919

Howard Johnson ($$)
7050 E 21st St
(46219) 317.352.0481

Knights Inn ($$)
9402 Haven Way
(46240) 800.843.5644

Knights Inn ($)
4909 Knights Way
(46217) 800.843.5644

La Quinta Inn ($$)
5316 W Southern Ave
(46241) 800.531.5900
call re: fees

La Quinta Inn ($$)
7304 E 21st St
(46219) 800.531.5900
call re: fees

Lees Inn ($$)
5011 Lafayette Rd
(46254) 317.297.8880

Motel 6 ($)
6330 Debonair Ln
(46224) 317.293.3220
1 small pet/room

Pickwick Farms ($$)
9300 Ditch Rd
(46260) 317.872.6506

Radisson Inn ($$$)
8787 Keystone Xing
(46240) 317.846.2700
small pets allowed

Red Roof Inn ($)
9520 Vaparaiso Ct
(46268) 800.843.7663

Red Roof Inn ($)
6415 Debonair Ln
(46224) 800.843.7663

Residence Inn
9765 Crosspoint Blvd
(46256) 800.331.3131

Super 8 ($)
4502 S Harding St
(46217) 800.800.8000
call re: fees

Super 8 ($$)
8850 E 21st St
(46219) 317.895.5402
call re: fees

The Canterbury Hotel ($$$$)
123 S Illinois St
(46225) 800.538.8186

● Jeffersonville ●
Ramada Inn ($$)
700 W Riverside Dr
(47130) 812.284.6711

● Kentland ●
Tri Way Inn ($)
611 E Dunlap St
(47951) 219.474.5141

● Kokomo ●
Comfort Inn ($$)
522 Essex Dr
(46901) 765.452.5050

Fairfield Inn ($$)
1717 E Lincoln Rd
(46902) 317.453.8822

Motel 6 ($)
2808 S Reed Rd
(46902) 317.457.8211
1 small pet/room

● La Porte ●
Pine Lake Hotel ($$)
444 Pine Lake Ave
(46350) 800.465.4329

● Lafayette ●
Days Inn ($$)
400 Sagamore Pkwy
(47905) 317.447.4131

Holiday Inn ($$)
201 Frontage Rd
(47905) 765.449.4808

Homewood Suites ($$$)
3939 Hwy 26E
(47905) 317.448.9700

Knights Inn ($)
4110 Hwy 26E
(47905) 800.843.5644

Radisson Inn ($$$)
4343 Hwy 26E
(47905) 800.333.3333

Red Roof Inn ($)
4201 Hwy 26E
(47905) 800.843.7663

● Lawrenceburg ●
Holiday Inn
765 Eads Pkwy
(47025) 812.537.2552

● Lebanon ●
Holiday Inn ($$)
I-65
(46052) 800.465.4329

Lees Inn ($$)
1245 Hwy 32W
(46052) 317.482.9611

● Logansport ●
Holiday Inn
3550 E Market
(46947) 219.753.6351

Holiday Inn ($$)
3550 US24
(46947) 800.465.4329

Super 8 ($$)
US 24
(46947) 800.800.8000
call re: fees

● Madison ●
Best Western ($$)
700 Clifty Dr Hwy 62
(47250) 812.273.5151
small pets

Pres Madison Motel ($)
906 E 1st St
(47250) 812.265.2361

● Marion ●
Broadmoor Motel ($)
1323 N Baldwin Ave
(46952) 317.664.0501

Holiday Inn ($$)
501 E 4th St
(46952) 317.668.8801
mgr preapproval reqd

● Martinsville ●
Lees Inn ($$)
50 Bills Blvd
(46151) 317.342.1842

● Merrillville ●
Carlton Lodge ($$$)
7850 Rhode Isalnd Ave
(46410) 219.756.1600

Days Inn
82nd St
(46410) 800.329.7466
$25 dep

Knights Inn ($)
8250 Louisiana St
(46410) 800.843.5644

La Quinta Inn ($)
8210 Louisiana St
(46410) 219.738.2071
call re: fees

Motel 6 ($)
8290 Louisiana St
(46410) 219.738.2701
1 small pet/room

Radisson Inn ($$$)
800 E 8Ust Ave
(46410) 219.769.6311

Red Roof Inn ($$)
8290 Georgia St
(46410) 800.843.7663

Residence Inn
8018 Delaware Pl
(46410) 800.331.3131

Super 8 ($$)
8300 Louisiana St
(46410) 800.800.8000
call re: fees

● Metamora ●
Thorpe House Inn
Box# 36
(47030) 317.647.5425

● Michigan City ●
City Manor Motel ($)
5225 Franklin St
(46360) 219.872.9149

Knights Inn ($)
201 W Kieffer Rd
(46360) 800.843.5644

Red Roof Inn ($)
110 W Kieffer Rd
(46360) 800.843.7663

● Middlebury ●
The Thayer House
14604 Cr 22
(46540) 219.825.7926

● Mishawaka ●
Hampton Inn ($$$)
445 W University Dr
(46545) 219.273.2309

● Monticello ●
1887 Black Dog Inn
2830 Untaluti
(47960) 219.583.8297

● Muncie ●
Comfort Inn ($$)
4011 W Bethel Ave
(47304) 765.282.6666

Days Inn ($$)
3509 N Everbrook Ln
(47304) 317.288.2311
$25 deposit

Lees Inn ($$)
3302 N Everbrook Ln
(47304) 317.282.7557

Radisson Inn ($$)
420 S High St
(47305) 317.741.7777

Super 8 ($)
3601 W Fox Ridge Ln
(47304) 800.800.8000
call re: fees

● Nappanee ●
Victorian House
302 E Market St
(46550) 219.773.4383

● Nashville ●
Salt Creek Inn ($$)
Box# 397
(47448) 812.988.1149

Story Inn
6404 S Hwy 135
(47448) 812.988.2273

● New Albany ●
Holiday Inn ($$)
411 S Spring St
(47150) 812.945.2771
mgr preapproval reqd

● New Castle ●
Best Western ($)
2836 S Hwy 3
(47362) 800.528.1234
under 15 lbs

Days Inn ($)
5343 S State Rd 3
(47362) 317.987.8205
$4

● Plymouth ●
Days Inn ($$)
2229 N Michigan St
(46563) 219.935.4276
$5

Holiday Inn
2550 N Michigan
(46563) 219.936.4013

Super 8 ($$)
2160 Oak
(46563) 800.800.8000
mgr preapproval reqd

● Portage ●
Days Inn ($$)
6161 Melton Rd
(46368) 219.762.2136

Indiana Dunes Motel ($$$)
6200 Melton Rd
(46368) 800.437.5145

Lees Inn ($$)
2300 Willowcreek Rd
(46368) 219.763.7177

● Remington ●
Days Inn ($$)
4252 W Hwy 24
(47977) 219.261.2178
$2/pets

● Rensselaer ●
Interstate Motel ($)
8530 W St Rd Hwy
(47978) 219.866.4164

● Reynolds ●
Park View Motel ($)
RR 1 Box# 4
(47980) 219.984.5380

● Richmond ●
Best Western ($)
3020 E Main St
(47374) 317.966.1505
small pets only

Comfort Inn ($$)
912 Mendleson Dr
(47374) 765.935.4766

Days Inn ($$)
540 W Eaton Pike
(47374) 317.966.7591
small pets $5 charge

Holiday Inn ($$)
5501 National Rd
(47374) 765.966.7511

Howard Johnson ($)
2525 Chester Blvd
(47374) 800.654.2000

Lees Inn ($$)
6030 National Rd
(47374) 317.966.6559

Ramada Inn ($$)
4700 National Rd
(47374) 800.272.6232

Villa Motel ($)
533 W Eaton Pike
(47374) 317.962.5202

● Rochester ●
Rose Dale Motel ($)
RR 1 Box# 280
(46975) 219.223.3185

● Scottsburg ●
Best Western ($$)
I-65
(47170) 812.752.2212
small pets

Campbells Motel ($)
300 N Gardner St
(47170) 812.752.4401

Mariann Travel Inn ($)
Box# 36
(47170) 812.752.3396

● Seymour ●
Days Inn ($$)
302 S Commerce Dr
(47274) 812.522.3678
$3/pets

Holiday Inn
2025 E Tipton St
(47274) 812.522.6767

Knights Inn ($)
207 N Frontage Rd
(47274) 800.722.7220

Lees Inn ($$)
2075 E Tipton St
(47274) 812.523.1850

Super 8 ($$)
Hwy 65 & 50
(47274) 800.800.8000
$3/day $25 dep

● Shelbyville ●
Lees Inn ($$)
2880 Hwy 44E
(46176) 317.392.2299

● South Bend ●
Best Inns ($)
425 N Dixie Way
(46637) 219.277.7700

Days Inn ($$)
52757 US 31
(46637) 219.277.0510
$3/pets

Hampton Inn ($$$)
52709 US 31 North
(46637) 219.277.9373

Holiday Inn ($$$)
515 N Dixie Way
(46637) 219.272.6600

Knights Inn ($)
236 N Dixie Way
(46637) 800.843.5644

Super 8 ($$$)
52825 US 31-33
(46637) 219.272.9000
call re: fees

University Park Inn ($)
52939 US 31 & 33
(46637) 219.272.1500
small & well trained

● Sullivan ●
Days Inn ($$)
RR #2
(47882) 812.268.6391

● Taylorsville ●
Comfort Inn ($$)
10330 US 31
(47280) 800.221.2222

● Tell City ●
Daystop ($)
Hwy 66 & 14th St
(47586) 812.547.3474

Ramada Inn ($$$)
235 Orchard Hill Dr
(47586) 812.547.3234

● Terre Haute ●
Best Western ($$)
3325 Dixie Bee Rd
(47802) 800.528.1234
mgr preapproval reqd

Holiday Inn
3300 US 41
(47802) 812.232.6081

Knights Inn ($$)
401 Margaret Ave
(47802) 800.843.5644

Mid Town Motel ($)
400 S 3rd St
(47807) 812.232.0383

Pear Tree Inn ($$)
3050 S US Hwy 41
(47802) 800.282.8733

Super 8 ($$)
3089 S 1st St
(47802) 812.232.4890
call re: fees

Thriftlodge ($)
530 S 3rd St
(47807) 812.232.7075
small pets only

Woodbridge Motel ($)
4545 Wabash Ave
(47803) 812.877.1571

● Vincennes ●
Holiday Inn ($$)
600 Wheatland Rd
(47591) 812.886.9900

Super 8 ($$)
609 Shirlee St
(47591) 812.882.5101
$3 fee $25 dep

Vincesses Lodge ($)
1411 Willow St
(47591) 812.882.1282

● Wabash ●
Around Window Inn
313 W Hill St
(46992) 219.563.6901

● Warsaw ●
Comfort Inn ($$)
2605 E Center St
(46580) 219.267.7337

Days Inn ($$)
3521 Lake City Hwy
(46580) 219.269.3031
$10

● West Lafayette ●
Holiday Inn
I-65 & SR43
(47906) 765.567.2131

Travelodge ($$)
200 Brown St
(47906) 317.743.9661

● Whiteland ●
Wishing Well Motel ($)
RR 1 Box# 93
(46184) 317.535.7548

● Zionsville ●
Brick Street Inn
175 S Main St
(46077) 317.873.9177

Iowa

● Albia ●
Indian Hills Inn ($)
Rt 1
(52531) 515.932.7181

● Algona ●
Burr Oak Motel ($)
Hwy 169
(50511) 515.295.7213

● Amana ●
Holiday Inn ($$)
I-80
(52203) 319.668.1175

● Ames ●
Best Western ($$)
2601 E 13th St
(50010) 515.232.9260
small pets only

Budgetel ($$)
2500 Elmwood Dr
(50010) 515.296.2500

Comfort Inn ($$)
1605 S Dayton Ave
(50010) 515.232.0689
mgr preapproval reqd

Heartland Inn ($$)
Hwy 30 & I-35
(50010) 515.233.6060

Holiday Inn
US30 & Elwood
(50014) 515.292.8600

Ramada Inn ($$)
1206 S Duff Ave
(50010) 515.232.3410

University Inn ($$)
316 S Duff Ave
(50010) 515.232.0280
$10 fee

● Ankeny ●
Best Western ($$)
133 SE Delaware Ave
(50021) 515.964.1717
smoking room

Days Inn ($$)
13 NE Delaware
(50021) 515.965.1995
$5

Super 8 ($$)
206 SE Delaware Ave
(50021) 515.964.4503
call re: fees

● Arnolds Park ●
Fillenwarth Ctges
87 Lake Shore Dr
(51331) 712.332.5646

● Atlantic ●
Econo Lodge ($$)
I-80 & US71
(50022) 712.243.4067

● Avoca ●
Capri Motel ($)
Box# 699
(51521) 712.343.6301

● Bettendorf ●
Econo Lodge ($)
2205 Kimberly Rd
(52722) 319.355.6471

Jumers Casle Lodge ($$$)
900 Spruce Hills Dr
(52722) 319.359.7141

Twin Bridges Inn ($$)
221 15th St
(52722) 319.355.6451

● Bloomfield ●
Southfork Inn ($)
Box# 155
(52537) 515.664.1063

● Boone ●
Super 8 ($$)
1715 S Story St
(50036) 515.432.8890
w/permission

● Burlington ●
Best Western ($$)
3001 Winegard Dr
(52601) 319.753.2223
mgr preapproval reqd

Comfort Inn ($)
3051 Kirkwood St
(52601) 319.753.0000
mgr preapproval reqd

Days Inn ($)
1601 N Roosevelt Ave
(52601) 319.754.1111
$5

Friendship Inn ($$)
2731 Mount Pleasant St
(52601) 319.754.7571

Ramada Inn ($$)
2759 Mount Pleasant St
(52601) 319.754.5781

● Carroll ●
71 30 Motel ($)
Jct US 30 & 71
(51401) 712.792.1100

Best Western ($)
Hwy 30 West
(51401) 712.792.9214
small pets only

Econo Lodge ($$)
1225 Plaza Dr
(51401) 712.792.5156

Super 8 ($$)
Hwy 71
(51401) 712.792.4753
pets w/permission

● Cedar Falls ●
Blackhawk Motel ($)
122 Washington St
(50613) 319.271.1161

Econo Lodge ($)
4117 University Ave
(50613) 319.277.6931

Holiday Inn ($$)
5826 University Ave
(50613) 319.277.1161
mgr preapproval reqd

Marquis Inn ($)
4711 University Ave
(50613) 319.277.1412

● Cedar Rapids ●
Collins Plaza Hotel ($$$)
1200 Collins Rd NE
(52402) 319.393.6600

Comfort Inn ($$)
390 33rd Ave SW
(52404) 319.363.7934

Comfort Inn ($$)
5055 Rockwell Dr NE
(52402) 319.393.8247
mgr preapproval reqd

Days Inn ($$)
3245 Southgate Pl SW
(52404) 319.365.4339

Days Inn
2501 Williams Blvd SW
(52404) 319.365.9441
$5

Econo Lodge ($$)
622 3Ord Ave SW
(52404) 319.363.8888

Exel Inn ($)
616 33rd Ave SW
(52404) 319.366.8888

Five Seasons Hotel ($$$)
350 1st Ave NE
(52401) 319.363.8161
small pets only

Hojo Inn ($$)
3233 S Ridge Dr SW
(52404) 319.363.9999

Ramada Inn ($$)
4011 16th Ave SW
(52404) 319.396.5000

Red Roof Inn ($)
3325 Southgate Ct SW
(52404) 319.366.7523
fees/limits may apply

Sheraton Inn ($$$)
525 33rd Ave SW
(52404) 319.366.8671

● Chariton ●
Royal Rest Motel ($)
Hwy 14 & 34
(50049) 515.774.5961

● Charles City ●
Hartwood Inn ($)
1312 Gilbert St
(50616) 515.228.4352

● Cherokee ●
Super 8 ($$)
1400 N 2nd St
(51012) 712.225.4278
call re: fees

Be
Discreet

● Clear Lake ●
Budget Inn ($$)
1306 N 25th St
(50428) 515.357.8700

Heartland Inn ($$)
1603 S Shore Dr
(50428) 515.357.5123

Super 8
I-35
(50428) 515.357.7521
call re: fees

● Clinton ●
Best Western ($$)
1522 Lincolnway St
(52732) 319.243.8841
mgr preapproval reqd

Ramada Inn ($)
1522 Lincolnway St
(52732) 319.243.6901

● Clive ●
Best Western ($$$)
11040 Hickman Rd
(50325) 515.287.6464

Budgetel ($$)
1390 NW 188th St
(50325) 515.221.9200

The Inn On University ($$)
11001 University Ave
(50325) 515.225.2222

● Columbus Junction ●
Columbus Motel ($)
Hwy 92
(52738) 319.728.8080

● Coralville ●
Best Western ($$)
704 1st Ave
(52241) 319.351.0400
mgr preapproval reqd

Best Western ($$)
1895 27th Ave
(52241) 319.354.7770
mgr preapproval reqd

Blue Top Motel ($)
1015 5th St
(52241) 319.351.0900

Comfort Inn ($$)
209 9th St
(52241) 319.351.8144
mgr preapproval reqd

Fairfield Inn ($$)
214 9th St
(52241) 319.337.8382
small in smoking rooms

Motel 6 ($)
810 1st Ave
(52241) 319.354.0030
1 small pet/room

University Inn
Hwy 6
(52241) 319.354.4400

● Council Bluffs ●
Best Western ($$)
2216 27th Ave
(51501) 712.322.3150

Days Inn ($$)
3619 9th Ave
(51501) 712.323.2200

Heartland Inn ($$)
1000 Woodbury Ave
(51503) 712.322.8400
$10 fee

Motel 6 ($)
1846 N 16th St
(51501) 712.328.8300
1 small pet/room

Motel 6 ($)
3032 S Expwy
(51501) 712.366.2405
1 small pet/room

Super 8 ($)
2712 S 24th St
(51501) 712.322.2888
pets w/permission

● Davenport ●
Best Western ($$$)
100 W 76th St
(52806) 319.386.6900
$3 small

Comfort Inn ($$)
7222 Northwest Blvd
(52806) 319.391.8222
mgr preapproval reqd

Days Inn ($$)
3202 E Kimberly Rd
(52807) 319.355.1190
pets allowed w/permission

Exel Inn ($)
6310 N Brady St
(52806) 319.386.6350
small pets only

Fairfield Inn ($$)
3206 E Kimberly Rd
(52807) 319.355.2264
smoking rooms

Fairfield Inn ($$)
3206 Kimberly Rd
(52807) 319.355.3364

Hampton Inn ($$)
3330 E Kimberly Rd
(52807) 319.354.3921

Hampton Inn ($$)
3330 E Kimberly Rd
(52807) 319.359.3921
under 20 lbs

Holiday Inn
5202 Brady
(52806) 319.391.1230

Motel 6 ($)
6111 N Brady St
(52806) 319.391.8997
1 small pet/room

Ramada Inn ($$)
6263 N Brady St
(52806) 319.386.1940
back bldg. only

Super 8 ($$)
410 E 65th St
(52807) 319.388.9810
call re: fees

● Decorah ●
Super 8
Hwy 9
(52101) 319.382.8771
call re: fees

● Denison ●
Best Western ($)
502 Boyer Valley Rd
(51442) 712.263.5081
small dogs only

Days Inn ($)
315 Chamberlin Dr
(51442) 712.263.2500

● Des Moines ●
Adventureland Inn ($$)
I-80 & Hwy 65
(50316) 515.265.7321

Archer Motel ($)
4965 Hubbell Ave
(50317) 515.265.0368

Best Western ($$)
929 3rd St
(50309) 515.282.5251
small

Best Western ($$)
5220 NE 14th St
(50313) 515.265.5611
small pets only

Best Western ($$)
5020 NE 14th St
(50313) 515.265.7511
attended

Best Western ($$)
1810 Army Post Rd
(50315) 515.287.6464
small pets only

Broadway Motel ($)
5100B Hubbell Ave
(50317) 515.262.5659

Comfort Inn ($$)
5231 Fleur Dr
(50321) 515.282.5251
mgr preapproval reqd

Days Inn ($$)
3501 E 14th St
(50316) 515.265.2541
small pets only $50 deposit

Embassy Suites ($$$$)
101 E Locust St
(50309) 515.244.1700

Fort Des Moines Hotel ($$$)
1000 Walnut St
(50309) 800.532.1466

Kirkwood Hotel ($$$)
400 Walnut St
(50309) 515.244.9191

Marriott Hotel ($$$)
700 Grand Ave
(50309) 515.245.5500

Motel 6 ($)
4817 Fleur Dr
(50321) 515.287.6364
1 small pet/room

Motel 6 ($)
4940 NE 14th St
(50313) 515.266.5456
1 small pet/room

Savery Hotel ($$$)
401 Locust St
(50309) 515.244.2151
under 20 lbs

Super 8 ($$)
4755 Merle Hay Rd
(50322) 515.278.8858
call re: fees

● Dubuque ●
Comfort Inn ($$)
4055 Dodge St
(52003) 319.557.8000
mgr preapproval reqd

Days Inn ($$)
1111 Dodge St
(52003) 319.583.3297

Fairfield Inn ($$)
3400 Dodge St
(52003) 319.588.2349

Holiday Inn
150 Main St
(52001) 319.556.2000

Motel 6 ($)
2670 Dodge St
(52001) 319.556.0880
1 small pet/room

● Early ●
Early Motel
403 Hwys 71 & 20
(50535) 712.273.5599

● Eldora ●
Village Motel ($)
2005 E Edington Ave
(50627) 515.858.3441

● Evansdale ●
Ramada Inn ($$)
450 Evansdale Dr
(50707) 319.235.1111

● Fairfield ●
Best Western ($$)
2200 W Burlington Ave
(52556) 515.472.2200
mgr preapproval reqd

Dream Motel ($)
US 34
(52556) 515.472.4161

● Fort Dodge ●
Best Western ($$)
Hwy 169
(50501) 515.575.7177
small pets only

Budget Host ($$)
US 20 & 169
(50501) 800.283.4678
mgr preapproval reqd

Comfort Inn ($$)
2938 5th Ave
(50501) 515.573.3731

Holiday Inn ($$)
2001 Hwy 169
(50501) 515.955.3621

● Fort Madison ●
Americana Motel
Hwy 61 & Hwy 2 West
(52627) 319.372.5123

Best Western ($$)
Hwy 61
(52627) 319.372.7510
mgr preapproval reqd

● Glenwood ●
Western Inn ($)
707 S Locust St
(51534) 712.527.3175

● Grinnell ●
Best Western ($$)
2210 West St
(50112) 515.236.6116

Days Inn ($$)
I-80 & Hwy 146
(50112) 515.236.6710
$5/pets

Super 8 ($$)
I-80 & Hwy 146 Ex 182
(50112) 515.236.7888
w/permission

● Hampton ●
Gold Key Motel ($)
RR 2 Box# 242
(50441) 515.456.2566

● Homestead ●
Die Heimat Inn ($$)
Box# 160
(52236) 319.622.3937

● Humboldt ●
Super 8 ($$)
Hwy 3
(50548) 515.332.1131
call re: fees

● Independence ●
Super 8 ($$)
2000 1st St
(50644) 319.334.7041
small in smoking rooms

● Indianola ●
Woods Motel
906 S Jefferson St
(50125) 515.961.5311

● Iowa City ●
Holiday Inn ($$$)
210 S Dubuque St
(52240) 319.337.4058

● Jefferson ●
Super 8
Hwy 30
(50129) 800.800.8000
call re: fees

● Johnston ●
Best Inns ($$)
5050 Merle Hay Rd
(50131) 515.270.1111

The Inn & Conference Ctr
($$)
5055 Merle Hay Rd
(50131) 515.276.5411

● Keokuk ●
Chief Motel ($)
2701 Main St Rd
(52632) 319.524.2565

Keokuk Motor Lodge ($)
Hwy 218 E Main St Rd
(52632) 800.252.2256

● Le Mars ●
Amber Inn ($)
635 8th Ave SW
(51031) 712.546.7066

● Mapleton ●
Maple Motel ($)
RR 1 Box# 1
(51034) 712.882.1271

● Maquoketa ●
Key Motel ($)
Hwy 61 & 64
(52060) 319.652.5131

● Marquette ●
The Frontier Motel ($)
101 S St St
(52158) 319.873.3497

● Marshalltown ●
Best Western ($$)
2009 S Center St
(50158) 515.752.3631
$10

Best Western ($$)
3303 S Center St
(50158) 515.752.6321
must be in dog kennels

Days Inn ($$)
403 E Church St
(50158) 515.753.7777
$10

● Mason City ●
Days Inn ($$)
2301 4th St SW
(50401) 515.424.0210
small pets allowed

Holiday Inn ($$)
2101 4th St SW
(50401) 515.423.1640
mgr preapproval reqd

Thriftlodge ($$)
24 5th St SW
(50401) 515.424.2910

IOWA, Missouri Valley

● Missouri Valley ●
Days Inn ($$)
1967 Hwy 30
(51555) 712.642.4003

● Mount Pleasant ●
Heartland Inn ($$)
Hwy 218
(52641) 319.385.2102

● Muscatine ●
Holiday Inn
2915 N Hwy 61
(52761) 319.264.5550

● New Hampton ●
Southgate Inn ($$)
2199 McCloud Ave
(50659) 515.394.4145

● Newton ●
Best Western ($$)
I-80
(50208) 515.792.4200

Days Inn ($$)
1605 W 19th St
(50208) 515.792.2330

Holiday Inn
1905 W 19th
(50208) 515.792.7722

Ramada Inn ($)
I-80 & Hwy 14
(50208) 515.792.8100

Super 8 ($$)
1635 S 12th Ave
(50208) 515.792.8868
call re: fees

Terrace Lodge Motel ($$)
Hwy 14 & I-80
(50208) 800.383.7722

● Okoboji ●
Country Club Motel ($)
1107 Sanborn Ave
(51355) 712.332.5617

● Onawa ●
Super 8 ($$)
I-29
(51040) 712.423.2101
call re: fees

● Osceola ●
Best Western ($$)
1520 Jeffreys Dr
(50213) 515.342.2133
small dogs

Blue Haven Motel ($)
325 S Main St
(50213) 515.342.2115

● Oskaloosa ●
Red Carpet Inn
2278 Hwy 63
(52577) 515.673.8641

Rodeway Inn ($$)
1315 A Ave
(52577) 515.673.8381

Traveler Budgetinn ($)
1210 A Ave
(52577) 515.673.8333

● Ottumwa ●
Colonial Motor Inn ($)
1534 Albia Rd
(52501) 515.683.1661

Days Inn ($$)
206 Church St
(52501) 515.682.8131
$25 deposit

Heartland Inn ($$)
125 W Joseph Ave
(52501) 515.682.8526
$10/day in smoking rms

● Pacific Junction ●
Bluff View Motel ($)
RR 1
(51561) 712.622.8191

● Sheldon ●
Sheldon Motel ($)
3 Blks W On US 18
(51201) 712.324.2568

● Shenandoah ●
Tall Corn Motel ($)
Sheridan Ave & US 59
(51601) 712.246.1550

● Sibley ●
Super 8 ($$)
1108 2nd Ave
(51249) 712.754.3603
$6/day per pet

● Sioux Center ●
Colonial Motel
1367 S Main Ave
(51250) 800.762.9149

Econo Lodge ($$)
86 9th Street Cir NE
(51250) 712.722.4000

● Sioux City ●
Best Western ($$)
130 Nebraska St
(51101) 712.277.1550

Fairfield Inn ($$)
4716 Southern Hills Dr
(51106) 712.276.5600

Hilton ($$$)
707 4th St
(51101) 712.277.4101

Marina Inn ($$$)
4th & B Sts
(51101) 800.798.7980

Motel 6 ($)
6166 Harbor Dr
(51111) 712.277.3131
1 small pet/room

Riverboat Inn ($$)
701 Gordon Dr
(51101) 712.277.9400

Super 8 ($$)
4307 Stone Ave
(51106) 712.274.1520
call re: fees

● Sloan ●
Rodeway Inn ($$)
1862 Hwy 141
(51055) 712.428.4280

● Spirit Lake ●
Oaks Motel ($)
1701 Chicago Ave
(51360) 712.336.2940

● Storm Lake ●
Cross Roads Motel ($$)
Hwys 3 & 71
(50588) 800.383.1456

Economy Inn ($)
1316 N Lake Ave
(50588) 712.732.2342

Palace Motel ($)
E Lake Shore Dr
(50588) 712.732.5753

● Story City ●
Viking Motor Inn ($$)
West Of I-35 Ex 124
(50248) 515.733.4306

● Stuart ●
Super 8 ($$)
I-80
(50250) 515.523.2888
call re: fees

● Toledo ●
Super 8 ($$)
Hwy 30
(52342) 515.484.5888
call re: fees

● Urbandale ●
Budget Host ($)
7625 Hickman Rd
(50322) 800.283.4678

Comfort Inn ($$)
5900 Sutton Pl
(50322) 515.270.1037
mgr preapproval reqd

Holiday Inn ($$)
5000 Merle Hay Rd
(50322) 515.278.0271
mgr preapproval reqd

● Walcott ●
Super 8 ($$)
Walcott I-80 Ind Prk
(52773) 319.284.5083
pets with deposit

● Walnut ●
Super 8 ($$)
Ex 46 I-80
(51577) 712.784.2221
call re: fees

● Washington ●
Super 8 ($$)
Hwy I & 92
(52353) 319.653.6621
$25 fee

● Waterloo ●
Best Western ($$)
214 Washington St
(50701) 319.235.0321
$5 fee

Comfort Inn ($$)
1945 La Porte Rd
(50702) 319.234.7411
mgr preapproval reqd

Days Inn ($$)
3141 La Porte Rd
(50702) 319.233.9191

Exel Inn ($)
3350 University Ave
(50701) 319.235.2165
small pets only

Fairfield Inn ($$)
2011 La Port Rd
(50702) 319.234.5452

Heartland Inn ($$)
3052 Marnie Rd
(50701) 319.232.7467
$10 fee

Heartland Inn ($$)
1809 La Porte Rd
(50702) 319.235.4461
$10 fee

Holiday Inn
205 W 4th St
(50701) 319.233.7560

Super 8 ($$)
1825 La Porte Rd
(50702) 319.233.1800
under 30 lbs

● Waverly ●
Best Western ($$)
1900 Heritage Way
(50677) 319.352.5330
small pets only

● Webster City ●
Super 8
305 Closz Dr
(50595) 515.832.2000
call re: fees

The Executive Inn ($$)
1700 Superior St
(50595) 515.832.3631

● West Bend ●
West Bend Motel ($)
West Of Hwy 15
(50597) 515.887.3611

● West Branch ●
Presidential Motel ($)
711 S Doney
(52358) 319.643.2526

● West Des Moines ●
Ramada Inn ($$)
1250 74th St
(50266) 515.223.6500

● West Liberty ●
Econo Lodge ($$)
1943 GarfieldAve
(52776) 319.627.2171

● West Union ●
Elms Motel
Hwy 150 South
(52175) 800.422.3843

● Williams ●
Best Western ($$)
I-35 Ex 144
(50271) 515.854.2281
small trained attended pets
only

● Williamsburg ●
Days Inn ($$)
2214 "U" Ave
(52361) 319.668.2097

Ramada Inn ($$)
I-80 & Hwy 149
(52361) 319.668.1000

Super 8 ($$)
2228 U Ave
(52361) 319.668.2800
$6 fee

● Windsor Heights ●
Hickman Motor Lodge ($)
6500 Hickman Rd
(50322) 515.276.8591

● Wyoming ●
Sunset Motel
RR #1
(52362) 319.488.2240

Kansas

● Abilene ●
Best Western ($$)
2210 N Buckeye Ave
(67410) 913.263.2050
small pets only

Best Western ($$$$)
1709 N Buckeye Ave
(67410) 913.263.2800
$20 dep

Spruce House ($$)
604 N Spruce St
(67410) 913.263.3900

Super 8
2207 Buckeye
(67410) 913.263.4545
call re: fees

● Arkansas City ●
Best Western ($$)
1617 N Summit St
(67005) 316.442.1400
small pets only

Heritage Regency Inn ($$)
3232 N Summit St
(67005) 316.442.7700

● Atchison ●
Atchison Motor Inn ($)
401 S 10th St
(66002) 913.367.7000

● Auburn ●
Lippincotts House ($$)
8720 W 85th St
(66402) 913.256.2436

● Baxter Springs ●
Baxter Inn 4 Less ($)
2451 Military Ave
(66713) 316.856.2106

● Belleville ●
Best Western ($$)
215 W US Hwy 36
(66935) 913.527.2231
small pets

● Beloit ●
Mainliner Inn ($)
RR 1 Box# 47
(67420) 913.738.3531

● Chanute ●
Guest House Inn ($)
1814 S Santa Fe St
(66720) 316.431.0600

Holiday Park Motel 65 ($)
3030 S Santa Fe St
(66720) 316.431.0850

Safari Inn ($)
3500 S Santa Fe St
(66720) 316.431.9460

● Chapman ●
Oak Creek Lodge ($$)
1787 Raim Road
(67431) 913.263.8755

● Clay Center ●
Cedar Court Motel ($)
905 Crawford St
(67432) 913.632.2148

● Coffeyville ●
Appletree Inn ($$)
820 E 11th St
(67337) 316.251.0002

Fountain Plaza Inn ($$)
104 W 11th St
(67337) 316.251.2250

● Colby ●
Best Western ($$)
2320 S Range Ave
(67701) 913.462.3943

Budget Host ($)
1745 W 4th St
(67701) 800.283.4678

Comfort Inn ($$)
2225 S Range Ave
(67701) 913.462.3833

Days Inn ($$)
1925 S Range Ave
(67701) 913.462.8691

Econo Lodge ($)
1985 S Range Ave
(67701) 800.424.4777

Ramada Inn ($$)
1950 S Range Ave
(67701) 800.272.6232

KANSAS, Colby

Super 8
1040 Zelfer Ave
(67701) 913.462.8248
call re: fees

● Columbus ●
Claytorne Lodge
RR 1 Box# 13
(66725) 316.597.2568

● Concordia ●
Best Western ($$)
89 Lincoln St
(66901) 913.243.4545
hunting dogs onsite kennels

● Cottonwood Falls ●
1874 Stonehouse Mulberry
Hill ($$$)
RR 1 Box# 67A
(66845) 316.273.8481

● Council Grove ●
Cottage House Hotel ($$)
25 N Neosho St
(66846) 316.767.6828

● Dodge City ●
Astro Motel ($$)
2200 Wyatt Earp Blvd
(67801) 316.225.9000

Best Western ($$)
1510 W Wyatt Earp Blvd
(67801) 316.227.2125
$10 pet deposit

Days Inn
2408 Wyatt Earp
(67801) 316.225.9900

Dodge House
2408 Wyatt Earp
(67801) 316.225.9900
guest rfd

Dodgen House Motel ($)
2408 W Wyatt Earp Blvd
(67801) 800.553.9901

Holiday Inn
2320 W Wyatt Earp
(67801) 316.227.5000

Super 8 ($$)
1708 W Wyatt Earp Blvd
(67801) 800.800.8000
call re: fees

● El Dorado ●
Best Western ($$)
2525 W Central Ave
(67042) 316.321.6900
attended pets only

Heritage Inn ($)
2515 W Central Ave
(67042) 316.321.6800

● Ellsworth ●
Best Western ($$)
Hwy 156
(67439) 913.472.3116
small pets

● Emporia ●
Budget Host ($)
1830 W Hwy 50
(66801) 800.283.4678

Comfort Inn ($)
2511 W 18th Ave
(66801) 316.343.7750

Days Inn ($$)
3032 W Hwy 50
(66801) 316.342.1787

Super 8
2913 Hwy 50
(66801) 316.342.7567
call re: fees

● Enterprise ●
Ehrsam Place ($$)
103 S Grant
(67441) 913.263.8747

● Erie ●
Ahs Motel ($)
700 W Canville
(66733) 316.244.5231

● Eureka ●
Blue Stem Lodge ($)
1314 E River St
(67045) 316.583.5531

● Florence ●
Holiday Motel ($)
630 W 5th St
(66851) 316.878.4246

● Fort Scott ●
Frontier Inn 4 Less ($)
2222 S Main St
(66701) 316.223.5330

Ranch House Motel
Hwy 54 West
(66701) 316.223.9734

● Garden City ●
Best Western ($$)
US 50 & US 8
(67846) 316.275.4164

Best Western ($$)
1311 E Fulton St
(67846) 316.276.2387

Budget Host ($)
123 Honeybee Ct
(67846) 800.283.4678

Continental Inn ($)
1408 Jones Ave
(67846) 316.276.7691

Days Inn ($$)
1818 Commanche Dr
(67846) 316.275.5095

Holiday Inn
2502 E Kansas Ave
(67846) 316.275.5900

National 9 ($)
1502 E Fulton
(67846) 316.276.2304

Plaza Inn ($$)
1911 E Kansas Ave
(67846) 800.875.5201

● Glasco ●
Rustic Remembrances ($)
RR 1 Box# 68
(67445) 913.546.2552

● Goodland ●
Super 8
2520 Hwy 27
(67735) 913.899.7566
call re: fees

● Great Bend ●
Best Western ($$)
2920 10th St
(67530) 316.792.3541
small pets only

Holiday Inn ($$)
3017 10th St
(67530) 316.792.2431

Inn 4 Less ($)
4701 10th St
(67530) 316.792.8235

Super 8
3500- 10th St
(67530) 316.793.8486
call re: fees

Travelers Budgetinn ($)
4200 10th St
(67530) 316.793.5448

● Greensburg ●
Best Western ($$)
515 W Kansas Ave
(67054) 316.723.2121
attended

Kansas Inn ($)
800 E Kansas Ave
(67054) 316.723.2141

● Hays ●
Best Western ($$)
2524 Vine St
(67601) 913.625.2511
attended

Budget Host ($)
810 E 8th St
(67601) 800.283.4678
small pets only

Days Inn ($$)
3205 Vine St
(67601) 913.628.8261

Days Inn
4701 - 10th
(67601) 316.792.8235

Hampton Inn ($$)
3801 Vine St
(67601) 913.625.8103

Holiday Inn ($$)
3603 Vine St
(67601) 913.625.7371

● Hiawatha ●
Heartland Inn ($)
1100 S 1st St
(66434) 913.742.7401

● Hutchinson ●
Comfort Inn ($$)
1621 Super Plz
(67501) 316.663.7822

Days Inn
100 -2nd Ave
(67501) 316.663.7100
$10 small

Quality Inn ($$)
15 W 4th Ave
(67501) 316.663.7822

Super 8 ($$)
1315 E 11th Ave
(67501) 316.662.6394
$50 deposit

● Independence ●
Appletree Inn ($$)
201 N 8th St
(67301) 316.331.5500

Best Western ($$)
US 75 & 160
(67301) 316.331.7300
deposit

● Junction City ●
Best Western ($)
110 E Flint Hills Blvd
(66441) 913.238.5188
smoking rooms

Days Inn ($$)
1024 S Washington St
(66441) 913.762.2727
mgr preapproval reqd

Dreamland Motel ($)
520 E Flint Hills Blvd
(66441) 913.238.1108

Econo Lodge ($)
211 E Flint Hills Blvd
(66441) 800.424.4777

Harvest Inn ($$)
1001 E 6th St
(66441) 800.762.0270

Holiday Inn
120 N East St
(66441) 913.762.4200

● Kansas City ●
Best Western ($$)
501 Southwest Blvd
(66103) 816.677.3060

Civic Centre Hotel ($$)
424 Minnesota Ave
(66101) 800.542.2983

Home & Hearth Inn ($)
3930 Rainbow Blvd
(66103) 913.236.6880

Kansas City KS Metro

● Lansing ●
Econo Lodge ($)
504 N Main St
(66043) 913.727.2777

● Lawrence ●
Days Inn ($$)
2309 Iowa St
(66046) 913.843.9100
mgr preapproval reqd

Ramada Inn ($$)
2222 W 6th St
(66049) 913.842.7030

Super 8 ($$)
515 McDonald Dr
(66049) 913.842.5721
call re: fees

Westminster Inn ($)
2525 W 6th St
(66049) 913.841.8410

● Leavenworth ●
Commanders Inn ($)
6th And Metropolitan
(66048) 913.651.5800

● Ottawa ●
Days Inn ($$)
1641 S Main St
(66067) 913.242.4842

Econo Lodge ($)
2331 S Cedar St
(66067) 800.424.4777

Royal Manor Motel ($)
1641 S Main St
(66067) 913.242.4842

Village Inn Motel ($)
2520 S Main St
(66067) 913.242.5512

● Shawnee Mission ●
Doubletree ($$$)
10100 College Blvd
(66210) 913.451.6100

Drury Inn ($$)
9009 Shawnee Mission Pkwy
(66202) 800.325.8300

Drury Inn ($$)
10951 Metcalf Ave
(66210) 800.325.8300

Embassy Suites ($$$$)
10601 Metcalf Ave
(66212) 913.649.7060

Holiday Inn
7240 Shawnee Mission
(66202) 913.262.3010

Howard Johnson ($$)
12381 W 95th St
(66215) 800.654.2000

La Quinta Inn ($$)
9461 Lenexa Dr
(66215) 800.221.4731
call re: fees

Marriott Hotel ($$$)
10800 Metcalf Ave
(66210) 913.451.8000

Red Roof Inn ($)
6800 W 108th St
(66211) 800.843.7663

Residence Inn ($$$)
6300 W 110th St
(66211) 800.331.3131

Kansas City MO Metro

● Blue Springs ●
Motel 6 ($)
901 W Jefferson St
(64015) 816.228.9133
1 small pet/room

Ramada Ltd ($$)
1110 NW State Route 7
(64014) 816.229.6363

● Independence ●
Howard Johnson ($$)
4200 S Noland Rd
(64055) 816.373.8856

Red Roof Inn ($$)
13712 E 42nd Ter S
(64055) 800.843.7663

Super 8 ($$)
4032 S Lynn Court Dr
(64055) 816.833.1888
small pets with deposit

● Kansas City ●
American Inn Motel ($)
1211 Armour Rd
(64116) 816.471.3451

Americana Hotel ($$)
1301 Wyandotte St
(64105) 816.221.8800

Budgetel ($$)
8601 Hillcrest Rd
(64138) 816.822.7000

Budgetel ($)
2214 Taney St
(64116) 816.221.1200

Days Inn
I-29
(64153) 800.329.7466
$5

Days Inn ($$)
11801 Blue Ridge Blvd
(64134) 816.765.1888
mgr preapproval reqd

Drury Inn ($$)
3830 Blue Ridge Cutoff
(64133) 800.325.8300

Embassy Suites ($$$)
7640 New Tiffany Sprgs
(64153) 816.891.7788

Historic Suites ($$$)
612 Central St
(64105) 816.842.6544

Holiday Inn
5701 Longview Rd
(64137) 816.765.4100

Inn Town Lodge ($$)
2620 NE 43Rd St
(64117) 816.453.6550

Marriott Hotel ($$$)
200 W 12th St
(64105) 816.421.6800

Marriott Hotel ($$)
775 Brasilia Ave
(64153) 816.464.2200

Motel 6 ($)
6400 E 87th St
(64138) 816.333.4468
1 small pet/room

Motel 6 ($)
8230 NW Prairie View Rd
(64151) 816.741.6400
1 small pet/room

Radisson Inn ($$$)
106 W 12th St
(64105) 800.333.3333

Ramada Inn ($)
7301 New Tiffany Spgs
(64153) 800.234.9501

Ramada Inn ($$)
1600 NE Parvin Rd
(64116) 816.453.5210

Red Roof Inn ($)
3636 Randolph Rd
(64161) 816.452.8585

Residence Inn ($$$$)
2675 Main St
(64108) 816.561.3000
$50 + $5 per day

Residence Inn ($$)
9900 NW Prairie View Rd
(64153) 816.891.9009
call for fee & availability

Super 8 ($$)
6900 NW 83Rd Ter
(64152) 816.587.0808
call re: fees

Travelodge ($$)
1051 N Cambridge St
(64120) 816.483.7900

Westin Hotel ($$$$)
1 E Pershing Rd
(64108) 816.474.4400
small pets accepted

● Lees Summit ●
Best Western ($$)
625 N Murray Rd
(64081) 816.525.1400

Comfort Inn ($$)
607 SE Oldham Pkwy
(64081) 816.524.8181

● Liberty ●
Super 8 ($$)
115 N Stewart Rd
(64068) 816.781.9400
25 lbs. or less

● Oak Grove ●
Days Inn ($$)
101 N Locust St
(64075) 816.625.8686
size limits & fees

Econo Lodge ($)
410 SE 1st St
(64075) 816.625.3681

● Platte City ●
Best Western ($$)
I-29
(64079) 816.858.4588
under 15 lbs

Comfort Inn ($$)
1200 Hwy 92
(64079) 816.858.5430

End of Kansas City MO Metro

● Kingman ●
Budget Host ($$)
1113 E Hwy 54
(67068) 316.532.3118
limited availability

Welcome Inn ($)
1101B E Hwy 54
(67068) 316.532.3144

● Lansing ●
Econo Lodge ($)
504 N Main St
(66043) 913.727.2777

● Larned ●
Best Western ($$)
123 E 14th St
(67550) 316.285.3114

● Lawrence ●
Days Inn ($$)
2309 Iowa St
(66046) 913.843.9100
mgr preapproval reqd

Holiday Inn ($$)
200 McDonald Dr
(66044) 913.841.7077

Ramada Inn ($$)
2222 W 6th St
(66049) 913.842.7030

Super 8 ($$)
515 McDonald Dr
(66049) 913.842.5721
call re: fees

Westminster Inn ($)
2525 W 6th St
(66049) 913.841.8410

● Leavenworth ●
Commanders Inn ($)
6th And Metropolitan
(66048) 913.651.5800

● Liberal ●
Best Western ($$)
229 W Pancake Blvd
(67901) 316.624.5601
small

Cimarron Inn ($)
564 E Pancake Blvd
(67901) 316.624.6203

Western Ho Motel ($)
754 E Pancake Blvd
(67901) 316.624.1921

Kansas Motel
310 E Pancake Blvd
(67901) 316.624.7215

Liberal Inn ($)
603 E Pancake Blvd
(67901) 316.624.7254
small pets only

Red Carpet Inn ($)
488 E Pancake Blvd
(67901) 316.624.5642

Thunderbird Inn ($)
2100 N Hwy 83
(67901) 316.624.7271

● Lindsborg ●
Coronado Motel
305 N Harrison St
(67456) 913.227.3943

● Louisburg ●
Red Maple Inn ($$)
201 S 11th St
(66053) 913.837.2840

● Lyons ●
Lyons Inn ($)
817 W Main St
(67554) 316.257.5185

● Manhattan ●
Best Western ($$)
100B Bluemont Ave
(66502) 913.776.4771
small pets only

Days Inn ($$)
1501 Tuttle Creek Blvd
(66502) 913.539.5391

Holiday Inn ($$$)
530 Richards Dr
(66502) 915.539.5311

Motel 6 ($)
510 Tuttle Creek Blvd
(66502) 913.537.1022
1 small pet/room

Ramada Inn ($$$)
17th & Anderson
(66502) 800.272.6232

● Mankato ●
Crest Vue Motel ($)
1/2 Mi East On US 36
(66956) 913.378.3515

Dreamliner Motel ($)
RR 2 Box# 8
(66956) 913.378.3107

● Marion ●
Country Dreams ($$)
RR 3 Box# 82
(66861) 316.382.2250

Be Discreet

• Marysville •
Best Western ($)
2005 Center St
(66508) 800.528.1234

Super 8
1155 Pony Express Rd
(66508) 913.562.5588
call re: fees

Thunderbird Motel ($)
Hwy 36W
(66508) 913.562.2373

• McPherson •
Best Western ($$)
2211 E Kansas Ave
(67460) 316.241.5343
small pets only

Red Coach Inn ($)
2111 E Kansas Ave
(67460) 316.241.6960

Super 8 ($$)
2110 E Kansas Ave
(67460) 316.241.8881
pets w/permission $50
deposit

• Meade •
Daltons Motel ($)
519 Carthage
(67864) 316.873.2131

• Ness City •
Derrick Inn ($)
Hwy 96
(67560) 913.798.3617

• Newton •
Best Western ($$)
1301 E 1st St
(67114) 316.283.9120
pets w/permission

Days Inn ($$)
105 Manchester Ave
(67114) 316.283.3300
$10

Super 8 ($$)
1620 E 2nd St
(67114) 316.283.7611
call re: fees

• Oakley •
Annie Oakley Motel ($)
428 Center Ave
(67748) 913.672.3223

Best Western ($$)
3506 US 40
(67748) 913.672.3254

First Travel Inn ($)
708 Center Ave
(67748) 913.672.3226

• Oberlin •
Frontier Motel ($)
207 E Frontier Pkwy
(67749) 913.475.2203

• Osborne •
Camelot Inn ($)
933 N 1st St
(67473) 913.436.5413

• Ottawa •
Days Inn ($$)
1641 S Main St
(66067) 913.242.4842

Econo Lodge ($)
2331 S Cedar St
(66067) 800.424.4777

Royal Manor Motel ($)
1641 S Main St
(66067) 913.242.4842

Village Inn Motel ($)
2520 S Main St
(66067) 913.242.5512

• Overbrook •
Pinemoore Inn ($$)
RR 1 Box# 44
(66524) 913.453.2304

• Parsons •
Townsman Motel ($)
Box# 813
(67357) 800.552.4008

• Phillipsburg •
Mark V Motel ($)
320 W State St
(67661) 800.219.3149

• Pittsburg •
Sunset Motel ($)
RR 3 Box# 737
(66762) 316.231.3950

• Pratt •
Best Western ($)
1336 E 1st St
(67124) 316.672.6407

Days Inn
1901 - 1st St
(67124) 316.672.9465
$3

Evergreen Inn ($)
20001 W Hwy 54
(67124) 800.456.6424

Holiday Inn
1401 W Hwy 54
(67124) 316.672.9433

Pratt Budget Inn ($)
1631 E 1st St
(67124) 316.672.6468

Red Carpet Inn
1401 E 1st St
(67124) 316.672.5588

Super 8 ($)
1906 E 1st St
(67124) 800.800.8000
call re: fees

• Quinter •
Budget Host ($$)
I-70 & 212
(67752) 913.754.3337

Q Motel ($)
Box# 398
(67752) 913.754.3337

• Russell •
Budget Host ($$)
1225 S Fossil St
(67665) 913.483.6660
small pets only

Red Carpet Inn
Hwy 281
(67665) 913.483.2107

Winchester Inn ($)
Frontage Rd Hwy 281
(67665) 913.483.6660

• Salina •
Airliner Motel ($)
781 N Broadway Blvd
(67401) 913.827.5586

Best Western ($$)
1846 N 9th St
(67401) 913.827.0356
small pets

Best Western ($$)
632 Westport Blvd
(67401) 913.827.9315
small attended pets

Budget Inn ($)
217 S Broadway Blvd
(67401) 913.825.7265

Budget King Motel ($)
809 N Broadway Blvd
(67401) 913.827.4477

Comfort Inn ($$)
1820 W Crawford St
(67401) 913.826.1711

Holiday Inn ($$)
1616 W Crawford St
(67401) 913.823.1791

Howard Johnson ($)
2403 S 9th St
(67401) 800.446.4656

Ramada Inn ($$)
1949 N 9th St
(67401) 800.272.6232

Red Coach Inn ($)
2020 W Crawford St
(67401) 913.825.2111

Super 8
1640 Crawford
(67401) 913.826.9215
call re: fees

• Seneca •
Starlite Motel ($)
410 North St
(66538) 913.336.2191

• Sharon Springs •
Heyls Traveler Motel
Jct US 40 & KS27
(67758) 913.852.4293

KANSAS, Shawnee Mission

● Shawnee Mission ●
Doubletree ($$$)
10100 College Blvd
(66210) 913.451.6100

Drury Inn ($$)
9009 Shawnee Mission Pkwy
(66202) 800.325.8300

Drury Inn ($$)
10951 Metcalf Ave
(66210) 800.325.8300

Embassy Suites ($$$$)
10601 Metcalf Ave
(66212) 913.649.7060

Holiday Inn
7240 Shawnee Mission
(66202) 913.262.3010

Howard Johnson ($$)
12381 W 95th St
(66215) 800.654.2000

La Quinta Inn ($$)
9461 Lenexa Dr
(66215) 800.221.4731
call re: fees

Marriott Hotel ($$$)
10800 Metcalf Ave
(66210) 913.451.8000

Red Roof Inn ($)
6800 W 108th St
(66211) 800.843.7663

Residence Inn ($$$)
6300 W 110th St
(66211) 800.331.3131

White Haven Motel ($)
8039 Metcalf Ave
(66204) 800.752.2892

● Smith Center ●
Modern Aire Motel ($)
117 W US 36
(66967) 800.727.7332

● South Hutchinson ●
Best Western ($$)
11 Des Moines Ave
(67505) 316.663.4444

● Tecumseh ●
Old Stone House ($$)
6033 SE Hwy 40
(66542) 913.379.5568

● Topeka ●
Best Western ($$)
2950 S Topeka Blvd
(66611) 913.267.1681
limited $5 charge

Comfort Inn ($$)
1518 SW Wanamaker Rd
(66604) 913.273.5365

Countryview Estate ($$)
5420 SW Fairlawn Rd
(66610) 913.862.0335

Days Inn ($$)
1510 SW Wanamaker Rd
(66604) 913.272.8538

Econo Lodge ($)
1240 SW Wanamaker Rd
(66604) 800.424.4777

Fairfield Inn ($$)
1530 SW Westport Dr
(66604) 800.348.6000

Holiday Inn
605 Fairlawn
(66606) 913.272.8040

Holiday Inn
914 SE Madisn
(66607) 913.232.7721

Liberty Inn ($$)
3839 S Topeka Blvd
(66609) 913.266.4700

Plaza Inn Motel ($$)
3802 S Topeka Blvd
(66609) 913.266.8880

Super 8 ($)
5968 SW 10th Ave
(66604) 800.800.8000
call re: fees

● Wa Keeney ●
Best Western ($$)
I-70 & US 283
(67672) 913.743.2118
small pets only

Budget Host ($)
I-70 & US283
(67672) 913.743.2121
small pets only

● Wamego ●
Summer Motel ($)
1215 Hwy 24
(66547) 913.456.2304

● Wathena ●
Capri Motel ($)
Box# 97
(66090) 913.365.0209

● Wichita ●
Air Cap Motel
6075 Air Cap Dr
(67219) 316.744.2071

Best Western ($$)
915 E 53rd St
(67219) 316.832.9387
small pets only

Deluxe Inn ($)
8401 Hwy 54W
(67209) 316.722.4221

Grand Palace Inn ($)
607 E 47th St
(67216) 316.529.4100

Hampton Inn ($$$)
9449 E Corporate Hills Dr
(67207) 316.686.3576

Harvey Hotel ($$$)
549 S Rock Rd
(67207) 316.686.7131

Holiday Inn ($$$)
5500 W Kellogg Dr
(67209) 316.943.2181

Holiday Inn ($$)
7335 E Kellogg Dr
(67207) 316.685.1281

Howard Johnson ($$)
6575 W Kellogg Dr
(67209) 316.943.8165

Inn At The Park ($$$)
3751 E Douglas Ave
(67218) 316.652.0500

La Quinta Inn ($$)
7700 E Kellogg Dr
(67207) 800.531.5900
call re: fees

Marriott Hotel ($$$)
9100 E Corporate Hills Dr
(67207) 316.651.0333

Red Carpet Inn ($$)
607 E 4Mth St
(67216) 316.529.4100

Wichita Royale Hotel ($$$)
125 N Market St
(67202) 800.876.0240

● Winfield ●
Comfort Inn ($$)
US77 At Quail Ridge
(67156) 316.221.7529

● Yates Center ●
Star Motel ($)
206 S Fry St
(66783) 316.625.2175

Townsman Motel ($)
609 W Mary St
(66783) 316.625.2131

Kentucky

● Ashland ●
Days Inn ($$)
12700 Hwy 180
(41101) 606.928.3600
$5 fee

Knights Inn ($)
7216 US 60
(41102) 800.843.5644

● Auburn ●
The Guest House
421 W Main St
(42206) 502.542.6019

● Bardstown ●
Holiday Inn
Hwy 31 & Bluegrass
(40004) 502.348.9253

Holiday Inn ($$)
Hwy 31
(40004) 800.465.4329

Old Bardstown Inn ($)
510 E Stephen Foster Ave
(40004) 502.349.0776

Old Kentucky Home ($)
414 W Stephen Foster Ave
(40004) 502.348.5979

Parkview Motel ($)
418 E Stephen Foster Av
(40004) 502.348.5983

Ramada Inn ($$)
523 N 3rd St
(40004) 502.349.0363

Red Carpet Inn ($$)
1714 New Haven Rd
(40004) 502.348.1112

● Belfry ●
Super 8
65 Hwy 292
(41514) 606.237.5898
call re: fees

● Benton ●
Cozy Cove Resort ($$)
917 Reed Rd
(42025) 502.354.8168

King Creek Resort
972N King Creek Rd
(42025) 502.354.8268

Southern Komfort
RR 4 Box# 348
(42025) 502.354.6422

● Berea ●
Days Inn ($$)
1202 Walnut Meadow Rd
(40403) 606.986.7373
$5/pets

Econo Lodge ($$)
1010 Paint Lick Rd
(40403) 800.424.4777

Holiday Motel ($$)
100 Jane St
(40403) 606.986.9311

Howard Johnson ($)
715 Chestnut St
(40403) 606.986.2384

Super 8 ($)
196 Prince Royal Dr
(40403) 606.986.8426
$4 fee

Tavern Hotel ($$)
Main & Prospect
(40404) 606.986.9358

● Bowling Green ●
Budgetel ($$)
165 Three Springs Rd
(42104) 502.843.3200

Holiday Inn ($$)
3240 Scottsville Rd
(42104) 502.781.1500

News Inn ($$)
3160 Scottsville Rd
(42104) 502.784.3460

Ramada Inn ($)
4767 Scottsville Rd
(42104) 502.781.3000

Scottish Inn ($)
3140 Scottsville Rd
(42104) 502.781.6550

● Burkesville ●
Riverfront Lodge ($$)
305 Kern St
(42717) 502.864.3300

● Cadiz ●
Country Inn ($$)
5909 Hgopkinsville Rd
(42211) 502.522.7007

● Campbellsville ●
Lakeview Motel ($)
1291 Old Lebanon Rd
(42718) 502.465.8139

Super 8 ($$)
100 Albion Way
(42718) 502.789.0808
mgr preapproval reqd

● Carrollton ●
Days Inn ($$)
61 Inn Rd
(41008) 502.732.9301
$45 deposit

Gables Court ($)
1501 Highland Ave
(41008) 502.732.4248

Holiday Inn ($$)
140 Inn Rd
(41008) 502.732.6661

Super 8 ($)
130 Slumber Ln
(41008) 502.732.0252
call re: fees

● Cave City ●
Caveland Motel ($)
451 Dixie Hwy
(42127) 502.773.2321

Comfort Inn ($$)
801 Mammoth Cave St
(42127) 502.773.2030
mgr preapproval reqd

Days Inn ($)
822 Mammoth Cave St
(42127) 502.773.2151
mgr preapproval reqd

Heritage Inn ($)
Box# 2048
(42127) 800.264.1514

Holiday Inn ($$)
Hwy 90 & I-65
(42127) 502.773.3101
mgr preapproval reqd

● Corbin ●
Budgetel ($$)
174 Adams Rd
(40701) 606.528.9040

Holiday Inn ($$)
2615 Cumberland Falls Hwy
(40701) 606.528.6301

Holiday Motel ($)
1304 S Main St
(40701) 606.528.6220

Knights Inn ($)
RR 11 Box# 256
(40701) 800.843.5644

Super 8 ($$)
171 W Cumberland Gap
Pkwy
(40701) 606.528.8888
$6

● Corinth ●
K & t Motel
Hwy 330 & I-75 Ex 144
(41010) 506.824.4371

● Covington ●
Embassy Suites ($$)
10 E Rivercenter Blvd
(41011) 606.261.8400

Holiday Inn
2100 Dixie Hwy
(41011) 606.331.1500

Quality Hotel ($$$)
666 W 5th St
(41011) 800.292.2079

Quality Hotel ($$$)
666 W 5th St
(41011) 606.491.1200

● Danville ●
Days Inn ($$)
Danville Bypass
(40422) 606.236.8601

Holiday Inn ($$)
96 Daniel Dr
(40422) 606.236.8600

Super 8 ($)
3663 Hwy 150/127 Bypass
(40422) 606.236.8881
call re: fees

● Dry Ridge ●
Super 8 ($$)
88 Blackburn Ln
(41035) 606.824.3700
call re: fees

● Eddyville ●
Eddy Bay Lodging ($$$)
75 Forest Glen Dr
(42038) 502.388.9960

● Elizabethtown ●
Best Western ($)
642 E Dixie Ave
(42701) 502.765.6139
small pets only

Comfort Inn ($$)
1043 Executive Dr
(42701) 502.769.3030

Days Inn ($)
2010 N Mulberry St
(42701) 502.769.5522
mgr preapproval reqd

Holiday Inn
US 62 & I-65
(42701) 502.769.2344

Lincoln Trail Motel ($)
905 N Mulberry St
(42701) 502.769.1301

Super 8 ($)
2028 N Mulberry St
(42701) 502.737.1088
$5

The Olde Bethlehem
Academy Inn ($$$)
7051 St. John Rd
(42701) 502.862.9003

Travelodge ($)
2009 N Mulberry St
(42701) 502.765.4166

● Erlanger ●
Howard Johnson ($$)
648 Donaldson Hwy
(41018) 606.342.6200

● Florence ●
Budget Host ($$)
8075 Steilen
(41042) 606.371.0277
attended only

Knights Inn ($)
8049 Dream St
(41042) 800.843.5644

Motel 6 ($)
7937 Dream St
(41042) 606.283.0909
1 small pet/room

Super 8 ($$)
7928 Dream St
(41042) 606.283.1221
designated rooms

● Frankfort ●
Bluegrass Inn ($)
635 Versailles Rd
(40601) 502.695.1800

Super 8 ($$)
1225 US Hwy 127
(40601) 502.875.3220
call re: fees

The Anchor Inn
790 E Main St
(40601) 502.227.7404

● Franklin ●
Comfort Inn ($$)
3794 Nashville Rd
(42134) 502.586.6100

Days Inn
103 Trotter
(42134) 502.586.5669
$5

Holiday Inn ($$)
3811 Nashville Rd
(42134) 502.586.5090
mgr preapproval reqd

Super 8 ($)
2805 Scottsville Rd
(42134) 502.586.8885
pets w/permission

● Ft Wright ●
Days Inn ($$)
1945 Dixie Hwy
(41011) 606.341.8801

● Georgetown ●
Days Inn ($)
385 Delaplain Rd
(40324) 502.863.5002
$4

Motel 6 ($)
401 Delaplain Rd
(40324) 502.863.1166
1 small pet/room

Shoneys Inn ($$)
200 Shoney Dr
(40324) 502.868.9800
$5 fee

Super 8 ($)
250 Shoney Dr
(40324) 502.863.4888
$6 & deposit

● Gilbertsville ●
Ramada Inn ($$)
Hwy 62
(42044) 502.362.4278

The Moors Resort
Hwy 963
(42044) 800.626.5472

● Glasgow ●
Glasgow Inn ($)
1003 W Main St
(42141) 502.651.5191

● Grand Rivers ●
Best Western ($$)
720 Complex Dr
(42045) 502.928.2700
small pets $5

● Hanson ●
Econo Lodge ($)
10530 Corduroy Rd
(42413) 419.836.2822

● Hardin ●
Cedar Lane Resort
Hwy 68 Rt 1 Box# 520
(42048) 502.474.8042

Early American Motel ($)
Rt 1
(42048) 502.474.2241

Fin N Feather
Rt 1 Hwy 68
(42048) 502.474.2351

● Harlan ●
Scottish Inn ($)
US 421 S Eugene Goss Hwy
(40831) 606.573.4660

● Harrodsburg ●
Best Western ($$)
1680 Danville Rd
(40330) 606.734.9431
small pets only

● Hazard ●
Days Inn
359 Morton Blvd
(41701) 606.436.4777
$6

● Hebron ●
Radisson Inn ($$$)
Cincinnati N Ky Airport
(41048) 606.371.6166

● Henderson ●
Days Inn ($$)
2044 US 41N
(42420) 502.826.6600
$5 fee

Scottish Inn ($)
2820 US 41N
(42420) 502.827.1806
$5 fee

Super 8 ($$)
2030 Hwy 41
(42420) 502.827.5611
deposit reqd

● Hopkinsville ●
Best Western ($$)
4101 Fort Campbell Blvd
(42240) 502.886.9000

Holiday Inn ($$)
2910 Ft Campbell
(42240) 502.886.4413

Rodeway Inn ($)
2923 Fort Campbell Blvd
(42240) 502.885.1126

● Kuttawa ●
Days Inn ($$)
Factory Outlet Ave
(42055) 502.388.5420
$10

● La Grange ●
Days Inn ($)
I-71 & Hwy 53
(40031) 502.222.7192

● Lebanon ●
Holly Hill Hotel
459 Main St
(40033) 502.692.2175

● Leitchfield ●
Country Side Inn ($)
Commerca Dr & W Ky
Pkwy
(42754) 502.259.4021

● Lexington ●
Days Inn ($$)
1987 N Broadway St
(40505) 606.299.1202
$7 charge small

Well
Behaved

Mortons Gap, KENTUCKY

Days Inn ($)
5575 Athens Boonesboro Rd
(40509) 606.263.3100
$3/pets

Econo Lodge ($)
5527 Athens Boonesboro Rd
(40509) 800.424.4777

Econo Lodge ($)
925 Newtown Rd
(40511) 800.424.4777

Fairfield Inn ($$)
3050 Lakecrest Cir
(40513) 606.224.3338

Greenleaf Motel ($$)
2280 Nicholasville Rd
(40503) 606.277.1191

Hampton Inn ($$$)
3060 Lakecrest Cir
(40513) 800.426.7866

Holiday Inn ($$)
5532 Athens-Boonesboro Rd
(40509) 606.263.5241

Holiday Inn ($$$)
1950 Newtown Rd
(40511) 606.233.0512

Howard Johnson ($)
2250 Elkhorn Rd
(40505) 606.299.8481

La Quinta Inn ($$)
1919 Stanton Way
(40511) 800.531.5900
call re: fees

Marriott Resort ($$$$)
1800 Newtown Rd
(40511) 606.231.5100

Quality Inn ($$)
1050 Newtown Rd
(40511) 606.233.0561

Radisson Inn ($$$$)
369 W Vine St
(40507) 800.333.3333

Red Roof Inn ($)
483 Haggard Ln
(40505) 800.843.7663

Red Roof Inn ($$)
2651 Wilhite Dr
(40503) 800.843.7663

Super 8 ($$)
2351 Buena Vista Rd
(40505) 606.299.6241
call re: fees

The Kentucky Inn ($$)
525 Waller Ave
(40504) 606.254.1177

Wilson Inn ($$)
2400 Buena Vista Dr
(40505) 606.293.6113

● London ●
Best Western ($$)
207 W Hwy 80
(40741) 606.864.2222
small pets

Days Inn ($)
285 W Hwy 80
(40741) 606.878.9800
$4

Holiday Inn
400 GOP
(40741) 606.878.7678

Ramada Inn ($$)
21035 Hwy 192
(40741) 800.272.6232

Westgate Inn Motel ($)
254 W Daniel Boone Pkwy
(40741) 606.878.7330

● Louisa ●
Best Western ($$)
117 E Madison St
(41230) 606.638.9417

● Louisville ●
Breckinridge Inn ($$$)
2800 Breckinridge Ln
(40220) 502.456.5050

Days Inn ($$$)
101 E Jefferson St
(40202) 502.585.2200
mgr preapproval reqd

Days Inn ($$)
4621 Shelbyville Rd
(40207) 502.896.8871
$6/pets

Days Inn ($$)
1850 Embassy Square Blvd
(40299) 502.491.1040
size limits & fees

Executive West ($$$)
830 Phillips Ln
(40209) 502.367.2251

Holiday Inn ($$)
1465 Gardiner Ln
(40213) 502.452.6361

Holiday Inn
1041 Zorn
(40207) 502.897.5101

Holiday Inn ($$$)
120 W Broadway
(40202) 502.582.2241

Holiday Inn ($$$)
3317 Fern Valley Rd
(40213) 502.966.3311

Holiday Inn ($$)
3255 Bardsrtown Rd
(40205) 502.454.0451

Holiday Inn ($$)
4110 Dixie Hwy
(40216) 502.448.2020

Hurstbourne Hotel ($$$)
9700 Bluegrass Pkwy
(40299) 502.491.4830

Ramada Inn ($$)
4805 Brownsboro Rd
(40207) 800.272.6232

Ramada Inn ($$$)
192 Bishop Ln
(40218) 800.272.6232

Red Roof Inn ($)
4704 Preston Hwy
(40213) 800.843.7663

Red Roof Inn ($)
9330 Blairwood Rd
(40222) 800.843.7663

Red Roof Inn ($)
3322 Newburg Rd
(40218) 800.843.7663

Residence Inn ($$$)
120 Hurstbourne Pkwy
(40222) 800.331.3131

Seelbach Hotel ($$$$)
200 S 4th Ave
(40202) 800.333.3399

Sleep Inn ($$)
3330 Preston Hwy
(40213) 502.368.9597
mgr preapproval reqd

Super 8 ($$)
4800 Preston Hwy
(40213) 502.968.0088
call re: fees

The Camberley Brown Hotel
($$$$)
335 W Broadway
(40202) 502.583.1234

Thrifty Dutchman ($)
3357 Fern Valley Rd
(40213) 502.968.8124

Wilson Inn ($$)
3209 Kemmons Dr
(40218) 800.945.7667

Wilson Inn ($$)
9802 Bunsen Way
(40299) 800.945.7667

● Madisonville ●
Days Inn ($$)
1900 Lantaff Blvd
(42431) 502.821.8620
$5/pets

● Mammoth Cave ●
Mammoth Cave Hotel ($$$)
I-65 & Hwy 70
(42259) 502.758.2225

● Middlesboro ●
Park View Motel ($)
202 1/2 N 12th St
(40965) 606.248.4516

● Mortons Gap ●
Best Western ($)
Pennyrile Pkwy
(42440) 502.258.5201

● Mount Sterling ●
Days Inn ($)
705 Maysville Rd
(40353) 606.498.4680
$5/pets

Scottish Inn ($)
517 Maysville Rd
(40353) 606.498.3424

● Mount Vernon ●
Best Western ($$)
US25 & 1 75
(40456) 800.528.1234
small cats & dogs

Days Inn ($)
1630 Richmond St
(40456) 606.256.3300

Econo Lodge ($)
Box# 1106
(40456) 800.424.4777

● Muldraugh ●
Golden Manor Motel ($$)
346 Dixie Hwy
(40155) 502.942.2800

● Murray ●
Days Inn ($$)
517 S 12th St
(42071) 502.753.6706
$4/pets

Murray Plaza Court ($)
S 12th St
(42071) 502.753.2682

Paradise Resort
RR 6 Box# 239
(42071) 502.436.2767

Shoneys Inn ($$)
1503 N 12th St
(42071) 502.753.5353
$4 fee

● New Concord ●
Missing Hill Resort
HC Box# 215-A
(42076) 502.436.5519

● Oak Grove ●
Days Inn
212 Auburn
(42262) 800.329.7466
$5

● Owensboro ●
Days Inn ($$)
3720 New Hartford Rd
(42303) 502.684.9621

Holiday Inn ($$)
3136 W 2nd St
(42301) 502.685.3941

Super 8 ($$)
1027 Goetz Dr
(42301) 502.685.3388
call re: fees

● Paducah ●
Best Inns ($$)
5001 Hinckleville Rd
(42002) 502.442.3334

Budget Host ($)
1234 Broadway St
(42001) 800.283.4678
mgr preapproval reqd

Days Inn ($$)
3901 Hinkleville Rd
(42001) 502.442.7501
$4 fee in smoking rooms

Drury Inn ($$)
3975 Hinkleville Rd
(42001) 800.325.8300

Drury Inn ($$$)
120 McBride Ln
(42001) 502.441.0024

Hampton Inn ($$$)
4930 Hinkleville Rd
(42001) 502.442.4500

Hickory House Motel
2504 Bridge St
(42003) 502.442.1601

Holiday Inn
3994 Hinkleville Rd
(42001) 502.442.8874

Pear Tree Inn ($$)
4910 Hinkleville Rd
(42001) 800.282.8733

Ramada Inn ($$)
727 Joe Clifton Dr
(42001) 502.443.7521

Royal Inn
2160 S Beltline
(42003) 502.442.6171

● Paintsville ●
Days Inn ($$)
512 S Mayo Trl
(41240) 606.789.3551

● Parkers Lake ●
Holiday Motor Lodge
Hwy 90 Box# 300
(42634) 606.376.2732

● Pikeville ●
Landmark Inn ($$)
146 S Mayo Trl
(41501) 606.432.2545

● Prestonsburg ●
Super 8
550 US 23
(41653) 606.886.3355
call re: fees

● Prospect ●
Melrose Inn ($$)
1330L US 42
(40059) 502.228.1136

● Radcliff ●
Econo Lodge ($)
261 N Dixie Blvd
(40160) 800.424.4777

Fort Knox Inn
1400 N Dixie Blvd
(40160) 502.351.3199

Super 8 ($$)
395 Redmar Blvd
(40160) 502.352.1888
mgr preapproval reqd

● Richmond ●
Days Inn ($$)
2109 Belmont Dr
(40475) 606.624.5769
$5/pets

Econo Lodge ($)
230 Eastern Byp
(40475) 800.424.4777

Hojo Inn ($)
1688 Northgate Dr
(40475) 800.446.4656

Motel 6 ($)
1698 Northgate Dr
(40475) 606.623.0880
1 small pet/room

Super 8 ($$)
107 N Keeneland Dr
(40475) 606.624.1550
call re: fees

Wise Motel ($)
105 N Killarney Ln
(40475) 606.623.8126

● Shelbyville ●
Best Western ($$)
115 Isaac Shelby Dr
(40065) 502.633.4400
small pets only

Days Inn ($$)
101 Howard Dr
(40065) 502.633.4005
mgr preapproval reqd

Shelbyville Motel
Box# 378 Hwy US 60
(40065) 502.533.3350

● Shepherdsville ●
Best Western ($$)
211 S Lakeview Dr
(40165) 502.543.7097
small pets only

Days Inn ($$)
Hwy 44 At Jct I-65
(40165) 502.543.3011

Motel 6 ($$)
144 Paraquet Springs Dr
(40165) 502.543.4400
1 small pet/room

● Smiths Grove ●
Bryce Motel ($)
592 S Main St
(42171) 502.563.5141

● Somerset ●
Cumberland Motel
6050 S Hwy 27
(42501) 606.561.5131

● Walton ●
Days Inn ($)
11177 Frontage Rd
(41094) 606.485.4151

Richwood Motel
10805 Dixie Hwy
(41094) 606.525.9525

● West Somerset ●
Beckett Motel
2001 Lees Ford Dock
(42564) 606.636.6411

● Whitesburg ●
Super 8 ($$)
377-A Hazard Rd
(41858) 606.633.8888
mgr preapproval reqd

● Williamsburg ●
Best Western ($)
Box# 204
(40769) 606.549.1500
small pets

Holiday Inn ($$)
30 W Hwy 92
(40769) 606.549.3450

● Williamstown ●
Days Inn ($$)
211 Hwy 36
(41097) 606.824.5025
$3

Hojo Inn ($)
10 Ksyway Dr
(41097) 800.446.4656

● Winchester ●
Holiday Inn ($$)
1100 Holiday Dr
(40391) 606.744.9111

Red Carpet Inn
1510 Lexington Ave
(40391) 606.744.9220

Louisiana

● Alexandria ● Best Western
($$)
2720 W Macarthur Dr
(71303) 318.445.5530

Rodeway Inn ($$)
742 Macarthur Dr
(71303) 318.448.1611

Travelodge ($$)
1146 Macarthur Dr
(71303) 318.443.1841

● Arcadia ●
Days Inn ($$)
1061 Hwy 151
(71001) 318.263.3555

● Bastrop ●
Country Inn ($)
1815 E Madison Ave
(71220) 318.281.8100

● Baton Rouge ●
Budgetel ($)
10555 Reiger Rd
(70809) 604.291.6600

Comfort Inn ($$)
2445 S Acadian
(70808) 504.927.5790

Days Inn
10245 Airline Hwy
(70816) 504.291.8152
$5

Hilton ($$$)
5500 Hilton Ave
(70808) 800.445.8667

La Quinta Inn ($$)
2333 S Acadian Thruway
(70808) 800.531.5900
call re: fees

Motel 6 ($)
9901 Gwenadele Ave
(70816) 504.924.2130
1 small pet/room

Red Roof Inn ($$)
11314 Broardwalk Dr
(70816) 800.843.7663

Shoneys Inn ($$)
9919 Gwenadele Ave
(70816) 800.222.2222

● Bossier City ●
Days Inn ($)
200 John Wesley Blvd
(71112) 318.742.9200
$5/pets - small pets only

Motel 6 ($)
210 John Wesley Blvd
(71112) 318.742.3472
1 small pet/room

Ramada Inn ($$)
750 Isle Of Capri Blvd
(71111) 318.746.8410

● Breaux Bridge ●
Best Western ($$)
2090 Rees St
(70517) 800.528.1234

● Chalmette ●
Quality Inn ($$)
5353 Paris Rd La 47
(70043) 504.277.5353

● Crowley ●
Best Western ($$)
9571 Egan Hwy
(70526) 318.783.2378

● Delhi ●
Best Western ($$)
35 Snider Rd
(71232) 318.878.5126

● Deridder ●
Best Western ($$)
1213 N Pine St
(70634) 318.462.3665
small pets

Red Carpet Inn ($)
806 N Pine St
(70634) 318.463.8605

● Franklin ●
Best Western ($$)
1909 Main St
(70538) 318.828.1810

● Gretna ●
Howard Johnson ($$)
100 Westbank Expwy
(70053) 504.366.8531

● Hammond ●
Best Western ($$)
14175 Hwy 190
(70401) 504.542.8555
small pets only

● Houma ●
Quality Inn ($$)
1400 W Tunnel Blvd
(70360) 504.879.4871

● Jackson ●
Asphodel Inn ($$)
RR 2 Box# 89A
(70748) 504.654.6868

● Jennings ●
Holiday Inn
603 Holiday Dr
(70546) 318.824.5280

● Kenner ●
Days Inn ($$)
1300 Vets Memorial
(70062) 504.469.2531
$8 fee

Hilton ($$$$)
901 Airline Hwy
(70062) 504.469.5000

● Kinder ●
Holiday Inn
11750 US 165
(70648) 318.738.3381

● Lafayette ●
Best Western ($$$)
1801 W Pinhook Rd
(70508) 318.233.8120

Comfort Inn ($$)
1421 SE Evangeline Thrwy
(70501) 318.232.9000

Days Inn ($$)
1620 N University & I-10
(70506) 318.237.8880
$5/small pets

Holiday Inn
2716 NE Evangeline
(70507) 318.233.0003

Holiday Inn
2503 SE Evangeline
(70508) 318.234.2000

La Quinta Inn ($$)
2100 NE Evangeline Thrwy
(70501) 800.531.5900
call re: fees

Quality Inn ($$)
1605 N University Ave
(70506) 318.232.6131

CALL AHEAD!

LOUISIANA, Lafayette

Red Roof Inn ($)
1718 N University Ave
(70507) 800.843.7663

Rodeway Inn ($$)
1801 NW Evangeline Thrwy
(70501) 318.233.5500

Super 8 ($)
2224 NE Evangeline Thrwy
(70501) 318.232.8826
call re: fees

● Lake Charles ●
Days Inn ($$)
1010 N Hwy 171
(70611) 318.433.1711
$4

Motel 6 ($)
335 Hwy 171
(70611) 318.433.1773
1 small pet/room

● Metairie ●
La Quinta Inn ($$)
3100 I-10 Service Rd
(70001) 504.835.8511
call re: fees

Quality Hotel ($$)
2261 N Causeway Blvd
(70001) 504.833.8213
mgr preapproval reqd

● Minden ●
Best Western ($$)
1411 Sibley Rd
(71055) 318.377.1001

● Monroe ●
Best Western ($$)
1475 Garrett Rd
(71202) 318.345.4000

Howard Johnson ($$)
5650 Frontage Rd
(71202) 318.345.2220

La Quinta Inn ($$)
1035 US 165S Bypass
(71203) 800.531.5900
call re: fees

Motel 6 ($)
1501 US Hwy 165 Bypass
(71202) 318.322.5430
1 small pet/room

● Natchitoches ●
Days Inn ($)
1000 College Ave
(71457) 318.352.4426
$4

Super 8
801 Hwy 1
(71457) 318.352.1700
call re: fees

● New Iberia ●
Best Western ($$)
2714 Hwy 14
(70560) 318.364.3030

Holiday Inn
2915 Hwy 14
(70560) 318.367.1201

● New Orleans ●
Best Western ($$)
2820 Tulane Ave
(70119) 504.822.0200
small pets $6/day

Scottish Inn
4200 Old Gentilly Rd
(70126) 504.944.0151

Sully Mansion ($$)
2631 Prytania St
(70130) 504.891.0457

The Maison Esplanade ($$)
1244 Esplanade Ave
(70116) 504.523.8080

Windsor Court Hotel ($$$$)
300 Gravier St
(70130) 504.523.6000

New Orleans Metro

● Chalmette ●
Quality Inn ($$)
5353 Paris Rd La 47
(70043) 504.277.5353

● Gretna ●
Howard Johnson ($$)
100 Westbank Expwy
(70053) 504.366.8531

● Hammond ●
Best Western ($$)
14175 Hwy 190
(70401) 504.542.8555
small pets only

● Houma ●
Quality Inn ($$)
1400 W Tunnel Blvd
(70360) 504.879.4871

● Kenner ●
Days Inn ($$)
1300 Vets Memorial
(70062) 504.469.2531
$8 fee

Hilton ($$$$)
901 Airline Hwy
(70062) 504.469.5000

● New Orleans ●
Best Western ($$)
2820 Tulane Ave
(70119) 504.822.0200
small pets $6/day

Scottish Inn
4200 Old Gentilly Rd
(70126) 504.944.0151

Sully Mansion ($$)
2631 Prytania St
(70130) 504.891.0457

The Maison Esplanade ($$)
1244 Esplanade Ave
(70116) 504.523.8080

Windsor Court Hotel ($$$$)
300 Gravier St
(70130) 504.523.6000

● Slidell ●
Econo Lodge ($$)
58512 Tyler Dr
(70459) 800.424.4777

La Quinta Inn ($$)
794 E I-10 Service Rd
(70461) 800.531.5900
call re: fees

Ramada Inn ($$)
798 E I-10 Service Rd
(70461) 504.653.9960

End of New Orleans Metro

● Opelousas ●
Best Western ($$)
1635 I-49 Service Rd
(70570) 318.942.5540

● Port Allen ●
Days Inn ($)
215 Lobdell Hwy
(70767) 504.387.0671
$5/pets

Newcourt Inn ($$)
I-10 & Hwy 415
(70767) 504.381.9134

● Rayville ●
Cottonland Inn ($)
Box# 29
(71269) 318.728.5985

● Ruston ●
Holiday Inn ($$)
401 N Service Rd
(71270) 318.255.5901

● Shreveport ●
Days Inn ($)
4935 W Monkhouse Dr
(71109) 318.636.0800
$5

Motel 6 ($)
4915 Monkhouse Dr
(71109) 318.631.9691
1 small pet/room

Red Roof Inn ($)
7296 Greenwood Rd
(71119) 800.843.7663

Residence Inn ($)
1001 Gould Dr
(71119) 318.747.6220

Super 8 ($$)
5204 Monkhouse Dr
(71109) 318.635.8888
call re: fees

● Slidell ●
Econo Lodge ($$)
58512 Tyler Dr
(70459) 800.424.4777

La Quinta Inn ($$)
794 E I-10 Service Rd
(70461) 800.531.5900
call re: fees

Ramada Inn ($$)
798 E I-10 Service Rd
(70461) 504.653.9960

● Sulphur ●
La Quinta Inn ($$)
2600 Ruth St
(70663) 800.531.5900
call re: fees

● Tallulah ●
Super 8 ($$)
1604 New Hwy 65
(71282) 318.574.2000
$10-$30 fee

● Thibodaux ●
Holiday Inn
400 W 1st
(70301) 504.446.0561

Howard Johnson ($$)
201 N Canal Blvd
(70301) 504.447.9071

● Vinton ●
Best Western ($$)
2267 Old Hwy 90
(70668) 318.589.7492

● West Monroe ●
Red Roof Inn ($$)
102 Constitution Dr
(71292) 800.843.7663

● Winnsboro ●
Best Western ($$)
4198 Front St
(71295) 318.435.2000

Maine
● Auburn ●
Auburn Inn ($$)
Washington St At Ex 12
(04210) 207.777.1777

● Augusta ●
Best Western ($$)
284 Western Ave
(04330) 207.622.5804
small pets only

Echo Lake Lodge
Rt 17 In Fayette
(04330) 207.685.9550

Motel 6 ($$)
18 Edison Dr
(04330) 207.622.0000
1 small pet/room

● Bangor ●
Best Western ($$)
155 Littlefield Ave
(04401) 207.862.3737

Best Western ($$)
155 Littlefield Ave
(04401) 207.862.9575

Comfort Inn ($$)
750 Hogan Rd
(04401) 207.942.7899
mgr preapproval reqd

Days Inn ($$)
250 Odlin Rd
(04401) 207.942.6272
$6

Econo Lodge ($)
327 Odlin Rd
(04401) 207.945.0111

Holiday Inn ($$)
500 Main St
(04401) 207.947.8651
mgr preapproval reqd

Holiday Inn ($$$)
404 Odlin Rd
(04401) 207.947.0101
mgr preapproval reqd

Motel 6 ($)
1100 Hammond St
(04401) 207.947.6921
1 small pet/room

Penopscott Inn ($$)
570 Main St
(04401) 207.947.0566

Red Carpet Inn ($)
480 Main St
(04401) 207.942.5282
mgr preapproval reqd

Riverside Inn ($$)
495 State St
(04401) 207.947.3800

Policies
Subject
to Change

Rodeway Inn ($$)
482 Odlin Rd
(04401) 207.942.6301
$5 charge not left alone

Scottish Inn ($)
1476 Hammond St
(04401) 207.945.2934

● Bar Harbor ●
Balance Rock Inn ($$$$)
21 Albert Mdws
(04609) 207.288.9900

Bayview Hotel
111 Eden St
(04609) 207.288.5861

Hutchins Mtn View ($$)
RR 1 Box# 1190
(04609) 207.288.4833

Wonderview Motor Lodge
Box# 25
(04609) 207.288.3358

● Bass Harbor ●
Gables Inn at Bass Harbor
($$$$)
Box# 396
(04653) 207.244.3699

● Bath ●
Fairhaven ($$)
North Bath Rd
(04530) 207.443.4391

Holiday Inn
139 Western Ave
(04530) 207.443.9741

New Meadows Inn ($)
Bath Rd
(04530) 207.443.3921

● Belfast ●
Belfast Motor Inn ($$$)
RR 2 Box# 21
(04915) 207.338.2740

Gull Motel ($)
RR 1 Box# 80
(04915) 207.338.4030

Meadows Inn ($$$)
90 Northport Ave
(04915) 207.338.5715

Ocean Inn ($)
RR 1 Box# 99A
(04915) 207.338.4260

● Bethel ●
Bethel Inn ($$$)
On The Common
(04217) 207.824.2175

Lauberge Country Inn ($$)
Mill Hill Rd
(04217) 207.824.2774

The Cameron House
Box# 468
(04217) 207.824.3219

● Bingham ●
Bingham Motor Inn ($)
Rte 201
(04920) 207.672.4135

● Boothbay ●
Hillside Acres Motel ($$)
Box# 300
(04537) 207.633.3411

White Anchor Motel ($)
RR 1 Box# 438
(04537) 207.633.3788

● Boothbay Harbor ●
Fishermans Wharf ($$)
40 Commercial St
(04538) 207.633.5090

The Pines Motel ($$)
Box# 693
(04538) 207.633.4555

Welch House Inn ($$)
36 McKown St
(04538) 207.633.3431

● Brewer ●
Brewer Motor Inn ($)
359 Wilson St
(04412) 207.989.4476

Rodeway Inn ($)
448 Wilson St
(04412) 207.989.3200
$5 fee

● Brunswick ●
Mainline Motel ($$)
133 Pleasant St
(04011) 207.725.8761

The Atrium Motel ($$)
Cooks Corner Ex
(04011) 207.729.5555

Viking Motor Inn ($)
287 Bath Rd
(04011) 207.729.6661
$5 per day

● Bucksport ●
Best Western ($$)
52 Main St
(04416) 207.469.3113
pets managers discretion

Bucksport Motor Inn ($)
151 Main St
(04416) 207.469.3111

Spring Fountain Motel ($)
RR 2 Box# 710
(04416) 207.469.3139

● Camden ●
Beloins Motel
HCr 60 Box# 3105 US 1
(04843) 207.236.3262

Blue Harbor House ($$$)
67 Elm St
(04843) 207.236.3196

Blue Harbor House ($$$$)
67 Elm St
(04843) 800.348.3196
referred resv a must

● Cape Elizabeth ●
Inn By The Sea ($$$)
40 Bowery Beach Rd
(04107) 207.799.3134

● Caribou ●
Caribou Inn ($$)
RR 3
(04736) 207.498.3733

● Castine ●
The Holiday House
Box# 215
(04421) 207.326.4335

The Manor ($$$)
Box# 276
(04421) 207.326.4861

● Center Lovell ●
Hewnoaks Cottages
RR 1 Box# 65
(04016) 207.925.6051

Westways ($$$)
Rt 5
(04016) 207.928.2663

● Damariscotta ●
County Fair Motel ($$)
RR 1 Box# 36
(04543) 207.563.3769

Oyster Shell Motel ($$$$)
Box# 267
(04543) 800.874.3747

● East Boothbay ●
Leeward Village ($$$)
Rt 96 Ocean Point Rd
(04544) 207.633.3681

Ocean Point Cabin
HC Box# 936
(04544) 207.633.2981

Smugglers Cove Motel ($$)
Smugglers Cove
(04544) 207.633.2800

● East Machias ●
Maineland Motel ($)
RR 2 East Machias
(04630) 207.255.3334

● East Winthrop ●
Lakeside Motel Cabins ($)
Box# 236
(04343) 800.532.6892

● Eastport ●
Todd House ($$)
Todd'S Head
(04631) 207.853.2328

● Edgecomb ●
Bay View Inn ($$)
Box# 117
(04556) 207.882.6911

The Edgecomb Inn ($$)
RR 1 Box# 51
(04556) 207.882.6343

● Ellsworth ●
Brookside Motel ($$)
High St
(04605) 207.667.2543

Colonial Motor Inn ($$)
Bar Harbor Rd
(04605) 207.667.5548

Comfort Inn ($$$)
130 High St
(04605) 207.667.1345
mgr preapproval reqd

Days Inn ($$)
RR 1 Box# 183
(04605) 207.667.9506
$25/pet

Sunrise Motel ($)
Bar Harbor Rd
(04605) 207.667.8452

The White Birches ($)
Box# 743
(04605) 207.667.3621

Twilite Motel ($)
US 1 & Hwy 3
(04605) 207.667.8165

● Farmington ●
Mount Blue Motel ($$)
RR 4 Box# 5260
(04938) 207.778.6004
$7 charge

● Freeport ●
Eagle Motel ($$)
291 US 1
(04032) 207.865.3106

Freeport Inn ($$)
335 US 1
(04032) 207.865.3106

Idyll Motor Inn
325 US Route 1
(04032) 207.865.4201

● Glen Cove ●
Sea View Motel ($$$)
Box# 101
(04846) 207.594.8479

● Greenville ●
Motel Kino ($$)
Rt 15 Box 514
(04441) 207.695.4470

Spencer Camps ($$)
HC 76 Box# 580
(04441) 207.695.2821
call for available space

● Greenville Junction ●
Chalet Moosehead ($$)
Box# 327
(04442) 207.695.2950

Greenwood Motel ($$)
Box# 307
(04442) 207.695.3321
$5 charge

● Holden ●
The Lucerne Inn ($$)
Bar Harbor Rd
(04429) 207.843.5123

● Houlton ●
American Motel ($)
RR 2 A Bangor Rd
(04730) 207.532.2236

Scottish Inn ($$)
RR 2 A Bangor Rd
(04730) 207.532.2233

Shiretown Motor Inn ($$)
RR 3 Box# 30
(04730) 207.532.9421

● Jackman ●
Briarwood Mtn Resort ($$)
Box# 490
(04945) 207.668.7756

Tuckaway Shores ($)
Forest St
(04945) 207.668.3351

● Jefferson ●
Housekeeping Cottage
($$$$)
RR 1 Box# 820 Jefferson
(04348) 207.832.7055

● Jonesboro ●
Windrise Farm
Box# 47
(04648) 207.434.2701

Be
Discreet

● Kennebunkport ●
Cabot Cove Lodge ($$$)
Box# 1082
(04046) 800.962.5424

Seaside Cottages ($$$)
Beach St Gooch'S Beach
(04046) 207.967.4461

The Colony ($$$$)
Box# 511
(04046) 207.967.3331
$15fee

Turbats Creek Lodge ($$)
Box# 2722
(04046) 207.967.8700

● Kingfield ●
The Herbert Hotel ($$)
Box# 67
(04947) 800.843.4372

● Kittery ●
Super 8 ($)
85 US Hwy 1
(03904) 207.439.2000
open summer only

● Leeds ●
The Angels Cove ($$$$)
Box# 29
(04263) 207.524.5041

● Lewiston ●
Holiday Motel ($)
1905 Lisbon Rd
(04240) 207.783.2277

Motel 6 ($)
516 Pleasant St
(04240) 207.782.6558
1 small pet/room

● Lincoln ●
Briarwood Motor Inn ($$)
Box# 628
(04457) 207.794.6731

Lincoln House ($)
85 Main St
(04457) 207.794.3096
small pets only

● Lincolnville ●
Pine Grove Cottages ($$)
RR 1
(04849) 207.236.2929

● Lubec ●
The Eastland Motel ($$)
Box# 220
(04652) 207.733.5501

● Machias ●
Machias Motor Inn ($$)
26 E Main St
(04654) 207.255.4861
$5 fee

The Bluebird ($$)
Box# 45
(04654) 207.255.3332

● Manset ●
Seawall Motel ($$)
Rt 102
(04656) 207.244.9250

● Matinicus ●
Tuckanuck Lodge ($$)
Shag Hollow Rd
(04851) 207.366.3830

● Medway ●
Gateway Inn ($$)
Rt 157
(04460) 207.746.3193

Katahdin Cabins ($)
Box# H
(04460) 207.746.9349

● Millinocket ●
Best Western ($$)
935 Central St
(04462) 207.723.9777
no pets unattended

Pamola Motor Lodge ($)
973 Central St
(04462) 207.723.9746

The Atrium Inn ($$$)
740 Central St
(04462) 207.723.4555

● Moody ●
Beach Motel ($$)
Box# 389
(04054) 207.646.2636

● New Harbor ●
The Mill Pond
Box# 447
(04554) 207.633.3270

● Newport ●
Bove House ($)
RR 1 Box# 147
(04953) 207.368.4311

● North Anson ●
Embden Lake Resort ($$$$)
RR 1 Box# 3395
(04958) 207.566.7501

● Norway ●
InnTown Motel ($$)
43 Paris St
(04268) 207.743.7706

Ledgewood Motel ($$)
RR 2 Box# 30
(04268) 207.743.6347

● Ogunquit ●
Norseman Motor Inn ($$)
Box# 896
(03907) 207.646.7024

Yellow Monkey House
168 Main St
(03907) 207.646.9056
pets welcome!

● Old Orchard Beach ●
Beau Rivage Motel ($$)
54 E Grand Ave
(04064) 207.934.4668

Flagship Motel ($)
54 W Grand Ave
(04064) 207.934.4866

Grand Beach Inn ($$$)
198 E Grand Ave
(04064) 800.926.3242

Old Colonial Motel
61 W Grand Ave
(04064) 207.934.9862

Waves Motor Inn ($$)
87 W Grand Ave
(04064) 207.934.4949
medium to small

● Orono ●
University Motel ($$)
5 College Ave
(04473) 207.866.4921

● Patten ●
Mt Chase Lodge
RR 1 Box# 281
(04765) 207.528.2183
call for pet rooms

Shin Pond Village ($)
RR 1 Box# 280
(04765) 207.528.2900

● Portland ●
Holiday Inn
88 Spring St
(04101) 207.775.2311

Holiday Inn ($$$)
81 Riverside St
(04103) 207.774.5601
mgr preapproval reqd

Howard Johnson ($$)
155 Riverside
(04103) 207.774.5861
$50 deposit

Inn At Portland ($$)
1150 Brighton Ave
(04102) 207.775.3711

Inn At St. John ($$)
939 Congress St
(04102) 207.773.6481
Reader referred

Motel 6 ($$)
1 Riverside St
(04103) 207.775.0111
1 small pet/room

Radisson Inn ($$$)
157 High St
(04101) 207.775.5411

Ramada Inn ($$$)
1230 Congress St
(04102) 207.774.5611

● Presque Isle ●
Keddys Motor Inn ($$)
Box# 270
(04769) 207.764.3321

Northern Lights ($)
692 Main St
(04769) 207.764.4441
$10 per day

● Princeton ●
The Hideaway
(04668) 207.427.6183

● Rangeley ●
Rangeley Inn ($$$)
Box# 160
(04970) 207.864.3341

Town & Lake Motel ($$)
Main St Box# 47
(04970) 207.864.3755

● Rockland ●
Navigator Motor Inn ($$)
520 Main St
(04841) 207.594.2131

Oakland Seashore ($)
RR 1 Box# 1449
(04841) 207.594.8104

Trade Winds Motel ($$)
2 Park View Dr
(04841) 207.596.6661

● Rockwood ●
Maynards Inn
Box# 228
(04478) 207.534.7702

The Birches Resort ($)
Box# 81
(04478) 207.534.7305

● Rumford ●
Linnell Motel ($$)
2 Mi W On US 2
(04276) 207.364.4511

Four Season Resort ($$$)
Rt 2 Box# 398
(04276) 207.364.7973

● Saco ●
Classic Motel ($$)
21 Ocean Park Rd
(04072) 207.282.5569

Saco Motel ($)
473 Main St
(04072) 207.284.6952

Tourist Haven Motel ($)
757 Portland Rd
(04072) 207.284.7251

● Sanford ●
Bar H Motel ($)
Hwy 109
(04073) 207.324.4662

● Searsport ●
Lights Motel ($)
Rfd Box# 349
(04974) 207.548.2405

● Skowhegan ●
Belmont Motel ($$)
Box# 160
(04976) 207.474.8315

Towne Motel ($$)
248 Madison Ave
(04976) 207.474.5151

● South Portland ●
Best Western ($$)
700 Main St
(04106) 800.528.1234

Howard Johnson ($$$)
675 Main St
(04106) 207.775.5343

Marriott Hotel ($$$)
200 Sable Oaks Dr
(04106) 207.871.8000
small sign release form

● Spruce Head ●
The Craig Inn ($$$)
Clark Island Rd
(04859) 207.594.7644

● Stratton ●
Spillover Motel ($$)
Box# 427
(04982) 207.246.6571

● Waterford ●
Waterford Inn ($$$)
Box# 149
(04088) 207.583.4037

● Waterville ●
Best Western ($$)
356 Main St
(04901) 207.873.3335

Budget Host ($)
400 Kennedy Memorial Dr
(04901) 800.876.2463
mgr preapproval reqd

Econo Lodge ($)
455 Kennedy Memorial Dr
(04901) 207.872.5577

Holiday Inn ($$)
375 Upper Main St
(04901) 207.873.0111
mgr preapproval reqd

The Atrium Motel ($$)
332 Main St
(04901) 207.873.2777

Waterville Motel ($)
320 Kennedy Memorial Dr
(04901) 207.873.0141

● Wells ●
The Garrison Motel ($$)
1099 Post Rd
(04090) 207.646.3497

Watercrest Cottages ($$$)
Box# 37
(04090) 207.646.2202

● West Boothbay Harbor ●
The Harborside ($$)
Box# 516
(04575) 207.633.5381
Reader referred

Policies
Subject
to Change

Be
Discreet

CALL
AHEAD!

● West Southport ●
Ocean Gate Motor Inn
Route 27
(04576) 207.633.3321

The Lawnmeer Inn ($$)
Rt 27
(04576) 207.633.2544

● Westbrook ●
Super 8 ($)
208 Larrabee Rd
(04092) 207.854.1881
mgr preapproval reqd

● Wilton ●
Whispering Pines ($$)
Box# 649
(04294) 207.645.3271

● Winterport ●
Colonial Inn ($$)
Box# 525
(04496) 207.223.5307

● Yarmouth ●
Down East Village Motel ($$)
31 US 1
(04096) 207.846.5161
Reader referred

● York ●
Commons Inn ($$)
RR 1
(03909) 207.363.8903

Well
Behaved

NO
Fleas

Maryland

• Aberdeen •
Days Inn ($$)
783 W Bel Air Ave
(21001) 410.272.8500

Econo Lodge ($)
820 W Bel Air Ave
(21001) 410.272.5500

Holiday Inn ($$$)
1007 Beards Hill Rd
(21001) 410.272.8100

Howard Johnson ($$)
793 W Bel Air Ave
(21001) 410.272.6000

Red Roof Inn ($$)
988 Hospitality Way
(21001) 410.273.7800
fees/limits may apply

• Annapolis •
Days Inn ($$)
1542 Whitehall Rd
(21401) 410.974.4440
small pets only

Econo Lodge ($$)
2451 Riva Rd
(21401) 410.224.4317

Holiday Inn ($$)
210 Holiday Ct
(21401) 410.224.3413

Loews Hotel ($$$$)
126 West St
(21401) 410.263.7777
vip pet program

Red Carpet Inn
101 Ferguson Rd
(21401) 410.757.3030

Residence Inn ($$$$)
170 Admiral Cochrane Dr
(21401) 410.573.0300
call for fee & availability

• Baltimore •
Comfort Inn ($$)
10 Wooded Way
(21208) 410.484.7700

Days Inn
1660 Whitehead Ct
(21207) 410.944.7400

Doubletree ($$$$)
4 W University Pkwy
(21218) 800.456.3396

Hampton Inn ($$$)
8225 Town Center Dr
(21236) 410.931.2200

Hampton Inn ($$$)
8225 Town Center Dr
(21236) 410.931.2200
small pets only

Holiday Inn ($$$)
6510 Frankford Ave
(21206) 410.485.7900

Holiday Inn ($$$)
1721 Reistertown Rd
(21208) 410.486.5600

Holiday Inn ($$)
1800 Belmont Ave
(21244) 410.265.1400

Holiday Inn
301 W Lombard
(21201) 410.685.3500

Motel 6 ($$)
1654 Whitehead Ct
(21207) 410.265.7660
1 small pet/room

Radisson Inn ($$$)
20 W Baltimore St
(21201) 800.333.3333

Ramada Inn ($$)
8712 Loch Raven Blvd
(21286) 410.823.8750

Sheraton Inn ($$$$)
300 S Charles St
(21201) 410.962.8300
small pets only

Sheraton Inn ($$$)
7032 Elm Rd
(21240) 410.859.3300

The Tremont Hotel ($$$)
8 E Pleasant St
(21202) 410.576.1200

Tremont Plaza Hotel ($$$)
222 Saint Paul Pl
(21202) 410.727.2222

Baltimore Metro

• Aberdeen •
Days Inn ($$)
783 W Bel Air Ave
(21001) 410.272.8500

Econo Lodge ($)
820 W Bel Air Ave
(21001) 410.272.5500

Holiday Inn ($$$)
1007 Beards Hill Rd
(21001) 410.272.8100

Howard Johnson ($$)
793 W Bel Air Ave
(21001) 410.272.6000

Red Roof Inn ($$)
988 Hospitality Way
(21001) 410.273.7800
fees/limits may apply

• Annapolis •
Days Inn ($$)
1542 Whitehall Rd
(21401) 410.974.4440
small pets only

Econo Lodge ($$)
2451 Riva Rd
(21401) 410.224.4317

Holiday Inn ($$)
210 Holiday Ct
(21401) 410.224.3413

Loews Hotel ($$$$)
126 West St
(21401) 410.263.7777
vip pet program

Red Carpet Inn
101 Ferguson Rd
(21401) 410.757.3030

Residence Inn ($$$$)
170 Admiral Cochrane Dr
(21401) 410.573.0300
call for fee & availability

• Baltimore •
Comfort Inn ($$)
10 Wooded Way
(21208) 410.484.7700

Days Inn
1660 Whitehead Ct
(21207) 410.944.7400

Doubletree ($$$$)
4 W University Pkwy
(21218) 800.456.3396

Hampton Inn ($$$)
8225 Town Center Dr
(21236) 410.931.2200

Hampton Inn ($$$)
8225 Town Center Dr
(21236) 410.931.2200
small pets only

Holiday Inn ($$$)
6510 Frankford Ave
(21206) 410.485.7900

Holiday Inn ($$$)
1721 Reistertown Rd
(21208) 410.486.5600

Holiday Inn ($$)
1800 Belmont Ave
(21244) 410.265.1400

Holiday Inn
301 W Lombard
(21201) 410.685.3500

Motel 6 ($$)
1654 Whitehead Ct
(21207) 410.265.7660
1 small pet/room

Radisson Inn ($$$)
20 W Baltimore St
(21201) 800.333.3333

Ramada Inn ($$)
8712 Loch Raven Blvd
(21286) 410.823.8750

Sheraton Inn ($$$$)
300 S Charles St
(21201) 410.962.8300
small pets only

Sheraton Inn ($$$)
7032 Elm Rd
(21240) 410.859.3300

The Tremont Hotel ($$$)
8 E Pleasant St
(21202) 410.576.1200

$=under $35 $$=$35-60 $$$=$60-100 $$$$=over $100

Tremont Plaza Hotel ($$$)
222 Saint Paul Pl
(21202) 410.727.2222

● Columbia ●
The Columbia Inn ($$$$)
10207 Wincopin Cir
(21044) 800.638.2817

● Edgewood ●
Best Western ($$)
1709 Edgewood Rd
(21040) 410.679.9700
small pets

Days Inn ($$)
2116 Emmorton Park Dr
(21040) 410.671.9990
$5 fee

● Glen Burnie ●
Holiday Inn
6323 RitchieHwy
(21061) 410.636.4300

Holiday Inn ($$$)
6600 Ritchie Hwy
(21061) 410.761.8300

● Hunt Valley ●
Marriott Hotel ($$$)
245 Shawan Rd
(21031) 410.785.7000

● Linthicum Heights ●
Hampton Inn ($$$)
829 Elkridge Landing Rd
(21090) 800.426.7866

Holiday Inn ($$$)
890 Elkridge Landing Rd
(21090) 410.859.8400

Motel 6 ($)
5179 RaynorAve
(21090) 410.636.9070
1 small pet/room

Red Roof Inn ($)
827 Elkridge Landing Rd
(21090) 800.843.7663

● Lutherville Timonium ●
Red Roof Inn ($)
111 W Timonium Rd
(21093) 800.843.7663

● Towson ●
Days Inn ($$)
8801 Loch Raven Blvd
(21286) 800.329.7466
$15

● Westminster ●
Comfort Inn ($$)
451 Westminster Dr
(21158) 410.857.1900

Days Inn ($$)
25 S Cranberry Rd
(21157) 410.857.0500
$5/pet

The Boston Inn ($)
533 Balimore Blvd
(21157) 410.848.9095

End of Baltimore Metro

● Beltsville ●
Holiday Inn ($$$)
4050 Powder Mill Rd
(20705) 301.937.4422
small pets only

Ramada Inn ($$)
4050 Powder Mill Rd
(20705) 301.572.7100

● Bethesda ●
Holiday Inn ($$$$)
8120 Wisconsin Ave
(20814) 301.652.2000

Marriott Hotel ($$$)
6711 Democracy Blvd
(20817) 301.897.5600
must call ahead

Ramada Inn ($$$)
8400 Wisconsin Ave
(20814) 301.654.1000

Residence Inn ($$$$)
7335 Wisconsin Ave
(20814) 301.718.0200
extra daily fee

● Boring ●
Econo Lodge ($$)
10100 York Rd
(21020) 410.667.4900

● Bowie ●
Econo Lodge ($$)
4502 NW Crain Hwy
(20718) 301.464.2200

● Capitol Heights ●
Days Inn ($$)
55 Hampton Park Blvd
(20743) 800.329.7466
mgr preapproval reqd

Econo Lodge ($)
100 Hampton Park Blvd
(20743) 800.424.4777

Motel 6 ($$)
75 Hampton Park Blvd
(20743) 301.499.0800
1 small pet/room

● Church Creek ●
Loblolly Lodge
2142 Liners Rd
(21622) 800.862.7452

● Clinton ●
Econo Lodge ($$)
7851 Malcolm Rd
(20735) 301.856.2800

● Cockeysville ●
Embassy Suites ($$$)
213 International Cir
(21030) 410.584.1400

Hampton Inn ($$)
11200 York Rd
(21030) 410.527.1500

Residence Inn ($$$)
10710 Beaver Dam Rd
(21030) 410.483.7370

● College Park ●
Park View Inn ($$)
9020 Baltimore Ave
(20740) 301.441.8110

● Columbia ●
The Columbia Inn ($$$$)
10207 Wincopin Cir
(21044) 800.638.2817

● Cumberland ●
Diplomat Motel ($)
17012 McMullen Hwy SW
(21502) 301.729.2311

Holiday Inn
100 S George St
(21502) 301.724.8800

● Easton ●
Days Inn
I-95
(21601) 410.822.4600
$6/day

Econo Lodge ($$)
US 50
(21601) 800.424.4777

The Tidewater Inn ($$$$)
101 E Dover St
(21601) 410.822.1300

● Edgewood ●
Best Western ($$)
1709 Edgewood Rd
(21040) 410.679.9700
small pets

Days Inn ($$)
2116 Emmorton Park Dr
(21040) 410.671.9990
$5 fee

● Elkton ●
Econo Lodge ($)
311 Belle Hill Rd
(21921) 410.392.5010

Motel 6 ($$)
223 Belle Hill Rd
(21921) 301.392.5020
1 small pet/room

● Frederick ●
Comfort Inn ($$)
420 Prospect Blvd
(21701) 301.695.6200

Hampton Inn ($$$)
5311 Buckeystown Pike
(21704) 301.698.2500

Holiday Inn ($$$)
999 W Patrick St
(21702) 301.662.5141

Holiday Inn
5400 Holiday Dr
(21703) 301.694.7500

$=under $35 $$=$35-60 $$$=$60-100 $$$$=over $100

Holiday Inn
5579 Spectrum Dr
(21703) 301.695.2881

Knights Inn ($$)
6005 Urbana Pike
(21704) 301.698.0555

Red Horse Inn ($$)
998 W Patrick St
(21703) 800.245.6701

● Frostburg ●
Charlies Motel
220 W Main St
(21532) 301.689.6557

Comfort Inn ($$)
Hwy 36
(21532) 301.689.2050

● Gaithersburg ●
Comfort Inn ($$)
16216 S Frederick Ave
(20877) 301.330.0023

Comfort Inn ($$)
16216 Frederick Rd
(20877) 800.221.2222

Econo Lodge ($$)
1875 N Frederick Ave
(20879) 301.963.3840

Hilton ($$$)
620 Perry Pkwy
(20877) 301.977.8900

Holiday Inn ($$$)
2 Montgomery Village Ave
(20879) 301.948.8900

Red Roof Inn ($$)
497 Quince Orchard Rd
(20878) 301.977.3311
fees/limits may apply

● Glen Burnie ●
Holiday Inn
6323 Ritchie Hwy
(21061) 410.636.4300

Holiday Inn ($$$)
6600 Ritchie Hwy
(21061) 410.761.8300

● Grantsville ●
Holiday Inn ($$)
US 219
(21536) 301.895.5993

● Greenbelt ●
Holiday Inn
7200 Hanover
(20770) 301.982.7000

Marriott Hotel ($$$)
6400 Ivy Ln
(20770) 301.441.3700
$25 fee

● Hagerstown ●
Best Western ($$)
431 Dual Hwy
(21740) 301.733.0830
small pets

Econo Lodge ($$)
18221 Mason-Dixon Rd
(21740) 301.791.3560
$2.50 charge

Motel 6 ($$)
11321 Massey Blvd
(21740) 301.582.4445
1 small pet/room

Sheraton Inn ($$)
1910 Dual Hwy
(21740) 301.790.3010

State Line Motel ($)
RR 6 Box# 195C
(21740) 301.733.8262

Super 8 ($$)
1220 Dual Hwy
(21740) 301.739.5800
small w/permission

● Halethorpe ●
Holiday Inn
1401 Bloomfield
(21227) 410.646.1700

● Hanover ●
Holiday Inn
7481 Ridge Rd
(21076) 410.684.3388

Red Roof Inn ($)
7306 Parkway Dr
(21076) 410.712.4070
fees/limits may apply

● Hunt Valley ●
Marriott Hotel ($$$)
245 Shawan Rd
(21031) 410.785.7000

● Hyattsville ●
Howard Johnson ($$)
5811 Annapolis Rd
(20784) 301.779.7700

● Jessup ●
Red Roof Inn
8000 Washington Blvd
(20794) 410.796.0380
fees/limits may apply

● La Plata ●
Travelodge ($)
Box# 1661
(20646) 301.934.1400

● Lanham ●
Best Western ($$)
5910 Princess Garden Pkwy
(20706) 800.528.1234

Days Inn
9023 Annapolis Rd
(20706) 301.459.6600

Red Roof Inn ($$)
9050 Lanham Severn Rd
(20706) 301.731.8830
fees/limits may apply

● Laurel ●
Motel 6 ($$)
3510 Old Annapolis Rd
(20724) 301.497.1544
1 small pet/room

Red Roof Inn
12525 Laurel Bowie Rd
(20708) 301.498.8811
fees/limits may apply

● Lexington Park ●
Days Inn ($$)
60 Main St
(20653) 301.863.6666

● Linthicum Heights ●
Hampton Inn ($$$)
829 Elkridge Landing Rd
(21090) 800.426.7866

Holiday Inn ($$$)
890 Elkridge Landing Rd
(21090) 410.859.8400

Motel 6 ($)
5179 Raynor Ave
(21090) 410.636.9070
1 small pet/room

Red Roof Inn ($)
827 Elkridge Landing Rd
(21090) 800.843.7663

● Lutherville Timonium ●
Red Roof Inn ($)
111 W Timonium Rd
(21093) 800.843.7663

● Mc Henry ●
Royal Oaks Inn
HC 2 Box# 11
(21541) 301.387.4200

● New Carrollton ●
Sheraton Inn ($$$)
8500 Annapolis Rd
(20784) 301.459.6700

● Oakland ●
Dreamland Motel
17848 Garrett Hwy
(21550) 301.387.6696

● Ocean City ●
Baysails Inn
102 60th St
(21842) 410.524.5634

Best Western ($)
6007 Coastal Hwy
(21842) 410.524.6100

Beach Motel
32nd St & Coastal Hwy
(21842) 410.289.1808

Econo Lodge ($)
6007 Coastal Hwy
(21842) 800.424.4777

Fenwick Inn ($$)
13801 Coastal Hwy
(21842) 800.492.1873

Georgia Belle Suites ($)
12000 Coastal Hwy
(21842) 410.250.4000

Well
Behaved

Rodeway Inn ($$)
2910 N Baltimore Ave
(21842) 301.567.8030

● Oxon Hill ●
Red Roof Inn ($)
6170 Oxon Hill Rd
(20745) 301.567.8030
fees/limits may apply

● Perryville ●
Comfort Inn ($$)
61 Heather Ln
(21903) 410.642.2866

● Pocomoke City ●
Days Inn ($$)
1540 Ocean Hwy
(21851) 410.957.3000

Quality Inn ($$)
825 Ocean Hwy
(21851) 410.957.1300

Red Carpet Inn
912 Ocean Hwy
(21851) 410.957.1030

● Princess Anne ●
Econo Lodge ($$)
10936 Market Ln
(21853) 410.651.9400

● Rockville ●
Days Inn ($$)
16001 Shady Grove Rd
(20850) 301.948.4300
small pets only

Woodfin Suites Hotel ($$$)
1380 Piccard Dr
(20850) 301.590.9880

● Salisbury ●
Budget Host ($$)
1510 S Salis Blvd
(21801) 410.742.3284

Comfort Inn ($$)
2701 N Salisbury Blvd
(21801) 410.543.4666

Econo Lodge ($)
712 N Salisbury Blvd
(21801) 410.749.7155

Hampton Inn ($$)
1735 N Salisbury Blvd
(21801) 800.426.7866

Holiday Inn ($$)
2625 N Salisbury Blvd
(21801) 410.742.7194

Lord Salisbury Motel ($$)
Rt 11 Box# 232
(21801) 410.742.3251

● Silver Spring ●
Econo Lodge ($$)
7990 Georgia Ave
(20910) 301.565.3444

● Solomons ●
Holiday Inn ($$$)
155 Holiday Dr
(20688) 410.326.6311

● Suitland ●
Motel 6 ($$)
5701 Allentown Rd
(20746) 301.702.1061
1 small pet/room

● Thurmont ●
Rambler Motel ($$)
US 15 & Jet Hwy 550
(21788) 301.271.2424

● Towson ●
Days Inn ($$)
8801 Loch Raven Blvd
(21286) 800.329.7466
$15

● Upper Marlboro ●
Forest Hills Motel ($$)
2901 Crain Hwy
(20774) 301.627.3969

● Waldorf ●
Days Inn ($$)
11370 Days Ct
(20603) 301.932.9200
$10 per pet

Econo Lodge ($$)
4 Business Park Dr
(20601) 301.645.0022
$15 fee

Hojo Inn ($$)
3125 Crain Hwy
(20603) 301.932.5090

Holiday Inn ($$)
1 Saint Patricks Dr
(20603) 301.843.7945

● Westminster ●
Comfort Inn ($$)
451 Wmc Dr
(21158) 410.857.1900

Days Inn ($$)
25 S Cranberry Rd
(21157) 410.857.0500
$5/pet

The Boston Inn ($)
533 Balimore Blvd
(21157) 410.848.9095

● Williamsport ●
Days Inn ($$)
310 E Potomac St
(21795) 301.582.3500
$4/pets

Wolfs End Farm ($$)
14940 Falling Waters Rd
(21795) 301.223.6888

Massachusetts
● Amherst ●
University Motel ($$)
345 N Pleasant St
(01002) 413.256.8111

● Andover ●
Andover Inn ($$$)
Chapel Ave
(01810) 508.475.5903

Marriott Hotel ($$$)
123 Old River Rd
(01810) 508.975.3600

● Attleboro ●
Days Inn ($$)
1116 Washington St
(02703) 508.761.4825
mgr preapproval reqd

● Auburn ●
Budgetel ($$)
444 Southbridge St
(01501) 508.832.7000

● Barnstable ●
Lamb & Lion Inn ($$$)
Box# 511
(02630) 508.362.6283

● Barre ●
Jenkins Inn ($$$)
7 West St
(01005) 508.335.6444

● Bedford ●
Stouffer Rennaissance
($$$$)
44 Middlesex Tpke
(01730) 617.275.5500

● Boston ●
Boston Harbor Hotel ($$$$)
70 Rowes Wharf
(02110) 617.439.7000

Copley Plaza Hotel ($$$$)
138 Saint James Ave
(02116) 617.267.5300

Hilton ($$$$)
40 Dalton St
(02115) 800.445.8667

Hilton ($$$$)
Logan Intl Airport
(02128) 617.569.9300

Howard Johnson ($$$)
200 Stuart St
(02116) 617.482.1800
small pets only

Howard Johnson ($$$)
575 Commonwealth Ave
(02215) 617.267.3100
if very discreet

Howard Johnson ($$$)
1271 Boylston St
(02215) 617.267.8300

Marriott Hotel ($$$$)
110 Huntington Ave
(02116) 617.236.5800

Newbury Guest House ($$$)
261 Newbury St
(02116) 617.437.7666

Sheraton Inn ($$$$)
39 Dalton St
(02199) 617.236.2000

Swissotel ($$$$)
1 Avenue De Lafayette
(02111) 617.451.2600

The Eliot Suite Hotel ($$$$)
370 Commonwealth Ave
(02215) 617.267.1607

Be Discreet

Boston Metro, MASSACHUSETTS

The Four Seasons ($$$$)
200 Boylston St
(02116) 800.332.3442

The Ritz Carlton ($$$$)
15 Arlington St
(02117) 617.536.5700

Westin Hotel ($$$$)
10 Huntington Ave
(02116) 617.262.9600
small pets accepted

Boston Metro

● Andover ●
Andover Inn ($$$)
Chapel Ave
(01810) 508.475.5903

Marriott Hotel ($$$)
123 Old River Rd
(01810) 508.975.3600

● Bedford ●
Stouffer Rennaissance
($$$$)
44 Middlesex Tpke
(01730) 617.275.5500

● Boston ●
Boston Harbor Hotel ($$$$)
70 Rowes Wharf
(02110) 617.439.7000

Copley Plaza Hotel ($$$$)
138 Saint James Ave
(02116) 617.267.5300

Hilton ($$$$)
40 Dalton St
(02115) 800.445.8667

Hilton ($$$$)
Logan Intl Airport
(02128) 617.569.9300

Howard Johnson ($$$)
200 Stuart St
(02116) 617.482.1800
small pets only

Howard Johnson ($$$)
575 Commonwealth Ave
(02215) 617.267.3100
if very discreet

Howard Johnson ($$$)
1271 Boylston St
(02215) 617.267.8300

Marriott Hotel ($$$$)
110 Huntington Ave
(02116) 617.236.5800

Newbury Guest House ($$$)
261 Newbury St
(02116) 617.437.7666

Sheraton Inn ($$$$)
39 Dalton St
(02199) 617.236.2000

Swissotel ($$$$)
1 Avenue De Lafayette
(02111) 617.451.2600

The Eliot Suite Hotel ($$$$)
370 Commonwealth Ave
(02215) 617.267.1607

The Four Seasons ($$$$)
200 Boylston St
(02116) 800.332.3442

The Ritz Carlton ($$$$)
15 Arlington St
(02117) 617.536.5700

Westin Hotel ($$$$)
10 Huntington Ave
(02116) 617.262.9600
small pets accepted

● Braintree ●
Days Inn ($$)
190 Wood Rd
(02184) 617.848.1260
mgr preapproval reqd

Motel 6 ($$)
125 Union St
(02184) 617.848.7890
1 small pet/room

● Burlington ●
Howard Johnson ($$$)
98 Middlesex Tpke
(01803) 617.272.6550
1 small caged pet

● Cambridge ●
Charles Harvard Square
($$$$)
1 Bennett St
(02138) 617.864.1200

Howard Johnson ($$$)
777 Memorial Dr
(02139) 617.492.7777

Morgan House Inn ($$)
33 Main St
(02142) 413.243.0181

Ramada Inn ($$)
165 Housatonic St
(02138) 800.272.6232

West Wind Cottages
41 Linnaean St
(02138) 617.868.6866

● Chelmsford ●
Howard Johnson ($$$)
187 Chelmsford St
(01824) 508.256.7511

● Danvers ●
Residence Inn ($$$$)
51 Newbury St
(01923) 508.777.7171
$75 deposit & $5/day

Super 8 ($$)
225 Newbury St
(01923) 508.774.6500
call re: fees

● Framingham ●
Motel 6 ($$)
1668 Worcester Rd
(01702) 508.620.0500
1 small pet/room

Red Roof Inn ($$)
650 Cochituate Rd
(01701) 508.481.3904

● Haverhill ●
Best Western ($$)
401 Lowell Ave
(01832) 508.373.1511
small pets welcome $10
deposit

● Kingston ●
Plymouth Bay Inn ($$)
149 Main St
(02364) 617.585.3831

● Lawrence ●
Hampton Inn ($$)
224 Winthrop Ave
(01843) 508.975.4050

● Lowell ●
Sheraton Inn ($$)
50 Warren St
(01852) 508.452.1200

● Mansfield ●
Motel 6 ($$)
60 Forbes Blvd
(02048) 508.339.2323
1 small pet/room

● Marlborough ●
Best Western ($$$)
181 Boston Post Rd
(01752) 800.528.1234

Super 8 ($$)
880 Donald J Lynch Bl
(01752) 800.800.8000
call re: fees

● Middleboro ●
Days Inn ($$)
Rt 105
(02346) 508.946.4400

● Needham ●
Sheraton Inn ($$$$)
100 Cabot St
(02194) 617.444.1110

● Peabody ●
Marriott Hotel ($$$)
8A Centennial Dr
(01960) 508.977.9700

● Randolph ●
Holiday Inn ($$$)
1374 N Main St
(02368) 617.961.1000

● Rockport ●
Sandy Bay Motel ($$$)
173 Main St
(01966) 508.546.7155

● Salem ●
Hawthorne Hotel ($$$)
18 Washington Sq
(01970) 508.744.4080
$10 fee

The Salem Inn ($$$)
7 Summer St
(01970) 508.741.0680
small $10 fee

● Saugus ●
Colonial Traveler ($$)
1753 Broadway
(01906) 617.233.6700

MASSACHUSETTS, Boston Metro

● Somerville ●
Pease Blueberry Farm ($$$)
Skyline Trail
(02143) 413.623.5519

● Tewksbury ●
Holiday Inn ($$)
4 Highwood Dr
(01876) 508.640.9000

Residence Inn ($$$)
1775 Andover St
(01876) 508.640.1003
$7 per night

● Wakefield ●
Best Western ($$)
595 North Ave
(01880) 800.528.1234

● Waltham ●
Boat House ($$$$)
15 Old N Wharf
(02254) 508.228.9552

Westin Hotel ($$$$)
70 3Rd Ave
(02154) 617.290.5600

● Woburn ●
Ramada Inn ($$)
15 Middlesex Canal Pk
(01801) 617.935.8760

Red Roof Inn ($$$)
19 Commerce Way
(01801) 800.843.7663

End of Boston Metro

● Boxborough ●
Holiday Inn
1 Adams Place
(01719) 508.263.8701

● Braintree ●
Days Inn ($$)
190 Wood Rd
(02184) 617.848.1260
mgr preapproval reqd

Motel 6 ($$)
125 Union St
(02184) 617.848.7890
1 small pet/room

● Brewster ●
Brewster Inn ($$$)
964 Sawtucket Rd
(02631) 508.896.3636

Pine Hills Cottages ($$$$)
Box# 75
(02631) 508.896.1999

● Burlington ●
Howard Johnson ($$$)
98 Middlesex Tpke
(01803) 617.272.6550
1 small caged pet

● Buzzards Bay ●
Best Western ($$)
100 Trowbridge Rd
(02532) 508.759.0800

Shipsway Motel
51 Canal Rd
(02532) 508.888.0206

The Bay Motor Inn ($$)
223 Main St
(02532) 508.759.3989

The Pond House ($$)
44 Monument Neck Rd
(02532) 508.759.1994

Yankee Thrift Motel
114 Trowbridge Rd
(02532) 508.759.3883

● Cambridge ●
Harvard Square ($$$$)
1 Bennett St
(02138) 617.864.1200

Howard Johnson ($$$)
777 Memorial Dr
(02139) 617.492.7777

Morgan House Inn ($$)
33 Main St
(02142) 413.243.0181

Ramada Inn ($$)
165 Housatonic St
(02138) 800.272.6232

West Wind Cottages
41 Linnaean St
(02138) 617.868.6866

● Centerville ●
Centerville Corners ($$)
Box# 507
(02632) 508.775.7223

● Chatham ●
Morgan Waterfront ($$$$)
444 Old Harbor Rd
(02633) 508.945.1870

Oceanfront Cottages
Seagull Ln
(02633) 508.945.5907

● Chelmsford ●
Howard Johnson ($$$)
187 Chelmsford St
(01824) 508.256.7511

● Chicopee ●
Best Western ($$)
463 Memorial Dr
(01020) 413.592.6171

Motel 6 ($$)
Rt 291
(01020) 508.774.8045
1 small pet/room

● Danvers ●
Residence Inn ($$$$)
51 Newbury St
(01923) 508.777.7171
$75 deposit & $5/day

Super 8 ($$)
225 Newbury St
(01923) 508.774.6500
call re: fees

● Dennis Port ●
Acorn Cottages
927 Main St
(02639) 508.760.2101

Bay Light Cottages
Box# 595
(02639) 508.398.5989

Beach House
DennisPort
(02639) 508.385.4588

Captains Row
257 Old Wharf Rd
(02639) 508.398.3117

Cricket Court ($$$$)
130 Route 28
(02639) 508.398.8400

Lamlighter Motel ($)
329 Main St
(02639) 508.398.8469

The Marine Cottage
15 North St
(02639) 508.398.2963

Town Cottages
319 Main St
(02639) 508.398.8469

Union Wharf Village
Dennis Port
(02639) 508.881.1381

● East Falmouth ●
Green Harbor ($$$)
134 Acapesket Rd
(02536) 508.548.4747

● East Sandwich ●
Azariah Snow House
Rt 6A
(02537) 508.888.6677

Cedar Cottages
59 Ploughed Neck Rd
(02537) 508.888.0464

Pine Grove Cottages
Rt 6A
(02537) 508.888.8179

The Sandwich Motor Inn ($$)
378 Route 6A
(02537) 508.888.1415

Wingscorton Farm
11 Wing Blvd
(02537) 508.888.0534
must call ahead

● Eastham ●
Blue Dolphin Inn ($$$)
Rt 6 Drawer
(02642) 508.255.1159

Cranberry Cottages ($$)
785 State Hwy
(02642) 508.255.0602

Gibson Cottages
Long Pond
(02642) 508.255.0882

CALL AHEAD!

$=under $35 $$=$35-60 $$$=$60-100 $$$$=over $100

Smith Hts Cottages
Box# 111
(02642) 508.255.5985

Town Crier Motel ($$)
Box# 457
(02642) 508.255.4000

● Fall River ●
Days Inn ($$$)
332 Milliken Blvd
(02721) 508.676.1991

● Falmouth ●
Falmouth Inn ($$)
824 Main St
(02540) 508.540.2500

Mariner Motel ($$)
555 Main St
(02540) 508.548.1331
dogs only

OceanView Motel ($$)
263 Grand Ave
(02540) 508.540.4120

Quality Inn ($$)
291 Jones Rd
(02540) 508.540.2000
mgr preapproval reqd

● Fiskdale ●
Econo Lodge ($$)
682 Main St
(01518) 508.347.2324

● Fitchburg ●
Royal Plaza Hotel ($$$)
150 Royal Plaza Dr
(01420) 508.342.7100

● Framingham ●
Motel 6 ($$)
1668 Worcester Rd
(01702) 508.620.0500
1 small pet/room

Red Roof Inn ($$)
650 Cochituate Rd
(01701) 508.481.3904

● Gloucester ●
Motel Cape Ann ($$)
33 Rockport Rd
(01930) 508.281.2900

Ocean View Inn ($$$)
171 Atlantic Rd
(01930) 508.283.6200

Spruce Manor Motel ($$)
141 Essex Ave
(01930) 508.283.0614

● Great Barrington ●
Court Motel
400 Stockbridge Rd
(01230) 413.528.2340

Chez Gabrielle ($$$)
320 State Rd
(01230) 413.528.2799

Chicadee Cottage ($$$)
27 Division St
(01230) 413.528.0002

Mountain View Motel ($$)
304 State Rd
(01230) 413.528.0250

Pines Inn ($$$)
142 Seekonk Cross Rd
(01230) 413.528.4192

Wainwright Inn ($$$)
518 Main St
(01230) 413.528.2062

● Greenfield ●
Candlelight Motel ($$)
208 Mohawk Trl
(01301) 413.772.0101
$5 night

● Hampden ●
Howard Johnson ($$)
401 Russell St
(01036) 413.586.0114

● Harwich Port ●
Coachman Motel ($$)
774 Main St
(02646) 508.432.0707

Harbor Walk House
6 Freeman St Harwich Port
(02646) 508.432.1675

● Haverhill ●
Best Western ($$)
401 Lowell Ave
(01832) 508.373.1511
small pets welcome $10
deposit

● Holyoke ●
Holiday Inn ($$$)
245 Whiting Farms Rd
(01040) 413.534.3311

● Housatonic ●
Brook Cove ($$$)
30 Linda Ln Housatonic
(01236) 413.274.6653

● Hyannis ●
Angel Motel ($$)
Rt 132
(02601) 508.775.2440

Colonial House Inn ($)
277 Main St Hyannis
(02601) 508.775.5225

Hyannis Inn By The Sea
182 Sea St
(02601) 508.775.1423

Hyannis Sands Motel
921 Route 132
(02601) 508.790.1700

Rainbow Motel ($$)
Rt 132
(02601) 508.362.3217

Snug Harbour Motor Inn
48 E Main St
(02601) 508.771.0699

The Country Squire ($)
206 Main St
(02601) 508.775.5225

● Hyannis Port ●
Harbor Village ($$$)
160 Marstons Ave
(02647) 508.775.7581

Sea Breeze Cottages ($$$$)
337 Sea St
(02647) 508.775.4269

● Kingston ●
Plymouth Bay Inn ($$)
149 Main St
(02364) 617.585.3831

● Lanesboro ●
Carraige House
Route 7
(01237) 413.458.5359

Lanesboro Motel
Box# 355
(01237) 413.442.6717

Mt View Motel ($)
499 S Main St
(01237) 413.442.1009

Weathervane Motel ($)
475 S Main St
(01237) 413.443.3230

● Lawrence ●
Hampton Inn ($$)
224 Winthrop Ave
(01843) 508.975.4050

● Lee ●
Hunters Motel ($)
89 Pleasant St
(01238) 413.243.0101

● Lenox ●
Seven Hills Inn
40 Plunkett St
(01240) 413.637.0060

Walker House Inn ($$$)
64 Walker St
(01240) 413.637.1271

● Leominster ●
Motel 6 ($$)
Commerical St
(01453) 508.537.8161
1 small pet/room

The Inn On The Hill ($$)
450 N Main St
(01453) 508.537.1661

● Lexington ●
Battle Green Inn ($$)
1720 Massachusetts Ave
(02173) 617.862.6100

Holiday Inn
440 Bedford St
(02173) 617.861.0850

● Lowell ●
Sheraton Inn ($$)
50 Warren St
(01852) 508.452.1200

• Malden •
New Englander Motel ($$)
551 Broadway
(02148) 617.321.0505

• Mansfield •
Motel 6 ($$)
60 Forbes Blvd
(02048) 508.339.2323
1 small pet/room

• Marlborough •
Best Western ($$$)
181 Boston Post Rd
(01752) 800.528.1234

Super 8 ($$)
880 Donald J Lynch Bl
(01752) 800.800.8000
call re: fees

• Middleboro •
Days Inn ($$)
Rt 105
(02346) 508.946.4400

• Nantucket •
Bartletts Beach Cottages
Box# 899
(02554) 508.228.2623

Corkish Cottages
320 Poplis Rd
(02554) 508.228.0258

Cottages Back-a-Bit
4 Walsh St
(02554) 508.228.3906

Far Island Cottages
41 Madaket Rd
(02554) 508.228.4227

Grey Lady ($$$)
34 Center St
(02554) 508.228.9552

Hallidays House
2 E York St
(02554) 508.228.9450

Jared Coffin House ($$$$)
29 Broad St
(02554) 508.228.2400

Nantucket Inn ($$$)
27 Macys Ln
(02554) 508.228.6900

Safe Harbor House ($$$$)
2 Harbor View Way
(02554) 508.228.3222

Ten Hussey Street ($$$)
10 Hussey St
(02554).508.228.9552

• Needham •
Sheraton Inn ($$$$)
100 Cabot St
(02194) 617.444.1110

• New Bedford •
Days Inn ($)
500 Hathaway Rd
(02740) 508.997.1231
mgr preapproval reqd

• Newburyport •
Morrill Place Inn ($$)
209 High St
(01950) 508.462.2808

•.North Adams •
Whitcomb Summit ($$)
229 Mohawk Trl
(01247) 413.662.2625

• North Attleboro •
Arns Park Motel ($$)
515 S Washington St
(02760) 508.222.0801

• North Truro •
Outer Reach Resort
Rt 6
(02652) 508.487.9500

Seascape Motor Inn
Rt 6A
(02652) 508.487.1225

• Northampton•
Days Inn ($$)
117 Conz St
(01060) 413.586.1500

Inn At Northampton
Rt 5 & Rt 91
(01060) 413.586.1211
$25 fee & $250 deposit

• Northborough •
Friendship Inn ($$)
At Jct Hwy 9 & 20
(01532) 508.842.8941

• Oak Bluffs •
Island Inn ($$$)
Beach Rd
(02557) 508.693.2002

• Orange •
Bald Eagle Motel ($)
110 Daniel Shays Hwy
(01364) 508.544.8864

• Orleans •
Orleans Holiday Motel ($$)
486 Cranberry Hwy
(02653) 508.255.1514

Skaket Beach Motel ($$)
203 Cranberry Hwy
(02653) 508.255.1020

• Otis •
Grouse House
Box# 70
(01253) 413.269.4446

• Peabody •
Marriott Hotel ($$$)
8A Centennial Dr
(01960) 508.977.9700

• Pittsfield •
Huntsman Motel
1350 W Housatonic St
(01201) 413.442.8714

Lakeview Cottage ($$$)
43 Thomas Rd
(01201) 413.445.7620

The Bonnie Bray ($$)
108 Broadway St
(01201) 413.442.3754

• Provincetown •
Holiday Inn ($$$)
Rt 6
(02657) 508.487.1711
closed nov-apr

The Breakwater Motel
Rt 6A
(02657) 508.487.1134

The Hargood House ($$$)
493 Commercial St
(02657) 508.487.9133

White Sands Motel
Rt 6A Box# 611
(02657) 508.487.0244

White Wind Inn
174 Commercial St
(02657) 508.487.1526

• Randolph •
Holiday Inn ($$$)
1374 N Main St
(02368) 617.961.1000

• Raynham •
Days Inn ($$)
Rt 44
(02767) 508.824.8647

• Readville •
Lake House
Ocean St
(02137) 413.442.6304

Lampost Motel
Box# 335
(02137) 413.443.2979

• Revere •
Howard Johnson ($$$)
407 Squire Rd
(02151) 617.284.7200

• Rockland •
Holiday Inn ($$$)
909 Hingham St
(02370) 617.871.5660
mgr preapproval reqd

• Rockport •
The Sandy Bay Motel ($$$)
173 Main St
(01966) 508.546.7155

• Rowley •
Country Garden Motel ($$)
101 Mai St
(01969) 508.948.7773

• Salem •
Hawthorne Hotel ($$$)
18 Washington Sq
(01970) 508.744.4080
$10 fee

The Salem Inn ($$$)
7 Summer St
(01970) 508.741.0680
small $10 fee

Policies
Subject
to Change

$=under $35 $$=$35-60 $$$=$60-100 $$$$=over $100

● Sandisfield ●
New Boston Inn ($$$)
Box# 166
(01255) 413.258.4477

● Sandwich ●
Sandwich Motel ($$$)
Box# 557
(02563) 508.888.2275
$15 fee

● Saugus ●
Colonial Traveler ($$)
1753 Broadway
(01906) 617.233.6700

● Scituate ●
Clipper Ship Lodge ($$$)
7 Beaver Dam Rd
(02066) 617.545.5550

● Seekonk ●
Motel 6 ($$)
821 Fall River Ave
(02771) 508.336.7800
1 small pet/room

Ramada Inn ($$)
940 Fall River Ave
(02771) 508.336.7300

● Sheffield ●
Bow Wow Road Inn
570 Bow Wow Rd
(01257) 413.229.3339

Depot Guest House ($$)
Box# 575
(01257) 413.229.2908

Ivanhoe Country House ($$)
254 S Undermountain Rd
(01257) 413.229.2143

Stagecoach Inn ($$)
854 S Undermountain Rd
(01257) 413.229.8585

● Shrewsbury ●
Days Inn ($$)
889 Boston Tpke
(01545) 508.842.8500
mgr preapproval reqd

● Somerset ●
Quality Inn ($$)
1878 Wilbur Ave
(02725) 508.678.4545
mgr preapproval reqd

● Somerville ●
The Blueberry Farms ($$$)
Skyline Trail
(02143) 413.623.5519

● South Deerfield ●
Motel 6 ($$)
Rt 5-10
(01373) 413.665.7161
1 small pet/room

● South Egremont ●
Swiss Hutte ($$$)
Route 23
(01258) 413.528.6200

● South Harwich ●
The Shoals Handkerchief
Motel ($$)
Mass 28
(02661) 508.432.2200

● South Orleans ●
Ocean Bay Cottages
Portanimicut Rd
(02662) 508.255.3344

● South Wellfleet ●
Green Haven Cottages
Rt 6 Box# 486
(02663) 508.349.1715

Oceanfront Cottages
Seagull Ln Chatham
(02663) 508.945.5907

● South Yarmouth ●
Brentwood Cottages
961 Route 28
(02664) 508.398.8812

Brentwood Inn ($)
Rt 28
(02664) 508.398.8812

Wayfarers Cottages ($$$$)
186 Seaview Ave
(02664) 508.771.4532

Windjammer Motel ($$)
192 S Shore Dr
(02664) 508.398.2370
ltd rooms call ahead

● Southborough ●
Red Roof Inn ($)
367 Turnpike Rd
(01772) 800.843.7663

● Stockbridge ●
High Meadows
Box# 976
(01262) 413.298.4652

● Sturbridge ●
Best Western ($$)
US 20
(01566) 508.347.9121
small pets

Host Hotel ($$$)
366 Main St
(01566) 800.582.3232

Publick House Resort ($$)
Hwy 131
(01566) 508.347.3313

Sturbridge Motor Inn ($$)
68 Old Rt 15
(01566) 508.347.3391

Super 8 ($$)
358 Main St
(01566) 508.347.9000
dep

● Tewksbury ●
Holiday Inn ($$)
4 Highwood Dr
(01876) 508.640.9000

Residence Inn ($$$)
1775 Andover St
(01876) 508.640.1003
$7 per night

● Wakefield ●
Best Western ($$)
595 North Ave
(01880) 800.528.1234

● Waltham ●
Boat House ($$$$)
15 Old N Wharf
(02254) 508.228.9552

Westin Hotel ($$$$)
70 3rd Ave
(02154) 617.290.5600

● Wellfleet ●
Breakwater Inn
Rt 6A Provincetown
(02667) 508.349.6923

Browns Landing
Box# 1017
(02667) 508.349.6923

Friendship Cottages
530 Chequessett Neck Rd
(02667) 508.349.3390

● West Dennis ●
Captain Varrieurs ($$$$)
Box# 1332
(02670) 508.394.4338

Elmwood Inn ($$)
57 Old Main St
(02670) 508.394.2798

Pine Cove Inn ($)
Rt 28 & Main St
(02670) 508.398.8511

Woodbine Village ($$$$)
Rt 28
(02670) 508.881.1381

● West Harwich ●
Barnaby Inn
36 Main St
(02671) 508.432.6789

Barnaby Inn
36 Main St
(02671) 508.432.9628

Claddagh Inn ($$$)
77 Main St
(02671) 508.432.9628

● West Springfield ●
Black Horse Motel ($$)
500 Riverdale St
(01089) 413.733.2161

Econo Lodge ($)
1533 Elm St
(01089) 413.734.8278

Goodlife Inn ($$$)
21 Baldwin St
(01089) 413.781.2300

MASSACHUSETTS, West Springfield

Hampton Inn ($$)
1011 Riverdale St
(01089) 800.426.7866

Motel 6 ($$)
106 Capital Dr
(01089) 413.788.4000
1 small pet/room

Red Roof Inn ($)
1254 Riverdale St
(01089) 413.731.1010
fees/limits may apply

● West Stockbridge ●
Pleasant Vly Motel ($)
Rt 102
(01266) 413.232.8511

● West Yarmouth ●
Ryans Cottage
19 Sandy Ln
(02673) 508.771.6387

Thunderbird Motel ($)
Rt 28
(02673) 508.775.2692

Town & Country Motel ($$$)
452 Main St
(02673) 508.771.0212

Yarmouth Shores
29 Lewis Bay Rd
(02673) 508.775.1944

● Westborough ●
Comfort Inn ($$)
399 Turnpike Rd
(01581) 508.366.0202

Marriott Hotel ($$$)
5400 Computer Dr
(01581) 508.366.5511

Residence Inn ($$$)
25 Connector Rd
(01581) 508.366.7700
call for pet room availability

● Westfield ●
Country Court Motel
480 Southampton Rd
(01085) 413.562.9790

● Westminster ●
Westminster Inn ($$$)
9 Village Inn Rd
(01473) 508.874.5351

● Williamstown ●
Cozy Corner Motel ($$)
284 Sand Sprin Grd
(01267) 413.458.8006

Jericho Valley Inn ($$)
Rt 13
(01267) 413.458.9511

The Villager Motel ($)
953 Simonds Rd
(01267) 413.458.4046

The Willows Motel ($$)
480 Main St
(01267) 413.458.5768

Williams Inn ($$$)
RR 2 & 7
(01267) 413.458.9371

● Woburn ●
Ramada Inn ($$)
15 Middlesex Canal Pk
(01801) 617.935.8760

Red Roof Inn ($$$)
19 Commerce Way
(01801) 800.843.7663

● Worcester ●
Econo Lodge ($$)
531 Lincoln St
(01605) 508.852.5800

Hampton Inn ($$$)
110 Summer St
(01608) 508.757.0400

● Yarmouth Port ●
Colonial House Inn ($$)
277 Main St Rt 6-A
(02675) 800.999.3416

Village Inn ($$)
Main St
(02675) 508.362.3182

Michigan
● Acme ●
Knollwood Motel ($$)
Box# 37
(49610) 616.938.2040

Sun N Sand Motel
Box# 307
(49610) 616.938.2190

● Albion ●
Best Western ($$)
400 B Dr
(49224) 517.629.3966
short hair

Days Inn
I-94
(49224) 517.629.9411

● Allegan ●
Budget Host
1580 Lincoln Rd
(49010) 800.283.4678

● Allen Park ●
Best Western ($$$)
3000 Enterprise Dr
(48101) 800.528.1234

● Alma ●
Petticoat Inn ($)
2454 W Monroe Rd
(48801) 517.681.5728

● Alpena ●
Amber Motel ($)
2052 State St
(49707) 517.354.8573

Bay Motel ($)
2107 US Hwy 23
(49707) 517.356.6137

Fireside Inn
18730 Fireside Hwy
(49707) 517.595.6369

Holiday Inn ($$$)
1000 Hwy 23N
(49707) 517.356.2151
mgr preapproval reqd

Parker House Motel ($$)
11505 Hwy 23N
(49707) 517.595.6484

Waters Edge Motel ($)
1000 State St
(49707) 517.354.5495

● Ann Arbor ●
Best Western ($$)
3505 S State St
(48108) 313.665.3500
small pets ok

Comfort Inn ($$$)
2455 Carpenter Rd
(48108) 313.973.6100
mgr preapproval reqd

Hampton Inn ($$)
2300 Green Rd
(48105) 313.996.4444

Hojo Inn ($$)
2424 E Stadium Blvd
(48104) 313.971.8000

Holiday Inn ($$$)
3600 Plymouth Rd
(48105) 313.769.9800
mgr preapproval reqd

Motel 6 ($$)
3764 S State St
(48104) 313.665.9900
1 small pet/room

Red Roof Inn ($$)
3621 Plymouth Rd
(48105) 313.996.5800
$3 charge

Residence Inn ($$$$)
800 Victors Way
(48108) 313.996.5666
addl chrg

● Au Gres ●
Point Au Gres Hotel ($)
3279 S Point Ln
(48703) 517.876.7217

● Auburn Hills ●
Hilton ($$$$)
2300 Featherstone Rd
(48326) 810.334.2222

Motel 6 ($$)
1471 N Opdyke Rd
(48326) 810.373.8440
1 small pet/room

● Baraga ●
Carlas Lake Shore ($)
RR 1 Box# 233
(49908) 906.353.6256

Super 8 ($$)
790 Michigan Ave
(49908) 906.353.6680
pets w/permission

CALL AHEAD!

$=under $35 $$=$35-60   **206** $$$=$60-100 $$$$=over $100

● Battle Creek ●
Appletree Inn ($$)
4786 Beckley Rd
(49015) 616.979.3561

Battle Creek Inn ($$)
5050 Beckley Rd
(49015) 616.979.1100

Days Inn
4786 Beckley Rd
(49017) 616.979.3561

Econo Lodge ($)
165 Capital Ave SW
(49015) 616.965.3976

Hampton Inn ($$)
1150 Riverside Dr
(49015) 616.979.5577

Holiday Inn
2590 Capitol Ave SW
(49015) 616.965.3201

Knights Inn ($)
2595 Capital Ave SW
(49015) 616.964.2600
size limits & fees

Michigan Motel ($)
20475 Capital Ave NE
(49017) 616.963.1565

Motel 6 ($)
4775 Beckley Rd
(49015) 616.979.1141
1 small pet/room

Super 8 ($$)
5395 Beckley Rd
(49015) 616.979.1828
call re: fees

● Bay City ●
Bay Valley Hotel ($$$)
2470 Old Bridge Rd
(48706) 517.686.3500

Delta Motel ($)
1000 S Euclid Ave
(48706) 517.684.4490

Holiday Inn ($$)
501 Saginaw St
(48708) 517.892.3501
mgr preapproval reqd

● Bear Lake ●
Bella Vista Motel
US #31 In Village
(49614) 616.864.3000

● Belding ●
Double R Ranch Resort ($)
4424 Whites Bridge Rd
(48809) 616.794.0520

● Bellaire ●
Windward Shore Motel
5812 E Torch Lake Dr
(49615) 616.377.6321

● Belleville ●
Red Roof Inn ($)
45501 I-94 N Expwy
(48111) 313.697.2244
fees/limits may apply

● Benton Harbor ●
Comfort Inn ($)
1598 Mall Dr
(49022) 616.925.1880
mgr preapproval reqd

Courtyard By Marriott ($$)
1592 Mall Dr
(49022) 616.925.3000

Days Inn ($$)
2699 Michigan Rt 139
(49022) 616.925.7021
$5 per day

Motel 6 ($)
2063 Pipestone Rd
(49022) 616.925.5100
1 small pet/room

Ramada Inn ($$)
798 Ferguson Dr
(49022) 616.927.1172

Red Roof Inn ($)
1630 Mall Dr
(49022) 616.927.2484
fees/limits may apply

Super 8 ($$)
1950 N Napier Ave
(49022) 616.926.1371
small pets only

● Bergland ●
Northwinds Motel ($)
1497 W M-28
(49910) 906.575.3557

● Beulah ●
Pine Knot Motel ($$)
171 N Center St
(49617) 616.882.7751

Sunnywoods Motel ($)
14065 US Hwy 31
(49617) 616.325.3952

● Birch Run ●
Market Street Inn ($$)
9087 Birch Run Rd
(48415) 517.624.9395

Super 8 ($$)
9235 Birch Run Rd
(48415) 517.624.4440
w/permission

● Blissfield ●
H D Ellis Inn ($$)
415 W Adrian St
(49228) 517.486.3155

● Bloomfield Hills ●
St Christopher Motel ($)
3915 Telegraph Rd
(48302) 810.647.1800

● Boyne Falls ●
Boyne Vue Motel ($)
Box# 12
(49713) 616.549.2822

● Branch ●
Lazy Days Motel ($)
Box# 104
(49402) 616.898.2252

● Bridgeport ●
Motel 6 ($)
6361 Dixie Hwy
(48722) 517.777.2582
1 small pet/room

● Bridgman ●
Bridgman Inn ($)
9999 Red Arrow Hwy
(49106) 616.465.3187

● Burton ●
Super 8 Motel ($)
G-1341 S Center Rd
(48509) 810.743.8850

● Cadillac ●
Best Western ($$)
845 S Mitchell St
(49601) 616.775.2458

Cadillac Sands Resort ($$)
6319 E M1115
(49601) 616.775.2407

Days Inn ($$)
6001 E M 115
(49601) 616.775.4414
mgr preapproval reqd

Pilgrims Village ($$)
181 S Lake Mitchell Dr
(49601) 616.775.5412

Pine Knoll Motel ($)
8072 Mackinaw Trl
(49601) 616.775.9471

South Shore Resort ($)
1246 Sunnyside Dr
(49601) 616.775.7641

Sunn Snow Motel ($)
301 S Lake Mitchell Dr
(49601) 616.775.9961

● Canton ●
Budgetel ($$)
41211 Ford Rd
(48187) 616.956.3300

Budgetel ($$)
41211 Ford Rd
(48187) 313.981.1808

Motel 6 ($)
41216 Ford Rd
(48187) 313.981.5000
1 small pet/room

● Caro ●
Kings Way Inn ($)
1057 E Caro Rd
(48723) 517.673.7511

● Caseville ●
Surf N Sand Motel ($$)
6006 Pt Austin Rd
(48725) 517.856.4400

MICHIGAN, Cass City

● Cass City ●
Wildwood Motel ($)
5986 Cass City Rd
(48726) 517.872.3366

● Cedarville ●
Comfort Inn ($$$)
210 Hwy 134
(49719) 906.484.2266

● Charlevoix ●
Capri Motel ($$)
1455 Bridge St
(49720) 616.547.2545

The Lodge Motel ($)
US 31
(49720) 616.547.6565

● Charlotte ●
Super 8 ($$)
I-69 & M-50
(48813) 517.543.8288
call re: fees

● Cheboygan ●
Birch Haus Motel ($)
1301 Mackinaw Ave
(49721) 616.627.5862

Cheboygan Motor Lodge ($)
1355 Mackinaw Ave
(49721) 616.627.3129

Continental Inn ($$)
613 N Main St
(49721) 616.627.7164

Monarch Motel ($)
1257 Mackinaw Ave
(49721) 616.627.2143

Pine River Motel ($)
102 Lafayette St
(49721) 616.627.5119

● Clare ●
Budget Host ($)
1110 N McEwan St
(48617) 517.386.7201
small w/ permission

Doherty Motor Hotel ($$)
604 N McEwan St
(48617) 517.386.3441

Lone Pine Motel ($$)
1508 N McEwan St
(48617) 517.386.7787

● Clio ●
Clio Motel ($$)
4254 W Vienna Rd
(48420) 810.687.0660

● Coldwater ●
Econo Lodge ($)
884 W Chicago Rd
(49036) 517.278.4501

Hampton Inn ($$)
4851 N Kickapoo
(49036) 405.275.1540

Little King Motel ($)
847 E Chicago St
(49036) 517.278.6660

Quality Inn ($$)
1000 Orleans Blvd
(49036) 517.278.2017
mgr preapproval reqd

Super 8 ($$)
600 Orleans Blvd
(49036) 517.278.8833
w/permission

● Coloma ●
Sweet Cherry Resort
3313 Chestnut Ave
(49038) 616.849.1233

● Comstock Park ●
Swan Inn Motel ($)
5182 Alpine Ave
(49321) 616.784.1224

● Cooks ●
Best Western ($$$)
7711 W Saginaw Hwy
(49817) 517.627.8471

● Copper Harbor ●
Astor House Resort ($$)
Box# 13
(49918) 906.289.4449

Bella Vista Motel ($$)
Box# 26
(49918) 906.289.4213

King Copper Motels ($$)
Box# 68
(49918) 906.289.4214

Norland Motel ($)
2 Mi E On US 41
(49918) 906.289.4815

● Cottrellville ●
Port Seaway Inn ($)
7623 River Rd
(48039) 810.765.4033

● Curtis ●
Seasons Motel ($)
Main St
(49820) 906.586.3078

● Dearborn ●
Marriott Hotel ($$$)
20301 Oakwood Blvd
(48124) 313.271.2700

Red Roof Inn ($$)
24130 Michigan Ave
(48124) 313.278.9732
fees/limits may apply

● Detroit ●
Hotel St Reig ($$$)
3071 W Grand Blvd
(48202) 313.873.3000

Ramada Inn ($$)
400 Bagley St
(48226) 313.962.2300

Residence Inn ($$$$)
5777 Southfield Dr
(48228) 313.441.1700
$100 charge & $7 per day

Shorecrest Motel ($$)
1316 E Jefferson Ave
(48207) 313.568.3000

Westin Hotel ($$$$)
Renaissance Center
(48243) 313.568.8000
small pets accepted

Detroit Metro

● Allen Park ●
Best Western ($$$)
3000 Enterprise Dr
(48101) 800.528.1234

● Ann Arbor ●
Best Western ($$)
3505 S State St
(48108) 313.665.3500
small pets ok

Comfort Inn ($$$)
2455 Carpenter Rd
(48108) 313.973.6100
mgr preapproval reqd

Hampton Inn ($$)
2300 Green Rd
(48105) 313.996.4444

Hojo Inn ($$)
2424 E Stadium Blvd
(48104) 313.971.8000

Holiday Inn ($$$)
3600 Plymouth Rd
(48105) 313.769.9800
mgr preapproval reqd

Motel 6 ($$)
3764 S State St
(48104) 313.665.9900
1 small pet/room

Red Roof Inn ($$)
3621 Plymouth Rd
(48105) 313.996.5800
$3 charge

Residence Inn ($$$$)
800 Victors Way
(48108) 313.996.5666
addl chrg

● Auburn Hills ●
Hilton ($$$$)
2300 Featherstone Rd
(48326) 810.334.2222

Motel 6 ($$)
1471 N Opdyke Rd
(48326) 810.373.8440
1 small pet/room

● Belleville ●
Red Roof Inn ($)
45501 I-94 N Expwy
(48111) 313.697.2244
fees/limits may apply

● Bloomfield Hills ●
St Christopher Motel ($)
3915 Telegraph Rd
(48302) 810.647.1800

Be
Discreet

208

$=under $35 $$=$35-60 $$$=$60-100 $$$$=over $100

● Canton ●
Budgetel ($$)
41211 Ford Rd
(48187) 616.956.3300

Budgetel ($$)
41211 Ford Rd
(48187) 313.981.1808

Motel 6 ($)
41216 Ford Rd
(48187) 313.981.5000
1 small pet/room

● Dearborn ●
Marriott Hotel ($$$)
20301 Oakwood Blvd
(48124) 313.271.2700

Red Roof Inn ($$)
24130 Michigan Ave
(48124) 313.278.9732
fees/limits may apply

● Detroit ●
Hotel St Reig ($$$)
3071 W Grand Blvd
(48202) 313.873.3000

Ramada Inn ($$)
400 Bagley St
(48226) 313.962.2300

Residence Inn ($$$$)
5777 Southfield Dr
(48228) 313.441.1700
$100 charge & $7 per day

Shorecrest Motel ($$)
1316 E Jefferson Ave
(48207) 313.568.3000

Westin Hotel ($$$$)
Renaissance Center
(48243) 313.568.8000
small pets accepted

● Farmington ●
Holiday Inn ($$$)
38123 W 10 Mile Rd
(48335) 810.477.4000
mgr preapproval reqd

Motel 6 ($)
38300 Grand River Ave
(48335) 810.471.0590
1 small pet/room

Red Roof Inn ($)
24300 Sinacola Ct
(48335) 810.478.8640
fees/limits may apply

● Harper Woods ●
Parkcrest Inn ($$)
20000 Harper Ave
(48225) 313.884.8800

● Hazel Park ●
Quality Inn ($$)
1 Nine Mile Rd
(48030) 810.399.5800
mgr preapproval reqd

● Livonia ●
Marriott Hotel ($$$)
17100 N Laurel Park Dr
(48152) 313.462.3100
sign waiver

Ramada Inn ($$)
30375 Plymouth Rd
(48150) 313.261.6800

● Madison Heights ●
Hampton Inn ($$)
32420 Stephenson Hwy
(48071) 810.585.8881

Knights Inn ($)
26091 Dequindre Rd
(48071) 800.843.5644

Motel 6 ($)
32700 Barrington St
(48071) 810.583.0500
1 small pet/room

Red Roof Inn ($)
32511 Concord Dr
(48071) 810.583.4700
fees/limits may apply

Residence Inn ($$$$)
32650 Stephenson Hwy
(48071) 810.583.4322
under 30 lbs. $75 charge

● New Baltimore ●
Lodge Keeper Inn
29101 23-Mile Rd
(48047) 810.949.4520
small pets only

● Novi ●
Fairlane Motel ($)
45700 Grand River Ave
(48374) 810.349.6410

Hilton ($$$)
21111 Haggerty Rd
(48375) 810.349.4000

● Plymouth ●
Red Roof Inn ($)
39700 Ann Arbor Rd
(48170) 313.459.3300
fees/limits may apply

● Port Huron ●
Best Western ($$)
2908 Pine Groce
(48060) 810.984.1522

Days Inn ($$)
2908 Pine Grove Ave
(48060) 810.984.1522
$5

Knights Inn ($$)
2160 Water St
(48060) 810.982.1022
size limits & fees

Mainstreet Lodge ($$)
514 Huron Ae
(48060) 810.984.3166

● Rochester Hills ●
Red Roof Inn ($$)
2580 Crooks Rd
(48309) 810.853.6400
fees/limits may apply

Rochester Motel ($$)
2070 S Rochester Rd
(48307) 810.651.8591

● Romulus ●
Budgetel ($$)
9000 Wickham St
(48174) 313.722.6000

Days Inn ($$$)
9501 Middlebelt Rd
(48174) 313.946.4300
$25 dep small

Howard Johnson ($$)
7600 Merriman Rd
(48174) 313.728.2430

Marriott Hotel ($$$)
30559 Flynn Dr
(48174) 313.729.7555

● Roseville ●
Budgetel ($$)
20675 E 13 Mile Rd
(48066) 810.296.6910

Georgian Inn ($$)
31327 Gratiot Ave
(48066) 810.294.0400

Red Roof Inn ($)
31800 Little Mack Ave
(48066) 810.296.0310
fees/limits may apply

● Southfield ●
Econo Lodge ($$)
23300 Telegraph Rd
(48034) 810.358.1800
small pets only

Hilton ($$$)
26000 American Dr
(48034) 810.357.1100

Holiday Inn ($$)
26555 Telegraph Rd
(48034) 810.353.7700
mgr preapproval reqd

Mariott Hotel ($$$)
27033 Northwestern Hwy
(48034) 313.356.7400

Ramada Inn ($$)
17017 W 9 Mile Rd
(48075) 810.557.4800

Red Roof Inn
27660 Northwestern Hwy
(48034) 810.353.7200
fees/limits may apply

Residence Inn ($$$$)
26700 Central Park Blvd
(48076) 810.352.8900

● Southgate ●
Budgetel ($$)
12888 Reeck Rd
(48195) 313.374.3000

Holiday Inn
17201 Northline Rd
(48195) 313.283.4400

209

MICHIGAN, Detroit Metro

● Taylor ●
Hoffmans Colonial ($)
10870 Telegraph Rd
(48180) 313.291.3000

Red Roof Inn ($)
21230 Eureka Rd
(48180) 313.374.1150
fees/limits may apply

● Troy ●
Drury Inn ($$$)
575 W Big Beaver Rd
(48084) 810.528.3330

Hilton ($$$)
5500 Crooks Rd
(48098) 810.879.2100

Holiday Inn ($$)
2537 Rochester Ct
(48083) 810.689.7500
mgr preapproval reqd

Marriott Hotel ($$$)
200 W Big Beaver Rd
(48084) 810.680.9797

Red Roof Inn ($)
235 Rochester Rd
(48083) 810.689.4391
fees/limits may apply

● Warren ●
Budgetel ($$)
30900 Van Dyke Ave
(48093) 810.574.0550

Homewood Suites ($$$)
30180 N Civi Center Blvd
(48093) 810.558.7870
$25 fee

Motel 6 ($)
8300 Chicago Rd
(48093) 313.826.9300
1 small pet/room

Red Roof Inn ($)
26300 Dequindre Rd
(48091) 810.573.4300
fees/limits may apply

Residence Inn ($$$$)
30120 N Civic Center Blvd
(48093) 810.558.8050
$50 fee + $8 per day

Van Dyke Park Hotel ($$)
31800 Van Dyke Ave
(48093) 800.321.1008

● Woodhaven ●
Knights Inn ($)
21880 West Rd
(48183) 313.676.8550
size limits & fees

End of Detroit Metro

● Douglas ●
Douglas Dunes Resort
333 Blue Star Hwy Douglas
(49406) 616.857.1401

Pines Motel ($)
56 Blue Star Hwy
(49406) 616.857.5211

● Drummond Island ●
Vechells Resort ($$$$)
Box# 175
(49726) 906.493.5381

● East China ●
Marine Bay Motel ($)
6000 River Rd E China
(48054) 810.765.8877

● East Jordan ●
Westbrook Motel ($$)
218 Elizabeth St
(49727) 616.536.2674

● East Lansing ●
Park Inn Intl ($$)
1100 Trowbridge Rd
(48823) 517.351.5500

Residence Inn ($$$)
1600 E Grand River Ave
(48823) 517.332.7711
call for fee & availability

● East Tawas ●
Carriage Inn ($)
1500 N US 23
(48730) 517.362.2831

Northland Beach Ctges
808 E Bay St
(48730) 517.362.2601

● Eastpointe ●
Eastland Motel ($)
21055 Gratiot Ave
(48021) 810.772.1300

● Elk Rapids ●
Camelot Inn ($$)
Box# 910
(49629) 616.264.8473

● Escanaba ●
Days Inn ($$)
2603 N Lincoln Rd
(49829) 906.789.1200
$35 deposit

Hiawatha Motel ($$)
2400 Ludington St
(49829) 906.786.1341

Sunset Motel ($)
Box# 343
(49829) 906.786.1213

● Farmington ●
Holiday Inn ($$$)
38123 W 10 Mile Rd
(48335) 810.477.4000
mgr preapproval reqd

Motel 6 ($)
38300 Grand River Ave
(48335) 810.471.0590
1 small pet/room

Red Roof Inn ($)
24300 Sinacola Ct
(48335) 810.478.8640
fees/limits may apply

● Flint ●
Days Inn ($$)
2207 W Bristol Rd
(48507) 810.239.4681
mgr preapproval reqd

Motel 6 ($)
2324 Austins Pkwy
(48507) 810.767.7100
1 small pet/room

Ramada Inn ($$)
G-4300 W Pierson Rd
(48504) 810.732.0400
small pets only

Red Roof Inn ($$)
G3219 Miller Rd
(48507) 810.733.1660
fees/limits may apply

Super 8
3033 Claude Ave
(48507) 810.230.7888
call re: fees

● Fountain ●
Christies Log Cabins ($$)
6503 E Sugar Grove Rd
(49410) 616.462.3218

● Frankfort ●
Chimney Crnrs Res ($$)
1602 Crystal Dr
(49635) 616.352.7522

● Freeland ●
Freeland Inn Motel
6840 Midland Rd
(48623) 517.695.9646

● Gaylord ●
Best Western ($$)
803 S Otsego Ave
(49735) 517.732.6451
pets in some rooms

Downtown Motel ($)
208 S Otsego Ave
(49735) 517.732.5010

Econo Lodge ($$)
2880 S Old Im
(49735) 517.732.5133

Holiday Inn ($$$)
833 Main
(49735) 517.732.2431

Michaywe Resort ($$$)
1535 Opal Lake Rd
(49735) 517.939.8914

Super 8 ($$)
1042 W Main St
(49735) 517.732.5193
w/permission

The Cedars Motel ($)
701 N Center Ave
(49735) 517.732.4525

Timberly Motel ($$)
881 S Old 27
(49735) 517.732.5166

• Gladstone •
Norway Pines Motel ($)
7111 US Hwy 2
(49837) 906.786.5119

• Gladwin •
Gladwin Motor Inn ($)
1003 W Cedar Ave
(48624) 517.426.9661

• Grand Blanc •
Scenic Inn ($)
G8308 S Saginaw Rd
(48439) 313.694.6611

• Grand Marais •
Budget Host ($$)
Canal Street
(49839) 906.494.2361

Budget Host ($)
Canal St
(49839) 800.283.4678

Hilltop Cabins ($$)
Box# 377
(49839) 906.494.2331

• Grand Rapids •
Cascade Inn ($)
2865 Broadmoor Ave SE
(49512) 616.949.0850

Days Inn ($$)
310 Pearl St NW
(49504) 616.235.7611
$10/pets

Econo Lodge ($$)
250 28th St SW
(49548) 616.452.2131

Exel Inn ($$)
4855 28th St SE
(49512) 616.957.3000
small pets only

Fairfield Inn
3930 Stahl Dr SE
(49546) 616.940.2700

Hampton Inn ($$)
4981 28th St SE
(49512) 616.956.9304
under 30 lbs

Holiday Inn
270 Ann St NW
(49504) 616.363.9001

Jim Williams Motel ($)
3821 S Division Ave
(49548) 616.241.5461

Knights Inn ($$)
5175 28th St SE
(49512) 616.956.6601

Motel 6 ($)
3524 28th St SE
(49512) 616.957.3511
1 small pet/room

Motel 6 ($)
777 3 Mile Rd NW
(49544) 616.784.9375
1 small pet/room

New England Suites ($$)
2985 Kraft Ave SE
(49512) 616.940.1777

Ramada Inn ($$)
65 28th St SW
(49548) 616.452.1461

Red Roof Inn ($$)
5131 28th St SE
(49512) 616.942.0800
fees/limits may apply

Residence Inn ($$$$)
2701 E Beltine SE
(49546) 616.957.8111
call for fee & availability

Rivera Motel ($)
4350 Remembrance Rd NW
(49544) 616.453.2404

Super 8 ($$)
727 44th St SW
(49509) 616.530.8588
w/permission

• Grayling •
Cedar Motel ($)
606 N James St
(49738) 517.348.5884

Holiday Inn ($$$)
2650 I-75
(49738) 517.348.7611

North Country Lodge ($$)
Box# 290
(49738) 517.348.8471

River Country Motel ($)
N I-75 Bus Loop
(49738) 517.348.8619

Super 8 ($$)
5828 Na Miles Pkwy
(49738) 517.348.8888
call re: fees

Woodland Motel ($)
267 I-75 Business Loop
(49738) 517.348.9094

• Harbor Beach •
The Train Station Motel ($$)
2044 N Lakeshore Rd
(48441) 517.479.3215

• Harbor Springs •
Harbor Springs Inn ($$)
145 Zoll St
(49740) 616.526.5431

• Harper Woods •
Parkcrest Inn ($$)
20000 Harper Ave
(48225) 313.884.8800

• Harrison •
Lakeside Motel ($)
South Business 27
(48625) 517.539.3796

Wagon Wheel Motel ($)
4294 N Clare Ave
(48625) 517.539.7065

• Hart •
Hart Motel
715 S State St
(49420) 616.873.2151

• Hazel Park •
Quality Inn ($$)
1 Nine Mile Rd
(48030) 810.399.5800
mgr preapproval reqd

• Hessel •
Lakeview Motel ($$)
Box# 277
(49745) 906.484.2474

• Hillsdale •
Bavarain Inn ($)
1728 Hudson Rd
(49242) 517.437.3367

• Holland •
Blue Mill Inn ($$)
409 US 31S
(49423) 616.392.7073

Days Inn ($$)
717 Hastings Ave
(49423) 616.392.7001
mgr preapproval reqd

Fairfield Inn ($$)
2854 W Shore Dr
(49424) 616.786.9700

Knights Inn ($$)
422 E 32nd St
(49423) 616.392.1000
limited availability

• Houghton •
Holiday Inn
1110 Century Way
(49931) 906.482.1066

• Houghton Lake •
Hillside Motel ($$)
3419 W Houghton Lk Dr
(48629) 517.366.5711

Holiday Inn ($$$)
9285 W Houghton Lake Dr
(48629) 517.422.5175
mgr preapproval reqd

Holiday On The Lake ($)
100 Clearview Dr
(48629) 517.422.5195

Lagoon Resort ($)
6578 W Houghton Lake Dr
(48629) 517.422.5761

Populars Resort ($$)
10360 Westshore Dr
(48629) 517.422.5132

Valhalla Motel ($)
9869 W Houghton Lake Dr
(48629) 517.422.5137

Policies Subject to Change

MICHIGAN, Houghton Lake

Way North Motel ($)
9052 N Old US 27
(48629) 517.422.5523

● Howell ●
Knights Inn ($$)
124 Holiday Ln
(48843) 517.548.2900

● Hudson ●
Sunset Acres Motel ($)
400 S Meridan US 127
(49247) 517.448.8968

● Hulbert ●
The Leeja Motel
2000 M28
(49748) 906.876.2323

● Imlay City ●
Super 8 ($$)
6951 Newark Rd
(48444) 810.724.8700
call re: fees

● Indian River ●
Caravan Motel Cottages ($$)
4904 Straits Hwy
(49749) 616.238.7537

Northwoods Lodge ($$)
2390 Straits Hwy
(49749) 616.238.7729

Reids Motor Court ($)
3977 Straits Hwy
(49749) 616.238.9353

Star Gate Motel ($)
4646 Straits Hwy
(49749) 616.238.7371

Woodlands Lodge ($$)
5115 Straits Hwy
(49749) 616.238.4137

● Ionia ●
Evergreen Motel ($)
2030 N State Rd
(48846) 616.527.0930

Midway Motel ($)
7076 S State Rd
(48846) 616.527.2080

Super 8 ($$)
7245 S State Rd
(48846) 616.527.2828
call re: fees

● Iron Mountain ●
Best Western ($$)
1518 S Stephenson Ave
(49801) 906.774.2040

Days Inn ($$)
W 8176 S US 2
(49801) 906.774.2181
$7

Edgewater Resort ($$)
N4128 U US 2
(49801) 906.774.6244

Howard Johnson ($$)
1609 S Stephenson Ave
(49801) 906.774.6220

Timbers Motor Lodge ($)
200 S Stephenson Ave
(49801) 906.774.7600

Woodlands Motel ($)
N 3957 North US 2
(49801) 906.774.6106

● Iron River ●
Iron River Motel ($)
3073 East US 2
(49935) 906.265.4212

● Ironwood ●
Armata Motel ($)
124 W Cloverland Dr
(49938) 906.932.4421

Blue Cloud Motel ($)
105 W Cloverland Dr
(49938) 906.932.0920

Super 8 ($$)
160 E Cloverland Dr
(49938) 906.932.3395
call re: fees

Twilight Time Motel ($)
930 E US 2
(49938) 906.932.3010

● Jackson ●
Budgetel ($$)
2035 N Service Dr
(49202) 517.789.6000

Fairfield Inn ($$)
2395 Shirley Dr
(49202) 517.784.7877

Holiday Inn ($$$)
2000 Holiday Inn Dr
(49202) 517.783.2681
small $15 fee

Motel 6 ($)
830 Royal Dr
(49202) 517.789.7186
1 small pet/room

Rodeway Inn ($$)
901 Rosehill Rd
(49202) 517.787.1111

● Jonesville ●
Pinecrest Motel ($)
516 W Chicago St
(49250) 517.849.2137

● Kalamazoo ●
Budgetel ($$)
2203 S 11th St
(49009) 616.372.7999

Hampton Inn ($$$)
1550 E Kilgore Rd # R
(49001) 616.344.7774

Holiday Inn ($$$)
2747 S 11th St
(49009) 616.375.6000
mgr preapproval reqd

La Quinta Inn ($$)
3750 Easy St
(49001) 616.388.3551
call re: fees

Red Roof Inn ($)
3701 E Cork St
(49001) 616.382.6350
fees/limits may apply

Red Roof Inn ($)
5425 W Michigan Ave
(49009) 616.375.7400
fees/limits may apply

Residence Inn ($$$$)
1500 E Kilgore Rd
(49001) 616.349.0855

Super 8 ($$)
618 Maple Hill Dr
(49009) 616.345.0146
call re: fees

● Lake City ●
Lake City Motel ($)
704 N Morey Rd
(49651) 616.839.4857

Northcrest Motel ($$)
1341 S Lakeshore Dr
(49651) 616.839.2075

● Lansing ●
Best Western ($$)
6133 S Pennsylvania Ave
(48911) 517.393.5500
small house pets

Days Inn ($$)
6501 S Pennsylvania Ave
(48911) 517.393.1650
mgr preapproval reqd

Fairfield Inn
810 Delta Commerce Dr
(48917) 517.886.1066

Hojo Inn ($)
6741 S Cedar St
(48911) 517.694.0454

Knights Inn ($)
1100 Ramada Dr
(48911) 800.843.5644

Marriott Hotel ($$$)
1275 Huron St
(48917) 313.487.2000

Motel 6 ($)
7326 W Saginaw Hwy
(48917) 517.321.1444
1 small pet/room

Motel 6 ($)
112 E Main St
(48933) 517.484.8722
1 small pet/room

Quality Suites ($$$)
901 Delta Commerce Dr
(48917) 517.886.0600

Red Roof Inn ($)
3615 Dunckel Dr
(48910) 517.332.2575
fees/limits may apply

Red Roof Inn ($)
7412 W Saginaw Hwy
(48917) 517.321.7246
fees/limits may apply

Residence Inn
922 Delta Commerce Dr
(48917) 517.886.5030

Sheraton Inn ($$$)
925 S Creyts Rd
(48917) 517.323.7100

● Lapeer ●
Town & Country Motel ($)
1275 Imlay City Rd
(48446) 810.664.9132

● Leland ●
Falling Waters Lodge ($$$)
Box# 345
(49654) 616.256.9832

● Lewiston ●
Fairway Inn ($$)
County Rd 489
(49756) 517.786.2217

● Livonia ●
Marriott Hotel ($$$)
17100 N Laurel Park Dr
(48152) 313.462.3100
sign waiver

Ramada Inn ($$)
30375 Plymouth Rd
(48150) 313.261.6800

● Ludington ●
Holiday Inn
5323 US 10
(49431) 616.845.7004

Marina Bay Motel ($)
604 W Ludington Ave
(49431) 616.845.5124

Naders Lake Shore ($$)
612 N Lakeshore Dr
(49431) 616.843.8757

Nova Motel ($)
472 S Old 31 Hwy
(49431) 616.843.3454

● Mackinaw City ●
Affordable Inns
206 Nicolet St
(49701) 616.436.8961
$3 fee

American Motel ($)
14351 S US 31
(49701) 616.436.5231

Beachcomber Motel ($)
1011 S Huron
(49701) 616.436.8451

Bells Melody Motel ($)
Box# 896
(49701) 616.436.5463

Budget Host ($)
517 N Huron
(49701) 616.436.5543

Capri Motel ($)
801 S Nicolet St
(49701) 616.436.5498

Econo Lodge ($)
412 Nicolet St
(49701) 616.436.5026

Knights Inn ($)
1009 S Huron
(49701) 616.436.5527
size limits & fees

Lamplighter Motel ($$)
303 Jamet St
(49701) 616.436.5350

Lovelands La Mirage ($)
699 N Huron
(49701) 616.436.5304

Ottawa Motel ($)
Box# 908
(49701) 616.436.8041

Parkside Inn ($$)
102 Nicolet St
(49701) 616.436.8301

Quality Inn ($$)
917 S Huron
(49701) 616.436.5051
small w/ approval

Starlite Budget Inns ($)
116 Old US 31
(49701) 616.436.5959

Surf Motel ($)
907 S Huron
(49701) 616.436.8831

The Beach House ($$)
1035 S Huron
(49701) 616.436.5353

Valu Motel ($)
Box# 521
(49701) 616.436.7691

● Madison Heights ●
Hampton Inn ($$$)
32420 Stephenson Hwy
(48071) 810.585.8881

Knights Inn ($)
26091 Dequindre Rd
(48071) 800.843.5644

Motel 6 ($)
32700 Barrington St
(48071) 810.583.0500
1 small pet/room

Red Roof Inn ($)
32511 Concord Dr
(48071) 810.583.4700
fees/limits may apply

Residence Inn ($$$$)
32650 Stephenson Hwy
(48071) 810.583.4322
under 30 lbs. $75 charge

● Mancelona ●
Mancelona Motel ($)
8306 US Hwy 131
(49659) 616.587.8621

Rapid River Motel ($)
7530 US 131
(49659) 616.258.2604

● Manistee ●
Carriage Inn ($)
200 Arthur St
(49660) 616.723.9949

Hillside Motel ($)
1599 US 31st
(49660) 616.723.2584

● Manistique ●
Econo Lodge ($)
E US 2
(49854) 906.341.6014

Hojo Inn ($$)
726 E Lakeshore Dr
(49854) 906.341.6981
$5 fee

Holiday Motel ($)
RR 1 Box# 1514
(49854) 906.341.2710

Ramada Inn ($$)
US 2 E Lakeshore Dr
(49854) 906.341.6911
a few rooms

● Manton ●
Green Mill Motel ($)
709 N Michigan Ave
(49663) 616.824.3504

Irish Inn Motel ($)
415 N Michigan Ave
(49663) 616.824.6988

● Marquette ●
Birchmont Motel ($)
2090 US 41S
(49855) 906.228.7538

Edgewater Motel ($)
2050 US 41
(49855) 906.225.1305

Holiday Inn
1951 US 41
(49855) 906.225.1351

Lamplighter Motel ($)
3600 US 41
(49855) 906.228.4004

Marquette Motel ($)
1010 M-28
(49855) 906.249.1712

Ramada Inn ($$$)
412 Washington
(49855) 906.228.6000

Tiroler House Motel ($$)
150 Carp River Hill
(49855) 906.226.7516

● Marshall ●
Arbor Inn ($$)
15435 W Michigan Ave
(49068) 616.781.7722

Well
Behaved

$=under $35 $$=$35-60   **213** $$$=$60-100 $$$$=over $100

Howards Motel ($)
14884 W Michigan Ave
(49068) 616.781.4201

Marshall Hts Motel ($)
16147 Old US 2M
(49068) 616.781.5659

● Mc Millan ●
Interlaken Lodge ($$$)
RR 3 Box# 2542
(49853) 906.586.3545

● Menominee ●
Hojo Inn ($$)
2516 10th St
(49858) 906.863.4431
small pets only

● Mesick ●
Indianhead Mtn Resort ($$)
500 Indianhead Rd
(49668) 906.229.5181

● Midland ●
Best Western ($$)
5221 Bay City Rd
(48642) 517.496.2700

Fairview Inn ($$)
2200 W Wackerly St
(48640) 517.631.0070

Holiday Inn ($$$)
1500 W Wackerly St
(48640) 517.631.4220
mgr preapproval reqd

Ramada Inn ($$)
1815 S Saginaw Rd
(48640) 517.631.0570

● Milan ●
Star Motel ($)
335 E Lewis Ave
(48160) 313.439.2448

● Milford ●
Milfords Motel ($)
640 N Milford Rd
(48381) 810.685.1020

● Mio ●
Mio Motel ($$)
415 N Morenci St
(48647) 517.826.3248

● Mohawk ●
Shoreline Resort ($$)
Box# 262
(49950) 906.289.4441

● Monroe ●
Holiday Inn ($$$)
1225 N Dixie Hwy
(48162) 313.242.6000
mgr preapproval reqd

Hometown Inn ($)
1885 Welcome Way
(48162) 313.289.1080

Knights Inn ($)
1250 N Dixie Hwy
(48162) 800.843.5644

● Moran ●
Chapel Hill Motel ($)
4422 US Hwy 2
(49760) 906.292.5521

● Mount Pleasant ●
Budgetel ($$)
5858 E Pickard Rd
(48858) 517.775.5555

Hampton Inn ($$)
5205 E Pickard Rd
(48858) 517.772.5500

Holiday Inn ($$$)
5665 E Pickard Rd
(48858) 517.772.2905
mgr preapproval reqd

● Munising ●
Best Western ($$)
M-28
(49862) 906.387.4864
under 10 lbs

Mirage ($$$)
Box# 276
(49862) 906.387.5292

Scottys Motel ($)
415 Cedar St
(49862) 906.387.2449

Star Lite Motel ($)
500 M-28E
(49862) 906.387.2291

Sunset Motel ($)
Box# 291
(49862) 906.387.4574

Terrace Motel ($)
420 Prospect St
(49862) 906.387.2735

Yule Log Resort ($$)
122 W Chocobay
(49862) 906.387.3184

● Muskegon ●
Bel Aire Motel ($$)
4240 Airline Rd
(49444) 616.733.2196

Super 8 ($$)
3380 Hoyt St
(49444) 616.733.0088
w/permission

● Naubinway ●
Wonderland Motel
80 West US 2
(49762) 906.292.5574

● Negaunee ●
Quartz Mountain Inn ($)
791 US 41
(49866) 906.475.7165

● New Baltimore ●
Lodge Keeper Inn
29101 23-Mile Rd
(48047) 810.949.4520
small pets only

● New Buffalo ●
Comfort Inn ($$)
11539 O'Brien Ct
(49117) 616.469.4440
mgr preapproval reqd

Edgewood Motel ($)
18716 La Porte Rd
(49117) 616.469.3345

Euroinn ($$$)
19265 S Lakeside Rd
(49117) 616.756.3141

Grand Beach Motel ($)
19189 US 12
(49117) 616.469.1555

● Newberry ●
Best Western ($$)
South Newberry Ave
(49868) 906.293.5114
pet not left alone

Gateway Motel
RR 4 Box# 980M123
(49868) 906.293.5651

Green Acres Motel ($$)
RR 1 Box# 736
(49868) 800.800.5398

Park Way Motel ($)
RR 4 Box# 966
(49868) 906.293.5771

Rainbow Lodge ($)
Box# 386
(49868) 906.658.3357

Zellars Village Inn
South Newberry Ave
(49868) 906.293.5114
owner rfd

● Niles ●
Ramada Inn ($$$)
930 S 11th St
(49120) 616.684.3000
small pets only

● Novi ●
Fairlane Motel ($)
45700 Grand River Ave
(48374) 810.349.6410

Hilton ($$$)
21111 Haggerty Rd
(48375) 810.349.4000

● Okemos ●
Holiday Inn
2187 University Park
(48864) 517.347.6690

● Onaway ●
Lakeside Motel
County Rd 489 Rt 1
(49765) 517.733.4298

● Onekama ●
Travelers Motel ($)
5606 8 Mile Rd # 97
(49675) 616.889.4342

● Ontonagon ●
Best Western ($$$)
120 Lincoln Ave
(49953) 906.885.5311
small managers discretion

Rainbow Motel ($$)
Box# 2900
(49953) 906.885.5348

Sunshine Motel ($)
1442 M-64
(49953) 906.884.2187

Superior Shores Res ($)
1823 M-64
(49953) 906.884.2653

● Oscoda ●
Anchorage Cottages ($$)
3164 N US 23
(48750) 517.739.7843

Aspen Motor Inn ($)
115 N Lake St
(48750) 517.739.9152

Blue Horizon Ct ($)
Box# 151
(48750) 517.739.8487

Cedar Lane Motel ($)
7404 N US 23
(48750) 517.739.9988

Northern Traveler ($)
5943 N US 23
(48750) 517.739.9261

Rainbow Resort
5764 N US 23
(48750) 517.739.5695

Surfside Motel ($$)
6504 N US 23
(48750) 517.739.5363

● Owosso ●
Owosso Motor Lodge ($)
2247 E Main St
(48867) 517.725.7148

● Paradise ●
Curleys Motel ($$)
Box# 57
(49768) 906.492.3445

● Paw Paw ●
Green Acres Motel
38245 W Red Arrow Hwy
(49079) 616.657.4037

Mroczek Inn ($)
139 Ampey Rd
(49079) 616.657.2578

● Perry ●
Hebs Inn Motel ($)
2811 Lansing Rd
(48872) 517.625.7500

● Petoskey ●
Coach House Motel ($$)
2445 Charlevoix Ave
(49770) 616.347.2593

Comfort Inn ($$)
1314 N US Hwy 31
(49770) 616.347.3220
mgr preapproval reqd

Days Inn ($$)
630 W Mitchell St
(49770) 616.347.8717
$10/pet

Econo Lodge ($$)
1858 S US Hwy 131
(49770) 616.348.3324

● Pinconning ●
Pinconning Trl Motel ($)
201 S M-13
(48650) 517.879.4219

● Plymouth ●
Red Roof Inn ($)
39700 Ann Arbor Rd
(48170) 313.459.3300
fees/limits may apply

● Port Austin ●
Lakeside Motor Lodge ($)
Box# 358
(48467) 517.738.5201

● Port Huron ●
Best Western ($$)
2908 Pine Groce
(48060) 810.984.1522

Days Inn ($$)
2908 Pine Grove Ave
(48060) 810.984.1522
$5

Knights Inn ($$)
2160 Water St
(48060) 810.982.1022
size limits & fees

Mainstreet Lodge ($$)
514 Huron Ae
(48060) 810.984.3166

● Portage ●
Days Inn
1912 Kilgore
(49002) 616.382.2303
$5

Motel 6 ($)
3704 Van Rick Rd
(49002) 616.344.9255
1 small pet/room

● Portland ●
Best Western ($$)
1625 E Grand River Ave
(48875) 517.647.2200

● Powers ●
Candle Lite Motel ($)
Box# 195
(49874) 906.497.5413

● Rapid River ●
The Right Bower Motel ($)
9912 US 2
(49878) 906.474.6078

● Redford ●
Coach & Lantern Motel ($)
25225 Grand River Ave
(48240) 313.533.4020

Dorchester Motel ($)
26825 Grand River Ave
(48240) 313.533.8400

● Rochester Hills ●
Red Roof Inn ($$)
2580 Crooks Rd
(48309) 810.853.6400
fees/limits may apply

Rochester Motel ($$)
2070 S Rochester Rd
(48307) 810.651.8591

● Romulus ●
Budgetel ($$)
9000 Wickham St
(48174) 313.722.6000

Days Inn ($$$)
9501 Middlebelt Rd
(48174) 313.946.4300
$25 dep small

Howard Johnson ($$)
7600 Merriman Rd
(48174) 313.728.2430

Marriott Hotel ($$$)
30559 Flynn Dr
(48174) 313.729.7555

● Roseville ●
Budgetel ($$)
20675 E 13 Mile Rd
(48066) 810.296.6910

Georgian Inn ($$)
31327 Gratiot Ave
(48066) 810.294.0400

Red Roof Inn ($)
31800 Little Mack Ave
(48066) 810.296.0310
fees/limits may apply

● Saginaw ●
Best Western ($$)
3325 Davenport Ave
(48602) 517.793.2080

Comfort Suites
5180 Fashion Square Blvd
(48604) 517.797.8000
mgr preapproval reqd

Fairfield Inn
5200 Fashion Square Blvd
(48604) 517.797.6100

Hampton Inn ($$)
2222 Tittabawassee Rd
(48604) 517.792.7666

Holiday Inn ($$$)
1408 S Outer Dr
(48601) 517.755.0461
mgr preapproval reqd

Knights Inn ($$)
2225 Tittabawassee Rd
(48604) 517.791.1411
size limits & fees

Knights Inn ($$)
1415 S Outer Dr
(48601) 517.754.4200

Red Roof Inn ($)
966 S Outer Dr
(48601) 517.754.8414
fees/limits may apply

Sheraton Inn ($$$$)
4960 Towne Centre Rd
(48604) 517.790.5050

Super 8 ($$)
4848 Town Cente Rd
(48603) 517.791.3003
w/permission

● Saint Ignace ●
Bay View Beach Front ($)
1133 N State St
(49781) 906.643.9444
$5fee open 5/15-10/15

Blue Bay Motel ($)
1071 N State St
(49781) 906.643.7414

Budget Host ($$)
700 N State St
(49781) 906.643.9666
w/permission

Cedars Motel ($)
2040 N Business Loop I-75
(49781) 906.643.9578

Howard Johnson ($$)
913 Boulevard Dr
(49781) 906.643.9700
$7 charge

Rockview Motel ($)
2055 N Business Loop I-75
(49781) 906.643.8839

Rodeway Inn ($$)
Box# 651
(49781) 906.643.8511

Silver Sands Resort ($$)
1519 US Hwy 2
(49781) 906.643.8635

The Driftwood Motel ($)
590 N State St
(49781) 906.643.7744

Wayside Motel ($)
751 N State St
(49781) 906.643.8944

● Saint Joseph ●
Best Western ($)
2723 Niles Ave
(49085) 616.983.6321
small pets

● Sandusky ●
Thumb Heritage Inn ($)
405 W Sanilac Rd
(48471) 810.648.4811

● Saugatuck ●
Ship N Shore ($$$)
528 Water St
(49453) 616.857.2194

● Sault Sainte Marie ●
Admirals Inn ($)
2701 I-75 Business Spur
(49783) 906.632.1130

Bavaria Motor Lodge ($)
2006 Ashmun St
(49783) 906.632.6864

Biltmore Motel ($)
331 E Portage Ave
(49783) 906.632.2119

Crestview Thrifty ($$)
1200 Ashmun St
(49783) 906.635.5213

Grand Motel ($$)
1100 E Portage Ave
(49783) 906.632.2141

Imperial Motor Inn
2216 Ashmun St
(49783) 906.632.7334

Kings Inn Motel ($)
3755 I-75 Business Spur
(49783) 906.635.5061

Laker Inn ($$)
1712 Ashmun St
(49783) 906.632.3581

Royal Motel ($)
1707 Ashmun St
(49783) 906.632.6323

Super 8 ($$)
3826 I-75 Business Spur
(49783) 906.632.8882
w/permission

● South Haven ●
Colonial Hotel ($$)
532 Dyckman Ave
(49090) 616.637.2887

Econo Lodge ($$)
09817 Hwy 140
(49090) 616.637.5141

● Southfield ●
Econo Lodge ($$)
23300 Telegraph Rd
(48034) 810.358.1800
small pets only

Hilton ($$$)
26000 American Dr
(48034) 810.357.1100

Holiday Inn ($$)
26555 Telegraph Rd
(48034) 810.353.7700
mgr preapproval reqd

Mariott Hotel ($$$)
27033 Northwestern Hwy
(48034) 313.356.7400

Ramada Inn ($$)
17017 W 9 Mile Rd
(48075) 810.557.4800

Red Roof Inn
27660 Northwestern Hwy
(48034) 810.353.7200
fees/limits may apply

Residence Inn ($$$$)
26700 Central Park Blvd
(48076) 810.352.8900

● Southgate ●
Budgetel ($$)
12888 Reeck Rd
(48195) 313.374.3000

Holiday Inn
17201 Northline Rd
(48195) 313.283.4400

● Standish ●
Standish Motel ($)
US 23 & M-76
(48658) 517.846.9571

● Stephenson ●
Stephenson Motel ($)
RR 2 Box# 20 Hwy 41
(49887) 906.753.2552

● Stevensville ●
Park Inn Intl ($$)
4290 Red Arrow Hwy
(49127) 616.429.3218

● Sturgis ●
The Inn Of Sturgis ($$$)
1300 S Centerville Rd
(49091) 616.651.7881

● Suttons Bay ●
Red Lion Inn ($$)
4290 S West Bay Shore Dr
(49682) 616.271.6694
call re: fees

● Tawas City ●
North Star Motel ($)
1119 S US 23
(48763) 517.362.2255

● Taylor ●
Hoffmans Colonial ($)
10870 Telegraph Rd
(48180) 313.291.3000

Red Roof Inn ($)
21230 Eureka Rd
(48180) 313.374.1150
fees/limits may apply

● Tecumseh ●
Tecumseh Inn ($$)
1445 W Chicago Blvd
(49286) 517.423.7401

● Three Rivers ●
Greystone Motel ($)
Box# 62
(49093) 616.278.1695

Three Rivers Inn ($$)
1200 W Broadway St
(49093) 616.273.9521

● Traverse City ●
Comfort Inn ($$)
1492 US 31
(49684) 616.929.4423
mgr preapproval reqd

Fox Haus Motel ($)
704 Munson Ave
(49686) 616.947.4450

$=under $35 $$=$35-60   CALL AHEAD! $$$=$60-100 $$$$=over $100

Holiday Inn ($$$)
615 E Front St
(49686) 616.947.3700
mgr preapproval reqd

Main Street Inns ($)
618 E Front St
(49686) 616.929.0410

Old Mission Inn
18599 Old Mision Rd
(49684) 616.223.7770

Rodeway Inn ($)
1582 US 31
(49686) 616.938.2080

● Trout Lake ●
McGowan Family Motel ($$)
Hwy 123
(49793) 906.569.3366

● Troy ●
Drury Inn ($$$)
575 W Big Beaver Rd
(48084) 810.528.3330

Hilton ($$$)
5500 Crooks Rd
(48098) 810.879.2100

Holiday Inn ($$)
2537 Rochester Ct
(48083) 810.689.7500
mgr preapproval reqd

Marriott Hotel ($$$)
200 W Big Beaver Rd
(48084) 810.680.9797

Red Roof Inn ($)
235 Rochester Rd
(48083) 810.689.4391
fees/limits may apply

● Walhalla ●
Timberlane Resort
7410 E US 10
(49458) 616.757.2142

● Warren ●
Budgetel ($$)
30900 Van Dyke Ave
(48093) 810.574.0550

Homewood Suites ($$$)
30180 N Civi Center Blvd
(48093) 810.558.7870
$25 fee

Motel 6 ($)
8300 Chicago Rd
(48093) 313.826.9300
1 small pet/room

Red Roof Inn ($)
26300 Dequindre Rd
(48091) 810.573.4300
fees/limits may apply

Residence Inn ($$$$)
30120 N Civic Center Blvd
(48093) 810.558.8050
$50 fee + $8 per day

Van Dyke Park Hotel ($$)
31800 Van Dyke Ave
(48093) 800.321.1008

● Waters ●
Northland Inn ($$)
9311 Old US 27
(49797) 517.732.4470

● Watersmeet ●
Vacationland Resort ($$)
E 19636 Herbert Rd
(49969) 906.358.4380

● West Branch ●
La Hacienda Motel
969 W Houghton Ave
(48661) 517.345.2345

Red Rose Motel ($$)
836 S M-33
(48661) 517.345.2136

Super 8 ($$)
2596 Austin Way
(48661) 517.345.8488
call re: fees

Welcome Motel ($)
3308 W M-76
(48661) 517.345.2896

● West Olive ●
The Four Seasons ($$$)
8841 Deadstream
(49460) 616.325.6992

● White Pigeon ●
Plaza Motel ($)
71410 US 131
(49099) 616.382.7285

● Whitmore Lake ●
Best Western ($$)
9897 Main St
(48189) 313.449.2058

Lakes Motel ($)
8365 Main St
(48189) 313.449.5991

● Woodhaven ●
Knights Inn ($)
21880 West Rd
(48183) 313.676.8550
size limits & fees

● Ypsilanti ●
Mayflower Motel ($)
5610 Carpenter Rd
(48197) 313.434.2200

Minnesota
● Aitkin ●
40 Club Inn ($$)
950 2nd St NW
(56431) 218.927.2903

Bills Resort
RR 2 Box# 521
(56431) 218.927.3841

Ripple River Motel ($)
701 Minnesota Ave
(56431) 219.927.3734

● Albert Lea ●
Bel Aire Motor Inn ($)
700US S Hwy 69
(56007) 507.373.3983

Best Western ($$)
2301 E Main St
(56007) 507.373.8291
pets $5

Days Inn ($$)
2306 E Main St
(56007) 507.373.6471

Lea Budget Inn ($)
2210 E Main St
(56007) 507.373.1496

Super 8 ($$)
2019 E Main St
(56007) 507.377.0591
pets with deposit

● Alexandria ●
Days Inn ($)
4810 Hwy 29
(56308) 612.762.1171

Holiday Inn
5637 State Hwy 29
(56308) 320.763.6577

L Motel ($)
910 Hwy 27
(56308) 612.763.5121

Red Carpet Inn
1903 Aga Dr
(56308) 612.762.0512

Skyline Motel
605 30th Ave
(56308) 612.763.3175

Super 8 ($$)
4620 Hwy 29
(56308) 612.763.6552
pets w/permission

● Anoka ●
Super 8 ($$)
1129 W Hwy 10
(55303) 612.422.8000
small dogs $25 deposit

● Appleton ●
Super 8 ($)
900 N Munsterman St
(56208) 320.289.2500
$3 w/permission

● Austin ●
Austin Motel ($)
805 21st St NE
(55912) 507.433.9254

Days Inn ($$)
700 16th Ave NW
(55912) 507.433.8600

Holiday Inn ($$)
1701 4th St NW
(55912) 507.433.1000

Rodeway Inn ($)
3303 W Oakland Ave
(55912) 507.437.7774

Super 8 ($$)
1401 14th St NW
(55912) 507.433.1801
pets with deposit

● Avon ●
Americinn Motel ($)
304 Blattner Dr
(56310) 612.356.2211

● Babbitt ●
Timber Bay Lodge ($$$$)
8347 Timber Bay Rd
(55706) 218.827.3682

● Baudette ●
Sportsmans Lodge ($$)
RR 1 Box# 167
(56623) 800.862.8602

● Baxter ●
Americinn Motel ($$)
600 Dellwood Dr
(56425) 800.634.3444

Twin Birch Motel ($)
2300 Fairview Rd
(56425) 218.829.2833

● Becker ●
Super 8 ($)
13804 1st St
(55308) 612.261.4440
call re: fees

● Bemidji ●
Bel Air Motel ($)
1350 Paul Bunyan Dr NW
(56601) 218.751.3222

Best Western ($$)
2420 Paul Bunyan Dr NW
(56601) 218.751.0390
small pets allowed

Comfort Inn ($$)
3500 Comfort Dr
(56601) 218.751.7700

Edgewater Motel ($)
1015 Paul Bunyan Dr NE
(56601) 218.751.3600

Holiday Inn
2422 Ridgeway Ave NW
(56601) 218.751.2487

Rutters Lodge ($$$)
530 Birchmont Bch
(56601) 218.751.1630

● Benson ●
Motel 1 ($)
620 Atlantic Ave
(56215) 612.843.4434

● Blackduck ●
American Motel ($$)
US 71 & Lake Rd
(56630) 218.835.4500

Drake Motel
305 N Pine
(56630) 218.835.4567

● Blue Earth ●
Super 8
1120 Grove
(56013) 507.526.7376
call re: fees

● Brainerd ●
Days Inn ($)
1630 Fairview Dr
(56401) 218.829.0391
mgr preapproval reqd

Dellwood Motel ($)
1302 S 6th St
(56401) 218.828.8756

Econo Lodge ($)
2655 Hwy 371
(56401) 218.828.0027

Holiday Inn ($$)
2115 S 6th St
(56401) 218.829.1441

● Breckenridge ●
Scottwood Motel ($)
821 Hwy 75
(56520) 218.643.9201

● Buffalo ●
Super 8 ($$)
303 10th Ave
(55313) 612.682.5930
pets w/permission

● Burnsville ●
Red Roof Inn ($)
12920 Aldrich Ave
(55337) 800.843.7663

Super 8 ($$)
1101 Brunsville Pkwy
(55337) 612.894.3400
call re: fees

● Cannon Falls ●
Country Quiet Inn ($$)
37295 112th Avenue Way
(55009) 612.258.4406

● Chanhassen ●
Chanhasen Inn Motel ($$)
531 W 79th St
(55317) 612.934.7373
$15 dep

Country Suites ($$$)
591 W 78th St
(55317) 612.937.2424

● Chatfield ●
Lunds Guest Houses ($$)
218 Winona St SE
(55923) 507.867.4003

● Chisago City ●
Super 8 ($)
11650 Lake Blvd
(55013) 612.257.8088
pets w/permission & deposit

● Clearwater ●
Budget Inn ($)
945 Hwy 24
(55320) 612.558.2221

● Cloquet ●
Americinn Motel ($$)
111 Big Lake Rd
(55720) 218.879.1231

Super 8 ($$)
Hwy 33 & Big Lake Rd
(55720) 218.879.1250
call re: fees

● Cold Spring ●
American Motel ($$)
118 3rd St
(56320) 612.685.4539

● Cook ●
Vermillion Dam Lodge
Box# 1105
(55723) 800.325.5780

Vermillon Dam Lodge
3276 Randa Rd
(55723) 218.666.5418

● Cottage Grove ●
Super 8 ($$)
7125 80th St
(55016) 612.458.0313
call re: fees

● Crane Lake ●
Olsons Borderland
7488 Crane Lake Rd
(55725) 218.993.2233

● Crookston ●
Northland Inn ($$)
2200 University Ave
(56716) 218.281.5210

● Deer River ●
Bahrs Motel ($)
Box# 614
(56636) 218.246.8271

Millers Resort
RR 1 Box# 266
(56636) 218.246.8951

● Deerwood ●
Country Inn ($$)
115 Front St
(56444) 218.534.3101

Deerwood Motel ($)
9 W Forest Rd
(56444) 218.534.3163

● Detroit Lakes ●
Budget Host ($)
895 Hwy 10
(56501) 218.847.4454

Castaway Inn
RR 4 Box# 15
(56501) 218.847.4449

Holiday Inn
Hwy 10
(56501) 218.847.2121

Inn On The Lake ($$)
Hwy 10E
(56501) 800.465.4329

Super 8 ($$)
400 Morrow Ave
(56501) 218.847.1651
attended dogs

$=under $35 $$=$35-60 $$$=$60-100 $$$$=over $100

● Dexter ●
Mill Inn Motel ($)
Box# 78A
(55926) 507.584.6440

● Dilworth ●
Howard Johnson ($$)
701 Center Ave
(56529) 218.287.1212

● Duluth ●
Allyndale Motel ($)
510 N 66th Ave
(55807) 218.628.1061

Best Western ($)
131 W 2nd St
(55802) 218.727.6851

Best Western ($$)
2400 London Rd
(55812) 218.728.3601
pets must be attended

Days Inn ($$)
909 Cottonwood Ave
(55811) 218.727.3110
smoking rooms

Fitgers Inn ($$)
600 E Superior St
(55802) 218.722.8826

Grand Motel
4312 Grand Ave
(55807) 218.624.4821

Park Inn Intl ($$)
250 Canal Park Dr
(55802) 218.727.8821

Radisson Inn ($$)
505 W Superior St
(55802) 218.727.8981
small pets allowed

Select Inn ($)
200 S 27th Ave
(55806) 218.723.1123

Voyageur Lakewald Inn ($)
333 E Superior St
(55802) 218.722.3911

Willard Munger Inn ($$)
7408 Grand Ave
(55807) 218.624.4814

● East Grand Forks ●
Comfort Inn ($$)
US 2-E
(56721) 218.773.9545

● Eden Prairie ●
Residence Inn ($$)
7780 Flying Cloud Dr
(55344) 612.829.0033
call for fee & availability

● Elk River ●
American Motel ($$)
17432 Hwy 10
(55330) 612.441.8554

Red Carpet Inn ($)
1729 Hwy 10
(55330) 612.411.2424

● Ely ●
Budget Host ($$)
1047 E Sheridan
(55731) 218.365.3237
w/permission

Olson Bay Cottages ($$$$)
2279 Grant McMahan Blvd
(55731) 800.777.4419

Silver Rapids Resort ($$)
HC 1 Box# 2992
(55731) 218.365.4877

Three Deer Haven ($$$)
1850 Deer Haven Dr
(55731) 218.365.6464

● Eveleth ●
Holiday Inn ($$$)
Hwy 53
(55734) 218.744.2703

Kokes Downtown Motel ($)
714 Fayal Rd
(55734) 218.744.4500

● Fairfax ●
Fairfax Motel
403 Lincoln Ave
(55332) 507.426.7266

● Fairmont ●
Comfort Inn ($$)
I-90/Hwy 15
(56031) 507.238.5444

Highland Court Motel ($)
1245 Lake Ave
(56031) 507.235.6686

Holiday Inn ($$)
I-90
(56031) 507.238.4771

Super 8 ($$)
1200 Torgerson
(56031) 507.238.9444
call re: fees

● Faribault ●
Best Western ($$)
1401 Hwy 60
(55021) 507.334.5508
small dogs ok

Faribault Motel
841 Faribault Rd
(55021) 507.334.1841

Select Inn ($)
4040 Hwy 60
(55021) 507.334.2051

● Fergus Falls ●
Americinn Motel ($$)
526 Western Ave
(56537) 218.739.3900

Motel 7 ($)
616 Frontier Dr
(56537) 218.736.2554

Super 8 ($)
2454 College Way
(56537) 218.739.3261
call re: fees

● Finlayson ●
Super 8 ($$)
2811 Hwy 23
(55735) 320.245.5284
fee designated rooms

● Forest Lake ●
Forest Motel ($)
7 6th Ave NE
(55025) 612.464.4077

● Fosston ●
Super 8 ($$)
Hwy 2 (56542) 218.435.1088
call re: fees

● Franklin ●
Maple Hill Cottage ($$)
RR 1 Box# 12
(55333) 507.557.2403

● Glencoe ●
Super 8 ($$)
717 Morningside Dr
(55336) 320.864.6191
pets w/permission

● Glenwood ●
Hi View Motel ($)
255 Hwy 55
(56334) 612.634.4541

● Grand Marais ●
Best Western ($$)
US Hwy 61
(55604) 218.387.2240

Clearwater Lodge ($$$$)
355 Gunflint Trl
(55604) 800.527.0554

Econo Lodge ($$)
US 61
(55604) 218.387.2500

Golden Eagle Lodge ($$$)
325 Gunflint Trl
(55604) 218.388.2203

Gunflight Lodge ($$$)
750 Gunflint Trail
(55604) 218.388.2294

Gunflint Pines
755 Gunflint Trail
(55604) 800.533.5814

Harbor Inn
207 Wisconsin St
(55604) 218.387.1191

Little Ollie Cabin ($$$$)
590 Gunflint Trl
(55604) 800.322.8327

Motel Wedgewood ($)
HC 1 Box# 100
(55604) 218.387.2944

Nor Wester Lodge
550 Gunflint Trl
(55604) 218.388.2252

Well
Behaved

MINNESOTA, Grand Marais

Sandgren Motel ($)
Box# 1056
(55604) 218.387.2975

Seawall Motel
Hwy 61 & 3rd Ave
(55604) 218.387.2095

Super 8 ($$)
Hwy 61
(55604) 218.387.2448
pets w/permission

Tomteboda Motel ($)
1800 Hwy 61
(55604) 218.387.1585

● Grand Rapids ●
Americana Motel
1915 W Hwy 2
(55744) 218.326.0369

Best Western ($$)
1300 US 169
(55744) 218.326.9655

Country Inn ($$)
2601 S Hwy 169
(55744) 218.327.4960

Days Inn ($$)
311 E Hwy 2
(55744) 218.326.3457
only reported small pets

Sawmill Inn ($$)
2301 S Pokegama Ave
(55744) 218.326.8501

● Granite Falls ●
Super 8 ($$)
845 Hwy 212
(56241) 612.564.4075
dep

● Hastings ●
A Country Rose ($$$)
13452 90th St
(55033) 612.436.2237

● Hendricks ●
Triple L Farm ($)
RR 1 Box# 141
(56136) 507.275.3740

● Hibbing ●
Days Inn ($)
1520 Hwy 37
(55746) 218.263.8306
small pets allowed

Kahler Park Hotel ($$$)
1402 E Howard St
(55746) 612.384.7751

Super 8 ($$)
1411 E 40th St
(55746) 218.263.8982
call re: fees

● Hinckley ●
Days Inn ($$)
104 Grindstone Ct
(55037) 320.384.7751
mgr preapproval reqd

Holiday Inn ($$)
604 Weber Ave
(55037) 320.384.7171

● Hutchinson ●
Best Western ($$)
1000 Hwy 7
(55350) 320.587.6030

● International Falls ●
Budget Host ($$)
10 Riverview Bl
(56649) 218.283.2577

Days Inn ($$)
2331 Hwy 53
(56649) 218.283.9441

Hilltop Motel ($)
2002 2nd Ave Wq
(56649) 218.283.2505

Holiday Inn ($$)
1500 Hwy 71W
(56649) 218.283.4451

Island View Lodge ($$)
HC 8 Box# 411
(56649) 218.266.3511

Northernaire Floating Lodges
Box# 510
(56649) 218.286.5221

● Jackson ●
Budget Host ($)
950 N US 71
(56143) 507.847.2020
w/permission

Super 8 ($$)
RR 3 Box# 21
(56143) 800.800.8000
$6

● Lake City ●
Lake Pepin Lodge ($$)
620 Central Point Rd
(55041) 612.345.5392

● Lakeville ●
Motel 6 ($)
11274 210th St
(55044) 612.469.1900
1 small pet/room

Super 8 ($$)
20800 Kenrick Ave
(55044) 612.469.1134
pets with prior approval &
attended

● Litchfield ●
Scotwood Motel ($$)
1017 E Frontage Rd
(55355) 612.693.2496

● Little Falls ●
Pine Edge Inn ($)
308 1st St
(56345) 612.632.6681

● Long Prairie ●
Budget Host ($)
417 Lake St
(56347) 612.732.6118
w/permission

● Lutsen ●
Best Western ($$)
Hwy 61
(55612) 218.663.7273
pets not unattended

Solbakken Resort ($$)
HC 3 Box# 170
(55612) 218.663.7566
need pet reservation

Thomason Beach ($$)
R3 Box# 470
(55612) 218.387.1532

● Luverne ●
Super 8 ($$)
I-90 & Hwy 75
(56156) 507.283.9541
call re: fees

● Mankato ●
Days Inn ($$)
1285 Range St
(56001) 507.387.3332
pets allowed w/permission

Holiday Inn ($$)
101 E Main St
(56001) 507.345.1248

Riverfront Inn ($)
1727 N Riverfront Dr
(56001) 507.388.1638

● Mantorville ●
Grand Old Mansion ($)
501 Clay St
(55955) 507.635.3231

● Marshall ●
Best Western ($$)
1500 E College Dr
(56258) 507.532.3221

Comfort Inn ($$)
1511 E College Dr
(56258) 507.532.3070
mgr preapproval reqd

Super 8 ($$)
1106 E Main St
(56258) 507.537.1461
pets with deposit

Travelers Lodge ($)
1425 E College Dr
(56258) 207.532.5751

● McGregor ●
Hillcrest Resort
HC 3 Box# 754
(55760) 218.426.3323

Town & Country Motel
Hwy 65 & 210
(55760) 218.768.3271

● Melrose ●
Super 8 ($$)
231 E Country Rd 173
(56352) 612.256.4261
$3/day w/permission

● Milaca ●
Rodeway Inn ($$)
215 10th Ave
(56353) 320.983.2660

● Minneapolis ●
Aqua City Motel ($)
5739 Lyndale Ave
(55419) 612.861.6061

Best Western ($$$)
405 S 8th St
(55404) 612.370.1400

Best Western ($$$)
5201 Central Ave NE
(55421) 612.571.9440
small pets only

Best Western ($$$)
2201 E 78th St
(55425) 612.854.3411

Best Western ($$$)
8151 Bridhe Rd
(55437) 612.830.1300

Budgetel ($$)
6415 James Cir
(55430) 612.561.8400

Budgetel ($$)
7815 Nicollet Ave
(55420) 612.881.7311

Country Suites ($$$)
155 Coon Rapids Blvd NW
(55433) 612.780.3797

Crown Sterling ($$$)
425 S 7th St
(55415) 800.433.4600

Crown Sterling ($$$$)
7901 34th Ave
(55425) 612.854.1000

Exel Inn ($$)
2701 E 78th St
(55425) 612.854.7200
small only with managers
approval

Hawthorne Suites ($$$)
3400 Edinborough Way
(55435) 612.893.9300

Holiday Inn
3000 Harbor Lane
(55447) 612.559.1222

Holiday Inn ($$$)
1500 Washington Ave
(55454) 612.233.4646

Hotel Sofitel ($$$$)
5601 W 78th St
(55439) 800.835.6303

Marquette ($$$)
710 Marquette Ave
(55402) 612.332.2351

Marriott Hotel ($$$)
2020 E 79th St
(55425) 612.854.7441

Metro Inn ($)
5637 Lyndale Ave
(55419) 612.861.6011

Hilton ($$$)
1001 Marquette Ave
(55403) 800.445.8667

Marriott ($$$)
30 S 7th St
(55402) 612.349.4000

Motel 6 ($$)
7640 Cedar Ave
(55423) 612.861.4491
1 small pet/room

Radisson Inn ($$$)
3131 Campus Dr
(55441) 612.559.6600
small pets allowed

Radisson Inn ($$$)
615 Washington Ave SE
(55414) 612.379.8888
small pets allowed

Radisson Inn ($$$)
7800 Normandie Blvd
(55439) 612.835.7800

Radisson Inn ($$$)
35 S 7th St
(55402) 612.339.4900

Red Roof Inn ($)
2600 Annapolis Ln
(55441) 800.843.7663

Regal Minneapolis ($$$)
1313 Nicollet Mall
(55403) 612.332.6000

Select Inn ($)
7851 Normandale Blvd
(55435) 612.835.7400

Sheraton Inn ($$$)
1330 Industrial Blvd NE
(55413) 612.331.1900

Sheraton Inn
1500 Park Place Blvd
(55416) 612.542.8600

Super 8 ($$)
7800 2nd Ave
(55420) 612.888.8800
pets w/permission

Wyndham Hotel ($$)
4460 W 78th St
(55435) 800.822.4200

Twin Cities Metro

● Anoka ●
Super 8 ($$)
1129 W Hwy 10
(55303) 612.422.8000
small dogs $25 deposit

● Burnsville ●
Red Roof Inn ($)
12920 Aldrich Ave S
(55337) 800.843.7663

Super 8 ($$)
1101 Brunsville Pkwy
(55337) 612.894.3400
call re: fees

● Chanhassen ●
Chanhasen Inn Motel ($$)
531 W 79th St
(55317) 612.934.7373
$15 dep

Country Suites ($$$)
591 W 78th St
(55317) 612.937.2424

● Eden Prairie ●
Residence Inn ($$)
7780 Flying Cloud Dr
(55344) 612.829.0033
call for fee & availability

● Elk River ●
American Motel ($$)
17432 Hwy 10
(55330) 612.441.8554

Red Carpet Inn ($)
1729 Hwy 10
(55330) 612.411.2424

● Glencoe ●
Super 8 ($$)
717 Morningside Dr
(55336) 320.864.6191
pets with permission

● Hastings ●
A Country Rose ($$$)
13452 90th St S
(55033) 612.436.2237

● Jackson ●
Budget Host ($)
950 N US 71
(56143) 507.847.2020
w/permission

Super 8 ($$)
RR 3 Box# 21
(56143) 800.800.8000
$6

● Lakeville ●
Motel 6 ($)
11274 210th St
(55044) 612.469.1900
1 small pet/room

Super 8 ($$)
20800 Kenrick Ave
(55044) 612.469.1134
pets with prior approval &
attended

● Minneapolis ●
Aqua City Motel ($)
5739 Lyndale Ave S
(55419) 612.861.6061

Best Western ($$$)
405 S 8th St
(55404) 612.370.1400

Best Western ($$$)
5201 Central Ave NE
(55421) 612.571.9440
small pets only

$=under $35 $$=$35-60 $$$=$60-100 $$$$=over $100

Best Western ($$$)
2201 E 78th St
(55425) 612.854.3411

Best Western ($$$)
8151 Bridhe Rd
(55437) 612.830.1300

Budgetel ($$)
6415 James Cir
(55430) 612.561.8400

Budgetel ($$)
7815 Nicollet Ave
(55420) 612.881.7311

Country Suites ($$$)
155 Coon Rapids Blvd NW
(55433) 612.780.3797

Crown Sterling ($$$)
425 S 7th St
(55415) 800.433.4600

Crown Sterling ($$$$)
7901 34th Ave S
(55425) 612.854.1000

Exel Inn ($$)
2701 E 78th St
(55425) 612.854.7200
small only with managers
approval

Hawthorne Suites ($$$)
3400 Edinborough Way
(55435) 612.893.9300

Hilton ($$$)
1001 Marquette Ave
(55403) 800.445.8667

Holiday Inn
3000 Harbor Lane
(55447) 612.559.1222

Holiday Inn ($$$)
1500 Washington Ave S
(55454) 612.233.4646

Hotel Sofitel ($$$$)
5601 W 78th St
(55439) 800.835.6303

Marquette ($$$)
710 Marquette Ave
(55402) 612.332.2351

Marriott ($$$)
30 S 7th St
(55402) 612.349.4000

Marriott Hotel ($$$)
2020 E 79th St
(55425) 612.854.7441

Metro Inn ($)
5637 Lyndale Ave S
(55419) 612.861.6011

Motel 6 ($$)
7640 Cedar Ave S
(55423) 612.861.4491
1 small pet/room

Radisson Inn ($$$)
3131 Campus Dr
(55441) 612.559.6600
small pets allowed

Radisson Inn ($$$)
615 Washington Ave SE
(55414) 612.379.8888
small pets allowed

Radisson Inn ($$$)
7800 Normandie Blvd
(55439) 612.835.7800

Radisson Inn ($$$)
35 S 7th St
(55402) 612.339.4900

Red Roof Inn ($)
2600 Annapolis Ln
(55441) 800.843.7663

Regal Minneapolis ($$$)
1313 Nicollet Mall
(55403) 612.332.6000

Select Inn ($)
7851 Normandale Blvd
(55435) 612.835.7400

Sheraton Inn ($$$)
1330 Industrial Blvd NE
(55413) 612.331.1900

Sheraton Inn
1500 Park Place Blvd
(55416) 612.542.8600

Super 8 ($$)
7800 2Nd Ave S
(55420) 612.888.8800
pets with permission

Wyndham Hotel ($$)
4460 W 78th St
(55435) 800.822.4200

● Monticello ●
Comfort Inn ($$)
200 Oakwood Dr
(55362) 612.295.1111
mgr preapproval reqd

● Rogers ●
Super 8 ($$)
21130 134th Ave
(55374) 612.428.4000
$3 deposit

● Saint Paul ●
Best Western ($$$)
161 Saint Anthony Ave
(55103) 612.227.8711

Best Western ($$)
1780 E Cr D
(55109) 800.528.1234

Country Inn ($$)
4940 Hwy 61
(55110) 612.429.5393

Crown Sterling ($$$)
175 10th St
(55101) 612.224.5400

Days Inn
1964 University Ave
(55104) 612.645.8681
dep

Days Inn ($$)
175 7th St
(55102) 612.292.8929

Exel Inn ($$)
1739 Old Hudson Rd
(55106) 612.771.5566
small pets only

Hampton Inn ($$$)
1450 Weir Dr
(55125) 612.578.2822

Hampton Inn ($$)
1000 Gramsie Rd
(55126) 800.465.4329

Holiday Inn
1010 Bandana Bl
(55108) 612.647.1637

Holiday Inn
1950 Rahncliff Ct
(55122) 612.681.9266

Holiday Inn ($$$)
2201 Burns Ave
(55119) 612.731.2220

Motel 6 ($)
2300 Cleveland Ave
(55113) 612.639.3988
1 small pet/room

Radisson Inn ($$$)
11 Kellogg Blvd
(55101) 612.292.1900
small pets allowed

Ramada Inn ($$)
1201 W Country Rd
(55112) 800.272.6232

Red Roof Inn ($$)
1806 Wooddale Dr
(55125) 800.843.7663

Residence Inn ($$$)
3040 Eagandale Pl
(55121) 612.688.0363
$150 cleaning fee

Sheraton Inn ($$$)
400 Hamline Ave
(55104) 612.642.1234
small pets only

● Shakopee ●
American Of Shakopee ($$)
1251 1st Ave
(55379) 800.634.3444

● Stillwater ●
Best Western ($$)
1750 Frontage Rd
(55082) 612.430.1300
managers discretion

End of Twin Cities Metro

● Montevideo ●
Best Western ($$)
207 N 1st St
(56265) 800.528.1234

CALL AHEAD!

$=under $35 $$=$35-60 $$$=$60-100 $$$$=over $100

Rochester, MINNESOTA

● Monticello ●
Comfort Inn ($$)
200 Oakwood Dr
(55362) 612.295.1111
mgr preapproval reqd

● Moorhead ●
Best Western ($$)
600 30th Ave
(56560) 218.233.6171

Guest House ($)
2107 SE Main Ave
(56560) 218.233.2471

Motel 75 ($)
810 Belsly Blvd
(56560) 218.233.7501

● Mora ●
Ann River Motel ($)
RR 2 Box# 279
(55051) 612.679.2972

● Morris ●
Best Western ($)
200 E Hwy 28
(56267) 320.589.3030

● Morton ●
Days Inn ($)
400 W Ledge
(56270) 507.697.6205

● Nevis ●
The Park Street Inn ($$)
254 Park St
(56467) 218.652.4500

● New Ulm ●
Colonial Inn Motel ($)
1315 N Broadway St
(56073) 507.354.3128

Holiday Inn
2101 S Broadway
(56073) 507.359.2941

Super 8 ($$)
1901 S Broadway St
(56073) 507.359.2400
$20 deposit

● New York Mills ●
Mills Motel ($)
Box# B
(56567) 218.385.3600

● Nisswa ●
Days Inn ($$)
45 Smiley Rd
(56468) 218.963.3500

Nisswa Motel ($$)
1426 Merrill Ave
(56468) 218.963.7611

● North Branch ●
Crossroads Motel ($)
1118 Main St
(55056) 612.674.7074

● Northome ●
Royal Shooks Motel
Hwy 1/72
(56661) 218.647.8379

● Olivia ●
Sheep Shedde Inn ($)
2425 W Lincoln Ave
(56277) 612.523.5000

● Onamia ●
Econo Lodge ($)
40993 US 169
(56359) 320.532.3838

● Owatonna ●
Budget Host ($)
745 State Ave
(55060) 507.451.8712
small pets only

Country Inn ($$)
130 Allan Ave
(55060) 507.455.9295

Days Inn ($)
205 N Oak Ave
(55060) 507.451.4620
mgr preapproval reqd

Oakdale Motel ($)
1416 S Oak Ave
(55060) 507.451.5480

Ramada Inn ($$)
1212 I-35
(55060) 507.455.0606
$10 per day

● Pine River ●
Trailside Inn ($$)
Hwy 371
(56474) 218.587.4499

● Pipestone ●
Kings Kourt
821 7th St SE
(56164) 507.825.3314

Super 8 ($$)
605 8th Ave SE
(56164) 507.825.4217
deposit

● Preston ●
Inn Town Lodge ($$)
205 Franklin St NW
(55965) 507.765.4412

● Princeton ●
Rum River Motel ($$)
510 19th Ave
(55371) 612.389.3120

● Red Wing ●
Americinn Motel ($$)
1819 Old Main
(55066) 612.385.9060

Best Western ($$$)
752 Withers Harbor Dr
(55066) 612.388.1577
some rooms only

Days Inn ($$)
955 E 7th St
(55066) 612.388.3568
$8

● Rochester ●
Best Western ($$)
20 5th Ave NW
(55901) 507.289.3987

Clinic View Inn ($$$)
93rd Ave NW
(55901) 507.289.8646

Colonial Hotel ($)
114 2nd St SW
(55902) 507.289.3363

Country Inn ($$)
4323 Hwy 52
(55901) 507.285.3335

Days Inn ($$)
111 28th St SW
(55902) 507.286.1001

Days Inn ($$)
61st Ave NW
(55901) 507.282.3801

Days Inn ($$)
17th Ave
(55902) 507.282.2733

Econo Lodge ($$)
519 3rd Ave SW
(55902) 507.288.1855

Fiksdal Motel ($)
1215 2nd St SW
(55902) 507.288.2671

Friendship Inn ($$)
116 5th St SW
(55902) 507.289.1628
a few rooms

Holiday Inn ($$)
220 S Broadway
(55904) 507.288.3231

Holiday Inn ($$)
1630 S Broadway
(55904) 507.288.1844

Howard Johnson ($$)
111 17th Ave SW
(55902) 507.289.1617

Kahler Plaza Hotel ($$)
101 1st Ave SW
(55902) 507.280.6000

Motel 6 ($)
2107 W Frontage Rd
(55901) 507.282.6625
1 small pet/room

Quality Inn ($$$)
1620 1st Ave SE
(55904) 507.282.8091
mgr preapproval reqd

Radisson Inn ($$)
150 S Broadway
(55904) 507.281.8000
$25 dep & advance notice

Ramada Inn ($$)
1625 S Broadway
(55904) 507.281.2211

$=under $35 $$=$35-60 $$$=$60-100 $$$$=over $100

Super 8 ($$)
1850 S Broadway
(55904) 507.282.9905
call re: fees

Super 8 ($$)
1230 S Broadway
(55904) 507.288.8288
call re: fees

Super 8 ($$)
1608 2nd St SW
(55902) 507.281.5100
call re: fees

The Kahler Hotel ($$)
20 2nd Ave SW
(55902) 507.282.2581

● Rogers ●
Super 8 ($$)
21130 134th Ave
(55374) 612.428.4000
$3 deposit

● Roseau ●
Americinn Motel ($)
1090 3rd St NW
(56751) 218.463.1045

Super 8 ($)
318 West Side
(56751) 218.463.2196
w/permission

● Saint Cloud ●
Budgetel ($)
70 37th Ave
(56301) 612.253.4444

Days Inn ($$)
420 Hwy 10
(56304) 612.253.0500

Fairfield Inn ($$)
4120 2nd St
(56301) 800.348.6000

Gateway Motel ($)
310 Lincoln Ave SE
(56304) 612.252.4050

Holiday Inn ($$)
75 37th Ave
(56301) 320.253.9000

Kleis Motel ($)
30 25th Ave
(56301) 612.251.7450

Super 8 ($$)
50 Park Ave
(56301) 320.253.5530
w/permission

● Saint James ●
Super 8 ($$)
Hwy 60
(56081) 507.375.4708
w/permission

● Saint Joseph ●
Super 8 ($$)
I-75
(56374) 612.363.7711
small w/permission

● Saint Paul ●
Best Western ($$$)
161 Saint Anthony Ave
(55103) 612.227.8711

Best Western ($$)
1780 E Cr D
(55109) 800.528.1234

Country Inn ($$)
4940 Hwy 61
(55110) 612.429.5393

Crown Sterling ($$$)
175 10th St
(55101) 612.224.5400

Days Inn
1964 University Ave
(55104) 612.645.8681
dep

Days Inn ($$)
175 7th St
(55102) 612.292.8929

Exel Inn ($$)
1739 Old Hudson Rd
(55106) 612.771.5566
small pets only

Hampton Inn ($$$)
1450 Weir Dr
(55125) 612.578.2822

Hampton Inn ($$)
1000 Gramsie Rd
(55126) 800.465.4329

Holiday Inn
1010 Bandana Bl
(55108) 612.647.1637

Holiday Inn
1950 Rahncliff Ct
(55122) 612.681.9266

Holiday Inn ($$$)
2201 Burns Ave
(55119) 612.731.2220

Motel 6 ($)
2300 Cleveland Ave
(55113) 612.639.3988
1 small pet/room

Radisson Inn ($$$)
11 Kellogg Blvd
(55101) 612.292.1900
small pets allowed

Ramada Inn ($$)
1201 W Country Rd
(55112) 800.272.6232

Red Roof Inn ($$)
1806 Wooddale Dr
(55125) 800.843.7663

Residence Inn ($$$)
3040 Eagandale Pl
(55121) 612.688.0363
$150 cleaning fee

Sheraton Inn ($$$)
400 Hamline Ave
(55104) 612.642.1234
small pets only

● Saint Peter ●
Americinn Motel ($$)
700 N Minnesota Ave
(56082) 507.931.6554

Viking Jr Motel
169 & 90 West
(56082) 507.931.3081

● Sanborn ●
Sod House On Prairie ($$$)
RR 2 Box# 75
(56083) 507.723.5138

● Sauk Centre ●
Econo Lodge ($$)
I-94 At Sauk Ctr
(56378) 320.352.6581

Gopher Prairie Motel ($)
I-94 & US71
(56378) 621.352.2275

Hillcrest Motel ($)
965 Main St
(56378) 612.352.2215

Palmer House Inn ($)
500 Sinclair Lewis Ave
(56378) 612.352.3431

● Sauk Rapids ●
Econo Lodge ($)
1420 2nd St
(56379) 800.251.1962

● Savage ●
Comfort Inn ($$)
4601 Hwy 13
(55378) 612.894.6124

● Schroeder ●
Lambs Resort
North Shore Dr Hwy 6
(55613) 218.663.7292

● Sebeka ●
Ks Motel
Hwy 71
(56477) 218.837.5162

● Shakopee ●
American Of Shakopee ($$)
1251 1st Ave
(55379) 800.634.3444

● Silver Bay ●
Mariner Motel ($)
46 Outer Dr
(55614) 218.226.4488

● Sleepy Eye ●
Best Western ($$)
1100 E Main St
(56085) 507.794.5390
rooms for small pets

● Spicer ●
Cazador Inn ($)
154 Lake St
(56288) 612.796.2091

● Spring Valley ●
66 Motel ($)
612 N Huron Ave
(55975) 507.346.9993

Policies
Subject
to Change

$=under $35 $$=$35-60 $$$=$60-100 $$$$=over $100

● Staples ●
Super 8 ($$)
109 2nd Ave
(56479) 218.894.3585
$3/day

● Stewartville ●
Americinn Motel ($$)
1700 2nd Ave NW
(55976) 507.533.4747

● Stillwater ●
Best Western ($$)
1750 Frontage Rd
(55082) 612.430.1300
managers discretion

● Sturgeon Lake ●
Sturgeon Lake Motel
I-35 & Country Rd 46
(55783) 218.372.3194

● Taylors Falls ●
Springs Inn ($)
90 Government Rd
(55084) 612.465.6565

● Thief River Falls ●
Super 8 ($$)
Hwy 59
(56701) 218.681.6205
deposit

● Tofte ●
Aspenwood Motel
130 Aspenwood
(55615) 218.663.7978

Bluffin Bay Motel ($$$)
Box# 2125
(55615) 800.258.3346

Chateau Le Veaux ($$)
Box# 115
(55615) 218.663.7223

Holiday Inn
Hwy 61
(55615) 218.663.7899

● Two Harbors ●
Country Inn ($$)
1204 7th Ave
(55616) 800.456.4000

Superior Shores Lodge ($$)
10 Superior Shores Rd
(55616) 218.834.5671

● Tyler ●
Babettes Inn ($$)
308 S Tyler St
(56178) 507.537.1632

● Virginia ●
Lakeshores Motor Inn ($)
404 N 6th Ave
(55792) 218.741.3360

Ski View Motel ($)
903 17th St
(55792) 218.744.8918

● Wabasha ●
The Anderson House ($)
333 Main St
(55981) 800.535.5467

● Waconia ●
Super 8 ($$)
301 E Frontage Rd
(55387) 612.442.5147
call re: fees

● Wadena ●
Best Western ($)
500 Ash Ave NW
(56482) 218.631.3725

● Waite Park ●
Motel 6 ($)
815 1st St
(56387) 612.253.7070
1 small pet/room

● Walker ●
Lakeview Inn
Box# 1359
(56484) 218.547.1212

● Warroad ●
Best Western ($)
406 Main Ave NE
(56763) 218.386.3807

The Patch Motel ($)
Hwy 11
(56763) 218.386.2723

● Willmar ●
Colonial Inn ($)
1102 1st St
(56201) 612.235.4444

Days Inn ($$)
225 28th St SE
(56201) 612.231.1275

Holiday Inn ($$)
2100 US 12
(56201) 320.256.0609

Super 8 ($)
US71
(56201) 800.800.8000
call re: fees

● Windom ●
Super 8
222 - 3rd Ave
(56101) 507.831.1120
call re: fees

● Winona ●
Best Western ($$)
900 Bruski Dr
(55987) 507.452.0606

Days Inn ($$)
420 Cottonwood Dr
(55987) 507.454.6930
small pets allowed

Sterling Motel
1450 Gilmore Ave
(55987) 507.454.1120

Super 8 ($$)
1025 Sugar Loaf Rd
(55987) 507.454.6066
pets with deposit

● Worthington ●
Best Western ($$)
1923 Dover St
(56187) 507.376.4146

Budget Host ($)
207 Oxford St
(56187) 800.283.4678
w/permission

Days Inn
207 Oxford St
(56187) 507.376.6155
$6

Super 8 ($$)
I-90
(56187) 507.372.7755
pets with deposit

● Zumbrota ●
Super 8 ($$)
Hwy 52
(55992) 507.732.7852
pets w/permission

Mississippi

● Aberdeen ●
Best Western ($$)
801 E Commerce St
(39730) 601.369.4343
small pets only

● Batesville ●
Batesville Skyline Motel ($)
311B Hwy 51
(38606) 601.563.7671

Comfort Inn ($$)
I-55 And Hwy 6
(38606) 601.563.1188

● Biloxi ●
Juls Beach Hotel ($$)
2428 Beach Blvd
(39531) 601.385.5555

Motel 6 ($$)
2476 Beach Blvd
(39531) 601.388.5130
1 small pet/room

Seaview Resort ($)
1870 Beach Blvd
(39531) 601.388.5512

● Brookhaven ●
Claridge Inn ($$)
1210 Brockway Blvd
(39601) 601.833.1341

● Clarksdale ●
Days Inn ($$)
1910 N State St
(38614) 601.624.4391
$8

Hampton Inn ($$)
710 State St
(38614) 601.627.9292

● Cleveland ●
Comfort Inn ($$)
721 N Davis Hwy 61
(38732) 800.221.2222

● Durant ●
Super 8 ($$)
RR 2 Box# 228
(39063) 601.653.3881
dep

MISSISSIPPI, Forest

● Forest ●
Best Western ($$)
I-20 & Hwy 35
(39074) 601.469.2640

● Greenville ●
Days Inn ($)
2500 Hwy 82
(38702) 601.335.1999
$3/pet

● Greenwood ●
Comfort Inn ($$)
401 US 82
(38930) 601.453.5974

Days Inn ($$)
335 Hwy 82-49
(38930) 601.453.4364
$5

● Grenada ●
Best Western ($$)
1750 Sunset Dr
(38901) 601.226.7816
small pets only

Holiday Inn ($$)
1796 Sunset
(38901) 601.226.2851

● Gulfport ●
Best Western ($$)
US 49 li-10
(39503) 601.864.0050
small pets only

Holiday Inn
9435 Hwy 49
(39503) 601.864.7222

Holiday Inn ($$)
9415 US Hwy 49
(39503) 601.865.9164

Motel 6 ($$)
9355US Hwy 49
(39503) 601.863.1890
1 small pet/room

Shoneys Inn ($$$)
9375 Hwy 49
(39503) 301.868.8500
small pets only

● Hattiesburg ●
Comfort Inn ($$)
6595 Hwy 49
(39401) 601.268.2170

Days Inn
6518 Hwy 49
(39401) 601.544.6300
$6

Hampton Inn ($$)
4301 Hardy St
(39402) 601.264.8080

Holiday Inn
6563 Hw 49
(39401) 601.268.2850

Howard Johnson ($$)
6553 U S Hwy 49
(39401) 601.268.2251
small pets only

Motel 6 ($)
6508 U S Hwy 49
(39401) 301.544.6096
1 small pet/room

● Iuka ●
Key West Inn ($$)
189 Cr 180
(38852) 601.423.9221

● Jackson ●
Best Western ($$)
1520 Ellis Ave
(39204) 601.355.7483
housebroken pets only

Best Western ($$)
5035 I-55
(39206) 601.939.8200

Days Inn ($$)
1035 Hwy 49
(39218) 601.932.5553
$5

Days Inn ($)
716 Hwy 80
(39208) 800.329.7466
$8

Edison Hotel ($$)
225 E Capitol St
(39201) 601.948.6161

Harvey Hotel ($$)
200 E Amite St
(39201) 800.922.9222

Holiday Inn ($$)
2649 Hwy 80
(39204) 601.355.3020

La Quinta Inn ($$)
150 Angle Dr
(39204) 800.531.5900
call re: fees

La Quinta Inn ($$)
616 Briarwood Dr
(39211) 800.531.5900
call re: fees

Motel 6 ($$)
6145 I-55
(39213) 601.956.8848
1 small pet/room

Red Roof Inn ($)
700 Larson St
(39202) 601.969.5006
fees/limits may apply

Residence Inn ($$$)
881 E River Pl
(39202) 601.355.3599
call for fee & availability

Scottish Inn ($)
2263US Hwy 80
(39204) 601.969.1144

Super 8 ($$)
2655 I-55
(39204) 601.372.1006
w/permission

● Kosciusko ●
Best Western ($$)
1052 Hwy 35 Byp
(39090) 301.289.6252

● Laurel ●
Days Inn ($)
Hwy 11 N I-59
(39442) 601.428.8421
$4

● Long Beach ●
Red Creek Inn ($$)
7416 Red Creek Rd
(39560) 601.452.3080

● Magee ●
Passport Inn
Hwy 49
(39111) 601.849.3250
$5.35 fee

● Mc Comb ●
Holiday Inn ($$)
1900 Delaware Ave
(39648) 601.684.6211

● Meridian ●
Budgetel ($)
1400 Roebuck Dr
(39301) 601.693.2300

Days Inn
I-59
(39301) 601.483.3812

Econo Lodge ($)
2405 S Frontage Rd
(39301) 301.693.9393

Holiday Inn ($$)
1401 Roebuck Dr
(39301) 601.693.4521

Motel 6 ($)
2309 S Frontage Rd
(39301) 601.482.1182
1 small pet/room

Ramada Inn ($$)
2915 Saint Paul St
(39301) 601.485.2722
small pets only

Rodeway Inn ($)
146 US 11/80
(39301) 800.228.2000

Scottish Inn ($)
1903 S Frontage Rd
(39301) 601.482.2487

● Natchez ●
Days Inn ($)
109US Hwy 61
(39120) 601.445.8291
small pets only

Howard Johnson ($$)
45 Prentiss St
(39120) 601.442.1691

$=under $35 $$=$35-60 $$$=$60-100 $$$$=over $100

Natchez Hotel ($$)
110 N Pearl St
(39120) 800.888.9140

Scottish Inn ($)
40 Sgt Prentiss Dr
(39120) 601.442.9141
small pets only

The Guest House Historic
Hotel ($$$)
201 N Pearl St
(39120) 601.442.1054

● New Albany ●
Holiday Inn
300 Hwy 30
(38652) 601.534.8870

● Newton ●
Days Inn ($$)
I-20 & Hwy 15
(39345) 601.683.3361
$8 on magrs approval

● Ocean Springs ●
Days Inn
7301 Washington Ave
(39565) 800.329.7466
$10/day per pet

● Oxford ●
Holiday Inn ($$)
400 N Lamar Blvd
(38655) 601.234.2834

● Pascagoula ●
La Font Inn ($$)
2703 Denny Ave
(39567) 601.762.7111

● Philadelphia ●
Days Inn ($$)
1009 Holland Ave
(39350) 601.650.3590
$5

Holiday Inn
1530 Hwy 16
(39350) 601.656.3553

Ramada Inn ($$)
1011 Holland Ave
(39350) 601.656.1223

● Ridgeland ●
Red Roof Inn ($$)
810 Adcock St
(39157) 601.956.7707
fees/limits may apply

● Sardis ●
Best Western ($$)
Box# 279
(38666) 301.487.2424
small pets only

● Southaven ●
Best Western ($$)
8945 Hamilton Rd
(38671) 800.528.1234

● Starkville ●
Hampton Inn ($$)
700 Hwy 12
(39759) 800.426.7866

Holiday Inn
Hwy 12 & Montgomery
(39759) 601.323.6161

Holiday Inn ($$)
Hwy 12
(39760) 800.465.4329

● Tupelo ●
Hampton Inn ($$)
1516 McCullough Blvd
(38801) 601.840.8300

● Vicksburg ●
Hampton Inn ($$)
3330 Clay St
(39180) 301.636.6100

Holiday Inn
3330 Clay St
(39180) 601.636.4551

Park Inn Intl ($$)
4137 I-20
(39180) 601.638.5811

Ramada Inn ($$)
4216 Washington St
(39180) 601.638.5750

Super 8 ($$)
4127 I-20 Frontage Rd
(39180) 601.638.5077
w/permission

Missouri

● Albany ●
Eastwood Motel ($)
US 136E
(64402) 816.726.5208

● Arnold ●
Drury Inn ($$)
1201 Drury Ln
(63010) 800.325.8300

● Aurora ●
Aurora Inn Motel ($$)
RR 3 Box# 200
(65605) 417.678.5035

● Bethany ●
Best Western ($$)
RR 1 Box# 249B
(64424) 816.425.7915
managers discretion

● Billings ●
Ramada Ltd ($$)
2316 Shepherd Hills Expy
(65610) 417.337.2207

Rodeway Inn ($$)
2422 Shep Of Hill Expy
(65610) 417.336.5577

● Birch Tree ●
Hickory House Motel ($)
Box# 306
(65438) 314.292.3232

● Blue Springs ●
Motel 6 ($)
901 W Jefferson St
(64015) 816.228.9133
1 small pet/room

Ramada Ltd ($$)
1110 NW State Route 7
(64014) 816.229.6363

● Bolivar ●
Super 8
1919 Killingsworth
(65613) 417.777.8888
call re: fees

● Bourbon ●
Budget Inn ($)
I-44 and Hwy C
(65441) 314.732.4626

● Branson ●
Barrington Hotel
263 Shep Of Hills Expy
(65616) 417.334.8866

Best Western ($)
403 W Main St
(65616) 417.334.6464

Big Valley Motel ($$)
2005 W Hwy 76
(65616) 417.334.7676

Branson Lodge ($$)
2456 Hwy 165
(65616) 417.334.3105

Brighton Place Motel ($$)
3514 W Hwy 76
(65616) 417.334.5510

Country Music Inn ($$)
3060 Green Mountain Dr
(65616) 417.336.3300

Days Inn ($$)
3524 Keeter St
(65616) 417.334.5544
small pets

Fairfield Inn ($)
220 Hwy 165
(65616) 417.336.5665

Grand Ramada ($$)
245 N Wildwood Dr
(65616) 417.336.6646

Good Shepherd Inn ($)
1023 W Hwy 76
(65616) 417.334.1695

Howard Johnson ($$$)
3027A W Hwy 76
(65616) 417.336.5151

Lakeshore Resort ($$)
1773 Lake Shore Dr
(65616) 417.334.6262
$5 dogs under 25 lbs

Lighthouse Inn ($$)
2375 Green Mountain Dr
(65616) 417.336.6161

Residence Inn ($$)
280 S Wildwood Dr
(65616) 417.336.4077

Settle Inn ($)
3050 Green Mountain Dr
(65616) 417.335.4700

Taney Motel ($)
311 N Hwy 65
(65616) 417.334.3143

Welk Resort Ctr ($$$)
1984 Hwy 165
(65616) 417.336.3575

White Wing Resort ($)
Lake Rd 76-60
(65616) 417.338.2318

● Branson West ●
Colonial Mtn Inn ($$)
Box# 2068
(65737) 417.272.8414

● Bridgeton ●
Bridgeport Inn ($)
4199 N Lindbergh Blvd
(63044) 314.739.4600

Econo Lodge ($)
4575 N Lindbergh Blvd
(63044) 314.731.3000

Howard Johnson ($$)
4530 N Lindbergh Blvd
(63044) 314.731.3800

Knights Inn ($)
12433 St Charles Rock
(63044) 800.843.5644

Motel 6 ($)
3655 Pennridge Dr
(63044) 314.291.6100
1 small pet/room

Ramada Inn ($$$)
4690 N Lindbergh Blvd
(63044) 314.731.3040

Scottish Inn ($)
4645 N Lindbergh Blvd
(63044) 314.731.1010

● Brookfield ●
Country Inn ($)
800 S Main St
(64628) 816.258.7262

● Butler ●
Super 8 ($$)
RR 3 Box# 74
(64730) 816.679.6183
call re: fees

● Camdenton ●
Lan O Lak Motel ($$)
Box# 619
(65020) 314.346.2256

● Cameron ●
Best Western ($$)
US 36
(64429) 816.632.2187
small pets

Budget Host ($$)
501 Northland Dr
(64429) 816.632.6623

Country Squire Inn ($)
501 Northland Dr
(64429) 816.632.6623

● Cape Girardeau ●
Drury Inn ($$)
104 Vantage Dr
(63701) 314.334.7151
small pets only

Drury Inn ($$$)
3303 Campster
(63701) 314.339.9500

Hampton Inn ($$)
103 Cape West Pkwy
(63701) 314.651.3000

Holiday Inn
3257 Williams St
(63701) 573.334.4491

Holiday Inn ($$$)
3257 Williams
(63702) 800.465.4329

Pear Tree Inn ($)
3248 William St
(63703) 314.334.3000

Sands Motel ($)
1448 N Kingshighway St
(63701) 314.334.2828

Victorian Inn ($$)
3249 William St
(63703) 314.651.4486

● Carthage ●
Days Inn ($)
2244 Grand Ave
(64836) 417.358.2499
mgr preapproval reqd

Econo Lodge ($$)
1441 W Central Ave
(64836) 417.358.3900

● Cassville ●
Holiday Motel ($)
85 Main St
(65625) 417.847.3163

Super 8 ($$)
Hwy 37
(65625) 417.847.4888
$20 deposit

Townhouse Motel ($)
HC 81 Box# 9570
(65625) 417.847.4196

● Centertown ●
Red Roof Inn ($)
201 E Texas Ave
(65023) 314.442.0145

● Charleston ●
Charleston Inn ($$)
310 S Story St
(63834) 314.683.2125

● Chesterfield ●
Residence Inn ($$$)
15431 Conway Rd
(63017) 314.537.1444
call for fee & availability

● Chillicothe ●
Best Western ($$)
1020 S Washington St
(64601) 816.646.0572

Grand River Inn ($$)
606 W Business 36
(64601) 816.646.6590

Travel Inn ($)
901 Hwy 36W
(64601) 816.646.0784

● Clarksville ●
Clarksville Inn ($)
2nd & Lewis Sts
(63336) 314.242.3324

● Clinton ●
Best Western ($)
On Mo 13 Bypass
(64735) 800.528.1234

Holiday Inn
Hwy 7 @ Rives
(64735) 816.885.6901

Safari Motel ($)
1505 N 2nd St
(64735) 816.885.3395

● Columbia ●
Budget Host ($)
900 Vandiver Dr
(65202) 800.283.4678
fee reqd

Budgetel ($)
2500 I-70 Dr SW
(65203) 573.445.1899

Days Inn ($)
1900 I-70 Dr SW
(65203) 573.445.8511
$10 deposit

Drury Inn ($$)
1000 Knipp St
(65203) 800.325.8300

Econo Lodge ($$)
900 I-70 Dr SW
(65203) 573.442.1191

Holiday Inn
801 Keene
(65201) 573.449.4422

Holiday Inn ($$)
1612 N Providence Rd
(65202) 573.449.2491

Holiday Inn ($$$)
2200 I-70 Dr SW
(65203) 573.445.8531

Motel 6 ($)
1718 N Providence Rd
(65202) 573.442.9390
1 small pet/room

Motel 6 ($)
1800 I-70 Dr SW
(65203) 573.445.8433
1 small pet/room

Be Discreet

$=under $35 $$=$35-60 $$$=$60-100 $$$$=over $100

Ramada Inn ($$)
111 E Broadway
(65203) 573.443.2090

Ramada Inn ($$)
1100 Vandiver Dr
(65202) 573.449.0051

Scottish Inn ($)
2112 Business Loop 70
(65201) 573.449.3771

● Concordia ●
Best Western ($$)
406 W Williams St
(64020) 816.463.2114
small pets only

Concordia Inn ($)
200 West St
(64020) 816.463.7987

● Cuba ●
Best Western ($)
RR 2 Box# 284
(65453) 573.885.7707
small pets only

● Dexter ●
Dexter Inn ($)
1707 Business 60W
(63841) 314.624.7465

● Doniphan ●
Econo Lodge ($)
109 Smith Dr
(63935) 800.424.4777

Tin Lizzie Motel
Hwy 160
(63935) 314.996.2101

● Eagle Rock ●
Eagle Rock Resort
HC 1 Box# 1593
(65641) 417.271.3222

Fletchers Devils
HC 1 Box# 8
(65641) 417.271.3396

Lazy Eagle Resort
Box# 141
(65641) 417.271.3390

Policies
Subject
to Change

● El Dorado Springs ●
El Dorado Motel
102 Hwy 54 East
(64744) 417.876.6888

● Ellington ●
Scenic Rivers Motel ($)
231 N 2nd St
(63638) 314.663.7722

● Eureka ●
Days Inn ($$)
15 Hilltop Vlg Ctr Dr
(63025) 314.938.5565
$5 fee

Oak Grove Inn ($)
1733 W 5th St
(63025) 314.938.4368
$10 deposit

Ramada Inn ($$)
4901 Allenton Rd
(63025) 314.938.6661

Red Carpet Inn
1725 - 5th St
(63025) 314.938.5348

● Farmington ●
Best Western ($$)
1627 W Columbia St
(63640) 573.756.8031
small pets only

● Fenton ●
Drury Inn ($$)
1088 S Hwy Dr
(63026) 800.325.8300

Motel 6 ($$)
1860 Bowles Ave
(63026) 314.349.1800
1 small pet/room

Pear Tree Inn ($$)
1100 S Hwy Dr
(63026) 314.343.8820

● Festus ●
Budgetel ($$)
1303 Veterans Blvd
(63028) 314.937.2888

Drury Inn ($$)
1001 Veterans Blvd
(63028) 800.325.8300

● Florissant ●
Red Roof Inn ($$)
307 Dunn Rd
(63031) 800.843.7663

● Foristell ●
Best Western ($)
Rt W Box# 10
(63348) 314.673.2900
$5 pet fee

● Fredericktown ●
Econo Lodge ($$)
740 Madison Plaza Dr
(63645) 573.783.2500

Longhorn Motel ($)
Box# 721
(63645) 314.783.3363

● Fulton ●
Budget Host ($)
422B Gaylord Dr
(65251) 800.283.4678

● Gravois Mills ●
Millstone Lodge ($$)
RR 1 Box# 515
(65037) 314.372.5111

● Hannibal ●
Days Inn ($)
4070 Market St
(63401) 314.248.1700

Howard Johnson ($)
3603 McMasters Ave
(63401) 314.221.7950

● Harrisonville ●
Best Western ($$)
US 71 & 291
(64701) 816.884.3200

Caravan Motel ($)
1705 Hwy 291
(64701) 816.884.4100

Slumber Inn Motel ($)
RR 3 Box# 611D
(64701) 816.884.3100

● Hayti ●
Drury Inn ($$)
I-55 & Rt 84
(63851) 800.325.8300

● Hazelwood ●
Budgetel ($$)
318 Taylor Rd # D
(63042) 314.731.4200

Ls Quinta Airport ($$)
5781 Campus Pkwy
(63042) 800.531.5900

● Higginsville ●
Best Western ($)
RR 2 Box# 231
(64037) 816.584.3646
small pets

Super 8 ($$)
I-70
(64037) 816.584.7781
pets with deposit

● Hollister ●
Econo Lodge ($)
US 65
(65672) 417.334.2770

Rock View Motel ($$)
1049 Parkview Dr
(65672) 417.334.4678

● Holts Summit ●
Ramada Inn ($$)
Hwy 54
(65043) 573.896.8787

● Independence ●
Howard Johnson ($$)
4200 S Noland Rd
(64055) 816.373.8856

Red Roof Inn ($$)
13712 E 42nd Ter
(64055) 800.843.7663

Super 8 ($$)
4032 S Lynn Court Dr
(64055) 816.833.1888
small pets with deposit

● Isabella ●
Lakepoint Resort ($$)
HC 1 Box# 1152
(65676) 417.273.4343

● Jackson ●
Days Inn
517 Jackson Blvd
(63755) 314.243.3577
$5

MISSOURI, Jefferson City

● Jefferson City ●
Capitol Plaza Hotel ($$$)
415 W McCarty St
(65101) 314.635.1234

Hotel Deville ($$)
319 W Miller St
(65101) 314.636.5231

Howard Johnson ($$)
422 Monroe St
(65101) 314.636.5101

Motel 6 ($)
1624 Jefferson St
(65109) 314.634.4220
1 small pet/room

● Joplin ●
Best Inns ($$)
3508 S Range Line Rd
(64804) 417.781.6776

Best Western ($$)
1611 N Range Line Rd
(64801) 417.624.8300

Capri Motel
3401 S Main St
(64804) 417.623.0391

Drury Inn ($$$)
3601 S Range Line Rd
(64804) 417.781.8000

Holiday Inn
3615 Range Line Rd
(64804) 417.782.1000

Howard Johnson ($$)
3510 S Range Line Rd
(64804) 417.623.0000
small pets only

Motel 6 ($)
3031 S Range Line Rd
(64804) 417.781.6400
1 small pet/room

Ramada Inn ($$)
3320 S Range Line Rd
(64804) 417.781.0500

Sleep Inn ($$)
I-44 & Hwy 43
(64804) 417.782.1212
mgr preapproval reqd

Super 8 ($$)
2830 E 36th St
(64804) 417.782.8765
w/permission

Tropicana Motel ($)
2417 S Range Line Rd
(64804) 417.624.8200

Westwood Motel ($)
170 W 30th St
(64804) 417.782.7212

● Kansas City ●
American Inn Motel ($)
1211 Armour Rd
(64116) 816.471.3451

Americana Hotel ($$)
1301 Wyandotte St
(64105) 816.221.8800

Budgetel ($$)
8601 Hillcrest Rd
(64138) 816.822.7000

Budgetel ($)
2214 Taney St
(64116) 816.221.1200

Days Inn
I-29
(64153) 800.329.7466
$5

Days Inn ($$)
11801 Blue Ridge Blvd
(64134) 816.765.1888
mgr preapproval reqd

Drury Inn ($$)
3830 Blue Ridge Cutoff
(64133) 800.325.8300

Embassy Suites ($$$)
7640 New Tiffany Sprgs
(64153) 816.891.7788

Historic Suites ($$$)
612 Central St
(64105) 816.842.6544

Holiday Inn
5701 Longview Rd
(64137) 816.765.4100

Inn Town Lodge ($$)
2620 NE 43rd St
(64117) 816.453.6550

Marriott Hotel ($$$)
200 W 12th St
(64105) 816.421.6800

Marriott Hotel ($$)
775 Brasilia Ave
(64153) 816.464.2200

Motel 6 ($)
6400 E 87th St
(64138) 816.333.4468
1 small pet/room

Motel 6 ($)
8230 NW Prairie View Rd
(64151) 816.741.6400
1 small pet/room

Radisson Inn ($$$)
106 W 12th St
(64105) 800.333.3333

Ramada Inn ($$)
7301 New Tiffany Spgs Rd
(64153) 800.234.9501

Ramada Inn ($$)
1600 NE Parvin Rd
(64116) 816.453.5210

Red Roof Inn ($)
3636 Randolph Rd
(64161) 816.452.8585

Residence Inn ($$$$)
2675 Main St
(64108) 816.561.3000
$50 + $5 per day

Residence Inn ($$)
9900 NW Prairie View Rd
(64153) 816.891.9009
call for fee & availability

Super 8 ($$)
6900 NW 83rd Ter
(64152) 816.587.0808
call re: fees

Travelodge ($$)
1051 N Cambridge St
(64120) 816.483.7900

Westin Hotel ($$$$)
1 E Pershing Rd
(64108) 816.474.4400
small pets accepted

Kansas City Metro

● Lansing ●
Econo Lodge ($)
504 N Main St
(66043) 913.727.2777

● Lawrence ●
Days Inn ($$)
2309 Iowa St
(66046) 913.843.9100
mgr preapproval reqd

Ramada Inn ($$)
2222 W 6th St
(66049) 913.842.7030

Super 8 ($$)
515 McDonald Dr
(66049) 913.842.5721
call re: fees

Westminster Inn ($)
2525 W 6th St
(66049) 913.841.8410

● Leavenworth ●
Commanders Inn ($)
6th And Metropolitan
(66048) 913.651.5800

● Ottawa ●
Days Inn ($$)
1641 S Main St
(66067) 913.242.4842

Econo Lodge ($)
2331 S Cedar St
(66067) 800.424.4777

Royal Manor Motel ($)
1641 S Main St
(66067) 913.242.4842

Village Inn Motel ($)
2520 S Main St
(66067) 913.242.5512

● Shawnee Mission ●
Doubletree ($$$)
10100 College Blvd
(66210) 913.451.6100

Drury Inn ($$)
9009 Shawnee Mission Pkwy
(66202) 800.325.8300

Well Behaved

Drury Inn ($$)
10951 Metcalf Ave
(66210) 800.325.8300

Embassy Suites ($$$$)
10601 Metcalf Ave
(66212) 913.649.7060

Holiday Inn
7240 Shawnee Mission
(66202) 913.262.3010

Howard Johnson ($$)
12381 W 95th St
(66215) 800.654.2000

La Quinta Inn ($$)
9461 Lenexa Dr
(66215) 800.221.4731
call re: fees

Marriott Hotel ($$$)
10800 Metcalf Ave
(66210) 913.451.8000

Red Roof Inn ($)
6800 W 108th St
(66211) 800.843.7663

Residence Inn ($$$)
6300 W 110th St
(66211) 800.331.3131

Kansas City MO Metro

● Blue Springs ●
Motel 6 ($)
901 W Jefferson St
(64015) 816.228.9133
1 small pet/room

Ramada Ltd ($$)
1110 NW State Route 7
(64014) 816.229.6363

● Independence ●
Howard Johnson ($$)
4200 S Noland Rd
(64055) 816.373.8856

Red Roof Inn ($$)
13712 E 42Nd Ter S
(64055) 800.843.7663

Super 8 ($$)
4032 S Lynn Court Dr
(64055) 816.833.1888
small pets with deposit

● Kansas City ●
American Inn Motel ($)
1211 Armour Rd
(64116) 816.471.3451

Americana Hotel ($$)
1301 Wyandotte St
(64105) 816.221.8800

Budgetel ($$)
8601 Hillcrest Rd
(64138) 816.822.7000

Budgetel ($)
2214 Taney St
(64116) 816.221.1200

Days Inn
I-29
(64153) 800.329.7466
$5

Days Inn ($$)
11801 Blue Ridge Blvd
(64134) 816.765.1888
mgr preapproval reqd

Drury Inn ($$)
3830 Blue Ridge Cutoff
(64133) 800.325.8300

Embassy Suites ($$$)
7640 New Tiffany Sprgs
(64153) 816.891.7788

Historic Suites ($$$)
612 Central St
(64105) 816.842.6544

Holiday Inn
5701 Longview Rd
(64137) 816.765.4100

Inn Town Lodge ($$)
2620 NE 43Rd St
(64117) 816.453.6550

Marriott Hotel ($$$)
200 W 12th St
(64105) 816.421.6800

Marriott Hotel ($$)
775 Brasilia Ave
(64153) 816.464.2200

Motel 6 ($)
6400 E 87th St
(64138) 816.333.4468
1 small pet/room

Motel 6 ($)
8230 NW Prairie View Rd
(64151) 816.741.6400
1 small pet/room

Radisson Inn ($$$)
106 W 12th St
(64105) 800.333.3333

Ramada Inn ($)
7301 New Tiffany Spgs Rd
(64153) 800.234.9501

Ramada Inn ($$)
1600 NE Parvin Rd
(64116) 816.453.5210

Red Roof Inn ($)
3636 Randolph Rd
(64161) 816.452.8585

Residence Inn ($$$$)
2675 Main St
(64108) 816.561.3000
$50 + $5 per day

Residence Inn ($$)
9900 NW Prairie View Rd
(64153) 816.891.9009
call for fee & availability

Super 8 ($$)
6900 NW 83Rd Ter
(64152) 816.587.0808
call re: fees

Travelodge ($$)
1051 N Cambridge St
(64120) 816.483.7900

Westin Hotel ($$$$)
1 E Pershing Rd
(64108) 816.474.4400
small pets accepted

● Lees Summit ●
Best Western ($$)
625 N Murray Rd
(64081) 816.525.1400

Comfort Inn ($$)
607 SE Oldham Pkwy
(64081) 816.524.8181

● Liberty ●
Super 8 ($$)
115 N Stewart Rd
(64068) 816.781.9400
25 lbs. or less

● Oak Grove ●
Days Inn ($$)
101 N Locust St
(64075) 816.625.8686
size limits & fees.

Econo Lodge ($)
410 SE 1st St
(64075) 816.625.3681

● Platte City ●
Best Western ($$)
I-29
(64079) 816.858.4588
under 15 lbs

Comfort Inn ($$)
1200 Hwy 92
(64079) 816.858.5430

End of Kansas City Metro

● Kearney ●
Econo Lodge ($)
505 Shanks Ave
(64060) 816.635.6000

● Kennett ●
Oxford Inn ($$)
110 Independence Ave
(63857) 314.888.9860

● Kimberling City ●
Best Western ($$)
Box# 429
(65686) 417.739.2461
not unattended

Best Western ($$)
Box# 429
(65686) 417.739.2461
not unattended

Kimberling Height ($$)
HC 4 Box# 980
(65686) 417.779.4158

● Kirksville ●
Best Western ($$)
Hwy 6 & 36
(63501) 816.665.8352
$15/day

Budget Host ($$)
1304 S Baltimore
(63501) 816.665.3722
$5

MISSOURI, Kirksville

Budget Host ($)
1304 S Baltimore St
(63501) 800.283.4678
$5/day each

Comfort Inn ($$)
2209 N Baltimore St
(63501) 816.665.2205

Days Inn
Hwy 63
(63501) 816.665.8244

● Knob Noster ●
Whiteman Inn ($)
2340 W Irish Ln
(65336) 816.563.3000

● Lake Ozark ●
Holiday Inn
Hwy 54 Business
(65049) 573.365.2334

● Lake Saint Louis ●
Days Inn ($$)
2560 S Outer Rd
(63367) 314.625.1711
$5/pets

● Lamar ●
Best Western ($)
65 SW 1st Ln
(64759) 417.682.3333

● Lebanon ●
Best Western ($$)
Loop 44
(65536) 417.532.6171
small pets not in rooms alone

Brentwood Motel ($)
1320 S Jefferson Ave
(65536) 417.532.6131

Econo Lodge ($)
Box# 972
(65536) 800.424.4777

Shepherd Hill Motel ($)
Box# 1100
(65536) 417.532.3133

● Lees Summit ●
Best Western ($$)
625 N Murray Rd
(64081) 816.525.1400

Comfort Inn ($$)
607 SE Oldham Pkwy
(64081) 816.524.8181

Fairfield Inn ($$)
1301 NE Windsor Dr
(64086) 816.524.7572

● Lexington ●
Lexington Inn ($)
Jct US 24 & Hwy 13
(64067) 816.259.4641

● Liberty ●
Super 8 ($$)
115 N Stewart Rd
(64068) 816.781.9400
25 lbs. or less

● Louisiana ●
Rivers Edge Motel ($)
201 Mansion St
(63353) 314.754.4522

● Macon ●
Best Western ($$)
28933 Sunset Dr
(63552) 816.385.2125
managers discretion

Super 8 ($$)
1420 N Rutherford St # 2A
(63552) 816.385.5788
call re: fees

● Maryland Heights ●
Best Western ($$$)
2434 Old Dorsett Rd
(63043) 314.291.8700

Budgetel ($$)
12330 Dorsett Rd
(63043) 314.878.1212

Drury Inn ($$)
12220 Dorsett Rd
(63043) 800.325.8300

● Maryville ●
Super 8 ($$)
Bus Hwy 71
(64468) 816.582.8088
pets with deposit

● Mexico ●
Best Western ($$)
1010 E Liberty St
(65265) 800.528.1234

● Moberly ●
Knoll Motel ($)
Box# 146
(65270) 816.263.5000

Ramada Inn ($$)
Jct US 24 & 63
(65270) 816.263.6540

● Monett ●
Hartland Lodge ($$$)
929 Hwy 60
(65708) 417.235.4000

Oxford Inn ($$)
868 Hwy 60
(65708) 417.235.8039

● Monroe City ●
Econo Lodge ($)
3 Gateway Sq
(63456) 573.735.4200

● Mound City ●
Audreys Motel ($)
RR 2 Box# 231
(64470) 816.442.3191

● Mount Vernon ●
Best Western ($$)
740 E Mount Vernon Blvd
(65712) 417.466.2111
small pets allowed

Budget Host ($)
RR 1 Box# 68
(65712) 800.283.4678
limited availability

● Mountain Grove ●
Best Western ($$)
111 E 17th St
(65711) 417.926.3152

Days Inn ($$)
300 E 19th St
(65711) 417.926.5555
$6 fee

● Neosho ●
Hartland Lodge ($$$)
1400 71S
(64850) 417.451.3784

Neosho Inn ($$)
2500 S 71 Hwy
(64850) 417.451.6500

● Nevada ●
Best Western ($$)
1401 E Austin Blvd
(64772) 417.667.3351
small pets only

Comfort Inn ($$)
2345 Martvel Dr
(64772) 417.667.6777

Ramseys Nevada Motel ($)
1514 E Austin Blvd
(64772) 417.667.5273

Super 8 ($$)
2301 E Austin
(64772) 417.667.8888
call re: fees

● Nixa ●
Super 8 ($$)
418 Massey Blvd
(65714) 417.725.0800
mgr preapproval reqd

● Oak Grove ●
Days Inn ($$)
101 N Locust St
(64075) 816.625.8686
size limits & fees

Econo Lodge ($)
410 SE 1st St
(64075) 816.625.3681

● Osage Beach ●
Scottish Inn
Rt 2
(65065) 573.348.3123

● Ozark ●
Days Inn ($$)
900 N 18th St
(65721) 417.581.5800
mgr preapproval reqd

Holiday Inn ($$)
1900 Evangel St
(65721) 417.485.6688
mgr preapproval reqd

Super 8 ($$)
299 N 20th
(65721) 417.581.8800
in smoking rooms no snakes
allowed

CALL
AHEAD!

$=under $35 $$=$35-60 $$$=$60-100 $$$$=over $100

• Palmyra •
Hillcrest Inn ($)
423 E Lafayette St
(63461) 314.769.2007

• Park Hills •
Roseners Inn ($)
Hwy 67
(63601) 314.431.4241

• Perryville •
Budget Host ($)
221 S Kingshighway St
(63775) 800.283.4678

• Platte City •
Best Western ($$)
I-29
(64079) 816.858.4588
under 15 lbs

Comfort Inn ($$)
1200 Hwy 92
(64079) 816.858.5430

• Poplar Bluff •
Drury Inn ($$)
2220 N Westwood Blvd
(63901) 800.325.8300

Holiday Inn ($$)
2115 N Westwood Blvd
(63901) 573.785.7711
small pets only

Pear Tree Inn ($$)
2218 N Westwood Blvd
(63901) 314.785.7100

• Portageville •
Teroy Motel ($)
903 Hwy 61
(63873) 314.379.5461

• Reeds Spring •
Kings Kove Resort ($$)
Rt 5 Box# 498A
(65737) 417.739.4513

Rustic Gate Inn ($)
US 76 & Hwy 13
(65737) 417.272.3326

• Rich Hill •
Apache Motel ($)
RR 3 Box# 309A
(64779) 417.395.2161

• Rock Port •
Rock Port Inn ($)
RR 4 Box# 218
(64482) 816.744.6282

• Rockaway Beach •
Eden Roc Resort ($)
607 Beach Blvd
(65740) 417.561.4163

Kennys Court ($)
Box# 87
(65740) 417.561.4131

• Rolla •
Best Western ($$)
1403 Martin Springs Dr
(65401) 573.341.2511

Bestway Inn ($)
1631 Martin Springs Dr
(65401) 314.341.2158

Days Inn ($$)
1207 Kingshighway St
(65401) 573.341.3700
$3/pets

Drury Inn ($$)
2006 N Bishop Ave
(65401) 800.325.8300

Econo Lodge ($)
1417 Martin Springs Dr
(65401) 573.341.3130

Holiday Inn
1507 Martin Springs Dr
(65401) 573.364.8200

Howard Johnson ($$)
127 H R Dr
(65401) 314.364.7111

Travelodge ($$)
1605 Martin Springs Dr
(65401) 314.341.3050

• Saint Ann •
Hampton Inn ($$$)
10800 Pear Tree Ln
(63074) 314.427.3400

• Saint Charles •
Budgetel ($)
1425 S 5th St
(63301) 314.946.6936

Comfort Inn ($$)
2750 Plaza Way
(63303) 314.949.8700

Comfort Inn
2750 Plaza Way
(63303) 314.949.8700
referred

Knights Inn ($)
3800 Harry S Truman Blvd
(63301) 800.843.5644

Monarch Budget Motel ($)
3717 I-70
(63303) 314.724.3717

Red Roof Inn ($)
2010 Zumbehl Rd
(63303) 314.947.7770

• Saint Clair •
Budget Lodging ($)
866 N Service Rd
(63077) 314.629.1000

• Saint Joseph •
Best Western ($$)
4502 S I-69
(64507) 816.232.2345

Days Inn ($)
4312 Frederick Ave
(64506) 816.279.1671
mgr preapproval reqd

Drury Inn ($$)
4213 Frederick Ave
(64506) 800.325.8300

Holiday Inn ($$)
102 S 3rd St
(64501) 816.279.8000

Motel 6 ($)
4021 Frederick Ave
(64506) 816.232.2311
1 small pet/room

Ramada Inn ($$)
4016 Frederick Ave
(64506) 816.233.6192

• Saint Louis •
Best Western ($$)
1200 S Kirkwood Rd
(63122) 800.528.1234

Best Western ($$$)
6224 Helmos Ind Pk
(63129) 314.961.1361

Comfort Inn ($$)
3730 S Lindbergh Blvd
(63127) 314.842.1200

Comfort Inn ($$)
12031 Lackland Rd
(63146) 314.878.1400

Days Inn ($$)
4545 Woodson Rd
(63134) 314.423.6770
$5 fee

Drury Inn ($$$)
711 N Broadway
(63102) 800.325.8300

Drury Inn ($$$)
201 S 20th St
(63103) 800.325.8300

Drury Inn ($$$)
10490 Natural Bridge Rd
(63134) 800.325.8300

Embassy Suites ($$$$)
901 N 1st St
(63102) 314.241.4200

Hampton Inn ($$$)
2211 Market St
(63103) 314.241.3200
smalll

Holiday Inn ($$)
5915 Wilson Ave
(63110) 314.645.0700

Holiday Inn ($$)
200 N 4th St
(63102) 314.621.8200

Holiday Inn ($$$)
4234 Butler Hill Rd
(63129) 314.894.0700

Marriott Hotel ($$$$)
I-70 At Lambert
(63134) 314.423.9700

Marriott Hotel ($$$$)
1 Broadway
(63102) 314.421.1776

Motel 6 ($$)
4576 Woodson Rd
(63134) 314.427.1313
1 small pet/room

Motel 6 ($)
1405 Dunn Rd
(63138) 314.869.9400
1 small pet/room

Motel 6 ($)
6500 S Lindbergh Blvd
(63123) 314.892.3664
1 small pet/room

Oak Grove Inn ($$)
6602 S Lindbergh Blvd
(63123) 314.894.9449

Quality Hotel ($$)
9600 Natural Bridge Rd
(63134) 314.427.7600

Red Roof Inn ($$)
11837 Lackland Rd
(63146) 314.991.4900

Red Roof Inn ($$)
5823 Wilson Ave
(63110) 314.645.0101

Residence Inn ($$)
1100 McMorrow Ave
(63117) 314.862.1900
$25&$10/day to 15 days

Residence Inn ($$$)
1881 Craigshire Rd
(63146) 314.469.0060
call for fee & availability

Seven Gables Inn ($$$)
26 N Meramec Ave
(63105) 314.863.8400
$25 fee must be well trained

Sheraton Inn ($$$)
191 Westport Plz
(63146) 314.878.1500

Summerfield Suites ($$$$)
1855 Craigshire Rd
(63146) 314.878.1555
$75 fee & $6 per day

Super 8 ($$)
2790 Target Dr
(63136) 314.355.7808
deposit

The Daniele ($$$)
216 N Meramec Ave
(63105) 314.721.0101

St Louis (IL) Metro

● Alton ●
Days Inn
1900 Hm Adams Pkwy
(62002) 618.463.0800
$10

Holiday Inn ($$$)
3800 Homer Adams Pkwy
(62002) 618.462.1220

Super 8
1800 Homer Adams Pkwy
(62002) 618.465.8888
call re: fees

● Collinsville ●
Best Western ($)
Rt 159
(62234) 618.345.5720
small pets

Days Inn ($$)
1803 Ramada Blvd
(62234) 618.345.8100

Howard Johnson ($)
301 N Bluff Rd
(62234) 618.345.1530

Innkeeper Motel
I-55-Rt 140
(62234) 618.633.2111

Motel 6 ($)
295A N Bluff Rd
(62234) 618.345.2100
1 small pet/room

Pear Tree Inn ($$)
552 Ramada Blvd
(62234) 618.345.9500

Super 8 ($$)
2 Gateway Dr
(62234) 618.345.8008
attended & in carrier

● Fairview Heights ●
Best Western ($$)
311 Salem Pl
(62208) 618.624.3636
under 20 lbs

Drury Inn ($$)
12 Ludwig Dr
(62208) 618.398.8530

Fairfield Inn ($$)
140 Ludwig Dr
(62208) 618.398.7124

Hampton Inn ($$)
150 Ludwig Dr
(62208) 618.397.9705

Ramada Inn ($$)
6900 N Illinois St
(62208) 618.632.4747

Super 8 ($$)
45 Ludwig Dr
(62208) 618.398.8338
sign waiver

Trailway Motel
10039 Lincoln Trl
(62208) 618.397.5757

● Granite City ●
Best Western ($$)
1240 Old Chain Rock
(62040) 618.931.2262
small pets only w/$10 deposit

Chain Of Rocks Motel
3228 W Chain Of Rocks Rd
(62040) 618.931.6660

Granite City Lodge
1200 19th St
(62040) 618.876.2600

Illni Motel
1100 Miedringhuas Ave
(62040) 618.877.7100

● Greenville ●
2 Acres Motel
I-70 & Rt 127
(62246) 618.664.3131

Budget Host ($)
I-70 & Rt 127
(62246) 618.664.1950
extra chg

Prairie House Inn
RR 4 Box# 47Aa
(62246) 618.664.3003

Uptown Motel
323 S 3Rd St
(62246) 618.664.3121

● Litchfield ●
Best Western ($$)
413 Columbian Blvd
(62056) 217.324.2181
small pets only

Super 8 ($$)
I-55
(62056) 217.324.7788
pets with permission

● O Fallon ●
Comfort Inn ($$)
1100 Eastgate Dr
(62269) 618.624.6060
mgr preapproval reqd

Ramada Inn ($$)
1313 Central Park Dr
(62269) 800.272.6232

St. Louis (MO) Metro

● Bridgeton ●
Bridgeport Inn ($)
4199 N Lindbergh Blvd
(63044) 314.739.4600

Econo Lodge ($)
4575 N Lindbergh Blvd
(63044) 314.731.3000

Howard Johnson ($$)
4530 N Lindbergh Blvd
(63044) 314.731.3800

Knights Inn ($)
12433 St Charles Rock
(63044) 800.843.5644

Motel 6 ($)
3655 Pennridge Dr
(63044) 314.291.6100
1 small pet/room

Ramada Inn ($$$)
4690 N Lindbergh Blvd
(63044) 314.731.3040

Scottish Inn ($)
4645 N Lindbergh Blvd
(63044) 314.731.1010

● Chesterfield ●
Residence Inn ($$$)
15431 Conway Rd
(63017) 314.537.1444
call for fee & availability

● Eureka ●
Days Inn ($$)
15 Hilltop Vlg Ctr Dr
(63025) 314.938.5565
$5 fee

Oak Grove Inn ($)
1733 W 5th St
(63025) 314.938.4368
$10 deposit

Ramada Inn ($$)
4901 Allenton Rd
(63025) 314.938.6661

Red Carpet Inn
1725 - 5th St
(63025) 314.938.5348

● Fenton ●
Drury Inn ($$)
1088 Hwy Dr
(63026) 800.325.8300

Motel 6 ($$)
1860 Bowles Ave
(63026) 314.349.1800
1 small pet/room

Pear Tree Inn ($$)
1100 Hwy Dr
(63026) 314.343.8820

● Florissant ●
Red Roof Inn ($$)
307 Dunn Rd
(63031) 800.843.7663

● Foristell ●
Best Western ($)
Rt W Box# 10
(63348) 314.673.2900
$5 pet fee

● Hazelwood ●
Budgetel ($$)
318 Taylor Rd # D
(63042) 314.731.4200

Ls Quinta Airport ($$)
5781 Campus Pkwy
(63042) 800.531.5900

● Lake Saint Louis ●
Days Inn ($$)
2560 S Outer Rd
(63367) 314.625.1711
$5/pets

● Maryland Heights ●
Best Western ($$$)
2434 Old Dorsett Rd
(63043) 314.291.8700

Budgetel ($$)
12330 Dorsett Rd
(63043) 314.878.1212

Drury Inn ($$)
12220 Dorsett Rd
(63043) 800.325.8300

● Saint Ann ●
Hampton Inn ($$$)
10800 Pear Tree Ln
(63074) 314.427.3400

● Saint Charles ●
Budgetel ($)
1425 S 5th St
(63301) 314.946.6936

Comfort Inn ($$)
2750 Plaza Way
(63303) 314.949.8700

Comfort Inn
2750 Plaza Way
(63303) 314.949.8700
referred

Knights Inn ($)
3800 Harry S Truman Blvd
(63301) 800.843.5644

Monarch Budget Motel ($)
3717 I-70
(63303) 314.724.3717

Red Roof Inn ($)
2010 Zumbehl Rd
(63303) 314.947.7770

● Saint Louis ●
Best Western ($$)
1200 S Kirkwood Rd
(63122) 800.528.1234

Best Western ($$$)
6224 Helmos Ind Pk
(63129) 314.961.1361

Comfort Inn ($$)
3730 S Lindbergh Blvd
(63127) 314.842.1200

Comfort Inn ($$)
12031 Lackland Rd
(63146) 314.878.1400

Days Inn ($$)
4545 Woodson Rd
(63134) 314.423.6770
$5 fee

Drury Inn ($$$)
711 N Broadway
(63102) 800.325.8300

Drury Inn ($$$)
201 S 20th St
(63103) 800.325.8300

Drury Inn ($$$)
10490 Natural Bridge Rd
(63134) 800.325.8300

Embassy Suites ($$$$)
901 N 1st St
(63102) 314.241.4200

Hampton Inn ($$$)
2211 Market St
(63103) 314.241.3200
smalll

Holiday Inn ($$)
5915 Wilson Ave
(63110) 314.645.0700

Holiday Inn ($$)
200 N 4th St
(63102) 314.621.8200

Holiday Inn ($$$)
4234 Butler Hill Rd
(63129) 314.894.0700

Marriott Hotel ($$$$)
I-70 At Lambert
(63134) 314.423.9700

Marriott Hotel ($$$$)
1 Broadway
(63102) 314.421.1776

Motel 6 ($$)
4576 Woodson Rd
(63134) 314.427.1313
1 small pet/room

Motel 6 ($)
1405 Dunn Rd
(63138) 314.869.9400
1 small pet/room

Motel 6 ($)
6500 S Lindbergh Blvd
(63123) 314.892.3664
1 small pet/room

Oak Grove Inn ($$)
6602 S Lindbergh Blvd
(63123) 314.894.9449

Quality Hotel ($$)
9600 Natural Bridge Rd
(63134) 314.427.7600

Red Roof Inn ($$)
11837 Lackland Rd
(63146) 314.991.4900

Red Roof Inn ($$)
5823 Wilson Ave
(63110) 314.645.0101

Residence Inn ($$)
1100 McMorrow Ave
(63117) 314.862.1900
$25&$10/day to 15 days

Residence Inn ($$$)
1881 Craigshire Rd
(63146) 314.469.0060
call for fee & availability

Seven Gables Inn ($$$)
26 N Meramec Ave
(63105) 314.863.8400
$25 fee must be well trained

Sheraton Inn ($$$)
191 Westport Plz
(63146) 314.878.1500

Summerfield Suites ($$$$)
1855 Craigshire Rd
(63146) 314.878.1555
$75 fee & $6 per day

Super 8 ($$)
2790 Target Dr
(63136) 314.355.7808
deposit

The Daniele ($$$)
216 N Meramec Ave
(63105) 314.721.0101

● Sullivan ●
Best Western ($$)
307 N Service Rd
(63080) 573.468.3136

Family Motor Inn ($)
209 N Service Rd
(63080) 314.468.4119

Super 8 ($$)
601 N Service Rd
(63080) 314.468.8076
pets allowed with deposit

● Villa Ridge ●
Best Western ($$)
581 Hwy 100
(63089) 314.742.3501

● Wentzville ●
Heritage Motel ($)
404 N Hwy 61
(63385) 314.327.6263
$10 fee prefer dogs

Holiday Inn
900 Corporate Pkwy
(63385) 314.327.7001

Howard Johnson ($$)
1500 Contintal Dr
(63385) 314.327.5212

Super 8
4 Pantera
(63385) 314.327.5300
small pets only

End of St Louis Metro

● Sainte Genevieve ●
Family Budget Inns ($)
17030 New Bremen Rd
(63670) 314.543.2272

● Salem ●
Scotish Inns ($)
1005 S Main St
(65560) 314.729.4191

● Sedalia ●
Best Western ($$)
3210 S 65 Hwy
(65301) 816.826.6100

● Shell Knob ●
Bass Haven Resort
HC 1 Box# 4480
(65747) 417.858.6401

● Sikeston ●
Best Western ($$)
220 S Interstate Dr
(63801) 573.471.9700

Drury Inn ($$)
2602 Rear East Malone
(63801) 800.325.8300

Hampton Inn ($$)
1330 S Main St
(63801) 573.471.3930

Holiday Inn ($$)
2602 Rear E Malone
(63801) 573.471.4100
mgr preapproval reqd

● Springfield ●
Bass Country Inn ($$)
2610 N Glenstone Ave
(65803) 417.866.6671

Best Western ($$)
203 S Glenstone Ave
(65802) 417.866.1963

Best Western ($$)
2535 N Glenstone Ave
(65803) 417.862.0701

Best Western ($$)
2745 N Glenstone Ave
(65803) 417.869.0001

Comfort Inn ($$)
2550 N Glenstone Ave
(65803) 800.221.2222

Courtyard By Marriott ($$$)
3370 E Battlefield St
(65804) 800.443.6000

Days Inn ($$)
2700 N Glenstone Ave
(65803) 417.865.5511

Days Inn ($$)
621 W Sunshine St
(65807) 417.862.0153
$10/day

Holiday Inn ($$)
333 Hammons Pkwy
(65803) 417.869.8246
small pets only

Markham Inn ($$)
2820 N Glenstone Ave
(65803) 417.866.3581

Motel 6 ($)
3114 N Kentwood Ave
(65803) 417.833.0880
1 small pet/room

Motel 6 ($)
2455 N Glenstone Ave
(65803) 417.869.4343
1 small pet/room

Mount Vernon Motel
2006 S Glenstone Ave
(65804) 417.881.2833

Red Roof Inn ($)
2655 N Glenstone Ave
(65803) 417.831.2100

Residence Inn ($$$)
1550 E Raynell Pl
(65804) 417.883.7300
$100 dep

Satellite Motel ($)
2305 N Glenstone Ave
(65803) 417.883.7300

Scottish Inn ($)
2933 N Glenstone Ave
(65803) 417.862.4301

Sheraton Inn ($$$)
2431 N Glenstone Ave
(65803) 417.831.3131

Skyline Motel ($)
2120 N Glenstone Ave
(65803) 417.866.4356

Super 8 ($)
3022 N Kentwood Ave
(65803) 417.833.9218
w/permission

● Strafford ●
Super 8 ($$)
315 E Chestnut St
(65757) 417.736.3883
call re: fees

● Sullivan ●
Best Western ($$)
307 N Service Rd
(63080) 573.468.3136

Family Motor Inn ($)
209 N Service Rd
(63080) 314.468.4119

Super 8 ($$)
601 N Service Rd
(63080) 314.468.8076
pets allowed with deposit

● Sweet Springs ●
Peoples Choice Motel ($)
1001 N Locust St
(65351) 816.335.6315

● Theodosia ●
Theodosia Marina Resort ($)
Hr 5 Box# 5020
(65761) 417.273.4444

● Tipton ●
Twin Pine Motel ($)
Hwy 50
(65081) 816.433.5525

● Van Buren ●
Hawthorne Motel ($)
Box# 615
(63965) 314.323.4275

● Villa Ridge ●
Best Western ($$)
581 Hwy 100
(63089) 314.742.3501

● Wappapello ●
Millers Motel ($)
Rt 2 Box# 2900
(63966) 314.222.8579

● Warrenton ●
Collier Inn ($)
2532 W Old Hwy 40
(63383) 314.456.7272

Days Inn ($)
220 Arlington Way
(63383) 314.456.4301
$8

● Waynesville ●
Best Western ($$)
14086 Hwy Z
(65583) 573.336.4299
no unattended pets

Days Inn ($$)
14125 Hwy Z
(65583) 573.335.5556

Econo Lodge ($)
HC 6 107 B
(65583) 314.336.3121

Econo Lodge ($)
309 Hwy 7
(65583) 573.336.7272

Howard Johnson ($$)
1083 7Issouri Ave
(65583) 314.336.5115

Ramada Inn ($$)
I-44 & Missouri Ave
(65583) 800.272.6232

Scottish Inn
25755 Hwy 17
(65583) 314.774.3600

Super 8 ($$)
I-44 & Hwy 28
(65583) 314.336.3036
mgr preapproval reqd

● Wentzville ●
Heritage Motel ($)
404 N Hwy 61
(63385) 314.327.6263
$10 fee prefer dogs

Holiday Inn
900 Corporate Pkwy
(63385) 314.327.7001

Howard Johnson ($$)
1500 Contintal Dr
(63385) 314.327.5212

Super 8
4 Pantera
(63385) 314.327.5300
small pets only

● West Plains ●
Best Western ($$)
220 US Hwy 63
(65775) 417.257.2711

Days Inn ($$)
Hwy 63
(65775) 417.256.4135

Ramada Inn ($$)
1301 Preacher Roe Blvd
(65775) 417.256.8191

Montana
● Alberton ●
River Edge Motel ($)
Box# 64
(59820) 406.722.4418

● Anaconda ●
Georgetown Lake Lodge ($$)
Dentons Point Rd
(59711) 406.563.7020

Pintlar Inn ($)
13902 Hwy I
(59711) 406.563.5072

Seven Gables ($$)
Hwy 1
(59711) 406.563.5052

● Augusta ●
Bunkhouse Inn ($)
122 Main St
(59410) 406.562.3387

● Babb ●
Thronsons Motel ($$)
Box# 169
(59411) 406.732.5530

Two Sisters Motel ($$)
Box# 262
(59411) 406.732.5535

● Baker ●
Roys Motel ($)
327 W Montana Ave
(59313) 406.778.3321

Sagebrush Inn ($$)
518 US 12
(59313) 406.778.3341

● Belgrade ●
Homestead Inn ($$)
6261 Jackrabbit Ln
(59714) 406.338.0800

● Big Sandy ●
Qs Motel ($)
US 87 & Hwy 236
(59520) 406.378.2389

● Big Sky ●
Best Western ($$$)
46625 Gallatin Rd
(59716) 406.995.4111

● Big Timber ●
Lazy 3 Motel ($$)
Hwy 10
(59011) 406.932.5533

Super 8 ($$)
I-90
(59011) 406.932.8888
deposit/w/permission

● Bigfork ●
Bayview Marina Resort
543 Yenne Point Rd
(59911) 800.775.3536

Gallery Suites ($$)
537 Electric Ave
(59911) 406.837.2288

Odauch Country Inn ($$)
675 Ferndale Dr
(59911) 406.837.6851

Timbers Motel ($)
8540 Hwy 35
(59911) 406.837.6200

Woods Bay Motel ($$)
26481 E Shore Rt
(59911) 406.837.3333

● Billings ●
Airport Metra Inn ($)
403 Main St
(59105) 406.245.6611

Best Western ($$)
5610 S Frontage Rd
(59101) 406.248.9800

Best Western ($$)
2511 1st Ave
(59101) 406.259.5511
small dogs

Billings Inn ($$)
880 N 2.th St
(59101) 406.252.6800

Cherry Tree Inn ($)
823 N Broadway
(59101) 406.252.5603

Clairon Hotel ($$)
1223 Mullowney L
(59101) 406.248.7151
pet rooms

Comfort Inn ($$)
2030 Overland Ave
(59102) 406.652.5200
mgr preapproval reqd

Days Inn ($$)
843 Parkway Ln
(59101) 406.252.4007

Dude Rancher Lodge ($$)
415 N 29th St
(59101) 406.259.5561

Fairfield Inn ($$)
2026 Overland Ave
(59102) 406.652.5330

Fireside Inn ($$)
1223 Mullowney Ln
(59101) 406.248.7151
pet rooms

Heights Inn Motel ($)
1206 Main St
(59105) 406.252.8451

Hilltop Inn ($$)
1116 N 28th St
(59101) 406.245.5000

Holiday Inn
5500 Midland Rd
(59101) 406.248.7701

Howard Johnson ($$)
S 27th St
(59101) 406.248.4656

Juniper Motel ($$)
1315 N 27th St
(59101) 406.245.4128

Kelly Inn ($$)
5425 Midland Rd
(59101) 406.252.2700

Lazy Kt Motel ($$)
1403 1st Ave
(59101) 406.252.6606

Motel 6 ($)
5353 Midland Rd
(59101) 406.248.7551
1 small pet/room

Motel 6 ($)
5400 Midland Rd
(59101) 406.252.0093
1 small pet/room

Picture Court Motel ($$)
5146 Laurel Rd
(59101) 406.252.8478

Quality Inn ($$)
2036 Overland Ave
(59102) 406.652.1320
mgr preapproval reqd

Radisson Inn ($$$)
19 N 28th St
(59101) 406.245.5121
small pets allowed

Ramada Ltd ($$)
1345 Ullowney Ln
(59101) 406.252.2584

Rimrock Inn ($$)
1203 N 27th St
(59101) 406.252.7107

Rimview Inn ($)
1025 N 27th St
(59101) 406.248.2622

Sheraton Inn ($$)
27 N 27th St
(59101) 406.252.7400

Super 8 ($$)
5400 Southgate Dr
(59101) 406.248.8842
call re: fees

War Bonnet Inn ($$)
2612 Belknap Ave
(59101) 406.248.7761

● Boulder ●
Castoria Motel ($)
211 S Monroe
(59632) 406.225.3549

E Z Motel ($)
114 N Main St
(59632) 406.225.3364

● Bozeman ●
Alpine Lodge ($)
1017 E Main St
(59715) 406.586.0356

Blue Sky Motel ($)
1010 E Main St
(59715) 406.587.2311

Bobcat Lodge ($$)
2307 W Main St
(59718) 406.587.5241

Bozemann Inn ($)
1235 N 7th Ave
(59715) 406.587.3176

Days Inn ($$)
1321 N 7th Ave
(59715) 406.587.5251

Fairfield Inn ($$)
828 Wheat Dr
(59715) 406.587.2222

Holiday Inn ($$)
5 E Baxter Ln
(59715) 406.587.4561
mgr preapproval reqd

Rainbow Motel ($)
510 N 7th Ave
(59715) 406.587.4201

Ramada Ltd ($$)
2020 Wheat Dr
(59715) 406.585.2626

Royal 7 Budget Inn ($$)
310 N 7th Ave
(59715) 406.587.3103

Super 8 ($$)
800 Wheat Dr
(59715) 406.586.1521
call re: fees

Western Heritage Inn ($$)
1200 E Main St
(59715) 406.586.8534

● Broadus ●
C J Motel ($$)
311 W Holt
(59317) 406.436.2671

Quaterhorse Motel ($)
101 N Park
(59317) 406.436.2626

● Browning ●
Glacier Motel ($$)
US 2
(59417) 406.338.7277

Red Eagle Motel ($$)
Star Rt Box# 896
(59417) 406.732.4453

St Mary Lodge ($$)
US 89
(59417) 406.732.4431

Western Motel ($$)
121 Central Ave
(59417) 406.338.7572

● Butte ●
Capri Motel ($$)
220 N Wyoming St
(59701) 406.723.4391

Comfort Inn ($$)
2777 Harrison Ave
(59701) 406.494.8850
mgr preapproval reqd

Days Inn ($$)
2700 Harrison Ave
(59701) 406.494.7000
mgr preapproval reqd

Mile Hi Motel ($$)
3499 Harrison Ave
(59701) 406.494.2250

Rose Motel ($)
920 S Montana St
(59701) 406.723.4346

Skookum Motel ($)
3541 Harrison Ave
(59701) 406.494.2153

Super 8 ($)
2929 Harrison Ave
(59701) 406.494.6000
w/permission dogs only

War Bonnet Inn ($$)
2100 Cornell Ave
(59701) 406.494.7800

● Cameron ●
West Fork Cabin Camp ($$)
1475 US 287
(59720) 406.682.4802

● Charlo ●
Allentown Motel ($)
41000 US 93
(59824) 406.644.2588

● Chinook ●
Chinook Motor Inn ($$)
100 Indiana Ave
(59523) 406.357.2248

● Choteau ●
Best Western ($$)
1005 N Main Ave
(59422) 406.466.5900

Big Sky Motel ($$)
209 S Main Ave
(59422) 406.466.5318

Western Star Motel ($)
426 Main Ave
(59422) 406.466.5737

● Circle ●
Travelers Inn ($)
Box# 78
(59215) 406.485.3323

● Clinton ●
Rock Creek Lodge ($)
I-90 Ex 126
(59825) 406.825.4868

● Columbia Falls ●
Glacier Inn Motel ($$)
1401 2nd Ave
(59912) 406.892.4341

Glacier Mountain ($$)
US 2 E & Hwy 206
(59912) 406.892.7686

● Columbus ●
Super 8 ($)
602 8th Ave
(59019) 406.322.4101
mgr preapproval reqd

● Conrad ●
Super 8 ($$$$)
215 Main St
(59425) 406.278.7676
pets w/permission $5 fee

● Cooke City ●
All Seasons Mine Co ($$)
US 212
(59020) 406.838.2251

Big Moose Resort ($$)
Colter Pass
(59020) 406.838.2393

Elkhorn Lodge ($$)
208 Main St
(59020) 406.838.2332

High Country Motel ($)
Box# 1146
(59020) 406.838.2272

● Culbertson ●
Diamond Willow Inn ($)
US 2 & Hwy 16
(59218) 406.787.6218

● Custer ●
D&L Motel ($)
Box# 105
(59024) 406.856.4128

● Cut Bank ●
Corner Motel ($)
201 E Main St
(59427) 406.873.5588

Glacier Gateway Inn ($$)
1121 E Railroad St
(59427) 406.873.5544

Parkway Motel ($)
73rd Ave
(59427) 406.873.4582

Point Motel ($)
1109 E Main St
(59427) 406.873.5433

Terrace Motel ($)
11 9th Ave SE
(59427) 406.873.5031

● Darby ●
Wilderness Motel ($)
308 S Mian St
(59829) 406.821.3405

● Deer Lodge ●
Down Towner Motel ($$)
506 4th St
(59722) 406.846.1021

Scharfs Motor Inn ($)
819 Main St
(59722) 406.846.2810

Super 8 ($$)
1150 N Main St
(59722) 406.846.2370
smoking rooms $5 fee

● Dillon ●
Best Western ($$)
650 N Montana St
(59725) 406.682.4214

Comfort Inn ($)
450 N Interchange
(59725) 406.683.6831
mgr preapproval reqd

Creston Motel ($)
335 S Atlantic St
(59725) 406.683.2341

Crosswinds Motel ($)
1004 S Atlantic St
(59725) 406.683.2378

Sacajawea Motel ($)
775 N Montana St
(59725) 406.683.2381

Sundowner Motel ($)
500 N Montana St
(59725) 406.683.2375

● Drummond ●
Drummond Motel ($)
170 W Front St
(59832) 406.288.3272

Sky Motel ($)
Front & Broadway
(59832) 406.288.3206

Wagon Wheel Motel ($)
Front & C Sts
(59832) 406.288.3201

● East Glacier Park ●
Jacobsons Cottages ($)
1204 Hwy 49
(59434) 406.226.4422

Porters Alpine Motel ($)
Box# 149
(59434) 406.226.4402

Sears Motel ($$)
1023 Hwy 49
(59434) 406.226.4432

● Elliston ●
Last Chance Motel ($)
Hwy 12
(59728) 406.492.7250

● Ennis ●
Fan Mountain Inn ($)
207 N Main
(59729) 40O.682.5200

Riverside Motel ($)
346 Main St
(59729) 406.682.4240

Silvertip Lodge ($)
301 Main St
(59729) 406.682.4384

Sportsmans Lodge ($$)
310 US 287
(59729) 406.682.4242

The El Western Motel ($$)
US 287
(59729) 406.682.4127

● Essex ●
Dennys Motel ($)
14297 US 2
(59916) 406.888.5720

● Eureka ●
Creek Side Cabins ($)
1333 US 93
(59917) 406.296.2361

Ksanka Motor Inn ($)
US 93 & Hwy 37
(59917) 406.296.3127

● Fairview ●
Korner Motel ($)
217 W 9th
(59221) 406.747.5259

● Forsyth ●
Best Western ($$)
1018 Front St
(59327) 406.356.2115
must declare

Rails Inn Motel ($$)
3rd & Front St
(59327) 406.356.2242

Restwel Motel ($)
810 Front St
(59327) 406.356.2771

Westwind Motor Inn ($)
Box# 5025
(59327) 406.356.2038

Whits Econo Lodge ($)
659 Front St
(59327) 406.356.7947

● Fort Benton ●
Fort Motel ($$)
1809 St Charles
(59442) 406.622.3312

● Galata ●
Galata Motel ($)
Box# 31
(59444) 406.432.2352

● Gallatin Gateway ●
320 Guest Ranch ($$)
205 Buffalo Horn
(59730) 406.995.4283

Castle Rock Inn
65840 Gallatin Rd
(59730) 406.763.4243

● Gardiner ●
Best Western ($$)
Hwy 89
(59030) 406.848.7311
in smoking rooms

Blue Haven Motel ($$)
Box# 952
(59030) 406.848.7719

Jim Bridger Court ($$)
Box# 325
(59030) 406.848.7371

Mile Hi Motel ($$)
Box# 1060
(59030) 406.848.7544

Wilson Yellowstone ($)
US 89
(59030) 406.848.7303

● Glasgow ●
Campbell Lodge ($)
534 3rd Ave
(59230) 406.228.9328

Cottonwood Inn ($$)
US 2
(59230) 406.228.8213

Well
Behaved

239

Koskis Motel ($)
320 US 2
(59230) 406.228.8282

Lacasa Motel ($)
238 1st Ave
(59230) 406.228.9311

Lakeridge Motel ($$)
Hwy 24 Hcr 1660
(59230) 406.526.3597

Star Lodge Motel ($)
US 2
(59230) 406.228.2494

● Glendive ●
Best Western ($$)
222 N Kendrick Ave
(59330) 406.365.5655
small pets $5

Budget Host ($)
HC 44 Hwy 18
(59330) 406.365.2349
mgr preapproval reqd

Days Inn ($)
2000 N Merrill Ave
(59330) 406.365.6011
small pets allowed

Jordon Motor Inn ($$)
223 N Merrill Ave
(59330) 406.365.3371

Kings Inn ($)
1903 N Merrill Ave
(59330) 406.365.5636

Super 8 ($$)
1904 N Merrill Ave
(59330) 406.365.5671
pets w/permission

● Great Falls ●
Budget Inn ($$)
2 Treasure State Dr
(59404) 406.453.1602

Central Motel ($)
715 Central Ave
(59404) 406.453.0161

Edelweiss Motel ($)
626 Central Ave
(59404) 406.452.9503

Fairfield Inn ($$)
1000 9th Ave
(59405) 406.454.3000

Great Falls Inn ($$)
1400 28th St
(59405) 406.453.6000

Holiday Inn ($$)
400 10th Ave
(59405) 406.727.7200
mgr preapproval reqd

Imperial Inn ($)
601 2nd Ave
(59401) 406.452.9581

Mid Town Motel ($$)
526 2nd Ave
(59401) 406.453.2411

Plaza Inn ($)
1224 10th Ave
(59405) 406.452.9594

Rendezvous 9 Motor Inn ($$)
Fox Farm Rd & 10th Ave
(59401) 406.452.9525

Skis Western Motel ($)
2420 10th Ave
(59405) 406.453.3281

Super 8 ($$)
1214 13th St
(59405) 406.727.7600
pets w/permission & deposit

Town & Country Motel ($)
2418 10th Ave
(59405) 406.452.5642

Townhouse Inns ($$)
1411 10th St
(59405) 406.761.4600

Triple Crown Motel ($)
621 Central Ave
(59401) 406.727.8300

Village Motor Inn ($)
726 10th Ave
(59405) 406.727.7666

● Greenough ●
Lorans Clearwtr Inn ($)
Box# 20
(59836) 406.244.9535

● Hamilton ●
Bitterroot Motel ($)
408 S 1st St
(59840) 406.363.1142

City Center Motel ($$)
W 415 Main
(59840) 406.363.1651

Comfort Inn ($$)
1115 N 1st St
(59840) 406.363.6000

Sportsman Motel ($)
410 N 1st St
(59840) 406.363.2411

● Hardin ●
Camp Custer Motel ($)
303 4th St
(59034) 406.665.2504

Lariat Motel ($)
709 N Center Ave
(59034) 406.665.2683

Western Motel ($$)
830 3rd St
(59034) 406.665.2296

● Harlowton ●
Corral Motel ($)
Box# 721
(59036) 406.632.4331

Countryside Inn ($)
309 3rd St NE
(59036) 406.632.4119

Troy Motel ($)
Box# 779
(59036) 406.632.4428

● Haugan ●
Silver $ Inn ($$)
I-90 Ex 16 Box#
(59842) 406.678.4242

● Havre ●
Budget Inn ($)
115 9th Ave
(59501) 406.265.8625

Circle Inn Motel ($)
3565 US 2
(59501) 406.265.9655

El Toro Inn ($$)
521 1st St
(59501) 406.265.5414

Rails Inn ($)
537 2nd St
(59501) 406.265.1438

Townhouse Inns ($$)
601 W 1st St
(59501) 406.265.6711

● Helena ●
Aladdin Motor Inn ($$)
2101 11th Ave
(59601) 406.443.2300

Comfort Inn ($$)
750 N Fee St
(59601) 406.443.1000
mgr preapproval reqd

Days Inn ($$)
2001 Prospect Ave
(59601) 406.442.3280
small $3 fee

Jorgensons Motel ($$)
Box# 857
(59624) 406.442.1770

Kings Carriage Inn ($$)
910 Last Chance Gulch
(59601) 406.442.6080

Knights Inn ($)
1831 Euclid Ave
(59601) 406.442.6384

Lamplighter Motel ($)
1006 Madison Ave
(59601) 406.442.9200

Park Plaza Hotel ($$)
22 N Last Chance Gulch St
(59601) 406.443.2200

Shilo Inn ($$)
2020 Prospect Ave
(59601) 406.442.0320
call re: fees

Super 8 ($$)
2200 11th Ave
(59601) 406.443.2450
call re: fees

CALL AHEAD!

$=under $35 $$=$35-60 $$$=$60-100 $$$$=over $100

● Hot Springs ●
Hot Springs Spa ($)
308 N Springs St
(59845) 406.741.2283

● Hungry Horse ●
Hungry Horse Motel ($$)
8808 US 2
(59919) 406.387.5443

Mini Golden Inn ($$)
8955 US 2
(59919) 406.387.4313

● Hysham ●
Treasure Vly Motel ($)
415 6th Ave
(59038) 406.342.5627

● Kalispell ●
Aero Inn ($$)
1830 US 93
(59901) 406.755.3798

Best Western ($$$)
1701 Hwy 93
(59901) 406.755.6100
small dogs

Big Chief Motel ($$)
1484 Hwy 35
(59901) 406.756.3434

Blue & White Motel ($$)
640 E Idaho St
(59901) 406.755.4311

Cavanaughs Kalipsell ($$)
20 N Main St
(59901) 406.752.6660

Diamond Lils Motel ($$$)
1680 Ujs 93
(59901) 406.752.3467

Glacier Gateway ($)
264 N Main St
(59901) 406.755.3330

Hilltop Inn ($$)
801 E Idaho St
(59901) 406.755.4455

Kalispell Grand Hotel ($)
100 Main St
(59901) 406.755.8100

Motel 6 ($)
1540 Hwy 93S
(59901) 406.752.6355
1 small pet/room

Red Lion Inn ($$$)
1330 Hwy 2W
(59901) 406.755.6700
call re: fees

Super 8 ($$)
1341 1stAve
(59901) 406.755.1888
call re: fees

The Four Seasons ($$)
350 N Main St
(59901) 406.755.6123

Vacationer Motel ($$)
285 7th Ave NE
(59901) 406.755.7144

White Birch Motel ($)
17 Shady Ln
(59901) 406.752.4008

● Laurel ●
Russell Motel ($$)
711 E Main St
(59044) 406.628.6821

● Lewistown ●
Motel Sunset ($)
115 NE Main St
(59457) 406.538.8741

Mountain View Motel ($)
1422 W Main St
(59457) 406.538.3457

Trails End Motel ($)
216 NE Main St
(59457) 406.538.5468

Yogo Inn ($$)
211 E Main St
(59457) 406.538.8721

● Libby ●
Budget Host ($$)
Hwy 2
(59923) 406.293.6201
limited availability

Mountain Magic Motel ($$)
919 Mineral Ave
(59923) 406.293.7795

Super 8 ($$)
448 US Hwy 2
(59923) 406.293.2771
pets w/permission

Venture Motor Inn ($$)
443 US Hwy 2
(59923) 406.293.7711

● Lima ●
Ex 15 Inn ($)
111 Baily St
(59739) 406.276.3535

● Lincoln ●
Blackfoot River Inn ($$)
Box# 295
(59639) 406.362.4255

Blue Sky Motel ($)
328 Main St
(59639) 406.362.4450

Three Bears Motel ($)
Box# 789
(59639) 406.362.4355

● Livingston ●
Budget Host ($)
1124 W Park St
(59047) 406.222.3840

Del Mar Motel ($)
Box# 636
(59047) 406.222.3120

Murray Hotel ($$)
201 W Park St
(59047) 406.222.1350

Paradise Inn ($)
Box# 684
(59047) 406.222.6320

Rainbow Motel ($$)
5574 E Park St
(59047) 406.222.3780

S S Motel ($$)
1 View Vista Dr
(59047) 406.222.0591

Yellowstone Motor Inn ($$)
1515 W Park St
(59047) 406.222.6110

● Lolo ●
Days Inn ($$)
11225 US 93
(59847) 406.273.2121

● Malta ●
Riverside Motel ($)
8 N Central
(59538) 406.654.2310

● Martin City ●
Middle Fork Motel ($$)
Box# 260237
(59926) 406.387.5900

● Martinsdale ●
Crazy Mountain Inn ($)
100 Main St
(59053) 406.572.3307

● Mc Allister ●
Crossroads Cabins ($)
5564 Ujs 287
(59740) 406.682.7652

● Melrose ●
Sportsman Motel ($$)
Frontage Rd
(59743) 406.835.2141

● Melstone ●
Terris Motel ($)
205 Main St
(59054) 406.358.2470

● Miles City ●
Best Western ($$)
1015 S Haynes Ave
(59301) 406.232.4560
@ mgrs discretion

Budget Host ($)
1209 S Haynes Ave
(59301) 406.232.5170
limited availability

Days Inn ($)
1006 S Haynes Ave
(59301) 406.232.3550
$6

Motel 6 ($)
1314 S Haynes Ave
(59301) 406.232.7040
1 small pet/room

$=under $35 $$=$35-60 $$$=$60-100 $$$$=over $100

Rodeway Inn ($$)
501 Main St
(59301) 406.232.2450
small pets only

Super 8 ($)
RR 2 Hwy 59
(59301) 406.232.5261
pets w/permission

● Missoula ●
4 Bs Inn North ($$)
4953 N Reserve St
(59802) 406.542.7550

4 Bs Inn South ($$)
3803 Brooks St
(59804) 406.251.2665

Bel Aire Motel ($)
300 E Broadway St
(59802) 406.543.3183

Best Western ($$$)
5290 Grant Creek Rd
(59802) 406.543.0700

Best Western ($$)
201 E Main St
(59802) 406.543.7221

Brooks St Motor Inn ($$)
3333 Brooks St
(59801) 406.549.5115

Brownies Plus Motel ($)
1540 W Broadway St
(59802) 406.543.6614

Budget Motel ($)
1135 W Broadway St
(59802) 406.549.2358

Campus Inn ($)
744 E Broadway St
(59802) 800.232.8013

Clark Fork Inn ($$)
1010 W Broadway St
(59802) 406.543.6619

Creekside Inn ($$)
630 E Broadway St
(59802) 406.549.2387

Days Inn ($$)
RR 2 US 93 N & I - 90
(59802) 406.721.9776
$5/pets

Downtown Motel ($)
502 E Broadway St
(59802) 406.549.5191

Econo Lodge ($)
1609 W Broadway St
(59802) 406.543.7231
$10 fee

Hampton Inn ($$$)
4805 N Reserve St
(59802) 406.549.1800

Holiday Inn ($$)
200 S Pattee St
(59802) 406.721.8550
mgr preapproval reqd

Hubbards Lodge ($$)
800 E Broadway St
(59802) 406.543.3102

Budget Inn ($$)
801 N Orange St
(59802) 406.721.3610

Red Lion Inn ($$)
700 W Broadway St
(59802) 406.728.3300
call re: fees

Red Lion Inn ($$)
100 Madison St
(59802) 406.728.3100
call re: fees

Redwood Lodge ($$)
8060 Hwy 93
(59802) 406.721.2110

Royal Motel ($)
338 Washington St
(59802) 406.542.2184

Rubys Reserve Inn ($$)
4825 N Reserve St
(59802) 406.721.0990

Sweet Rest Motel ($)
1135 W Broadway St
(59802) 406.549.2350

Thunderbird Motel ($)
1009 E Broadway St
(59802) 406.543.7251

Travelers Inn ($)
4850 N Reserve St
(59802) 406.728.8330

● Noxon ●
Noxon Motel ($)
2 Klakken Rd
(59853) 406.847.2600

● Ovando ●
Lake Upsata Ranch ($$$$)
135 Lake Upsala Rd
(59854) 800.594.7687

● Philipsburg ●
The Inn At Philipsburg ($)
915 W Broadway
(59858) 406.859.3959

● Plains ●
Tops Motel ($$)
340 E Railroad
(59859) 406.826.3412

● Plentywood ●
Sherwood Inn ($)
515 W 1st Ave
(59254) 406.549.6484

● Polson ●
Days Inn ($)
914 Hwy 93
(59860) 406.883.3120
$10/small pet

● Ramsay ●
Hibernation Station ($$$)
Box# 821
(59748) 406.646.4200
$10 nightly fee

Kelly Inn ($$$)
104 Canyon St
(59748) 406.646.4544

Ramsey Lake View Cabins
($$)
15570 Hebgenlake
(59748) 406.646.7257

Ranch Motel ($$)
235 Canyon
(59748) 406.646.7388

Weary Rest Motel ($$)
601 US 20
(59748) 406.646.7633

● Red Lodge ●
Becks Alpine Motel ($$)
Box# 471
(59068) 406.446.2213

Best Western ($$)
702 S Hauser
(59068) 406.446.1321
dogs: small attended

Eagles Nest Motel ($)
702 S Braodway
(59068) 406.446.2312

Super 8 ($)
1223 S Broadway
(59068) 406.446.2288
pets w/permission

Valli Hi Motor Lodge ($)
320 S Broadway
(59068) 406.446.1414

Yodeler Motel ($)
601 S Broadway
(59068) 406.446.1435

● Ronan ●
Starlite Motel ($)
18 Main St SW
(59864) 406.676.7000

● Roundup ●
Big Sky Motel ($)
740 Main St
(59072) 406.323.2303

● Saint Ignatius ●
Sunset Motel ($)
Main Hwy Access
(59865) 406.745.3900

● Saint Regis ●
Little River Motel ($)
I-90 Ex 33
(59866) 406.649.2713

Super 8 ($$)
9 Old Hwy 10
(59866) 406.649.2422
pets with deposit

● Saint Xavier ●
Royal Bighorn Lodge ($$)
Box# 181
(59075) 406.666.2340

Be
Discreet

$=under $35 $$=$35-60 $$$=$60-100 $$$$=over $100

• Scobey •
Cattle King Motor Inn ($$)
Box# 750
(59263) 406.487.5332

• Seeley Lake •
Duck Inn Motel ($$)
Hwy 83 At Mm 15
(59868) 406.677.2335

Wilderness Gateway Inn ($)
Box# 661
(59868) 406.677.2095

• Shelby •
Beacon Motel ($$)
722 1st St
(59474) 406.434.2721

Comfort Inn ($$)
50 Frontage Rd
(59474) 406.434.2212
mgr preapproval reqd

Crossroads Inn ($$)
1200 Hwy 2
(59474) 406.434.5134

Glacier Motel ($)
744 US 2
(59474) 406.434.5181

Ohaire Manor Motel ($)
204 2nd St
(59474) 406.434.5555

• Sheridan •
Mill Creek Inn ($$)
Box# 155
(59749) 406.842.5422

• Sidney •
Lone Tree Motel ($$)
900 S Central Ave
(59270) 406.482.4520

Richland Motor Inn ($$)
1200 S Central Ave
(59270) 406.482.6400

• Silver Gate •
Park View Cabins ($$)
Hwy 212 HC 84
(59081) 406.838.2371

• Stanford •
Sundown Motel ($)
Box# 126
(59479) 406.566.2316

• Stevensville •
St Marys Motel ($$)
3889 US 93
(59870) 406.777.2838

• Superior •
Budget Host ($$)
103 4th Ave
(59872) 406.822.4831

• Three Forks •
Broken Spur Motel ($$)
124 W Elm
(59752) 406.285.3237

Fort Three Forks Motel ($)
10776 Hwy 287
(59752) 406.285.3233

Sacajawea Inn ($$)
5 N Main St
(59752) 406.285.6515

• Townsend •
Lake Townsend Motel ($)
413 N Pine St
(59644) 406.266.3461

Mustang Motel ($$)
412 N Front St
(59644) 406.266.3491

• Trout Creek •
Trout Creek Motel ($$)
Box# 1441
(59874) 406.827.3268

• Twin Bridges •
Kings Motel ($)
307 S Main
(59754) 406.684.5639

Stardust Country Inn ($)
409 N Main
(59754) 406.684.5648

• Valier •
Atkins Inn ($)
412 Teton
(59486) 406.279.3476

• Virginia City •
Daylight Creek Motel ($$)
Box# 338
(59755) 406.843.5377

Fairweather Inn ($$)
315 W Wallace
(59755) 406.843.5377

Nevada City Hotel ($$)
Box# 338
(59755) 406.843.5377

• West Glacier •
Apgar Village Lodge ($$)
Box# 398
(59936) 406.888.5484

River Bend Motel ($$)
200 Going To The Sun Rd
(59936) 406.888.5662

• West Yellowstone •
Best Western ($)
103 Gibbon Ln
(59758) 406.646.7373
must declare pets

Best Western ($)
133 Canyon
(59758) 406.646.7376

Best Western ($$$)
236 Dunraven
(59758) 406.646.7681
must declare pets

Best Western ($)
201 Firehole Ln
(59758) 406.646.9557

Big West Pine Motel ($)
234 Firehole Ln
(59758) 406.646.7622

Buckboard Motel ($)
119 Electric St
(59758) 406.646.9020

Circle R Motel ($)
321 Madison Ln
(59758) 406.646.7641

Days Inn ($$)
118 Electric St
(59758) 406.646.7656
mgr preapproval reqd

Evergreen Motel ($)
229 Firehole Ln
(59758) 406.646.7655

Three Bear Annex ($)
24 Dunraven
(59758) 406.646.7394

Three Bear Motel ($)
217 Yellowstone Ave
(59758) 406.646.7353

Travelers Lodge ($$)
225 Yellowstone Ave
(59758) 406.646.9561

• White Sulphur Springs •
Chico Hot Springs Lodge
($$)
Box# 127
(59645) 406.333.4933

Spa Hot Springs Motel ($)
202 Mayn Rd
(59645) 406.547.3366

Tenderfoot Hiland ($)
301 Mayn Rd
(59645) 406.547.3303

• Whitefish •
Allens Motel ($$)
6540 US 93
(59937) 406.862.3995

Best Western ($$)
6510 US 93
(59937) 406.862.2569

Chalet Motel ($)
6430 US 93
(59937) 406.862.5581

Comfort Inn ($)
6590 US 93
(59937) 406.862.4020
not unattended

Mountain Holiday ($$)
6595 US 93
(59937) 406.862.2548

Quality Inn ($$)
920 Spokane Ave
(59937) 406.862.7600
mgr preapproval reqd

MONTANA, Whitefish

Super 8 ($$)
800 Spokane Ave
(59937) 406.862.8255
pets w/permission $2.50 per
day

Whitefish Athletic Club ($$)
224 Spokane Ave
(59937) 406.862.2535

. Whitefish Motel ($$)
620 8th St
(59937) 406.862.3507

● Whitehall ●
Chief Motel ($$)
303 E Legion
(59759) 406.287.3921

Super 8 ($$)
515 N Whitehall St
(59759) 406.287.5588
call re: fees

● Wibaux ●
Super 8 ($)
400 2nd Ave
(59353) 406.759.2666
call re: fees

● Wisdom ●
Nez Pierce Motel ($)
Box# 123
(59761) 406.689.3254

● Wolf Point ●
Homestead Inn ($)
101 US 2
(59201) 406.653.1300

Sherman Motor Inn ($)
200 E Main St
(59201) 406.653.1100

● Yellowtail ●
Bighorn Angler Motel ($$)
Rt 313
(59035) 406.666.2233

Quill Gordon Motel ($$)
Box# 7597
(59035) 406.666.2253

● Zortman ●
Buckhorn Cabins ($)
Box# 501
(59546) 406.673.3162

Nebraska

● Ainsworth ●
Lazy A Motel ($)
1120 E 4th St
(69210) 402.387.2600

Remington Arms Motel ($)
1000 E 4th St
(69210) 402.387.2220

● Alliance ●
Holiday Inn
1420 West 3rd
(69301) 308.762.7600

McCarrolls Motel ($)
1028 E 3rd St
(69301) 308.762.3680

Sunset Motel ($$)
1210 E Hwy 2
(69301) 308.762.8660

Super 8 ($$)
1419 W 3rd St
(69301) 308.762.8300
under 20 lbs

West Way Motel ($$)
1207 W Hwy 2 & 385
(69301) 308.762.4040

● Alma ●
Super Outpost Motel ($)
N Hwy 183 & 136
(68920) 308.928.2116

● Arapahoe ●
Arapahoe Motel ($)
W Hwys 6 & 34
(68922) 308.962.7948

● Auburn ●
Auburn Inn ($)
517 J St
(68305) 402.274.3143

Palmer House Motel ($)
1918 J St
(68305) 402.274.3193

● Aurora ●
Budget Host ($)
1515 11th St
(68818) 402.694.3141
small pets only

Hamilton Motor Inn ($)
Rt 3 Box# 41A
(68818) 402.694.6961

Kens Motel ($)
1515 11th St
(68818) 402.694.3141

● Beatrice ●
Beatrice Inn ($)
3500 N 6th St
(68310) 402.223.4074

Holiday Villa Motel ($)
1820 N 6th St
(68310) 402.223.4036

● Bellevue ●
American Family Inn ($)
1110 Fort Crook Rd
(68005) 402.291.0804
$7 fee

Offutt Motor Court ($)
3618 S Fort Crook Rd
(68123) 402.291.4333

● Blair ●
Blair House Motel ($)
W Hwy 30
(68008) 402.426.4801

● Bridgeport ●
Bell Motor Inn ($)
Box# 854
(69336) 308.262.0557

● Broken Bow ●
Wm Penn Lodge ($)
853 E South E St
(68822) 308.872.2412

● Burwell ●
Calamus Country Motel ($)
HC 79 Box# 18A
(68823) 308.346.4729

Rodeo Inn ($)
Hwys 91 & 11
(68823) 308.346.4408

● Callaway ●
Motel 4 ($)
106 E Kimball St
(68825) 308.836.2205

● Cambridge ●
Bunkhouse Motel ($)
E Hwy 6 & 34
(69022) 308.697.4540

Medicine Creek Lodge ($)
RR 2 Box# 93
(69022) 308.697.3774

● Central City ●
Crawford Motel ($)
RR 1 Box# 270
(68826) 308.946.3051

Crest Motel ($)
E Hwy 30
(68826) 308.946.3077

● Chadron ●
Best Western ($$)
1100 W 10th St
(69337) 308.432.3305
@ mgrs discretion

Blaine Motel ($)
159 Bordeaux St
(69337) 308.432.5568

● Columbus ●
Gembols Motel ($)
3220 8th St
(68601) 402.564.2729

Seven Knights Motel ($)
2222 23rd St
(68601) 402.563.3533

New World Inn ($$)
265 33rd Ave
(68601) 402.564.1492
quiet pets only

● Cozad ●
Budget Host ($)
440 S Meridan
(69130) 308.784.2290

Budget Host ($)
440 Meridian
(69130) 800.283.4678

● Crawford ●
Butte Ranch ($$)
803 W Ash Creek Rd
(69339) 308.665.2364

Policies
Subject
to Change

$=under $35 $$=$35-60 $$$=$60-100 $$$$=over $100

Hilltop Motel ($$)
304 McPherson St
(69339) 308.665.1144

Town Line Motel ($)
Hwys 2 & 20
(69339) 308.665.1450

● Crete ●
Villa Madrid Motel ($)
Hwy 33
(68333) 402.826.4341

● Crofton ●
Bogners Motel ($)
Hwys 12 & 121
(68730) 402.388.4626

● Davenport ●
Check In Motel ($)
1901 Fulton St
(68335) 402.245.2433

● David City ●
Fiesta Motel ($)
N Hwy 15
(68632) 402.356.3129

● Doniphan ●
USA Inns ($)
7000 S Nine Bridge Rd
(68832) 308.381.0111

● Edgar ●
Hotel Edgar ($)
Box# 217
(68935) 402.225.3228

● Elm Creek ●
First Interstate Inn ($)
I-80 & Hwy 183
(68836) 308.856.4652

● Elwood ●
J Js Marina ($$)
4 Lakeview Acres DR14
(68937) 308.785.2836

● Fairbury ●
Capri Motel ($)
1100 14th St
(68352) 402.729.3317

● Falls City ●
Stehenson Motel ($)
2621 Harlan St
(68355) 402.245.2459

● Franklin ●
Planks Plunk N Bunk ($)
Hwy 10 & 136
(68939) 308.425.6269

● Fremont ●
Holiday Lodge ($$)
1220 E 23rd St
(68025) 402.727.1110

Super 8 ($$)
1250 E 23rd St
(68025) 402.727.4445
mgr preapproval reqd

● Gering ●
Circle S Lodge ($)
400 M St
(69341) 308.426.2157

● Gibbon ●
5 Star Motel ($)
I-80 Ex 285
(68840) 308.468.5256

● Gordon ●
Gordon Hills Motel
107 West Hwy 20
(69343) 308.282.1795

● Gothenburg ●
Travel Inn ($)
501 S Lake Ave
(69138) 308.537.3638

Western Motor Inn ($)
1102 21st St
(69138) 308.537.3622

● Grand Island ●
Best Western ($$)
3333 Ramada Rd
(68801) 800.528.1234

Budget Host ($)
2311 S Locust St
(68801) 308.382.1815
mgr preapproval reqd

Conoco Motel ($)
2107 W 2nd St
(68803) 308.384.2700

Holiday Inn
I-80 & Hwy 281
(68802) 308.384.7770

Holiday Inn ($$)
I-80
(68802) 308.384.1330

Lazy Y Motel ($)
2703 E Hwy 30
(68801) 308.384.0700

Motel 6 ($)
3021 S Locust St
(68801) 308.384.4100
1 small pet/room

Oak Grove Inn ($)
3205 S Locust St
(68801) 308.384.1333

Super 8 ($$)
2603 S Locust St
(68801) 308.384.4380
pets w/permission

● Greenwood ●
Days Inn ($)
13006 238th St
(68366) 402.944.3313

● Hastings ●
Econo Lodge ($$)
2903 Osborne Dr
(68901) 800.424.4777

Holiday Inn
2205 Osborne Dr
(68901) 402.463.6721

Holiday Inn ($$)
2205 Osborne
(68902) 402.463.6721

Midlands Lodge ($)
910 W J St
(68901) 402.463.2428

Rainbow Motel ($)
1400 W J St
(68901) 402.463.2989

Super 8 ($$)
2200 N Kansas Ave
(68901) 402.463.8888
call re: fees

USA Inns ($$)
2434 Osborne Dr
(68901) 402.463.1422

Wayfair Motel ($)
101 Eat J St
(68901) 402.463.2434

X L Motel ($)
1400 W J St
(68901) 402.463.3148

● Hayes Center ●
Midway Motel ($)
Hwy 25
(69032) 308.286.3253

● Hebron ●
Riverside Motel ($)
S Hwy 81
(68370) 402.768.7366

Wayfarer Motel ($)
104 N 13th St
(68370) 402.768.7226

● Henderson ●
Wayfarer Motel ($)
Jct I-80 & S-93A
(68371) 800.543.0577

● Holdrege ●
Plains Motel ($)
619 W Hey 6
(68949) 308.995.8646

Tower Motel
413 W 4th Ave
(68949) 308.995.4488

● Kearney ●
Best Western ($$)
1013 3rd Ave
(68847) 308.237.5185

Budget Motel South ($)
411 2nd Ave
(68847) 308.237.5991

Fort Kearny Inn ($)
Box# 16881 I-80 Ex 272
(68848) 308.234.2541

Holiday Inn
301 2nd Ave
(68848) 308.237.3141

Kearney Inn 4 Less ($)
709 2nd Ave
(68847) 308.237.2671

Super 8 ($$)
15 W 8th St
(68847) 308.234.5513
call re: fees

Western Inn ($)
510 3rd Ave
(68847) 308.234.1876

Western Motel ($)
824 E 25th St
(68847) 308.234.2408

● Kimball ●
First Interstate Inn ($)
RR 1 Box# 136
(69145) 308.235.4601

Finer Motel ($)
RR 1 Box# 126
(69145) 308.235.4878

Motel Kimball ($)
RR 1 Box# 131
(69145) 308.235.4606

Western Motel ($$)
914 W Hwy 30
(69145) 308.235.4622

● Laurel ●
Big Red Motel ($)
202 Hwy 20
(68745) 402.256.9952

● Lewellen ●
Gander Inn Motel ($)
S Main St
(69147) 308.778.5616

● Lexington ●
Budget Host ($$)
801 S Plumb Creek Hwy
(68850) 308.324.5544
w/permission

Days Inn ($)
Hwy 285 & Commerce Rd
(68850) 308.324.6440
$6 smoking rooms no cats

Econo Lodge ($)
I-80 At US 283
(68850) 308.324.5601

Green Valley Motel ($)
311 S 5th
(68850) 308.324.3216

Minute Man Motel ($)
801 S Bridge St
(68850) 308.324.5540

Toddleb Inn Motel ($)
2701 Plum Creek Pkwy
(68850) 308.324.5595

● Lincoln ●
Airport Lodge ($)
2410 NW 12th St
(68521) 402.474.1311

Best Western ($$$)
5200 O St
(68510) 402.464.9111

Best Western ($$)
1200 Cornhusker Hwy
(68521) 402.475.9541

Comfort Inn ($$)
2940 NW 12th St
(68521) 402.464.2200
mgr preapproval reqd

Comfort Suites ($$)
4231 Industrial Ave
(68504) 402.464.8080
mgr preapproval reqd

Congress Inn ($)
2001 W O St
(68528) 402.477.4488

Econo Lodge ($)
5600 Cornhusker Hwy
(68507) 402.464.5971

Fairfield Inn ($$)
4221 Industrial Ave
(68504) 402.476.6000

Guesthouse Inn ($)
3245 Cornhusker Hwy
(68504) 402.466.2341

Holiday Inn ($$)
1101 W Bond St
(68521) (800)HOLIDAY

Inn 4 Less ($)
1140 W Cornhusker Hwy
(68521) 402.475.4511

Kings Inn Motel ($)
3510 Cornhusker Hwy
(68504) 402.466.2324

Motel 6 ($)
3001 NW 12th St
(68521) 402.475.3211
1 small pet/room

Ramada Inn ($$)
2301 NW 12th St
(68521) 402.475.4400
$25 deposit

Residence Inn ($$$)
200 S 68th Pl
(68510) 402.483.4900
$50 charge + $50 deposit

Senate Inn Motel ($)
2801 W O St
(68528) 402.475.4921

Starlite Motel ($$)
5200 Cornhusker Hwy
(68504) 402.466.1902

Town House Motel ($$)
174J M St
(68508) 402.475.3000

● Loup City ●
Colony Inn ($)
RR 1 Box# 184
(68853) 308.745.0164

● Mc Cook ●
Cedar Motel ($)
1400 E C St
(69001) 308.345.7091

Holiday Inn
1 Holiday Bison Rd
(69001) 308.345.4505

Red House Motel ($)
E Hwys 6 & 34
(69001) 308.345.2800

Super 8 ($)
1103 E B St
(69001) 308.345.1141
w/permission

● Minden ●
Pioneer Village Motel ($)
224 W Hwy 6
(68959) 308.832.2750

● Nebraska City ●
Apple Inn ($)
502 S 11th St
(68410) 402.873.5959

● Neligh ●
Deluxe Motel ($)
Hwy 275
(68756) 402.887.4628

West Hillview Motel ($)
RR 2 Box# 43
(68756) 402.887.4186

● Niobrara ●
Two Rivers Hotel ($)
254-12 Park Ave
(68760) 402.857.3340

● Norfolk ●
Blue Ridge Motel ($)
916 S 13th St
(68701) 402.371.0530

Norfolk Country Inn ($$)
Box# 181
(68701) 402.371.4430

● North Platte ●
First Interstate Inn ($)
I-80 & Hwy
(69101) 308.532.6980

Bar M Motel ($)
905 N Jeffers St
(69101) 308.532.0664

Best Western ($$)
920 N Jeffers St
(69101) 308.532.2313
small pets

Blue Spruce Motel ($)
821 S Dewey St
(69101) 308.534.2600

$=under $35 $$=$35-60 $$$=$60-100 $$$$=over $100

Camino Inn Suites ($$)
2102 S Jeffers St
(69101) 308.532.9090

Country Inn ($)
321 S Dewey St
(69101) 308.532.8130

Green Acres ($$)
4601 Rodeo Rd
(69101) 308.532.6654

Holiday Inn
300 Holiday Frontage Rd
(69103) 308.532.9500

Motel 6 ($)
1520 S Jeffers St
(69101) 308.534.6200
1 small pet/room

Park Motel ($)
1302 N Jeffers St
(69101) 308.532.6834

Pioneer Motel ($)
902 S Dewey St
(69101) 308.232.8730

Rambler Inn ($)
1420 Rodeo Rd
(69101) 308.532.9290

Sands Motor Inn ($)
501 Halligan Dr
(69101) 308.532.0151

Stanford Motel ($)
1400 E 4th St
(69101) 308.532.9380

Stockman Inn ($$)
1402 S Jeffers St
(69101) 308.534.3630

Super 8 ($)
220 W Eugene Ave
(69101) 308.532.4224
pets w/permission & $10
deposit

Travelers Inn ($)
602 E 4th St
(69101) 308.534.4020

● Ogallala ●
First Interstate Inn ($)
108 Prospector Dr
(69153) 308.285.2056

Best Western ($$)
201 Stagecoach Trl
(69153) 308.284.3656
@mgrs discretion

Days Inn ($)
601 Stagecoach Trl
(69153) 608.284.6365
$6 smoking rms no cats

Kingsley Lodge ($)
R.2 Box# 62-0
(69153) 308.284.2775

Lakeway Lodge ($)
918 N Spruce St
(69153) 308.284.4431

Plaza Inn ($$)
311 E 1st St
(69153) 308.284.8416

Ramada Ltd ($$)
201B Chuckwagon Rd
(69153) 308.284.3623
smoking rooms

Sunset Motel ($)
1021 W 1st St
(69153) 308.284.4264

Super 8 ($)
500 A St
(69153) 308.284.2076
pets w/permission & $10
deposit

Western Paradise ($)
221 E 1st St
(69153) 308.284.3684

● Omaha ●
American Star Inn ($$)
1715 S 11th St
(68108) 402.873.6656

Ben Franklin Motel ($$)
10308 Sapp Brothers Dr
(68138) 402.895.2200

Be
Discreet

Budgetel ($$)
10760 M St
(68127) 402.592.5200

Comfort Inn ($$)
10919 J St
(68137) 402.592.2882
mgr preapproval reqd

Econo Lodge ($$)
7833 W Dodge Rd
(68114) 402.391.7100

Hampton Inn ($$)
10728 L St
(68127) 402.593.2380

Hawthorn Suites ($$)
11025 M St
(68137) 402.331.0101

La Quinta Inn ($$)
3330 N 104th Ave
(68134) 402.493.1900
call re: fees

Marriott Hotel ($$$$)
10220 Regency Cir
(68114) 402.399.9000

Motel 6 ($)
10708 M St
(68127) 402.331.3161
1 small pet/room

Park Inn Intl ($$)
9305 S 145th St
(68138) 402.895.2555

Ramada Inn ($$)
Abbott Dr & Locust St
(68110) 402.342.5100

Ramada Inn ($$$)
7007 Grover St
(68106) 402.391.7030

Residence Inn ($$$)
6990 Dodge St
(68132) 402.553.8898
$25 1-6 days

Satellite Motel ($)
6006 L St
(68117) 402.733.7373

Sheraton Inn ($$$$)
4888 S 118th St
(68137) 402.895.1000

Townhouse Inn ($$)
13929 Gold Cir
(68144) 402.333.3777

● Oneill ●
Budget Host ($)
929 E Douglas St
(68763) 402.336.3403

Capri Motel ($)
14020 E Douglas St
(68763) 402.336.2765

Elms Motel ($)
E Hwys 20 & 275
(68763) 402.336.3800

Golden Hotel ($)
406 E Douglas St
(68763) 402.336.4436

Innkeeper ($)
725 E Douglas St
(68763) 402.336.1640

● Orchard ●
Orchard Motel ($)
E Hwy 20
(68764) 402.893.2165

● Oshkosh ●
S & S Motel ($)
Hwy 26 & Hwy 27
(69154) 308.772.3350

● Pawnee City ●
Pawnee Inn ($)
1021 F St
(68420) 402.852.2238

● Paxton ●
Days Inn
I-80
(69155) 308.239.4510
pre-approval reqd

● Plattsmouth ●
Browns Family Motel ($$)
1913 Hwy 34
(68048) 402.296.9266

● Randolph ●
Cedar Motel ($)
107 East Hwy 20
(68771) 402.337.0500

● Red Cloud ●
McFarland Hotel ($)
137 West 14th Abe
(68970) 402.746.3591

● Republican City ●
Gateway Motel ($)
147 Hwy 136
(68971) 308.799.2815

● Rushville ●
Antlers Motel ($)
607 East 2nd St
(69360) 308.327.2444

Nebraskaland Motel ($)
Box# 377
(69360) 308.327.2277

● Saint Paul ●
Kellers Korner Motel ($)
1517 2nd St
(68873) 308.754.4451

Super 8 ($$)
116 Howard Ave
(68873) 308.754.4554
call re: fees

● Schuyler ●
Johnnies Motel ($)
222 W 16th
(68661) 402.352.5454

Valley Court Motel ($)
320 W 16th St
(68661) 402.352.3326

● Scottsbluff ●
Capri Motel ($)
2424 Avenue I
(69361) 308.635.2057
small $3 fee

Lampligher Motel ($)
606 E 27th St
(69361) 308.632.7108

Sands Motel ($)
814 W 27th St
(69361) 308.632.6191

Scottsbluff Inn ($$)
1901 21st Ave
(69361) 308.635.3111

● Seward ●
East Hill Motel ($)
131 E Hwy 34
(68434) 402.643.3679

Super 8 ($$)
Hwy 15
(68434) 402.643.3388
$3 fee w/ permission

● Sidney ●
Days Inn ($$)
3042 Silverberg Dr
(69162) 308.254.2121
mgr preapproval reqd

Fort Sidney Inn ($)
935 9th Ave
(69162) 308.254.5863

Generic Motel ($)
11552 Hwy 30
(69162) 308.254.4527

Holiday Inn
664 Chase Blvd
(69162) 308.254.2000

Sidney Motor Lodge ($)
2031 Illinois St
(69162) 308.254.4581

Super 8 ($$)
2115 Illinois St
(69162) 308.254.2081
pets w/permission

● South Sioux City ●
Econo Lodge ($)
4402 Dakota Ave
(68776) 402.494.4114

Park Plaza Motel ($)
1201 1st Ave
(68776) 402.494.2021

The Marina Inn ($$)
4th & B Sts
(68776) 402.494.4000

Travelodge ($$)
400 Dakota Ave
(68776) 402.494.3046

● Spencer ●
Skyline Motel ($)
Hwys 281 & 12
(68777) 402.589.1300

● Sutherland ●
Park Motel ($)
1110 1st St
(69165) 308.386.4384

● Sutton ●
Sutton Motel ($)
208 N French
(68979) 402.773.4803

● Thedford ●
Rodeway Inn ($$)
HC 58 Box# 1-D
(69166) 308.645.2284

● Valentine ●
Ballard Motel ($)
227 S Hall St
(69201) 402.376.3300

Fountain Inn ($$)
237 S Cherry St
(69201) 402.376.2300

Merritt Resort ($$)
HC 32 Box# 23
(69201) 402.376.3437

Motel Raine ($)
W Hwy 20
(69201) 402.676.2030

Trade Winds Lodge ($)
HC 37 Box# 2
(69201) 402.676.1600

Valentine Motel ($)
Hwy 20 & 83
(69201) 402.376.2450

● Wahoo ●
Bills Wahoo Motel ($)
Hwy 77 92 & 109
(68066) 402.443.9933

● Wausa ●
Commercial Hotel ($)
Main St
(68786) 402.586.2377

● Wayne ●
K D Inn Motel
311 E 7th St
(68787) 402.375.1770

● West Point ●
Super 8 ($$)
1211 N Lincoln St
(68788) 402.372.3998
call re: fees

● Wisner ●
Midwest Motel ($)
1612 Avenue
(68791) 402.529.6910

● Wood River ●
Wood River Motel ($)
11774 S Hwy 11
(68883) 308.583.2256

● Wymore ●
D&M Motel ($)
601 S 14th St
(68466) 402.645.3801

● York ●
Best Western ($$)
2426 S Lincoln Ave
(68467) 402.362.5585
small pets

Staehr Motel ($)
RR 4 Box# 49
(68467) 402.362.4804

Super 8 ($$)
I-80
(68467) 402.362.3388
pets w/permission

USA Inns ($)
4817 S Lincoln Ave
(68467) 402.362.6885

Nevada
● Alamo ●
Little Aleinn ($)
Hcr Box# 45 Hwy 375
(89001) 702.729.2515

Meadow Lane Motel ($)
US Hwy 93
(89001) 702.725.3371

● Amargosa Valley ●
Longstreet Inn ($$)
Hwy 373
(89020) 702.372.1777

• Austin •
Mountain Motel ($)
Box# 91
(89310) 702.964.2471

Pony Canyon Motel ($)
Box# 209
(89310) 702.964.2605

The Pony Express House ($)
115 NW Main St
(89310) 702.964.2306

• Baker •
Border Inn
Hwy 50 & 6
(89311) 702.234.7300

Silverjack Motel ($)
Box# 166
(89311) 702.234.7323

• Battle Mountain •
Best Western ($$)
434 W Front St
(89820) 702.635.2416

Colt Service Center Motel
($$)
650 W Front St
(89820) 702.635.5424
Dogs ok

Del Court Motel ($)
292 E Front St
(89820) 702.635.2569

Ho Motel ($)
150 W Front St
(89820) 702.635.5101

Nevada Hotel ($)
36 E Front St
(89820) 702.635.2453

• Beatty •
Stagecoach Hotel ($)
Box# 836
(89003) 702.553.2419

• Blue Diamond •
Bonnie Springs Motel
1 Bonnie Springs Rd
(89004) 702.875.4191

• Boulder City •
Desert Inn ($)
800 Nevada Hwy
(89005) 702.293.2827

Flamingo Inn Motel ($)
804 Nevada Hwy
(89005) 702.293.3565

Lake Mead Resort ($$)
322 Lakeshore Rd
(89005) 702.293.2074

Starview Motel ($)
1017 Nevada Hwy
(89005) 702.293.1658

• Caliente •
Caliente Hot Springs ($)
Hwy 93
(89008) 702.726.3777

Longhorn Cattle Ranch ($$$$)
Rainbow Canyon Rd
(89008) 702.388.9955

Rainbow Cyn Motel ($)
884 A St
(89008) 702.726.3291

Shady Motel ($)
450 Front St
(89008) 702.726.3274

• Carson City •
Best Western ($$)
1300 N Carson St
(89701) 702.883.7300
very small dogs

Carson Motor Lodge ($)
1421 N Carson St
(89701) 702.882.3572

Days Inn ($$)
3103 N Carson St
(89706) 702.883.3343
$5/day per pet

Desert Hills Motel
1010 S Carson St
(89701) 702.882.1932

Motel 6 ($)
2749 S Carson St
(89701) 702.885.7710
1 small pet/room

Motel Orleans ($)
2731 S Carson St
(89701) 702.882.2007

Pioneer Motel ($)
907 S Carson St
(89701) 702.882.3046

Round House Inn ($)
1400 N Carson St
(89701) 702.882.3446

Royal Crest Inn
1930 N Carson St
(89701) 702.882.1785

Sierra Sage Motel ($)
801 S Carson St
(89701) 702.882.1419

Sierra Vista Motel ($)
711 S Plaza St
(89701) 702.883.9500

• Denio •
Denio Junction Motel ($)
Box# 10
(89404) 702.941.0371

• Elko •
Best Western ($$)
837 Idaho St
(89801) 702.738.7261
managers discretion

Best Western ($$$)
2050 Idaho St
(89801) 702.738.8421

Centre Motel ($)
475 3rd St
(89801) 702.738.3226

Elko Motel ($)
1243 Idaho St
(89801) 702.738.4433

Esquire Motel Lodge ($)
505 Idaho St
(89801) 702.738.3157

Holiday Inn ($$)
3015 Idaho St
(89801) 702.738.8425

Jiggs Guest Ranch ($$$$)
HC 30 Box# 197
(89801) 702.744.2277

Louis Motel ($)
2100 Idaho St
(89801) 702.738.3536

Motel 6 ($)
3021 Idaho St
(89801) 702.738.4337
1 small pet/room

Red Lion Inn ($$$)
2065 Idaho St
(89801) 800.547.8010
call re: fees

Ruby Chest Ranch ($$$$)
HC 30 Box# 197
(89801) 702.744.2277

Shilo Inn ($$$)
2401 Mountain City Hwy
(89801) 800.222.2244

Thunderbird Motel ($$)
345 Idaho St
(89801) 702.738.7115

Towne House Motel ($)
500 W Oak St
(89801) 702.738.7269

Travelers Motel ($)
1181 Idaho St
(89801) 702.738.4048

• Ely •
Best Western ($$)
930 Aultman St
(89301) 702.289.4497
small

Best Western ($$)
1101 Aultman St
(89301) 702.289.4529
small

El Rancho Motel ($)
1400 Aultman St
(89301) 702.289.3644

Fireside Inn ($)
McGill Hwy
(89301) 702.289.3765

Grand Central Motel ($)
1498 Lyons Ave
(89301) 702.289.6868

NEVADA, Ely

Great Basin Inn ($)
701 Avenue F
(89301) 702.289.4468

Hotel Nevada ($)
501 Aultman St
(89301) 702.289.6665

Idle Inn Motel ($)
150 4th St
(89301) 702.289.4411

Lanes Ranch Motel ($)
HC 34 Box# 34145
(89301) 702.238.5246

Motel 6 ($)
7th St & Ave O
(89301) 792.289.6671
1 small pet/room

Ramada Inn ($$)
701 Avenue I
(89301) 702.289.4884

Rustin Inn ($)
1555A Aultman St
(89301) 702.289.4404

Sure Rest Motel ($)
1550 High St
(89301) 702.289.2512

White Pine Motel ($)
1301 Aultman St
(89301) 702.289.3800

● Eureka ●
Colonade Hotel ($)
Clark & Monroe Sts
(89316) 702.237.9988

Eureka Motel ($)
10289 Main St
(89316) 702.237.5247

Ruby Hill Motel ($)
Box# 281
(89316) 702.237.5339

Sundown Lodge ($)
Box# 324
(89316) 702.237.5334

● Fallon ●
Budget Inn ($)
1705 S Taylor St
(89406) 702.423.2277

Nevada Belle Motel ($)
25 N Taylor St
(89406) 702.423.4648

Western Motel ($)
125 S Carson St
(89406) 702.423.5118

● Fernley ●
Best Western ($$)
1405 Newlands Dr
(89408) 702.575.6776

Rest Rancho Motel
350 Main
(89408) 702.575.4452

Truck Inn ($)
485 Truck Inn Way
(89408) 702.351.1000

● Gabbs ●
Gabbs Motel ($)
100 S Main St
(89409) 702.285.4019

● Gardnerville ●
Best Western ($$)
1795 Ironwood Dr
(89410) 702.782.7766

Nenzel Mansion ($$$)
1431 Ezell St
(89410) 702.782.7644

Topaz Lodge ($$)
1979 US 3955
(89410) 702.266.3338

Westerner Motel ($)
1353 US 395S
(89410) 702.782.3602

● Hawthorne ●
Anchor Motel ($)
965 Sierra Way
(89415) 702.945.2573

Best Western ($$)
1402 E Fifth St
(89415) 702.945.2600

El Capital Motel ($)
540 F St
(89415) 702.945.3321

Hawthorne Motel ($)
720 Sierra Hwy 95
(89415) 702.945.2544

Holiday Lodge ($)
Fifths & J Sts
(89415) 702.945.3316

Monarch Motel ($)
1291 E Fifth St
(89415) 702.945.3117

Rocket Motel ($)
694 Sierra Way
(89415) 702.945.2143

Sand N Sage Motel ($)
Box# 2325
(89415) 702.945.3352

Wright Motel ($)
W Fifth & I Sts
(89415) 702.945.2213

● Henderson ●
Bobby Motel ($)
2100 Boulder Hwy
(89015) 702.565.9711

Outpost Motel ($$)
1104 N Boulder Hwy
(89015) 702.564.2664

● Indian Springs ●
Indian Springs Motel ($)
Box# 270
(89018) 702.897.3700

● Jackpot ●
Bartons ($)
Box# 523
(89825) 702.755.2341

Horseshue Hotel ($)
Hwy 93 (Dice Rd)
(89825) 702.755.7777

● Jarbidge ●
Outdoor Inn
Main St
(89826) 702.488.2311

● Lamoille ●
Pine Lodge Hotel ($$)
Box# 281208
(89828) 702.753.6363

● Las Vegas ●
Best Western ($$)
1000 N Main St
(89101) 702.382.3455
pets $7

Best Western ($$)
5330 E Craig Rd
(89115) 702.643.6111
dogs

Best Western ($$)
4975 S Valley View Blvd
(89118) 702.798.7736

Bestern Western ($$)
905 Las Vegas Blvd
(89101) 702.385.1213
small pets $6

Center Strip Inn ($)
3688 Las Vegas Blvd
(89109) 702.739.6066

City Center Motel ($)
700 Fremont St
(89101) 702.382.4766

Convention Inn ($$)
735 E Desert Inn Rd
(89109) 702.737.1555

Crowne Plaza ($$$)
4255 Paradise Rd
(89109) 702.369.4400

Daisy Motel ($)
415 S Main St
(89101) 702.382.0707

Desert Rose ($$)
On Strip
(89193) 702.739.6739
guest rid

Desert Star Motel ($)
1210 Las Vegas Blvd Sa
(89104) 702.382.1066

E Z 8 Motel ($)
5201 Industrial Rd
(89118) 702.735.9513

Fergusons Motel ($)
1028 Fremont St
(89101) 702.382.3500

Gateway Motel ($)
928 Las Vegas Blvd
(89101) 702.382.2146

Gatewood Motel ($)
3075 Fremont St
(89104) 702.457.3600

Glass Pool Inn
4613 Las Vegas Blvd
(89119) 800.527.7118

Golden Inn
120 Las Vegas Blvd
(89101) 702.384.8204

Holiday Inn ($$)
8669 W Sahara Ave
(89117) 702.256.3766
mgr preapproval reqd

Holiday Royale Apartment
Suite
4505 Paradise Rd
(89109) 702.733.7676

Imperial Motel ($$$)
1326 S Main St
(89104) 702.384.8069

La Quinta Inn ($$)
3782 Las Vegas Blvd
(89109) 800.531.5900

La Quinta Inn ($$$)
3970 Paradise Rd
(89109) 702.796.9000
call re: fees

Meadows Inn ($)
525 E Bonanza Rd
(89101) 702.366.0456

Motel 6 ($)
194 E Tropicana Ave
(89109) 702.798.0728
1 small pet/room

Motel 6 ($)
5085 Industrial Rd
(89118) 702.739.6747
1 small pet/room

Motel 6 ($)
4125 Boulder Hwy
(89121) 702.457.8051
1 small pet/room

Motel Monaco ($)
3072 Las Vegas Blvd
(89109) 702.735.9222

Normandie Motel ($)
708 Las Vegas Blvd
(89101) 702.382.1002

Paradise Resort Inn ($$)
3450 Paradise Rd
(89109) 702.733.3900

Regency Motel ($)
700 N Main St
(89101) 702.382.2332

Residence Inn ($$$$)
3225 Paradise Rd
(89109) 800.331.3131

Sita Inn ($)
1322 Fremont St
(89101) 702.385.1150

Tam Oshanter Motel ($$)
3317 Las Vegas Blvd
(89109) 702.735.7331

Vacation Village Hotel ($)
6711 Las Vegas Blvd
(89119) 702.897.1700

Vagabond Inn ($$)
3265 Las Vegas Blvd
(89109) 702.735.5102
$15fee& $50 deposit

Vagabond Motel ($)
1919 Fremont St
(89101) 702.387.1650

Valley Motel ($)
1313 Fremont St
(89101) 702.384.6890

● Laughlin ●
Bayshore Inn ($$)
1955 S Casino Dr
(89029) 702.299.9010

Riverside Resort ($)
1650 Casino Dr
(89029) 702.298.2535

● Lovelock ●
Best Western ($)
1420 Cornell Ave
(89419) 702.273.2971

Cadillac Inn ($)
1395 Cornell Ave
(89419) 702.273.2798

Covered Wagon Motel ($$)
945 Dartmouth Ave
(89419) 702.273.2961

Desert Haven Motel ($)
885 Dartmouth Ave
(89419) 702.273.2339

Desert Plaza Inn
1435 Cornell Ave
(89419) 702.273.2500

Lovelock Inn ($$)
55 Cornell Ave
(89419) 702.273.2937

National 9 ($)
1390 Cornell Ave
(89419) 702.273.2224

Sierra Motel ($)
14th & Dartmouth Sts
(89419) 702.273.2798

Sunset Motel
1145 Cornell Ave
(89419) 702.273.7366

The Sage Motel ($)
1335 Cornell Ave
(89419) 702.273.0444

● Mc Dermitt ●
Diamond A Motel ($)
140 S US 95
(89421) 702.532.8551

McDermitt Motel
US Hwy 95
(89421) 702.532.8588

● Mesquite ●
Desert Palms Motel ($)
Mesquite Blvd
(89024) 702.346.5756

Valley Inn Motel ($)
791 W Mesquite Blvd
(89027) 702.346.5281

Virgin River Hotel ($)
Box# 1620
(89024) 702.346.7777

● Minden ●
Holiday Lodge ($)
1591 US 395N
(89423) 702.782.2288

● Mountain City ●
Chambers Motel ($)
Box# 188
(89831) 702.763.6626

Mountain City Motel
Hwy 225
(89831) 702.763.6622

● North Las Vegas ●
Barker Motel
26001 Las Vegas Blvd
(89030) 702.642.1138

Comfort Inn ($$)
910 E Cheyenne Ave
(89030) 702.399.1500
mgr preapproval reqd

Knotty Pine Motel ($)
1900 Las Vegas Blvd
(89030) 702.642.8300

Vegas Chalet Motel ($)
2401 Las Vegas Blvd
(89030) 702.642.2115

● Overton ●
Echo Bay Resort ($$$)
On Lake Mead
(89040) 702.394.4000

● Pahrump ●
Charlotta Inn Motel ($)
1201 S Hwy 160
(89048) 702.727.5445

Days Inn ($$)
Hwy 160
(89041) 702.727.5100
$4/pets

● Pioche ●
Hutchings Motel ($)
Box# 353
(89043) 702.962.5404

Motel Pioche ($)
100 Lacour St
(89043) 702.962.5551

● Reno ●
Bananza Inn
215 W 4th St
(89501) 702.322.8632

Castaway Inn
525 W 2nd St
(89503) 702.329.2555

Coach Inn ($)
500 N Center St
(89501) 702.323.3222

Days Inn ($)
701 E 7th St
(89512) 702.786.4070
$10

Donner Inn Motel ($)
720 W 4th St
(89503) 702.323.1851

El Patio Motel ($)
3495 S Virginia St
(89502) 702.825.6666

El Ray Motel ($)
330B N Arlington Ave
(89501) 702.329.6669

El Tavern Motel ($)
1801 W 4th St
(89503) 702.322.4504

Farris Motel
1752 E 4th St
(89512) 702.322.3190

Gateway Inn
1275 Stardust St
(89503) 702.747.4220

Gold Coin Motel ($)
2555 E Fourth Srt
(89512) 702.323.0237

Hampton Inn ($$)
175 Second St
(89501) 702.788.2300

Harrahs Hotel ($$$)
219 N Center St
(89501) 702.786.3232

Holiday Inn ($$)
1000 E 6th St
(89512) 702.786.5151
mgr preapproval reqd

In Town Motel ($)
260 W 4th St
(89501) 702.323.1421

Keno Motel ($)
322 N Arlington Ave
(89501) 702.322.6281

La Quinta Inn ($$)
4001 Market St
(89502) 702.348.6100
call re: fees

Martin Lodge ($)
6950 S Virginia St
(89511) 702.853.6504

Motel 500 ($)
500 S Center St
(89501) 702.786.2777

Motel 6 ($)
1901 S Virginia St
(89502) 702.827.0255
1 small pet/room

Motel 6 ($)
1400 Stardust St
(89503) 702.747.7390
1 small pet/room

Motel 6 ($)
666 N Wells Ave
(89512) 702.329.8681
1 small pet/room

Motel 6 ($)
866 N Wells Ave
(89512) 702.786.9852
1 small pet/room

Olympic Hotel ($$)
195 W 2nd St
(89501) 702.323.0726

Ox Bow Motor Lodge ($)
941 S Virginia St
(89502) 702.786.3777

Plaza Motor Lodge ($)
11 E Plaza St
(89501) 702.786.1077

Ponderosa Motel ($)
595 N Lake St
(89501) 702.786.3070

Ramada Inn ($$)
567 W 4th St
(89503) 702.322.8181

Reno Inn ($$)
5851 S Virginia St
(89502) 702.825.2940

River House Motel ($)
Box# 2425
(89505) 702.329.0036

Rodeway Inn ($$)
2050 Market St
(89502) 702.786.2500
$5 fee

Seasons Inn ($)
495 West St
(89503) 702.322.6000

Silver State Lodge
1791 W 4th St
(89503) 702.322.1380

Sundance Motel ($)
850 N Virginia St
(89501) 702.329.9248

Travelodge ($$)
655 W 4th St
(89503) 702.329.3451

Truckee River Lodge ($)
501 W 1st St
(89503) 800.635.8950
$10 per day or $50 per week

Vagabond Inn ($$)
3131 S Virginia St
(89502) 702.825.7134

● Searchlight ●
El Rey Motel
Box# 1235
(89046) 702.297.1144

● Sparks ●
Blue Fountain Inn
1590 B St
(89431) 702.359.0359

Inncal ($)
255 N McCarran Blvd
(89431) 702.358.2222

Motel 6 ($)
2405 Victorian Ave
(89431) 702.358.1080
1 small pet/room

Pony Express Lodge ($)
2406 Prater Way
(89431) 702.358.7110

Super 8 ($$)
E Greg St
(89431) 800.800.8000
call re: fees

● Stateline ●
Best Western ($$)
670 W Winnemucca Blvd
(89449) 702.623.3684

Harrahs Hotel ($$$$)
Box# 8
(89449) 702.588.6611

Horizon Casino ($$$)
Box# C
(89449) 702.588.6211

● Tonopah ●
Best Western ($$)
320 Main St
(89049) 702.482.3511
over 1 yr. old & attended

Golden Hills Motel
826 E Main St
(89049) 702.482.6238

Jim Butler Motel ($)
100 S Main St
(89049) 800.635.9455

Mizpah Hotel ($)
100 Main St
(89049) 702.482.6202

Oik Corral Inn ($)
Hwy 95
(89049) 702.482.8202

Silver Queen Motel ($)
Box# 311
(89049) 702.482.6291

Sundowner Motel ($)
700 Hwy 95
(89049) 702.482.6224

Tonopah Motel ($)
325 Main St
(89049) 702.482.3987

● Virginia City ●
Comstock Lodge ($$)
875 South C St
(89440) 702.847.0233

CALL AHEAD!

Sugar Loaf Motel ($$)
430 South C St
(89440) 702.857.0505

Virginia City Motel
675 South C St
(89440) 702.847.0277

● Walker Lake ●
Cliff House Lakeside ($)
1 Cliff House Rd
(89415) 702.945.2444

● Wells ●
Best Western ($)
576 6th St
(89835) 702.752.3353
small managers discretion

Cottonwood Ranch ($$$)
HC 62 Box# 1300
(89835) 702.752.3604

Lone Star Motel
676 6th St
(89835) 702.752.3632

Motel 6 ($)
US 40 & US 93
(89835) 702.752.2116
1 small pet/room

Oasis Motel ($)
I-80 Ex 378
(89835) 702.478.5113

Overland Hotel ($)
Box# 79
(89835) 702.752.3373

Restinn Suites ($$)
1250 E 6th St
(89835) 702.752.2277

Sharon Motel ($)
633 6th St
(89835) 702.752.3232

Shellcrest Motel
575 6th St
(89835) 702.752.3755

Wagon Wheel Motel ($)
326 Sixth St
(89835) 702.752.2151

Wells Chinatown ($)
455 S Humboldt Ave
(89835) 702.752.2101

● Wendover ●
Super 8 ($)
1325 Wendover Blvd
(89883) 702.664.2888
mgr preapproval reqd

● Winnemucca ●
Best Western ($$)
921 W Winnemucca Blvd
(89445) 702.623.6999

Bull Head Motel ($)
500 E Winnemucca Blvd
(89445) 702.623.3636

Cozy Motel ($)
344 E Winnemucca Blvd
(89445) 702.622.2615

Days Inn ($$)
511 E Winnemucca Blvd
(89445) 702.623.3661
$10

Downtown Motel ($)
251 E Winnemucca Blvd
(89445) 702.623.2394

Frontier Motel ($$)
410 E Winnemucca Blvd
(89445) 702.623.2915

Holiday Inn
1987 W Winnemucca Blvd
(89445) 702.625.3100

La Villa Motel ($$)
390 Lay St
(89445) 702.623.2334

Model T Motel ($)
112 Winnemucca Blvd
(89445) 702.623.0222

Motel 6 ($)
1600 W Winnemucca Blvd
(89445) 702.623.1180
1 small pet/room

Nevada Motel ($)
635 W Winnemucca Blvd
(89445) 702.623.5281

Park Motel ($)
740 W Winnemucca Blvd
(89445) 702.623.2810

Ponderosa Motel ($)
705 W Winnemucca Blvd
(89445) 702.623.4898

Pyrenes Motel ($$)
714 W Winnemucca Blvd
(89445) 702.623.1116

Scott Shady Court ($)
400 W 1st St
(89445) 702.623.3646

Scottish Inn
333 N Winnemucca Blvd
(89445) 702.623.3703

Super 8 ($$)
1157 W Minnemucca Blvd
(89445) 702.625.1818
call re: fees

Thunderbird Motel ($$)
511 W Minnemucca Blvd
(89445) 702.623.3661

Value Inn ($$)
125 E Winnemucca Blvd
(89445) 702.623.5248

Winners Hotel ($$)
185 W Winnemucca Blvd
(89445) 702.623.2511

● Yerington ●
Casino West ($$)
11 N Main St
(89447) 702.463.2481

In Town Motel ($)
111 S Main St
(89447) 702.463.2164

Ranch House Motel ($)
311 W Bridge St
(89447) 702.463.2200

● Zephyr Cove ●
Zephry Cove Resort
760 Hwy 50
(89448) 702.588.6644

**Policies
Subject
to Change**

New Hampshire

● Alton ●
Eve Joy Cottages
Roberts Cove Rd
(03809) 603.569.4973

● Alton Bay ●
Horse & Buggy Cottages ($$)
Bay Hill Rd
(03810) 603.875.5600

Lemays
Rt 28A Box# 127
(03810) 603.875.3629

● Antrim ●
The Maplehurst Inn ($$)
155 Main St
(03440) 603.588.8000

● Ashland ●
Black Horse Motel
RR 1 Box# 46RT3
(03217) 603.968.7116

● Bartlett ●
North Colony Motel ($)
Box# 1
(03812) 603.374.6679

The Villager Motel ($)
Box# 427
(03812) 603.356.2878

● Bennington ●
Econo Lodge ($$)
634 Francestown Rd
(03442) 603.588.2777

● Berlin ●
Traveler Motel ($)
25 Pleasant St
(03570) 603.752.2500

● Bradford ●
Bradford Inn
RR 1 Box# 40
(03221) 603.938.5309

● Center Conway ●
Saco River Motel ($$)
Rt 302 Box# 9A
(03813) 603.447.3720

● Center Harbor ●
Lakeshore Motel
RR 2 Box# 16T
(03226) 603.253.6244

The Meadows ($$)
Box# 204
(03226) 603.253.4347

● Claremont ●
Claremont Motor Lodge ($)
Beauregard St
(03743) 603.542.2540

The Dell East Motel ($)
24 Sullivan St
(03743) 603.542.9567

● Colebrook ●
Northern Comfort ($$)
RR 1 Box# 520
(03576) 603.237.4440

The Grand Resort ($$$$)
Off Hwy 26
(03576) 603.255.3400

● Concord ●
Brick Tower Motor Inn ($$)
414 S Main St
(03301) 603.224.9565

Comfort Inn ($$)
71 Hall St
(03301) 603.226.4100
$10 deposit

Econo Lodge ($$)
Gulf St
(03301) 603.224.4011

Holiday Inn ($$$)
172 N Main St
(03301) 603.224.9534

Holiday Inn
172 N Main
(03301) 603.224.9534

● Conway ●
Sunnybrook Place
Rt 16 Box# 1429
(03818) 603.447.3922

The Tablewood Motel
Rt 16 Box# 108
(03818) 603.447.5932

● Dover ●
Days Inn ($$)
481 Central Ave
(03820) 603.742.0400

● East Swanzey ●
The Coach Motor Inn
755 Manadnock Inn
(03446) 603.357.3705

● Exeter ●
Best Western ($$)
137 Portsmouth Ave
(03833) 603.772.3794
managers discretion

Exeter Inn ($$$)
Box# 508
(03833) 603.772.5901
small pets only

● Francestown ●
Inn At Crotched Mountain
($$)
Mountain Rd
(03043) 603.588.6840

● Franconia ●
Gale River Motel ($$)
1 Main St
(03580) 603.823.5655

Lovetts Inn ($$$)
Route 18
(03580) 800.356.3802

The Horse & Hound Inn ($$$)
205 Wells Rd
(03580) 603.823.5501

● Gilmanton ●
Temperance Inn ($$)
Hwy 140 & 107
(03237) 603.267.7349

● Glen ●
The RedApple Inn ($$)
Box# 103
(03838) 603.383.9680

● Gorham ●
Gorham Motor Inn ($$)
324 Main St
(03581) 603.466.3381

Northern Peaks Motel ($)
289 Main St
(03581) 603.466.3374

Philbrook Farm Inn ($$$$)
North Rd
(03581) 603.466.3831

Royalty Inn ($$$)
130 Main St
(03581) 603.466.3312

Top Notch Motel ($)
265 Main St
(03581) 603.466.5496

Town & Country Motel ($$)
Box# 220
(03581) 800.325.4386

● Hampton ●
Lamies Inn ($$)
490 Lafayette Rd
(03842) 603.926.0330

The Villager Motor Inn ($)
308 Lafayette Rd
(03842) 603.926.3964

● Hampton Falls ●
Hampton Falls Inn ($$)
11 Lafayette Rd
(03844) 603.926.9545

● Hanover ●
Hanover Inn ($$$$)
Dartmouth College
(03755) 603.643.4300

● Henniker ●
Heinniker Motel ($$)
Box# 622
(03242) 603.428.3536

● Hillsboro ●
1830N House Motel ($$)
626 W Main St
(03244) 603.478.3135

● Holderness ●
Olde Colonial Eagle ($$$)
Box# R
(03245) 603.968.3233

● Intervale ●
Riverside Inn ($$)
Rt 16A
(03845) 603.356.9060

Swiss Chalets Motel ($$)
Rt 16A
(03845) 800.831.2727

● Jackson ●
Dana Place Inn ($$$)
Box# L
(03846) 603.383.6822

Wentworth Hotel ($$$)
Box# M
(03846) 603.383.9700

Whitneys Inn ($$)
Box# 822
(03846) 603.383.8916

● Jaffrey ●
Woodbound Inn ($$$)
Woodbound Rd
(03452) 800.688.7770

● Keene ●
Best Western ($$$)
401 Winchester St
(03431) 603.357.3038

Days Inn ($$)
175 Key Rd
(03431) 603.352.7616
small pets allowed $10
deposit

The Motor Inn Motel
921 Main St Rt 12
(03431) 603.352.4138

Valley Green Motel ($)
379 West St
(03431) 603.352.7350

Winding Brook Lodge ($)
Box# 372
(03431) 603.352.3111

● Laconia ●
Tin Whistle Inn
1047 Union Ave
(03246) 603.528.4185

● Lancaster ●
Lancaster Motor Inn ($)
Box# 543
(03584) 603.788.4921

Pinetree Motel ($)
RR 2 Box# 281
(03584) 603.636.2479

Woodpile Inn ($)
39 Portland St
(03584) 603.788.2096

● Lincoln ●
Parkers Motel ($)
Rt 3 Box# 100
(03251) 603.745.8341

● Lisbon ●
The Hilltop Inn ($$)
Main St
(03585) 603.823.5695

The Homestead Inn
Sunset Hill Rd
(03585) 603.823.5564

● Littleton ●
Eastgate Motor Inn ($$)
RR 1
(03561) 303.444.3971

The Continental ($$)
Lisbon Rd
(03561) 603.444.5366

● Lyme ●
Loch Lyme Lodge ($)
NH 10
(03768) 800.423.2141

● Manchester ●
Days Hotel ($$$)
55 John E Devine Dr
(03103) 603.668.6110

Econo Lodge ($$)
75 W Hancock St
(03102) 603.624.0111

Holiday Inn ($$$)
700 Elm St
(03101) 603.625.1000

Howard Johnson ($$$)
298 Queen City Ave
(03102) 303.668.2600

● Merrimack ●
Residence Inn ($$$)
246 Daniel Webster Hwy
(03054) 603.424.8100
$100 dep & $10/night

Be
Discreet

● Mirror Lake ●
Nineteen Mile Bay Lodges
Hwy Contract 69/Box# 110
(03853) 603.569.3507

● Moultonborough ●
Rob Roy Motel ($$)
Box# 420
(03254) 603.476.5571

● Nashua ●
Holiday Inn ($$)
9 Northeastern Blvd
(03062) 603.888.1551

Marriott Hotel ($$$)
2200 Southwood Dr
(03063) 603.880.9100

Motel 6 ($$)
2 Progress Ave
(03062) 603.889.4151
1 small pet/room

Red Roof Inn ($)
77 Spit Brook Rd
(03060) 603.888.1893

● Newbury ●
Best Western ($$$)
1403 Route 103
(03255) 603.763.2010

● North Conway ●
Maple Leaf Motel
Box# 917 Rt 16
(03860) 603.356.5388

North Conway Mtn Inn ($$$)
Main St
(03860) 603.356.2803

● North Woodstock ●
Pitres Cabins
Rt 112 West
(03262) 603.745.8646

● Northwood ●
Lake Shore Farm ($$$$)
Jenness Pond Rd
(03261) 603.942.5921

● Ossipee ●
Pine Cove Motel ($$)
Rts 16 & 28
(03864) 603.539.4491

● Pittsburg ●
The Glen ($$$)
77 The Glen Rtd
(03592) 603.538.6500

● Portsmouth ●
Anchorage Inn ($$)
417 Woodbury Ave
(03801) 800.370.8111

Howard Johnson ($$)
Interstate Traffic Cir
(03801) 603.436.7600

The Port Motor Inn ($)
Portsmouth Cir
(03801) 800.282.7678

The Wrens Nest ($$)
3548 Lafayette Rd
(03801) 603.436.2481

● Rochester ●
Anchorage Inn ($$)
Box# 7325
(03839) 603.332.3350

● Salem ●
Holiday Inn ($)
1 Keewaydin Dr
(03079) 603.893.5511
mgr preapproval reqd

Red Roof Inn ($)
15 Red Roof Ln
(03079) 603.898.6422
small

● Sunapee ●
Burkehaven Resort ($$)
173 Burkehaven Hill Rd
(03782) 603.763.2788

Dexters Inn ($$$)
Box# 703A
(03782) 603.763.5571

The Old Governors House
Lower Main St
(03782) 603.763.9918

● Tamworth ●
The Tamworth Inn ($$$)
Main St
(03886) 603.323.7721

● Troy ●
East Hill Farm Inn
Mountain Rd
(03465) 603.242.6495

● Twin Mountain ●
Charlmont Motor Inn ($)
Rt 3 Box# G
(03595) 603.846.5549

● West Lebanon ●
Economy Inn ($$)
7 Airport Rd
(03784) 603.298.8888

Radisson Inn ($$$)
Airport Rd
(03784) 800.333.3333

● Wilton ●
Stepping Stones
Bennington Trail
(03086) 603.654.9048

● Winnisquam ●
Lynnmere Motel ($)
850 Laconia Rd
(03289) 603.524.0912

● Wolfeboro ●
Museum Lodges ($$$)
HC 69 Box# 680
(03894) 603.569.1551

● Woodstock ●
Wheelock Motor Court
Rt 3
(03293) 603.745.8771

● Woodsville ●
The All Seasons Motel ($)
30 Smith St
(03785) 603.747.2157

New Jersey

● Absecon ●
Days Inn ($$)
224 E White Horse Pk
(08201) 609.652.2200
$10

● Atlantic City ●
Howard Johnson ($$$)
Broadwalk Chelsea Ave
(08401) 609.344.7071

$=under $35 $$=$35-60 $$$=$60-100 $$$$=over $100

NEW JERSEY, Atlantic City

Red Carpet Inn
1630 N Albany Ave
(08401) 609.348.3171

● Beach Haven ●
Engleside Inn ($$$)
30 Engleside Ave
(08008) 609.492.1251

● Bellmawr ●
Howard Johnson ($$)
341 S Black Horse Pike
(08031) 609.931.0700

● Blackwood ●
Hojo Inn ($$$)
832 N Black Horse Pike
(08012) 609.228.4040

● Bordentown ●
Best Western ($$$)
1068 US 296
(08505) 609.298.8000

Days Inn ($$)
1073 US 206
(08505) 609.298.6100

Econo Lodge ($$)
187 US 130
(08505) 609.298.5000

Ramada Inn ($$)
1083 Route 206
(08505) 609.298.3200

● Cape May ●
The Marquis ($$$)
501 Beach Dr
(08204) 609.884.3500

● Carteret ●
Holiday Inn ($$$)
1000 Roosevelt Ave
(07008) 908.541.9500

● Cherry Hill ●
Holiday Inn
Rt 70
(08002) 609.663.5300

Residence Inn ($$$$)
1821 Old Cuthbert Rd
(08034) 609.429.6111
minimum 7 night stay and fee

● Clifton ●
Howard Johnson ($$$)
680 W Rt 2
(07014) 201.471.3800

Ramada Inn ($$$)
265 Rt 3
(07014) 201.778.6500

● Clinton ●
Holiday Inn
111 Rt 173
(08809) 908.735.5111

● East Brunswick ●
Motel 6 ($$)
244 Rt 18
(08816) 908.390.4545
1 small pet/room

● East Hanover ●
Ramada Inn ($$$)
130 Rt 10
(07936) 201.386.5622

● East Rutherford ●
Sheraton Inn ($$$)
2 Meadowlands Plz
(07073) 201.896.0500

● Eatontown ●
Crystal Motel ($$)
170-174 Hwy 35
(07724) 908.542.4900

Red Roof Inn ($$)
11 Center Plz
(07724) 908.389.4646

Residence Inn ($$$$)
90 Park Rd
(07724) 908.389.8100
$150 fee plus $6 per day

Sunrise Suites ($$$)
3 Center Plz
(07724) 908.389.4800

● Edison ●
Clarion Hotel ($$$)
2055 Lincoln Hwy
(08817) 908.287.3500

Crowne Plaza ($$$$)
125 Raritan Center Pkwy
(08837) 908.225.8300

Red Roof Inn ($)
860 New Durham Rd
(08817) 908.248.9300
small pets only

Wellesley Inn ($$)
831 US 1S
(08817) 908.287.0171
smoking rooms

● Elizabeth ●
Holiday Inn ($$$)
1000 Srping St
(07201) 908.355.1700
mgr preapproval reqd

● Englewood ●
Radisson Inn ($$$)
401 S Van Brunt St
(07631) 201.871.2020

● Fairfield ●
Best Western ($$$)
216-234 Rt 46
(07004) 201.575.7700

Radisson Inn ($$$$)
690 US 46
(07004) 201.227.9200

Ramada Inn ($$$)
38 Two Bridges Rd
(07004) 201.575.1742

● Flemington ●
Ramada Inn ($$$)
Route 202 & 31
(08822) 908.782.7472

● Hazlet ●
Wellesley Inn ($$)
3215 Hwy 35
(07730) 908.888.2800

● Hightstown ●
Days Inn ($$)
460 Route 33
(08520) 609.448.3200

Ramada Inn ($$)
399 Monmouth St
(08520) 609.448.7000
w/permission

Town House Motel ($$)
Hwy 33
(08520) 609.448.2400

● Hope ●
Inn At Millrace Pond ($$$)
Rt 519
(07844) 908.459.4884

● Jersey City ●
Econo Lodge ($$)
750 Tonnelle Ave
(07302) 201.420.9040

● Lakewood ●
Best Western ($$$)
1600 Route 70
(08701) 908.367.0900
housebroken pets

● Lyndhurst ●
Novotel ($$$)
1 Polito Ave
(07071) 201.896.6666
small & well behaved

● Mahwah ●
Ramada Inn ($$$)
180 Rt 17
(07430) 201.529.5880

Sheraton Inn ($$$$)
1 Int'L Blvd
(07495) 201.529.1660

● Maple Shade ●
Motel 6 ($$)
Rt 73
(08052) 609.235.3550
1 small pet/room

The Landmark Inn ($$)
Rts 73 & 38
(08052) 609.235.6400

● Marmora ●
Econo Lodge ($)
119 US 95
(08223) 800.424.4777

● Mc Afee ●
Days Inn ($$)
Rt 23 & Rt 94
(07428) 201.827.4666

● Middletown ●
Howard Johnson ($$$)
750 Hwy 35
(07748) 908.671.3400

● Millville ●
Millville Motel ($$)
Rt 47 Delseas Dr
(08332) 800.428.4373

● Monmouth Junction ●
Red Roof Inn ($)
208 New Rd
(08852) 908.821.8800

● Mount Holly ●
Best Western ($$)
2020 Route 541
(08060) 609.261.3800
pets $5

Howard Johnson ($$)
Mt Holly Rd
(08060) 609.267.6550

● Mount Laurel ●
Red Roof Inn ($)
603 Fellowship Rd
(08054) 609.234.5589
small pets only

● New Brunswick ●
Econo Lodge ($$)
26 US 1
(08901) 908.828.8000

● Newark ●
Marriott Hotel ($$$)
Newark Intl Airport
(07114) 201.623.0006

Radisson Inn ($$$)
128 Frontage Rd
(07114) 201.690.5500

Ramada Inn ($$$)
550 Rt 1
(07114) 201.824.4000

Newark Metro
● Carteret ●
Holiday Inn ($$$)
1000 Roosevelt Ave
(07008) 908.541.9500

● Clifton ●
Howard Johnson ($$$)
680 W Rt 2
(07014) 201.471.3800

Ramada Inn ($$$)
265 Rt 3
(07014) 201.778.6500

● East Hanover ●
Ramada Inn ($$$)
130 Rt 10
(07936) 201.386.5622

● East Rutherford ●
Sheraton Inn ($$$)
2 Meadowlands Plz
(07073) 201.896.0500

● Edison ●
Clarion Hotel ($$$)
2055 Lincoln Hwy
(08817) 908.287.3500

Crowne Plaza ($$$$)
125 Raritan Center Pkwy
(08837) 908.225.8300

Red Roof Inn ($)
860 New Durham Rd
(08817) 908.248.9300
small pets only

Wellesley Inn ($$)
831 US 1S
(08817) 908.287.0171
smoking rooms

● Elizabeth ●
Holiday Inn ($$$)
1000 Srping St
(07201) 908.355.1700
mgr preapproval reqd

● Englewood ●
Radisson Inn ($$$)
401 S Van Brunt St
(07631) 201.871.2020

● Fairfield ●
Best Western ($$$)
216-234 Rt 46
(07004) 201.575.7700

Radisson Inn ($$$$)
690 US 46
(07004) 201.227.9200

Ramada Inn ($$$)
38 Two Bridges Rd
(07004) 201.575.1742

● Jersey City ●
Econo Lodge ($$)
750-762 Tonnelle Ave
(07302) 201.420.9040

● Lyndhurst ●
Novotel ($$$)
1 Polito Ave
(07071) 201.896.6666

● Newark ●
Marriott Hotel ($$$)
Newark Intl Airport
(07114) 201.623.0006

Radisson Inn ($$$)
128 Frontage Rd
(07114) 201.690.5500

Ramada Inn ($$$)
550 Rt 1 S
(07114) 201.824.4000

● Paramus ●
Howard Johnson ($$$)
393 Sr 17
(07652) 201.265.4200

Radisson Inn ($$$$)
601 From Rd
(07652) 201.262.6900

Red Carpet Inn ($$)
211 Rt 17
(07652) 201.261.8686

● Parsippany ●
Days Inn ($$)
3159 Route 46
(07054) 201.355.0200

Hilton ($$$)
1 Hilton Ct
(07054) 201.267.7373
sign waiver

Howard Johnson ($$)
625 Route 46
(07054) 201.882.8600

Ramada Inn ($$$)
949 Route 46
(07054) 201.263.0404

Red Roof Inn ($$)
855 Route 46
(07054) 201.334.3737

● Piscataway ●
Motel 6 ($$)
1012B Stelton Rd
(08854) 908.981.9200
1 small pet/room

● Plainfield ●
Howard Johnson ($$)
US 22
(07060) 908.753.6500

● Ramsey ●
Howard Johnson ($$)
1255 Rt 17 S
(07446) 201.327.4500

Wellesley Inn ($$)
946 Rt 17
(07446) 201.934.9250
$3 charge

● Rochelle Park ●
Marriott Hotel ($$$)
I-80 & Grdn State Pkwy
(07662) 201.843.9500
$25fee balcony rms only

● Rockaway ●
Howard Johnson ($$$)
Green Pond Rd
(07866) 201.625.1200

Ramada Inn ($$)
375 W Passaic St
(07866) 201.845.3400

● Saddle Brook ●
Holiday Inn ($$$)
50 Kenny Pl
(07663) 201.843.0600
mgr preapproval reqd

● Secaucus ●
Courtyard By Marriott ($$$$)
455 Harmon Meadow Blvd
(07094) 201.617.8888

Ramada Inn ($$$)
350 Mill Creek Dr
(07094) 201.863.8700

Red Roof Inn ($$)
15 Meadowlands Pkwy
(07094) 201.319.1000

NEW JERSEY, South Plainfield

● South Plainfield ●
Comfort Inn ($$)
Stelton Rd
(07080) 908.561.4488

Holiday Inn ($$)
4701 Stelton Rd
(07080) 908.753.5500
mgr preapproval reqd

● Springfield ●
Holiday Inn ($$$)
304 Route 22
(07081) 201.376.9400
mgr preapproval reqd

● Wayne ●
Howard Johnson ($$$)
1850 Rt 23 & Ratzer Rd
(07470) 201.696.8050

● Whippany ●
Howard Johnson ($$$)
1255 Rt 10
(07981) 201.539.8350

End of Newark Metro

● Ocean City ●
Crossings Motor Inn ($$)
3420 Haven Ave
(08226) 609.396.4433

● Paramus ●
Howard Johnson ($$$)
393 Hwy 17
(07652) 201.265.4200

Radisson Inn ($$$$)
601 From Rd
(07652) 201.262.6900

Red Carpet Inn ($$)
211 Rt 17
(07652) 201.261.8686

● Park Ridge ●
Marriott Hotel ($$$)
300 Brae Blvd
(07656) 201.307.0800

● Parsippany ●
Days Inn ($$)
3159 Route 46
(07054) 201.355.0200

Hilton ($$$)
1 Hilton Ct
(07054) 201.267.7373
sign waiver

Howard Johnson ($$)
625 Route 46
(07054) 201.882.8600

Ramada Inn ($$$)
949 Route 46
(07054) 201.263.0404

Red Roof Inn ($$)
855 Route 46
(07054) 201.334.3737

● Penns Grove ●
Wellesley Inn
517 Pennsville Auburn
(08069) 609.299.3800

● Piscataway ●
Motel 6 ($$)
1012B Stelton Rd
(08854) 908.981.9200
1 small pet/room

● Plainfield ●
Howard Johnson ($$)
US 22
(07060) 908.753.6500

● Princeton ●
Novotel Hotel ($$$)
100 Independence Way
(08540) 609.520.1200

Residence Inn ($$$)
4225 Rt 1
(08543) 908.329.9600
$10 per day

Summerfield Suites ($$$)
4375 US 1
(08543) 609.951.0009

● Ramsey ●
Howard Johnson ($$)
1255 Rt 17
(07446) 201.327.4500

Wellesley Inn ($$)
946 Rt 17
(07446) 201.934.9250
$3 charge

● Rio Grande ●
The Pineapple Inn ($)
1225 Aquidneck Ave
(08242) 401.847.8400

● Rochelle Park ●
Marriott Hotel ($$$)
I-80 & Garden State Pkwy
(07662) 201.843.9500
$25 fee balcony rooms only

● Rockaway ●
Howard Johnson ($$$)
Green Pond Rd
(07866) 201.625.1200

Ramada Inn ($$)
375 W Passaic St
(07866) 201.845.3400

● Runnemede ●
Holiday Inn ($$)
109 E 9th Ave
(08078) 609.939.4200
mgr preapproval reqd

● Saddle Brook ●
Holiday Inn ($$$)
50 Kenny Pl
(07663) 201.843.0600
mgr preapproval reqd

● Seaside Heights ●
Scottish Inn
50 Lincoln Ave
(08751) 908.793.6999

● Secaucus ●
Courtyard By Marriott ($$$$)
455 Harmon Meadow Blvd
(07094) 201.617.8888

Ramada Inn ($$$)
350 Mill Creek Dr
(07094) 201.863.8700

Red Roof Inn ($$)
15 Meadowlands Pkwy
(07094) 201.319.1000

● Somers Point ●
Residence Inn ($$$)
900 Mays Landing Rd
(08244) 609.927.6400
small $150 deposit $50 non-refundable

● Somerset ●
Holiday Inn
195 Davidson
(08873) 908.356.1700

Ramada Inn ($$$)
60 Cottontail Ln
(08873) 908.560.9880

Summerfield Suites ($$$$)
260 Davidson Ave
(08873) 908.356.8000

● South Plainfield ●
Comfort Inn ($$)
Stelton Rd
(07080) 908.561.4488

Holiday Inn ($$)
4701 Stelton Rd
(07080) 908.753.5500
mgr preapproval reqd

● Springfield ●
Holiday Inn ($$$)
304 Route 22
(07081) 201.376.9400
mgr preapproval reqd

● Sussex ●
High Point Inn ($$)
1328 Hwy 23
(07461) 201.702.1860

● Toms River ●
Holiday Inn ($$$)
290 Hwy 37
(08753) 908.244.4000
mgr preapproval reqd

Howard Johnson ($$$)
Rt 37 Hooper Ave
(08753) 908.244.1000

Ramada Inn ($$$)
2373 Route 9
(08755) 908.905.2626

● Trenton ●
Howard Johnson ($$$)
2995 Brunswick Ave
(08648) 800.654.2000

Red Roof Inn ($$)
3203 Brunswick Ave
(08648) 609.896.3388

● Vineland ●
Ramada Inn ($$)
2216 W Landis Ave
(08360) 609.696.3800
$5 per day

● Voorhees ●
Hampton Inn ($$$)
121 Laurel Oak Rd
(08043) 609.346.4500

● Wayne ●
Howard Johnson ($$$)
1850 Rt 23 & Ratzer Rd
(07470) 201.696.8050

● Weehawken ●
Ramada Inn ($$$$)
500 Harbor Blvd
(07087) 201.617.5600

● Whippany ●
Howard Johnson ($$$)
1255 Rt 10
(07981) 201.539.8350

● Wildwood ●
New England Motel ($$)
106 W 11th Ave
(08260) 609.522.7250

New Mexico

● Alamogordo ●
All American Inn ($)
508 S White Sands Blvd
(88310) 505.437.1850

Best Western ($$)
1021 S White Sands Blvd
(88310) 505.437.2110

Holiday Inn ($$)
1401 S White Sands Blvd
(88310) 505.437.7100
mgr preapproval reqd

Satellite Inn ($)
2224 N White Sands Blvd
(88310) 505.437.8454

Super 8 ($)
3204 N White Sands Blvd
(88310) 505.434.4205
w/permission

● Albuquerque ●
Hotel Four Seasons ($$$)
2500 Carlisle Blvd NE
(87110) 505.888.3311

Amberley Suite Hotel ($$$)
7620 Pan American Fwy NE
(87109) 800.333.9806

Best Western ($$$)
2910 Yale Blvd SE
(87106) 505.843.7000

Best Western ($$)
12999 Central Ave NE
(87123) 505.298.7426
$5 pet fee

Budgetel ($$)
7439 Pan American Fwy NE
(87109) 505.345.0010

Comfort Inn ($$)
13031 Central Ave NE
(87123) 505.294.1800
mgr preapproval reqd

Comfort Inn ($$)
2300 Yale Blvd SE
(87106) 505.243.2244
mgr preapproval reqd

Days Inn ($$)
6031 Lliff Rd NW
(87105) 505.836.3297
$5 fee

Days Inn ($$)
13317 Central Ave NE
(87123) 505.294.3297
$5/pets

Days Inn ($$)
10321 Hotel Ave NE
(87123) 505.275.0599
$5/pets

De Anza Motor Lodge ($)
4302 Central Ave NE
(87108) 505.255.1654

Econo Lodge ($)
13211 Central Ave NE
(87123) 505.292.7600

Hampton Inn ($$)
5101 Ellison St NE
(87109) 505.344.1555
under 25 lbs

Hojo Inn ($$)
7640 Central Ave SE
(87108) 505.265.9309

Holiday Inn ($$)
10330 Hotel Ave NE
(87123) 505.275.8900
mgr preapproval reqd

Howard Johnson ($$)
15 Hotel Cir NE
(87123) 505.296.4852

Howard Johnson ($$)
7630 Pan Amer Fwy NE
(87109) 505.828.1600

La Quinta Inn ($$)
2424 San Mateo Blvd NE
(87110) 505.884.3591
call re: fees

La Quinta Inn ($$)
2116 Yale Blvd SE
(87106) 505.243.5500
call re: fees

La Quinta Inn ($$)
5241 San Antonio Dr NE
(87109) 505.821.9000
call re: fees

Lorlodge Motel East ($)
801 Central Ave NE
(87102) 505.243.2891

Motel 6 ($)
5701 Lliff Rd NW
(87105) 505.831.8888
1 small pet/room

Motel 6 ($)
3400 Prospect Ave NE
(87107) 505.883.8813
1 small pet/room

Motel 6 ($)
13141 Central Ave NE
(87123) 505.294.4600
1 small pet/room

Motel 6 ($)
1701 University Blvd NE
(87102) 505.843.9228
1 small pet/room

Motel 6 ($)
6015 Lliff Rd NW
(87121) 505.831.3400
1 small pet/room

Motel 6 ($)
1000 Stadium Blvd SE
(87102) 505.243.8017
1 small pet/room

Park Inn Intl ($)
601 Paisano St NE
(87123) 505.293.4444

Plaza Inn ($$$)
900 Medical Arts Ave NE
(87102) 505.243.5693

Radisson Inn ($$)
1901 University Blvd SE
(87106) 505.247.0512

Ramada Inn ($$$)
25 Hotel Cir NE
(87123) 505.271.1000

Ramada Ltd ($$)
Yale & Ross Blvd
(87106) 505.325.1191

Residence Inn ($$$$)
3700 Prospect NE
(87107) 505.881.2661

Rio Grande Inn ($$)
1015 Rio Grande Blvd NW
(87104) 800.959.4726

Royal Hotel ($)
4119 Central Ave NE
(87108) 800.843.8572

Super 8 ($$)
2500 University Blvd NE
(87107) 505.888.4884
mgr preapproval reqd

Travelodge ($$)
13139 Central Ave NE
(87123) 505.292.4878
$5 night

Travelodge ($$)
1635 Candelaria Rd NE
(87107) 505.344.5311

Well Behaved

$=under $35 $$=$35-60 $$$=$60-100 $$$$=over $100

NEW MEXICO, Alto

● Alto ●
High Country Lodge ($$)
N Hwy 48
(88312) 505.336.4321

La Junta Ranch ($$$)
Box# 139
(88312) 800.443.8423
must have reservation

● Artesia ●
Artesia Inn ($)
1820 S 1st St
(88210) 505.746.9801

● Aztec ●
The Step Back Inn ($$)
103 W Aztec Blvd
(87410) 505.334.1200

● Belen ●
Best Western ($$)
2101 Sosimo Padilla Blvd
(87002) 505.861.0980

● Bloomfield ●
Super 8 ($$)
525 W Broadway Ave
(87413) 505.632.8886
call re: fees

● Carlsbad ●
Best Western ($$)
1829 S Canal St
(88220) 505.887.2851

Continental Inn ($)
3820 National Parks Hwy
(88220) 505.887.0341

Days Inn ($$)
3910 National Parks Hwy
(88220) 505.887.7800

Lor Lodge ($)
2019 S Canal St
(88220) 505.887.1171

Motel 6 ($)
3824 National Parks Hwy
(88220) 505.885.0011
1 small pet/room

Parkview Motel ($)
401 E Greene St
(88220) 505.885.3117

Quality Inn ($$)
3706 National Parks Hwy
(88220) 505.887.2861

Stagecoach Inn ($)
1819 S Canal St
(88220) 505.887.1148

Travelodge ($)
3817 National Parks Hwy
(88220) 505.887.8888

● Chama ●
Elk Horn Motel ($$)
Rte 1 Box# 45
(87520) 800.532.8874

● Cimarron ●
Cimarron Inn ($)
Box# 623
(87714) 505.376.2268

● Clayton ●
Best Western ($$)
702 S 1st St
(88415) 505.374.2589

Thriftlodge ($)
Hwy 87 NW
(88415) 505.374.2558

● Cloudcroft ●
Summit Inn Motel ($$)
Box# 627
(88317) 505.682.2814

● Clovis ●
Days Inn ($)
1720 Mabry Dr
(88101) 505.762.2971
$3/pets

Holiday Inn
2700 E Mabry Dr
(88101) 505.762.4491

Holiday Inn ($$)
2700 Mabry
(88102) 800.465.4329

Motel 6 ($)
2620 Mabry Dr
(88101) 505.762.2995
1 small pet/room

● Deming ●
Best Western ($$)
1500 W Pine St
(88030) 505.546.4544

Days Inn ($)
1709 E Spruce St
(88030) 505.546.8813

Deming Motel ($)
500 W Pine St
(88030) 505.546.2737

Grand Motor Inn ($$)
1721 E Spruce St
(88030) 505.546.2632

Holiday Inn
I-10 Ex 85
(88031) 505.546.2661

Holiday Inn ($$)
I-10
(88031) 800.465.4329

Motel 6 ($)
I-10 & Motel Dr
(88031) 505.546.2623
1 small pet/room

Wagon Wheel Motel ($)
12109 W Pine St
(88030) 505.546.2681

● Dulce ●
Best Western ($$)
US 64 & Hawks Dr
(87528) 505.759.3663

● Elephant Butte ●
Elephant Butte Inn ($$)
Box#
(87935) 505.744.5431

● Espanola ●
Chamesa Inn ($$)
920 Riverside Dr
(87532) 505.753.7291

Comfort Inn ($$)
604B Riverside Dr
(87532) 505.753.2419

Super 8 ($$)
811 S Riverside Dr
(87532) 505.753.5374
$5 charge

● Farmington ●
Best Western ($$$)
700 Scott Ave
(87401) 505.327.5221

Comfort Inn ($$)
555 Scott Ave
(87401) 505.325.2626

Holiday Inn ($$)
600 E Broadway
(87401) 505.327.9811

La Quinta Inn ($$)
675 Scott Ave
(87401) 800.531.5900
call re: fees

Motel 6 ($)
1600 Bloomfield Hwy
(87401) 505.326.4501
1 small pet/room

Motel 6 ($)
510 Scott Ave
(87401) 505.327.0242
1 small pet/room

● Gallup ●
Ambassador Motel ($)
1601US W 66th
(87301) 505.722.3843

Best Western ($$)
3009 W US 66
(87301) 505.722.2221
small pets

Blue Spruce Lodge ($)
1119US E 66th
(87301) 505.863.5211

Colonial Motel ($)
1007 W Coal Ave
(87301) 505.863.6821

Comfort Inn ($$)
3208 US 66
(87305) 505.722.0982
$5/pet

Days Inn ($$)
1603US W 66th
(87301) 505.863.3891
$3/pets

Days Inn ($)
3201US W 66th
(87301) 505.863.6889
$3/pets

Econo Lodge ($$)
3101US W 66th
(87301) 505.722.3800

Economy Inn ($)
1709US W 66th
(87301) 505.863.9301
under 20 lbs

El Capitan Motel ($)
1300US E 66th
(87301) 505.863.6828

El Rancho Hotel ($$)
1000US E 66th
(87301) 505.863.9311

Holiday Inn ($$)
2915 W 66th
(87301) 505.722.2201

Motel 6 ($)
3306US W 66th
(87301) 505.863.4492
1 small pet/room

Road Runner Motel ($)
3012US E 66th
(87301) 505.863.3804

Roseway Inn ($)
2003 W Hwy 66
(87301) 800.454.5444

Sleep Inn ($$)
3820 US 66
(87301) 505.863.3535

● Glenwood ●
Los Olmos Guest Ranch ($$)
Box# 127
(88039) 505.539.2311

● Grants ●
Best Western ($$)
1501 E Santa Fe Ave
(87020) 505.287.7901

Days Inn ($$)
1504 E Santa Fe Ave
(87020) 505.287.8883

Holiday Inn ($$)
1496 E Santa Fe Ave
(87020) 505.285.4676
mgr preapproval reqd

Leisure Lodge ($)
1204 E Santa Fe Ave
(87020) 505.287.2991

Motel 6 ($)
1505 E Santa Fe Ave
(87020) 505.285.4607
1 small pet/room

Ramada Inn ($$)
1509 E Santa Fe Ave
(87020) 505.287.7700

Sands Motel ($)
112 Mc Arthur St
(87020) 505.287.2996

● Hobbs ●
Best Western ($$)
1301 E Broadway St
(88240) 505.393.4101

Days Inn ($)
211 N Marland Blvd
(88240) 505.397.6541

Econo Lodge ($)
619 N Marland Blvd
(88240) 505.397.3591

Holiday Inn
3610 N Lovington Hwy
(88240) 505.392.8777

Motel 6
1505 N Marland Blvd
(88240) 505.393.0221
1 small pet/room

Ramada Inn ($$)
501 N Marland Blvd
(88240) 505.397.3251

Super 8 ($)
722 N Marland Blvd
(88240) 505.397.7511
call re: fees

Zia Motel ($)
619 N Marland Blvd
(88240) 505.397.3591

● Las Cruces ●
Best Western ($$)
1765 S Main St
(88005) 505.524.8591

Best Western ($$)
901 Avenida De Mesilla
(88005) 505.524.8603
small pets ok

Days Inn ($$)
2600 S Valley Dr
(88005) 505.526.4441
$10

Desert Lodge Motel ($)
1900 W Picacho Ave
(88005) 505.524.1925

Hampton Inn ($$)
755 Avenida De Mesilla
(88005) 505.526.8311

Hilton ($$$)
705 S Telshor Blvd
(88011) 505.522.4300

Holiday Inn ($$$)
201 E University Ave
(88005) 905.526.4411

Holiday Inn
2200 S Valley Dr
(88005) 505.527.9947

La Quinta Inn ($$)
790 Avenida De Mesilla
(88005) 800.531.5900
call re: fees

Motel 6 ($)
235 La Posada Ln
(88005) 505.525.1010
1 small pet/room

Plaza Suites
201 E University Ave
(88005) 505.526.4411

Royal Host Motel ($)
2146 W Picacho Ave
(88005) 505.524.8536

Super 8 ($$)
245 La Posada Ln
(88005) 505.523.8695
call re: fees

Western Inn ($)
2155 W Picacho Ave
(88005) 505.523.5399

● Las Vegas ●
El Caminio Motel ($)
1152 Grand Ave
(87701) 505.425.5994

Historic Plaza Hotel ($$)
230 Old Town Plaza
(87701) 505.425.3591

Inn On Santa Fe Trail
1133 Grand Ave
(87701) 505.425.6791
$3 fee

Scottish Inn
1216 Grand Ave
(87701) 505.425.9357

Town House Motel ($)
1215 Grand Ave
(87701) 505.425.6717

● Lordsburg ●
Best Western ($$)
994 E Motel Dr
(88045) 505.542.3591

Best Western ($$)
1303 Main St
(88045) 505.542.8807

Desert West Motel ($$)
Box# 2005
(88045) 505.542.8801

● Los Alamos ●
Bandeller Inn ($$)
Center Hwy 4
(87544) 505.672.3838

Hilltop House Motel ($$$)
Trinity Dr At Central
(87544) 505.662.2441

● Lovington ●
Days Inn ($)
1600 W Avenue D
(88260) 505.396.5346
$50 dep

$=under $35 $$=$35-60 $$$=$60-100 $$$$=over $100

• Moriarty •
Days Inn ($$)
US 66
(87035) 505.832.4451
pets allowed with charge &
deposit

Howard Johnson ($)
1316 Central Ave
(87035) 505.832.4457

Sunset Motel ($)
501 Old Rt 66
(87035) 505.832.4234

Super 8 ($$)
1611 W Old Rt 66
(87035) 505.832.6730
mgr preapproval reqd

• Portales •
Dunes Motel ($)
1613 W 2nd St
(88130) 505.356.6668

Portales Inn ($)
218 W 3rd St
(88130) 505.359.1208

• Raton •
Capri Motel ($)
304 Canyon Dr
(87740) 505.445.3641

Harmony Motor Motel ($$)
351 Clayton Rd
(87740) 505.445.2763

Melody Lane Motel ($)
136 Canyon Dr
(87740) 505.445.3655

Motel 6 ($)
1600 Cedar St
(87740) 505.445.2777
1 small pet/room

Super 8 ($$)
1610 Cedar St
(87740) 505.445.2355
w/permission

• Red River •
Rio Colorado Lodge
East Main St
(87558) 505.754.2212

Tall Pine Resort ($$)
Box# 567
(87558) 505.754.2241

Terrace Towers Lodge ($)
Box# 149
(87558) 800.695.6343

• Rio Rancho •
Best Western ($$)
1465 Rio Rancho Dr SE
(87124) 505.892.1700
pets ok

Days Inn ($$)
4200 Crestview Dr SE
(87124) 505.892.8800

• Roswell •
Best Western ($$)
2205 N Main St
(88201) 505.622.2721

Best Western ($$$)
2000 N Main St
(88201) 505.622.6430
small pets only

Budget Inn ($)
2101 N Main St
(88201) 800.752.4667

Budget Inn ($)
2200 W 2nd St
(88201) 505.623.3811

Comfort Inn ($$)
3581 Main
(88201) 800.228.5150

Days Inn ($$)
1310 N Main St
(88201) 505.623.4021

Frontier Motel ($)
3010 N Main St
(88201) 505.622.1400

Leisure Inns ($)
2700 W 2nd St
(88201) 505.622.2575

National 9 ($)
2001 N Main St
(88201) 505.622.0110

Ramada Inn ($$)
2803 W 2nd St
(88201) 505.623.9440
small pets only

• Ruidoso •
Best Western ($$)
1451 Mechem Dr
(88345) 505.258.3333

Holiday Inn
400 W Hwy 70
(88345) 505.257.3736

Village Lodge ($$)
1000 Mechem Dr
(88345) 505.258.5442

• Ruidoso Downs •
Bestway Inn ($)
2052 Hwy 70
(88346) 505.378.8000

Inn At Pine Springs ($$)
Box# 2100
(88346) 505.378.8100

• Santa Fe •
527 Santa Fe Motel ($$$)
320 Artist Rd
(87501) 505.982.6636

Days Inn ($$)
3650 Cerrillos Rd
(87505) 505.438.3795
mgr preapproval reqd

Doubletree ($$$$)
3347 Cerrillos Rd
(87505) 505.473.2800

El Paradero Inn ($$)
220 W Manhattan Ave
(87501) 505.988.1177

Eldorado Hotel ($$$$)
309 W San Francisco St
(87501) 505.988.4455

Holiday Inn ($$$$)
4048 Cerrillos Rd
(87505) 505.473.4646

Homewood Suites ($$$$)
400 Griffin St
(87501) 505.988.3000

Hotel Santa Fe ($$$$)
1501 Paseo De Peralta
(87501) 800.825.9876

Inn Of The Anasazi ($$$$)
113 Washington Ave
(87501) 800.688.8140

Inn On The Alameda ($$$$)
303 E Alameda St
(87501) 800.289.2122

La Quinta Inn ($$)
4298 Cerrillos Rd
(87505) 800.531.5900
call re: fees

Motel 6 ($$)
3007 Cerrillos Rd
(87505) 505.473.1380
1 small pet/room

Motel 6 ($$)
3695 Cerrillos Rd
(87505) 505.471.4140
1 small pet/room

Park Inn Intl ($$)
2900 Cerrillos Rd
(87505) 505.473.4281

Preston House ($$)
106 E Faithway St
(87501) 505.982.3465

Quality Inn ($$$)
3011 Cerrillos Rd
(87505) 505.471.1211

Ramada Inn ($$$)
2907 Cerrillos Rd
(87505) 505.471.3000

Residence Inn ($$$)
1698 Galisteo St
(87505) 505.988.7300

• Santa Rosa •
Best Western ($$)
1501 E Will Rogers Dr
(88435) 505.472.3446
small housebroken pets

Best Western ($$)
3022 E Will Rogers Dr
(88435) 505.472.5877

CALL AHEAD!

$=under $35 $$=$35-60 $$$=$60-100 $$$$=over $100

Days Inn ($$)
1830 Will Rogers Dr
(88435) 505.472.5985

Holiday Inn
3202 Will Rogers Dr
(88435) 505.472.5411

Motel 6 ($)
3400 Will Rogers Dr
(88435) 505.472.3045
1 small pet/room

Scottish Inn
860 Will Rogers Dr
(88435) 505.472.3466

Super 8 ($)
1201 Will Rogers Dr
(88435) 505.472.5388
mgr preapproval reqd

● Silver City ●
Bear Mtn Guest Ranch ($$$)
2251 Bear Mt Rd
(88061) 505.538.2538

Days Inn ($$)
3420 US Hwy 180
(88061) 505.538.3711

Super 8 ($$)
1040 Hwy 180
(88061) 505.388.1983
call re: fees

The Drifter Motel ($$)
711 Silver Heights Blvd
(88061) 505.538.2916

● Socorro ●
Best Western ($$)
507 N California St
(87801) 505.835.0230
pets @ mgrs discretion

Econo Lodge ($)
713 NW California St
(87801) 505.835.1550

Holiday Inn
1100 California NE
(87801) 505.838.0556

Motel 6 ($)
807 US Hwy 85
(87801) 505.835.4300
1 small pet/room

● Taos ●
El Monte Lodge ($$)
317 Kit Carson Rd
(87571) 505.758.3171

El Pueblo Lodge ($$)
412 Paseo Del Pueblo
(87571) 505.758.8700

Holiday Inn
1005 Paseo Del Pueblo Sur
(87571) 505.758.4444

Inn On The Rio ($$)
910 E Kit Carson Rd
(87571) 505.758.7199

Quality Inn ($$)
1043 Paseo Del Pueblo Sur
(87571) 505.758.2200

Ramada Inn ($$$)
615 Paseo Del Pueblo Sur
(87571) 505.758.2900

Sagebrush Inn ($$)
Paseo Del Pueblo Sur
(87571) 800.428.3626

Sun God Lodge ($$)
919 Paseo Del Pueblo Sur
(87571) 505.758.3162

Taos Motel
Hwy 68
(87571) 800.323.6009

● Taos Ski Valley ●
Austing Haus Inn ($$$)
Box# 8
(87525) 800.748.2932

● Truth Or Consequ's ●
Ace Lodge Motel ($)
1302 N Date St
(87901) 505.894.2151

Best Western ($$)
2270 N Date St
(87901) 505.894.6665
@ mgrs discretion

Super 8 ($$)
2151 N Date St
(87901) 505.894.7888
mgr preapproval reqd

● Tucumcari ●
Americana Motel ($)
406 E Tucumcari Blvd
(88401) 505.461.0431

Apache Motel ($)
1106 E Tucumcari Blvd
(88401) 505.461.3367

Best Western ($$)
801 W Tucumcari Blvd
(88401) 505.461.0500
must be attended

Best Western ($$)
1700 E Tucumcari Blvd
(88401) 505.461.3335
pets ltd. to managers
discretion

Buckaroo Motel ($)
1315 W Tucumcari Blvd
(88401) 505.461.1650

Budget Host ($)
1620 E TumcUmcAri
(88401) 505.461.1212

Comfort Inn ($$)
2800 E Tucumcari Blvd
(88401) 505.461.4094

Days Inn ($)
2623 S 1st St
(88401) 505.461.0330

Econo Lodge ($)
3400 E Tucumcari Blvd
(88401) 505.461.4194

Friendship Inn ($)
315 E Tucumcari Blvd
(88401) 800.424.4777

Holiday Inn ($$)
3716 E Tucumcari Blvd
(88401) 505.461.3780

Motel 6 ($)
2900 E Tucumcari Blvd
(88401) 505.461.4791
1 small pet/room

Relax Inn ($)
1010 E Tucumcari Blvd
(88401) 505.461.3862

Rodeway Inn ($$)
1302 W Tucumcari Blvd
(88401) 505.461.3140

Royal Palacio Motel ($)
1602 E Tucumcari Blvd
(88401) 505.461.1212

Safari Motel ($)
722 E Tucumcari Blvd
(88401) 505.461.3642

Super 8 ($)
4001 E Tucumcari Blvd
(88401) 505.461.4444
pets w/permission

Travelodge ($)
1214 E Tucumcari Blvd
(88401) 505.461.1401

● Vaughn ●
Bel Air Motel ($)
Box# 68
(88353) 505.584.2241

● Whites City ●
Best Western ($$)
17 Carlsbad Caverns Hwy
(88268) 505.785.2291

New York
● Albany ●
Econo Lodge ($)
1632 Central Ave
(12205) 518.456.8811

Howard Johnson ($$)
1375 Washington Ave
(12206) 518.459.3100

Howard Johnson ($$$)
416 Southern Blvd
(12209) 518.562.6555

Marriott Hotel ($$$$)
189 Wolf Rd
(12205) 518.458.8444

Motel 6 ($$)
100 Watervioliet Ave
(12206) 518.438.7447
1 small pet/room

Ramada Inn ($$$)
300 Broadway
(12207) 518.434.4111

Ramada Ltd ($$)
1630 Central Ave
(12205) 518.456.0222

Red Roof Inn ($$)
188 Wolf Rd
(12205) 518.459.1197

● Alexandria Bay ●
Riveredge Resort ($$$)
17 Holland St
(13607) 315.482.9917

● Altmar ●
Cannons Place
Road 48
(13302) 315.298.5054

Fox Hollow
2740 Hwy 13
(13302) 315.298.2876

Jayhawkers Bunkhouse
Box# 132
(13302) 315.964.2557

The Brenda Motel
644 Cr 48
(13302) 315.298.2268

● Amenia ●
Deer Run ($$)
Box# 302
(12501) 914.373.9558

● Amsterdam ●
Holiday Inn
10 Market St
(12010) 518.843.5760

Valley View Motel ($)
Rts 5 S & 30
(12010) 518.842.5637

● Armonk ●
Ramada Inn ($$$)
94 Business Park Dr
(10504) 914.273.9090

● Auburn ●
Days Inn ($$)
37 William St
(13021) 315.252.7567

Holiday Inn ($$$)
75 North St
(13021) 315.252.4531

● Avoca ●
The Goodrich Motel ($)
8620 State Route 415
(14809) 607.566.2216

● Bainbridge ●
The Algonquin Motel
Rds Box# 45 Rt 7
(13733) 607.967.5911

● Ballston Lake ●
Westwood Motel ($$)
1012 Saratoga Rd
(12019) 518.339.3612

● Ballston Spa ●
Post Road Lodge
2865 Rt 9
(12020) 518.584.4169

Riviera Motel
2539 Rt 9
(12020) 518.899.2600

● Batavia ●
Best Western ($$)
8204 Park Rd
(14020) 716.343.1000

Days Inn ($$)
200 Oak St
(14020) 716.343.1440

Rodeway Inn ($$)
8212 Park Rd
(14020) 716.343.2311
$3 per day

● Bath ●
The Old Nat'l Hotel ($$)
13 E Steuben St
(14810) 607.776.4104

● Berlin ●
The Sedgwick Inn ($$$)
Box# 250
(12022) 518.658.2334

**Policies
Subject
to Change**

● Bernhards Bay ●
Snug Harbor
Rt 9 Box# 44
(13028) 315.675.3527

● Binghamton ●
Hojo Inn ($$)
690 Front St
(13905) 607.724.1341

Holiday Inn ($$$)
2-8 Hawley St
(13901) 607.722.1212

Motel 6 ($$)
1012 Front St
(13905) 607.771.0400
1 small pet/room

Super 8 ($$)
Upper Court St
(13904) 607.775.3443
call re: fees

● Bolton Landing ●
Timberlane Cottages ($$$$)
Box# 562
(12814) 518.644.5901
$4 owner referred

● Boonville ●
Headwaters Motel ($$)
Box# 404
(13309) 315.952.4493

● Bowmansville ●
Red Roof Inn ($)
146 Maple Dr
(14026) 716.633.1100

● Brockport ●
Econo Lodge ($$)
6575 4th Section Rd
(14420) 716.637.3157

● Buffalo ●
Buffalo Motor Lodge ($$)
475 Dingens St
(14206) 716.896.2800

Heritage House Inn ($$)
8261 Main St
(14221) 716.633.4900

Hilton ($$$$)
120 Church St
(14202) 800.445.8667

Holiday Inn ($$$)
601 Dingens St
(14206) 716.896.2900
small pets only

Lord Amherst Hotel ($$)
5000 Main St
(14226) 800.544.2200

Marriott Hotel
1340 Millersport Hwy
(14221) 716.689.6900
small pets only $50 charge

Microtel ($)
50 Freemand Rd
(14221) 716.633.6200

Motel 6 ($$)
4400 Maple Rd
(14226) 716.834.2231
1 small pet/room

Radisson Inn ($$$$)
4243 Genesee St
(14225) 716.634.2300

Red Roof Inn ($$)
42 Flint Rd
(14226) 716.689.7474
small pets only

Residence Inn ($$$)
100 Maple Rd
(14221) 800.331.3131

Wellesley Inn ($$)
4630 Genesee St
(14225) 716.631.8966
$3 charge

● Calcium ●
Microtel ($$$$)
8000 Virginia Smith
(13616) 315.629.5000

● Cambridge ●
Blue Willow Motel ($)
51 S Park St
(12816) 518.677.3552

Town House Motel ($$)
16 W Main St
(12816) 518.677.5524

● Canandaigua ●
Econo Lodge ($$)
170 Eastern Blvd
(14424) 716.394.9000

The Inn On The Lake ($$$)
770 S Main St
(14424) 716.394.7800

● Canastota ●
Days Inn ($$)
Nys Rte 13
(13032) 315.697.3309

● Castleton On Hudson ●
Bel Air Motel ($$)
1036 Route 9
(12033) 518.732.7744

● Catskill ●
Days Inn ($$)
I-87 Ex 21
(12414) 518.943.5800

● Cazenovia ●
Lincklaen House ($$$)
79 Albany St
(13035) 315.655.3461

● Central Square ●
Town & Country Motel
1436 Brewerton Rd
(13036) 315.668.6751

● Chaffee ●
Brookside Motel ($)
Hwy 16 & 39
(14030) 716.496.5057

● Cicero ●
Rodeway Inn ($$)
901 S Bay Rd
(13039) 315.458.3510

● Clayton ●
Westwinds Motel ($$)
RR 2 Box# 56
(13624) 315.686.3352

● Clifton Park ●
Comfort Inn ($$)
41 Fire Rd
(12065) 518.234.4321
mgr preapproval reqd

● Cobleskill ●
Best Western ($$)
12 Campus Dr
(12043) 800.528.1234

● Cohoes ●
Hampton Inn ($$$)
981 New Loudon Rd
(12047) 518.785.0000

The Century Inn ($$$)
997 New Loudon Rd
(12047) 518.785.0931

● Cold Spring ●
Hudson House ($$$)
2 Main St
(10516) 914.265.9355

● Cooperstown ●
Aalsmeer Motel ($$$)
RR 2 Box# 790
(13326) 607.547.8819

Best Western ($$)
50 Commons Dr
(13326) 607.547.9439

● Corfu ●
Econo Lodge ($$)
8593 Hwy 77
(14036) 716.599.4681

● Corning ●
Radisson Inn ($$$)
125 Denison Pkwy
(14830) 800.333.3333

● Cortland ●
Econo Lodge ($$)
3775 US 11
(13045) 607.753.7594

Super 8 ($$)
188 Clinton Ave
(13045) 607.756.5622
call re: fees

● Croton On Hudson ●
Waterfalls Motel ($$)
Rt 9 A & Furnace Dock Rd
(10520) 914.271.4322

● Dansville ●
Daystop ($$)
I-390 Ex 5
(14437) 716.335.6023
$5/pets

● Delhi ●
Buena Vista Motel ($$)
Box# 212
(13753) 607.746.2135

● Deposit ●
Alexanders Inn ($$)
770 Oquaga Lake Rd
(13754) 607.467.6023

● Dover Plains ●
Old Drovers Inn ($$$)
Old Rt 22
(12522) 914.832.9311

● Dunkirk ●
Drakes Motor Inn
5361 W Lake Rd
(14048) 716.672.4867

Rodeway Inn ($$)
310 Lake Shore Dr
(14048) 716.366.2200

Sheraton Inn ($$$)
30 Lake Shore Dr
(14048) 716.366.8350

● Durham ●
Rose Motel
Rt 145
(12422) 518.239.8496

● East Greenbush ●
Mount Vernon Motel
576 Columbia Tpke
(12061) 518.477.9352

● East Norwich ●
East Norwich Inn ($$$)
Hwy 25A & Hwy 106
(11732) 516.922.1500

● East Syracuse ●
Embassy Suites ($$$)
6646 Old Collamer Rd
(13057) 315.446.3200

Holiday Inn ($$$)
6501 College Dr
(13057) 315.437.2761

Marriott Hotel ($$$)
6302 Carrier Pkwy
(13057) 315.432.0200

Microtel ($)
6608 Old Collamer Rd
(13057) 315.437.3500

Motel 6 ($)
6577 Court Street Rd
(13057) 315.433.1300
1 small pet/room

Residence Inn ($$$)
6420 Yorktown Cir
(13057) 315.432.4488
call for fee & availability

● Elbridge ●
Cozy Cottage
4987 Kingston Rd
(13060) 315.689.2082

● Elmira ●
Coachman Motel ($$)
908 Pennsylvania Ave
(14904) 607.733.5526
$10 per day

Holiday Inn
1 Holiday Plaza
(14901) 607.734.4211

New Plantation Motel
2046 Rt 17
(14901) 607.737.9008

Red Jacket Motel ($)
Box# 489
(14902) 607.734.1616

● Endicott ●
Best Western ($$)
749 W Main St
(13760) 800.528.1234

● Fairport ●
Trail Break Motel ($$)
7340 Pittsford-Palmyra Rd
(14450) 716.223.1710

● Falconer ●
Motel 6 ($$)
1980 E Main St
(14733) 716.665.3670
1 small pet/room

● Farmington ●
Best Western ($)
6037 Rt 6
(14425) 800.800.8000

● Fishkill ●
Residence Inn ($$$)
2481 Route 9
(12524) 914.896.5210

Wellesley Inn ($$)
2477 Route 9
(12524) 914.896.4995

● Flushing ●
Marriott Hotel ($$$$)
102-05 Ditmars Blvd
(11369) 718.565.8900

Quality Hotel ($$$)
9500 Ditmars Blvd
(11369) 800.221.2222

● Fredonia ●
Days Inn ($$)
10455 Bennett Rd
(14063) 716.673.1351

● Freeport ●
Freeport Motor Inn ($$$)
445 S Main St
(11520) 516.623.9100

● Fulton ●
192 Executive Suites
192 S 1st St
(13069) 315.593.6631

Fulton Motor Lodge ($$)
163 S 1st St
(13069) 315.598.6100

Mini Motel
RR 8 Box# 160
(13069) 315.592.7238

Quality Inn ($$$)
930 S 1st St
(13069) 315.593.2444

● Fultonville ●
The Poplars Inn ($$)
Riverside Dr
(12072) 518.853.4511

● Gansevoort ●
McGregor Inn Motel
Rt 9
(12831) 518.587.1394

● Garden City ●
The Garden City Hotel
($$$$)
45 7th St
(11530) 516.747.3000

● Gasport ●
Hartland Motel
8464 Ridge Rd
(14067) 716.772.2266

● Geneva ●
Daystop ($)
Rt 14 & 318
(14456) 315.789.4510

Motel 6 ($$)
485 Hamilton St
(14456) 315.789.4050
1 small pet/room

● Gilboa ●
Golden Acres Farm ($$$)
Windy Ridge Rd
(12076) 607.588.7329

● Grand Island ●
Chateau Motor Lodge ($)
1810 Grand Island Blvd
(14072) 716.773.2868

● Greenport ●
Silver Sands Motel ($$$)
Box# 285
(11944) 516.477.0011

● Hamburg ●
Hojo Inn ($$)
5245 Camp Rd
(14075) 716.648.2000

Howard Johnson ($$)
5245 Camp Rd
(14075) 800.446.4656

Red Roof Inn ($)
5370 Camp Rd
(14075) 716.648.7222

● Hammondsport ●
Vinehurst Motel
Box# 203 Rt 54
(14840) 607.569.2300

● Hancock ●
Smiths Colonial ($$)
Rt 97 Box# 172-D
(13783) 607.637.2989

● Hauppauge ●
Radisson Inn ($$$$)
3635 Express Dr
(11788) 800.333.3333

● Henrietta ●
Microtel ($)
905 Lehigh Station Rd
(14467) 716.334.3400

Red Roof Inn ($)
4820 W Henrietta Rd
(14467) 800.843.7663

● Hensonville ●
Point Lookout Inn ($$)
Rt 23 Box# 33
(12439) 518.734.3381

● Herkimer ●
Glen Ridge Motel
Rt 5
(13350) 315.866.4149

Herkimer Motel ($$)
100 Marginal Rd
(13350) 315.866.0490

Inn Towne Motel ($)
227 N Washington St
(13350) 315.866.1101

● Highland Falls ●
Best Western ($$$)
Hwy 218
(10928) 914.446.9400

● Hillsdale ●
Linden Valley Inn ($$$$)
E On Ny 23
(12529) 518.325.7100

Swiss Hutte Motel ($$$)
Rt 23
(12529) 518.325.3333

● Holbrook ●
Red Carpet Inn
4444 Vets Mem Hwy
(11741) 516.588.7700

● Horseheads ●
Best Western ($)
3527 Watkins Glen Rd
(14845) 607.739.3891
$4 charge

Howard Johnson ($$)
2671 Corning Rd
(14845) 607.739.5636

Motel 6 ($$)
4133 Rt 17
(14845) 607.739.2525
1 small pet/room

● Hunter ●
Evergreen Cottages
Box# 161
(12442) 518.263.4932

● Ilion ●
Whiffletree Motel ($$)
345 E Main St
(13357) 315.895.7777

● Ithaca ●
Best Western ($$$)
1020 Ellis Hollow Rd
(14850) 072.726.100'

Collegetown Motel ($$)
312 College Ave
(14850) 800.745.3542

Econo Lodge ($$)
2303 N Triphammer Rd
(14850) 607.257.1400

Economy Inn ($)
658 Elmira Rd
(14850) 607.277.0370

Holiday Inn ($$$)
222 S Cayuga St
(14850) 607.272.1000

Howard Johnson ($$)
2300 N Triphammer Rd
(14850) 607.257.1212

La Tourelle Inn ($$$)
1150 Danby Rd
(14850) 607.273.2734

Be
Discreet

Meadow Court Inn ($)
529 S Meadow St
(14850) 607.273.3885

Ramada Inn ($$$)
2310 N Triphammer Rd
(14850) 607.257.3100

Spring Water Motel ($$)
Rt 366
(14850) 607.272.3721

● Jamaica ●
Plaza Hotel
13530 140th St
(11436) 718.659.6003

Travelodge ($$$)
Belt Pkwy & Van Wyck
(11430) 718.995.9000
$30 fee

● Jamestown ●
Comfort Inn ($$)
2800 N Main Street Ext
(14701) 716.664.5920
mgr preapproval reqd

Holiday Inn ($$$)
150 W 4th St
(14701) 716.664.3400
mgr preapproval reqd

● Johnson City ●
Best Western ($$)
569 Harry L Dr
(13790) 607.729.9194

Red Roof Inn ($$)
590 Fairview St
(13790) 607.729.8940

● Johnstown ●
Holiday Inn ($$)
308 N Comrie Ave
(12095) 518.762.4686
mgr preapproval reqd

● Kingston ●
Holiday Inn ($$$)
503 Washington Ave
(12401) 914.338.0400
mgr preapproval reqd

Super 8 ($$)
487 Washington Ave
(12401) 914.338.3078
call re: fees

● Lake George ●
Balmoral Motel ($)
444 Canada St
(12845) 518.668.2673

Diamond Cove Cottages ($$)
Lake Shore Dr
(12845) 518.668.5787

The Green Haven ($)
RR 2 Box# 2384
(12845) 518.668.2489

● Lake Placid ●
Best Western ($$)
150 Main St
(12946) 518.523.3353
small in smoking rooms

Devlins Motor Hotel ($$)
350 Main St
(12946) 518.523.3700
call for approval

Edge O' The Lake Motel ($$)
56 Saranac Ave
(12946) 518.523.9430

Holiday Inn ($$)
1 Olympic Dr
(12946) 518.523.2556
mgr preapproval reqd

Howard Johnson ($$$)
90 Saranac Ave
(12946) 518.523.9555

Ramada Inn ($$)
8-12 Saranac Ave
(12946) 518.523.2587

The Northway Motel ($$)
5 Wilmington Rd
(12946) 518.523.3500

Town & Country Motel ($$)
67 Saranac Ave
(12946) 518.523.9268

● Latham ●
Comfort Inn ($$)
866 Albany Shaker Rd
(12110) 518.783.1900
mgr preapproval reqd

Holiday Inn ($$$)
946 New Loudon Rd
(12110) 518.783.6161

Howard Johnson ($$)
611 Troy Schenectady Rd
(12110) 518.785.5891

Microtel ($)
7 Rensselaer Ave
(12110) 518.782.9161

Quality Inn ($$)
622 Hwy 155
(12110) 518.785.1414
mgr preapproval reqd

Residence Inn ($$$$)
1 Residence Inn Dr
(12110) 518.783.0600

● Liberty ●
Holiday Inn ($$)
7 Rt 52
(12754) 914.292.7171
mgr preapproval reqd

● Little Falls ●
Best Western ($$)
20 Albany St
(13365) 315.823.4954
deposit required

● Liverpool ●
Days Inn ($$$)
400 7th North St
(13088) 315.451.1511

Econo Lodge ($$$)
401 7th North St
(13088) 315.451.6000

Econo Lodge ($$)
401 7th North St
(13088) 315.451.6000
$3 per day

Four Points Hotel ($$$)
441 Electronics Pkwy
(13088) 315.457.1122
small pets only

Friendship Inn ($$)
629 Old Liverpool Rd
(13088) 800.424.4777

Hampton Inn ($$)
417 7th North St
(13088) 315.457.9900

Homewood Suites ($$$)
275 Elwood Davis Rd
(13088) 315.451.3800

Knights Inn ($$)
430 Electronics Pkwy
(13088) 315.453.6330
call for size limits & fees

● Livingston Manor ●
Lanza Inn ($$)
RR 2 Box# 446
(12758) 914.439.5070

● Lockport ●
Twin Oaks Motel
4660 Ridge Rd
(14094) 716.433.2447

● Long Lake ●
Journeys End Cottage
Deerland Rd Rt 30
(12847) 518.624.5381

● Lowman ●
Fountain Motel
Rt 17 Box# 11
(14861) 607.732.8617

● Malone ●
Econo Lodge ($$)
227 W Main St
(12953) 518.483.0500

Flanagan Hotel ($)
1 Elm St
(12953) 518.483.1400

Super 8 ($$)
Finny Blvd Rt 30
(12953) 518.483.8123
mgr preapproval reqd

The Four Seasons ($$)
236 W Main St
(12953) 518.483.3490

● Manchester ●
Rodeway Inn ($$)
Hwy 96 & 21
(14504) 716.289.3811

● Masonville ●
Mason Inn ($$)
Rt 206 Box# 81
(13804) 607.265.3287

● Massena ●
Bobs Motel
RR 2 Box# 301
(13662) 315.769.9497

Hillside Motel
15 Smith Rd
(13662) 315.769.5403

New Flanders Inn
Main & W Orvis Sts
(13662) 315.769.2441

Park Inn Intl
528 Cr 42
(13662) 315.769.7799

● Mexico ●
Strike King Lodge
286 Hwy 104B
(13114) 315.963.7826

Waltons Motel
3210 US Route 11 # 92
(13114) 315.963.7120

● Middle Grove ●
Daybreak Motel ($)
2909 Rt 9
(12850) 518.882.6838

● Middleport ●
Canal Country Inn
4021 Peet St
(14105) 716.735.7572

● Middletown ●
Middletown Motel ($$)
501 Rt 211
(10940) 914.342.2535

Super 8 ($$)
563 Rt 211
(10940) 914.692.5828
pets w/permission

● Millbrook ●
Cottonwood Motel ($$)
RR 2 Box# 25
(12545) 914.677.3283

● Montauk ●
Surfsound ($$$)
Ditch Plains Rd
(11954) 516.668.2215

● Montgomery ●
Super 8 ($$)
207 Montgomery Rd
(12549) 914.457.3143
pets w/permission

● Montour Falls ●
Falls Motel ($)
239 N Genesee St
(14865) 607.535.7262

Relax Inn ($)
100 Clawson Blvd
(14865) 607.535.7183

● Mount Kisco ●
Holiday Inn
1 Holiday Inn Dr
(10549) 914.241.2600

● Nanuet ●
Econo Lodge ($$)
367 Hwy 59
(10954) 914.623.3838

● New Hampton ●
Days Inn ($$)
Rt 17 M
(10958) 914.374.2411

● New York ●
Delmonico Hotel ($$$$)
502 Park Ave
(10022) 212.486.0509

Hilton ($$$$)
1335 Ave Of Americas
(10019) 800.445.8667

Hotel Pierre ($$$$)
2 E 61st St
(10021) 212.838.8000
pet friendly special treatment

Hotel Plaza Athenee ($$$$)
37 E 64th St
(10021) 212.734.9100
small dogs @
mgr's discretion

Le Parker Meridien
118 W 57th St
(10019) 212.245.5000

Loews Hotel ($$$$)
569 Lexington Ave
(10022) 212.752.7000
small pets only

Marriott Hotel ($$$$)
1535 Broadway
(10036) 212.393.1900

Mayfair Hotel ($$$$)
610 Park Ave
(10021) 212.288.0800
small pets only

Millenium Hotel ($$$$)
145 W 44th St
(10036) 212.768.4400

Morgans Hotel ($$$$)
237 Madison Ave
(10016) 212.686.0300

Novotel New York ($$$$)
226 W 52nd St
(10019) 212.315.0100

Renaissance Hotel ($$$$)
714 7th Ave
(10036) 212.765.7676

Sheraton Inn ($$$$)
790 7th Ave
(10019) 212.581.3300

Sheraton Inn ($$$$)
811 7th Ave
(10019) 212.581.1000

The Carlyle ($$$$)
35 E 76th St
(10021) 212.744.1600
$10 per day

The Essex House ($$$$)
160 Central Park
(10019) 212.247.0300

The Four Seasons ($$$$)
57 E 57th St
(10022) 212.758.5700
small pets only

The Lowell ($$$$)
28 E 63rd St
(10021) 212.838.1400

The Mayflower ($$$$)
150 Central Park
(10023) 212.265.0060
pet fee

The Peninsula ($$$$)
700 5th Ave
(10019) 212.247.2200
$20/day

The Plaza Hotel ($$$$)
5th Ave At 59th St
(10019) 212.759.3000
small pets accepted

The Regency Hotel ($$$$)
540 Park Ave
(10021) 212.759.4100
sign agreement

The Royalton Hotel ($$$$)
44 W 44th St
(10036) 212.869.4400

The Stanhope ($$$$)
995 5th Ave
(10028) 212.288.5800

The Waldorf Astoria ($$$$)
301 Park Ave
(10022) 212.355.3000

Westbury Hotel ($$$$)
15 E 69th St
(10021) 212.535.2000
small only

● Newark ●
Quality Inn ($$$)
125 N Main St
(14513) 315.331.9500
mgr preapproval reqd

● Newburgh ●
Howard Johnson ($$$)
95 Route 17
(12550) 914.564.4000

The Kelsay
1 Scenic Dr
(12550) 914.562.1477
small only

● Newfane ●
Lake Ontario Motel
3330 Lockport Olcott Rd
(14108) 716.778.5004

● Niagara Falls ●
Best Western ($$$)
7001 Buffalo Ave
(14304) 716.283.7612
small pets with notice

Best Western ($$)
9500 Niagara Falls Blvd
(14304) 716.297.5050
small pets with notice

268

Caravan Motel
6730 Niagara Falls Blvd
(14304) 716.236.0752

Days Inn ($$)
201 Rainbow Blvd
(14303) 716.285.9321

Dunes Motel
5655 Niagara Falls Blvd
(14304) 716.283.6114

Econo Lodge ($$)
7708 Niagara Falls Blvd
(14304) 716.283.0621

Falls Motel
5820 Buffalo Ave
(14304) 716.283.3239

Hospitality Inn
6734 Niagara Falls Blvd
(14304) 716.283.8611

Howard Johnson ($$)
454 Main St
(14301) 716.285.5261

Juniors Motor Inn
5647 Niagara Falls Blvd
(14304) 716.283.4914

Niagara Rainbow Motel ($)
7900 Niagara Falls Blvd
(14304) 716.283.1760

Paris Motel
9890 Niagara Falls Blvd
(14304) 716.297.1710

Pelican Motel ($)
6817 Niagara Falls Blvd
(14304) 716.283.2278

Plaza Court Motel
7680 Niagara Falls Blvd
(14304) 716.283.2638

Radisson Inn ($$$)
3rd St & Old Falls
(14303) 716.285.3361

Sunrise Inn
6225 Niagara Falls Blvd
(14304) 716.283.9952

The Coachman Motel ($$)
523 3rd St
(14301) 716.285.2295

The Travel Budget Inn ($)
9001 Niagara Falls Blvd
(14304) 716.297.3228

Travelodge ($$)
200 Rainbow Blvd
(14303) 716.285.7316

Trift Lodge
200 Rainbow Blvd
(14303) 716.285.7316
guest rfd

● North Creek ●
Black Mtn Lodge ($$)
Star Rt
(12853) 518.251.2800

Gore Mountain Inn ($$)
Peaceful Valley Rd
(12853) 518.251.2111

● North Tonawanda ●
Royal Motel
3333 Niagara Falls Bld
(14120) 716.692.2724

Starfire Motel
3466 Niagara Falls Blvd
(14120) 716.694.3600

● Norwich ●
Howard Johnson ($$)
75 N Broad St
(13815) 607.334.2200

● Ogdensburg ●
Alta Courts Motel ($)
Riverside Dr
(13669) 315.393.6860

Days Inn ($$)
1200 Patterson St
(13669) 315.393.3200
$7

Quality Inn ($$)
RR 4
(13669) 315.393.4550

Rodeway Inn ($$)
RR 4 Box# 84
(13669) 315.393.3730
$8 per day

Stonefence Hotel ($$)
RR 4 Box# 29
(13669) 315.393.1545

● Old Forge ●
Sunset Motel ($$)
Rt 28 Box# 261
(13420) 315.369.6836

● Oneonta ●
Celtic Motel
112 Oneida St
(13820) 607.432.0860

Holiday Inn
Rt 23
(13820) 607.433.2250

Holiday Inn ($$$)
Rt 23
(13820) 800.465.4329

Super 8 ($$)
Rt 23 South
(13820) 607.432.9505
w/permission

● Oswego ●
Chestnut Grove Inn
7096 Hwy 104
(13126) 315.342.2547

Econo Lodge ($$)
70 E 1st St
(13126) 315.343.1600

K&G Lodge
94 Creamery Rd
(13126) 315.343.8171

Sunset Cabins
RR 10 Box# 43
(13126) 315.343.2166

The Thomas Inn
309 W Seneca St
(13126) 315.343.4900

Twin Pines Cabins
1881 Cr 1
(13126) 315.343.2475

● Owego ●
Sunrise Motel ($)
3778 Waverly Rd
(13827) 607.687.5666

● Painted Post ●
Best Western ($$)
US 15 & Hwy 17
(14870) 607.962.2456

Econo Lodge ($$)
200 Robert Dann Blvd
(14870) 800.424.4777

Econo Lodge ($$)
200 Robert Dann Blvd
(14870) 607.962.4444

Lampliter Motel ($)
9316 Victory Hwy
(14870) 607.962.1184

Stiles Motel ($)
9239 Victory Hwy
(14870) 800.331.3290

Stiles Motel ($)
9329 Victory Hwy
(14870) 607.962.5221

● Palenville ●
Hickory Notch Cabins
Box# 279
(12463) 518.678.3259

● Parish ●
Montclair Motel ($)
Rt 69
(13131) 315.625.7100

● Parksville ●
Best Western ($$)
Tanzman Rd
(12768) 914.292.6700

● Peekskill ●
Peekskill Inn ($$$)
634 Main St
(10566) 914.739.1500

● Penn Yan ●
Viking Motel ($$)
680 E Lake Rd
(14527) 315.536.7061

● Pine City ●
Rufus Tanner House
60 Sagetown Rd
(14871) 607.732.0213

● Pittsford ●
The Depot Inn ($$$)
41 N Main St
(14534) 716.381.9900

$=under $35 $$=$35-60 $$$=$60-100 $$$$=over $100

● Plainview ●
Residence Inn ($$$$)
9 Gerhard Rd
(11803) 516.433.6200
fee/day & cleaning fee

● Plattsburgh ●
Econo Lodge ($$)
610 Upper Cornelia St
(12901) 518.561.1500

Howard Johnson ($$)
446 Rt 3 Cornelia St
(12901) 518.561.7750

Plattsburgh Hotel ($$$)
412 Route 3
(12901) 518.561.5000

Super 8 ($$)
7129 Route 9
(12901) 518.562.8888
pets w/permission

● Port Jefferson ●
Danfords Inn ($$$)
25 E Broadway
(11777) 800.332.6367

● Port Jervis ●
Comfort Inn ($$$)
Rt 23 & Greenville Tpk
(12771) 914.856.6611
mgr preapproval reqd

● Poughkeepsie ●
Econo Lodge ($$)
426 South Rd
(12601) 914.452.6600

Holiday Inn ($$$)
341 South Rd
(12601) 914.473.1151
mgr preapproval reqd

● Pulaski ●
Big A Lodge
7542 Salina St
(13142) 315.298.5509

Clark Cottages
Rd 2 Lake Rd
(13142) 315.298.4778

Double Eagle Lodge
3268 Hwy 13
(13142) 315.298.3326

Driftwood Motel
5240 US Route 11
(13142) 315.298.5000

Fish Hawk Lodge
1091 Albion Cross Rd
(13142) 315.298.5841

Golden Fish Cabins
Rd 1 Rt 3
(13142) 315.298.6556

Laurdon Heights
7489 Lewis St
(13142) 315.298.6091

Mannings Pt Ontario
Rt 3
(13142) 315.298.2509

Maple Grove Sport
2870 Hwy 13
(13142) 315.298.7256

Port Lodge Motel
7469 Scenic Hwy
(13142) 315.298.6876

Rainbow Shores Hotel
RR 2
(13142) 315.298.9982

Rainbow Shores Motel
348 Rainbow Shores Rd
(13142) 315.298.4407

Redwood Motel
Box# 315
(13142) 315.298.4717

The Angler Lodge
Rt 13
(13142) 315.298.4773

The Trading Post
7539 Rome St
(13142) 315.298.4042

Whitakers Motel
7700 Rome Rd
(13142) 315.298.6162

Wild Bills Lodge
7453 Lewis St
(13142) 315.298.2461

● Purling ●
Bavarian Manor Inn
Cr 24
(12470) 518.622.3261

● Queensbury ●
Wakita Court Motel ($$)
RR 5 Box# 228
(12804) 518.792.0326

● Rensselaer ●
Fort Crailo Motel ($)
110 Columbia Tpke
(12144) 518.472.1360

● Rhinebeck ●
Rhinebeck Motel ($$)
117 Rt 9
(12572) 914.876.5900

Whistle Wood Farm ($$$)
11 Pells Rd
(12572) 914.876.6838

● Ripley ●
Budget Host ($)
Shortman Rd
(14775) 716.736.8000

● Rochester ●
Comfort Inn ($)
395 Buell Rd
(14624) 716.436.4400

Comfort Inn ($$)
1501 Ridge Rd
(14615) 716.621.5700

Econo Lodge ($$)
940 Jefferson Rd
(14623) 716.427.2700

Hampton Inn ($$)
500 Center Place Dr
(14615) 716.663.6070

Hampton Inn ($$$)
717 E Henrietta Rd
(14623) 716.272.7800

Holiday Inn
911 Brooks Ave
(14624) 716.328.6000

Marriott Hotel ($$$)
1890 Ridge Rd
(14615) 716.225.6880
sign waiver on 1st floor

Motel 6 ($$)
155 Buell Rd
(14624) 716.436.2170
1 small pet/room

Radisson Inn ($$$)
175 Jefferson Rd
(14623) 716.475.1910
pet fee

Ramada Inn ($$)
1273 Chili Ave
(14624) 716.464.8800

Residence Inn ($$$)
1300 Jefferson Rd
(14623) 716.272.8850

Towpath Motel ($$)
2323 Monroe Ave
(14618) 716.271.2147

Wellesley Inn ($$)
797 E Henrietta Rd
(14623) 716.427.0130
small $3 per day

Wellesley Inn ($$)
1635 Ridge Rd
(14615) 716.621.2060

● Rock Hill ●
Howard Johnson ($$)
Box# 469
(12775) 914.796.3000

● Rockville Centre ●
Holiday Inn ($$$)
173 Sunrise Hwy
(11570) 516.678.1300
mgr preapproval reqd

● Rome ●
Adirondack Pines ($)
7353 River Rd
(13440) 315.337.4930

American Heritage Inn ($)
799 Lower Lawrence St
(13440) 315.339.3610

Family Inns ($$)
145 E Whitesboro St
(13440) 315.337.9400

Uniondale, NEW YORK

The Paul Revere ($$)
7900 Turin Rd
(13440) 315.336.1776

● Roscoe ●
Roscoe Motel ($$)
Box# 608
(12776) 607.498.5220

● Sackets Harbor ●
Ontario Place Hotel ($$)
103 General Smith Dr
(13685) 315.646.8000

● Salamanca ●
Dudley Hotel ($$)
132 Main St
(14779) 716.945.3200

● Sandy Creek ●
Harris Lodging
Box# 547
(13145) 315.387.5907

Tug Hill Lodge
216 Salisbury St
(13145) 315.387.5326

● Saranac Lake ●
Adirondack Motel ($$)
23 Lake Flower Ave
(12983) 518.891.2116

Comfort Inn ($$)
148 Lake Flower Ave
(12983) 800.221.2222

Hotel At Saranac ($$)
101 Main St
(12983) 518.891.2200

Lake Side Motel ($$)
27 Lake Flower Ave
(12983) 518.891.4333

Placid Motel ($)
120 Lake Flower Ave
(12983) 518.891.2729

The Point ($$$$)
HC 1 Box# 65
(12983) 518.891.5674

● Saratoga Springs ●
Adirondack Motel ($$)
230 West Ave
(12866) 518.584.3510

Community Court Motel ($$)
248 Broadway
(12866) 518.584.6666

Country Club Motel ($$)
306 Church St
(12866) 518.882.6838

Grand Union Motel ($$)
92 S Broadway
(12866) 518.584.9000
$10 fee

Holiday Inn ($$)
232 Broadway
(12866) 518.584.4550
mgr preapproval reqd

Robin Hood Motel
2205 Route 50
(12866) 518.885.8899

Sheraton Inn ($$$)
534 Broadway
(12866) 518.584.4000

St Charles Motel ($$)
160 Broadway
(12866) 518.584.2050

St Francis Motel ($$)
177 Broadway
(12866) 518.548.1275

Thorobred Motel
Box# 195
(12866) 518.583.4903

● Saugerties ●
Hojo Inn ($$)
2764 Route 32
(12477) 914.246.9511

● Schenectady ●
Best Western ($$)
2788 Hamburg St
(12303) 518.355.1111

Holiday Inn ($$$)
100 Nott Ter
(12308) 518.393.4141
mgr preapproval reqd

Super 8 ($$)
3083 Carman Rd
(12303) 518.355.2190
mgr preapproval reqd

● Schroon Lake ●
Blue Ridge Motel ($$)
RR 1 Box# 321
(12870) 518.532.7521

D-R Cabins ($$)
Rt 9 Box# 535
(12870) 518.532.7277

Rawlins Motel
Box# 9
(12870) 518.532.7907

● Shelter Island Heights ●
Beach House Inn ($$$)
Box# 648
(11965) 516.749.0264

● Sidney ●
Country Motel
Rt 7 & E Of Rt 8
(13838) 607.563.1035

● Southampton ●
Cold Spring Bay Resort ($$$)
Country Rd 39
(11968) 516.283.7600

● Spring Glen ●
Gold Mountain Resort ($$$$)
Box# 456
(12483) 914.647.4332

● Spring Valley ●
Econo Lodge ($$)
Rt 59
(10977) 800.424.4777

● Suffern ●
Wellesley Inn ($$)
17 N Airmont Rd
(10901) 914.368.1900

● Syracuse ●
Best Western ($$$)
701 E Genesee St
(13210) 315.479.7000

Best Western ($$$)
Hancock Airport
(13212) 315.455.7362

Days Inn ($$)
6609 Thompson Rd
(13206) 315.437.5998
$5

Holiday Inn
6701 Buckley Rd
(13212) 315.457.7877

Holiday Inn ($$)
100 Farrell Rd
(13209) 315.457.8700

Milton Inn ($)
6578 Thompson Rd
(13206) 315.463.8555

Ramada Ltd ($$)
6590 Thompson Rd
(13206) 315.463.0202
$10 fee

Red Roof Inn ($$)
6614 Thompson Rd
(13206) 315.437.3309

● Ticonderoga ●
Circle Court Motel ($$)
440 Montcalm St
(12883) 518.585.7660

Rancho House ($$$)
RR 1 79 Baldwin Rd
(12883) 518.585.6596

● Tonawanda ●
Microtel ($$)
1 Hospitality Centre Way
(14150) 716.693.8100

● Troy ●
Best Western ($$)
1800 6th Ave
(12180) 518.274.3210

● Tupper Lake ●
Pine Terrace Motel ($$)
Moody Rd
(12986) 518.359.9258

Red Top Inn ($$)
90 Moody Rd
(12986) 518.359.9209

Sunset Park Motel ($$)
De Mars Blvd
(12986) 518.359.3995

● Uniondale ●
Marriott Hotel ($$$$)
101 James Doolittle Blvd
(11553) 516.794.3800

$=under $35 $$=$35-60 $$$=$60-100 $$$$=over $100

NEW YORK, Upper Jay

● Upper Jay ●
Grand View Motel ($$)
Hwy 86
(12987) 518.946.2209

● Utica ●
A 1 Motel ($)
238 N Genesee St
(13502) 315.735.6698

Best Western ($$$)
175 N Genesee St
(13502) 315.732.4121

Happy Journey Motel ($)
300 N Genesee St
(13502) 315.738.1959

Howard Johnson ($$)
302 N Genesee St
(13502) 315.724.4141

Motel 6 ($$)
150 N Genesee St
(13502) 315.797.8743
1 small pet/room

Radisson Inn ($$$)
200 N Genesee St
(13502) 800.333.3333

Red Roof Inn ($$)
20 Weaver St
(13502) 315.724.7128
small pets only

Super 8 ($$)
309 N Genesee St
(13502) 315.797.0964
call re: fees

● Vestal ●
Holiday Inn
4105 Vestal Pkwy
(13850) 607.729.6371

Howard Johnson ($)
3601 Vestal Pkwy
(13850) 607.729.6181

Residence Inn ($$$)
4610 Vestal Pkwy
(13850) 607.770.8500

● Victor ●
Microtel ($)
7498 Main St Fishers
(14564) 716.924.9240

● Waddington ●
Riverview Motel ($$)
RR 1 Box# 14
(13694) 315.388.5912

● Waterloo ●
Holiday Inn ($$)
2568 Hwy 414
(13165) 315.539.5011
mgr preapproval reqd

● Watertown ●
City-Line Motel ($)
19226 US Route 11
(13601) 315.782.9619

Econo Lodge ($$)
1030 Arsenal St
(13601) 315.762.5500

New Parrot Motel ($)
5791 Outer Washington St
(13601) 315.788.5080

Quality Inn ($$)
1190 Arsenal St
(13601) 315.788.6800

Rainbow Motel
RR 6 Box# 20
(13601) 315.788.2830

Super 8 ($)
104 Breen Ave
(13601) 315.786.6666
call re: fees

● Watkins Glen ●
Chalet Leon ($$)
Box# 388
(14891) 607.546.7171

Glen Motor Inn ($$$)
3380 Rt 14
(14891) 607.535.2706

● Waverly ●
Obriens Inn ($$)
6312 Cr 60
(14892) 607.565.2817

● Weedsport ●
Best Western ($$)
2709 Erie Dr
(13166) 315.834.6623
small pets

Port Forty Motel ($)
9050 Rt 24
(13166) 315.834.6198

● West Nyack ●
Nyack Motor Lodge ($$)
Rt 303
(10994) 914.358.4100

● West Point ●
Hotel Thayer
West Point
(10996) 914.446.4731

● Westbury ●
Island Inn ($$$)
Old Country Rd
(11590) 516.228.9500

● Westmoreland ●
Carriage Motor Inn ($)
Box# 379
(13490) 315.853.3561

● White Plains ●
Residence Inn
5 Barker Ave
(10601) 914.761.7700

White Plains Hotel ($$)
S Broadway
(10601) 914.761.8100

● Whitehall ●
Apple Orchard Inn ($$$)
Old Fairhaven Rd
(12887) 518.499.0180

● Wilmington ●
High Valley Motel ($$)
HC 2 Box# 13
(12997) 518.946.2355

Holiday Lodge ($)
Box# 38
(12997) 518.946.2251

Ledge Rock Motel ($$)
HC 2 Box# 34
(12997) 518.946.2302

The Hungry Trout Motel ($$)
W Rt 86
(12997) 518.946.2217
must call ahead

Winkelman Motel ($$)
NY 86
(12997) 518.946.7761

● Woodbury ●
Ramada Ltd ($$)
8030 Jericho Tpke
(11797) 516.921.8500

● Woodstock ●
Pinecrest Lodge
Woodstock
(12498) 914.679.2814
guest reader referred

● Youngstown ●
River Loft
425 Main St
(14174) 716.745.3217

Well Behaved

CALL AHEAD!

NO Fleas

Policies Subject to Change

Be Discreet

North Carolina

● Aberdeen ●
Best Western ($$$)
1500 Sandhills Blvd
(28315) 910.944.2367

Bryant House ($$)
214 N Poplar St
(28315) 919.944.3300
mgmt requests reservation

Motel 6 ($)
1408 Sandhills Blvd
(28315) 910.944.5633
1 small pet/room

● Albemarle ●
Rodeway Inn ($$)
200 Henson St
(28001) 704.982.3939

● Asheville ●
Econo Lodge ($$)
190 Tunnel Rd
(28805) 704.254.9521

Glen&Ednas Cottage
Box# 98
(28801) 704.684.9938
rfd

Holiday Inn ($$)
1450 Tunnel Rd
(28805) 704.298.5611
mgr preapproval reqd

Motel 6 ($)
1415 Tunnel Rd
(28805) 704.299.3040
1 small pet/room

Red Roof Inn ($)
16 Crowell Rd
(28806) 704.667.9803

● Banner Elk ●
Beech Mtn Chalets
503 Beech Mount' Pkwy
(28604) 704.387.4251

Last Recluse
816 Burma Rd
(28604) 704.963.5710
owner referred

● Battleboro ●
Days Inn ($$)
RR 1 Box# 155
(27809) 919.446.0621
$3 per day

Masters Economy Inn ($)
RR 1 Box# 162
(27809) 919.442.8075

Motel 6 ($)
RR 1 Box# 162A
(27809) 919.977.3505
1 small pet/room

● Biscoe ●
Days Inn
531 Main
(27209) 910.428.2525
$5

● Black Mountain ●
Super 8 ($$)
101 Flat Creek Rd
(28711) 704.669.8076
call re: fees

● Boone ●
Scottish Inn ($)
782 Blowing Rock Rd
(28607) 704.264.2483

● Burlington ●
Comfort Inn ($$)
978 Plantation Dr
(27215) 910.227.3681
mgr preapproval reqd

Motel 6 ($)
2155 W Hanford Rd
(27215) 910.226.1325
1 small pet/room

● Buxton ●
Whalebone Motel
Mile 17 Beach Rd
(27920) 919.441.7423
$5/day or $30/wk

● Cashiers ●
High Hampton Inn ($$$)
Box# 338
(28717) 704.743.2411

● Charlotte ●
Bradley Motel ($)
4200 I-85S
(28214) 704.392.3206
small pets only

Comfort Inn ($$)
5111 N Service Rd
(28269) 704.598.0007

Cricket Inn ($)
219 Archdale Dr
(28217) 704.527.8500

Days Inn
601 Tryon St
(28202) 704.333.4733

Days Inn
1408 Sugar Creek
(28213) 704.597.8110
$5

Econo Lodge ($$)
I-85 Sugar Creek Rd
(28213) 704.597.0470

Holiday Inn
212 Woodlawn Rd
(28217) 704.525.8350

Holiday Inn ($$$)
8520 University Park
(28262) 704.547.0999
mgr preapproval reqd

Hyatt Hotel ($$$)
5501 Carnegie Blvd
(28209) 704.554.1234

La Quinta Inn ($$)
3100 I-85 S Service Rd
(28208) 704.393.5306
call re: fees

La Quinta Inn ($$)
7900 Nations Ford Rd
(28217) 704.522.7110
call re: fees

Motel 6 ($)
3430 Saint Vardell Ln
(28217) 704.527.0144
1 small pet/room

Red Roof Inn ($)
3300 I-85
(28208) 704.392.2316

Red Roof Inn ($)
5116 I-85
(28206) 704.596.8222

Red Roof Inn ($)
131 Red Roof Dr
(28217) 704.529.1020

Residence Inn ($$$)
8503 N Tryon St
(28262) 704.547.1122
small pets

Sheraton Inn ($$$$)
3315 I-85
(28208) 704.392.1200
small pets only

● Cherokee ●
Hampton Inn ($$$)
Box# 1926
(28719) 704.497.3115

● Concord ●
Holiday Inn
1601 US 29
(28025) 704.786.5181

● Cornelius ●
Holiday Inn ($$$)
19901 Holiday Ln
(28031) 704.842.9120
mgr preapproval reqd

● Dunn ●
Best Western ($$)
603 Spring Branch Rd
(28334) 910.892.2162
small pets

Days Inn ($$)
1125 E Broad St
(28334) 910.892.1293

Econo Lodge ($$)
513 Spring Branch Rd
(28334) 910.892.6181

● Durham ●
Best Western ($$)
5400 US 70
(27705) 919.383.2508

Carolina Duke Motel ($)
2517 Guess Rd
(27705) 919.286.0771

NORTH CAROLINA, Durham

Days Inn ($$)
I-85 & Redwood Rd
(27704) 919.688.4338
in kennel /crate

Hampton Inn ($$$)
1816 Hillandale Rd
(27705) 919.471.6100

Howard Johnson ($$)
1800 Hillandale Rd
(27705) 919.477.7381

Red Roof Inn ($$)
2000 I-85 Service Rd
(27705) 919.471.9882

Red Roof Inn ($)
5623 Durham (27707)
919.489.9421

Red Roof Inn ($)
4405 Hwy 55
(27713) 919.361.1950

Residence Inn ($$$$)
1919 Hwy 54
(27713) 919.361.1266

● Fayetteville ●
Howard Johnson ($$)
1965 Cedar Creek Rd
(28301) 910.323.8282

Motel 6 ($)
2076 Cedar Creek Rd
(28301) 910.485.8122
1 small pet/room

● Garner ●
Hampton Inn ($$$)
US 70 & 110
(27529) 919.772.6500

● Gastonia ●
Days Inn ($)
1700 N Chester St
(28052) 704.864.9981
$5 per day

Motel 6 ($)
1721 Broadcast St
(28052) 704.868.4900
1 small pet/room

● Goldsboro ●
Best Western ($$)
801 US 70 E Byp
(27534) 919.735.7911
small pets @ mgrs discretion

Motel 6 ($)
701 US 70 E Byp
(27534) 919.734.4542
1 small pet/room

● Graham ●
Econo Lodge ($)
640 E Harden St
(27253) 910.228.0231

● Greensboro ●
Days Inn ($$)
501 S Regional Rd
(27409) 910.668.0476

Howard Johnson ($$)
3030 High Point Rd
(27403) 910.294.4920

Motel 6 ($)
605 S Regional Rd
(27409) 910.668.2085
1 small pet/room

Motel 6 ($)
831 Greenhaven Dr
(27406) 910.854.0993
1 small pet/room

Red Roof Inn ($$)
615 S Regional Rd
(27409) 910.271.2636

Red Roof Inn ($)
2101 W Meadowview Rd
(27403) 910.852.6560

Scottish Inn ($)
2608 Preddy Blvd
(27407) 910.299.6131

● Greenville ●
Howard Johnson ($$)
702 S Memorial Dr
(27834) 919.758.0643

Red Roof Inn ($$)
301 Greenville Blvd SE
(27858) 919.756.2792

● Henderson ●
Days Inn ($)
I-85 & Ruin Creek Rd
(27536) 919.492.4041
mgr preapproval reqd

● Hendersonville ●
Comfort Inn ($$)
206 Mitchelle Dr
(28792) 704.693.8800
mgr preapproval reqd

Quality Inn ($$)
201 Sugarloaf Rd
(28792) 704.692.7231
mgr preapproval reqd

● Hickory ●
Econo Lodge ($$)
325 US 70 SW
(28603) 704.328.2111

Howard Johnson ($$)
483 Hwy 70 & 321
(28601) 704.322.1600

Red Roof Inn ($)
1184 Lenoir Rhyne Blvd SE
(28602) 704.323.1500

● High Point ●
Howard Johnson ($$)
2000 Brentwood St
(27263) 910.886.4141

Motel 6 ($)
200 Ardale Dr
(27260) 910.841.7717
1 small pet/room

● Jacksonville ●
Onslow Inn ($$)
201 Marine Blvd
(28540) 800.763.3151

Super 8 ($$)
2149 N Marine Blvd
(28546) 910.455.6888
call re: fees

● Kenly ●
Econo Lodge ($)
Box# 577
(27542) 919.284.1000

● Kill Devil Hills ●
Budget Host ($$)
Outer Banks
(27948) 919.441.2503

Hampton Inn ($$)
804 Virginia Dare Tr
(27948) 919.441.0411

Ramada Inn ($$)
1701 Virginia Dare Tr
(27948) 919.441.2151
ground floor

● Kinston ●
Hampton Inn ($$)
1403 Richlands Rd
(28504) 919.523.1400

● Laurinburg ●
Hampton Inn ($$)
115 Hampton Cir
(28352) 910.277.1516

● Lenoir ●
Days Inn ($$)
206 Blowing Rock Blvd
(28645) 704.754.0731

● Lumberton ●
Best Western ($$)
201 Jackson Ct
(28358) 910.618.9799

Days Inn ($$)
3030 N Roberts Ave
(28358) 910.738.6401
$5 in kennel

Econo Lodge ($)
3591 Lackey St
(28358) 800.424.4777

Howard Johnson ($)
3530 Capuano St
(28358) 910.738.4281

Motel 6 ($)
2361 Lackey St
(28358) 910.738.2410
1 small pet/room

Quality Inn ($)
3608 Kahn Dr
(28358) 910.738.8261
mgr preapproval reqd

● Marion ●
Econo Lodge ($$)
2035 US 221
(28752) 704.659.7940

● Mooresville ●
Ramada Ltd ($$)
I-77 At Hwy 150
(28115) 704.664.6556

● Morganton ●
Holiday Inn ($$)
2400 S Sterling St
(28655) 704.437.0171
mgr preapproval reqd

Red Carpet Inn ($$)
2217 S Sterling St
(28655) 704.437.6980

● Morrisville ●
Budgetel ($$)
1001 Aerial Center Pkwy
(27560) 919.481.3600

● Murphy ●
Comfort Inn ($$)
114 US 64
(28906) 704.837.8030
mgr preapproval reqd

● Nags Head ●
Whalebone Motel
Box# 185
(27959) 919.441.7423

● Raeford ●
Days Inn ($$)
Hwy 401 Byp & Teal Dr
(28376) 910.904.1050
$4

● Raleigh ●
Best Western ($$$)
6619 Glenwood Ave
(27612) 919.782.8650

Days Inn ($$)
6329 Glenwood Ave
(27612) 919.781.7904

Econo Lodge ($$)
5110 Holly Ridge Dr
(27612) 919.782.3201

Howard Johnson ($)
3120 New Bern Ave
(27610) 919.231.3000

Motel 6 ($)
3921 Arrow Dr
(27612) 919.782.7071
1 small pet/room

Motel 6 ($$)
1401 Buck Jones Rd
(27606) 919.467.6171
1 small pet/room

Red Roof Inn ($)
3520 Maitland Dr
(27610) 919.231.0200

Sundown Inn North ($$)
3801 Capital Blvd
(27604) 919.790.8480

The Plantation Inn ($$)
6401 Capital Blvd
(27616) 919.876.1411
guest referred

Velvet Cloak Inn ($$$)
1505 Hillsborough St
(27605) 800.334.4372

● Roanoke Rapids ●
Holiday Inn ($$$)
100 Holiday Dr
(27870) 919.537.1031
mgr preapproval reqd

Motel 6 ($)
1911 Weldon Rd
(27870) 919.537.5252
1 small pet/room

● Rowland ●
Days Inn ($)
RR 2 Box# 187
(28383) 910.422.3366
pets in kennels only

● Roxboro ●
Days Inn ($)
1006 N Madison Blvd
(27573) 910.599.9276

● Rutherfordton ●
Carrier Houses ($$)
423 N Main St
(28139) 704.287.4222

● Salisbury ●
Days Inn ($)
1810 Lutheran Synod Dr
(28144) 704.633.4211
$5/pets

Hampton Inn ($$)
1001 Klumac Rd
(28147) 704.637.8000

Holiday Inn ($$$)
530 Jake Alexander Blvd
(28144) 704.637.3100
mgr preapproval reqd

Rodeway Inn ($$)
321 Bendix Dr
(28146) 704.636.7065

● Sanford ●
Palomino Motel ($)
Box# 777
(27331) 919.776.7531

● Selma ●
Days Inn ($)
I-95 & 70
(27576) 919.965.3762
in kennel

● Smithfield ●
Howard Johnson ($)
I-96& US70
(27577) 919.934.7176

Log Cabin Motel ($$)
RR 2 Box# 447
(27577) 919.934.1534

● Southport ●
Port Motel ($$)
4821 Long Beach Rd
(28461) 910.457.4800

● Statesville ●
Holiday Inn
740 Sullivan Rd
(28677) 704.872.4101

Red Roof Inn ($)
1508 E Broad St
(28677) 704.878.2051

Super 8 ($$)
1125 Greenland Dr
(28677) 704.878.9888
small under 35 lbs. w/
permission

● Tarboro ●
Lady Ann ($$)
1205 N Main St
(27886) 919.641.1438

● Wade ●
Days Inn ($$)
RR 1 Box# 216Bb
(28395) 910.323.1255
$6 kennel

● Wadesboro ●
Days Inn
209 Caswell
(28170) 704.694.7070
$4

● Washington ●
Econo Lodge ($)
1220 W 5th St
(27889) 919.946.7781

● Weldon ●
Days Inn ($$)
1611 Roanoke Rapids Rd
(27890) 919.536.4867

Interstate Inn ($)
1606 Roanoke Rapids Rd
(27890) 919.536.4111

● Williamston ●
Holiday Inn
Hwy 17 & 64
(27892) 919.792.3184

● Wilmington ●
Motel 6 ($)
2828 Market St
(28403) 910.762.0120
1 small pet/room

Waterway Lodge ($$)
7246 Wrightsville Ave
(28403) 910.256.3771

● Wilson ●
Holiday Inn
1815 Hwy 301
(27893) 919.243.5111

Quality Inn ($$)
Hwy 301S
(27893) 919.243.5165
mgr preapproval reqd

Well
Behaved

NORTH CAROLINA, Winston Salem

● Winston Salem ●
Hawthorne Inn ($$$)
420 High St
(27101) 910.777.3000

Holiday Inn ($$$)
3050 University Pkwy
(27105) 910.723.2911
mgr preapproval reqd

Motel 6 ($)
3810 Patterson Ave
(27105) 910.767.8240
1 small pet/room

Ramada Ltd ($$)
128 N Cherry St
(27101) 910.723.8861

Residence Inn ($$$)
7835 N Point Blvd
(27106) 910.759.0777
$75 fee

Salem Inn ($$)
127 S Cherry St
(27101) 910.725.8561

North Dakota
● Beach ●
Buckboard Inn ($)
HC 2 Box# 109A
(58621) 701.872.4794

● Bismarck ●
Best Western ($$)
122 E Thayer Ave
(58501) 701.255.1450
small pets

Bismarck Motor Hotel ($)
Box# 1724
(58502) 701.223.2474

Comfort Inn ($$)
1030 Interstate Ave
(58501) 701.223.1911

Days Inn ($)
1300 E Capitol Ave
(58501) 701.223.9151
small pets allowed

Expressway Inn ($)
200 Bismarck Expwy
(58504) 701.222.2900

Fairfield Inn ($$)
1120 Century Ave
(58501) 701.223.9077

Holiday Inn ($$)
605 E Broadway Ave
(58501) 701.255.6000
mgr preapproval reqd

Kelly Inn ($$)
1800 N 12th St
(58501) 701.233.8001

Motel 6 ($)
2433 State St
(58501) 701.255.6878
1 small pet/room

Radisson Inn ($$$)
800 S 3rd St
(58504) 701.258.7700
small pets allowed

Select Inn ($)
1505 Interchange Ave
(58501) 701.223.8060

Super 8 ($$)
1124 E Capitol Ave
(58501) 701.255.1314
call re: fees

● Bowman ●
Budget Host ($)
704 Hwy 12
(58623) 701.523.3243

L-View Motel
Hwy 12 & Hwy 85
(58623) 800.521.0379

North Winds Lodge ($)
Box# 346
(58623) 701.523.5641

Super 8 ($$)
Hwys 12&85
(58623) 701.523.5613
call re: fees

● Carrington ●
Chieftain Motor Lodge ($)
Hwy 281
(58421) 701.652.3131

● Devils Lake ●
Comfort Inn ($$)
215 Hwy 2
(58301) 701.662.6760
mgr preapproval reqd

Days Inn ($$)
RR 5 Box# 8
(58301) 701.662.5381
$3/pet deposit required

Super 8 ($)
1001 Hwy
(58301) 701.662.8656
small pets w/permission

Trails West Motel ($)
Box# 1113
(58301) 701.662.5011

● Dickinson ●
Budget Inn ($)
529 12th St
(58601) 701.225.9123

Comfort Inn ($)
493 Elk Dr
(58601) 701.264.7300
mgr preapproval reqd

Hospitality Inn ($$)
Box# 1778
(58602) 701.227.1853

Nodak Motel ($)
600 E Villard St
(58601) 701.225.5119

Rodeway Inn ($)
1000 W Villard St
(58601) 701.225.6703

Select Inn ($)
642 12th St
(58601) 701.227.1891

● Drayton ●
Motel 6 ($)
Box# 116
(58225) 701.454.6464
1 small pet/room

● Fargo ●
Americinn Motel ($$)
1423 35th St SW
(58103) 701.234.9946

Best Western ($$$)
3333 13th Ave
(58103) 701.253.3333

Best Western ($$)
3800 Main Ave
(58103) 701.282.2143
small pets only

Comfort Inn ($$)
1407 35th St
(58103) 701.280.9666
mgr preapproval reqd

Comfort Inn ($$)
3825 9th Ave SW
(58103) 701.282.9596
mgr preapproval reqd

Comfort Suites ($$)
1415 35th St
(58103) 701.280.9666
mgr preapproval reqd

Country Suites ($$$)
3316 13th Ave
(58103) 701.234.0565

Days Inn ($$)
1507 19th Ave
(58102) 701.232.0000
$15 dep

Econo Lodge ($)
1401 35th St
(58103) 701.232.3412

Fairfield Inn ($$)
3902 9th Ave
(58103) 701.281.0494

Holiday Inn ($$$)
3803 13th Ave
(58103) 701.282.2700
mgr preapproval reqd

Holiday Inn
1040 40th St
(58103) 701.282.2000

Motel 6 ($)
1202 36th St
(58103) 701.232.0251
1 small pet/room

Motel 75 ($)
3402 14th Ave
(58103) 701.232.1321

Be Discreet

Radisson Inn ($$$)
201 5th St
(58102) 701.232.7363
small pets allowed

Rodeway Inn ($)
2202 S University Dr
(58103) 701.239.8022

Select Inn ($)
1025 38th St SW
(58103) 701.282.6300

Super 8 ($$)
301 3rd Ave
(58102) 701.232.8851
call re: fees

Super 8 ($)
3518 Interstate Blvd
(58103) 701.232.9202
$3/day w/permission

Super 8 ($)
825 Main Ave
(58078) 701.282.7121
pets w/permission

● Garrison ●
Garrison Motel ($)
Box# 99
(58540) 701.463.2858

● Grafton ●
Leonard Motel
Hwy 17 West
(58237) 701.352.1730

● Grand Forks ●
Comfort Inn ($$)
3251 30th Ave
(58201) 701.775.7503
mgr preapproval reqd

Country Inn ($$)
3350 32nd Ave
(58201) 701.775.5000

Days Inn ($$)
3101 S 34th St
(58201) 701.775.0060

Econo Lodge ($)
900 N 43rd St
(58203) 701.746.4444

Fairfield Inn ($$)
3051 S 34th St
(58201) 701.775.7910
smoking rooms

Plainsman Motel ($)
2201 Gateway Dr
(58203) 701.775.8134
call ahead

North Star Inn ($)
2100 S Washington St
(58201) 701.772.8151

Rodeway Inn ($)
4001 Gateway Dr
(58203) 701.795.9960

Select Inn ($)
1000 N 42nd St
(58203) 701.775.0555

Super 8 ($$)
1122 N 43rd St
(58203) 701.775.8138
pets w/permission

● Jamestown ●
Best Western ($$)
Hwy 281
(58401) 701.252.3611

Comfort Inn ($$)
811 20th St SW
(58401) 701.252.7125
mgr preapproval reqd

Gladstone Select ($$)
Box# 989
(58402) 701.252.0700

Ranch House Motel ($)
408 Business Loop
(58401) 701.252.0222

● Lakota ●
Sunlac Inn ($)
Box# 648
(58344) 701.701.2487

● Langdon ●
Langdon Motor Inn ($)
210 9th Ave
(58249) 701.256.3600

● Linton ●
Willows Motel ($)
Box# 882
(58552) 701.254.4555

● Mandan ●
Best Western ($$)
2611 Old Red Trl
(58554) 701.663.7401

● Minot ●
Best Western ($$)
1510 26th Ae SW
(58701) 701.852.4300

Casa Motel ($)
1900 US 2 & 52 Byp
(58701) 701.852.2352

Comfort Inn ($$)
1515 22nd Ave SW
(58701) 701.852.2201
mgr preapproval reqd

Days Inn ($$)
2100 4th St SW
(58701) 701.852.3646
small pets allowed

Fairfield Inn ($$)
900 24th Ave SW
(58701) 701.838.2424
small in smoking rooms

Holiday Inn ($$)
2200 Burdick Expy
(58702) 701.852.2504
mgr preapproval reqd

Mid Town Motel ($)
906 E Main St
(58702) 701.845.2830

Select Inn ($)
Box# 460
(58702) 701.852.3411

Super 8 ($)
1315 N Broadway
(58703) 701.852.1817
call re: fees

● Oriska ●
Ashland Motel ($)
2300 W Lakeshore Dr
(58063) 715.682.5503

● Parshall ●
Parshall Motor Inn
Box# 38
(58770) 701.862.3127

● Rolla ●
Northern Lights
Hwy 5 East
(58367) 701.477.6164

● Rugby ●
Econo Lodge ($$)
US 2
(58368) 701.776.5776

● Steele ●
Lone Steer Motel
I-94 Hwy #3
(58482) 701.475.2221

O K Motel
301 3rd Ave Northest
(58482) 701.475.2440

● Valley City ●
Wagon Wheel Inn ($)
930 4th Ae SW
(58072) 701.845.5333

● Wahpeton ●
Comfort Inn ($)
209 13th St
(58075) 701.642.1115
mgr preapproval reqd

Holiday Inn
1800 Two Ten Dr
(58075) 701.642.5000

Super 8 ($$)
995 21st Ave
(58075) 701.642.8731
very small & deposit

● Washburn ●
Scotwood Motel ($)
Box# 1183
(58577) 701.462.8191

● Watford City ●
McKenzie Inn ($)
120 3rd St SW
(58854) 701.842.3980

● West Fargo ●
Days Inn ($)
525 Main Ave
(58078) 701.281.0000

$=under $35 $$=$35-60 $$$=$60-100 $$$$=over $100

● Williston ●
Airport Int'L Inn ($$)
US Rt
(58802) 701.744.0241

El Rancho Motel ($)
Box# 4277
(58802) 701.572.6321

Select Inn ($)
213 35th SW
(58801) 701.572.4242

Super 8 ($)
2324 2nd Ave
(58801) 701.572.8371
pets w/permission

Ohio

● Akron ●
Days Inn ($$)
3237 S Arlington Rd
(44312) 216.644.1204
size limits & fees

Days Inn
3150 Market
(44333) 330.869.9000
small $25 dep

Hampton Inn ($$)
80 Springside Dr
(44333) 330.666.7361

Holiday Inn ($$$)
I-77 & Arlington Rd
(44312) 330.644.7126

Red Roof Inn ($)
2939 S Arlington Rd
(44312) 216.644.7748

Residence Inn ($$$)
120 W Montrose Ave
(44321) 216.666.4811
call for pet room availability

● Alliance ●
Comfort Inn ($$)
2500 W State St
(44601) 330.821.5555
mgr preapproval reqd

● Amherst ●
Motel 6 ($)
704 N Leavitt Rd
(44001) 216.988.3266
1 small pet/room

Travelodge ($$)
934 N Leavitt Rd
(44001) 216.985.1428

● Ashland ●
Amerihost Inn ($$)
741 US 250E
(44805) 419.281.8090

Days Inn ($$)
1423 Cr 1575
(44805) 419.289.0101
mgr preapproval reqd

Travelodge ($$)
736 US 250
(44805) 419.281.0567

● Ashtabula ●
Ho Hum Motel ($)
3801 N Ridge
(44004) 419.358.7000

● Austinburg ●
Holiday Inn
1860 Austinburg
(44010) 216.275.2711

● Bellefontaine ●
Holiday Inn
1134 N Main
(43311) 937.593.8515

● Bowling Green ●
Best Western ($$)
1450 E Wooster St
(43402) 419.352.4671

Buckeye Budget Inn ($$)
1740 E Wooster St
(43402) 419.352.1520

Holley Modge ($$)
1630 E Wooster St
(43402) 419.352.2521

● Broadview Heights ●
Days Inn ($$)
4501 E Royalton Rd
(44147) 216.526.0640
mgr preapproval reqd

● Brookville ●
Days Inn ($$)
100 Parkview Dr
(45309) 513.833.4003
$5/pets

● Bucyrus ●
Days Inn ($$)
1515 N Sandusky Ave
(44820) 419.562.3737
$10

● Burbank ●
Motel Plaza ($)
Rt 1 Box# 8
(44214) 216.624.3012

● Cambridge ●
Fairdale Inn ($)
6405 Glenn Hwy
(43725) 614.432.2304

Holiday Inn
2248 Southgate Pkwy
(43725) 614.432.7313

● Canton ●
Best Suites ($$$)
4914 E Everhard Rd
(44718) 216.499.1011

Canton Fairfield Inn ($$)
5285 Broadmoor Cir NW
(44709) 330.493.7373

Days Inn ($$)
3970 Convenience Cir NW
(44718) 330.493.8883
small w/permission & deposit

Holiday Inn ($$$)
4520 Everhard Rd NW
(44718) 330.494.2770
sign waiver

Red Roof Inn ($)
5353 Inn Circle Ct NW
(44720) 216.499.1970

Residence Inn ($$)
5280 Broadmoor Cir NW
(44709) 330.493.0004

Super 8 ($$)
3950 Convenience Cir NW
(44718) 330.492.5030
call re: fees

● Chillicothe ●
Christopher Inn ($$$)
30 N Plaza Blvd
(45601) 614.774.6835

Comfort Inn ($$)
20 N Plaza Blvd
(45601) 614.775.3500

Days Inn ($$)
1250 N Bridge St
(45601) 614.775.7000
$5

Travelodge ($$)
1135 E Main St
(45601) 614.775.2500

● Cincinnati ●
Amerisuites ($$)
12001 Chase Plaza
(45240) 513.825.9035

Best Western ($$$)
5901 Pfeiffer Rd
(45242) 513.793.4500
$10 fee

Budgetel ($$)
12150 Springfield Pike
(45246) 513.671.2300

Comfort Inn ($$)
9011 Fields-Ertel Rd
(45249) 513.683.9700
mgr preapproval reqd

Days Inn ($$)
US 42 Ex 46
(45241) 513.554.1400
mgr preapproval reqd

Days Inn ($$)
4056 Mt Carmel Tobasco
(45255) 513.528.3800

Holiday Inn ($$$)
3855 Hauck Rd
(45241) 513.563.8330
mgr preapproval reqd

Holiday Inn ($$$)
4501 Eastgate Blvd
(45245) 513.752.4400
mgr preapproval reqd

Holiday Inn ($$$)
2235 E Sharon Rd
(45241) 513.771.0700
mgr preapproval reqd

Homewood Suites ($$$)
2670 E Kemper Rd
(45241) 513.772.8888
under 40 lbs

Howard Johnson ($$)
400 Glensprings Dr
(45246) 513.825.3129

Imperial House West ($$)
5510 Rybolt Rd
(45248) 513.574.6000

Marriott Hotel ($$$)
11320 Chester Rd
(45246) 513.772.1720

Motel 6 ($$)
3960 Nine Mile Rd
(45255) 513.752.2262
1 small pet/room

Motel 6 ($)
3850 Hauck Rd
(45241) 513.563.1123
1 small pet/room

Motel 6 ($)
2000 E Kemper Rd
(45241) 513.772.5944
1 small pet/room

Quality Hotel ($$$)
4747 Montgomery Rd
(45212) 513.351.6600

Red Roof Inn ($$)
5300 Kenney Dr
(45213) 513.531.6589

Red Roof Inn ($)
2301 E Sharon Rd
(45241) 800.843.7663

Red Roof Inn ($)
11345 Chester Rd
(45246) 513.771.5141

Red Roof Inn ($)
4035 Mt Carmel Tobasco
(45255) 513.528.2741

Red Roof Inn ($$)
5900 Pfefifer Rd
(45242) 513.793.8811

Regal Hotel ($$$)
150 W 5th St
(45202) 513.352.2100
under 20 lbs

Residence Inn ($$$)
11401 Reed Hartman Hwy
(45241) 513.530.5060
fee between $70 & $150

Residence Inn ($$)
11689 Chester Rd
(45246) 513.771.2525
call for fee & availability

Sheraton Inn ($$$)
11911 Sheraton Ln
(45246) 513.671.6600
charge

Travelodge ($$)
3244 Central Pkwy
(45225) 513.559.1800

Villager Lodge ($)
7313 Kingsgate Way
(45225) 513.777.5170

Westin Hotel ($$$$)
Fountain Square
(45202) 513.621.7700
small pets accepted

Cincinnati Metro
● Cincinnati ●
Amerisuites ($$)
12001 Chase Plaza
(45240) 513.825.9035

Best Western ($$$)
5901 Pfeiffer Rd
(45242) 513.793.4500
$10 fee

Budgetel ($$)
12150 Springfield Pike
(45246) 513.671.2300

Comfort Inn ($$)
9011 Fields-Ertel Rd
(45249) 513.683.9700
mgr preapproval reqd

Days Inn ($$)
US 42 Exit 46
(45241) 513.554.1400
mgr preapproval reqd

Days Inn ($$)
4056 Mt Carmel Tobasco
(45255) 513.528.3800

Holiday Inn ($$$)
3855 Hauck Rd
(45241) 513.563.8330
mgr preapproval reqd

Holiday Inn ($$$)
4501 Eastgate Blvd
(45245) 513.752.4400
mgr preapproval reqd

Holiday Inn ($$$)
2235 E Sharon Rd
(45241) 513.771.0700
mgr preapproval reqd

Homewood Suites ($$$)
2670 E Kemper Rd
(45241) 513.772.8888
under 40 lbs

Howard Johnson ($$)
400 Glensprings Dr
(45246) 513.825.3129

Imperial House West ($$)
5510 Rybolt Rd
(45248) 513.574.6000

Marriott Hotel ($$$)
11320 Chester Rd
(45246) 513.772.1720

Motel 6 ($$)
3960 Nine Mile Rd
(45255) 513.752.2262
1 small pet/room

Motel 6 ($)
3850 Hauck Rd
(45241) 513.563.1123
1 small pet/room

Motel 6 ($)
2000 E Kemper Rd
(45241) 513.772.5944
1 small pet/room

Quality Hotel ($$$)
4747 Montgomery Rd
(45212) 513.351.6600

Red Roof Inn ($$)
5300 Kenney Dr
(45213) 513.531.6589

Red Roof Inn ($)
2301 E Sharon Rd
(45241) 800.843.7663

Red Roof Inn ($)
11345 Chester Rd
(45246) 513.771.5141

Red Roof Inn ($)
4035 Mt Carmel Tobasco
(45255) 513.528.2741

Red Roof Inn ($$)
5900 Pfefifer Rd
(45242) 513.793.8811

Regal Hotel ($$$)
150 W 5th St
(45202) 513.352.2100
under 20 lbs

Residence Inn ($$$)
11401 Reed Hartman Hwy
(45241) 513.530.5060
fee between $70 & $150

Residence Inn ($$)
11689 Chester Rd
(45246) 513.771.2525
call for fee & availability

Sheraton Inn ($$$)
11911 Sheraton Ln
(45246) 513.671.6600
charge

Travelodge ($$)
3244 Central Pkwy
(45225) 513.559.1800

Villager Lodge ($)
7313 Kingsgate Way
(45225) 513.777.5170

Westin Hotel ($$$$)
At Fountain Square
(45202) 513.621.7700
small pets accepted

● Franklin ●
Comfort Inn ($$)
3458 Commerce Dr
(45005) 513.420.9378

$=under $35 $$=$35-60 $$$=$60-100 $$$$=over $100

Knights Inn ($)
8500 Claude Thomas Rd
(45005) 800.843.5644

Oakbrook Inn ($)
6147 W Sr 122
(45005) 513.424.1201

Super 8 ($$)
3553 Commerce Dr
(45005) 513.422.4888
mgr preapproval reqd

● Lebanon ●
Best Western ($)
674 N Broadway St
(45036) 513.932.4111
small pets

● Mason ●
Best Western ($)
9847 Escort Dr
(45040) 513.398.3633

Days Inn ($$)
9735 Mason Montg'ry
(45040) 513.398.3297

● Middletown ●
Fairfield Inn ($$)
6750 Roosevelt Ave
(45044) 513.424.5444

Holiday Inn
6575 Terhune Dr
(45044) 513.727.8440

● Oxford ●
College View Motel ($)
4000 Oxford Millville Rd
(45056) 513.523.6311

Scottish Inn ($$)
5235 College Corner Rd
(45056) 513.523.6306

End of Cincinnati Metro

● Circleville ●
Hometown Inn ($)
23897 US 23S
(43113) 614.474.6006

Montecello Motel ($)
21530 US 23S
(43113) 614.474.8884

Travelodge ($$)
24701 US 23S
(43113) 614.474.7511

● Cleveland ●
Budgetel ($$)
1421 Golden Gate Blvd
(44124) 216.442.8400

Budgetel ($$)
4222 W 150th St
(44135) 216.251.8500

Embassy Suites ($$$$)
1701 E 12th St
(44114) 216.523.8000
small pets allowed

Marriott Hotel ($$$$)
4277 W 150th St
(44135) 216.252.5333
$50 fee

Marriott Hotel ($$$$)
127 Public Sq
(44114) 216.696.9200

Motel 6 ($)
7210 Engle Rd
(44130) 216.234.0990
1 small pet/room

Red Roof Inn ($$)
17555 Bagley Rd
(44130) 216.243.2441

Residence Inn ($$$$)
17525 Rosbough Blvd
(44130) 216.234.6688
call for fee & availability

● Clyde ●
Plaza Motel ($)
500 E McPherson Hwy
(43410) 419.547.6514

● Columbus ●
Amerisuties ($$$)
7490 Vantage Dr
(43235) 614.846.4355

Days Inn ($)
5930 Scarborough Blvd
(43232) 614.868.9290
small pets allowed

Days Inn ($)
1700 Clara Ave
(43211) 614.299.4300

Days Inn ($$)
3160 Olentangy River Rd
(43202) 614.261.0523
$5 fee

Days Inn ($)
1559 W Broad St
(43222) 614.275.0388
size limits & fees

Econo Lodge ($)
920 N Wilson Rd
(43204) 614.274.8581

Hampton Inn ($$)
1100 Mediterranean Ave
(43229) 614.848.9686

Holiday Inn
175 Hutchinson
(43235) 614.885.3334

Holiday Inn ($$$)
328 W Lane Ave
(43201) 614.294.4848
mgr preapproval reqd

Homewood Suites ($$$)
115 Hutchinson Ave
(43235) 614.785.0001

Howard Johnson ($$)
1070 Dublin Grandview Ave
(43215) 614.486.4554

Knights Inn ($$)
1300 Dublin Granville
(43229) 614.846.7635
size limits & fees

Knights Inn ($)
4320 Groves Rd
(43232) 614.864.0600

Marriott Hotel ($$$$)
6500 Doubletree Ave
(43229) 614.885.1885

Microtel ($)
7500 Vantage Dr
(43235) 614.436.0556

Motel 6 ($)
5500 Renner Rd
(43228) 614.870.0993
1 small pet/room

Motel 6 ($)
5910 Scarborough Blvd
(43232) 614.755.2250
1 small pet/room

Motel 6 ($$)
1289 Dublin Granville
(43229) 614.846.9860
1 small pet/room

Parke University Hotel ($$)
3025 Olentangy River Rd
(43202) 614.267.1111

Quality Inn ($$)
4801 E Broad St
(43213) 614.861.0321
mgr preapproval reqd

Radisson Inn ($$$)
4900 Sinclair Rd
(43229) 614.846.0300
small pets allowed

Ramada Inn ($$)
I-70 & Hamilton
(43232) 614.861.7220

Ramada Inn ($$)
4601 W Broad St
(43228) 614.878.5301

Red Roof Inn ($)
750 Morse Rd
(43229) 614.846.8520

Red Roof Inn ($$)
5001 Renner Rd
(43228) 614.878.9245

Red Roof Inn ($)
441 Ackerman Rd
(43202) 614.267.9941

Residence Inn ($$$$)
6191 Zumstein Dr
(43229) 614.431.1819
call for pet room availability

Residence Inn ($$$$)
2084 S Hamilton Rd
(43232) 614.864.8844
daily chrg; call re pets

Policies Subject to Change

$=under $35 $$=$35-60 $$$=$60-100 $$$$=over $100

Travelodge ($)
7480 N High St
(43235) 614.431.2525

Village Lodge ($$)
5950 Scarborough Blvd
(43232) 614.864.4670

Columbus Metro

● Circleville ●
Hometown Inn ($)
23897 US 23S
(43113) 614.474.6006

Montecello Motel ($)
21530 US 23S
(43113) 614.474.8884

Travelodge ($$)
24701 US 23S
(43113) 614.474.7511

● Columbus ●
Amerisuties ($$$)
7490 Vantage Dr
(43235) 614.846.4355

Days Inn ($)
5930 Scarborough Blvd
(43232) 614.868.9290
small pets allowed

Days Inn ($)
1700 Clara Ave
(43211) 614.299.4300

Days Inn ($$)
3160 Olentangy River Rd
(43202) 614.261.0523
$5 fee

Days Inn ($)
1559 W Broad St
(43222) 614.275.0388
size limits & fees

Econo Lodge ($)
920 N Wilson Rd
(43204) 614.274.8581

Hampton Inn ($$)
1100 Mediterranean Ave
(43229) 614.848.9686

Holiday Inn
175 Hutchinson
(43235) 614.885.3334

Holiday Inn ($$$)
328 W Lane Ave
(43201) 614.294.4848
mgr preapproval reqd

Homewood Suites ($$$)
115 Hutchinson Ave
(43235) 614.785.0001

Howard Johnson ($$)
1070 Dublin Grandview Ave
(43215) 614.486.4554

Knights Inn ($$)
1300 Dublin Granville
(43229) 614.846.7635
size limits & fees

Knights Inn ($)
4320 Groves Rd
(43232) 614.864.0600

Marriott Hotel ($$$$)
6500 Doubletree Ave
(43229) 614.885.1885

Microtel ($)
7500 Vantage Dr
(43235) 614.436.0556

Motel 6 ($)
5500 Renner Rd
(43228) 614.870.0993
1 small pet/room

Motel 6 ($)
5910 Scarborough Blvd
(43232) 614.755.2250
1 small pet/room

Motel 6 ($$)
1289 Dublin Granville
(43229) 614.846.9860
1 small pet/room

Parke University Hotel ($$)
3025 Olentangy River Rd
(43202) 614.267.1111

Quality Inn ($$)
4801 E Broad St
(43213) 614.861.0321
mgr preapproval reqd

Radisson Inn ($$$)
4900 Sinclair Rd
(43229) 614.846.0300
small pets allowed

Ramada Inn ($$)
I-70 & Hamilton
(43232) 614.861.7220

Ramada Inn ($$)
4601 W Broad St
(43228) 614.878.5301

Red Roof Inn ($)
750 Morse Rd
(43229) 614.846.8520

Red Roof Inn ($$)
5001 Renner Rd
(43228) 614.878.9245

Red Roof Inn ($)
441 Ackerman Rd
(43202) 614.267.9941

Residence Inn ($$$$)
6191 Zumstein Dr
(43229) 614.431.1819
call for pet room availability

Residence Inn ($$$$)
2084 S Hamilton Rd
(43232) 614.864.8844
daily chrg; call re pets

Travelodge ($)
7480 N High St
(43235) 614.431.2525

Village Lodge ($$)
5950 Scarborough Blvd
(43232) 614.864.4670

● Delaware ●
Travelodge ($$)
1001 US 23
(43015) 614.369.4421

● Dublin ●
Budgetel ($$)
6145 Parkcenter Cir
(43017) 614.792.8300

Red Roof Inn ($)
5125 Post Rd
(43017) 614.764.3993

Residence Inn ($$$$)
435 Metro Pl S
(43017) 614.791.0403
call for fee & availability

Stouffer ($$$)
600 Metro Pl
(43017) 614.764.2200

Woodfin Suites Hotel ($$$)
4130 Tuller Rd
(43017) 614.766.7762

● Grove City ●
Best Western ($$)
4026 Jackpot Rd
(43123) 614.875.7770
small pets only w/$5 fee

Red Roof Inn ($)
1900 Stringtown Rd
(43123) 614.875.8543

● Lancaster ●
Best Western ($$)
1858 N Memorial Dr
(43130) 614.653.3040

Knights Inn ($$)
1327 River Valley Blvd
(43130) 614.687.4823
call for size limits & fees

● Newark ●
Holiday Inn ($$)
733 Hebron Rd
(43056) 614.522.1165

Hometown Inn ($$)
1266 Hebron Rd
(43056) 614.522.6112

Howard Johnson ($$)
775 Hebron Rd
(43056) 614.522.3191

Mount Vernon Inn ($$)
601 W High St
(43058) 614.392.9881

Super 8 ($$)
1177 Hebron Rd
(43056) 800.800.8000
call re: fees

● Reynoldsburg ●
Best Western ($$)
2100 Brice Rd
(43068) 614.864.1280

La Quinta Inn ($$)
2447 Brice Rd
(43068) 614.866.6456
call re: fees

OHIO, Columbus Metro

Lenox Inn ($$)
Box# 346
(43068) 614.861.7800

Red Roof Inn ($)
2449 Brice Rd
(43068) 614.864.3683

● Westerville ●
Knights Inn ($$)
32 Heatherdown Dr
(43081) 614.890.0426
size limits & fees

End of Columbus Metro

● Copley ●
Red Roof Inn ($$)
99 Rothrock Rd
(44321) 216.666,0566

● Coshocton ●
Travelodge ($$)
275 S Whitewoman St
(43812) 614.622.98

● Dayton ●
Comfort Inn ($$)
7125 Miller Ln
(45414) 937.890.9995

Econo Lodge ($$)
2140 S Edwin C Moses Blvd
(45408) 513.223.0166
$10 per day

Howard Johnson ($$)
7575 Poe Ave
(45414) 513.454.0550

Knights Inn ($)
3663 Maxton Rd
(45414) 800.843.5644

Marriott Hotel ($$$)
1414 S Patterson Blvd
(45409) 513.223.1000

Motel 6 ($)
7130 Miller Ln
(45414) 513.898.3606
1 small pet/room

Radisson Inn ($$$)
2401 Needmore Rd
(45414) 513.278.5711
small pets allowed

Ramada Inn ($$)
4079 Little York Rd
(45414) 513.890.9500

Red Roof Inn ($)
7370 Miller Ln
(45414) 513.898.1054
small pets only

Residence Inn ($$$$)
7070 Poe Ave
(45414) 513.898.7764
call for fee & availability

Stouffer ($$$)
5th & Jefferson Sts
(45402) 513.224.0800

Travelodge ($)
7911 Brandt Pike
(45424) 513.236.9361
deposit

Dayton Metro

● Dayton ●
Comfort Inn ($$)
7125 Miller Ln
(45414) 937.890.9995

Econo Lodge ($$)
2140 S Edwin C Moses Blvd
(45408) 513.223.0166
$10 per day

Howard Johnson ($$)
7575 Poe Ave
(45414) 513.454.0550

Knights Inn ($)
3663 Maxton Rd
(45414) 800.843.5644

Marriott Hotel ($$$)
1414 S Patterson Blvd
(45409) 513.223.1000

Motel 6 ($)
7130 Miller Ln
(45414) 513.898.3606
1 small pet/room

Radisson Inn ($$$)
2401 Needmore Rd
(45414) 513.278.5711
small pets allowed

Ramada Inn ($$)
4079 Little York Rd
(45414) 513.890.9500

Red Roof Inn ($)
7370 Miller Ln
(45414) 513.898.1054
small pets only

Residence Inn ($$$$)
7070 Poe Ave
(45414) 513.898.7764
call for fee & availability

Stouffer ($$$)
5th & Jefferson Sts
(45402) 513.224.0800

Travelodge ($)
7911 Brandt Pike
(45424) 513.236.9361
deposit

● Englewood ●
Motel 6 ($)
1212 S Main St
(45322) 513.832.3770
1 small pet/room

● Fairborn ●
Fairfield Inn ($$)
2500 Paramount Pl
(45324) 513.427.0800

Hampton Inn ($$$)
2550 Paramount Pl
(45324) 513.429.5505

Holiday Inn ($$$)
2800 Presidential Dr
(45324) 513.426.7800
mgr preapproval reqd

Homewood Suites ($$$$)
2750 Presidential Dr
(45324) 513.429.0600
$10 per day

Ramada Inn ($$)
800 N Broad St
(45324) 513.879.3920

Red Roof Inn ($$)
2580 Col Glenn Hwy
(45324) 513.426.6116

● Miamisburg ●
Motel 6 ($)
8101 Springboro Pike
(45342) 513.434.8750
1 small pet/room

Red Roof Inn ($$)
222 Byers Rd
(45342) 513.866.0705

Residence Inn ($$$$)
155 Prestige Pl
(45342) 513.434.7881
call for fee & availability

● Piqua ●
Howard Johnson ($)
902 Scott Dr
(45356) 513.773.2314

● Sidney ●
Econo Lodge ($$)
2009 Michigan St
(45365) 513.492.9164

Holiday Inn ($$)
400 Folkerth Ave
(45365) 513.492.1131
mgr preapproval reqd

● Vandalia ●
Park Inn Intl ($$)
75 Corporate Center Dr
(45377) 513.898.8321

● Xenia ●
Best Western ($$)
600 Little Main St
(45385) 513.372.9954

End of Dayton Metro

● Defiance ●
Days Inn ($$)
1835 N Clinton St
(43512) 419.782.5555

● Delaware ●
Travelodge ($$)
1001 US 23
(43015) 614.369.4421

● Dover ●
Knights Inn ($$)
889 Commercial Pkwy
(44622) 330.364.7724
size limits & fees

● Dublin ●
Budgetel ($$)
6145 Parkcenter Cir
(43017) 614.792.8300

Red Roof Inn ($)
5125 Post Rd
(43017) 614.764.3993

Residence Inn ($$$$)
435 Metro Pl
(43017) 614.791.0403
call for fee & availability

Stouffer ($$$)
600 Metro Pl
(43017) 614.764.2200

Woodfin Suites Hotel ($$$)
4130 Tuller Rd
(43017) 614.766.7762

● Eaton ●
Econo Lodge ($)
I-70 & US 127
(45320) 513.456.5959

● Elyria ●
Comfort Inn ($$)
739 Leona St
(44035) 216.324.7676
mgr preapproval reqd

Howard Johnson ($$)
1724 Lorain Blvd
(44035) 216.323.1515

● Englewood ●
Motel 6 ($)
1212 S Main St
(45322) 513.832.3770
1 small pet/room

● Fairborn ●
Fairfield Inn ($$)
2500 Paramount Pl
(45324) 513.427.0800

Hampton Inn ($$$)
2550 Paramount Pl
(45324) 513.429.5505

Holiday Inn ($$$)
2800 Presidential Dr
(45324) 513.426.7800
mgr preapproval reqd

Homewood Suites ($$$$)
2750 Presidential Dr
(45324) 513.429.0600
$10 per day

Ramada Inn ($$)
800 N Broad St
(45324) 513.879.3920

Red Roof Inn ($$)
2580 Col Glenn Hwy
(45324) 513.426.6116

● Fairlawn ●
Hilton ($$$)
3180 W Market St
(44333) 216.867.5000

● Findlay ●
Econo Lodge ($)
316 Emma St
(45840) 419.422.0154
medium

Fairfield Inn ($$)
2000 Tiffin Ave
(45840) 419.424.9940

Findlay Inn ($$)
200 E Main Cross St
(45840) 419.422.5682

Hampton Inn ($$)
921 Interstate Dr
(45840) 419.422.5252

Ramada Inn ($$)
820 Trenton Ave
(45840) 419.423.8212

● Fostoria ●
Days Inn ($$)
601 Findlay St
(44830) 419.435.6511
small pets only

● Franklin ●
Comfort Inn ($$)
3458 Commerce Dr
(45005) 513.420.9378

Knights Inn ($)
8500 Claude Thomas Rd
(45005) 800.843.5644

Oakbrook Inn ($)
6147 W S R 122
(45005) 513.424.1201

Super 8 ($$)
3553 Commerce Dr
(45005) 513.422.4888
mgr preapproval reqd

● Fremont ●
Fremont Tunrpike Motel ($)
520 Cr 89
(43420) 419.332.6489

Holiday Inn ($$$)
3422 Port Clinton Rd
(43420) 419.334.2682
mgr preapproval reqd

Travelodge ($$)
1750 Cedar S R
(43420) 419.334.9517
deposit

● Galion ●
Hometown Inn ($$)
172 Portland Way
(44833) 419.468.9909

● Gallipolis ●
Best Western ($)
918 2nd Ave
(45631) 614.446.3373
1 small pet

Holiday Inn
577 S R 7N
(45631) 614.446.0090

● Girard ●
Days Inn ($$)
1610 Motor Inn Dr
(44420) 330.759.3410
$5 per day

Econo Lodge ($)
1615 E Liberty St
(44420) 330.759.9820

Motel 6 ($)
1600 Motor Inn Dr
(44420) 216.759.7833
1 small pet/room

● Grove City ●
Best Western ($$)
4026 Jackpot Rd
(43123) 614.875.7770
small pets only w/$5 fee

Red Roof Inn ($)
1900 Stringtown Rd
(43123) 614.875.8543

● Hamilton ●
Hamiltonian Hotel ($$$)
1 Riverfront Plz
(45011) 513.896.6200

● Hebron ●
Regal Inn ($)
4756 Keller Rd
(43025) 614.927.8011

● Hilliard ●
Comfort Inn ($$$)
3831 Park Mill Run Dr
(43026) 614.529.8118
mgr preapproval reqd

Homewood Suites ($$$)
3841 Park Mill Rd
(43026) 614.529.4100

Motel 6 ($)
3950 Parkway Ln
(43026) 614.771.1500
1 small pet/room

● Holland ●
Red Roof Inn ($)
1214 Corporate Dr
(43528) 419.866.5512

Residence Inn ($$$$)
6101 Trust Dr
(43528) 419.867.9555
call for fee & availability

● Hudson ●
Days Inn
344 Hines Hill Rd
(44236) 216.650.1100
$10

● Huron ●
Plantation Motel ($)
2815 Cleveland Rd
(44839) 419.433.4790

● Independence ●
Budgetel ($$)
6161 Quarry Ln
(44131) 216.447.1133

$=under $35 $$=$35-60 $$$=$60-100 $$$$=over $100

Hilton ($$$)
6200 Quarry Ln
(44131) 216.447.1300
$25 daily fee

Red Roof Inn ($$)
6020 Quarry Ln
(44131) 216.447.0030

Residence Inn ($$$)
5101 W Creek Rd
(44131) 216.520.1450

● Jackson ●
Comfort Inn ($$)
605 E Main St
(45640) 614.286.7581
mgr preapproval reqd

● Kent ●
Knights Inn ($$)
4423 S R 43
(44240) 216.678.5250
size limits & fees

The Inn Of Kent ($$)
303 E Main St
(44240) 216.673.3411

● Kings Mills ●
Holiday Inn
5589 Kings Mill Rd
(45034) 513.398.8075

● Lakeside Marblehead ●
Surf Motel ($$)
230 E Main St
(43440) 419.798.4823

● Lakewood ●
Days Inn ($$)
12019 Lake Ave
(44107) 216.226.4800

● Lancaster ●
Best Western ($$)
1858 N Memorial Dr
(43130) 614.653.3040

Knights Inn ($$)
1327 River Valley Blvd
(43130) 614.687.4823
call for size limits & fees

● Lebanon ●
Best Western ($)
674 N Broadway St
(45036) 513.932.4111
small pets

● Lima ●
Days Inn ($)
1250 Neubrecht Rd
(45801) 419.227.6515

Econo Lodge ($$)
1201 Neubrecht Rd
(45801) 419.222.0596
$5 night

Knights Inn ($)
2285 N Eastown Rd
(45807) 419.331.9215
size limits & fees

Motel 6 ($)
1800 Harding Hwy
(45804) 419.228.0456
1 small pet/room

Ramada Inn ($$)
3600 E Bluelick Rd
(45801) 800.272.6232

● Logan ●
Shawnee Inn ($)
30916 Lake Logan Rd
(43138) 614.385.5674

● Loudonville ●
Little Brown Inn Motel ($$)
940 S Market St
(44842) 419.994.5525

● Macedonia ●
Knights Inn ($)
240 Highland Rd
(44056) 216.467.1981
size limits & fees

Motel 6 ($$)
311 Highland Rd
(44056) 216.468.1670
1 small pet/room

● Mansfield ●
42 Motel ($)
2444 Lexington Ave
(44907) 419.884.1315

Best Western ($$)
880 Laver Rd
(44905) 419.589.2200

Comfort Inn ($$)
500 N Trimble Rd
(44906) 419.529.1000
mgr preapproval reqd

Econo Lodge ($$)
1017 Roogle Rd
(44903) 419.589.3333

Fairfield Inn ($$$)
1065 Lexington
(44906) 419.747.2200

Knights Inn ($$)
555 N Trimble Rd
(44906) 419.529.2100
size limits & fees

Park Place Hotel ($$)
191 Park Ave
(44902) 419.522.7275

Super 8 ($$)
2425 Interstate Cir
(44903) 419.746.8875
call re: fees

Travelodge ($$)
90 W Hanley Rd
(44903) 419.756.7600

● Marietta ●
Best Western ($$)
279 Muskingum Dr
(45750) 614.374.7211

Econo Lodge ($$)
702 Pike St
(45750) 614.374.8481

Knights Inn ($)
506 Pike St
(45750) 614.373.7373
size limits & fees

Lafayette Hotel ($$$)
101 Front St
(45750) 614.373.5522

● Marion ●
Comfort Inn ($$)
256 Jamesway
(43302) 614.398.5552

Fairfield Inn ($$)
227 James Way
(43302) 614.389.6636

Harding Motor Lodge ($$)
1065 Delaware Ave
(43302) 614.383.6771
$5 fee

L K Motel ($)
1838 Marion-Mt Gilead Rd
(43302) 614.389.4651
$5 charge

Travelodge ($$)
1952 Marion Mt Gilead
(43302) 614.389.4671
$5 night

● Mason ●
Best Western ($)
9847 Escort Dr
(45040) 513.398.3633

Days Inn ($$)
9735 Mason Montgomery
(45040) 513.398.3297

● Maumee ●
Country Inn ($$)
541 Dussel Dr
(43537) 419.893.8576

Days Inn ($$)
150 Dussel Dr
(43537) 419.893.9960
under 20 lbs

Knights Inn ($)
1520 Holland Sylvania
(43537) 419.865.1380
size limits & fees

Red Roof Inn ($)
1570 Reynolds Rd
(43537) 419.893.0292

Theraldson Inn ($$)
521 Dussel Dr
(43537) 419.897.0865

● Mentor ●
Knights Inn ($$)
7677 Reynolds Rd
(44060) 216.946.0749
call for size limits & fees

Be Discreet

Knights Inn ($$)
8370 Broadmoor Rd
(44060) 216.953.8835
size limits & fees

• Miamisburg •
Motel 6 ($)
8101 Springboro Pike
(45342) 513.434.8750
1 small pet/room

Red Roof Inn ($$)
222 Byers Rd
(45342) 513.866.0705

Residence Inn ($$$$)
155 Prestige Pl
(45342) 513.434.7881
call for fee & availability

• Middletown •
Fairfield Inn ($$)
6750 Roosevelt Ave
(45044) 513.424.5444

Holiday Inn
6575 Terhune Dr
(45044) 513.727.8440

• Milan •
Comfort Inn ($$)
11020 Milan Rd
(44846) 419.499.4681
mgr preapproval reqd

• Montpelier •
Holiday Inn ($$$)
RR 3
(43543) 419.485.5555
mgr preapproval reqd

• Mount Gilead •
Derrick Motel ($$)
5898 S R 95
(43338) 419.946.6010

• Mount Vernon •
Curtis Motor Hotel ($$)
6 Public Sq
(43050) 614.397.4334

• Napoleon •
Paramount Hotel ($$)
Box# 68
(43545) 419.592.5010

• New Philadelphia •
Motel 6 ($$)
181 Bluebell Dr
(44663) 216.339.6446
1 small pet/room

Travelodge ($$)
1256 W High Ave
(44663) 330.339.6671

• Newark •
Holiday Inn ($$)
733 Hebron Rd
(43056) 614.522.1165

Hometown Inn ($$)
1266 Hebron Rd
(43056) 614.522.6112

Howard Johnson ($$)
775 Hebron Rd
(43056) 614.522.3191

Mount Vernon Inn ($$)
601 W High St
(43058) 614.392.9881

Super 8 ($$)
1177 Hebron Rd
(43056) 800.800.8000
call re: fees

• North Baltimore •
Crown Inn ($)
Box# 82
(45872) 419.257.3821

• North Canton •
Motel 6 ($)
6880 Sunset Strip Ave NW
(44720) 216.216.4947
1 small pet/room

• North Lima •
Economy Inn ($$)
10145 Market St
(44452) 330.549.3224

• North Ridgeville •
Travelers Inn ($)
32751 Lorain Rd
(44039) 216.327.6311

• Norwalk •
L K Motel ($)
283 Benedict Ave
(44857) 419.668.8255

• Oregon •
Comfort Inn ($$)
2930 Navarre Ave
(43616) 419.691.8911
mgr preapproval reqd

• Orrville •
Orrville Inn ($)
10355 Lincoln Way
(44667) 330.682.4080

• Oxford •
College View Motel ($)
4000 Oxford Millville Rd
(45056) 513.523.6311

Scottish Inn ($$)
5235 College Corner Rd
(45056) 513.523.6306

• Painesville •
Riderinn ($$$)
792 Mentor Ave
(44077) 216.354.8200

• Peninsula •
Virginia Motel ($)
5374 Akron Cleveland Rd
(44264) 216.650.0449

• Perrysburg •
Days Inn ($$)
I-75 & US 20
(43551) 419.874.8771
mgr preapproval reqd

Holiday Inn ($$$)
10621 Fremont Pike
(43551) 419.874.3101
mgr preapproval reqd

Howard Johnson ($)
I-280 & Hanley Rd
(43551) 419.837.5245

• Piqua •
Howard Johnson ($)
902 Scott Dr
(45356) 513.773.2314

• Port Clinton •
L K Inn ($)
1811 E Perry St
(43452) 419.732.2111

• Put In Bay •
Perry Holiday Hotel ($$$)
99 Concord Ave
(43456) 419.285.2107

• Reynoldsburg •
Best Western ($$)
2100 Brice Rd
(43068) 614.864.1280

La Quinta Inn ($$)
2447 Brice Rd
(43068) 614.866.6456
call re: fees

Lenox Inn ($$)
Box# 346
(43068) 614.861.7800

Red Roof Inn ($)
2449 Brice Rd
(43068) 614.864.3683

• Richfield •
Howard Johnson ($$)
5171 Brecksville Rd
(44286) 216.659.6116

• Rio Grande •
College Hill Motel ($)
10987 S R 588
(45674) 614.245.5326

• Rossford •
Knights Inn
1120 Buck Rd
(43460) 800.843.5644

• Saint Clairsville •
Fischer Motel ($)
Box# 63
(43950) 614.782.1715

Knights Inn ($)
51260 National Rd
(43950) 614.695.5038

Red Roof Inn ($)
68301 Red Roof Ln
(43950) 614.695.4057

Super 8 ($$)
68400 Matthew Dr
(43950) 614.695.1994
w/permission

Twin Pines Motel
46079 National Rd
(43950) 614.695.3720

Well
Behaved

$=under $35 $$=$35-60 $$$=$60-100 $$$$=over $100

OHIO, St Marys

● Saint Marys ●
S&W Motel ($$)
1321 Celina Rd
(45885) 419.394.2341

● Sandusky ●
Best Budget Inn ($)
5918 Milan Rd
(44870) 419.625.7252

Best Western ($$)
1530 Cleveland Rd
(44870) 419.625.9234

Mecca Motel ($$)
2227 Cleveland Rd
(44870) 419.626.1284

Radisson Inn ($$$)
2001 Cleveland Rd
(44870) 419.627.2500
small pets allowed $50
deposit

Rodeway Inn ($)
2905 Milan Rd
(44870) 419.625.1291

Sheraton Inn ($$)
1119 Sandusky Mall Blvd
(44870) 419.625.6280

● Seaman ●
Rodeway Inn ($$)
55 Stern Dr
(45679) 513.386.2511

● Seville ●
Howard Johnson ($)
I-71 & I-76
(44273) 216.769.2053

● Shelby ●
Lodge Keeper Motel
178 Mansfield Ave
(44875) 419.347.2141

● Sidney ●
Econo Lodge ($$)
2009 Michigan St
(45365) 513.492.9164

Holiday Inn ($$)
400 Folkerth Ave
(45365) 513.492.1131
mgr preapproval reqd

● South Point ●
Best Western ($$)
803 Solida Rd
(45680) 614.894.3391
small pets $6 each day

Grandview Inn ($$)
154 County Rd
(45680) 614.377.4388

● Springfield ●
Fairfield Inn ($$$)
1870 W 1st St
(45504) 513.323.9554

Ramada Ltd ($$)
319 E Leffel Ln
(45505) 513.328.0123

Townhouse Motel ($$)
2850 E Main St
(45503) 513.325.7661

● Steubenville ●
Holiday Inn ($$)
1401 University Blvd
(43952) 614.282.0901
mgr preapproval reqd

● Stow ●
Stow Inn ($$)
4601 Darrow Rd
(44224) 216.688.3508

● Strongsville ●
Days Inn ($)
9029 Pearl Rd
(44136) 216.234.3575
$5 fee

Holiday Inn
15471 Royalton
(44136) 216.238.8800

Red Roof Inn ($)
15385 Royalton Rd
(44136) 216.238.0170

● Tiffin ●
Tiffin Motel
315 W Market St
(44883) 419.447.7411

● Toledo ●
Budget Inn ($)
2450 S Reynolds Rd
(43614) 419.865.0201

Clarion Hotel ($$$)
3536 Secor Rd
(43606) 419.535.7070
mgr preapproval reqd

Comfort Inn ($$)
3560 Secor Rd
(43606) 419.531.2666
mgr preapproval reqd

Crown Inn ($$)
1727 W Alexis Rd
(43613) 419.473.1485

Holiday Inn
2340 S Reynolds Rd
(43614) 419.865.1361

Radisson Inn ($$$)
101 N Summit St
(43604) 419.241.3000
small pets allowed

Ramada Inn ($$$)
2429 S Reynolds Rd
(43614) 419.381.8765

Red Roof Inn ($)
3530 Executive Pkwy
(43606) 419.536.0118

● Troy ●
Hampton Inn ($$)
45 Troy Town Rd
(45373) 513.339.7801

Knights Inn ($$)
30 Troy Town Rd
(45373) 513.339.1515
size limits & fees

Motel 6 ($)
1210 Brukner Dr
(45373) 513.335.0013
1 small pet/room

● Twinsburg ●
Super 8 ($$)
8848 Twin Hills Pkwy
(44087) 216.425.2889
mgr preapproval reqd

● Upper Sandusky ●
Amerihost Inn ($$)
1726 E Wyandot Ave
(43351) 419.294.3919

● Urbana ●
Logan Lodge Motel ($$)
2551 S R 68
(43078) 513.652.2188

● Van Wert ●
Days Inn ($$)
820 N Washington St
(45891) 419.238.5222

Lodge Keeper Inn
875 N Washington St
(45891) 419.238.3700

● Vandalia ●
Park Inn Intl ($$)
75 Corporate Center Dr
(45377) 513.898.8321

● Wadsworth ●
Knights Inn ($$)
810 High St
(44281) 330.336.6671
size limits & fees

● Wapakoneta ●
Days Inn ($)
1659 Bellefontaine St
(45895) 419.738.2184
$5/pet

Holiday Inn ($$)
1510 Saturen
(45895) 419.738.8181

Super 8 ($$)
511 Lunar Dr
(45895) 419.738.8810
call re: fees

● Warren ●
Best Western ($$)
777 Mahoning Ave NW
(44483) 216.392.2515
1 room for pets

● Washington Court House ●
Knights Inn ($$)
1820 Columbus Ave
(43160) 614.335.9133
size limits & fees

● Wauseon ●
Arrowhead Motel ($$)
8225 S R 108
(43567) 419.335.5811

$=under $35 $$=$35-60 $$$=$60-100 $$$$=over $100

● Westerville ●
Knights Inn ($$)
32 Heatherdown Dr
(43081) 614.890.0426
size limits & fees

● Westlake ●
Red Roof Inn ($$)
29595 Clements Rd
(44145) 216.892.7920

Residence Inn ($$$$)
30100 Clemens Rd
(44145) 216.892.2254
$7/day plus cleaning fee

● Wickliffe ●
Plaza Motel ($)
29152 Euclid Ave
(44092) 216.943.0546

● Willard ●
Lodge Keeper Inn
117 E Walton St
(44890) 419.935.6321

● Willoughby ●
Red Roof Inn ($$)
4166 S R 306
(44094) 216.946.9872

● Wilmington ●
L K Motel ($$)
264 W Curry Rd
(45177) 513.382.6605

● Wooster ●
Econo Lodge ($$)
2137 E Lincoln Way
(44691) 330.264.8883

The Wooster Inn ($$)
801 E Wayne Ave
(44691) 330.264.2341

● Xenia ●
Best Western ($$)
600 Little Main St
(45385) 513.372.9954

● Youngstown ●
Best Western ($$)
870 N Canfield-Niles Rd
(44515) 330.544.2378

Days Inn ($)
8392 Market St
(44512) 216.758.2371
$4/pets

Fairfield Inn ($$)
7397 Tiffany
(44514) 330.726.5979

Microtel ($$)
7393 South Ave
(44512) 330.758.1816

Super 8 ($$)
4250 Belmont Ave
(44505) 330.793.7788
call re: fees

Wagon Wheel Motel ($)
7015 Market St
(44512) 216.758.4551

● Zanesville ●
Fairfield Inn ($$)
725 Zane St
(43701) 614.453.8770

Holiday Inn ($$)
4645 East Pike
(43701) 614.453.0771
mgr preapproval reqd

Super 8 ($$)
2440 National Rd
(43701) 614.455.3124
pets w/permission

Oklahoma
● Ada ●
Holiday Inn
400 NE Richardson Loop
(74820) 405.332.9000

● Altus ●
Days Inn ($)
3202 N Main St
(73521) 405.477.2300

Ramada Inn ($$)
2515 E Broadway St
(73521) 405.477.3000

● Alva ●
Ranger Inn Motel ($)
420 E Oklahoma Blvd
(73717) 405.327.1981

Whartons Vista Motel ($)
1330 Oklahoma Blvd
(73717) 405.327.3232

● Apache ●
Andarko Motel ($)
1301 E Central
(73006) 405.247.3315

● Ardmore ●
Best Western ($$)
6 Holliday Dr
(73401) 405.223.7525

Comfort Inn ($$)
2700 W Broadway St
(73401) 405.226.1250
mgr preapproval reqd

Days Inn ($$)
2432 Veterans Blvd
(73401) 405.223.7976
small $5/pet charge

Holiday Inn ($$)
2705 Holiday Dr
(73401) 405.223.7130
mgr preapproval reqd

Motel 6 ($)
120 Holliday Dr
(73401) 405.226.7666
1 small pet/room

Super 8 ($)
2120 Veterans Blvd
(73401) 405.223.2201
call re: fees

● Atoka ●
Best Western ($$)
2101 S Mississippi Ave
(74525) 405.889.7381
small pets

● Bartlesville ●
Best Western ($$)
222 SE Washington Blvd
(74006) 918.335.7755
pets @ mgrs discretion

Holiday Inn ($$)
1410 SE Washington Blvd
(74006) 918.333.8320
mgr preapproval reqd

Super 8 ($$)
211 SE Washington Blvd
(74006) 918.335.1122
call re: fees

● Blackwell ●
Days Inn ($)
4302 W Doolin Ave
(74631) 405.363.2911

● Boise City ●
Townsman Motel ($)
1205 E Main
(73933) 405.544.2506

● Broken Arrow ●
Econo Lodge ($$)
1401 N Elm Pl
(74012) 918.258.6617

Holiday Inn
2600 N Aspen
(74012) 918.258.7085

Stratford House Inn ($)
1301 N Elm Pl
(74012) 918.258.7556

● Broken Bow ●
Charles Wesley Motel ($)
302 N Park Dr
(74728) 405.584.3303

End Of Trail Motel
11 N Park Dr
(74728) 405.584.3350

● Catoosa ●
Travelers Inn ($)
19250 Timbercrest Cir
(74015) 918.266.7000

● Chandler ●
Econo Lodge ($$)
600 N Price Ave
(74834) 405.258.2131
$20 deposit

● Checotah ●
Best Western ($$)
I-40
(74426) 918.473.2376
sm. housebroken pets only

**Policies
Subject
to Change**

Budget Host ($)
I-40 Ex 265
(74426) 918.473.2331

Days Inn Rt 2
(74426) 918.689.3999
$5

I 40 Inn
Old 69 Hwy & I-40
(74426) 918.473.2331

● Chickasha ●
Best Western ($$)
2101 S 4th St
(73018) 405.224.4890

Days Inn ($$)
2701 S 4th St
(73018) 405.222.5800
$5

Super 8 ($)
2728 S 4th St
(73018) 405.222.3710
call re: fees

● Claremore ●
Best Western ($$)
940 S Lynn Riggs Blvd
(74017) 918.341.4410

Days Inn ($$)
Hwy 66 & Country Club Dr
(74017) 918.343.3297
$10

Motel Claremore ($)
812 E Will Rogers Blvd
(74017) 918.341.3254

● Clinton ●
Best Western ($$)
2128 W Gary Blvd
(73601) 405.323.2610

Park Inn Intl ($)
2140 W Gary Blvd
(73601) 405.323.2010

Relax Inn ($)
1116 S 10th St
(73601) 405.323.1888

● Crowder ●
Hojo Inn ($)
Hwy 75 & Trudgeon St
(74430) 918.652.4448

● Duncan ●
Duncan Inn ($)
3402 N US 81
(73533) 405.252.5210

Hillcrest Motel ($)
1417 S 81 Byp
(73533) 405.255.1640

Holiday Inn ($$)
1015 N US 81
(73533) 405.252.1500

● Durant ●
Best Western ($$)
2401 W Main St
(74701) 405.924.7676
small housebroken pets

Durant Inn ($)
2121 W Main St
(74701) 405.924.5432

● Edmond ●
Seasons Inn ($$)
1005 Waterwood Pkwy
(73034) 800.322.4686

● El Reno ●
Best Western ($$)
I-40 & Country Club Rd
(73036) 405.262.6490
small pet

Days Inn ($$)
2700 S Country Club Rd
(73036) 405.262.8720

Ramada Ltd ($)
2851 S Hwy 81
(73036) 405.262.1022

Red Carpet Inn ($)
2640 S Country Club Rd
(73036) 405.262.1526

Super 8 ($)
2820 S Hwy 81
(73036) 405.262.8240
call re: fees

● Elk City ●
Best Western ($)
2015 W 3rd St
(73644) 405.225.2331
1 small pet only

Budget Host ($)
I-40 Ex 41
(73644) 405.225.4020

Days Inn ($)
1100 Hwy 34
(73644) 405.225.9210

Econo Lodge ($)
108 Meadowridge Dr
(73644) 405.225.5120

Flamingo Inn ($)
2000 W 3rd St
(73644) 405.225.1811

Hojo Inn ($)
2604 E Hwy 66
(73644) 405.225.2241
small pets - $3 fee

Holiday Inn ($$)
I-40
(73648) 405.225.6637

Motel 6 ($)
2500 E Hwy 66
(73644) 405.225.6661
1 small pet/room

Quality Inn ($)
102 Bj Hughes
(73648) 405.225.8140

Super 8 ($)
2801 E Hwy 66
(73644) 405.225.9430
call re: fees

Travelodge ($)
301 Sleepy Hollow Ct
(73644) 405.243.0150

● Enid ●
Econo Lodge ($)
2523 Mercer Dr
(73701) 405.237.3090

Holiday Inn ($)
2901 S Van Buren St
(73703) 405.237.6000

Ramada Inn ($$)
3005 W Garriott Rd
(73703) 405.234.0440

● Erick ●
Days Inn ($$)
I-40 & Hwy 30
(73645) 405.526.3315
$5

● Frederick ●
Scottish Inn ($)
1015 S Main St
(73542) 405.335.2129
small dogs

● Glenpool ●
Best Western ($$)
14831 S Casper St
(74033) 405.282.8831

● Guthrie ●
Best Western ($$)
2323 Territorial Tr
(73044) 405.282.8831

Harrison House Inn ($$)
124 W Harrison Ave
(73044) 405.282.1000

Town House Motel ($)
221 E Oklahoma Ave
(73044) 405.282.2000

● Guymon ●
Ambassador Inn ($$)
Box# 5
(73942) 405.338.5555

Best Western ($$)
212 NE Hwy 54
(73942) 405.338.6556
small pets only

Econo Lodge ($$)
923 E Hwy 54
(73942) 405.338.5431

Super 8 ($$)
1201 E Hwy 54
(73942) 405.338.0507
call re: fees

$=under $35 $$=$35-60 $$$=$60-100 $$$$=over $100

● Hooker ●
Sunset Motel ($)
710 Hwy 54
(73945) 405.652.3250

● Kingston ●
Lake Texoma Resort ($$$)
Box# 41
(73439) 800.654.8240

● Lawton ●
Best Western ($$)
2202 N Hwy 277
(73507) 405.353.0310
managers discretion

Executive Inn ($$)
3110 NW Cache Rd
(73505) 405.353.3104
$5 charge

Hospitality Inn ($)
202 E Lee Blvd
(73501) 405.355.9765

Howard Johnson ($$)
1125 E Gore Blvd
(73501) 405.353.0200

● Lone Wolf ●
Quartz Mtn Resort ($$)
RR 1
(73655) 800.654.8240

● McAlester ●
Comfort Inn ($$)
1215 George Nigh Expwy
(74502) 918.426.0115
mgr preapproval reqd

Days Inn ($$)
1217 S George Nigh Expy
(74501) 918.426.5050
$15

Holiday Inn ($$)
1500 S George Nigh Ex
(74501) 918.423.7766

Super 8 ($)
2400 S Main Bus 69
(74501) 918.426.5400
call re: fees

● Miami ●
Best Western ($$)
2225 E Steve Owens Blvd
(74354) 918.542.6681

● Muskogee ●
Best Western ($$)
534 S 32nd St
(74401) 918.683.2951

Days Inn ($$)
900 S 32nd St
(74401) 918.683.3911
$5 fee

Econo Lodge ($)
2018 W Shawnee St
(74401) 800.424.4777

Motel 6 ($)
903 S 3lnd St
(74401) 918.683.8369
1 small pet/room

Ramada Inn ($$)
800 S 32nd St
(74401) 918.682.4341

● Norman ●
Days Inn ($$)
609 N Interstate Dr
(73069) 405.360.4380
mgr preapproval reqd

Residence Inn ($$$)
2681 Jefferson St
(73072) 405.366.0900

The Stratford House Inn ($)
225 N Interstate Dr
(73069) 405.329.7194

● Oklahoma City ●
Appletree Suites ($)
6022 1/2 NW 23rd St
(73127) 405.495.3881

Best Western ($$)
2600 N Broadway St
(73160) 405.794.6611

Carlyle Motel ($)
3600 NW 29th Expwy
(73112) 405.946.3355

Century Center Hotel ($$$$)
1 N Broadway Ave
(73102) 800.285.2780

Clarion Hotel ($$$)
4345 N Lincoln Blvd
(73105) 405.528.2741

Comfort Inn ($$)
5653 Tinker Diagonal
(73110) 405.733.1339
mgr preapproval reqd

Comfort Inn ($$)
4017 NW 39th Expwy
(73112) 405.947.0038
mgr preapproval reqd

Comfort Inn ($$)
7800 C A Henderson Blvd
(73139) 800.221.2222
mgr preapproval reqd

Days Inn ($$)
122nd St
(73131) 405.478.2554

Days Inn
1701 Moore Ave
(73160) 405.794.5070
$10

Days Inn ($$)
4712 W I-40
(73128) 405.947.8721
$5/pets

Days Inn ($$)
2801 NW 39th St
(73112) 405.946.0741
pets ok w/deposit & some
restrictions

Days Inn ($$)
2616 S I-35
(73129) 405.677.0521
$15/pet

Econo Lodge ($)
8200 W I-40
(73128) 405.787.7051

Econo Lodge ($)
820 S Macarthur Blvd
(73128) 405.947.8651
deposit

Embassy Suites ($$$)
1815 S Meridian Ave
(73108) 405.682.6000
under 20 lbs

Governors Suites Hotel ($$)
2308 S Meridian Ave
(73108) 405.682.5299

Hampton Inn ($$$)
1833 Center Dr
(73110) 405.732.5500

Hampton Inn ($$$)
13500 Plaza Ter
(73120) 405.752.7070

Holiday Inn ($$)
801 S Meridian Ave
(73108) 405.942.8544
mgr preapproval reqd

Holiday Inn
5301 N Lincoln
(73105) 405.528.7563

Holiday Inn
13520 Plaza Terrace
(73120) 405.755.8686

Howard Johnson ($$)
400 S Meridian Ave
(73108) 405.943.9841

Howard Johnson ($$)
1629 S Prospect Ave
(73129) 405.677.0551

La Quinta Inn ($$)
5501 Tinker Diagonal St
(73115) 405.672.0067
call re: fees

La Quinta Inn ($$)
8315 S I-35
(73149) 405.631.8661
call re: fees

Marriott Hotel ($$$$)
3233 NW Expwy
(73112) 405.842.6633

Motel 6 ($)
6821 SE 29th St
(73110) 405.737.8880
1 small pet/room

Motel 6 ($)
12121 NE Expwy
(73131) 405.478.4030
1 small pet/room

Motel 6 ($)
1417 N Moore Ave
(73160) 405.799.6616
1 small pet/room

OKLAHOMA, Norman

Motel 6 ($)
820 S Meridian Ave
(73108) 405.946.6662
1 small pet/room

Motel 6 ($)
11900 NE Expwy
(73131) 405.478.8666
1 small pet/room

Motel 6 ($)
4200 I-40
(73108) 405.947.6550
1 small pet/room

Radisson Inn ($$)
401 S Meridian Ave
(73108) 800.333.3333

Ramada Inn ($$)
6800 S I-35
(73149) 405.631.3321

Ramada Ltd ($$)
3709 NW 39th Expwy
(73112) 405.942.7730

Ramada Ltd ($$)
1400 NE 63rd St
(73111) 405.478.5221

Red Carpet Inn ($)
8217 S I-35
(73149) 405.632.0807

Residence Inn ($$$)
4361 W Reno Ave
(73107) 405.942.4500
call for fee & availability

Richmond Suites ($$$)
1600 NW Expwy
(73118) 405.840.1440

Rodeway Inn ($$)
4601 SW 3rd St
(73128) 405.947.2400

Southgate Inn
5245 S I 35
(73129) 405.672.5561

● Okmulgee ●
Best Western ($$)
3499 N Wood Dr
(74447) 918.756.9200

Days Inn
1221 Wood Dr
(74447) 918.758.0660
$10

● Pauls Valley ●
Days Inn ($$)
RR 3 Box# 295C
(73075) 405.238.7548
$10

Garden Inn Motel ($)
Box# 931
(73075) 405.238.7313

● Pawnee ●
Motel 6 ($)
136 Taos St
(74058) 504.649.7925
1 small pet/room

● Perry ●
Best Western ($$)
I-35
(73077) 405.336.2218
small & deposit

Dan D Motel ($)
515 Fir St
(73077) 405.336.4463

First Interstate Inn ($)
Box# 833
(73077) 405.336.2277

● Ponca City ●
Days Inn ($)
1415 Bradley Ave
(74604) 405.767.1406
$10

Holiday Inn
2215 N 14th St
(74601) 405.762.8311

● Poteau ●
Best Western ($$)
3111 N Broadway St
(74953) 918.647.4001

● Pryor ●
Days Inn ($$)
Hwy 69 S & 69A
(74362) 918.825.7600
$10

Holiday Motel ($)
701 S Mill St
(74361) 918.825.1204

Pryor House Motor Inn ($)
123 S Mill St
(74361) 918.825.6677

● Purcell ●
Econo Lodge ($$$)
2500 Hwy 74
(73080) 405.527.5603

● Sallisaw ●
Best Western ($)
706 S Kerr Blvd
(74955) 918.775.6294

Days Inn ($$)
RR 2 Box# 13
(74955) 918.775.4406
$8

Econo Lodge ($$)
2403 E Cherokee St
(74955) 918.775.7981

Golden Spur Inn ($)
Box# 828
(74955) 918.775.4443

McKnight Motel ($)
1611 W Ruth St
(74955) 800.842.9442

Ramada Ltd ($$)
1300 E Cherokee St
(74955) 918.775.7791

Super 8 ($)
924 S Kerr Blvd
(74955) 918.775.8900
$5 fee w/permission

● Sapulpa ●
Super 8 ($)
1505 New Sapulpa Rd
(74066) 918.227.3300
w/permission

● Savanna ●
Budget Host ($)
US Hwy 69
(74565) 918.548.3506

Budget Host ($)
Hwy69
(74565) 800.283.4678

● Shawnee ●
Best Western ($$)
623 Kickapoo Spur St
(74801) 405.273.7010

Motel 6 ($)
4981 N Harrison St
(74801) 405.275.5310
1 small pet/room

Rodeway Inn ($)
12510 Valley View Rd
(74801) 405.275.1005

● Stillwater ●
Best Western ($$)
600 E McElroy Rd
(74075) 405.377.7010

Days Inn ($)
5010 W 6th Ave
(74075) 405.743.2570

Holiday Inn ($$)
2515 W 6th Ave
(74074) 405.372.0800
mgr preapproval reqd

Motel 6 ($)
5122 W 6th Ave
(74075) 405.624.0433
1 small pet/room

● Stroud ●
Best Western ($$)
1200 N 8th Ave
(74079) 918.968.9515
small pets

● Sulphur ●
Super 8 ($$)
2110 W Broadway St
(73086) 405.622.6500
pets w/permission

● Tahlequah ●
Tahlequah Motel ($)
2501 S Muskogee Ave
(74464) 918.456.2350

● Tonkawa ●
Western Inn ($)
RR 1 Box# 130
(74653) 405.628.2577

$=under $35 $$=$35-60 $$$=$60-100 $$$$=over $100

• Tulsa •
Best Western ($$)
3337 E Skelly Dr
(74135) 918.743.7931
small pets only

Camelot Hotel ($$)
4956 S Peoria Ave
(74105) 918.747.8811

Comfort Inn ($$)
4717 S Yale Ave
(74135) 918.622.6776
mgr preapproval reqd

Days Inn ($)
5525 W Skelly Dr
(74107) 918.446.1561
$4

Days Inn
8201 Skelly Dr
(74129) 918.665.6800
deposit

Days Inn ($$)
1016 N Garnett Rd
(74116) 918.438.5050
$10 small pets allowed

Doubletree ($$$)
616 W 7th St
(74127) 918.587.8000
$25 fee & $50 deposit

Doubletree ($$$)
6110 S Yale Ave
(74136) 918.495.1000
$100 deposit

Hawthorn Suites ($$)
3509 S 79th East Ave
(74145) 918.663.3900

Holiday Inn
9010 E 71st St
(74133) 918.459.5321

Holiday Inn ($$)
1010 N Garnett Rd
(74116) 918.437.7660

Holiday Inn ($$)
8181 E Skelly Dr
(74129) 800.465.4329
mgr preapproval reqd

Howard Johnson ($$)
17 W 7th St
(74119) 918.585.5898

Howard Johnson ($$)
4724 S Yale Ave
(74135) 918.496.1760

La Quinta Inn ($$)
10829 E 41st St
(74146) 918.665.0200
call re: fees

La Quinta Inn ($$)
35 N Sheridan Rd
(74115) 918.836.3931
call re: fees

La Quinta Inn ($$)
12525 E 5Ind St
(74146) 918.254.1626
call re: fees

Motel 6 ($)
1011 S Garnett Rd
(74128) 918.234.6200
1 small pet/room

Motel 6 ($)
5828 W Skelly Dr
(74107) 918.445.0223
1 small pet/room

Residence Inn ($$$)
8181 E 41st St
(74145) 918.664.7241
extra chrg

• Vinita •
Park Hills Motel ($)
RR 4 Box# 292
(74301) 918.256.5511

Super 8 ($)
30954 S Hwy 69
(74301) 800.800.8000
call re: fees

• Wagoner •
Indian Lodge Motel ($)
RR 2 Box# 393
(74467) 918.485.3184

Super 8 ($)
805 S Dewey Ave
(74467) 918.485.4818
call re: fees

Western Hills Ranch ($$)
Box# 509
(74477) 918.772.2545

• Watonga •
Roman Nose Resort ($$)
RR 1
(73772) 405.623.7281

• Weatherford •
Best Western ($$)
525 E Main St
(73096) 405.772.3325
1 pet only not unattended

Scottish Inn ($)
616 E Main St
(73096) 405.772.3349

Travel Inn ($)
3401 E Main St
(73096) 405.772.6238

• Webbers Falls •
Super 8 ($)
I-40 & Hwy 100
(74470) 918.464.2272
call re: fees

• Woodward •
Hospitality Inn ($)
4120 Williams Ave
(73801) 405.254.2964

Northwest Inn ($$)
Hwy 270 & 1st St
(73801) 405.256.7600

Wayfarer Inn ($)
2901 Williams Ave
(73801) 405.256.5553

• Yukon •
Comfort Inn ($$)
321 N Mustang Rd
(73099) 405.324.1000
mgr preapproval reqd

Oregon
• Agness •
Lucas Pioneer Lodge ($)
3904 Cougar Ln
(97406) 541.247.7443

Singing Sprgs Resort ($)
34501 Agness Illahe Rd
(97406) 541.247.6162

• Albany •
Best Western ($$$)
315 Airport Rd SE
(97321) 541.928.6322
small pets allowed

Budget Inn ($$)
2727 Pacific Blvd SE
(97321) 541.926.4246

City Center Motel ($)
1730 Pacific Blvd SE
(97321) 541.926.8442

Comfort Inn ($$)
251 Airport Rd SE
(97321) 541.928.0921
mgr preapproval reqd

Holiday Inn ($$)
1100 Price Rd SE
(97321) 541.928.5050

Marco Polo Motel ($)
2410 Pacific Blvd SE
(97321) 541.926.4401

Motel Orleans ($$)
1212 Price Rd SE
(97321) 541.926.0170

Pioneer Villa Plaza ($)
Ex 216 I-5
(97321) 541.369.2801

Stardust Motel ($)
2735 E Pacific Blvd
(97321) 541.926.4233

Valu Inn ($$)
3125 Santiam Hwy SE
(97321) 541.926.1538

• Arlington •
Village Inn Motel ($$)
131 Beech St
(97812) 541.454.2646

• Ashland •
Ashland Motel ($)
1145 Siskiyou Blvd
(97520) 541.482.2561

Ashland Valley Inn ($$)
1193 Siskiyou Blvd
(97520) 541.482.2641

$=under $35 $$=$35-60 $$$=$60-100 $$$$=over $100

OREGON, Ashland

Best Western ($$)
132 N Main St
(97520) 541.482.0049
$10 charge

Best Western ($$)
434 Valley View Rd
(97520) 541.482.6932

Cedarwood Inn ($$$)
1801 Siskiyou Blvd
(97520) 541.488.2000

Green Springs Inn ($$)
11470 Hwy 66
(97520) 541.482.0614

Knights Inn ($)
2359 Hwy 66
(97520) 541.482.5111

Quality Inn ($$)
2520 Ashland St
(97520) 541.488.2330
mgr preapproval reqd

Windmills Inn ($$)
2525 Ashland St
(97520) 541.482.8310

● Astoria ●
Bayshore Motor Inn ($$)
555 Hamburg Ave
(97103) 503.325.2205

Crest Motel ($$$)
5366 Leif Erickson Dr
(97103) 503.325.3141

Crest Motel
5366 Leif Erickson
(97103) 503.325.3141
owners have dogs

Lamplighter Motel ($)
131 W Marine Dr
(97103) 503.325.4051

Red Lion Inn ($$$)
400 Industry St
(97103) 503.325.7373
call re: fees

Rosebriar Inn ($$)
636 14th St
(97103) 503.325.7427

● Baker City ●
Baker City Motel ($)
880 Elm St
(97814) 541.523.6391

El Dorado Motel ($$)
695 Campbell St
(97814) 541.523.6494

Geiser Grand Hotel ($$$)
1996 Main St
(97814) 541.523.1889

Green Gables Motel ($)
2533 10th St
(97814) 541.523.5588

Oregon Trail Motel ($)
211 Bridge St
(97814) 541.523.5844

Quality Inn ($$)
810 Campbell St
(97814) 541.523.2244
mgr preapproval reqd

The Western Motel ($)
3055 10th St
(97814) 541.523.3700

Trail Motel
2815 10th St
(97814) 541.523.4646

● Bandon ●
Bandon Beach Motel ($$)
1140 Beach Loop Rd
(97411) 541.347.4430

Caprice Motel ($$)
RR 1 Box# 530
(97411) 541.347.4494

Driftwood Motel ($)
460 Hwy 101
(97411) 541.347.9022

La Kris Motel ($)
Hwy 101 S At 9th St
(97411) 541.347.3610

Sunset Oceanfront ($$)
Box# 373
(97411) 541.347.2453

Table Rock Motel ($)
840 Beach Loop Rd
(97411) 541.347.2700

The Inn At Face Rock Motel
($$)
3225 Beach Loop Rd
(97411) 541.347.9441

● Beaverton ●
Greenwood Inn ($$$)
10700 SW Allen Blvd
(97005) 503.643.7444

Peppertree Motel ($$)
10720 SW Allen Blvd
(97005) 503.641.7477

Val U Inn Motel ($$)
12255 SW Canyon Rd
(97005) 503.643.6621

● Bend ●
Bend Riverside Motel ($$)
1565 NW Hill St
(97701) 541.389.2363

Best Western ($$)
721 NE 3rd St
(97701) 541.382.1515

Best Western ($$)
19221 Century Dr
(97702) 541.382.4080

Cascade Motel Lodge ($$)
420 SE 3rd St
(97702) 541.382.2612

Cascade View Ranch ($$$$)
60435 Tekampe Rd
(97702) 541.388.5658

Chalet Motel ($)
510 SE 3rd St
(97702) 541.382.6124

Cimarron Motor Inn ($$)
437 NE 3rd St
(97701) 541.382.7711

Comfort Inn ($$)
61200 S Hwy 97
(97702) 541.388.2227
mgr preapproval reqd

Cultus Lake Resort ($$)
Box# 262
(97709) 541.389.3230

Deschutes River Ranch
($$$$)
20210 Swalley Rd
(97701) 541.382.7240

Hampton Inn ($$)
15 NE Butler Market
(97701) 541.388.4114

Holiday Motel ($)
880 SE 3rd St
(97702) 541.382.4620

Motel West ($$)
228 NE Irving Ave
(97701) 541.389.5577

Palmers Cottages ($)
645 NE Greenwood Ave
(97701) 541.382.1197

Pines Lodge ($$)
61405 S Hwy 97
(97702) 541.389.5910

Plaza Motel ($)
1430 NW Hill St
(97701) 541.389.0235

Red Lion Inn ($$$)
849 NE 3rd St
(97701) 541.382.8384
call re: fees

Shilo Inn ($$$)
3105 NE O B Riley Rd
(97701) 541.389.9600
call re: fees

Sonoma Lodge ($)
450 SE 3rd St
(97702) 541.382.4891

Super 8 ($$)
1275 S Hwy 97
(97702) 541.388.6888
deposit

The Riverhouse Resrot ($$$)
3075 N Hwy 97
(97701) 541.389.3111

Twin Lakes Resort ($$$)
11200 S Century Dr
(97707) 541.593.6526

Village Propertie ($$$)
Box# 3055
(97707) 541.593.1653

$=under $35 $$=$35-60 $$$=$60-100 $$$$=over $100

● Blue River ●
The Country Place ($$$)
56245 Delta Dr
(97413) 541.822.6008

● Boardman ●
Dodge City Inn ($$)
1st Front St
(97818) 541.481.2451

Nugget Inn ($$)
15 Front St SW
(97818) 541.481.2375

Riverview Motel ($)
200 Front St NE
(97818) 541.481.2775

● Brookings ●
Beaver State Motel ($$)
437 Chetco Ave
(97415) 541.469.5361

Best Western ($$$)
16008 Boat Basin Rd
(97415) 541.469.7779

Bonn Motel ($$)
1216 Cehtco Ave
(97415) 541.469.2161

Harbor Inn Motel ($$)
15991 Hwy 101
(97415) 541.469.3194

Pacific Sunset Inn ($)
1144 Chetco Ave
(97415) 541.469.2141

● Brothers ●
Travelers Inn ($)
375 N Hwy 97
(97712) 541.382.2211

● Burns ●
Best Western ($$)
577 W Monroe St
(97720) 541.573.2047

Royal Inn ($$)
999 Oregon Ave
(97720) 541.573.5295

● Camp Sherman ●
Black Butte Resort ($$)
35 Suttle-Sherman Rd
(97730) 541.595.6514

Cold Springs Resrot ($$$)
Cold Springs Resort Ln
(97730) 541.595.6271

Twin View Resort ($$)
HcR2126
(97730) 541.595.6125

● Cannon Beach ●
Cannon Beach Lodge ($$)
208 8th St
(97110) 503.436.2776

Cannon Vlg Motel ($$$)
3163 S Hemlock St
(97110) 503.436.2317

Hallmark Resort ($$$)
1400 S Hemlock St
(97110) 503.436.1566
$25 fee & $3 per day

Haystack Resort ($$$)
3339 S Hemlock St
(97110) 503.436.1577

McBee Motel Cottages ($$)
888 S Hemlock St
(97110) 503.436.2569

Quiet Cannon Lodge ($$$)
372 N Spruce St
(97110) 503.436.1405

Surfs And Resort ($$$$)
Oceanfront & Gower St
(97110) 503.436.2274

Tolovana Inn ($$$)
3400 S Hemlock St
(97110) 503.436.2211

Viking Motel ($$$$)
Matanuska & S Pacific
(97110) 503.436.2274

● Canyonville ●
Leisure Inn ($$)
Box# 869
(97417) 541.839.4278

● Cascade Locks ●
Best Western ($$)
735 Wanapa St
(97014) 541.374.8777

Bridge Of Gods Motel ($$)
630 Wanapa St
(97014) 541.374.8628

Scandian Motel ($)
Box# 217
(97014) 541.374.8417

● Cave Junction ●
Country Hills Resort ($$)
7901 Caves Hwy
(97523) 541.592.3406

● Chemult ●
Chemult Motel ($$)
US Hwy 97
(97731) 541.365.2228

Crater Lake Motel ($)
Box# 190
(97731) 541.365.2241

● Chiloquin ●
Meliths Motel ($)
39500 Hwy 97
(97624) 541.783.2401

Spring Creek Motel ($)
47600 Hwy 97
(97624) 541.783.2775

● Clackamas ●
Clackamas Inn ($$)
16010 SE 82nd Dr
(97015) 503.650.5340

● Clatskanie ●
Westport Motel ($$)
Hwy 30
(97016) 503.455.2212

● Coos Bay ●
Best Western ($$)
411 N Bayshore Dr
(97420) 541.269.5111
small pets only

Edgewater Inn ($$$)
275 E Johnson Ave
(97420) 541.267.0423
$4 charge

Lazy J Motel
1143 Hill St
(97420) 541.269.9666

Motel 6 ($)
1445 N Bayshore Dr
(97420) 541.267.7171
1 small pet/room

Plainview Motel ($)
2760 Cape Arago Hwy
(97420) 541.888.5166

Sea Psalm Motel ($)
125 Cape Arago Hwy
(97420) 541.888.9053

Timber Lodge Motel
1001 N Bayshore Dr
(97420) 541.267.7066

● Coquille ●
Myrtle Lane Motel ($)
787 N Central St
(97423) 541.396.2102

● Corvallis ●
Budget Inn ($)
1480 SW 3rd St
(97333) 541.752.8756

Econo Lodge ($$)
345 NW 2nd St
(97330) 541.752.9601

Jason Inn ($$)
800 NW 9th St
(97330) 541.753.7326

Motel Orleans ($$)
935 NW Garfield Ave
(97330) 541.758.9125

Shanico Inn ($$)
1113 NW 9th St
(97330) 541.754.7474

Super 8 ($$)
407 NW 2nd St
(97330) 541.758.8088
call re: fees

Towne House Motel ($$)
350 SW 4th St
(97333) 541.753.4496

● Cottage Grove ●
Best Western ($$)
725 Row River Rd
(97424) 541.942.2491

City Center Motel ($)
737 Hwy 99
(97424) 541.942.8322

Be Discreet

Comfort Inn ($$)
845 Gateway Blvd
(97424) 541.942.9747
mgr preapproval reqd

Holiday Inn ($$)
1601 Gateway Blvd
(97424) 800.465.4329
mgr preapproval reqd

Rainbow Motel ($)
1030 Pacific Hwy 99
(97424) 541.942.5132

River Country Inn ($$$)
71864 London Rd
(97424) 541.942.9334

Stardust Motel ($)
455 Beac Creek Rd
(97424) 541.942.5706

Stardust Motel ($$$)
455 Bear Creek Rd
(97424) 541.942.5706

● Crater Lake ●
Holiday Village Motel ($)
Box# 95
(97604) 541.365.2394

Whispering Pines ($)
Diamond Lake Jet
(97604) 541.365.2259

● Crescent ●
Woodsman Motel ($)
Hwy 97
(97733) 541.433.2170

● Crescent Lake ●
Crescent Creek Ctges ($)
Hwy 58 Milepost 71
(97425) 541.433.2324

Odell Lake Resort ($$)
Hwy 58 Milesport L7
(97425) 541.433.2540

Shelter Cove Resort ($$$)
W Odell Lake Rd Hwy 58
(97425) 541.433.2548

Williamette Pass Inn ($$)
Hwy 8 Milepost 69
(97425) 541.433.2221

● Dallas ●
Rivreside Motel ($)
517 Main St
(97338) 541.623.8163

● Dayton ●
Wine Country Farm ($$$)
6855 Breyman Orchards
(97114) 503.864.3446

● Dayville ●
Fish House Inn ($$)
110 Franklin Hwy 26
(97825) 541.987.2124

● Depoe Bay ●
Holiday Surf Lodge ($$)
939 NW Hwy 101
(97341) 541.765.2133

Inn At Arch Rock ($$)
70 NW Sunset St
(97341) 541.765.2560

Whale Inn ($$)
416 Hwy 101
(97341) 541.765.2789

● Detroit ●
All Seasons Motel ($$)
130 Breitenbrush Rd
(97342) 503.854.3421

● Diamond ●
Westward Ho Motel ($)
94 SE Third St
(97722) 541.382.2111

● Elgin ●
City Centre Motel ($$)
Box# 207
(97827) 541.437.2441

Minam Motel
7260 Hwy 72
(97827) 541.437.4475

● Enterprise ●
Boucher Guest Cottage ($$)
83162 W Dorrance Ln
(97828) 541.426.3209

Ponderosa Motel ($$)
102 SE Greenwood
(97828) 541.426.3186

Shilo Inn ($$)
84570 Bartlett Rd
(97828) 503.828.7741
call re: fees

Wilderness Inn ($$)
301 W North St
(97828) 541.426.4335

● Eugene ●
Angus Inn Motel ($$)
2121 Franklin Blvd
(97403) 541.342.1243

Barrons Motor Inn ($$)
1859 Franklin Blvd
(97403) 541.342.6383

Best Western ($$)
1655 Franklin Blvd
(97403) 541.683.3669

Campus Inn ($$)
390 E Broadway
(97401) 541.343.3376

Classic Residence Inn ($)
1140 W 6th Ave
(97402) 541.343.0730

Country Squire Inn ($$)
33100 Van Duyn Rd
(97408) 541.484.2000

Courtesy Inn ($$)
345 W 6th Ave
(97401) 541.345.3391

Eugene Motor Lodge ($)
476 E Broadway
(97401) 541.344.5233

Eugene Travelers Inn ($)
540 E Broadway
(97401) 541.342.1109

Hilton ($$$)
66 E 6th & Oak Sts
(97401) 541.342.2000
$25 fee

Phoenix Inn ($$)
850 Franklin Blvd
(97403) 541.344.0001

Red Lion Inn ($$$)
205 Cobury Rd
(97401) 541.342.5201
call re: fees

Rodeway Inn ($$)
3840 Hutton St
(97477) 541.746.8471

Sixty Six Motel ($)
755 E Broadway
(97401) 541.342.5041

The Valley River Inn ($$$)
100 Valley River Way
(97440) 541.687.0123

Timbers Motel ($)
1015 Pearl St
(97401) 541.343.3345

● Florence ●
Gull Haven Lodge ($)
94770 Hwy 101
(97439) 541.547.3583

Mercer Lake Resort ($$)
88875 Bayberry Ln
(97439) 541.997.3633

Money Saver Motel ($)
170 Hwy 101
(97439) 541.997.7131

Ocean Breeze Motel ($$)
85165
(97439) 541.997.2642

Park Motel ($)
85034 Hwy 101
(97439) 541.997.2634
$5 per day

Silver Sands Motel ($)
1449 Hwy 101
(97439) 541.997.3459

Villa West Motel ($)
901 Hwy 101
(97439) 541.997.3457

● Forest Grove ●
Holiday Motel ($)
3224 Pacific Ave
(97116) 541.357.7411

● Fort Klamath ●
Crater Lake Resort ($)
50711 Hwy 62
(97626) 541.381.2349

Wilsons Cottages ($)
57997 Hwy 62
(97626) 541.381.2209

● Garibaldi ●
Harbor View Inn ($$)
302 Mooring Basin Rd
(97118) 503.322.3251

Tilla Bay Motel ($$)
8th & Hwy 101
(97118) 541.322.3405

● Gladstone ●
Budget Inn ($)
19240 McLoughlin Blvd
(97027) 503.656.1955

● Gold Beach ●
Best Western ($$)
29266 Ellensburg Ave
(97444) 541.247.6691
must be approved by
manager

Breaker House ($$$)
32864 Neskia Beach Rd
(97444) 541.247.6670

City Center Motel ($$)
150 Harlow St
(97444) 541.247.6675

Drift In Motel ($$)
715 No Ellensburg
(97444) 541.247.4547

Inn At Gold Beach ($)
1435 S Ellesburg
(97444) 541.247.6606

Irelands Lodges ($)
1120 S Ellensburg Ave
(97444) 541.247.7718

Jots Resort ($$)
94360 Wedderbnurn Loop Rd
(97444) 541.247.6676

Kimbell Creek Bend ($$)
97136 N Bank Rogue
(97444) 541.247.7580

Oregon Trail Lodge ($)
550 N Ellesburg Ave
(97444) 541.247.6030

River Bridge Inn ($$)
1010 Jerry'S Flat Rd
(97444) 503.247.4533

Rogue Landing ($)
94749 Jerrys Flat Rd
(97444) 541.247.6105

Sand n Sea Motel ($$)
1040 S Ellensburg Ave
(97444) 541.247.6658

Tu Tu Tun Lodge ($$$)
96550 N Bank Rogue
(97444) 541.247.6664
make reservations on
voicemail

Western Village Motel ($)
975 S Ellensburg Ave
(97444) 541.247.6611

● Government Camp ●
Mt Hood Inn ($$$)
87450 Gov't Camp
(97028) 800.443.7777

Shamrock Forest Inn ($$)
59550 E Hwy 26
(97028) 503.622.4003

● Grants Pass ●
Budget Inn ($$)
1253 NE 6th St
(97526) 541.479.2952

City Center Motel
741 NE 6th St
(97526) 541.476.6134

Flamingo Inn ($)
728 NW 6th St
(97526) 541.476.6601

Golden Inn ($$)
1950 Vine St
(97526) 541.479.6611
$2 per pet

Holiday Inn ($$)
105 NE Agnes Ave
(97526) 541.471.6144
mgr preapproval reqd

Knights Inn ($$)
104 SE 7th St
(97526) 541.479.5595

Motel Orleans ($$)
1889 NE 6th St
(97526) 541.479.8301

Redwood Motel ($)
815 NE 6th St
(97526) 541.476.0878
$5 fee

Regal Lodge ($)
1400 NW 6th St
(97526) 541.479.3305

Riverside Inn ($$)
971 SE 6th St
(97526) 541.476.6873
$15 fee

Rod -N- Reel Motel ($$)
7875 Rogue River Hwy
(97527) 541.582.1516

Rogue River Inn ($)
6285 Rogue River Hwy
(97527) 541.582.1120

Rogue Valley Motel ($$)
7799 Rogue River Hwy
(97527) 541.582.3762

Shilo Inn ($$$)
1880 NW 6th St
(97526) 541.479.8391
call re: fees

Super 8 ($$)
1949 NE 7th St
(97526) 541.474.0888
deposit

Thriftlodge
748 SE 8th St
(97526) 541.476.7793

Weasku Inn ($$$)
748 Rogue River Hwy
(97527) 541.476.4190

● Halfway ●
Clear Creek Farm ($$)
RR 1 Box# 138
(97834) 541.742.2238

● Hermiston ●
Sands Motel ($)
835 North First
(97838) 541.567.5516

The Way Inn ($)
635 S Hwy 395
(97838) 541.567.5561

● Hood River ●
Columbia Gorge Hotel ($$$$)
4000 Westcliff Dr
(97031) 541.386.5566

Hood River Hotel ($$)
102 Oak St
(97031) 541.386.1900

Lost Lake Resort ($$)
Mt Mood National Forest
(97031) 541.386.6366

Meredith Gorge Motel ($)
4300 Westcliff Dr
(97031) 541.386.1515

Sunset Motel ($$)
2300 Cascade Ave
(97031) 541.386.6027

The Upper Rooms ($$)
344 Avalon Dr
(97031) 541.386.2560

Vagabond Lodge ($)
4070 Westcliff Dr
(97031) 503.386.2992
fee

● Idleyld Park ●
North Umpqua Resort ($)
23885 N Umpqua Hwy
(97447) 541.496.0149

● Jacksonville ●
The Stage Lodge ($$)
830 N 5th St
(97530) 541.899.3953

● John Day ●
Best Western ($$)
315 S Main
(97845) 541.575.1700
managers dis. w/$3 charge

Budget 8 Motel ($$)
711 W Main St
(97845) 541.575.2155

Budget Inn ($$)
250 E Main St
(97845) 541.575.2100

Dreamers Lodge ($$)
144 N Canyon Blvd
(97845) 541.575.0526

Well
Behaved

$=under $35 $$=$35-60 $$$=$60-100 $$$$=over $100

Sunset Inn ($$)
390 W Main St
(97845) 800.452.4899

● Joseph ●
Indian Lodge Motel ($$)
201 S Main St
(97846) 541.432.2651

Steins Cabins ($$)
84681 Ponderosa Ln
(97846) 541.432.2391

● Junction City ●
Guest House Motel ($$)
1335 Ivy St
(97448) 541.998.6524

● Kerby ●
Holiday Motel ($$)
24810 Redwood Hwy
(97531) 503.592.3003

● Klamath Falls ●
Best Western ($$)
4061 S 6th St
(97603) 541.882.1200

Cimarron Motor Inn ($$)
3060 S 6th St
(97603) 541.882.4601

Diamond Lake Resort ($$)
Diamond Lake
(97601) 541.793.3333

Hill View Motel ($$)
5543 S 6th St
(97603) 541.883.7771

Maverick Motel ($)
1220 Main St
(97601) 541.882.6688

Olympic Lodge ($$)
3006 Greensprings Dr
(97601) 541.883.8800

Oregon Motel 8 ($)
Kiik Hwy 97
(97601) 541.883.3431

Red Lion Inn ($$)
3612 S 6th St
(97603) 541.882.8864
call re: fees

Shilo Inn ($$$)
2500 Almond St
(97601) 541.885.7980

Super 8 ($$)
3805 N Hwy 97
(97601) 800.800.8000
call re: fees

● La Grande ●
Best Western ($$$)
2612 Island Ave
(97850) 541.963.7195

Broken Arrow Lodge ($)
2215 Adams Ave
(97850) 541.963.7116

Greenwell Motel ($)
305 Adams Ave
(97850) 541.963.4134

Moon Motel
2116 Adams Ave
(97850) 541.963.2724

Orchard Motel ($)
2206 Adams Ave
(97850) 541.963.6160

Quail Run Motor Inn ($)
2400 Adams Ave
(97850) 541.963.3400

Stardust Lodge ($)
402 Adams Ave
(97850) 541.963.4166

Wendells Corner
2309 Adams Ave
(97850) 541.963.4424

● La Pine ●
East Lake Resort ($$)
Box# 95
(97739) 541.536.2230

Highlander Motel
51511 Hwy 97
(97739) 541.536.2131

Lampliter Motel ($)
51526 Hwy 97
(97739) 541.536.2931

Pauline Lake Resort ($$)
Box# 7
(97739) 541.536.2240

Timbercrest Inn ($)
52560 Hwy 97
(97739) 541.536.1737

Westview Motel ($$)
51371 Hwy 97
(97739) 541.536.2115

● Lake Oswego ●
Best Western ($$)
15700 Upper Boones Fry
(97034) 503.620.2980
small dogs $5 per day

Crowne Plaza ($$$)
14811 Kruse Oaks Blvd
(97035) 503.624.8400

Howard Johnson ($$$)
14811 Kruse Oaks Blvd
(97035) 800.654.2000

Phoenix Inn ($$)
14905 SW Bangy Rd
(97034) 503.624.7400

Residence Inn ($$$$)
15200 Bangy Rd
(97035) 503.684.2603
call for fee & availability

● Lakeside ●
Lakeshore Lodge ($)
290 S 8th St
(97449) 541.759.3161

Seadrift Motel ($$)
11022 Coast Hwy 101
(97449) 541.759.3102

● Lakeview ●
Aa Motel ($)
411 N F St
(97630) 541.947.2201

Hunters Hot Springs ($$)
Hwy 395
(97630) 541.648.4800

Interstate 8 Motel ($)
354 N K St
(97630) 541.947.3341

Lakeview Lodge ($)
301 N G St
(97630) 541.947.2181

Rim Rock Motel ($)
727 S F St
(97630) 541.947.2185

● Lebanon ●
Cascade City Motel ($)
1296 S Main St
(97355) 541.258.8154

Shanico Inn ($$)
1840 S Main St
(97355) 541.259.2601

● Lincoln City ●
Anchor Motel ($$)
4417 SW Hwy 101
(97367) 541.996.3810

Bel Aire Motel
2945 NW Hwy 101
(97367) 541.994.2984

Best Western ($$$)
535 NW Inlet Ave
(97367) 541.994.4227

Blue Heron Landing ($$)
4006 West Devils Lake
(97367) 541.994.4708

Captain Cook Inn ($$)
2626 NE Hwy 101
(97367) 541.994.2522

City Center Motel ($)
1014 NE Hwy 101
(97367) 541.994.2612

Coho Inn ($$$)
1635 NW Harbor Ave
(97367) 541.994.3684

Edgecliff Motel ($$)
3733 SW Hwy 101
(97367) 541.996.2055

Ester Lee Motel ($$)
3803 SW Hwy 101
(97367) 541.996.3606

Hideaway Motel
810 SW 10th St
(97367) 541.994.8874

Holiday Inn
1091 SE 1st
(97367) 541.996.4400

Overlook Motel
3521 SW Anchor Dr
(97367) 541.996.3300

Rodeway Inn ($$)
861 SW 51st St
(97367) 541.996.3996

Sailor Jack Motel ($$)
1035 NW Harbor Ave
(97367) 541.994.3696

Sea Echo Motel ($)
3510 NE Hwy 101
(97367) 541.994.2575

Sea Horse Motel ($$)
2039 N Harbor Dr
(97367) 541.994.2101

Sea Rest Motel
1249 NW 15th St
(97367) 541.994.3053

Seagull Beachfront ($$)
1511 NW Harbor Ave
(97367) 541.994.2948

Shilo Inn ($$)
1501 NW 40th St
(97367) 541.994.3655
call re: fees

Surftides Beach Resort ($$)
2945 NW Jetty Ave
(97367) 541.994.2191

Westshore Oceanfront ($$)
3127 SW Anchor Ave
(97367) 541.996.2091

Whistling Winds
3264 NW Jetty Ave
(97367) 541.994.6155

● Madras ●
Best Western ($)
12 SW 4th St
(97741) 541.475.6141

Goffys Motel ($)
Hwy 26
(97741) 541.475.4633

Juniper Motel
414 N Hwy 26
(97741) 541.475.6186

Royal Dutch Motel ($)
1101 SW Hwy 97
(97741) 541.475.2281

Sonnys Motel ($$)
1539 SW Hwy 97
(97741) 541.475.7217

● Manzanita ●
Sunset Surf Motel ($$)
248 Ocean Rd
(97130) 541.368.5224

● Maupin ●
Deschutes Motel ($)
RR 1 Box# 10 Hwy 197
(97037) 541.395.2626

The Oasis Resort ($)
609 Hwy 197
(97037) 541.395.2611

● McMinnville ●
Best Western ($$$)
2035 SW 99W
(97128) 503.472.4900

Paragon Motel ($$)
2065 Hwy 99 West
(97128) 503.472.9493

● Medford ●
Best Western ($$)
585 S Columbia River Hwy
(97501) 503.397.3000

Best Western ($$$)
2340 Crater Lake Hwy
(97504) 541.779.2011
small pets

Capri Motel ($)
250 E Barnett Rd
(97501) 541.773.7796

Cedar Lodge Motel ($$)
518 N Riverside Ave
(97501) 541.773.7361

Horizon Motel ($$)
1150 E Barnett Rd
(97504) 541.779.5085

Motel Orleans ($)
850 Alba Dr
(97504) 541.779.6730

Pear Tree Inn ($$)
3730 Fern Valley Rd
(97504) 541.535.4445

Red Lion Inn ($$$)
200 N Riverside Ave
(97501) 541.779.5811
call re: fees

Reston Hotel ($$)
2300 Crater Lake Hwy
(97504) 541.779.3141

Travelodge ($$)
2111 Biddle Rd
(97504) 541.620.6574

Village Inn Motel ($)
535 S Hwy 30
(97501) 503.397.1490

Windmill Inn ($$)
1950 Biddle Rd
(97504) 541.779.0050

● Milton Freewater ●
Out West Motel ($)
Hwy 11
(97862) 541.938.6647

● Molalla ●
Stage Coach Motel ($$)
415 Grange St
(97038) 503.829.4382

● Monmouth ●
Courtesy Inn ($$)
270 Pacific Ave
(97361) 541.838.4438

● Myrtle Point ●
Hyrtle Trees Motel ($)
1010 8th St
(97458) 541.572.5811

● Neskowin ●
The Breakers Condominums
($$$)
48060 Breakers Blvd
(97149) 503.392.3417

● Netarts ●
Terimore Lodging ($$)
5105 Crab Ave
(97143) 503.842.4623

● Newberg ●
Shilo Inn ($$)
501 Sitka Ave
(97132) 503.537.0303

● Newport ●
Agate Beach ($$$)
175 NW Gilbert Way
(97365) 541.265.8746

Best Western ($$$)
744 SW Elizabeth St
(97365) 541.265.2600

City Center Motel ($$)
538 SW Coast Hwy
(97365) 541.265.7381

Driftwood Village ($$)
7947 N Coast Hwy
(97365) 541.265.5738

Money Saver Motel
861 SW Coast Hwy # 101
(97365) 541.265.2277

Newport Motor Inn ($$)
1311 N Hwy 101
(97365) 541.265.8516

Pennysaver Motel ($$)
710 N Hwy 101
(97365) 541.265.6631

Sands Motor Lodge ($$)
206 N Coast Hwy
(97365) 541.265.5321

Shilo Inn ($$$)
536 SW Elizabeth St
(97365) 541.265.7701
call re: fees

Surfn Sand Motel ($$$)
8143 N Hwy 101
(97365) 541.265.2215

Tides Inn Motel ($)
715 SW Bay St
(97365) 541.265.7202

Vikings Cottages ($$)
729 NW Coast St
(97365) 541.265.2477

Waves Motel ($$)
820 NW Coast St
(97365) 541.265.4661

$=under $35 $$=$35-60 $$$=$60-100 $$$$=over $100

West Wind Motel ($$)
747 SW Coast Hwy
(97365) 541.265.5388

Whaler Motel ($$$)
155 SW Elizabeth St
(97365) 541.265.9261

Willers Motel ($$)
754 SW Coast Hwy
(97365) 541.265.2241

● North Bend ●
Bay Bridge Motel ($$)
33 US 101
(97459) 541.756.3151

Parkside Inn
1480 Sherman Ave
(97459) 541.756.4124

Pony Village Motel ($$)
Virginia Ave
(97459) 541.756.3191

● North Powder ●
Powder River Motel
850 2nd St
(97867) 541.898.2829

● Oakridge ●
Arbor Inn ($)
48229 Hwy 58
(97463) 541.782.2611

Best Western ($$)
47433 Hwy 58
(97463) 541.782.2212
small pets & fee

Oakridge Motel ($)
48197 Hwy 58
(97463) 541.782.2432

● Ontario ●
Budget Inn ($)
1737 N Oregon St
(97914) 541.889.3101

Carlile Motel ($)
589 N Oregon St
(97914) 541.889.8658

Holiday Inn
1249 Tayadera Ave
(97914) 541.889.8621

Holiday Motor Inn ($)
615 E Idaho Ave
(97914) 541.889.9188

Howard Johnson ($$)
1249 Tapadera Ave
(97914) 541.889.8621

Oregon Trail Motel ($)
92 E Idaho Ave
(97914) 541.889.8633

Regency Crest Inn ($)
88 N Oregon St
(97914) 541.889.6449

Stockmans Motel ($)
81 SW 1st St
(97914) 541.889.4446

● Oregon City ●
Val U Inn Motel ($$)
1900 Clackamette Dr
(97045) 503.655.7141

● Otter Rock ●
Alpine Chalets ($$$)
7045 Otter Crest Loop
(97369) 541.765.2572

● Pacific City ●
Anchorage Motel ($)
6585 Pacific Ave
(97135) 503.965.6773

Inn At Pacific City ($$)
35215 Brooten Rd
(97135) 503.965.6366

● Pendleton ●
7 Inn ($)
I-84 Ex 202
(97801) 541.276.4111

Chaparral Motel ($$)
620 Tutuilla Rd
(97801) 541.276.8654

Leter Buck Motel ($)
205 SE Dorion Ave
(97801) 541.276.3293

Longhorn Motel ($)
411 SW Dorion Ave
(97801) 541.276.7531

Red Lion Inn ($$$)
304 SE Nye Ave
(97801) 541.276.6141
call re: fees

Super 8 ($$)
601 SE Nye Ave
(97801) 541.276.8881
call re: fees

Tapadera Motel ($)
105 SE Court Ave
(97801) 541.276.3231

● Pilot Rock ●
Pilot Rock Motel
362 NE 4th St
(97868) 541.443.2851

● Plush ●
Dock Of The Bay
1116 SW 51st St
(97637) 541.996.2124

● Port Orford ●
Castaway By The Sea ($$)
545 W 5th St
(97465) 541.332.4502

Sea Crest Motel ($)
Box# C
(97465) 541.332.3040

Shoreline Motel ($)
206 6th
(97465) 541.332.2903

● Portland ●
4th Avenue Motel ($$)
1889 SW 4th Ave
(97201) 503.226.7646

Aladdin Motor Inn ($)
8905 SW 30th Ave
(97219) 503.246.8241

Best Value Inn ($)
3310 SE 82nd Ave
(97266) 503.777.4786

Best Western ($$)
4319 NW Yeon Ave
(97210) 503.497.9044

Best Western ($$)
1215 N Hayden Meadows Dr
(97217) 503.286.9600

Best Western ($$)
17993 Lower Boones Fry
(97224) 503.620.2030

Best Western ($$)
420 NE Holladay St
(97232) 503.233.6331

Budget Value Viking ($$)
6701 N Interstate Ave
(97217) 503.285.6687

Cascade Motel ($$)
10308 SE 82nd Ave
(97266) 503.775.1571

Center Apartments
200 SW Harrison St
(97201) 503.224.3030

Comfort Inn ($$)
431 NE Multnomah St
(97232) 503.233.7933
mgr preapproval reqd

Cypress Inn ($$$)
9040 SE Adams
(97266) 503.655.0062

Cypress Inn ($$)
809 SW King Ave
(97205) 503.252.8247

Days Inn ($$)
3828 NE 2nd Ave
(97220) 503.256.2550
$10

Days Inn ($$$)
1414 SW 6th Ave
(97201) 503.221.1611
mgr preapproval reqd

Delta Inn ($$)
9930 N Whitaker Rd
(97217) 503.289.1800

Embassy Suites ($$$$)
9000 Washington Square
(97223) 503.644.4000

Fifth Avenue Suite ($$$$)
521 SW 5th Ave
(97204) 503.222.0001

Historic Hotel ($$$$)
422 SW Broadway
(97205) 503.228.1212

$=under $35 $$=$35-60 $$$=$60-100 $$$$=over $100

Holiday Inn ($$)
2323 NE 181st Ave
(97230) 503.492.4000

Holiday Motel ($)
8050 Ml King
(97211) 503.285.3661

Howard Johnson ($$$)
7101 NE 82nd Ave
(97220) 503.255.6722

Imperial Hotel ($$$)
400 Broadway
(97205) 503.228.7221

Mallory Hotel ($$$)
729 SW 15th Ave
(97205) 503.223.6311

Marriott Hotel ($$$$)
1401 SW Naito Pkwy
(97201) 503.226.7600

Mels Motor Inn ($$)
5205 N Interstate Ave
(97217) 503.285.2556

Milwaukie Inn ($)
14015 SE McLoughlin Blvd
(97267) 503.659.2125

Motel 6 ($$)
17950 SW McEwan Ave
(97224) 503.620.2066
1 small pet/room

Motel 6 ($)
17959 SW McEwan Ave
(97224) 503.684.0760
1 small pet/room

Oxford Suites ($$$)
12226 N Jantzen Dr
(97217) 503.283.3030

Quality Inn ($$$)
8247 NE Sandy Blvd
(97220) 503.256.4111
mgr preapproval reqd

Quality Inn ($$)
7300 SW Hazelfern Rd
(97224) 503.620.3460
mgr preapproval reqd

Ranch Inn Motel ($)
10138 SW Barbur Blvd
(97219) 503.246.3375

Red Lion Inn ($$$$)
1401 N Hayden Isld Dr
(97217) 503.283.2111
call re: fees

Red Lion Inn ($$$)
310 SW Lincoln St
(97201) 503.221.0450
call re: fees

Red Lion Inn ($$$)
909 N Hayden Island Dr
(97217) 503.283.4466
call re: fees

Red Lion Inn ($$)
1224 N Thunderbird Way
(97227) 503.235.8311
call re: fees

Residence Inn ($$$)
18855 NW Tanasbourne Dr
(97229) 503.531.3200

River Place Hotel ($$$$)
1510 SW Harbor Way
(97201) 503.228.3233
$10 fee

Riverside Inn ($$$)
50 SW Morrison St
(97204) 503.221.0711

Rodeway Inn ($$)
1506 NE 2nd Ave
(97232) 503.231.7665

Rose Manor Inn ($)
4546 SE McLoughlin Blvd
(97202) 503.236.4175

Rose Motel
8920 SW Barbur Blvd
(97219) 503.244.0107

Shilo Inn ($$$)
9900 SW Canyon Rd
(97225) 503.297.2551
call re: fees

Shilo Inn ($$)
10830 SW Greenbrg Rd
(97223) 800.222.2244

Silver Spur Motel ($)
789 N Broadway
(97220) 541.573.2077

Sixth Venue Motel ($$)
2221 SW 6th Ave
(97201) 503.226.2979

The Benson Hotel ($$$$)
309 SW Broadway At Oak
(97205) 503.228.2000

The Mark Spencer Hotel ($$)
409 SW 11th Ave
(97205) 503.224.3293

Value Inn ($)
415 SW Montgomery St
(97201) 503.226.4751

● Prairie City ●
Strawberry Mtn Inn ($$)
HC 77 940 Hwy 26
(97869) 541.820.4522

● Prineville ●
Carolina Motel ($)
1050 E 3rd St
(97754) 541.447.4152

City Center Motel ($)
509 E 3rd St
(97754) 541.447.5522

Ochoco Inn ($$)
123 E 3rd St
(97754) 541.447.6231

Rustlers Roost Motel ($$)
960 W 3rd St
(97754) 541.447.4185

● Prospect ●
Prospect Hotel ($$)
391 Mill Creek Dr
(97536) 541.560.3664

● Redmond ●
Hub Motel ($$)
1128 N Hwy 97
(97756) 541.548.2101

Redmond Inn ($$)
1545 Hwy 97
(97756) 541.548.1091

● Reedsport ●
Anchor Bay Inn ($)
1821 Winchester Ave
(97467) 541.271.2149

Best Budget Inn ($)
1894 Winchester Ave
(97467) 541.271.3686

Best Western ($$)
1400 Hwy Ave 101
(97467) 541.271.4831

Fir Grove Motel ($)
2178 Winchester Ave
(97467) 541.271.4848

Friendship Inn ($$)
390 Broadway Ave
(97467) 541.271.4871

Salbasgeon Inn ($$$)
45209 S R 38
(97467) 541.271.2025

Salty Seagull Motel ($)
1806 Winchester Ave
(97467) 541.271.3729

Tropicana Motel ($)
1593 Hwy Ave
(97467) 541.271.3671

● Rockaway Beach ●
101 Motel ($)
530 Hwy 101
(97136) 503.355.2420

Broadwater Rentals ($$)
438 Hwy 101
(97136) 503.355.2248

Getaway Motel ($$)
621 S Pacific Dr
(97136) 503.355.2501

Ocean Locomotion Motel
($$)
19130 Alder St
(97136) 503.355.2093

Ocean Spray Motel ($$)
505 N Pacific St
(97136) 503.355.2237

Sand Dollar Motel ($$)
105 NW 23rd Ave
(97136) 503.355.2301

Sea Treasures Inn ($$)
301 N Miller St
(97136) 503.355.8220

$=under $35 $$=$35-60 $$$=$60-100 $$$$=over $100

OREGON, Rockaway Beach

Silver Sands Motel ($$$)
215 S Pacific
(97136) 503.355.2206

Surfside Resort Motel ($$)
101 NW 11th Ave
(97136) 503.355.2312

Tradewinds Motel ($$)
523 N Pacific St
(97136) 503.355.2112

● Roseburg ●
Best Western ($$)
511 SE Stephens St
(97470) 541.673.6625

Best Western ($$)
760 NW Garden Valley Blvd
(97470) 541.672.1601
pets @ mgrs discretion

Budget 16 Motel ($$)
1067 NE Stephens St
(97470) 541.673.5556

Casa Loma Motel ($)
1107 NE Stephens St
(97470) 541.673.5569

Dunes Motel ($$)
Madrone St
(97470) 541.672.6684

Holiday Inn ($$)
375 Harvard Blvd
(97470) 541.673.7517

Howard Johnson ($$)
978 NE Stephens St
(97470) 541.673.5082

Motel Orleans ($$)
427 NW Garden Valley Blvd
(97470) 541.673.5561

Ranch Motel ($)
581 John Long Rd
(97470) 541.849.2126

Sycamore Motel
1627 SE Stephens St
(97470) 541.672.3354

Windmill Inn ($$)
1450 NW Mulholland Dr
(97470) 541.673.0901

● Salem ●
City Centre Motel ($$)
510 Libertyst SE
(97301) 503.364.0121

Grand Motel ($$)
1555 State St
(97301) 503.581.2466

Holiday Lodge ($$)
1400 HawthorneAve NE
(97301) 503.585.2323

Motel 6 ($)
2250 Mission St SE
(97302) 503.588.7191
1 small pet/room

Phoenix Inn ($$)
4370 Commercial St SE
(97302) 503.588.9220

Quality Hotel ($$$)
3301 Market St NE
(97301) 503.370.7888
$10 fee

Tiki Lodge Motel ($)
3705 Market St NE
(97301) 503.581.4441

Travelodge ($)
1875 Fisher Rd NE
(97305) 503.588.5423
ground floor

● Sandy ●
Best Western ($$)
37465 Hwy 26
(97055) 503.668.7100

Mt Hood Motel ($)
59550 E Hwy 26
(97055) 503.622.4911

● Seaside ●
Best Western ($$$)
414 N Promenade
(97138) 503.738.3334

City Center Motel ($$)
250 1st Ave # 97138
(97138) 503.738.6377

Coast River Inn ($$)
800 S Holladay Dr
(97138) 503.738.8474

Comfort Inn ($$$)
545 Broadway St
(97138) 503.738.3011
mgr preapproval reqd

Country River Inn ($$)
1020 N Holladay Dr
(97138) 503.738.8049

Edgewater Inn ($$$)
341 S Promenade
(97138) 503.738.4142

Gearhart By The Sea ($$$)
10th & N Marion
(97138) 503.738.8331

Inn On The Promenade ($$)
361 S Promenade
(97138) 503.738.5241

Seasider Motel ($)
210 N Downing St
(97138) 503.738.7622

Seasider Motel ($)
110 5th Ave
(97138) 503.738.7764

Seaview Inn ($$)
1421 Division
(97138) 509.328.6054

The Lanai Motel ($$)
3140 Sunset Blvd
(97138) 503.738.6343

Windjammer Motel ($$)
4301 Hwy 101
(97138) 503.738.3250

● Sisters ●
Best Western ($$$)
500 Hwy 20
(97759) 541.549.1234

Blue Lake Resort ($$$)
Blue Lake Dr Hwy 20/126
(97759) 541.595.6671

Cascade Country Inn ($$$)
15870 Barclay Dr
(97759) 541.549.4666

● Springfield ●
Red Lion Inn ($$$)
3280 Gateway St
(97477) 541.726.8181
call re: fees

Rodeway Inn ($$)
3480 Hutton St
(97477) 541.746.8471

Shilo Inn ($$)
3350 Gateway St
(97477) 541.747.0332
call re: fees

Sutton Motel ($)
1152 Main St
(97477) 541.747.5621

Village Inn Motel ($$)
1875 Mohawk Blvd
(97477) 541.747.4546

● Sublimity ●
Best Western ($$)
300 SW Sublimity Blvd
(97385) 503.769.9579

● Summer Lake ●
The Lodge At Summer Lake
($)
36980 Hwy 31
(97640) 541.943.3993

● Sutherlin ●
Town & Country Motel ($$)
1386 W Central Ave
(97479) 541.459.9615

● Sweet Home ●
Porta Via Motel ($$)
805 Long St
(97386) 541.367.5137

Willow Motel ($)
3026 Hwy 20
(97386) 541.367.2206

● The Dalles ●
Best Eastern ($$)
200 W 2nd St
(97058) 541.296.9111

Best Western ($$)
112 W 2nd St
(97058) 541.296.9107

Captain Grays House ($$)
210 W 4th St
(97058) 541.298.2222

Days Inn ($$)
2500 W 6th St
(97058) 541.296.1191
$10

$=under $35 $$=$35-60 $$$=$60-100 $$$$=over $100

Lone Pine Motel ($$)
351 Lone Pine Dr
(97058) 541.298.2800

Quality Inn ($$)
2114 W 6th St
(97058) 541.298.5161
mgr preapproval reqd

Shamrock Motel ($)
118 W 4th St
(97058) 541.296.5464

Shilo Inn ($$)
3223 Bret Clodfelter Way
(97058) 541.298.5502
call re: fees

The Inn At The Dalles ($)
3550 SE Frontage Rd
(97058) 541.296.1167

● Tillamook ●
Shilo Inn ($$$)
2515 N Main St
(97141) 800.222.2244

Three Capes Inn ($$)
4800 Netarts Hwy
(97141) 503.842.4003

Western Royal Inn ($$)
1125 N Main St
(97141) 503.842.8844

● Troutdale ●
Phoenix Inn ($$)
477 NW Phoenix Dr
(97060) 503.669.6500

Shilo Inn ($$)
2522 NE 238th Dr
(97060) 503.667.1414
call re: fees

● Tualatin ●
Sweetbrier Inn ($$)
7125 SW Nyberg Rd
(97062) 503.692.5800

● Umatilla ●
Heather Inn ($$)
705 Willamette St
(97882) 541.922.4871

Rest A Bit Motel ($)
1370 6th St
(97882) 541.922.3271

● Vida ●
Wayfarer Resort ($$$)
46725 Goodpasture Rd
(97488) 541.896.3613

● Waldport ●
Alsea Manor Motel ($$)
190 SW Hwy 101
(97394) 541.563.3249

Edgewater Cottages ($$)
3978 SW 101
(97394) 541.563.2240

Sea Stones Cottages ($)
6317 SW 101
(97394) 541.547.3118

Sundown Motel ($$)
5050 SW Pch 101
(97394) 541.563.3018

Waldport Motel ($)
170 SW Arrow
(97394) 541.563.3035

● Wallowa ●
Mingo Motel ($$)
102 N Alder
(97885) 541.886.2021

● Warm Springs ●
Kah Nee Ta Village ($$$)
100 Main St
(97761) 541.553.1112

● Warrenton ●
Rays Motel ($)
45 NE Skipanon Dr
(97146) 503.861.2566

Shilo Inn ($$$)
1609 E Harbor St
(97146) 503.861.2181
call re: fees

● Welches ●
Mt Hood Village
65000 E Hwy 26
(97067) 503.622.4011

● Westlake ●
Siltcoos Lake Resort ($$)
82855 Fir St
(97493) 541.997.3741

● Wheeler ●
Wheeler On The Bay ($$$)
580 Marine Dr
(97147) 503.368.5858

● Wilsonville ●
Motel Orleans ($)
8815 SW Sun Pl
(97070) 503.682.3184

● Wolf Creek ●
Sunny Valley Motel ($)
I-5 Ex 71
(97497) 541.476.9217

● Woodburn ●
Comfort Inn ($$)
120 Arney Rd NE
(97071) 503.982.1727
mgr preapproval reqd

Fairway Inn ($)
2450 Country Club Ct
(97071) 503.981.3211

Holiday Inn ($$)
2887 Newberg Hwy
(97071) 503.982.6515
mgr preapproval reqd

● Yachats ●
Fireside Motel ($$)
1881 Hwy 101
(97498) 541.547.3636

Gull Haven Lodge ($)
94770 Hwy 101
(97498) 541.547.3583

Shamrock Lodgettes ($$$$)
105 US 101
(97498) 503.547.3312
cabins only guest rfd

The Adobe Resort ($$)
1555 Hwy 101
(97498) 541.547.3141

Pennsylvania
● Adamstown ●
Black Forest Inn ($$)
Box# 457
(19501) 717.484.4801

● Allentown ●
Allenwood Motel ($$)
1058 Hausman Rd
(18104) 215.395.3707

Days Inn ($$)
Rt 22 & 309
(18104) 610.395.3731
$15

Econo Lodge ($$)
2115 Downyflake Ln
(18103) 610.797.2200

Holiday Inn
Rt 22
(18104) 610.435.7880

Holiday Inn
3620 Hamilton Blvd
(18104) 610.437.9255

Howard Johnson ($$)
3220 Hamilton Blvd
(18103) 610.439.4000

Microtel ($$)
1880 Steelstone Rd
(18103) 610.266.9070

Red Roof Inn ($$)
1846 Catasauqua Rd
(18103) 610.264.5404

● Altoona ●
Econo Lodge ($$)
2906 Pleasant Valley Blvd
(16602) 814.944.3555

Hojo Inn ($$)
1500 Sterling St
(16602) 814.946.7601

● Bartonsville ●
Comfort Inn ($$)
S R 611
(18321) 717.476.1500

Holiday Inn ($$$)
Rt 611 & I-80
(18321) 717.424.6100
mgr preapproval reqd

● Beaver Falls ●
Beaver Valley Motel ($$)
S R 18
(15010) 412.843.0630

Policies Subject to Change

$=under $35 $$=$35-60 $$$=$60-100 $$$$=over $100

PENNSYLVANIA, Beaver Falls

Holiday Inn
Rt 18
(15010) 412.846.3700

Holiday Inn ($$$)
Rt 18
(15010) 412.646.3700

● Bedford ●
Econo Lodge ($)
RR 2 Box 28
(15522) 814.623.5174

Janey Lynn Motel ($)
RR 5 Box# 367
(15522) 814.623.9515

Motel Town House ($)
200 S Richard St
(15522) 814.623.5138

Quality Inn ($$)
RR 2 Box# 171
(15522) 814.623.5188
mgr preapproval reqd

Super 8 ($$)
Bus Rt 220
(15522) 814.849.8840
call re: fees

● Bensalem ●
Comfort Inn ($$)
3660 Street Rd
(19020) 800.221.2222

● Berwyn ●
Residence Inn ($$$)
600 W Swedesford Rd
(19312) 610.640.9494
$100 fee & $6 per day

● Bethlehem ●
Comfort Inn ($$)
3191 Highfield Dr
(18017) 610.865.6300
mgr preapproval reqd

Comfort Suites ($$$)
120 W 3rd St
(18015) 610.882.9700
mgr preapproval reqd

● Bloomsburg ●
Econo Lodge ($$)
189 Columbia Mall Dr
(17815) 717.387.0490
$10 per day

Magees Main Street ($$)
20 W Main St
(17815) 800.331.9815

Quality Inn ($$)
7 Buckhorn Rd
(17815) 717.784.5300

The Inn At Turkey Hill ($$$)
991 Central Rd
(17815) 717.387.1500

● Breezewood ●
Penn Aire Motel ($$)
Box# 156
(15533) 814.735.4351

Wiltshire Motel ($)
HC 2 Box# 1
(15533) 814.735.4361

● Bridgeville ●
Knights Inn ($)
111 Hickory Grade Rd
(15017) 412.221.8110
size limits & fees

● Brookville ●
Budget Host ($)
RR 3 Box# 358
(15825) 800.283.4678

Days Inn ($$)
230 Allegheny Blvd
(15825) 814.849.8001

Howard Johnson ($$)
245 Allegheny Blvd
(15825) 814.849.3335

Ramada Ltd ($$)
235 Allegheny Blvd
(15825) 814.849.8381
$5 fee

● Butler ●
Days Inn
139 Pittsburgh Rd
(16001) 412.287.6761

Super 8 ($$)
138 Pittsburgh Rd
(16001) 412.287.8888
pets w/permission

● Camp Hill ●
Radisson Inn ($$$)
1150 Camp Hill Baypass
(17011) 800.333.3333

● Carlisle ●
Albright Motel ($)
1165 Harrisburg Pike
(17013) 717.249.4380

Best Western ($$)
1245 Harrisburg Pike
(17013) 717.243.5411

Budget Host ($$)
1252 Harrisburg Pike
(17013) 717.243.8585

Days Inn ($$)
101 Alexander Spring Rd
(17013) 717.258.4147
$6

Econo Lodge ($$)
1460 Harrisburg Pike
(17013) 717.249.7775
$5 per day

Holiday Inn ($$)
1450 Harrisburg Pike
(17013) 717.245.2400
mgr preapproval reqd

Howard Johnson ($$)
1255 Harrisburg Pike
(17013) 717.243.6000

Rodeway Inn ($$)
1239 Harrisburg Pike
(17013) 717.249.2800
pet rooms

● Chadds Ford ●
Brandywine River Hotel ($$$)
US 1 & S R 100
(19317) 610.388.1200

● Chambersburg ●
Days Inn ($$)
30 Falling Spring Rd
(17201) 717.263.1288

Friendship Inn ($)
1620 Lincoln Way
(17201) 717.264.4108
small pets

Holiday Inn ($$)
1095 Wayne Ave
(17201) 717.263.3400

Travelodge ($$)
565 Lincoln Way
(17201) 717.264.4187
small pets only

● Chester ●
Howard Johnson ($$)
1300 Providence Ave
(19013) 610.876.7211

● Clarion ●
Days Inn ($$)
Rt 68 & I-80
(16214) 814.226.8682

Holiday Inn ($$$)
Rt 68 & I-80
(16214) 814.226.8850
mgr preapproval reqd

Super 8 ($$)
RR 3 & Rt 68
(16214) 814.226.4550
size limits & fees

● Clarks Summit ●
Summit Inn ($)
649 Northern Blvd
(18411) 717.586.1211
$3 charge

● Clearfield ●
Best Western ($$)
Po Obx 286
(16830) 814.765.2441
1 small housebroken pet

Best Western ($$)
I-80
(16830) 814.765.2441
small pets only

Days Inn ($$)
RR 2 Box# 245B
(16830) 814.765.5381

Royal 9 Motor Inn ($)
Rt 322
(16830) 814.765.2639

Super 8 ($$)
RR 2 Box# 242-C
(16830) 814.768.7580
call re: fees

Well
Behaved

$=under $35 $$=$35-60 $$$=$60-100 $$$$=over $100

• Cooksburg •
Forest View Cabins
Box# 105
(16217) 814.744.8413

• Coopersburg •
Travelodge ($$)
321 S 3rd St
(18036) 610.282.1212

• Coraopolis •
Embassy Suites ($$$)
550 Cherrington Pkwy
(15108) 412.269.9070

Holiday Inn
1406 Beers School Rd
(15108) 412.262.3600

La Quinta Inn ($$)
1433 Beers School Rd
(15108) 412.269.0400
call re: fees

Marriott Hotel ($$$)
100 Aten Rd
(15108) 412.788.8800

Motel 6 ($$)
1170 Thorn Run Rd
(15108) 412.269.0990
1 small pet/room

Red Roof Inn ($$)
1454 Beers School Rd
(15108) 412.264.5678

Royce Hotel Airport ($$$$)
1160 Thorn Run Rd
(15108) 412.262.2400

• Cranberry Twp •
Residence Inn
1306 Freedom Rd
(16066) 412.779.1000

• Danville •
Red Roof Inn ($)
300 Red Roof Inn Rd
(17821) 717.275.7600

• Delmont •
Super 8 ($$)
180 Sheffield Dr
(15626) 412.468.4888
call re: fees

• Denver •
Black Horse Lodge ($$)
2180 N Reading Rd
(17517) 717.336.7563

Comfort Inn ($)
2015 N Reading Rd
(17517) 717.336.4643
mgr preapproval reqd

Holiday Inn
Rt 272 & 222
(17517) 717.336.7541

Pennsylvania Dutch ($$)
2275 N Reading Rd
(17517) 717.267.5559

• Douglassville •
Econo Lodge ($$)
387 Ben Franklin Hwy
(19518) 610.385.3016

• Drums •
Jecono Lodge ($$)
S R 309 I-80
(18222) 717.788.4121

• Du Bois •
Dubois Manor Motel ($)
525 Liberty Blvd
(15801) 814.371.5400

Holiday Inn ($$)
US 219 & I-80
(15801) 814.371.5100
mgr preapproval reqd

Ramada Inn ($$)
Rt 255 & I-80 Ex 17
(15801) 814.371.7070

• East Stroudsburg •
Super 8 ($$)
340 Greentree Dr
(18301) 717.424.7411
pets w/permission

• Easton •
Best Western ($$)
185 S 3rd St
(18042) 610.253.9131

Days Inn ($$)
2555 Nazareth Rd
(18045) 610.253.0546
$5

• Ebensburg •
Comfort Inn ($$)
SR22
(15931) 814.472.6100
mgr preapproval reqd

The Cottage Inn ($$)
RR 4 Box# 50
(15931) 814.472.8002

• Edinboro •
Ramada Inn ($$$)
Rt 6N
(16412) 814.734.5650

• Enola •
Quality Inn ($$)
501 N Enola Rd
(17025) 717.732.0785

• Ephrata •
Smithton Ctry Inn ($$)
900 W Main St
(17522) 717.733.6094

• Erie •
Days Inn ($$)
7415 Schultz Rd
(16509) 814.868.8521
$5

Holiday Inn ($$$)
8040 Perry Hwy
(16509) 814.864.4911
mgr preapproval reqd

Howard Johnson ($$)
7575 Peach St
(16509) 814.864.4811

Microtel ($)
8100 Peach St
(16509) 814.864.1010

Ramada Inn ($$)
6101 Wattsbury Rd
(16509) 814.825.3100
$5 charge

Red Roof Inn ($$)
7865 Perry Hwy
(16509) 814.868.5246

Super 8 ($$)
8052 Perry Hwy
(16509) 800.800.8000
call re: fees

• Essington •
Econo Lodge ($$)
600 S R 291
(19029) 610.521.3900

Holiday Inn ($$$)
45 Industrial Hwy
(19029) 610.521.2400
mgr preapproval reqd

Motel 6 ($$)
43 Industrial Hwy
(19029) 215.521.6650
1 small pet/room

Red Roof Inn ($$)
49 Industrial Hwy
(19029) 610.521.5090

• Exton •
Comfort Inn ($$)
5 N Pottstown Pike
(19341) 610.524.8811
mgr preapproval reqd

Holiday Inn ($$$)
815 N Pottstown Pike
(19341) 610.363.1100
mgr preapproval reqd

Holiday Inn
120 N Pottstown Pike
(19341) 610.524.7259

• Fayetteville •
Rite Spot Motel ($)
5651 Lincoln Way
(17222) 717.352.2144

• Feasterville Trevose •
Red Roof Inn ($$)
3100 Lincoln Hwy
(19053) 215.244.9422

• Fogelsville •
Cloverleaf Motel ($$)
327 Star Srd
(18051) 610.395.3367

• Frackville •
Econo Lodge ($$)
501 S Middle St
(17931) 717.874.3838

PENNSYLVANIA, Franklin

● Franklin ●
Franklin Motel
1421 Liberty St
(16323) 814.437.3061

● Freemansburg ●
Hotel Bethlehem
437 Main St
(18017) 215.867.3711
small pets only

● Galeton ●
Ox Yoke Inn
Rd 1 Route 6
(16922) 814.435.6522

Pine Log Motel ($)
Box# 151
(16922) 814.435.6400

● Gettysburg ●
Budget Host ($$)
205 Steinwehr Ave
(17325) 800.729.6564

Econo Lodge ($)
945 Blatimreo Pike
(17325) 800.424.4777

Heritage Motor Lodge ($)
64 Steinwehr Ave
(17325) 717.334.9281

Holiday Inn ($$)
516 Baltimore St
(17325) 717.334.6211
mgr preapproval reqd

Howard Johnson ($$)
301 Steinwehr Ave
(17325) 717.334.1188

Quality Inn ($$)
380 Steinwehr Ave
(17325) 717.334.1103
mgr preapproval reqd

● Glen Rock ●
Rocky Ridge Motel ($)
Rt 216 Steaks Run Rd
(17327) 717.235.5646

● Greencastle ●
Econo Lodge ($)
735 Buchanan Trl
(17225) 800.424.4777

● Harrisburg ●
Best Western ($$)
150 Nationwide Dr
(17110) 717.545.9089

Best Western ($$$)
765 Eisenhower Blvd
(17111) 717.558.9500

Best Western ($$$)
300 N Mountain Rd
(17112) 717.652.7180

Budgetel ($)
990 Eisenhower Blvd
(17111) 717.939.8000

Budgetel ($$)
200 N Mountain Rd
(17112) 717.540.9339

Comfort Inn ($$)
4021 Union Deposit Rd
(17109) 717.561.8100
mgr preapproval reqd

Hojo Inn ($$)
1450 N 7th St
(17102) 800.446.4656

Holiday Inn ($$$$)
4751 Lindle Rd
(17111) 800.637.4817
mgr preapproval reqd

Red Roof Inn ($$)
400 Corporate Cir
(17110) 717.657.1445

Red Roof Inn ($)
950 Eisenhower Blvd
(17111) 717.939.1331

Residence Inn ($$$)
4480 Lewis Rd
(17111) 717.561.1900

Sheraton Inn ($$$)
800 E Park Dr
(17111) 717.561.2800

Super 8 ($$)
4125 N Front St
(17110) 717.233.5891
w/permission

● Harrisville ●
Dys Inn ($$)
I-80 & Rd 8
(16038) 814.786.7901

● Hazleton ●
Best Western ($$)
RR 1 Box# 37
(18201) 717.454.2494

Comfort Inn ($$$)
RR 1 Box# 301
(18201) 717.455.9300
mgr preapproval reqd

Forest Hill Inn ($$)
RR 1 Box# 262
(18201) 717.459.2730

Hampton Inn ($$)
RR 1 Box# 273A
(18201) 717.454.3449

Holiday Inn ($$$)
Rt 309
(18201) 717.455.1451
mgr preapproval reqd

Mount Laurel Motel ($$)
1039 S Church St
(18201) 717.455.6391

● Hermitage ●
Royal Motel ($)
301 S Hermitage Rd
(16148) 412.347.5546

● Hershey ●
Econo Lodge ($$)
115 Lucy Ave
(17033) 717.533.2515

● Honesdale ●
Fife&Drum Motel ($)
100 Terrace St
(18431) 717.253.1392

● Horsham ●
Residence Inn ($$$$)
3 Walnut Grove Dr
(19044) 215.443.7330
call for room availability

● Huntingdon ●
Days Inn ($$)
RR 1 Box# 353
(16652) 814.643.3934
$5/pets

Huntington Motel ($)
Box# 353
(16652) 814.643.1133

● Indiana ●
Holiday Inn
1395 Wayne Ave
(15701) 412.463.3561

● Johnstown ●
Holiday Inn
250 Market
(15901) 814.535.7777

Holiday Inn ($$)
1440 Scalp Ave
(15904) 814.266.8789
mgr preapproval reqd

● Kane ●
Kane View Motel ($)
RR 1 Box# 91A
(16735) 814.837.8600

● King Of Prussia ●
Motel 6 ($$)
815 W Dekalb
(19406) 610.265.7200
1 small pet/room

● Kittanning ●
Rodeway Inn ($$)
422 E Friendship Plaza
(16201) 412.543.1100

● Kulpsville ●
Holiday Inn ($$$)
1750 Sumneytown Pike
(19443) 215.368.3800
mgr preapproval reqd

● Kutztown ●
Campus Inn ($$)
15080 Kutztown Rd
(19530) 610.683.8271

Lincoln Motel ($)
RR 4 Box# 171
(19530) 610.683.3456

● Lancaster ●
Best Western ($$$)
222 Eden Rd
(17601) 717.569.6444

Brunswick Hotel ($$)
Box# 749
(17608) 717.397.4801

Be Discreet

Comfort Inn ($$)
500 Centerville Rd
(17601) 717.898.2431
under 30 lbs

Mountain Meadows ($$$)
Redmond/Fall Hwy
(17601) 206.392.9222
pets get great care

Super 8 ($)
2129 Lincoln Hwy
(17602) 717.393.8888
w/permission

Travelodge ($$)
2101 Columbia Ave
(17603) 717.397.4201

● Langhorne ●
Red Roof Inn ($$)
3100 Cabot Blvd
(19047) 215.750.6200

● Lemoyne ●
Friendship Inn ($)
US 15 & 11
(17043) 800.424.4777

● Lenhartsville ●
Top Motel
RR 1 Box# 834
(19534) 215.756.6021

● Lewisburg ●
Days Inn ($$)
US Rt 15
(17837) 717.523.1171
mgr preapproval reqd

● Lewistown ●
Gables Inn ($$)
900 Main St
(17044) 717.248.4242
owner rfd

● Lititz ●
General Sutter Inn ($$$)
14 E Main St
(17543) 717.626.2115

● Lock Haven ●
Best Western ($$)
101 E Walnut St
(17745) 717.748.3297
$3/pets

● Manheim ●
Mt Hope Motel ($)
2845 Lebanon Rd
(17545) 717.665.3118

Rodeway Inn ($$)
2931 Lebanon Rd
(17545) 717.665.2755

● Mansfield ●
Comfort Inn ($$)
300 Gateway Dr
(16933) 717.662.3000
mgr preapproval reqd

Mansfield Inn ($$)
26 S Main St
(16933) 717.662.2136

Oasis Motel ($)
RR 1 Box# 90
(16933) 717.659.5576

Wests Deluxe Motel ($)
RR 1 Box# 97
(16933) 717.659.5141

● Mars ●
Days Inn ($$)
909 Sheraton Dr
(16046) 412.772.2700

Motel 6 ($)
Rt 19 Box# 1316
(16046) 412.776.4333
1 small pet/room

Oak Leaf Motel
US Rt 19
(16046) 412.776.1551

Red Roof Inn ($$)
20009 Rd 19
(16046) 800.843.7663

● Matamoras ●
Best Western ($$)
900 Rt 6 & 209 Matamoras
(18336) 717.491.2400

● Meadville ●
Days Inn ($$)
240 Conneaut Lake Rd
(16335) 814.337.4264
$5/pets

Super 8 ($$)
17259 Conneaut Lake Rd
(16335) 814.333.8883
pets w/permission

● Mechanicsburg ●
Days Inn
1012 Wesley Dr
(17055) 717.766.3700
$25/pet

Econo Lodge ($)
650 Gettysburg Rd
(17055) 717.766.4728

Holiday Inn ($$$)
5401 Carlisle Pike
(17055) 717.697.0321
mgr preapproval reqd

● Middletown ●
Days Inn
800 Eisenhower Blvd
(17057) 717.939.4147

● Milesburg ●
Holiday Inn
I-80 & US 150
(16853) 814.355.7521

● Milford ●
Red Carpet Inn
RR2
(18337) 717.296.9444

● Monroeville ●
Days Inn
2727 Mosside Blvd
(15146) 412.856.1610
$5/day

Holiday Inn
2750 Mosside Blvd
(15146) 412.372.1022

● Moosic ●
Days Inn
4130 Birney Ave
(18507) 717.457.6713
$5

● Morgantown ●
Holiday Inn
Ex 22 Pa Tumpke
(19543) 610.286.3000

● Myerstown ●
Motel Of Frystown ($)
90 Fort Motel Dr
(17067) 717.933.4613

● New Columbia ●
Colonial Inn ($$)
Box# 62
(17856) 717.568.8000

● New Cumberland ●
Days Inn ($$)
353 Lewisberry Rd
(17070) 717.774.4156
$5

Holiday Inn
I-83 & Pa Turnpike
(17070) 717.774.2721

Knights Inn ($)
300 Commerce Dr
(17070) 717.774.5990
size limits & fees

Motel 6 ($)
200 Commerce Dr
(17070) 717.774.8910
1 small pet/room

Ramada Inn ($$)
Pa Trpk Ex 18 & 1
(17070) 717.657.1445

● New Kensington ●
Days Inn ($$)
300 Tarentum Bridge Rd
(15068) 412.335.9171

● New Stanton ●
Cardinal Motel ($)
Box# B
(15672) 412.925.2162

Howard Johnson ($$)
112 W Byers Ave
(15672) 412.925.3511

● North East ●
Red Carpet Inn
12264 Main
(16428) 814.725.4554

Policies Subject to Change

● Oakdale ●
Comfort Inn ($$)
7011 Old Stuebenville
(15071) 412.787.2600
mgr preapproval reqd

Howard Johnson ($$)
2101 Montour Church
(15071) 412.923.2244

● Oil City ●
Holiday Inn ($$$)
1 Seneca St
(16301) 814.677.1221
mgr preapproval reqd

● Philadelphia ●
Barclay Hotel ($$$$)
237 S 18th St
(19103) 800.421.6662

Chestnut Hill Hotel ($$$$)
8229 Germantown Ave
(19118) 215.242.5905

Hilton ($$$$)
4509 Island Ave
(19153) 215.365.4150

Residence Inn ($$$)
4630 Island Ave
(19153) 215.492.1611

The Four Seasons ($$$$)
1 Logan Sq
(19103) 215.963.1500
small pets allowed

The Rittenhouse Hotel ($$$$)
210 W Rittenhouse Sq
(19103) 215.546.9000

Travelodge ($$)
2015 Penrose Ave
(19145) 215.755.6500

● Philipsburg ●
Harbor Inn ($$)
Rts 322 & 53
(16866) 814.342.0250

Main Liner Motel ($)
RR 3 Box# 115
(16866) 814.342.2004

● Pine Grove ●
Comfort Inn ($$)
Rt 443 & I-81
(17963) 717.345.8031
mgr preapproval reqd

Econo Lodge ($$)
RR 1 Box# 581
(17963) 717.345.4099

● Pittsburgh ●
Days Inn ($)
100 Kisow Dr
(15205) 412.922.0120

Days Inn
Rt 28
(15238) 412.828.5400

Hampton Inn ($$$)
3315 Hamlet Pl
(15213) 412.681.1000

Hampton Inn ($$$)
555 Trumbull Dr
(15205) 412.922.0100

Hawthorn Suites ($$$$)
700 Mansfield Ave
(15205) 412.279.6300
$50 deposit

Hilton ($$$)
Gateway Center
(15222) 412.391.4600

Holiday Inn ($$$$)
100 Lytton Ave
(15213) 412.682.6200

Holiday Inn ($$$)
401 Holiday Dr
(15220) 412.922.6100
mgr preapproval reqd

Holiday Inn ($$)
4859 McKnight Rd
(15237) 412.366.5200
mgr preapproval reqd

Holiday Inn
915 Brinton Rd
(15221) 412.247.2700

Holiday Inn ($$$)
164 Fort Couch Rd
(15241) 412.833.5300
mgr preapproval reqd

Howard Johnson ($$$)
5300 Clairton Blvd
(15236) 412.884.6000

Marriott Hotel ($$$)
101 Marriott Dr
(15205) 412.922.8400

Motel 6 ($)
211 Beecham Dr
(15205) 412.922.9400
1 small pet/room

Red Roof Inn ($)
6404 Steubenville Pike
(15205) 412.787.7870

Super 8 ($$)
Rt 286
(15239) 800.800.8000
call re: fees

Travelodge ($)
4800 Steubenville Pike
(15205) 412.922.6900

Westin Hotel ($$$$)
530 William Penn Pl
(15219) 412.281.7100
small pets accepted

● Pittston ●
Holiday Inn
30 Concorde Dr
(18641) 717.654.3300

Howard Johnson ($$)
347 Rt 15
(18640) 717.654.3301

Knights Inn ($)
310 Rt 315
(18640) 717.654.6020
size limits & fees

● Pottstown ●
Comfort Inn ($$)
99 Robinson St
(19464) 610.326.5000
mgr preapproval reqd

Days Inn ($$)
29 High St
(19464) 610.970.1101
$10/pet charge

Holiday Inn ($$)
1600 Industrial Hwy
(19464) 610.327.3300
mgr preapproval reqd

● Punxsutawney ●
Country Villa Motel ($)
RR 1 Box# 77
(15767) 814.938.8330

Pantall Hotel ($$)
135 E Mahoning St
(15767) 814.938.6600

● Quakertown ●
Econo Lodge ($$)
1905 Route 663
(18951) 215.538.3000

Rodeway Inn ($)
1920 S R 663
(18951) 215.536.7600

● Reading ●
Canyon Motel ($)
18 East Ave
(19601) 717.724.1681

Dutch Colony Inn ($$)
4635 Perkiomen Ave
(19606) 610.779.2345

Econo Lodge ($$)
2310 Fraver Dr
(19605) 610.378.1145

Econo Lodge ($)
635 Spring St
(19610) 610.378.5105
$3 charge

Holiday Inn ($$$)
2545 N 5th St
(19605) 610.929.4741
mgr preapproval reqd

Sheraton Inn ($$$)
422 W Papermill Rd
(19610) 610.376.3811

The Inn At Reading ($$$)
1040 N Park Rd
(19610) 610.372.7811

Wellesley Inn
910 Woodland Rd
(19610) 610.374.1500
$3 charge

$=under $35 $$=$35-60 $$$=$60-100 $$$$=over $100

● Saint Marys ●
Best Western ($$)
1002 Earth Rd & Rt 255
(15857) 814.834.0000

● Scranton ●
Days Inn ($$)
1100 O'Neill Hwy
(18512) 717.348.6101
$3/pets

Econo Lodge ($)
1175 Kane St
(18505) 717.346.8782

Holiday Inn
200 Tigue St
(18512) 717.343.4771

● Shamokin Dam ●
Days Inn
Rt 11 & 15
(17876) 717.743.1111

● Shippensburg ●
Budget Host ($$)
I-81 Ex 10
(17257) 717.530.1234

Budget Host ($$)
720 Walnut Bottom Rd
(17257) 717.532.7311
ltd rooms

● Somerset ●
Budget Host ($)
799 N Central Ave
(15501) 814.445.7988

Days Inn
I-70/76
(15501) 814.445.9200

Holiday Inn
202 Shaffer St
(15501) 814.445.9611

Super 8 ($$)
I-70 76 Ex
(15501) 814.445.8788
call re: fees

● State College ●
Days Inn ($$)
240 S Pugh St
(16801) 814.238.8454
$7

Hampton Inn ($$)
1101 E College Ave
(16801) 814.231.1590

● Strasburg ●
Strasburg Inn ($$)
1 Historic Dr
(17579) 717.687.7691

● Stroudsburg ●
Howard Johnson ($$$$)
1220 Main St
(18360) 714.424.1930

● Tannersville ●
Howard Johnson ($$)
I-80 & Rt 715
(18372) 717.629.4100

● Towanda ●
Towanda Motel ($$)
383 York Ave
(18848) 717.265.2178

● Ulysses ●
Pine Log Motel ($)
RR 1 Box# 15
(16948) 814.435.6400

● Uniontown ●
Holiday Inn
700 W Main St
(15401) 412.437.2816

● Warren ●
Holiday Inn ($$)
210 Ludlow St
(16365) 814.726.3000
mgr preapproval reqd

Super 8 ($$)
204 Struthers St
(16365) 814.723.8881
pets w/permission

● Washington ●
Knights Inn ($$)
125 Knights Inn Dr
(15301) 800.843.5644

Motel 6 ($$)
1283 Motel 6 Dr
(15301) 412.223.8040
1 small pet/room

Red Roof Inn ($$)
1399 W Chestnut St
(15301) 412.228.5750

● Waynesboro ●
Best Western ($$)
239 W Main St
(17268) 717.762.9113

● Waynesburg ●
Econo Lodge ($$)
350 Miller Ln
(15370) 412.627.5544

Super 8 ($$)
80 Miller Ln
(15370) 412.627.8880
call re: fees

● Wellsboro ●
Sherwood Motel ($)
2 Main St
(16901) 717.724.3424

● West Chester ●
Abbey Green Motel ($$)
1036 Wilmington Pike
(19382) 610.692.3310

● West Middlesex ●
Comfort Inn ($$)
Rt 18 & Wilson Rd
(16159) 412.342.7200
mgr preapproval reqd

Holiday Inn ($$$)
3200 S Hermitage Rd
(16159) 412.981.1530
mgr preapproval reqd

Radisson Inn ($$$)
Box# 596
(16159) 412.528.2501

● Wexford ●
Econo Lodge ($$)
107 Vip Dr
(15090) 800.424.4777

● White Haven ●
Days Inn ($$)
Rt 940
(18661) 717.443.0391
$5 small

Pocono Mtn Lodge ($$)
Rt 940 White Haven
(18661) 800.443.4049

● Wilkes Barre ●
Best Western ($$$$)
77 E Mark St
(18701) 717.823.6152

Days Inn ($$)
760 Kidder St
(18702) 717.826.0111

Hampton Inn ($$)
1063 Hwy 315
(18702) 717.825.3838

Holiday Inn
880 Kidder St
(18702) 717.824.8901

Red Carpet Inn ($)
400 Kidder St
(18702) 717.823.2171

Red Roof Inn ($$)
1035 Hwy 315
(18702) 717.829.6422

● Williamsport ●
Bings Motel ($)
2961 Lycoming Creek Rd
(17701) 717.494.0601

City View Inn ($$)
RR 4 Box# 550
(17701) 717.326.2601

Econo Lodge ($$)
2401 E 3rd St
(17701) 717.326.1501

Genetti Hotel ($)
200 W 4th St
(17701) 717.326.6600

Holiday Inn ($$$$)
1840 E 3rd St
(17701) 717.326.1981
mgr preapproval reqd

Ridgemont Motel ($)
RR 4 Box# 536
(17701) 717.321.5300

Well Behaved

Sheraton Inn ($$$)
100B Pine St
(17701) 717.327.8231

● Wind Gap ●
Travel Inn ($$)
499 E Moorestown Rd
(18091) 610.863.4146

● York ●
Days Inn ($$)
222 Arsenal Rd
(17402) 717.843.9971

Hampton Inn ($$$)
1550 Mount Zion Rd
(17402) 717.840.1500

Holiday Inn ($$$)
2600 E Market St
(17402) 717.755.1966
mgr preapproval reqd

Holiday Inn
2000 Loucks Rd
(17404) 717.846.9500

Motel 6 ($)
125 Arsenal Rd
(17404) 717.846.6260
1 small pet/room

Red Roof Inn ($$)
323 Arsenal Rd
(17402) 717.843.8181

Super 8 ($)
40 Arsenal Rd
(17404) 717.852.8686
call re: fees

Travelodge ($)
132-140 N Georgia St
(17401) 717.843.8974

Rhode Island
● Cranston ●
Days Inn ($$)
101 New London Ave
(02920) 401.942.4200

● Middletown ●
Budget Host ($$$)
1185 W Main Rd
(02842) 401.849.4700
closed nov-apr

Howard Johnson ($)
351 W Main Rd
(02842) 401.849.2000

● Newport ●
Annas Victorian
5 Fowler Ave
(02840) 401.849.2489

Harbor Base Pineapple Inn
($)
372 Coddington Hwy
(02840) 401.847.2600

Motel 6 ($)
249 Jt Connell Hwy
(02840) 401.848.0600
1 small pet/room

● Portsmouth ●
Founders Brook Motel ($$)
314 Boyds Ln
(02871) 401.683.1244

● Providence ●
Marriott Hotel ($$$$)
Charles & Orms Sts
(02904) 401.272.2400

Providence Biltmore ($$$$)
Kennedy Plaza
(02903) 401.421.0700

Westin Hotel ($$$)
1 W Exchange St
(02903) 401.598.8000

● Rumford ●
New Yorker Motel
400 Newport Ave
(02916) 401.434.8000

● Wakefield ●
Larshwood Inn ($$$)
521-522 Main St
(02879) 401.783.5454

● Warwick ●
Holiday Inn ($$$$)
801 N Greenwich Ave
(02886) 401.732.6000

Master Host
2138 Post Rd
(02886) 401.737.7400

Motel 6 ($$)
20 Jefferson Blvd
(02888) 401.467.9800
1 small pet/room

● Westerly ●
The Villa Inn ($$$)
190 Shore Rd
(02891) 800.722.9240

South Carolina
● Aiken ●
Days Inn ($)
1204 Richland Ave
(29801) 803.649.5524
$5/day ltd rms must reserve

Deluxe Inn ($)
Box# 2875
(29802) 803.642.2840

Ramada Inn ($$)
Hwy 19 & I-20
(29801) 803.648.4272

Ramada Ltd ($)
1850 Richland Ave
(29801) 803.648.6821

Wilcox Inn ($$$)
100 Colleton Ave SW
(29801) 803.649.1377

● Anderson ●
Days Inn ($$)
1007 Smith Mill Rd
(29625) 803.375.0375

Holiday Inn ($$)
3025 N Main St
(29621) 864.226.6051
mgr preapproval reqd

La Quinta Inn ($$)
3430 Clemson Blvd
(29621) 864.225.3721
call re: fees

Royal Amer'n Motel ($)
4515 Clemson Blvd
(29621) 803.226.7236

Super 8 ($$)
3302 Cinema Ave
(29621) 864.225.8384
call re: fees

● Beaufort ●
Battery Creek Inn ($$$)
102 B Marina Blvd
(29902) 803.521.1441

Days Inn ($$)
1809 S Rabaut
(29902) 803.524.1551

Holiday Inn ($$)
2001 Boundary St
(29902) 803.524.2144
mgr preapproval reqd

Howard Johnson ($$)
3651 Trask Pkwy
(29902) 803.524.6020

Ramada Ltd ($$)
US Hwy 21 & Sc 170
(29903) 803.524.3322

Scottish Inn ($)
262 Hwy 21
(29902) 803.521.1555
$5 per day

● Bishopville ●
Econo Lodge ($)
1153 S Main St
(29010) 805.428.3200

● Camden ●
Colony Inn ($)
2020 W Dekalb St
(29020) 803.342.5508

Greenleaf Inn ($$)
1310B N Broad St
(29020) 803.425.1806

Parkview Motel ($)
1039 Dekalb St
(29020) 803.432.7687

● Cayce ●
Knights Inn ($)
1987 Airport Blvd
(29033) 803.794.0222
size limits & fees

Masters Economy Inn ($)
2125 Commerce Dr
(29033) 803.791.5850

$=under $35 $$=$35-60 $$$=$60-100 $$$$=over $100

Tremont Inn ($)
111 Knox Abbott Dr
(29033) 803.796.6240

● Charleston ●
Best Western ($$)
1540 Savannah Hwy
(29407) 803.571.6100
small pets only

Comfort Inn ($)
5055 N Arco Ln
(29418) 803.554.6485
mgr preapproval reqd

Days Inn ($$)
2998 W Montague Ave
(29418) 803.747.4101
$6

Econo Lodge ($$)
3668 Dorchester Rd
(29405) 803.747.0961

Hawthorn Suites ($$$)
181 Church St
(29401) 803.577.2644

Hojo Inn ($)
3640 Dorchester Rd
(29405) 803.554.4140

Holiday Inn
6099 Fain St
(29406) 803.744.1621

Holiday Inn ($$)
2070 McMillan Ave
(29405) 803.554.1600

Holiday Inn ($$)
301 Savannah Hwy
(29407) 803.556.7100
mgr preapproval reqd

Howard Johnson ($)
2512 Ashley Phosphate
(29418) 803.797.6864

La Quinta Inn ($$)
2499 La Quinta Ln
(29420) 803.797.8181
call re: fees

Marriott Hotel ($$$)
4770 Goer Dr
(29406) 803.747.1900

Masters Economy Inn ($$)
6100 Rivers Ave
(29406) 800.633.3434

Middleton Inn ($$$$)
Ashley River Rd
(29414) 803.446.0500

Motel 6 ($)
2551 Ashley Phosphate Rd
(29418) 803.572.6590
1 small pet/room

Motel 6 ($)
2058 Savannah Hwy
(29407) 803.556.5144
1 small pet/room

Orchard Inn ($$)
4725 Saul White Blvd
(29418) 803.747.3671

Red Roof Inn ($)
7480 Northwoods Blvd
(29406) 800.843.7663

Residence Inn ($$$)
7645 Northwoods Blvd
(29406) 803.572.5757

Rodeway Inn ($$)
5020 Rivers Ave
(29406) 803.554.4982

Super 8 ($$)
2311 Ashley Phosphate
(29406) 803.572.2228
call re: fees

Town & Country Inn ($$)
2008 Savannah Hwy
(29407) 803.571.1000

● Cheraw ●
Inn Cheraw ($$)
321 2nd St
(29520) 803.537.2011

● Clemson ●
Days Inn ($$)
1387 Tiger Blvd
(29631) 864.653.4411
mgr preapproval reqd

Holiday Inn ($$)
894 Tiger Blvd
(29631) 864.654.4450
mgr preapproval reqd

● Clinton ●
Days Inn ($$)
I-26 & S R 56
(29325) 803.833.6600
$4/pets

Holiday Inn
Hwy 56 & I-26
(29325) 864.833.4900

● Columbia ●
Adams Mark Hotel ($$$)
1200 Hampton St
(29201) 803.771.7000
sign waiver

Amerisuites ($$)
7525 Two Notch Rd
(29223) 803.736.6666

Budgetel ($$)
1538 Horseshoe Dr
(29223) 803.736.6400

Budgetel ($)
911 Bush River Rd
(29210) 803.798.3222

Comfort Inn ($$)
2025 Main St
(29201) 803.252.6321
mgr preapproval reqd

Days Inn ($)
133 Plumbers Rd
(29203) 803.754.4408

Days Inn ($)
827 Bush River Rd
(29210) 803.772.9672
$5 per day

Days Inn
7128 Parklane Rd
(29223) 803.736.0000
$4

Economy Inn ($$)
1776 Burning Tree Dr
(29210) 803.798.9210

Hampton Inn ($$)
7333 Garners Ferry Rd
(29209) 803.783.5410

Holiday Inn
773 St Andrews Rd
(29210) 803.772.7275

Holiday Inn ($$)
630 Assembly St
(29201) 803.779.7800
mgr preapproval reqd

Holiday Inn ($$$)
7510 Two Notch Rd
(29223) 803.736.3000
mgr preapproval reqd

Knights Inn ($)
1803 Bush River Rd
(29210) 803.772.0022
size limits & fees

La Quinta Inn ($$)
1335 Garner Ln
(29210) 803.798.9590
call re: fees

Red Roof Inn ($)
7580 Two Notch Rd
(29223) 803.736.0850

Red Roof Inn ($)
10 Berryhill Rd
(29210) 803.798.9220

Residence Inn ($$$)
150 Stoneridge Dr
(29210) 803.779.7000

Super 8 ($$)
5719 Fairfield Rd
(29203) 803.735.0008
call re: fees

● Dillon ●
Days Inn ($)
818 Rudford Blvd
(29536) 803.774.6041
$5/pets

Holiday Inn ($$)
RR 1 Box# 73
(29536) 803.774.5111
mgr preapproval reqd

Super 8 ($$)
I-95 Ex 193
(29536) 803.774.4161
call re: fees

● Easley ●
Days Inn ($$)
121 Days Inn Dr
(29640) 803.859.9902
$5/pets under 35 lbs

$=under $35 $$=$35-60 $$$=$60-100 $$$$=over $100

● Florence ●
Days Inn ($)
2111 W Lucas St
(29501) 803.665.4444

Days Inn ($)
I-95
(29502) 803.665.8550
$4/pets

Econo Lodge ($)
I-95 & US 52
(29502) 803.665.8558

Econo Lodge ($)
3932 W Palmetto St
(29501) 803.662.7712

Hampton Inn ($$$)
1826 W Lucas St
(29501) 803.662.7000

Hojo Inn ($)
3821 Bancroft Rd
(29501) 803.664.9494

Motel 6 ($)
1834 W Lucas St
(29501) 803.667.6100
1 small pet/room

Park Inn Intl ($)
831 S Irby St
(29501) 803.662.9421

Quality Inn ($)
3024 TV Rd
(29501) 803.669.1715

Ramada Inn ($$)
I-95 & US 52 Ex 164
(29501) 803.669.4241

Red Roof Inn ($)
2690N David McLeod Blvd
(29501) 803.678.9000

Shoneys Inn ($$)
I-95 & US 52
(29501) 803.669.1921

Super 8 ($$)
1832 W Lucas St
(29501) 803.661.7267
mgr preapproval reqd

Thunderbird Motel ($)
Box# 3909
(29502) 803.669.1611

Youngs Plantation Inn($)
Box# 3806
(29502) 803.669.4171

● Fort Mill ●
Days Inn ($)
3482 Carowinds Blvd
(29715) 803.548.8000
$5

Ramada Inn ($$$)
225 Carowinds Blvd
(29715) 803.548.2400

● Gaffney ●
Comfort Inn ($$)
143 Corona Dr
(29341) 864.487.4200
mgr preapproval reqd

Days Inn ($$)
136 Peachoid Rd
(29341) 803.489.7172

● Georgetown ●
Seasons Motel
412 Saint James St
(29440) 803.546.4117

● Greenville ●
Days Inn ($)
3905Augusta Rd
(29605) 803.277.4010
small $5/pets

Days Inn ($$)
831 Congaree Rd
(29607) 803.288.6221
$10

Holiday Inn ($$)
27 S Pleasantburg Dr
(29607) 864.232.3339
$10 charge

Holiday Inn ($$)
4295Augusta Rd
(29605) 864.277.8921

Howard Johnson ($$)
2756 Laurens Rd
(29607) 803.588.6900

La Quinta Inn ($$$$)
31 Old Country Rd
(29607) 803.297.3500
call re: fees

Motel 6 ($)
224 Bruce Rd
(29605) 803.277.8630
1 small pet/room

Quality Inn ($$)
50 Orchard Park Dr
(29615) 864.297.9000

Ramada Inn ($$)
1001 S Church St
(29601) 803.232.7666
$15 fee

Ramada Ltd ($$)
1314 S Pleasantburg Dr
(29605) 803.277.3734

Red Roof Inn ($)
2801 Laurens Rd
(29607) 803.297.4458

Residence Inn ($$$)
48 McPrice Ct
(29615) 803.297.0099
$50 fee & $5 per day

The Phoenix Inn ($$)
Box# 5064
(29606) 864.233.4651

● Greenwood ●
Econo Lodge ($$)
719 Byp 25 NE
(29646) 864.229.5329

Holiday Inn
1014 Montague
(29649) 864.223.4231

● Hardeeville ●
Days Inn ($$)
I-95 & US 17
(29927) 803.784.2281
$5

Economy Inn ($)
101 Frontage Rd
(29927) 803.784.2201

Howard Johnson ($)
I-95 & US Hwy 17
(29927) 803.784.2271

Ramada Ltd ($)
I-95 & Rd 88 Ex 98
(29927) 803.784.3192

Super 8 ($)
Hwy 17 & I-95
(29927) 803.784.2151
call re: fees

Thunderbird Lodge ($)
Box# 1126
(29927) 803.784.2196

● Hartsville ●
Landmark Inn ($$)
1301 S 4th St
(29550) 803.332.2611

● Hilton Head Island ●
Motel 6 ($$)
830Wm W Hilton Pkwy
(29928) 803.785.2700
1 small pet/room

Red Roof Inn ($)
5 Regency Pkwy
(29928) 803.686.6808

Shoneys Inn ($$$)
200 Museum St
(29926) 803.681.3655

● Lancaster ●
Days Inn ($$)
1100 N Main St
(29720) 803.286.6441

● Latta ●
Patrick Henry Motel ($)
203 N Richardson St
(29565) 803.752.5861

● Little River ●
Harbour Inn ($)
1564 US 17 Hwy
(29566) 800.292.0404

● Lugoff ●
Days Inn ($$)
529 Hwy 601
(29078) 803.438.6990
$5/pet

Holiday Inn
Hwy 1
(29078) 803.438.9441

Santee, SOUTH CAROLINA

• Manning •

Budget Inn ($)
I-95 & US 301
(29102) 803.473.2561

Comfort Inn ($$)
I-95
(29102) 803.473.7550

Days Inn ($)
RR 5 Box# 442
(29102) 803.473.2596

Economy Inn ($)
Box# 490
(29102) 803.473.4021

• Mount Pleasant •

Comfort Inn ($$)
310 Hwy 17 Byp
(29464) 803.884.5853
mgr preapproval reqd

Days Inn ($$)
261 Johnnie Dodds Blvd
(29464) 803.881.1800
$5/pets

Guilds Inn ($$$)
101 Pitt St
(29464) 803.881.0510

Masters Economy Inn ($$)
300 Wingo Way
(29464) 803.884.2814

• Myrtle Beach •

Days Inn ($$)
3650 Hwy 501
(29577) 803.236.1950
$10

El Dorado Motel ($)
2800 S Ocean Blvd
(29577) 803.626.3559

Knights Inn ($)
3622 Hwy 501
(29577) 803.236.7400
size limits & fees

Mariner Motel ($)
7003 N Ocean Blvd
(29572) 803.449.5281

Motel Catoe Villa ($)
506 N Ocean Blvd
(29577) 803.448.5706

Red Roof Inn ($$)
2801 S Kings Hwy
(29577) 803.626.4444

Sea Mist Resort ($)
1200 S Ocean Blvd
(29577) 803.448.1551

St Johns Inn ($)
6803 N Ocean Blvd
(29572) 803.449.5251

Super 8 ($$)
3450 Hwy 17S Byp
(29577) 803.293.6100
call re: fees

Waterside Inn ($$$)
2000 N Ocean Blvd
(29577) 803.448.5935

• Newberry •

Best Western ($$)
11701 S Hwy 34
(29108) 803.276.5850

Days Inn ($)
RR 1 Box# 407B
(29108) 803.276.2294
$4/pets

• Orangeburg •

Best Western ($$)
826 John C Calhoun Dr
(29115) 803.534.7630
managers discretion

Holiday Nn ($$)
415 John C Calhoun Dr
(29115) 803.531.4600
small pets only

Howard Johnson ($$)
3608 Old St Matthews Rd
(29115) 803.531.4900

Rusell Street Inn ($)
491 N Russell St
(29115) 803.531.2030

Sun Inn ($)
895 John C Calhoun Dr
(29115) 800.488.5368

• Richburg •

Days Inn ($)
I-77 Ex 65
(29729) 803.789.5555
$3/small pets

Econo Lodge ($)
RR 1 Box# 182
(29729) 803.789.3000

Relax Inn ($)
Rt 1 Box# 1830
(29729) 803.789.6363

Super 8 ($$)
RR 1 Box# 181-C
(29729) 803.789.7888
call re: fees

• Ridgeland •

Comfort Inn ($$)
I-95
(29936) 800.726.2121

Econo Lodge ($$)
516 E Main St
(29936) 800.424.4777

Palms Motel ($)
Box# 547
(29936) 803.726.5511

• Ridgeway •

Ridgeway Motel ($)
Box# 472
(29130) 803.337.3238

• Rock Hill •

Best Western ($$)
1106 N Anderson Rd
(29730) 803.329.1330

Econo Lodge ($$)
962 Riverview Rd
(29730) 803.329.3232

Holiday Inn ($$)
2640 Cherry Rd
(29730) 803.329.1122
mgr preapproval reqd

Howard Johnson ($$)
2625 Cherry Rd
(29730) 803.329.3121

Rodeway Inn ($)
656 N Anderson Rd
(29730) 803.329.2100

• Saint George •

Best Western ($$)
I-95
(29477) 803.563.2277
small pets $5

Econo Lodge ($)
I-95 & US 78
(29477) 803.563.4027

Economy Motel ($)
125 Motel Dr
(29477) 803.563.2360

Holiday Inn ($$)
I-95 & US 78
(29477) 803.563.4581

Southern Inn ($)
Box# 375
(29477) 803.563.3775

St George Motor Inn ($)
215 S Parler Ave
(29477) 803.563.3029

Super 8 ($)
114 Winningham Rd
(29477) 803.563.5551
call re: fees

• Santee •

Clarks Inn ($$)
114 Bradford Blvd
(29142) 800.345.7888

Comfort Inn ($$)
265 Britain St
(29142) 803.854.3221
mgr preapproval reqd

Days Inn ($$)
I-95
(29142) 803.854.2175
$6/pets

Economy Inn ($)
626 Bass Dr
(29142) 803.854.2107

Howard Johnson ($)
I-95 Ex 102 Rd 400
(29142) 803.478.7676

Ramada Inn ($$)
Rt 6 Box# 501
(29142) 803.854.2191

Super 8 ($)
9125 Old Hwy 6
(29142) 803.854.3456
small in smoking rooms

$=under $35 $$=$35-60   **311** $$$=$60-100 $$$$=over $100

● Spartanburg ●
Best Western ($$)
I-85 Bus At Ex 6
(29303) 864.578.5400
small pets only

Days Inn ($)
578 N Church St
(29303) 864.585.4311
$10

Econo Lodge ($)
710 Sunbeam Rd
(29303) 864.578.9450

Motel 6 ($)
105 Jones Rd
(29303) 803.573.6383
1 small pet/room

Quality Hotel ($$)
7136 Asheville Hwy
(29303) 864.503.0780
mgr preapproval reqd

Ramada Inn ($$)
1000 Hearon Cir
(29303) 864.503.9048

Residence Inn ($$)
9011 Fairforest Rd
(29301) 803.576.3333

Wilson World Hotel ($$$)
9027 Fairforest Rd
(29301) 803.574.2111

● Summerton ●
Summerton Inn ($)
Box# 640
(29148) 803.485.2635

● Summerville ●
Econo Lodge ($$)
110 Holiday Inn Dr
(29483) 803.875.3022

Holiday Inn ($$)
120 Holiday Inn Dr
(29483) 803.875.3300
mgr preapproval reqd

● Sumter ●
Economy Inn ($)
Box# 704
(29151) 803.469.4740

Ramada Inn ($$)
226 N Washington St
(29150) 803.775.2323

● Turbeville ●
Ex Inn ($)
Box# 289
(29162) 803.659.8060

● Walterboro ●
Best Western ($$)
1140 Sniders Hwy
(29488) 803.538.3600
small pets

Comfort Inn ($$)
1109 Sniders Hwy
(29488) 803.538.5403
mgr preapproval reqd

Econo Lodge ($)
1057 Sniders Hwy
(29488) 803.538.3830

Holiday Inn ($$)
1120B Sniders Hwy
(29488) 803.538.5473
mgr preapproval reqd

Howard Johnson ($)
1305 Bells Hwy
(29488) 803.538.3948

Rice Planters Inn ($)
Box# 529
(29488) 803.538.8964

Super 8 ($)
RR 3 Box# 760
(29488) 803.538.5383
call re: fees

Thunderbird Inn ($)
Box# 815
(29488) 803.538.2503

● West Columbia ●
Holiday Inn ($$$)
500 Chris Dr
(29169) 803.794.9440
mgr preapproval reqd

● Winnsboro ●
Days Inn ($)
Hwy 34 & 321 Byp
(29180) 803.635.1447
$5

Fairfield Motel ($)
115 S 32N Byp
(29180) 800.292.1509

● Yemassee ●
Days Inn ($)
Hct US 17 & I-95
(29945) 803.726.8156
$3/pets

Palmetto Lodge ($)
Box# 218
(29945) 803.589.2361

Southern Comfort Inn ($)
Box# 574
(29945) 803.589.2015

Super 8 ($)
Hwy 68 & I-95
(29945) 803.589.2177
call re: fees

● York ●
Days Inn ($$)
1568 Alexander Love Hwy
(29745) 803.684.2525
$5

South Dakota
● Aberdeen ●
Best Western ($$)
1400 8th Ave NW
(57401) 605.229.4040

Breeze Inn Motel ($)
1216 6th Ave SW
(57401) 605.225.4222
small pets only

Budget Saver Motel
1409 6th Ave SE
(57401) 605.225.5300

Comfort Inn ($$)
2923 6th Ave SE
(57401) 605.226.0097
mgr preapproval reqd

Holiday Inn
2727 6th Ave
(57401) 605.225.3600

Holiday Inn ($$)
2727 6th
(57402) 800.465.4329

Super 8 ($$)
2405 6th Ave SE
(57401) 605.229.5005
pets w/permission

Super 8 ($)
770 NW Hwy 281
(57401) 605.226.2288
w/permission

Super 8 ($)
714 S Hwy 281
(57401) 605.225.1711
w/permission

White House Inn ($)
500 6th Ave SW
(57401) 605.225.5000

● Belle Fourche ●
Ace Motel ($)
109 6th Ave
(57717) 605.892.2612

Best Western ($)
518 National St
(57717) 605.892.2691

Motel Lariat ($)
1033 Elkhorn St
(57717) 605.892.2601

Sunset Motel ($)
HC 30 Box# 65
(57717) 605.892.2508

Super 8 ($)
501 National St
(57717) 605.892.3361
call re: fees

● Beresford ●
Crosroads Motel ($)
1409 W Cedar St
(57004) 605.763.2020

● Brandon ●
Holiday Inn
1105 N Splirock Bl
(57005) 605.582.2901

● Brookings ●
Best Western ($$)
2515 6th St
(57006) 605.692.9421
attended pets only

Holiday Inn ($$)
2500 6th St
(57006) 800.465.4329

Super 8 ($$$)
3034 Lefevre Dr
(57006) 605.692.6920
call re: fees

Wayside Motel ($)
1430 6th St
(57006) 800.658.4577

● Buffalo ●
Tipperary Lodge ($)
Box# 247
(57720) 605.375.3721

● Canistota ●
Best Western ($)
130 Ash St
(57012) 605.296.3466
small dogs

Motel 6 ($)
1309 S Ohlman St
(57012) 605.996.0530
1 small pet/room

● Canova ●
Skoglund Farms Inn/B&B
Rt 1
(57321) 605.247.3445
owner rfd

● Chamberlain ●
Bel Aire Motel ($)
312 E King Ave
(57325) 605.734.5595

Lake Shore Motel ($)
115 N River St
(57325) 605.734.5566

Radisson Inn ($$$)
101 G Mickleson
(57325) 605.734.6376

● Corsica ●
Parkway Motel ($)
Hwy 281
(57328) 605.946.5230

● Custer ●
American Pres Cabins ($)
Box# 446
(57730) 605.673.3373

Bavarian Inn Motel ($)
Box# 152
(57730) 605.673.2802

Blue Bell Lodge ($$$)
HC 83 Box# 63
(57730) 605.255.4531
in cabins $5 fee

Chief Motel ($)
120 Mount Rushmore Rd
(57730) 605.673.2318
small dogs

Legion Lake Resort ($$$)
HC 83 Box# 67
(57730) 800.658.3530
$5 fee

Rocket Motel ($)
211 Mount Rushmore Rd
(57730) 605.673.4401

The Roost Resort ($)
HC 83 Box# 120
(57730) 605.673.2326

● Deadwood ●
Days Inn ($)
68 Main St
(57732) 605.578.3476

Deadwood Gulch Resort ($$)
Box# 643
(57732) 605.578.1294

First Gold Hotel ($$)
270N Main St
(57732) 605.578.9777

● Eagle Butte ●
Super 8 ($$)
Hwy 212
(57625) 605.964.8888
call re: fees

● Eureka ●
Lakeview Motel ($)
RR 1 Box# 49
(57437) 605.284.2681

● Faith ●
Prairie Vista Inn ($$)
Box# 575
(57626) 605.967.2343

● Faulkton ●
Super 8 ($)
700 Main St
(57438) 605.598.4567
w/permission

● Fort Pierre ●
Fort Pierre Motel ($)
211 S First St
(57532) 605.223.3111

● Freeman ●
Fensels Motel ($)
Hwy 81
(57029) 605.925.4204

● Gettysburg ●
Trail Motel ($)
211 E Garfield Ave
(57442) 605.765.2482

● Hill City ●
Best Western ($)
106 Main St
(57745) 605.574.2577

Lantern Inn Motel ($$)
Box# 744
(57745) 605.574.2582

Palmer Gulch Lodge ($$$)
Box# 295
(57745) 605.574.2525

Robins Roost Cabins
HC 87 Box# 62
(57745) 605.574.2252

● Hot Springs ●
Best Western ($$)
602 W River St
(57747) 605.745.4292
small pets only

Bison Motel
646 S 5th St
(57747) 605.745.5191

Comfort Inn ($$)
737 S 6th St
(57747) 605.745.7378
mgr preapproval reqd

El Rancho Motel ($)
640 S 6th St # T
(57747) 800.341.8000

Super 8 ($$)
800 Mammoth St
(57747) 605.745.3888
pets with deposit

● Huron ●
Best Western ($$)
2000 Dakota Ave
(57350) 605.352.2000

Holiday Inn
100 21st St
(57350) 605.352.6655

The Crossroads Hotel ($$)
100 4th Sdt SW
(57350) 605.352.3204

Traveler Motel
241 Lincoln Ave NW
(57350) 605.352.6401

● Interior ●
Badlands Inn ($)
Box# 103
(57750) 605.433.5401

Budget Host ($$)
HC 54 Box# 115
(57750) 605.433.5335

Cedar Pass Lodge ($)
Box# 5
(57750) 605.433.5460

● Kadoka ●
Best Western ($$)
I-90
(57543) 605.837.2287
under 25 lbs

Cuckleburr Motel ($)
Box# 575
(57543) 605.837.2151

Hilltop Motel ($)
E 225 Hwy 16
(57543) 605.837.2216

Dakota Inn ($)
I-90 Ex 150
(57543) 605.837.2151

West Motel ($)
Box# 247
(57543) 605.837.2427

$=under $35 $$=$35-60 $$$=$60-100 $$$$=over $100

SOUTH DAKOTA, Kennebec

• Kennebec •
Kings Motel ($)
HC 81 Box# 30
(57544) 605.869.2270

• Keystone •
Best Western ($$)
Hwy 16A
(57751) 605.666.4472
small $10/day

Econo Lodge ($)
S R 40
(57751) 605.666.4417

Kelley Inn ($)
Box# 654
(57751) 605.666.4483

Powder House Lodge ($)
Box# 714
(57751) 605.666.4646

Rushmore Manor Inn ($$)
115 Swanzey St
(57751) 605.666.4443

The First Lady Inn ($$)
Box# 677
(57751) 800.252.2119

Triple R Ranch
Hwy 16A
(57751) 605.666.4605

• Kimball •
Travelers Motel ($)
Box# 457
(57355) 605.778.6215

• Lake City •
La Quinta Inn ($$)
1625 Regal Row
(57247) 214.630.5701
call re: fees

• Lead •
Best Western ($$$)
900 Miners Ave
(57754) 605.584.1800

• Lemmon •
Prairie Motel ($)
115 E 10Tj
(57638) 605.374.3304

• Lower Brule •
Golden Buffalo Resort ($$)
120 Crazy Horse St
(57548) 605.473.5506

• Madison •
Lake Park Motel ($)
Box# 47
(57042) 605.256.3524

Super 8 ($)
Hwys 34&81
(57042) 605.256.6931
pets w/permission

• Marvin •
Lantern Motel ($)
RR 2 Box# 281
(57251) 605.432.4591

• Milbank •
Manor Motel ($)
Box# 26
(57252) 605.432.4527

• Mitchell •
Best Western ($)
1001 S Burr St
(57301) 605.996.5536
small pets must register

Budget Host ($)
1313 S Ohlman St
(57301) 605.996.6647
prior approval reqd

Holiday Inn ($$)
1525 W Havens St
(57301) 605.996.6501
mgr preapproval reqd

Siesta Motel ($)
1210 W Havens St
(57301) 605.996.5544

• Mobridge •
Wrangler Motor Inn ($$)
820 W Grand Xing
(57601) 605.645.3641

Super 8 ($)
Hwy 12
(57601) 605.845.7215
pets w/permission

• Murdo •
Anderson Motel
408 Lincoln
(57559) 605.669.2448

Best Western ($)
301 W 5th St
(57559) 605.669.2441
managers discretion

Hospitality Inn ($)
302 W 5th St
(57559) 605.669.2425

Super 8 ($)
604 E 5th
(57559) 605.669.2437
$5/day

• North Sioux City •
Country Inn ($$)
151 Tower Rd
(57049) 605.232.3500

Super 8 ($$)
1300 River Dr
(57049) 605.332.4716
call re: fees

• Oacoma •
Days Inn ($)
I-90 Ex 260
(57365) 605.734.4100

Oasis Inn ($)
Box# 39
(57365) 605.734.6061

Oacoma Inn ($)
Box# 38
(57365) 605.734.5593

• Pickstown •
Fort Randall Inn ($)
Box# 108
(57367) 605.487.7801

• Piedmont •
Elk Creek Resort ($)
Box# 8486
(57769) 800.846.2267

• Pierre •
Best Western ($$)
920 W Sioux Ave
(57501) 605.224.6877

Budget Host ($)
640 N Euclid Ave
(57501) 605.224.5896
small pets only

Capitol Inn Motel ($)
815 E Wells Ave
(57501) 800.658.3055

Days Inn ($)
520 W Sioux Ave
(57501) 605.224.0411
small pets only

Governors Inn ($$)
700 W Sioux Ave
(57501) 605.224.4200

Kelly Inn ($$)
713 W Sioux Ave
(57501) 605.224.4140

Super 8 ($)
320 W Sioux Ave
(57501) 605.224.1617
pets w/permission

• Plankinton •
Super 8 ($$)
801 S Main
(57368) 605.942.7722
call re: fees

• Platte •
Kings Inn ($)
Box# 54
(57369) 605.337.3385

• Presho •
Hutchs Motel ($)
Box# 449
(57568) 605.895.2591

• Rapid City •
Big Sky Motel ($)
4080 Tower Rd
(57701) 605.348.3200

Castle Inn ($)
15 E North St
(57701) 800.658.5464

Days Inn ($$)
125 Main St
(57701) 605.343.5501
$15 fee

Be Discreet

$=under $35 $$=$35-60 $$$=$60-100 $$$$=over $100

Econo Lodge ($)
625 E Disk Dr
(57701) 605.342.6400

Fair Value Inn ($)
1607 La Crosse St
(57701) 605.342.8118

Foothilsl Inn ($)
1625 La Crosse St
(57701) 605.348.5640

Gold Nugget Motel ($$)
13470 S Hwy 16
(57701) 605.348.2082

Gold Star Motel ($)
801 E North St
(57701) 605.341.7051

Hillside Cottages ($)
13315 S Hwy 16
(57701) 605.342.4121

Hiltop Inn ($$$)
445 Mount Rushmore Rd
(57701) 605.348.8300
$25 deposit

Lazy U Motor Lodge ($)
2215 Mount Rushmore Rd
(57701) 605.343.4242

Motel 6 ($)
620 E Latrobe St
(57701) 605.343.3687
1 small pet/room

Ramada Inn ($$)
1721 La Crosse St
(57701) 605.342.1300
very seasonal rates

Rockerville Motel ($)
13525 Main St
(57701) 605.341.4880

Super 8 ($)
2124 La Crosse St
(57701) 605.348.8070
pets w/permission

Thrifty Motor Inn ($)
1303 La Crosse St
(57701) 605.342.0551

Tip Top Motor Hotel ($)
405 Saint Joseph St
(57701) 605.343.3901

Tradewinds Motel
420 E North St
(57701) 605.342.4153

● Redfield ●
Coachman Inn ($)
826 W 4th St
(57469) 800.382.8000

● Selby ●
Super 8 ($$)
5000 Hwy 12 & 83
(57472) 605.649.7979
call re: fees

● Sioux Falls ●
Best Western ($$)
400 S Main Ave
(57104) 605.336.2740

Best Western ($$$$)
2400 N Louise Ave
(57107) 605.336.0650
small pets only

Brimark Inn ($$)
3200 W Russell St
(57107) 605.332.2000

Budget Host ($$)
2620 E 10th
(57103) 605.336.1550
w/permission

Budgetel ($)
3200 S Meadow Ave
(57106) 605.362.0835

Comfort Inn ($)
5100 N Cliff Ave
(57104) 605.331.4490
mgr preapproval reqd

Comfort Inn ($$)
3216 S Carolyn Ave
(57106) 605.361.2822
mgr preapproval reqd

Comfort Suites ($$)
3208 S Carolyn Ave
(57106) 605.362.9711
mgr preapproval reqd

Exel Inn ($)
1300 W Russell St
(57104) 605.331.5800
small pets only

Fairfield Inn ($$)
4501 W Empire Pl
(57106) 605.361.2211

Kelly Inn ($$)
3101 W Russell St
(57107) 605.338.6242

Motel 6 ($)
3009 W Russell St
(57107) 605.336.7800
1 small pet/room

Ramada Inn ($$)
1301 W Russell St
(57104) 605.336.1020

Ramada Ltd ($)
12th & South Lyons Ave
(57104) 605.330.0000

Residence Inn ($$$)
4509 W Empire Pl
(57106) 605.361.2202

Rodeway Inn ($$)
809 N West Ave
(57104) 605.336.0230

Select Inn ($)
3500 S Gateway Blvd
(57106) 605.361.1864

Super 8 ($$)
1508 W Russia St
(57104) 605.339.9330
w/permission

● Sisseton ●
Holiday Motel ($)
E Of Jct US 127
(57262) 605.698.7644

I 29 Motel ($)
I-29 Jct Sd 10E
(57262) 605.698.4314

Viking Motel
West Hwy 10
(57262) 605.698.7663

● Spearfish ●
Best Western ($)
2431 S Junction
(57783) 605.347.3604

Best Western ($$)
346 W Kansas St
(57783) 605.642.4676
1 cat or 1 dog

Fairfield Inn ($$)
2720 1st Ave
(57783) 605.642.3500

Holiday Inn
I-90 Ex 14
(57783) 605.642.4683

Kelly Inn ($$)
540 E Jackson Blvd
(57783) 605.642.7795

Queens Motel ($)
305 N Main St
(57783) 605.642.2631
small pets only

Ramada Inn ($$)
I-90 & Ex 14
(57783) 605.642.4683

Royal Rest Motel ($)
444 N Main St
(57783) 605.642.3842

Shady Pines Cabins
514 W Mason St
(57783) 800.551.8920

Sherwood Lodge
231 W Jackson Blvd
(57783) 605.642.4688

● Sturgis ●
Junction Inn ($)
1802 Junction Ave
(57785) 605.347.5675

National 9 ($)
2426 Junction Ave
(57785) 605.347.2506

Super 8 ($)
HC 55
(57785) 605.347.4447
pets with deposit

● Vermillion ●
Budget Host ($$$)
1313 W Cherry
(57069) 605.624.2601

Well
Behaved

SOUTH DAKOTA, Vermillion

Comfort Inn ($$)
701 W Cherry St
(57069) 605.624.8333
mgr preapproval reqd

Super 8 ($$)
1208 E Cherry St
(57069) 605.624.8005
$5

● Wall ●
Best Western ($$)
712 Glenn St
(57790) 605.279.2145
pets must be registered

Elk Motwel ($)
South Bend
(57790) 605.279.2127

Hitching Post Motel ($)
211 10th Ave
(57790) 605.279.2133

Kings Inn Motel ($)
608 Main St
(57790) 605.279.2178

Sands Motor Inn ($)
804 Glenn St
(57790) 605.279.2121

● Watertown ●
Best Western ($$)
1901 9th Ave SW
(57201) 605.886.8011

Budget Host ($$)
309 8th Ave
(57201) 605.886.8455

Comfort Inn ($$)
800 35th Cir SE
(57201) 605.886.3010
mgr preapproval reqd

Drake Motor Inn ($)
Box# 352
(57201) 800.821.8695

Guest House Inn ($)
Box# 1147
(57201) 605.886.8061

Travel Host Motel ($)
1714 9th Ave SW
(57201) 605.886.6120
small dog

● Webster ●
Super 8 ($)
Hwy 12
(57274) 605.345.4701
pets w/permission

● Winner ●
Bufffalo Trail Motel ($)
950 W 1st St
(57580) 605.842.2212

Super 8 ($)
902 W Hey 44
(57580) 605.842.0991
pets w/permission

Warrior Inn Motel ($)
Hwy 44 & 118
(57580) 800.658.4705

● Yankton ●
Broadway Motel ($)
1210 Broadway St
(57078) 605.665.7805

Comfort Inn ($$)
2118 Broadway St
(57078) 605.665.8053
mgr preapproval reqd

Lewis&Clark Resort ($)
Box# 754
(57078) 605.665.2680

Mulberry Inn ($)
512 Mulberry St
(57078) 605.665.7116

Super 8 ($)
RR 4 Box# 36
(57078) 605.665.6510
pets w/permission

Yankton Inn ($$)
1607 E Hwy 50
(57078) 605.665.2906

Tennessee
● Alcoa ●
Comfort Inn ($$)
2306 Airport Hwy Alcoa
(37701) 423.970.3140
mgr preapproval reqd

● Antioch ●
Days Inn ($$)
I-24 Bell Rd
(37013) 615.731.7800
$5/pets

Hampton Inn ($$)
210 Crossings Pl
(37013) 615.731.0229

Holiday Inn
201 Crossing Place
(37013) 615.731.2361

Quarters Motor Inn ($$)
1100 Bell Rd
(37013) 615.731.5990

● Ashland City ●
Birdsong Country Inn
1306 Hwy 49
(37015) 615.792.4005

● Athens ●
Days Inn
2541 Decatur Pike
(37303) 423.745.5800

Holiday Inn ($)
I-75 & Mt Verd Rd
(37303) 423.745.1212
mgr preapproval reqd

Homestead Inn ($)
1827 Holiday Dr
(37303) 423.744.9002
$2 charge

Homestead Inn ($)
2808 Decatur Pike
(37303) 423.745.9002

Scottish Inn
2620 Decatur Pike
(37303) 423.744.8200
$3 fee

Super 8 ($$)
2539 Decatur Pike
(37303) 423.745.4500
call re: fees

● Brentwood ●
Amerisuites ($$$)
202 Summit View Dr
(37027) 615.661.9477

Hilton ($$$)
9000 Overlook Blvd
(37027) 615.370.0111
deposit

Residence Inn ($$$)
206 Ward Cir
(37027) 615.371.0100
$75 fee

● Bristol ●
Econo Lodge ($$)
3281 W State St
(37620) 423.968.9119

Hojo Inn ($$)
975 Volunteer Pkwy
(37620) 423.968.9474

Quality Inn ($$)
I-81
(37621) 423.968.9119

● Brownsville ●
Days Inn ($$)
2530 Anderson Ave
(38012) 901.772.3297
$5/pets

● Buchanan ●
Cypress Bay Resort
110 Cypress Resort Loop
(38222) 901.232.8221

Paris Landing Motel
RR 1 Box# 84B
(38222) 901.642.5590

Shamrock Resort
220 Shamrock Rd
(38222) 901.232.8211

● Camden ●
Birdsong Resort
255 Marina Rd
(38320) 901.584.7880

● Carthage ●
Defeated Creek Marina
156 Marina Ln
(37030) 615.774.3131

● Caryville ●
Budget Host ($)
101 Tennessee Dr
(37714) 423.562.9595

$=under $35 $$=$35-60 $$$=$60-100 $$$$=over $10

Holiday Inn ($$)
RR 1 Box# 14
(37714) 423.562.8476
mgr preapproval reqd

● Celina ●
Cedar Hill Resort ($)
2371 Cedar Hill Rd
(38551) 615.243.3201

Dale Hollow Marina
99 Arlon Webb Dr
(38551) 615.243.2211

● Chattanooga ●
Best Western ($$)
6650 Ringgold Rd
(37412) 423.894.1860

Best Western ($$)
7641 Lee Hwy
(37421) 423.899.3311
small pets only

Comfort Inn ($$)
7717 Lee Hwy
(37421) 423.894.5454
mgr preapproval reqd

Days Inn ($$)
7725 Lee Hwy
(37421) 615.899.2288
$4 night

Days Inn
101 - 20th St
(37408) 423.267.9761
$4

Days Inn ($$)
3801 Cummings Hwy
(37419) 615.821.6044
$7

Days Inn ($$)
901 Carter St
(37402) 423.266.7331
mgr preapproval reqd

Diamond Motel ($)
1407 NW 3rd St
(37410) 913.263.2360

Econo Lodge ($)
1417 Saint Thomas St
(37412) 423.894.1417
small & caged

Holiday Inn ($$$)
7024 McCutcheon Rd
(37421) 423.490.8560
mgr preapproval reqd

Holiday Inn ($$$)
2345 Shallowford Vlg
(37421) 423.855.2898
mgr preapproval reqd

Holiday Inn ($$)
6700 Ringgold Rd
(37412) 423.893.8100
mgr preapproval reqd

Kings Lodge Motel ($)
2400 Westside Dr
(37404) 423.698.8944

Motel ($)
7707 Laa Hwy
(37421) 615.892.7707
1 small pet per room

Ramada Inn ($$)
100 W 21st St
(37408) 423.265.3151

Ramada Inn ($$)
6639 Capehart Ln
(37412) 423.894.6110

Red Roof Inn ($$)
7014 Shallowford Rd
(37421) 423.899.0143

Super 8 ($$)
1401 N Mack Smith Rd
(37412) 423.892.3888
call re: fees

● Clarksville ●
A&W Motel
1505 Madison St
(37040) 615.647.3545

Days Inn ($$)
1100 Hwy 76
(37043) 615.358.3194

Holiday Inn ($$)
3095 Wilma Rudolph Blvd
(37040) 615.648.4848
mgr preapproval reqd

Ramada Inn ($$)
50 College St
(37040) 615.552.3331
under 10 lbs

Ramada Ltd ($$)
3100 Wilma Rudolph Blvd
(37040) 615.552.0098

Skyway Motel ($)
2581 Fort Campbell Blvd
(37042) 615.431.5225

Travelodge ($$)
3075 Wilma Rudolph Blvd
(37040) 615.645.1400

● Cleveland ●
Best Western ($$)
156 James Asbury Dr NW
(37312) 423.457.2233

Budgetel ($)
107 Interstate Dr NW
(37312) 615.339.1000

Colonial Inn ($)
1555 25th St NW
(37311) 423.472.6845

Days Inn ($)
2550 Georgetwn Rd NW
(37311) 423.476.2112
$5/pet

Holiday Inn ($$)
I-75 & S R 60
(37320) 423.472.1504
mgr preapproval reqd

Ramada Inn ($$)
I-75 & S R 64
(37320) 423.479.4531
small pets only

Red Carpet Inn ($)
1501 25th St NW
(37311) 423.476.6514
$4 fee

Travel Inn ($)
3000 Valley Hills Trl NW
(37311) 615.472.2185

● Collierville ●
Plantation Inn ($$)
1230 W Poplar Ave
(38017) 901.853.1235

● Columbia ●
Econo Lodge ($$)
1548 Bear Creek Pike
(38401) 615.381.1410

James K Polk Motel ($)
1111 Nashville Hwy
(38401) 615.388.4913

Oak Springs Inn
151I Williamsport Pike
(38401) 615.388.7539

Ramada Inn ($$)
1208 Nachville Hwy
(38401) 615.388.2720

● Cookeville ●
Best Western ($)
900 S Jefferson Ave
(38501) 615.526.7115
pets allowed except no-
smoke rooms

Days Inn ($)
1292 Bunker Hill Rd
(38501) 615.528.1511

Eastwood Inn
1646 E Spring St
(38506) 615.526.6158

Holiday Inn
970 S Jefferson
(38501) 615.526.7125

● Cordova ●
Best Suites ($$$)
8166 Vanavas Dr
(38018) 901.386.4600

● Covington ●
Best Western ($$)
873 Hwy 51
(38019) 901.476.8561

● Crossville ●
Capri Terrace Motel
714 N Main St
(38555) 615.484.7561

Executive Inn
3114 N Main St
(38555) 615.484.9691

Heritage Inn
317 Hwy 127
(38555) 615.484.9505

$=under $35 $$=$35-60 $$$=$60-100 $$$$=over $100

Crossville, TENNESSEE

Ramada Inn ($$)
S R 127 & I-40
(38555) 615.484.7581

● Cumberland Gap ●
Cumberland Gap Inn ($$)
630B Brooklyn St
(37724) 423.869.9172

Holiday Inn
US 25
(37724) 423.869.3631

● Dandridge ●
Mountain Harbor Inn ($$)
1199 Hwy 139
(37725) 423.397.3345

Tennesee Mtn Inn ($)
531 Patriot Dr
(37725) 423.397.9437

● Dayton ●
Best Western ($$)
7835 Rhea County Hwy
(37321) 423.775.6560

Days Inn ($$)
3914 Rhea County Hwy
(37321) 423.775.9718

● Denmark ●
Econo Lodge ($)
Jackson West
(38391) 901.427.2778
deposit

● Dickson ●
Days Inn ($)
Hwy 46 & I-40
(37055) 615.446.7561
$5/pets

Holiday Inn ($$)
2420 Hwy 46
(37055) 615.446.9081
mgr preapproval reqd

● Dyersburg ●
Ramada Inn ($)
2331 Lake Rd
(38024) 901.287.0044

● Elizabethton ●
Days Inn
505 Elk Ave
(37643) 423.543.3344

● Elkton ●
Economy Inn
I-65 P Bryson Rd
(38455) 615.468.2594

● Fayetteville ●
Best Western ($$)
3021 Thornton Taylor
(37334) 615.433.0100
sign damage waiver

Days Inn ($$)
1651 Huntsville Hwy
(37334) 615.433.6121
only small pets allowed

● Franklin ●
Best Western ($$)
1308 Murfreesboro Rd
(37064) 615.790.0570
small pets $5/day

Budgetel ($$)
4207 Franklin Commons Ct
(37064) 615.791.7700

Days Inn ($$)
4217 S Carothers Rd
(37067) 615.790.1140

Goosecreek Inn
2404 Goose Creek Byp
(37064) 615.794.7200

● Gallatin ●
Shoneys Inn ($$)
221 W Main St
(37066) 615.452.5433

● Gatlinburg ●
Alto Motel ($$)
US 321
(37738) 615.436.5175

Bon Air Mtn Inn ($$)
950 Parkway
(37738) 423.436.4857

Coxs Gateway Motel ($$)
1100 Parkway
(37738) 615.436.5656

Creekstone Motel ($)
104 Oglewood Ln
(37738) 800.572.7770

Grandview Inn ($$$)
335 E Holly Ridge Rd
(37738) 615.436.3161

Highland Motor Inn ($)
131 Parkway
(37738) 423.436.4110

Holiday Inn ($$)
520 Airport Rd
(37738) 423.436.9201
mgr preapproval reqd

Margies Chalets
Box# 288
(37738) 615.436.9475

Microtel ($)
211 Airport Rd
(37738) 615.436.0107

Park Vista Hotel ($$$)
Box# 30
(37738) 423.436.9211

Ramada Inn
756 Parkway
(37738) 423.436.7881

Rodeway Inn ($$)
1109 Parkway
(37738) 423.436.5811

● Goodlettsville ●
Budgetel ($$)
120 S Cartwright Ct
(37072) 615.851.1891

Econo Lodge ($)
320B Long Hollow Pike
(37072) 615.859.4988
small pets only

Master Host
622- 2Mile Pkwy
(37072) 615.859.2861

Motel 6 ($)
323 Cartwright St
(37072) 615.859.9674
1 small pet/room

Rodeway Inn ($)
650 Wade Cir
(37072) 615.859.1416
$3 per day

● Greeneville ●
Andrew Johnson Inn ($)
2145 E Andrew Johnson Hwy
(37745) 423.638.8124

Days Inn ($)
935 E Andrew Johnson Hwy
(37745) 615.639.2156
$10

● Harriman ●
Best Western ($$)
I-40
(37748) 423.882.6200
small $2 charge

Holiday Inn
I-40 & US27
(37748) 423.882.5340

Scottish Inn ($)
1867 S Roane St
(37748) 423.882.6600

● Hermitage ●
Hermitage Inn ($)
4144 Lebanon Rd
(37076) 615.883.7444

Ramada Ltd ($$)
I-40 E & Old Hickory Blvd
(37076) 615.889.8940

● Hornbeak ●
Bill Nations Camp
244 W Lakeview Dr
(38232) 901.538.2177

Boardsmans Resort
813 Lake Dr
(38232) 901.538.2112

Hamiltons Resort
4992 Hamilton Rd
(38232) 901.538.2325

● Huntsville ●
Holiday Inn ($$)
11597 Scott Hwy
(37756) 423.663.4100
mgr preapproval reqd

$=under $35 $$=$35-60 $$$=$60-100 $$$$=over $100

• Hurricane Mills •
Best Western ($$)
1554I Hwy 13
(37078) 615.296.4251
small

Days Inn ($$)
15415 Hwy 13
(37078) 615.296.7647
deposit

Super 8 ($)
RR 1 Box# 79
(37078) 615.296.2432
call re: fees

• Jackson •
Best Western ($$)
1849 Hwy 45 Byp
(38305) 901.668.4222

Budgetel ($)
2370 N Highland Ave
(38305) 901.664.1800

Days Inn ($)
1919 US 45 Byp
(38305) 901.688.3444

Days Inn ($)
2239 Hollywood Dr
(38305) 901.668.4840
spayed cats & clean dogs
with permissi

Econo Lodge ($)
1936 US 45
(38305) 901.664.3030

Hampton Inn ($$)
340 Interstate Dr
(38301) 615.520.1117

Super 8 ($)
2295 N Highland Ave
(38305) 901.668.1145
call re: fees

The Travelers Motel ($)
2244 N Highland Ave
(38305) 901.668.0542

• Jasper •
Days Inn ($)
Hwy 72 Dixie Lee Jct
(37347) 423.837.7933
$4 fee

• Jellico •
Days Inn
I-75
(37762) 423.784.7281
$5

• Joelton •
Days Inn ($)
201 Gifford Pl
(37080) 615.876.3261

• Johnson City •
Comfort Inn ($$)
1900 S Roan St
(37601) 423.928.9600
mgr preapproval reqd

Days Inn ($$)
2312 Brown'S Mill Rd
(37601) 423.282.3211
$5

Garden Plaza Hotel ($$$)
211 Mockingbird Ln
(37604) 423.929.2000

Hampton Inn ($$)
508 St Franklin
(37604) 423.929.8000

Holiday Inn ($$$)
101 S Springbrook Dr
(37604) 423.282.4611
mgr preapproval reqd

Red Roof Inn ($)
210 Broyles St
(37601) 423.282.3050

Super 8 ($)
108 Wesley St
(37601) 432.282.8818
call re: fees

• Kingsport •
Comfort Inn ($$)
100 Indian Center Ct
(37660) 423.378.4418
mgr preapproval reqd

Econo Lodge ($$)
1704 E Stone Dr
(37660) 423.245.0286

La Quinta Inn ($$)
10150 Airport Pkwy
(37663) 423.323.0500
call re: fees

Microtel ($$)
1708 Stone Dr
(37660) 615.378.9220

• Kingston •
Days Inn
495 Gallaher Rd
(37763) 423.376.2069
$5

Howard Johnson ($)
1200 N Kentucky St
(37763) 615.376.3477

• Kingston Springs •
Econo Lodge ($)
123 Luyben Hills Rd
(37082) 615.952.2900

Scottish Inn ($)
116 Luyden Hills Rd
(37082) 615.952.3115

• Knoxville •
Best Western ($$)
500 Lovell Rd
(37932) 423.675.7666
small pets only

Budgetel ($$)
11341 Campbell Lakes Dr
(37922) 423.671.1010

Days Inn ($$)
1706 Cumberland Ave
(37916) 423.521.5000
$15

Days Inn ($$)
200 Lovell Rd
(37922) 423.966.5801
$5/pets

Econo Lodge ($$)
5505 Merchants Center
(37912) 423.687.5680

Hampton Inn ($$)
119 Cedar Ln
(37912) 423.689.1011

Holiday Inn ($$$)
1315 Kirby Rd
(37909) 423.584.3911
mgr preapproval reqd

Howard Johnson ($$)
118 Merchants Dr
(37912) 423.688.3141
$25 deposit

La Quinta Inn ($$)
258 N Peters Rd
(37923) 423.690.9777
call re: fees

Microtel ($$)
309 N Peters Rd
(37922) 615.531.8041

Motel 6 ($)
402 Lovell Rd
(37922) 423.675.7200
1 small pet/room

Quality Inn ($)
6712 Central Avenue Pike
(37912) 423.689.6600
mgr preapproval reqd

Ramada Inn ($$)
323 N Cedar Bluff Rd
(37923) 423.693.7330

Ramada Inn ($)
1500 Cherry St NE
(37917) 423.547.7110

Ramada Ltd ($$)
11748 Snyder Rd
(37932) 423.675.5566

Ramada Ltd ($)
722 Brakebill Rd
(37924) 423.546.7271

Red Roof Inn ($)
5640 Merchants Center
(37912) 423.689.7100

Red Roof Inn ($)
209 Advantage Pl
(37922) 423.691.1664

Rodeway Inn ($)
6730 Central Avenue Pike
(37912) 423.687.3500

Scottish Inn
301 Callahan
(37912) 615.689.7777

$=under $35 $$=$35-60 $$$=$60-100 $$$$=over $100

TENNESSEE, Knoxville

Scottish Inn
9340 Park West Blvd
(37923) 423.693.6061
$5 fee

Super 8 ($)
6200 Papermill Rd
(37919) 423.584.8511
call re: fees

● Kodak ●
Best Western ($)
3426 Winfield Dunn Pkwy
(37764) 423.933.3467
small pets

● Lake City ●
The Lambs Inn ($)
602 N Marin St
(37769) 423.426.2171

● Lebanon ●
Days Inn ($)
231 Murfreesboro Rd
(37087) 615.444.5635
$5/pets

Hampton Inn ($$)
704 S Cumberland St
(37087) 615.444.7400

Holiday Inn ($$)
641 S Cumberland St
(37087) 615.444.7020
mgr preapproval reqd

Super 8 ($)
914 Murfreesboro Rd
(37090) 615.444.5637
$5

● Loudon ●
Holiday Inn ($$)
12452 Hwy 72nd
(37774) 423.458.5668
mgr preapproval reqd

Knights Inn ($)
15100 Hwy 72
(37774) 423.458.5855

● Louisville ●
Crossroads Inn ($)
1110 Hwy 321N
(37777) 423.986.2011

Policies Subject to Change

● Madison ●
Rodeway Inn ($$)
625 Gallatin Rd
(37115) 615.865.2323

● Manchester ●
Ambassador Inn ($)
RR 6 Box# 6022
(37355) 800.237.9228

Days Inn ($)
I-24 & Hwy 53
(37355) 615.728.6023

Econo Lodge ($)
RR 8 Box# 8131
(37355) 615.728.9530
$3 per day

Hampton Inn ($$)
RR 6 Box# 6009
(37355) 615.728.3300

Holiday Inn ($$)
I-24 & US 41
(37355) 615.728.9651
mgr preapproval reqd

Scottish Inn ($)
2457 Hillsboro Blvd
(37355) 615.728.0506
$4 fee

Super 8 ($)
2430 Hillsboro Blvd
(37355) 615.728.9720
small pets only

● Martin ●
University Lodge ($$)
Box# 50
(38237) 901.587.9577

● Mc Kenzie ●
Howard Johnson ($)
2021 E Spring St
(38201) 615.526.3333

McKenzie Motor Inn
121 Highland Dr
(38201) 901.352.3325

Star Motor Inn
1115 S Willow Ave
(38201) 615.526.9511

● Mc Minnville ●
Scottish Inn ($)
1105 Sparta St
(37110) 615.473.2181
$4 charge

Shoneys Inn ($$)
508 Sunnyside Hts
(37110) 615.473.4446

● Memphis ●
Best Inns ($$)
7787 Wold River Blvd
(38138) 901.757.7800

Best Western ($$)
340 W Illinois Ave
(38106) 901.948.9005

Best Western ($$$)
5024 Hwy 78
(38118) 901.363.8430

Brownestone Hotel ($$$)
300 N 2nd St
(38105) 901.525.2511

Budgetel ($$)
6020 Shelby Oaks Dr
(38134) 901.377.2233

Budgetel ($$)
3005 Millbrank Rd
(38116) 901.396.5411

Comfort Inn ($$)
1581 E Brooks Rd
(38116) 901.345.3344
mgr preapproval reqd

Comfort Inn ($$)
5877 Poplar Ave
(38119) 901.767.6300
mgr preapproval reqd

Country Suites ($$$)
4300 American Way
(38118) 901.366.9333

Days Inn ($$)
3839 Elvis Presley Blvd
(38116) 901.346.5500
small dogs $5 fee

Days Inn ($$)
1533 E Brooks Rd
(38116) 901.345.2470
$5

Drury Inn
1556 Sycamore View Rd
(38134) 800.325.8300

Hampton Inn ($$)
33 Humphreys Center Dr
(38120) 901.747.3700

Hampton Inn
5320 Poplar Ave
(38119) 901.683.8500

Holiday Inn ($$$)
5795 Poplar Ave
(38119) 901.682.7881
mgr preapproval reqd

Holiday Inn ($$$)
1837 Union Ave
(38104) 901.278.4100
mgr preapproval reqd

Hometown Suites ($$$)
7855 Wold River Blvd
(38138) 901.751.2500

Homewood Suites ($$$)
5811 Poplar Ave
(38119) 901.763.0500

Howard Johnson ($$)
1541 Sycamore View Rd
(38134) 901.388.1300

La Quinta Inn ($$)
2745 Airways Blvd
(38132) 901.396.1000
call re: fees

La Quinta Inn ($$)
6068 Macon Cv
(38134) 901.382.2323
call re: fees

La Quinta Inn ($$)
42 S Camilla St
(38104) 901.526.1050
call re: fees

Memphis Airport Hotel ($$)
2240 Democrat Rd
(38132) 901.332.1130

Memphis Inn East ($)
6050 Macon Cv
(38134) 901.375.9898

$=under $35 $$=$35-60 $$$=$60-100 $$$$=over $100

Motel 6 ($)
1117 E Brooks Rd
(38116) 901.346.0992
1 small pet/room

Motel 6 ($)
1321 Sycamore View Rd
(38134) 901.382.8572
1 small pet/room

Red Roof Inn ($$)
210 S Pauline St
(38104) 901.528.0650

Red Roof Inn ($$)
6055 Shelby Oaks Dr
(38134) 901.388.6111

Red Roof Inn ($$)
3875 American Way
(38118) 901.363.2335

Residence Inn ($$$$)
6141 Poplar Pike
(38119) 901.685.9595

Super 8 ($$)
3280 Elvis Presley Blvd
(38116) 901.345.1425
small $5 fee

Super 8 ($$)
4060 Lamar Ave
(38118) 800.800.8000
$5

Super 8 ($$)
6015 Macon Cove Rd
(38134) 501.373.4888
w/permission

● Milan ●
Ramada Ltd
US Hwy 70/79 & 45
(38358) 901.686.3345
small to medium size

● Millington ●
Best Western ($$)
7726 Hwy 51
(38053) 901.873.2222
small pets

Econo Lodge ($)
8193 Hwy 51
(38053) 901.873.4400

● Monteagle ●
Adams Edgeworth Inn ($$$$)
Montegle Assembly
(37356) 615.924.4000

Budget Host ($$$)
I-24 Ex 134
(37356) 615.924.2221
$3

Days Inn ($)
742 Dixie Lee Ave
(37356) 615.924.2900
small pets $6 per day

Jim Olivers Smokehse ($)
US Hwy 64-41A
(37356) 615.924.2268

● Morristown ●
Days Inn ($)
2512 E Andrew Johnson Hwy
(37814) 423.587.2200
mgr preapproval reqd

Ramada Inn ($$)
I-81 & US 25
(37815) 423.587.2400

Super 8 ($$)
2430 E Andrew Johnson Hwy
(37814) 423.586.8880
under 30 lbs w/permission

● Mountain City ●
Days Inn ($$)
Hwy 421 Rt 4
(37683) 615.727.7311
$6

● Murfreesboro ●
Best Western ($$)
168 Chaffin Pl
(37129) 615.895.3818

Days Inn ($)
2036 S Church St
(37130) 615.893.1090

Garden Plaza Hotel ($$$)
1850 Old Fort Pkwy
(37129) 615.895.5555

Hampton Inn ($$)
2230 Old Fort Pkwy
(37129) 615.896.1172
under 20 lbs

Howard Johnson ($$)
2424 S Church St
(37127) 615.896.5522

Motel 6 ($)
114 Chaffin Pl
(37129) 615.890.8524
1 small pet/room

Murfreesboro Motel ($)
1150 NW Broad St
(37129) 615.893.2100

Quality Inn ($)
118 Westgate Blvd
(37128) 615.848.9030
mgr preapproval reqd

Ramada Ltd ($$)
1855 S Church St
(37130) 615.896.5080
$5/pet

Scottish Inn ($)
2029 S Church St
(37130) 615.896.3210
$3 fee

Travelodge ($$)
2025 S Church St
(37130) 615.896.2320

● Nashville ●
Best Suites ($$$)
2521 Elm Hill Pike
(37214) 615.391.3919

Best Western ($$)
701 Stewarts Ferry Pike
(37214) 615.889.9199

Budgetel ($$)
531 Donelson Pike
(37214) 615.885.3100

Budgetel ($$)
5612 Lenox Ave
(37209) 615.353.0700

Comfort Inn ($)
2306 Brick Church Pike
(37207) 615.226.9560
mgr preapproval reqd

Days Inn ($)
1400 Brick Church Pike
(37207) 615.228.5977
$5 fee

Drury Inn ($$)
837 Briley Pkwy
(37217) 615.361.6999

Drury Inn ($$)
341B Harding Pl
(37211) 615.834.7170

Econo Lodge ($)
24030 Brick Church Pike
(37207) 800.424.4777

Econo Lodge ($$)
2460 Music Valley Dr
(37214) 615.889.0090
under 10 lbs

Embassy Suites ($$$)
10 Century Blvd
(37214) 615.871.0033

Hampton Inn ($$$)
2530 Elm Hill Pike
(37214) 615.871.0222
small pets only

Hojo Inn ($$)
323 Harding Pl
(37211) 615.834.0570

Holiday Inn
2401 Brick Church Pike
(37207) 615.226.4600

Holiday Inn ($$)
2516 Music Valley Dr
(37214) 615.889.0086
mgr preapproval reqd

Holiday Inn ($$)
981 Murfreesboro Pike
(37217) 615.327.9150
mgr preapproval reqd

Howard Johnson ($$)
6834 Charlotte Pike
(37209) 615.352.7080

Howard Johnson ($$)
2600 Music Valley Dr
(37214) 615.889.8235
$10 per day

Howard Johnson ($$)
970 Murfreesboro Pike
(37217) 615.367.6119

La Quinta Inn ($$)
2001 Metrocenter Blvd
(37228) 615.259.2130
call re: fees

La Quinta Inn ($$)
4311 Sidco Dr
(37204) 615.834.6900
call re: fees

La Quinta Inn Airport ($$)
2345 Atrium Way
(37214) 615.885.3000

Motel 6 ($$)
420 Metroplex Dr
(37211) 615.833.8887
1 small pet/room

Motel 6 ($)
311 W Trinity Ln
(37207) 615.227.9696
1 small pet/room

Motel 6 ($$)
95 Wallace Rd
(37211) 615.333.9933
1 small pet/room

Nashville Med Cntr ($$$)
1909 Hayes St
(37203) 615.329.1000

Pear Tree ($$)
343N Harding Pl
(37211) 615.834.4242

Ramada Inn ($$)
2425 Atrium Way
(37214) 615.883.5201

Red Roof Inn ($$)
510B Claridge Dr
(37214) 615.872.0735

Red Roof Inn ($$)
4271 Sidco Dr
(37204) 615.832.0093

Residence Inn ($$$)
2300 Elm Hill Pike
(37214) 615.889.8600

Scottish Inn
1501 Dickerson Rd
(37207) 615.226.6940

Sheraton Inn ($$$$)
777 McGavock Pike
(37214) 615.885.2200
small pets only

Shoneys Inn
15421 Demonbreun St
(37203) 615.255.9977

Super 8 ($$)
412 Robertson Ave
(37209) 615.356.0888
pets w/permission

Super 8 ($$)
350 Harding Pl
(37211) 615.834.0620
mgr preapproval reqd

Travel Park ($)
2572 Music Valley Dr
(37214) 615.889.4225

Twelve Oaks Motel
656 W Iris Dr
(37204) 615.385.1323

Union Station Hotel ($$$)
1001 Broadway
(37203) 615.726.1001

Wyndham Hotel ($$$)
1112 Airport Center Dr
(37214) 615.889.9090

● Newport ●
Best Western ($$)
I-40
(37821) 423.623.8713
small pets only

Holiday Inn ($$)
I-40 & Hwy 32
(37821) 423.623.8622
mgr preapproval reqd

Relax Inn ($)
1848 W Knoxville Hwy
(37821) 615.625.1521

● Normandy ●
Paris Patch Inn
625 Cortner Rd
(37360) 615.857.3017

● Oak Ridge ●
Comfort Inn ($$)
433 S Rutgers Ave
(37830) 423.481.8200
mgr preapproval reqd

Days Inn ($$)
206 S Illinois Ave
(37830) 423.483.5615
$4/pets

Garden Plaza Hotel ($$$)
215 S Illinois Ave
(37830) 423.481.2468

Super 8 ($$)
1590 Oak Ridge Tpke
(37830) 423.483.1200
$5 charge

● Oneida ●
The Galloway Inn ($)
Box# 4525
(37841) 423.569.8835

● Only ●
Bucksnort Motel
I-40 Ex 152
(37140) 615.729.5450

● Ooltewah ●
Super 8 ($$)
5111 Hunter Rd
(37363) 423.238.5951
$2 fee

● Paris ●
Avalon Motel
1315 Wood St
(38242) 901.642.4121

Best Western ($$)
1297 E Wood St
(38242) 901.642.8881

● Pigeon Forge ●
Econo Lodge ($$$)
2440 Parkway
(37863) 423.438.1231

Heartlander Resort ($)
2385 Parkway
(37863) 423.456.4106

Microtel ($$)
202 Emert St
(37863) 423.429.0150

The Grand Hotel ($)
3171 Parkway
(37863) 423.453.1000
small $10 fee

● Portland ●
Budget Host ($)
5339 Long Rd
(37148) 615.325.2005
$5

● Powell ●
Comfort Inn ($$)
323 Emory Rd
(37849) 423.938.5500
mgr preapproval reqd

● Pulaski ●
Sands Motor Hotel ($)
Box# 408
(38478) 615.363.4501

Super 8 ($$)
2400B Hwy 64
(38478) 615.363.4501
$5

● Riceville ●
Relax Inn ($)
RR 2 Box# 278-A
(37370) 615.745.5893

● Samburg ●
Duck Inn
218 Church
(38254) 901.538.2364

Samburg Motel
100 Lakeview St
(38254) 901.538.2467

● Savannah ●
Savannah Motel
105 Adam St
(38372) 901.925.3392

Shaws Komfort Motel
2302 Wayne Rd
(38372) 901.925.3977

$=under $35 $$=$35-60 $$$=$60-100 $$$$=over $100

Amarillo, TEXAS

• Sevierville •
Spring Gap Log Cabins ($$$)
3054 Kulpan Way
(37862) 423.453.0829

• Shelbyville •
Best Western ($$)
724 Madison St
(37160) 615.684.2378

Shelbyville Inn ($$)
317 N Cannon Blvd
(37160) 615.684.6050

• Smyrna •
Days Inn ($$)
1300 Plaza Dr
(37167) 615.355.6161
$10/small pets only

• Spring Hill •
Holiday Inn
104 Kedron Rd
(37174) 615.486.1234

• Sweetwater •
Budget Host ($)
207 Hwy 68
(37874) 423.337.9357
$2

Comfort Inn ($)
RR 5 Box# 48
(37874) 423.337.3353
mgr preapproval reqd

Days Inn ($)
RR 5 Box# 46
(37874) 423.337.4200

Quality Inn ($$)
1421 Murray'S Chapel
(37874) 423.337.3541
small pets only

Sweetwater Hotel ($$)
180 Hwy 68
(37874) 615.337.3511

• Tiptonville •
Gravys Camp
RR 1 Box# 280
(38079) 901.253.7813

Rays Camp
RR 1 Box# 5B-1
(38079) 901.253.7765

• Townsend •
Best Western ($)
Hwy 321
(37882) 423.448.2237

Days Inn
Hwy 321
(37882) 423.448.9111

Days Inn ($)
Hwy 321
(37882) 423.448.2211

Wears Motel ($$)
8270 Hwy 73
(37882) 423.448.2296

• Union City •
Cultra Motor Inn
1221 Reelfoot Ave
(38261) 901.885.6610

Hampton Inn
2201 Reelford Ave
(38261) 901.885.8850

Super 8 ($$)
1400 Vaden St
(38261) 901.885.4444
w/permission

• White House •
Holiday Inn
I-65 & Hwy 76
(37188) 615.672.7200

• White Pine •
Days Inn ($$)
3670 Roy Messer Hwy
(37890) 423.674.2573
$7

• Wildersville •
Best Western ($)
21045 Hwy 22
(38388) 901.968.2532

• Winchester •
Frassrand Terrace ($)
700 S College St
(37398) 615.967.3856

Texas
• Abilene •
Best Western ($$)
3210 Pine St
(79601) 915.677.2683

Best Western ($$)
3950 Ridgemont Dr
(79606) 915.695.1262
small pets only

Days Inn ($$)
17021 I-20
(79601) 915.672.6433

Econo Lodge ($)
1633 W Stamford St
(79601) 915.673.5424

Embassy Suites ($$$)
4250 Ridgemont Dr
(79606) 915.698.1234
$15 fee

Fairfield Inn ($$)
3902 Turner Plz
(79606) 915.695.2448

Hampton Inn ($$)
3917 Ridgemont Dr
(79606) 915.695.0044

Holiday Inn ($$)
1625 S R 351
(79601) 915.673.5271
mgr preapproval reqd

Kiva Motel ($$)
5403 S 1st St
(79605) 915.695.2150

La Quinta Inn ($$)
3501 W Lake Rd
(79601) 915.676.1676
call re: fees

Motel 6 ($)
4951 W Stamford St
(79603) 915.672.8462
1 small pet/room

Quality Inn ($$)
505 Pine St
(79601) 915.676.0222
mgr preapproval reqd

Ramada Inn ($$)
3450 S Clack St
(79606) 915.675.7700

Red Carpet Inn ($)
2202 I-20
(79603) 915.677.2463

Royal Inn ($)
5695 S 1st St
(79605) 915.692.3022

Super 8 ($)
1525 E I-20
(79601) 915.673.5251
call re: fees

• Alice •
Days Inn ($)
555 N Johnson St
(78332) 512.664.8016

Kings Inn Motel ($)
815 Hwy 281
(78332) 512.664.4351

• Alpine •
Best Western ($$$)
2401 E Hwy 90
(79830) 915.837.1530

Days Inn ($)
2000 W Hwy 90
(79830) 915.837.3417

Highland Inn ($$)
1404 E Hwy 90
(79830) 915.837.5811

Longhorn Ranch Motel ($$)
HC 65 Box# 267
(79830) 915.371.2541

Ramada Ltd ($$)
2800 W Hwy 90
(79830) 915.837.1100

Sunday House Motel ($)
Box# 578
(79831) 915.837.3363

Terlingua Ranch ($$)
HC 65 Box# 220
(79830) 915.371.2416

• Alvin •
Homeplace Inn ($$)
1588 S Hwy 35 Byp
(77511) 743.331.0335

• Amarillo •
Best Western ($$)
4600 I-40
(79103) 806.372.1885

```

_navigation">
$=under $35   $$=$35-60   **323**   $$$=$60-100   $$$$=over $100
```

Budget Host ($$)
2915 I-40
(79104) 806.372.8101

Comfort Inn ($$)
2100 Coulter Dr
(79106) 806.358.6141
mgr preapproval reqd

Crowne Plaza ($$$)
3100 I-40
(79102) 806.358.6161

Econo Lodge ($)
1803 Lakeside Dr
(79120) 806.335.1561

Hampton Inn ($$)
1700 I-40 E
(79103) 806.372.1425

Holiday Inn ($$$)
1911 I-40 At Rossosage
(79102) 806.372.8741
mgr preapproval reqd

La Quinta Inn ($$)
2108 S Coulter St
(79106) 806.352.6311
call re: fees

La Quinta Inn ($$)
1708 I-40
(79103) 806.373.7486
call re: fees

Motel.6 ($)
4301 I-40
(79104) 806.373.3045
1 small pet/room

Motel 6 ($)
2032 Paramount Blvd
(79109) 806.355.6554
1 small pet/room

Motel 6 ($)
3930 I-40
(79103) 806.374.6444
1 small pet/room

Motel 6 ($)
6040 I-40
(79106) 806.359.7651
1 small pet/room

Radisson Inn ($$$)
7090 I-40
(79103) 806.373.3303

Ramada Inn ($$$)
2501 I-40
(79104) 806.379.6555

Ramada Inn ($$)
6801 I-40
(79106) 806.358.7881

Rodeway Inn ($)
6005 W Amarillo Blvd
(79106) 806.355.3321

The Big Texan Motel ($$)
7701 I-40
(79103) 806.372.5000

Travelodge ($)
3205 I-40
(79104) 806.372.8171

● Angleton ●
Homeplace Inn ($$)
1235 N Velasco St
(77515) 409.849.2465

● Anthony ●
Super 8 ($$)
100 Park North Dr
(79821) 915.886.2888
call re: fees

● Aransas Pass ●
Homeport Inn ($)
1515 W Wheeler Ave
(78336) 512.758.3213

● Archer City ●
Value Lodge Motel ($)
Rt 3 Box# 319
(76351) 817.386.8959

● Arlington ●
Best Western ($$)
3501 E Division St
(76011) 817.640.7722
small pets

Budgetel ($$)
2401 Diplomacy Dr
(76011) 800.428.3438

Days Inn ($)
1195 N Watson Rd
(76011) 817.648.8881

Days Inn ($)
910 N Collins St
(76011) 817.261.8444
$5/pets

Days Inn ($$)
2001 E Copeland Rd
(76011) 817.461.1122

Hawthorn Suites ($$$)
2401 Brookhollow Plaza Dr
(76006) 817.640.1188
small to medium size $50
charge $250 dep

Howard Johnson ($$$)
903 N Collins St
(76011) 817.261.3621

Inn Towne Lodge ($)
1181 N Watson Rd
(76011) 817.649.0993

Lester Motor Inn ($)
2725 W Division St
(76012) 817.275.5496

Motel 6 ($)
2626 E Rando Mill Rd
(76011) 817.649.0147
1 small pet/room

Oasis Motel ($)
818 W Division St
(76012) 817.274.1616

Park Inn Intl ($)
703 N Benge Dr
(76013) 817.860.2323

Ramada Inn ($$)
700 E Lamar Blvd
(76011) 817.265.7711
under 10 lbs

Residence Inn ($$$)
1050 Brookhollow Plaza Dr
(76006) 817.640.5151

Value Inn ($)
820 N Watson Rd
(76011) 817.640.5151

● Athens ●
Spanish Trace Motel ($$)
716 E Tyler St
(75751) 903.675.5173

● Atlanta ●
The Butlers Inn ($)
1100 W Main St
(75551) 903.796.8235

● Austin ●
Balcor Suites ($$)
11215 Research Blvd
(78759) 512.343.0584

Bel Air Motel ($)
3400 S Congress Ave
(78704) 512.444.5973

Best Western ($$)
3401 I-35
(78741) 512.448.2444
small pets only

Best Western ($$)
4323 I-35
(78744) 512.447.5511
small pets only

Best Western ($$)
7928 Gessner Dr
(78753) 512.339.7311
small pets only

Capitol Motor Inn ($$)
2525 I-35
(78741) 512.441.0143

Carringtons Inn ($$$)
1900 David St
(78705) 512.479.0638

Corporate Suites ($$$)
4815 W Braker Ln
(78759) 512.345.8822

Country Inn ($)
5656 I-35
(78751) 512.452.1177

Courtyard By Marriott ($$$)
5660 I-35
(78751) 512.458.2340

Days Inn ($)
8210 I-35
(78753) 512.835.2200

Be
Discreet

$=under $35 $$=$35-60 $$$=$60-100 $$$$=over $100

Doubletree ($$$)
303 W 15th St
(78701) 512.478.7000

Doubletree ($$$)
6505 I-35
(78752) 512.454.3737

Drury Inn ($$)
919 E Koenig Ln
(78751) 512.454.1144

Econo Lodge ($$)
6201 US 290
(78723) 512.458.4759

Embassy Suites ($$$$)
5901 I-35
(78723) 512.454.8004

Exel Inn ($)
2711 I-35
(78741) 512.462.9201
small pets only

Fosons Regent Hotel ($$$$)
98 San Jacinto Blvd
(78701) 512.478.4500
small pets allowed

Greenshores ($$$)
6900 Greenshores Dr
(78730) 512.346.0011

Habitat Suites Hotel ($$$)
500 E Highland Mall Blvd
(78752) 512.467.6000

Hawthorn Suites ($$$)
935 La Posada Dr
(78752) 512.459.3335
$50 fee

Hawthorne Suites ($$$)
4020 I-35
(78704) 512.440.7722
$100 fee plus $5 per day

Heart Of Texas Motel ($$)
5303N US 290
(78735) 512.892.0644

Hilton ($$$)
6000 Middle Fiskville Rd
(78752) 512.451.5757
$25 charge

Holiday Inn ($$$)
6911 I-35
(78752) 512.459.4251
mgr preapproval reqd

Holiday Inn ($$$)
3401 I-35
(78741) 512.448.4999
mgr preapproval reqd

Holiday Inn ($$$)
8901 Business Park Dr
(78759) 512.343.0888
mgr preapproval reqd

Howard Johnson ($$)
7800 I-35
(78753) 512.836.8520

La Quinta Inn ($$$)
300 E 11th St
(78701) 512.476.1166
call re: fees

La Quinta Inn ($$)
4200 I-35
(78745) 512.443.1774
call re: fees

La Quinta Inn ($$)
5812 I-35
(78751) 512.459.4381
call re: fees

La Quinta Inn ($$)
7100 I-35
(78752) 512.422.9401
call re: fees

La Quinta Inn ($$)
1603 E Oltorf St
(78741) 512.447.6661
call re: fees

Master Host ($$)
7300 I-35
(78752) 512.452.9371

Motel 6 ($)
5330 Interrigional Hwy
(78751) 512.467.9111
1 small pet/room

Motel 6 ($)
8010 I-35
(78753) 512.837.9890
1 small pet/room

Motel 6 ($)
9420 I-35
(78753) 512.339.6161
1 small pet/room

Motel 6 ($)
2707 Interrigional Hwy
(78741) 512.444.5882
1 small pet/room

New Austin Motel ($)
2607 I-35
(78741) 512.443.4242

Omni Southpark Hotel ($$$$)
4140 Governors Row
(78744) 512.448.2222

Quality Inn ($$)
909 E Koenig Ln
(78751) 512.452.4200
mgr preapproval reqd

Quality Inn ($$)
2200 I-35
(78704) 512.444.0561
mgr preapproval reqd

Ramada Inn ($$$)
1212 W Ben White Blvd
(78704) 512.447.0151
under 20 lbs

Ramada Ltd ($$)
5526 I-35
(78751) 512.451.7001

Red Lion Inn ($$$)
6121 I-35
(78752) 512.323.5466
call re: fees

Stouffer Hotel ($$$$)
9721 Arboretum Blvd
(78759) 512.343.2626

Residence Inn ($$$)
4537 I-35
(78744) 512.912.1100

Residence Inn ($$$)
3713 Tudor Blvd
(78759) 512.502.8200

Stars Passport Inn ($)
3105 I-35
(78722) 512.478.1631

Town Lake Motel ($)
2915 I-35
(78741) 512.444.8432

Travelodge ($$)
8300 I-35
(78752) 512.835.5050

Walnut Forest Motel ($)
11506 I-35
(78753) 512.835.0864

● Ballinger ●
Ballinger Motel ($)
1005N Hutchings
(76821) 915.365.5717

Desert Inn Motel ($)
Hwy 67
(76821) 915.365.2518

Stonewall Motel ($)
201 N Broadway St
(76821) 915.895.7760

● Bandera ●
Cool Water Acres ($$)
Rt 1 Box# 785
(78003) 210.796.4866

River Front Motel ($$)
Box# 2609
(78003) 210.796.3093

● Bastrop ●
Bastrop Inn Motel ($)
102 Childers Dr
(78602) 512.321.3949

● Baytown ●
Best Western ($$)
5021 I-10
(77521) 713.421.2233

Budgetel ($$)
5215 I-10E
(77521) 713.421.7300

La Quinta Inn ($$)
4911 I-10
(77521) 713.421.5566
call re: fees

Motel 6 ($)
8911 N Hwy 146
(77520) 713.576.5777
1 small pet/room

● Beaumont ●
Best Western ($$)
2155 N 11th St
(77703) 409.898.8150

Best Western ($$)
1610B I-10
(77707) 409.842.0037

Big Tree Inn ($)
HC 04 Box# 146
(77710) 512.729.8708

Days Inn ($)
30 I-10
(77702) 409.838.0581
$5/pet charge

Econo Lodge ($)
1155 I-10
(77701) 409.835.5913

Grand Duerr ($$$)
2298 McFaddin St At 7th
(77701) 409.833.9600

Hilton ($$$)
2355 I-10
(77705) 409.842.3600
$50 deposit

Holiday Inn ($$$)
3950 I-10
(77705) 409.842.5995
mgr preapproval reqd

Holiday Inn ($$)
2095 N 11th St
(77703) 409.892.2222
mgr preapproval reqd

J&J Motel ($)
6675 Eastex Fwy
(77706) 409.892.4241

La Quinta Inn ($$)
220 I-10
(77702) 409.838.9991
call re: fees

Quality Inn ($$)
1295 N 11th St
(77702) 409.892.7722
mgr preapproval reqd

Ramada Inn ($$)
2525 N 11th St
(77703) 409.898.2111

Road Runner Motel ($)
3985 College St
(77707) 409.842.4420

Rodeway Inn ($)
4085 I-10
(77705) 409.842.9341

Sea Gun Resort ($$)
5868 I-35
(77710) 512.729.3292

● Bedford ●
La Quinta Inn ($$)
1450 Airport Fwy
(76022) 817.267.5200
call re: fees

● Beeville ●
Best Western ($$)
400 US 181
(78102) 512.358.4000

El Camino Motel ($)
150 N Washington St
(78102) 512.358.2141

Executive Inn ($$)
1601 N Saint Marys St
(78102) 512.358.0022

● Belton ●
Best Western ($)
1414 E 6th Ave
(76513) 817.939.5711
small pets

Budget Host ($)
1520 I-35
(76513) 817.939.0744

Ramada Ltd ($)
1102 E 2nd Ave
(76513) 817.939.3745

● Big Bend National Park ●
Chisos Mountains Lodge ($$)
Basin Rural Station
(79834) 915.477.2291

● Big Spring ●
Days Inn ($$)
300N Tulare Ave
(79720) 915.263.7621

Econo Lodge ($$)
804 I-20
(79720) 915.263.5200

Motel 6 ($)
600 I-20
(79720) 915.267.1695
1 small pet/room

Ponderosa Motor Inn ($)
2701 S Gregg St
(79720) 915.267.5237

● Blanco ●
Swiss Lodge ($$)
1206 N Main
(78606) 210.833.5528

● Boerne ●
Best Western ($$)
35150 I-10
(78006) 210.249.9791

Boerne Lake Lodge ($$$$)
310 Lake View Dr
(78006) 210.816.6060

Key To The Hills Motel ($$)
1228 S Main St
(78006) 210.249.3562

● Bonham ●
Days Inn ($$)
1515 Old Ector Rd
(75418) 903.583.3121

● Borger ●
The Inn Place Of Borger ($$)
100Building Blvd
(79007) 806.273.9556

● Bowie ●
Days Inn ($)
RR 5 Box# 138
(76230) 817.872.5426

Park Lodge ($)
708 Park Ave
(76230) 817.872.1111

● Brady ●
Plateau Motel ($)
2023 S Bridge St
(76825) 915.597.2185

Sunset Inn ($$)
2108 S Bridge St
(76825) 915.597.0789

● Breckenridge ●
Ridge Motel ($)
Box# 312
(76424) 817.559.2244

● Brenham ●
The Brenham Inn ($$)
2217 S Market St
(77833) 409.836.1300

● Broaddus ●
Country Inn ($)
Box# 428 Hwy 147
(75929) 409.872.3691

● Brookshire ●
Budget Inn ($)
542 Koomey Rd
(77423) 713.934.4477

Days Inn ($$)
Rm 359 & I-10
(77423) 713.934.3122

● Brownfield ●
Best Western ($$)
321 Lubbock Rd
(79316) 806.637.9471
small pets only

● Brownsville ●
Holiday Inn ($$$)
1900 E Elizabeth St
(78520) 210.546.2201
mgr preapproval reqd

Howard Johnson ($$)
1945 N Expwy
(78520) 210.546.4591

La Quinta Inn ($$)
55 Sam Perl Blvd
(78520) 210.546.0381
call re: fees

Well
Behaved

Motel 6 ($)
2250 N Expwy
(78521) 210.546.4699
1 small pet/room

Sheraton Inn ($$$)
3777 N Expwy
(78520) 210.350.9191

● Brownwood ●
Best Western ($$)
410 E Commerce St
(76801) 915.646.3511

Days Inn ($$)
1204 C C Woodson Rd
(76802) 915.643.5611

Gate I Motor Inn ($)
4410B Hwy 377
(76801) 915.643.5463

Gold Key Inn Motel ($)
515 E Commerce St
(76801) 915.646.2551

● Bryan ●
Fairfield Inn ($$)
4613 S Texas Ave
(77802) 409.268.1552

Preference Inn ($)
1601 S Texas Ave
(77802) 409.822.6196

● Buffalo ●
Best Western ($$)
US 79
(75831) 903.322.5831
small pets

● Burleson ●
Days Inn ($$)
329 S Burleson Blvd
(76028) 817.447.1111
$10/pet deposit

● Burnet ●
Rocky Rest Inn ($$)
404 S Water St
(78611) 512.756.2600

● Caldwell ●
The Surrey Inn ($$)
403 E Hwy 21
(77836) 409.567.3221

Varsity Inn Caldwell ($)
705 Hwy 36
(77836) 409.567.4661

● Cameron ●
Varsity Motel ($)
1004 E 1st St
(76520) 817.697.6446

● Canton ●
Best Western ($$)
RR 2 Box# 6-B
(75103) 903.567.6591

Days Inn ($)
Hwy 19 I-20
(75103) 903.567.6588
$5.55 per day

● Canyon Lake ●
Maricopa Ranch ($$)
Box# 1659
(78130) 210.964.3731

● Carrollton ●
Red Roof Inn ($)
1720 S Broadway St
(75006) 214.245.1700

● Carthage ●
Carthage Motel ($)
321 S Shelby Motel
(75633) 903.693.3814

● Castroville ●
Best Western ($$)
1650 Hwy 90
(78009) 210.538.2262

● Center ●
Best Western ($$)
1005 Hurst Inn
(75935) 409.598.3384

● Center Point ●
Mariannes ($$$)
Rt 1 Box# 527
(78010) 210.634.7489

● Centerville ●
Days Inn ($)
I-45
(75833) 903.536.7175
$10/pet

● Channelview ●
Best Western ($)
15919 I-10
(77530) 713.452.1000
2 per rm w/$20 dep

Days Inn ($$)
15545 I-10
(77530) 713.457.3000

Holiday Inn
15157 I-10
(77530) 281.452.7304

● Childress ●
Best Western ($$)
1805 Avenue F NW
(79201) 817.937.6353
small pets only

Comfort Inn ($$)
1804 Avenue F NW
(79201) 817.937.6363
mgr preapproval reqd

Econo Lodge ($)
1612 Avenue F NW
(79201) 817.937.3695

● Cisco ●
Oak Motel ($)
300I-20
(76437) 817.442.2100

Rodeway Inn ($$)
1898 Hwy 206
(76437) 817.442.3735

● Clarendon ●
Western Skies Motel ($)
800 W 2nd St
(79226) 806.874.3501

● Claude ●
L A Motel ($)
200 E 1st
(79019) 806.226.4981

● Cleburne ●
Budget Host ($$)
2107 N Main St
(76031) 817.556.3631

Days Inn ($$)
101 N Ridgeway Dr
(76031) 817.645.8836

● Clute ●
La Quinta Inn ($$)
1126 Hwy 332
(77531) 409.265.7461
call re: fees

Motel 6 ($)
1000 Hwy 332
(77531) 409.265.4764
1 small pet/room

● Coldspring ●
San Jacinto Inn ($)
Box# 459
(77331) 409.653.3008

● College Station ●
Hilton ($$$)
801 University Dr
(77840) 409.693.7500
small pets only

Holiday Inn ($$)
1503 Texas Ave
(77840) 409.693.1736
mgr preapproval reqd

La Quinta Inn ($$)
607 Texas Ave
(77840) 409.696.7777
call re: fees

Manor House Motel ($$)
2504 Texas Ave
(77840) 409.764.9540

Motel 6 ($)
2327 Texas Ave
(77840) 409.696.3379
1 small pet/room

Ramada Inn ($$)
1502 Texas Ave
(77840) 409.693.9891
caged & $10 fee

● Colorado City ●
Days Inn ($)
RR 1 Box# 293
(79512) 915.728.2638

Villa Inn Motel ($)
2310 Hickory St
(79512) 915.728.5217

• Columbus •

Columbus Inn ($$)
2208 S Hwy 71
(78934) 409.732.5723

Homeplace Inn ($$)
2436 S Hwy 71
(78934) 409.732.6293

• Comanche •

Guesthouse Heritage Hill
($$)
Hwy 36 E Rt 3
(76442) 915.356.3397

• Comfort •

Motor Inn Comfort ($$)
32 Hwy 87 & I-10
(78013) 210.995.3822

• Conroe •

Heathers Glen ($$$)
200 E Phillips St
(77301) 409.441.6611

Holiday Inn ($$)
1601 I-45
(77301) 409.756.8941
mgr preapproval reqd

Motel 6 ($)
820 I-45
(77304) 409.760.4003
1 small pet/room

Ramada Inn ($$$)
1520 S Frazier St
(77301) 409.756.8939

• Corpus Christi •

Best Western ($$)
11217 I-37
(78410) 512.241.6675

Days Inn ($)
901 Navigation Blvd
(78408) 512.888.8599
$6/pets

Drury Inn ($$)
2021 N Padre Island Dr
(78408) 512.289.8200

Embassy Suites ($$$$)
4337 S Padre Island Dr
(78411) 512.853.7899
$10 deposit

Fairfield Inn ($$)
5217 Blanche Moore Dr
(78411) 512.985.8393

Gulf Beach 2 Motel ($$)
3500 Surfside Blvd
(78402) 512.882.3500

Hampton Inn ($$)
5501 I-37
(78408) 512.289.5861

Hampton Inn ($$)
5209 Blanche Moore Dr
(78411) 512.985.8395

Holiday Inn ($$$)
5549 Leopard St
(78408) 512.289.5100
mgr preapproval reqd

Holiday Inn ($$$)
1102 S Shoreline Blvd
(78401) 512.883.5731
mgr preapproval reqd

Holiday Inn ($$$)
1520 Windward Dr
(78418) 512.949.8041
mgr preapproval reqd

Howard Johnson ($$$)
300 N Shoreline Blvd
(78401) 512.883.5111
small pets allowed

La Quinta Inn ($$)
5155 I-37
(78408) 512.888.5721
call re: fees

La Quinta Inn ($$)
6225 S Padre Island Dr
(78412) 512.991.5730
call re: fees

Motel 6 ($)
8202 S Padre Island Dr
(78412) 512.991.8858
1 small pet/room

Motel 6 ($)
845 Lantana St
(78408) 512.289.9397
1 small pet/room

Red Roof Inn ($)
6301 I-37
(78409) 512.289.6925
$25 deposit

Residence Inn ($$$$)
5229 Blanche Moore Dr
(78411) 512.985.1113

Surfside Apartment ($$$)
15005 Windward Dr
(78418) 512.949.8128

Travelodge ($$)
910 Corn Products Rd
(78409) 512.289.5666

Val U Inn ($$)
5224 I-37 Navigation Blvd
(78407) 512.883.2951

• Cotulla •

Rodeway Inn ($$)
1100 Fm 468
(78014) 210.879.2311

• Crockett •

Crockett Inn ($)
1600 E Loop 304
(75835) 409.544.5611

Embers Motor Inn ($)
1401 E Loop 304
(75835) 409.544.5681

• Cuero •

Sands Motel ($)
2117 N Esplanade St
(77954) 512.275.3437

• Dalhart •

Best Western ($)
623 Denver Ave
(79022) 806.249.4538
small pets at managers
discretion

Best Western ($)
Hwy 87
(79022) 806.249.5637

Days Inn ($$)
701 Liberal St 54
(79022) 806.249.5246

Econo Lodge ($)
123 Liberal St
(79022) 806.249.6464

Friendship Inn ($)
400 Liberal St
(79022) 806.249.4557

Sands Motel ($)
301 Liberal St
(79022) 806.249.4568

Super 8 ($)
E Hwy 54
(79022) 806.249.8526
pets w/permission

• Dallas •

Best Western ($$)
13333 N Stemmons Fwy
(75234) 214.241.8521
small pets only

Best Western ($$$$)
6104 LBJ Frwy
(75240) 214.458.2626

Bristol Suites ($$$)
7800 Alpha Rd
(75240) 214.233.7600

Crescent Court Hotel ($$$$)
400 Crescent Ct
(75201) 214.871.3200

Days Inn ($$)
8312 S Lancaster Rd
(75241) 214.224.3196

Days Inn ($$)
4150 N Central Expwy
(75204) 214.827.6080

Doubletree ($$)
8250 N Central Expwy
(75206) 214.691.8700

Doubletree ($$$)
1590 LBJ Frwy
(75234) 214.869.4300

Drury Inn ($$)
2421 Walnut Hill Ln
(75229) 214.484.3330

Econo Lodge ($$)
Airport I-35
(75234) 214.243.5500

CALL AHEAD!

$=under $35 $$=$35-60 $$$=$60-100 $$$$=over $100

Embassy Suites ($$$$)
13131 N Central Expwy
(75243) 214.234.3300
$25 deposit

Executive Inn ($$)
3232 W Mockingln Ln
(75235) 214.357.5601

Exel Inn ($$)
8510 Thornton Fwy
(75228) 214.328.5500

Hampton Inn ($$$)
1015 Elm St
(75202) 214.742.5678

Hampton Inn ($$)
4154 Preferred Pl
(75237) 214.298.4747
small pets only

Hampton Inn ($$)
4555 Beltway Dr
(75244) 214.991.2800

Hampton Inn ($$)
11069 Composite Dr
(75229) 214.484.6557

Harvey Hotel ($$)
14315 Midway Rd
(75244) 214.980.8877

Harvey Hotel ($$$)
7050 N Stemmons Fwy
(75247) 214.630.8500

Harvey Hotel ($$)
7815 LBJ Frwy Colt Rd
(75240) 214.960.7000

Harvey Hotel ($$$)
400 Olive St
(75201) 214.922.8000

Hawthorn Suites ($$$)
7900B Brookriver Dr
(75247) 214.688.1010

Holiday Inn
1933 Main St
(75201) 214.741.7700

Holiday Inn
2370 W Northwest Hwy
(75220) 214.350.5577

Homewood Suites ($$$)
4451 Belt Line Rd
(75244) 214.788.1342

Hyatt Hotel ($$$)
300 Reunion Blvd
(75207) 214.651.1234

La Quinta Inn ($$)
13685 N Central Expwy
(75243) 214.234.0682
call re: fees

La Quinta Inn ($$)
1001 N Central Expwy
(75231) 214.361.8200
call re: fees

La Quinta Inn ($$)
13235 N Stemmons Fwy
(75234) 214.620.7333
call re: fees

La Quinta Inn ($$)
4440 N Central Expwy
(75206) 214.821.4220
call re: fees

La Quinta Inn ($$)
8303 E Thornton Frwy
(75228) 214.324.3731
call re: fees

Marriott Hotel ($$$)
14901 Dallas Pkwy
(75240) 214.661.2800

Marriott Hotel ($$$)
7750 LBJ Frwy
(75251) 214.233.4421

Motel 6 ($)
2660 Forest Ln
(75234) 214.484.9111
1 small pet/room

Motel 6 ($)
2753 Forest Ln
(75234) 214.620.2828
1 small pet/room

Motel 6 ($)
4325 Belt Line Rd
(75244) 214.386.4577
1 small pet/room

Motel 6 ($)
4220 Independence Dr
(75237) 214.296.3331
1 small pet/room

Plaza Americas Hotel ($$$$)
650 N Pearl St
(75201) 214.979.9000

Grand Hotel ($$$$)
1914 Commerce St
(75201) 214.747.7000

Radisson Inn ($$$)
2330 W Northwest Hwy
(75220) 214.351.4477
small pets allowed

Radisson Inn ($$)
1893 W Mockingbird Ln
(75235) 214.634.8850
fee

Raidsson Central ($$$)
6060 N Central Expwy
(75206) 214.750.6060
small pets allowed

Ramada Inn ($$)
1011 S Akard St
(75215) 214.421.1083

Ramada Inn ($$$)
1055 Regal Row
(75247) 214.634.8550

Red Roof Inn ($)
8108 E Thornton Frwy
(75228) 214.388.8741

Red Roof Inn ($)
1550 Empire Central
(75235) 214.638.5151

Red Roof Inn ($)
10335 Gardner Rd
(75220) 214.506.8100

Residence Inn ($$$)
10333 N Central Expwy
(75231) 214.750.8220
$50 fee

Residence Inn ($$$)
6950 N Stemmons Fwy
(75247) 214.631.2472
$50 fee

Residence Inn ($$$)
13636 Goldmark Dr
(75240) 214.669.0478
call for fee & availability

Rodeway Inn ($$)
2026 Market Center Blvd
(75207) 214.748.2243

Sheraton Inn ($$$$)
4440 W Carpenter Frwy
(75261) 214.929.8400

Sheraton Inn ($$$)
12720 Merit Dr
(75251) 214.385.3000
deposit

Stouffer Renaissance ($$$)
2222 N Stemmons Fwy
(75207) 214.631.2222

Travelodge ($$)
3140 W Mockingbird Ln
(75235) 214.357.1701

Westin Hotel ($$$$)
13340 Dallas Pkwy
(75240) 214.934.9494
small pets accepted

Dallas Metro

● Carrollton ●
Red Roof Inn ($)
1720 S Broadway St
(75006) 214.245.1700

● Dallas ●
Best Western ($$)
13333 N Stemmons Fwy
(75234) 214.241.8521
small pets only

Best Western ($$$$)
6104 LBJ Frwy
(75240) 214.458.2626

Bristol Suites ($$$)
7800 Alpha Rd
(75240) 214.233.7600

Crescent Court Hotel ($$$$)
400 Crescent Ct
(75201) 214.871.3200

Policies Subject to Change

$=under $35 $$=$35-60 $$$=$60-100 $$$$=over $100

TEXAS, Dallas Metro

Days Inn ($$)
8312 S Lancaster Rd
(75241) 214.224.3196

Days Inn ($$)
4150 N Central Expwy
(75204) 214.827.6080

Doubletree ($$)
8250 N Central Expwy
(75206) 214.691.8700

Doubletree ($$$)
1590 LBJ Frwy
(75234) 214.869.4300

Drury Inn ($$)
2421 Walnut Hill Ln
(75229) 214.484.3330

Econo Lodge ($$)
Airport I-35
(75234) 214.243.5500

Embassy Suites ($$$$)
13131 N Central Expwy
(75243) 214.234.3300
$25 deposit

Executive Inn ($$)
3232 W Mockington Ln
(75235) 214.357.5601

Exel Inn ($$)
8510 E R L Thornton Fwy
(75228) 214.328.5500

Hampton Inn ($$$)
1015 Elm St
(75202) 214.742.5678

Hampton Inn ($$)
4154 Preferred Pl
(75237) 214.298.4747
small pets only

Hampton Inn ($$)
4555 Beltway Dr
(75244) 214.991.2800

Hampton Inn ($$)
11069 Composite Dr
(75229) 214.484.6557

Harvey Hotel ($$)
14315 Midway Rd
(75244) 214.980.8877

Harvey Hotel ($$$)
7050 N Stemmons Fwy
(75247) 214.630.8500

Harvey Hotel ($$)
7815 LBJ Frwy Colt Rd
(75240) 214.960.7000

Harvey Hotel ($$$)
400 Olive St
(75201) 214.922.8000

Hawthorn Suites ($$$)
7900B Brookriver Dr
(75247) 214.688.1010

Holiday Inn
1933 Main St
(75201) 214.741.7700

Holiday Inn
2370 W Northwest Hwy
(75220) 214.350.5577

Homewood Suites ($$$)
4451 Belt Line Rd
(75244) 214.788.1342

Hyatt Hotel ($$$)
300 Reunion Blvd
(75207) 214.651.1234

La Quinta Inn ($$)
13685 N Central Expwy
(75243) 214.234.0682
call re: fees

La Quinta Inn ($$)
1001 N Central Expwy
(75231) 214.361.8200
call re: fees

La Quinta Inn ($$)
13235 N Stemmons Fwy
(75234) 214.620.7333
call re: fees

La Quinta Inn ($$)
4440 N Central Expwy
(75206) 214.821.4220
call re: fees

La Quinta Inn ($$)
8303 E Thornton Frwy
(75228) 214.324.3731
call re: fees

Marriott Hotel ($$$)
14901 Dallas Pkwy
(75240) 214.661.2800

Marriott Hotel ($$$)
7750 LBJ Frwy
(75251) 214.233.4421

Motel 6 ($)
2660 Forest Ln
(75234) 214.484.9111
1 small pet/room

Motel 6 ($)
2753 Forest Ln
(75234) 214.620.2828
1 small pet/room

Motel 6 ($)
4325 Belt Line Rd
(75244) 214.386.4577
1 small pet/room

Motel 6 ($)
4220 Independence Dr
(75237) 214.296.3331
1 small pet/room

Plaza Americas Hotel ($$$$)
650 N Pearl St
(75201) 214.979.9000

Grand Hotel ($$$$)
1914 Commerce St
(75201) 214.747.7000

Radisson Inn ($$$)
2330 W Northwest Hwy
(75220) 214.351.4477
small pets allowed

Radisson Inn ($$)
1893 W Mockingbird Ln
(75235) 214.634.8850
fee

Raidsson Central ($$$)
6060 N Central Expwy
(75206) 214.750.6060
small pets allowed

Ramada Inn ($$)
1011 S Akard St
(75215) 214.421.1083

Ramada Inn ($$$)
1055 Regal Row
(75247) 214.634.8550

Red Roof Inn ($)
8108 E Thornton Frwy
(75228) 214.388.8741

Red Roof Inn ($)
1550 Empire Central
(75235) 214.638.5151

Red Roof Inn ($)
10335 Gardner Rd
(75220) 214.506.8100

Residence Inn ($$$)
10333 N Central Expwy
(75231) 214.750.8220
$50 fee

Residence Inn ($$$)
6950 N Stemmons Fwy
(75247) 214.631.2472
$50 fee

Residence Inn ($$$)
13636 Goldmark Dr
(75240) 214.669.0478
call for fee & availability

Rodeway Inn ($$)
2026 Market Center Blvd
(75207) 214.748.2243

Sheraton Inn ($$$$)
4440 W Carpenter Frwy
(75261) 214.929.8400

Sheraton Inn ($$$)
12720 Merit Dr
(75251) 214.385.3000
deposit

Stouffer Renaissance ($$$)
2222 N Stemmons Fwy
(75207) 214.631.2222

Travelodge ($$)
3140 W Mockingbird Ln
(75235) 214.357.1701

Westin Hotel ($$$$)
13340 Dallas Pkwy
(75240) 214.934.9494
small pets accepted

• Duncanville •
Holiday Inn ($$)
711 E Camp Wisdom Rd
(75116) 972.298.8911

Motel 6 ($)
202 Jellison Blvd
(75116) 214.296.0345
1 small pet/room

• Ennis •
Holiday Inn
600 I 45
(75119) 972.875.6990

• Garland •
Days Inn ($$)
6222 Beltline Rd
(75043) 214.226.7621
$10/pet

La Quinta Inn ($$)
12721 I-635
(75041) 214.271.7581
call re: fees

Motel 6 ($)
436 W I-30 & Beltline
(75043) 214.226.7140
1 small pet/room

• Grand Prairie •
Hampton Inn ($$$)
2050 N Hwy 360
(75050) 214.988.8989

La Quinta Inn ($$)
1410 NW 19th St
(75050) 214.641.3021
call re: fees

Motel 6 ($)
406 E Safari Pkwy
(75050) 214.642.9424
1 small pet/room

Ramada Inn ($$)
402 E Safari Pkwy
(75050) 214.263.4421

• Greenville •
Best Western ($$)
1216 I-30
(75402) 903.454.1792

Holiday Inn ($$)
1215 I-30
(75401) 903.454.7000
mgr preapproval reqd

Motel 6 ($)
5109 I-30 & US 69
(75402) 903.455.0515
1 small pet/room

Royal Inn ($)
I-30 & US 69
(75401) 903.455.9600

• Irving •
Comfort Inn ($$)
8205 Esters Blvd
(75063) 972.929.0066
$25 deposit

Days Inn ($$)
2200 E Airport Fwy
(75062) 214.438.6666

Drury Inn ($$$)
4210 W Airport Fwy
(75062) 214.986.1200
small pets only

Hampton Inn ($$$)
4340 W Airport Fwy
(75062) 214.986.3606

Harvey Hotel ($$$)
4545 W John Carpenter Fwy
(75063) 214.929.4500
$25 fee

Harvey Suites ($$$)
4550 W John Carpenter
(75063) 214.929.4499

Homewood Suites ($$$)
4300 Wingren Dr
(75039) 214.556.0665
$50 fee

Irving Inn Suites ($)
909 W Airport Fwy
(75062) 214.255.7108

La Quinta Inn ($$)
4105 W Airport Fwy
(75062) 214.252.6546
call re: fees

Motel 6 ($)
510 S Loop 12
(75060) 214.438.4227
1 small pet/room

Red Roof Inn ($$)
8150 Esters Blvd
(75063) 214.929.0020

Red Roof Inn ($$)
2611 W Airport Fwy
(75062) 214.570.7500

Residence Inn ($$$)
950 W Walnut Hill Ln
(75038) 214.580.7773
$50 deposit

Skyway Inn ($)
110 W Airport Fwy
(75062) 214.438.2000

Suites Inn ($)
1701 W Airport Fwy
(75062) 214.255.1133

The Four Seasons ($$$$)
4150 N Macarthur Blvd
(75038) 214.717.0700
small pets allowed

Wilson World Hotel ($$$)
4600 W Airport Fwy
(75062) 214.513.0800

• Lewisville •
Comfort Suites ($$$)
755A Vista Ridge Mall Dr
(75067) 972.315.6464

Country Inn ($$)
755 Vista Ridge Mall Dr
(75067) 214.315.6565

Days Inn ($$)
1401 S Stemmons Fwy
(75067) 214.436.0080

La Quinta Inn ($$)
1657 N Stemmons Fwy
(75067) 214.221.7525
call re: fees

• Mesquite •
Days Inn ($)
3601 E Hwy 80
(75150) 214.279.6561

Motel 6 ($)
3629 E Hwy 80
(75150) 214.613.1662
1 small pet/room

• Plano •
Best Western ($$$)
640 E Park Blvd
(75074) 214.578.2243

Comfort Inn ($$)
621 E Central Pkwy
(75074) 972.424.5568
small pets only

Harvey Hotel ($$)
1600 N Central Expwy
(75074) 214.578.8555

La Quinta Inn ($$)
1820 N Central Expwy
(75074) 214.423.1300
call re: fees

Motel 6 ($)
2550 N Central Expwy
(75074) 214.578.1626
1 small pet/room

• Richardson •
Clarion Hotel ($$)
1981 N Central Expwy
(75080) 972.644.4000

Hawthorn Suites ($$$)
250 Municipal Dr
(75080) 214.669.1000

Omni Hotel ($$$)
701 E Campbell Rd
(75081) 214.231.9600

Sleep Inn ($$)
2650 N Central Expwy
(75080) 972.470.9440

**End of Dallas
Metro**

● De Soto ●
Holiday Inn ($$$)
1515 N Beckley Rd
(75115) 972.224.9100

● Decatur ●
Best Western ($)
1801 S Hwy 287
(76234) 817.627.5982

Comfort Inn ($$)
1709 S R 287
(76234) 817.627.6919

● Del Rio ●
Amistad Lodge Motel ($)
Hwy 90 W Hcr 3 Box# 25
(78840) 210.775.8591

Anglers Lodge Motel ($)
Hwy 90 W Hcr 3 Box# 25
(78840) 210.775.1586

Best Western ($$)
2000 Avenue F
(78840) 800.528.1234

Best Western ($$)
810 Avenue F
(78840) 210.775.7511
small pets only

Days Inn ($)
3808 W Hwy 90
(78840) 210.775.1511

Del Rio Motor Lodge ($)
1300 Avenue F
(78840) 210.775.2486

Desert Hills Motel ($)
1912 Avenue F
(78840) 210.775.3548

Holiday Inn
3616 Ave F
(78840) 210.775.2933

La Quinta Inn ($$)
2005 Avenue F
(78840) 210.775.7591
call re: fees

Lakeview Inn ($)
Hwy 90 W Hcr 3 Box# 38
(78840) 210.775.9521

Motel 6 ($)
2115 Avenue F
(78840) 210.774.2115
1 small pet/room

Red Top Inn/Economy Inn ($)
3811 W Hwy 90
(78840) 210.775.7414

Rough Canyon Motel ($)
Hwy 277 N RR 2
(78840) 210.774.6266

Western Motel ($)
1203 Avenue F
(78840) 210.774.4661

● Denison ●
Ramada Inn ($$)
1600 S Austin Ave
(75020) 903.465.6800

● Denton ●
Days Inn ($$)
601 I-35
(76205) 817.566.1990

Denton Inn ($$)
820 S I-35
(76205) 817.387.0591

Desert Sands Motel ($)
611 S I-35
(76205) 817.387.6181

Econo Lodge ($)
3116 Bandera St
(76207) 800.424.4777

Exel Inn ($)
4211 N I-35
(76201) 817.383.1471
small pets only

Holiday Lodge ($)
1112 E University Dr
(76201) 817.382.9688

La Quinta Inn ($$)
700 Fort Worth Dr
(76201) 817.387.5840
call re: fees

Motel 6 ($)
5125 N I-35
(76207) 817.566.4798
1 small pet/room

Royal Hotel ($)
1210 N I-35
(76205) 817.383.2007

Western Inn ($)
3116 Bandera St
(76207) 817.383.1681

● Dumas ●
Best Western ($$)
1712 S Dumas Ave
(79029) 806.935.6441

Days Inn ($$)
1701 S Dumas Ave
(79029) 806.935.9644

Econo Lodge ($)
1719 S Dumas Ave
(79029) 806.935.9098

Holiday Inn ($$)
1525 S Dumas Ave
(79029) 806.935.4000
mgr preapproval reqd

Phillips Manor Motel ($)
18721 S Dumas Ave
(79029) 806.935.9281

Super 8 ($)
119 W 17th St
(79029) 806.935.6222
$5 charge/w/permission

● Duncanville ●
Holiday Inn ($$)
711 E Camp Wisdom Rd
(75116) 972.298.8911

Motel 6 ($)
202 Jellison Blvd
(75116) 214.296.0345
1 small pet/room

● Eagle Lake ●
The Farris 1912 Inn ($$)
201 N McCarty Ave
(77434) 409.234.2546

● Eagle Pass ●
Best Western ($$$)
1923 Loop 431
(78852) 210.758.1234

Eagle Pass Inn ($)
2150 N Hwy 277
(78852) 210.773.9531

Royal Hotel ($)
1210 N I-35
(76205) 817.383.2007

Holly Inn ($$)
2421 E Main St
(78852) 210.773.9261

La Quinta Inn ($$)
2525 E Main St
(78852) 210.773.7000
call re: fees

● Eastland ●
Budget Host ($)
I-20
(76448) 817.629.2655

Econo Lodge ($)
2001 I-20
(76448) 817.629.3324

Super 8 ($)
3900 I-20
(76448) 817.629.3336
call re: fees

● El Campo ●
El Campo Inn ($)
210 W Hwy 59
(77437) 409.543.1110

● El Paso ●
Americana Inn ($)
14387 Gateway Blvd
(79927) 915.852.3025

Best Western ($$)
7144 Gateway Blvd
(79915) 915.779.7700
small pets

Budget Lodge Motel ($)
1301 N Mesa St
(79902) 915.533.6821

Budgetel ($$)
7620 N Mesa St
(79912) 915.585.2999

Camino Real Hotel ($$$$)
101 S El Paso St
(79901) 915.534.3000

Comfort Inn ($$)
900 N Yarbrough Dr
(79915) 915.594.9111
small pets only

Days Inn ($$)
9125 Gateway Blvd
(79925) 915.593.8400

$=under $35 $$=$35-60 $$$=$60-100 $$$$=over $100

Econo Lodge ($$)
6363 Montana Ave
(79925) 915.779.6222

Embassy Suites ($$$)
6100 Gateway Blvd
(79905) 915.779.6222
$50 fee

Hilton ($$$)
2027 Airway Blvd
(79925) 915.778.4241
small under 25 lbs

Howard Johnson ($$)
8887 Gateway Blvd
(79925) 915.591.9471

International Hotel ($$)
113 W Missouri Ave
(79901) 915.544.3300

La Quinta Inn ($$)
6140 Gateway Blvd
(79905) 915.778.9321
call re: fees

La Quinta Inn ($$)
11033 Gateway Blvd
(79935) 915.591.2244
call re: fees

La Quinta Inn ($$)
7550 RemcOn Cir
(79912) 915.833.2522
call re: fees

Marriott Hotel ($$)
1600 Airway Blvd
(79925) 915.779.3300
small pets only

Motel 6 ($)
1330 Lomaland Dr
(79935) 915.592.6386
1 small pet/room

Motel 6 ($)
4800 Gateway Blvd
(79905) 915.533.7521
1 small pet/room

Motel 6 ($)
11049 Gateway Blvd
(79935) 915.594.8533
1 small pet/room

Motel 6 ($)
7840 N Mesa St
(79932) 915.584.2129
1 small pet/room

Pear Tree Apartments ($$)
222 Bartlett Dr
(79912) 915.833.7327

Quality Inn ($$)
6201 Gateway Blvd
(79925) 915.778.6111
mgr preapproval reqd

● Ennis ●
Holiday Inn
600 I 45
(75119) 972.875.6990

● Euless ●
La Quinta Inn ($$)
1001 Airport Fwy
(76040) 817.540.0233
call re: fees

Motel 6 ($)
110 Airport Fwy
(76039) 817.545.0141
1 small pet/room

Ramada Inn ($$)
2155 Airport Fwy
(76040) 817.283.2400

● Falfurrias ●
Days Inn ($$)
Hwy 281
(78355) 512.325.2515

● Fort Davis ●
Historic Kimpia Hotel ($$)
Box# 822
(79734) 915.426.3237

● Fort Hancock ●
Fort Hancock Motel ($)
Box# 250
(79839) 915.769.3981

● Fort Stockton ●
Best Western ($$)
3201 W Dickinson Blvd
(79735) 915.336.8521
1 small pet&deposit

Comfort Inn ($)
3200 W Dickinson Blvd
(79735) 915.336.8531
mgr preapproval reqd

Days Inn ($$)
1408 N Hwy 285
(79735) 915.336.7500

Econo Lodge ($$)
800 E Dickinson Blvd
(79735) 915.336.9711
$5 fee

La Quinta Inn ($$)
2601 I-10 West
(79735) 915.336.9781
call re: fees

Motel 6 ($)
3001 W Dickinson Blvd
(79735) 915.336.9737
1 small pet/room

Sands Motel ($)
1801 W Dickinson Blvd
(79735) 915.336.2274

● Fort Worth ●
Best Western ($$)
7301 West Fwy
(76116) 817.244.7444
small pets only

Caravan Motor Hotel ($)
Box# 10128
(76114) 817.626.1951

Days Inn ($$)
1010 Houston Ts
(76102) 817.336.2011
$6/pet charge

Days Inn ($$)
8500 I-30
(76108) 817.246.4961
pets with $5 deposit

Green Oaks Inn ($$$)
6901 West Fwy
(76116) 817.738.7311

Hampton Inn ($$$)
4799 SW Loop 820
(76132) 817.346.7845

Holiday Inn
2540 Meacham Bl
(76106) 817.625.9911

La Quinta Inn ($$)
7888 I-30
(76108) 817.246.5511
call re: fees

Motel 6 ($)
1236 Oakland Blvd
(76103) 817.834.7361
1 small pet/room

Motel 6 ($)
3271 I-35
(76106) 817.625.4359
1 small pet/room

Motel 6 ($)
4433 South Fwy
(76115) 817.921.4900
1 small pet/room

Motel 6 ($)
6600 South Fwy
(76134) 817.293.8595
1 small pet/room

Motel 6 ($)
8701 I-30
(76116) 817.244.9740
1 small pet/room

Radisson Inn ($$$)
815 Main St
(76102) 817.870.2100

Ramada Inn ($$$)
1701 Commerce St
(76102) 817.335.7000

Ramada Inn ($$)
1401 S University Dr
(76107) 817.336.9311

Residence Inn ($$$)
1701 S University Dr
(76107) 817.870.1011
call for fee & availability

Royal Western Suites ($$)
8401 I-30
(76116) 817.560.0060

Be
Discreet

Super 8 ($$)
7960 I-30
(76108) 817.246.7168
mgr preapproval reqd

Worthington Hotel ($$$$)
200 Main St
(76102) 817.870.1000

● Fredericksburg ●
Alleganis Horse Inn ($$$)
307 S Creek St
(78624) 210.997.7448

Best Western ($$)
501 E Main St
(78624) 210.997.4484
small pets under 10 lbs

Budget Host ($)
901 E Main St
(78624) 210.997.3344

Comfort Inn ($$)
908 S Adams St
(78624) 210.997.9811
mgr preapproval reqd

Country Inn ($)
Hwy 290
(78624) 210.997.2185

Dietzel Motel ($)
909 W Main St
(78624) 210.997.3330

Dietzel Motel
US 290 & 87
(78624) 201.997.3330
owner rfd pets welcome

Econo Lodge ($$)
810 S Adams St
(78624) 210.997.3437

Fredericksburg Inn ($$)
201 S Washington St
(78624) 210.977.0202

Frontier Inn Motel ($)
RR 2 Box# 99
(78624) 210.997.4389

Millers Inn Motel ($$)
910 E Main St
(78624) 210.997.2244

Peach Tree Inn ($)
401 S Washington St
(78624) 210.997.2117

River View Inn ($$)
Hwy 16
(78624) 210.997.8555

Save Inn Motel ($$)
514 E Main St
(78624) 210.997.6568

Settlers Crossing ($$$)
RR 1 Box# 315
(78624) 210.997.2722

Stonewall Valley Ranch ($$$)
104 N Adams St
(78624) 210.990.8455

Strackbein Roeders ($$$)
231 W Main St
(78624) 210.997.5612

Sunset Inn ($)
900 S Adams St
(78624) 210.997.9581

Watkins Hill ($$$)
608 E Creek St
(78624) 210.997.6739

● Freeport ●
Anchor Motel ($)
1302 Blue Water Hwy
(77541) 409.239.3543

Country Hearth Inn ($$)
1015 W 2nd St Velasco
(77541) 409.239.1602

● Fulton ●
Best Western ($$)
3902 I-35
(78358) 512.729.8351
small pets accepted with
deposit

Harbor Lights Ctges ($$)
108 Laurel
(78358) 512.729.6770

Kontiki Beach Motel ($$)
2290 Fulton Bch Rd
(78358) 512.729.4975

Reef Motel ($$)
3rd & Broadway
(78358) 512.729.6955

Sportsman Manor ($$)
4170 I-35
(78358) 512.729.5331

● Gainesville ●
Best Western ($)
2103 I-35
(76240) 817.665.7737
no unattended pets

Budget Host ($)
RR 2 Box# 120
(76240) 817.665.2856
mgr preapproval reqd

Comfort Inn ($$)
1936 I-35
(76240) 817.665.5599
mgr preapproval reqd

Days Inn ($)
RR 2 Box# 13A
(76240) 817.665.5555

Holiday Inn ($$)
600 Fair Park Blvd
(76240) 817.665.8800
mgr preapproval reqd

● Galveston ●
Econo Lodge ($)
2825 61st St
(77551) 409.744.7133

Hilltop Motel ($)
8828 Seawall Blvd
(77554) 409.744.4423

La Quinta Inn ($$$)
1402 Seawall Blvd
(77550) 409.763.1224
call re: fees

Motel 6 ($)
7404 Ave J Broadway
(77554) 409.740.3794
1 small pet/room

● Garland ●
Days Inn ($$)
6222 Beltline Rd
(75043) 214.226.7621
$10/pet

La Quinta Inn ($$)
12721 I-635
(75041) 214.271.7581
call re: fees

Motel 6 ($)
436 W I-30 & Beltline
(75043) 214.226.7140
1 small pet/room

● Gatesville ●
Best Western ($)
2501 E Main St
(76528) 817.865.2281
small pets only

● Georgetown ●
Comfort Inn ($$)
1005 Leander Rd
(78628) 512.863.7504
mgr preapproval reqd

Days Inn ($)
209 I-35
(78628) 512.863.5572

La Quinta Inn ($$)
333 I-35
(78628) 512.869.2541
call re: fees

● Giddings ●
Best Western ($)
3556 E Austin St
(78942) 409.542.5791
small housebroken pets

Econo Lodge ($)
RR 3 Box# 461
(78942) 409.542.9666

Giddings Sands Motel ($)
1600 E Austin St
(78942) 409.542.3111

● Graham ●
Gateway Inn ($)
1401 Hwy 16
(76450) 817.549.0222

Rodeway Inn ($)
1919 Hwy 16
(76450) 817.549.8320

● Granbury ●
Best Western ($$)
1209 N Plaza Dr
(76048) 817.573.8874

Days Inn ($$)
1339 N Plaza Dr
(76048) 817.573.2691

Plantation Inn ($$)
1451 E Pearl St
(76048) 817.573.8846

● Grand Prairie ●
Hampton Inn ($$$)
2050 N Hwy 360
(75050) 214.988.8989

La Quinta Inn ($$)
1410 NW 19th St
(75050) 214.641.3021
call re: fees

Motel 6 ($)
406 E Safari Pkwy
(75050) 214.642.9424
1 small pet/room

Ramada Inn ($$)
402 E Safari Pkwy
(75050) 214.263.4421

● Greenville ●
Best Western ($$)
1216 I-30
(75402) 903.454.1792

Holiday Inn ($$)
1215 I-30
(75401) 903.454.7000
mgr preapproval reqd

Motel 6 ($)
5109 I-30 & US 69
(75402) 903.455.0515
1 small pet/room

Royal Inn ($)
I-30 & US 69
(75401) 903.455.9600

● Groom ●
Chalet Inn ($)
Fm 2300 I-40
(79039) 806.248.7524

● Groves ●
Motel 6 ($)
5201 E Parkway St
(77619) 409.962.6611
1 small pet/room

● Harlingen ●
Best Western ($$)
6779 US 83 W Expwy
(78552) 210.425.7070

Days Inn ($$)
1901 W Tyler St
(78550) 210.425.1810

La Quinta Inn ($$)
1002 US 83 S Expwy
(78552) 210.428.6888
call re: fees

Motel 6 ($)
224 US 77 S Expwy
(78550) 210.421.4200
1 small pet/room

Super 8 ($$)
1115 US 77 & 83 S Expwy
(78550) 210.412.8873
small pets only

● Hearne ●
Executive Inn ($)
Hwy 6 At Fm 485
(77859) 409.279.5345

● Hebbronville ●
Texas Executive Inn ($$)
1302 N Smith Ave
(78361) 512.527.4082

● Henderson ●
Best Western ($$)
1500 Hwy 259
(75652) 903.657.9561

● Hereford ●
Best Western ($)
830 W 1st St
(79045) 806.364.0540
small pet ok

● Hillsboro ●
Best Western ($$)
307 W Service Rd
(76645) 817.582.8465
small pets

Ramada Inn ($$)
I-35 & Hwy 22
(76645) 817.582.3493

● Hondo ●
Whitetail Lodge ($$)
Box# 110 Hwy 90
(78861) 210.426.3031

● Houston ●
Days Inn ($$)
4640 Main St
(77002) 713.523.3777

Days Inn ($$)
9041 Westheimer Rd
(77063) 713.783.1400

Days Inn ($$)
8500 Kirby Dr
(77054) 713.796.8383

Days Inn ($$)
9025 North Fwy
(77037) 713.820.1500
pets allowed w/deposit

Days Inn ($$)
9799 Katy Fwy
(77024) 713.468.7801

Doubletree ($$$$)
5353 Westheimer Rd
(77056) 713.961.9000

Doubletree ($$$)
400 Dallas St
(77002) 713.759.0202

Drury Inn ($$$)
1615 W Loop 610
(77027) 713.963.0700

Drury Inn ($$$)
7902 Mosley Rd
(77061) 713.941.4300

Drury Inn ($$)
1000 Hwy 6
(77079) 713.558.7007

Econo Lodge ($)
9535 Katy Fwy
(77024) 713.467.4411

Fairfield Inn ($$$)
3131 West Loop
(77027) 713.961.1690

Hampton Inn ($$)
10155 East Fwy
(77029) 713.675.2711

Hampton Inn ($$)
828 Mercury Dr
(77013) 713.673.4200

Harvey Hotel ($$)
2712 Southwest Fwy
(77098) 713.523.8448

Hawthorn Suites ($$$$)
6910 Southwest Fwy
(77074) 713.785.3415
call for fee & availability

Hilton ($$$)
4800 Calhoun Rd
(77004) 713.743.2610

Hojo Inn ($$)
4602 Katy Fwy
(77007) 713.861.9000

Holiday Inn ($$)
7787 Katy Fwy
(77024) 713.681.5000
mgr preapproval reqd

Holiday Inn ($$$)
15222 JFK Blvd
(77032) 713.449.2311
mgr preapproval reqd

Holiday Inn ($$$)
6701 Main St
(77030) 713.797.1110
mgr preapproval reqd

Howard Johnson ($$)
7777 Airport Blvd
(77061) 713.644.1261

Howard Johnson ($$)
4225 North Fwy
(77022) 713.695.6011

Hyatt Hotel ($$$$)
1200 Louisiana St
(77002) 713.654.1234

Well
Behaved

TEXAS, Houston

Interstate Lodge ($)
13213 I-10
(77015) 713.453.6353

J W Marriott ($$$$)
5150 Westheimer Rd
(77056) 713.961.1500
$50 deposit

La Quinta Inn ($$)
6 N Belt Dr
(77060) 713.447.6888
call re: fees

La Quinta Inn ($$)
9911 Buffalo Speedway
(77054) 713.668.8082
call re: fees

La Quinta Inn ($$)
11002 Northwest Fwy
(77092) 713.688.2581
call re: fees

La Quinta Inn ($$)
13290 Fm 1960 Rd
(77065) 713.469.4018
call re: fees

La Quinta Inn ($$)
11999 East Fwy
(77029) 713.453.5425
call re: fees

La Quinta Inn ($$$)
4015 Southwest Fwy
(77027) 713.623.4750
call re: fees

La Quinta Inn ($$)
9902 Gulf Fwy
(77034) 713.941.0900
call re: fees

La Quinta Inn ($$)
17111 North Fwy
(77090) 713.444.7500
call re: fees

La Quinta Inn ($$)
8201 Southwest Fwy
(77074) 713.772.3626
call re: fees

La Quinta Inn ($$)
10552 Southwest Fwy
(77074) 713.270.9559
call re: fees

La Quinta Inn ($$)
11113 Katy Fwy
(77079) 713.932.0808
call re: fees

La Quinta Inn ($$)
8017 Katy Fwy
(77024) 713.688.8941
call re: fees

Marriott Hotel ($$)
255 N Sam Houston Pkwy
(77060) 713.875.4000

Marriott Hotel ($$$)
1750 West Loop
(77027) 713.960.0111

Marriott Hotel ($$$$)
13210 Katy Fwy
(77079) 713.558.8338
$20 deposit

Medallion Hotel ($$$$)
3000 North Loop
(77092) 713.688.0100

Motel 6 ($)
16884 Northwest Fwy
(77040) 713.937.7056
1 small pet/room

Motel 6 ($)
5555 W 34th St
(77092) 713.682.8588
1 small pet/room

Motel 6 ($)
14833 Katy Fwy
(77094) 713.497.5000
1 small pet/room

Motel 6 ($)
3223 South Loop
(77025) 713.664.6425
1 small pet/room

Motel 6 ($)
8800 Airport Blvd
(77061) 713.941.0990
1 small pet/room

Motel 6 ($)
9638 Plainfield St
(77036) 713.778.0008
1 small pet/room

Omni Houston ($$$$)
4 Riverway
(77056) 713.871.8181

Quality Inn ($$)
6115 Will Clayton Pkwy
(77205) 281.446.9131
$15 fee

Radisson Inn ($$$)
1400 Old Spanish Trl
(77054) 713.796.1000
small pets allowed

Ramada Inn ($$$)
2100 S Braeswood Blvd
(77030) 713.797.9000

Ramada Inn ($$$)
1301 Nasa Rd 1
(77058) 713.488.0220
very small pets

Ramada Inn ($$$)
12801 Northwest Fwy
(77040) 713.462.9977

Ramada Ltd ($$)
15725 Bammel Village Dr
(77014) 713.893.5224

Red Roof Inn ($$$)
9005 Airport Blvd
(77061) 713.943.3300

Residence Inn ($$$)
525 Bay Area Blvd
(77058) 713.486.2424
$50 fee & $6 per day

Residence Inn ($$$)
7710 Main St
(77030) 713.660.7993
call for fee & availability

Residence Inn ($$$)
2500 McCue Rd
(77056) 713.840.9757

Rodeway Inn ($$)
3135 Southwest Fwy
(77098) 713.526.1071

Sheraton Inn ($$$$)
2525 West Loop
(77027) 713.961.3000

Shoneys Inn
12323 Katy Fwy
(77079) 713.493.5626

Shoneys Inn
2364 South Loop
(77054) 713.799.2436

Stouffer Renaissance ($$$)
6 E Greenway Plz
(77046) 713.629.1200

The Four Seasons ($$$)
1300 Lamar St
(77010) 713.650.1300
small pets allowed

The Lancaster Hotel ($$$)
701 Texas
(77002) 713.228.9500

Travelodge ($)
4204 Hwy 6
(77084) 713.859.2233

Travelodge ($$)
4726 1960 Rd
(77069) 713.587.9171

Westin Oaks ($$$$)
5011 Westheirner Rd
(77056) 713.960.8100
small pets accepted

Houston Metro

● Baytown ●
Best Western ($$)
5021 I-10
(77521) 713.421.2233

Budgetel ($$)
5215 I-10E
(77521) 713.421.7300

La Quinta Inn ($$)
4911 I-10
(77521) 713.421.5566
call re: fees

Motel 6 ($)
8911 Hwy 146
(77520) 713.576.5777
1 small pet/room

$=under $35 $$=$35-60 $$$=$60-100 $$$$=over $100

● Brookshire ●
Budget Inn ($)
542 Koomey Rd
(77423) 713.934.4477

Days Inn ($$)
Rm 359 & I-10
(77423) 713.934.3122

● Channelview ●
Best Western ($)
15919 I-10
(77530) 713.452.1000
2 per rm w/$20 dep

Days Inn ($$)
15545 I-10
(77530) 713.457.3000

Holiday Inn
15157 I-10
(77530) 281.452.7304

● Conroe ●
Heathers Glen ($$$)
200 E Phillips St
(77301) 409.441.6611

Holiday Inn ($$)
1601 I-45 S
(77301) 409.756.8941
mgr preapproval reqd

Motel 6 ($)
820 I-45 S
(77304) 409.760.4003
1 small pet/room

Ramada Inn ($$$)
1520 S Frazier St
(77301) 409.756.8939

● Houston ●
Days Inn ($$)
4640 Main St
(77002) 713.523.3777

Days Inn ($$)
9041 Westheimer Rd
(77063) 713.783.1400

Days Inn ($$)
8500 Kirby Dr
(77054) 713.796.8383

Days Inn ($$)
9025 North Fwy
(77037) 713.820.1500
pets allowed w/deposit

Days Inn ($$)
9799 Katy Fwy
(77024) 713.468.7801

Doubletree ($$$$)
5353 Westheimer Rd
(77056) 713.961.9000

Doubletree ($$$)
400 Dallas St
(77002) 713.759.0202

Drury Inn ($$$)
1615 W Loop 610 S
(77027) 713.963.0700

Drury Inn ($$$)
7902 Mosley Rd
(77061) 713.941.4300

Drury Inn ($$)
1000 Hwy 6
(77079) 713.558.7007

Econo Lodge ($)
9535 Katy Fwy
(77024) 713.467.4411

Fairfield Inn ($$$)
3131 West Loop S
(77027) 713.961.1690

Hampton Inn ($$)
10155 East Fwy
(77029) 713.675.2711

Hampton Inn ($$)
828 Mercury Dr
(77013) 713.673.4200

Harvey Hotel ($$)
2712 Southwest Fwy
(77098) 713.523.8448

Hawthorn Suites ($$$$)
6910 Southwest Fwy
(77074) 713.785.3415
call for fee & availability

Hilton ($$$)
4800 Calhoun Rd
(77004) 713.743.2610

Hojo Inn ($$)
4602 Katy Fwy
(77007) 713.861.9000

Holiday Inn ($$)
7787 Katy Fwy
(77024) 713.681.5000
mgr preapproval reqd

Holiday Inn ($$$)
15222 JFK Blvd
(77032) 713.449.2311
mgr preapproval reqd

Holiday Inn ($$$)
6701 Main St
(77030) 713.797.1110
mgr preapproval reqd

Howard Johnson ($$)
7777 Airport Blvd
(77061) 713.644.1261

Howard Johnson ($$)
4225 North Fwy
(77022) 713.695.6011

Hyatt Hotel ($$$$)
1200 Louisiana St
(77002) 713.654.1234

Interstate Lodge ($)
13213 I-10
(77015) 713.453.6353

J W Marriott ($$$$)
5150 Westheimer Rd
(77056) 713.961.1500
$50 deposit

La Quinta Inn ($$)
6 N Belt Dr
(77060) 713.447.6888
call re: fees

La Quinta Inn ($$)
9911 Buffalo Speedway
(77054) 713.668.8082
call re: fees

La Quinta Inn ($$)
11002 Northwest Fwy
(77092) 713.688.2581
call re: fees

La Quinta Inn ($$)
13290 Fm 1960 Rd
(77065) 713.469.4018
call re: fees

La Quinta Inn ($$)
11999 East Fwy
(77029) 713.453.5425
call re: fees

La Quinta Inn ($$$)
4015 Southwest Fwy
(77027) 713.623.4750
call re: fees

La Quinta Inn ($$)
9902 Gulf Fwy
(77034) 713.941.0900
call re: fees

La Quinta Inn ($$)
17111 North Fwy
(77090) 713.444.7500
call re: fees

La Quinta Inn ($$)
8201 Southwest Fwy
(77074) 713.772.3626
call re: fees

La Quinta Inn ($$)
10552 Southwest Fwy
(77074) 713.270.9559
call re: fees

La Quinta Inn ($$)
11113 Katy Fwy
(77079) 713.932.0808
call re: fees

La Quinta Inn ($$)
8017 Katy Fwy
(77024) 713.688.8941
call re: fees

Marriott Hotel ($$)
255 N Sam Houston Pkwy
(77060) 713.875.4000

Marriott Hotel ($$$)
1750 West Loop S
(77027) 713.960.0111

Marriott Hotel ($$$$)
13210 Katy Fwy
(77079) 713.558.8338
$20 deposit

Medallion Hotel ($$$$)
3000 North Loop
(77092) 713.688.0100

$=under $35 $$=$35-60 $$$=$60-100 $$$$=over $100

Motel 6 ($)
16884 Northwest Fwy
(77040) 713.937.7056
1 small pet/room

Motel 6 ($)
5555 W 34th St
(77092) 713.682.8588
1 small pet/room

Motel 6 ($)
14833 Katy Fwy
(77094) 713.497.5000
1 small pet/room

Motel 6 ($)
3223 South Loop
(77025) 713.664.6425
1 small pet/room

Motel 6 ($)
8800 Airport Blvd
(77061) 713.941.0990
1 small pet/room

Motel 6 ($)
9638 Plainfield St
(77036) 713.778.0008
1 small pet/room

Omni Houston ($$$$)
4 Riverway
(77056) 713.871.8181

Quality Inn ($$)
6115 Will Clayton Pkwy
(77205) 281.446.9131
$15 fee

Radisson Inn ($$$)
1400 Old Spanish Trl
(77054) 713.796.1000
small pets allowed

Ramada Inn ($$$)
2100 S Braeswood Blvd
(77030) 713.797.9000

Ramada Inn ($$$)
1301 Nasa Rd 1
(77058) 713.488.0220
very small pets

Ramada Inn ($$$)
12801 Northwest Fwy
(77040) 713.462.9977

Ramada Ltd ($$)
15725 Bammel Village Dr
(77014) 713.893.5224

Red Roof Inn ($$$)
9005 Airport Blvd
(77061) 713.943.3300

Residence Inn ($$$)
525 Bay Area Blvd
(77058) 713.486.2424
$50 fee & $6 per day

Residence Inn ($$$)
7710 Main St
(77030) 713.660.7993
call for fee & availability

Residence Inn ($$$)
2500 McCue Rd
(77056) 713.840.9757

Rodeway Inn ($$)
3135 Southwest Fwy
(77098) 713.526.1071

Sheraton Inn ($$$$)
2525 West Loop S
(77027) 713.961.3000

Shoneys Inn
12323 Katy Fwy
(77079) 713.493.5626

Shoneys Inn
2364 South Loop
(77054) 713.799.2436

Stouffer Renaissance ($$$)
6 E Greenway Plz
(77046) 713.629.1200

The Four Seasons ($$$)
1300 Lamar St
(77010) 713.650.1300
small pets allowed

The Lancaster Hotel ($$$)
701 Texas At Louisiana
(77002) 713.228.9500

Travelodge ($)
4204 Hwy 6
(77084) 713.859.2233

Travelodge ($$)
4726 Fm 1960 Rd
(77069) 713.587.9171

Westin Oaks ($$$$)
5011 Westheimer Rd
(77056) 713.960.8100
small pets accepted

● Humble ●
Days Inn ($$)
17607 Eastex Fwy
(77396) 713.446.4611
$10/pets

● Katy ●
Best Western ($$)
22455 I-10
(77450) 713.392.9800
small pets

Holiday Inn
22108 Katy Fwy
(77450) 281.395.4800

Super 8 ($$)
22157 Katy Fwy
(77450) 713.395.5757
call re: fees

● La Porte ●
La Quinta Inn ($$)
1105 Hwy 146 S
(77571) 713.470.0760
call re: fees

● Pasadena ●
Econo Lodge ($$)
823 W Pasadena Fwy
(77506) 713.477.4266

Ramada Inn ($$)
114 Richey St
(77506) 713.477.6871

● Richmond ●
Executive Inn ($)
26035 Southwest Fwy
(77469) 713.342.5387

● Rosenberg ●
Best Western ($)
28382 Southwest Fwy
(77471) 713.342.6000
small pets

● Spring ●
La Quinta Inn ($$)
28673 I-45
(77381) 713.367.7722
call re: fees

Motel 6 ($)
19606 Cypresswood Ct
(77388) 713.350.6400
1 small pet/room

Red Roof Inn ($$)
24903 I-45
(77380) 713.367.5040

The Woodlands Resort
($$$$)
2301 N Millbend Dr
(77380) 713.367.1100

● Stafford ●
La Quinta Inn ($$)
12727 Southwest Fwy
(77477) 713.240.2300
call re: fees

● Sugar Land ●
Shoneys Inn
14444 Southwest Fwy
(77478) 713.565.6655

● Webster ●
Motel 6 ($)
1001 W Nasa Blvd
(77598) 713.332.4581
1 small pet/room

End of Houston Metro

● Humble ●
Days Inn ($$)
17607 Eastex Fwy
(77396) 713.446.4611
$10/pets

● Huntsville ●
Econo Lodge ($)
1501 I-45
(77340) 409.295.6401

Motel 6 ($)
1607 I-45
(77340) 409.291.6927
1 small pet/room

Park Inn Intl ($$)
1407 I-45
(77340) 409.295.6454

Rodeway Inn ($)
3211 I-45 S Ex 114
(77340) 409.295.7595

CALL AHEAD!

$=under $35 $$=$35-60 $$$=$60-100 $$$$=over $100

Kingsville, TEXAS

Sam Houston Inn ($$)
3296 I-45 S Ex 114
(77340) 409.295.9151

● Ingram ●
Hunter House Motel ($$)
310 Hwy 39
(78025) 210.367.2377

● Irving ●
Comfort Inn ($$)
8205 Esters Blvd
(75063) 972.929.0066
$25 deposit

Days Inn ($$)
2200 E Airport Fwy
(75062) 214.438.6666

Drury Inn ($$$)
4210 W Airport Fwy
(75062) 214.986.1200
small pets only

Hampton Inn ($$$)
4340 W Airport Fwy
(75062) 214.986.3606

Harvey Hotel ($$$)
4545 W John Carpenter Fwy
(75063) 214.929.4500
$25 fee

Harvey Suites ($$$)
4550 W John Carpenter Fwy
(75063) 214.929.4499

Homewood Suites ($$$)
4300 Wingren Dr
(75039) 214.556.0665
$50 fee

Irving Inn Suites ($)
909 W Airport Fwy
(75062) 214.255.7108

La Quinta Inn ($$)
4105 W Airport Fwy
(75062) 214.252.6546
call re: fees

Motel 6 ($)
510 S Loop 12
(75060) 214.438.4227
1 small pet/room

Red Roof Inn ($$)
8150 Esters Blvd
(75063) 214.929.0020

Red Roof Inn ($$)
2611 W Airport Fwy
(75062) 214.570.7500

Residence Inn ($$$)
950 W Walnut Hill Ln
(75038) 214.580.7773
$50 deposit

Skyway Inn ($)
110 W Airport Fwy
(75062) 214.438.2000

Suites Inn ($)
1701 W Airport Fwy
(75062) 214.255.1133

The Four Seasons ($$$$)
4150 N Macarthur Blvd
(75038) 214.717.0700
small pets allowed

Wilson World Hotel ($$$)
4600 W Airport Fwy
(75062) 214.513.0800

● Jacksboro ●
Jacksboro Inn ($)
704 S Main St
(76458) 817.567.3751

● Jacksonville ●
Best Western ($$)
1407 E Rusk St
(75766) 903.586.9842

● Jasper ●
Best Western ($$)
205 W Gibson St
(75951) 409.384.7767

Ramada Inn ($$)
239 E Gibson St
(75951) 409.384.9021

● Jefferson ●
Best Western ($$)
400 S Walcott St
(75657) 903.665.3983

● Johnson City ●
Save Inn Motel ($$)
107 Hwy 281 & 290
(78636) 210.868.4044

● Junction ●
Best Western ($$)
HC 10 Box# 138
(76849) 915.446.3331

Carousel Inn ($)
1908 Main St
(76849) 915.446.3301

Days Inn ($$)
111st Martinez St
(76849) 915.446.3730
$4/pet charge

La Vista Motel ($)
2040 Main St
(76849) 915.446.2191

The Hills Motel ($)
1520 Main St
(76849) 915.446.2567

● Katy ●
Best Western ($$)
22455 I-10
(77450) 713.392.9800
small pets

Holiday Inn
22108 Katy Fwy
(77450) 281.395.4800

Super 8 ($$)
22157 Katy Fwy
(77450) 713.395.5757
call re: fees

● Kerrville ●
Best Western ($$)
2124 Sidney Baker St
(78028) 210.896.1313

Flagstaff Inn ($$)
906 Junction Hwy
(78028) 210.792.4449

Hillcrest Inn ($)
1508 Sidney Baker St
(78028) 210.896.7400

Holiday Inn ($$$)
2033 Sidney Baker St
(78028) 210.257.4440
mgr preapproval reqd

Inn Of Hills River ($$)
1001 Junction Hwy
(78028) 210.895.5000

Ramada Inn ($$)
2127 Sidney Baker St
(78028) 210.896.1511

Save Inn Motel ($)
1804 Sidney Baker St
(78028) 210.896.8200

Shoneys Inn ($)
2145 Sidney Baker St
(78028) 210.896.1711
small pets only

● Kilgore ●
Ramada Inn ($$)
3501 Hwy 259
(75662) 903.983.3456

● Killeen ●
La Quinta Inn ($$)
1112 S Fort Hood St
(76541) 817.526.8331
call re: fees

Ramada Inn ($$)
1100 S Fort Hood St
(76541) 817.634.3101

● Kingsville ●
Best Western ($$)
2402 E King Ave
(78363) 512.595.5656
1 small pet

Howard Johnson ($$)
105 Hwy 77
(78363) 512.592.6471

La Cupula Motor Inn ($$)
3430 Hwy 77
(78363) 512.595.5753

Motel 6 ($)
101 Hwy 77
(78363) 512.592.5106
1 small pet/room

Motel 77 ($)
716 S 14th St
(78363) 512.592.4322

Motel Carby ($)
1415 S 14th St
(78363) 512.592.5214

$=under $35 $$=$35-60   **339** $$$=$60-100 $$$$=over $100

● Kountze ●
Little House Timber Ridge
($$$)
Box# 115
(77625) 409.246.3107

● La Grange ●
Northpointe Suites ($$)
202 Northpointe Ave
(78945) 409.968.6406

● La Porte ●
La Quinta Inn ($$)
1105 Hwy 146
(77571) 713.470.0760
call re: fees

● Lake Jackson ●
Best Western ($$)
915 Hwy 332
(77566) 409.297.3031

Ramada Inn ($$$)
925 Hwy 332
(77566) 409.297.1161
small pets only

● Lamesa ●
Shilo Inn ($)
1707 Lubbock Hwy
(79331) 806.872.6721

● Lampasas ●
Circle Motel ($$)
1502 S Key Ave
(76550) 512.556.6201

Saratoga Motel ($)
1408 S Key Ave
(76550) 512.556.6244

● Laredo ●
Best Western ($$)
5240 San Bernardo Ave
(78041) 210.723.3603

Family Gardens Inn ($$)
5830 San Bernardo Ave
(78041) 210.723.5300

Holiday Inn
800 Garden St
(78040) 210.727.5800

Holiday Inn ($$)
1 S Main Ave
(78040) 210.722.2411
mgr preapproval reqd

La Quinta Inn ($$)
3610 Santa Ursula Ave
(78041) 210.722.0511
call re: fees

Motel 6 ($)
5920 San Bernardo Ave
(78041) 210.722.8133
1 small pet/room

Motel South ($)
5310 San Bernardo Ave
(78041) 210.725.8187
1 small pet per room

● League City ●
South Shore Resort ($$$$)
2500 S Shore Blvd
(77573) 713.344.1000

● Lewisville ●
Comfort Suites ($$$)
755A Vista Ridge Mall Dr
(75067) 972.315.6464

Country Inn ($$)
755 Vista Ridge Mall Dr
(75067) 214.315.6565

Days Inn ($$)
1401 S Stemmons Fwy
(75067) 214.436.0080

La Quinta Inn ($$)
1657 N Stemmons Fwy
(75067) 214.221.7525
call re: fees

● Littlefield ●
Crescent Park Motel ($)
2000 Hall Ave
(79339) 806.385.4464

● Livingston ●
Econo Lodge ($)
117 Hwy 59 At Hwy 190
(77351) 409.327.2451

Park Inn Intl ($)
2500 Hwy 59
(77351) 409.327.2525

● Llano ●
Best Western ($$)
901 W Young St
(78643) 915.247.4101
small pets only

● Lockhart ●
Best Western ($$)
2001 Hwy 183
(78644) 512.398.4911

Lockhart Inn ($)
1207 Hwy 183
(78644) 512.398.5201

● Longview ●
Comfort Suites ($$)
3307 N 4th St
(75605) 903.663.4991
mgr preapproval reqd

Days Inn ($$)
3103 Estes Pkwy
(75602) 903.758.1113
small pets ok

Econo Lodge ($$)
3120 Estes Pkwy
(75602) 903.753.4884

Fairfield Inn ($$)
3305 N 4th St
(75605) 903.663.1995

Hampton Inn ($$$)
112 S Access Rd
(75603) 903.758.0959

Holiday Inn ($$)
3119 Estes Pkwy
(75602) 903.758.0700
mgr preapproval reqd

La Quinta Inn ($$)
502 S Access Rd
(75602) 903.757.3663
call re: fees

Longview Inn ($$)
605 N Access Rd
(75602) 903.753.0350

Motel 6 ($)
110 W Access Rd
(75603) 903.758.5256
1 small pet/room

● Lubbock ●
Best Western ($$)
6624 I-27
(79404) 806.745.2208

Hampton Inn ($$)
4003 S Loop 289
(79423) 806.795.1080

Holiday Inn ($$$)
801 Avenue Q
(79401) 806.763.1200
mgr preapproval reqd

Holiday Inn ($$$)
3201 S Loop 289
(79423) 806.797.3241
mgr preapproval reqd

Motel 6 ($)
909 66th St
(79412) 806.745.5541
1 small pet/room

Residence Inn ($$$)
2551 S Loop 289
(79423) 806.745.1963
$75 fee

Sheraton Inn ($$$)
505 Avenue Q
(79401) 806.747.0171

Super 8 ($$)
501 Avenue Q
(79401) 806.762.8726
$25 dep $5 per pet

Super 8 ($$)
5410 2-27
(79412) 806.762.8400
$25 dep

● Lufkin ●
Best Western ($$)
4200 N Medford Dr
(75901) 409.632.7300
small dogs/cats only

Days Inn ($$)
2130 S 1st St
(75901) 409.639.3301

Holiday House Motel ($)
308 N Timberland Dr
(75901) 409.634.6626

**Policies
Subject
to Change**

$=under $35 $$=$35-60 $$$=$60-100 $$$$=over $100

Holiday Inn ($$)
4306 S 1st St
(75901) 409.639.3333
mgr preapproval reqd

La Quinta Inn ($$)
2119 S 1st St
(75901) 409.634.3351
call re: fees

Motel 6 ($)
1110 S Timberland Dr
(75901) 409.637.7850
1 small pet/room

● Lytle ●
Best Western ($$)
19525 McDonald St
(78052) 210.772.4777

● Madisonville ●
Best Western ($$)
3305 E Main St
(77864) 409.348.3636

● Mansfield ●
Days Inn ($)
1560 E Broad St
(76063) 817.473.6118

● Marathon ●
The Gage Hotel ($$)
102 Hwy 90
(79842) 915.386.4205

● Marble Falls ●
Best Western ($$)
1403 Hwy 281
(78654) 210.693.5122

Tropical Hideway ($$$)
604 Highcrest St
(78654) 210.598.9896

● Marshall ●
Best Western ($$)
5555 E End Blvd
(75672) 903.935.1941

Economy Inn ($)
6002 E End Blvd
(75672) 903.935.1184

La Maison Malfacon ($$)
700 E Rusk St
(75670) 903.938.3600

Motel 6 ($)
300 I-20
(75670) 903.935.4393
1 small pet/room

Ramada Inn ($$)
5301 E End Blvd
(75672) 903.938.9261

● Mathis ●
Mathis Motor Inn ($)
1223 N Front St
(78368) 512.547.3272

● Mc Kinney ●
Comfort Inn ($$)
2104 N Central Expy
(75070) 972.548.8888

Woods Motel ($)
1431 N Tennessee St
(75069) 214.542.4469

● McAllen ●
Doubletree ($$$)
101 Main St
(78501) 210.653.1101

Drury Inn ($$)
612 W Expwy 83
(78501) 210.687.5100

Hampton Inn ($$)
300 W Expwy 83
(78501) 210.682.4900
small pets only

Holiday Inn ($$)
2000 S 10th St
(78503) 210.686.1741
mgr preapproval reqd

La Quinta Inn ($$)
1100 S 10th St
(78501) 210.687.1101
call re: fees

Motel 6 ($)
700 Hwy 83 Expwy
(78501) 210.687.3700
1 small pet/room

Rodeway Inn ($$)
1421 S 10th St
(78501) 210.686.1586

Thrifty Inn ($$)
620 Hwy 83 Expwy
(78501) 210.631.6700

● Memphis ●
Best Western ($$)
Hwy 287
(79245) 806.259.3583
small pets in certain rooms
only

● Mercedes ●
Days Inn ($$)
Mile 2 W & Expwy 83
(78570) 210.565.3121

● Mesquite ●
Days Inn ($)
3601 E Hwy 80
(75150) 214.279.6561

Motel 6 ($)
3629 E Hwy 80
(75150) 214.613.1662
1 small pet/room

● Midland ●
Best Western ($$)
3100 W Wall St
(79701) 915.699.4144
small pets only

Days Inn ($)
4714 W Hwy 80
(79703) 915.699.7727

Hampton Inn ($$)
3904 W Wall St
(79703) 915.694.7774

Holiday Inn ($$)
4300 W Wall St
(79703) 915.697.3181
mgr preapproval reqd

La Quinta Inn ($$)
4130 W Wall St
(79703) 915.697.9900
call re: fees

Lexington Hotel ($$)
1003 S Midkiff Rd
(79701) 915.697.3155

Motel 6 ($)
1003 S Midkiff Rd
(79701) 915.697.3197
1 small pet/room

Ramada Inn ($$)
100 S Airport Plza Dr
(79711) 915.561.8000

Super 8 ($)
1000 I-20
(79701) 915.684.8888
small pets only

● Midlothian ●
Best Western ($$)
220 N Hwy 67
(76065) 214.775.1891

● Mineral Wells ●
12 Oaks Inn Motel ($$)
4103 Hwy 180
(76067) 817.325.6956

Days Inn ($$)
3701 E Hubbard
(76067) 817.325.6961

Hojo Inn ($$)
2809 Hwy 180
(76067) 817.328.1111

● Mission ●
Mission Inn ($$)
1786 W Hwy 83
(78572) 210.581.7451

● Monahans ●
Best Western ($$)
702 I-20
(79756) 915.943.4345

● Mount Pleasant ●
Days Inn ($$)
2501 W Ferguson Rd
(75455) 903.577.0152

Lakewood Motel ($)
2214 Lakewood Dr
(75455) 903.572.9808

● Mountain Home ●
Y O Ranch ($$$)
Hwy 41
(78058) 210.640.3222
with prior approval

● Muleshoe ●
Heritage House Inn ($$)
2301 W American Blvd
(79347) 806.272.7575

Be Discreet

$=under $35 $$=$35-60 $$$=$60-100 $$$$=over $100

● Nacogdoches ●
Best Western ($$)
3428 South St
(75964) 409.560.4900

Econo Lodge ($$)
2020 NW Stallings Dr
(75964) 409.569.0880

Hardemans Guest House
($$$)
316 N Church St
(75961) 409.569.1947
w/mgmt approval

La Quinta Inn ($$)
3215 South St
(75964) 409.560.5453
call re: fees

The Fredonia Hotel ($$)
200 N Fredonia St
(75961) 409.564.1234

● Navasota ●
Best Western ($)
818 Hwy 6 Loop
(77868) 409.825.7775
1 small pet/room w/fee

● Nederland ●
Best Western ($$)
200 Memorial Hwy 69
(77627) 409.727.1631

● New Boston ●
Best Western ($$)
1024 N Center St
(75570) 903.628.6999

● New Braunfels ●
Camp Huaco Cabins ($)
1405 Gruene Rd
(78130) 210.625.5411

Holiday Inn ($$$)
1051 I-35
(78130) 210.625.8017
mgr preapproval reqd

Ramada Ltd ($)
815 I-35
(78130) 210.625.6201

Rodeway Inn ($$)
1209 I-35
(78130) 210.629.6991

● Nocona ●
Nocona Hills Motel ($)
100 E Huron Cir
(76255) 817.825.3161

● North Richland Hills ●
La Quinta Inn ($$)
7920 Bedford Euless Rd
(76180) 817.485.2750
call re: fees

Lexington Inn ($$)
8709 Airport Fwy
(76180) 817.656.8881

Motel 6 ($)
7804 Bedford Euless Rd
(76180) 817.485.3000
1 small pet/room

● Odem ●
Days Inn ($)
1505 Voss Ave
(78370) 512.368.2166
$5/pets

● Odessa ●
Best Western ($$)
110 I-20
(79761) 915.337.3006

Classic Suites ($)
3031 I-20 E Business
(79761) 915.333.9678

Days Inn ($$)
3075 E Hwy 80
(79761) 915.335.8000
pets allowed w/small deposit

Econo Lodge ($)
1518 S Grant Ave
(79761) 915.333.1485

Holiday Inn
3001 E Business US20
(79761) 915.333.3931

Holiday Inn ($$)
6201 E Hwy 80
(79762) 915.362.2311
mgr preapproval reqd

La Qunta Inn ($$)
5001 E Hwy 80
(79761) 915.333.2820
call re: fees

Motel 6 ($)
200 E I-20 Service Rd
(79766) 915.333.4025
1 small pet/room

Parkway Inn ($)
3071 E Hwy 80
(79761) 915.332.4242

Super 8 ($)
6713 2-20
(79762) 915.363.8281
small pets only

Villa West Inn ($)
300 I-20
(79760) 915.335.5055

● Orange ●
Best Western ($$)
2630 I-10
(77630) 409.883.6616

Holiday Inn ($$)
2900 I-10
(77630) 409.883.9981
mgr preapproval reqd

Kings Inn Motel ($$)
2208 I-10
(77630) 409.883.6701

Motel 6 ($)
4407 27th St
(77632) 409.883.4891
1 small pet/room

Ramada Inn ($$)
26101 I-10
(77630) 409.993.0231

● Ozona ●
Daystop ($)
820 Loop 466
(76943) 915.392.2631

Flying W Lodge ($)
8 -11th St
(76943) 915.392.2656

● Palestine ●
Best Western ($$)
1601 W Palestine Ave
(75801) 903.723.4655
small pets

Days Inn ($$)
1100 E Palestine Ave
(75801) 903.729.3151

● Panhandle ●
S&S Motor Inn ($)
Rt 2 Box# 58
(79068) 806.537.5111

● Paris ●
Best Western ($)
3755 NE Loop 286
(75460) 903.785.5566
pets must be on leash

Days Inn ($)
2650 N Main St
(75460) 903.784.8164

Holiday Inn ($$)
3560 NE Loop 286
(75460) 903.785.5545
mgr preapproval reqd

Victorian Inns ($)
425 35th St NE
(75460) 903.785.3871

● Pasadena ●
Econo Lodge ($$)
823 W Pasadena Fwy
(77506) 713.477.4266

Ramada Inn ($$)
114 Richey St
(77506) 713.477.6871

● Pearsall ●
Executive Inn ($)
613 N Oak St
(78061) 210.334.3693

● Pecos ●
Best Western ($)
900 Palmer St
(79772) 915.447.2215
1 small pet

Motel 6 ($)
3002 S Cedar St
(79772) 915.445.9034
1 small pet/room

342

$=under $35 $$=$35-60 $$$=$60-100 $$$$=over $100

● Plainview ●
Best Western ($$)
600 2-27
(79072) 806.293.9454
small pets only

Days Inn ($)
3600 Olton Rd
(79072) 806.293.2561

Holiday Inn ($$)
4005 Olton Rd
(79072) 806.293.4181
mgr preapproval reqd

● Plano ●
Best Western ($$$)
640 E Park Blvd
(75074) 214.578.2243

Comfort Inn ($$)
621 E Central Pkwy
(75074) 972.424.5568
small pets only

Harvey Hotel ($$)
1600 N Central Expwy
(75074) 214.578.8555

La Quinta inn ($$)
1820 N Central Expwy
(75074) 214.423.1300
call re: fees

Motel 6 ($)
2550 N Central Expwy
(75074) 214.578.1626
1 small pet/room

● Port Aransas ●
Beachgate Condos ($)
2000 On The Beach
(78373) 512.749.6138

Executive Keys ($$)
820 Access Rd 1A
(78373) 512.749.6272

Harbor View Motel ($)
121 W Cotter Ave
(78373) 512.749.6391

Paradise Isle Motel ($$)
314 Cut Off Rd
(78373) 512.749.6993

Rock Cottages ($$)
603 E Avenue G
(78373) 512.749.6360

Sea Horse Lodge ($$$)
503 E Avenue G
(78373) 512.749.5513

Sea&Sands Cottages ($$)
410 10th St
(78373) 512.749.5191

Seaside Motel ($$)
500 Sandcastle Dr
(78373) 512.749.4105

Sunday Villas ($$$)
1900 S 11th St
(78373) 512.749.6480

Tropic Island Motel ($$)
315 Cut Off Rd
(78373) 512.749.6128

● Port Arthur ●
Ramada Inn ($$)
3801 Hwy 73
(77642) 409.962.9858
small pets only

● Port Isabel ●
Southwind Inn ($)
600 E Davis St
(78578) 210.943.3392

Yacht Club Hotel ($)
700 Yturria St
(78578) 210.943.1301

● Port Lavaca ●
Days Inn ($$)
2100 N Byp 35
(77979) 512.552.4511

● Portland ●
Comfort Inn ($$)
1703 N Hwy 181
(78374) 512.643.2222
mgr preapproval reqd

● Quanah ●
Quanah Parker Inn ($)
1405 W 11th St
(79252) 817.663.6366

● Queen City ●
Days Inn ($)
301 Hwy 59
(75572) 903.796.7191

● Ranger ●
Days Inn ($$)
I-20 Ex 349 Box# 160C
(76470) 817.647.1176

● Richardson ●
Clarion Hotel ($$)
1981 N Central Expwy
(75080) 972.644.4000

Hawthorn Suites ($$$)
250 Municipal Dr
(75080) 214.669.1000

Omni Hotel ($$$)
701 E Campbell Rd
(75081) 214.231.9600

Sleep Inn ($$)
2650 N Central Expwy
(75080) 972.470.9440

● Richmond ●
Executive Inn ($)
26035 Southwest Fwy
(77469) 713.342.5387

● Roanoke ●
Marriott Hotel ($$)
5 Village Cir
(76262) 817.430.3848

● Robstown ●
Days Inn ($)
320 S Hwy 77
(78380) 512.387.9416

Econo Lodge ($$)
2225 Hwy 77
(78380) 512.387.9444

● Rockport ●
Anchor Motel ($$)
1204 E Market St
(78382) 512.729.3249

Bay Front Cottages ($$)
309 S Fulton Beach Rd
(78382) 512.729.6693

Days Inn ($$)
1212 E Laurel St
(78382) 512.729.6379
small pet only

Del Camino Motel ($$$)
1009 I-35
(78382) 512.729.2510

Holiday Lodge Motel ($)
1406 I-35
(78382) 512.729.3433

Hunts Court Motel ($$)
901 S Water St
(78382) 512.729.2273

Key Allegro Rentals ($$$$)
1798 Bayshores
(78382) 512.729.2333

Laguna Reef Motel ($$)
1021 S Water St
(78382) 512.729.1742

Las Brizas Motel ($)
1151 I-35
(78382) 512.729.9112

Ocean View Motel ($)
1131 S Water St
(78382) 512.729.3326

Pelican Motel ($$)
1011 E Market St
(78382) 512.729.3837

Rockporter Inn ($$)
813 S Church St
(78382) 512.729.9591

Rod And Reel Motel ($)
1105 E Market St
(78382) 512.729.2028

Sandollar Motel ($$)
HC 1 Box# 30
(78382) 512.729.2381

Sandra Bay Cottages ($$)
1801 Broadway St
(78382) 512.729.6257

Sun Tan Motel ($$)
1805 Broadway St
(78382) 512.729.2179

$=under $35 $$=$35-60 $$$=$60-100 $$$$=over $100

Sunset Inn ($)
800 S Church St
(78382) 512.729.4792

● Rockwall ●
Lailias Pet B&B
2411 Rochell Rd
(75087) 214.771.5049
referred

● Rosenberg ●
Best Western ($)
28382 Southwest Fwy
(77471) 713.342.6000
small pets

● Round Rock ●
La Quinta Inn ($$)
2004 I-35
(78681) 512.255.4437
call re: fees

● San Angelo ●
Best Western ($$)
415 W Beauregard Ave
(76903) 915.653.2995
small pets

Days Inn ($)
4613 S Jackson St
(76903) 915.658.6594

El Patio Motel ($)
1901 W Beauregard Ave
(76901) 915.655.5711

Hampton Inn ($$$)
2959 Loop 306
(76904) 915.942.9622

Holiday Inn ($$)
441 Rio Concho Dr
(76903) 915.658.2828
mgr preapproval reqd

Inn Of The Conchos ($$)
2021 N Bryant Blvd
(76903) 915.658.2811

La Quinta Inn ($$)
2307 Loop 306
(76904) 915.949.0515
call re: fees

Motel 6 ($)
311 N Bryant Blvd
(76903) 915.658.8061
1 small pet/room

Ole Coach Motor Inn ($)
4205 S Bryant Blvd
(76903) 915.653.6966

Santa Fe Jct Motel ($)
410 W Avenue L
(76903) 915.655.8101

Super 8 ($$)
1601 S Bryant Blvd
(76903) 915.653.1323
call re: fees

● San Antonio ●
Aloha Inn ($)
1435 Austin Hwy
(78209) 210.828.0933

Best Western ($$)
6815 Hwy 90
(78227) 210.675.9690

Best Western ($$)
6855 NW Loop 410
(78238) 210.520.8080
small pets only

Best Western ($$)
13535 I-10
(78249) 210.697.9761
small pet/room

Coachman Inn ($$)
3180 Gollard Rd
(78223) 210.337.7171

Comfort Inn ($$)
4403 I-10
(78219) 210.333.9430
mgr preapproval reqd

Comfort Inn ($$)
4 Plano Pl
(78229) 210.684.8606
mgr preapproval reqd

Comfort Suites ($$)
6530 I-35
(78218) 210.646.6600
mgr preapproval reqd

Comfort Suites ($$$)
14202 US 281
(78232) 210.494.9000

Days Inn ($$)
11202 I-35
(78233) 210.655.4311

Days Inn ($)
439 E Houston St
(78205) 210.333.9100

Days Inn ($)
3443 I-35
(78219) 210.225.4521

Drury Inn ($$)
8300 I-35
(78239) 210.654.1144

Drury Inn ($$$)
8811 Jones Maltsberger Rd
(78216) 210.308.8100

Embassy Suites ($$$$)
10110 Hwy 281
(78216) 210.525.9999

Executive Guesthouse ($$$)
12828 Hwy 281
(78216) 210.494.7600

Family Gardens Suites ($$$)
2383 NE Loop 410
(78217) 210.599.4204

Hampton Inn ($$$)
8818 Jones
(78216) 210.366.1800

Hampton Inn ($$$)
4900 Crestwind Dr
(78239) 210.657.1107

Hawthorn Suites ($$$)
4041 Bluemel Rd
(78240) 210.561.9660

Hilton ($$$$)
611 NW Loop 410
(78216) 210.340.6060

Hilton ($$$$)
200 S Alamo St
(78205) 210.222.1400
small pets only

Holiday Inn
320 Bonham
(78205) 210.225.6500

Holiday Inn
11939 N I-35
(78233) 210.599.0999

Holiday Inn ($$$)
318 W Durango Blvd
(78204) 210.225.3211
mgr preapproval reqd

Holiday Inn ($$$)
95 NE Loop 410
(78216) 210.308.6700
mgr preapproval reqd

Holiday Inn ($$)
3855 I-35
(78219) 210.226.4361
mgr preapproval reqd

Holiday Inn ($$$$)
217 N Saint Marys St
(78205) 210.224.2500
mgr preapproval reqd

Howard Johnson ($)
9603 I-35
(78233) 210.655.2120

Hyatt Hotel ($$$$)
9800 Hyatt Resort Dr
(78251) 210.647.1234

Hyatt Hotel ($$$$)
123 Losoya St
(78205) 210.222.1234

La Mansion Del Rio ($$$$)
112 College St
(78205) 210.225.2581

La Quinta Inn ($$$)
333 NE Loop 410
(78216) 210.828.0781
call re: fees

La Quinta Inn ($$)
219 NE Loop 410
(78216) 210.342.4291
call re: fees

La Quinta Inn ($$$)
1001 E Commerce St
(78205) 210.222.9181
call re: fees

La Quinta Inn ($$$)
7134 NW Loop 410
(78238) 210.680.8883
call re: fees

$=under $35 $$=$35-60 $$$=$60-100 $$$$=over $100

La Quinta Inn ($$)
6511 W Military Dr
(78227) 210.674.3200
call re: fees

La Quinta Inn ($$$)
900 Dolorosa
(78207) 210.271.0001
call re: fees

La Quinta Inn ($$$)
12822 I-35
(78233) 210.657.5500
call re: fees

La Quinta Inn ($$)
5922 NW Expwy
(78201) 210.734.7931
call re: fees

La Quinta Inn ($$)
64101 I-35
(78218) 210.653.6619
call re: fees

La Quinta Inn ($$)
9542 I-10
(78230) 210.593.0338
call re: fees

Marriott Hotel ($$$$)
101 Bowie St
(78205) 210.233.1000

Marriott Hotel ($$$$)
711 E River Walk St
(78205) 210.224.4555

Motel 6 ($)
138 NW White Rd
(78219) 210.333.1850
1 small pet/room

Motel 6 ($)
16500 2-10
(78257) 210.697.0731
1 small pet/room

Motel 6 ($)
5522 N Pan Am Expressway
(78218) 210.661.8791
1 small pet/room

Motel 6 ($)
95031 I-35
(78233) 210.650.4419
1 small pet/room

Motel 6 ($)
4621 Rittiman Rd
(78218) 210.665.8088
1 small pet/room

Motel 6 ($$)
9400 Wurzbach Rd
(78240) 210.593.0013
1 small pet/room

Motel 6 ($$)
211 N Pecos
(78207) 210.225.1111
1 small pet/room

Motel 6 ($)
2185 SW Loop 410
(78227) 210.673.9020
1 small pet/room

Oak Motor Lodge ($)
150 Humphrey Ave
(78209) 210.826.6368

Pear Tree Inn ($$$)
143 NE Loop 410
(78216) 210.366.4300

Plaza San Antonio ($$$$)
555 S Alamo St
(78205) 210.229.1000
small pets only

Quality Inn ($$)
3817 N Pam Am Expwy
(78219) 210.224.3030
mgr preapproval reqd

Ramada Inn ($$$)
1111 NE Loop 410
(78209) 210.828.9031
one small pet seasonal rates

Ramada Ltd ($$)
6370 I-35
(78218) 210.646.6336
size limits & fees

Relay Station Motel ($)
5530 I-10
(78219) 210.662.6691

Residence Inn ($$$$)
628 S Santa Rosa
(78204) 210.231.6000

Residence Inn ($$$)
1014 NE Loop 410
(78209) 210.805.8118

Rodeway Inn ($$)
900 N Main Ave
(78212) 210.223.2951

Rodeway Inn ($$)
6804 NW Expwy
(78201) 210.734.7111

Rodeway Inn ($$)
1500 I-35
(78204) 210.271.3334
small with $20 deposit

Rodeway Inn ($$)
19793 I-10
(78257) 210.698.3991

Scotsman Inn East ($$)
211 N Ww White Rd
(78219) 210.359.7268

Seven Oaks Resort ($$)
1400 Austin Hwy
(78209) 210.824.5371

Shoneys Inn ($$)
8600 Jones Maltsberger Rd
(78216) 210.342.1400

St Anthony Hotel ($$$$)
300 E Travis St
(78205) 210.227.4392

Super 8 ($)
11027 I-35
(78233) 210.637.1022
call re: fees

Super 8 ($$)
5336 Wurzbach Rd
(78238) 210.520.0888
call re: fees

Super 8 ($$)
3617 N Pan Am
(78219) 210.227.8888
mgr preapproval reqd

Super 8 ($$)
5319 Casa Bella
(78249) 210.696.6916
mgr preapproval reqd

Terrell Castle Inn ($$)
950 E Grayson St
(78208) 210.271.9145

Thrifty Inn ($$)
9806 I-10
(78230) 210.696.0810

La Quinta Inn South ($$)
7202 S Pan American Expwy
(78224) 210.922.2111
call re: fees

● San Marcos ●
Days Inn ($)
1005 I-35
(78666) 512.353.5050

Executive House ($)
1433 I-35
(78666) 512.353.7770

Holiday Inn ($$)
108 I-35
(78666) (800)HOLIDAY

Homeplace Inn ($$)
1429 I-35
(78666) 512.396.0400

La Quinta Inn ($$$)
1619 I-35
(78666) 512.392.8800
call re: fees

Motel 6 ($)
1321 I-35
(78666) 512.396.8705
1 small pet/room

Rodeway Inn ($)
801 I-35
(78666) 512.353.1303

● Sanderson ●
Desert Air Motel ($)
Box# 326
(79848) 915.345.2572

● Schulenburg ●
Oakridge Motel ($$)
Box# 43
(78956) 409.743.4192

● Sealy ●
Rodeway Inn ($)
2021 Meyer St
(77474) 409.885.7407

TEXAS, Seguin

● Seguin ●
Econo Lodge ($)
3013 N Hwy 123 Byp
(78155) 210.372.3990

● Seminole ●
Seminole Inn ($)
2000 Hobbs Hwy
(79360) 915.758.9881

● Shamrock ●
Best Western ($$)
301 I-40
(79079) 806.256.2106

Econo Lodge ($)
1006 E 12th St
(79079) 806.256.2111

The Western Motel ($)
104 E 12th St
(79079) 806.256.3244

● Sherman ●
Best Western ($$)
2105 Texoma Pkwy
(75090) 903.892.2161
$20 deposit

Crossroads Inn ($)
2424 Texoma Pkwy
(75090) 903.893.0184

Economy Inn ($)
1530 Texoma Pkwy
(75090) 903.893.7666

Holiday Inn ($$)
3605 S Hwy 75
(75090) 903.868.0555
mgr preapproval reqd

Sherwood Inn ($$)
401 S Sam Rayburn Fwy
(75090) 903.893.6581

● Snyder ●
Purple Sage Motel ($)
1501 E Coliseum Dr
(79549) 915.573.5491

Willow Park Inn ($$)
1137 E Hwy 180 & 84
(79549) 915.573.1961

● Sonora ●
Devils River Motel ($)
1312 N Service Rd
(76950) 915.387.3516

Holiday Host Motel ($)
Hwy 290
(76950) 915.387.2532

Twin Oaks Motel ($)
907 N Crockett Ave
(76950) 915.387.2551

● South Padre Island ●
Best Western ($$)
5701 Padre Blvd
(78597) 210.761.4913
$25 deposit

Castaways ($$$)
3700 Gulf Blvd
(78597) 210.761.1903

Continental ($$$)
4908 Gulf Blvd
(78597) 210.761.1306

Days Inn ($$)
3913 Padre Blvd
(78597) 210.761.7831
$25 fee for pets

La International ($$$)
5008 Gulf Blvd
(78597) 210.761.1306

Motel 6 ($$)
4013 Padre Blvd
(78597) 210.761.7911
1 small pet/room

Palms Resort ($$)
3616 Gulf Blvd
(78597) 210.761.1316

Radisson Inn ($$$)
500 Padre Blvd
(78597) 210.761.6511
small cats & dogs

Sand Castle Motel ($$)
200 W Kingfish St
(78597) 210.761.1321

Service 24 Condos ($$$)
108 W Pompano St
(78597) 210.761.1487

The Tiki Hotel ($$$)
6608 Padre Blvd
(78597) 210.761.2694

● Spring ●
La Quinta Inn ($$)
286731 I-45
(77381) 713.367.7722
call re: fees

Motel 6 ($)
19606 Cypresswood Ct
(77388) 713.350.6400
1 small pet/room

Red Roof Inn ($$)
24903 I-45
(77380) 713.367.5040

The Woodlands Resort
($$$$)
2301 N Millbend Dr
(77380) 713.367.1100

● Stafford ●
La Quinta Inn ($$)
12727 Southwest Fwy
(77477) 713.240.2300
call re: fees

● Stephenville ●
Best Western ($$)
1625 W South Loop
(76401) 817.968.2114
pets @ mgrs discretion

Days Inn ($)
701 S Loop
(76401) 817.968.3392

Holiday Inn ($$)
2865 W Washington St
(76401) 817.968.5256
mgr preapproval reqd

● Sugar Land ●
Shoneys Inn
14444 Southwest Fwy
(77478) 713.565.6655

● Sulphur Springs ●
Holiday Inn ($$)
1495 Industrial Dr
(75482) 915.236.6887
mgr preapproval reqd

● Sweetwater ●
Best Western ($$)
701 SW Georgia Ave
(79556) 915.235.4853

Holiday Inn ($$)
500 NW Georgia Ave
(79556) 915.236.6887
mgr preapproval reqd

Motel 6 ($)
510 NW Georgia Ave
(79556) 915.235.4387
1 small pet/room

Ranch House Motel ($)
301 SW Georgia Ave
(79556) 915.236.6341

● Temple ●
Best Western ($$)
2625 S 31st St
(76504) 817.778.5511

Econo Lodge ($)
1001 N General Bruce Dr
(76504) 817.771.1688

Fairfield Inn ($$)
1402 SW H K Dodgen
(76504) 817.771.3030

Hampton Inn ($$)
1414 SW H K Dodgen
(76504) 817.778.6700

La Quinta Inn ($$)
1604 W Barton Ave
(76504) 817.771.2980
call re: fees

Motel 6 ($)
1100 N General Bruce Dr
(76504) 817.778.0272
1 small pet/room

Rodeway Inn ($$)
400 H K Dodgen
(76504) 817.773.1515

Super 8 ($)
5505 S General Bruce Dr
(76502) 817.778.0962
call re: fees

● Terlingua ●
Big Ben Motor Inn ($$)
Box# 336
(79852) 915.371.2218

Chisos Mining Co Motel ($)
Box# 228
(79852) 915.371.2254

Lajitas ($$)
HC 70 Box# 400
(79852) 915.424.3471

● Terrell ●
Best Western ($$)
309 I-20
(75160) 214.563.2676
1 small pet allowed

Days Inn ($$)
1618 Hwy 34
(75160) 214.551.1170

● Texarkana ●
Comfort Inn ($$)
5105 N State Line Ave
(75503) 903.792.6688
mgr preapproval reqd

Holiday Inn ($$)
5401 N State Line Ave
(75503) 903.792.3366
mgr preapproval reqd

La Quinta Inn ($$)
5201 N State Line Ave
(75503) 501.794.1900
call re: fees

La Quinta Inn ($$)
5201 N State Line Ave
(75503) 903.794.1900
call re: fees

Motel 6 ($)
1924 Hampton Rd
(75503) 903.793.1413
1 small pet/room

Ramada Inn ($$)
I-30 & Summerhill Rd
(75503) 501.794.3131

Sheraton Inn ($$)
5301 N State Line Ave
(75503) 501.792.3222

Shoneys Inn ($$)
5210 N State Line Ave
(75504) 501.772.0070

● Texas City ●
Hampton Inn ($$)
2320 Fm 2004 Rd
(77591) 409.986.6686

La Quinta Inn ($$)
1121 Hwy 146
(77590) 409.948.3101
call re: fees

● Three Rivers ●
Nolan Ryans Bass Inn ($$)
HC 71 Box# 390
(78071) 512.786.3521

● Tomball ●
Best Western ($$)
30130 State Hwy 249
(77375) 713.351.9700

● Tulia ●
Best Western ($$)
RR 1 Box# 60
(79088) 806.995.2738

● Tyler ●
Best Western ($$)
2828 W Northwest Loop 323
(75702) 903.595.2681
small with fee

Days Inn ($$)
3300 Mineola Hwy
(75702) 903.595.2451

Econo Lodge ($)
3209 W Gentry Pkwy
(75702) 903.593.0103
$2 per pet

Fairfield Inn ($$)
1945 W Southwest Loop 323
(75701) 903.561.2535

Holiday Inn ($$)
3310 Troup Hwy
(75701) 903.593.3600
mgr preapproval reqd

● Van Horn ●
Holiday Inn
1905 SW Frontage Rd
(79855) 915.283.7444

Howard Johnson ($)
Box# 776
(79855) 915.283.2780

Rodeway Inn ($)
1805 W Broadway
(79855) 915.283.2992

Super 8 ($$)
1807 E Service Rd
(79855) 915.283.2282
deposit

● Vega ●
Best Western ($$)
1800 Vega Blvd
(79092) 806.267.2131
small cats & dogs only

● Vernon ●
Best Western ($$)
1615 Expressway
(76384) 817.552.5417
small pets only

Days Inn ($$)
3110 Expwy
(76384) 817.552.9982

Econo Lodge ($$)
4100 Hwy 287 NW
(76384) 817.553.3384

Greentree Inn ($)
3029 Morton St
(76384) 817.552.5421

Super 8 ($)
1829 Exp Hwy 287
(76384) 817.552.9321
$20 dep $5 per pet

Western Motel ($)
715 Wilbarger St
(76384) 817.552.2531

● Victoria ●
Fairfield Inn ($$)
7502 N Navarro St
(77904) 512.582.0660

Hampton Inn ($$)
3112 E Houston Hwy
(77901) 512.578.2030

Holiday Inn ($$)
2705 Houston Hwy
(77901) 512.575.0251
mgr preapproval reqd

La Quinta Inn ($$)
7603 N Navarro St
(77904) 512.572.3585
call re: fees

Motel 6 ($)
3716 Houston Hwy
(77901) 512.573.1273
1 small pet/room

Ramada Inn ($$)
3901 Houston Hwy
(77901) 512.578.2723
very samll

● Waco ●
Best Western ($$)
I-35 & 4th St
(76703) 817.753.0316

Econo Lodge ($)
500 I-35
(76704) 817.756.5371

Hilton ($$$)
113 S University Parks Dr
(76701) 817.754.8484
small notify with advance
reservation

Holiday Inn ($$)
1001 Lake Brazos Dr
(76704) 817.753.0261
mgr preapproval reqd

La Quinta Inn ($$)
1110 S 9th St
(76706) 817.752.9741
call re: fees

Motel 6 ($)
3120 Jack Kultgen Frwy
(76706) 817.662.4622
1 small pet/room

Motel 6 ($)
1509 Hogan Ln
(76705) 817.799.4967
1 small pet/room

TEXAS, Waco

Ramada Inn ($$)
4201 Franklin Ave
(76710) 817.772.9440

Riverplace Inn ($)
101 I-35
(76704) 817.752.8333

● Waxahachie ●
Comfort Inn ($$)
200 N I-35
(75165) 972.937.4202

Ramada Ltd ($)
795 S I-35
(75165) 214.937.4982

Travelodge ($$)
803 S I-35
(75165) 214.937.8223

● Weatherford ●
Best Western ($$)
1927 Santa Fe Dr
(76086) 817.594.7401
small pets

Comfort Inn ($$)
809 Palo Pinto St
(76086) 817.599.8683
mgr preapproval reqd

Super 8 ($$)
111 I-20
(76087) 817.594.8702
call re: fees

● Webster ●
Motel 6 ($)
1001 W Nasa Blvd
(77598) 713.332.4581
1 small pet/room

● West Columbia ●
Homeplace Inn ($$)
714 S Columbia Dr
(77486) 409.345.2399

● Wharton ●
Homeplace Inn ($$)
1808 Fm 102 Rd
(77488) 409.532.1152

● Wichita Falls ●
Best Western ($)
1601 8th St
(76301) 817.322.1182
small pets only

Days Inn ($$)
1211 Central Expwy
(76305) 817.723.5541
$5/pets

Fairfield Inn ($$)
4414 Westgate Dr
(76307) 817.691.1066

La Quinta Inn ($$)
1128 Central Fwy
(76305) 817.322.6971
call re: fees

La Quinta Inn ($$)
4414 Westgate Dr
(76307) 817.322.6971
call re: fees

Motel 6 ($)
1812 Maurine St
(76304) 817.322.8817
1 small pet/room

Sheraton Inn ($$)
100 Central Fwy
(76305) 817.761.6000
$5 fee

● Wimberley ●
7A Ranch ($$)
333 Wayside Dr
(78676) 512.847.2517

● Winnie ●
Best Western ($$)
46310 I-10
(77665) 409.296.9292
deposit

● Woodville ●
Woodville Inn ($)
201 N Magnolia St
(75979) 409.283.3741

● Woodway ●
Best Western ($$)
6624 W Hwy 84
(76712) 817.776.3194
small pets

Fairfield Inn ($$)
5805 Woodway Dr
(76712) 817.776.7821

● Zapata ●
Best Western ($)
HC 1 Box# 252
(78076) 210.765.8403

Falcon Executive ($$)
Box# 686
(78076) 210.765.6982

Policies Subject to Change

Be Discreet

Well Behaved

CALL AHEAD!

$=under $35 $$=$35-60 $$$=$60-100 $$$$=over $100

Utah

● Altamont ●
Moon Lake Resort ($$)
Box# 70
(84001) 801.454.3475

● Beaver ●
Beaver Lodge
Box# 406
(84713) 801.438.2462

Best Western ($$)
161 S Main
(84713) 801.438.2438
managers discretion

Best Western ($$)
1451 N 300
(84713) 801.438.2455

Country Inn ($$)
1450 N 300
(84713) 801.438.2484

Delano Motel ($)
480 N Main St
(84713) 801.438.2418

Granada Inn ($$)
Box# K
(84713) 801.438.2292

Pace Mansfield Motel ($$)
Box# 777
(84713) 801.438.2410

● Bicknell ●
Aquarius Motel ($)
240 W Main St
(84715) 801.425.3835

Capitol Reef Inn ($$)
Box# 100
(84715) 801.425.3271

Sunglow Motel ($)
63 E Main St
(84715) 801.425.3821

● Big Water ●
Warm Creek Motel ($$)
Box# 410004
(84741) 801.675.9199

● Blanding ●
Best Western ($$)
88 E Center St
(84511) 801.678.2278
pets must be attended

● Bluff ●
Burchs Trading Co ($$)
Box# 310
(84512) 801.683.2221

Kokopelli Inn ($$)
Hwy 191
(84512) 801.672.2322

Recapture Lodge ($$)
Box# 309
(84512) 801.672.2281

Sunset Inn ($$)
88 W Center Box# 119-3
(84512) 801.723.8511

● Boulder ●
Boulder Mtn Lodge ($$)
Box# 1397
(84716) 801.335.7460

Boulder Mtn Ranch ($$)
Box# 1373
(84716) 801.335.7480

Circle Cliffs Motel ($$)
Box# 1399
(84716) 801.335.7353

● Brigham City ●
Bushnell Lodge ($$)
115 E 700
(84302) 801.723.8575

Crystal Inn ($$$)
480 Westland Dr
(84302) 801.723.0440

Howard Johnson ($$)
1167 S Main St
(84302) 801.723.8511

● Bryce ●
Best Western ($$)
Hwy 63 Box# 1
(84764) 801.834.5341
pets with advanced notice

● Bryce Canyon ●
Pink Cliffs Village ($$$)
13550 E Hwy 12
(84717) 801.834.5351

● Castle Dale ●
Village Inn Motel ($$)
Box# 1244
(84513) 801.381.2309

● Cedar City ●
Astro Budget Inn ($)
323 S Main St
(84720) 801.586.6557

Comfort Inn ($)
250 N 1100
(84720) 801.586.2082
mgr preapproval reqd

Economy Hotel ($)
443 S Main St
(84720) 801.586.4461

Holiday Inn ($$)
1575 W 200
(84720) 801.586.8888
mgr preapproval reqd

Raycap Motel ($)
2555 N Main St
(84720) 801.586.7435

Rodeway Inn ($$)
281 S Main St
(84720) 801.586.9916

Super 8 ($$)
145 N 1550
(84720) 801.586.8880
call re: fees

Valu Inn ($)
344 S Main St
(84720) 801.586.9114

● Circleville ●
The Bunkhouse ($$)
Box# 85
(84723) 801.577.2522

● Clearfield ●
Super 8 ($$)
572 Main
(84015) 801.825.8000
w/permission

● Delta ●
Best Western ($$)
527 Topaz Blvd
(84624) 801.864.3882
deposit required

Budget Motel ($)
75 S 350
(84624) 801.864.4533

● Draper ●
Econo Lodge ($$)
12605 Minuteman Dr
(84020) 801.571.1122

● Duchesne ●
Rio Damian Motel ($$$$)
23 W Main St
(84021) 801.738.2217

● Duck Creek Village ●
Duck Creek Inn ($$)
Box# 1149
(84762) 801.682.2568

Meadeau View Lodge ($$)
Box# 1331
(84762) 801.682.2495

Whispering Pines ($$$)
116 Color Country Rd
(84762) 801.682.2378

● Dutch John ●
Red Canyon Lodge ($$$)
790 Red Canyon Rd
(84023) 801.889.3759

● Echo ●
Kozy Motel ($)
24 Echo Main St
(84024) 801.336.5641

● Ephraim ●
Iron Horse Motel ($$)
670 N Main St # 226
(84627) 801.283.4223

Travel Inn Motel ($$)
330 N Main St
(84627) 801.283.4071

● Escalante ●
Circle D Motel ($$)
475 W Main St
(84726) 801.826.4297

Quiet Falls Motel ($$)
75 S 100 W 84726
(84726) 801.826.4250

● Fairview ●
Skyline Motel ($$)
236 N State St
(84629) 801.427.3312

CALL AHEAD!

$=under $35 $$=$35-60 $$$=$60-100 $$$$=over $100

● Fillmore ●
Best Western ($$)
1025 N Main St
(84631) 801.743.6895
small pets allowed

Fillmore Motel ($)
61 N Main St
(84631) 801.743.5454

Spinning Wheel ($)
65 S Main St
(84631) 801.743.6260

● Garden City ●
Bear Lake Motel ($$)
50 S Bear Lake Blvd
(84028) 801.946.3271

Blue Water Resort ($$$)
2126 S Bear Lake Blvd
(84028) 801.946.3333

Harbor Village ($$$)
900 N Bear Lake Blvd
(84028) 801.946.3448

● Green River ●
Budget Host ($)
395 E Main
(84525) 801.561.3406
$5

Budget Inn ($)
60 E Main
(84525) 801.564.3441

Mancos Rose Motel ($$)
20 W Main
(84525) 801.564.9660

Motel 6 ($)
946 E Main
(84525) 801.564.3436
1 small pet/room

National 9 ($$)
456 W Main
(84525) 801.564.8237

● Hanksville ●
Poor Boy Motel ($$)
264 E 100
(84734) 801.542.3471

● Hatch ●
Galaxy Motel ($$)
216 N Main
(84735) 801.735.4327

Mt Ridge Motel ($$)
106 S Main
(84735) 801.735.4258

New Bryce Motel ($$)
227 W Main
(84735) 801.735.4265

Riverside Motel ($)
Box# 521
(84735) 801.735.4223

● Heber City ●
Danish Viking Lodge ($$)
999 S Main St
(84032) 801.654.2202

Hy Lander Motel ($)
425 S Main St
(84032) 801.654.2150

Swiss Alps Inn ($)
167 S Main St
(84032) 801.654.0722

● Huntington ●
Village Inn Motel ($$)
307 S Main
(84528) 801.687.9888

● Huntsville ●
Jackson Fork Inn ($$$)
7345 E 900
(84317) 801.745.0051

● Hurricane ●
Best Western ($$)
280 W State St
(84737) 801.635.4647
small pets $5

Hot Springs ($$)
825 North 800 Hwy
(84737) 801.635.2353

Park Villa Motel ($)
650 W State St
(84737) 801.635.4010

● Junction ●
Junction Motel ($$)
300 S Main
(84740) 801.577.2629

● Kanab ●
A National 9 ($)
79 W Center St
(84741) 801.644.2625

Bunkhouse Motel ($$)
6676 E Hwy 89
(84741) 801.644.8805

Color Country Inn ($$)
1550 S Hwy 89A
(84741) 501.644.2164

Coral Sands Motel ($$)
60 S 100
(84741) 801.644.2616

Highway Host Motel ($$)
Box# 4
(84741) 801.675.3731

K Motel ($$)
330 S 100
(84741) 801.644.2611

Parry Lodge ($$)
89 E Center St
(84741) 801.644.2601
$5 fee

Riding Quail ($)
125 N 300
(84741) 801.644.2639

Shilo Inn ($$$)
296 W 100
(84741) 801.644.2562
call re: fees

Sun N Sand Motel ($$)
347 S 100
(84741) 801.644.5050

The Four Seasons ($$)
36 N 300
(84741) 801.644.2635

Treasure Trail Motel ($$)
150 W Center St
(84741) 801.644.2687

● Koosharem ●
Grass Valley Motel ($$)
Box# 440071
(84744) 801.638.7322

● Lake Powell ●
Defiance House ($$$)
Bullfrog Marina
(84533) 801.684.2233

● Layton ●
La Quinta Inn ($$)
1965 N 1200
(84041) 801.776.6700
call re: fees

Valley View Motel ($$)
1560 N Main St
(84041) 801.825.1632

● Lehi ●
Best Western ($$$)
195 S 850
(84043) 801.768.1400

● Manila ●
Nikis Inn ($)
Box# 340
(84046) 801.784.3117

Vacation Inn ($$)
Hwy 43
(84046) 801.784.3259

● Manti ●
Manti Cntry Village ($$)
145 N Main St
(84642) 801.835.9300

Manti Motel ($$)
445 N Main St
(84642) 801.835.8533

● Marysvale ●
Marysvale Miners Lodge ($$)
315 N Main St
(84750) 801.326.4258

● Mexican Hat ●
River House Inn ($$)
Box# 310252
(84531) 801.672.2217

San Juan Inn ($$)
US 163 Box# 535
(84531) 801.683.2220

● Midvale ●
La Quinta Inn ($$$)
530 Catalpa Rd
(84047) 801.566.3291
call re: fees

Motel 6 ($$)
496 Catalpa Rd
(84047) 801.561.0058
1 small pet/room

● Milford ●
The Station Motel ($$)
485 S 100
(84751) 801.387.2481

● Moab ●
Apache Motel ($)
166 S 400
(84532) 801.259.5755

Arches Inn ($$)
41 W 100
(84532) 801.259.5191

Bowen Motel ($)
169 N Main St
(84532) 801.259.7132

Comfort Suites ($$$)
800 S Main St
(84532) 801.259.5252
mgr preapproval reqd

Entrada Ranch ($$)
Box# 567
(84532) 801.259.5796

Hotel Off Center ($$)
96 E Center St
(84532) 801.259.4244

Kokopelli Lodge ($$)
72 S 100
(84532) 801.259.7615

Moab Valley Inn ($$$)
711 S Main St
(84532) 801.259.4419

Pack Creek Ranch ($$$)
La Sal Pass Rd
(84532) 801.259.5505

Red Stone Inn ($$)
535 S Main St
(84532) 801.259.3500

Rose Tree Inn ($$)
481 Rosetree Ln
(84532) 801.259.4305

Slickrock Cabins ($$)
1301 1/2 N Hwy 191
(84532) 801.259.4152

Sunset Motel ($$)
41 W 100
(84532) 801.259.5192

The Virginian Motel ($)
70 E 200
(84532) 801.259.5951
$4 per day

● Monticello ●
Canyonlands Motel ($)
197 N Main
(84535) 801.587.2266

● Mount Carmel ●
Best Western ($$)
Hwy 9 & 89
(84755) 801.648.2203

Golden Hills Motel ($)
125 E State St
(84755) 801.648.2268

● Nephi ●
Best Western ($$)
1025 S Main St
(84648) 801.623.0642

Safari Hotel ($)
413 S Main St
(84648) 801.623.1071

Starlite Motel ($$)
675 S Main St
(84648) 801.623.1937

Temple View Lodge ($$$)
260 E Main
(84648) 801.623.2047

● North Salt Lake ●
Best Western ($$$)
10695 S Auto Mall Dr
(84054) 801.523.8484

● Ogden ●
Best Western ($)
Big Z Motel
(84401) 801.394.6632

Best Western ($$)
1335 W 12th St
(84404) 801.391.9474

Colonial Motel ($$)
1269 Washington Blvd
(84404) 801.399.5851

Comfort Suites ($$)
1150 W 2150
(84401) 801.621.2545
mgr preapproval reqd

Flying J Inn ($$)
1206 W 21 St St
(84404) 801.393.8644

Millstream ($$)
1450 Washington Blvd
(84404) 801.394.9425

Motel 6 ($)
1455 Washington Blvd
(84404) 801.627.4560
1 small pet/room

Motel 6 ($)
1500 W Riverdale Rd
(84405) 801.627.2880
1 small pet/room

Sleep Inn ($$)
1155 S 1700
(84404) 801.731.6500
mgr preapproval reqd

Super 8 ($$)
1508 W 2100
(84401) 801.731.7100
pets w/permission

Travelodge ($$)
2110 Washington Blvd
(84401) 801.394.4563
$10 fee

Western Colony Inn ($$)
234 24th St
(84401) 801.627.1332

● Orderville ●
Parkway Motel ($$)
74 E State St
(84758) 801.648.2380

Starlite Motel ($$)
Hwy 89
(84758) 801.648.2060

● Panguitch ●
Blue Pine Motel ($)
130 N Main St
(84759) 801.676.8197

Bryce Way Motel ($)
429 N Main St
(84759) 801.676.2400

Cameron Motel ($$)
78 W Center St
(84759) 801.676.8840

Color Country Motel ($)
526 N Main
(84759) 801.676.2386

Deer Trail Lodge ($$)
Box# 647
(84759) 801.676.2211

Horizon Motel ($)
730 N Main St
(84759) 801.676.2651

Marianna Inn Motel ($)
699 N Main
(84759) 801.676.8844

Rustic Lodge ($$)
186 S Westshore Rd
(84759) 801.676.2627

Sands Motel
390 N Main
(84759) 801.676.8874

Sportsmans Cabins
Box# 655
(84759) 801.676.8348

● Park City ●
Best Western ($$$)
6560 N Landmark Dr
(84060) 801.649.7300

Blue Church Lodge ($$$$)
424 Park Ave
(84060) 801.649.8009
small pets $10 per day

Radisson Inn ($$$)
2121 Park Ave
(84060) 801.649.5000
small pets $10 per day

● Parowan ●
Best Western ($$)
580 N Main St
(84761) 801.477.3391

Days Inn ($$)
625 West 200
(84761) 801.477.3326

● Payson ●
Comfort Inn ($$$)
830 N Main St
(84651) 801.465.4861
mgr preapproval reqd

$=under $35 $$=$35-60 $$$=$60-100 $$$$=over $100

UTAH, Pine Valley

● Pine Valley ●
Pine Valley Lodge ($$)
960 E Main St
(84781) 801.574.2544

● Price ●
Budget Host ($$)
145 N Carbondale Rd
(84501) 801.637.2424
$5

Greenwell Inn ($)
655 E Main St
(84501) 801.637.3520

National 9 ($)
641 W Price River Dr
(84501) 801.637.7000
$5 fee

Shaman Lodge ($$$)
3769 W Garden Creek Rd
(84501) 801.637.7489

● Provo ●
Colony Inn Suites ($)
1380 S University Ave
(84601) 801.374.6800

Comfort Inn ($$)
1555 N Canyon Rd
(84604) 801.374.6020
mgr preapproval reqd

Days Inn ($$)
1675 N 200 W # Orth
(84604) 801.375.8600

Hampton Inn ($$$)
1511 S 40
(84606) 801.377.6396

Howard Johnson ($$$)
1292 S University Ave
(84601) 801.374.2500

Motel 6 ($$)
1600 S University Ave
(84601) 801.375.5064
1 small pet/room

Provo Park Hotel ($$$)
101 W 100
(84601) 801.377.4700

Residence Inn
295 W 2230
(84604) 800.331.3131

Sleep Inn ($$)
1505 S 40
(84606) 801.377.6396
mgr preapproval reqd

Uptown Motel ($)
469 W Center St
(84601) 801.373.8248

Valley Inn Motel ($$)
1425 S State St
(84606) 801.377.3804

● Richfield ●
Best Western ($$)
145 S Main St
(84701) 801.896.5481
managers discretion

Budget Host ($)
69 S Main St
(84701) 800.525.9024
limited availability

Days Inn ($$)
333 N Main St
(84701) 801.896.6476

Grand Western Hotel ($$)
575 S Main St
(84701) 801.896.6948

Jensen Motel ($$)
290 S Main St
(84701) 801.896.5447

Montair Motel ($$)
190 S Main St
(84701) 801.896.4415

New West Motel ($$)
447 S Main St
(84701) 801.896.4076

Romanico Inn ($)
1170 S Main St
(84701) 801.896.8471

Weston Inn ($$)
647 S Main St
(84701) 801.896.9271

● Roosevelt ●
Best Western ($$)
RR 2 Box# 2860
(84066) 801.722.4644
small dogs

Frontier Motel ($)
75 S 200 East St
(84066) 801.722.3640

Western Hills Motel ($$)
737 S 200
(84066) 801.722.5115

● Saint George ●
Ancestor Inn ($)
60 W Saint George Blvd
(84770) 801.673.4666

Budget Inn ($$)
1221 S Main St
(84770) 801.673.6661

Desert Edge Inn
525 E Saint George Blvd
(84770) 801.673.6137

Econo Lodge ($$)
460 E Saint George Blvd
(84770) 801.673.4861

Hilton ($$)
145 Hilton Dr
(84770) 801.628.0463

Holiday Inn ($$$)
850 S Bluff St
(84770) 801.628.4235
mgr preapproval reqd

Motel 6 ($)
205 N 1000
(84770) 801.628.7979
1 small pet/room

Sands Motel ($$)
581 E Saint George Blvd
(84770) 801.673.3501

Singletree Inn ($$)
260 E Saint George Blvd
(84770) 801.673.6161

Southside Inn ($$)
750 E Saint George Blvd
(84770) 801.628.9000

Sun Time Inn ($$)
420 E St Goerge Blvd
(84770) 801.673.3232

Super 8 ($$)
915 S Bluff St
(84770) 801.628.4251
pets w/permission

The Bluffs Motel ($$)
1140 Bluff
(84770) 801.628.6699

The Olde Penny Farthing
($$)
278 N 100A
(84770) 801.673.7755

Thunderbird Lodge ($$)
150 N 1000
(84770) 801.673.6123

Travelodge ($)
175 N 1000 East St
(84770) 801.673.4621
no large pets

● Salina ●
Budget Host ($)
75 E 1500
(84654) 801.529.7483
$6

Safari Motel ($)
1425 S State St
(84654) 801.529.7447

The Hideaway ($)
60 N State St
(84654) 801.529.7467
$10 deposit

● Salt Lake City ●
All Star ($$)
754 W North Temple
(84116) 801.531.7300

Colonial Village ($$)
1530 S Main St
(84115) 801.486.8171

Comfort Inn ($$$)
200 Admiral Byrd Rd
(84116) 801.537.7444
mgr preapproval reqd

Continental Motel ($$)
819 W North Temple
(84116) 801.363.4546

Covered Wagon Motel ($$)
230 W North Temple
(84103) 801.533.9100

Days Inn ($$)
1900 W North Temple
(84116) 801.539.8538

Be
Discreet

$=under $35 $$=$35-60 $$$=$60-100 $$$$=over $100

Days Inn ($$)
315 W 33rd
(84115) 801.486.8780
small pets only

Econo Lodge ($$)
715 W North Temple
(84116) 801.363.0062
$20 deposit

Hilton ($$$)
5151 Wiley Post Way
(84116) 801.539.1515
$25 deposit

Hilton ($$$)
150 W 500
(84101) 801.532.3344

Howard Johnson ($$$)
122 W South Temple
(84101) 801.521.0130

Majestic Rockies ($$)
8901 S State
(84111) 801.255.2313

Marriott Hotel ($$$)
75 S West Temple
(84101) 801.531.0800

Motel 6 ($)
1990 W North Temple
(84116) 801.364.1053
1 small pet/room

Motel 6 ($$)
176 W 6th South St
(84101) 801.531.1252
1 small pet/room

Quality Inn ($$)
154 W 600
(84101) 801.521.2930
mgr preapproval reqd

Ramada Inn ($$$)
230 W 600
(84101) 801.364.5200

Red Lion Inn ($$$)
255 S West Temple
(84101) 801.328.2000
call re: fees

Residence Inn ($$$$)
765 E 400
(84102) 801.532.5511
under 25 lbs & pet fee

Reston Hotel ($$)
5335 College Dr
(84123) 801.264.1054

Royal Executive Inn ($$)
121 N 300
(84103) 801.521.3450

Shilo Inn ($$$)
206 S West Temple
(84101) 800.222.2244

Skyline Inn ($$)
2475 E 1700
(84108) 801.582.5350

Sleep Inn ($$)
3440 S 2200
(84119) 801.975.1888
mgr preapproval reqd

Super 8 ($$)
616 S 200
(84101) 801.534.0808
mgr preapproval reqd

Super 8 ($$$)
223 Jimmy Doolittle Rd
(84116) 801.533.8878
call re: fees

Travelodge ($$)
524 S West Temple
(84101) 801.531.7100
always caged

● Scipio ●
Hotel Scipio ($$)
195 N State Box# 75
(84656) 801.758.2450

● South Jordan ●
Super 8 ($$)
10722 S 300
(84095) 801.553.8888
call re: fees

● Spanish Fork ●
Ideal Motel ($$)
150 S Main St
(84660) 801.798.1900

● Springdale ●
Best Western ($$)
1515 Zion Park Blvd
(84767) 801.772.3262
small managers discretion

Canyon Ranch Motel ($$)
668 Zion Park Blvd
(84767) 801.772.3357

Cliffrose Lodge ($$)
281 Zion Park Blvd
(84767) 801.772.3234

El Rio Lodge ($$)
995 Zion Park Blvd
(84767) 801.772.3205

Zion Park Inn ($$)
1215 Zion Park Blvd
(84767) 801.772.3200

● Toquerville ●
Chuck Wagon Lodge ($$)
12 W Main
(84774) 801.425.3335

Luna Mesa Oasis ($$)
Box# 140
(84774) 801.456.9122

Rim Rock Rustic Inn ($$)
Hwy 24 Box# 750264
(84774) 801.425.3843

Torrey Trading Post ($$)
75 W Main St
(84774) 801.425.3716

Your Inn ($$)
650 Spring Dr
(84774) 801.635.9964

● Torrey ●
Capitol Reef Inn ($$)
360 W Main St
(84775) 801.425.3271

● Tremonton ●
Marble Motel ($)
116 N Tremont St
(84337) 801.257.3524

Sandman Motel ($)
585 W Main St
(84337) 801.257.7149

● Tropic ●
Bryce Pioneer Village ($$)
Box# 119
(84776) 801.679.8654

Dougs Country Inn Motel
($$)
141 N Main
(84776) 801.679.8600

World Host Inn ($$)
200 N Main St
(84776) 801.723.8511

● Vernal ●
Econo Lodge ($)
311 E Main St
(84078) 801.789.2000

Rodeway Inn ($$)
590 W Main St
(84078) 801.789.8172

Split Mountain Motel ($$)
1015 E Hwy 40
(84078) 801.789.9020

● Wellington ●
National 9 ($)
50 S 700
(84542) 801.637.7980

● Wendover ●
Heritage Motel ($$)
505 E Wendover
(84083) 801.665.7744

Motel 6 ($)
561 E Wendover
(84083) 801.665.2267
1 small pet/room

Western Ridge Motel ($$)
895 E Wendover
(84083) 801.665.2211

● Woods Cross ●
Hampton Inn ($$$$)
2393 S 800
(84087) 801.296.1211

Motel 6 ($)
2433 S 800
(84087) 801.298.0289
1 small pet/room

Vermont
● Arlington ●
Cutleaf Maple Motel
Rt 7A
(05250) 802.375.2725

$=under $35 $$=$35-60 $$$=$60-100 $$$$=over $100

VERMONT, Arlington

Hill Farm Inn ($$$)
RR 2 Box# 2015
(05250) 802.375.2269

Valhalla Motel
Historia Rt 7A
(05250) 802.375.2212

● Barnet ●
Maplemont Farm ($$$)
RR 5
(05821) 802.633.4880

● Barre ●
Budget Inn ($)
573 N Main St
(05641) 802.479.3333

Hojo Inn ($$)
571 N Main St
(05641) 802.479.3333

Hollow Inn ($$)
278 S Main St
(05641) 802.479.3333

● Barton ●
Pine Crest Motel ($)
RR 1 Box# 279
(05822) 802.525.3472

● Bellows Falls ●
Whippowil Cottage
US Rt 5
(05101) 802.463.3442

● Bennington ●
Appley Valley Inn ($)
Rt 7
(05201) 802.442.6588

Bennington Motor Inn ($$)
143 Main St
(05201) 802.442.5479
$10 fee

Fife N Drum Motel ($)
Rt 7S RR 1 Box# 4340
(05201) 802.442.4074

Knotty Pine Motel ($$)
130 Northside Dr
(05201) 802.442.5487

Pleasant Vly Motel ($$)
Pleasant Valley Rd
(05201) 802.442.6222

Ramada Inn ($$$)
US 7 At Kocher Dr
(05201) 802.442.8145

South Gate Motel ($)
Box# 1073
(05201) 802.447.7525

Vermonter Motel ($$)
RR 1 Box# 2377
(05201) 802.442.2529

● Bethel ●
Greenhurst Inn
River St Rd 2
(05032) 802.234.9474

● Bondville ●
Bromley View Inn ($$)
Rt 30 Box# 161
(05340) 802.297.1459

● Bradford ●
Bradford Motel ($)
Box# 250
(05033) 802.222.4467

● Brandon ●
Brandon Motor Lodge ($$)
Rt 7 South
(05733) 802.247.9594

Gingerbread House ($$)
RR 3 Rt 73E Box# 3241
(05733) 802.247.3380

● Brattleboro ●
Brattleboro Inn ($$$$)
1380 Putney Rd
(05301) 802.254.8701

Colonial Motel ($)
Putney Rd
(05301) 802.257.7733

Molly Stark Motel ($$)
829 Marlboro Rd
(05301) 802.254.2440
small pets only

Motel 6 ($$)
Putney Rd Rt 5N
(05301) 802.254.6007
1 small pet/room

● Bridgewater Corners ●
The Corners Inn ($$)
Rt 4 & Upper Rd
(05035) 802.672.9968

● Bristol ●
Bristol Commons Inn ($$)
Jct 17 & 116
(05443) 802.453.2326

● Brownsville ●
The Pond House ($$$)
Box# 234
(05037) 802.484.0011

● Burlington ●
Super 8 ($)
1016 Shelburne Rd
(05403) 802.862.6421
call re: fees

Town&Country Motel ($)
490 Shelburne Rd
(05401) 802.862.5786

● Canaan ●
Lake Wallace Motel
Rt 114
(05903) 802.266.3311

● Chester ●
Inn At High View ($$$)
East Hill Rd
(05143) 802.875.2724

● Colchester ●
Days Inn ($)
23 College Pkwy
(05446) 802.655.0900

Hampton Inn ($$$)
8 Mountain View Dr
(05446) 802.655.6177

● Craftsbury Common ●
The Inn On The Common
($$$$)
Main St
(05827) 802.586.9619

● Danby ●
Tucker Inn ($$)
RR 1 Box# 100
(05739) 802.293.5835

● Derby ●
The Border Motel ($$)
135 N Main
(05829) 802.766.2088

● Dorset ●
Barrows House ($$$$)
Rt 30
(05251) 802.867.4455

● East Burke ●
Old Cutter Inn ($$)
RR 1 Box# 52
(05832) 802.626.5152

● East Hardwick ●
Brick House Guests ($$)
2 Brick House Rd
(05836) 802.472.5512

● Essex Junction ●
The Wilson Inn ($$$)
10 Kellogg Rd
(05452) 802.879.1515

● Fairlee ●
Silver Maple Inn ($$)
RR 1 Box# 8
(05045) 802.333.4326

● Grafton ●
The Hayes House
Bear Hill Rd
(05146) 802.843.2461

● Jeffersonville ●
Deer Run Motor Inn ($$)
RR 1 Box# 260
(05464) 802.644.8866

The Highlander Motel ($$)
RR 1 Box# 436
(05464) 802.644.2725

The Jefferson House
Box# 288
(05464) 802.644.2030

● Killington ●
Butternut Mtn ($$)
Box# 306
(05751) 802.422.2000

Cedarbrook Motel ($)
US 4 & S R 100
(05751) 802.422.9666

Cortina Inn ($$$$)
US Rte 4
(05751) 802.773.3333

Well
Behaved

$=under $35 $$=$35-60 $$$=$60-100 $$$$=over $100

Cortina Inn ($$$$)
Hcr 34
(05751) 800.451.6108
owner referred

Edelweiss Motel ($$)
US Rt 4
(05751) 802.775.5577

Mendon Mtn Resort ($$)
Rt 4E Box# 32 Hcr
(05751) 802.773.4311

The Cascades Lodge ($$)
RR 1 Box# 2848
(05751) 802.422.3731

● Londonderry ●
White Pine Lodge
Rt 11 West
(05148) 802.824.3909

● Ludlow ●
Cavendish Pointe ($$)
Rt 103
(05149) 802.226.7688

Happy Trails Motel ($$)
Rt 103
(05149) 802.228.8888

The Family Inn ($$$)
953 E Lake Rd
(05149) 802.228.8799

Timber Inn Motel ($$)
RR 1 Box# 1003
(05149) 802.228.8666

● Lyndonville ●
Lynburke Motel ($)
RR 1 Box# 37M
(05851) 802.626.3346

● Manchester ●
Avalanche Motor Lodge ($$)
RR 11
(05254) 802.362.2622

● Manchester Center ●
Brittany Inn Motel ($$)
Rt 7A Box# 760
(05255) 802.362.1033

Wedgewood Motel ($$)
RR 1 Box# 2295
(05255) 802.362.2145

● Marlboro ●
Whetstone Inn ($)
Off Hwy 9
(05344) 802.254.2500

● Middlebury ●
Motel Sugar House ($$)
Rural Rt 7
(05753) 802.388.2770

The Middlebury Inn ($$$)
Court Square
(05753) 802.388.4961
$6fee

● Montpelier ●
Econo Lodge ($$)
101 Northfield St
(05602) 802.223.5258
small pets only

● Newfane ●
Four Columns Inn ($$$)
230 West St
(05345) 802.365.7713

● Newport ●
Top O Hills Motel ($$)
HC 61 Box# 14
(05855) 802.334.2452

● North Springfield ●
The Abby Lyn Motel ($$)
RR 1 Box# 80
(05150) 802.886.2223
2 small or 1 large dog

● Pittsfield ●
Clear River Inn ($$)
Rt 100
(05762) 802.746.7916

● Putney ●
Putney Inn ($$)
Depot Rd
(05346) 802.387.5517

● Richmond ●
Trailside Condos ($$$$)
HC 33 Box# 751
(05477) 802.434.2769

● Rochester ●
Mountainview Inn ($)
RR 1 Box# 53
(05767) 802.767.4273

● Rutland ●
Days Inn ($$)
253 S Main St
(05701) 802.773.3361

Econo Lodge ($$)
RR 4 Box# 7650
(05701) 802.773.6644

Green Mont Motel ($)
138 Main St
(05701) 802.775.2575

Highlander Motel ($$)
203 N Main St
(05701) 802.773.6069

Hojo Inn ($$)
378 S Main St
(05701) 802.775.4303

Holiday Inn ($$$)
411 S Main St
(05701) 802.775.1911
mgr preapproval reqd

Red Clover Country Inn
($$$$)
Woodward Rd
(05701) 802.775.2290
must call ahead

Sunset Motel ($)
238 S Main St
(05701) 802.773.2784

Tyrol Motor Inn ($$)
RR 2 Box# 7602
(05701) 802.773.7485

● Saint Albans ●
Cadillac Motel ($$)
213 Main St
(05478) 802.524.2191

Econo Lodge ($$)
287 S Main St
(05478) 800.424.4777

● Saint Johnsbury ●
Aimes Motel ($)
RR 1 Box# 332
(05819) 802.748.3194

● Saxtons River ●
The Inn At Saxtons River
($$$)
27 Main St
(05154) 802.869.2100

● Shaftsbury ●
Bay Berry Motel ($$)
Rt 7 A Box# 137
(05262) 802.447.7180

Hillbrook Motel ($)
Rt 7 A
(05262) 802.447.7201

Kimberly Cottage ($$)
Box# 345
(05262) 802.442.4354

Serenity Motel ($$)
RR 1 Box# 281
(05262) 802.442.6490

● Sharon ●
Columns Motor Lodge ($$)
Rt 14
(05065) 802.763.7040

● Shelburne ●
Econo Lodge ($$)
1961 Shelburne Rd
(05482) 802.985.3377
$5 charge

● South Burlington ●
Anchorage Inns ($$)
108 Dorset St
(05403) 802.863.7000

Econo Lodge ($$)
1076 Williston Rd
(05403) 802.863.1125
$5 fee

Ethan Allen Motel
1611 Williston Rd
(05403) 802.863.4573

Friendship Inn ($)
1860 Shelburne Rd
(05403) 800.424.6423

Harbor Sunset Motel ($)
1700 Shelburne Rd
(05403) 802.864.5080

Ho Hum ($)
1660 Williston Rd
(05403) 802.863.4551

Holiday Inn ($$$)
1068 Williston Rd
(05403) 802.863.6363
mgr preapproval reqd

VERMONT, South Burlington

Howard Johnson ($$$)
1720 Shelburne Rd
(05403) 802.860.6000

Howard Johnson ($$)
1 Dorset St
(05403) 802.863.5541

Ramada Inn ($$)
1117 Williston Rd
(05403) 802.658.0250

Rodeway Inn ($$)
1860 Shelburne Rd
(05403) 802.862.0230

Sheraton Hotel ($$$)
870 Williston Rd
(05403) 802.865.6600

● South Hero ●
Sandbar Motor Inn ($$)
US Rt 2
(05486) 802.372.6911

● South Londonderry ●
Birkenaus Hotel ($$)
Stratton Mt Rd
(05155) 802.297.2000

Liftline Lodge ($$)
Stratton Mtn Rd
(05155) 802.297.2600

● South Woodstock ●
Kedron Valley Inn ($$$)
Rt 106
(05071) 802.457.1473

● Springfield ●
Holiday Inn
818 Charlestown Rd
(05156) 802.885.4516

Pa Lo Mar Motel ($)
2 Linhale Rd
(05156) 802.885.4142

● Stowe ●
Anderson Lodge ($$)
3430 Mountain Rd
(05672) 802.253.7336

Burgundy Rose Motel ($$)
Rt 100
(05672) 802.253.7768

Commodores Inn ($$)
Rt 100
(05672) 802.253.7131

Golden Kitz Lodge ($)
1965 Mountain Rd
(05672) 802.253.4217

Green Mountain Inn ($$$)
Main St
(05672) 802.253.7301

Hob Knob Inn ($$)
2364 Mountain Rd
(05672) 802.253.8549

Innsbruck Inn ($$)
4361 Mountain Rd
(05672) 802.253.8582

Stowe Away ($$)
3148 Mountain Rd
(05672) 802.253.7574

Mountain Rd Resort ($$)
1007 Mountain Rd
(05672) 802.253.4566

Mountaineer Inn ($)
3343 Mountain Rd
(05672) 802.253.7525

Notch Brook Condos ($$)
1229 Notchbrook Rd
(05672) 802.253.4882

Stowe Inn ($$)
123 Mountain Rd
(05672) 802.253.4836

Stowe Mountain Resort ($$$)
5781 Mountain Rd
(05672) 802.253.3000

Ten Acres Lodge ($$)
14 Barrows Rd
(05672) 802.253.7638

Topnotch Stowe Resort
($$$$)
4000 Mountain Rd
(05672) 802.253.8585
under 30 lbs

Ye Olde England Inne ($$$)
433 Mountain Rd
(05672) 802.253.7558

● Vergennes ●
Harbor Club Resort ($$$$)
Basin Harbor Rd
(05491) 802.475.2311

Whitford House Inn ($$$)
RR 1 Box# 1490
(05491) 802.758.2704

● Waitsfield ●
Millbrook Inn
Rfd Box# 62
(05673) 802.496.2405

The Garrison Hotel ($$)
Box# 539C
(05673) 802.496.2352

Tucker Hill Lodge ($$)
Rt 17 Box# 147
(05673) 802.496.3984

● Warren ●
Golden Lion Inn ($)
Sugarbush Access Rd
(05674) 802.496.3084

Powderhound Resort ($$$$)
Rt 100 Box# 369
(05674) 802.496.5100

Sugarbush Resort
RR 1 Box# 35
(05674) 802.583.3333

Sugarbush Vlg Condos
RR 1 Box# 68-12
(05674) 802.583.3000

● Waterbury ●
Holiday Inn ($$$)
I-89
(05676) 802.244.7822
$30 fee in smoking rooms

● Waterbury Center ●
1836 Cabins ($$$)
128 Stowe Rd
(05677) 802.244.8533

● West Danville ●
Injun Joe Motel ($$)
US Rt 2 Box# 12
(05873) 802.684.3430

● White River Junction ●
Best Western ($$)
Rt 5 I-91 Ex 11
(05001) 802.295.3015

Holiday Inn ($$$)
Holiday Inn Dr
(05001) 802.295.3000
mgr preapproval reqd

Hotel Coolidge
17 S Main St
(05001) 802.295.3118

● Wilder ●
Wilder Motel
319 Hartford Ave
(05088) 802.295.9793

● Williamstown ●
The Autumn Crest Inn ($$$)
RR 1 Box# 1540
(05679) 802.433.6627

● Williston ●
Residence Inn ($$$)
1 Hurricane Ln
(05495) 802.878.2001

● Wilmington ●
Vintage Motel ($)
Rt 9
(05363) 802.464.8824

● Woodstock ●
Braeside Motel ($$)
Box# 411
(05091) 802.457.1366

Virginia
● Alexandria ●
Alexandria Hotel
801 N Fairfax St
(22314) 703.549.1000

Comfort Inn ($$)
5716 S Van Dorn St
(22310) 703.922.9200
mgr preapproval reqd

Comfort Inn ($$)
7212 Richmond Hwy
(22306) 703.765.9000
mgr preapproval reqd

Days Inn ($$)
6100 Richmond Hwy
(22303) 703.329.0500
small pets allowed

Policies
Subject
to Change

$=under $35 $$=$35-60 $$$=$60-100 $$$$=over $100

Days Inn ($$)
110 S Bragg St
(22312) 703.354.4950
$5/pets

Doubletree ($$$)
100 S Reynolds St
(22304) 703.370.9600
$10 per day

Econo Lodge ($$)
8849 Richmond Hwy
(22309) 703.780.0300
$50 deposit

Econo Lodge ($$)
700 N Washington St
(22314) 703.836.5100

Holiday Inn ($$$)
2460 Eisenhower Ave
(22314) 800.465.4329
mgr preapproval reqd

Holiday Inn ($$$)
480 King St
(22314) 703.549.6080
mgr preapproval reqd

Howard Johnson ($$)
5821 Richmond Hwy
(22303) 703.329.1400
small with mgrs approval

Howard Johnson ($$)
5821 Richmond Hwy
(22303) 703.329.1400
small with mgrs approval

Ramada Inn ($$$$)
901 N Fairfax St
(22314) 703.683.6

Ramada Inn ($$$)
4641 Kenmore Ave
(22304) 703.751.4510

Ramada Inn ($$$)
901 N Fairfax St
(22314) 703.683.6000
small pets only

Red Roof Inn ($$)
5975 Richmond Hwy
(22303) 703.960.5200
fees/limits may apply

Sheraton Inn ($$$)
801 N St Asaph St
(22314) 703.836.4700
w/permission from mgr

● Altavista ●
Comfort Suites ($$)
1558 Main St
(24517) 804.369.4000
mgr preapproval reqd

● Appomattox ●
Budget Inn ($)
714 W Confederate Blvd
(24522) 804.352.7451

Super 8 ($$)
RR 4 Box# 100
(24522) 804.352.2339
w/permission

● Arlington ●
Best Western ($$)
2480 S Glebe Rd
(22206) 703.979.4400

Best Western ($$$)
1850 Fort Myer Dr
(22209) 703.522.0400
small pets only

Doubletree ($$$)
300 Army Navy Dr
(22202) 800.222.8733

Econo Lodge ($)
3335 Lee Hwy
(22207) 800.424.4777

Holiday Inn
1489 Jefferson Davis Hwy
(22202) 800.465.4329
mgr preapproval reqd

Holiday Inn
1900 N Ft Meyer
(22209) 703.807.2000

Howard Johnson ($$$)
2650 Jefferson Davis Hwy
(22202) 703.684.7200

Hyatt Hotel ($$$)
1325 Wilson Blvd
(22209) 703.525.1234

Marriott Hotel ($$$$)
1700 Jefferson Davis Hwy
(22202) 703.920.3230

Marriott Hotel ($$$$$)
1401 Lee Hwy
(22209) 703.524.6400

Ramada Inn ($$$$)
950 N Stafford St
(22203) 703.528.6000

Stouffer ($$$)
2399 Jefferson Davis Hwy
(22202) 703.418.6800
if small enough to carry

● Ashland ●
Comfort Inn ($$)
101 Cottage Greene Dr
(23005) 804.752.7777
mgr preapproval reqd

Econo Lodge ($)
I-95 & S R 54
(23005) 804.798.9221

● Bedford ●
Best Western ($$)
921 Blue Ridge Ave
(24523) 540.586.8266

● Big Stone Gap ●
Country Inn ($)
627 Gilley Ave
(24219) 703.523.0374

● Blacksburg ●
Best Western ($$)
900 Plantation Rd
(24060) 540.552.7770

Brush Mountain Inn
3030 Mount Tabor Rd
(24060) 703.951.7530

Budget Host ($)
3333 S Main St
(24060) 540.951.4242
small

Comfort Inn ($$)
3705 S Main St
(24060) 540.951.1500
mgr preapproval reqd

Holiday Inn ($$)
3503 Holiday Lnn
(24060) 540.951.1330
mgr preapproval reqd

Marriott Hotel ($$$)
900 Prices Fork Rd
(24060) 703.552.7001

● Bland ●
Big Walker Motel ($)
Box# 155
(24315) 703.688.3331

● Boyce ●
River House
RR 2 Box# 135
(22620) 703.837.1476

● Bracey ●
Days Inn ($$)
2850 Hwy 903
(23919) 804.689.2000

● Bristol ●
Econo Lodge ($$$)
912 Commonwealth Ave
(24201) 540.466.2112

La Quinta Inn ($$)
1014 Old Airport Rd
(24201) 540.669.9353
call re: fees

Red Carpet Inn
15589 Lee Hwy
(24202) 703.669.1151

Skyland Motel ($)
15545 Lee Hwy
(24202) 703.669.0160

Super 8 ($$)
2139 Lee Hwy
(24201) 540.466.8800
small with $10 deposit &
permission

● Buchanan ●
Wattstull Inn ($$)
RR 1 Box# 21
(24066) 703.254.1551

● Buena Vista ●
Buena Vista Motel ($$)
477 E 29th St
(24416) 703.261.2138

● Cape Charles ●
Days Inn ($$)
29106 Lankford Hwy
(23310) 804.331.1000

$=under $35 $$=$35-60 $$$=$60-100 $$$$=over $100

VIRGINIA, Chatilly

● Chantilly ●
Washington Dulles ($$)
333 W Service Rd
(22021) 703.471.9500

● Charlottesville ●
Best Western ($$)
1613 Emmet St
(22901) 804.296.5501

Best Western ($$)
105 Emmet St
(22905) 804.296.8111
pets with a reservation

Boars Head Inn
200 Ednam Dr
(22903) 800.476.1988

Camps&Cottages
RR 6 Box# 260
(22902) 804.293.2529

Econo Lodge ($$)
400 Emmet St
(22903) 804.296.2104

Econo Lodge ($$)
2014 Holiday Dr
(22901) 804.295.3185

English Inn
2000 Morton Dr
(22903) 804.971.9900

Holiday Inn ($$)
1600 Emmet
(22901) 804.293.9111

Knights Inn ($$)
1300 Seminole Trl
(22901) 804.973.8133
size limits & fees

Omni
235 W Main St
(22902) 804.971.5500

Quality Inn ($$)
1600 Emmet St
(22901) 804.971.3746
mgr preapproval reqd

Super 8 ($$)
390 Greenbrier Dr
(22901) 804.973.0888
small w/permission

● Chesapeake ●
Days Inn ($)
1439 Washington Hwy
(23323) 804.487.8861

Econo Lodge ($$)
2222 S Military Hwy
(23320) 804.543.2200
$5.48 pet fee

Econo Lodge ($$)
3244 Western Branch Blvd
(23321) 804.484.6143

Econo Lodge ($)
4725 W Military Hwy
(23321) 804.488.4963

Motel 6 ($$)
701 Woodlake Dr
(23320) 804.420.2976
1 small pet/room

Red Roof Inn ($)
724 Woodlake Dr
(23320) 804.523.0123
small pets only

Super 8 ($$)
100 Red Cedar Ct
(23320) 804.547.8880
pets w/permission

Wellesley Inn ($$)
1750 Sara Dr
(23320) 804.366.0100
$5 fee

● Chester ●
Comfort Inn ($$)
2100 W Hundred Rd
(23831) 804.751.0000
mgr preapproval reqd

Days Inn ($$)
I-95
(23831) 804.748.5871
$6/pets

Howard Johnson ($$)
2401 W Hundred Rd
(23831) 804.748.6321

Red Carpet Inn
2300 Hundred Rd
(23831) 804.748.2237

Super 8 ($$)
2421 Southland Dr
(23831) 804.748.0050
confined

● Chincoteague ●
Beach Road Motel ($)
6151 Maddox Blvd
(23336) 804.336.6562

● Christiansburg ●
Days Inn ($$)
I-81
(24073) 540.382.0261
$5/pets

Econo Lodge ($$)
2430 Roanoke St
(24073) 540.382.6161

Howard Johnson ($)
100 Bristol Dr
(24073) 540.381.0150

Super 8 ($$)
55 Laurel St
(24073) 540.382.5813
w/permission

● Collinsville ●
Dutch Inn Motel ($$)
633 S Virginia Ave
(24078) 540.647.3721

Econo Lodge ($)
800 S Virginia Ave
(24078) 540.647.3941

● Colonial Beach ●
Days Inn ($$)
30 Colonial Ave
(22443) 804.224.0404

● Colonial Heights ●
Days Inn ($$)
2310 2Ndian Hill Rd
(23834) 804.520.1010
$5/pets

Travelodge ($)
2201 Ruffin Mill Rd
(23834) 804.526.4611

● Covington ●
Best Western ($$$)
820 E Madison St
(24426) 540.962.4951

Comfort Inn ($$)
203 Interstate Dr
(24426) 540.962.2141
$10 fee

Knights Inn ($$)
908 Valley Ridge Rd
(24426) 540.962.7600
size limits & fees

● Culpeper ●
Comfort Inn ($$)
890 Willis Ln
(22701) 540.825.4900
mgr preapproval reqd

Holiday Inn ($$)
Rt 29
(22701) 540.825.1253

Super 8 ($$)
889 Willis Ln
(22701) 540.825.8088
w/permission

● Danville ●
Days Inn ($$)
1390 Piney Forest Rd
(24540) 804.836.6745

Super 8 ($$)
2385 Riverside Dr
(24540) 804.799.5845
call re: fees

● Doswell ●
Best Western ($)
I-95
(23047) 804.876.3321

● Dumfries ●
Holiday Inn ($$)
17133 Dumfries Rd
(22026) 703.221.1141
mgr preapproval reqd

● Emporia ●
Comfort Inn ($$)
1411 Skippers Rd
(23847) 804.348.3282
mgr preapproval reqd

Days Inn ($$)
921 W Atlantic St
(23847) 804.634.9481
$5/pets

358

$=under $35 $$=$35-60 $$$=$60-100 $$$$=over $100

Econo Lodge ($)
3173 Sussett Dr
(23847) 804.535.8535
small pets only

Hampton Inn ($$)
1207 W Atlantic St
(23847) 804.634.9200

Holiday Inn ($$)
311 Florida Ave
(23847) 804.634.4191

Red Carpet Inn ($)
1586 Skippers Rd
(23847) 804.634.4181

• Fairfax •
Holiday Inn ($$$)
11787 Lee Jackson Hwy
(22033) 703.352.2525
mgr preapproval reqd

Holiday Inn ($$$)
3535 Chain Bridge Rd
(22030) 703.591.5500
mgr preapproval reqd

Hyatt Hotel ($$)
12777 Fair Lakes Cir
(22033) 703.818.1234
small on lower level

Wellesley Inn ($$)
10327 Lee Hwy
(22030) 703.359.2888
$3 charge

• Falls Church •
Econo Lodge ($$)
5666 Columbia Pike
(22041) 703.820.5600

Marriott Hotel ($$$$)
3111 Fairview Park Dr
(22042) 703.849.9400
small pets only

Quality Inn ($$)
6111 Arlington Blvd
(22044) 703.534.9100
mgr preapproval reqd

Ramada Inn ($$$)
7801 Leesburg Pike
(22043) 703.893.1340
small pets only

Ramada Inn ($$$)
7801 Leeburg Pike
(22043) 703.675.3693

• Farmville •
Super 8 ($$)
HC 6 Box# 1755
(23901) 804.392.8196
pets w/permission

• Fredericksburg •
Best Western ($$)
2205 William St
(22401) 703.786.5050

Best Western ($$)
3000 Plank Rd
(22401) 703.786.7404
small pets

Best Western ($)
543 Warrenton Rd
(22406) 540.373.0000

Days Inn ($$)
14 Simpson Rd
(22405) 540.373.5340
$5/pets

Days Inn ($$)
5316 Jefferson Davis Hwy
(22408) 540.898.6800

Dunning Mills Inn ($$)
2305 Jefferson Davis Hwy
(22401) 703.373.1256

Econo Lodge ($$)
5321 Jefferson Davis Hwy
(22408) 540.898.5440

Hampton Inn ($$)
2310 Plank Rd
(22401) 703.371.0220

Heritage Inn ($)
5308 Jefferson Davis Hwy
(22408) 540.898.1000

Holiday Inn
564 Warrentown Rd
(22405) 540.371.5550

Holiday Inn ($$)
5324 Jefferson Davis Hwy
(22408) 540.898.1102
mgr preapproval reqd

Howard Johnson ($)
386 Warrenton Rd
(22405) 540.371.6000

Howard Johnson ($$)
5327 Jefferson Davis Hwy
(22408) 540.898.1800

Motel 6 ($)
401 Warrenton Rd
(22405) 540.371.5443
1 small pet/room

Ramada Inn ($$)
I-95 Ex 130-B
(22404) 540.786.8361

Sheraton Inn ($$)
Box# 618
(22404) 703.786.8321

Super 8 ($$)
3002 Mall Dr
(22401) 540.786.8881
w/permission

• Front Royal •
Budget Inn ($)
1122 N Royal Ave
(22630) 540.635.2196

Center City Motel ($)
416 S Royal Ave
(22630) 540.635.4050

Scottish Inn ($$)
533 S Royal Ave
(22630) 540.636.6168

Super 8 ($$)
111 South St
(22630) 540.636.4888
w/permission

• Glade Spring •
Economy Inn ($)
Box# 453
(24340) 703.429.5131

• Glen Allen •
Amerisuites ($$$)
4100 Cox Rd
(23060) 804.747.9644

• Goshen •
The Hummingbird Inn ($$$)
Box# 147
(24439) 800.397.3214

• Hampton •
Arrow Inn ($$)
7 Semple Farm Rd
(23666) 804.865.0300

Coliseum Inn
2000 W Mercury Blvd
(23666) 804.838.7070

Days Inn ($$)
1918 Coliseum Dr
(23666) 804.826.4810
$5/pets

Econo Lodge ($)
2708 W Mercury Blvd
(23666) 804.826.8970

Hampton Inn ($$)
1813 W Mercury Blvd
(23666) 804.838.8484

La Quinta Inn ($$)
2138 W Mercury Blvd
(23666) 804.827.8680
call re: fees

Quality Inn ($$$)
1809 W Mercury Blvd
(23666) 757.838.5011

Red Roof Inn ($)
1925 Coliseum Dr
(23666) 804.838.1870

Sheraton Inn ($$)
1215 W Mercury Blvd
(23666) 804.838.5011

• Harrisonburg •
Comfort Inn ($$)
1440 E Market St
(22801) 540.433.6066
mgr preapproval reqd

Days Inn ($$)
1131 Forest Hill Rd
(22801) 540.433.9353
$5/pet

Econo Lodge ($$)
US 33 & I-81
(22801) 540.438.2576

Hojo Inn ($$)
605 Port Republic Rd
(22801) 540.434.6771

$=under $35 $$=$35-60 $$$=$60-100 $$$$=over $100

VIRGINIA, Harrisonburg

Knights Inn
10 Linda Ln
(22801) 703.433.2538

Motel 6 ($$)
10 Linda Ln
(22801) 703.433.6939
1 small pet/room

Ramada Inn ($)
1 Pleasant Valley Rd
(22801) 540.434.9981

Red Carpet Inn ($)
3210 S Main St
(22801) 703.434.6704

Rockingham Motel ($)
4035 S Main St
(22801) 703.433.2538

Scottish Inn ($)
RR 11
(22801) 703.434.5301
$5 fee

Sheraton Inn ($$)
1400 E Market St
(22801) 703.433.2521

Super 8 ($$)
3330 S Main St
(22801) 540.433.8888
w/permission

Village Inn ($)
RR 1 Box# 76
(22801) 703.434.7355

● Herndon ●
Hilton ($$$)
13869 Park Center Rd
(20171) 703.478.2900

Residence Inn ($$)
315 Elden St
(20170) 703.435.0044

Summerfield Suites
13700 Coppermine Rd
(20171) 703.713.6800

● Hillsville ●
Econo Lodge ($)
I-77 & US 58
(24343) 540.728.9118

Holiday Inn ($$)
RR 1 Box# 361
(24343) 540.728.2120
mgr preapproval reqd

The Groundhog ($$$$)
189 Blue Ridge Pkwy
(24343) 703.398.2212

● Hopewell ●
Innkeeper
3852 Courthouse Rd
(23860) 804.458.2600

● Hot Springs ●
Roseloe Motel ($)
RR 2 Box# 590
(24445) 540.839.5373

● Irvington ●
Tides Inn ($$$$)
Box# 480
(22480) 804.438.5000

Tides Lodge ($$$$)
Box# 309
(22480) 804.438.6000

● Keysville ●
Sheldons Motel ($$)
RR 2 Box# 189
(23947) 804.736.8434

● Leesburg ●
Best Western ($$)
726 E Market St
(20176) 703.777.9400

Colonial Inn
19 S King St
(20175) 703.777.5000

Days Inn ($$)
721 E Market St
(20176) 703.777.6622

Laurel Brigage Inn
20 W Market St
(20176) 703.777.1010

Leesburg Hotel
59 Club House Dr SW
(20175) 703.777.1910

Little Rock Motel
RR 4 Box# 608
(20176) 703.777.3499

Piedmont Motel
RR 2 Box# 230
(20175) 703.777.3361

● Lexington ●
Days Inn ($$)
RR 6 Box# 31
(24450) 540.463.2143

Econo Lodge ($$)
I-64 & US 11
(24450) 540.463.7371

Holiday Inn ($$)
I-64 Ex 55
(24450) 540.463.7351
mgr preapproval reqd

Howard Johnson ($$)
I-81 & US 11
(24450) 540.463.9181

Ramada Inn ($$)
US 11 Rt I-81 & A5
(24450) 540.463.6400

Red Oak Inn
US 11 Ex 53
(24450) 703.463.9131

Super 8 ($$)
RR 7 Box# 99
(24450) 540.463.7858
w/permission

The Keep
116 Lee Ave
(24450) 703.463.3560

Thrifty Inn ($)
820 S Main St
(24450) 540.463.2151

● Luray ●
Best Western ($$)
410 W Main St
(22835) 540.743.6511

Cardinal Motel
US Bus 211
(22835) 703.743.5010

Luray Caverns Motel
US 211 Bypass
(22835) 703.743.4536

Luray Inn
Box# 389
(22835) 703.743.4521
$10 nightly pet charge

● Lynchburg ●
Comfort Inn ($$)
Odd Fellows Rd
(24506) 804.847.9041
mgr preapproval reqd

Holiday Inn ($$$)
3436 Oddfellows Rd
(24506) 804.847.4424
smoking rooms

Holiday Inn ($$$)
601 Main St
(24504) 804.528.2500
mgr preapproval reqd

Howard Johnson ($$)
US 29
(24506) 804.845.7041

Ramada Ltd ($$)
1500 Main St
(24504) 804.845.5975

● Manassas ●
Red Roof Inn ($$)
10610 Automotive Dr
(20109) 703.335.9333

● Marion ●
Best Western ($$$)
1424 N Main St
(24354) 540.783.3193

Budget Host ($)
435 S Main St
(24354) 540.783.8511
$5

Virginia House Motel ($$)
419 N Main St
(24354) 703.783.5112

● Martinsville ●
Best Western ($$)
220 N
(24114) 540.632.5611

Super 8 ($$)
960 Memorial Blvd
(24112) 540.666.8888
w/permission

Be Discreet

$=under $35 $$=$35-60 $$$=$60-100 $$$$=over $100

• Max Meadows •
Gateway Motel ($)
RR 3 Box# 488
(24360) 703.637.3119

• Mc Kenney •
Scottish Inn ($)
21723 Boydton Plank Rd
(23872) 804.478.4481

• Mc Lean •
The Ritz Carlton ($$$$)
1700 Tysons Blvd
(22102) 703.506.4300
small pets only

Tysons Westpark Hotel ($$)
8401 Westpark Dr
(22102) 703.734.2800
waiver

• Meadows Of Dan •
Woodberry Inn
Box# 908
(24120) 703.593.2567

• Melfa •
Captains Quarters Motel
Rt 13 Box# D
(23410) 804.787.4545

• Millboro •
Fort Lewis Lodge
HC 3 Box# 21A
(24460) 703.925.2314

• Montross •
The Inn At Montross ($$$)
Box# 908
(22520) 804.493.9097

• Mount Jackson •
Best Western ($$)
250 Conickville Rd
(22842) 703.477.2911

The Widow Kips Country Inn
($$$)
335 Orchard Dr
(22842) 540.477.2400

• Natural Bridge •
Budget Inn ($)
US 11
(24578) 703.291.2143

Fancy Hill Motel
US 11
(24578) 703.291.2143

Wattstull Inn
Blue Ridge Pkwy
(24578) 703.254.1551

• New Church •
Garden Of The Sea ($$$)
Rt 710
(23415) 804.824.0672
owner rfd pet lovers

• New Market •
Budget Inn ($)
2192 Old Valley Pike
(22844) 540.740.3105

Days Inn ($$)
9360 Collins Pkwy
(22844) 540.740.4100

• Newport News •
Comfort Inn ($$)
12330 Jefferson Ave
(23602) 757.249.0200

Days Inn ($$)
14747 Warwick Blvd
(23608) 757.874.0201

Host Inn ($$)
985 J Clyde Morris Blvd
(23601) 804.599.3303

King James Motel ($)
6045 Jefferson Ave
(23605) 804.245.2801

Motel 6 ($)
797 J Clyde Morris Blvd
(23601) 804.595.6336
1 small pet/room

Travelodge ($$)
6128 Jefferson Ave
(23605) 804.826.4500
make prior reservations with
manager

• Norfolk •
Anchorage Inn
929 E Ocean View Ave
(23503) 804.583.2605

Beachcomber Motel
2090 E Ocean View Ave
(23503) 804.583.2605

Comfort Inn ($)
930 E Virginia Beach Blvd
(23504) 757.623.5700
$20 fee

Days Inn ($$)
1631 Bayville St
(23503) 757.583.4521

Days Inn ($$)
5701 Chambers St
(23502) 804.461.0100
$5/pets

Econo Lodge ($$)
865 N Military Hwy
(23502) 804.461.4865

Econo Lodge ($$)
9601 4th View St
(23503) 804.480.9611
$50 deposit

Econo Lodge ($)
1850 E Little Creek Rd
(23518) 804.588.8888

Econo Lodge ($)
3343 N Military Hwy
(23518) 804.855.3116

Econo Lodge
9601 -4th View St
(23503) 804.480.9611
referred

Hotel 6 ($$)
853 N Military Hwy
(23502) 804.461.2380

Howard Johnson ($$)
700 Monticello Ave
(23510) 804.627.5555
small pets only

Lafayette
4233 Granby St
(23504) 804.622.5383

Lodge At Little Creek
7969 Shore Dr
(23518) 804.588.3600

Marriott Hotel
235 E Main St
(23510) 804.627.4200
under 35 lbs with $35 fee

Quality Inn ($$)
6280 Northampton Blvd
(23502) 757.461.6251

Sheraton Inn
Military Hwy
(23518) 804.461.9192

• Norton •
Holiday Inn
551 Hwy 58E
(24273) 540.679.7000

Super 8 ($$)
425 Wharton Ln
(24273) 540.679.0893
w/permission

• Onley •
Anchor Motel ($$)
Box# 69
(23418) 804.787.8000

• Orange •
Best Western ($$)
15 Windigrove Dr
(22960) 800.528.1234

• Petersburg •
American Inn ($)
2209 Country Dr
(23803) 804.733.2800

Best Western ($$)
405 E Washington St
(23803) 804.733.1776
small pets only

California Inn
2214 Country Dr
(23803) 804.732.5500

Comfort Inn ($$)
11974 S Crater Rd
(23805) 804.732.2900
mgr preapproval reqd

Days Inn ($$)
I-95
(23805) 804.733.4400
$5/pets

Econo Lodge ($)
16905 Parkdale Rd
(23805) 804.862.2717

Flagship Inn ($)
815 S Crater Rd
(23803) 804.861.3470

Quality Inn ($)
12205 Crater Rd
(23805) 804.733.0600
$5 night

Ramada Inn ($$)
501 E Washington St
(23803) 804.733.0730

Star Motel
39 S Crater Rd
(23803) 804.733.3600

Super 8 ($)
555 E Wythe St
(23803) 804.861.0793
small pets w/permission

• Port Haywood •
Inn At Tabbs Creek
Box# 219
(23138) 804.725.5136

• Portsmouth •
Days Inn ($)
1031London Blvd
(23704) 757.399.4414
$5/night

Holiday Inn ($$$)
8 Crawford Pkwy
(23704) 804.393.2573
mgr preapproval reqd

Super 8 ($$)
925 London Blvd
(23704) 804.398.0612
pets allowed

• Pulaski •
Red Carpet Inn ($)
I-81 Ex 94
(24301) 703.980.2230
small pets only

• Radford •
Best Western ($$)
1501 Tyler Ave
(24141) 540.639.3000
pets under 15 lbs

Comfort Inn ($$)
1501 Tyler Ave
(24141) 540.639.4800
mgr preapproval reqd

Dogwood Lodge ($)
7073 Lee Hwy
(24141) 540.639.9338

Super 8 ($$)
1600 Tyler Ave
(24141) 540.731.9355
mgr preapproval reqd

• Raphine •
Days Inn ($)
RR 2 Box# 438
(24472) 540.377.2604

• Richmond •
Days Inn ($$)
1600 Robin Hood Rd
(23220) 804.353.1287
$2/pets

Days Inn ($$)
2100 Dickens Rd
(23230) 804.282.3300

Econo Lodge ($)
2125 Willis Rd
(23237) 804.271.6031

Econo Lodge ($)
6523 Midlothian Tpke
(23225) 804.276.8241

Hojo Inn ($$)
801 E Parham Rd
(23227) 804.266.8753

Holiday Inn
3207 North Blvd
(23230) 804.359.9441

Holiday Inn
4303 Commerce Rd
(23234) 804.275.7891

Howard Johnson ($$$)
4303 Commerce Rd
(23234) 800.446.4656

Marriott Hotel ($$$)
500 E Broad St
(23219) 804.643.3400
under 25 lbs

Park Suites Hotel
9th & Bank St
(23219) 804.343.7300

Ramada Inn ($$)
2126 Willis Rd
(23237) 804.271.1281

Ramada Ltd ($)
5221 Brook Rd
(23227) 800.272.6232

Red Roof Inn ($)
100 Greshamwood Pl
(23225) 804.745.0600

Red Roof Inn ($)
4350 Commerce Rd
(23234) 804.271.9240

Residence Inn ($$$)
2121 Dickens Rd
(23230) 804.285.8200
$50 fee & $5 per day

Sheraton Inn ($$)
4700 S Laburnum Ave
(23231) 804.226.4300
small pets only

Sheraton Inn ($$)
9901 Midlothian Tpke
(23235) 804.323.1144

Super 8 ($$)
5615 Chamberlayne Rd
(23227) 804.262.8880
w/permission

Super 8 ($$)
5110 Williamsburg Rd
(23231) 804.222.8008
small pets w/permission $25
deposit

Super 8 ($$)
8620 Midlothian Tpke
(23235) 804.320.2823
w/permission

Super 8 ($$)
7200 W Broad St
(23294) 804.672.8128
w/permission prefer smaller

• Roanoke •
Comfort Inn ($$)
3695 Thirlane Rd NW
(24019) 540.563.0229

Days Inn ($$)
501 Orange Ave NE
(24016) 540.342.8961

Holiday Inn ($$$)
4468 Starkey Rd
(24014) 540.774.4400
mgr preapproval reqd

Marriott Hotel ($$)
2801 Hershberger Rd NW
(24017) 540.563.9300

Ramada Inn ($$)
1927 Franklin Rd SW
(24014) 540.343.0121

Roanoker Motel ($)
7645 Williamson Rd
(24019) 540.362.3344

Rodeway Inn ($$)
526 Orange Ave NE
(24016) 540.981.9341

Sheraton Inn ($$$)
2727 Ferndale Dr NW
(24017) 540.372.4500

Super 8 ($$)
6616 Thirlane Rd NW
(24019) 540.563.8888
w/permission

• Rocky Mount •
Budget Host ($)
Hwy 220
(24151) 540.483.9757
w/permission

Franklin Motel ($)
Rfd 1
(24151) 540.483.9962

• Ruther Glen •
Days Inn ($)
Box# 70
(22546) 804.448.2011
$5 per day

Howard Johnson ($$)
23786 Rogers Clark Blvd
(22546) 804.448.2499

• Salem •
Budget Host ($)
5399 W Main St
(24153) 540.380.2080
permission $5

Holiday Inn
1671 Skyview Rd
(24153) 540.389.7061

Virginia Beach, VIRGINIA

Knights Inn ($$)
301 Wildwood Rd
(24153) 540.389.0280
call for size limits & fees

Quality Inn ($$)
179 Sheraton Dr
(24153) 540.562.1912
mgr preapproval reqd

Super 8 ($$)
300 Wildwood Rd
(24153) 540.389.0297
w/permission

● Sandston ●
Best Western ($$)
5700 Williamsburg Rd
(23150) 804.222.2780

Days Inn ($$)
5500 Williamsburg Rd
(23150) 804.222.2041

Econo Lodge ($)
5408 Williamsburg Rd
(23150) 804.222.1020

Holiday Inn
5203 Williamsburg Rd
(23150) 804.222.6450

Knights Inn
5252 Airport Square Ln
(23150) 804.226.4519

Motel 6 ($)
5704 US Hwy 60
(23150) 804.222.7600
1 small pet/room

● Scottsville ●
Chester Inn
RR 4 Box# 57
(24590) 804.286.2218

High Meadows Inn ($$$)
High Meadows Ln
(24590) 804.286.2218

● Skippers ●
Econo Lodge ($)
I-95 S & S R 629
(23879) 804.634.6124

**Policies
Subject
to Change**

● South Boston ●
Best Western ($$)
2001 Seymour Dr
(24592) 804.572.4311
small housebroken pets

Super 8 ($$)
1040 Bill Tuck Hwy
(24592) 804.572.8868
w/permission

● South Hill ●
Best Western ($$$)
US 58
(23970) 804.447.3123

Econo Lodge ($$)
623 E Atlantic St
(23970) 804.447.7116
dogs

Super 8 ($$)
922 E Atlantic St
(23970) 804.447.7655
small w/permission

● Springfield ●
Econo Lodge ($$)
6868 Springfield Blvd
(22150) 703.491.5196

Ramada Inn ($$)
6868 Springfield Blvd
(22150) 703.644.5311

● Stanley ●
Jordan Hollow Farm Inn
RR 2 Box# 375
(22851) 703.778.2209

● Staunton ●
Comfort Inn ($$)
1302 Richmond Ave
(24401) 540.886.5000
mgr preapproval reqd

Days Inn ($$)
RR 2 Box# 414
(24401) 540.337.3031
$4/pets

Econo Lodge ($)
RR 2 Box# 364
(24401) 540.337.1231
advance notice req'd

Econo Lodge ($$)
1031 Richmond Ave
(24401) 540.885.5158

Holiday Inn
Rt 275 & I-81
(24402) 540.248.6020

● Sterling ●
Holiday Inn
1000 Sully Rd
(20166) 703.471.7411

● Strasburg ●
Hotel Strasburg ($$$)
201 S Holliday St
(22657) 540.465.9191

● Syria ●
Graves Mtn Lodge ($$$)
Hwy 670
(22743) 703.923.4231

● Trout Dale ●
Fox Hill Inn
RR 2 Box# 1A1
(24378) 703.677.3313

● Troutville ●
Comfort Inn ($$)
2654 Lee Hwy
(24175) 540.992.5600
mgr preapproval reqd

Howard Johnson ($$)
Box# 100
(24175) 703.992.3000

Travelodge ($$)
2444 Le Hwy
(24175) 703.992.6700

● Verona ●
Scottish Inn ($)
I-81
(24482) 703.248.8981
for 1 night

● Vienna ●
Residence Inn ($$$$)
8616 Westwood Center Dr
(22182) 800.331.3131

Marriott Hotel ($$)
8028 Leesburg Pike
(22182) 703.734.3200

● Virginia Beach ●
Alicias Cottages
304-306 24th St
(23451) 804.340.8890

Angies Guest Cottage
302 24th St
(23451) 804.428.4690

Aquarius Motel
20th & Coeanfront
(23451) 804.425.0650

Beach Cabana
23rd & Oceanfront
(23451) 804.428.8188

Coral Sand Motel
23rd & Pacific
(23451) 804.425.0872

Econo Lodge ($$)
2968 Shore Dr
(23451) 804.481.0666

Econo Lodge ($)
3637 Bonney Rd
(23452) 804.486.5711

Econo Lodge ($)
5819 Northampton Blvd
(23455) 804.464.9306

Executive Inn ($)
717 S Military Hwy
(23464) 804.420.2120

Holly Cove
395 Norfolk Ave
(23451) 804.425.8374

Howard Johnson ($$)
1801 Atlantic Ave
(23451) 804.437.9100

La Coquille Motel ($$)
314 16th St
(23451) 804.422.3889

La Quinta Inn ($$)
192 Newtown Rd
(23462) 804.497.6620
call re: fees

Lakeside Motel
2572 Virginia Beach Blvd
(23452) 804.340.3211

Mardi Gras Motel
28th & Atlantic
(23451) 804.428.3434

Ocean Holiday Hotel ($$)
2417 Atlantic Ave
(23451) 804.425.6920

363

$=under $35 $$=$35-60 $$$=$60-100 $$$$=over $100

VIRGINIA, Virginia Beach

Ramada Inn ($$)
5725 Northampton Blvd
(23455) 804.464.9351

Red Carpet Inn ($$)
2700 Pacific Ave
(23451) 804.425.9330

Red Roof Inn ($)
196 Ballard Ct
(23462) 804.490.0225

Sandpiper Motel
1112 Pacific Ave
(23451) 804.422.0001

Sundowner Motel
27th & Pacific Ave
(23451) 804.428.3011

Thunderbird Motel ($)
35th & Oceanfront
(23451) 804.428.3024

Travelodge ($)
4600 Bonney Rd
(23462) 804.473.9745

● Warm Springs ●
Meadow Lane Lodge
Star Rt A Box# 110
(24484) 703.839.5959

Three Hills Inn ($$)
Box# 9
(24484) 540.839.5381

● Warrenton ●
Hampton Inn ($$)
501 Blackwell Rd
(20186) 540.349.4200

Hojo Inn ($)
6 Broadview Ave
(20186) 703.347.4141

● Warsaw ●
Best Western ($$)
4522 Richmond Rd
(22572) 800.528.1234

● Waynesboro ●
Comfort Inn ($$)
640 W Broad St
(22980) 540.942.1171
mgr preapproval reqd

Days Inn ($$)
2060 Rosser Ave
(22980) 703.942.1171

Deluxe Bduge Motel ($)
2112 W Main St
(22980) 540.949.8253

Super 8 ($$)
2045 Rosser Ave
(22980) 540.943.3888
w/permission

● Williamsburg ●
Best Western ($$)
900 Capitol Landing Rd
(23185) 804.229.1655

Best Western ($$)
111 Penniman Rd
(23185) 804.253.1222

Best Western ($)
1600 Richmond Rd
(23185) 800.528.1234

Best Western ($$)
Rt 60 & Hwy 199
(23187) 804.229.3003
small pets only

Best Western ($$)
York & Page Sts
(23187) 804.229.9540
small pets only

Commonwealth Inn ($)
1233 Richmond Rd
(23185) 804.253.1087

Days Inn ($)
902 Richmond Rd
(23185) 757.229.5060
$5/pets

Days Inn ($)
6488 Richmond Rd
(23188) 804.565.0900

Econo Lodge ($)
1900 Richmond Rd
(23185) 804.229.6600

Econo Lodge ($)
7051 Richmond Rd
(23188) 804.564.3341

George Washington Inn ($$)
500 Merrimac Trl
(23185) 804.220.1410

Governors Inn ($$)
504 N Henry St
(23185) 804.229.1000

Heritage Inn ($)
1324 Richmond Rd
(23185) 804.229.6220

Holiday Inn ($$)
3032 Richmond Rd
(23185) 804.565.2600
mgr preapproval reqd

Motel 6 ($)
3030 Richmond Rd
(23185) 804.565.3433
1 small pet/room

Quarterpath Inn ($)
620 York St
(23185) 804.220.0960

Ramada Inn ($)
351 York St
(23185) 804.220.0960

Ramada Inn ($$)
351 York St
(23185) 804.229.4100
$10 per stay

Super 8 ($$)
304 2nd St
(23185) 804.229.0500
call re: fees

Thomas Jefferson Inn
7247 Pocahontas Trl
(23185) 804.220.2000

Travelodge ($)
1420 Richmond Rd
(23185) 804.229.2981

● Willis Wharf ●
Ballard House ($$)
12527 Ballard Dr
(23486) 804.442.2206

● Winchester ●
Best Western ($$)
711 Millwood Ave
(22601) 540.662.4154

Budgetel ($$)
800 Millwood Ave
(22601) 540.678.0800

Days Inn ($$)
2951 Valley Ave
(22601) 540.667.1200

Echo Village Motel
US Rt 1
(22603) 703.869.1900

Holiday Inn ($$)
1017 Millwood Pike
(22602) 540.667.3300
mgr preapproval reqd

Howard Johnson ($)
2549 Valley Ave
(22601) 540.662.2521

Mohawk Motel ($)
2754 Northwestern Pike
(22603) 540.667.1410

Quality Inn ($$)
603 Millwood Ave
(22601) 540.667.2250
mgr preapproval reqd

Super 8 ($$)
1077 Millwood Pike
(22602) 540.665.4450
call re: fees

Tourist City Motel ($)
214 Millwood Ave
(22601) 540.662.9011

Travelodge ($$)
160 Front Royal Pike
(22602) 540.665.0685

● Woodbridge ●
Days Inn ($$)
14619 Potomac Mills Rd
(22192) 703.494.4433
small pets allowed

Econo Lodge ($$)
13317 Gordon Blvd
(22191) 703.491.5196

Friendship Inn ($$)
13964 Jefferson Davis Hwy
(22191) 703.494.4144

$=under $35 $$=$35-60 $$$=$60-100 $$$$=over $1

Scottish Inn ($$)
951 Annapolis Way
(22191) 703.490.3400

● Woodstock ●
Budget Host ($)
1290 S Main St
(22664) 540.459.4086

● Wytheville ●
Best Western ($$)
355 Nye Rd
(24382) 540.228.7300

Days Inn ($$)
150 Malin Dr
(24382) 540.228.5500
$5/pets

Econo Lodge ($)
1190 E Main St
(24382) 540.228.5517

Holiday Inn
US 11
(24382) 540.228.5483

Intersate Lodge ($)
705 Chapman Rd
(24382) 540.228.8618

Motel 6 ($)
220 Lithia Rd
(24382) 540.228.7988
1 small pet/room

Red Carpet Inn ($)
280 Lithia Rd
(24382) 540.228.5525

Super 8 ($$)
130 Nye Cir
(24382) 540.228.6620
call re: fees

Washington
● Aberdeen ●
Central Park Motel ($)
6504 Olympic Hwy
(98520) 360.533.1210

Nordic Inn ($)
1700 S Boone St
(98520) 360.533.0100
smoking rooms

Olympic Inn ($$)
616 W Heron St
(98520) 360.533.4200

Red Lion Inn ($$)
521 W Wishkah St
(98520) 360.532.5210
call re: fees

Thunderbird Motel ($$)
410 W Wishkah St
(98520) 360.532.3153

Towne Motel
712 W Wishkah St
(98520) 360.533.2340

Travelure Motel ($$)
623 W Wishkah St
(98520) 360.532.3280

● Airway Heights ●
Heights Motel
13504 W Hwy 2
(99001) 509.244.2072

Lantern Park Motel ($)
W 13820 Sunset Hwy
(99001) 509.244.3653

● Amanda Park ●
Amanda Park Motel ($)
Box# 624
(98526) 800.410.2237

● Anacortes ●
Anacortes Inn ($$)
3006 Commercial Ave
(98221) 360.293.3153
$10-$30 fee

Islands Inn ($$)
3401 Commercial Ave
(98221) 360.293.4644
$5 fee

San Juan Motel ($)
1103 6th St
(98221) 360.293.5105

Ship Harbor Inn ($$)
536 Ferry Terminal Rd
(98221) 360.293.5177

● Arlington ●
Arlington Motor Inn ($$)
2214 S R 530 NE
(98223) 360.652.9595

Smokey Point Motel ($$)
17329 Smokey Point Dr
(98223) 360.659.8561

● Ashford ●
Cabins At The Berry
37221 Hwy 706
(98304) 360.569.2628

Mt Rainier Cabins ($$)
38624 S R 706
(98304) 360.569.2355

● Auburn ●
Best Western ($$$)
1521 D St NE
(98002) 206.939.5950
small pets allowed

Val U Inn ($$)
9 14th St NW
(98001) 206.735.9600

● Bellevue ●
Best Western ($$$)
11211 Main St
(98004) 206.455.5240
$30 fee

Kanes Motel ($$)
14644 SE Eastgate SE Way
(98007) 206.746.8201

La Residence Suites
475 100th Ave NE
(98004) 206.455.1475

Red Lion Inn ($$$)
818 112th Ave NE
(98004) 206.455.1515
call re: fees

Residence Inn ($$$)
14455 NE 29th Pl
(98007) 206.882.1222
$50 fee $5 per day

West Coast Hotel ($$$)
625 116th Ave NE
(98004) 206.455.9444

● Bellingham ●
Ays Inn ($$)
125 E Kellogg Rd
(98226) 360.671.8200

Bay City Motor Inn
116 N Samish Way
(98225) 360.676.0332

Bell Motel
208 N Samish Way
(98225) 360.733.2520

Coachman Inn
120 N Samish Way
(98225) 360.671.9000

Lions Inn Motel ($$)
2419 Elm St
(98225) 360.733.2330

Macs Motel
1215 E Maple St
(98225) 360.734.7570

Motel 6 ($)
3701 Byron St
(98225) 360.671.4494
1 small pet/room

Park Motel ($$)
101 N Samish Way
(98225) 360.733.8280

Quality Inn ($$)
100 E Kellogg Rd
(98226) 360.647.8000
mgr preapproval reqd

Rodeway Inn ($$)
3710 Meridian St
(98225) 360.738.6000

Shamrock Motel
4133 W Maplewood Ave
(98226) 360.676.1050

Shangri La Motel ($)
611 E Holly St
(98225) 360.733.7050

Val U Inn ($$)
805 Lakeway Dr
(98226) 360.671.9600

● Bingen ●
City Center Motel
208 W Steuben
(98605) 509.493.2445

● Blaine ●
Northwoods Motel ($)
288 D St
(98230) 360.332.5603

The Inn At Semiahmoo
($$$$)
9565 Semiahmoo Pkwy
(98230) 360.371.2000

WASHINGTON, Blaine

Westview Motel
1300 Peace Portal Dr
(98230) 360.332.5501

● Bothell ●
Residence Inn ($$$)
11920 NE 195th St
(98011) 206.485.3030
$10 per day

● Bremerton ●
Dunes Motel ($$)
3400 11th St
(98312) 360.377.0093
$25 fee

Flagship Inn ($$)
4320 Kitsap Way
(98312) 360.479.6566

Midway Inn ($$)
2909 Wheaton Way
(98310) 360.479.2909

Oyster Bay Inn ($$)
4412 Kitsap Way
(98312) 360.377.5510

Quality Inn ($$$)
4303 Kitsap Way
(98312) 360.405.1111

Super 8 ($$)
5068 Kitsap Way
(98312) 360.377.8881
call re: fees

The Chieftan Motel
600 National Ave
(98312) 206.479.3111

● Brewster ●
Brewster Motel ($)
801 S Bridge St
(98812) 509.689.2625

● Bridgeport ●
Stirling Motell
1717 Foster Creek Ave
(98813) 509.686.4821

● Buckley ●
Mt View Inn ($$)
29405 Hwy 410
(98321) 360.829.1100

● Burlington ●
Sterling Motor Inn ($)
866 S Burlington Blvd
(98233) 206.757.0071

● Carson ●
Carson Mineral Hot Sprgs ($)
Box# 1169
(98610) 509.427.8292

● Castle Rock ●
7 West Motel
864 Walsh Ave NE
(98611) 360.274.7526

Mt St Helens Motel ($)
1340 Mt St Helens
(98611) 360.274.7721

Timberland Inn ($$)
1271 Mt St Helens
(98611) 360.274.6002

● Cathlamet ●
Nassa Point Motel ($)
851 E Hwy 4
(98612) 360.795.3941

● Centralia ●
Days Inn ($$)
702 Harrison Ave
(98531) 360.736.2875

Ferrymans Inn ($$)
1003 Eckerson Rd
(98531) 360.330.2094
$ fee

Lake Shore Motel
1325 Lakeshore Dr
(98531) 360.736.9344

Motel 6 ($)
1310 Belmont Ave
(98531) 360.330.2057
1 small pet/room

Park Motel ($)
1011 Belmont Ave
(98531) 206.736.9333
small pets only

Peppertree Motel ($)
1208 Alder St
(98531) 360.736.1124

● Chehalis ●
Relax Inn ($)
550 SW Parkland Dr
(98532) 360.748.8608

● Chelan ●
4 Motel ($)
2138 Columbia
(98816) 509.686.2002

Cabana Motel ($$$)
420 Manson Rd
(98816) 509.682.2233

Kellys Resort ($$$)
12801 S Lakeshore Rd
(98816) 509.687.3220

Lake Chelan Motel
2044 W Woodin Ave
(98816) 509.682.2742

Midtowner Motel
721 Woodin Ave
(98816) 509.682.4051

● Cheney ●
Rosebrook Inn
304 W 1st St
(99004) 509.235.6538

Willow Springs Motel ($$)
5 B St
(99004) 509.235.5138

● Chewelah ●
49Er Motel
311 S Park St
(99109) 509.935.8613

Nordlig Motel ($)
101 W Grant Ave
(99109) 509.935.6704

● Clarkston ●
Astor Motel
1201 Bridge St
(99403) 509.758.2509

Golden Key Motel
1376 Bridge St
(99403) 509.758.5566

Hacienda Lodge Motel
812 Bridge St
(99403) 800.600.5583

Motel 6 ($)
222 Bridge St
(99403) 509.758.1631
1 small pet/room

Sunset Motel
1200 Bridge St
(99403) 800.845.5223

● Cle Elum ●
Bonita Motel
906 E 1st St
(98922) 509.674.2380

Cedars Motel ($$)
1001 E 1st St
(98922) 509.674.5535

Chalet Motel
800 E 1st St
(98922) 509.674.2320

Mus Motel ($)
521 E 1st St
(98922) 509.674.2551

The Stewart Lodge ($$)
805 W 1st St
(98922) 509.674.4548

The Wind Blew Inn
811 Hwy 970
(98922) 509.674.2294

Timber Lodge Motel ($$)
301 W 1st St
(98922) 509.674.5966

● Colville ●
Beaver Lodge Resort
2430 Hwy 20
(99114) 509.684.5657

Bennys Colville Inn ($$)
915 S Main St
(99114) 509.684.2517

Downtown Motel ($)
369 S Main St
(99114) 509.684.2565

● Conconully ●
Conconully Lake Resort ($$)
102 Sinlahekin Rd
(98819) 800.850.0813

Conconully Motel
Box# 181
(98819) 509.826.1610

Gibsons North Fork Lodge
100 W Boone
(98819) 509.826.1475

Liars Cove Resort ($$)
1835 A Conconully Rd
(98819) 800.830.1288

Shady Pines Resort ($$)
125 Fork Salmon Creek
(98819) 800.552.2287

● Connell ●
The M&M Motel
730 S Columbia Ave
(99326) 509.234.8811

Tumblewood Motel ($)
433 S Columbia
(99326) 509.234.2081

● Copalis Beach ●
Low Tide Motel ($)
14 McCullough Rd
(98535) 360.289.3450

Rods Beach Resort
2961 S R 109
(98535) 360.289.2222

Shades Sea Motel ($)
3208 Hwy 109
(98535) 360.289.3358

● Copalis Crossing ●
Beachwood Resort
S R 109
(98536) 360.289.2177

● Coulee City ●
Blue Top Motel ($)
109 N 6th St
(99115) 509.632.5596

Coulee Lodge Resort ($)
33017 Park Lake Rd NE
(99115) 509.632.5565

Lakeview Motel
HC 1 Box# 11
(99115) 509.632.5792

Laurent Sun Village ($$)
33575 Park Lake Rd NE
(99115) 509.632.5664

Be Discreet

● Coulee Dam ●
Coulee House Motel ($$)
110 Roosevelt Way
(99116) 509.633.1101
only in 2 rooms

Ponderosa Motel ($$)
10 Lincoln Ave
(99116) 509.633.2100

● Curlew ●
Blue Cougar Mtoel
2141 Hwy 21
(99118) 509.779.4817

● Cusick ●
The Outpost Resort
405351 Hwy 20
(99119) 509.445.1317

● Dayton ●
Blue Mountain Motel
414 W Main St
(99328) 509.382.3040

The Weinhard Hotel ($$$)
235 E Main St
(99328) 509.382.4032

● Deming ●
Glacier Creek Motel
10036 Mt Baker Hwy
(98244) 360.599.2991

Mt Baker Chalet ($$)
9857 Mt Baker Hwy
(98244) 360.599.2405

The Logs Resort
9002 Mt Baker Hwy
(98244) 360.599.2711

● Des Moines ●
Kings Arms Motel
23226 30th Ave
(98198) 206.824.0300

Legend Motel
22204 Pacific Hwy
(98198) 206.878.0366

● East Wenatchee ●
Nendels Auburn ($$)
102 15th St NE
(98802) 206.833.8007

The Four Seasons ($$)
11 Grant Rd
(98802) 509.884.6611

● Eastsound ●
North Beach Inn ($$$)
Box# 80
(98245) 360.376.2660

North Shore Cottage ($$$$)
Box# 1273
(98245) 360.376.5131

Rosario Resort ($$$)
1 Rosario Way
(98245) 800.562.8820

West Beach Resort ($$$)
RR 1 Box# 510
(98245) 360.376.2240

● Eatonville ●
Henleys Silver Lake
40718 Silver Lake Rd
(98328) 360.832.3580

● Edmonds ●
K&e Motor Inn ($$)
23921 Hwy 99
(98026) 206.778.2181

● Elbe ●
Hobo Inn ($$$)
Box# 20
(98330) 360.569.2500

● Elk ●
Jerrys Resort
41114 N Lake Shore Rd
(99009) 509.292.2337

● Ellensburg ●
Best Western ($$)
1700 Canyon Rd
(98926) 509.925.9801

Harolds Motel ($)
601 N Water St
(98926) 509.925.4141

I 90 Inn Motel ($)
1390 N Dolarway Rd
(98926) 509.925.9844

Nites Inn Motel ($$)
1200 S Ruby St
(98926) 509.962.9600
$6 per day

Regal Lodge ($)
300 W 6th Ave
(98926) 509.925.3116

Super 8 ($$)
1500 Canyon Rd
(98926) 509.962.6888
pets with deposit

Thunderbird Motel ($)
403 W 8th Ave
(98926) 800.843.3492

● EnumcLaw ●
Alta Crystal Resort ($$$)
68317 S R 410
(98022) 360.663.2500

Best Western ($$$)
1000 Griffin Ave
(98022) 360.825.4490
small pets

The Inn At The Ranch Cabin
($$$)
16423 Mountain Side Dr
(98022) 360.663.2667

● Ephrata ●
Columbia Motel ($)
1257 Basin St SW
(98823) 509.754.5226

Lariat Motel
1639 Basin St SW
(98823) 509.754.2437

● Everett ●
Cherry Motel ($)
8421 Evergreen Way
(98208) 206.347.1100

Cypress Inn ($$)
12619 4th Ave
(98204) 206.347.9099

Holiday Inn
101 128th St SE
(98208) 206.337.2900

Howard Johnson ($$$)
3501 Pine St
(98201) 206.339.3333

Motel 6 ($)
10006 Everett Way
(98204) 206.347.2060
1 small pet/room

Motel 6 ($$)
224 128th St SW
(98204) 206.353.8120
1 small pet/room

Ramada Inn ($$)
9602 19th Ave SE
(98208) 206.337.9090

Travelodge ($$)
3030 Broadway
(98201) 206.259.6141

Waits Motel ($)
1301 Lombard Ave
(98201) 206.252.3166

Welcome Motor Inn ($$)
1205 Broadway
(98201) 206.252.8828

● Federal Way ●
Best Western ($$$)
21611 20th Ave
(98003) 206.941.6000

Roadrunner Motel
1501 S 350th St
(98003) 800.828.7202

Super 8 ($$)
1688 S 348th St
(98003) 206.838.8808
call re: fees

● Ferndale ●
Super 8 ($$)
5788 Barrett Rd
(98248) 360.384.8881
call re: fees

● Forks ●
Forks Motel ($$)
351 Forks Ave
(98331) 360.374.6243

Hoh Humm Ranch
171763 Hwy 101
(98331) 360.374.5337

Kalaloch Lodge ($$$)
15715 Hwy 101
(98331) 360.962.2271

Manitou Lodge ($$)
Box# 600
(98331) 360.374.6295

Three Rivers Resort ($)
7764 La Push Rd
(98331) 360.374.5300

Town Motel
HC 80 Box# 350
(98331) 360.374.6231

● Freeland ●
Harbour Inn Motel ($)
1606 E Main St
(98249) 360.331.6900

● Friday Harbor ●
Friday Harbor Housel ($$$$)
130 West St
(98250) 360.378.8455

Inn At Friday Harbor ($$)
410 Spring St
(98250) 360.378.4000

Inn At Friday Harbor ($$)
680 Spring St
(98250) 360.378.3031

Lakedale Lodge ($$$)
2627 Roche Harbor Rd
(98250) 800.617.2267

Snug Harbor Resort ($)
2371 Mitchell Bay Rd
(98250) 360.378.4762

Sun Juan Inn ($$$)
50 Spring St
(98250) 360.378.2070

● Gig Harbor ●
Westwynd Motel
6703 144th St NW
(98332) 206.857.4047

● Goldendale ●
Barchris Motel
128 N Academy Ave
(98620) 509.773.4325

Ponderosa Motel ($$)
775 E Broadway St
(98620) 509.773.5842

● Grand Coulee ●
Trail West Motel ($)
108 Spokane Way
(99133) 509.633.3155

Umbrella Motel ($)
404 Spokane Way
(99133) 509.633.1691

● Grandview ●
Grandview Motel ($)
522 E Wine Country Rd
(98930) 509.882.1323

● Grayland ●
Grayland Motel
2013 Hwy 105
(98547) 360.267.2395

Ocean Spray Motel ($$)
1757 Hwy 105
(98547) 360.267.2205

Surf Motel ($$)
2029 Hwy 105
(98547) 360.267.2244

Walsh Motel
1593 Hwy 105
(98547) 360.267.2191

● Greenacres ●
Alpine Motel ($)
18815 E Cataldo Ave
(99016) 509.928.2700

● Hoodsport ●
Canal Creek Motel ($$)
N 27131 Hwy 101
(98548) 360.877.6770

Sunrise Motel
N 24520 Hwy 101
(98548) 360.877.5301

● Hoquiam ●
Snore&whisker Motel ($)
3031 Simpson Ave
(98550) 360.532.5060

Stoken Motel
504 Perry Ave
(98550) 360.532.4300

Timberline Inn ($)
415 Perry Ave
(98550) 360.533.8048

West Wood Inn ($$)
910 Simpson Ave
(98550) 360.532.8161
$10 fee

● Ilwaco ●
A Coho Motel
Port Of Ilwaco
(98624) 360.642.3333

Col Pacific Motel
Box# 34
(98624) 360.642.3177

Heidis Inn Motel ($$)
126 Spruce St
(98624) 360.642.2387

● Inchelium ●
Hartmans Resort
Hcr 156 Twin Lakes
(99138) 509.722.3543

Rainbow Beach Resort
HC 1 Box# 146
(99138) 509.722.5901

● Index ●
Bush House Inn
300 5th St
(98256) 360.793.2312

● Ione ●
Ione Motel ($)
301 S 2nd
(99139) 509.442.3213

Pend Oreille Inn
107 Riverside
(99139) 509.442.3418

Plaza Motel ($)
103 S 2nd
(99139) 509.442.3534

● Issaquah ●
Motel 6 ($$)
1885 15th Pl NW
(98027) 206.392.8405
1 small pet/room

● Kalama ●
Columbia Inn Motel ($)
602 N Frontage Rd
(98625) 360.673.2855

● Kelso ●
Best Western ($$)
310 Long Ave
(98626) 360.425.9660
managers discretion

Budget Inn ($)
505 N Pacific Ave
(98626) 360.636.4610

$=under $35 $$=$35-60 $$$=$60-100 $$$$=over $100

Long Beach, WASHINGTON

Motel 6 ($$)
106 N Minor Rd
(98626) 360.425.3229
1 small pet/room

Super 8 ($$)
250 Kelso Dr
(98626) 360.423.8880
call re: fees

● Kennewick ●
Cavanaughs Columbia ($$$)
1101 Columbia Center
(99336) 509.783.0611

Clearwater Inn ($$)
5616 W Clearwater Ave
(99336) 509.735.2242

Comfort Inn ($$)
7801 W Quinault St
(99336) 509.783.8396
mgr preapproval reqd

Green Gable Motel
515 W Columbia Dr
(99336) 509.582.5811

Holiday Inn ($$)
4220 W 27th Ave
(99337) 509.736.3326
mgr preapproval reqd

Nendels Inn
2811 W 2nd Ave
(99336) 509.735.9511

Shaniko Inn ($$)
321 N Johnson St
(99336) 509.735.6385

Super 8 ($$)
626 Columbia Center
(99336) 509.736.6888
call re: fees

Tapadera Budget Inn ($$)
311 N Ely Hwy 395
(99336) 509.783.6191

● Kent ●
Best Western ($$$)
1233 Central Ave
(98032) 206.852.7224
$20 deposit

Cypress Inn ($$$)
22218 84th Ave
(98032) 206.395.0219

Days Inn ($$)
1711 W Meeker St
(98032) 206.854.1950

Golden Kent Motel ($$)
22203 84th Ave
(98032) 206.872.8372

Homecourt All Suite Hotel
($$$)
6329 S 212th St
(98032) 800.426.0670

The Best Inn ($$)
23408 30th Ave
(98032) 206.870.1280

Val U Inn ($$)
22420 84th Ave
(98032) 206.872.5525
$5 fee

● Kettle Falls ●
Barneys Motel
395 & 20 Jct
(99141) 509.738.6546

Bull Hill Ranch ($$$)
3738 Bull Hill Rd
(99141) 509.732.4355

Grandview Inn Motel
978 Hwy 395
(99141) 509.738.6733

Kettle Falls Inn ($$)
205 E 3rd Ave
(99141) 509.738.6514

● Kingston ●
Smileys Colonial ($)
11067 Hwy 104
(98346) 360.297.3622

● Kirkland ●
Best Western ($$)
12223 116th Ave NE
(98034) 206.822.2300
deposit required

La Quinta Inn ($$$)
10530 Northup Way
(98033) 206.828.6585
call re: fees

Motel 6 ($$)
12010 120th Pl NE
(98034) 206.821.5618
1 small pet/room

● La Conner ●
La Conner Inn ($$$)
107 S 2nd St
(98257) 360.466.3101

● La Grande ●
Lagrande Motel
46719 Mt Hwy East
(98348) 206.832.4912

● La Push ●
Ocean Park Resort ($$)
700 Main St
(98350) 800.487.1267

● Lacey ●
Capitol Inn Motel ($$)
120 College St SE
(98503) 360.493.1991
$5 per day

Days Inn ($$)
120 College St SE
(98503) 360.493.1991
$5 per day

Super 8 ($$)
4615 Martin Way
(98516) 360.459.8888
call re: fees

● Leavenworth ●
Bayern On The River ($$)
1505 Alpensee Strasse
(98826) 509.548.5875

Budget Host ($$$)
185 Hwy 2
(98826) 509.548.7992
$10

Der Ritterhof Inn ($$$)
Box# 307
(98826) 509.548.5845

Lake Wenatchee Hideaways
($$$)
2511 Kinnikinnick Dr
(98826) 800.883.2611

Natapoc Lodging ($$$$)
12338 Bretz Rd
(98826) 509.763.3313

Obertal Motor Inn ($$$)
922 Commercial St
(98826) 509.548.5208

Rivers Edge Lodge ($$)
8401 Hwy 2
(98826) 509.548.7612
smoking rooms

Saimons Hide A Ways ($$$)
16408 River Rd
(98826) 800.845.8638

Squirrel Tree Inn
15251 Hwy 2
(98826) 509.763.3157

The Evergreen Inn ($$)
1117 Front St
(98826) 509.548.5515

Ritz Hotel ($$)
633 Front St
(98826) 509.548.5455

● Lilliwaup ●
Bonaparte Lake Resort
695 Bonaparte Lake Rd
(98555) 509.486.2828

Mikes Beach Resort
N 38470 Hwy 101
(98555) 800.231.5324

● Long Beach ●
Anchorage Court ($$)
2209 Blulevard
(98631) 360.642.2351

Arcadia Court Motel ($$)
401 Blulevard
(98631) 360.642.2613

Boulevard Motel ($)
301 Ocean Blvd
(98631) 360.642.2434

Breakers Motel ($$)
26th St & Hwy 103
(98631) 800.288.8890

Chautauqua Lodge ($$)
305 14th St NW
(98631) 800.869.8401

Light House Motel ($$)
RR 1 Box# 527
(98631) 360.642.3622

Long Beach Motel
12th South & Pacific
(98631) 206.642.3500

$=under $35 $$=$35-60   **369** $$$=$60-100 $$$$=over $100

WASHINGTON, Long Beach

Ocean Lodge ($$)
101 Boulevard
(98631) 360.642.2777

Our Place At The Beach ($$)
1309 Boulevard
(98631) 360.642.3793

Pacific View Motel ($$)
203 Bolstad St
(98631) 360.642.2415

Ridge Court Motel ($)
201 Boulevard
(98631) 360.642.2412

Sand Lo Motel
1910 Pacific Ave
(98631) 360.642.2600

Shaman Motel ($$)
115 3rd St SW
(98631) 800.753.3750

The Sands Motel
RR 1 Box# 531
(98631) 360.642.2100

Whales Tale Motel ($$)
Box# 418
(98631) 360.642.3455

• Longview •
Holiday Inn
723 7th Ave
(98632) 360.414.1000

Hudson Manor Motel ($)
1616 Hudson St
(98632) 360.425.1100

Red Lion Inn ($$$)
510 Kelso Dr
(98632) 360.636.4400
call re: fees

The Townhouse ($)
744 Washington Way
(98632) 360.423.7200

Town Chalet Motel ($)
1822 Washington Way
(98632) 360.423.2020
$3/night

• Loon Lake •
Shore Acres Resort
41987 Shore Acres Rd
(99148) 800.900.2474

• Lynden •
Windmill Inn ($)
8022 Guide Meridian Rd
(98264) 360.354.3424

• Lynnwood •
Best Western ($$$)
4300 200th St SW
(98036) 206.775.7447
small pets only

Residence Inn ($$$)
18200 Alderwood Mall Pkwy
(98037) 206.771.1100
call for fee & availability

Rose Motel
20222 Hwy 99
(98036) 206.771.9962

Silver Cloud Inn ($$)
19332 36th Ave
(98036) 206.775.7600

• Marysville •
Village Motor Inn ($$)
235 Beach Ave
(98270) 360.659.0005

• Mazama •
Lost River Resort ($$)
Harts Pass Hwy
(98833) 800.996.2537

• Mercer Island •
Mercer Isle Hideaway ($$)
8820 SE 63rd St
(98040) 206.232.1092

• Metaline Falls •
Circle Motel ($)
Hcz Box# 616 Hwy 31
(99153) 509.446.4343

• Moclips •
Barnacle Motel
4816 Pacific Ave
(98562) 360.276.4318

Hi Tide Beach Resort ($$$)
4890 Railroad Ave
(98562) 360.276.4142

Moclips Motel
4852 Pacific Ave
(98562) 360.276.4228

Moonstone Bch Motel
4849 Pacific Ave
(98562) 360.276.4346

Weekender Motel
4675 Hwy 109
(98562) 360.276.4670

• Monroe •
Best Western ($$)
19223 Hwy 2
(98272) 360.794.3111

Brookside Motel
19930 Hwy 2
(98272) 360.794.8832

Fairgrounds Inn
18950 Hwy 2
(98272) 360.794.5401

• Montesano •
Monte Square Motel
518 1/2 1st St
(98563) 206.249.4424

• Morton •
Evergreen Motel
121 Front St
(98356) 360.496.5407

Resort Of Mtns
1130 Morton Rd
(98356) 360.496.5885

Roys Motel
161 2nd St Hwy 7
(98356) 360.496.5000

Seasons Motel ($$)
200 Westlake
(98356) 360.496.6835

Stiltner Motel
30 Morton Rd
(98356) 360.496.5103

• Moses Lake •
El Rancho Motel ($)
1214 S Pioneer Way
(98837) 509.765.7193

Holiday Inn ($$$)
1745 Kittleson Rd
(98837) 509.766.2000

Interstate Inn ($$)
2801 W Broadway Ave
(98837) 509.765.1777

Lake Shore Motel ($)
3206 W Lakeshore Dr
(98837) 509.765.9201
$ 5 charge

Lakeside Motel
802 W Broadway Ave
(98837) 509.765.8651

Maples Motel
1006 W 3rd Ave
(98837) 509.765.5665

Motel 6 ($)
2822 W Wapato Dr
(98837) 509.766.0250
1 small pet/room

Oasis Budget Inn
466 Melva Ln
(98837) 509.765.8636

Sage N Sand Motel ($)
1011 S Pioneer Way
(98837) 800.336.0454

Shilo Inn ($$$)
1819 Kittleson Rd
(98837) 509.765.9317
call re: fees

Sunland Motor Inn ($)
309 E 3rd Ave
(98837) 509.765.1170

Super 8 ($$)
449 Melva Ln
(98837) 509.765.8886
pets with deposit

Travelodge ($$)
316 S Pioneer Way
(98837) 509.765.8631

• Mount Vernon •
Best Western ($$)
300 W College Way
(98273) 360.424.4287
mgr discr

Best Western ($$$)
2300 Market St
(98273) 360.428.5678

Days Inn ($)
2009 Riverside Dr
(98273) 360.424.4141

Policies Subject to Change

370

$=under $35 $$=$35-60 $$$=$60-100 $$$$=over $100

Hillside Motel
2300 Bonnieview Rd
(98273) 360.445.3252

The White Swan Inn ($$$)
1388 Moore Rd
(98273) 206.445.6805

West Winds Motel
2020 Riverside Dr
(98273) 360.424.4224

Whispering Firs
1957 Kanako Ln
(98274) 360.428.1990

● Naches ●
Game Ridge Motel ($$)
27350 Hwy 12
(98937) 509.672.2212

Silver Beach Motel
40380 Hwy 12
(98937) 509.672.2500

Squaw Rock Resort
15070 S R 410
(98937) 509.658.2926

Trout Lodge ($$)
27090 Hwy 12
(98937) 509.672.2211

● Neah Bay ●
Silver Salmon Resort
Bayview & Roosevelt
(98357) 360.645.2388

The Cape Motel
Bay View Ave
(98357) 360.645.2250

Tyee Motel
Box# 193
(98357) 360.645.2233

● Newport ●
Golden Spur Motel
924 W Hwy 2
(99156) 509.447.3823

Marshall Lk Resort
1301 Marshall Alke Rd
(99156) 509.447.4158

● North Bend ●
Edgewick Inn ($$)
14600 468th Ave SE
(98045) 206.888.9000

● Oak Harbor ●
Acorn Motor Inn ($$)
8066 80th St NW
(98277) 360.675.6646
$5 charge

Best Western ($$$)
33175 S R 20
(98277) 360.679.4567

● Ocean Park ●
Coastal Cottages ($$)
Box# 888
(98640) 360.665.4658

Ocean Park Resort ($$)
259th R St
(98640) 360.665.4585

Shakti Cove Cottages ($$)
253rd At Park
(98640) 360.665.4000

Shakti Cove Cottages ($$$)
Box# 385
(98640) 360.665.4000
friendly & peaceful

Sunset View Resort ($$$)
Box# 399
(98640) 360.665.4494
small $10 fee

Westgate Motel ($$)
20803 Pacific Way
(98640) 360.665.4211

● Ocean Shores ●
Beach Front ($$$)
759 Ocean Shores Blvd
(98569) 800.544.8887

Casa Del Oro Motel ($$$)
665 Brown Ave NW
(98569) 360.289.2281

Chalet Village Motel ($$$)
659 Ocean Shores Blvd
(98569) 360.289.4297

Discovery Inn ($$)
1031 Discovery Ave SE
(98569) 360.289.3371

Ebb Tide Motel
839 Ocean Shores Blvd
(98569) 360.289.3700

Nautilus Condos ($$$)
835 Ocean Shores
(98569) 800.221.4511

North Beach Motel ($)
2601 S R 109
(98569) 360.289.4116

Ocean Shores Motel ($$)
681 Ocean Shores Blvd
(98569) 360.289.3351

Pacific Sands Motel ($$)
2687 S R 109
(98569) 360.289.3588

Royal Pacific Motel ($$)
781 Ocean Shores Blvd NW
(98569) 360.289.3306

Sands Resort ($$)
801 Ocean Shores Blvd
(98569) 360.289.2444

Silver King Motel ($$)
1070 Discovery Ave SE
(98569) 360.289.3386

Surfview Condos ($$)
656 Ocean Court
(98569) 360.289.3077

The Grey Gull ($$$)
651 Ocean Shores Blvd
(98569) 360.289.3381

West Winds Motel ($)
Rt 4 Box# 160
(98569) 360.289.3448

Westerly Motel ($)
870 Ocean Shores
(98569) 360.289.3711

● Odessa ●
Odessa Motel ($$)
601 E First Ave
(99159) 509.982.2412

● Okanogan ●
Cariboo Inn Motel
233 Queen St
(98840) 509.422.6109

Cedars Inn ($$)
1 Appleway
(98840) 509.422.6431

Ponderose Motor Lodge ($$)
1034 2nd Ave
(98840) 509.422.0400

U&I Motel
838 2nd Ave
(98840) 509.422.2920

● Olga ●
Doe Bay Vlge Resort ($$)
HC 1 Box# 85
(98279) 360.376.2291

● Olympia ●
Bailey Motor Inn
3333 Martin Way
(98506) 360.491.7515

Best Western ($$)
900 Capitol Way
(98501) 360.352.7200
small pets

Deep Lake Resort ($$)
12405 Tilley Rd
(98512) 360.352.7388

Holiday Inn ($$$)
2300 Evergreen Park Dr SW
(98502) 360.943.4000
mgr preapproval reqd

Holly Motel
2816 Martin Way
(98506) 360.943.3000

Motel 6 ($)
400 W Lee St
(98501) 360.754.7320
1 small pet/room

● Omak ●
Omak Inn ($$)
912 Koala Ave
(98841) 509.826.3822

Royal Motel
514 E Riverside Dr
(98841) 509.826.5715

Stampede Motel
215 W 4th St
(98841) 800.639.1161

Thriftlodge ($)
122 N Main
(98841) 800.578.7878

Well Behaved

371

WASHINGTON, Oroville

● Oroville ●
Red Apple Inn ($)
1815 Main St
(98844) 509.476.3694

● Othello ●
Aladdin Motor Inn ($)
1020 E Cedar St
(99344) 509.488.5671

Cabana Motel ($)
665 E Windsor St
(99344) 800.442.4581

Mar Don Resort
8198 Hwy 262
(99344) 509.346.2651

● Pacific Beach ●
Sand Dollar Motel ($$)
53 Central
(98571) 360.276.4525

Sandpiper Resort ($$)
4159 S R 109
(98571) 360.276.4580

Shoreline Motel ($$)
12 1st St
(98571) 800.233.3365

● Packwood ●
Mountain View Motel ($)
13163 Hwy 12
(98361) 360.494.5555

Tatoosh Meadows Res ($$$)
102 E Main
(98361) 800.294.2311

● Pasco ●
Airport Motel
2532 N 4th Ave
(99301) 509.545.1460

King City Motel ($$)
2100 E Hillsboro St
(99301) 509.547.3475

Motel 6 ($)
1520 N Oregon Ave
(99301) 509.546.2010
1 small pet/room

Red Lion Inn ($$$)
2525 N 20th Ave
(99301) 509.547.0701
call re: fees

Sage N Sun Motel ($)
1232 S 10th Ave
(99301) 800.391.9188

The Vineyard Inn ($$)
1800 W Lewis St
(99301) 509.547.0791

Thunderbird Motel
414 W Columbia St
(99301) 509.547.9506

Travel Inn Motel
725 W Lewis St
(99301) 509.547.7791

Tri Mark Motel
720 W Lewis St
(99301) 509.547.7766

● Pateros ●
Lake Pateros Motel ($$)
115 Lakeshore Dr
(98846) 509.923.2207

● Peshastin ●
Timberline Hotel
8284 Hwy 2
(98847) 509.548.7415

● Pomeroy ●
Pioneer Motel ($)
1201 Main St
(99347) 509.843.1312

● Port Angeles ●
Aggies Inn ($$)
602 E Front St
(98362) 360.457.0471

Chinook Motel
1414 E 1st St
(98362) 360.452.2336

Dan Dee Motel
132 E Lauridsen Blvd
(98362) 206.457.5404

Historic Lake Lodge ($$$)
416 Lake Crescent Rd
(98363) 360.928.3211

Indian Valley Motel
7020 Hwy 101
(98362) 206.928.3266

Lake Crescent Lodge ($$$)
HC 62 Box# 11
(98362) 360.928.3211
$5 charge

Log Cabin Resort ($$)
3183 E Beach Rd
(98363) 360.928.3325

Log Cabin Resort ($$)
6540 E Beach Rd
(98363) 360.928.3325

Red Lion Inn ($$$)
221 N Lincoln St
(98362) 360.452.9215
call re: fees

Sol Duc Hot Springs ($$$)
Box# 2169
(98362) 360.327.3583

Super 8 ($$)
2104 E 1st St
(98362) 360.452.8401
$25 deposit

The Pond Motel ($)
1425 W Hwy 101
(98363) 360.452.8422

Uptown Motel ($)
101 E 2nd St
(98362) 360.457.9434

● Port Hadlock ●
Port Hadlock Inn
201 Alcohol Loop Rd
(98339) 206.385.5801

● Port Ludlow ●
Aladdin Motor Inn ($$)
2333 Wasington
(98365) 360.385.3747

Commanders House
Getaway ($$)
Point House
(98365) 360.385.2828

Gajas Getaway ($$)
4343 Haines
(98365) 360.385.1194

Inn At Ludlow Bay ($$$$)
1 Heron Rd
(98365) 360.437.0411

North Beach Retreat ($$)
510 56th St
(98365) 360.385.1621

Pilot House Getaway ($$)
327 Jackson
(98365) 360.379.0811

Point Hudson Resort ($$)
Point Hudson
(98365) 360.385.2828

The Cabin Getaway ($$$)
839 Jacob Miller
(98365) 360.385.5571

● Port Orchard ●
Cedar Hollow House ($$$)
3875 Ocker Rd
(98366) 360.871.1527

Vista Motel ($)
1090 Bethel Ave
(98366) 360.876.8046

● Port Townsend ●
Aladdin Motor Inn
2333 Washington St
(98368) 360.385.3747

Bishop Victorian ($$)
714 Washington St
(98368) 360.385.6122

Harborside Inn ($$$)
330 Benedict St
(98368) 800.942.5960

James Swan Hotel
222 Monroe St
(98368) 800.776.1718

Point Hudson Resort ($$)
Point Hudson Harbor
(98368) 800.826.3854

Port Townsend Inn ($$)
2020 Washington St
(98368) 360.385.2211

Puffin&gull Motel
825 Washington St
(98368) 360.385.1475

The Tides Inn ($$)
1807 Water St
(98368) 360.385.0595

$=under $35 $$=$35-60 $$$=$60-100 $$$$=over $100

Water Street Hotel ($$)
635 Water St
(98368) 360.385.5467

● Poulsbo ●
Cypress Inn ($$)
19801 7th Ave NE
(98370) 360.697.2119

Poulsbo Inn ($$)
18680 Hwy 305
(98370) 360.779.3921

● Prosser ●
Best Western ($$)
225 Merlot Dr
(99350) 509.786.7977
pets at mgrs discretion

Prosser Motel ($)
120 Wine Country
(99350) 509.786.2555

● Pullman ●
American Travel Inn ($)
515 S Grand Ave
(99163) 509.334.3500

Holiday Inn ($$$)
SE 1190 Bishop
(99163) 509.334.4437
mgr preapproval reqd

Manor Lodge Motel
SE 455 Paradise
(99163) 509.334.2511

Quality Inn ($$)
SE 1050 Bishop
(99163) 509.332.0500
mgr preapproval reqd

● Puyallup ●
Motel Puyallup ($$)
1412 Meridian St
(98371) 206.845.8825

Northwest Motor Inn ($$)
1409 Meridian St
(98371) 206.841.2600
$5 charge

● Quilcene ●
Maple Grove Motel ($$)
61 Maple Grove Rd
(98376) 360.765.3410

● Quinault ●
Lake Quinault Lodge ($$$)
345 S Shore Rd
(98575) 360.288.2571

● Quincy ●
The Sundowner Motel
414 F St SE
(98848) 509.787.3587

Traditional Inns ($$)
500 F St SW
(98848) 509.787.3525

● Randle ●
Medici Motel ($$)
471 Cispus Rd
(98377) 360.497.7700

Tall Timber
10023 Hwy 12
(98377) 360.497.5908

● Raymond ●
Maunus Mt Castle ($)
524 3rd St
(98577) 360.942.5571

Willis Motel
425 3rd St
(98577) 360.942.5313

● Redmond ●
Redmond Inn ($$)
17601 Redmond Way
(98052) 800.634.8080

Silver Cloud Inn ($$)
15304 NE 21st St
(98052) 206.746.8200

Silver Cloud Inn ($$$)
15304 NE 21st
(98052) 206.746.8200
small pets only

● Renton ●
Nendels Inn ($$)
3700 E Valley Rd
(98055) 206.251.9591

Silver Cloud Inn ($$)
1850 SE Maple Valley Hwy
(98055) 206.226.7600

● Republic ●
Fishermans Cove ($)
1157 Fishermans Cove Rd
(99166) 509.775.3641

Frontier Inn Hotel ($)
979 S Clark Ave
(99166) 509.775.3361

Klondike Motel
150 N Clark St
(99166) 509.775.3555

Tifanys Resort ($$)
1026 Tiffany Rd
(99166) 509.775.3152

● Richland ●
Bali Hi Motel ($$)
1201 Washington Way
(99352) 509.943.3101

Columbia Center Dunes ($)
1751 Fowler St
(99352) 509.783.8181

Nendels Inn ($$)
615 Jadwin Ave
(99352) 509.943.4611
$5 charge

Red Lion Inn ($$$)
802 George Washington Way
(99352) 509.946.7611
call re: fees

Shilo Inn ($$)
50 Comstock St
(99352) 509.946.4611

Vagabond Inn ($)
515 George Washington Way
(99352) 509.946.6117

● Ritzville ●
Best Western ($$)
1405 Smittys Blvd
(99169) 509.659.1007
pets in some rooms

Colwell Motor Inn ($$)
501 W 1st Ave
(99169) 509.659.1620

Cottage Motel
508 E 1st Ave
(99169) 509.569.0721

Top Hat Motel ($)
210 E 1st Ave
(99169) 509.659.1100

West Side Motel
407 W 1st Ave
(99169) 509.659.1164

● Rockport ●
Clarks Skagit Cabins ($$)
5675 Hwy 20
(98283) 360.873.2250

Diablo Lake Resort
Hwy 20 Mile 127 1/2
(98283) 206.386.4429

Totem Trail Motel ($)
5551 Hwy 20
(98283) 360.873.4535

● Roslyn ●
The Roslyn Inns
Box# 386
(98941) 509.649.2936

● Seatac ●
Best Western ($$$)
20717 Pacific Hwy
(98198) 206.878.3300

Continental Court ($$)
17223 32nd Ave
(98188) 800.233.1501

Hilton ($$$$)
17620 Pacific Hwy
(98188) 206.244.4800

La Quinta Inn ($$)
2824 S 188th St
(98188) 206.241.5211
call re: fees

Marriott Hotel ($$$)
3201 S 176th St
(98188) 206.241.2000

Motel 6 ($)
16500 Pacific Hwy
(98188) 206.246.4101
1 small pet/room

Motel 6 ($)
18900 47th Ave
(98188) 206.241.1648
1 small pet/room

Motel 6 ($$)
20651 Military Rd
(98198) 206.824.9902
1 small pet/room

Red Lion Inn ($$$$)
18740 Pacific Hwy
(98188) 206.433.1881
call re: fees

Shadow Motel
2930 S 176th St
(98188) 206.246.9300

Super 8 ($$$)
3100 S 192nd St
(98188) 206.433.8188
call re: fees

Thriftlodge ($)
17108 Pacific Hwy
(98188) 206.244.1230
$10 large pets

● Seattle ●
Aurora Nites Inn
11746 Aurora Ave
(98133) 206.365.3216

Aurora Seafair Inn ($$)
9100 Aurora Ave
(98103) 206.522.3754

Best Western ($$$)
200 Taylor Ave
(98109) 206.448.9444
small housebroken pets

Cavanaughs Fifth Ave
1415 5th Ave
(98101) 800.843.4667

City Center Motel
226 Aurora Ave
(98109) 206.441.0266

Days Inn ($$$)
2205 7th Ave
(98121) 206.448.3434
$3 under 25 lbs

Emerald Inn ($$)
8512 Aurora Ave
(98103) 206.522.5000

Executive Residence ($$)
2601 Elliott Ave
(98121) 800.428.3867

Executive Resort ($$$$)
2400 Elliott Ave
(98121) 206.329.8000

Geisha Motor Inn
9613 Aurora Ave
(98103) 206.524.8880

Holiday Inn
19631 International Blvd
(98188) 206.824.3200

Mayflower Park ($$$$)
405 Olive Way
(98101) 206.623.8700

Quality Inn ($$$)
2224 8th Ave
(98121) 206.624.6820
mgr preapproval reqd

Ramada Inn ($$$$)
2140 N Northgate Way
(98133) 206.365.0700
seasonal rates

Residence Inn ($$$)
800 Fairview Ave
(98109) 206.624.6000
$20 fee

Rodeside Lodge ($$)
12501 Aurora Ave
(98133) 206.364.7771

Sandpiper Villas ($$)
11000 1st Ave SW
(98146) 206.242.8883

Sea Tac Crest Motel ($$)
18845 Intl Blvd
(98188) 206.433.0999

Seattle Inn
225 Aurora Ave
(98109) 206.728.7666
$6

Sun Hill Motel
8517 Aurora Ave
(98103) 20O.525.1205

The Alexis Hotel ($$$$)
1007 1st Ave
(98104) 206.624.4844

The Four Seasons ($$$$)
411 University St
(98101) 206.621.1700
small pets allowed

Travelodge ($$$)
200 6th Ave
(98109) 206.441.7878
$25 fee

Vagabond Inn ($$)
325 Aurora Ave
(98109) 206.441.0400

Warwick Hotel ($$$)
401 Lenora St
(98121) 206.443.4300

Westcoast Roosevelt
1531 7th Ave
(98101) 206.621.1200

Westin Hotel ($$$$)
1900 5th Ave
(98101) 206.728.1000

Seattle Metro
● Arlington ●
Arlington Motor Inn ($$)
2214 Sr 530 NE
(98223) 360.652.9595

Smokey Point Motel ($$)
17329 Smokey Point Dr
(98223) 360.659.8561

● Auburn ●
Best Western ($$$)
1521 D St NE
(98002) 206.939.5950
small pets allowed

Val U Inn ($$)
9 14th St NW
(98001) 206.735.9600

● Bellevue ●
Best Western ($$$)
11211 Main St
(98004) 206.455.5240
$30 fee

Kanes Motel ($$)
14644 SE Eastgate SE Way
(98007) 206.746.8201

La Residence Suites
475 100th Ave NE
(98004) 206.455.1475

Red Lion Inn ($$$)
818 112th Ave NE
(98004) 206.455.1515
call re: fees

Residence Inn ($$$)
14455 NE 29th Pl
(98007) 206.882.1222
$50 fee $5 per day

West Coast Hotel ($$$)
625 116th Ave NE
(98004) 206.455.9444

● Bothell ●
Residence Inn ($$$)
11920 NE 195th St
(98011) 206.485.3030
$10 per day

● Bremerton ●
Dunes Motel ($$)
3400 11th St
(98312) 360.377.0093
$25 fee

Flagship Inn ($$)
4320 Kitsap Way
(98312) 360.479.6566

Midway Inn ($$)
2909 Wheaton Way
(98310) 360.479.2909

Oyster Bay Inn ($$)
4412 Kitsap Way
(98312) 360.377.5510

Quality Inn ($$$)
4303 Kitsap Way
(98312) 360.405.1111

Super 8 ($$)
5068 Kitsap Way
(98312) 360.377.8881
call re: fees

The Chieftan Motel
600 National Ave
(98312) 206.479.3111

● Des Moines ●
Kings Arms Motel
23226 30th Ave S
(98198) 206.824.0300

Legend Motel
22204 Pacific Hwy S
(98198) 206.878.0366

● EnumcLaw ●
Alta Crystal Resort ($$$)
68317 Sr 410
(98022) 360.663.2500

Seattle, WASHINGTON

Best Western ($$$)
1000 Griffin Ave
(98022) 360.825.4490
small pets

The Inn At The Ranch Cabin
($$$)
16423 Mountain Side Dr
(98022) 360.663.2667

● Everett ●
Cherry Motel ($)
8421 Evergreen Way
(98208) 206.347.1100

Cypress Inn ($$)
12619 4th Ave
(98204) 206.347.9099

Holiday Inn
101 128th St SE
(98208) 206.337.2900

Howard Johnson ($$$)
3501 Pine St
(98201) 206.339.3333

Motel 6 ($)
10006 Everett Way
(98204) 206.347.2060
1 small pet/room

Motel 6 ($$)
224 128th St SW
(98204) 206.353.8120
1 small pet/room

Ramada Inn ($$)
9602 19th Ave SE
(98208) 206.337.9090

Travelodge ($$)
3030 Broadway
(98201) 206.259.6141

Waits Motel ($)
1301 Lombard Ave
(98201) 206.252.3166

Welcome Motor Inn ($$)
1205 Broadway
(98201) 206.252.8828

● Federal Way ●
Best Western ($$$)
21611 20th Ave S
(98003) 206.941.6000

Roadrunner Motel
1501 S 350th St
(98003) 800.828.7202

Super 8 ($$)
1688 S 348th St
(98003) 206.838.8808
call re: fees

● Gig Harbor ●
Westwynd Motel
6703 144th St NW
(98332) 206.857.4047

● Issaquah ●
Motel 6 ($$)
1885 15th Pl NW
(98027) 206.392.8405
1 small pet/room

● Kent ●
Best Western ($$$)
1233 Central Ave
(98032) 206.852.7224
$20 deposit

Cypress Inn ($$$)
22218 84th Ave S
(98032) 206.395.0219

Days Inn ($$)
1711 W Meeker St
(98032) 206.854.1950

Golden Kent Motel ($$)
22203 84th Ave S
(98032) 206.872.8372

Homecourt All Suite Hotel
($$$)
6329 S 212th St
(98032) 800.426.0670

The Best Inn ($$)
23408 30th Ave S
(98032) 206.870.1280

Val U Inn ($$)
22420 84th Ave S
(98032) 206.872.5525
$5 fee

● Kirkland ●
Best Western ($$)
12223 116th Ave NE
(98034) 206.822.2300
deposit required

La Quinta Inn ($$$)
10530 Northup Way
(98033) 206.828.6585
call re: fees

Motel 6 ($$)
12010 120th Pl NE
(98034) 206.821.5618
1 small pet/room

● Lynnwood ●
Residence Inn ($$$)
18200 Alderwood Mall Pkwy
(98037) 206.771.1100
call for fee & availability

● Marysville ●
Village Motor Inn ($$)
235 Beach Ave
(98270) 360.659.0005

● Mercer Island ●
Mercer Isle Hideaway ($$)
8820 SE 63Rd St
(98040) 206.232.1092

● Monroe ●
Best Western ($$)
19223 Hwy 2
(98272) 360.794.3111

Brookside Motel
19930 Hwy 2
(98272) 360.794.8832

Fairgrounds Inn
18950 Hwy 2
(98272) 360.794.5401

● North Bend ●
Edgewick Inn ($$)
14600 468th Ave SE
(98045) 206.888.9000

● Puyallup ●
Motel Puyallup ($$)
1412 Meridian St S
(98371) 206.845.8825

Northwest Motor Inn ($$)
1409 Meridian St S
(98371) 206.841.2600
$5 charge

● Redmond ●
Redmond Inn ($$)
17601 Redmond Way
(98052) 800.634.8080

Silver Cloud Inn ($$)
15304 NE 21st St
(98052) 206.746.8200

Silver Cloud Inn ($$$)
15304 NE 21st
(98052) 206.746.8200
small pets only

● Renton ●
Nendels Inn ($$)
3700 E Valley Rd
(98055) 206.251.9591

Silver Cloud Inn ($$)
1850 SE Maple Valley Hwy
(98055) 206.226.7600

● Seatac ●
Best Western ($$$)
20717 Pacific Hwy S
(98198) 206.878.3300

Motel 6 ($$)
20651 Military Rd S
(98198) 206.824.9902
1 small pet/room

● Seattle ●
Aurora Nites Inn
11746 Aurora Ave
(98133) 206.365.3216

Aurora Seafair Inn ($$)
9100 Aurora Ave
(98103) 206.522.3754

Best Western ($$$)
200 Taylor Ave
(98109) 206.448.9444
small housebroken pets

Cavanaughs Fifth Ave
1415 5th Ave
(98101) 800.843.4667

City Center Motel
226 Aurora Ave
(98109) 206.441.0266

Days Inn ($$$)
2205 7th Ave
(98121) 206.448.3434
$3 under 25 lbs

Emerald Inn ($$)
8512 Aurora Ave
(98103) 206.522.5000

$=under $35 $$=$35-60   **375** $$$=$60-100 $$$$=over $100

WASHINGTON, Seattle

Executive Residence ($$)
2601 Elliott Ave
(98121) 800.428.3867

Executive Resort ($$$$)
2400 Elliott Ave
(98121) 206.329.8000

Geisha Motor Inn
9613 Aurora Ave
(98103) 206.524.8880

Holiday Inn
19631 International Blvd
(98188) 206.824.3200

Mayflower Park ($$$$)
405 Olive Way
(98101) 206.623.8700

Quality Inn ($$$)
2224 8th Ave
(98121) 206.624.6820
mgr preapproval reqd

Ramada Inn ($$$$)
2140 N Northgate Way
(98133) 206.365.0700
seasonal rates

Residence Inn ($$$)
800 Fairview Ave
(98109) 206.624.6000
$20 fee

Rodeside Lodge ($$)
12501 Aurora Ave
(98133) 206.364.7771

Sandpiper Villas ($$)
11000 1st Ave SW
(98146) 206.242.8883

Sea Tac Crest Motel ($$)
18845 Intl Blvd
(98188) 206.433.0999

Seattle Inn
225 Aurora Ave
(98109) 206.728.7666
$6

Sun Hill Motel
8517 Aurora Ave
(98103) 200.525.1205

The Alexis Hotel ($$$$)
1007 1st Ave
(98104) 206.624.4844

The Four Seasons ($$$$)
411 University St
(98101) 206.621.1700
small pets allowed

Travelodge ($$$)
200 6th Ave
(98109) 206.441.7878
$25 fee

Vagabond Inn ($$)
325 Aurora Ave
(98109) 206.441.0400

Warwick Hotel ($$$)
401 Lenora St
(98121) 206.443.4300

Westcoast Roosevelt
1531 7th Ave
(98101) 206.621.1200

Westin Hotel ($$$$)
1900 5th Ave
(98101) 206.728.1000

● Tacoma ●
Best Western ($$$)
5700 Pacific Hwy
(98424) 206.922.0080

Best Western ($$$)
5700 Pacific Hwy
(98424) 800.938.8500

Best Western ($$$)
8726 S Hosmer St
(98444) 206.535.2880

Best Western ($$)
6125 Motor Ave SW
(98499) 206.584.2212

Blue Spruce Motel
12715 Pacific Ave S
(98444) 206.531.6111

Budget Inn
9915 S Tacoma Way
(98499) 206.588.6615

Comfort Inn ($$)
5601 Pacific Hwy
(98424) 206.926.2301
mgr preapproval reqd

Corporate Suites
219 E Division Ct
(98404) 800.255.6058

Days Inn ($$)
3021 Pacific Hwy
(98424) 206.922.3500

Econo Lodge ($)
3518 Pacific Hwy
(98424) 206.922.0550

Golden Lion Motel
9021 S Tacoma Way
(98499) 206.588.2171

Hometel Inn ($)
3520 Pacific Hwy
(98424) 800.258.3520

Howard Johnson ($$)
8702 S Hosmer St
(98444) 206.535.3100
under 20 lbs

Kings Motor Inn
5115 Pacific Hwy
(98424) 800.929.3509

La Quinta Inn ($$$)
1425 E 27th St
(98421) 206.383.0146
call re: fees

Madigan Motel ($$)
12039 Pacific Hwy SW
(98499) 206.588.8697

Motel 6 ($)
5201 20th St
(98424) 206.922.1270
1 small pet/room

Motel 6 ($)
1811 S 76th St
(98408) 206.473.7100
1 small pet/room

Ramada Inn ($$$)
2611 E E St
(98421) 206.572.7272
$15 deposit

Royal Coachman Inn ($$)
5805 Pacific Hwy
(98424) 206.922.2500

Sheraton Inn ($$$$)
1320 Broadway
(98402) 206.572.3200

Shilo Inn ($$$)
7414 S Hosmer St
(98408) 206.475.4020
call re: fees

Western Inn ($$)
9920 S Tacoma Way
(98499) 206.588.5241
End of Seattle Metro

● Seaview ●
Seaview Coho Motel ($$)
3701 Pacific Hwy
(98644) 360.642.2531

Sou Western Lodge ($)
Beach Access Rd 38th Pl
(98644) 360.642.2542

● Sedro Woolley ●
Skagit Motel
1977 Hwy 20
(98284) 360.856.6001

Three Rivers Motel ($$)
210 Ball St
(98284) 360.855.2626

● Sekiu ●
Curleys Resort
291 Front St
(98381) 360.963.2281

Olsons Resort ($$)
Front St 444
(98381) 360.963.2311

Straitside Motel ($)
241 Front St
(98381) 360.963.2100

Van Ripers Resort
Front & Rice St
(98381) 360.963.2334

● Sequim ●
Best Western ($$)
268522 Hwy 101
(98382) 360.683.0691

Econo Lodge ($$)
801 E Washington St
(98382) 360.683.7113

Juan De Fuca Cottages ($$$)
182 Marine Dr
(98382) 360.683.4433

$=under $35 $$=$35-60 $$$=$60-100 $$$$=over $100

Red Ranch Inn ($$)
830 W Washington St
(98382) 360.683.4195

Sundowner Motel ($$)
364 W Washington St
(98382) 206.683.5532

• Shelton •
City Center Motel ($)
128 E Alder St
(98584) 360.426.3397

Lake Nahwatzel Resort ($)
12900 Shelton Matlock
(98584) 360.426.8323

Super 8 ($$)
2943 N View Cir
(98584) 360.426.1654
pets with deposit

• Shoreline •
Shoreline Motel
16526 Aurora Ave
(98133) 206.542.7777

• Silver Creek •
Lake Mayfield Motel
2911 US Hwy 12
(98585) 360.985.2484

• Silverdale •
Seabreeze Ctges ($$$$)
16609 Olympic Vw NW
(98383) 360.692.4648

• Silverlake •
Silver Lake Motel ($)
3201 Spirit Lake Hwy
(98645) 360.274.6141

• Skykomish •
Skyriver Inn ($$)
333 River Dr
(98288) 360.677.2261

The Skymoish Hotel
102 Railroad Ave
(98288) 360.677.2477

• Snoqualmie •
Salish Lodge ($$$$)
37807 SE Fall City
(98065) 206.888.2556

• Snoqualmie Pass •
Best Western ($$$)
S R 906
(98068) 206.434.6300

• Soap Lake •
Royal View Motel
Hwy 17 & 4th St
(98851) 509.246.1831

• South Bend •
H&h Motel
Box# 613
(98586) 360.875.5523

Seaquest Motel
801 W First St
(98586) 800.624.7006

• Spokane •
Als Motel
6217 N Division St
(99207) 509.487.1619

Appletree Inn
9508 N Division St
(99218) 800.323.5796

Arnolds Motel
6217 N Division St
(99207) 509.487.1619

Bel Air Motel ($)
1303 E Sprague Ave
(99202) 509.535.1677

Bell Motel
9030 W Sunset Hwy
(99224) 800.223.1388

Best Western ($$)
120 W 3rd Ave
(99204) 509.747.2011

Best Western ($$)
3033 N Division St
(99207) 509.326.5500

Best Western ($$)
9601 N Newport Hwy
(99218) 509.468.4201

Broadway Motel ($$$)
6317 E Broadway Ave
(99212) 509.535.2442

Carrolls Budget Saver ($)
1234 E Sprague Ave
(99202) 509.534.0669

Cavanaughs At Park ($$$)
303 W North River Dr
(99201) 509.326.8000

Cavanaughs Fourth Ave ($$)
110 E 4th Ave
(99202) 509.838.6100

Cavanaughs Value Inns ($)
1203 W 5th Ave
(99204) 800.843.4667

Cavanaughs River Inn ($$$)
700 N Division St
(99202) 509.326.5577

Clinic Center Motel
702 S McClellan St
(99204) 509.747.6081

Comfort Inn ($$)
6309 E Broadway Ave
(99212) 509.535.7185
mgr preapproval reqd

Comfort Inn ($$)
7111 N Division St
(99208) 509.467.7111

Comfort Inn ($$$)
905 Sullivan
(99037) 509.924.3838

Days Inn ($$)
1919 N Hutchinson Rd
(99212) 509.926.5399
small $10 fee

Liberty Motel ($$)
6801 N Division St
(99208) 509.467.6000

Mapletree Motel ($)
4824 E Sprague Ave
(99212) 509.535.5810

Motel 6 ($)
1508 S Rustle St
(99204) 509.459.6120
1 small pet/room

Nendels Valu Inn ($$$)
1420 W 2nd Ave
(99204) 509.838.2026

Quality Inn ($$$)
8923 Mission
(99212) 509.928.5218

Ramada Inn ($$)
Spokane Intl Airport
(99219) 509.838.5211

Ranch Motel ($)
1609 S Lewis St
(99224) 800.871.8919

Red Lion Inn ($$$)
322 N Spokane Falls Ct
(99201) 509.455.9600
call re: fees

Red Lion Inn ($$$)
N 1100 Sullivan Rd
(99220) 509.925.9000
call re: fees

Red Top Motel ($$)
7217 E Trent Ave
(99212) 509.926.5728

Rodeway Inn ($$)
4301 W Sunset Hwy
(99210) 509.838.1471

Rodeway Inn ($$)
827 W 1st Ave
(99204) 509.838.8271

Royal Scot Motel
20 W Houston Ave
(99208) 509.467.6672

Shamrock Motel ($$)
1629 E Sprague Ave
(99202) 509.535.0388

Shangri La Motel ($)
2922 W Government Way
(99224) 509.747.2066

Sheraton Hotel
322 N Spokane Falls Ct
(99201) 800.848.9600

Shilo Inn ($$)
923 E 3rd Ave
(99202) 509.535.9000
call re: fees

Suntree Inn ($$)
211 S Division St
(99202) 509.838.6630

Suntree Inn ($)
123 S Post St
(99204) 800.888.6630

WASHINGTON, Spokane

Super 8 ($$)
2020 N Argonne Rd
(99212) 509.928.4888
w/permission

Super 8 ($$)
11102 W Westbow Blvd
(99224) 509.838.8800
call re: fees

The Westcoast ($$)
515 W Sprague Ave
(99204) 509.838.2711

Wolff Lodging ($)
1825 N Hutchison Rd
(99212) 800.528.9519

● Sprague ●
Last Roundup Motel
312 E First
(99032) 509.257.2593

Purple Sage Motel
405 W First
(99032) 509.257.2507

● Steilacoom ●
Salishan Lodge ($$$$)
7760 Hwy 101
(98388) 431.764.2371

● Stevenson ●
Econo Lodge ($$)
40 NE 2nd St
(98648) 509.427.5628

● Sultan ●
Dutch Cup Motel ($$)
918 Main St
(98294) 360.793.2215

● Sunnyside ●
Red Apple Motel
412 Yakima Valley Hwy
(98944) 509.839.2100

Sun Valley Inn ($)
724 Yakima Valley Hwy
(98944) 509.837.4721

Town House Motel ($$)
509 Yakima Valley Hwy
(98944) 509.837.5500
$25 fee

Travelodge ($$)
408 Yakima Valley Hwy
(98944) 509.837.7878

● Tacoma ●
Best Western ($$$)
5700 Pacific Hwy
(98424) 206.922.0080

Best Western ($$$)
5700 Pacific Hwy
(98424) 800.938.8500

Best Western ($$$)
8726 S Hosmer St
(98444) 206.535.2880

Best Western ($$)
6125 Motor Ave SW
(98499) 206.584.2212

Blue Spruce Motel
12715 Pacific Ave
(98444) 206.531.6111

Budget Inn
9915 S Tacoma Way
(98499) 206.588.6615

Comfort Inn ($$)
5601 Pacific Hwy
(98424) 206.926.2301
mgr preapproval reqd

Corporate Suites
219 E Division Ct
(98404) 800.255.6058

Days Inn ($$)
3021 Pacific Hwy
(98424) 206.922.3500

Econo Lodge ($)
3518 Pacific Hwy
(98424) 206.922.0550

Golden Lion Motel
9021 S Tacoma Way
(98499) 206.588.2171

Hometel Inn ($)
3520 Pacific Hwy
(98424) 800.258.3520

Howard Johnson ($$)
8702 S Hosmer St
(98444) 206.535.3100
under 20 lbs

Kings Motor Inn
5115 Pacific Hwy
(98424) 800.929.3509

La Quinta Inn ($$$)
1425 E 27th St
(98421) 206.383.0146
call re: fees

Madigan Motel ($$)
12039 Pacific Hwy SW
(98499) 206.588.8697

Motel 6 ($)
5201 20th St
(98424) 206.922.1270
1 small pet/room

Motel 6 ($)
1811 S 76th St
(98408) 206.473.7100
1 small pet/room

Ramada Inn ($$$)
2611 E E St
(98421) 206.572.7272
$15 deposit

Royal Coachman Inn ($$)
5805 Pacific Hwy
(98424) 206.922.2500

Sheraton Inn ($$$$)
1320 Broadway
(98402) 206.572.3200

Shilo Inn ($$$)
7414 S Hosmer St
(98408) 206.475.4020
call re: fees

Western Inn ($$)
9920 S Tacoma Way
(98499) 206.588.5241

● Tenino ●
Holiday Inn
685 Ocean Shores Blvd
(98589) 360.289.4900

● Thorp ●
Circle H Holiday Resort
810 Watt Canyon Rd
(98946) 509.964.2000

● Tokeland ●
Tradewinds Bay Motel
4305 Pomeroy Ave
(98590) 360.267.7500

● Toledo ●
Cowlitz Motel
162 Cowlitz Loop Rd
(98591) 360.864.6611

● Tonasket ●
Rainbow Resort
761 Loomis Hwy
(98855) 509.223.3700

Red Apple Inn ($$)
Hwy 97 & 1st St
(98855) 509.486.2119

Spectacle Falls Motel
879 Loomis Hwy
(98855) 509.233.4141

Spectacle Lake Resort ($)
10 McCammon Rd
(98855) 509.223.3433

● Toppenish ●
El Corral Motel ($)
61731 Hwy 97
(98948) 509.865.2365

Oxbow Motor Inn ($$)
511 S Elm St
(98948) 509.865.5800

Toppenish Motel ($$)
515 S Elm St
(98948) 509.865.7444

● Tukwila ●
Best Western ($$$)
15901 W Valley Hwy
(98188) 206.226.1812

Doubletree ($$$)
205 Strander Blvd
(98188) 206.575.8220
$25 fee

Econo Lodge ($$)
13910 Pacific Hwy
(98168) 209.922.0550

Embassy Suites ($$$$)
15920 W Valley Hwy
(98188) 206.227.8844

Hampton Inn ($$$)
7200 S 156th St
(98188) 206.228.5800

CALL AHEAD!

$=under $35 $$=$35-60 $$$=$60-100 $$$$=over $10

Homewood Suites ($$$$)
6955 Fort Dent Way
(98188) 206.433.8000
$175 fee

Residence Inn ($$$$)
16201 W Valley Hwy
(98188) 800.331.3131

Residence Inn ($$$$)
16201 W Valley Hwy
(98188) 206.226.5500
call for fee & availability

South City Motel
14242 Pacific Hwy
(98168) 206.243.0222

Town&country Suites ($$)
14800 Interurban Ave
(98168) 206.246.2323

● Tumwater ●
Best Western ($$)
5188 Capitol Blvd
(98501) 360.956.1235
$5 charge-small pets only

Lee Street Suites
348 Lee St SW
(98501) 360.943.8391

Shalimar Suites
5895 Capitol Blvd
(98501) 360.943.8391

Tyee Hotel ($$$)
500 Tyee Dr SW
(98512) 360.352.0511

● Twisp ●
Idle A While Motel ($$)
505 North Hwy 20
(98856) 509.997.3222

Sportsman Motel
1010 E Hwy 20
(98856) 509.997.2911

Wagon Wheel Motel
HC 73 Box# 57
(98856) 509.997.4671

● Union ●
Aldebrook Resort ($$)
E 7101 Hwy 106
(98592) 360.898.2200

Robin Hood Village ($$)
106
(98592) 360.898.2163

● Union Gap ●
Days Inn ($$)
2408 Rudkin Rd
(98903) 509.248.9700

La Casa Motel
2703 Main St
(98903) 509.457.6147

● Usk ●
The Inn At Usk
410 River Rd
(99180) 509.445.1526

● Valley ●
Teals Waitts Resort
3365 Waitts Lake Rd
(99181) 509.937.2400

● Vancouver ●
Best Western ($$$$)
780 NE Greenwood Dr
(98662) 360.254.3100

Best Western ($$)
7901 NE 6th Ave
(98665) 360.574.2151
$3 charge

Red Lion Inn ($$$)
100 Columbia St
(98660) 360.694.8341
call re: fees

Residence Inn ($$$$)
8005 NE Park Way Dr
(98662) 360.253.4800

Rodeway Inn ($$)
221 NE Chalkov Dr
(98684) 360.256.7044

Shilo Inn ($$)
401 E 13th St
(98660) 360.696.0411
call re: fees

Shilo Inn ($$)
13206 NE Hwy 99
(98686) 360.573.0511

Sunnyside Motel
12200 NE Hwy 99
(98686) 206.573.4141

The Fort Motel
500 E 13th St
(98660) 360.694.3327

Value Motel
708 NE 78th St
(98665) 360.574.2345

Vancouver Lodge ($$)
601 Broadway St
(98660) 360.693.3668

● Vashon ●
Sojourn House
27415 94th Ave SW
(98070) 206.463.5193

Swallows Nest Cottages ($$)
6030 SW 248th St
(98070) 206.463.2646

● Waitsburg ●
Waitsburg Motel
711 Coppei Ave
(99361) 509.337.8103

● Walla Walla ●
A&h Motel
2599 E Isaacs Ave
(99362) 509.529.0560

Best Western ($$)
7 E Oak St
(99362) 509.525.4700

Capri Motel ($$)
2003 E Melrose St
(99362) 509.525.1130

City Center Motel
627 W Main St
(99362) 509.529.2660

Comfort Inn ($$)
520 N 2nd Ave
(99362) 509.525.2522
mgr preapproval reqd

Pony Solider Motel ($$$)
326 E Main St
(99362) 509.529.4360

Super 8 ($$)
2315 Eastgate St
(99362) 509.525.8800
deposit

Tapadera Budget Inn ($)
211 N 2nd Ave
(99362) 800.722.8277

Whitman Inn ($$)
107 N 2nd Ave
(99362) 509.525.2200

● Washougal ●
Econo Lodge ($$)
544 6th St
(98671) 360.835.8591

● Wenatchee ●
Avenue Motel ($)
720 N Wenatchee Ave
(98801) 509.663.7161

Best Western ($$$)
1905 N Wenatchee Ave
(98801) 509.664.6565

Chieftan Motel ($$)
1005 N Wenatchee Ave
(98801) 509.663.8141

Hill Crest Motel
2921 School St
(98801) 509.663.5157

Holiday Lodge ($$)
610 N Wenatchee Ave
(98801) 509.662.8167

Motel Lyles ($$)
924 N Wenatchee Ave
(98801) 800.582.3788

Orchard Inn ($$)
1401 N Miller St
(98801) 509.662.3443

Red Lion Inn ($$$)
1225 N Wenactchee Ave
(98801) 509.663.0711
call re: fees

The Uptowner Motel
101 N Mission St
(98801) 509.288.5279

Vagabond Inn ($)
700 N Wenatchee Ave
(98801) 509.663.8133

West Coast Hotel ($$$)
201 N Wenatchee Ave
(98801) 509.663.1234

NO Fleas

$=under $35 $$=$35-60 $$$=$60-100 $$$$=over $100

● Westport ●
Albatross Motel ($$)
200 E Dock St
(98595) 360.268.9235

Breakers Motel
971 S Montesano St
(98595) 360.268.0848

Chinook Motel
707 N Montesano
(98595) 360.268.9623

Cranberry Motel
920 S Montesano St
(98595) 360.268.0807

Frank L Motel
725 S Montesano St
(98595) 360.268.9200

Harbor Resort
871 Neddie Rose Dr
(98595) 360.268.0169

Mariners Cove Inn ($$)
303 Ocean Ave
(98595) 360.268.0531

Ocean Ave Inn
275 Ocean Ave
(98595) 360.268.9278

Sands Motel
1416 S Montesano St
(98595) 800.654.5250

Shipwreck Motel
2653 Nyhus
(98595) 360.268.9151

● Wilbur ●
Settle Inn ($)
303 NE Main
(99185) 509.647.2100

● Winlock ●
Sunrise Motel ($$)
663 S R 505
(98596) 360.785.4343

● Winthrop ●
The Chewuch Inn Motel ($$)
223 White Ave
(98862) 509.996.3107

The Virginian Resort ($$)
808 N Cascase Hwy
(98862) 509.996.2535

Winthrop Inn ($$)
E Thinthrop Hwy 20
(98862) 509.996.2217

Wolfridge Resort
412B Wolf Creek Rd
(98862) 509.996.2828

● Woodland ●
Hansens Motel
1215 Pacific Ave
(98674) 360.225.7018

Lakeside Motel
785 Lake Shore Dr
(98674) 360.225.8240

Lewis River Inn ($$)
1100 Lewis River Rd
(98674) 360.225.6257

Scandia Motel ($$)
1123 Hoffman St
(98674) 360.225.8006

Woodlander Inn ($$)
1500 Atlantic Ave
(98674) 360.225.6548

● Yakima ●
Bali Hai Motel ($)
710 N 1st St
(98901) 509.452.7178

Cavanaughs Yakima Ctr ($$)
607 E Yakima Ave
(98901) 509.248.5900

Colonial Motor Inn ($$)
1405 N 1st St
(98901) 509.453.8981

Holiday Inn ($$$)
9 N 9th St
(98901) 509.452.6511
mgr preapproval reqd

Motel 6 ($)
1104 N 1st St
(98901) 509.454.0080
1 small pet/room

RedApple Motel
416 N 1st St
(98901) 509.248.7150

Red Lion Inn ($$)
818 N 1st St
(98901) 509.453.0391
call re: fees

Red Lion Inn ($$$)
1507 N 1st St
(98901) 509.248.7850
call re: fees

Tourist Motor Inn
1223 N 1st St
(98901) 509.452.6551

Vagabond Inn ($$)
510 N 1st St
(98901) 509.457.6155
$10 per day

● Yelm ●
Prairie Motel
700 Prairie Park Ln
(98597) 360.458.8300

West Virginia
● Beckley ●
Beckley Hotel ($$$$)
1940 Harper Rd
(25801) 800.274.6010

Best Western ($$)
1939 Harper Rd
(25801) 304.252.0671
$5 fee

Charles House Motel
223 S Heber St
(25801) 304.253.8318

Comfort Inn ($$)
1909 Harper Rd
(25801) 304.255.2161
mgr preapproval reqd

Howard Johnson ($$)
1907 Harper Rd
(25801) 800.446.4656

Super 8 ($$)
2014 Harper Rd
(25801) 304.253.0802
pets w/permission

● Berkeley Springs ●
Park Haven Motel
RR 1 Box# 298
(25411) 304.258.1734

● Bluefield ●
Econo Lodge ($$)
3400 E Cumberland Rd
(24701) 304.327.8171

Holiday Inn ($$)
US 460
(24701) 800.465.4329
mgr preapproval reqd

Ramada Inn ($$)
3175 E Cumberland Rd
(24701) 304.325.5421

● Bridgeport ●
Hedges Motel
Rt 50
(26330) 304.842.2811

Holiday Inn ($$)
100 Lodgeville Rd
(26330) 304.842.5411
mgr preapproval reqd

Knights Inn ($$)
1235 W Main St
(26330) 304.842.7115
size limits & fees

Super 8 ($$)
S R 2
(26330) 304.842.7381
$7/pet

● Buckhannon ●
Baxa Hotel Motel ($)
21 N Kanawha St
(26201) 304.472.2500

Colonial Motel
24 N Kanawha St
(26201) 304.472.3000

● Burnsville ●
Burnsville Motel ($)
5th & Main
(26335) 304.853.2918

● Chapmanville ●
Rodeway Inn ($$)
Box# 4545
(25508) 304.855.7182

● Charleston ●
Days Inn ($$)
6400 Maccorkle Ave SE
(25304) 304.925.1010

Be
Discreet

Martinsburg, WEST VIRGINIA

Hampton Inn ($$$)
1 Preferred Pl
(25309) 304.746.4646

Holiday Inn
600 Kanawha Bl
(25301) 304.344.4092

Knights Inn ($$)
6401 Maccorkle Ave SE
(25304) 304.925.0451
size limits & fees

Microtel ($)
600 Second St
(25303) 304.744.4900

Motel 6 ($)
6311 Maccorkle Ave SE
(25304) 304.925.0471
1 small pet/room

Motel 6 ($)
330 Goff Mountain Rd
(25313) 304.776.5911
1 small pet/room

Ramada Inn ($$)
2nd Ave & B St
(25303) 304.744.4641

Red Roof Inn ($$)
6305 Maccorkle Ave SE
(25304) 304.925.6953

Red Roof Inn ($$)
4006 Maccorkle Ave SW
(25309) 304.744.1500

Shoneys Inn
2033 Harper Rd
(25313) 304.255.9091

● Clarksburg ●
Terrace Motel
1202 E Pike St
(26301) 304.622.6161

● Davis ●
Deerfield Vlg Resort ($$$$)
Cortland Ln
(26260) 304.866.4698

Highland Village ($)
Box# 656
(26260) 304.259.5551

● Dunbar ●
Super 8 ($$)
911 Dunbar Ave
(25064) 304.768.6888
call re: fees

● Elkins ●
Best Western ($$)
Rt 219
(26241) 304.636.7711
small $5/day

Cheat River Lodge
RR 1 Box# 115
(26241) 304.636.2301

Cheat River Lodge ($$)
Rt 1
(26241) 304.636.2301
$4 owner rfd

Days Inn ($$)
1200 Harrison Ave
(26241) 304.637.4667

Econo Lodge ($$)
RR 1 Box# 15
(26241) 304.636.5311

Mountain Splendor
Box# 1802
(26241) 304.636.8111

Super 8 ($$)
RR 3 Box# 284
(26241) 304.636.6500
call re: fees

● Fairmont ●
Country Club Motel ($)
1499 Locust Ave
(26554) 304.366.4141

Econo Lodge ($$)
226 Middletown Rd
(26554) 304.366.5995

Holiday Inn ($$)
I-79 & E Grafton Rd
(26554) 304.366.5500
mgr preapproval reqd

Red Roof Inn ($)
50 Middletown Rd
(26554) 304.366.6800
small pets only

● Dunbar ●

Super 8 ($$)
I-79 Kingmont Ex
(26554) 800.800.8000
call re: fees

● Fayetteville ●
Comfort Inn ($)
US 19& Laurel Creek Rd
(25840) 304.574.3443
mgr preapproval reqd

● Franklin ●
Mt State Motel
Rt 220
(26807) 304.358.2084

● Ghent ●
Econo Lodge ($$)
I-77 Ex 28 Odd Rd
(25843) 304.787.3250

● Harpers Ferry ●
Cliffside Inn ($$)
US Rt 340
(25425) 800.786.9437

● Hillsboro ●
The Current
Denmar Rd
(24946) 304.653.4722

● Huntington ●
Days Inn ($)
5196 US 60
(25705) 304.529.1331

Radisson Inn ($$$)
1001 3rd Ave
(25701) 304.525.1001
small pets allowed

Red Roof Inn ($$)
5190 US 60
(25705) 304.733.3737

● Hurricane ●
Ramada Ltd ($)
419 Hurricane Creek Rd
(25526) 304.562.3346

Red Roof Inn ($)
I-64 At S R 34
(25526) 304.757.6392

● Jane Lew ●
Wilderness Plantation ($$)
Box# 96
(26378) 304.884.7806

● Keyser ●
Econo Lodge ($$)
US 220
(26726) 304.788.0913

● Lewisburg ●
Brier Inn ($$)
540 N Jefferson St
(24901) 304.645.7722

Budget Host ($)
204 N Jefferson St
(24901) 304.645.3055
$5

Days Inn ($$)
635 N Jefferson St
(24901) 304.645.2345

General Lewis Inn ($$)
301 E Washington St
(24901) 304.645.2600

Super 8 ($$)
550 N Jefferson St
(24901) 304.647.3188
w/permission

● Logan ●
Super 8 ($$)
316 Riverview Ave
(25601) 304.752.8787
w/permission

● Martinsburg ●
Days Inn ($$)
209 S Viking Way
(25401) 304.263.1800

Econo Lodge ($$)
I-81 & Spring Mills Rd
(25401) 304.274.2181

Holiday Inn ($$$)
301 Foxcroft Ave
(25401) 304.267.5500
mgr preapproval reqd

Knights Inn ($$)
1599 Edwin Miller Blvd
(25401) 304.267.2211
call for size limits & fees

Krista Lite Motel ($)
Rt 1
(25401) 304.267.2900

Policies Subject to Change

381

$=under $35 $$=$35-60 $$$=$60-100 $$$$=over $100

Pikeside Motel ($)
2138 Winchester Pike
(25401) 304.263.5189

Scottish Inn ($)
1024 Winchester Ave
(25401) 304.267.2935

● Morgantown ●
Econo Lodge ($$)
3506 Monongahela Blvd
(26505) 304.599.8181

Friendship Inn ($$)
452 Country Club Dr
(26505) 304.599.4850

Holiday Inn ($$)
1400 Saratoga St
(26505) 304.599.1680
mgr preapproval reqd

● New Creek ●
Toll Gate Motel ($)
HC 72 Box# 121
(26743) 304.788.5100

● Nitro ●
Best Western ($$)
4115 1st Ave
(25143) 304.755.8341
small mgrs discretion

● Oceana ●
Oceana Motel
Cook Parkway
(24870) 304.682.6186

● Parkersburg ●
Best Western ($$)
US 50
(26101) 304.485.6511

Econo Lodge ($)
US 50
(26101) 800.424.4777

Red Roof Inn ($$)
3714 E 7th St
(26101) 304.485.1741
small pets only

The Stables Lodge
3604 7th St
(26101) 304.424.5100

● Pence Springs ●
Pence Springs Hotel ($$)
Box# 90
(24962) 304.445.2606

● Princeton ●
Budget Host ($$)
1115 Oakvale
(24740) 304.425.8711
small only

Days Inn ($$)
Rt 469
(24740) 304.425.8100
$5/pets

Town&country Motel ($)
805 Oakvale Rd
(24740) 304.425.8156

● Ravenswood ●
Scottish Inn
Rt 2
(26164) 304.273.2830

● Richwood ●
The Four Seasons
39-55 Rt Marlinton
(26261) 304.846.4605

● Ripley ●
Econo Lodge ($$)
1 Hospitality Dr
(25271) 304.372.5000

Super 8 ($$)
102 Duke St
(25271) 304.372.8880
pets w/permission

● Saint Albans ●
Days Inn ($$)
6210 Maccorkle Ave
(25177) 304.766.6231
small dog

● Summersville ●
Best Western ($$)
1203 Broad St
(26651) 304.872.6900
small

Comfort Inn ($$)
903 N Industrial Dr
(26651) 304.872.6500
mgr preapproval reqd

Sleep Inn ($$)
701 Professional Park Dr
(26651) 304.872.4500
mgr preapproval reqd

Super 8 ($$)
306 Merchants Walk
(26651) 304.872.4888
call re: fees

● Sutton ●
Elk Motor Court
35 Camden Ave
(26601) 304.765.7173

● Triadelphia ●
Days Inn ($$)
RR 1 Box# 292
(26059) 800.329.7466

● Weston ●
Comfort Inn ($$)
I-79 & US 33
(26452) 304.269.7000
mgr preapproval reqd

Super 8 ($$)
12 Market Place Mall
(26452) 304.269.1086
w/permission

● Wheeling ●
Wilson Lodge ($$$)
S R 88
(26003) 304.243.4000

● White Sulphur Springs ●
Budget Inn ($)
830 E Main St
(24986) 304.536.2121

Old White Motel ($)
865 E Main St
(24986) 304.536.2441

Wisconsin
● Abbotsford ●
Cedar Crest Motel ($)
207 N 4th St
(54405) 715.223.3661

Home Motel ($)
412 N 4th St
(54405) 715.223.6343

● Abrams ●
Foster Farm House ($$)
4991 Hwy 41
(54101) 414.826.7570

● Algoma ●
Algoma Beach Motel ($)
1500 Lake St
(54201) 414.487.2828

Harbor Inn Motel ($$)
99 Michigan St
(54201) 414.487.5241

River Hills Motel ($)
820 N Water St
(54201) 414.487.3451

Scenic Shore Inn ($)
2221 Lake St
(54201) 414.487.3214

West Wind Shores ($$)
N6870 Hwy 42
(54201) 414.487.5867

● Alma ●
Reidts Motel ($)
S1638 S R 35
(54610) 608.685.4843

● Amery ●
Amerys Camelot Motel ($)
359 Keller Ave
(54001) 715.268.8194

Forrest Inn Motel ($$)
1045 Riverplace Dr
(54001) 715.268.4100

● Antigo ●
Super 8 ($$)
535 Century Ave
(54409) 715.623.4188
pets w/permission

● Appleton ●
Best Western ($$$)
3033 W College Ave
(54914) 414.731.4141

Budgetel ($$)
3920 W College Ave
(54914) 414.734.6070
call for fees & size
restrictions

$=under $35 $$=$35-60 $$$=$60-100 $$$$=over $100

Comfort Suites ($$$)
3809 W Wisconsin Ave
(54914) 414.730.3800
mgr preapproval reqd

Exel Inn ($$)
20 N Westhill Blvd
(54914) 414.733.5551
small pets only

Fairfield Inn ($$)
132 N Mall Dr
(54915) 414.954.0202

Residence Inn
310 N Metro Dr
(54915) 414.954.0570

Roadstar Inn ($)
3623 W College Ave
(54914) 414.731.5271

Snug Inn Motel ($)
3437 N Richmond St
(54911) 414.739.7316

Woodfield Suites ($$$)
3730 W College Ave
(54914) 414.734.7777

● Arcadia ●
Rkd Motel ($)
915 E Main Hwy 95
(54612) 608.323.3338

● Ashland ●
Andersons Motel ($)
2200 Lake Shore Dr
(54806) 715.682.4658

Bayview Motel ($)
2419 Lake Shore Dr
(54806) 715.682.5253

Best Western ($$)
Hwy 12 Lakeshore Dr
(54806) 715.682.5235
small pets

Crest Motel ($$)
Sanborn Ave & Hwy 2
(54806) 715.682.6603

Harbor Motel ($)
1200 Lake Shore Dr
(54806) 715.682.5211

Hotel Chequamegon ($$)
101 Lakeshore Dr
(54806) 715.682.9095

Lake Aire Motor Inn ($)
US 2 & Hwy 13
(54806) 715.682.4551

Super 8 ($$)
1610 Lake Shore Dr
(54806) 715.682.9377
w/permission

Town Motel ($$)
920 Lake Shore Dr
(54806) 715.682.5555

● Baileys Harbor ●
Journey End Motel ($$)
2528 Cty Rd F
(54202) 414.839.2887

Parent Motel ($$)
8404 Hwy 57
(54202) 414.839.2218

Ridges Resort ($$)
8252 Hwy 57
(54202) 414.839.2288

Sands Resort Motel ($$)
2371 Ridge Dr
(54202) 414.839.2401
$5 charge seasonal

● Baldwin ●
Colonial Motel ($)
I-94 & US 63
(54002) 715.684.3351

● Balsam Lake ●
Balsam Lake Motel ($)
501 W Main St
(54810) 715.485.3501

Fox Den Motel ($)
101 County Rd 1
(54810) 715.485.3400

● Baraboo ●
4 Winds Motel ($)
4090 Hwy 12
(53913) 608.356.0963

Best Western ($$)
725 W Pine St
(53913) 608.356.1100

Howard Johnson ($)
750 W Pine St
(53913) 608.356.8366

Spinning Wheel Motel ($)
809 8th St
(53913) 608.356.3933

Swansons Motel ($)
414 8th Ave
(53913) 608.835.4005

Thunderbird Motel ($$)
1013 8th St
(53913) 608.356.7757

● Bayfield ●
Appletree Inn ($$$)
RR 1 Box# 251
(54814) 715.779.5572

Bay Villa Motel ($$)
RR 1 Box# 33
(54814) 715.779.3252

Harbors Edge Motel ($$)
33 N Front St
(54814) 715.779.3962

Seagull Bay Motel ($)
Hwy13
(54814) 715.779.5558

Winfield Inn ($)
RR 1 Box# 33
(54814) 715.779.5180

● Beaver Dam ●
Grand View Motel ($)
1510 N Center St
(53916) 414.885.9208

Super 8 ($$)
711 Park Ave
(53916) 414.887.8880
$50 deposit

● Belgium ●
Quarry Inn Motel ($)
690 Hwy D
(53004) 414.285.3475

● Beloit ●
Comfort Inn ($$)
2786 Milwaukee Rd
(53511) 608.362.2666
mgr preapproval reqd

Driftwood Motel ($)
1826 Riverside Dr
(53511) 608.364.4081

Econo Lodge ($)
2956 Milwaukee Rd
(53511) 608.364.4000

Ikes Motel ($)
114 Dearborn St
(53511) 608.362.3423

● Berlin ●
Travelers Rest Motel ($)
227 Ripon Rd
(54923) 414.361.4441

● Black River Falls ●
American Budget Inn ($$)
919 Hwy 54
(54615) 715.284.4333

Best Western ($$)
I-94 Hwy 54
(54615) 715.284.9471

Falls Economy Motel ($)
512 E 2nd St
(54615) 715.284.9919

Pines Motor Lodge ($)
I-94 & Hwy 12N
(54615) 715.284.5311

River Crest Resort ($$)
N6978 Hwy 12
(54615) 152.844.763

● Bloomer ●
Oaside Motel ($)
2407 Woodard Dr
(54724) 715.568.3234

● Boscobel ●
Hubbell Motel ($)
RR 2 Hwy 60
(53805) 608.375.4277

● Boulder Junction ●
Wildcat Lodge ($$)
Hwy M
(54512) 715.385.2421

Zastrows Lynx Lodge ($$$$)
Box# 277
(54512) 715.686.2249

Well Behaved

WISCONSIN, Brantwood

● Brantwood ●
Palmquists Farm ($$)
RR 1 Box# 134
(54513) 715.564.2558

● Brillion ●
Sandman Motel ($)
550 W Ryan St
(54110) 414.756.2106

● Brookfield ●
Marriott Hotel ($$$)
375 S Moorland Rd
(53005) 414.786.1100

Motel 6 ($)
20300 W Bluemound Rd
(53045) 414.786.7337
1 small pet/room

Residence Inn ($$$)
950 Pinehurst Ct
(53005) 414.782.5990
$175fee & $6/day per pet

● Burlington ●
Rainbow Motel ($$)
733 Milwaukee Ave
(53105) 414.763.2491

● Cable ●
Alpine Resort Motel ($$)
HC 60 Box# 48
(54821) 715.798.3603

Lakewoods Resort ($$)
HC 73 Box# 715
(54821) 715.792.2561

● Camp Douglas ●
K&K Motel ($)
RR 2 Box# 242
(54618) 608.427.3100

● Campbellsport ●
Melke Mauk House ($$)
W 977 Hwy F
(53010) 414.533.8602

Newcastle Pines ($$$)
N1499 Highwayh 45
(53010) 414.533.5252

● Cascade ●
Hoefts Resort ($$$)
W9070 Crooked Lake Dr
(53011) 414.626.2221

Timberlake Inn ($$)
311 Madison Ave
(53011) 414.528.8481

● Cassville ●
Eagles Roost Resort ($)
1034 Jack Oak Rd
(53806) 608.725.5553

Sand Bar Motel ($)
1115 E Bluff St
(53806) 608.725.5300

The Geiger House ($$)
401 Denniston St
(53806) 608.725.5419

● Chilton ●
Thunderbird Motel ($$)
121 E Chestnut St
(53014) 414.846.4216

● Chippewa Falls ●
Americinn Motel ($$)
11 W South Ave
(54729) 715.723.5711

Country Villa Motel ($)
RR 3 Box# 40
(54729) 715.288.6376

Indianhead Motel ($)
501 Summit Ave
(54729) 715.723.9171

Lake Aire Motel ($)
5732 183rd St
(54729) 715.723.2231

● Clear Lake ●
Athletic Club Motel ($)
200 Digital Dr
(54005) 715.263.3111

● Clintonville ●
Clintonville Motel
297 S Main St # T
(54929) 715.823.6565

● Columbus ●
Dering House ($)
251 W James St
(53925) 414.632.2015

● Crandon ●
Lakeland Motel ($)
400 S Lake Ave
(54520) 715.478.2423

Rustic Haven Resort ($$)
RR 1 Box# 93
(54520) 715.478.2255

● Crivitz ●
Bonnie Bell Motel ($)
1450 US Hwy 141
(54114) 715.854.7395

Shaffer Park Motel ($$)
RR 3
(54114) 715.854.2186

The Pines Motel ($)
7968 N Hwy 141
(54114) 715.854.7987

● Darlington ●
Towne Motel
245 W Harriet St
(53530) 608.776.2661

● Dickeyville ●
Plaza Motel ($)
203 S Main
(53808) 608.568.7562

● Dodgeville ●
Best Western ($$$)
Hwy 18 Johns St
(53533) 800.528.1234

Super 8 ($$)
1308 N Johns St
(53533) 618.935.3888
pets w/ permission & $50
refundable dep

● Dresser ●
Valley Motel ($)
211 State Road 35
(54009) 715.755.2781

● Dunbar ●
Richards Motel ($)
11466 W Hwy 8
(54119) 715.324.5444

● Durand ●
Durand Motel ($)
610 11th Ave
(54736) 715.755.2781

● Eagle River ●
American Budget Inn ($$)
780 Hwy 45
(54521) 715.479.5151

Eagle River Inn ($$$)
5260 Hwy 70
(54521) 715.479.2000

Gypsy Villa Resort ($$$$)
950 Circle Dr
(54521) 800.232.9714

Riverside Motel
5012 Hwy 70
(54521) 800.530.0019
depends-type of pet&season

The Edgewater Inn ($$)
5054 Hwy 70
(54521) 715.479.4011

White Eagle Motel ($)
4948 Hwy 70
(54521) 715.479.4426
small pets only

● Eau Claire ●
Best Western ($$)
1828 S Hastings Way
(54701) 715.832.8356
small

Comfort Inn ($$)
3117 Craig Rd
(54701) 715.833.9798
mgr preapproval reqd

Days Inn ($$)
6319 Truax Ln
(54703) 715.874.5550

Eau Claire Motel ($)
3210 E Clairemont Ave
(54701) 715.835.5148

Exel Inn ($)
2305 Craig Rd
(54701) 715.834.3193
small pets only

Heartland Inn ($$)
4075 Commonwealth Ave
(54701) 715.839.7100
smoking rooms

Highlander Inn ($)
1135 W Macarthur Ave
(54701) 715.835.2261

Holiday Inn ($$)
2703 Craig Rd
(54701) 715.835.2211
mgr preapproval reqd

$=under $35 $$=$35-60 $$$=$60-100 $$$$=over $100

Holiday Inn ($$$)
205 S Barstow St
(54701) 715.835.6121

Maple Manor Motel ($)
2507 S Hasings Way
(54701) 715.834.2618

Quality Inn ($$)
809 W Clairemont Ave
(54701) 715.834.6611
mgr preapproval reqd

Roadstar Inn ($)
1151 W Macarthur Ave
(54701) 715.832.9731
$25 deposit

Super 8 ($$)
6260 Teaco Dr
(54703) 715.874.6868
$5 fee w/permission

● Edgerton ●
Towne Edge Motel ($)
1104 N Main St
(53534) 608.884.9328

● Egg Harbor ●
The Alpine Inn ($$$)
7715 Alpine Rd
(54209) 414.868.3000

● Ellison Bay ●
Andersons Retreat ($$)
12621 Woodland Dr
(54210) 414.854.2746

Ellison Bay Ctges ($$)
12039 Hwy 42
(54210) 414.854.4109

Harbor House Inn ($$)
12666 S R 42
(54210) 414.854.5196

Windside Cottages ($$)
12714 Hwy 42
(54210) 414.854.4871

● Elroy ●
Elroy Valley Inn ($)
Hwy 80 & 82
(53929) 608.462.8251

● Fennimore ●
Fenmore Hills Motel ($$)
5814 Hwy 18
(53809) 608.822.3281

● Ferryville ●
Grandview Motel ($)
RR 1 Box# 280
(54628) 608.734.3235

● Fond Du Lac ●
Budgetel ($$)
77 Holiday Ln
(54937) 414.921.4000

Days Inn ($$)
107 N Pioneer Rd
(54935) 414.923.6790

Econo Lodge ($$)
649 W Johnson St
(54935) 414.923.2020

Holiday Inn ($$$)
625 W Rolling Meadows Dr
(54937) 414.923.1440
$100 deposit

Motel 6 ($)
738 W Johnson St
(54935) 414.923.0678
1 small pet/room

Northway Motel ($)
301 S Pioneer Rd
(54935) 414.921.7975

Super 8 ($$)
391 Pioneer Rd
(54935) 414.922.1088
call re: fees

Travelers Inn ($)
1325 S Main St
(54935) 414.923.0223

● Frederic ●
Frederic Motel
Hwy 35
(54837) 715.327.4496

● Germantown ●
Super 8 ($$)
17490 County Q
(53022) 414.255.0880
pets with deposit

● Grafton ●
Best Western ($$)
135 E Grand Ave
(53024) 414.284.9461

● Grantsburg ●
Wood River Inn ($)
703 W S R 70
(54840) 715.463.2541

● Green Bay ●
Barths Tower Motel ($$)
2625 Humboldt Rd
(54311) 414.468.1242

Bay Motel ($)
1301 S Military Ave
(54304) 414.494.3441

Best Western ($$)
321 S Washington St
(54301) 414.437.8771

Budgetel ($$)
2840 S Oneida St
(54304) 414.494.7887

Comfort Inn ($$)
2841 Ramada Way
(54304) 414.498.2060
mgr preapproval reqd

Days Inn ($$)
1978 Gross St
(54304) 414.498.8088
small pets allowed

Days Inn ($$)
406 N Washington St
(54301) 414.435.4484

Exel Inn ($$)
2870 Ramada Way
(54304) 414.499.3599
small pets only

Holiday Inn ($$$)
200 Main St
(54301) 414.437.5900
mgr preapproval reqd

Motel 6 ($)
1614 Shawano Ave
(54303) 414.494.6730
1 small pet/room

Residence Inn ($$$)
335 W Saint Joseph St
(54301) 414.435.2222
$25 deposit & $5 per day

Super 8 ($$)
2868 S Oneida St
(54304) 414.494.2042
pets w/permission

Valley Motel ($)
116 N Military Ave
(54303) 414.494.3455

● Hartford ●
Super 8 ($$)
1539 E Summer St
(53027) 414.673.7431
deposit

● Hayward ●
Country Inn ($$)
Box# 1010
(54843) 715.634.4100

Northwoods Motel ($$)
RR 6 Box# 6453
(54843) 715.634.8088

Ross Teal Lodge ($$$$)
RR 7
(54843) 715.462.3631

Super 8 ($$)
317 S Hwy 27
(54843) 715.634.2646
w/permission

● Hazelhurst ●
Hazelhurst Inn ($$)
6941 Hwy 51
(54531) 715.356.6571

● Hillsboro ●
Tiger Inn ($$)
629 High Ave
(54634) 608.489.2918

● Hudson ●
Best Western ($$)
1616 Crest View Dr
(54016) 715.386.2394

Comfort Inn ($$)
811 Dominion Dr
(54016) 715.386.6355
mgr preapproval reqd

Super 8 ($$)
808 Dominion Dr
(54016) 715.386.8800
w/permission

$=under $35 $$=$35-60 $$$=$60-100 $$$$=over $100

WISCONSIN, Andalusia

● Hurley ●
American Budget Inn ($$)
850 10th Ave
(54534) 715.561.3500

Holiday Inn ($$)
1000 10th Ave
(54534) 715.561.3030
mgr preapproval reqd

● Janesville ●
Budgetel ($$)
616 Midland Rd
(53546) 608.758.4545

Motel 6 ($)
3907 Milton Ave
(53546) 608.756.1742
1 small pet/room

Select Inn ($)
3520 Milton Ave
(53545) 608.754.0251

Super 8 ($$)
3430 Milton Ave
(53545) 608.756.2040
w/permission

● Johnson Creek ●
Colonial Inn Motel ($)
Hwy 26
(53038) 414.699.3518

Days Inn ($$)
W 4545 Linmar Ln
(53038) 414.699.8000

● Kaukauna ●
Settle Inn ($$)
1201 Maloney Rd
(54130) 414.766.0088

● Kenosha ●
Budgetel ($$)
7540 118th Ave
(53142) 414.857.7911

Days Inn ($$)
12121 75th St
(53142) 414.857.2311
small & caged

Holiday Inn
5125 6th Ave
(53140) 414.658.3281

Knights Inn ($$)
7221 122nd Ave
(53142) 414.857.2622
size limits & fees

● Kewaskum ●
The Doctors Inn ($$)
1121 Fond Du Lac Ave
(53040) 414.626.2666

● La Crosse ●
Bluff View Inn ($)
3715 Mormon Coulee Rd
(54601) 608.788.0600

Days Inn ($$)
101 Sky Harbour Dr
(54603) 608.783.1000

Exel Inn ($)
2150 Rose St
(54603) 608.781.0400
small pets only

Radisson Inn ($$$)
200 Harborview Plz
(54601) 608.784.6680
small pets allowed

Roadstar Inn ($)
2622 Rose St
(54603) 608.781.3070

Super 8 ($$)
1625 Rose St
(54603) 608.781.8880
w/permission

● La Pointe ●
Madeline Isle Motel ($$)
Box# 51
(54850) 715.747.3000

● Lac Du Flambeau ●
Dillmans Sand Lodge ($$)
330K Sand Lake Ln
(54538) 715.588.3143

● Ladysmith ●
Americinn Motel ($$)
800 College Ave
(54848) 715.532.6650

Best Western ($$)
8500 W Flambeau Ave
(54848) 715.532.6666

Evergreen Motel ($)
Hwy 8 W Of Hwy 27
(54848) 715.532.5611

● Lake Geneva ●
Lakewood Inn Motel ($)
1150 S Wells St
(53147) 414.248.6773
advance reservations req'd

● Land O Lakes ●
Sunrise Lodge ($$)
5900 W Shore Rd
(54540) 715.547.3684

● Lodi ●
Lodi Valley Suites ($$)
N 1440 Hwy 113
(53555) 608.592.7331

● Luck ●
Luck Country Inn ($$)
Hwy 35 & 48
(54853) 715.472.2000

● Luxemburg ●
Gypsy Villa Resort ($$$)
950 Circle Dr
(54217) 715.479.8644

Hiawatha Motor Inn ($)
1982 N Hwy 45
(54217) 715.479.6431

Pine Aire Resort ($$$)
4443 Chain O'Lakes Rd
(54217) 715.479.9208

Sunset Beach Motel ($$)
8931 N Hwy 57
(54217) 414.866.2978

● Madison ●
Best Western ($$)
650 Grand Canyon Dr
(53719) 608.833.4200

Budgetel ($$)
8102 Excelsior Dr
(53717) 608.831.7711

Days Inn ($$)
4402 E Broadway
(53716) 608.223.1800

East Towne Suites ($$$)
4801 Annamark Dr
(53704) 608.244.2020

Econo Lodge ($$)
4726 E Washington Ave
(53704) 608.241.4171

Edgewater Hotel ($$$$)
666 Wisconsin Ave
(53703) 608.256.9071

Exel Inn ($)
4202 E Towne Blgd
(53704) 608.241.3861
small pets only

Exel Inn ($$)
722 John Nolen Dr
(53713) 608.255.7400

Holiday Inn ($$$)
4402 E Washington Ave
(53704) 800.465.4329
mgr preapproval reqd

Homewood Suites ($$$)
501 D'Onofrio Dr
(53719) 608.833.8333
$250 deposit

Madison Hotel ($$$)
1 W Dayton St
(53703) 608.257.6000

Motel 6 ($)
1754 Thierer Rd
(53704) 608.241.8101
1 small pet/room

Motel 6 ($)
6402 E Broadway
(53704) 608.221.0415
1 small pet/room

Quality Inn ($$$)
4916 E Broadway
(53716) 608.222.5501

Ramada Ltd ($$)
3841 E Washington Ave
(53704) 608.244.2481

Red Roof Inn ($)
4830 Hayes Rd
(53704) 608.241.1787

Residence Inn ($$$)
4862 Hayes Rd
(53704) 608.244.5047

$=under $35 $$=$35-60 $$$=$60-100 $$$$=over $100

Roadstar ($$)
6900 Seybold Rd
(53719) 608.274.6900

Select Inn ($)
4845 Hayes Rd
(53704) 608.249.1815

Super 8 ($$)
1602 W Beltine Hwy
(53713) 608.258.8882
pets with deposit

University Inn ($$)
441 N Frances St
(53703) 608.257.4881

● Manitowish Waters ●
Voss Birchwood Lodge ($$)
Box# 456
(54545) 715.543.8441

● Manitowoc ●
Comfort Inn ($$)
2200 S 44th St
(54220) 414.683.0220
mgr preapproval reqd

Days Inn ($$)
908 Washington St
(54220) 414.682.8271

Westmoor Motel ($)
4626 Calumet Ave
(54220) 414.684.3374

Inn On Maritime Bay ($$$)
101 Maritime Dr
(54220) 414.682.7000

● Marinette ●
Chalet Motel ($)
1301 Marinette Ave
(54143) 715.735.6687

Super 8 ($$)
1508 Marinette Ave
(54143) 715.735.7887
pets w/permission

● Marshfield ●
Best Western ($$)
2700 S Roddis Ave
(54449) 715.387.1761

Downtown Motel ($$)
750 S Central Ave
(54449) 715.387.1111

Marshfield Inn ($$)
116 W Ives St
(54449) 715.387.6381

● Mauston ●
Country Inn ($$)
Box# 25
(53948) 608.847.5959

● Medford ●
Medford Inn ($)
321 N 8th St
(54451) 715.748.4420

● Menomonie ●
Bolo Country Inn ($$)
207 Pine Ave
(54751) 715.235.5596

Cedar Trail House ($$)
E4761 County Road C
(54751) 715.664.8828

Super 8 ($$)
1622 Broadway St
(54751) 715.235.8889
w/permission

● Mequon ●
Breeze Inn Chalet ($$)
10401 Pt Washington
(53092) 414.241.4510

Port Zedler Motel ($)
10036 Pt Washington
(53092) 414.241.5850

● Mercer ●
Great Northern Motel ($$)
Hwy 51S
(54547) 715.476.2440

● Milton ●
Chase On The Hill ($$)
11624 N State Road 26
(53563) 608.868.6646

● Milwaukee ●
Budgetel ($$)
5110 N Port Washington Rd
(53217) 414.964.8484

Budgetel ($$)
5442 N Lovers Lane Rd
(53225) 414.535.1300

Be
Discreet

Econo Lodge ($)
6541 W 13th St
(53221) 414.764.2510

Exel Inn ($)
115 Mayfair Rd
(53226) 414.257.0140
small pets only

Exel Inn ($$)
5485 N Port Washington Rd
(53217) 414.961.7272
small pets only

Holiday Inn ($$$)
6331 S 13th St
(53221) 414.764.1500
mgr preapproval reqd

Hotel Wisconsin ($$)
720 N Old World 3rd St
(53203) 414.271.4900

Motel 6 ($)
5037 S Howell Ave
(53207) 414.482.4414
1 small pet/room

Port Motel ($)
9717 W Appleton Ave
(53225) 414.466.4728

Ramada Inn ($$)
6401 S 13th St
(53221) 414.764.5300

Residence Inn ($$$$)
7275 N Port Washington Rd
(53217) 414.352.0070
$175 fee & $6 per day

Super 8 ($$)
8698 N Servite Dr
(53223) 414.354.5354
call re: fees

Super 8 ($$)
5253 S Howell Ave
(53207) 414.481.8488
call re: fees

● Minocqua ●
Aqua Aire Motel ($)
806 Hwy 51
(54548) 715.356.3433

Best Western ($)
311 Park St & Hwy 51
(54548) 715.356.5208

Comfort Inn ($$)
8729 Hwy 51
(54548) 715.358.2588
mgr preapproval reqd

Cross Trails Motel ($)
8644 Hwy 51
(54548) 715.356.5202

Super 8 ($$)
Hwy 51 & 70
(54548) 715.356.9541
w/permission

● Nekoosa ●
Shermalot Motel ($)
1148 W Queens Way
(54457) 715.325.2626

● New Glarus ●
Swiss Aire Motel ($$)
1200 Hwy 69
(53574) 608.527.2138

● New Lisbon ●
Edge O Wood Motel ($)
W7396 Frontage Rd
(53950) 608.562.3705

● Oak Creek ●
Budgetel ($$)
7141 S 13th St
(53154) 414.762.2266

Knights Inn ($$)
9420 S 20th St
(53154) 414.761.3807
size limits & fees

Red Roof Inn ($)
6360 S 13th St
(53154) 414.764.3500

● Oconomowoc ●
Holiday Inn
1350 Royale Mile Rd
(53066) 414.567.0311

Inn At Pine Terrace ($$)
351 E Lisbon Rd
(53066) 800.421.4667

Olympia Resort ($$)
1350 Royale Mile Rd
(53066) 800.558.9573

● Onalaska ●
Comfort Inn ($$)
1223 X'ssing Meadows
(54650) 608.781.7500
mgr preapproval reqd

Holiday Inn
9409 Hwy 16
(54650) 608.783.6555

Onalaska Inn ($)
651 2nd Ave
(54650) 608.783.2270

Shadow Run Lodge ($)
710 2nd Ave
(54650) 608.783.0020

● Oshkosh ●
Budgetel ($$)
1950 Omro Rd
(54901) 414.233.4190

Fairfield Inn ($$)
1800 S Koeller St
(54901) 414.233.8504

Hilton ($$$)
1 N Main St
(54901) 414.231.5000
small pets only

Howard Johnson ($$)
1919 Omro Rd
(54901) 414.233.1200
small pets only

Motel 6 ($)
1015 S Washburn St
(54904) 414.235.0265
1 small pet/room

Super 8 ($$)
Hwy 41
(54903) 414.426.2885
w/permission

● Osseo ●
Budget Host ($)
1994 E 10th St
(54758) 715.597.3114
mgr preapproval reqd

Rodeway Inn ($$)
Box# 7
(54758) 715.597.3175

● Park Falls ●
Northway Motor Lodge ($$)
Hwy 135
(54552) 715.762.2406

Super 8 ($$)
1212 Hwy 13S
(54552) 715.762.3383
w/permission kept in crate

● Pembine ●
Grand Motel ($)
Jct 8 & 141
(54156) 715.324.5417

● Phillips ●
Skyline Motel ($$)
804 N Pake Ave
(54555) 715.339.3086

Timber Inn ($$)
606 N Lake Ave
(54555) 715.339.3071

● Platteville ●
Best Western ($$)
W Hwy 151
(53818) 608.348.2301
small pets only

Mound View Inn ($)
1755 E Hwy 151
(53818) 608.348.9518

Super 8 ($$)
100 Hwy 80-81
(53818) 608.348.8800
pets w/ permission & $10
charge

● Plover ●
Days Inn ($$)
5253 Harding Ave
(54467) 715.341.7300

Elizabeth Inn ($)
5246 Harding Ave
(54467) 715.341.3131

● Plymouth ●
Beverlys Log Guest House
($$$)
W6926 Stoney Ridge Ln
(53073) 414.892.6064

● Port Washington ●
Port Washington Inn ($$$)
308 W Washington St
(53074) 414.284.5583

● Portage ●
Ridge Motor Inn ($)
2900 New Pinery Rd
(53901) 608.742.5306

Super 8 ($$)
3000 New Pinery Rd
(53901) 608.742.8330
call re: fees

● Poynette ●
Jamieson House ($$$)
407 N Franklin St
(53955) 608.635.4100

● Prairie Du Chien ●
Best Western ($$$)
Hwy 18/35 & 60
(53821) 608.326.4777
some rooms only

Bridgeport Inn ($$$)
Hwy 18/35 & 60
(53821) 608.326.6082

Brisbois Motor Inn ($$)
533 N Marquette Rd
(53821) 608.326.8404

Delta Motel ($)
Hwy 18 & 35
(53821) 608.326.4951

Holiday Motel ($)
1010 S Marquette Rd
(53821) 608.326.2448

Prairie Motel ($)
1616 S Marquette Rd
(53821) 608.326.6461

Super 8 ($$)
Hwy 18/35 & 60
(53821) 608.326.8777
w/permission & $15 fee

● Prentice ●
Best Nights Inn ($)
303 W Wisconsin St
(54556) 608.269.3066

Countryside Motel ($)
W 5370 Greenberg Rd
(54556) 715.428.2333

● Racine ●
Fairfield Inn ($$)
6421 Washington Ave
(53406) 414.886.5000

Holiday Inn ($$)
3700 Northwestern Ave
(53405) 800.465.4329
mgr preapproval reqd

Knights Inn ($$)
1149 Oakes Rd
(53406) 800.843.5644

Marriott Hotel ($$)
711 Washington Ave
(53403) 414.886.6100

Super 8 ($$)
7141 Kinzie Ave
(53406) 414.884.0486
call re: fees

● Reedsburg ●
Copper Springs Motel ($)
E7278 Hwy 23 & 33
(53959) 608.524.4312

Motel Reedsburg ($)
1133 E Main St
(53959) 608.524.2306

● Rhinelander ●
Best Western ($$)
70 N Stevens St
(54501) 715.362.7100

Feases Shady Rest ($$$$)
8440 Shady Rest Rd
(54501) 715.282.5231

Holiday Acres ($$)
4060 S Shore Pkwy
(54501) 715.369.1500

Kafkas Resort ($$$)
4281 W Lake George Rd
(54501) 715.369.2929

Super 8 ($$)
667 W Kemp St
(54501) 715.369.5880
pets w/permission

● Rib Lake ●
Olkives Lakeview
N9503 Spirit Lake Rd
(54470) 715.427.3344

Well
Behaved

388

Trevor, WISCONSIN

• Rice Lake •
Curriers Lakeview ($$)
2010 E Sawyer St
(54868) 715.234.7474

Super 8 ($$)
2401 S Main St
(54868) 715.234.6956
deposit

• Richland Center •
Starlite Motel ($)
RR 2 Hwy 147 East
(53581) 608.647.6158

Super 8 ($$)
100 Foundry Dr
(53581) 608.647.8988
call re: fees

• River Falls •
Super 8 ($$)
1207 Saint Croix St
(54022) 715.425.8388
w/permission

• Saint Croix Falls •
Dallas House Motel ($$)
Hwy 8 & Hwy 35
(54024) 715.483.3206
small pets only

• Saint Germain •
St Germain Motel
170 Hwy 70
(54558) 715.542.3535

• Sayner •
Froelichs Lodge ($$)
Box# 100
(54560) 715.542.3261

• Shawano •
Super 8 ($$)
211 S Waukechon St
(54166) 715.526.6688
pets w/permission

• Sheboygan •
Budgetel ($$)
2932 Kohler Memorial Dr
(53081) 414.457.2321

Comfort Inn ($$)
4332 N 40th St
(53083) 414.457.7724

Parkway Motel ($$)
3900 Motel Rd
(53081) 414.458.8338

Ramada Inn ($$)
723 Center Ave
(53081) 414.458.1400

Select Inn ($)
930 N 8th St
(53081) 414.458.4641
$25 pet deposit

• Siren •
Pine Wood Motel ($)
23862 Hwy 35
(54872) 715.349.5225

• Sister Bay •
Edge Of Town Motel ($)
11092 Hwy 42
(54234) 414.854.2012

• Sparta •
Country Inn ($$)
737 Avon Rd
(54656) 800.456.4000

Dotwntown Motel ($)
509 S Water St
(54656) 608.269.3138

Heritage Motel ($)
704 W Wisconsin St
(54656) 608.269.6991

• Spooner •
American Budget Inn ($$)
101 Maple St
(54801) 715.635.9770

Country House Motel ($)
717 S River St
(54801) 715.635.8271

Green Acres Motel ($$)
N 4809 Hwy 63 S & 253
(54801) 715.635.2177

• Stevens Point •
Budgetel ($)
4917 Main St
(54481) 715.344.1900

Holiday Inn ($$$)
1501 Northpoint Dr
(54481) 715.341.9446
mgr preapproval reqd

Point Motel ($)
209 Division St
(54481) 715.344.8312
$3 night/$10 weekly

Traveler Motel ($)
3350 Church St
(54481) 715.344.6455

• Stockholm •
Pine Creek Lodge ($$$)
N447 244th St
(54769) 715.448.3203

• Stoddard •
Waters Edge Motel
201 N Pearl St
(54658) 608.457.2126

• Sturgeon Bay •
Carls Old Bridge ($)
114 N Madison Ave
(54235) 414.743.1245

Comfort Inn ($$)
923 Green Bay Rd
(54235) 414.743.7486
mgr preapproval reqd

Holiday Motel ($)
29 N 2nd Ave
(54235) 414.743.5571

Nightengale Motel ($)
1547 Egg Harbor Rd
(54235) 414.743.7633

Quiet Cottage ($$$)
4608 Glidden Dr
(54235) 414.743.4526

Snug Harbor Inn ($$)
1627 Memorial Dr
(54235) 414.743.2337

• Sun Prairie •
McGoverns Motel ($)
820 W Main St
(53590) 608.837.7321

• Superior •
Best Western ($$)
1405 Susquehanna Ave
(54880) 715.392.7600

Budget Uptown Motel ($$)
104 E 5th St
(54880) 715.394.4449

Driftwood Inn ($)
2200 E 2nd St
(54880) 715.398.6661

Stockade Motel ($)
1610 E 2(d St
(54880) 715.398.3585

Superior Inn ($)
525 Hammond Ave
(54880) 715.394.7706

• Three Lakes •
Oneida Village Inn ($)
1785 Superior St
(54562) 715.546.3373

• Tomah •
Budget Host ($)
Hwys 12 & 16
(54660) 608.372.5946
$4 w/reservations

Comfort Inn ($$)
305 Wittig Rd
(54660) 608.372.6600
mgr preapproval reqd

Cranberry Suites ($$)
319 Wittig Rd
(54660) 608.374.2801

Econo Lodge ($)
2005 N Superior Ave
(54660) 800.424.4777

Howard Johnson ($$)
I-90 & Hwy 131
(54660) 608.372.4500

Lark Inn ($$)
229 N Superior Ave
(54660) 608.372.5981

Park Motel ($)
1515 Kilbourn Ave
(54660) 608.372.4655

Super 8 ($$)
I-94
(54660) 608.372.3901
pets w/permission

• Trevor •
State Line Motel
23610 128th St
(53179) 414.396.9561

$=under $35 $$=$35-60   **389** $$$=$60-100 $$$$=over $100

WISCONSIN, Two Rivers

● Two Rivers ●
Cool City Motel ($)
3009 Lincoln Ave
(54241) 414.793.2244

Village Inn Motel ($$)
3310 Memorial Dr
(54241) 414.794.8818

● Viroqua ●
Doucettes Motel ($)
S R 27 & 82
(54665) 608.637.3104

● Washburn ●
Redwood Motel ($)
26 W Bayfield St
(54891) 715.373.5512

Super 8 ($$)
Harbor View Dr
(54891) 715.373.5671
call re: fees

● Washington Island ●
Dor Cros Chalet Motel ($$)
Box# 249
(54246) 414.847.2126

Findlays Inn ($$)
Detroit Harbor
(54246) 414.847.2526

Viking Village Motel ($$)
Box# 135
(54246) 414.847.2551

● Watertown ●
Flags Inn Motel
N627 Hwy 26
(53098) 414.261.9400

Heritage Inn ($$)
700 E Main St
(53094) 414.261.9010

Holiday Inn
101 Aviation Way
(53094) 414.262.1910

Karlshuegel Inn ($$)
749 N Church St
(53098) 414.261.3980

Super 8 ($$)
1730 S Church St
(53094) 414.261.1188
deposit

● Waupaca ●
Village Inn Motel ($$)
1060 W Fulton St
(54981) 715.258.8526

● Wausau ●
Ace Motel
2211 Stewart Ave
(54401) 715.845.4261

Best Western ($$$)
2901 Martin Ave
(54401) 715.842.1616
small caged pets $10

Budgetel ($$)
1910 Stewart Ave
(54401) 715.842.0421

Exel Inn ($)
116 S 17th Ave
(54401) 715.842.0641
small pets only

Marlene Motel ($)
2010 Stewart Ave
(54401) 715.845.6248

Rib Mountain Inn ($$)
2900 Rib Mountain Way
(54401) 715.848.2802

Ski Inn Hotel ($$)
201 N 17th Ave
(54401) 715.845.4341

Wausau Inn ($$)
2001 N Mountain Rd
(54401) 800.928.7281

● Wautoma ●
Super 8 ($$)
Hwys 21&73
(54982) 414.787.4811
w/deposit

● West Bend ●
Super 8 ($$)
2433 W Washington St
(53095) 414.335.6788
call re: fees

● Westby ●
Westby House ($$)
200 W State St
(54667) 608.634.4112

● Weyerhaeuser ●
Country View Motel ($)
W1469 Hwy 8
(54895) 715.353.2780

● White Lake ●
Jesses Wolf Lodge ($$$)
N2119 Taylor Rd
(54491) 715.882.2182

● Whitewater ●
Black Stallion Inn
RR 1 US Hwy 12
(53190) 414.473.7700

● Willard ●
The Barn Of Clark County
($$)
N7890 Bachelors Ave
(54493) 715.267.3215

● Windsor ●
Super 8 ($$)
4506 Lake Cir
(53598) 608.846.3971
deposit

● Wisconsin Dells ●
International Motel ($)
1311 Broadway
(53965) 608.254.2431

Super 8 ($$)
800 Co Hwy H
(53965) 608.254.6464
pets w/permission

● Wisconsin Rapids ●
Best Western ($$)
911 Huntington Ave
(54494) 715.423.3211
small pets with mgrs
approval

Camelot Motel ($)
9210 Hwy 13
(54494) 715.325.5111

Mead Inn ($$)
451 E Gran Ave
(54494) 715.423.1500

Super 8 ($$)
3410 8th St
(54494) 715.423.8080
w/permission

Wyoming

● Afton ●
Best Western ($$)
Hwy 89
(83110) 307.886.3856
small pets

Mountain Inn ($$)
US 89 Rt 1
(83110) 307.886.3156
small- medium size

The Corral ($)
689 S Washington
(83110) 307.886.5424

● Alpine ●
Alpen Haus Hotel ($$)
Hwy 89 & 26
(83128) 307.654.7545

Best Western ($$$)
Hwy 89 & 26
(83128) 307.654.7561
pets with prior approval

Lakeside Motel
Box# 238
(83128) 307.654.7507

Three Rivers Motel
US Hwy 89
(83128) 307.654.7551

● Baggs ●
Drifters Inn
Hwy 789
(82321) 307.383.2015

● Basin ●
Lilac Motel
710 W C St
(82410) 307.568.3355

● Bondurant ●
Hoback Village Motel
Hwy 191
(82922) 307.733.3631

Smiling S
Box# 171
(82922) 307.733.3457

Triangle F Lodge
Box# 159
(82922) 307.733.2836

$=under $35 $$=$35-60 $$$=$60-100 $$$$=over $10

• Buffalo •

Arrowhead Motel ($)
749 Fort St
(82834) 307.684.9453

Blue Gables Motel
662 N Main St
(82834) 307.684.7822

Crossroads Inn ($)
75 N Bypass Rd
(82834) 307.684.2256

Econo Lodge ($)
333 Hart St
(82834) 307.684.2219

Z Bar Motel ($)
626 Fort St
(82834) 307.684.5535

Mansion House Motel
313 N Main St
(82834) 307.684.2218

Mountain View Motel ($)
585 Fort St
(82834) 307.684.2881

South Fork Inn
US 16
(82834) 307.684.9609

Wyoming Motel ($)
610 E Hart St
(82834) 307.684.5505

• Casper •

Best Western ($$)
2325 E Yellowstone Hwy
(82609) 307.234.3541

Comfort Inn ($$)
480 Lathrop
(82601) 307.235.3038
mgr preapproval reqd

Commercial Inn
5755 Cy Ave
(82604) 307.235.6688

First Interstate Inn ($)
205 E Wyoming Blvd
(82601) 307.234.9125

Hampton Inn ($$)
400 W F St
(82601) 307.235.6668
$6/pets

Hilton ($$$)
I-25 P N Poplar
(82601) 307.266.6000

Holiday Inn ($$$)
300 W F St
(82601) 307.235.2531
mgr preapproval reqd

Kelly Inn ($$)
821 N Poplar St
(82601) 307.266.2400

La Quinta Inn ($)
301 E E St
(82601) 307.234.1159
call re: fees

Motel 6 ($)
1150 Wilkins Cir
(82601) 307.234.3903
1 small pet/room

Parkway Plaza ($$)
123 W E St
(82601) 307.235.1777

Ranch House Motel
1130 E F St
(82601) 307.266.4044

Red Arrow Motel
W Yellowstone & Wyo Blvd
(82601) 307.234.5293

Royal Inn ($)
440 E A St
(82601) 307.234.3501

Shilo Inn ($$)
739 Luker Ln
(82601) 307.237.1335

Showboat Motel ($)
100 W F St
(82601) 307.235.2711

Super 8 ($)
3838 Cy Ave
(82604) 307.266.3480
pets w/permission

Topper Motel
728 E A St
(82601) 307.237.8407

Traveler Motel ($)
500 E 1st St
(82601) 307.237.9343

Virginian Motel
830 E A St
(82601) 307.266.9731

Westridge Motel ($$)
855 Cy Ave
(82601) 307.234.8911

Yellowstone Motel
1610 E Yellowstone Hwy
(82601) 307.234.9174

• Centennial •

Centennial Valley Trading
Post
2755 Hwy 130
(82055) 307.721.5074

Friendly Fly Motel
Box# 195
(82055) 307.742.6033

Old Corral Mtn Lodge
Main St
(82055) 307.745.5918

Rainbow Vly Resort
75 Rainbow Valley Rd
(82055) 307.745.0368

Snowy Mountain Lodge
3474 Hwy 130
(82055) 307.742.7669

• Cheyenne •

Atlas Motel
1524 W Lincolnway
(82001) 307.632.9214

Best Western ($$)
1700 W Lincolnway
(82001) 307.638.3301

Big Horn Motel
2004 E Lincolnway
(82001) 307.632.3122

Cheyenne Motel
1601 E Lincolnway
(82001) 307.778.7664

Comfort Inn
2245 Etchepare Cir
(82007) 307.632.3122
mgr preapproval reqd

Days Inn ($)
2360 W Lincolnway
(82001) 307.778.8877

Fairfield Inn ($$)
1415 Stillwater Ave
(82009) 307.637.4070

Firebird Motel
1905 E Lincolnway
(82001) 307.632.5505

Frontier Motel
1400 W Lincolnway
(82001) 307.634.7961

Holiday Inn ($$$)
204 W Fox Farm Rd
(82007) 307.638.4468
mgr preapproval reqd

Home Ranch Motel
2414 E Lincolnway
(82001) 307.634.3575

Knights Inn
3839 E Lincolnway
(82001) 307.634.2171

La Quinta Inn ($$)
2410 W Lincolnway
(82001) 307.632.7117
call re: fees

Lincoln Court ($$)
1700 W Lincolnway
(82001) 307.638.3307

Motel 6 ($)
1735 Westland Rd
(82001) 307.635.6806
1 small pet/room

Quality Inn
5401 Walker Rd
(82009) 307.632.8901
mgr preapproval reqd

Ranger Motel
909 W 16th St
(82001) 307.634.7995

Roundup Motel
403 S Greeley Hwy
(82007) 307.634.7741

Sapp Brothers
I-80 & Archer
(82001) 307.632.6000

Stagecoach Motel
1515 W Lincolnway
(82001) 307.634.4495

Cheyenne, WYOMING

Super 8 ($$)
1900 W Lincolnway
(82001) 307.635.8741
under 30 lbs w/permission

Twin Chimneys Motel
2405 E Lincolnway
(82001) 307.632.8921

Windy Hills House ($$$)
393 Happy Jack Rd
(82007) 307.632.6423

Wyoming Motel
1401 W Lincolnway
(82001) 307.632.8104

● Chugwater ●
Buffalo Lodge ($$)
100 Buffalo Rd
(82210) 307.422.3248

● Cody ●
Best Bet Inn
1701 17th St
(82414) 307.567.9009

Best Western ($)
1601 8th St
(82414) 307.587.4265
small managers discretion

Best Western ($$)
1407 8th St
(82414) 307.587.5566
small pets

Big Bear Motel ($)
139 W Yellowstone Ave
(82414) 307.587.3117

Carriage House Motel
1816 8th St
(82414) 307.587.2572

Carter Mtn Motel
1701 Central Ave
(82414) 307.587.4295

Gateway Motel
203 Yellowstone Ave
(82414) 307.587.2561

Goff Creek Lodge ($$)
Box# 155
(82414) 307.587.3753

High Country Motel
405 Yellowstone Ave
(82414) 307.527.5505

Kelly Inn
405 Yellowstone Ave
(82414) 307.587.5960

Mountain View Inn ($$)
N Fork Star Rt
(82414) 307.587.2081

Seven Ks Motel
232 W Yellowstone Ave
(82414) 307.587.5890

Shoeshone Lodge ($$)
Box# 790
(82414) 307.587.4044
open may - october

Skyline Motor Inn ($)
1919 17th St
(82414) 307.587.4201

Stage Stop
502 Yellowstone Ave
(82414) 307.587.2804

Super 8 ($)
730 Yellowstone Ave
(82414) 307.527.6214
w/permission

Trail Inn
2750 N Fork Hwy
(82414) 307.587.3741

Trout Creek Inn ($)
Yellowstone Hwy
(82414) 307.587.6288

Uptown Motel
1562 Sheridan Ave
(82414) 307.587.4245

Western 6 Gun Motel
423 Yellowstone Ave
(82414) 307.587.4835

Wise Choice Inn ($$$)
2908 N Fork Hwy
(82414) 307.587.6288

Yellowstone Vly Inn
3324 N Fork Hwy
(82414) 307.587.3961
$5 fee

● Cokeville ●
Hideout Motel
245 S Hwy 30
(83114) 307.279.3281

Valley Hi Motel
Hwy 30 & 89
(83114) 307.279.3251

● Dayton ●
Foothills Motel
101 Nmain
(82836) 307.655.2547

● Diamondville ●
Energy Inn ($)
Box# 494
(83116) 307.877.6901

● Douglas ●
4 Winds Motel
615 Richards St
(82633) 307.358.2322

Alpine Inn
2310 Richards St
(82633) 307.358.4780

Best Western ($$)
1450 Riverbend Dr
(82633) 307.358.9790

Chieftain Motel ($)
815 Richards St
(82633) 307.358.2673

First Interstate Inn ($)
2349 Richards St
(82633) 307.358.2833

Plains Motel
628 Richards St
(82633) 307.358.4484

Super 8 ($$)
314 Russell Ave
(82633) 307.358.6800
pets w/permission

Vagabond Motel
430 Richards St
(82633) 307.358.9414

● Dubois ●
Black Bear Inn ($)
505 N Ramshorn St
(82513) 307.455.2344

Branding Iron Motel ($)
401 N Ramshorn St
(82513) 307.455.2893

Chicook Winds Motel ($)
640 S 1st St
(82513) 307.455.2987

Lazy L&B Ranch ($$$$)
Rte 66
(82513) 307.455.2839

Pinnacle Buttes ($)
3577 Hwy 26
(82513) 307.455.2506

Rendezvous Motel ($$)
1349 W Ramshorn St
(82513) 307.455.2844

Stagecoach Motel ($)
103 E Ramshorn St
(82513) 307.455.2303
$2 per day

Twin Pines Lodge ($)
218 W Ramshorn St
(82513) 307.455.2600

Wind River Motel
519 W Ramshorn St
(82513) 307.455.2611

● Edgerton ●
Teapot Motor Lodge
Hwy 387
(82635) 307.437.6541

● Encampment ●
Elk Horn Motel
Box# 666
(82325) 307.327.5110

Riverside Cabins
Star Rt Box# 15
(82325) 307.327.5361

● Evanston ●
Alexander Motel
Off I-80
(82931) 307.789.2346

Bear River Inn
261 Bear River Dr
(82930) 307.789.0791

Best Western ($$)
1601 Harrison Dr
(82930) 307.780.3770

$=under $35 $$=$35-60 $$$=$60-100 $$$$=over $10

Big Horn Motel ($)
202 Bear River Dr
(82930) 307.789.6830

Days Inn ($$)
339 Wasatch Rd
(82930) 307.789.2220

Pine Gables Inn
1049 Center St
(829300 307.789.2220
small only

Prairie Inn Motel ($)
264 Bear River Dr
(82930) 307.789.2920

Super 8 ($)
70 Bear River Dr
(82930) 307.789.7510
pets w/permission

Weston Plaza Hotel ($$)
1983 Harrison Dr
(82930) 307.789.0783

Weston Super Budget
1936 Harrison Dr
(82930) 307.789.2810

● Evansville ●
Shilo Inn ($$)
739 Luker Ln
(82636) 800.222.2244

● Farson ●
Sitzmans Motel
Box# 25
(82932) 307.273.9241

● Fort Bridger ●
Wagon Wheel Motel
270 N Main
(82933) 307.782.6361

● Gillette ●
Arrowhead Motel
202 S Emerson Ave
(82716) 307.686.0909

Best Western ($$)
109 N Hwy 14-16
(82716) 307.686.2210

Circle L Motel
410 E 2nd
(82716) 307.682.9375

Days Inn ($$)
910 E Boxfelder Rd
(82718) 800.329.7466

Holiday Inn ($$$)
2009 S Douglas Hwy 59
(82716) 307.686.3000
mgr preapproval reqd

Motel 6 ($)
2105 Rodgers Dr
(82716) 307.686.8600
1 small pet/room

Mustang Motel
922 E 3rd St
(82716) 307.682.4784

Ramada Ltd ($)
608 E 2nd St
(82716) 307.682.9341
smoking rooms

Rodeway Inn ($$)
1020 Hwy 51
(82716) 307.682.5111

Rolling Hills Motel
409 Butler Spaeth Rd
(82716) 307.682.4757

Super 8 ($)
208 Decker Ct
(82716) 307.682.8078
pets w/permission

Thirfty Inn
1004 E Hwy 14-16
(82716) 307.621.2616

● Glenrock ●
Glenrock Motel
108 S 3rd St
(82637) 307.436.2772

● Green River ●
Coachman Inn ($)
470 E Flaming Gorge Way
(82935) 307.875.3681

Desmond Motel ($)
140 N 7th West St
(82935) 307.875.3701

Falming Gorge Motel
316 E Flaming Gorge Way
(82935) 307.875.4190

Super 8 ($)
280 E Flaming Gorge Way
(82935) 307.875.9330
pets w/permission

Western Motel ($)
890 Flaming Gorge Way
(82935) 307.875.2840

● Greybull ●
Antler Motel ($)
1116 N 6th St
(82426) 307.765.4404

Cassidy Inn Motel
326 Nolan Ave
(82426) 307.738.2250

K Bar Motel ($)
300 Greybull Ave
(82426) 307.765.4426

Sage Motel ($)
1135 N 6th St
(82426) 307.765.4443

Wheels Motel
1324 N 6th St
(82426) 307.765.2105

Yellowstone Motel ($)
247 Greybull Ave
(82426) 307.765.4456

● Guernsey ●
Bunkhouse Hotel ($)
380 W Whalen
(82214) 307.836.2356

Bunkhouse Motel
Hwy 26
(82214) 307.826.2356
owner referred

● Hanna ●
Golden Rule Motel
305 S Adams
(82327) 307.325.6525

● Hulett ●
Hulett Motel
202 Main St
(82720) 307.467.9900

Motel Pioneer ($)
119 Hunter
(82720) 307.467.5656

● Jackson ●
Alipine Motel
70 Jean St
(83001) 307.739.3200

Antler Motel ($$$)
43 W Pearl St
(83001) 307.733.2535

Dont Fence Me Inn
2350 N Moose Wilson Rd
(83001) 307.733.7979

Elk Country Inn
480 W Pearl St
(83001) 307.733.2364

Forty Niner Motel ($$)
330 W Pearl St
(83001) 307.733.7550

Jackson Hole Lodge ($$$)
40 W Broadway
(83001) 307.733.2992

Jacksonhole Racquetclub
Star Rt 362A
(83001) 307.733.3990

Mad Dog Ranch
Box# 1645
(83001) 307.733.3729

Motel 6 ($)
600 S Hwy 89
(83001) 307.733.1620
1 small pet/room

Painted Buffalo Inn ($$)
400 W Broadway
(83001) 307.733.4340

Snow King Resort ($$$)
400 E Snow King Ave
(83001) 307.733.5200

Teton Gables Motel
Jct 191-189 22
(83001) 307.733.3723

Virginian Motel ($$)
750 W Broadway
(83001) 307.733.2792
limited pet rooms

Wilson Motel
980 E Pearl St
(83001) 307.733.2956

$=under $35 $$=$35-60 $$$=$60-100 $$$$=over $100

WYOMING, Jackson

Wyoming Inn ($$$)
930 W Broadway
(83001) 307.734.0035

● Kaycee ●
Siesta Motel
255 Nolan Ave
(82639) 307.738.2291

● Kemmerer ●
Antler Motel
419 Coral St
(83101) 307.877.4461

Fairview Motel ($)
Hwy N 30 At 89
(83101) 307.877.3578

Fossil Butte Motel
1424 Central Ave
(83101) 307.877.3996

Lake Via Naughton
Hwy 233
(83101) 307.877.9669

Railway Inn Motel
1427 W 5th Ave
(83101) 307.877.3544

● Lagrange ●
Bear Mtn Back Trails
Box# 37
(82221) 307.834.2281

● Lander ●
Atlantic City Merc
100 Main St
(82520) 307.332.5143

Best Western ($$)
260 Grandview Dr
(82520) 307.332.2847

Budget Host ($$)
150 E Main St
(82520) 307.332.3940

Downtown Motel
569 Main St
(82520) 307.332.5220

Holiday Lodge ($)
210 McFarland Dr
(82520) 307.332.2511
$2 charge

Maverick
808 W Main St
(82520) 307.332.2821

Pronghorn Lodge ($)
150 E Main St
(82520) 307.332.3940
smoking room

Silver Spur Motel ($)
340 N 10th St
(82520) 307.332.5189

Teton Motel
586 Main St
(82520) 307.332.3582

● Laramie ●
Best Western ($$)
960 N 3rd St
(82070) 307.742.6616

Best Western ($$)
1561 Snowsy Range Rd
(82070) 307.742.8371

Downtown Motel ($)
165 N 3rd St
(82070) 307.742.6671
in only 2 smoking rooms

Econo Lodge ($)
1470 N McCue St
(82070) 307.745.8900

Holiday Inn ($$)
2313 Soldier Springs Rd
(82070) 307.742.6611
mgr preapproval reqd

Laramie Inn ($)
421 Boswell Dr
(82070) 307.742.3271

Motel 6 ($)
621 Plaza Ln
(82070) 307.742.2307
1 small pet/room

Motel 8
501 Boswell Dr
(82070) 307.745.4856

Ranger Motel
453 N 3rd St
(82070) 307.742.6677

Sunset Inn ($)
1104 S 3rd St
(82070) 307.742.3741

Thunderbird Lodge
1369 N 3rd St
(82070) 307.745.4871

University Inn ($)
1720 E Grand Ave
(82070) 307.721.8855

● Lovell ●
Cattlemen Motel ($$)
470 Montana Ave
(82431) 307.548.2296

Horseshoe Bend Motel ($)
375 E Main St
(82431) 307.548.2221

Super 8 ($)
595 E Main St
(82431) 307.548.2725
pets w/permission

Western Motel
1808 W Main St
(82431) 307.548.2781

● Lusk ●
Rawhide Motel
805 S Main St
(82225) 307.334.2440

Sage&cactus Village
Star Rt 1 Box# 158
(82225) 307.663.7653

Town House Motel ($)
525 S Main St
(82225) 307.334.2376

Trail Motel ($)
305 W 8th St
(82225) 307.334.2530

● Lyman ●
Valley West Motel
Main St
(82937) 307.787.3700

● Medicine Bow ●
Trampas Lodge
Box# 66
(82329) 307.379.2280

Virginian Hotel
Box# 127
(82329) 307.379.2377

● Meeteetse ●
Oasis Motel
1702 State St
(82433) 307.868.2551

Vision Quest Inn
2207 Stte St
(82433) 307.868.2512

● Moorcroft ●
Keyhole Motel Marina
213 McKean Rd
(82721) 307.756.9529

Moorcourt Motel ($)
Hwy 14 & Devils Tower Rd
(82721) 307.756.3411

● Moran ●
Atkinsons Motel
Box# 108
(83013) 307.543.2442

Colter Bay Village ($$)
Box# 240
(83013) 307.543.2811

Flagg Ranch Village ($$$)
Box# 187
(83013) 307.543.2861

Jackson Lake Lodge ($$$)
Box# 240
(83013) 307.543.2855

Singal Mtn Lodge ($$$)
Box# 50
(83013) 307.543.2831

Togwotee Mtn Lodge ($$)
Box# 91
(83013) 800.543.2847

● Newcastle ●
Auto Inn Motel
2503 W Main St
(82701) 307.746.2734

Flying V Cambria Inn
23726 Hwy 85
(82701) 307.746.2096

$=under $35 $$=$35-60 $$$=$60-100 $$$$=over $10

Fountain Inn Crystal Pk
Resort ($$)
2 Fountain Plz
(82701) 307.746.4426
in smoking rooms

Four Corners
24713 N US Hwy 85
(82701) 307.746.4776

Hill Top Motel
1121 S Summit Ave
(82701) 307.746.4494

Mallo Resort
Box# 233
(82701) 307.746.4094

Morgan Motel
205 S Spokane Ave
(82701) 307.746.2715

Pines Motel ($)
248 E Wentworth St
(82701) 307.746.4334

Sage Motel ($)
1227 S Summit Ave
(82701) 307.746.2724

Stardust Motel
833 S Summit Ave
(82701) 307.746.4719

Sundowner Inn
451 W Main St
(82701) 307.746.2796

● Parkman ●
Foothills Ranch
521 Pass Creek Rd Parkman
(82838) 307.655.9362

● Pine Bluffs ●
Gators Travelyn Motel
515 W 7th St
(82082) 307.245.3226

Sunset Motel
316 W 3rd
(82082) 307.245.3591

● Pinedale ●
Best Western ($$)
850 W Pine St
(82941) 307.367.6869

Boulder Lake Lodge
Box# 1100
(82941) 307.537.4300

Camp O Pines Motel
38 N Fremont
(82941) 307.367.4536

Half Moon Lodge Motel
46 N Sublett Ave
(82941) 307.367.2851

Lakeside Lodge
99 S R 111
(82941) 307.367.2221

Log Cabin Motel
49 E Magnolia
(82941) 307.367.4579

Pine Creek Inn
650 W Pine St
(82941) 307.367.2191

Rivera Lodge
442 W Marilyn
(82941) 307.367.2424

Sun Dance Motel ($)
148 E Pine
(82941) 307.367.4336

Teton Court Motel
123 E Magnolia St
(82941) 307.367.4137

The Zzzz Inn ($$)
327 Hwy 191
(82941) 307.367.2121

● Powder River ●
Hells Half Acre Motel
Hwys 20 & 26
(82648) 307.472.0018

● Powell ●
Best Choice Motel
337 E 2nd St
(82435) 307.754.2243

Best Western ($$)
777 E 2nd St
(82435) 307.754.5117
small pets only

Joann Ranch
137 Road 8Ve
(82435) 307.645.3109

Park Motel
715 E 2nd St
(82435) 307.754.2233

Super 8 ($)
845 E Coulter Ave
(82435) 307.754.7231
w/permission

● Ranchester ●
Western Motel ($)
350 Dayton St
(82839) 307.655.2212

● Rawlins ●
Best Western ($$)
23rd & Spruce
(82301) 307.324.2737
mgrs discretion

Days Inn ($$)
2222 E Cedar St
(82301) 307.324.6615
$4/pets

Key Motel ($)
1806 E Cedar St
(82301) 307.324.2728

Rawlins Motel ($)
905 W Spruce St
(82301) 307.324.3456

Sunset Motel ($)
1302 W Spruce St
(82301) 307.324.3448

Weston Inn
1801 E Cedar St
(82301) 307.324.2783

● Riverton ●
Days Inn ($)
909 W Main St
(82501) 307.856.9677

Hi Lo Motel ($)
414 N Federal Blvd
(82501) 307.856.9223

Jack Pine Motel
120 S Federal Blvd
(82501) 307.856.9251

Mountain Veiw Motel
720 W Main St
(82501) 307.856.2418

Sundowner Station ($$)
1616 N Federal Blvd
(82501) 307.856.6503

Super 8 ($)
1040 N Federal Blvd
(82501) 307.857.2400
w/permission

Thunderbird Motel ($)
302 E Fremont Ave
(82501) 307.856.9201

Wyoming Motel
319 N Federal Blvd
(82501) 307.856.6549

● Rock Springs ●
Comfort Inn ($$)
1670 Sunset Dr
(82901) 307.382.9490
mgr preapproval reqd

Days Inn ($$)
1545 Elk St
(82901) 307.362.5646

Econo Lodge ($)
1635 Elk St
(82901) 307.382.4217

Holiday Inn ($$)
1675 Sunset Dr
(82901) 307.382.9200
mgr preapproval reqd

Irwin Hotel
138 Elk St
(82901) 307.382.9817

La Quinta Inn ($$)
2717 Dewar Dr
(82901) 307.362.1770
call re: fees

Motel 6 ($)
2615 Commercial Way
(82901) 307.362.1850
1 small pet/room

Motel 8
108 Gateway Blvd
(82901) 307.362.8200

Rodeway Inn ($$)
1004 Dewar Dr
(82901) 307.362.6673

$=under $35 $$=$35-60 $$$=$60-100 $$$$=over $100

Springs Motel ($)
1525 9th St
(82901) 307.362.6683

The Inn At Rock Springs ($$)
2518 Foothill Blvd
(82901) 307.362.9600

● Saratoga ●
Carys Sage&sand Motel
311 S 1st
(82331) 307.326.8339

Hacienda Motel ($)
Hwy 130
(82331) 307.326.5751

Riviera Lodge
303 N 1st
(82331) 307.326.5651

Saratoga Inn
Box# 869
(82331) 307.326.5261

Silver Moon
412 E Bridge
(82331) 307.326.5974

● Shell ●
Wagon Wheel Lodge
Hwy 14
(82441) 307.765.2561

● Sheridan ●
Alamo Motel
1326 N Main St
(82801) 307.672.2455

Bramble Motel
2366 N Main St
(82801) 307.674.4902

Evergreen Inn
580 E 5th St
(82801) 307.672.9757

Holiday Inn ($$)
1809 Sugarland Dr
(82801) 307.672.8931
mgr preapproval reqd

Holiday Lodge
625 Coffeen Ave
(82801) 307.672.2407

Guest House Motel ($)
2007 N Main St
(82801) 307.674.7496

Parkway Motel
2112 Coffeen Ave
(82801) 307.674.7259

Rancher Motel
1552 Coffeen Ave
(82801) 307.672.2428

Rock Trim Motel ($)
449 Coffeen Ave
(82801) 307.672.2464

Super 8 ($)
2435 N Main St
(82801) 307.672.9725
pets w/permission

Super Saver Inn
1789 N Main St
(82801) 307.672.0471

Trails End Motel ($)
2125 N Main St
(82801) 307.672.2477

Triangle Motel
540 Coffeen Ave
(82801) 307.674.8031

X-L Motel
907 Broadway St
(82801) 307.674.6458

● Shoshoni ●
Desert Inn Motel
605 W 2nd
(82649) 307.876.2273

● Story ●
Wagon Box Inn
Box# 248
(82842) 307.683.2444

● Sundance ●
Best Western ($)
26 Hwy 585
(82729) 307.283.2800
small pets with $15 deposit

● Ten Sleep ●
Circle S Motel
Box# 50
(82442) 307.366.2320

Flagstaff Motel
Box# 376
(82442) 307.366.2745

Meadowlark Resort
Box# 86
(82442) 307.366.2424

● Teton Village ●
Crystal Springs Inn ($$)
3285 W McCollister Dr
(83025) 307.733.4423

The Hostel
Box# 546
(83025) 307.733.3415

● Thermopolis ●
El Rancho Motel ($)
924 Shoshoni St
(82443) 307.864.2341

Holiday Inn ($$)
115 Park
(82443) 307.864.3131

Plaza Inn The Park
116 Park St
(82443) 307.864.2251

Rainbow Motel
408 Park St
(82443) 307.864.2129

Roundtop Mtn Motel
412 N 6th St
(82443) 307.864.3126

Super 8 ($$)
Lane 5 Hwy 20
(82443) 307.864.5515
call re: fees

● Torrington ●
Blue Lantern Motel
1402 Main St
(82240) 307.532.8999

Kings Inn ($$)
1555 Main St
(82240) 307.532.4011

Maverick Motel ($)
US 26 & 85
(82240) 307.532.4064

Oregon Trail Lodge
710 E Valley Rd
(82240) 307.532.2101

● Veteran ●
Wind River Motel
501 S 6th St
(82243) 307.864.2325

● Wapiti ●
Absaroka Mtn Ranch ($$)
1231 Yellowstone Park Hwy
(82450) 307.587.3963

Elephant Head Lodge ($$)
1170 Yellowstone Park Hwy
(82450) 307.587.3980

Half Mile Creek Ranch ($$)
Box# 48
(82450) 307.587.9513

● Wheatland ●
Best Western ($$)
1809 16th St
(82201) 307.322.4070

Blackbird Inn
1101 11th St
(82201) 307.322.4540

Plains Motel
208 16th St
(82201) 307.322.3416

Vimbos Motel ($)
203 16th St
(82201) 307.322.3842

West Winds Motel ($)
1756 South St
(82201) 307.322.2705

Wyoming Motel
1101 9th St
(82201) 307.322.5383

● Worland ●
Best Western ($$)
2200 Big Horn Ave
(82401) 307.347.8201

Days Inn ($)
500 N 10th St
(82401) 307.347.4251

Super 8 ($)
2500 Big Horn Ave
(82401) 307.347.9236
w/permission

Town House Motel
119 N 10th St
(82401) 307.347.2426

Town&Country Motel
1021 Russell Ave
(82401) 307.347.3249

● Yellowstone Nat'l Park ●
Canyon Village Lodge ($$)
Yellowstone National Park
(82190) 303.297.2757
limited kennels, call ahead,
fee

Grant Villae ($$)
Yellowstone National Park
(82190) 303.297.2757
limited kennels, call ahead,
fee

Lake Lodge ($$)
Yellowstone National Park
(82190) 303.297.2757
limited kennels, call ahead,
fee

Lake Yellowstone Hotel ($$)
Yellowstone National Park
(82190) 303.297.2757
limited kennels, call ahead,
fee

Mammoth Hot Spgs ($)
Yellowstone National Park
(82190) 303.297.2757
limited kennels, call ahead,
fee

Old Faithful Inn ($$)
Box# 165
(82190) 307.344.7311
june - august

Old Faithful Cabins ($)
Box# 165
(82190) 307.344.7311
open june - august

$=under $35 $$=$35-60 $$$=$60-100 $$$$=over $100

ZIPS 00000-10000

01002	MA Amherst
01035	MA Hadley
01040	MA Holyoke
01060	MA Northhampton
01089	MA West Springfield
01104	MA Springfield
01301	MA Greenfield
01373	MA South Deerfield
01518	MA Sturbridge
01545	MA Shrewsbury
01581	MA Westborough
01608	MA Worcester
01701	MA Framingham
01742	MA Concord
01752	MA Marlborough
01772	MA Southborough
01801	MA Woburn
01803	MA Burlington
01810	MA Andover
01832	MA Haverhill
01843	MA Lawrence
01852	MA Lowell
01876	MA Tewksbury
01880	MA Wakefield
01906	MA Saugas
01923	MA Danvers
01970	MA Salem
02048	MA Mansfield
02115	MA Boston
02139	MA Cambridge
02162	MA Newton
02184	MA Braintree
02194	MA Needham
02346	MA Middleboro
02364	MA Kingston
02368	MA Randolph
02540	MA Cape Cod
02540	MA Falmouth
02563	MA Sandwich
02657	MA Provincetown
02664	MA South Yarmouth
02721	MA Fall River
02740	MA New Bedford
02767	MA Raynham
02790	MA Westport
02840	RI Middletown
02840	RI Newport
02886	RI Warwick
02903	RI Providence
03054	NH Merrimack
03063	NH Nashua
03079	NH Salem
03103	NH Manchester
03264	NH Plymouth
03301	NH Concord
03431	NH Keene
03581	NH Gorham
03801	NH Portsmouth
03820	NH Dover
03833	NH Exeter
03867	NH Rochester
03874	NJ Seabrook
03904	ME Kittery
03907	ME Ogunquit
04011	ME Brunswick
04032	ME Freeport
04046	ME Kennebunkport
04062	ME Windham
04064	ME Old Orchard Bch
04073	ME Sanford
04103	ME Portland
04106	ME South Portland
04240	ME Lewiston
04276	ME Rumford
04330	ME Augusta
04401	ME Bangor
04412	ME Brewer
04416	ME Bucksport
04442	ME Greenville
04457	ME Lincoln
04462	ME Millinocket
04605	ME Trenton
04650	ME Ellsworth
04654	ME Machias
04769	ME Presque Isle
04841	ME Rockland
04846	ME Glen Cove
04901	ME Waterville
04938	ME Farmington
05001	VT White River Jct.
05059	VT Quechee
05071	VT Woodstock
05150	VT North Springfield
05156	VT Springfield
05201	VT Bennington
05250	VT Arlington
05254	VT Manchester
05301	VT Brattleboro
05346	VT Putney
05403	VT Burlington
05446	VT Colchester
05482	VT Shelburne
05602	VT Montpelier
05672	VT Stowe
05674	VT Warren
05676	VT Waterbury
05701	VT Rutland
05751	VT Killington
05753	VT Middlebury
05855	VT Newport
06051	CT New Britain
06066	CT Vernon
06082	CT Enfield
06088	CT East Windsor
06089	CT Simsbury
06095	CT Windsor
06096	CT Windsor Locks
06108	CT Hartford
06109	CT Wethersfield
06320	CT New London
06333	CT Niantic
06360	CT Norwich
06416	CT Cromwell
06450	CT Meriden
06460	CT Milford
06473	CT North Haven
06484	CT Shelton
06489	CT Southington
06804	CT Brookfield
06810	CT Danbury
06820	CT Darien
06854	CT Norwalk
07008	NJ Carteret
07013	NJ Clifton
07047	NJ North Bergen
07054	NJ Parsippany
07060	NJ North Plainfield
07066	NJ Clark
07073	NJ East Rutherford
07080	NJ South Plainfield
07081	NJ Springfield
07094	NJ Secaucus
07114	NJ Newark
07201	NJ Elizabeth
07446	NJ Ramsey
07652	NJ Paramus
07662	NJ Rochelle Park
07662	NJ Saddle Brook
07724	NJ Tinton Falls
07866	NJ Rockaway
07936	NJ East Hanover
08016	NJ Mount Holly
08034	NJ Cherry Hill
08043	PA Voorhees
08054	NJ Mount Laurel
08232	NJ W. Atlantic City
08244	NJ Somers Point
08360	NJ Vineland
08520	NJ East Windsor
08540	NJ Lawrenceville
08543	NJ Princeton
08562	NJ Wrightstown
08648	NJ Trenton
08701	NJ Lakewood
08810	NJ Dayton
08837	NJ Edison
08854	NJ Piscataway
08865	NJ Phillipsburg
08873	NJ Somerset

ZIPS 10001-20000

10021	NY Manhattan
10021	NY New York
10504	NY Armonk
10523	NY Elmsford
10549	NY Mount Kisco
10928	NY Highland Falls
10954	NY Nanuet
10958	NY Middletown
10977	NY Spring Valley
11369	NY East Elmhurst
11430	NY Jamaica
11550	NY Hempstead
11570	NY Rockville Centre
11747	NY Melville
11788	NY Hauppauge
11797	NY Woodbury
11803	NY Plainview
12110	NY Albany
12110	NY Latham
12308	NY Schenectady
12401	NY Kingston
12430	NY Fleischmanns
12477	NY Saugerties
12549	NY Montgomery
12550	NY Newburgh
12601	NY Poughkeepsie
12754	NY Liberty
12771	NY Port Jervis
12824	NY Diamond Point
12845	NY Lake George
12866	NY Saratoga Springs
12901	NY Plattsburgh
12946	NY Lake Placid
13021	NY Auburn
13032	NY Canastota
13057	NY East Syracuse
13088	NY Liverpool
13101	NY McGraw
13143	NY New Hartford
13165	NY Waterloo
13166	NY Weedsport
13203	NY Syracuse
13365	NY Little Falls
13502	NY Utica
13601	NY Watertown
13617	NY Canton
13669	NY Ogdensburg
13760	NY Endicott
13820	NY Oneonta
13905	NY Binghamton
14020	NY Batavia
14048	NY Dunkirk
14063	NY Fredonia
14075	NY Hamburg
14202	NY Buffalo
14221	NY Amherst
14304	NY Niagara Falls
14437	NY Dansville
14456	NY Geneva
14624	NY Rochester
14701	NY Jamestown
14810	NY Bath
14845	NY Horseheads
14850	NY Ithaca
14904	NY Elmira
15017	PA Bridgeville
15071	PA Oakdale
15071	PA Pittsburgh
15108	PA Coraopolis
15205	PA Greentree

15301 PA Washington	18507 PA Moosic	21502 MD La Vale	23901 VA Farmville
15370 PA Waynesburg	18512 PA Dunmore	21532 MD Frostburg	23970 VA Shouth Hill
15401 PA Uniontown	18631 PA Mifflinville	21536 MD Grantsville	23970 VA South Hill
15501 PA Somerset	18640 PA Pittston	21601 MD Easton	24014 VA Roanoke
15522 PA Bedford	18640 PA Scranton	21613 MD Cambridge	24060 VA Blacksburg
15533 PA Breezewood	18661 PA Lake Harmony	21663 MD St. Michaels	24073 VA Christiansburg
15601 PA Greensburg	18702 PA Wilkes-Barre	21701 MD Frederick	24112 VA Martinsville
15601 PA Irwin	19020 PA Philadelphia	21740 MD Hagerstown	24141 VA Radford
15672 PA New Stanton	19029 PA Essington	21795 MD Williamsport	24153 VA Salem
15801 PA Dubois	19034 PA Ft. Washington	21801 MD Salisbury	24175 VA Troutville
15825 PA Brookville	19044 PA Horsham	21842 MD Ocean City	24203 VA Bristol
15904 PA Johnstown	19053 PA Trevose	21851 MD Pocomoke	24244 VA Duffield
16001 PA Butler	19057 PA Levittown	21851 MD Pocomoke City	24273 VA Norton
16038 PA Barkeyvillle	19312 PA Berwyn	21921 MD Elkton	24301 VA Pulaski
16046 PA Mars	19341 PA Downingtown	22021 VA Chatilly	24382 VA Wytheville
16046 PA Warrendale	19341 PA Exton	22030 VA Fairfax	24401 VA Staunton
16101 PA New Castle	19406 PA King of Prussia	22041 VA Baileys	24426 VA Covington
16137 PA Mercer	19443 PA Kulpsville	Crossroads	24450 VA Lexington
16159 PA West Middlesex	19464 PA Pottstown	22043 VA Falls Church	24482 VA Verona
16214 PA Clarion	19610 PA Reading	22071 VA Herndon	24504 VA Lynchburg
16301 PA Oil City	19702 DE Newark	22075 VA Leesburg	24522 VA Appomattox
16335 PA Meadville	19720 DE New Castle	22102 VA McLean	24523 VA Bedford
16365 PA Warren	19801 DE Wilmington	22110 VA Manassas	24541 VA Danville
16509 PA Erie	19901 DE Dover	22150 VA Springfield	24592 VA South Boston
16601 PA Altoona		22170 VA Sterling	24701 WA Bluefield
16652 PA Huntingdon		22182 VA Vienna	24701 WV Bluefield
16801 PA State College	**ZIPS 20001-30000**	22186 VA Warrenton	24740 WV Princeton
16830 PA Clearfield		22192 VA Woodbridge	24901 WV Lewisburg
16853 PA Milesburg	20601 MD Waldorf	22202 VA Arlington	25143 WV Nitro
16933 PA Mansfield	20619 MD Lexington Park	22303 VA Alexandria	25177 WV St. Albans
17009 PA Burnham	20705 MD Beltsville	22310 DC Washington	25271 WV Ripley
17013 PA Carlisle	20706 MD Lanham	22401 VA Fredericksburg	25304 WV Charleston
17025 PA Enola	20707 MD Laurel	22480 VA Irvington	25401 WV Martinsburg
17028 PA Grantville	20743 MD Capitol Heights	22546 VA Carmel Church	25601 WV Logan
17055 PA Mechanicsburg	20745 MD Oxon Hill	22554 VA Stafford	25705 WV Huntington
17070 PA New Cumberland	20746 MD Camp Springs	22560 VA Tappahannock	25801 WV Beckley
17109 PA Harrisburg	20770 MD Greenbelt	22601 VA Winchester	25840 WV Fayetteville
17201 PA Chambersburg	20784 MD Cheverly	22630 VA Front Royal	26059 WV Wheeling
17268 PA Waynesboro	20784 MD New Carrollton	22701 VA Culpeper	26101 WV Parkersburg
17325 PA Gettysburg	20794 MD Jessup	22801 VA Harrisonburg	26241 WV Elkins
17402 PA York	20815 MD Chevy Chase	22835 VA Luray	26330 WV Bridgeport
17517 PA Denver	20817 MD Bethesda	22842 VA Mt. Jackson	26330 WV Clarksburg
17601 PA Lancaster	20850 MD Rockville	22844 VA New Market	26452 WV Weston
17701 PA Williamsport	20879 MD Gaithersburg	22901 VA Charlottesville	26505 WV Morgantown
17745 PA Lock Haven	20910 MD Silver Spring	22980 VA Waynesboro	26554 WV Fairmont
17751 PA Mill Hall	21001 MD Aberdeen	23005 VA Ashland	26651 WV Summersville
17815 PA Bloomsburg	21030 MD Cockeysville	23150 VA Sandston	27105 NC Winston-Salem
17821 PA Danville	21030 MD Hunt Valley	23185 VA Williamsburg	27260 NC High Point
17856 PA New Columbia	21040 MD Edgewood	23220 VA Richmond	27288 NC Eden
17876 PA Shamokin Dam	21044 MD Columbia	23320 VA Chesapeake	27409 NC Greensboro
17901 PA Pottsville	21061 MD Glen Burnie	23434 VA Suffolk	27514 NC Chapel Hill
18017 PA Bethlehem	21076 MD Hanover	23462 VA Virginia Beach	27534 NC Goldsboro
18042 PA Easton	21078 MD Havre De Grace	23504 VA Norfolk	27576 NC Selma
18104 PA Allentown	21090 MD Linthicum	23602 VA Newport News	27612 NC Raleigh
18201 PA Hazleton	21093 MD Timonium	23666 VA Hampton	27705 NC Durham
18201 PA West Hazelton	21113 MD Odenton	23704 VA Portsmouth	27809 NC Battleboro
18301 PA East Stroudsburg	21157 MD Westminster	23805 VA Petersburg	27815 TN Morristown
18336 PA Matamoras	21204 MD Towson	23831 VA Chester	27834 NC Greenville
18360 PA Stroudsburg	21208 MD Pikesville	23834 VA Colonial Heights	27870 NC Roanoke Rapids
18436 PA Hamlin	21225 MD Baltimore	23847 VA Emporia	27892 NC Williamston
18436 PA Lake Ariel	21401 MD Annapolis	23851 VA Franklin	27893 NC Wilson
	21502 MD Cumberland		

27948 NC Kill Devil Hills	**ZIPS 30001-40000**	31647 GA Sparks
28024 TN Dyersburg		31701 GA Albany
28031 NC Cornelius		31714 FL Ashburn
28052 NC Gastonia	30001 GA Austell	31714 GA Ashburn
28112 NC Monroe	30034 GA Decatur	31717 GA Bainbridge
28144 NC Salisbury	30058 GA Lithona	31728 GA Cairo
28262 NC Charlotte	30067 GA Marietta	31733 GA Chula
28314 NC Fayetteville	30067 GA Roswell	31792 GA Thomasville
28315 NC Aberdeen	30080 GA Smyrna	31794 GA Tifton
28315 NY Aberdeen	30084 GA Tucker	31833 GA West point
28334 NC Dunn	30093 GA Norcross	31907 GA Columbus
28383 NC Rowland	30101 GA Acworth	32052 FL Jasper
28395 NC Wade	30120 GA Cartersville	32053 FL Jennings
28604 NC Banner Elk	30144 GA Atlanta	32055 FL Ellisville
28613 NC Conover	30144 GA Kennesaw	32055 FL Lake City
28642 NC Jonesville	30161 GA Rome	32084 FL Augustine Beach
28655 NC Morganton	30174 GA Suwanee	32084 FL St. Augustine
28677 NC Statesville	30180 GA Villa Rica	32091 FL Starke
28734 NC Franklin	30184 GA White	32096 FL White Springs
28739 NC Hendersonville	30201 GA Alpharetta	32114 FL Daytona Beach
28752 NC Marion	30223 GA Griffin	32118 FL Daytona
28801 NC Asheville	30236 GA Jonesboro	32174 FL Ormond Beach
29033 SC Cayce	30240 GA LaGrange	32234 FL Baldwin
29078 SC Lugoff	30248 GA Locust Grove	32256 FL Jacksonville
29102 SC Manning	30260 GA Morrow	32301 FL Tallahassee
29108 SC Newberry	30263 GA Newnan	32401 FL Panama City
29115 SC Orangeburg	30281 GA Stockbridge	32425 FL Bonifay
29142 SC Santee	30344 GA East Point	32428 FL Chipley
29148 SC Summerton	30349 GA College Park	32433 FL Defuniak Springs
29151 SC Sumter	30354 GA Hapeville	32446 FL Marianna
29169 SC West Columbia	30458 GA Statesboro	32504 FL Pensacola
29203 SC Columbia	30474 GA Vidalia	32536 FL Crestview
29303 SC Spartanburg	30503 GA Gainesville	32541 FL Destin
29325 SC Clinton	30513 GA Blue Ridge	32548 FL Ft. Walton
29340 SC Gaffney	30529 GA Commerce	32578 FL Niceville
29418 SC Charleston	30601 GA Athens	32608 FL Gainesville
29418 SC North Charleston	30605 FL Athens	32615 FL Alachua
29456 SC Ladson	30701 GA Calhoun	32639 FL Crystal River
29464 SC Mt. Pleasant	30720 GA Dalton	32667 FL Micanopy
29477 SC St. George	30736 GA Ringgold	32675 FL Ocala
29488 SC Aberdeen	30907 GA Augusta	32688 FL Silver Springs
29488 SC Walterboro	31008 GA Byron	32714 FL Altamonte Sprgs
29501 SC Florence	31015 GA Cordele	32724 FL Deland
29536 SC Dillon	31029 GA Forsyth	32763 FL Orange City
29577 SC Myrtle Beach	31040 GA Dublin	32771 FL Sanford
29605 SC Greenville	31061 GA Milledgeville	32778 FL Tavares
29621 SC Anderson	31069 GA Perry	32796 FL Titusville
29631 SC Clemson	31091 GA Unadilla	32809 FL Orlando
29640 SC Easley	31093 GA Warner Robins	32836 FL Lake Buena Vista
29715 SC Ft. Mill	31204 GA Macon	32903 FL Indiatlantic
29720 SC Lancaster	31322 GA Pooler	32904 FL Melbourne
29729 SC Richburg	31324 GA Richmond Hill	32909 FL Palm Bay
29730 SC Rock Hill	31331 GA Townsend	32926 FL Cocoa
29801 SC Aiken	31419 GA Savannah	32931 FL Cocoa Beach
29902 SC Beaufort	31501 GA Waycross	32937 FL Satellite Beach
29927 SC Hardeeville	31520 GA Brunswick	32966 FL Vero Beach
29928 SC Hilton Head	31520 GA Jekyll Island	33004 FL Dania
29935 SC Port Royal	31533 GA Douglas	33004 FL Dania Beach
29945 SC Point South	31548 GA Kingsland	33030 FL Homestead
29945 SC Yemassee	31602 GA Valdosta	33034 FL Florida City
	31620 GA Adel	33040 FL Key West
	31636 GA Lake Park	

33050 FL Marathon
33069 FL Pompano Beach
33142 FL Miami
33160 FL Miami Beach
33166 FL Miami Springs
33183 FL Kendall
33311 FL Ft. Lauderdale
33404 FL Riviera Beach
33404 FL Singer Island
33407 FL W. Palm Beach
33410 FL Palm Beach
33442 FL Deerfield Beach
33462 FL Lantana
33467 FL Lake Worth
33487 FL Boca Raton
33566 FL Plant City
33570 FL Rushkin
33572 FL Apollo Beach
33612 FL Tampa
33619 AL Tillmans Corner
33706 FL Treasure Island
33805 FL Lakeland
33844 FL Lake Hamilton
33845 FL Haines City
33852 FL Lake Placid
33853 FL Lake Wales
33903 FL Myers
33904 FL Cape Coral
33907 FL Ft. Myers
33942 FL Naples
33950 FL Punta Gorda
33952 FL Port Charlotte
34208 FL Bradenton
34222 FL Ellenton
34224 FL Englewood
34228 FL Longboat Key
34234 FL Sarasota
34293 FL Venice
34620 FL Clearwater
34652 FL New Port Richey
34665 FL Pinellas Park
34666 FL St. Petersburg
34668 FL Port Richey
34684 FL Palm Harbor
34689 FL Tarpon Springs
34691 FL Holiday
34746 FL Kissimmee
34748 FL Leesburg
34785 FL Wildwood
34945 FL Ft. Pierce
35020 AL Bessemer
35045 AL Clanton
35055 AL Cullman
35216 AL Hoover
35223 AL Birmingham
35405 AL Tuscaloosa
35476 AL Northport
35601 AL Decatur
35611 AL Athens
35630 AL Florence
35653 AL Russellville

35660 AL Sheffield	37762 TN Jellico	40475 KY Richmond	44010 OH Austinburg
35661 AL Muscle Shoals	37763 TN Kingston	40505 KY Lexington	44035 OH Elyria
35758 AL Madison	37764 TN Kodak	40601 KY Frankfort	44056 OH Macedonia
35768 AL Scottsboro	37774 TN Loudon	40701 KY Corbin	44060 OH Mentor
35816 AL Huntsville	37821 TN Newport	40741 KY London	44087 OH Twinsburg
35901 AL Gadsden	37830 TN Knoxville	40769 KY Williamsburg	44092 OH Wickliffe
35954 AL Attalla	37830 TN Oak Ridge	40831 KY Harlan	44122 OH Beachwood
35957 AL Boaz	37863 TN Pidgeon Forge	40965 KY Middlesboro	44130 OH Middleburg Hts
35976 AL Guntersville	37863 TN Pigeon Forge	41008 KY Carrollton	44136 OH Strongsville
36027 AL Eufaula	37874 TN Sweetwater	41011 KY Covington	44145 OH Cleveland
36037 AL Greenville	37882 TN Townsend	41011 KY Ft. Wright	44147 OH Broadview Hghts
36075 AL Shorter	38012 TN Brownsville	41017 KY Ft. Mitchell	44240 OH Brimfield
36123 AL Montgomery	38053 TN Millington	41018 KY Erlanger	44240 OH Kent
36203 AL Anniston	38116 TN Memphis	41042 KY Florence	44241 OH Streetsboro
36203 AL Oxford	38261 TN Union City	41094 KY Walton	44256 OH Medina
36302 AL Dothan	38305 TN Jackson	41097 KY Williamstown	44281 OH Wadsworth
36310 AL Abbeville	38320 TN Camden	41101 KY Ashland	44286 OH Richfield
36330 AL Enterprise	38358 TN Milan	41503 KY South Williamson	44321 OH Montrose
36361 AL Ozark	38388 TN Wildersville	42001 KY Paducah	44333 OH Akron
36460 AL Monroeville	38391 TN Denmark	42044 KY Gilbertsville	44420 OH Girard
36535 AL Foley	38402 TN Columbia	42045 KY Grand Rivers	44446 OH Niles
36561 AL Orange Bch	38501 TN Cookeville	42071 KY Murray	44483 OH Warren
36605 AL Mobile	38555 TN Crossville	42104 KY Bowling Green	44512 OH Boardman
36701 AL Selma	38666 MS Sardis	42127 KY Cave City	44515 OH Austintown
36732 AL Demopolis	38671 MS Southaven	42134 KY Franklin	44515 OH Youngstown
36784 AL Thomasville	38701 MS Greenville	42240 KY Hopkinsville	44601 OH Alliance
36801 AL Opelika	38801 MS Tupelo	42301 KY Owensboro	44622 OH Dover
37027 TN Brentwood	38901 MS Grenada	42401 KY Fulton	44663 OH New Philadelphia
37043 TN Clarksville	38930 MS Greenwood	42420 KY Henderson	44691 OH Wooster
37055 TN Dickson	39074 MS Forest	42431 KY Madisonville	44709 OH Canton
37064 TN Franklin	39111 MS Magee	42701 KY Elizabethtown	44718 OH North Canton
37072 TN Goodlettesville	39120 MS Natchez	42718 KY Campbellsville	44820 OH Bucyrus
37078 TN Hurricane Mills	39157 MS Ridgeland	42749 KY Horse Cave	44830 OH Fostoria
37080 TN Joelton	39180 MS Vicksburg	43015 OH Delaware	44870 OH Sandusky
37087 TN Lebanon	39236 MS Jackson	43017 OH Dublin	44903 OH Mansfield
37110 TN McMinnville	39301 MS Meridian	43040 OH Marysville	45005 OH Franklin
37115 TN Madison	39345 MS Newton	43056 OH Newark	45036 OH Lebanon
37130 TN Murfreesboro	39401 MS Hattiesburg	43068 OH Reynoldsburg	45040 OH Mason
37172 TN Springfield	39503 MS Gulfport	43123 OH Grove City	45056 OH Oxford
37174 TN Spring Hill	39531 MS Biloxi	43130 OH Lancaster	45241 OH Blue Ash
37188 TN Whitehouse	39567 MS Pascagoula	43160 OH Wash. Ct. House	45241 OH Cincinnati
37211 TN Antioch	39601 MS Brookhaven	43202 OH Columbus	45241 OH Sharonville
37211 TN Nashville	39648 MS McCombs	43302 OH Marion	45246 OH Springdale
37303 TN Athens	39701 MS Columbus	43311 OH Bellefontaine	45309 OH Brookville
37311 TN Cleveland	39730 MS Aberdeen	43402 OH Bowling Green	45320 OH Eaton
37321 TN Dayton		43420 OH Fremont	45322 OH Englewood
37326 TN Ducktown	ZIPS 40001-50000	43447 OH Millbury	45324 OH Fairborn
37334 TN Fayetteville		43452 OH Port Clinton	45342 OH Miamisburg
37347 TN South Pittsburg	40004 KY Bardstown	43512 OH Defiance	45356 OH Piqua
37355 TN Manchester	40031 KY LaGrange	43528 OH Holland	45365 OH Sidney
37356 TN Monteagle	40065 KY Shelbyville	43537 OH Maumee	45373 OH Troy
37363 TN Ooltewah	40160 KY Radcliff	43537 OH Toledo	45385 OH Zenia
37421 TN Chattanooga	40165 KY Shepherdsville	43543 OH Montpelier	45414 OH Dayton
37620 TN Bristol	40207 KY Louisville	43545 OH Napolean	45601 OH Chillicothe
37643 TN Elizabethton	40324 KY Georgetown	43551 OH Perrysburg	45631 OH Gallipolis
37660 TN Kingsport	40330 KY Harrodsburg	43616 OH Oregon	45640 OH Jackson
37701 TN Alcoa	40353 KY Mt. Sterling	43701 OH Zanesville	45662 OH Portsmouth
37714 TN Caryville	40391 KY Winchester	43725 OH Cambridge	45680 OH South Point
37724 TN Cumberland Gap	40403 KY Berea	43950 OH St. Clairsville	45750 OH Marietta
37738 TN Gatlinburg	40422 KY Danville	43952 OH Steubenville	45764 OH Nelsonville
37748 TN Harriman	40456 KY Mt. Vernon	44001 OH Amherst	45801 OH Lima

401

ZIP INDEX

ZIPS 50001-60000

45822 OH Celina	48131 MI Dundee
45840 OH Findlay	48150 MI Livonia
45891 OH Van Wert	48154 MI Detroit
45895 OH Wapakoneta	48161 MI Monroe
46013 IN Anderson	48167 MI Northville
46017 IN Daleville	48170 MI Plymouth
46038 IN Fishers	48174 MI Romulus
46052 IN Lebanon	48180 MI Taylor
46120 IN Cloverdale	48183 MI Woodhaven
46131 IN Franklin	48187 MI Canton
46176 IN Shelbyville	48195 MI Southgate
46219 IN Indianapolis	48309 MI Rochester Hills
46224 IN Speedway	48312 MI Sterling Heights
46250 IN Castleton	48415 MI Birch Run
46324 IN Hammond	48444 MI Imlay City
46350 IN La Porte	48507 MI Flint
46360 IN Michigan City	48601 MI Saginaw
46368 IN Portage	48617 MI Clare
46410 IN Merrillville	48629 MI Houghton Lake
46514 IN Elkhart	48640 MI Midland
46526 IN Goshen	48708 MI Bay City
46563 IN Plymouth	48823 MI East Lansing
46580 IN Warsaw	48836 MI Fowlerville
46637 IN South Bend	48843 MI Howell
46825 IN Ft. Wayne	48858 MI Mt. Pleasant
46901 IN Kokomo	48864 MI Okemos
46947 IN Logansport	48911 MI Lansing
47112 IN Corydon	49002 MI Kalamazoo
47129 IN Clarksville	49015 MI Battle Creek
47130 IN Jeffersonville	49022 MI Benton Harbor
47170 IN Scottsburg	49036 MI Coldwater
47201 IN Columbus	49085 MI St. Joseph
47250 IN Madison	49117 MI New Buffalo
47274 IN Seymour	49120 MI Niles
47305 IN Muncie	49202 MI Jackson
47374 IN Richmond	49224 MI Albion
47401 IN Bloomington	49423 MI Holland
47523 IN Dale	49431 MI Ludington
47546 IN Jasper	49444 MI Muskegon
47591 IN Vincennes	49504 MI Grand Rapids
47711 IN Evansville	49504 MI Walker
47802 IN Terre Haute	49509 MI Grand Rapids
47882 IN Sullivan	49601 MI Cadillac
47905 IN Lafayette	49684 MI Traverse City
47906 IN West Lafayette	49701 MI Mackinaw City
47933 IN Crawfordsville	49707 MI Alpena
47977 IN Remington	49721 MI Cheboygan
48017 MI Clawson	49735 MI Gaylord
48024 MI Farmington	49738 MI Grayling
48034 MI Southfield	49770 MI Petoskey
48047 MI New Baltimore	49781 MI St. Ignace
48050 MI Novi	49783 MI Sault Ste. Marie
48057 MI Auburn Hills	49801 MI Iron Mountain
48060 MI Port Huron	49829 MI Escanaba
48066 MI Roseville	49854 MI Manistique
48071 MI Madison Heights	49855 MI Marquette
48083 MI Troy	49858 MI Menominee
48093 MI Warren	49862 MI Munising
48108 MI Ann Arbor	49868 MI Newberry
48111 MI Belleville	49908 MI Baraga
48124 MI Dearborn	49953 MI Silver City

50010 IA Ames	53598 WI Windsor
50022 IA Atlantic	53704 WI Madison
50036 IA Boone	53818 WI Platteville
50112 IA Grinnell	53821 WI Prairie Du Chien
50131 IA Johnston	53913 WI Baraboo
50158 IA Marshalltown	53913 WI West Baraboo
50208 IA Newton	53916 WI Beaver Dam
50213 IA Osceola	53965 WI Wisconsin Dells
50248 IA Story City	54016 WI Hudson
50271 IA Williams	54022 WI River Falls
50321 IA Des Moines	54024 WI St. Croix Falls
50322 IA Clive	54143 WI Marinette
50322 IA Urbandale	54166 WI Shawano
50401 IA Mason City	54202 WI Baileys Harbor
50428 IA Clear Lake	54301 WI Green Bay
50501 IA Ft. Dodge	54401 WI Wausau
50613 IA Cedar Falls	54409 WI Antigo
50644 IA Independence	54449 WI Marshfield
50702 IA Waterloo	54481 WI Stevens Point
51012 IA Cherokee	54501 WI Rhinelander
51054 IA Sergeant Bluff	54521 WI Eagle River
51106 IA Sioux City	54534 WI Hurley
51401 IA Carroll	54548 WI Minocqua
51442 IA Dennison	54552 WI Park Falls
51501 IA Council Bluffs	54603 WI La Crosse
52001 IA Dubuque	54615 WI Black River Falls
52101 IA Decorah	54650 WI Onalaska
52203 IA Amana	54656 WI Sparta
52240 IA Iowa City	54660 WI Tomah
52241 IA Coralville	54701 WI Eau Claire
52361 IA Williamsburg	54729 WI Chippewa Falls
52402 IA Cedar Rapids	54751 WI Menomonie
52501 IA Ottumwa	54758 WI Osseo
52556 IA Fairfield	54806 WI Ashland
52601 IA Burlington	54843 WI Hayward
52627 IA Ft. Madison	54847 WI Iron River
52632 IA Keokuk	54848 WI Ladysmith
52641 IA Mount Pleasant	54868 WI Rice Lake
52732 IA Clinton	54880 WI Superior
52761 IA Muscatine	54891 WI Washburn
52773 IA Walcott	54901 WI Oshkosh
52806 IA Davenport	54914 WI Appleton
53005 WI Brookfield	54935 WI Fond Du Lac
53022 WI Germantown	54971 WI Ripon
53027 WI Hartford	54982 WI Wautoma
53074 WI Port Washington	55013 MN Chisago City
53081 WI Sheboygan	55021 MN Faribault
53094 WI Watertown	55037 MN Hinckley
53142 WI Kenosha	55044 MN Lakeville
53147 WI Lake Geneva	55060 MN Owatonna
53154 WI Oak Creek	55066 MN Red Wing
53186 WI Waukesha	55082 MN Stillwater
53190 WI Whitewater	55102 MN St. Paul
53217 WI Glendale	55112 MN Arden Hills
53217 WI Milwaukee	55113 MN Roseville
53405 WI Racine	55119 MN Maplewood
53511 WI Beloit	55121 MN Eagan
53533 WI Dodgeville	55125 MN Woodbury
53545 WI Janesville	55126 MN Shoreview
	55303 MN Anoka
	55313 MN Buffalo

55317 MN Chanhassen	57325 SD Oacoma	ZIPS 60001-70000
55318 MN Chaska	57362 SD Miller	
55330 MN Elk River	57401 SD Aberdeen	60005 IL Arlington Heights
55336 MN Glencoe	57438 SD Faulkton	60007 IL Elk Grove Village
55337 MN Burnsville	57501 SD Pierre	60008 IL Chicago
55344 MN Eden Prairie	57543 SD Kadoka	60008 IL Rolling Meadows
55362 MN Monticello	57559 SD Murdo	60014 IL Crystal Lake
55374 MN Rogers	57580 SD Winner	60015 IL Deerfield
55403 MN Brooklyn Center	57601 SD Mobridge	60018 IL Rosemont
55421 MN Fridley	57701 SD Rapid City	60025 IL Glenview
55423 MN Richfield	57717 SD Belle Fourche	60060 IL Mundelein
55425 MN Bloomington	57730 SD Custer	60062 IL Northbrook
55441 MN Plymouth	57732 SD Deadwood	60067· IL Palatine
55454 MN Minneapolis	57745 SD Hill City	60069 IL Lincolnshire
55604 MN Grand Marais	57747 SD Hot Springs	60070 IL Prospect Heights
55612 MN Lusten	57750 SD Badlands Nat Pk	60077 IL Skokie
55734 MN Eveleth	57751 SD Keystone	60085 IL Waukegan
55735 MN Finlayson	57783 SD Spearfish	60098 IL Woodstock
55744 MN Grand Rapids	57785 SD Sturgis	60115 IL Dekalb
55746 MN Hibbing	57790 SD Wall	60123 IL Elgin
55801 MN Duluth	57938 SD Lemmon	60126 IL Elmhurst
55904 MN Rochester	58075 ND Wahpeton	60137 IL Glen Ellyn
55912 MN Austin	58078 ND West Fargo	60148 IL Lombard
55987 MN Winona	58103 ND Fargo	60162 IL Hillside
55992 MN Zumbrota	58201 ND Grand Forks	60173 IL Schaumberg
56001 MN Mankato	58301 ND Devils Lake	60176 IL Schiller Park
56003 MN N Mankato	58421 ND Carrington	60181 IL Oakbrook Terrace
56007 MN Albert Lea	58501 ND Bismarck	60195 IL Hoffman Estates
56031 MN Fairmont	58554 ND Mandan	60426 IL Harvey
56073 MN New Ulm	58601 ND Dickinson	60429 IL East Hazelcrest
56081 MN St. James	58623 ND Bowman	60430 IL Homewood
56085 MN Sleepy Eye	58701 ND Minot	60435 IL Joliet
56164 MN Pipestone	58801 ND Williston	60438 IL Lansing
56187 MN Worthington	59011 MT Big Timber	60445 IL Crestwood
56201 MN Willmar	59019 MT Columbus	60450 IL Morris
56208 MN Appleton	59030 MT Gardiner	60455 IL Bridgeview
56258 MN Marshall	59047 MT Livingston	60462 IL Orland Park
56265 MN Montevideo	59068 MT Red Lodge	60473 IL South Holland
56301 MN St. Cloud	59101 MT Billings	60515 IL Downers Grove
56308 MN Alexandria	59301 MT Miles City	60521 IL Oak Brook
56352 MN Melrose	59327 MT Forsyth	60521 IL Willowbrook
56374 MN St. Joseph	59330 MT Glendive	60525 IL La Grange
56401 MN Brainerd	59405 MT Great Falls	60532 IL Lisle
56468 MN Nisswa	59425 MT Conrad	60542 IL Aurora
56482 MN Wadena	59434 MT E. Glacier Park	60563 IL Naperville
56501 MN Detroit Lakes	59501 MT Havre	60648 IL Niles
56537 MN Fergus Falls	59601 MT Helena	60658 IL Alsip
56601 MN Bemidji	59701 MT Butte	60901 IL Kankakee
56679 MN Int'l Falls	59714 MT Belgrade	60938 IL Gilman
56701 MN Thief River Falls	59715 MT Bozeman	60970 IL Watseka
56751 MN Roseau	59716 MT Big Sky	61021 IL Dixon
56763 MN Warroad	59722 MT Deer Lodge	61032 IL Freeport
57006 SD Brookings	59725 MT Dillon	61036 IL Galena
57012 SD Canistota	59758 MT W. Yellowstone	61071 IL Rock Falls
57042 SD Madison	59758 MT Yellowstone	61108 IL Rockford
57069 SD Vermillion	59802 MT Missoula	61265 IL Moline
57078 SD Yankton	59860 MT Polson	61342 IL Mendota
57106 SD Sioux Falls	59866 MT St. Regis	61354 IL Peru
57201 SD Watertown	59901 MT Kalispell	61401 IL Galesburg
57274 SD Webster	59923 MT Libby	61455 IL Macomb
57301 SD Mitchell	59937 MT Whitefish	61571 IL Washington

61611 IL East Peoria
61614 IL Peoria
61701 ID Bloomington
61701 IL Bloomington
61752 IL Le Roy
61754 IL McLean
61761 IL Normal
61764 IL Pontiac
61801 IL Urbana
61821 IL Champaign
61832 IL Danville
61866 IL Rantoul
61874 IL Savoy
61938 IL Mattoon
61953 IL Tuscola
62002 IL Alton
62025 IL Edwardsville
62040 IL Pontoon Beach
62056 IL Litchfield
62208 IL Fairview Heights
62233 IL Chester
62234 IL Collinsville
62246 IL Greenville
62269 IL O'Fallon
62271 IL Okawville
62301 IL Quincy
62401 IL Effingham
62411 IL Altamont
62454 IL Robinson
62471 IL Vandalia
62526 IL Decatur
62535 IL Forsyth
62650 IL Jacksonville
62656 IL Lincoln
62703 IL Springfield
62812 IL Benton
62864 IL Mt. Vernon
62881 IL Salem
62901 IL Carbondale
62959 IL Marion
62965 IL Muddy
62992 IL Ullin
63017 MO Chesterfield
63025 MO Eureka
63026 MO Fenton
63042 MO Hazelwood
63044 MO Bridgeton
63077 MO St. Clair
63080 MO Sullivan
63089 MO Villa Ridge
63134 MO St. Louis
63301 MO St. Charles
63348 MO Foristell
63385 MO Wentzville
63401 MO Hannibal
63501 MO Kirksville
63552 MO Macon
63640 MO Farmington
63701 MO Cape Girardeau
63755 MO Jackson
63775 MO Perryville

ZIP INDEX

63801 MO Sikeston	67401 KS Salina	71635 AR Crossett	73644 OK Elk City
64015 MO Blue Springs	67401 KS Salinas	71701 AR Camden	73645 OK Erick
64020 MO Concordia	67410 KS Abilene	71730 AR El Dorado	73701 OK Enid
64029 MO Grain Valley	67439 KS Ellsworth	71753 AR Magnolia	73942 OK Guymon
64037 MO Higginsville	67460 KS McPherson	71801 AR Hope	74006 OK Bartlesville
64055 MO Independence	67501 KS Hutchinson	71901 AR Hot Springs	74012 OK Broken Arrow
64068 MO Liberty	67530 KS Great Bend	71923 AR Arkadelphia	74017 OK Claremore
64075 MO Oak Grove	67550 KS Larned	71953 AR Mena	74033 OK Glenpool
64079 MO Platte City	67601 KS Hays	72015 AR Benton	74033 OK Tulsa
64081 MO Lee's Summit	67654 KS Norton	72021 AR Brinkley	74066 OK Sapulpa
64093 MO Warrensburg	67672 KS Wakeeney	72023 AR Cabot	74074 OK Stillwater
64137 MO Kansas City	67701 KS Colby	72024 AR Carlisle	74079 OK Stroud
64424 MO Bethany	67735 KS Goodland	72032 AR Conway	74354 OK Miami
64429 MO Cameron	67801 KS Dodge City	72076 AR Jacksonville	74401 OK Muskogee
64468 MO Maryville	67846 KS Garden City	72110 AR Morrilton	74426 OK Checotah
64506 MO St. Joseph	67901 KS Liberal	72114 AR North Little Rock	74437 OK Henryetta
64701 MO Harrisonville	68005 NE Bellevue	72160 AR Stuttgart	74501 OK McAlester
64735 MO Clinton	68025 NE Fremont	72209 AR Little Rock	74525 OK Atoka
64772 MO Nevada	68124 NE Omaha	72301 AR Clinton	74631 OK Blackwell
64804 MO Joplin	68434 NE Seward	72301 AR West Memphis	74701 OK Durant
65065 MO Osage Beach	68467 NE York	72316 AR Blytheville	74801 OK Shawnee
65101 MO Jefferson	68521 NE Lincoln	72335 AR Forrest City	74834 OK Chandler
65203 MO Columbia	68601 NE Columbus	72346 AR Heth	74955 OK Sallisaw
65233 MO Boonville	68701 NE Norfolk	72354 AR Marion	75043 TX Garland
65270 MO Moberly	68776 NE South Sioux City	72365 AR Marked Tree	75050 TX Grand Prairie
65301 MO Desalia	68801 NE Grand Island	72370 AR Osceola	75050 TX Grand Prarie
65401 MO Rolla	68848 NE Kearney	72401 AR Jonesboro	75062 TX Irving
65453 MO Cuba	68901 NE Hastings	72455 AR Pocahontas	75067 TX Lewisville
65536 MO Lebanon	69001 NE McCook	72601 AR Harrison	75074 TX Plano
65583 MO St. Robert	69101 NE North Platte	72632 AR Eureka Springs	75080 TX Richardson
65583 MO Waynesville	69145 NE Kimball	72653 AR Mountain Home	75090 TX Sherman
65616 MO Branson	69153 NE Ogallala	72703 AR Fayetteville	75103 TX Canton
65625 MO Cassville	69162 NE Sidney	72712 AR Bentonville	75150 TX Mesquite
65686 MO Kimberling City	69301 NE Alliance	72762 AR Springdale	75160 TX Terrell
65711 MO Mountain Grove	69337 NE Chadron	72801 AR Russellville	75228 TX Thornton Fwy.
65712 MO Mt. Vernon	69361 NE Scottsbluff	72801 AR Russellville	75234 TX Forest Lane
65721 MO Ozark		72830 AR Clarksville	75244 TX Addison
65775 MO West Plains	**ZIPS 70001-80000**	72901 AR Ft. Smith	75401 TX Greenville
65806 MO Springfield		72956 AR Van Buren	75418 TX Bonham
66043 KS Lansing	70062 LA Kenner	73023 OK Chickasha	75455 TX Mt. Pleasant
66048 KS Leavenworth	70063 LA New Orleans	73036 OK El Reno	75460 TX Paris
66049 KS Lawrence	70360 LA Houma	73044 OK Guthrie	75482 TX Sulphur Springs
66061 KS Olathe	70401 LA Hammond	73069 OK Norman	75502 AR Texarkana
66067 KS Ottawa	70458 LA Slidell	73075 OK Pauls Valley	75503 TX Texarkana
66202 KS Merriam	70506 LA Lafayette	73077 OK Perry	75551 TX Atlanta
66211 KS Overland Park	70560 LA New Iberia	73080 OK Purcell	75602 TX Longview
66215 KS Lenexa	70601 LA Lake Charles	73086 OK Sulpher	75662 TX Henderson
66441 KS Junction City	70634 LA DeRidder	73096 OK Weatherford	75662 TX Kilgore
66502 KS Manhattan	70663 LA Sulphur	73110 OK Midwest City	75670 TX Marshall
66508 KS Marysville	70668 LA Vinton	73112 OK Oklahoma City	75702 TX Tyler
66604 KS Topeka	70767 LA Port Allen	73115 OK Del City	75766 TX Jacksonville
66720 KS Chanute	70775 LA St. Francisville	73160 OK Moore	75801 TX Palestine
66801 KS Emporia	70816 LA Baton Rouge	73160 OK Moore,	75831 TX Buffalo
66901 KS Concordia	71052 LA Mansfield	73401 OH Ardmore	75901 TX Lufkin
66935 KS Belleville	71109 LA Shreveport	73401 OK Ardmore	75935 TX Center
67005 KS Arkansas City	71112 LA Bossier City	73505 OK Lawton	75951 TX Jasper
67042 KS El Dorado	71202 LA Monroe	73521 OH Altus	75961 TX Nacogdoches
67054 KS Greenburg	71291 LA West Monroe	73521 OK Altus	76011 TX Arlington
67114 KS Newton	71301 LA Alexandria	73533 OK Duncan	76011 TX Dallas
67124 KS Pratt	71457 LA Natchitoches	73542 OK Frederick	76022 TX Bedford
67216 KS Wichita	71601 AR Pine Bluff	73601 OK Clinton	76028 TX Burleson

76040 TX Euless	78363 TX Kingsville	80601 CO Brighton	82935 WY Green River
76053 TX Hurst	78370 TX Odem	80620 CO Evans	82941 WY Pinedale
76067 TX Mineral Wells	78382 TX Rockport	80631 CO Greeley	83001 WY Jackson
76086 TX Weatherford	78409 TX Corpus Christi	80701 CO Ft. Morgan	83110 WY Afton
76102 TX Ft. Worth	78501 TX McAllen	80723 CO Brush	83128 WY Alpine
76117 TX Haltom City	78521 TX Brownsville	80751 CO Sterling	83201 ID Pocatello
76201 TX Denton	78550 TX Harlingen	80807 CO Burlington	83254 ID Montpelier
76234 TX Decatur	78597 TX S. Padre Island	80836 CO Stratton	83301 ID Twin Falls
76240 TX Gainsville	78624 TX Fredricksburg	80920 CO Colorado Springs	83402 ID Idaho Falls
76301 TX Whichita Falls	78666 TX San Marcos	81008 CO Pueblo	83422 ID Driggs
76305 TX Wichita Falls	78681 TX Round Rock	81050 CO La Junta	83440 ID Rexburg
76384 TX Vernon	78741 TX Austin	81052 CO Lamar	83501 ID Lewiston
76401 TX Stephenville	78801 TX Uvalde	81054 CO Las Animas	83638 ID Mccall
76504 TX Temple	78840 TX Del Rio	81082 CO Trinidad	83651 ID Nampa
76513 TX Belton	78852 TX Eagle Pass	81089 CO Walsenburg	83705 ID Boise
76528 TX Gatesville	78942 TX Giddings	81101 CO Alamosa	83814 ID Coeur D'Alene
76541 TX Killeen	79022 TX Dalhart	81144 CO Monte vista	83843 ID Moscow
76645 TX Hillsboro	79029 TX Dumas	81147 CO Pagosa Springs	83864 ID Sandpoint
76705 TX Bellmead	79045 TX Hereford	81201 CO Salida	84015 UT Clearfield
76710 TX Waco	79072 TX Plainview	81212 CO Canon City	84041 UT Layton
76712 TX Vaco	79079 TX Shamrock	81227 CO Monarch	84060 UT Park City
76849 TX Junction	79092 TX Vega	81230 CO Gunnison	84066 UT Roosevelt
76903 TX San Angelo	79102 TX Amarillo	81301 CO Durango	84078 UT Vernal
76943 TX Ozona	79201 TX Childress	81321 CO Cortez	84083 UT Wendover
76950 TX Sonora	79245 TX Memphis	81323 CO Dolores	84116 UT Salt Lake City
77024 TX Houston	79316 TX Brownfield	81401 CO Montrose	84302 UT Brigham City
77030 TX Greenbrier	79401 TX Lubbock	81416 CO Delta	84404 UT Ogden
77032 TX Houston Airport	79512 TX Colorado City	81501 CO Grand Junction	84501 UT Price
77304 TX Conroe	79556 TX Sweetwater	81601 CO Glenwood Sprgs	84511 UT Blanding
77340 TX Huntsville	79601 TX Abilene	81611 CO Aspen	84525 UT Green River
77381 TX Woodlands	79703 TX Midland	81615 CO Snowmass Viilg	84532 UT Moab
77450 TX Katy	79720 TX Big Springs	81620 CO Avon	84532 UT Moad
77471 TX Rosenberg	79735 TX Ft. Stockton	81625 CO Craig	84536 UT Monument Valley
77521 TX Baytown	79756 TX Monahans	81635 CO Parachute	84542 UT Wellington
77530 TX Channelview	79761 TX Odessa	81657 CO Vail	84604 UT Provo
77531 TX Clute	79772 TX Pecos	82001 WY Cheyene	84624 UT Delta
77550 TX Galveston	79834 TX Big Bend Nat Pk	82007 WY Cheyenne	84631 UT Filmore
77566 TX Lake Jackson	79855 TX Van Horn	82070 WY Laramie	84648 UT Nephi
77568 TX La Marque	79925 TX El Paso	82190 WY Yellowstone Pk	84651 UT Payson
77571 TX LaPorte		82201 WY Wheatland	84654 UT Salina
77590 TX Texas City	**ZIPS 80001-90000**	82240 WY Torrington	84701 UT Richfield
77598 TX Webster		82301 WY Rawlins	84713 UT Beaver
77619 TX Groves	80012 CO Aurora	82401 WY Worland	84720 UT Cedar City
77630 TX Orange	80033 CO Wheat Ridge	82414 WY Cody	84737 UT Hurricane
77642 TX Port Arthur	80104 CO Castle Rock	82426 WY Greybull	84741 UT Kanab
77702 TX Beaumont	80112 CO Englewood	82431 WY Lovell	84741 UT Kenab
77840 TX College Station	80156 UT Midvale	82435 WY Powell	84755 UT Mt. Carmel Jct.
77864 TX Madisonville	80207 CO Denver	82443 WY Thermopolis	84759 UT Panguitch
77868 TX Navasota	80215 CO Lakewood	82501 WY Riverton	84764 UT Bryce
77901 TX Victoria	80221 CO Thornton	82513 WY Bubois	84767 UT Springdale
77979 TX Port Lavaca	80233 CO Northglenn	82520 WY Lander	84770 UT St. George
78006 TX Boerne	80234 CO Westminster	82601 WY Casper	85008 AZ Phoenix
78028 TX Kerrville	80302 CO Boulder	82633 WY Douglas	85202 AZ Mesa
78040 TX Laredo	80401 CO Golden	82636 WY Evansville	85220 AZ Apache Junction
78076 TX Zapata	80435 CO Dillon	82701 WY Newcastle	85222 AZ Casa Grande
78104 TX Beeville	80443 CO Frisco	82716 WY Gillette	85251 AZ Scottsdale
78148 TX Universal City	80477 CO Steamboat Spgs	82729 WY Sundance	85282 AZ Tempe
78155 TX Seguin	80501 CO Longmont	82801 WY Sheridan	85334 AZ Ehrenberg
78219 TX San Antonio	80517 CO Estes Park	82834 WY Buffalo	85337 AZ Gila bend
78332 TX Alice	80524 CO Ft. Collins	82901 WY Rock Springs	85338 AZ Goodyear
78358 TX Fulton	80537 CO Loveland	82930 WY Evanston	85358 AZ Wickenburg

ZIP INDEX

85363 AZ Sun City
85363 AZ Youngtown
85364 AZ Yuma
85539 AZ Miami
85546 AZ Safford
85607 AZ Douglas
85614 AZ Green Valley
85621 AZ Nogales
85635 AZ Sierra Vista
85638 AZ Tombstone
85643 AZ Wilcox
85714 AZ Tucson
85935 AZ Pinetop
86001 AZ Flagstaff
86023 AZ Grnd Cyn Nat Pk
86025 AZ Holbrook
86040 AZ Page
86046 AZ Williams
86047 AZ Winslow
86301 AZ Prescott
86326 AZ Cottonwood
86336 AZ Sedona
86401 AZ Kingman
86403 AZ Lake Havasu
86430 AZ Bullhead City
86442 AZ Laughlin
86502 AZ Chambers
87020 NM Grants
87035 NM Moriarty
87107 NM Albuquerque
87110 NJ Albuquerque
87124 NM Rio Ranch
87301 NM Gallup
87401 NM Farmington
87501 NM Santa Fe
87532 NM Espanola
87571 NM Taos
87701 NM Las Vegas
87740 NM Raton
87801 NM Socorro
87901 NM Truth/Con.
88001 NM Las Cruces
88003 NM Deming
88021 TX El Paso West
88045 NM Lordsburg
88101 NM Clovis
88201 NM Roswell
88240 NM Hobbs
88280 NM Carlsbad
88310 NM Alamogordo
88345 NM Ruidoso
88401 NM Tucumcari
88435 NM Santa Rosa
89041 NV Pahrump
89049 NV Tonopah
89109 NV Las Vegas
89301 NV Ely
89406 NV Fallon
89410 NV Minden
89431 NV Sparks
89445 NV Winnemucca

89449 NV Stateline
89512 NV Reno
89701 NV Carson City
89801 NV Elko
89820 NV Battle Mountain
89835 NV Wells
89883 AZ Wendover

ZIPS OVER 90000

90028 CA Hollywood
90040 CA Commerce
90210 CA Bel Air
90212 CA Beverly Hills
90227 CA Redondo Beach
90241 CA Downey
90245 CA El Segundo
90266 CA Manhattan Beach
90291 CA Marina Del Rey
90304 CA Inglewood
90304 CA Los Angeles
90401 CA Santa Monica
90503 CA Torrance
90606 CA Whittier
90622 CA Buena Park
90638 CA La Mirada
90680 CA Stanton
90706 CA Bellflower
90710 CA Harbor City
90731 CA San Pedro
90815 CA Long Beach
91006 CA Arcadia
91016 CA Monrovia
91107 CA Pasadena
91204 CA Glendale
91301 CA Agoura Hills
91303 CA Canoga Park
91306 CA San Fernando
91311 CA Chatsworth
91320 CA Newbury Park
91342 CA Sylmar
91345 CA Mission Hills
91355 CA Valencia
91364 CA Woodland Hills
91381 CA Santa Clarita
91384 CA Castaic
91505 CA Burbank
91706 CA Baldwin Park
91710 CA Chino
91711 CA Claremont
91719 CA Corona
91731 CA El Monte
91748 CA Rowland Heights
91764 CA Ontario
91768 CA Pomona
91770 CA Rosemead
91773 CA San Dimas
91791 CA West Covina
91942 CA La Mesa
91945 CA Lemon Grove
91950 CA National City

92008 CA Carlsbad
92010 CA Chula Vista
92020 CA El Cajon
92025 CA Escondido
92028 CA Fallbrook
92037 CA La Jolla
92054 CA Oceanside
92073 CA San Ysidro
92083 CA Vista
92118 CA Coronado
92123 CA San Diego
92127 CA Rancho Bernardo
92201 CA Bermuda Dunes
92201 CA Indio
92225 CA Blythe
92240 CA Desert Hot Sprgs
92243 CA El Centro
92262 CA Palm Springs
92270 CA Rancho Mirage
92284 CA Yucca Valley
92301 CA Adelanto
92311 CA Barstow
92315 CA Big Bear
92324 CA Colton
92335 CA Fontana
92343 CA Hemet
92345 CA Hesperia
92352 CA Lake Arrowhead
92363 CA Needles
92374 CA Redlands
92388 CA Moreno Valley
92390 CA Rancho Calif.
92392 CA Victorville
92407 CA San Bernardino
92501 CA Riverside
92549 CA Idyllwild
92590 CA Temecula
92626 CA Costa Mesa
92631 CA Fullerton
92648 CA Huntington Bch
92660 CA Newport Beach
92668 CA Orange
92670 CA Placentia
92672 CA San Clemente
92675 CA San Juan Cap
92683 CA Westminister
92701 CA Santa Ana
92701 CA Santa Anna
92708 CA Fountain Valley
92714 CA Irvine
92805 CA Anaheim
93001 CA Ventura
93010 CA Camarillo
93013 CA Carpinteria
93022 CA Oakview
93023 CA Ojai
93030 CA Oxnard
93065 CA Simi Valley
93103 CA Santa Barbara
93108 CA Montecito
93206 CA Buttonwillow

93210 CA Coalinga
93215 CA Delano
93245 CA Lemoore
93249 CA Lost Hills
93257 CA Porterville
93271 CA Three Rivers
93274 CA Tulare
93277 CA Visalia
93309 CA Bakersfield
93401 CA San Luis Obispo
93420 CA Arroyo Grande
93422 CA Atascadero
93427 CA Buellton
93436 CA Lompoc
93442 CA Morro Bay
93446 CA Paso Robles
93449 CA Pismo Beach
93452 CA San Simeon
93454 CA Santa Maria
93460 CA Santa Ynez
93463 CA Solvang
93501 CA Mojave
93514 CA Bishop
93517 CA Bridgeport
93534 CA Lancaster
93545 CA Lone Pine
93546 CA Mammoth Lakes
93551 CA Palmdale
93555 CA Ridgecrest
93561 CA Tehachapi
93635 CA Los Banos
93637 CA Madera
93644 CA Oakhurst
93662 CA Selma
93709 CA Fresno
93905 CA Salinas
93922 CA Carmel
93930 CA King City
93930 CA King city
93933 CA Marina
93940 CA Monterey
93950 CA Pacific Grove
93955 CA Seaside
94010 CA Burlingame
94019 CA Half Moon Bay
94030 CA Millbrae
94030 CA San Francisco
94040 CA Mountain View
94063 CA Redwood City
94080 CA S. San Francisco
94086 CA Sunnyvale
94086 CA Sunnyvale
94306 CA Palo Alto
94402 CA San Mateo
94510 CA Benicia
94520 CA Concord
94523 CA Pleasant Hill
94533 CA Fairfield
94536 CA Fremont
94541 CA Hayward
94550 CA Livermore

ZIP INDEX

94558 CA Napa
94560 CA Newark
94564 CA Pinole
94565 CA Pittsburg
94583 CA San Ramon
94588 CA Pleasanton
94589 CA Vallejo
94596 CA Walnut Creek
94608 CA Emeryville
94621 CA Oakland
94901 CA San Rafael
94928 CA Rohnert Park
94954 CA Petaluma
95008 CA Campbell
95020 CA Gilroy
95035 CA Milpitas
95037 CA Morgan Hill
95051 CA Santa Clara
95060 CA Santa Cruz
95066 CA Scotts Valley
95076 CA Watsonville
95121 CA San Jose
95207 CA Stockton
95240 CA Lodi
95322 CA Santa Nella
95340 CA Merced
95351 CA Modesto
95376 CA Tracy
95380 CA Turlock
95387 CA Westley
95403 CA Santa Rosa
95448 CA Healdsburg
95476 CA Sonoma
95482 CA Ukiah
95501 CA Eureka
95521 CA Arcata
95531 CA Crescent City
95540 CA Fortuna
95542 CA Garberville
95567 CA Smith River
95603 CA Auburn
95616 CA Davis
95620 CA Dixon
95630 CA Folsom
95642 CA Jackson
95660 CA North Highlands
95667 CA Placerville
95669 CA Plymouth
95670 CA Rancho Cordova
95678 CA Roseville
95682 CA Cameron Park
95688 CA Vacaville
95695 CA Woodland
95726 CA Pollock Pines
95729 CA S. Lake Tahoe
95737 CA Truckee
95814 CA Sacramento
95926 CA Chico
95937 CA Dunnigan
95965 CA Oroville
95967 CA Paradise

95987 CA Williams
95988 CA Willows
95991 CA Yuba City
96003 CA Redding
96007 CA Anderson
96021 CA Corning
96025 CA Dunsmuir
96067 CA Mount Shasta
96080 CA Red Bluff
96097 CA Yreka
96101 CA Alturas
96157 CA Lake Tahoe
97030 OR Gresham
97031 OR Hood River
97035 OR Lake Oswego
97058 OR The Dalles
97060 OR Troutdale
97060 OR Wood Village
97070 OR Wilsonville
97071 OR Woodburn
97103 OR Astoria
97110 OR Cannon Beach
97124 OR Hillsboro
97132 OR Newberg
97138 OR Seaside
97141 OR Tillamook
97146 OR Warrenton
97220 OR Portland
97222 OR Milwaukee
97224 OR Tigard
97302 OR Salem
97321 OK Albany
97321 OR Albany
97339 OR Corvallis
97365 OR Newport
97367 OR Lincoln City
97401 OR Eugene
97415 OR Harbor
97420 OR Coos Bay
97424 OR Cottage Grove
97439 OR Florence
97444 OR Gold Beach
97463 OR Oakridge
97470 OR Roseburg
97477 OR Springfield
97504 OR Medford
97520 OR Ashland
97526 OR Grants Pass
97603 OR Klamath Falls
97630 OR Lakeview
97701 OR Bend
97702 OK Bend
97720 OR Burns
97801 OR Pendleton
97814 OR Baker City
97828 OR Enterprise
97845 OR John Day
97914 OR Ontario
98002 WA Auburn
98007 WA Bellevue
98011 WA Bothell

98022 WA Enumclaw
98027 WA Issaquah
98032 WA Kent
98033 WA Kirkland
98037 WA Lynnwood
98063 WA Federal Way
98104 WA Seattle
98188 WA South Seattle
98188 WA Tukwila
98198 WA Sea-Tac
98204 WA Everett
98221 WA Anacortes
98225 VA Bellingham
98225 WA Bellingham
98233 WA Burlington
98271 WA Marysville
98273 WA Mount Vernon
98277 WA Oak Harbor
98310 WA Bremerton
98362 WA Port Angeles
98371 WA Puyallup
98382 WA Sequim
98424 WA Fife
98424 WA Tacoma
98501 WA Tumwater
98501 WA Turnwater
98503 WA Lacey
98503 WA Olympia
98520 WA Aberdeen
98531 WA Centralia
98550 WA Hoquiam
98569 WA Ocean Shores
98584 WA Shelton
98626 WA Kelso
98631 WA Long Beach
98632 WA Longview
98640 WA Ocean Park
98665 WA Vancouver
98801 WA Wenatchee
98801 WA Yakima
98826 WA Leavenworth
98837 WA Moses Lake
98840 WI Okanogan
98903 WA Union Gap
98922 WA Cle Elum
98926 WA Ellensburg
98944 WA Sunnyside
99037 WA Spokane
99116 WA Coulee Dam
99163 WA Pullman
99169 WA Ritzville
99301 WA Pasco
99302 WA Kennewick
99350 WA Prosser
99352 WA Richland
99362 WA Walla Walla
99403 WA Clarkston
99501 AK Anchorage
99603 AK Homer
99669 AK Soldonta
99701 AK Fairbanks

99801 AK Juneau
99827 AK Haines
99835 AK Sitka
99901 AK Ketchikan

Always
Call
Ahead!

ACCOMMODATIONS IN CANADA

Rules for Successful Pet Travel

US and Canada share the longest unfortified border in the world. If your plans to cross the border include travel with your pet cat or dog, you will need a veterinarian-signed Pet Health Certificate for Dogs and Cats. This certificate provides a description of your pet and verifies required vaccinations, such as rabies and distemper. The certificate requires a visit to your vet within 30 days of travel.

The US requires the same valid certificate for reentry of your pets. Restrictions may apply for stays over 30 days. Pets, Wildlife and U.S. Customs, an informative booklet, can be obtained at any U.S. Customs Office or from U.S. Customs, PO Box# 7407, Washington, D.C. 20044

ALBERTA

Best Western
453 Marten St
• Banff • T0L 0C0
800.528.1234

Castle Mountain Village
Box 1655
• Banff • T0L 0C0
403.762.3868
$20

Johnston Cyn Resort
Hwy 1A
• Banff • T0L 0C0
403.762.2971

Red Carpet Inn
425 Banff Ave Box 1800
• Banff • T0L 0C0
403.762.4184
small

Rocky Mtn Resort
1020 Banff Ave
• Banff • T0L 0C0
403.762.5531

Douglas Ctry Inn
Hwy 1
• Brooks • T1R 1B5
403.362.2873
in heated kennels

Heritage Inn
13033 - 2nd St
• Brooks • T1R 1B8
403.362.6666
$5

Best Western
1947 18th Ave NE
• Calgary • T2E 7T8
403.250.5015
small

Best Western
1330 -8th St
• Calgary • T2R 1B6
403.228.6900
small pets

Best Western
1804 Chowchild Trail
• Calgary • T2M 3Y7
403.289.0241
small pets

Blackfoot Inn
5940 Blackfoot Tr
• Calgary • T2H 2B5
403.222.2533

Budget Host
4420 16 Ave NW
• Calgary • T3B 0M4
800.661.3772
small

Carriage House
9030 Macleod Tr
• Calgary • T2H 0M4
403.253.1101
$5

Clarion Hotel Airport
4804 Edmonton Trail NE
• Calgary • T2E 3V2
800.221.2222

Coast Plaza
1316 - 33Rdst
• Calgary • T2A 6B6
403.248.8888
$20 dep

Crowne Plaza
10111 Bellamy Hill
• Calgary • T5J 1N7
403.428.6611
small pets

Days Inn
2369 Banff Trail NW
• Calgary • T2M 4L2
403.289.5571
small

Econo Lodge
101 St & Trans Canada Hwy
• Calgary • T2M 4N3
800.424.4777

Econo Lodge
2440 16th Ave NW
• Calgary • T2M 0M5
403.289.2561

Econo Lodge
5307 Macleod Trail S
• Calgary • T2H 0J3
403.258.1064

ALBERTA

CANADA

ALBERTA

Econo Lodge
2231 Banff Trail
• Calgary • T2M 4L2
403.289.1921
$10

Flamingo
7505 Macleod Tr
• Calgary • T2H 0L8
403.252.4401
small pets

Glenmore Inn
2720 Glenmore Tr
• Calgary • T2C 2Ec
403.279.8611
small & $10 fee

Highlander
1818 -16th Ave
• Calgary • T2M 0L8
403.289.1961
$10

Holiday Inn
4206 Macleod Tr
• Calgary • T2G 2R7
403.287.2700
small ground flr

Holiday Inn
2227 Banff Tr
• Calgary • 72M 4L2
403.289.6600
small 1st flr

Howard Johnson
4510 S Macleod Trail
• Calgary • T2G 0A4
403.243.1700

Palliser Hotel
133 9th Ave
• Calgary • T2P 2M3
403.262.1234
small pets

Quality Inn
2359 Banff Trail NW
• Calgary • T2M 4L2
800.661.4667
small

Ramada Hotel
708 8th Ave SW
• Calgary • T2P 1H2
800.661.8684
small

Ramada Inn
5353 Crowchild Tr NW
• Calgary • T3A 1W9
403.288.5353
small

Ramada Inn
1250 McKinnon Dr NE
• Calgary • T2E 7T7
800.228.5151
small

Relax Inn
2750 Sunridge Blvd NE
• Calgary • T1Y 3C2
800.667.3529

Relax Inn
9206 McLeod Trail S
• Calgary • T2J 0P5
800.667.3529

Sandman Hotel
888 7th Ave
• Calgary • T2P 3J3
800.663.6900

Sheraton Cavalier
2620 32nd Ave NE
• Calgary • T1Y 6B8
800.325.3535

Super 8 Motel
1904 Crowchild Tr NW
• Calgary • T2M 3Y7
403.289.9211
small

Travel Lodge
2750 Sunridge Blvd
• Calgary • T1Y 3C2
403.291.1260
small pets

Travel Lodge
9206 Macleod Tr
• Calgary • T2J 0P5
403.253.1260
small pets

Westin Hotel
320 4th Ave SW
• Calgary • T2P 2S6
800.228.3000
small

Lady Macdonald
1201 Bow Valley
• Canmore • T0L 0M0
403.678.3665
small pets

Quality Resort
1720 Bow Valley
• Canmore • T0L Omo
403.678.6699
$10

Rocky Mtn Ski Ldg
Hwy 1A
• Canmore • T0L 0M0
403.678.5445

Rundle Ridge Chalet
Hwy 1
• Canmore • T0L 0M0
403.678.5387

Stockage Cabins
Hwy 1
• Canmore • T0L 0M0
403.678.5212
$10

Flamingo
848 Main
• Cardston • Tok Oko
403.653.3952
$5

Trail's End
37- 8th Ave
• Cardston • Tok Oko
403.653.4481
$5

Bluebird Motel
5505-1St St
• Claresholm • Tol Oto
403.625.3395

Bow River Inn
3 Westside Dr
• Cochrane • T0L 0W0
403.932.7900
small pets

New Frontier
1002 - 8th Ave
• Cold Lake • Toa Ovo
403.639.3030
small

Pidgeon Mtn Motel
Hwy 1
• Deadmans Flat • Tol Omo
403.678.5756
small pets

Green Acres
Hwy 1
• Deanmans Flats • Tol Omo
403.678.5344
small

Super 8
1714 -20th Ave
• Didsbury • Tom Owo
403.335.8088

Best Western
1103 Hwy 9 S
• Drumheller • T0J 0Y.0
403.823.7700

Alberta Place
10049 - 103rd St
• Edmonton • T5J 2W7
403.423.1565
small pets

Best Western
11310 109 St
• Edmonton • T5G 2T7
403.479.2042

Best Western
5116 Calary Tr
• Edmonton • T6H 2H4
403.434.7411
small pets

Campus Tower
11145 - 87th Ave
• Edmonton • T6G OY1
403.439.6060

Chateau Louis
11721 Kingsway
• Edmonton • T5G 3A1
403.452.7770
small

Comfort Inn
17510 100th Ave
• Edmonton • T5S 1S9
800.221.2222

Continental Inn
16625 Stony Plain
• Edmonton • T5P 4A8
403.484.7751
small

409

Convention Inn
4404 Calgary Tr
• Edmonton • T6H 5C2
403.434.6415
small

Days Inn
10041 106 St
• Edmonton • T5J 1G3
403.423.1925
$8

Delta Edmonton
10222 - 102nd
• Edmonton • T5J 4C5
403.429.3900
small pets

Econo Lodge
4009 Calgary Trail N
• Edmonton • T6J 5H2
403.435.4877

Econo Lodge
10209 100th Ave
• Edmonton • T5J 0A1
403.428.6442

Edmonton House
10205 - 100th Ave
• Edmonton • T5J 4B5
403.420.4000
small

Edmonton Inn
11830 Kingsway
• Edmonton • T5G 0X5
403.454.9521
small pets

Holiday Inn
101 St At Bellamy Hill
• Edmonton • T5J 1H7
800.465.4329

Holiday Inn
4235 Calgary Tr
• Edmonton • T6J 5H2
403.438.1222
small

Hotel Macdonald
10065-100th St
• Edmonton • T5J 0N6
403.424.5181
$20 in cage

Quality Inn
10209 100th Ave
• Edmonton • T5J 0A1
800.221.2222

Relax Travelodge
18320 Stony Plain Rd
• Edmonton • T5S 1A7
800.661.9563

Royal Inn
10010 - 178th St
• Edmonton • T5S 1T3
403.484.6000
small pets

Travel Lodge
3414 -118th Ave
• Edmonton • T5W OZ4
403.474.0456
small pets

Travelodge
3414 118 Ave
• Edmonton • T5W 0Z4
800.255.3050

Westin Hotel
10135 100th St
• Edmonton • T5J 0N7
800.228.3000
small

Guest House
4411 - 4th Ave
• Edson • T73 1B8
403.723.4486
small

Super 8 Motel
4300 2nd Ave Box 6867
• Edson • T7E 1V2
403.723.2500

Dj Motel
416 Main
• Ft Macleod • Tol Ozo
403.553.4011
$5

Fort Motel
451 Main
• Ft Macleod • Tol Ozo
403.553.3606
small pets

Kozy Motel
433 - 24th St
• Ft Macleod • Tol Ozo
403.553.3606
$5

Sunset Motel
104 Hwy 3
• Ft Macleod • Tol Ozo
403.553.4448

Super 8 Motel
10050 116 Ave
• Grand Prairie • T8V 4K5
403.532.8288

Canadian Inn
10901 - 100th Ave
• Grande Prairie • T8V 3J9
403.532.1680
$5

Stanford Inn
11401 - 100th Ave
• Grande Prairie • T8V 5M6
403.539.5678
$5

Crestwood Hotel
678 Carmichael
• Hinton • T7V 1S9
403.865.4001
small

Greentree Lodge
393 Gregg Ave
• Hinton • T7V 1X7
403.865.3321
small pets

Jasper Park
Hwy 16
• Jasper • Toe 1E0
403.852.3301
$30

Lobstick Lodge
94 Geikie
• Jasper • Toe 1Eo
403.852.4431

Marmot Lodge
86 Connaught
• Jasper • Toe 1Eo
403.852.4471
small pets

Pat Lake Bungalow
Patricia Lake Rd
• Jasper • Toe 1Eo
403.852.3560
small pets

Sunwapta Falls
Hwy 93
• Jasper • Toe 1Eo
403.852.4852

Tekarra Lodge
Hwy 93
• Jasper • Toe 1Eo
403.852.3058
$5

Relax Inn
5705 50th St Box 3538
• Leduc • T9E 6M3
800.667.3529

Days Inn
100 3rd Ave S
• Lethbridge • T1J 4L2
403.327.6000

Lethbridge Lodge
320 Scenic Dr
• Lethbridge • T1J 4B4
403.328.1123
small pets

Parkside Inn
1008 Myr Macgrath
• Lethbridge • Tik 2P7
403.328.2366
small pets

Pepper Tree Inn
1142 Myr Macgrath
• Lethbridge • Tik 2P8
103.328.4436
$5

Sundance Inn
1030 Myr Macgrath
• Lethbridge • Tik 2P8
403.328.6636
$5

Super 8 Motel
2210 7th Ave S
• Lethbridge • T1J 1M7
403.329.0100
small

410

ALBERTA

CANADA

BRITISH COLUMBIA

Travel Lodge
526 Myr Macgrath
• Lethbridge • Tij 3M2
403.327.5701

Lodge Motel
6301 44 St
• Lloydminster • T9V 2G6
403.875.1919

Tropical Inn
5621 - 44th St
• Lloydminster • T9V 0B2
403.875.7000
small pets

Wayside Inn
5411 -44th
• Lloydminster • T9V OA9
403.875.4404
$5

West Harvest Inn
5620 44 St
• Lloydminster • T9V 0B6
403.875.6113

Best Western
722 Redcliff Dr
• Medicine Hat • T1A 5E3
800.528.1234
small

Quality Inn
954 7th St SW
• Medicine Hat • T1A 7R7
800.221.2222

Ranchman Motel
1617 Bomford Cresc
• Medicine Hat • T1A 5E7
403.527.2263

Super 8 Motel
1280 Trans Canada Way
• Medicine Hat • T1B 1J5
403.528.8888
small

Sheep River Inn
59 River Gate
• Okotoks • T0L 1T0
403.938.1999
$5

Best Western
Hwy 27 & Hwy 2A
• Olds • T4H 1P7
403.556.5900

Travelers Motel
8510 - 100th St
• Peace River • T8S 1S9
403.624.3621
small pets

Super 8 Motel
1307 Freebairn Ave Box
1628
• Pincher Creek • T0K 1W0
403.627.5671

Heritage Inn
919 Waterton Ave
• Pincher Crk • Tok Iwo
403.627.5000
small pets

Friendship Inn
4124 Gaetz Ave
• Red Deer • T4N 3Z2
403.342.6969

Travelodge Hotel
2807 50 Ave
• Red Deer • T4R 1H6
403.346.2011
small

Holiday Inn
6500 - 67th St
• Reed Deer • T4P 1A2
403.342.6567
small pets

Chinook Inn
59th Ave
• Rocky Mtn House • Tom
1T0
403.845.2833
$15

St Albert Inn
156 St Albert
• St Albert • T8N OP5
403.459.5551

Stony Motor Inn
4620 48th St
• Stony Plain • T7Z 1L4
403.963.9492
small

Stony Plain Hwy Inn
3301 - 43rd
• Stony Plain • T7Z 1L1
403.963.0222
$4

Best Western
550 Hwy 1
• Strathmore • T1P 1M6
403.934.5777

Heritage Inn
4830 - 46th
• Taber • Tig 2A4
403.223.4424
small pets

Bayshore Inn
111 Waterton Ave
• Waterton Park • Tok 2Mo
403.859.2211

Wayside Inn
4103 - 56th St
• Wetaskiwin • T9A 1V2
403.352.5996

Green Gables Inn
Hwy 43
• Whitecourt • T7S 1P3
403.778.4537
small pets

100 Mile House Slumber
Lodge
350 Cariboo Hwy 2 Box 1328
• (one) 100 Mile House •
V0K 2E0
800.663.2831

99 Mile Motel
896 Alpine Hwy 97 Box 2140
• (one) 100 Mile House •
V0K 2E0
250.395.2255

Best Western
Telqua Dr RR 1 Comp 2 108
Rnch
• (one) 100 Mile House •
V0K 2E0
250.791.5211

Imperial Motel
250 Hwy 97 Box 113
• (one) 100 Mile House •
V0K 2E0
250.395.2471

BRITISH
COLUMBIA

Econo Lodge
32111 Marshall Rd
• Abbotsford • V2T 1A3
604.859.3171

Quality Inn
1881 Sumas Way
• Abbotsford • V2S 4L5
800.221.2222
$5

Mnt Springs Motel
Hwy 235
• Barriere • Voe 1Eo
250.672.0090
$5

Heli Ski Vlg
Harwood Dr
• Blue River • Voe Ijo
250.673.8381
small pets

Sandman Inn
Hwy 5 Box 31
• Blue River • V0E 1J0
800.726.3626

Canyon Alpine Motel
50530 Trans Canada Hwy
Box 395
• Boston Bar • V0K 1C0
604.867.9295

Whitewater Motel
50885 Trans Canada Hwy
Box 352
• Boston Bar • V0K 1C0
604.867.8831

Holiday Inn
4405 Central Blvd
• Burnaby • V5H 4M3
800.465.4395

Burns Lake Inn
Yellowhead Hwy
• Burns Lake • Voj Ieo
250.692.7545
$5

Bonaparte Motel
1395 Hwy 97
• Cache Creek • 97N 1Ho
250.457.9693
small

Sandman Inn
Hwy 1 Box 278
● Cache Creek ● V0K 1H0
800.726.3626

Slumber Lodge
1085 Trans Canada Hwy Box
158
● Cache Creek ● V0K 1H0
800.663.2831

Tumbleweed Motel
Hwy 97
● Cache Creek ● Vok Iho
250.457.6522
small pets

Anchor Inn
261 Island Hwy
● Campbell River ● V9W
2B3
800.663.7227
$5

Best Western
462 South Island Hwy
● Campbell River ● V9W
1A5
250.923.4231
small

Campbell Rvr Lodge
1760 Island Hwy
● Campbell River ● V9W
2E7
250.287.7446
small

Super 8 Motel
340 S Island Hwy
● Campbell River ● V9W
1A5
800.800.8000

Sandman Inn
1944 Columbia Ave
● Castlegar ● V1N 2W7
800.726.3626

Twin Rivers Motel
1485 Columbia Ave
● Castlegar ● V1N 1H8
604.365.6900

Chase Ctry Inn
576 Coburn Rd
● Chase ● Voe Imo
250.679.3333
small

Quaaout Lodge
Little Shuswap Rd
● Chase ● Voe Imo
250.679.3090
$5

Pinecone Motor Inn
5224 53rd Ave Box 686
● Chemainus ● V0C 1J0
800.663.8082

Stagecoach Inn
5413 S Access Rd Box 927
● Chemainus ● V0C 1J0
800.663.2744

Fuller Lake Motel
9300 Transcan Hwy
● Cheminus ● Vor Iko
250.246.3282
small

Stagecoach Inn
5413 Access Rd
● Chetwynd ● Voc 1Jo
250.788.9666
small pets

Best Western
43971 Industrial Way
● Chilliwack ● V2R 3A4
604.795.3828

Holiday Inn
45920 1St Ave
● Chilliwack ● V2P 7K1
604.795.4788

Travelodge
45466 Yale Rd W
● Chilliwack ● V2R 1A3
604.792.4240

Lakeview Motel
1658 Hwy 3 Box 296
● Christina Lake ● V0H 1E0
604.447.9358

Totem Resort
61 Kingsley Rd Box 6
● Christina Lake ● V0H 1E0
604.447.9322

Clearwater Country Inn
449 Yellowhead Hwy 5 RR 1
● Clearwater ● V0E 1N0
604.674.3121

Dutch Lake Motel
333 Roy Rd Bx 5116 RR 2
● Clearwater ● V0E 1N0
604.674.3325

Sylvan Court Motel
734 Clearwater Vlge Rd Bx
1104
● Clearwater ● V0E 1N0
604.674.2334

Days Inn
725 Brunette Ave
● Coquitlam ● V3K 1C3
800.325.2525

Coast Westerly
1500 Cliffe Ave
● Courtenay ● V9N 2K4
250.338.7741
small

Collingwood Inn
1675 Cliffe Ave
● Courtenay ● V9N 2K6
250.338.1464
small

Quality Suites
4330 Island Hwy
● Courtenay ● V9N 8H9
250.338.1323
small

Sleepy Hollow Inn
1190 Cliffe Ave
● Courtenay ● V9N 2K1
604.334.4476

The Economy Inn
2605 Island Hwy
● Courtenay ● V9N 2L8
604.334.4491

Travel Lodge
2605 Island Hwy
● Courtenay ● V9N 2Lb
250.334.4491
small

Kilpahlas Resort
1681 Botwood
● Cowichan Bay ● Vor 1N0
250.748.6222
$10

Best Western
1417 Cranbrook St N
● Cranbrook ● V1C 3S7
800.528.1234

Inn Of The South
803 Cranbrook
● Cranbrook ● V1C 3T1
250.489.4301
small pets

Model A Inn
1908 Cranbrook
● Cranbrook ● V1C 3T1
250.489.4600
small

Ponderosa Motel
500 Van Home
● Cranbrook ● V1C 4H3
250.426.6114
small

Sandman Inn
405 Cranbrok St N
● Cranbrook ● V1C 3R7
800.726.3626

Travellers Motel
2000 Cranbrook St
● Cranbrook ● V1C 3T1
604.426.4208

Budget Host Sunset Motel
2705 Hwy 3 Box 2186
● Creston ● V0B 1G0
800.663.7082

City Center Motel
220 - 15th Ave
● Creston ● Vob 1Go
250.428.2257

Creston Valley Motel
1809 Canyon St Bx 1699
● Creston ● V0B 1G0
604.428.9823

Downtowner
1218 Canyon St
● Creston ● Vob 1Go
250.428.2238
$4

Siesta Motel
320 20th Ave S Box 1188
● Creston ● V0B 1G0
604.428.2640

Sunset Motel
2705 Canyon St
• Creston • Vob 1Go
250.428.2229
small

Dawson Creek Travellers Inn
800 112th Ave
• Dawson Creek • V1G 2Y2
604.782.5551

Econo Lodge
832 103rd Ave
• Dawson Creek • V1G 2E8
604.782.9181

North Country Inn
800 120th Ave
• Dawson Creek • V1G 4P9
604.782.9404

Trail Inn
1748 Alaska Ave
• Dawson Creek • V1G 1P4
250.782.8595

Voyageur Motel
801 111 Ave
• Dawson Creek • V1G 2Z1
604.782.1020

Best Western
1665 56th St
• Delta • V4L 2B2
604.943.8221

Best Western
6464 Trans Canada Hwy
• Duncan • V9L 3W8
800.528.1234
small

Falcon Crest Motel
5867 Transcan Hwy
• Duncan • V9L 3R9
250.748.8188
small

Silver Bridge Inn
140 Transcan Hwy
• Duncan • V9L 3P7
250.748.4311
$5-10

York Town Inn
5325 Trans Canada Hwy Box 395
• Duncan • V9L 3X5
604.748.0331

Cedar Motel
1101 - 7th Ave
• Fernie • Vob 1Mo
250.423.4622

Park Place
742 Hwy 3
• Fernie • Vob 1Mo
250.423.6871
small pets

Super 8 Motel
Hwy 3
• Fernie • VOB 1M1
604.423.6788

Kicking Horse Ldg
100 Centre St
• Field • Voa 1Go
250.343.6303
small

Coachouse Inn
4711 50th Ave S Box 27
• Fort Nelson • V0E 1R0
604.774.3911
small

Four Seasons Motor Inn
9810 100th St
• Fort St John • V1J 3Y1
604.785.6647

Northwoods Inn
10627 Alaska Rd
• Fort St John • V1J 5P4
800.663.8316

Pioneer Inn
9830 100th Ave
• Fort St John • V1J 1Y5
800.663.8312

Cedars Inn
895 Coast Hwy
• Gibsons • Von 1Vo
640.886.3008
small. $10

Sunshine Lodge
679 North Rd Box 1768
• Gibsons • VON 1N0
604.886.3321

Uptown Motel
710 North Rd Box 425
• Gibsons • VON 1V0
604.886.2957

Best Western
1024 11th St N
• Golden • V0A 1H0
250.344.2333

Golden Gate
Hwy 95
• Golden • Voa 1Ho
250.344.2252

Golden Rim Inn
1416 Golden View
• Golden • Voa 1Ho
250.344.2216
small

Super 8 Motel
1047 Trans Cn Hwy
• Golden • V0A 1H0
604.344.0888

The Big Bend Hotel
429 North 9th Ave
• Golden • V0A 1H0
604.344.5951

Imperial Motel
7389 Riverside Box 2558
• Grand Forks • V0H 1H0
604.442.8236

Western Traveller Motel
1591 Central Ave Box 1780
• Grand Forks • V0H 1H0
604.442.5566
small

Hot Springs Hotel
100 Esplanade
• Harrison Hot Spgs • Vom 1Ko
604.796.2244
small pets

Alpine Motel
505 Hope-Princeton
• Hope • V0X 1Lo
604.869.9931
small pets

Continental
860 Fraser Ave
• Hope • Vox 1Lo
604.869.9726
small pets

Holiday Motel
63950 Old Yale Rd
• Hope • V0X 1L0
604.869.5352

Imperial Motel
350 Hope Princeton Hwy
• Hope • V0X 1L0
604.869.9951

Inn-Towne Motel
510 Transcan Hwy
• Hope • Vox 1Lo
604.869.7276
$4

Quality Inn
350 Hope-Princeton
• Hope • Vox 1Lo
604.869.9951
small

Red Goat Lodge
Hwy 37
• Iskut • Voj 1Ko
250.234.3261

Best Western
1310 - 7th Ave
• Ivermere • Voa 1Ko
250.342.9246

Days Inn
1285 Transcan
• Kamloops • V2E 2J7
250.374.5911
$10

Quality Inn
650 Victoria St
• Kamloops • V2C 2B4
800.221.2222

Roche Lake Resort
Hwy 5A
• Kamloops • V2C 5L7
250.828.2007
small

Sandman Inn
550 Columbia St
• Kamloops • V2C 1V1
800.726.3626

Stay 'N Save
1325 Transcan
• Kamloops • V2C 6P4
250.374.8877
small pets

Super 8 Motel
1521 Hugh Allan Dr
• Kamloops • V1S 1P4
604.374.8688

Thompson Hotel
650 Victoria
• Kamloops • V2C 2B4
250.374.1999

Travelodge Hotel
430 Columbia St
• Kamloops • V2C 2T5
800.255.3050
small

Mariner Inn Hotel
430 Front St Box 606
• Kaslo • V0G 1M0
604.353.7171

Sunny Bluffs Motel
434 N Marine Dr Box 1060
• Kaslo • V0G 1M0
604.353.2277

Days Inn
2649 Hwy 79 N
• Kelowna • V1X 4J6
250.868.3297

Oasis Motor Inn
1884 Gordon Dr
• Kelowna • V1Y 3H7
250.763.5396
small

Sandman Inn
2130 Harvey Ave
• Kelowna • V1Y 6G8
800.726.3626

Siesta Motel
3152 Lakeshore
• Kelowna • V1W 3T1
250.763.5013

Stay 'N Save
1140 Harvey
• Kelowna • Viy 6E7
250.862.8888
small

The Park Lake Hotel
1675 Abbott St
• Kelowna • V1Y 8S3
250.860.7900

Thrift Inn
2592 Hwy 97 N
• Kelowna • V1X 4J4
250.762.8222

Town & Country
2629 Hwy 97
• Kelowna • V1X 4J6
250.860.7121
small

Western Budget Motel
2679 Hwy 97 N
• Kelowna • V1X 4J6
250.763.2484

Elk Motel
310 7th Ave RR 1 Hwy 3W
Bx 361
• Keremeos • V0X 1N0
604.499.2043

Kimberley Palace Hotel
2665 Warren Ave
• Kimberley • V1A 1T6
604.427.7848

Sylvia Motel
455 Ross St
• Kimberley • V1A 2C5
604.427.2203

Loyalist B&b
10890 Chemainus
• Ladysmith • Xor 2E0
250.245.2590
small pets

Travelodge
20470 88th Ave
• Langley • V1M 2Y6
604.888.4891

Manning Resort
Hwy 3
• Manning Park • Vox 1R0
250.840.8822
$3 in cabins

Best Western
21735 Lougheed Hwy 7
• Maple Ridge • V2X 2S2
800.528.1234

Travelodge
21650 Lougheed Hwy
• Maple Ridge • V2X 2S1
800.255.3050

North Ctry Ldg
Hwy 16
• McBride • Voj 2E0
250.569.0001
pet rooms

Sandman Inn
Hwy 16 Box 548
• McBride • V0J 2E0
800.726.3626

Days Inn
3350 Voght St
• Merritt • V1K 1C7
250.378.2292

Merrit Motel
3561 Vought
• Merritt • Vok 2Bo
250.378.9422
small pets

Travel Lodge
3561 Vought
• Merritt • Vok 2Bo
250.378.8830
small pets

Best Western
6450 Metral Dr
• Nanaimo • V9T 2L8
800.661.0061
small

Days Inn
809 Island Hwy S
• Nanaimo • V9R 5K1
250.754.8171
small

Harbourview Days Inn
809 Island Hwy S RR 1
• Nanaimo • V9R 5K1
800.325.2525

Travel Lodge
96 Terminal
• Nanaimo • V9S 4K1
250.754.6355

Falcon Motel
7106 62nd Ave Hwy 3 E RR
1
• Osoyoos • V0H 1V0
604.495.7544

Highland Inn
5912 62nd Ave RR 1 Box 6
• Osoyoos • V0H 1V0
604.495.6919

Richter Pass Motor Inn
7506 62nd Ave Box 480
• Osoyoos • V0H 1V0
604.495.7229

Riviera Motel
6512 64th Ave RR 1
• Osoyoos • V0H 1V0
604.495.6551

Holiday Inn
424 Island Hwy
• Parksville • V9P 1K8
250.248.2232
small pets

Davis Cove Resort
3701 Beach Ave RR 2 Site
22 #5
• Peachland • V0H 1X0
250.767.2355

Peachland Motel
5956 Hwy 97 S Box 798
• Peachland • V0H 1X0
250.767.2205

Clarion
21 Lakeshore Dr
• Penticton • V2A 7M5
250.493.8221
$20

Crown Motel
950 Lakeshore Dr
• Penticton • V2A 1C1
604.492.4092

Golden Sands Condos
1028 Lakeshore
• Penticton • V2A 1C1
250.492.4210
small

Ramada Courtyard Inn
1050 Eckhardt Ave W
• Penticton • V2A 2C3
604.492.8926

Sandman Inn
939 Burnaby Ave W
• Penticton • V2A 1G7
800.726.3626

Harbour Way Motel
3805 Redford St
• Port Alberni • V9Y 3S2
604.723.9405

Redford Motor Inn
3723 Redford St
• Port Alberni • V9Y 3S3
604.724.0121

BRITISH COLUMBIA   CANADA   MANITOBA

Tyee Village Motel
4151 Redford St
● Port Alberni ● V9Y 3R6
800.663.6876

Best Western
1545 Lougheed Hwy
● Port Coquitlam ● V3B 1A5
604.941.6216

Hyatt Motor Lodge
6255 Marine Ave
● Powell River ● V8A 4K6
604.483.3113

Holiday Inn
444 George St
● Prince George ● V2L 1R6
800.465.4329

Ramada Hotel Downtown
444 George St
● Prince George ● V2L 1R6
604.563.0055

Sandman Inn
1650 Central St
● Prince George ● V2M 3C2
800.726.3626

Sandman Inn
Hwy 3 Box 421
● Princeton ● V0X 1W0
800.726.3626

Good Knight Inn
176 Davie St
● Quesnel ● V2J 2S7
800.663.1585

Best Western
1901 Laforme
● Revelstoke ● V0E 2S0
800.528.1234

Sandman Inn
1821 Fraser
● Revelstoke ● V0E 2S0
800.726.3626

Best Western
7551 Westminster Hwy
● Richmond ● V6X 1A3
800.663.0299

Best Western
Transcan Hwy
● Rogers Pass ● V0E 2S0
800.528.1234

Super 8 Motel
2477 Mt Newton Cross Rd
● Saanichton ● V8M 2B7
250.652.6888

Best Western
61 10th St SW
● Salmon Arm ● V1E 4M2
800.528.1234

Super 8 Motel
2901 10th Ave NE
● Salmon Arm ● V1E 4N1
250.832.8812

Best Western
43971 Industrial Wy
● Sardis ● V2R 1A9
604.795.3828

Comfort Inn
45405 Luckakuck Way
● Sardis ● V2R 3C7
800.221.2222

Best Western
2306 Beacon Ave
● Sidney ● V8L 1X2
250.656.4441
$20

Travelodge
2280 Beacon Ave
● Sidney ● V8L 1X1
800.255.3050
small

Sandman Inn
3932 Hwy 16 Box 935
● Smithers ● V0J 2N0
800.726.3626

Ramada Limited
19225 Hwy 10
● Surrey ● V3S 8V9
604.576.8388
small

Alpine House
4326 Lakelse Ave
● Terrace ● V8G 1N8
250.635.7216
$5

Coast In
4620 Lakelse
● Terrace ● V8G 1R1
250.638.8141
small pets

Sandman Inn
4828 Hwy 16 W
● Terrace ● V8G 1L6
800.726.3626

Chalet Cont
1450 5th Ave
● Valemount ● Voe 2Z0
250.566.9787
$5

Four Seasons Hotel
791 W Georgia St
● Vancouver ● V6C 2T4
800.332.3442
small

Holiday Inn
1110 Howe St
● Vancouver ● V6Z 1R2
800.465.4329
small

Holiday Inn
711 W Broadway Ave
● Vancouver ● V5Z 3Y2
800.465.4329

Quality Inn
1335 Howe St
● Vancouver ● V6Z 1R7
800.221.2222
small

Quality Inn
3484 Kingsway
● Vancouver ● V5R 5L6
800.221.2222

Sandman Hotel
180 W Georgia St
● Vancouver ● V6B 4P4
800.726.3626

Travelodge
2060 Marine Dr
● Vancouver ● V7P 1V7
604.985.5311

Travelodge
1304 Howe St
● Vancouver ● V6Z 1R6
604.682.2767

Westin
1601 Georgia St
● Vancouver ● V6G 2V4
800.228.3000
small

Best Western
3914 32 St
● Vernon ● V1T 5P1
250.545.3385
$10

Sandman Inn
4201 32nd St
● Vernon ● V1T 5P3
800.726.3626

Travelodge
3000 28th Ave
● Vernon ● V1T 1W1
800.255.3050
$5

Quality Hotel
4550 Cordova Bay Rd
● Victoria ● V8X 3V5
800.221.2222

Ramada Inn
3010 Blanshard St
● Victoria ● V8T 5B5
800.228.2828

Best Western
4121 Village Green
● Whistler ● V0N 1B4
604.932.1133

Sandman Inn
664 Oliver St
● Williams Lake ● V2G 1M6
800.726.3626

Super 8 Motel
1712 Broadway Ave S
● Williams Lake ● V2G 2W4
800.800.8000
small

MANITOBA

Comfort Inn
925 Middleton Ave
● Brandon ● R7C 1A8
800.221.2222

Rodeway Inn
300 18th St N
● Brandon ● R7A 6Z2
204.728.7230
$3

Super 8 Motel
Hwy 1 & 10
● Brandon ● R7C 1A7
800.800.8000

Rodeway Inn
Box 602
• Dauphin • R7N 2V4
204.638.5102
small

Hi-Way Motel
2010 Saskatchewan
• Portage La Prairie • R1N
0P2
204.857.8771

Westgate Inn
1010 Saskatchewan
• Portage La Prairie • R1N
0K1
204.239.5200
small

Westward Village
2401 Saskatchewan
• Portage La Prairie • R1N
3L5
204.857.9745

Two-Morrows Inn
1570 Main
• Stony Mountain • R0L 1Z0
204.734.3451

Washenfelders
703 Main St
• Stony Mountain • R0L 1Z0
204.734.2058

Manigaming Motel
137 Ta-Wa-Pit
• Wasagaming • R0J 2H0
204.848.2459

Best Western
220 Carlton St
• Winnipeg • R3C 1P5
800.528.1234

Best Western
1808 Wellington Ave
• Winnipeg • R3H 0G3
800.528.1234
$5

Comfort Inn
3109 Pembina Hwy
• Winnipeg • R3T 4R6
800.221.2222

Comfort Inn
1770 Sargent Ave
• Winnipeg • R3H 0C8
800.221.2222

Country Inns
730 King Edward St
• Winnipeg • R3H 1B4
800.456.4000
small

Crowne Plaza
350 St Marys Ave
• Winnipeg • R3C 3J2
800.465.4329

Holiday Inn
1330 Pembina Hwy
• Winnipeg • R3T 2B4
800.465.4329

Ramada
331 Smith St
• Winnipeg • R3B 2G9
204.942.6411
small

Ramada Inn
1824 Pembina Hwy
• Winnipeg • R3T 2G2
800.268.8998
small

Rodeway Inn Downtown
367 Ellice Ave
• Winnipeg • R3B 1Y1
800.221.2222

Sheraton Winnipeg
161 Donald St
• Winnipeg • R3C 1M3
800.325.3535

Super 8 Motel
1484 Niakwa Rd E
• Winnipeg • R2J 3T3
204.253.1935
$20 dep

Travelodge Hotel Downtown
360 Colony St
• Winnipeg • R3B 2P3
800.667.3529
small

Westin Hotel
2 Lombard Pl
• Winnipeg • R3B 0Y3
800.228.3000

NEW BRUNSWICK

Best Western
St Peter Ave W Po Box 180
• Bathurst • E2A 3Z2
800.528.1234

Comfort Inn
1170 St Peter Ave
• Bathurst • E2A 2Z9
800.221.2222

Country Inn & Suites
777 St Peter Ave
• Bathurst • E2A 1Y9
800.456.4000
small

Keddys Le Chateau
80 Main St
• Bathurst • E2A 2Y9
506.546.0015
small pets

Norwood B&b
Rt 715
• Cambridge-Narrows •
506.488.2681
small

Best Western
385 Adelaide St
• Campbellton • E0K 1B0
506.684.5681
small

Comfort Inn
3 Sugarloaf
• Campbellton • E3N 3G9
800.221.2222

Howard Johnson
157 Water St
• Campbellton • E3N 3H2
506.753.4133
small

Auberge Wandlyn Inn
919 Canada Rd
• Edmundston • E3V 3K5
506.735.5525

Comfort Inn
5 Bateman Ave
• Edmundston • E3V 3L1
800.221.2222

Howard Johnson
100 Rice St
• Edmundston • E3V 1T4
800.654.2000

Auberge Wandlyn Inn
58 Prospect St
• Fredericton • E3B 2T8
506.452.8937

Carriage House
230 University Ave
• Fredericton • E3B 4H7
506.452.9924
small

Comfort Inn
255 Prospect St W
• Fredericton • E3B 5Y4
800.221.2222

Comfort Inn
Hwy 2
• Fredericton • E3B 5Y4
506.453.0800
small

Country Inn
445 Prospect St
• Fredericton • E3B 6B8
506.459.0035
$50 deposit

Howard Johnson
Transcan Hwy
• Fredericton • E3B 5E3
506.472.0480

Keddys Inn
368 Forest Hill
• Fredericton • E3B 5G2
506.454.4461

Keddys Lord Beaver
659 Queen St
• Fredericton • E3B 5A6
506.455.3371

Best Western
RR 6
• Grand Falls • E0J 1M0
506.473.1300
small

Beacon Light
Mountain Rd
• Moncton • E1C 2T1
506.384.1734

Best Western
499 Paul St
• Moncton • E1A 6S5
506.858.8584
small

Colonial Inn
42 Highfield St
• Moncton • E1C 8T6
506.382.3395
small

Comfort Inn
20 Maplewood Dr
• Moncton • E1A 6P9
800.221.2222
$50 dep

Comfort Inn
2495 Mountain Rd
• Moncton • E1C 8K2
800.221.2222

Country Inn & Suites
2475 Mountain Rd
• Moncton • E1C 8J3
800.456.4000
$50 dep

Keddys Hotel
1005 Main St
• Moncton • E1C 8N6
506.854.6340

Travelodge
434 Main St
• Moncton • E1C 1B9
506.382.1664

Auberge Wandlyn Inn
365 Water St
• Newcastle • E1V 3M5
506.622.3870

Comfort Inn
201 Edward St
• Newcastle • E1V 2Y7
800.221.2222

Country Inn
333 King George Hwy
• Newcastle • E1V 2Y7
506.627.1999
small

Shadow Lawn Inn
Rt 100
• Rothesay • E2E 5A3
506.847.7539

Marshlands Inn
59 Bridge St
• Sackville • E0A 3C0
506.536.0170
w/permission

Comfort Inn
1155 Fairville
• Saint John • E2M 5E6
800.221.2222

Country Inn & Suites
1011 Fairville
• Saint John • E2M 4Y2
800.456.4000
$50 dep

Fundy Line Motel
2149 Ocean West
• Saint John • E2M 5H6
506.672.2493

Fundy Line Motel
532 Rothesay Ave
• Saint John • E2J 2C7
506.633.7733

Howard Johnson
400 Main St
• Saint John • E2K 4N5
506.642.2622

Best Western
218 Water St
• St Andrews • E0G 2X0
800.528.1234

Best Western
218 Water St
• St Andrews • E0G 2X0
506.529.8877
small pets

Fundy Lodge
Hwy 1
• St George • E0G 2Y0
506.755.2963
$7 fee

Granite Town Hotel
Rt 772
• St George • E0G 2Y0
506.755.6415
$10 fee

Colonial Inn
175 City Rd
• St John • E2L 3T5
506.652.3000
small

Hilton
1 Market Sq
• St John • E2L 4Z6
506.693.8484

Keddys
10 Portland St
• St John • E2K 4H8
506.657.7320

Park Plaza
607 Rothesay
• St John • E2H 2G9
506.633.4100

Regent Motel
2121 Ocean West Wy
• St John • E2M 5H6
506.672.8273
small

Terrace Motel
2131 Ocean Way West
• St John • E2M 5H6
506.672.9670

Auberge Wandlyn Inn
99 King St
• St Stephen • E3L 2C6
506.466.1814

Fundy Line Motel
198 King St
• St Stephen • E3L 2E2
506.466.2130

Loon Bay Lodge
Rt 745
• St Stephen • E3L 2W9
506.466.1240

Pine Cone Motel
Hwy 2
• Sussex • E0E 1L0
506.433.3958

Quality Inn
Hwy 1
• Sussex • E0E 1P0
506.433.3470

Auberge Wandlyn Inn
Po Box 1191
• Woodstock • E0J 2B0
506.328.8876

Panorama Motel
Hwy 2
• Woodstock • E0J 2B0
506.328.3315

Stiles Motels
827 Upper Main
• Woodstock • E0J 2B0
506.328.6671
small

NEWFOUNDLAND

Holiday Inn
Trans Canada Hwy Rt 1
• Clarenville • A0E 1J0
800.465.4329

Best Western
Maple Valley Rd Box 787 Rt 1
• Corner Brook • A1H 6G7
709.639.8901

Comfort Inn
41 Maple Valley Rd Po Bx 1142
• Corner Brook • A2H 6P2
800.221.2222

Holiday Inn
48 West St
• Corner Brook • A2H 2Z2
800.465.4329

Deer Lake Motel
Hwy 430
• Deer Lake • A0K 2E0
709.635.2108
small

Country Inn
315 Gander Bay Rd Box 154
• Gander • A1V 1W6
709.256.4005

Holiday Inn
1 Caldwell St
• Gander • A1V 1T6
800.465.4329

Best Western
199 Kenmount Rd
• St Johns • A1B 3P9
800.528.1234

Delta St Johns Hotel
120 New Gower St
• St Johns • A1C 6K4
709.739.6404
small

Holiday Inn
180 Portugal Cove Rd
• St Johns • A1B 2N2
800.465.4329

Quality Hotel
2 Hill O Chips
● St Johns ● A1C 6B1
800.221.2222

Radisson Plaza Hotel
120 New Gower St
● St Johns ● A1C 6K4
800.333.3333

NOVA SCOTIA

Auberge Wandlyn Inn
Box 275 Hwy 104
● Amherst ● B4H 3Z2
902.667.3331

Comfort Inn
143 S Albion St
● Amherst ● B4H 2X2
800.221.2222

Auberge Wandlyn
P O Box 628
● Annapolis Royal ● B0S 1A0
902.532.2323

Auberge Wandlyn Inn
158 Main St
● Antigonish ● B2G 2B7
902.863.4001
small

Silver Dart Lodge
Rt 205
● Baddeck ● B0E 1B0
902.295.2340
small

Coastal Inn
771 Bedford Hwy
● Bedford ● B4A 1Eg
902.835.3367
small

Days Inn
636 Bedford Hwy
● Bedford ● B3M 2Lb
902.443.3171
small

Travelers Motel
773 Bedford Hwy
● Bedord ● B4A 1A4
902.835.3394

Grandview Motel
Hwy 3
● Black Point ● B0J 1B0
902.857.9776
small

Auberge Wandlyn Inn
50 North St Box 40
● Bridgewater ● B4V 2W6
902.543.7131

Comfort Inn
49 North St
● Bridgewater ● B4V 2V7
800.221.2222

Windjammin Motel
Rt 3
● Chester ● B0J 1Jo
902.275.3567
large grounds

Lauries Inn
Main St
● Cheticamp ● B0E 1H0
902.224.2400

Parkview Motel
Cabot Trail
● Cheticamp ● B0E 1H0
902.224.3232

Auberge Wandlyn Inn
739 Windmill Rd
● Dartmouth ● B3B 1C1
902.469.0810

Best Western
313 Prince Albert Rd
● Dartmouth ● B2Y 1N3
902.469.5850
small

Comfort Inn
456 Windmill Rd
● Dartmouth ● B3A 1J7
800.221.2222

Comfort Inn
456 Windmill Rd
● Dartmouth ● B3A 1J7
902.463.9900

Country Inn & Suites
P O Box 57
● Dartmouth ● B2Y 3Y2
800.456.4000

Future Inns
20 Highfield Park Dr
● Dartmouth ● B3A 4S8
902.465.6555
small

Keddys
9 Braemar Dr
● Dartmouth ● B2Y 3H6
902.469.0331

Ramada
240 Brownlow Ave
● Dartmouth ● B3B 1X6
902.468.8888
small

Siesta Motel
81 Montague Row Box 250
● Digby ● B0V 1A0
902.245.2568

The Markland
Cabot Trail
● Dingwall ● B0C 1G0
902.383.2246

Auberge Wandlyn Inn
50 Bedford Hwy
● Halifax ● B3M 2J2
902.443.0416

Chateau Halifax
1990 Barrington
● Halifax ● B3J 1P2
902.425.6700

Days Inn
636 Bedford Hwy
● Halifax ● B3M 2L8
902.443.3171

Delta Barrington
1875 Barrington
● Halifax ● B3J 3L6
902.429.7410

Doubletree Chateau Halifax
1990 Barrington St
● Halifax ● B3J 1P2
800.828.7447

Econo Lodge
560 Bedford Hwy
● Halifax ● B3M 2L8
800.424.4777
small

Hilton
1181 Hollis St
● Halifax ● B3H 2P6
800.268.9275
small

Holiday Inn
99 Wyse Rd
● Halifax ● B3A 1L9
800.465.4329

Holiday Inn
1980 Robie St
● Halifax ● B3H 3G5
800.465.4329

Holiday Inn Exp
133 Kearney Lake
● Halifax ● B3M 4P3
902.445.1100
small

Lord Nelson Hotel
1515 S Park St Box 700
● Halifax ● B3J 2T3
800.565.2020

Prince George Hotel
1725 Market
● Halifax ● B3J 3N9
902.425.1986
small

Sheraton Halifax
1919 Upper Water St
● Halifax ● B3J 3J5
800.325.3535
small

The Citadel
1960 Brunswick
● Halifax ● B3J 2G7
902.422.1391

Comfort Inn
740 Westville Rd
● New Glasgow ● B2H 2J8
800.221.2222
small

Auberge Wandlyn Inn
689 Reeves St Box 759
● Port Hawkesbury ● B0E 2V0
902.625.0320
small

Comfort Inn
368 Kings Rd
• Sydney • B1S 1A8
800.221.2222

Holiday Inn
480 Kings Rd
• Sydney • B1S 1A8
800.465.4329

Best Western
150 Willow St
• Truro • B2N 4Z6
.800.528.1234
small

Comfort Inn
12 Meadow Dr
• Truro • B2N 5V4
800.221.2222

Best Western
545 Main St
• Yarmouth • B5A 1J6
800.528.1234
small

Comfort Inn
96 Starrs Rd
• Yarmouth • B5A 2T5
800.221.2222

ONTARIO

White Otter Inn
710 Mackenzie Ave E Box 27
• Atikokan • P0T 1C0
807.597.2747

Best Western
146 Hastings St N Box 28
• Bancroft • K0L 1C0
800.528.1234
small

Best Western
35 Hart Dr
• Barrie • L4N 5M3
800.528.1234
small

Comfort Inn
75 Hart Dr
• Barrie • L4N 5M3
800.221.2222

Holiday Inn
20 Fairview Rd
• Barrie • L4M 6E7
800.465.4329

Best Western
387 Front St N
• Belleville • K8P 3C8
613.969.1112
small

Comfort Inn
200 Park St N
• Belleville • K8P 2Y9
800.221.2222

Quality Inn
407 Front St N
• Belleville • K8P 3C8
800.221.2222

Ramada Inn
11 Bay Bridge Rd Hwy 62
• Belleville • K8N 4Z1
800.228.2828
small

Friendship Inn
181 Causley St Hwy 1
• Blind River • P0R 1B0
705.356.2249

Riverside Lodge
84 Front St E Box 903
• Bobcaygeon • K0M 1A0
705.738.2193

Holiday Inn
30 Peel Centre Dr
• Brampton • L6T 4G3
800.465.4329

Best Western
19 Holiday Dr Box 1900
• Brantford • N3T 5W5
800.528.1234
small

Comfort Inn
58 King George Rd
• Brantford • N3R 5K4
800.221.2222

Days Inn
460 Fairview Dr
• Brantford • N3R 7A9
519.759.2700
small

Quality Inn
666 Colborne St E
• Brantford • N3S 3P8
800.221.2222

Travelodge
664 Colborne St
• Brantford • N3S 3P8
519.753.7371
small

Comfort Inn
7777 Kent Blvd
• Brockville • K6V 5V5
800.221.2222

Comfort Inn
3290 S Service Rd
• Burlington • L7N 3M6
800.221.2222
small

Holiday Inn
3063 S Service Rd
• Burlington • L7N 3E9
800.465.4329

Travelodge Burlington
950 Walkers Line
• Burlington • L7N 2G2
800.255.3050

Comfort Inn
220 Holiday Inn Dr
• Cambridge • N3C 1Z4
800.221.2222
except pet shows

Days Inn
650 Hespeler Rd
• Cambridge • N1R 6J8
519.622.1070

Holiday Inn
200 Holiday Inn Dr
• Cambridge • N3C 1Z4
800.465.4329

Chatham Motel
659 Grand Ave E
• Chatham • N7L 1X6
519.352.4670

Comfort Inn
1100 Richmond St
• Chatham • N7M 5J5
800.221.2222
small

Kent Motel
420 Grand Ave E
• Chatham • N7L 1X2
519.352.9222

Best Western
930 Burnham St
• Cobourg • K3A 2X9
800.528.1234

Comfort Inn
121 Densmore Rd
• Cobourg • K9A 4J9
800.221.2222

Highwayman Inn
1 Balsam St
• Collingwood • L9Y 3J4
705.444.2144

Mariner Motor Hotel
305 Hume St
• Collingwood • L9Y 1W2
705.445.3330

Sea & Ski Motel
530 First St
• Collingwood • L9Y 1C1
705.445.2061

Best Western
1515 Vincent Massey Dr
• Cornwall • K6H 5R6
613.932.0451

Comfort Inn
1625 Vincent Massey Dr
• Cornwall • K6H 5R6
800.221.2222

Econo Lodge
1750 Vincent Massey Dr
• Cornwall • K6H 5R8
800.424.4777

Holiday Inn
805 Brookdale Ave
• Cornwall • K6J 4P3
800.465.4329
1st floor

Travelodge Hotel
1142 Brookdale Ave
• Cornwall • K6J 4P4
800.255.3050

Best Western
349 Government Rd
• Dryden • P8N 2Z5
800.528.1234

Comfort Inn
522 Government Rd
• Dryden • P8N 2P5
800.221.2222
small

Town & Country Motel
500 Government Rd
• Dryden • P8N 2P7
807.223.2377

Trans Canada Motel
149 Third St
• Dryden • P8N 2V8
807.223.2251

Queensway Motel
287 Queensway Rd
• Espanola • P0P 1C0
705.869.1065

Ramada Hotel Airport
2 Holiday Dr
• Etobicoke • M9C 2Z7
416.621.2121

Sundial Motel
157 Lindsay St
• Fenelon Falls • K0M 1N0
705.887.2400

Comfort Inn
1 Journeys End Dr
• Fort Erie • L2A 6G1
800.221.2222

Lakeview Inn Motel
139 Garrison Rd
• Fort Erie • L2A 1M3
416.871.6806

Quality Inn
20 Central Ave S
• Fort Erie • L2A 6C1
800.221.2222

Midtown Motel
417 Portage Ave
• Fort Frances • P9A 2A1
807.274.9814

Appleby Motel
480 King St E
• Gananoque • K7G 1G8
613.382.4402

Can-Am Motor Lodge
641 King St E
• Gananoque • K7G 1H4
613.382.3311

Colonial Resort
780 King St W
• Gananoque • K7G 2H5
613.382.4677

Crown & Anchor Motel
1801 Main St
• Geraldton • P0T 1M0
807.854.1211

Gold Nugget Motel
509 Main St
• Geraldton • P0T 1M0
807.854.0740

Travelodge
1486 Innes Rd
• Gloucester • K1B 3V5
613.745.1133

Bedford Arms Motel
242 Bayfield Rd
• Goderich • N7A 3G6
519.524.7348

Gardiners Motel
400 Bayfield Rd
• Goderich • N7A 4E7
519.524.7302

Best Western
106 Carden St
• Guelph • N1H 3A3
613.632.5941
small

Comfort Inn
480 Silvercreek Pkwy
• Guelph • N1H 7R5
800.221.2222
1st floor

Days Inn
785 Gordon St
• Guelph • N1G 1Y8
519.822.9112
$10

Holiday Inn
601 Scottsdale Rd
• Guelph • N1G 3E7
800.465.4329

Howard Johnson
112 E King St
• Guelph • L8N 1A8
905.546.8111

Best Western
51 Keefer Crt
• Hamilton • L8E 4V4
416.578.1212

Comfort Inn
183 Centennial Pkwy N
• Hamilton • L8E 1H8
800.221.2222
small

Holiday Inn
150 King St E
• Hamilton • L8N 1B2
800.465.4329

Howard Johnson
1333 E Weber St
• Hamilton • N2A 1C2
519.893.1234

Howard Johnson
112 E King St
• Hamilton • L8N 1A8
905.546.8111

Ramada Hotel
150 King St E
• Hamilton • L8N 1B2
905.528.3451

Sheraton Hotel
116 King St W
• Hamilton • L8P 4V3
800.325.3535

Best Western
1575 Tupper St
• Hawkesbury • K6A 3E1
800.528.1234

Comfort Inn
86 King William St
• Huntsville • P0A 1K0
800.221.2222

Rainbow Motel
32 King William St
• Huntsville • P0A 1K0
705.789.5514

Raymor Motel
117 Main St W
• Huntsville • P0A 1K0
705.789.6784

Comfort Inn
222 Hearst Way
• Kanata • K2L 3A2
800.221.2222

Chain Of Lakes Motel
470 Government Rd
• Kapuskasing • P5N 2X7
705.335.2213

Comfort Inn
172 Government Rd E
• Kapuskasing • P5N 2W9
800.221.2222

Best Western
920 Hwy 17 E
• Kenora • P9N 3X1
800.528.1234

Comfort Inn
1230 Hwy 17
• Kenora • P9N 1L9
807.221.2222
in smoking rm

Days Inn
920 Hwy 17 E
• Kenora • P9N 1L9
807.468.2003

Kenora Inn Motel
1429 River St
• Kenora • P9N 1K6
807.468.5261

Kenora Travelodge
800 Sunset Strip
• Kenora • P9N 1L9
800.255.3050

Comfort Inn
1454 Princess St
• Kingston • K7M 3E5
800.221.2222

Comfort Inn
55 Warne Crescent
• Kingston • K7L 4V4
800.221.2222

Econo Lodge
2327 Princess St
• Kingston • K7M 3G1
613.546.2691

Holiday Inn
1 Princess St
• Kingston • K7L 1A1
613.546.4411
small

Howard Johnson
237 Ontario St
● Kingston ● K7L 2Z4
800.654.2000

Comfort Inn
455 Government Rd W
● Kirkland Lake ● P0K 1A0
800.221.2222

Comfort Inn
2899 King St E
● Kitchener ● N2A 1A6
800.221.2222
small

Holiday Inn
30 Fairway Rd S
● Kitchener ● N2A 2N2
800.465.4329
$50 dep

Howard Johnson
Hwy 2 Po Box 1140
● Kitchener ● K0C 1X0
613.543.3788

Howard Johnson
1333 E Weber St
● Kitchener ● N2A 1C2
519.893.1234

Rodeway Suites
55 New Dundee Rd
● Kitchener ● N2G 3W5
519.895.2272

Comfort Inn
279 Erie St S
● Leamington ● N8H 3C4
800.221.2222
$5

Manerys Motel
161 Talbot St E
● Leamington ● N8H 1L8
519.326.3336

Best Western
591 Wellington Rd S
● Lombardy ● N6C 4R3
800.528.1234
$5

Econo Lodge
1170 Wellington Rd S
● Lombardy ● N6E 1M3
800.424.4777

Howard Johnson Hotel
1150 Wellington Rd S
● Lombardy ● N6E 1M3
800.446.4656
small

Quality Inn
1156 Wellington Rd
● Lombardy ● N6E 1M3
800.221.2222

Quality Suites
1120 Dearness Dr
● Lombardy ● N6E 1N9
519.680.1024

Quality Suites Downtown
374 Dundas St
● Lombardy ● N6B 1V7
519.661.0233

Radisson Hotel
300 King St
● Lombardy ● N6B 1S2
800.333.3333

Ramada Hotel Downtown
186 King St
● Lombardy ● N6A 1C7
800.228.2828

Ramada Inn
817 Exeter Rd
● Lombardy ● N6E 1W1
519.681.4900

Sheraton Armouries Hotel
325 Dundas St
● Lombardy ● N6B 1T9
519.679.6111

Howard Johnson
555 Cochrane Dr
● Markham ● L3R 8E3
416.479.5000

Bel Air Motel
351 4th Ave Box 219
● Matheson ● P0K 1N0
705.273.2757

Fishermans Wharf Motel
12 Bayfield St Box 374
● Meaford ● N0H 1Y0
519.538.1390

Hilltop Motel
300 Sykes St S Box 609
● Meaford ● N0H 1Y0
519.538.1700

Comfort Inn
980 King St
● Midland ● L4R 4K5
800.221.2222

Kings Motel
751 King St Box 23
● Midland ● L4R 4K8
705.526.7744

Comfort Inn
1230 Journeys End Cir
● Mississauga ● L3Y 7V1
800.221.2222
$30 dep

Ramada Hotel
2501 Argentia Rd
● Mississauga ● L5N 4G8
905.858.2424

Howard Johnson
Hwy 2 Box 1140
● Morrisburg ● K0C 1X0
613.543.3788

Napanee Motel
361 Dundas St W
● Napanee ● K7R 2B5
613.354.5200

Twin Peaks Motel
353 Dundas St W
● Napanee ● K7R 2B5
613.354.4066

Waterfront Inn
2 Cedar St Box 2734
● New Liskeard ● P0J 1P0
705.647.8711

Best Western
5551 Murray St
● Niagara Falls ● L2G 2J4
416.356.0551
small

Clarion Inn
5425 Robinson St
● Niagara Falls ● L2G 7L6
416.357.1234

Comfort Inn
5640 Stanley Ave
● Niagara Falls ● L2G 3X5
800.221.2222

Comfort Inn
4009 River Rd
● Niagara Falls ● L2E 3E4
905.356.3306

Days Inn
4029 River Rd
● Niagara Falls ● L2E 3E5
416.356.6666

Ramada Coral Inn
7429 Lundys Lane
● Niagara Falls ● L2H 1G9
905.356.6116
small

Siesta Motel
5703 Thorold Stone
● Niagara Falls ● L2J 1A1
416.356.7299

Thriftlodge
6000 Stanley Ave
● Niagara Falls ● L2G 3Y1
905.358.6243

Best Western
700 Lakeshore Dr
● North Bay ● P1A 2G4
800.528.1234

Comfort Inn
676 Lakeshore Dr
● North Bay ● P1A 2G4
800.221.2222

Comfort Inn
1200 Obrien St
● North Bay ● P1B 9B3
800.221.2222

Howard Johnson
425 Fraser St
● North Bay ● P1B 3X1
705.472.8200

Howard Johnson
425 Fraser St
● North Bay ● P1B 3X1
705.472.8200

Relax Inn
1525 Seymour St Box 748
● North Bay ● P1B 8J8
800.667.3529

Holiday Inn
360 Iroquois Shore Rd
● Oakville ● L6H 1M4
800.465.4329

Howard Johnson
590 Argus Rd
● Oakville ● L6J 3J3
800.654.2000

Comfort Inn
75 Progress Dr
● Orillia ● L3V 6V7
800.221.2222

Holiday Motel
436 Laclie St
● Orillia ● L3V 4P6
705.325.1316

Knights Inn
285 Memorial Ave
● Orillia ● L3V 5X8
705.326.3554

Comfort Inn
605 Bloor St W
● Oshawa ● L1J 5Y6
800.221.2222

Holiday Inn
1011 Bloor St E
● Oshawa ● L1H 7K6
800.465.4329

Rodeway Suites
1910 SimcOe St N
● Oshawa ● L1G 4Y3
905.404.8700

Travelodge
940 Champlain Ave
● Oshawa ● L1J 7A6
800.255.3050

Comfort Inn
1242 Michael St
● Ottawa ● K1J 7T1
800.221.2222

Hilton
150 Albert St
● Ottawa ● K1P 5G2
613.238.1500

Holiday Inn
350 Dalhousie St
● Ottawa ● K1N 7E9
800.465.4329

Howard Johnson
140 Slater St
● Ottawa ● K1P 5H6
800.654.2000

Quality Hotel
290 Rideau St
● Ottawa ● K1N 5Y3
800.221.2222
in smoking rms

Radisson Hotel Ottawa
Centre
100 Kent St
● Ottawa ● K1P 5R7
800.333.3333

Ramada Hotel & Suites
111 Cooper St
● Ottawa ● K2P 2E3
613.238.1331

Relax Hotel Ottawa
Downtown
402 Queen St
● Ottawa ● K1R 5A7
800.667.3529

Travelodge
2098 Montreal Rd
● Ottawa ● K1J 6M8
613.745.1531

Westin Hotel
11 Colonel By Dr
● Ottawa ● K1N 9H4
800.228.3000
small

Comfort Inn
955 9th Ave E
● Owen Sound ● N4K 6N4
800.221.2222

Econo Lodge
485 9th Ave E
● Owen Sound ● N4K 3E2
519.371.3011
small

Holiday Inn
950 6th St E
● Owen Sound ● N4K 1H1
800.465.4329

Comfort Inn
118 Bowes St
● Parry Sound ● P2A 2L7
800.221.2222

Georgian Inn
48 Joseph St
● Parry Sound ● P2A 2G5
705.746.2118

Travellers Motor Hotel
36 Mary St
● Parry Sound ● P2A 1E4
705.746.9307

Best Western
1 International Dr
● Pembroke ● K8A 6X9
800.567.2378
small

Comfort Inn
959 Pembroke St E
● Pembroke ● K8A 3M3
800.221.2222

Travellers Inn
1044 Pembroke St E
● Pembroke ● K8A 6Z3
613.732.9901

Friendship Inn
125 Dufferin St
● Perth ● K7H 3A5
613.267.3300

Comfort Inn
1209 Landsdowne St
● Peterborough ● K9J 7M2
800.221.2222
small

Holiday Inn
150 George St N
● Peterborough ● K9J 3G5
800.465.4329

Quality Inn
1074 Landsdowne St
● Peterborough ● K9J 1Z9
800.221.2222

Ramada Inn
100 Charlotte St
● Peterborough ● K9J 7L4
705.743.7272

Colonial Motel
235 Goderich St S
● Port Elgin ● N0H 2C1
519.832.2021

Jk Motel
764 Goderich St S
● Port Elgin ● N0H 2C0
519.389.4837

Comfort Inn
Po Box 86
● Port Hope ● L1A 3V9
800.221.2222
small

Days Inn
Box 355
● Renfrew ● K7V 4A4
613.432.3636

Sunset Motel
409 Stewart St N
● Renfrew ● K7V 1Y4
613.432.5801

Best Western
1400 Venetian Blvd
● Sarnia ● N7T 7W6
519.337.7577

Comfort Inn
505 Harbour Rd
● Sarnia ● N7T 5R8
800.221.2222

Holiday Inn
1498 Venetial Blvd Box 2290
● Sarnia ● N7T 7W6
800.465.4329

Comfort Inn
333 Great Northern Rd
● Sault Ste Marie ● P6B 4Z8
800.221.2222

Holiday Inn
208 St Marys River Dr
● Sault Ste Marie ● P6A 5V4
800.465.4329

Ramada Inn
229 Great Northern Rd
● Sault Ste Marie ● P6B 4Z2
800.228.2828

Travellers Motel
859 Trunk Rd
● Sault Ste Marie ● P6A 3T3
705.946.6433

Birch Grove Motel
316 Walker St Box 277
● Schreiber ● P0T 2S0
807.824.2800

Cliffside Motel
106 Quebec St Box 332
● Schreiber ● P0T 2S0
807.824.2754

Best Western
203 Queensway W
● SimcOe ● N3Y 2M9
519.426.2125

Comfort Inn
85 The Queensway E
● SimcOe ● N3Y 4M5
800.221.2222

Comfort Inn
2 Dunlop Dr
● St Chatharines ● L2R 1A2
800.221.2222

Holiday Inn
2 N Service Rd
● St Chatharines ● L2N 4G9
800.465.4329

Howard Johnson
89 Meadowvale Dr
● St Chatharines ● L2N 3Z8
800.654.2000

Comfort Inn
100 Centennial Ave
● St Thomas ● N5R 5B2
800.221.2222

Champlain Motel
155 Front St Box 1078
● Sturegon Falls ● P0H 2G0
705.753.1300

Moulin Rouge Motel
175 Front St Box 38
● Sturegon Falls ● P0H 2G0
705.753.2020

Comfort Inn
440 2nd Ave N Box 2490 Stn A
● Sudbury ● P3A 4S9
800.221.2222

Comfort Inn
2171 Regent St S
● Sudbury ● P3E 5V3
800.221.2222

Holiday Inn
85 St Anne Rd Box 1033
● Sudbury ● P3E 4S4
800.485.4329

Howard Johnson
390 S Elgin St
● Sudbury ● P3B 1B4
705.675.1273

Ramada Inn City Centre
85 Ste Anne Rd
● Sudbury ● P3E 4S4
705.675.1123

Relax Inn
1401 Paris St
● Sudbury ● P3E 3B6
800.667.3529

Best Western
655 W Arthur St
● Thunder Bay ● P7E 5R6
800.528.1234
small

Comfort Inn
660 W Arthur St
● Thunder Bay ● P7E 5R8
800.221.2222

Holiday Inn
375 Kingsway Ave
● Thunder Bay ● P7E 2A6
807.623.2514

Venture Inn
450 Memorial Ave
● Thunder Bay ● P7B 3Y7
807.345.2343

Super 8 Motel
92 SimcOe St
● Tillsonburg ● N4G 2J1
519.842.7366

Best Western
1800 Riverside Dr
● Timmins ● P4N 7J5
705.267.6241

Comfort Inn
939 Algonquin Blvd E Bx 1190
● Timmins ● P4N 7J5
800.221.2222
small

Venture Inn Timmins
730 Algonquin Blvd E
● Timmins ● P4N 7G2
705.268.7171

Best Western
33 Carlston Crt
● Toronto ● M9W 6H5
416.675.1234
small

Best Western
30 Norfinch Dr
● Toronto ● M3N 1X1
416.665.3500

Comfort Inn
5 Rutherford Rd S
● Toronto ● L6W 3J3
800.221.2222

Comfort Inn
66 Norfinch Dr
● Toronto ● M3N 1X1
800.221.2222

Comfort Inn
8330 Woodbine Ave
● Toronto ● L3R 2N8
800.221.2222

Comfort Inn
533 Kingstn Rd
● Toronto ● L1V 3N7
800.221.2222

Comfort Inn
1500 Matheson Blvd
● Toronto ● L4W 3Z4
800.221.2222

Comfort Inn
3306 Kingston Rd
● Toronto ● M1M 1P8
800.221.2222

Days Inn
30 Carlton St
● Toronto ● M5B 2E9
800.325.2525

Days Inn
4635 Tomken Rd
● Toronto ● L4W 1J9
800.325.2525

Four Seasons Hotel
21 Avenue Rd
● Toronto ● M5R 2G1
800.332.3442

Four Seasons Inn On The Park
1100 Eglinton Ave E
● Toronto ● M3C 1H8
800.332.3442

Hilton
5875 Airport Rd
● Toronto ● L4V 1N1
416.677.9900

Holiday Inn
2125 N Sheridan Way
● Toronto ● L5K 1A3
418.855.2000

Holiday Inn
89 Chestnut St
● Toronto ● M5G 1R1
800.465.4329

Holiday Inn
970 Dixon Rd
● Toronto ● M9W 1J9
800.465.4329

Holiday Inn
2 Holiday Inn Dr
● Toronto ● M9C 2Z7
800.465.4329

Holiday Inn
22 Metropolitan Rd
● Toronto ● M1R 2T6
800.465.4329

Hotel Inter-Continental
220 Bloor St W
● Toronto ● M5S 1T8
416.960.5200

Howard Johnson
2420 Surveyor Rd
● Toronto ● L5N 4E6
416.858.8600

Howard Johnson
40 Progress Crt
● Toronto ● M1G 3T5
800.446.4656

Howard Johnson
475 Younge St
● Toronto ● M4Y 1X7
416.924.0611

Howard Johnson
2737 Keele St
● Toronto ● M2M 2E9
416.636.4656

Howard Johnson
600 Dixon Rd
● Toronto ● M9W 1J1
416.240.7511

Howard Johnson
555 Cochrane Dr
● Toronto ● L3R 8E3
905.479.5000

ONTARIO CANADA PRINCE EDWARD IS

Howard Johnson
15520 Yonge St
● Toronto ● L4G 1P2
905.727.1312

Howard Johnson
430 Ouellette Ave
● Toronto ● N9A 1B2
519.256.4656

Marriott Hotel
901 Dixon Rd
● Toronto ● M9W 1J5
416.674.9400

Quality Hotel
2180 Islington Ave
● Toronto ● M9P 3P1
800.221.2222

Quality Hotel
111 Lombard St
● Toronto ● M5C 2T9
800.221.2222

Quality Hotel
280 Bloor St
● Toronto ● M5S 1V8
800.221.2222

Quality Suites
262 Carlingview Dr
● Toronto ● M9W 5G1
800.221.2222

Radisson Hotel
1250 Eglinton Ave E
● Toronto ● M3C 1J3
800.333.3333

Ramada Hotel Airport
5444 Dixie Rd
● Toronto ● L4W 2L2
800.854.7854

Ramada Inn
1677 Wilson Ave
● Toronto ● M3L 1A5
800.228.2828

Relax Hotel Toronto Airport
445 Rexdale Blvd
● Toronto ● M9W 6K5
800.667.3529

Relax Inn
20 Milner Business Crt
● Toronto ● M1B 3C6
800.667.3529

Relax Inn
50 Forfinch Dr
● Toronto ● M3N 1X1
800.667.3529

Relax Inn
5599 Ambler Dr
● Toronto ● L4W 3Z1
800.667.3529

Sheraton Centre Hotel
123 Queen St W
● Toronto ● M5H 2M9
800.325.3535

Sheraton Toronto Towers
2035 Kennedy Rd
● Toronto ● M1T 3G2
416.299.1500

Venture Inn
50 Estate Dr
● Toronto ● M1H 2Z1
416.439.9666

Venture Inn
89 Avenue Rd
● Toronto ● M5R 2G3
416.964.1220

Westin Harbour Castle
1 Harbour Sq
● Toronto ● M5J 1A6
800.228.3000

Comfort Inn
68 Monogram Pl
● Trenton ● K8V 6E6
800.221.2222
not during pet sho

Days Inn
10 Trenton St
● Trenton ● K8V 4M9
613.392.9291

Ramada Inn
Hwy 401 & Glen Miller Rd Bx 70
● Trenton ● K8V 5R1
800.228.2828

Auberge Owens Inn
Box 178
● Val Rita ● P0L 2G0
705.335.8575

Bayview Motel
35 Spruce St
● Vermillion Bay ● P0V 2V0
807.227.2603

Comfort Inn
190 Weber St N
● Waterloo ● N2J 3H4
800.221.2222

Lakeview Htel
25 Broadway Ave Box 265
● Wawa ● P0S 1K0
705.856.2625

Sportsman Motel
45 Mission Rd Box 219
● Wawa ● P0S 1K0
705.856.2272
small

Best Western
300 Prince Charles Dr
● Welland ● L3C 7B3
800.528.1234

Comfort Inn
870 Niagara St
● Welland ● L3C 1M3
800.221.2222

Quality Suites
1700 Champlain Ave
● Whitby ● L1N 6A7
800.221.2222
small

Shenstone Motor Inn
RR 1
● Wiarton ● N0H 2T0
519.534.1831

Spirit Rock Motel
877 Berford St
● Wiarton ● N0H 2T0
519.534.1645

Best Western
430 Ouellette Ave
● Windsor ● N9A 1B2
519.253.7281

Comfort Inn
2765 Huron Church Rd
● Windsor ● N9E 3Y7
800.221.2222
small

Comfort Inn
2955 Dougall Ave
● Windsor ● N9E 1S1
800.221.2222

Hilton Windsor
277 Riverview Dr W
● Windsor ● N9A 5K4
519.973.5555

Quality Inn & Con Ctr
580 Bruin Blvd
● Windsor ● N4S 7Z5
800.221.2222

Quality Suites
250 Dougall Ave
● Windsor ● N9A 7C6
800.221.2222

Ramada Inn
480 Riverside Dr W
● Windsor ● N9A 5K6
800.268.8998
small

Relax Hotel
33 Riverside Dr E
● Windsor ● N9A 2S4
800.667.3529

Relax Inn
2330 Huron Chruch Rd W
● Windsor ● N9E 3S6
800.667.3529

PRINCE EDWARD ISLAND

Auberge Wandlyn Inn
Box 9500
● Charlottetown ● C1A 8L4
902.892.1201

Best Western
238 Grafton St
● Charlottetown ● C1A 1L5
800.528.1234
small

Comfort Inn
112 Transcan Hwy
● Charlottetown ● C1E 1E7
800.221.2222
small

Doubletree
18 Queen St
● Charlottetown ● C1A 8B9
800.828.7447

424

Holiday Island Motor Lodge
307 University Ave
• Charlottetown • C1A 4M5
902.892.4141

Thriftlodge
Highway 1
• Charlottetown • C1A 7L3
902.892.2481

Travelodge
Hwys 1 & 2
• Charlottetown • C1A 8C2
902.894.8566
small

Shady Rest Motel
RR 2
• Montague • C0A 1R0
902.838.4298

The Sulky Inn
4 Rink St Box 286
• Montague • C0A 1R0
902.838.4100

Travellers Inn
80 All Weather Hwy
• St Eleanors • C1N 5L3
902.436.9100

Best Western
311 Market St
• Summerside • C1N 1K8
800.528.1234

Quality Inn
618 Water St E
• Summerside • C1N 2V5
800.221.2222

QUEBEC

Comfort Inn
870 Ave Du Pont St
• Alma • G8B 2V8
800.221.2222

Comfort Inn
1255 Boul Duplessis
• Ancienne Lorette • G2G
2B4
800.221.2222

Comfort Inn
745 Boul Lafleche
• Bai Comeau • G5C 1C6
800.221.2222

Comfort Inn
240 Boul Sainteanne
• Beauport • G1E 3L7
800.221.2222

Motel Colonial
142 Du Manege
• Beauport • G1E 5H5
418.667.3652

Comfort Inn
96 Boul De Mortagne
• Boucherville • J4B 5M7
800.221.2222
small

Travelodge
115 Rue Copin
• Charlemagne • J52 4P8
514.582.5933

Comfort Inn
1595 Boul Talbot
• Chicoutimi • G7H 4C3
800.221.2222

Days Inn
250 Des Saguneens
• Chicoutimi • G7H 3A4
418.545.8326

Aubuerge La Diligence
414 De La Friche
• Dolbeau • G8L 2R1
800.463.9651

Comfort Inn
340 Ave Michel Jasmin
• Dorval • H9P 1C1
800.221.2222

Quality Hotel Airport
770 Cote De Liesse
• Dorval • H4T 1E7
800.221.2222

Quality Inn Airport
6755 Cote De Liesse
• Dorval • H4T 1E5
800.221.2222
small

Comfort Inn
1055 Rue Hains
• Drummondville • J2C 5L3
800.221.2222

Auberge Des Commandants
Cp 470
• Gaspe • G0C 1R0
418.368.3355

Comfort Inn
630 Boul La Gappe
• Gatineau • J8T 9Z6
800.221.2222

Quality Inn
131 Rue Laurier
• Hull • J8X 3W3
800.221.2222

Auberge Evasion
80 Tour Du Lac
• Lac Simon • J0V 1E0
819.428.4444

Comfort Inn
2055 D'Laurentides
• Laval • H7S 1Z6
800.221.2222
small

Quality Suites
2035 D'Laurentides
• Laval • H7S 1Z6
800.221.2222
small

Relax Hotel
2900 Le Carrefour
• Laval • H7T 2K9
800.667.3529

Sheraton Laval
2440 D'Laurentides
• Laval • H7T 1X5
800.325.3535

Comfort Inn
10 Du Vallon
• Levis • G0R 2K0
800.221.2222
small

Holiday Inn
999 De Serigny
• Longueuil • J4K 2T1
800.465.4329

Ramada Hotel
999 De Serigny
• Longueuil • J4K 2T1
514.670.3030

Econo Lodge
700 Paquette
• Mont Laurier • J9L 1L4
819.623.6465

Crowne Plaza
420 Sherbrooke St W
• Montreal • H3A 1B4
800.465.4329
small

Crowne Plaza
505 Sherbrooke
• Montreal • H2L 1K2
800.465.4329
small

Days Inn
4545 Cote Vertu
• Montreal • H4S 1C8
800.329.2525

Four Seasons Hotel
1050 Sherbrooke St W
• Montreal • H3A 2R6
800.332.3442

Howard Johnson
475 Sherbrooke
• Montreal • H3A 2L9
514.842.3961
small

Howard Johnson
6600 Cote D'Liesse
• Montreal • H4T 1E3
514.735.7788

Le Westin Mont-Royal
1050 Sherbrooke St W
• Montreal • H3A 2R6
514.284.1110

Ramada Renaissance
3625 Ave Du Parc
• Montreal • H2X 3P8
800.228.2828

Ritz Carlton
1228 Sherbrooke St
• Montreal • H3G 1H6
800.363.0366

Thriftlodge
1600 St Hubert
• Montreal • H2L 3Z3
514.849.3214

Travelodge
1010 Herron Rd
● Montreal ● H9S 1B3
514.631.4537

Travelodge Hotel
50 Renelevesque
● Montreal ● H2Z 1A2
514.874.9090
small

Comfort Inn
700 Saint Jean
● Pointe Claire ● H9R 3K2
800.221.2222
small

Holiday Inn
6700 Transcan Hwy
● Pointe Claire ● H9R 1C2
800.465.4329
small

Quality Suites
6300 Transcan Hwy
● Pointe Claire ● H9R 1B9
800.221.2222
small

Days Inn
7300 Wilfredhamel
● Quebec City ● G2R 1C8
418.877.2226

Hilton
3 Place Quebec
● Quebec City ● G1K 7M9
800.268.9275

Holiday Inn
395 Couronne
● Quebec City ● G1K 8Y2
800.465.4329

Loews
1225 Place Montcalm
● Quebec City ● G1R 4W6
800.463.5256

Quality Suites
1600 Rue Bouvier
● Quebec City ● G2K 1N8
800.221.2222

Ramada Downtown
395 Couronne
● Quebec City ● G1K 8Y2
418.647.2611

Aubergo Stewart
4333 Ch Brennan
● Rawdon ● J0K 1S0
514.834.8210

Comfort Inn
455 St Germain
● Rimouski ● G5L 3P2
800.221.2222

Comfort Inn
85 Boul Cartier
● Riviere-Du-Loup ● G5R 4X4
800.221.2222
small

Days Inn
182 Fraser
● Riviere-Du-Loup ● G2R 1C8
418.862.6354

Comfort Inn
4295 Bourque
● Rock Forest ● J1N 1C3
800.221.2222

Comfort Inn
1295 Lariviere
● Rouyn-Noranda ● J9X 6M6
800.221.2222

Holiday Inn
7300 Cote D'Liesse
● Seigneurie ● H4T 1E7
800.465.4329

Comfort Inn
854 Boul Laure
● Sept Iles ● G4R 1Y7
800.221.2222

Auberge
186 St Julien
● St Ferreol ● G0A 3R0
418.826.2663

Auberge
18255 Lacroix
● St Georges ● G5Y 5C4
800.361.6162

Comfort Inn
700 Rue Gadbois
● St Jean Sur Richelieu ● J3A 1V1
800.221.2222

Econo Lodge
6755 Cote D'Liesse
● St Laurent ● H4T 1E5
514.735.5702

Ramada Hotel Airport
7300 Cote D'Liesse
● St Laurent ● H4T 1E7
514.733.8818

Econo Lodge
4645 Metropolitan
● St Leonard ● H1R 1Z4
514.725.3671

Comfort Inn
7320 Wil Hamel
● Ste Foy ● G2G 1C1
800.221.2222

Days Inn
410 Couture
● Ste Helene ● J0H 1M0
514.791.2580

Motel Canadien
1821 Notre-Dame
● Ste Marthe ● G8T 8B2
819.375.5542

Motel Le Havre
1360 Notre-Dame
● Ste Marthe ● G8T 4J3
819.378.4597

Comfort Inn
123 Boul Smith
● Thetford Mines ● G6G 7S7
800.221.2222

Comfort Inn
7075 De La Plaza
● Tracy ● J3R 4X9
800.221.2222

Comfort Inn
6255 Rue Corbeil
● Trois-Rivieres ● G8Z 4P8
800.221.2222

Radisson
1480 Rte 117
● Trois-Rivieres ● J0T 2N0
819.322.2727

Comfort Inn
1665 Sieme Ave
● Val D'Or ● J9P 1V9
800.221.2222

SASKATCHEWAN

Assinboia Motel
137 Centre
● Assiniboia ● S0H 0B0
306.642.3515

Assiniboia Lodge
122 3rd Ave W
● Assiniboia ● S0H 0B0
306.642.3386

Franklin Motor Hotel
137 Centre St Box 640
● Assiniboia ● S0H 0B0
306.642.3515

Biggar Hotel
1St Ave W Box 1647
● Biggar ● S0K 0M0
306.948.3641

Homestyle Motel
801 Main St Box 935
● Biggar ● S0K 0M0
306.948.2225

Circle 6 Motel
206 4th St
● Estevan ● S4A 0T6
306.634.2637

Estevan Motel
905 4th St
● Estevan ● S4A 0W2
306.634.2609

Ambassador Hotel
Main St Box 30
● Goodsoil ● S0H 1X0
306.648.3550

Mayfair Motel
4th Ave E Box 930
● Goodsoil ● S0H 1X0
306.648.3138

Gull Motel
Hwy 1 Box 630
● Gull Lake ● S0N 1A0
306.672.4184

Best Western
Box 1657
● Kindersley ● S0L 1S0
800.528.1234
small

SASKATCHEWAN CANADA SASKATCHEWAN

Drifters Motel
Hwy 2 Box 303
• La Ronge • S0J 1L0
306.425.2224

Harbour Inn
1327 La Ronge Ave Box 1140
• La Ronge • S0J 1L0
800.667.4097

Riverside Motel
Hwy 2 Box 255
• La Ronge • S0J 1L0
306.425.2150

Cedar Inn Motel
4526 44th St
• Lloydminster • S9V 0G4
306.825.6155

The Good Knight Inn
4729 44th St
• Lloydminster • S9V 0G6
306.825.0124

Voyageur Motel
4724 44th St
• Lloydminster • S9V 0G6
306.825.2248

Commercial Hotel
Hwy 21 Pacific Ave Box 1959
• Maple Creek • S0N 1N0
306.662.2673

Maple Grove Motel
Hwy 21 Box 34
• Maple Creek • S0N 1N0
306.662.2658

Capri Motor Inn
101 1St St E Box 327
• Meadow Lake • S0M 1V0
306.236.3101

Best Western
45 Athabasca St E
• Moose Jaw • S6H 0L3
800.528.1234

Best Western
1590 Main St N Box 2020
• Moose Jaw • S6H 7N7
800.528.1234
$25 dep

Moose Jaw Inn
24 Fairford St E
• Moose Jaw • S6H 0C7
306.691.5440

Super 8 Motel
1706 Main St N Box 452
• Moose Jaw • S6H 4P1
306.692.8888

Avenue Hotel
101 1St St W Box 786
• Nipawin • S0E 1E0
306.862.9877

Kingfisher Inn
Hwy 35 S Box 849
• Nipawin • S0E 1E0
306.862.9801

Battlefords Inn
11212 Railway Ave N
• North Battleford • S9A 2R7
306.445.1515

Capri Motor Hotel
992 101St St
• North Battleford • S9A 2Z6
306.445.9425

Super 8 Motel
Hwy 16
• North Battleford • S9A 3W2
306.446.8888

Raylen Motel
522 McKenzie St Box 400
• Outlook • S0L 2N0
306.867.8661

Red Wheel Motel
509 Saskatchewan Ave E Box 613
• Outlook • S0L 2N0
306.867.8374

Ponteix Motor Inn
120 Centre St Box 697
• Ponteix • S0N 1Z0
306.625.3501

Journeys End Motel
3863 2nd Ave W
• Prince Albert • S6W 1A1
800.668.4200

Marlboro Inn
67 13th St E
• Prince Albert • S6V 1C7
800.661.7666

Prince Albert Inn
3680 2nd Ave W
• Prince Albert • S6V 5G2
306.922.5000

South Hill Inn
3245 2nd Ave W
• Prince Albert • S6V 5G1
306.922.1333

Best Western
777 Albert St
• Regina • S4R 2P6
306.757.0121

Comfort Inn
3221 E Eastgate Dr
• Regina • S4Z 1A4
800.221.2222

Country Inn & Suites
3321 Eastgate Bay
• Regina • S4Z 1A4
800.456.4000
small

Howard Johnson
1717 Victoria Ave
• Regina • S4P 0P9
306.569.4656

Imperial 400 Motel
4255 Albert St S
• Regina • S4S 3R6
306.584.8800

Relax Inn
1110 E Victoria Ave
• Regina • S4N 7A9
800.667.3529

Relax Inn
4025 Albert St
• Regina • S4S 3R6
800.667.3529

Siesta Motel
641 Victoria Ave E
• Regina • S4N 0P1
306.525.8142

Super 8 Motel
2730 Victoria Ave E
• Regina • S4N 6M5
306.789.8833
$10

Travelodge
1110 Victoria Ave
• Regina • S4N 7A9
306.565.0455

Best Western
1715 Idylwyld Dr N
• Saskatoon • S7L 1B4
800.528.1234

Comfort Inn
2155 Northridge Dr
• Saskatoon • S7L 6X6
800.221.2222
small

Country Inn & Suites
617 Cynthia St
• Saskatoon • S7L 6B7
800.456.4000
small

Holiday Inn
90 22nd St E
• Saskatoon • S7K 3X6
800.465.4329

Imperial 400 Motel
610 Idylwyld Dr N
• Saskatoon • S7L 0Z2
306.244.2901

Ramada Hotel
90 22nd St E
• Saskatoon • S7K 3X6
306.244.2311

Ramada Renaissance Hotel
405 20th St E
• Saskatoon • S7K 6X6
800.268.9889

Relax Inn
102 Cardinal Cres
• Saskatoon • S7L 6H6
800.667.3529

Sheraton Cavalier
612 Spadina Cres E
• Saskatoon • S7K 3G9
800.325.3535

427

Best Western
105 George St W
● Swift Current ● S9H 0K4
306.773.4660

Comfort Inn
1510 Service Rd
● Swift Current ● S9H 3X6
800.221.2222

Friendship Inn
160 Begg St W
● Swift Current ● S9H 0K4
800.424.4777

Imperial 400 Motel
1150 Begg St E
● Swift Current ● S9H 3X6
306.773.2033
small

Rodeway Inn
1200 Begg St E
● Swift Current ● S9H 3X6
306.773.4664
small

Countryside Inn
Hwy 3
● Tisdale ● S0E 1T0
306.873.5603

Tisdale Hotel
1001 100th Ave Box 1748
● Tisdale ● S0E 1T0
306.873.2134

Viscount Hotel
306 Amhurst Ave Box 68
● Viscount ● S0K 4M0
306.944.4262

Circle 6 Motel
140 Sims Ave
● Weyburn ● S4H 2H5
306.842.4528

El Rancho Motel
53 Government Rd S
● Weyburn ● S4H 2A2
306.842.1411

Weyburn Inn
5 Government Rd
● Weyburn ● S4H 0N8
306.842.6543

Holiday Inn
100 Broadway
● Yorkton ● S3N 2V6
800.667.1585

Imperial 400 Motel
207 Broadway E
● Yorkton ● S3N 2V6
306.783.6581

YUKON

Fort Yukon Hotel
2163 2nd Ave
● Whitehorse ● Y1A 3T7
403.667.2595

Regina Hotel
102 Wood St
● Whitehorse ● Y1A 2E3
403.667.7801

Town & Mtn Hotel
401 Main St
● Whitehorse ● Y1A 2B6
403.668.7644
$10/night

Yukon Inn
4220 4th Ave
● Whitehorse ● Y1A 1K1
800.661.0454

ACCOMMODATIONS IN MEXICO

Rules for Successful Pet Travel

We do not encourage travel with pets in Mexico. However, we realize that there are times when you may choose to do so, such as extended work assignments.

You will need a veterinarian-signed Pet Health Certificate for Dogs and Cats. This certificate provides a description of your pet and verifies required vaccinations, such as rabies and distemper. The certificate requires a visit to your vet within 30 days of travel. Consult the Mexican Consulate in the U.S. if you have any special questions.

The US requires the same valid certificate for reentry of your pets. Restrictions may apply for stays over 30 days and may require quarantine to reenter the US. Pets, Wildlife and U.S. Customs, an informative booklet, can be obtained at any U.S. Customs Office or from U.S. Customs, PO Box# 7407, Washington, D.C. 20044 Consult a Mexican consulate for regulations concerning all other animals, as some may not be allowed across the border.

There are many ABKA kennels listed in this directory in border cities such as El Paso, Laredo, Brownsville and Tucson. You may wish to consider boarding your pet in the U.S. while you travel in Mexico.

BC
Casa Del Sol (US$55)
1001 Ave Lopez Mateos
● Ensenada ● (22800)
617/8-1570
small only

Rancho Sereno B&B
(US$45)
W of Hwy 1
● San Quintin ● (gendelvry)
9099827087
designated rooms

BCS
Club El Morro (US$40)
Blvd Alberto Aramburro
● La Paz ● (23010)
112/2-4084
designated rms only

Melia Cabo Beach Resort
(US$185)
KM 19.5 Carretera Tranpen
● San Jose Del Cabo ●
(23400)
114/4-0000

CHI
Lodge at Creel (US$80)
Ave Lopez Mateo 61
● Creel ● (33200)
145-60071

Margaritas Plaza (US$40)
Elefido Batista
● Creel ● (33200)
145/6-0245

COA
Camino Real Hotel (US$75)
Mex 57, Box 55
● Saltillo ● (25000)
84/30-0000

DF
Internacional Havre (US$60)
Havre 21
● Mexico City ● (06600)
5/211-0082
pets by prior arrangment

Jardin Amazonas (US$45)
Rio Amazonas 73
● Mexico City ● (06500)
5/533-5950

Radisson Paraiso (US$150)
Cuspide 53
● Mexico City ● (14020)
5/606-4211
small pets only

Ramada (US$80)
Blvd Puerto Aereo 502
● Mexico City ● (15500)
5/785-8522
in certain rooms

GTO

Mi Casa B & B (US$65)
Canal 58 APDO 496
● San Miguel De Allende ●
(37700)
415/2-2492

Motel La Siesta (US$28)
Mex 49, Box 72
● San Miguel De Allende ●
(37700)
415/2-0207

JAL

La Nueva Posada (US$50)
Donato Guerra 9, Box 30
● Ajijic ● (3766-1444)
376/6-1344

NL

Ancira Radisson Plaza
(US$110)
Plaza Hidalgo, Box 697
● Monterrey ● (64000)
8/345-1060
small pets only

Crowne Plaza Holiday Inn
(US$188)
Constitution 300 Ote
● Monterrey ● (64000)
8/319-6000

SIN

Motel Los Arcos (US$55)
Rodolfo Loaiza 214
● Mazatlan ● (82110)
69/13-5066
small only

SLP

Hotel Valles (US$40)
Blvd N 36
● Ciudad Valles ● (79050)
138/2-0050

Motel El Dorado (US$20)
Mex, 57, Box 78700
● Matehuala ● (78700)
488/2-0174

Holiday Inn (US$85)
Mex 57, Box F-1893
● San Luis Potosi ● (78090)
48/18-1312

SON

Casa De Los Tesoros
(US$65)
Calle A Obregon 10
● Alamos ● (85760)
642/8-0010

Casa Encantada (US$70)
Ave Juarez 20
● Alamos ● (85763)
642/8-0482

Hotel La Mansion (US$50)
Calle Obregon 2
● Alamos ● (85763)
642/8-0021

La Hacienda Perico (US$50)
2 De Abril
● Alamos ● (85763)
642/8-0045

TMP

Camino Real Motel (US$55)
Ave Hidalgo 2000
● Tampico ● (89140)
12/13-8811

KENNEL INFORMATION AT MAJOR TOURIST ATTRACTIONS

You shouldn't have any problem with petcare at many of the tourist attractions across the nation. Many have on-site kennels or have made arrangements with nearby kennels to accommodate their visitor's pets. However you MUST call ahead to reserve space especially during busy times.

Always remember to bring your pet's health certificate and proof of kennel cough and rabies vaccinations. Reputable kennels will not board pets without these and to avoid exposure to contagious conditions, you will not want to board your pet in a kennel that does not require them.

Listed below in alphabetical state order are the attractions that either have on-site kennels or refer to kennels nearby. This information was supplied by the parks and is subject to change. So always call ahead to avoid disappointment and to **RESERVE** space.

Grand Canyon National Park South Rim Village, Grand Canyon National Park

(602) 638-2631
Pets are permitted in the park but are not permitted on the trails below the rim. Pets can be kenneled in the South Rim Village for a daily fee.

Disneyland 1313 Harbor Blvd. Anaheim, CA 92803 (714) 999-4565 For a daily fee, an on site pet care center available.

Knott's Berry Farm 8039 Beach Blvd., Box 5002, Buena Park CA 90620 (714) 827-1776 No on-site pet care available but they will refer you to nearby kennels.

San Diego Zoo, Zoological Society of San Diego, Box 551, San Diego, CA, 92112 Pets are not permitted in the zoo but they will refer you to nearby kennels.

Sea World, 1720 S. Shores Rd., San Diego, CA 92109 (619) 222-6363 Pets are not permitted but they will refer you to nearby kennels.

Universal Studios Hollywood, 100 Universal City Plaza, Universal City, CA 91608 (818) 622-3801 Kennels available.

Six Flags Magic Mountain, Box 5500, Valencia, CA, 91355 (805) 255-4100 Your pet can stay free in the on-site kennel.

Weeki Wachee Spring & Buccaneer Bay, PO Box 97, Brookville, FL 34605 (352) 596-2062 kennels available.

Busch Gardens, 3605 Bougainvillea, Tampa FL, 33674, (813) 987- 5082 For a fee your pet can stay in the on-site kennel.

Universal Studios Florida, 1000 Universal Studios Plaza, Orlando, FL 32819 (407) 363-8000 kennels available.

Silver Springs & Wild Waters, PO Box 370, Silver Springs, FL 32688 (352) 236-2121 Kennels available.

Cypress Gardens, Winter Haven, FL, 34787 (941) 324-2111 For a fee your pet can stay in the on-site kennel.

Kennedy Space Center, Cape Canaveral, FL 32920 On-site kennel available at no charge.

Walt Disney World, Box 10000, Lake Buena Vista, FL 32830-1000, (407) 824-2222 For a daily fee, an on site pet care center is available.

Six Flags Over Georgia, 7561 Six Flags Pkwy, Mapleton, GA 30378 (770) 739-3400 A fee is charged at their Park-a-Pet Kennel.

Six Flags Great America, Grand Ave., Gurnee, IL 60031 (847) 249-1776. A fee is charged at the kennel.

Holiday World, PO Box 179, Santa Claus, IN 47579, (800) GO-SANTA, (812) 937-4401. Kennels available.

Six Flags Over Mid-America, 1-44 & Allenton, Eureka, MO 63025 (314) 938-5300 Free kennels are available on-site.

Worlds of Fun, 4545 Worlds of Fun Ave., Kansas City, MO 64161, (816) 454-4545 Free kennels are available on-site.

Six Flags Great Adventure, Box 120, Route 537, Jackson, NJ 08527 (908) 928-2000 Free kennels are available on-site.

Carlsbad Caverns National Park, 31 Carlsbad Hwy., White City, NM 88268 (505) 785-2291 or 1- (800) CAVERNS
A fee is charged to stay in their facilities.

Cedar Point, Sandusky, OH (419) 626-8006 $6 charge for your pet to stay at Pet Check.

Kings Island, 6300 Kings Island Dr., Kings Island, OH 45034 (513) 241-5600 On-site pet care available.

Sea World of Ohio, 1100 Sea World Dr., Aurora, OH 44202 (216) 562-8101 No on-site kennel. Nearby kennel's number is (216) 562-7011.

Hersheypark, 100 W. Hersheypark Dr., Hershey, PA 17033 (717) 534-3900 On-site kennels available.

Dollywood, 700 Dollywood Lane, Pidgeon Forge.
TN 37863 (423) 428-9488
Pets are permitted in the park if they are leashed.
Because the park is all paved however, their paws may
get hot. Dollywood has an arrangement with a kennel
a half mile away. The "Loving Care Kennels" will
come to the gate to pick up your pet.

Opryland USA, 2802 Opryland Dr., Nashville, TN,
37214 (615) 889-6700 A fee is charged at the kennel.

Six Flags Over Texas, 2201 Road to Six Flags, Arlington, TX 76010 (817) 640-8900 Your pet can stay in
their kennel for $6/day.

Sea World of Texas, 10500 Sea World Drive, San
Antonio, TX 78251, (800) 722-2762 ,
(210) 523-6311.

Kings Dominion, 1-95 & Routes 30, Doswell, VA
23047 (804) 876-5000 A $2 fee is charged for your pet
to stay in their on-site kennels.

Busch Gardens, 7901 Pocahontas Trail, Williamsburg,
VA, 23185, (804) 253-3350.

TIPS FOR BOARDING S.U.C.C.E.S.S.

There is no reason to fear kenneling your pet, BUT, you must make the time to plan and prepare for Boarding **S.U.C.C.E.S.S.** Remember to make your reservations early! And, before you commit to a particular kennel, be sure that you go in for an inspection. Discuss things such as their boarding rates, policies, agreements or contracts, location of nearby veterinarians, hours-of-operation and so forth. The following points will help you to prepare for boarding.

Safety/Security

The kennel must be well-maintained with sturdy fencing to prevent pets from escaping. Be sure to let the kennel know if your pet has a tendency toward jumping, climbing, or digging its way out of confined situations so extra precautions can be taken.

Unhealthy

Does the kennel require "proof of immunization" and "health certificates" before admitting pets? Without proof you run the risk of boarding your pet with other animals who are not immunized. Also ask if they have a method of controlling fleas and ticks, such as a pre-entry exam. Find out about access to veterinary service. Some have on-site services, others will use your pet's regular vet. If your pet needs medication, some kennels won't take pets who require a lot of medication and special attention.

Cuisine

Check to make sure each pet has its own container of clean drinking water which is changed frequently throughout the day. Ask the kennel what their policy is on supplying food. Some provide food. Others require that you bring your pet's food. If your pet is choosey, be sure to provide their regular food.

Clean/Comfortable

The kennels should look and smell neat and clean. Fecal debris and dirt should be cleaned up regularly and there should be a set schedule of chemical disinfection to combat parasites and odors.

Be sure the kennel can maintain a temperature that will be comfortable for your pet and that is has a good ventilation system. Air conditioning is a must in some areas. And, good ventilation helps to cut down on the spread of bacteria and viruses.

Exercise

If you are boarding a dog, make sure it has space to run and that the exercise area has protection from the wind, rain, snow and sun. Also, find out how frequently your dog will be exercised to determine if it will be adequate for your dog's needs.

While cats don't need "exercise areas" per se, be sure your cat's enclosure is roomy enough to permit movement and stretching and that the litter box is cleaned regularly.

Supervision

Find out how many times your pet will be checked and petted throughout the day. Be sure the personnel are well trained in handling pets and are able to spot signs of distress and able to determine when pets need veterinary attention.

Sleeping

Be sure cages are large enough for your pet to move around in comfortably. Determine whether the kennel provides bedding or if you'll need to bring your own, and whether they restrict what you bring. Being able to leave a familiar item from home, like a blanket or article of clothing, can help your pet feel more comfortable.

If you have additional questions about choosing the right boarding kennel for your pet, you can call or write:

American Boarding Kennel Association
4575 Galley Road, Suite 400A
Colorado Springs, CO 80915
(719) 591-1113

ALABAMA
Oporto Pet Hotel
Birmgham 205.836.5229

Pet Lodge
Birngham 205.823.5473

Hi Cotton Knls
Clanton205.755.7011

Waggy Tail
Daphne 334.626.2259

Kountry K-9 Knls
Hope Hull 334.288.6933

Brding Ark Pet Resort
Millbrook 334.285.5557

Copeland's Pet Motel
Mobile 334.661.5021

Harvard's K-9 Center
Opelika 334.298.0414

Kirsten's Dog Training
Toney 205.828.9006

ALASKA
Rabbit Creek Knls
Anchorage 907.345.1152

ARIZONA
Canine Country Club
Cottonwd 520.639.1624

Cinder Hills Brdg Knl
Flagstaff 602.526.3812

Fred Harvey Knl
Grand Cyn 602.638.2631

Scales' Arizona Brdg
Hereford 520.366.5578

Pet Resort&Hotel
Lk Havasu 520.855.2888

Applewood Knls
ParadiseVly602.596.1190

AAA Companion Care
Phoenix 602.244.8171

Ace Knls
Phoenix 602.894.0494

PetsTowne Resort
Scottsdale602.488.0948

Raintree Pet Resort
Scottsdale 602.991.3371

Bark 'N Purr Pet Care
Sedona 602.282.4108

Sun City Anml Hospital
Sun City 602.974.3691

University Brding
Tempe 602.968.9275

Creature Comforts
Tucson 520.792.4500

Sabino Cnyon Pet Resort
Tucson 602.290.8181

Triple Crown Dog Acdmy
Tucson 520.760.0150

Wiseman Hosp./ Knl
Tucson 520.296.2388

ARKANSAS
Lancaster Doggie Ranch
Hot Spring 501.767.8867

Fairview Knls
Little Rock 501.225.1391

Timberlane Pet Motel
Mtn Home 501.425.3227

Russellville Anml Clinic
Russellville 501.967.7777

CALIFORNIA
Stonewall Retrievers
Acampo 209.366.2816

My Little Cat House
Arroyo Grd 805.481.0238

McKays Lazy Daze Knl
Bakersfield 805.399.2180

Four Paws Inn
Banning 909.349.1462

Bonita Brding Knl
Bonita 619.475.3850

L'Amoreaux's Pet Resort
Brentwood 510.516.0754

Seacrest Knls
Carlsbad 619.438.2469

K-9 Dog Ranch
Carpinteria 805.684.3223

Canine Spa
Cathedral 619.328.0876

Country Cattery
Cedar Rdg 916.477.1003

Meridian Knls
Chico 916.343.4551

Breton's Dogs&Cats
Danville 510.736.6231

Glennroe Knls
Danville 510.837.4077

Airport Knl Inn
El Segundo310.322.6506

Duckpond Knls
Elk Grove 916.456.5683

Amy's Pet Care
Encinitas 619.942.0714

Anml Keeper
Encinitas 619.753.9366

Holiday Pet Hotel
Encinitas 619.753.6754

Anml Care Cntr
Escondido 619.747.4100

Dog House
Exeter 209.592.6354

Regency Pet Hotel
Fontana 909.829.0626

Elaine's Anml Inn
Fresno 209.227.5959

Anml Inns Of America
Garden Grv714.636.4455

Highland Labradors
Gustine 209.854.3855

Hayward Pet Complex
Hayward 510.886.1522

Dog Lodge
La Habra 310.691.1152

Waiterock Knls
Lafayette 510.284.4729

A.J. Country Knls
Lemoore 209.582.5108

Knl Kare
Long Bch 562.597.9587

Camp Best Friends
LA 310.473.8585

Knl Club of So. Calif
LA 310.338.9166

Lori's Love Em Pets
Mariposa 209.966.4818

Farrington Knls
Martinez 510.228.6288

Pet Bazaar
Midway 714.892.5008

Cat's Nest Brdg
Milpitas 408.262.5498

Nat'l. Inst. of Dog Trng.
MontereyPk818.571.4900

SidRose Knls
Moorpark 805.523.0325

American Canine Knl
Mtn View 415.964.4422

Aloha Brding
Murphys 209.736.6989

Clip&Snip Knls
Murrieta 909.677.6031

Silverado Brding
Napa 707.224.7970

Porter Pet Hospital
Northridge 818.349.8387

Postmore Knls
Novato 415.897.5892

Anml Keeper
Oceanside 619.941.3221

Oceanside Knl
619.757.2345

Inglis Pet Hotel
Oxnard 805.647.1990

Pacific Palisades Vet ctr
Pac Pal 310.573.7707

CA

Shamrock Ranch Knl
Pacifica 415.359.1627

Buffs Pets N' More
Palm Desert
619.346.8511

Pleasanton Pet Hotel
Pleasanton 510.484.3030

Dogwood Pet Ranch
Prunedale 408.663.3647

Helen WoodwardAn Ctr
Rancho Santa Fe
619.756.4117

Country-Aire Pet Resort
Redding 916.549.3335

Classic Knls
Roseville 916.771.0202

O'Briens Brdg
Roseville 916.991.3007

Peninsula Pet Resort
San Carlos 415.592.2441

Best Friends Pet Resort
San Diego 619.565.8455

Fon Jon Knls
San Diego 619.273.2266

Happy Pets Inn
San Fran 415.584.8370

Aspen Glen Knls
San Martin 408.683.2163

Je Neill Knls
Santa Clara408.988.3118

Capitola Knls
Santa Cruz408 462.0784

Santa Cruz Anml Care
Santa Cruz408.475.1580

Sea Breeze Knls
Snta Maria 805.925.2825

Bayside Knls
Santa Rosa707.578.8196

Shiloh Knls
Santa Rosa707.584.9115

Springdale Knls
Saratoga 408.281.1965

West Valley Pet Lodge
Saratoga 408.379.6820

Pet Resort
Sepulveda 818.891.4472

Balcom Canyon Pet Ldg
Somis 805.523.7076

Aberglen Knls
Sonoma 707.938.2657

Ronakers Knls
Sonoma 707.938.1173

Spring Crk Knl&Cattery
Spring Vly 619.463.1722

Mission Gate Knls
Stanton 714.527.0422

Happiness Cntry Knls
Sunol 510.657.7753

Knl Club Resort/Spa
Torrance 310.539.2201

Gln-Be's Pet Motel
29 Palms 619.362.5154

Pampered Pets
Vacaville 707.453.1995

Canine Castle
Vista 619.726.2068

CeCe Belle Pet Hotel
Vista 619.758.7322

Canonwyck Knls
Walnut Crk 510.934.4090

North Main Pet Lodge
Walnut Crk 510.256.0646

Westlake Pet Motel
WestlakeVlg805.497.8669

Don O'Brien Knls
Wilton 916.687.8638

Granite Bay Pet Resort
Wilton 916.687.8001

Country Care Pet Resort
YorbaLinda714.985.1330

Vinjon's Knl
YorbaLinda714.528.8734

Hi Dez Knls
Yucca Valley 619.365.3111

COLORADO
Terroux Training Knl
Arvada 303.424.7703

Tenaker Knl&Vet.
Aurora 303.366.2376

Cottonwood Knls
Boulder 303.442.2602

Dry Crk Anml Hosp/Knl
Broomfield 303.469.7387

Shady Greenhorn Knl
Colo. City 719.676.3437

NorthwestAnml Hosp
Colo. Spgs 719.593.8582

Countryside Knl
Colo Spgs 719.495.3678

Top Hat Knl
Conifer 303.838.4147

SoutheastArea Vet Med
Denver 303.751.4954

Doggy Day Camp
Englewd 303.680.4001

Wingate Knls
Englewd 303.771.8620

Grand Paw's Knl
Falcon 718.683.3887

Andelt's Pet Motel
Ft Collins 970.484.5776

Land of Ahs Knl
Fountain 917.382.1126

Cntry Squire Pet Resort
Ft. Collins 970.484.3082

Critter Sitters&Outfitters
Gunnison 970.641.0460

The Greater Dog&Cats
Littleton 303.791.4525

Creature Comforts Pet
Loveland 970.669.2084

Pet Lodge
Monument 719.488.2500

Silveracres Knl
Morrison 303.697.4479

Star Brding Knl
Sedalia 303.688.8569

Pet Village
Wheat Rdg303.422.2055

CONNECTICUT
Ansonia Pet Resort
Ansonia 203.735.5454

Keystone Knls
Bethany 203.393.3126

Marta's Vineyard Resort
Brookfield 203.775.4404

Roaring Brook Knls
Canton 860.693.0603

Cromwell Knls
Cromwel 203.635.2984

Oronoque Knl
Derby 203.735.3624

New Inn Knls
E. Haddam 860.873.8149

Pet Palace
E.Hartford 860.289.7585

Harlan Ridge Knl
Eastford 203.974.0256

Sand RoadAnml Hosp
Falls Vlg 203.824.5223

Candlewick Knls
Glastonbury 860.633.6878

Lone Pine Knl
Greenwich 203.661.4739

Maple Ridge Knls
Groton 860.445.4999

Connecticut Valley Dog
Meriden 203.237.6499

Pieper-Olson Bet
Middletwn 203.347.1122

Snowflake Pet Care
Milford 203.878.3117

Merryall Knls
New Milford860.355.2732

Cassio Knls
Newtown 203.426.2881

Silver Trails Anml Inn
N.Stonington203.599.1784

Best Friends Pet Resort
Norwalk 203.846.6730

Best Friends Pet Resort
Norwalk 203.846.3360

Norwichtown Brdg
Norwich 203.822.6342

Hemlock Trails Brdg
Old Lyme 203.434.2771

Severn/Brodny Knls
Pomfret Ctr860.928.3978

Wayfarer Knl
Portland 860.342.1067

Prospect Brding
Prospect 203.758.4405

Brding House
S. Norwalk 203.866.2383

Bark Inn Knl
Stafford Spgs 203.684.7436

Holiday Pet Lodge .
Wallingford 203.269.4222

Canine College
W. Redding203.938.2124

Silver Trails Anml Inn
Westbrook 860.399.7673

Winding Way Lodging
Westbrook 860.399.7572

Knl Schulhof
Westport 203.226.0781

Town House Dogs &Cats
Westport 203.227.3276

Day Hill Knls
Windsor 203.688.2370

DELAWARE
Home Away From Home
Lewes 302.684.8576

Never Never Land Knl
Lewes 302.645.6140

Kirkwood Anml Brdg
Newark 302.738.1738

Branch Oaks Knl
RehbothBch 302.227.8268

Heavenly Hound Hotel
Selbyville 302.436.2926

Anml Inn .
Smyrna 302.653.5560

Wilmington An Hospital
Wilmgton 302.762.2694

Windcrest AnHospital
Wilmgton 302.998.2995

FLORIDA
Greenbrier Knl
Apopka 407.886.2620

ABCD Knl
Belleview 352.245.9410

Sleepy Hollow Brding
Belleview 352.245.9500

Chateau du Chien
Bradenton 941.746.5060

Anml Acres Pet Resort
Brooksville 352.796.4715

B-Well Knls
Brooksville 520.799.6002

For Fours Acres
Brooksville 352.796.2441

Sweet 'N Lo Pet Motel
Brooksville 352.796.7788

Gulf Bay Pet Resort
Clearwater 813.797.6688

V.I.P. Knls
Daytona Bch 904.756.2313

Shady Lane Knls
Ft Walton Bch 904.862.7432

Bobbi's World Knls
Ft Lauderdale 954.491.8189

Holly Acres Knl
Ft Lauderdale 954.434.1535

Hollydogs .
Hollywood 305.925.7758

El Saba Knls
Homestead 305.248.8013

Creature Comforts Pet
Resort
Jacksonville 904.389.9008

Bass Knls
Kissimmee 407.396.6031

EPCOT Knl
Lk BuenaVista 407.939.3746

Ft. Wilderness Knl
Lk BuenaVista 407.939.3746

Hideaway Knls
Lk Wales 813.676.1987

Lake Worth Anl Hospital
Lk Worth 521.582.3364

Anml House
Lantana 407.439.2246

Paradise Pet Motel
Largo 813.581.6831

Driftwood Brding
Laurel 941.485.6672

J D P Knl
Lecanto 352.746.3302

Magic Kingdom Knl
Lk BuenaVista 407.939.3746

MGM Studios Knl
Lk BuenaVista 407.939.3746

Eau Gallie Vet Hosp
Melbourne 407.259.8492

A Country Cat House
Miami 305.279.9770

Brower Knl
N. Ft Myers 941.656.4433

Collier Pet Care
Naples 941.643.5808

Anml Inn
New PtRichey 813.847.7480

Kritter Knls .
Niceville 904.678.6121

Canine Estates .
Palm Bay 305.723.3703

Just Like Home Knl
Palm City 561.220.2239

Parkway Pet Hotel
Panama City 904.763.8387

Rogue's Run Knls
Pensacola 904.477.1425

Home Alone Pet Palace
Plantation 954.584.6261

Pompano Pet Lodge
Pompano Bch 954.972.5584

Dog House
Pompano Bch 954.941.9391

Adorable Dogs Brding&Grmg
Punta Gorda 941.637.9888

A Country Cat House
Riverview 813.654.2287

Oakhurst Knls
Seminole 813.397.8844

Four Paws Brdg
Spring Hill 352.596.5607

Suncoast Knls .
Spring Hill 813.857.0300

Happy Dog Inn
St. Augustine 904.446.8443

Kellogg's Knl
St Petersburg 813.526.5507

Pasadena Pet Motel
St Petersburg 813.345.2852

Sunrise Knl Club
Sunrise 305.748.1900

Air Anml Hosp.
Tampa 813.879.3210

Holiday Pet Inn
Tampa 813.289.9214

Whyte House
Tampa 813.664.9820

Anml Inn Pet Resort
Tarpon Spgs 813.942.3691

Lake-Land Knls
Umatilla 352.669.6960

Almost Home Pet Resort
Valrico 813.654.1166

Anml Inn Of Palm Beaches
W. Palm Bch 561.833.3303

Ed's Pet Motel
Winter Haven 941.293.0295

Little Wolfe's Pet Resort
Winter Haven 941.293.7327

GEORGIA
Four Paws Inn
Albany 912.883.1618

Atlanta Pet Resort
Alpharetta 770.475.4656

Alpharetta Pet
770.475.9220

Pet Lodge
Alpharetta 770.475.3455

Alpha Academy
Atlanta 404.874.5224

Buckwood Pet Hotel
Atlanta 404.351.3246

Atlanta Dogworks
Ball Grnd 404.592.9916

Back Acre Knls
Boston 912.498.7321

Hog Mountain Pet Resort
Dacula 770.932.4977

Indian Shoals Pet Resort
Dacula 770.995.9123

North Hall Knls .
Dahlonega 770.535.7829

Cloud 9 Pet Resort
Ellenwood 404.981.9512

Professional Brdg Knl
Ft. Oglethorpe 706.866.8228

Reigning Cats&Dogs
Ft. Oglethorpe 706.858.0362

Mountain Vu Pet Lodge
Jasper 706.692.6604

Kennesaw Pet Center
Kennesaw 770.428.5454

Brookside Knl .
Lawrencevl 770.962.1117

Bay Creek Knls
Loganville 404.466.8944

AA Pet Resort
Marietta 770.977.5542

Mont Royal Knl
Monroe 770.464.4188

The Dog House Knl
Newnan 770.253.7234

Bremer Bet Clinic
Savannah 912.897.3300

Camelot Knls
Stone Mtn 770.469.9533

Winding Creek Knls
Winder 770.725.2700

HAWAII
Bar-King Dog Knl
Keaau 808.966.8733

IDAHO
ADA Brding Knl
Boise 208.362.5288

We Care Knls
Idaho Falls 208.524.7287

Sun Valley Anml Center
Ketchum 208.726.7777

Gem Crest Knls
Meridian 208.375.4398

ILLINOIS
Heidanes Hidden Timbers
Altamont 618.483.5179

Twyneff Knls
Antioch 847.395.0554

Apolda Knls
Aurora 708.898.2947

Barrington Brding Knls
Barrington 847.381.6009

Rowens Knls
Brighton 618.372.3837

Bel-Kon Knl
Darien 630.968.2406

Lynnwood Knls
Davis Jct 815.645.8585

Countryside Pet Motel
Dekalb 815.758.3074

Allikats Country Dog Inn
Dunlap 309.243.7130

Brewster Creek Knls
Elgin 708.697.1525

Country Lane Pet Lodge
Freeport 815.232.3915

Timber Hill Knl
Freeport 815.235.8999

Carriage Hill Knls
Glenview 708.724.0270

Tanglewood Knl
Glenview 708.724.2282

Casey Road Pet Motel
Grayslake 847.362.3567

Kountry Knls
Hampshire 847.741.5434

Bark 'N' Town Knls
Ingleside 815.385.0632

Lake Forest Knl
Lake Forest 708.234.3120

Cha/Dai Pet Care
Lincoln 217.732.1529

Cindy's Critter Camp
Maryville 618.344.4096

Topono Pet Resort
Momence 815.472.6836

Naperville Kountry Knls
Naperville 708.983.6656

Nat'l Dog&Cat Hotel
Northbrook 847.824.4455

Preiser Brding Knl
Northbrook 708.827.5200

Green Meadow Knls
Oak Brook 708.968.3343

Kibbles N Klips
Olney 618.869.2642

Top Notch Knls
Oswego 708.554.9001

Anml Ark
Palos Heights 708.448.4275

King Knls
Riverwoods 708.945.9592

Airport Pet Lodge
Rockford 815.397.4597

Country Lane Knls
Rockford 815.885.3622

Tail Waggers Pet Chateau
Savoy 217.359.4212

Dal Acres Bding Knl
Springfield 217.522.1047

Tanglewood Knls
St. Charles 630.365.2388

Doggone Grming/Brding
St. Jacob 618.644.5823

Poochi's
Steger 708.747.7074

Countryside Anml Clinic
Streator 815.672.4576

Paw Print Knl
W. Chicago 630.231.1117

Frisco Knls
Zion 708.746.2849

INDIANA
Spring Valley Knls
Anderson 317.643.8444

Canine Companion
Bloomington 812.331.0665

Wayport Knls
Bloomington 812.876.2098

Best Friends Pet Resort
Carmel 317.848.7387

Belmar Farms Knls
Columbus 812.376.3858

Windy Hill Pet Ranch
Crawfordsvl 317.362.3239

Windsong Pet Care
Elkhart 219.262.2019

Beverly's Precious Pets
Fishers 317.842.1647

Sojourn Knl
Fishers 317.849.4446

Sleepy Hollow Pet Ranch
Indianapolis 317.787.8040

Petsburgh/Paw Prints Anml
Hosp
Lafayette 317.423.5500

Anml Den
Lebanon 317.769.5948

Top Dog Brding
Manilla 317.525.6484

Pet Pals
Michigan City 219.879.2898

Hurstacres Knl
Muncie 317.284.0903

Klondike Knls
W. Lafayette 317.463.1603

IOWA
Avondale Pet Resort
Des Moines 515.262.7297

Vista Knls
Des Moines 515.262.0309

A+ Brding Knl
Eldridge 319.285.9977

Mite-Win-Knls
Mason City 515.423.4851

KANSAS
High Halo Knls .
Goddard 316.794.2203

Knl Crest
Lawrence 913.887.6230

Morning Star Pet Care
Lawrence 913.842.9979

Majesty Knls
Leavenworth 913.683.4160

Mission Pet Mart
Mission 913.362.9573

Kathy's Kanine boarding
Pittsburg 316.232.1710

L D'S Knl
Valley Ctr 316.755.4054

Chisholm Creek Knls
Wichita 316.744.0191

KENTUCKY
Almost Home Pet Resort
Covington 606.356.8181

Sundance Knls
Independence 606.356.7900

Keshlyn Knls
Lexington 606.272.4412

Sheabel Knl
Lexington 606.269.6377

Dogwood Knls
Louisville 502.245.9740

Minirosa Knls
Louisville 502.499.1910

Royalton Knls
Louisville 502.239.0827

Vine Crest Knls
Louisville 502.425.5145

All Creatures' Inn
Nicholasville 606.233.9000

Andick Knls
Richmond 606.527.3893

Joyland Knl
Union 606.371.2043

Companion Knls
Verona 606.485.6432

Woodford Vet. Clinic/Knl
Versailles 606.873.1595

Canine Companion Brdg
Walton 606.356.6457

LOUISIANA
Alexandria Pet Inn
Alexandria 318.445.7333

K-9 Security
Lafayette 318.232.3952

All Creatures Cntry Club
Mandeville 504.626.9664

Good Going Pet Resort
Mooringsport 318.929.2435

MAINE
Carden Knls
Bangor 207.942.2161

Green Acres Knl
Bangor 207.945.6841

Jacamar Knl
Bangor 207.848.5613

Acadia Woods Knl
Bar Harbor 207.288.9766

G&S Pet Services
Benton 207.453.9490

Safe Harbor Knl
Bremen 207.529.4127

Bear Brook Knl
Brewer 207.989.7979

Cedarosen Knl
Cornville 207.474.6691

Haggett Hill Knls
Edgecomb 207.882.6709

Downeast Brding
Ellsworth 207.667.3062

Fairfield Knls
Fairfield 207.465.7801

Creature Comforts
Kittery 207.439.6674

Aussie-Magic Knl
Leeds 207.524.3835

Lewiston Bet
Lewiston 207.782.8121

Deb's Barnyard
New Glouchester
207.926.3037

Pussy's Port O'Call
Northport 207.338.6050

Clover Acres
Windham 207.892.6108

York Country Knls
York 207.363.7950

MARYLAND
Oak Park Knls
Baltimore 410.242.8735

Fieldstone Knl
Berlin 301.647.6516

Country Lane Pet Camp
Bethesda 301.365.7510

Rivermist Knls .
Brinklow 301.774.3100

Linda's Dog Design
Brookville 301.977.2873

Happy Run Knl
Chestertown 410.778.5158

Preston Ctry Club Pets
Columbia 301.596.7387

Happy Tails Pet Resort
Crownsville 410.923.1131

Captain's Quarters Pets
Elkton 410.398.8320

Potomac Knls .
Gaithersbg 301.948.2202

Anml Chalet
Germantwn 301.540.5931

Germantown Pet
Germantwn 301.972.9730

Pets Vacationland
Hagerstwn 301.797.4147

Bed&Bones
Highland 301.854.9761

Riviera Brding Knls
Hughesvill 301.274.4456

Cherry Lane Knls .
Laurel 800.233.6093

Pet Salon
Millersvill 410.647.3505

Tamira Knls
Millersvill 301.987.4535

Belquest Knls
Mt. Airy 301.831.7507

Country Knl
Mt. Airy 301.831.7766

TedJoi Knls
Mt. Airy 301.829.0152

Countryside Knls .
Owings 301.855.8308

Deer Park Knls
Owings Mills 410.655.8330

Tricrown Inn For Pets
Oxford 410.822.1921

El Taro Knls
Poolesville 301.428.8091

Lipsitt Trng/Sugarland Knls
Poolesville 301.428.8300

Wonmore Knl
Port Deposit 301.658.4919

Canine Country Club
Queenstown 410.827.4245

Wye River Knl
Queenstown 410.827.9474

Debendale Knls
Reisterstown 410.833.4762

Reisterstown Brding
Reisterstown 410.833.2090

Carol's Pet Brdg
Rockville 301.340.2547

Pet Dominion
Rockville 301.258.0333

Doghouse
Salisbury 800.644.4380

Columbia Knls
Seabrook 301.577.1090

Interlude
St. Leonard 410.586.1843

Country Comfort Knls
Street 410.692.5055

Pinewood Knls
Sudlersville 410.758.2942

Rhapsody Acres Knls
Temple Hills 301.449.3720

Dog&Cat Hotel .
Towson 410.825.8880

Precious Pup Knls
Upr Marlboro 301.952.0318

QueenAnne Knls
Upr Marlboro 301.249.1210

Happy Tracks Brdg
Waldorf 301.893.0028

Amberlyn Knl
Walkersville 301.898.3106

Happy Hollow Knl
Westminster 410.876.1235

Shady Spring Brdg Knls
Woodbine 410.795.1957

MASSACHUSETTS
Palmer Knls
Acton 508.263.4979

Pet Quarters
Ashland 508.881.7557

Fox Run Knl
Barre 508.355.6800

Shady Glen Brding
Belchertown 413.323.7349

Petcetera Knls
Belmont 617.484.6133

Skipton Knl
Boston 617.442.0747

Weloset Knls
Boxford 508.887.5760

Holiday Knls
Brockton 508.583.8555

Rover Room
Cambridge 617.441.8646

Sutter Creek Knl .
Chartley 508.222.4752

Cohasset Knl
Cohasset 617.383.1475

Wignall Anml Hospital
Dracut 508.454.8272

Greengate Knls
Duxbury 617.837.5125

Cloverleaf Knl
Cape Cod 508.540.7387

Porter Road Pet Care
E. Longmdw 413.525.3532

Anml Inn .
Forestdale 508.477.0990

Hickory Hill Knl
Gill 413.863.9753

Valley Inn For Pets
Hadley 413.584.1223

Harvard Knls
Harvard 508.772.4242

Family Bet Center
Haydenville 413.268.8387
Canine College
Holbrook 617.767.3908

Pampered Cats
Manomet 508.224.7085

Red Dog Inn
Mansfield 508.339.5912

Tee Emm's Knls
Methuen 508.683.5795

Rufco Knls
Millbury 508.791.2145

Natick Anml Clinic
Natick 508.653.5020

Northborough Knls
Northbrough 508.393.6040

Lake Farm Brding
Orleans 508.255.7214

Hospice Knl
Oxford 508.987.2927

Muddy Creek Care Cntr
Rowley 508.948.2345

Ramson Knl
Salisbury 508.388.0826

Wintergreen Knls
Southampton 413.562.9478

Southboro Knls
Southboro 508.485.5136
Champion Knls
Sterling 508.422.3100

Blue Moon Knl
Stockbridge 413.274.6674

Great Scott Knl
Stoughton 617.344.2581

Cape Cod Farm Knls
Barnstable 508.428.2322

Fairlawn Knls
Wakefield 617.245.1237

Continental Shoppe
W. Roxbury 617.323.9511

Ven-Elger Pet Care Center
Westport 508.636.8143

Woburn Anl Hosp/
Ledgebrook Knl
Woburn 617.933.0170

MARYLAND
Anchors
Accokeek 301.283.2626

Arnold Pet Station .
Arnold 410.544.1130

MICHIGAN
Arbor Hills Pet Care/Trng Ctr
Ann Arbor 313.475.2296

Copper Country Pet Srvc
Calumet 906.337.1111

Halliday's Knls
Canton 313.397.8899

Pet Club
Charlevoix 616.582.6800

Kamber Knls
Clinton 810.792.3000

Brady Knls
Fowlerville 517.223.3939

Windy Acres Knls
Freeland 517.695.5994

Double 'B' Knls
Gaylord 517.732.5766

Anml Inn
Gwinn 906.346.5945

Bay Pines Brding
Harbor Spg 616.347.1383

Caraway Knls
Haslett 517.655.4178

Hill's Knls
Ironwood 906.932.5810

Hallas Doghouse Acres
Jackson 517.529.9305

Woodland Vet Clinic
Kentwood 616.942.6780

Orion Knl Club
Lake Orion 810.391.4200

Wag'n Tails Pet Motel
Lansing 517.482.7799

Belle Creek Knls
Livonia 313.421.1144

Fruit Hill Farm Assoc.
Livonia 313.462.0588

Wingford Knl
Marysville 810.385.5335

Whistle Lake Pet Resort
Metamora 810.678.3159

Country Knl Pet Care
Milan 313.429.2375

Wayback Knl
Montrose 810.639.7776

Bittersweet Pet Resort
Niles 616.684.7361

Shady Oaks Farm
Niles 616.683.7387

Springfield Pet Resort/Trng
North Street 810.385.7007

Common Scents Canine Ctr
Ortonville 810.627.2929

Birch Haven Knl
Ottawa Lake 313.856.6858

Eve's Groom 'N Room
Paw Paw 616.657.3463

Blue Water Brding Knls
Port Huron 810.984.2330

Deb's Knl
Portland 517.647.4951

Rockford 616.866.2294

Bill Wells Knls
Romulus 313.721.2329

AAA Dog&Cat Motel
Taylor 313.946.5555

Classic Canine
Traverse City 616.946.3646

Rexpointe Knls .
Troy 248.879.0940

Union Lake Pet Services
Waterford 810.363.6262

Anml Medical Cntr/Wyoming
Wyoming 616.531.7387

MINNESOTA
Pet Watchers' Brding Knl
Austin 507.433.4950

American Brding Knls
Burnsville 612.894.5100

Diamond Paradise Pet
Styling
Chisago City 612.257.2466

White Buck Farm
Glencoe 320.864.6342

Northcote Brding
Hallock 218.843.3516

Anml Inn Brding Knl
Lake Elmo 612.777.0255

Dog House Brding Knls .
Long Lake 612.473.9026

Maplewood Care Brding
Maplew'd 612.770.8373

Cathy's Pet Care
Moose Lake 218.485.8170

Oak Ridge Knls
Mound 612.472.3702

Lake Shady Knls
Oronoco 507.367.4782

Plymouth Heights Pet Hosp
Plymouth 612.544.4141

Paw Prints Pet Care
Red Wing 612.388.2729

K-9 Knls .
Rochester 507.289.2470

Pensinger's Bluff High
Savage 612.890.6010

Jan's Doghouse .
St. Cloud 612.253.7555

Silver Dog Bed&Biscuit
St. Paul 612.455.1558

Goldwood Knls
White Bear 612.429.0648

Fancy Coats Pet Grmg&Inn
Willmar 612.382.6270

Mar-Lar Brding Knls
Winona 507.457.0310

Lone Lake Knls .
Woodbury 612.459.2234

Camp Comfort Knl
Wyoming 612.462.4614

MISSISSIPPI
Lamay's Knl
Bay St. Louis 601.467.5281

Butler's Brding Knl
Biloxi 601.388.4093

Town&Country Brding
Gulfport 601.832.7188

Whispering Pines
Gulfport 601.831.3566

Okatoma All Breed Brdg Knl
Hattiesburg 601.582.4153

Pet's Night Out
Madison 601.856.5242

Bienville Anml Medical Cntr
Ocean Springs 601.872.1231

MISSOURI
Master Canine
Branson 417.335.6800

Petropolis
Chesterfield 314.537.2322

Ann Gafke's Teacher's Pet
Columbia 573.443.0716

Fenwick Knl
Columbia 314.657.6100

Pet Fair
Columbia 314.445.7783

Sorenson Knl
Defiance 314.828.5149

Hideaway Knl
Harrisonville 816.380.5387

Serenity Acres Farm Knl
Harrisonville 816.380.6196

Dog House .
High Ridge 314.677.3131

Nancy Crane Pet Care
High Ridge 314.343.2182

Imperial Anml Hosp. .
Imperial 314.464.0777

Honey Creek Pet Brding
Jefferson City 573.496.3138

Country Knls
Kansas City 816.353.5675

Country Lane Knl
Kansas City 816.322.6666

Red Bridge Hideaway Knl
Kansas City 816.942.6800

Country Acres
Manchester 314.227.1919

Country Lane Knl
St. Charles 314.447.4488

Pet Tender's Brding Knl
St. Clair 314.629.3413

Knlwood Village .
St. Louis 314.429.2100

Silver Maple Farm
St. Louis 314.965.1630

MONTANA
Guardian Knls
Clancy 406.443.1117

Carol's Knls&Dog Grmg
Glendive 406.687.3745

F&L Pet Resort
Great Falls 406.452.6828

Grooming Room&Doggy
Daycare
Havre 406.265.9646

AnimaLodge/Laurel
Laurel 406.628.4683

NEBRASKA
Hilltop Pet Clinic
Kearney 308.236.5912

Kenl Inn
Lincoln 402.488.8190

Clearview Pet Care Centre
Omaha 402.493.5151

NEVADA
Paws 'N Claws Anml Lodge
Henderson 702.565.7297

Anml Inn/Am.Anml Services
Las Vegas 702.736.0036

Canine Country Club
Minden 702.267.2251

Chaparral Anml Spa
Las Vegas 702.649.6383

NEW HAMPSHIRE
Auburn Groom&Brd
Auburn 603.668.8551

Country Road Knls&Trng
Cntr
Brentwood 603.772.4049

Village Sentry Knl
Hollis 603.465.7553

Littleton Pet Center&Knl
Littleton 603.444.6285

Sendaishi Pet Resort
Manchester 603.622.9684

State Line Bet Hospital
Nashua 603.888.2751

Upwind Farms
New Durham 603.859.4171

Bittersweet Knls
Newfields 603.772.5453

Marcoda-Chantur Pet Knl
N. Hampton 603.964.8514

Saddleback Pet Services
Northwood 603.942.5988

Stillwater Knls
Rochester 603.335.6424

Woodlawn Knl
Warner 603.746.4201

Crosshaven Knl
W. Swanzey 603.352.8809

Cherry Mountain Knl
Whitefield 603.837.2448

NEW JERSEY
Northcliff Knls
Andover 201.786.5250

Lyndell Knls
Annandale 908.730.8977

Beth&Kens Pet Hotel
Atco 609.753.7744

Bed&Biscuit Inn
Belle Mead 908.874.7748

Bernardsville Country Knls
Bernardsville 908.766.3929

Hope's Knls
Blairstown 908.459.5380

Cedarview Knl
Bridgeton 609.451.0350

Hal Wheeler's Sch For Dogs
Cedar Grove 201.256.0694

Best Friends Pet Resort
Cinnaminson 609.611.0707

Knls At Columbus
Columbus 609.298.4600

Cream Ridge Pet Care Cntr
Cream Ridge 609.758.7777

T. Blumig Knls
E Brunswick 908.251.3210

Hi-Crest Knls
Edison 908.561.7098

Mansion House Knls
Fredon 201.579.1476

Pet Country Club
Frenchtown 908.996.7200

Willow Run Knls
Frenchtown 908.782.7218

Hay Hill Knls
Green Brook 908.968.2265

Highland Knls
Howell 908.364.4443

Knl Club
Iselin 908.283.2110

Lake Hopatcong Knls
LkHopatcong 201.663.1111

Top Dog Trng/Puppy Day
Care
Lanoka Hbr 609.971.9669

Whitehouse Knls
Lebanon 908.534.2444

Anml Inn Pet Hotel
Ledgewood 201.691.2662

Country Knl
Lindenwold 609.784.4559

Falkenturm Knls
Livingston 201.992.6194

Kountry Knls K-9 Resort
Montague 201.948.0624

Allen's Knl .
Moorestown 609.235.0196

Morris Anml Inn
Morristown 201.539.0377

A-1Knls
Randolph 201.442.1112

Somers Point Knls
Somers Pt 609.927.5118

Woodland Knls
Sussex 201.875.3908

Purr 'N Pooch .
Tinton Falls 908.842.4949

Lotta LuvAnml Lodge
Vineland 609.696.4965

Roxdane Knls .
Warren 908.755.0227

Kauffman Knls .
Windsor 609.448.3114

NEW MEXICO
Academy Brding Knls
Albuquerque 505.884.7878

Canine Country Club
Albuquerque 505.898.0725

Luv N' Care
Albuquerque 505.255.8749

Capitan Knls
Capitan 505.354.2509

Valley Pet Lodge and Salon
Farmington 505.326.2237

Coyote Knls
Roswell 505.622.0004

Best Friends
Santa Fe 505.471.6140

Paw Print Knls
Santa Fe 505.471.7194

Santa Fe Cats
Santa Fe 505.983.8573

NEW YORK
Pinekroff Knls
Allegany 716.372.0961

Windsong Farms Pet Brding
Auburn 315.252.5241

Shield Crest Knl
Ballston Spa 518.885.1738

Northwood Knls .
Bedford 914.234.3771

Locust Grove Knls
Bloomfield 716.657.6249

Pet Barbers
Brooklyn 718.258.2342

Woofs 'N Whiskers
Brooklyn 718.237.0298

Camillus Hills Pet Lodge
Camillus 315.672.5154

Timber Ridge Knls
Campbell Hall 914.427.9925

Wyeland Knl
Carthage 315.493.1886

Evergreen Knls
Churchville 716.293.1920

Windy Knoll Knls
Collins 716.532.4194

Blue Jay Knls
Corning 607.524.6603

Willow Pet Hotel
Deer Park 516.667.8924

Kliffside Knl
Eagle Bay 315.357.3607

Delta Pond Knl
East Nassau 518.766.5103

Valley View Knl
Elmira 607.734.8160

Pet Pleasers
Fishkill 914.896.2133

Anml Inn
Glen Cove 516.759.2662

Whispering Pines Brdg Knl
Glenfield 315.376.8349

Reigning Cats And Dogs
Glenmont 518.432.1030

Heatherstone Knls
Grand Isld 716.773.4296

Balmoral Knls
Harrison 914.967.1721

Add-En-On Knls
Honeoye Falls 716.624.1155

Country Acres Knls
Huntington Stn 516.427.6077

Bed and Biscuit
Ithaca 607.277.3481

Club Pet
Lk Katrine 914.336.5893

Cedar Brook Knls
Lansing 607.533.4535

Cathy's Clip &Brdg
Massena 315.764.1273

Dakola Knls&Cattery
Middletown 914.342.2005

Rock Ridge Knls
Monticello 914.791.7444

Lohr's "Country" Brding
Munnsville 315.495.5781

Bihari Knls
Nanuet 914.356.1658

Pet Superette II
New York 212.534.1732

Run Spot .
New York 212.996.6666

Sutton Dog Parlour
New York 212.355.2850

We Kare Knls .
New York 212.567.2100

Hudson Valley Pet Resort
Newburgh 914.566.0469

Northport Brding Knl
Northport 516.754.0566

Schaffer Knls
N Tonawanda 716.694.6070

Eagle Ridge Brdg Knl
Orchard Park 716.662.5302

Cedar Hill Knls
Palmyra 315.597.6552

Paumanok Bet Hosp.P.C.
Patchogue 516.475.1312

Saint C. Knls
Portville 716.933.6218

Uhrbabe Knls Ltd
Port Crane 607.648.3883

Almost Home Knls
Putnam Vly 914.528.3000

R&R Knls
Rome 315.337.2344

Liberty Canine Care Center
Round Lake 518.899.5098

Rye Country Brdg Knls .
Rye 914.967.4577

Emerald Acres Pet Motel
Schenectady 518.355.1749

Country Estate Knls
Staten Island718.356.3933

Rondout Valley Knls
Stone Ridge 914.687.7619

New Hartford Anml Hosp/
Care
Washington Mills
315.737.7387

Reigning Dogs&Cats
Waterloo 315.539.4003

Eagle Hill Pet Care
Westmoland 315.853.8523

Stonybrook Knls
White Plains 914.946.0961

NORTH CAROLINA
Apex Anml Care Center
Apex 919.362.1123

Green Level Knl
Apex 919.362.7877

Town&Country Anml Care
Ctr
Apex 919.387.7833

Avery Creek Knl
Arden 704.684.2161

Pet's Companion Inn
Bahama 919.477.0618

Greenwood Pet Motel
Bolivia 800.569.6970

Granbar Knls
Charlotte 704.596.8941

Horky's Paws Inn
Charlotte 704.399.1609

Sunnybrook Knls
Concord 704.788.8800

Shady Grove Knl
Durham 919.596.0235

Haus Schura Knl
Fayetteville 910.425.1774

Hideaway Hills Knl
Flat Rock 704.685.3149

Redmond Knls
Fletcher 704.684.9938

River Ridge Bed&Biscuit
Franklin 704.524.0700

Hatteras Island Pet Resort
Frisco 919.995.5476

Beechline Knls
Greensboro 919.855.8292

Best Friends Bed&Biscuit
Greensboro 910.643.9096

Guil-Rand Pet Inn
High Point 910.885.8129

Horse Shoe Knls
Horse Shoe 704.891.3705

Four Seasons Pet Care
Jacksonville 919.347.5298

Salty Dog Grooming&Brding
Kill Devil Hills 919.441.6501

Wilkinson Anml Hospital
Lowell 704.824.9876

Anml Knl Care
Matthews 704.545.5192

Bed And Bone
Mebane 919.563.4756

Cedar Creek Knl
Mocksville 910.940.3740

V.I.P. Knl
Monroe 704.289.1659

Kustom Kare Knl
Morganton 704.438.4126

Lynaire Knls
New Bern 919.633.4333

Custom K-9
Oxford 919.492.4500

Country Side Brdg Knl
Pfafftown 910.945.9321

Armadale Farm Knl
Raleigh 919.847.0389

Pinebrook Knls
Raleigh 919.851.1554

Reidsville Bet Hospital
Reidsville 910.349.3194

Wishingwell Farm Knl
Rocky Mount 919.442.9474

Riverbend Knls
Sanford 919.499.2233

Creature Comforts/W.
Carolina
Waynesville704.452.0160

Rahama Knl and Cattery
Waynesville704.452.2176

Arbor Creek Knls
Weaverville704.645.7775

All Creatures Great&Small
Whiteville 910.640.1909

Sylvia's Pet Care Center
Wilmington 910.799.2375

Briarwood Knl
Winston Salem 919.769.2649

Legacy Brdng Knls
Winston Salem 910.764.1828

Almost Home Brdg&Grmg
Knl
Winston-Salem
910.377.2160

Groomingdales/A Cut Above
Winston-Salem
910.768.3645

Hoffman-Haus Knls
Winterville 919.355.4663

NORTH DAKOTA
Lunn's Knl Club
Bismarck 701.222.1056

Fargo Brdg&Grmg Svc
Fargo 701.282.0197

Dakota Hunting Club&Knl
Grand Forks 701.775.2074

Crown Butte Knls
Mandan 701.663.6141

OHIO

Doggie Depot
Alliance 216.823.8866

Hayden Run Knls
Amlin 614.876.7974

Pearl's TLC Brding Knl
Beaver 614.226.2116

Pine Meadow Knl
Bristolville 330.889.9944

Anml Ark Pet Resort
Cincinnati 513.825.7387

Blue Ridge Knl
Cincinnati 513.528.0382

Breezy Acres Knls
Cincinnati 513.474.2222

Briarwood Pet Motel
Cincinnati 513.489.6300

Country Cottage Knl
Cincinnati 513.574.7960

Tail Waggers Trng&Dog Care
Columbus 614.794.0568

Balmorhea Knls
Dayton 513.233.2577

Big Times Knl .
Dayton 513.885.3427

Paws Inn Anml Hospital
Dayton 937.435.1500

Torok Knls
Dayton 513.233.6281

Oakshadows Knl Plus
Dover 216.343.7233

Findlay Anml Care Center
Findlay 419.423.4445

Puppy Love Brdg Knl/Cattery
Hartville 330.877.8877

Pine View Knls
Hoytville 419.278.7145

Chalet Knl
Hudson 216.656.2823

Home Away From Home Knl
Huntsville 513.686.6365

Tannenberg Knls
Kettering 513.293.9233

Mentor TLC Pet Lodge
Mentor 216.975.9789

Colonial Acres Knl .
Middletown 513.777.2266

Pineland Farm Knls
Milford 513.575.4000

Country Lane Brding Knls
Moscow 513.553.4513

Promway Knls
North Canton 216.494.8100

Kenilridge Knl&Kattery
N. Ridgeville 216.327.8281

Pet Holiday Knls
Northwood 419.691.7201

Braemar Brding Knls
Norwalk 419.668.4073

Brown Woof Inn
Painesville 216.254.4676

Country Knl
Plymouth 419.687.8880

Ohio Valley Knls
Reno 614.374.5373

Benchmark Pet Services
Reynoldsbg 614.866.9738

Paws Awhile Knl&Grmg
Richfield 216.659.9450

Rushville Brding Knl
Rushville 614.536.7007

Country-Side Brding Knl
Sidney 513.492.7199

Neal Knls
Springfield 513.324.3205

Sunshine Knls
Union 513.836.1244

Karnik Inn Of Waterville
Waterville 419.878.9796

OKLAHOMA
Moore Pet Center
Duncan 405.255.6051

Delmar Smith Knls
Edmond 405.478.1171

Cedar Acres Knl
Enid 405.233.6706

Four Paws Rooming
Grove 918.786.3402

Country Knl Bed&Biskit
Guthrie 405.340.4454

Redwind Knls
Norman 405.329.9129

Anne's Country Club for Pets
Oklahoma City 405.478.2303

Best Friends Pet Resort
Oklahoma City 405.751.1944

DeShane Knls
Tulsa 918.437.3343

Woodland West Brdg&Grmg
Tulsa 918.299.5720

OREGON
Claymore Waggin' Inn
Alvadore 541.688.3260

Albany Anml Bed 'n' Beauty
Albany 541.926.9351

Cooper Mountain Knls
Beaverton 503.649.4956

Forest Glen Knl .
Beaverton 503.590.2300

Bend Pet Resort
Bend 541.388.0435

Ranch Knls
Bend 541.382.3634

Grand Rond Valley Brdg Knl
Cove 541.963.7927

Oak Tree School For Dogs
Eagle Pt 541.830.8800

Klassic Tails Inn
Elmira 503.935.1180

Countryside Pet Spa
Gresham 503.663.3370

Hammond Knls
Hammond 503.861.1601

Rock Creek Knls .
Hillsboro 503.645.2912

Double-C Dog Training
Klamath Falls 541.882.5959

LaPine Pet Bed and Bath
LaPine 503.536.2907

Fletcher's Knls .
Portland 503.761.2091

Nottingham/Cheyenne
Portland 503.257.3752

Townhouse Pet Care Center
Portland 503.230.9596

Pampered Pets
Prineville 541.416.1653

Pet Village LTD.
Salem 503.363.3647

Archer's Brding Knls
Sherwood 503.639.2343

Von Shambis Knl
Sutherlin 541.459.1302

PENNSYLVANIA
Honeybrook Knl
Aliquippa 412.375.0192

Groomingdale's Country Knls
Allison Park 412.443.8989

Holzland Knls
Ashland 717.875.6355

Critter Sitters
Benton 717.925.2284

Bernville Bet Pet Spa
Bernvile 610.488.0166

Bucks County Pet Care
Buckingham 215.794.0423

Whispering Winds Brdg Knl
Butler 412.789.7672

Anml Inn
Carlisle 717.243.4250

Country-Aire Knls
Carlisle 717.249.3809

Stewards Pet Resort
Chadds Ford 215.459.2724

Hickorybrook Farm Knls
Chalfont 215.348.4454

Hickory Sprgs Farm Knls Ltd
Chester Spgs 610.933.9584

Town and Country Dogs
Claysville 412.225.9035

Parkway Knls
Coraopolis 412.262.2727

Pet Care Associates .
Dallas 717.675.1621

Tender Loving Care Knls
Dauphin 717.921.2851

All Breeds Grooming&Brdg
Doylestown 215.348.7605

Holiday House Pet Resort
Doylestown 215.345.6960

Bolingbroke Knls
Edinboro 814.734.5255

Brizes Brding Knl
Elizabeth 412.384.6445

K-9 Kampus
Fogelsvill 610.285.6711

Anmls' Choice
Freedom 412.728.1484

Vir-Del Knl
GreatBend 717.879.2709

Laurel Hill Knls
Hanover 717.632.1440

Anderson's Knls
Indiana 412.349.0311

Connie Winters Knl/Stable
Indiana 412.465.6120

Fox Chase Inn Brding Knl
Johnstown 814.288.5241

Stone Ridge Knls
Lake Ariel 717.689.4244

Spotlight Knl
Lancaster 717.393.7192

Town&Country Knls
Langhorne 215.752.3661

Anml Crackers
Lansdale 215.855.8378

Molly's Run Country Knls .
Lansdale 610.584.6515

Roselynde Knls .
Lansdale 215.855.8026

Gochenauer Knls
Lititz 717.569.6151

Cloud Nine Country Knl
Macungie 610.845.7330

Hunting Hill Farm Pet Care
Malvern 610.644.7561

Brickyard Knls
Mars 412.625.1475

Kel-View Knls
Mechncsbg 717.790.9465

Mehoopany Pet Lodge
Mehoopany 717.833.2000

Grocott's Hayastan Farm Knl
Millville 717.458.5915

Country Road Knl
Moontwnship 412.264.5836

Springbrook Knls
Moscow 717.842.4502

Happy Tails Farm
Mnt Top 717.868.5082

Poochie's
Huntingdon 412.824.8440

Cat's Meow Cattery
New Alexandria
412.668.0002

Tree-Berri Farms Brdg Knls
Newville 717.249.6799

Country Lane Pet Htl Ctr
N. Versaille 412.824.7991

Ridge Crest Farm
Pennsburg 215.679.8606

World Wide Grooming
Phildlphia 215.624.7300

Golden Bone Pet Resort
Pittsburgh 412.661.7001

Hickory Bet Hospital
Plymouth Mtg 610.828.3054

Harmony Farm Knls
Pt Allegany 814.642.7167

Noah's Pet Motel
Pottstown 610.323.2206

Brierwood Brding Knl/Cattery
Pottsville 717.544.9663

Acorn Valley Pet Brding
Quakertn 215.536.5100

An Inn On Rippling Run
Sewickley 412.364.4447

Kennel
Sewickley 412.741.2407

Misty Pines Pet Care Trng
Ctr
Sewickley 412.364.4122

Oak Hill Knls
Sewickley 412.741.6421

Barmyre Knls
Shippensburg 717.532.7588

Rovin' Hollow Knls
Shoemakrville 610.926.4046

Skimeister Knls
Shrewsbury 717.235.3312

Sweda
Silver Spring 717.285.2494

Grandma's Hse For Pets
Stewartstwn 717.993.6336

Sandy Hill Knls
Valencia 412.898.2895

Graysland Knl
Waterford 814.796.2234

Warrior Run Petcare Center
Watsontwn 717.538.2393

Braxton's Anml Works
Wayne 610.688.0769

Rustic Ridge Knl
Wexford 412.935.1736

Tan-Zar Brding Knls
Wexford 412.935.2185

Dona-Shirl Pet Motel
Windber 814.487.5288

Yardley Anml Knl .
Yardley 215.493.2717

Locust Run Knls
York 717.252.2653

Meadows Pet Resort
York 717.266.7044

Ba Mar Farm Knl
Zelienple 412.452.4714

RHODE ISLAND
Ashe Pond Farm
Ashaway 401.377.2764

East Bay Knls
Bristol 401.253.0082

Delmyra Knls .
Exeter 401.294.3247

Kandy Kane Knls
Foster 401.647.2130

Mini Manor Knl .
N Kingstown 401.295.1222

Compatipup Canine Services
Tiverton 401.625.5953

SOUTH CAROLINA
Powderhouse Knls
Aiken 803.648.0779

Chapin Pet Lodge
Chapin 803.345.5082

Charleston Pet Resort
Charleston 803.763.0985

Primrose Acres
Chesnee 864.461.3003

Wag-N-Train Knl
Columbia 803.781.8825

Haywood Road Pet Motel .
Greenville 803.288.7472

Top Dog Ltd
Greenville 864.288.7282

Airport Knls
Greenwood 864.942.0040

College Park Road Brdg Knl
Ladson 803.764.0049

Palmetto Knls
Lancaster 803.285.1809

Red Barn Knl
Lexington 803.359.9045

Four Paws Pet Place
Liberty 864.843.0333

K-9 Country Club
Little Rvr 803.280.4350

Best Friends Brding
Mt Pleasant 803.856.7829

Sun-Glo Knls
N. Myrtle Bch 803.249.1263

Man's Best Friend LLC
Piedmont 864.299.0540

SanteeAnml Hospital
Santee 803.854.3351

Allcare Knl
Spartanbrg 864.579.0391

Noah's Ark Knls
Spartanbrg 803.576.0760

Westbury Pet Care Center
Summerville 803.873.2761

My Buddy Brdg. Inn For Pets
Sumpter 803.773.2501

Anml World Pet Lodge
W Columbia 803.794.9071

Deer Springs Knls
Westville 803.432.2980

SOUTH DAKOTA
Radar's Bed&Biscuit
Lennox 605.368.5123

Dakota Hills Vet. Clinic
Rapid City 605.342.7498

Pine Lake Pet Care
Sioux Falls 605.332.2151

TENNESSEE
Copyright Pet Resort
Cookeville 615.528.8007

Franklin Knls
Franklin 615.794.2333

Countryview Knls
Jackson 901.427.8585

All Kreatures Pet Care
Knoxville 423.675.0799

Groomingdales W'sdeKnl
Knoxville 615.966.1734

Claridge Knls
Memphis 901.365.3500

Pleasant View Knls
Memphis 901.386.3232

Custom Kare Knls
Murfrsbro 615.893.8959

Cuts Limited Knls
Murfrsbro 615.890.3732

Pampered Pets of Donelson
Nashville 615.889.1500

Crikett Lane
Walland 615.983.1322

TEXAS
Abilene Pet Regency ·
Abilene 915.677.7387

Ambassador Pet Resort
Austin 512.832.1012

Bed and Biscuit
Austin 512.343.0723

Canine Hilton
Austin 800.392.1021

Exmoor Knls
Austin 512.443.9393

Hill Country Knl
Austin 512.288.4696

Pet Connection
Big Spring 915.267.7387

Critter Camp
Canyon 806.655.8444

Toothacres Pet Care Center
Carrollton 214.492.3711

Anml Inn
Clodine 281.277.2727

Anml America
Colleyville 817.498.6410

Cats Aboard
Colleyville 817.577.2287

Texas Pet Bed&Breakfast
Coppr Cyn 817.241.3052

Boykin Knl
Dallas 214.330.1500

Cat Connection
Dallas 214.386.6369

First Class Prof. Pet
Services
Dallas 214.320.2902

Countryside Knls
Frisco 972.625.5420

Canine Fitness Camp
Granbury 817.573.1207

Man's Best Friend
Grd Prairie 214.988.0991

Lanehaus Knls
Harlingen 210.428.5976

Valley Pet Motel
Harlingen 512.428.5400

ABC Pet Grooming&Knls
Houston 713.444.9414

Bubbles&Bows Pet Salon
Houston 713.462.0234

Cat's Pajamas
Houston 713.558.2287

Ean's Pet .
Houston 713.721.6945

ABKA KENNELS

Pet Hotel
Houston 713.664.6111

Shadow Rock Pet Resort
Houston 713.280.0682

Spring Branch Pet Knl
Houston 713.465.2816

TLC Regency Knls
Houston 713.464.9852

Atascocita Brdg/Grmg
Humble 713.852.7387

All Pets Anml. Hosp./ Cuddly
Canine
Katy 281.579.7083

Katy 713.392.7373

Roomin 'N' Groomin
Killeen 817.634.8076

Happy Pets Cottage
LeagueCity 281.332.0130

Sea Dog Inn
League City 713.554.2068

Foster Ranch Knls
Los Fresno 210.233.5553

Anml Keepers
McAllen 210.686.4196

Cottondale Knls
Richmond 281.342.8407

Pecan Grove Knl
Richmond 281.342.7946

Knl Kare
Roanoke 817.379.0737

J.D. Knls
Royse City 214.636.9494

Green Heron&Co Anm Lodge
San Angelo 915.651.1323

Best Friends Pet Resort
San Antonio 210.822.0003

Char-Rich Knl
SanAntonio210.494.5334

Northport Knls
SanAntonio210.822.1425

Rob Cary Pet Resort
SanAntonio210.494.7787

Candyland Farm
Spring 713.320.1187

Elkin Knls
Spring 713.353.4835

Lexington Blvd Anml Hos
SugarLand 713.980.3737

Holiday Pet Hotel
Tomball 713.351.5441

Quail Creek Knl
Waco 817.662.5620

Clearlake Knls
Webster 281.332.4870

Wimberley Valley Knl
Wimberley 512.847.3990

TLC Knls
Winters 915.767.3822

UTAH
Don's Pet Care
Ogden 801.393.5143

Pet Care
Ogden 801.479.3000

Willow Creek Pet Center
Sandy 801.942.0777

VERMONT
Middlebury Brdg&Grmg
Middlebry 802.388.9643

Deja Vu Knls
Milton 802.893.4124

Tavern Hill Pet Care Cntr
Putney 802.387.5073

Doggie Daycare
Williston 802.860.1144

VIRGINIA
Woodlawn Knl
Alexandria 703.360.6161

Suncrest Knls
Amherst 804.277.5916

Locust Grove Brding Knl
Amissville 703.937.3511

Yopaka Knls
Ashland 804.798.8248

Deja Vu Knl
Bealeton 540.439.3416

Clarke's Country Knl
Burnpass 540.872.3928

Club Pet International
Chantilly 703.471.7818

Pleasant Valley Knl
Chantilly 703.471.9617

Pampered Pets Boutique
Charltsville 804.973.7387

Dominion Knls
Chesapeak 757.547.5922

Las Gaviotas Pet Hotel
Chesapeak 757.548.0049

Alpha Knls
Culpeper 540.825.1247

Mountain Run Knl
Culpeper 540.547.2961

Danville Pet Lodge
Danville 804.836.1245

Dulles Pet Center
Dulles 703.709.1111

Cedarcrest Anml Clinic
Fishrsvill 703.943.7599

Calypso Brding Knls .
Fredrkbrg 703.720.0050

Dog House/Kee Rocka Knl
Fredrkbrg 540.898.7560

Pathfinder Knls
Fredrkbrg 540.786.2005

Commonwealth Knl Ltd
Glen Allen 804.360.2065

Holiday Barn Pet Hotels
Glen Allen 804.672.2200

Armistead Anml Inn
Hampton 804.723.8571

Puppy Luv
Harrisnbrg 540.833.6901

Blue Ridge Knls
Lynchburg 804.237.5777

Lake Jackson Knls
Manassas 703.361.7550

PetCentre Brding
Manassas 703.368.9241

Great Falls Brdg Knls
McLean 703.759.2620

Old Dominion Anml Hosp
McLean 703.893.2441

Fursman Knls
Middlebrg 703.687.6990

Broughton's Knl
Midlothian 804.794.6923

Midlothian Anml Clinic
Midlothian 804.794.2099

Anml Lovers
Mineral 804.747.0229

Pet Styles
Tazewell 540.988.8014

Eastern Shore Anml Hosp.
Painter 804.442.3150

Countryside Knl
Powhatan 804.794.8702

Holiday Barn Pet Hotel
Richmond 804.794.5400

Aberdeen Acres Pet Ctr.
Stephenson540.667.7809

Crest Hill Anml Inn
Troutville 540.992.3950

Bayside Knls
Virginia Bch 804.499.7697

Owl Creek Pet Hotel
Virginia Bch 804.425.5349

Anml Clinic
Williamsburg 757.253.0812

WASHINGTON
Creature Comforts Knl
Auburn 206.833.5177

Plush Pooch
Bellingham 360.676.0430

Tails-A-Waggin Dog Inn
Bothell 206.481.3214

Fairinall Knls
Bremerton 360.830.4427

Jee Jac Knls
Burlington 360.757.0520

Pantara Pet Care Center
Centralia 360.736.4460

Longview Kitty Inn
Coupeville 206.678.4285

Anml Inn
Friday Hbr 206.378.4735

Prison Pet Partnership .
Gig Harbor 206.858.4240

Cowlitz Anml Inn .
Kelso 360.577.1679

Happy Camp Knls
Kennewik 509.582.8244

Paran Tree Knl
Mica 509.924.8101

Devonshire Pet Lodge
Montesano 360.249.2500

TLC Brding Knl
Napavine 360.262.9195

Anml Care Center
Oak Harbor 360.675.0737

Sunset Knl
Oak Harbor360.675.7288

Peninsula Pet Lodge
Olalla 206.857.5990

Cleaner Dog
Olympia 360.866.7290

Sagemoor Knls
Pasco 509.544.9682

Aardvarks To Zebras Pet
Pt Angeles 360.452.1099

Bar-King Brding Knls
Richland 509.946.4487

Atwood's Pet Resort
Seattle 206.241.0880

Sylvan Pet Lodge
Shelton 206.426.3052

Marcinda Knls
Spokane 509.928.6662

Atwood's Pet Resort
Tacoma 206.531.0779

Pacific Ave. Bet Hosp
Tacoma 206.537.0242

Susie's Country Inn
Vancouver 360.576.5959

Kitty's Royal Court
Winlock 360.785.3088

Cascade Knls
W'dinville 206.483.9333

Paradise Pet Lodge
Woodinville 206.483.3647

WEST VIRGINIA
Camp Critter Creek
Charleston 304.345.8944

Shamrock Stables Brdgl
Charleston 304.744.1101

Tender Loving Pet Care
Gerrardstwn304.229.2222

Brackenbriar Knls .
Kearneysville304.725.0554

Greensburg Bed&Biscuit
Martinsburg304.263.4485

Mountaineer Pet Care
Morgantown 304.296.1677

Winding Rd. Brding Knl
Parkersburg 304.428.3518

Blue Diamond Knls
S Ch'leston304.768.7181

Windamere Facility
St. Marys 304.684.1090

WISCONSIN
Ker-Mor Knls
Belgium 414.994.4523

All Aboard Knl
Big Bend 414.662.2323

4-Paws Brding Knl
Blair 608.989.9083

Circle C Sommer Camp
Bristol 414.857.7353

Anml Motel
Butler 414.781.5200

Bryerlane Pet Resort
Caledonia 414.835.2444

Critter Sitters
Chilton 414.439.1849

Best Friends Pet Care
Dodgeville 608.935.7573

Kenlyn Knls
Edgerton 608.884.8355

Calico Knls
Egg Harbor414.868.3804

Mecca Knls
Elk Mound 715.874.6863

Countryaire Knls .
Germantown414.242.3154

Golrusk Pet Care Center
Green Bay 414.468.7956

Timberlawn Pet Care Center
Hayward 715.634.8712

Cedar Creek Pet Resort
Jackson 414.677.4500

Loving Paws Pet Salon
Kenosha 414.652.4643

Shel-Ray Pet Shalet
Kenosha 414.857.2163

Camp K-9 Pet Care Ctr
Madison 608.249.3939

Clay Banks Knls
Manitowoc 414.758.2666

Barking Spot
Marinette 715.732.4023

Pet Clips&More
Menomonie 715.235.8669

Allens Pet Lodge
Middleton 608.831.8000

Puppy Lodge/Pet Lawn
Cemetery
Milwaukee 414.353.9387

Barkshire Pet Care Center
Neenah 414.729.6382

Cherokee Knls
Oregon 608.835.5250

Dog House&Pet Center
Oshkosh 414.231.5232

Rodak Knl
Rubicon 414.542.3209

Complete Canine Care
Shawano 715.524.2838

Countryside Brding Knls
Solon Spgs 715.378.2900

Almost Home K-9 Condos
Suamico 414.434.3377

Silverwood Knl
Superior 715.398.7188

Decorah Anml Hospital
W. Bend 414.334.5551

WYOMING
Broadmoor Brding
Cheyenne 307.632.6607

PETSITTERS

Even the best traveling pets must sometimes be left behind. Until recently, when you needed to leave your pet while you traveled, your choices were to send them to a kennel or to entrust them to the care of a friend or neighbor. Since some pets don't respond well to kennels and since friends and neighbors are not always willing or able to look after pets, you now have the alternative of hiring a pet sitter.

Pet Sitting is a service that allows your pet to remain in the comfort and security of their own home and still have their needs attended to while you are away. Typically a petsitter comes to your home and can provide a number of services during an average 30-45 minute visit.

Naturally, these mainly include feeding and watering your pet and then walking or playing with your pet. Additionally some pet sitters will bring in the mail, water plants, open and close drapes, turn lights on and off and in general give your home an occupied look. Some pets sitters will even sleep at your home though this service will cost more.

Pet sitting fees vary widely. In general, the fee for an average daytime visit of about a half hour duration will be between $10-$15. Depending on your pet's individual needs you can arrange daily, twice daily or even more frequent visits. In some cases you can even arrange live-in care.

The best way to find a reputable, reliable pet sitter is by word of mouth. Call your vet or groomer or local pet shops for recommendations. Ask your pet loving friends and neighbors. Local animal welfare organizations or the humane society might also know of local pet sitters. You can also look in the Yellow Pages under Pet Sitting or House Sitting.

It is best to select a petsitter in person. Have a sheet of information and instructions prepared prior to the interview. The instructions should outline your pet's routine including: feeding, exercising, medication and so forth. The "information sheet" should provide emergency listings of friends, neighbors, relatives, your veterinarian and the numbers where you can be reached while you are away.

Ask that the petsitter comes and visits prior to your departure so they can get to know your pet, your home and your neighborhood or the area where your pet goes for walks or play. Note whether your pet appears comfortable with the petsitter and whether the petsitter appears capable and compassionate with your pet.

Also go over your pet's routine, feeding schedule, play habits and so forth. Be as specific as possible about what your pet likes. For example, tell the petsitter where your pet is and isn't allowed in the house, what your pet is and isn't allowed to do, what your pet is afraid of, favorite toys and so forth.

Discuss how often you would like the pet sitter to visit, for how long, and what the associated fees would be. Also discuss what procedures they should follow in case of emergency. Also, ask for references. A reputable pet sitter will gladly provide them.

Following is a list of both national and regional organizations that may be able to help you find a pet sitter in your area.

NATIONAL RESOURCES

National Assn. of Pet Sitters (202) 393-3317

REGIONAL RESOURCES

Pet Sitters Assn. Southern California (714) 964-5884

Pet Sitting Referral of New Jersey (908) 706-1200

Following is a list of pet sitters from across the U.S.

ALASKA
Critter Care By Ronnie
Petersburg 907.772.3305

The Clip Joint
Petersburg 907.772.4404

ALABAMA
Domestic Tranquility
Decatur 205.350.4357

Domestic Tranquility
Florence 205.766.7177

Albrights Pet-Stg
Huntsville 205.883.4884

Pet Pals Pet Stg
Montgomery 334.272.9100

The Knl Alternative
Montgomery 334.260.8089

Kritter Kare
Pinson 205.680.9850

ARKANSAS
Creature Comforts
Farmington 501.267.3989

Kritter Keepers Plus
Fort Smith 501.646.1169

Dogwood Brdng Knls
Mena 501.394.5947

Critter Sitters
Springdale 501.361.2567

ARIZONA
Tender Loving Care
Fountain Hls 602.816.1890

Happy Paws
Mesa 602.832.3503

Neighbors & Friends
Mesa 602.844.0589

The Kitty Sitter
Mesa 602.396.5123

Pet Stg Day & Night
Phoenix 602.496.0087

Waggin Tails Pet Stg
Phoenix 602.277.3440

West Side Pet Parents
Waddell 602.935.9345

CALIFORNIA
Pampered Paws HouseStg
Agoura Hills 818.597.9347

All Seasons Pet Sitters
Alta Loma 909.944.5513

Hse Calls Pet & Home Svc
Anderson 916.357.4040

Hse Calls Pet & Home Svc
Antioch 510.778.1611

Trinidad Kanine Academy
Arcata 707.826.1511

Ursulas Pet Stg
Arroyo Grande 805.489.4630

Majestic K-9
Auburn 916.885.7264

Accipiter Knls
Bakersfield 805.845.8955

Cherry Ave Knls
Bakersfield 805.589.7313

Critter Sitters
Bakersfield 805.324.9810

Proud Pooch
Bakersfield 805.322.4542

Solano Pet Shop
Berkeley 510.525.4190

Cannon Pacific Svcs
Big Bear Lk 909.866.3284

Hometenders
Bonsall 619.728.5000

Rancho Del Rey Knls
Bonsall 619.724.0926

Theres No Pl Like Home Pet
Boulder Creek 408.338.2253

Cat Hotel
Burbank 818.845.0222

Being There Petcare
Cardiff 619.942.8880

Betty & The Beasts
Carmel 408.625.5329

Creature Comfort
Carmel 408.626.1118

Pets at Home
408.625.1338

Kenar Pet Resort
Carmichael 916.487.5221

Elite Home Svcs
Chatsworth 818.886.5837

Little Darlins
Claremont 909.625.7562

Paw Partners
Clayton 510.672.7297

Aardvark Ambulances Hybrid
Concord 510.689.1942

Wolffs Pet Stg
Concord 510.827.3262

Copper Anml Nannies
Copperopolis 209.785.4954

Critter Care
Cupertino 408.241.2416

Pet Pals
Davis 916.753.7069

Rent-A-Friend
Davis 916.758.5815

Free Flight
Del Mar 619.481.3148

Menagerie Minders In Home
Del Mar 619.481.2253

Precious Pet Home Care
Diamond Bar 909.861.6918

Pets R People Too
Diamond Spgs 916.642.2526

Heavenly Poodle
Dublin 510.828.0444

Hse Calls Pet & Home Svc
Dublin 510.828.3338

Caring Critter Companions
El Cajon 619.579.3888

Creature Cmfrt In Your Home
El Cajon 619.444.6265

Hse Sitters International
El Cajon 619.469.5700

Home Stg Svcs Bay Area
El Cerrito 510.236.4764

Piccadilly Farms
Elk Grove 916.682.3229

A Pampered Pet
Encinitas 619.436.7387

All Creatures Pet Stg Svc
Encinitas 619.753.3379

Critters Content
Encinitas 619.794.4086

Holiday Pet & Home
Encinitas 619.753.3137

Pet Cruzin Travel
Fair Oaks 916.536.9859

T L C Professional Pet Stg
Fair Oaks 916.649.0322

Furry Finned & Feathered
Fairfield 707.421.9401

On Call Svcs
Fallbrook 619.723.3445

Barbara L Shull
Fort Bragg 707.964.9651

Anml Hse
Fremont 510.792.5611

Home & Pet Companions
Fresno 209.434.7387

Caretakers Pet Stg
Galt 209.339.4186

S Bay Pet Inn
Gardena 310.515.5432

While Your Away Pet Stg
Glen Ellen 707.935.9339

Creatures Comfort
Granada Hills 818.891.1316

Happy At Home Petcare
Granite Bay 916.791.6270

Tlc Pet Svcs
Grass Valley 916.477.7387

Candys Pampered Pets
Hayward 510.581.8781

Hayward Pet Complex
Hayward 510.886.1522

Noahs Ark
Hermosa 310.318.1812

Castle Caretakers
Huntington Bh 714.374.4828

Chrissys Critter Care
Huntington Bh 714.840.7005

Claws & Paws Pet Sitting
Huntington Bh 800.274.7297

Lady N Waiting Your Prsnl
Huntington Bh 714.841.9996

The Dirty Dog Grming
Indio 619.342.9844

Creature Comfort
La Jolla 619.581.1131

La Mesa Pet Stg
La Mesa 619.698.7297

Royal Pet Stg
Lafayette 510.283.7018

Canine Care Company
Laguna Beach 714.494.0300

Mobile Pet Svcs
Laguna Beach 714.376.1540

The Dog Hse
Laguna Beach 714.494.5285

Connies Pet Stg Laguna
Laguna Niguel 714.249.8844

Phils Pet Setters
Laguna Niguel 714.249.6656

Pet Huggers
Lancaster 805.723.5683

Smart Bay
Lancaster 805.945.0035

Pet Watchers
Lodi 209.368.1134

Your Pets Pal
Lodi 209.368.3373

The Pet Spa
Los Gatos 408.379.8911

Marys Pet Stg
Martinez 510.229.2757

Specialized Home Svcs
Menlo Park 415.368.7940

Creature Comforts
Merced 209.723.2339

For Pets Sake
Mill Valley 415.456.8241

Tlc Pet Svcs
Mill Valley 415.389.8214

The Cats Nest
Milpitas 408.262.5498

Cats And Tails Sitters
Modesto 209.572.2287

Marys Petcare
Modesto 209.527.1827

Vacation Watch
Moorpark 805.523.8643

Peninsula Pet Stg
Mountain View 415.968.0603

Critter Care Pet Plnt
Newark 510.790.1845

Sitters Unltd Agcy
Newport Beach 714.650.1166

Pet Mom
Nipomo 805.489.7380

Dees Pet Stg
Norco 909.685.7749

E Bay Petcare
Oakland 510.895.1454

Classy Clips
Oceanside 619.721.1562

Wadsworths Pet Stg
Orland 916.865.7368

Home Away From Home
Pacific Grove 408.375.1215

All-Ways At Your
Palm Desert 619.776.1818

Ritzi Rover Pet Grming
Palm Desert 619.341.4133

Carin For Critters & Cottages
Palo Cedro 916.547.3887

Prds For Pets Stg & Brdng
Pasadena 818.797.6842

Quality Home Care
Placerville 916.622.6086

Pet & Home Care
Pleasant Hill 510.825.8881

Ashworth Pet Stg
Pleasanton 510.485.4915

For Pets Sake
Pollock Pines 916.644.7387

Good Dog Training School
Poway 619.748.7943

Suzzetes Ryl Knls & Grm
Prunedale 408.663.3709

Ltl Darlins
Rch Cucamonga
909.625.7562

Pet Sitters
Rch Cucamonga
909.989.7775

The Critter Sitter
Rcho Santa Fe 619.756.9635

Professional Assistant
Redondo 310.376.3772

Affordable Grming
Redwood City 415.365.1594

Hse Calls Pet & Home Svc
Redwood City 415.364.4017

Pet Connections
Redwood City 415.369.1039

Boyles At Home Pet Stg
Riverside 909.780.9495

Boyles At Home Pet Stg
Riverside 909.781.6866

We Care Pet Sitters
Rohnert Park 707.795.1230

Paws Claws & Hooves
Rolling Hills 310.833.1333

N Bay Petcare
Ross 415.456.9896

The North Connection
S Lk Tahoe 916.577.3099

Alexis Friends
Sacramento 916.689.5715

Crown & Associates
Sacramento 916.443.1500

Gladies All Breed Grming
Sacramento 916.366.0858

Lisas Housekeeping
Sacramento 916.452.5080

The Anmls Nanny
Sacramento 916.920.5304

Like Family
San Bruno 415.697.6270

K-9 Companion
San Carlos 415.595.5958

Super Scoopers
San Carlos 415.598.0706

Anything But Elephants
San Clemente 714.492.7585

Best Friends Petcare
San Diego 619.565.8455

Greens All Critter Care
San Diego 619.279.3457

Corys Pet Stg
San Diego 619.487.0993

For Pets Sake
San Diego 619.284.5656

Hse Sitters International
San Diego 619.451.1617

Pet-Tenders
San Diego 619.298.3033

Pets Best Frnd Pet Stg Svc
San Diego 619.565.9317

Point Loma Pet Sitter
San Diego 619.226.7387

Professional Pet Grming
San Diego 619.483.4680

The Pet Valet
San Diego 619.538.8577

Vickis Pampered Petcare
San Diego 619.583.0730

Wags N Whiskers Pet Svcs
San Diego 619.224.7297

Pet-Tenders
San Dimas 909.592.6979

Adrians Urban Anml
San Francisco 415.553.3966

Alpha Pet
San Francisco 415.931.7387

At Your Beckon Call
San Francisco 415.239.5520

Claws & Paws Pet Stg Svc
San Francisco 415.921.1577

Dog Walking San Fran
San Francisco 415.731.0120

Hse Calls Pet & Home Svc
San Francisco 415.387.9373

Ladies And The Tramp
San Francisco 415.923.1943

Pet Pals
San Francisco 415.334.1585

Safe At Home
San Francisco 415.665.0856

The Hometender
San Francisco 415.337.8944

The Pet Grming HQ
San Fran 415.771.1811

Top Quality Obedience
San Francisco 415.566.4141

All Dog Yard Cleanup
San Jose 408.247.7963

Calero Pet Retreat
San Jose 408.268.7171

Cats N Dogs Pet Stg
San Jose 408.267.3472

Critter Sitter
San Jose 408.972.0269

Home Alone Pet And Plant
Care
San Jose 408.379.2033

W Vly Dog Sln & Pet Stg
San Jose 408.725.0340

Paws-N-Claws
San Juan Cap 714.661.7252

Pet Sitters
San Juan Cap 714.240.4440

J Witt Creations
San Marcos 619.744.2115

Woof Waggin Tails
San Marino 800.454.woof

In Lieu Of You Pet
San Mateo 415.347.0627

Teds Pet Sitting
San Pedro 310.832.9733

Pets-R-Us
San Rafael 415.459.6090

Hse Calls Pet & Home Svc
San Ramon 510.328.0500

Grming Boutique
Sanger 209.875.1477

Aunt Susies Kingdom Care
Santa Ana 714.832.2293

The Dog Tub
Santa Cruz 408.476.1709

Creature Comforts
Santa Rosa 707.542.3133

Petcare Pro
Santa Rosa 707.838.2716

The Dog Walker-Sitter
Santa Rosa 707.538.5590

Doggie-Doo Disposal
Santee 619.449.3301

Quality Petcare
Santee 619.449.2273

Home Stg Svcs
Saratoga 408.253.5489

Ggs Pals
Sebastopol 707.824.0100

Ace Hse Stg
Sepulveda 818.894.5500

Happy Tails
Sn Luis Obisp 805.546.0587

Perfect Pet Salon
Solana Beach 619.755.3308

Helping Hands Home Svcs
Sonora 209.536.1660

Pams Grm Sln & Pet Stg
Sunnyvale 408.736.1640

Paws N Tails
Sunnyvale 408.733.7297

Pets & Plants
Tahoe City 916.583.6550

Canine Estates
Thermal 619.399.0048

WestLk Pet Motels
Thousand Oaks
805.497.8669

Gretlo Knls
Torrance 310.328.1688

Paw Partners
Torrance 310.214.3834

For Pets Sake
Tracy 209.836.8981

Critter Sitters
Tulare 209.687.1815

Paws & Claws
Turlock 209.632.9624

Love & Protection Dog Trng
Tustin 714.544.6405

Pet Nannies Pet Stg Svc
Vallejo 707.553.2608

Berube Home Petcare
Ventura 805.643.3657

Caseys In Hse Petcare
Ventura 805.647.8366

Grants Home & Critter Sitters
Ventura 805.652.2054

Most Valuable Pet
Ventura 805.648.5638

Grming By Alexis
Vista 619.724.1708

Knl Alternative
Vista 619.598.6250

Paws-A-Walking
Walnut Creek 510.934.4073

Fur-Friend-Z
Woodland 916.661.6080

Cat Stg At Home
Yorba Linda 714.692.8228

COLORADO
Homewatch International
Denver 303.758.7290

Aardvarks To Zebras Pet
Estes Park 970.586.8416

CONNECTICUT
Pet Pals
Bloomfield 860.242.5854

Mary & Wes
Bridgeport 203.374.2488

Round The Clock
Canaan 860.824.0172

Critter Sitter
Canton 860.693.1095

Noahs Ark
Canton 860.693.9551

Errands Plus Pet Stg
Danbury 203.790.9329

Critter Sitters
Darien 203.972.7173

Executive Pet Stg
Essex 860.767.0526

Just Critters
Fairfield 203.367.6878

Paws & Claws Etc
Fairfield 203.255.4787

Meadow Winds Farm
Farmington 860.677.6509

Hse Pet Plant Stg Co
New Canaan 203.966.8914

A Passion For Pets
Newtown 203.426.1644

Cassio Knls
Newtown 203.426.2881

Debbies Home & Petcare
Old Greenwich 203.698.2136

Pet Pals
Pawcatuck 860.599.2478

redacare
Stamford 203.348.4143

Robins Nest
Torrington 860.489.6795

Village Pet Spa
Wallingford 203.269.3554

No Place Like Home
Waterford 860.437.0800

Kitty Komforts
W Haven 203.937.5803

DISTRICT OF COLUMBIA
Companions Pet Shop
Washington 202.797.3663

Sit-A-Pet
Washington 202.362.8900

Zoolatry
Washington 202.547.9255

DELAWARE
Heavenly Hound Hotel
Selbyville 302.436.2926

Zoo Keeper Ltd
Wilmington 302.239.2961

FLORIDA
Claudia Pauletti
Boca Raton 561.487.3962

Tender Loving Care Pet
Boca Raton 561.750.0359

Pampered Pets Stg
Boynton Bch 561.737.7269

The Pet Nanny
Boynton Bch 561.731.1909

Chateau Du Chien Knl
Bradenton 941.746.5060

Hills Critter Care
Bradenton 941.753.9740

Loving Petcare
Bradenton 941.758.1375

Quality Petcare
Bradenton 941.748.6522

The Critter Shop
Bradenton 941.795.8150

Pets-N-Partners
Casselberry 407.699.7387

Mans Best Friend
Clearwater 813.530.7733

Steppin Out Grming Salon
Clearwater 813.572.8594

Paradise Pet Shop
Cocoa 407.636.5998

Precious Pets Pet Stg Svc
Cocoa 407.633.4099

Doggie Care
Cocoa Beach 407.784.0106

Pattis Pals
Cocoa Beach 407.783.6622

Pampered Pets Stg
Coconut Creek 954.428.4221

Critter Care
Cooper City 954.680.5815

Dawn Okelleys Canine
Design
Coral Spgs 954.804.9668

Art Art Pet Stg
Davie 954.370.7718

Avi Pet Sitters
Davie 352.587.8913

Love Your Pet
Davie 954.423.3971

A-Pet-Agree-Above
Daytona Beach
904.255.5150

Canine Communication
Deerfield Bch 954.570.3647

Deborah Yng Kritter Sitters
Deerfield Bch 954.421.4573

Kimberlys Pet Btq
Delray Beach 561.272.1303

Luv Dat Dog
Delray Beach 561.279.9300

Shamoon
Delray Beach 561.274.8688

Critter Care
Dunedin 813.738.1400

Above & Beyond Pet Grming
Edgewater 904.428.1905

Pampered Pooch
Fernandina 904.277.3075

Trishs Petcare
Flagler Beach 904.439.7527

Touch Of Class Mbl Grm S
Florida City 305.247.4555

Critter Sitter
Ft Lauder 954.523.0169

Hounds Tooth Pet Stg
Ft Lauderdale 954.563.3565

Pet Sitters
Ft Lauderdale 954.424.3415

Linda's PetStg Svc
Ft Myers 941.590.0158

Creature Care Plus
Green Cv Spgs
904.284.7912

Tyner Pet Stg
Hallandale 407.458.4639

Top Dog Brding & Train Ctr
Hudson 813.868.7514

Critter Sitters Space Coast
Ind Hbr Bch 407.773.5116

Klip N Dip
Jacksonville 904.751.3809

Odies Pet Stg
Jacksonville 904.739.2539

Pet Chauffeur
Jacksonville 904.268.7041

A Purrr-Fect Choice
Jupiter 561.743.3510

Pats Petcare
Jupiter 561.745.1704

Bass Pet Motel
Kissimmee 407.396.6031

All Anml Pet Sitters
Lakeland 941.648.5870

Clip In Time
Lakeland 941.853.2757

Lk Gibson Pet Grming Shop
Lakeland 941.859.3470

Home Bodies Pet Stg
Land O Lakes 813.996.0603

Discount Pet Stg By Pat
Largo 813.530.7301

Bravo Grming
Longwood 407.862.1481

Cntry Club Pet Wld Grm
Longwood 407.332.8000

Love Em & Leave Em Pet Sit
Longwood 407.339.7401

A Trusted Frnd Pet Stg Svc
Loxahatchee 561.793.3011

Ryl Petcare Ctr Mbl Grm
Melbourne 407.952.9918

A Country Cat Hse
Miami 305.279.9770

Coris Creative Grming
Miami 305.858.8633

Exotic Pet Sitters & Hse
Miami 305.238.4100

For Ferrets Only
Miami 305.378.8877

Ntrl Habitat Petcare Svc
Miami 305.477.1812

Pets Are People Too
Miami Bch 305.531.2431

Paws And Claws
Mims 407.267.7635

Fur Feathers & Friends
New Prt Rchy 813.376.8959

Prisco Enterprise Mgmt
New Prt Rchy 813.849.7919

Puppy Love
New Prt Rchy 813.849.7338

Karlenes Krite Kare
New Smyrna 904.426.1559

Total Petcare
N Port 941.423.0539

Neighborhood Pet Nannies
Oakland Park 954.561.0765

Beauregards Grming Salon
Orlando 407.855.2690

Critter Sitter
Orlando 407.660.2371

Helping Hands Pet Svcs
Orlando 407.296.2138

Creature Comfort
Oviedo 407.359.2198

Quality Pet
Palatka 904.329.9037

Lois M Praizner Pet Stg
Palm Bch Gdns
561.625.4253

Pga Pet Pals
Palm Bch Gdns
561.694.8099

Criter Care & Catering
Palm City 561.220.7325

Kathis Pet Motel
Panama City 904.769.1099

Naju Brding & Grming
Panama City 904.871.1785

Creighton Road All Breed
Pensacola 904.478.2032

Pines Pampered Pet Sitters
Pmbk Pines 954.436.6264

Crazy For Cats
Pompano Bch 954.785.2002

Noahs Ark Pet Stg
Pompano Beach
954.943.2578

Pet-Kare
Ponte Vedra 904.273.9000

Bryn Knls
Port Orange 904.761.3647

Reigning Cats & Dogs
Port Orange 904.760.6011

Grming Post Dog Grming
Port Richey 813.869.1993

Pet Set Grm Shp
Port Richey 813.842.6485

Wags & Whiskers
Ruskin 813.645.3644

A Pet Solution
Safety Harbor 813.725.0206

Caroles Critter Sitters
St Cloud 407.892.6366

A Mobile Grmer
Sarasota 941.924.2433

Desario Knls
Sarasota 941.379.4200

Pattys Pampered Pets
Sarasota 941.379.8927

Pampered Paws
Satellite Bch 407.777.4214

All Pets-Sitters
St Petersburg 813.343.1964

Dog Gone Purrfect Petcare
St Pete 813.522.8506

Fins Feathers & Fur
St Petersburg 813.327.1835

Rent-A-Hand
St Petersburg 813.347.3424

Wags N Whiskers Pet Stg
St Petersburg 813.367.5453

Bay Area Prof Svcs
Tampa 813.985.1619

K 9 Educl Train Ctr
Tampa 813.881.0770

Pets @ Home
Tampa 813.973.4397

The Whyte Hse
Tampa 813.664.9820

Home Pet Watch
Valrico 813.654.7387

Blunks Pet
Venice 941.497.7458

Caring Hands Svcs
Vero Beach 561.589.6399

Angelic Pet Sitters
W Palm Bch 561.659.0405

Anml Inn
W Palm Bch 561.833.9228

C Cs Comfort Care
W Palm Bch 561.547.1316

Home Care For Pets
W Palm Bch 407.854.7353

Klassy Klips
W Palm Bch 561.439.6767

Pet Sitters Palm Beaches
W Palm Bch 561.965.1622

Homebodies PetStg
Winter Park 407.647.1278

Not Fur-Gotten Pet Stg
Winter Park 407.678.2443

Apple Of My Eye
Winter Spgs 407.699.8577

Knl & Grming Center
Zephyrhills 813.788.4870

GEORGIA
Crittercare
Albany 912.883.7387

Sitters For Critters
Athens 706.543.2979

Barbaras Grming
Atlanta 404.256.0129

Canine Acdmy & Playschool
Atlanta 404.875.3647

Home Sweet Home Petcare
Atlanta 770.640.6487

Our Place Or Yours Pet
Atlanta 404.248.1096

Pet Stg By Ann
Atlanta 404.897.1820

Sit-A-Spell Pet Sitters
Atlanta 770.451.8610

Best Friends Pet Stg
Augusta 706.737.3820

Herbert J Swords
Blakely 912.723.4876

Anml Friend Pet Stg
Brunswick 912.261.2456

My Little Helper
Chamblee 770.986.9847

Pet Peoples
Chamblee 770.451.3424

Pets Home Alone
Columbus 706.596.1578

Town & Country Pet Salon
Columbus 706.327.2047

Dalton Kritter-Sitters
Dalton 706.217.6940

For Your Cats Only
Decatur 404.320.9777

Oak Grove Pet Partners
Decatur 404.315.9041

Tall Tails Pet Stg
Decatur 404.286.6569

Anml Lovers Pet Stg
Doraville 770.938.1963

My Concierge
Eatonton 706.485.5620

Waterwood Knl
Fayetteville 770.461.9893

Pet Nanny
Gainesville 770.531.9920

Mare-Z-Doats
Jackson 770.775.0478

Quality Pet Companions
Kingsland 912.882.9015

Kaymis Anml Tending Svc
Loganville 770.466.6411

Precious Pups Grming
Macon 912.471.7414

Lovin Petcare
Marietta 770.426.7477

Sittin Pretty Pet Stg Svc
Marietta 770.928.3384

Tend-A-Pet
Marietta 770.977.6587

Grimes Dog Grming
Milledgeville 912.452.4188

Doggie Waggin & Kitty Cart
Pet
Powder Spgs 770.943.0301

Mayhers Professional Pet
Svc
Roswell 770.643.9925

No Pl Like Home Pet Stg
Roswell 770.640.0266

Paws & Claws Pet
Roswell 770.569.4988

Professional Anml Watcher
Smyrna 770.437.8969

TLC Sitters
Smyrna 770.435.6250

Carolyns Companion Care
St Simons Is 912.634.6150

Purrs & Wags
Stone Mtn 404.299.6130

Stay Home Pet
Valdosta 912.242.1070

Luvn Stuff Pet Sitters
Woodstock 770.516.7387

HAWAII
No Fleez Pleez
Hilo 808.934.8544

Honolulu Pet Sitters
Honolulu 808.946.1038

Personalized Petcare
Kailua 808.254.3357

Comfy Critters Pet Stg
Mountain View 808.968.8744

ILLINOIS
Lady Kenworth
Algonquin 847.658.3969

A 1 Pet Watchers
Antioch 847.395.1633

Anml Attraction
Arlington Hts 847.253.7387

Apolda Knls
Aurora 630.898.2947

Pets Care Unlimited
Barrington 847.358.1455

Critter Care
Bartlett 630.736.8226

Anml Lovers
Batavia 630.879.0343

Baker Hollow Knls
Canton 309.647.9439

The Country Knls
Canton 309.647.5940

William R Pfaff Knls
Carol Stream 630.668.5272

A Paw Above
Chicago 312.944.3525

Anml Care
Chicago 773.282.1631

Castle Keepers Realty
Chicago 312.922.2854

Chgo HouseStg & Petcare
Chicago 773.477.0136

David Burns
Chicago 773.874.8283

David Burns
Chicago 773.921.0151

Exoticare
Chicago 773.274.9682

Home Swt Home Pet Stg
Chicago 312.587.8790

Homebuddies Pet Stg Svc
Chicago 773.525.7111

Kitty City
Chicago 312.335.0207

Pet And Plant Care
Chicago 312.266.8689

House-Pet Stg
Clarendon Hls 630.920.1603

The Pet Pal
Clarendon Hls 630.323.1203

Labest
Collinsville 618.344.7387

Your Pets Best Friend
Crete 708.754.6000

Star Bright Petcare
Crystal Lk 815.459.3903

Gwyaine Brding Knls
Decatur 217.865.2504

Sawgrass Knls
Decatur 217.877.8733

Susies Sitter
Decatur 217.428.7488

Elizabeth Carpenter Ltd
Downers Grove
630.969.0101

Pretty Pups Pet Grming
E Peoria 309.694.7877

United Pet Resort
Edwardsville 618.692.6399

Pet Loving Care
Elk Grove Vlg 847.437.8383

Lk County Pet Sitters
GraysLk 847.223.1071

Canine Care
Hanover Park 630.289.9596

Four Paws
Hinsdale 708.325.3647

Pampered Paws
Indian Creek 847.816.6494

Northern Illinois Pet Sitter
Ingleside 847.587.6477

Paws And Tails
Joliet 815.722.7297

The Critter Connection
Joliet 815.436.1704

Puppy Tender & Adult
Petcare
Libertyville 847.549.1822

The Pet Sitters Of America
Libertyville 847.816.4744

For Pets Sake
Lisle 630.964.7322

The Pet Nanny
Lisle 630.964.5164

Emmies Ark
Lk Barrington 847.304.1636

Leaveum Ease Pet Stg
Lockport 847.301.2244

Meyers Pet
Maryville 618.344.9033

Cozy Cats Inn
Mc Henry 815.344.8911

Pats Professional Pet Stg
New Lenox 815.485.1048

Kitty Care Pet Sitters
Niles 847.588.2287

Canine Designing
Norridge 708.456.2288

Dependable Pet
Northbrook 847.272.8333

Flos Critter Sitters
O Fallon 618.632.9028

Paws On Vacation
O Fallon 618.624.7297

Always There Pet
Oak Forest 708.535.0375

All Around Anml Care
Oak Lawn 708.422.5794

Tender Loving Knls
Oak Lawn 708.857.8078

Spikes Hotel
Oak Park 708.386.9881

Almost Home Pet Motel
Oakley 217.763.6333

Pet Svcs Unlimited
Ottawa 815.433.6660

Critter Sitter
Palatine 847.358.0818

Joanns Allbreed Grming
Palatine 847.991.4044

Puppy Love Petcare
Park Ridge 847.823.2011

Fishin Times
Pekin 309.353.7171

Home Petcare Svcs
Pekin 309.353.2190

Canine Design
Peoria 309.691.0801

The Clipp Joint
Peoria 309.688.6321

Canine & Abel
Rockford 815.962.6544

Pet Stg And Training Ctr
Rockford 815.637.6264

Safe & Happy Pet Sitters
Round Lk Bch 847.740.3954

Pets Delight
Savoy 217.355.1508

Anml Nannys
Skokie 847.679.7387

Pet Tenders
S Holland 708.333.8390

Auntie Ms Company
Springfield 217.698.0487

Bow Wow Barber Shop
Springfield 217.528.9540

Pampered Pets Plus
Springfield 217.787.3454

Blitzen Canine Academy
Tinley Park 708.532.0939

Kastle Kare
Tinley Park 708.614.1066

Lance Knls
Tremont 309.925.5125

A A Petsitters In Your Home
Wheaton 630.653.1050

Pampered Pet
Wheaton 630.690.0811

Peppy Paws
Wheaton 630.665.2610

Pet Watchers NorthW
Wheeling 847.520.3277

Cat Calls
Winfield 630.510.4001

INDIANA
Bloomington Pet Sitters
Bloomington 812.333.1789

In Good Hands
Bloomington 812.333.5108

Marthas Petcare Plus
Bloomington 812.334.3002

Waggintails Petcare
Brazil 812.442.1016

Ambassador Pet Stg
Brownsburg 317.858.0090

Best Friends Pet Resort &
Sln
Carmel 317.848.7387

Creature Comforts
Carmel 317.843.2422

Pet Watch
Carmel 317.582.1667

Catered Critters
Dyer 219.865.1548

Birdland Breeding Farm
Elkhart 219.262.4284

Abc Pet Sitters
Fort Wayne 219.436.6535

Pet Sitters
Fort Wayne 219.432.1751

The Pet Nanny
Fort Wayne 219.747.7943

Maloys Pet & Helper
Fremont 219.833.3309

Critter Sitters
Indianapolis 317.885.1942

Home Stg Seniors
Indianapolis 317.255.5056

Kastle Keepers Pet Stg
Indianapolis 317.636.5050

Kitten Sittin
Indianapolis 317.466.7877

Paw Prints Exclusive
Indianapolis 317.231.9763

Pet Guardians
Indianapolis 317.253.7630

Pet Minders
Indianapolis 317.259.8975

The Cat Nanny
Indianapolis 317.255.7297

Theres No Place Like Home
Indianapolis 317.845.4140

Cozy Comfort Pet Stg
Kendallville 219.347.3349

Mes Creatures
Kokomo 317.452.0006

The Gold Clipper
La Porte 219.324.5000

S R Pet Hotel
Madison 812.866.5381

Critter Sitters
Michigan City 219.874.7387

Prestwick Pet Sitters
Plainfield 317.745.9900

Love Therm Pets
Plymouth 219.935.9331

Pampered Pets
St John 219.365.9750

Greenacre Knls
Seymour 812.445.3446

Dees Pet & Home Care
Valparaiso 219.531.0842

Kritter Sitters
Valparaiso 219.477.5186

Cozy Cat Pet Stg
W Lafayette 317.463.1254

KANSAS
Critter Sitters
Derby 316.788.9584

Wildcat Pet Resort
Manhattan 913.539.1515

Pet Pals
PV 913.385.7257

Best Friends Pet Stg Svc
Salina 913.827.3754

Amore Pet Stg
Shawnee Msn 913.642.9356

Happy Tails Peet Svcs
Shawnee Msn 913.492.4746

Johnson Cnty Pet Ride &
Prsnl
Shawnee Msn 913.722.4005

Pet PlayHse
Topeka 913.478.3555

Big Hearted Pet Stg
Wichita 316.263.7387

Cozy Companions Petcare
Wichita 316.634.9869

Doggy Day Care
Wichita 316.263.0060

Housewatchers
Wichita 316.721.2233

Pet Nanny
Wichita 316.941.4500

The Brder Patrol
Wichita 316.683.9339

KENTUCKY
Petaway Pet Stg
Frankfort 502.223.2329

Cozy Creature Pet Sitters
Lexington 606.271.8962

Creature Comforts
Lexington 606.278.3025

Pet Connection
Lexington 606.223.9136

Tender Petcare
Lexington 606.269.0072

Minirosa Knls
Louisville 502.499.1910

Bullitt County Pet Stg
Mt Washington 502.538.7332

Fantasy Pet Land & Spa
Owensboro 502.926.7387

LOUISIANA
Champagnes Special
Petcare
Baton Rouge 504.343.8228

Critter Care
Baton Rouge 504.769.4160

Critter Care
Baton Rouge 504.766.4151

Mans Best Friend
Baton Rouge 504.334.0583

Marlanas Pet Stg Svc
Denham Spgs 504.664.7431

Pup-Go
Destrehan 504.764.2871

All Creatures Country Club
Mandeville 504.626.9664

Home Alone Pet Stg
Metairie 504.456.6236

Pampered Pets Bed &
Breakfast
Metairie 504.734.7387

Preferred Pet And Home
Care
Metairie 504.837.8187

Safe Harbor Pet Stg
Metairie 504.885.3632

Creature Comfort
Shreveport 318.861.4028

MASSACHUSETTS
Sit-A-Pet
Allston 617.489.3951

Critter Sitters
Amesbury 508.463.8616

River Valley Pet Stg
Amherst 413.253.1559

Doodys Anml Inn
Ashby 508.386.2412

Pampered Pets
Ayer 508.772.5833

Vip Sitters
Bedford 617.275.2369

Wishing Well Knls
Bellingham 508.966.7654

In Good Hands Pro In Home
Belmont 617.484.5399

Parade Of Pets
Belmont 617.489.0635

Pet-Estrian Svcs
Belmont 617.484.2489

Sit-A-Pet
Belmont 617.489.3951

Boston Pet Sitters
Boston 617.247.7387

Gone To The Dogs
Boston 617.424.0706

Weloset Knl
Boxford 508.887.5760

Anything For Anmls
Brewster 508.896.4606

Weir Pet Mbl Pet Taxi &
Sittng
Carver 508.866.7620

Aandora Knls
Chelmsford 508.454.8718

Your Pets Pal
Clinton 508.368.0997

Four Paws Only
Dracut 508.957.7387

Pet Stg & More
Fall River 508.676.1210

Dog Days
Falmouth 508.540.8532

Behavior Modification &
Canine
Gloucester 508.281.3141

Pooch Paws-2
Hanover 617.826.0081

Happy Tails/Doggy
Playground
Hudson 508.562.1123

All Pet Pet Stg & Taxi Svc
Hyde Park 617.337.4777

Dipn Clip
Ipswich 508.356.5340

New England Center Canine
Hygn
Leominster 508.840.6565

Pawsitive Loving Petcare
Leominster 508.348.2288

The Dog Sitter
Leominster 508.534.7001

A Reli Frnd Pet Stg Svc
Malden 617.388.9234

Betwixt & Between
Marblehead 617.631.6593

Puss & Boots Pet Stg Svc
Marlborough 508.460.1996

The Mutt Hut
Marlborough 508.485.8569

Pawsltive Pleasures
Medford 617.396.7387

Fluff & Puff Dog Grming
Medway 508.533.5800

Dog Data
Milford 508.473.0606

Creature Care Pet Stg
Milton 617.696.9667

Creature Comfors Home Pet
Needham 617.323.1652

Sundown Sitters
Newburyport 508.463.3214

Tlc Pet Svcs
Newton 617.969.0225

A As Pet Nstuff
N Reading 508.664.9921

Critter Comfort
Northampton 413.586.7178

Northampton Pet Stg
Northampton 413.584.7387

Companion Pet Stg
Northborough 508.393.5307

Pet Nannys And More
Northborough 508.393.4599

Luv-In-Home Pet Stg
Quy 617.472.0444

Angels Pet Stg
Randolph 617.331.7877

Jakes Loving Care Pet Stg
Rehoboth 508.336.2281

Purr Fect Companion Pet
Revere 617.286.6666

A Daily Dog Walk
Roslindale 617.325.2030

Mary Pawpins Pet Stg
Roslindale 617.323.1624

Paws For Applause
Saugus 617.233.9299

Moriartys Pet Stg
Seekonk 508.761.7990

Ashmont Farm Pet Stg Svc
Sherborn 508.651.3974

Pet Companions
Somerville 617.623.2758

Pet Partners Pet Stg Svc
Somerville 617.776.0833

The Watchful Eye
Stoneham 617.279.4444

Pet-Serve Plus
Sudbury 508.443.0270

Chien Elegant Grming
Swampscott 617.581.9377

Pawsn Purrs Salon
Swampscott 617.581.7080

Bayview Knls
W Barnstble 508.362.6506

Best Friend
Wakefield 617.246.8407

Sharons Pet Svcs
Wakefield 617.246.1504

T L Kittycare Pet Stg Svc
Watertown 617.923.3554

The Grm Room
W Yarmouth 508.778.0939

Lindas Doggie Playland
Westborough 508.366.7364

Mary Pops
Weston 617.647.1459

Pet Ercise
Westwood 617.326.3085

Angels Pet Stg
Weymouth 617.331.7877

Puppy Patrol
Woburn 617.935.5559

Walk A Pet/Feed A Pet
Worcester 508.795.0021

Critter Care
Wrentham 508.384.5940

MARYLAND
Bonnie-Brae Knls
Annapolis 410.757.1555

Tender Loving Care Pet
Arnold 410.544.2279

Aunt Pollys Pet Stg
Baltimore 410.265.6832

Claws & Paws Stg
Baltimore 410.931.0811

Purrfect Pets
Bel Air 410.836.5399

Red Baron Pet Stg
Bel Air 410.569.7793

Paradise For Pets
Beltsville 301.776.6353

Pampered Pets & Plants
Bishopville 410.352.5403

Robins Pet Stg
Chesapeake Cy
410.885.2450

Pooh Bears Pet Stg
Clinton 301.868.5669

Pet Companions
College Park 301.474.0904

Pats Pet-A-Go Go
Columbia 301.596.3208

Preston Country Club For
Pets
Columbia 301.596.7387

Anml Lovers
Cumberland 301.729.2955

Professional Pet Svcs
Easton 410.819.0559

Rock Spring Knls
Forest Hill 410.838.6960

Dog Gone But Not Forgotten
Pet
Frederick 301.662.9045

Pet Serve
Gaithersburg 301.963.9747

Potomac Knls
Gaithersburg 301.948.2202

Tender Loving Cat Care
Gaithersburg 301.258.7745

Happy Pet
Grasonville 410.827.5735

Associated Pet Sitters
Hagerstown 301.797.1626

Spoiled Pets
Highland 301.854.0287

Country Comfort Knls
Jarrettsville 410.692.5055

Jarrettsville Vet Ctr
Jarrettsville 410.692.6171

Pets Unlimited Pet Stg
Joppa 410.679.0030

Ripleys Results Pet Svcs
Laurel 301.953.1840

Creature Comfort
Middletown 301.371.4460

Baskervilles Pro Pet & Hse
Mitchellville 301.464.1033

Pals For Pets
New Market 301.831.6349

Terris Grming
Odenton 410.551.9820

Pet Friends
Olney 301.570.1700

Deer Park Brding Knls
Owings Mills 410.655.8330

Jimmies PetStg
Parkville 410.882.0424

Paradise Pet Stg
Pasadena 410.360.5950

Privileged Pet Sitters
Potomac 301.983.8343

Pet Sitters Plus
Reisterstown 410.526.0371

Pet Taxi & Stg Svc By C
Rockville 301.330.7999

Rockville Pet Hotel
Rockville 301.340.3376

The Family Cat
Salisbury 410.860.2280

Rhapsody Acres Knls
Temple Hills 301.449.3720

Amberlyn Knls
Walkersville 301.898.3106

MAINE
Home Petcare
Auburn 207.783.6184

Hse Holders
Bangor 207.942.3003

Catnapszzz Feline Rooms
Berwick 207.698.5000

Bear Brook Knls
Brewer 207.989.7979

Elizabeth Cape Pet Svcs
Cape Eliz 207.767.8190

Canines & Cats
Oakland 207.465.4420

Critters Sitters Etc
S Portland 207.767.7260

Furry Friends Dog Walking
S Portland 207.767.3740

The Cats Meow
Scarborough 207.883.9611

MICHIGAN
Carols At Your
Ann Arbor 313.663.2127

Pets First
Ann Arbor 313.769.0188

The Pet Companion
Ann Arbor 313.662.6176

Pet Nanny
Battle Creek 616.964.3330

Alternative Pet Svcs
Belleville 313.699.8080

Precious Pet
Belleville 313.753.5665

Pet Watcher
Berkley 810.548.5668

Birmingham Dog Obedience
Schl
Birmingham 810.258.5004

Ken-Care
Birmingham 810.644.3763

Scales To Tails Petsitters
Brighton 810.220.0287

Town & Country Pet Salon
Burton 810.742.4240

Hallidays Knls
Canton 313.397.8899

Pet Number For Pets
Center Line 810.756.6634

Affectionate Pet & Home
Clarkston 810.625.1144

Fifi & Fido Cake Removal
Clawson 810.435.6265

Canine Workshop
Clinton Twp 810.792.8533

The Urban Zookeeper
Dexter 313.426.5161

Pampered Pets Brding Grm
E Leroy 616.979.5581

Pet Watch
Edwardsburg 616.663.5401

Yuppy Puppy Day Care
Farmingtn Hls 810.442.2224

Pets Home Alone
Farmington 810.615.1752

Dirty Dog Gone & The Cats
Meow
Flint 810.743.3958

Happy Home Petcare
Flushing 810.659.6601

Blue Water Pet Patrol
Fort Gratiot 810.385.7940

Setters Sitters
Fort Gratiot 810.385.4842

Caretakers
Fowlerville 517.546.6413

Pet Sitters Plus
Grand Rapids 616.241.0337

Time Away Svcs
Grand Rapids 616.454.6330

No Place Like Home Cat
Care
Grandville 616.261.2287

Island Pet Sitters
Grosse Ile 313.675.5994

Pet Sitter
Hanover 517.563.2405

Professional Pet Sitters
Howell 517.546.4337

Advanced K-9 Academy
Jackson 517.783.3770

Pet Friends
Jackson 517.787.8375

Topdog Pet Clinic
Jackson 517.783.1000

Critter Care
Kalamazoo 616.373.6222

Derspinna Knls
Kalamazoo 616.372.2746

The Critter Sitter
Kalamazoo 616.382.3466

Irish Sitters
Lk Orion 810.693.4701

R & D Pet Stg
Lk Orion 810.693.9060

Pampered Pet Plant & Home
Care
Lambertville 313.856.6240

Pet Nanny
Lansing 517.694.4400

Pet Nanny Of America
Lansing 517.336.8622

Baybreeze Knls
Linwood 517.697.5222

Home Pet Stg Svcs
Livonia 313.425.7661

Trainers Academy
Madison Hts 810.616.6500

Pet Nanny Of Trav City
Maple City 616.228.7387

Community Anml Clinic
Marlette 517.635.7095

Pet Keepers
Marquette 906.249.3456

Anml Lovers Pet Stg Svc
Marysville 810.364.6122

Critter Sitters
Marysville 810.364.2750

A Good Hair Day Dog
Grming
Midland 517.832.5171

Debs Pet Stg Svc
Midland 517.832.5732

V I P Knls Llc
Midland 517.839.0223

Monroe Knls
Monroe 313.243.0070

Pet Pal-Sal
Monroe 313.241.0022

Happy Hearts
Mt Clemens 810.463.3965

Wags By Holly
Mount Clemens
810.468.4333

Kaley Park Knls
Muskegon 616.798.3968

Paws For Pets
Muskegon 616.744.3809

The Pet Sitters
Negaunee 906.475.7387

Pet Love
Niles 616.684.0224

Critter Care Pet Stg Svc
Northville 810.348.6370

D Cs Pet Pal
Novi 810.349.7755

No Pl Like Home Pet Stg
Oakland Twp810.652.6596

Comfy Critters Pet & Home
Oxford 810.628.1653

Total Petcare
Pontiac 810.253.9650

Kitty Stans Kare
Portage 616.324.0300

A Beastly Bus Pro Pet Sitters
Rochester 810.652.0520

Privileged Petcare
Rochester Hls 810.652.7691

Michael Willett Laurie
Rockford 616.874.8482

Tlc Pet Sitters
Roscommon 517.275.5768

Noahs Ark-In-Home Petcare
Royal Oak 810.545.6767

Preferred Pet Sitters
Saginaw 517.792.1522

Sparkys Doggie Barn
Saginaw 517.781.1401

Bow Wow Btq Dog & Cat
Grm
St Louis 517.681.4127

Cindys Pet Stg
Saline 313.944.1837

Lizs Anml Kingdom
St Clair Shrs 810.445.0605

Martys Pet & Hse Stg Svc
Traverse City 616.929.3174

Premier Pet Sitters
Troy 810.680.0733

Creature Comfort
W Bloomfield 810.737.2622

Paws & Claws Pet Stg
W Bloomfield 810.363.7337

Daritz Grming
Waterford 810.666.9928

Purr Fect Companion Cat
Care
Waterford 810.674.2287

Home Alone Svcs
Whitmore Lk 313.449.2770

Brd No More
Williamston 517.655.6700

Anmlz Pet Svcs
Wyandotte 313.284.7985

All Creatures Great & Small
Ypsilanti 313.483.4838

MISSOURI
Country Acres
Ballwin 314.227.1919

Mans Best Friend
Belton 816.331.4364

Vetrnry Grp Chesterfield
Chesterfield 314.537.3915

Baronwood Knls
Florissant 314.838.2021

Pets Are Inn
Florissant 314.838.1999

Heart To Heart Nanny Svcs
Glencoe 314.458.8400

Lil Critters
Hollister 417.337.5166

The Grm Room
Hollister 417.336.6685

D-Js Knl
Imperial 314.464.1316

In-Home Petcare
Jackson 573.243.6868

Pet Partners
Joplin 417.782.5474

All-Ways At Your
Kansas City 816.363.3373

Joey Loves Cats
Maryland Hts 314.291.8728

54 Pet Stop
Mexico 573.581.6620

Cedar Lane Equine Clinic
New Haven 573.237.6111

Critter Sitters N More
St Charles 314.922.7387

Petsmart
St Charles 314.925.1611

Critter Sitters & Company
St Louis 314.962.6776

Gateway Pet Stg & More
St Louis 314.481.7387

Hse Sitters
St Louis 314.781.4722

Kastle Keepers
St Louis 314.721.0819

Love My Pet-Stg
St Louis 314.428.5122

Nanny Care For Pets
St Louis 314.997.5750

Peace Mind Hse & Pet Stg
St Louis 314.781.1243

Pet Sitters
St Louis 314.993.5093

Pet Tending & Transportation
St Louis 314.968.8790

Petkeepers Ltd
St Louis 314.535.3182

Pets Are Inn
St Louis 314.822.7387

Rose-The Grmer
St Louis 314.524.2456

Creature Comforts Pet Stg
Wright City 314.926.9985

MISSISSIPPI
Pet-N-Nanny
Jackson 601.372.5221

All Creatures Great And
Small
Madison 601.853.9423

Noahs Nanny
Madison 601.856.8347

Hawkins Brding Knl
Petal 601.582.5974

MONTANA
Four Footers Vacation Spa
Missoula 406.726.3823

Muirs Brding Knls
Missoula 406.251.2540

NORTH CAROLINA
Kritter Kare
Albemarle 704.982.7482

Creature Comfort Pet Stg
Asheville 704.254.1493

Pet Guardians
Asheville 704.254.8988

Morrison Anml Clinic Pa
Burnsville 704.682.7710

Canine Companions
Cary 919.460.1096

Pet Pals
Cary 919.460.0370

Pupsi
Cary 919.460.9909

Amys Pampered Pooches
Charlotte 704.552.8245

B C D E Pet Stg
Charlotte 704.563.1430

Blue Velvet Poodle Parlor
Charlotte 704.332.8662

Charlotte Care Svcs
Charlotte 704.335.0501

Critter Sitters Of Carolinas
Charlotte 704.643.0002

Partners In Pet Stg
Charlotte 704.376.0842

Pet Nannies
Charlotte 704.948.9229

Pet Peeves
Charlotte 704.392.8020

Pampered Pets
Concord 704.784.5606

Critter Sitters
Durham 919.477.6876

Paw Pals
Durham 919.490.6844

Pets Companion Inn Knls
Durham 919.477.0618

Very Important Pets Pro Pet
Durham 919.419.1647

Hideaway Hills Pet Center
Flat Rock 704.685.3149

Redmond Kennels
704.684.9938

Pampered Pets
Fletcher 704.684.4512

Anml Artistry
Garner 919.662.0937

Day By Day Home & Pet
Sitters
Garner 919.779.3670

Happy Home Petcare
Goldsboro 919.734.8008

Pampered Pups
Greensboro 910.856.7877

Peace Of Mind Pet Sitters
Kannapolis 704.932.4685

New Beginnings
King 910.983.2444

Pampered Paws Pet Stg Svc
Lumberton 910 671.0908

At Home Petcare
Raleigh 919.571.0993

Homesitters Of Raleigh &
Cary
Raleigh 919.571.7387

Kitty Kare Pet Stg
Raleigh 919.231.9999

Rockingham Anml Hospital
Reidsville 910.349.4918

Tree Tops Farm
Reidsville 910.342.9523

Collins Critter Sitters
Rockingham 910.997.4296

The Pet Sitters Of Iredell
Statesville 704.878.6060

Critter Companions
Waxhaw 704.843.1447

Natures Nanny Pet Stg Svc
Waxhaw 704.843.2929

Victorias Grming Parlor
Winston Salem 910.922.1555

NEW HAMPSHIRE
All Paws Everywhere
Barrington 603.664.7297

Auntie Ms Pet Care
Barrington 603.664.9010

Catlove
Bedford 603.472.5889

Lyonking Pet Sitters
Concord 603.224.8931

Tahcas Pet Svcs
Concord 603.774.7387

Country Anml Tender
Deerfield 603.463.7388

Furry Friends Pet Stg
Dover 603.743.4023

Patricks Pet Stg
E Swanzey 603.357.1541

Dogworks
Hollis 603.883.6654

T L C Sitters
Manchester 603.625.1738

The Center For Dog
Management
Manchester 603.625.2512

Chrismas Acres Critter Salon
Newport 603.863.6975

Nothin Fancy Pet Grming
Newport 603.863.0028

Pet Devotion
Northfield 603.286.3033

Hse Calls
Portsmouth 603.436.0322

Happy Trails Pet Stg Svc
Salem 603.890.6302

Pawsitive Results Pet Stg
Stratham 603.772.6977

Passtime Pet
Windham 603.894.4675

NEW JERSEY
The Hap Hoofer Pet Stg Svc
Bayonne 201.437.7387

Pet Sitters
Bloomfield 201.743.5330

Klassy K9
Brick 908.785.1200

Walk The Dog
Brick 908.920.7019

While U R Away Pet Stg Svc
Budd Lk 201.691.5834

Pet Stg In Cape May County
Cape May 609.886.5288

Creature Comforts Pet Stg
Cherry Hill 609.661.0078

Best Friends Pet Resort &
Sln
Cinnaminson 609.661.0707

No Place Like Home-Pet
Sitters
Clifton 201.458.1616

Critter Sitters
E Hanover 201.887.2539

Donnas Pampered Paws
Eatontown 908.389.8908

Worry Free Petcare
Englewood 201.568.1010

Creature Comfort By Megan
Far Hills 908.953.0633

Bone Voyage Pet Stg Svc
Freehold 908.866.6645

Rainbow Home Stg Seniors
Glassboro 609.863.0003

Calypsos Companions
Glen Rock 201.447.4443

Fur Feather & Fin
Glen Rock 201.427.6633

Hay Hill Knls
Green Brook 908.968.2265

Creature Comforts Pet Stg
Haddonfield 609.427.0402

Alternative Pet Sitters
Jersey City 201.653.3343

Anml Inn Pet Hotel
Ledgewood 201.691.2662

Always There Pet Stg
Loln Park 201.305.1061

Country Knl
Lindenwold 609.784.4559

Lk Hopatcong Knls
Lk Hopatcong 201.663.1111

Purrfect Pals
Manalapan 908.617.0994

Home But NotAlone
Manasquan 908.528.0407

Love Your Pet
Manville 908.722.1228

Maywood Pet Center
Maywood 201.845.3331

Lindas Happy Tails
Middletown 908.706.0600

At Home Petcare
Millington 908.604.0055

Looking Good Pet Grming
Morris Plains 201.540.9561

Pgells Knls
Mount Laurel 609.235.7475

Village Pet Center
New Providnce 908.464.8507

Pet Pals
N Bergen 201.866.2557

Cut Above For Pets Only
Nutley 201.667.7381

Anml Attraction Pet Stg
Palmyra 609.786.0542

Roxdane Knls Petcare Ctr
Plainfield 908.755.0227

While U R Away Pet Stg Svc
Randolph 201.927.5834

V I P In Your Home Pet
Rockaway 201.625.2033

The Preppy Pup
Summit 908.522.1630

Four Winds Anml Inn
Tuckerton 609.296.2131

Champion Cat Care
Vineland 609.692.1667

Happy Tails Pet Stg Svc
W Milford 201.208.0654

4 Paws Pet Stg & Dog
Westfield 908.232.5239

NEW YORK
Chateau Du Chien
NYC 212.759.8126

NEVADA
Personal Touch
Henderson 702.565.4788

Birds Nest
Las Vegas 702.259.4885

Cats Cradle
Las Vegas 702.457.0370

Critter Care
Las Vegas 702.228.1297

Happy Tails To You
Las Vegas 702.255.2611

In Charge Home Pet Stg S
Las Vegas 702.870.0055

Akers Petcare
Reno 702.852.7387

Amys Pet Grming Boutique
Reno 702.324.4107

The Pet Set
Reno 702.322.6285

Professional Sitter
Sparks 702.356.7823

NEW YORK
Dog Gone Beautiful Grm Svc
Adams 315.232.3593

Barking Boutique The Pet
Albany 518.454.9663

The Housesitter
Albany 518.482.3997

Wash-N-Grm Doggie Saloon
Angola 716.549.0672

Luv Em N Leave Em
Bald'ville 315.622.7387

Foxwood Brding Knl
Ballston Spa 518.399.7434

Happy Tails Pet Stg
Ballston Spa 518.885.0484

Christophers Pooch Mobile
Bay Shore 516.968.6697

Kitties Kanines & Kritters
Bay Shore 516.666.3503

Critter Care Broome
Binghamton 607.723.6544

N Country Danes
Boonville 315.942.6616

Pet Safe Pet Stg
Brewerton 315.676.7233

A Tailored Pet
Brooklyn 718.875.7387

City Critters
Brooklyn 718.834.1777

K 9 Control
Brooklyn 718.769.7278

Noahs Ark Petcare &
Transport
Brooklyn 212.255.8939

Anml Associates Stg Svc
Buffalo 716.877.8113

Happy Pets
Buffalo 716.876.9047

Anmls-R-Us
Clay 315.698.1338

Whiskers Watchers
Clifton Park 518.383.4605

Critter Care Corning & Elmira
Corning 607.962.7929

The Pet Sitter
Cross River 914.763.5924

Dream Pet
Croton Hdsn 914.271.3532

Entirely Errands
E Amherst 716.636.5999

Pet Huggers
E Amherst 716.688.0304

Wagging Tails
Elmhurst 718.592.9673

Creature Comforts
Elmira 607.735.0470

Concierge Svcs
Endicott 607.748.1324

Contented Critters
Fishkill 914.896.7002

Critter Care Of Queens
Flushing 718.263.3770

Pet Minders
Fonda 518.853.3171

L I Housesitters
Freeport 516.223.1151

Pet Pals
Hartsdale 914.725.7387

Petminders
Holbrook 516.567.5479

Grand-Paws
Huntingtn Sta 516.427.8076

Grand-Paws
Huntington 516.271.6350

Pet Minders
Johnstown 518.725.9776

Critters Choice
Latham 518.783.2273

Feline Fantasies
Latham 518.783.2297

Hse Of Dogs Etc
Latham 518.783.0725

Pooch Protectors
Lewiston 716.754.4669

All Suffolk Dog Grming
Lindenhurst 516.957.2319

Canine Club
Long Is City 718.729.0664

Northern Pine Knls
Lorraine 315.232.3232

A Cut Above
Mamaroneck 914.698.4704

Exotic Wings
Marcy 315.733.6659

Smittys
Middle Island 516.345.0000

Dakola Knls & Cattery
Middletown 914.342.2005

Kayceys Pro Pet Sitters
Monroe 914.782.6209

Candys Critter Citters
Mount Vernon 914.667.6369

At-Home Petcare
N Tonawanda 716.693.3835

Ronald Alessandroni
New Rochelle 914.636.8368

American Dog Trainers
Network
New York 212.727.7257

Amsterdam Aquarium & Pet
Shop
New York 212.724.0536

Cat-Care
New York 212.947.6190

Cat-Care
New York 212.838.2996

Family Affair Petcare
New York 212.249.0839

Fur Fin & Feather Pet Svcs
New York 212.529.0658

Pet Get-Away
New York 212.534.7924

Pets Please
New York 212.873.2724

Puddles Pet
New York 212.410.7338

Puppy Paths
New York 212.369.1500

Purrfect Cat Care
New York 212.362.2175

Tail Waggers Home Petcare
Svc
New York 212.683.1108

The Dog Wash
New York 212.673.3290

The K-9 Club
New York 212.410.3764

W Side Dog Spa
New York 212.222.7022

Emilys PetStg Svc
Niagara Falls 716.283.7387

Calgary Knls
Oswego 315.342.0525

Hand Helping
Peekskill 914.736.3078

About Town Pet & Home
Sitters
Plattsburgh 518.563.7387

Best In Show
Plattsburgh 518.561.2640

Trialfast Knl
Poestenkill 518.283.1251

Pet Watchers
Port Jervis 914.856.2489

Clendon Brook Petcare Plus
Queensbury 518.792.0303

Educated Dog
Rhinebeck 914.876.3671

Professional Petcare
Rhinebeck 914.876.0815

Loyal Companion
Rochester 716.254.7414

Comforts Of Home
Saugerties 914.247.0669

Carois Petcare
Schenectady 518.347.1472

Lots Of Love Pro Pet Sitters
Schenectady 518.382.1605

The Pets Platter
Shrub Oak 914.245.9343

Kcc Pet Stg
Staten Island 718.317.1464

Soft Paws Pet Stg Svc
Staten Island 718.980.7297

Grand-Paws Pet Stg Svce
Syosset 516.921.8871

Anything For Anmls
Syracuse 518.425.7008

Basically Puppies
Syracuse 315.673.3333

Pet Svcs
Syracuse 315.437.2103

Anml Associates
Tonawanda 716.877.8113

Dogs Best Friend
Vestal 607.748.9422

Affordable Grming & Brding
Wallkill 914.564.3597

Critter Care Pet Stg Svc
Warwick 914.986.7826

Hillside Knls
Watertown 315.788.2844

Anml Respite Kare/A R K
Waverly 607.565.3007

Critter Sitter
W Chazy 518.562.0549

Canine 1St Academy
White Plains 914.428.5789

Greenridge Pet Grming
White Plains 914.761.2557

Pet Companions
White Plains 914.948.5977

Whitestone Pet Brdng
Whitestone 718.767.7452

Tlc Knls
Willseyville 607.272.1317

Pet Watch Plus
Woodstock 914.679.6070

Ltl Darlings Pet Stg Svce
Yonkers 914.476.7387

Noahs Critters
Yorktown Hts 914.245.7935

OHIO
Doggie Depot
Alliance 330.823.8866

Pet Pals
Ashtabula 216.964.3246

Petigrees & Greeneries
Aurora 216.562.6095

Avon Lk Anml Care Center
Avon Lk 216.933.7774

At Home Critter Care
Brecksville 216.526.9432

Birdie Brders
Broadview Hts 216.546.0646

Pet Nannies
Canton 330.493.9944

Pets Home Alone
Canton 330.493.1009

Summer Wind Stables &
Tack Shp
Chesterland 216.729.7430

Pets To Posies
Cleveland 216.481.7387

American Care Options
Columbus 614.759.2729

Bills Pet Stg
Columbus 614.759.7770

Toni Sits Pets
Columbus 614.262.8333

Pet Stg By Lucille
Crestline 419.683.3644

C K Pet Sitters
Dayton 937.277.7034

The Pet Sitters
Dayton 937.890.0164

Pampered Pups
Delaware 614.369.9247

Paws Place Clip & Care
Fostoria 419.435.7387

Jolly Knls
Geneva 216.466.8200

Critter Crossing Pet Store
Gibsonburg 419.862.3834

Critter Sitters
Hilliard 614.876.6912

Hse & Pet Companions
Hilliard 614.876.2337

Pampered Pet Plant & Home
Ctr
Holland 419.470.7690

Pretty Coat Junction
Lakewood 216.521.7297

Creature Comforts Of
Cleveland
Lyndhurst 216.461.7387

Tlc Pet Stg
Marietta 614.373.0804

Pups N People Dog Training
Maumee 419.893.4110

Chippewa Knls & Grming
Medina 330.725.8529

Home Swt Home Pet Stg
Svc
Medina 330.722.3714

Pet Patrol
Moreland Hls 216.247.1136

Windmill Knl
New Holland 614.495.5277

A Knl Alternative
Painesville 216.350.1811

Pamper Your Pets
Piqua 937.773.4324

Paws Of Purrfection
Powell 614.764.5857

Perfect Idea
Rockbridge 614.380.2301

Critter Sitters
Stewart 614.662.3904

Pet Nanny W
Strongsville 216.846.7387

Dependable Home Petcare
Sylvania 419.841.4663

Dog Poop Patrol
Sylvania 419.882.5743

Adorable Pet Stg
Toledo 419.472.7834

Fifi Chere Grming Salon
Toledo 419.472.1415

Karnik Inn
Toledo 419.841.6621

We Care Pet Stg
Toledo 419.726.7387

Cjs Country Grming & Knls
Toronto 614.537.5551

Dapper Dogs
Vandalia 937.890.3695

Pets Unlimited-Petcare
Wadsworth 330.334.7387

Wilmington Pet Sitters
Wilmington 937.382.4033

Walk-N-Feed
Youngstown 330.270.1500

OKLAHOMA
Browns Stg
Glenpool 918.291.1960

Rock Creek Knl Pet Hotel
McAlester 918.823.4600

Elite Dog Grming
Ninnekah 405.222.2992

Best Friends Pet Resort
Oklahoma City 405.751.1944

Home Chaperones
Oklahoma City 405.842.9427

Red Dog Salon & BathHse
Oklahoma City 405.728.9274

Waggin Tails
Tulsa 918.695.5445

OREGON
Pacific Pet Sitters
Forest Grove 503.357.7593

Happy Cats
Hillsboro 503.640.0465

Critter Sitters
Lk Oswego 503.697.1970

Cambridge Food For Life
Portland 503.644.8224

Fur Fins & Feathers
Portland 503.690.7780

Silverton Petcare
Silverton 503.873.7387

Pets & More
Tigard 503.620.2093

OR PETSITTERS PA

Kitty Kare
Troutdale 503.667.8813

Companion Care Cat Sitters
Wilsonville 503.682.2273

PENNSYVANIA
Critter Care Plus
Allentown 610.797.5150

Paws To Learn
Allentown 610.432.1144

T L C Pet Stg
Ardmore 610.649.2321

Tiara Knls
Bath 610.759.8806

E Js Brding Knl
Beaver Falls 412.846.6745

Kathies Resdntl Pet Stg
Beaver Falls 412.846.6745

Walkers Pet Watchers
Berlin 814.267.4688

Pet Sitters Of S Hills
Bethel Park 412.831.1444

All Gods Creatures Pro Pet
Bloomfield 412.682.5636

The Zoo Crew
Bradford 814.368.7436

Noahs Ark Pet Svcs
Bristol 215.781.0554

The Grm Room
Brockway 814.265.0255

Home Stg Svc Main Ln
Bryn Mawr 610.525.6114

The Pet Professionals
Bryn Mawr 610.527.0540

Pets And Plants
Camp Hill 717.737.7241

Hickory Springs Farm
Chester Sprgs 610.933.9584

Brandywine Pet Supplies
Coatesville 610.384.6340

Embreeville Mill
Coatesville 610.486.6369

Lees Pampered Pets
Coatesville 610.383.6211

The Dog Hse
Coatesville 610.384.3702

Parkway W Petcare
Coraopolis 412.262.2727

Janet Jones Pet Grming
Derry 412.694.8489

Home Sweet Home Pet
Sitters
Dickson City 717.383.2693

Brandywine Country Living
Downingtown 610.873.3081

Pet Recess
Downingtown 610.458.2529

All Breeds Knls
Doylestown 215.348.7605

Bobbies Pet Stg
Du Bois 814.375.8983

Abracadabra Pet Stg Svc
Easton 610.258.9838

Daugherty Brding Knls
Edinburg 412.652.7715

Foxs Pet Grming
Ellwood City 412.758.6620

Secure Home Of Lower
Bucks
Fairless Hls 215.736.3355

Safe & Sound Pet Stg
Fairview 814.474.2659

Creature Comforts Plus
Fountainville 215.249.1926

Stg Pretty
Fstrvl Trvose 215.355.6862

Robins Pet Connection
Glenolden 610.461.4747

Creature Comforts Pet Stg
Glenside 215.657.7387

Pollys Pet Svcs
Harrison City 412.744.4593

Pet Watch Svcs
Hollidaysburg 814.696.6500

Pampered Pets Stg
Jeannette 412.837.8013

Pro Home Petcare
Jessup 717.383.9844

LynneAunt Pampers Pets
Kng Of Prussa 610.688.2622

Pet Sitters Unlimited
Kng Of Prussa 610.272.0849

Companions For Pets
Lancaster 717.293.0401

Home Stg Svc Lancaster
Lancaster 717.293.1584

Pets Are Inn
Lansdale 215.412.7387

J E M Pet Stg
Lebanon 717.865.6422

Barbs Clip & Dip
Lemoyne 717.737.0733

Mrs Macs Pet Sitters
Malvern 610.644.0718

Riverfront Brding & Knls
Mc Veytown 814.542.3490

Tlc Pet Sitters
Meadville 814.337.4205

Home Helper
Mechanicsburg 717.796.1121

Sudzy Puppy
Mechanicsburg
717.796.9576

Critter Companions
Media 610.565.2781

Home And Pet Watch
Media 610.566.4558

Precious Pet Pro Pet Stg
Morrisville 215.736.9558

Puppy Luv
Murrysville 412.337.6582

Cats In The Cradle
New Kensingtn 412.339.2480

Noahs Bark
Newtown Sq 610.356.0159

Dog Talk Puppy & Dog
Training
Norristown 610.277.8975

Home Support Svcs
Norristown 610.630.1099

Trooper Vet Hospital
Norristown 610.539.6820

C & L Pet Sitters
Oakdale 412.788.2661

Kid Hearts Kritter Kare
Pa Furnace 814.237.7631

Critter Care
Paoli 610.296.5352

Errands And Concierges
Express
Paoli 610.408.0535

Creature Comports At
Runaway
Pennsburg 215.679.6205

Precious Pet Stg
Pennsburg 215.541.4820

Anml Care Svcs
Philadelphia 215.763.3309

Chambley & Co
Philadelphia 215.545.6730

Creature Comforts Petcare
Philadelphia 215.438.2769

Endless Paws-Abilities
Philadelphia 215.247.7297

Pampered Pet Stg
Philadelphia 215.849.6960

Priceless Pets
Philadelphia 215.624.2461

Jacks Dog Farm
Pipersville 215.766.8802

Amshels Home Pet Stg
Pittsburgh 412.963.6933

Home Stg Svcs Wstrn Pa
Pittsburgh 412.561.4424

470

Pet Sitter
Pittsburgh 412.241.7737

Pet Tender
Pittsburgh 412.884.2679

Pets At Home
Pittsburgh 412.885.2275

Pittsburgh N Pet Sitters
Pittsburgh 412.366.6277

Purrfect Petsitters
Pittsburgh 412.881.4402

Critter Watchers
Point Marion 412.725.0729

Acorn Valley Pet Brding
Quakertown 215.536.5100

Hansens Personal Svcs
Quakertown 215.538.7798

We Care Petcare
Quakertown 215.538.3676

Critter Sitter
Reading 610.775.5102

Frames Knls
Ridley Park 610.521.1123

Knls Raydon
Rochester 412.774.8541

Pampered Pawn Pet Stg
Sellersville 215.453.3888

Home Alone Pets
Sharon Hill 610.586.3950

Precious Pets Pet Stg Svc
Sinking Spg 610.777.9920

Penns Valley Knls
Spring Mills 814.422.8638

Pet Sitters
State College 814.234.8911

Lov-In-Care
Trevose 215.355.9023

Theres No Pl Like Home Frm
Warminster 215.957.9550

The Noble Pet
Washington 412.228.2095

High Steppin Knls & Game
Waynesburg 412.852.1430

Pet Tenders
W Chester 610.793.1113

Penn Line Security
Williamsport 717.327.0721

Pet Sitter Plus
Wilmerding 412.823.7780

Carols Pet
York 717.840.0019

Critter Sitters
York 717.792.4207

Errands Etc A Unique
York 717.854.9227

Errands Plus
York 717.764.2511

Zephyr Petcare
York 717.764.5840

RHODE ISLAND
A & L Pet Stg
Bristol 401.253.7297

Kitty Stg
Coventry 401.822.2518

Tri-State Multi Svcs
Coventry 401.828.6210

Creature Comfort Pet-Stg
Narragansett 401.782.4777

Compati Pup Canine Svcs
Tiverton 401.625.5953

Paws Petcare Svc & Day Care
Warwick 401.737.7804

Your Home PetStg
W Warwick 401.828.7096

Happy Tails
Woonsocket 401.765.0550

SOUTH CAROLINA
Carolina Grming
Charleston 803.556.1604

The Petsitter
Columbia 803.256.2776

Professional Pet Setting
Darlington 803.395.0802

Pet & Co
Elgin 803.736.4806

Pampered Paws
Greenville 864.370.0277

The Roaming Trainer
Greer 864.895.7826

Spoil Rotten Pets
Myrtle Beach 803.238.8387

My Concierge
Salem 864.944.9008

The Pet Nanny
Simpsonville 864.963.3037

Robins Pro Pet Stg Svc
Sumter 803.469.2117

Care N Company
Surfside Bch 803.238.7387

SOUTH DAKOTA
Lynns Pet Motel
Custer 605.673.3347

TENNESSEE
Creature Comfort Pet Stg
Chattanooga 423.877.3996

Sandys Pet-Care
Concord 423.966.2130

Pet Sitters
Franklin 615.794.7555

Dog Hse Pleasers
Germantown 901.757.5228

Paws-R-Us
Grandview 423.365.6397

Superpetz
Knoxville 423.558.8438

The Pet Pacifier
Knoxville 423.690.2882

Claws And Paws Pet Sitters
Memphis 901.382.7541

Critter Sitters
Memphis 901.388.6126

Vacation Svcs
Memphis 315.689.9151

Best Friends Pet Stg Svc
Nashville 615.385.0518

Critter Care
Nashville 615.333.2782

Pampered Pets Of Donelson
Nashville 615.889.1500

Pet Stg Tlc
Nashville 615.662.2216

Smiths Critter Keepers
Nashville 615.834.9063

Paws & More PetStg
Smyrna 615.355.0983

Tomjo Knls
White Hse 615.672.4886

Pet Watchers
Woodbury 615.563.6875

TEXAS
The Critter Sitter
Abilene 915.695.4179

Pitter Patter Pets
Amarillo 806.355.7736

Happy Pets Stg
Arlington 817.860.1191

Alexanders Particular Pets
Austin 512.441.6370

Anmlia Petcare
Austin 512.292.0796

Lovin Petcare
Austin 512.835.4085

Midtown Grming Pet Stg
Austin 512.477.8079

Pampered Pets & Places
Austin 512.335.3040

Personalized Petcare
Austin 512.280.7455

Your Secret
Austin 512.474.2007

Windy Valley Brding Knls
Brenham 409.836.3105

Purelove Pet Sitters
Carrollton 972.418.7124

Cats ABrd
Colleyville 817.577.2287

In-Hse Pet And Home Care
Colleyville 817.571.3981

Top Cat Care
Copperas Cove
817.547.0569

All Pets Bathe & Grm
Crp Christi 512.939.9597

Critter Sitters
Crp Christi 512.991.3523

Claws And Paws
Dallas 972.484.3793

Landmark Associated Svcs
Dallas 972.733.1878

Otter Crk Pet Ldg & Cntry
Club
Dallas 214.521.0073

Pet Watch
Dallas 972.243.3388

Pets R Us
Dallas 972.614.7397

Anml Lovers
Fort Worth 817.788.8810

Critter Companion
Fort Worth 817.292.0377

Critter Sitters Unltd
Fort Worth 817.788.2275

Maid For Pets
Fort Worth 817.626.7387

My Sitter Etc
Fort Worth 817.244.9316

Nghbrhd Stg Svc Hse & Pet
Fort Worth 817.732.6776

The Pet Valet
Fort Worth 817.281.0171

Best Friends Pet Resort &
Houston 713.664.6111

Cat Tenders
Houston 713.644.2696

Creatures Comforts
Houston 713.862.1844

Critter Companion Formerly
Houston 713.522.7222

Georges Pampered Paws
Houston 713.695.3142

Marks Tlc In Home Pet
Houston 713.988.0959

Puppy Love Brding
Houston 281.580.6918

Critter Sitters
Humble 281.360.7722

The Caretaker
Lufkin 409.632.9776

Pampered Paws
Mansfield 817.473.6862

Aall Around Referral
Mesquite 972.613.6886

Sassys Pet Nanny
Midland 915.684.0814

Country Club Grming
Missouri City 281.499.8772

Triangle Pet Sitters
Nederland 409.729.7387

P S S T
Plano 972.517.0482

Pet Plus
Plano 972.618.3559

Preferred Pet Sitters
Rosenberg 281.232.2341

Bark & Purr Pet Sitters
San Antonio 210.599.7387

Best Friends Pet Resort &
Sln
San Antonio 210.822.0003

Companion Keepers
San Antonio 210.545.5333

The Dog Hse Pet Salon
San Antonio 210.822.0365

The Creature Keeper
Seguin 210.379,3073

Cross Country Care
Tomball 281.351.5559

Pet Sitters
Victoria 512.573.2466

ALEXANDRIA
Alexandria Pet Stg
Alexandria 703.823.9225

Bencelia Knls
Alexandria 703.354.6700

Paws & Claws Pet
Alexandria 703.780.8767

Pet Au Pair
Alexandria 703.836.0229

Woodlawn Knls
Alexandria 703.360.6161

Julies Pooch Pad
Arlington 703.820.7387

Paw In Hand
Arlington 703.271.1955

Grand Paws Petcare
Blacksburg 540.552.0116

Tinas Hse & Pet Stg Svc
Bluemont 540.554.2436

Teddys Tender Care
Burke 703.455.4517

Club Pet International
Chantilly 703.471.7818

Chester Grming Cottage
Chester 804.748.6856

Alpha Knls
Culpeper 540.825.1247

Jills Pet Stg
Culpeper 540.547.4138

Happy At Home
Fredericksbrg 540.785.0385

Pied Piper
Great Falls 703.759.4922

Pet Stg By Mitzie
Harrisonburg 540.432.6899

Critter Sitters
Herndon 703.437.4100

Critter Cmfrt Pet Care
Manassas 703.369.6802

Marilyns Pampered Pets
Manassas 703.361.7728

Yappie Cuttery
Manassas 703.361.1363

Great Falls Brdng Knls
Mc Lean 703.759.2620

Canine College
Middleburg 540.687.5251

All For Paws
Newport 540.552.3673

Accomack Anml Hospital
Onley 757.787.3112

Powhatan Pet Professional
Powhatan 804.598.8728

Blue Ridge Vet Assocs
Purcellville 540.338.7387

Gentle Touch Mobile Grm
Richmond 804.745.4437

Purely Pets
Richmond 804.323.4275

Clip & Dip Pro Dog Grm
Roanoke 540.774.3461

Mothers Love Pet Stg Svc
Roanoke 540.772.7487

Pet And Hse Sitters
Roanoke 540.774.4299

All Pets Care
Springfield 703.644.7905

While Youre Away
Springfield 703.807.2929

A Dogs Delite Pet Sitters
Stafford 540.659.2927

Ursulas Pet Sitter
Stephens City 540.869.2902

Aberdeen Acres Knl
Stephenson 540.667.7809

Pet Sitters
Tabb 757.867.7387

Loving Care Pet Resort
Verona 540.248.6816

Time Savers
Virginia Bch 757.463.8789

Tlc Pet Stg
Whester 540.722.4664

Loving Cat Care
Woodbridge 703.490.5300

VERMONT
Creature Comforts
Manchestr Ctr 802.362.0189

Make A Moment
Montpelier 802.229.0817

The Crate Escape
Richmond 802.434.6411

Home Alone Anml Care Svc
Rutland 802.773.4663

Maggie Maes Petcare
S Burlington 802.658.5323

Doggie Daycare
Williston 802.860.1144

WASHINGTON
Pet Pals
Anacortes 360.293.1311

Cc Canin Enterprises
Bellingham 360.671.0116

Mountain Vet Hospital
Bellingham 360.592.5113

Muttleys
Bellingham 360.671.3647

Pets Western Inn
Bellingham 360.738.1302

Sharons Pet Pals
Bellingham 360.647.2545

Flos Pet Stg Serv
E Wenatchee 509.884.7644

Kensington Knls
Friday Harbor 360.378.5432

Vacation Petcare
Gig Harbor 206.265.8500

Barbandale
Kirkland 206.822.5604

In Your Home Petcare
Kirkland 206.827.3654

Family Affair Too
Long Beach 360.642.5501

Beastly Endeavors
Lynnwood 206.743.6130

Park Place Pet Sitter
Monroe 360.794.1458

A-1 Petcare
MountLk Ter 206.776.2365

Whiskers & Tails
Mukilteo 206.347.0322

Von Schultz Knls
Newport 509.447.3543

Aloha Petcare & Home Svcs
Redmond 206.236.4641

Pampered Paws
Richland 509.946.1683

Critter Sitter
Seattle 206.324.7441

Cstm Care For Companion
Shoreline 206.368.0503

Conway Knl
Stanwood 360.445.6901

For Petes Sake
Wenatchee 509.665.0234

WISCONSIN
Becky Chase
Appleton 414.731.1854

All ABrd Knl
Big Bend 414.662.2323

Fin Fur & Feathers Pet Stg
Burlington 414.763.2114

Vip Stg
Delafield 414.646.4944

Sunset Dog Brding Knls
Florence 715.589.2157

Reichland Knls
Fort Atkinson 414.563.7080

Golrusk Petcare Center
Green Bay 414.468.7956

Maid For Pets
Green Bay 414.499.7839

Town & Country Pet Sitters
Green Bay 414.432.1111

Always There Petcare
Kenosha 414.859.2907

For Pets Sake
Kenosha 414.942.1188

Collettes Bow Wowserie Grm
La Crosse 608.784.9676

Your Home Petcare
La Crosse 608.788.9654

Armdll Pet & Hse Stg Svc
Madison 608.256.7387

Park Ur Pooch
Madison 608.249.6660

Cathys In-HomePetcare
Manitowoc 414.682.1555

Castlerocks Critters Cafe
Marshfield 715.389.1118

Angelcare Pet Resort
Racine 414.886.8728

Pet Friends
Racine 414.554.7470

WEST VIRGINIA
Cleaners Helpers & More
Barboursville 304.733.2149

Home Alone Critter Care
Beckley 304.253.7297

Pet Check
Bridgeport 304.623.2273

Tender Loving Petcare
Gerrardstown 304.229.2222

Pet Sitters
Hurricane 304.562.7619

Posh Pet Knls
Martinsburg 304.264.4647

Howladay In Home Pet
Tenders
Washington 304.863.8533

If your pet becomes ill during travel, go to a vet at once. Find a vet in the area where you are in by using our 2,500+ listings, the local yellow pages or call the American Animal Hospital Association (AAHA) at (800) 252-2242. AAHA can give you the location of a nearby veterinary clinic during the hours of 9 - 5 Mountain Time, Monday through Friday.

If your pet is sick at other times, don't wait for weekday hours. Take your pet to a close-by emergency clinic. DO NOT DELAY CARE FOR YOUR PET.

ALASKA
College Village Anml Clnc
Anchorage 907.274.5623

Northern Lights Anml Clnc
Anchorage 907.276.2340

VCA E Anchorage Anml
Hosp
Anchorage 907.337.1561

Mt McKinley Anml Hosp
Fairbanks 907.452.6104

Wasilla Vet Clnc
Wasilla 907.376.3993

ALABAMA
Jones Vet Hosp
Andalusia 334.222.4713

Village Vet Clnc
Auburn 334.821.7730

Central Park Anml Hosp
Birmingham 205.787.8601

Hoke Anml Clnc
Birmingham 205.956.6096

Kelley Anml Hosp
Birmingham 205.833.9400

Kents Anml Hosp
Birmingham 205.323.1536

Oxmoor Anml Clnc
Birmingham 205.871.6010

Riverview Anml Clnc
Birmingham 205.991.9580

Roebuck Dog&Cat Hosp
Birmingham 205.833.7104

Osborne Anml Clnc
Decatur 205.353.4339

Care Anml Hosp
Dothan 334.794.6333

Green Springs Anml Clnc
Homewood 205.942.5144

Anml Med Clnc
Huntsville 205.837.9700

Bentley Anml Hosp
Huntsville 205.852.4121

Renfroe Anml Hosp Clnc
Huntsville 205.533.4411

Whitesburg Anml Hosp
Huntsville 205.882.0950

McAdory Vet Associates
Mc Calla 205.424.7387

Azalea Anml Hosp
Mobile 334.479.4566

W Mobile Vet Clnc
Mobile 334.633.3608

Brown Sternenberg Anml
Hosp
Montgomery 334.281.0415

Goodwin Anml Hosp
Montgomery 334.279.7456

Northwood Vet Clnc
Northport 205.339.3200

Gulf Coast Vet Hosp
Orange Beach 334.974.5633

Companion Anml Hosp
Phenix City 334.297.2316

Anml Health Care
Rainbow City 205.442.2967

Trussville Anml Hosp
Trussville 205.655.8538

ARKANSAS
Congo Road Anml Clnc
Benton 501.778.4000

Reynolds Road Anml Clnc
Bryant 501.847.5300

Petcare Vet Clnc
Cabot 501.941.7387

Maul Road Anml Clnc
Camden 501.836.4371

Ralston Anml Hosp
El Dorado 501.863.4194

E 16 Anml Hosp
Fayetteville 501.443.5221

Stanton Anml Hosp
Fayetteville 501.443.4544

All Anml Health Cntr
Fort Smith 501.452.5154

Ozark Vet Hosp
Harrison 501.741.1664

Lake Hamilton Anml Hosp
Hot Springs 501.767.8503

Canterbury Vet Clnc
Jacksonville 501.982.2536

Vetcare
Jonesboro 501.972.5320

Col Glenn Stagecoach Vet
Little Rock 501.562.1256

Hillcrest Anml Hosp
Little Rock 501.663.1284

Pleasant Valley Vet Clnc
Little Rock 501.225.2600

Sherwood Pet Clnc
N Little Rock 501.834.3434

Hope New Anml Hosp
Rogers 501.631.0880

Hubbs Anml Clnc
Van Buren 501.474.6898

ARIZONA
Anml Health Services
Buckeye 602.386.2532

Casa Grande Anml Hosp
Casa Grande 520.836.5979

Dr Leslie Wootton
Chandler 602.732.0018

First Regional Anml Hosp
Chandler 602.732.0018

Kennel Care Vet Svc
Chandler 602.940.0066

Circle L Anml Clnc
Chino Valley 520.636.4421

Alpine Anml Hosp
Flagstaff 520.774.9441

Caring Hearts Anml Clnc
Gilbert 602.545.8921

43 Avenue Anml Hosp
Glendale 602.843.5452

Acdmy W Anml Hosp
Glendale 602.938.8650

Dr Jim Prater
Glendale 602.938.2707

Glenn Anml Care Hosp
Glendale 602.937.4004

Samaritan Vet Cntr
Globe 520.425.5797

The Anml Clnc
Green Valley 520.625.7566

Novak Anml Care Cntr
Lk Havasu Cty 520.855.0588

Dr Ray C Anderson
Mesa 602.838.3682

Mesa Verde Anml Hosp
Mesa 602.969.0900

Mesa Vet Hosp Ltd
Mesa 602.833.7330

Petsmart Vet Services
Mesa 602.898.3100

Petsmart Vet Services
Mesa 602.641.9000

Sysel Anml Hosp
Mesa 602.964.9601

Petsmart Vet Services
Peoria 602.486.9600

AAA Clncs
Phoenix 602.942.4308

AAA Clncs
Phoenix 602.273.7387

Ahwatukee Commons Vet Hosp
Phoenix 602.893.8423

Amigo Anml Clnc
Phoenix 602.971.3561

Anml Care Hosp & Clnc
Phoenix 602.955.5757

Central Phoenix Anml Hosp
Phoenix 602.277.5155

Cortez Anml Hosp
Phoenix 602.973.0709

Desert View Anml Hosp
Phoenix 602.955.5500

Dr Rita J Roberts
Phoenix 602.996.3540

Loln View Anml Hosp
Phoenix 602.944.1585

Lookout Mountain Vet Clnc
Phoenix 602.993.1660

Moon Valley Anml Hosp
Phoenix 602.942.8850

Palo Verde Anml Hosp
Phoenix 602.944.9661

Quail Run Anml Hosp
Phoenix 602.996.0966

Southside Anml Hosp
Phoenix 602.276.5505

Westridge Anml Hosp
Phoenix 602.846.5635

Thump Butte Anml Hosp
Prescott 520.445.2331

Anml Med Ctr Scottsdale
Scottsdale 602.945.7692

Aztec Anml Hosp
Scottsdale 602.945.8671

Emer Anml Clnc Ltd
Scottsdale 602.949.8001

Estrella Anml Hosp
Scottsdale 602.877.1088

Pets Plus
Scottsdale 602.991.2858

Scottsdale Ranch Anml Hosp
Scottsdale 602.391.3699

Sonora Vet Surg & Oncology
Scottsdale 602.483.6677

Oak Creek Small Anml Clnc
Sedona 520.282.1195

Buena Vet Clnc
Sierra Vista 520.458.5841

Sun Lakes Anml Clnc
Sun Lakes 602.895.7633

El Mirage Anml Hosp
Surprise 602.583.9335

Anml Care Cntr
Tempe 602.966.1580

Petsmart Vet Cntr
Tempe 602.961.3377

Univ Vet Hosp & Brdng Knl
Tempe 602.968.9275

AAA Clncs
Tucson 520.321.0277

Ajo Vet Clnc
Tucson 520.623.5728

Amphi-Pet Hosp
Tucson 520.887.6363

Canada Hills Anml Hosp
Tucson 520.544.4734

Companion Anml Clnc
Tucson 520.327.5763

Desert Small Anml Hosp
Tucson 520.888.8586

Dr J W Percell
Tucson 520.795.4612

Encanto Pet Clnc
Tucson 520.881.3221

NorthW Pet Clnc
Tucson 520.742.4148

Pantano Anml Clnc
Tucson 520.885.3594

Plaza Pet Clnc
Tucson 520.544.2080

St Marys Anml Clnc
Tucson 520.623.8439

Valley Anml Hosp
Tucson 520.327.0331

Vet Specialists
Tucson 520.885.2364

Kritter Kare
Winslow 520.289.3273

Ironwood Vet Clnc
Yuma 520.726.5432

CALIFORNIA
VCA Agoura Meadows Anml Hosp
Agoura Hills 818.889.0810

Alamo Anml Hosp
Alamo 510.837.7246

Diablo Horse Clnc
Alamo 510.939.8700

Alhambra Vet Hosp
Alhambra 818.289.9227

Ball-Hurst Anml Hosp
Anaheim 714.533.6441

E Hills Anml Hosp
Anaheim 714.921.2500

Nohl Ranch Anml Hosp
Anaheim 714.637.9730

Auburn Blvd Vet Hosp
Antelope 916.349.2755

Antioch Vet Hosp
Antioch 510.757.2233

Bear Valley Anml Hosp
Apple Valley 619.240.5228

Arcadia Small Anml Hosp
Arcadia 818.447.8144

Arcata Anml Hosp
Arcata 707.822.2402

VCA S County Anml Hosp
Arroyo Grande 805.489.1361

N Fork Vet Clnc
Auburn 916.888.8788

Azusa Hills Anml Hosp
Azusa 818.969.2266

Bakersfield Vet Hosp
Bakersfield 805.834.6005

Kern Anml Emer Clnc
Bakersfield 805.322.6019

Olive Drive Anml Hosp
Bakersfield 805.393.1213

Stiern Vet Hosp
Bakersfield 805.327.5571

Banning Vet Hosp
Banning 909.849.3864

Belmont Pet Hosp
Belmont 415.593.3161

Beverly Hills Small Anml
Hosp
Beverly Hills 310.276.7113

Brea Vet Hosp
Brea 714.529.4988

Specifically Eqn Vet Svc
Buellton 805.688.2825

Buena Anml Clnc
Buena Park 714.522.2020

M S Anml Hosp
Burbank 213.849.3420

Calistoga Pet Clnc
Calistoga 707.942.0404

Goldorado Anml Hosp
Cameron Park 916.677.8387

Camino Anml Hosp
Camino 916.644.6011

Central Anml Hosp
Campbell 408.377.4043

Pets Rx
Campbell 408.378.8133

The Cat Hosp
Campbell 408.866.6188

Companion Anml Hosp
Canoga Park 818.340.1569

Adobe Vet Hosp
Canyon Cntry 805.251.3710

Carlsbad Anml Hosp
Carlsbad 619.729.4431

Anml Hosp At Mid Valley
Carmel 408.624.8509

Blue Cross Pet Hosp
Carmichael 916.944.3850

Carpinteria Vet Hosp
Carpinteria 805.684.3617

Valencia Vet Group
Castaic 805.257.6363

Bay Area Spay Neuter
Castro Valley 510.582.6705

Date Palm Anml Hosp
Cathedral Cty 619.328.3330

Cerritos S Vet Clnc
Cerritos 310.860.7747

Anml Med Ctr Chatsworth
Chatsworth 818.709.8659

Cozycroft Pet Hosp
Chatsworth 818.341.3040

Acacia Vet Hosp
Chico 916.345.1338

Evers Vet Clnc
Chico 916.343.0713

Otay Lake Vet Clnc
Chula Vista 619.482.2000

All About Pets
Citrus Hts 916.722.0400

Pets Rx
Citrus Hts 916.725.2200

Claremont Vet Hosp
Claremont 909.621.0900

Vet Smart Care Clnc
Clovis 209.297.9350

All Bay Anml Hosp
Concord 510.687.7346

Clayton Valley Pet Hosp
Concord 510.689.4600

Crown Vet Hosp
Coronado 619.435.6624

All Creatures Care
Csta Mesa 714.642.7151

Bayshore Anml Hosp
Costa Mesa 714.646.1664

Newport Harbor Anml Hosp
Costa Mesa 714.631.1030

Newport-Mesa Anml Hosp
Costa Mesa 714.642.2100

Cotati Large Anml Hosp
Cotati 707.795.4356

Anml Med Cntr
Covina 818.339.5401

Cypress Ave Anml Hosp
Covina 818.331.0775

Culver City Anml Hosp
Culver City 310.836.4551

A B C Anml Hosp
Cypress 714.995.8033

Aids Pet Cntr
Daly City 415.994.9907

Dana Niguel Vet Hosp
Dana Point 714.661.6375

General Pet Hosp
Diamond Bar 909.861.4116

Dixon Vet Clnc
Dixon 916.678.2377

Se Area Anml Cntrl Athrty
Downey 310.803.3301

Tri Valley Vet Emer Clnc
Dublin 510.828.0654

Abc Vet Hosps
El Cajon 619.590.6160

Anml Care Clnc
El Cajon 619.670.8700

Vet Hosp
El Sobrante 510.223.0740

Bradshaw Vet Clnc
Elk Grove 916.685.2494

Hatton Vet Hosp
Elk Grove 916.689.1688

N Coast Vet Medl Grp
Encinitas 619.632.1072

Encino Vet Clnc
Encino 818.783.7387

Companion Anml Clnc
Escondido 619.743.2751

Hazel Ridge Vet Clnc
Fair Oaks 916.965.8200

Brook-Ellis Pet Hosp
Fountain Vly 714.963.0440

Westhaven Vet Hosp
Fountain Vly 714.775.5544

Ctrl Vet Hosp & Emer Svc
Fremont 510.797.7387

Irvington Pet Hosp
Fremont 510.657.4060

Kings Canyon Vet Hosp
Fresno 209.251.8482

L H Krum & Associates
Fresno 209.266.1327

Vet Smart Care Clnc
Fresno 209.271.0437

Aspen Pet Clnc
Fullerton 714.870.9497

Anml Dermatology Clnc
Garden Grove 714.971.6211

Garden Grove Dog & Cat
Hosp
Garden Grove 714.537.8800

Golden State Humane
Society
Garden Grove 714.638.8111

California Vet Hosp
Gardena 310.323.6867

Gavilan Anml Hosp
Gilroy 408.842.0393

Orchard Vet Hosp
Gilroy 408.842.1333

Westwood Anml Hosp
Gilroy 408.848.3443

Anml Emer Clnc Glendale
Glendale 818.247.3973

Rafael M Villicana
Glendale 213.256.5840

Elwood Anml Clnc
Glendora 818.914.5671

La Concepcion Anml Hosp
Goleta 805.685.4513

Brighton Greens Vet Hosp
Grass Valley 916.477.6863

Brunswick Vet Clnc
Grass Valley 916.477.2287

Greenbrae Pet Hosp
Greenbrae 415.924.3493

Oak Park Vet Clnc
Grover Beach 805.481.6641

Anml Clnc W
Harbor City 310.534.0315

Anml Med Cntr
Hawthorne 310.978.4065

Chabot Vet Clnc & Hosp
Hayward 510.538.2330

Noble Vet Clnc
Hayward 510.537.3292

Acacia Anml Hosp
Hemet 909.658.3219

Coast Pet Clnc
Hermosa Beach
310.318.2436

Highland Village Pet Hosp
Highland 909.864.7387

Hollister Vet Clnc
Hollister 408.637.2580

Beach Blvd Pet Hosp
Huntington Bh 714.847.1291

Hamilton Anml Hosp
Huntington Bh 714.964.4744

Huntington Pet-Vet
Huntington Bh 714.969.0211

Irvine Vet Services
Irvine 714.786.0990

Northwood Anml Hosp
Irvine 714.559.1992

Woodbridge Hosp For Anmls
Irvine 714.551.0304

Foothill Vet Clnc
Jackson 209.223.3131

Crescenta-Canada Pet Hosp
La Crescenta 818.248.3963

Gregg Anml Hosp
La Habra 310.691.7751

The Anml Hosp
La Jolla 619.459.2665

El Cerrito Vet Hosp
La Mesa 619.466.0533

Fletcher Hills Pet Clnc
La Mesa 619.463.6604

Parkway Pet Hosp
La Mesa 619.463.9151

Imperial Anml Hosp
La Mirada 310.941.0284

La Puente Pet Hosp
La Puente 818.330.4558

La Verne Anml Hosp
La Verne 909.593.4340

Mt Diablo Vet Medl Ctr
Lafayette 510.284.1350

Laguna Beach Anml Hosp
Laguna Beach 714.494.9721

El Toro All Anml Hosp
Lake Forest 714.837.5222

Saddleback Anml Care Cntr
Lake Forest 714.586.4250

Lakeside Vet Hosp
Lakeside 619.390.2342

Hawthorne Dog & Cat Hosp
Lawndale 310.675.3328

Adobe Pet Hosp
Livermore 510.449.4228

Narbonne Anml Clnc
Lomita 310.325.5850

Ambassador Dog & Cat
Hosp
Long Beach 310.427.7933

Belmont Shore Anml Clnc
Long Beach 310.433.9986

Jaymor Anml Hosp
Long Beach 310.597.5533

Spring Street Anml Hosp
Long Beach 310.421.8463

Loomis Basin Vet Ctr Lrge
Loomis 916.652.7645

Ambassador Dog & Cat
Hosp
Los Angeles 213.384.1255

Angeles City Anml Medl Ctr
Los Angeles 213.933.8406

Angeles Vista Pet Med Ctr
Los Angeles 213.292.0387

Century Vet Group
Los Angeles 310.559.2500

L A Central Anml Hosp
Los Angeles 213.225.4228

Petville Anml Hosp
Los Angeles 310.313.9118

Rancho Park Vet Clnc
Los Angeles 310.474.3398

Sunset Anml Hosp
Los Angeles 213.850.6952

El Gato Vet Hosp
Los Gatos 408.356.2181

Los Gatos Dog&Cat Hosp
Los Gatos 408.354.6474

Oak Mdw Vet Hosp & Brdng
Los Gatos 408.354.0838

Anml Med Group
Manhattan Bch 310.546.5731

Bay Cities Vet Hosp
Marina Dl Rey 310.821.4967

Anml Eye Clnc
Menlo Park 415.321.1218

Mid-Peninsula Anml Hosp
Menlo Park 415.325.5671

Atwater Vet Clnc
Merced 209.358.4469

Middletown Anml Hosp
Middletown 707.987.2000

Tamalpais Pet Hosp
Mill Valley 415.388.3315

Capuchino Vet Clnc
Millbrae 415.583.1500

Granada Vet Clnc
Mission Hills 818.361.0125

Portola Plaza Vet Hosp
Mission Viejo 714.859.2101

Stanislaus Feline Practice
Modesto 209.524.5226

Sylvan Vet Clnc
Modesto 209.551.4527

Vet Emer Clnc
Modesto 209.527.8844

Montebello Vet Hosp
Montebello 213.726.1525

Aguajito Vet Hosp
Monterey 408.372.8151

Spca Monterey Cnty
Humane Scty
Monterey 408.373.2631

Sunnymead Anml Hosp
Moreno Valley 909.242.3118

Mt Shasta Anml Hosp
Mount Shasta 916.926.5266

California Oaks Vet Clnc
Murrieta 909.698.8919

Murrieta Equine Associates
Murrieta 909.676.5587

California Pet Hosp
Napa 707.255.6832

Frontier Pet Clnc
Napa 707.252.3390

Evergreen Anml Hosp
Newhall 805.254.5102

Newport Hills Anml Hosp
Newport Beach 714.759.1911

Norco Equine Hosp
Norco 909.734.0084

Northridge Pet Hosp
Northridge 818.885.8323

Kirk Anml Clnc
Oak View 805.649.4094

Oakland Vet Hosp
Oakland 510.530.1353

The Lake Vet Hosp
Oakland 510.452.1255

Lone Star Vet Hosp
Oceanside 619.722.4840

Temple Heights Anml Hosp
Oceanside 619.630.3590

Matilija Vet Hosp
Ojai 805.646.5539

Chino Valley Vet Assocs
Ontario 909.947.3529

Orange Vet Hosp
Orange 714.978.6260

Orange Villa Vet Hosp
Orange 714.637.3660

Pet Hosp
Orange 714.771.3261

Butte Oroville Vet Hosp
Oroville 916.533.1194

Linda Mar Vet Hosp
Pacifica 415.359.6471

Vet Oncology Splty
Pacifica 415.359.3132

Anml Med Clnc
Pacoima 818.896.9770

Dsrt Anml Hosp
Palm Springs 619.323.1794

Antelope Valley Anml Hosp
Palmdale 805.273.1234

Palo Alto Pet Hosp
Palo Alto 415.323.8558

Stanford Pet Clnc
Palo Alto 415.493.4233

Clark Road Vet Hosp
Paradise 916.872.5111

A Breed Apart Vet Ctrs
Pasadena 818.795.4444

Foothill Vet Hosp
Pasadena 818.792.1187

A E Z R Pet Hosp
Petaluma 707.778.7521

Brandner Vet Hosp
Petaluma 707.762.3549

VCA Bay Area Anml Hosp
Piedmont 510.654.8375

Anml Hosp Of Pittsburg
Pittsburg 510.432.0818

Placentia Vet Clnc
Placentia 714.528.3145

Hillcrest Vet Clnc
Pleasant Hill 510.676.1909

Amador Valley Vet Hosp
Pleasanton 510.462.3646

Pomona Valley Vet Hosp
Pomona 909.623.2602

Anml Med Hosp Poway
Poway 619.748.5989

Valley Vet Clnc
Red Bluff 916.527.5259

Hilltop Vet Hosp
Redding 916.221.6733

Panorama Farm Vet Medcn
Redding 916.221.7004

Anml Med Cntr Redlands
Redlands 909.793.4775

P V Pet Hosp
Redondo Beach
310.540.5656

River Oak Vet Hosp
Riverbank 209.869.3692

Arlington Anml Hosp
Riverside 909.689.0440

Canyon Crest Anml Hosp
Riverside 909.684.2121

Pedley Vet Hosp
Riverside 909.685.5224

Cntr Anml Hosp
Rllng Hls Est 310.377.5548

Folsom Blvd Pet Hosp
Rncho Cordova
916.363.6561

Vetsmart Pet Hosp & Hlth Ctr
Rncho Cordova
916.853.1351

All Pets Vet Hosp
Rncho Pls Vrd 310.547.2784

Expressway Vet Hosp
Rohnert Park 707.584.4848

Placer Vet Clnc
Roseville 916.786.5711

All Our Pets Hosp
Sacramento 916.452.2685

Anml Den Annex
Sacramento 916.456.4723

Arden Anml Hosp
Sacramento 916.485.5412

Broadway Vet Hosp
Sacramento 916.446.6154

Discovery Plaza Vet Clnc
Sacramento 916.920.1555

Pocket S Pet Hosp
Sacramento 916.395.7387

S Sacramento Pet Hosp
Sacramento 916.421.0619

Large Anml Vet Corp
Salinas 408.455.1808

Romie Lane Pet Hosp
Salinas 408.424.0863

White & Ivie Small Anml
Hosp
San Bruno 415.583.5039

San Clemente Vet Hosp
San Clemente 714.492.5777

Avian & Reptile Medl Clnc
San
San Diego 619.299.6020

Bay Park Pet Clnc
San Diego 619.276.1616

Bernardo Westwood Vet Clnc
San Diego 619.485.7570

Boulevard Anml Clnc
San Diego 619.582.7250

Carmel Mtn Rnch Vet Hosp
San Diego 619.592.9779

Clairemont Square Anml
Hosp
San Diego 619.274.1760

Friars Road Pet Hosp
San Diego 619.282.7677

Grand Anml Hosp
San Diego 619.272.1320

Mesa Pet Hosp
San Diego 619.279.3000

Palm Ridge Pet Hosp
San Diego 619.690.2272

Peninsula Vet Clnc
San Diego 619.223.7145

Shelter Island Vet Clnc
San Diego 619.222.0597

Arrow Anml Hosp
San Dimas 909.592.1931

Dill Vet Hosp
San Fernando 818.899.5287

Arguello Pet Hosp
San Francisco 415.751.3242

Avenues Pet Hosp
San Francisco 415.681.4313

Ocean Avenue Vet Hosp
San Francisco 415.586.5327

Small Anml Hosp
San Jacinto 909.654.7396

Almadale Anml Hosp
San Jose 408.227.1661

Pets Rx
San Jose 408.268.0289

Pets Rx
San Jose 408.227.0416

Saratoga Pet Clnc
San Jose 408.253.6717

VCA Crocker Anml Hosp
San Jose 408.272.1330

San Juan Anml Hosp
San Juan Capo
714.493.1147

Alameda County Emer Pet Clnc
San Leandro 510.352.6080

San Lorenzo Vet Hosp
San Lorenzo 510.276.7234

Levitt Anml Hosp
San Marcos 619.744.5242

San Martin Vet Hosp
San Martin 408.683.4777

Nthrn Pen Vet Emer Clnc
San Mateo 415.348.2575

Rolling Hills Anml Hosp
San Pedro 310.831.1209

Dog & Cat House Calls
San Ramon 510.735.7387

San Ramon Vet Hosp
San Ramon 510.837.0526

Alton Centre Anml Hosp
Santa Ana 714.540.3105

Grnd Ave Pet Hosp
Santa Ana 714.558.7622

A B C Vet Hosp
Santa Barbara 805.564.1464

Pets Rx
Santa Clara 408.246.1893

A-1 Vet Services
Santa Clarita 805.255.7767

Anml Hosp Of Soquel
Santa Cruz 408.475.0432

La Mirada Anml Hosp
Santa Fe Spgs 310.921.3539

Anml Clnc Of Santa Maria
Santa Maria 805.937.7671

Santa Monica Dog & Cat Hosp
Santa Monica 310.453.5459

Vet Cntrs Of Amer
Santa Monica 310.392.9599

Coddingtown Vet Clnc
Santa Rosa 707.546.4646

Ron Valley Anml Hosp
Santa Rosa 707.539.1262

Sequoia Valley Vet Hosp
Santa Rosa 707.545.7387

Moblvet Vet Hosp
Sausalito 415.332.2212

McConnell Vet Service
Scotts Valley 408.438.0751

Jack Long Vmd
Sebastopol 707.823.7312

Adler Vet Group
Sepulveda 818.893.6366

Angeles Anml Hosp
Simi Valley 805.527.6877

Santa Susana Vet Medl Hosp
Simi Valley 805.526.3455

Murieta Anml Hosp
Sloughhouse 916.354.0511

Highland Avenue Vet Clnc
Sn Bernrdno 909.889.0093

Loma Linda Anml Hosp
Sn Bernrdno 909.825.3144

Anml Care Clnc
Sn Luis Obisp 805.545.8212

Stenner Creek Anml Hosp
Sn Luis Obisp 805.543.2500

Academy Anml Hosp
Solana Beach 619.755.1511

Humphrey & Giacopuzzi Vet
Somis 805.386.4291

S Gate Dog & Cat Hosp
S Gate 213.564.6913

Paradise Valley Road Pet Hosp
Spring Valley 619.263.0345

Walker Vet Hosp
Stockton 209.478.8883

W Lane Pet Hosp
Stockton 209.465.5414

Studio City Anml Hosp
Studio City 818.769.1338

Not Just 4 Paws Anml Hosp
Sun City 909.244.4199

Shadow Hills Pet Clnc
Sun Valley 818.767.3904

Verdugo Pet Hosp
Sunland 818.353.8508

Pets Friend Anml Clnc
Sunnyvale 408.739.2688

Serra Vet Hosp
Sunnyvale 408.739.3545

Conejo Valley Vet Clnc
Thousand Oaks
818.889.1415

Anml Emer Clnc Dsrt
Thousand Plms
619.343.3438

Clarmar Anml Hosp
Torrance 310.371.2474

Country Hills Anml Clnc
Torrance 310.539.3851

Sierra Pet Clnc Of Truckee
Truckee 916.587.7200

Cross Street Vet Clnc
Tulare 209.688.0631

Lander Vet Clnc
Turlock 209.634.5801

Tustin Santa Ana Pet Hosp
Tustin 714.544.3124

Mendocino Anml Hosp
Ukiah 707.462.8833

Foothill Anml Hosp
Upland 909.985.1988

All Creatures Vet Hosp
Vallejo 707.642.4405

Anml Med Cntr
Van Nuys 818.786.1651

Mission Anml Hosp
Ventura 805.643.5479

Care Vet Clnc Visalia
Visalia 209.625.8549

Lone Oak Vet Clnc
Visalia 209.732.4818

Tri-City Vet Clnc
Vista 619.758.2091

Sacramento Anml Medl Grp
W Sacramento 916.371.8900

Cottage Vet Hosp
Walnut Creek 510.935.9080

Valley Vet Hosp
Walnut Creek 510.932.2420

E Lake Anml Clnc
Watsonville 408.724.6391

W Covina Pet Hosp
W Covina 818.337.2023

Magnolia Anml Hosp
Westminster 714.848.9114

SouthE Pet Clnc
Whittier 310.944.6296

Whittier Dog & Cat Hosp
Whittier 310.698.0264

Clinton Keith Vet Hosp
Wildomar 909.678.7800

VCA W Los Angeles Anml Hosp
Wla 310.473.2951

Yolo Vet Clnc
Woodland 916.666.3366

VCA Parkwood Anml Hosp
Woodland Hls 818.884.5506

E Lake Anml Hosp
Yorba Linda 714.777.1661

Equine Vet Associates
Yorba Linda 310.691.8160

COLORADO
Arvada Flats Vet Hosp
Arvada 303.467.9212

Jefferson Anml Clnc
Arvada 303.423.3370

Altos Vet Clnc
Aurora 303.343.8796

Chambers Point Vet Clnc
Aurora 303.751.5593

Pet Palace Vet Clnc
Aurora 303.699.0477

Petsvet
Aurora 303.360.0760

Seven Hills Vet Cntr
Aurora 303.699.1600

Lone Rock Vet Clnc
Bailey 303.674.8020

Boulder Vet Hosp
Boulder 303.442.6262

Marshall Road Anml Clnc
Boulder 303.499.5505

Planned Pethood Plus
Boulder 303.444.9859

Kenline Vet Clnc
Canon City 719.275.2081

Aspen Anml Hosp
Carbondale 970.963.2826

Anml Med Services
Colorado Spgs 719.591.1022

Anml Surgical Splty Clnc
Colorado Spgs 719.591.9643

Chapel Hills Anml Clnc
Colorado Spgs 719.593.1336

Cheyenne Mountain Anml
Hosp
Colorado Spgs 719.475.1314

Nw Anml Hosp & Pet Care
Ctr
Colorado Spgs 719.593.8582

Westside Anml Clnc
Colorado Spgs 719.632.6111

Anml Med Specialists
Denver 303.733.2440

Colfax E Anml Hosp
Denver 303.393.0510

Northglenn Vet Clnc
Denver 303.451.1333

Planned Pethood Plus
Denver 303.433.3291

Se Area Vet Medl Ctr
Denver 303.751.4954

The Vets Anml Hosp
Denver 303.429.6594

University Hills Anml Hosp
Denver 303.757.5638

Dr James K Morrow
Durango 970.247.3174

Anml Hosp Ctr Emer Svc
Englewood 303.794.2200

Reference Surgcl Vet Prac
Englewood 303.794.1188

Hiwan Anml Hosp
Evergreen 303.670.0838

Lemay Anml Hosp
Fort Collins 970.482.9840

S Mesa Vet Hosp
Fort Collins 970.226.6526

Welsh Anml Clnc
Fort Collins 970.493.1818

Belcaro Anml Hosp
Glendale 303.756.3653

Golden Anml Hosp
Golden 303.279.6601

Tiara Rado Anml Hosp
Grand Jct 970.243.4007

Anml Care Hosp
Greeley 970.352.7611

W Ridge Anml Hosp
Greeley 970.330.7283

Colorado Vet Clnc
La Junta 719.384.8111

VCA Anderson Anml Hosp
Lakewood 303.922.1127

Anml Clnc At The Festival
Littleton 303.850.9393

Arapahoe Vet Hosp
Littleton 303.794.5574

Cherry Hills Anml Hosp
Littleton 303.730.3248

Deer Creek Anml Hosp
Littleton 303.973.4200

Dr Terry Swanson
Littleton 303.794.6359

Petsmart Vet Svc Co
Littleton 303.971.0070

Nelson Road Vet Clnc
Longmont 303.678.8387

Anmlhouse Vet Clnc
Louisville 303.666.4888

Allard Anml Hosp
Loveland 970.667.9230

Montrose Vet Clnc
Montrose 970.249.5469

Rocky Mountain Equine Clnc
Monument 719.481.2749

Squires Large Anml Practice
Parker 303.841.3099

Pets & Friends Anml Hosp
Pueblo 719.542.2022

Steamboat Vet Hosp
Steamboat Spr 970.879.1041

Wheat Ridge Anml Hosp
Wheat Ridge 303.424.3325

CONNECTICUT
Mountain View Anml Hosp
Llc
Avon 860.675.2134

Fairport Anml Hosp
Bridgeport 203.333.2195

Bristol Vet Associates
Bristol 860.583.4641

Chester Vet Clnc
Chester 860.526.5313

Cromwell Vet Hosp
Cromwell 860.635.1979

Plumtrees Anml Hosp
Danbury 203.748.8878

Darien Anml Hosp
Darien 203.655.1449

Greenfield Anml Hosp
Fairfield 203.254.0700

Highway Anml Hosp
Fairfield 203.366.6733

Gales Ferry Anml Hosp
Gales Ferry 860.464.7286

Glastonbury Vet Hosp
Glastonbury 860.633.3588

Brook Salmon Vet Hosp
Granby 860.653.7238

Noank Mystic Vet Hosp
Groton 860.536.6656

Merryfield Hosp For Anmls
Hamden 203.281.3811

Anml Med Clnc
Manchester 860.646.1110

Connecticut Vly Vet Assocs
Marlborough 860.295.8381

Meriden Anml Hosp
Meriden 203.235.1131

Milford Vet Hosp & Anml
Milford 203.877.3221

Ragged Mountain Anml Hosp
New Britain 860.826.1545

New Hvn Ctrl Hosp For Vet
New Haven 203.865.0878

Candlewood Anml Hosp
New Milford 860.355.3008

Hartford Vet Hosp
Newington 860.666.1447

Mt Pleasant Hosp For Anmls
Newtown 203.426.8585

Ridgehill Anml Hosp
N Haven 203.288.3307

Broad River Anml Hosp
Norwalk 203.846.3495

Norwalk Anml HospClnc
Norwalk 203.846.8146

Norwalk Vet Hosp
Norwalk 203.838.8421

Old Canal Vet Clnc
Plainville 860.747.2759

Apple Valley Veterinarians
Plantsville 860.628.9635

Wolcott Vet Clnc
Prospect 203.758.6601

Anml Hosp Of Rocky Hill
Rocky Hill 860.563.1027

Anml Health Clnc
S Glastonbury 860.633.7388

Valley Vet Hosp
S Windsor 860.528.2178

Southbury Vet Hosp
Southbury 203.264.6569

Davis Anml Hosp
Stamford 203.327.0300

The Pet Hosp Of Stratford
Stratford 203.381.9488

Suffield Vet Hosp
Suffield 860.668.4041

Michael Reid
Trumbull 203.261.9223

Vet Specialists Of Ct
W Hartford 860.236.3273

Mattatuck Anml Hosp
Waterbury 203.754.2105

New London Vet Hosp
Waterford 860.442.0611

Winsted Hosp For Anmls
Winsted 860.379.0701

DISTRICT OF COLUMBIA
Adams Morgan Anml Clnc
Washington 202.638.7470

DELAWARE
Dover Anml Hosp
Dover 302.674.1515

Atlantic Vet Associates
Hockessin 302.234.3275

Middletown Vet Hosp
Middletown 302.378.2342

Milford Anml Hosp
Milford 302.422.3502

Red Lion Vet Hosp
New Castle 302.834.2250

The Pet Practice
Newark 302.737.8100

Anml Kingdom
Wilmington 302.475.2228

Brandywine Hundred Vet
Wilmington 302.792.2777

FLORIDA
Altamonte Vet Hosp
Altamonte Spg 407.339.1922

Spring Run Vet Hosp
Altamonte Spg 407.862.7579

Anml Hosp Of Hunt Club
Apopka 407.862.0595

Piedmont Anml Hosp
Apopka 407.880.7387

Atlantic E Pet Cntr
Atlantic Bch 904.246.8300

Bluffs Anml Hosp Belleair
Belleair Blf 813.585.5682

Belleview Vet Hosp
Belleview 352.347.7331

Countryside Anml Clnc
Beverly Hills 352.746.7171

Anml Hosp At Msn Bay Plz
Boca Raton 561.479.2997

Boca Village Anml Hosp
Boca Raton 561.391.2266

Bonita Vet Clnc
Bnita Spgs 941.498.0100

Coral Breeze Anml Hosp
Boynton Beach
561.738.9400

Pet-Vet
Boynton Beach
561.732.2222

Manatee Vet Clnc
Bradenton 941.746.7902

Palma Sola Anml Clnc
Bradenton 941.794.3275

Santa Cruz Anml Clnc
Brandon 813.685.7751

Brooksville Vet Clnc
Brooksville 352.796.5181

County Line Anml Hosp
Brooksville 352.799.1025

Baywood Vet Hosp
Cape Coral 941.549.2949

Elizabeth Smith
Cape Coral 941.945.2279

Clearwater Anml Clnc
Clearwater 813.584.1151

Murphy Anml Hosp
Clearwater 813.796.2552

Skycrest Anml Hosp
Clearwater 813.461.4960

Tampa Bay Vet Emer Svc
Clearwater 813.531.5752

S Lake Anml Clnc
Clermont 352.394.2202

Coral Springs Anml Hosp
Coral Springs 305.753.1800

Ramblewood Anml Hosp
Coral Springs 954.753.6220

The Pet Practice
Coral Springs 954.752.6270

Wagn Tails Anml Hosp
Davie 954.434.1029

Driftwood Anml Hosp
Daytona Beach
904.255.1407

Imperial Point Anml Hosp
Deerfield Bch 954.426.1234

Lund Anml Hosp
Delray Beach 561.499.5520

Anml Hosp Of Dunedin
Dunedin 813.733.9351

Rainbow River Anml Hosp
Dunnellon 352.489.5121

Apalachicola Bay Anml Clnc
Eastpoint 904.670.8306

Coral Vet Clnc
Fort Myers 941.481.4746

Miracle Mile Anml Clnc
Fort Myers 941.936.0177

San Carlos Park Anml Hosp
Fort Myers 941.267.7711

Briggs Vet Hosp
Fort Pierce 561.461.2739

Andrews Anml Hosp
Ft Lauderdale 954.522.5478

Indian Trace Anml Hosp
Ft Lauderdale 954.384.7147

Promenade Anml Hosp
Ft Lauderdale 954.748.9600

Aalatash Anml Hosp
Gainesville 352.372.5391

Millhopper Vet Medl Ctr
Gainesville 352.373.8055

Shores Anml Hosp
Gainesville 352.372.8502

Green Cove Anml Hosp
Green Cv Spgs
904.284.5624

Amimal Med Cntr
Gulf Breeze 904.932.6085

Parkway Anml Hosp
Gulf Breeze 904.932.5534

Heart Of Florida Anml Hosp
Haines City 941.422.0210

Hialeah Miami Lakes Anml
Clnc
Hialeah 305.821.3160

Palm Springs Anml Hosp
Hialeah 305.821.7801

Treasure Coast Wildlife Hosp
Hobe Sound 561.546.8281

Broward Anml Hosp
Hollywood 954.925.2467

Advanced Pet Care Cntr
Homestead 305.248.6538

S Patrick Anml Hosp
Ind Hbr Bch 407.773.3111

Anml Care Cntr
Jacksonville 904.646.9414

Cornerstone Anml Hosp
Jacksonville 904.766.3089

Hidden Hills Anml Hosp
Jacksonville 904.641.3384

Mandarin Anml Hosp
Jacksonville 904.731.5341

Parkway Anml Hosp
Jacksonville 904.724.6644

San Jose Beauclerc Anml
Hosp
Jacksonville 904.733.5022

Timuquana Anml Hosp
Jacksonville 904.779.0311

Beaches Anml Clnc
Jaxville Bch 904.246.2045

Shoreline Vet Hosp
Jaxville Bch 904.249.8277

Lower Keys Anml Clnc
Key W 305.294.6335

Shewmaker Anml Hosp
Labelle 941.675.2441

Lake Emma Anml Hosp
Lake Mary 407.333.2901

Rdg Vet Hosp
Lk Wales 941.676.8240

Lake Worth Anml Clnc
Lk Worth 561.582.3364

Military Trail Anml Clnc
Lake Worth 561.967.5195

The Pet Practice
Lake Worth 561.964.4448

All Creatures Anml Clnc
Lakeland 941.646.5683

Kraft Anml Hosp
Lakeland 941.646.2241

Lakeland Vet Hosp
Lakeland 941.665.1811

Land O Lakes Anml Hosp
Land O Lakes 813.996.2021

Avian & Anml Hosp
Bardmoor
Largo 813.398.1928

Longboat Key Anml Hosp
Longboat Key 941.383.8816

River Oaks Anml Hosp
Longwood 407.774.1515

Briarwood Vet Hosp
Marianna 904.526.3680

Courtenay Anml Hosp
Merritt Is 407.452.3647

Cabrera Anml Hosp
Miami 305.261.2374

Clnca Veterinaria Latina
Miami 305.264.1335

Companion Anml Hosp
Miami 305.232.6661

Coral Reef Anml Clnc
Miami 305.233.2920

Country Club Anml Hosps
Miami 305.254.6000

Dixie Anml Hosp
Miami 305.238.5161

Greater Miami Anml Hosp
Miami 305.444.4741

Quail Roost Anml Hosp
Miami 305.235.4991

South W Anml Hosp
Miami 305.661.7765

Wander Anml Hosp
Miami 305.598.1425

Black Creek Vet Hosp
Middleburg 904.282.0499

Lake Vet Clnc
Mount Dora 352.357.6040

Noahs Anml Hosp
N Miami Beach
305.651.8681

All Anmls Hosp Gldn Gate
Naples 941.353.3644

Gulfshore Anml Hosp
Naples 941.262.3633

Westcoast Vet Svc
Naples 941.598.2202

All Pets Hosp
New Prt Rchy 813.376.6767

Glencoe Vet Hosp
New Smyrna 904.427.4149

Pky Vet Hosp & Pet Care
Niceville 904.678.9733

PGA Anml Clnc
N Palm Beach 561.626.5020

Brandt Vet Clnc
Nokomis 941.485.1555

Biscayne Anml Hosp
N Miami 305.891.4323

Anml Hosp At Merryfield
Oakland Park 954.771.1198

Anml Hosp Of Ft Laudle
Oakland Park 954.561.8777

Shank Anml Hosp
Oakland Park 954.564.1263

Peterson Smith Matthews
Hahn
Ocala 352.237.6151

S Ocala Anml Clnc
Ocala 352.622.5253

Okeechobee Vet Hosp
Okeechobee 941.763.2523

Willowdale Vet Cntr
Orange Park 904.269.8866

Conway Anml Hosp
Orlando 407.851.4752

E Orange Anml Hosp
Orlando 407.275.3856

E Orlando Anml Hosp
Orlando 407.277.3497

John Young Parkway Anml
Hosp
Orlando 407.295.4482

Kirkman Road Vet Clnc
Orlando 407.297.7528

Kirkpatrick Vet Hosp
Orlando 407.841.3407

Powers Drive Anml Hosp
Orlando 407.299.4850

S Orlando Anml Hosp
Orlando 407.855.1297

Trail Anml Clnc
Orlando 407.855.1350

Underhill Anml Hosp
Orlando 407.277.0927

Shadow Lakes Anml Hosp
Ormond Beach 904.673.0333

Anml Med Clnc
Palatka 904.328.4613

Anml Med Clnc
Palm Bay 407.676.3350

Gardens Anml Hosp
Palm Bch Gdns
561.622.6300

Palmetto Anml Clnc
Palmetto 941.722.2456

Gulf Coast Anml Hosp
Panama City 904.785.0549

Parkway Anml Hosp
Panama City 904.763.8387

Scenic Hills Vet Hosp
Pensacola 904.477.6225

Pinellas Anml Hosp Clnc
Pinellas Park 813.546.0005

Lakeside Anml Hosp
Plantation 954.474.8808

Boulevard Anml Hosp
Pmbk Pines 954.966.0600

Flamingo Anml Clnc
Pmbk Pines 954.435.5555

S Pompano Collins Anml
Hosp
Pompano Beach
954.946.4700

The Pet Practice
Pompano Beach
954.428.5599

Halifax Vet Clnc
Port Orange 904.322.0108

Bayonet Point Anml Clnc
Port Richey 813.863.2435

Companion Anml Hosp
Port Richey 813.862.5938

N Port Anml Hosp
Port St Lucie 561.878.4818

Charlotte Anml Hosp
Pt Charlotte 941.625.6111

Punta Gorda Anml Hosp
Punta Gorda 941.639.8717

Royal Palm Bch Cmnty Anml
Hosp
Ryl Palm Bch 561.798.5508

St Cloud Vet Clnc
St Cloud 407.892.3415

Seminole Vet Hosp
Sanford 407.322.8465

Ashton Anml Clnc
Sarasota 941.927.2700

Lockwood Ridge Anml Clnc
Sarasota 941.359.3800

Pine Island Anml Clnc
St James City 941.283.1244

NorthW Vet Clnc
St Petersburg 813.541.4496

Pasadena Vet Hosp
St Petersburg 813.381.3739

VCA St Petersburg Anml
Hosp
St Petersburg 813.527.5803

Town & Country Vet Clnc
Starke 904.964.6411

Atlantic Anml Clnc
Stuart 561.692.0242

Anml Hosp Of Univ Dr
Sunrise 954.741.3114

Northeast Anml Hosp
Tallahassee 904.893.5636

Shannon Lakes Anml Clnc
Tallahassee 904.668.9333

Westwood Anml Hosp
Tallahassee 904.576.4168

Tamarac Anml Hosp
Tamarac 954.731.5500

Baycrest Anml Clnc
Tampa 813.886.9866

Beach Park Anml Clnc
Tampa 813.289.3925

Citrus Park Anml Hosp
Tampa 813.920.6656

Skipper Anml Hosp
Tampa 813.971.6105

Sunshine Anml Hosp
Tampa 813.885.7071

Vetcare Anml Hosp
Tampa 813.961.6699

Vet Med Clnc
Tampa 813.289.4086

Dunn Anml Hosp
Titusville 407.269.0677

Garden Street Anml Hosp
Titusville 407.267.4615

Suncoast Vet Clnc
Valrico 813.689.1228

Village Anml Clnc
Vero Beach 561.569.4553

Maybeck Anml Hosp
W Melbourne 407.723.5911

Baker Vet Clnc
W Palm Bch 561.642.9972

Pet Emer & Critical Care
Clnc
W Palm Bch 561.691.9999

River Bridge Anml Hosp
W Palm Bch 561.966.1171

Arbor Pet Hosp
Wilton Manors 954.565.1896

Dunham Anml Hosp Clnc
Winter Haven 941.293.0850

Losey Anml Hosp & Feed
Winter Haven 941.965.2548

Affiliated Vet Spec
Winter Park 407.644.1287

Winter Park Vet Clnc
Winter Park 407.644.2676

Bells Falls Vet Hosp
Acworth 770.926.5311

Companion Anml Hosp
Albany 912.888.7181

GEORGIA
Country Place Anml Hosp
Alpharetta 770.475.4159

Jones Bridge Anml Hosp
Alpharetta 770.410.0044

Buckhead Anml Clnc
Atlanta 404.873.3771

Dogwood Hosp For Anmls
Atlanta 404.636.0363

Inman Anml Hosp
Atlanta 404.584.8761

Lawrence Anml Hosp
Atlanta 404.636.9444

M Lnc Hirsh Vet Ctr
Atlanta 770.840.9679

Mhew Anml Hosp
Atlanta 404.255.9345

N Springs Anml Clnc
Atlanta 770.393.9889

Petsmart Vet Svc
Atlanta 404.237.4601

Wieuca Anml Clnc
Atlanta 404.252.8676

Paradise Anml Hosp
Augusta 706.860.4544

Disque Anml Clnc
Brunswick 912.267.6002

Vet Med Clnc
Brunswick 912.265.8668

Buford Anml Hosp
Buford 770.945.6757

Anml Med Cntr
Canton 770.479.0111

Carrollton Anml Hosp
Carrollton 770.834.6671

Peachtree Anml Hosp
Chamblee 770.457.2591

Anml Emer Cntr
Columbus 706.324.6659

Anml General Hosp
Columbus 706.568.4848

Anml General Hosp
Columbus 706.561.3341

Brown & Holton Vet Clnc
Columbus 706.323.0736

Commerce Vet Hosp
Commerce 706.335.5111

E Paulding Anml Hosp
Dallas 770.445.7300

Chapel Woods Anml Hosp
Decatur 404.289.3178

Dearborn Anml Hosp
Decatur 404.377.6477

Pleasant Hill Anml Hosp
Duluth 770.476.9339

Dunwoody Anml Hosp
Dunwoody 770.394.4030

Dunwoody Anml Med Cntr
Dunwoody 770.698.9227

Eatonton Vet Svc
Eatonton 706.485.4017

Fairview Anml Hosp
Ellenwood 770.389.9757

Flat Creek Anml-Clnc
Fayetteville 770.487.5354

Lafayette Cntr Anml Hosp
Fayetteville 770.460.0090

Browns Bridge Anml Hosp
Gainesville 770.536.8831

S Hall Vet Hosp
Gainesville 770.532.4449

Jefferson Anml Hosp
Jefferson 706.367.5161

Wolfe Anml Hosp
Jesup 912.427.3212

Jonesboro Anml Hosp
Jonesboro 770.478.5521

Boones Pet First
Kennesaw 770.422.0112

Shiloh Vet Hosp
Kennesaw 770.426.6900

Anml Medl Ctr Lawrenceville
Lawrenceville 770.963.7363

Beaver Crossing Anml Hosp
Lilburn 770.921.4981

Mountain Pk Anml Hosp
Lilburn
Lilburn 770.921.2965

Brantley&Jordan Anml Hosp
Macon 912.757.1600

Hudspeth Anml Hosp
Macon 912.742.8766

Anml Health Cntr
Marietta 770.439.1994

Fair Oaks Vet Clnc
Marietta 770.432.7155

Grtr Atlanta Vet Refrl
Marietta 770.424.6663

Johnson Ferry Anml Hosp
Marietta 770.973.1500

Lassiter Anml Hosp
Marietta 770.998.5100

Sprayberry Anml Hosp
Marietta 770.977.8300

Terrell Mill Anml Hosp
Marietta 770.952.9300

Westside Vet Hosp
Marietta 770.427.0033

Acute Care Vet Clnc
Martinez 706.868.7955

Eagles Landing Vet Hosp
Mc Donough 770.954.1414

Lake Harbin Anml Hosp
Morrow 770.961.5036

Matthews Vet Hosp
Moultrie 912.985.9744

Coweta Anml Hosp
Newnan 770.253.8013

Indian Trail Anml Hosp
Norcross 770.925.4884

Medlock Brdge An Hosp
Norcross 770.242.9272

Anml Med Clnc
Peachtree Cty 770.487.1338

Powder Springs Anml Clnc
Powder Spgs 770.943.1811

Catoosa Vet Clnc
Ringgold 706.937.4171

Three Counties Anml Hosp
Riverdale 770.471.6046

Culbreth Carr Watson Anml
Clnc
Rome 706.234.9243

Chattahoochee Anml Clnc
Roswell 770.993.6329

N Fulton Vet Hosp
Roswell 770.993.4043

Washington County Anml
Hosp
Sandersville 912.552.3170

Southside Hosp For Anmls
Savannah 912.925.7925

VCA Greater Savannah Anml
Hosp
Savannah 912.355.8898

Cumberland Anml Clnc
Smyrna 770.433.1414

Gwinnett Anml Hosp
Snellville 770.972.0447

Westside Vet Hosp
Statesboro 912.489.1998

Mainstreet Veterinarians
Stone Mtn 770.498.4620

Falcon Village Anml Hosp
Suwanee 770.962.8326

Thomaston Anml Hosp
Thomaston 706.648.2146

Thomasville Anml Hosp
Thomasville 912.226.4561

Dekalb Anml Hosp Pc
Tucker 770.938.3900

Pets Are People Too
Tucker 770.493.1001

Warner Robins Anml Hosp
Warner Robins 912.923.3139

Winterville Anml Clnc
Winterville 706.742.5108

Trickum Ridge Anml Hosp
Woodstock 770.516.1111

HAWAII
VCA Kaneohe Anml Hosp
Kaneohe 808.236.2414

Gentry-Waipio Pet Clnc
Waipahu 808.676.2205

IOWA
Belmond Vet Clnc
Belmond 515.444.4161

Brooklyn Vet Clnc
Brooklyn 515.522.7055

Carroll Vet Clnc
Carroll 712.792.4338

Taylor Vet Hosp
Cedar Falls 319.277.1883

All Pets Vet Clnc
Cedar Rapids 319.396.7759

Frey Pet Hosp
Cedar Rapids 319.364.7149

Eastridge Anml Cntr
Chariton 515.774.8486

Strohbehn Vet Clnc
Co Bluffs 712.366.0556

Kimberly Crest Vet Hosp
Davenport 319.386.4676

N Brady Anml Hosp
Davenport 319.391.9522

Avondale Anml Hosp
Des Moines 515.262.6111

Grand Avenue Vet Hosp
Des Moines 515.280.3051

Highland Park Vet Clnc
Des Moines 515.243.4665

Starch Pet Hosp
Des Moines 515.283.1576

Vanderloo & White Vet
Dubuque 319.556.3013

N Central Vet Ctr
Dumont 515.857.3871

Risius & Assoc
Eldridge 319.285.7891

Tri-Vet Associates
Farley 319.744.3341

Town & Country Vet Ctr
Fort Dodge 515.955.8591

Fort Madison Vet Clnc
Fort Madison 319.372.9000

Adair County Vet Clnc
Greenfield 515.743.2138

Harlan Vet Associates
Harlan 712.755.5466

All Creatures Small Anml
Hosp
Indianola 515.961.7882

All Pets Vet Clnc
Iowa City 319.338.8625

Le Mars Vet Clnc
Le Mars 712.546.6040

Anml Clnc-The Vet
Marshalltown 515.753.5486

Monte Vet Clnc
Montezuma 515.623.5471

Orange City Vet Clnc
Orange City 712.737.4474

Thomas Vet Clnc
Ottumwa 515.683.1835

Tri-County Vet Clnc
Pella 515.628.4040

Sheldon Vet Clnc
Sheldon 712.324.3014

Fremont County Vet Clnc
Sidney 712.374.2721

Central Vet Medl Clnc
Sioux Cntr 712.722.1087

Fourth Street Vet Clnc
Vinton 319.472.5590

Vet Medl Grp Des Moines
W Des Moines 515.224.4368

All Pets Anml Clnc
Waterloo 319.234.7511

Logan Anml Hosp
Waterloo 319.233.7526

IDAHO
Blackfoot Anml Clnc
Blackfoot 208.785.1960

Ada Anml Hosp Annex
Boise 208.362.5329

All Pet Complx Hosp & Hlth
Ctr
Boise 208.853.1000

Eastgate Pet Clnc
Boise 208.336.3278

NorthW Anml Hosp
Boise 208.375.2700

Bonners Ferry Vet Clnc
Bonners Ferry 208.267.7502

Blayney Vet Clnc
Caldwell 208.459.6167

Larue Vet Clnc
Filer 208.326.8646

Eastside Pet Clnc
Idaho Falls 208.529.2217

Sunnyside Vet Clnc
Idaho Falls 208.523.2513

Dairy Health Services/Mps
Jerome 208.324.8100

Kellogg Anml Hosp
Kellogg 208.784.1381

Orchards Pet Hosp
Lewiston 208.743.5432

Treasure Valley Vet Hosp
Meridian 208.888.4844

Ashton-Clark Vet Clnc
Payette 208.642.9391

Alpine Anml Hosp
Pocatello 208.237.1111

Blue Cross Vet Clnc
Salmon 208.756.3331

ILLINOIS
Aledo Vet Clnc
Aledo 309.582.2622

Geoffrey Connell
Byron 815.234.5424

Cambridge Vet Service
Cambridge 309.937.5719

Lakeside Vet Hosp
Carbondale 618.529.2236

Brush College Anml Hosp
Decatur 217.422.9393

Edwardsville Pet Hosp
Edwardsville 618.656.7656

Geneseo Vet Service
Geneseo 309.944.4343

Jersey Calhoun Vet Clnc
Jerseyville 618.498.2413

Lena Vet Clnc
Lena 815.369.2400

Colonial Manor Anml Hosp
Lockport 815.838.8800

Mon-Clair Anml Hosp
Millstadt 618.476.3786

Abel Keppy Anml Health Ctr
Moline 309.762.0515

Anml Clnc At New Lenox
New Lenox 815.485.4477

Bureau Valley Vet Serv
Preton 815.875.1621

Anml Medl Clnc & Chry Vale
Rockford 815.398.4410

Hillcrest Anml Hosp
Rockford 815.398.9313

Bremen Anml Hosp Ltd
Tinley Park 708.532.5577

INDIANA
Devonshire Vet Clnc
Anderson 317.644.3628

Bedford Vet Med Ctr
Bedford 812.279.7501

Blue Sky Vet Clnc
Bloomington 812.336.8029

Combs Vet Clnc
Bloomington 812.825.4464

Bremen Anml Clnc
Bremen 219.546.2472

Companion Anml Hosp &
Clnc
Carmel 317.844.0049

Woodland Anml Hosp
Carmel 317.844.2696

Best Friends Anml Care
Columbus 812.342.1233

Corydon Anml Hosp
Corydon 812.738.8216

NorthW Vet Hosp Pc
Crawfordsvlle 317.362.4699

Horizon Vet Service
Delphi 317.564.3400

Georgetown Vet Clnc
Georgetown 812.951.3388

Sugar Creek Anml Hosp
Greenfield 317.462.1218

Meridian Vet Clnc
Greenwood 317.888.4405

Anml Emer Clnc
Indianapolis 317.849.4925

Avian & Exotic Anml Clnc
Indianapolis 317.879.8633

Brookville Road Anml Hosp
Indianapolis 317.353.6143

Decatur Vet Clnc
Indianapolis 317.856.4000

Eastwood Anml Clnc
Indianapolis 317.255.6627

Geckler Vet Hosp
Indianapolis 317.271.3000

Noahs Anml Hosp
Indianapolis 317.253.1327

Paw Patch
Indianapolis 317.356.7148

Paw Patch
Indianapolis 317.293.8363

Pet Pals Hosp & Hse Calls
Indianapolis 317.257.1761

Sixteenth Street Vets
Indianapolis 317.352.1277

Blue Cross Anml Hosp
Indianapolis 317.634.3494

Jefferson Road An Hosp
Kokomo 317.457.5521

Creekside Anml Hosp
Lafayette 317.742.0140

Lakeville Vet Clnc
Lakeville 219.784.8869

Lapel Anml Clnc
Lapel 317.534.3142

Southway Anml Hosp
Marion 317.674.4361

Martinsville Vet Hosp
Martinsville 317.342.0544

Boyce Anml Hosp
Muncie 317.288.1877

Rlm Vet Services
N Vernon 812.346.8008

Anml Clnc Of Plainfield
Plainfield 317.839.8154

Plymouth Vet Clnc
Plymouth 219.936.2232

Janssen Vet Clnc
Sheridan 317.873.5353

Roseland Anml Hosp
S Bend 219.272.6100

Greenwood Anml Hosp
Tell City 812.547.7087

Heritage Anml Hosp
Terre Haute 217.466.1155

King Anml Care Clnc
Topeka 219.593.2482

Michigan Road Anml Hosp
Zionsville 317.873.1833

KANSAS
Atchison Anml Clnc
Atchison 913.367.0427

Auburn Anml Clnc
Auburn 316.256.2476

Augusta Anml Clnc
Augusta 316.775.7061

Ripple & Liebl
Dodge City 316.227.2751

Emporia Vet Hosp
Emporia 316.342.6515

Ark Valley Vet Hosp
Great Bend 316.793.5457

Junction City Anml Hosp
Junction City 913.238.5513

Welborn Pet Hosp
Kansas City 913.334.6770

Lawrence Vet Hosp
Lawrence 913.841.9956

Chem-Tronics
Leavenworth 913.651.3930

Town&Country Anml Clnc
Newton 316.283.1650

Olathe W Vet Care
Olathe 913.829.3275

The Anml Hosp
Plainville 913.434.7222

Leawood Plaza Anml Hosp
Shawnee Msn 913.491.6665

Oak Park Vet Clnc
Shawnee Msn 913.888.3939

Overland Park Vet Ctr
Shawnee Msn 913.642.9371

Roeland Park Vet Cntr
Shawnee Msn 913.432.2050

Companion Anml Clnc
Topeka 913.271.7387

Gage Anml Hosp
Topeka 913.272.8876

Blair Doon Vet Hosp
Wichita 316.685.7300

E Central Vet Clnc
Wichita 316.686.7418

Indian Hills Anml Clncs
Wichita 316.942.3900

KENTUCKY
Central Kentucky Anml Clnc
Bardstown 502.348.9098

Greystone Pet Hosp
Bowling Green 502.843.1558

Bevins Anml Hosp Frankfort
Frankfort 502.695.1144

Crocker Anml Clnc
Franklin 502.586.9000

Vet Med Cntr
Glasgow 502.651.5444

Appalachian Anml Hosp Psc
Hazard 606.436.1197

Hartland Anml Hosp
Horse Cave 502.786.5545

Chevy Chase Small Anml
Clnc
Lexington 606.266.0449

Anml Emer Cntr
Louisville 502.456.6102

Criti Care Vet Services
Louisville 502.339.9594

Fegenbush Lane Anml Clnc
Louisville 502.239.8530

Kentucky Vet Spec
Louisville 502.339.9594

Plantation Anml Clnc
Louisville 502.426.1016

Shelbyville Road Vet Clnc
Louisville 502.245.6352

The Audubon Group
Louisville 502.933.1818

Anml Med Cntr
Madisonville 502.821.6349

Town & Country Vet
Maysville 606.759.5496

Kentuckiana Anml Clnc Psc
Owensboro 502.684.2949

Paducah Vet Clnc
Paducah 502.443.8835

Pewee Valley Vet Cntr
Pewee Valley 502.241.8834

Bullitt County Vet Ctr
Shepherdsvlle 502.543.3001

Springfield Anml Clnc
Springfield 606.336.9923

Fenwick Anml Clnc
St Matthews 502.896.0331

Woodford Vet Clnc
Versailles 606.873.7361

LOUISIANA
Lester Vet Hosp
Alexandria 318.448.8710

All Pets Hosp
Baton Rouge 504.767.2462

Armstrong Vet Hosp
Baton Rouge 504.928.4540

Associated Vet Services
Baton Rouge 504.928.4417

Perkins Road Vet Hosp
Baton Rouge 504.766.0550

Woodlawn Anml Hosp
Baton Rouge 504.753.1120

Buccaneer Villa Vet Hosp
Chalmette 504.271.1234

Anml Med Cntr
Covington 504.893.1616

Dodge City Vet Hosp
Denham Spgs 504.664.6441

Companion Anml Hosp
Gretna 504.365.0098

Walther Anml Clnc
Houma 504.872.1771

Jennings Anml Hosp
Jennings 318.824.6551

Broussard Vet Clnc
Lafayette 318.988.5022

Monticello Anml Clnc
Lake Charles 318.477.1325

Airline Anml Hosp
Metairie 504.834.4422

Veterans Vet Hosp
Metairie 504.888.1261

W Esplanade Vet Clnc
Metairie 504.455.6386

Lefebvre Vet Medl Ctr
Monroe 318.361.9395

Audubon Vet Hosp
New Orleans 504.891.0685

De Gaulle Vet Clnc
New Orleans 504.367.8680

Maple Small Anml Clnc
New Orleans 504.866.6316

The Cat Practice
New Orleans 504.525.6369

Haas Anml Hosp
Pineville 318.640.7153

Tioga Anml Clnc
Pineville 318.640.4450

Marcello Anml Hosp
Raceland 504.532.2937

Summer Grove Anml Hosp
Shreveport 318.686.1320

University Vet Hosp
Shreveport 318.797.5522

Anml Med Clnc
Slidell 504.649.0660

Gause Boulevard Vet Hosp
Slidell 504.641.3922

Maplewood Anml Hosp
Sulphur 318.625.2575

Anml Care Clnc
Terrytown 504.393.0825

MASSACHUSETTS
Adams Vet Clnc
Adams 413.743.4000

Amesbury Anml Hosp
Amesbury 508.388.3636

Ashland Anml Hosp
Ashland 508.881.2400

Bellingham Anml Hosp
Bellingham 508.966.1000

Belmont Anml Hosp
Belmont 617.484.5197

The Boston Cat Hosp
Kenmore Sq
Boston 617.266.7877

Brighton Anml Hosp
Brighton 617.787.1500

Carlisle Anml Hosp
Carlisle 508.369.9364

Cntrysd Vet Hosp
Chelmsford 508.256.9555

Dennis Anml Hosp
Dennis 508.385.8323

E Longmeadow Anml Hosp
E Longmeadow
413.788.9657

Woodland Anml Clnc
E Freetown 508.763.8029

Fitchburg Anml Clnc
Fitchburg 508.342.5892

Slade Vet Hosp
Framingham 508.875.7086

Acorn Anml Hosp
Franklin 508.528.1135

Pioneer Valley Vet Hosp
Greenfield 413.773.7511

Hanson Anml Hosp
Hanson 617.293.2511

N Valley Anml Hosp
Haverhill 508.373.3251

Family Vet Cntr
Haydenville 413.268.8387

Old Derby Anml Clnc
Hingham 617.749.2800

Hudson Anml Hosp
Hudson 508.562.2868

Srh Vet Services
Ipswich 508.356.1119

Leominster Anml Hosp
Leominster 508.534.0936

Lexington Bedford Vet Hosp
Lexington 617.862.3670

Linwood Anml Hosp
Lowell 508.453.1784

Heritage Hill Vet Clnc
Medfield 508.359.4392

Pleasant Valley Anml Hosp
Methuen 508.686.4998

Mass Scty For Prvntn
Cruelty
Nantucket 508.228.1491

Northboro Vet Clnc
Northborough 508.393.8339

Anml Hosp Of Orleans
Orleans 508.255.1194

Pepperell Vet Hosp
Pepperell 508.433.8613

House Calls Ltd
Pittsfield 413.443.7387

Pilgrim Anml Hosp
Plymouth 508.746.5003

Abbott Anml Hosp
Rehoboth 508.336.4430

Coastal Anml Clnc
Salisbury 508.463.3309

Driftway Anml Hosp
Scituate 617.545.0952

Porter Square Veterinarian
Somerset 617.628.5588

Mspca Rowley Merrl Anml
Hosp
Springfield 413.785.1221

Sudbury Anml Hosp
Sudbury 508.443.2839

W Springfield Anml Hosp
W Springfield 413.781.5275

The Windhover Vet Ctr
Walpole 508.668.4520

New England Anml Med Ctr
W Boylston 508.835.6258

Hyannis Anml Hosp
W Yarmouth 508.775.4521

S Weymouth Anml Care Ctr
Weymouth 617.331.6620

Whester Vet Grp
Whester 617.721.0707

Abbott Anml Hosp
Worcester 508.853.3350

MARYLAND
Aberdeen Vet Clnc
Aberdeen 410.272.0655

Anne Arundel Vet Emer Clnc
Annapolis 410.224.0331

Arnold Vet Hosp
Arnold 410.757.7645

Aardmore Veterinarian
Baltimore 410.889.2230

Carney Anml Hosp
Baltimore 410.665.5255

Cat Hosp At Towson
Baltimore 410.377.7900

Everhart Anml Hosp
Baltimore 410.355.3131

Pulaski Vet Clnc
Baltimore 410.686.6310

Vinson Anml Hosp At Towson
Baltimore 410.828.7676

Westview Anml Hosp
Baltimore 410.744.4800

Benson Anml Hosp
Bethesda 301.652.8818

The Pet Practice
Bowie 301.262.8590

Hyattsville Anml Hosp
Brentwood 301.864.2325

Choptank Anml Hosp
Cambridge 410.221.0444

Paradise Anml Hosp
Catonsville 410.744.4224

Churchville Vet
Churchville 410.838.0085

Lavale Vet Hosp
Cumberland 301.729.6084

Dundalk Dog & Cat Clnc
Dundalk 410.282.2250

S Arundel Vet Hosp
Edgewater 410.956.2932

Dunloggin Vet Hosp
Ellicott City 410.465.6218

Howard County Anml Hosp
Ellicott City 410.465.0639

Frederick W Vet Hosp
Frederick 301.473.4478

Gaithersburg Sq Vet Clnc
Gaithersburg 301.840.9477

Germantown Vet Clnc
Germantown 301.972.9730

Vet Smart Pet Hosp & Hlth
Ctr
Glen Burnie 410.863.1100

Cumberland Valley Vet Clnc
Hagerstown 301.739.3121

Green Valley Anml Hosp
Ijamsville 301.831.6930

Kensington Vet Hosp
Kensington 301.933.5010

New Carrollton Vet Hosp
Lanham 301.552.3800

Town & Country Anml Clnc
Olney 301.774.7111

Reggie Cox
Pasadena 410.768.3620

Somerset Anml Hosp
Press Anne 410.651.1044

Frederick Pre Anml Hosp
Prnc Frederck 410.535.2590

Main Street Vet Hosp
Reisterstown 410.526.7500

Reisterstown 24 Hr Vet
Reisterstown 410.833.0500

Lynn Anml Hosp
Riverdale 301.779.1184

Metropolitan Emer Anml
Rockville 301.770.5225

Petvacx
Rockville 301.838.9506

Johnson-McKee Anml Hosp
Salisbury 410.749.9422

Four Corners Anml Hosp
Silver Spring 301.593.6330

Marymont Anml Hosp
Silver Spring 301.384.1223

Norbeck Anml Clnc
Silver Spring 301.924.3616

New Hampshire Avenue
Anml Hosp
Takoma Park 301.270.2050

Timonium Anml Hosp
Timonium 410.252.8820

Squire Vet Clnc
Uppr Marlboro 301.627.4664

St Charles Anml Hosp
Waldorf 301.645.2550

Woodsboro Vet Clnc
Woodsboro 301.898.7272

MAINE
Broadway Vet Clnc
Bangor 207.942.2281

The Vet Ctr Cape Elizabeth
Cape Eliz 207.799.6952

Cumberland Anml Clnc
Cumberlnd Ctr 207.829.5078

Fryeburg Vet Hosp
Fryeburg 207.935.2244

Mann Memorial Clnc For
Anmls
Kennebunk 207.985.4774

Casco Bay Vet Hosp
Portland 207.761.8033

Lakeview Vet Hosp
Rockland 207.594.2581

Oxford Hills Vet Hosp
S Paris 207.743.9271

Anml Hosp Of Waterville
Waterville 207.873.2759

MICHIGAN
Ironwood Vet Clnc
Ironwood 906.932.2060

Lawton Anml Hosp
Lawton 616.624.4711

MINNESOTA
Cedar View Anima Hosp
Apple Valley 612.432.4928

Battle Lake Vet Clnc
Battle Lake 218.864.5695

Belle Plaine Vet Svc
Belle Plaine 612.873.8387

S Hyland Pet Hosp
Bloomington 612.884.1868

Lakeland Vet Hosp
Brainerd 218.829.1709

Brookdale Anml Hosp
Brooklyn Park 612.560.6906

Vet Associates
Caledonia 507.724.2779

Park Grove Pet Hosp
Cottage Grove 612.459.9663

Duluth Vet Hosp
Duluth 218.728.3616

Eagan Pet Clnc
Eagan 612.454.5684

Anderson Lakes Anml Hosp
Eden Prairie 612.942.5506

Barrington Oaks Vet Hosp
Elk River 612.441.4000

S Shore Vet Hosp
Forest Lake 612.464.4210

Skyline Vet Hosp
Fridley 612.574.9892

Glencoe Vet Clnc
Glencoe 320.864.3414

Glacial Ridge Vet Clnc
Glenwood 320.634.3558

Golden Valley Anml Hosp
Golden Valley 612.544.4286

Clearwater Vet Svc Ltd
Gonvick 218.487.5227

Inver Grove Heights Anml
Hosp
Inver Grove 612.451.4404

Lakeland Vet Hosp
Lakeland 612.436.6146

Minn-I-Kota Vet Clnc
Luverne 507.283.8507

Grove Square Pet Hosp
Maple Grove 612.420.7958

Gehrman Anml Hosp
Maple Plain 612.479.1550

Hillcrest Anml Hosp
Maplewood 612.484.7211

SouthW Vet Svc Ltd
Marshall 507.532.5235

Melrose Albany Upsala Vet
Melrose 320.256.4252

Amc
Minneapolis 612.374.4414

Belt Line Pet Hosp Ltd
Minneapolis 612.533.2746

Blue Cross Anml Hosp Ltd
Minneapolis 612.822.2149

Brooklyn Pet Hosp
Minneapolis 612.537.3669

Kenwood Pet Clnc
Minneapolis 612.377.5551

Woodlake Vet Hosp
Minneapolis 612.861.7461

Nicollet New Ulm Vet Clnc
Nicollet 507.225.3401

Vet Clnc Clara Cy & Olivia
Olivia 320.523.5550

River Valley Vet Svc
Prior Lake 612.447.4118

Northern Valley Anml Clnc
Rochester 507.282.0867

Rogers Pet Clnc
Rogers 612.428.8688

Suburban Anml Hosp
Roseville 612.633.5700

Feist Anml Hosp
St Paul 612.646.7257

Minnesota Vet Hosp
St Paul 612.484.3331

Sauk Centre Vet Clnc
Sauk Centre 320.352.2264

Springfield Morgan Vet
Springfield 507.723.5211

Park Pet Hosp Ltd
St Louis Pk 612.926.2703

Stillwater Vet Clnc
Stillwater 612.770.6167

Drs S Skadron
W St Paul 612.451.6421

Norman Mett Ofc
W Concord 507.527.2559

Birch Lake Anml Hosp
White Bear Lk 612.426.2246

Hudson Road Anml Hosp
Woodbury 612.739.0117

Vet Med Cntr
Worthington 507.372.2957

Zimmerman Vet Clnc
Zimmerman 612.856.4848

MISSOURI
Rolling Meadows Anml Hosp
Adrian 816.297.2006

County Anml Hosp Ltd
Ballwin 314.256.8387

Ellisville Vet Hosp
Ballwin 314.227.7154

Sulphur Springs Vet Clnc
Ballwin 314.394.3227

Ericson Vet Hosp
Blue Springs 816.229.8255

Rolling Hills Vet Hosp
Columbia 573.449.7387

Farmington Anml Hosp
Farmington 573.756.3301

Cross Keys Anml Clnc
Florissant 314.837.4617

Callaway Cnty Vet Clnc
Fulton 573.642.3724

Equine Med Associates
Glencoe 314.458.3311

Hermann Vet Clnc
Hermann 573.486.2515

Schondelmeyer Anml Hosp
Independence 816.833.1300

Lea Merry Anml Clnc
Jackson 573.243.3200

Parkview Anml Hosp
Joplin 417.781.0906

Anml Med Cntr
Kansas City 816.333.9000

Antioch Dog & Cat Hosp
Kansas City 816.453.7272

Crest Anml Hosp
Kansas City 816.763.1313

Platte Woods Anml Hosp
Kansas City 816.741.8600

Small Anml Hosp
Kansas City 816.931.5989

Kennett Vet Clnc
Kennett 573.888.2255

Terra Vet Services
Lebanon 417.532.9147

Chipman Rd Anml Clnc
Lees Summit 816.524.1886

Liberty Anml Hosp & Clnc
Liberty 816.781.1414

Saline County Vet Svc
Marshall 816.886.6812

Anml Med Cntr
Marshfield 417.468.3484

All Creatures Anml Hosp
O Fallon 314.240.8387

Homestead Equine Hosp
Pacific 314.451.4655

Jackson Anml Clnc
Platte City 816.858.3112

St Charles Anml Hosp & Clnc
St Charles 314.723.2400

Binder Anml Hosp
St Louis 314.892.5406

Florissant Anml Hosp
St Louis 314.921.0500

Grantview Anml Hosp
St Louis 314.842.0403

Humane Society Of Missouri
St Louis 314.647.8800

Kirkwood Anml Hosp & Pet
Ctr
St Louis 314.965.2660

Tesson Ferry Vet Hosp
St Louis 314.842.3377

Webster Groves Anml Hosp
St Louis 314.968.4310

Cottage Vet Hosp
Springfield 417.869.1103

Country Club Vet Hosp
Springfield 417.881.2263

Espey Vet Clnc
Tarkio 816.736.5722

Loln County Anml Hosp
Troy 314.528.5099

Washington Vet Clnc
Washington 314.239.5445

MISSISSIPPI
S Panola Vet Hosp
Batesville 601.563.4870

All Pet Care Anml Clnc
Biloxi 601.392.3295

Greenville Anml Clnc
Greenville 601.335.1183

Handsboro Anml Hosp
Gulfport 601.896.3613

Rogers Vet Hosp
Hattiesburg 601.268.2696

Forest Hill Anml Hosp
Jackson 601.922.8393

Anml Care Hosp
Long Beach 601.868.9479

Anml Med Cntr
Natchez 601.442.7407

Big Ridge Vet Hosp
Ocean Springs 601.872.2088

A Anml Clnc Of Oxford
Oxford 601.234.8022

Anml Med Cntr
Starkville 601.323.2547

Terry Anml Clnc
Terry 601.878.5950

All Anml Hosp
Tupelo 601.844.4955

Vicksburg Anml Hosp
Vicksburg 601.636.8112

MONTANA
Heath Vet Hosp
Billings 406.245.4772

Vet Clnc W
Billings 406.656.6320

Montana Vet Hosp & Brdng
Bozeman 406.586.2019

Anml Medl Clnc Carl
McQueary
Butte 406.494.3630

Associated Vet Services
Great Falls 406.727.0477

Big Sky Anml Clnc
Helena 406.442.0980

E Side Anml Clnc
Helena 406.443.1862

Laurel E Vet Service
Laurel 406.628.4683

NORTH CAROLINA
Village Way Vet Hosp
Advance 910.998.0263

Arden Anml Hosp
Arden 704.684.6372

Asheboro Anml Hosp
Asheboro 910.625.4077

Biltmore Vet Associates
Asheville 704.665.4399

Redwood Anml Hosp
Asheville 704.298.1846

Skyland Anml Hosp Asheville
Asheville 704.252.8644

Blue Ridge Anml Hosp
Black Mtn 704.669.8719

Appalachian New Riv Vet
Boone 704.264.5621

Vet Hosp Of Burgaw
Burgaw 910.259.8686

Alamance Vet Hosp
Burlington 910.228.1773

Anml Hosp Carrboro
Carrboro 919.967.9261

Cary Vet Hosp
Cary 919.469.0947

Cornerstone Vet Hosp
Cary 919.319.1555

Northwoods Anml Hosp
Cary 919.481.2987

Legion Road Anml Clnc
Chapel Hill 919.933.3331

Armstrong Anml Clnc
Charlotte 704.334.1996

Carmel Anml Hosp
Charlotte 704.541.0043

Clear Creek Anml Hosp
Charlotte 704.537.8405

Metrolina Expo
Charlotte 704.596.4643

Parker Vet Hosp
Charlotte 704.399.8304

Vet Med Clnc
Clinton 910.592.3338

Foster Anml Hosp
Concord 704.786.0104

The Beard House
Cornelius 704.892.3761

E Loln Anml Hosp
Denver 704.483.2931

Cornwallis Road An Hosp
Durham 919.489.9194

Guess Road Anml Hosp
Durham 919.471.6472

N Paw Anml Hosp
Durham 919.471.1471

Shelton Anml Hosp
Durham 919.477.1161

Fuquay Vet Hosp
Fuquay Varina 919.552.7200

Anml Med Hosp
Gastonia 704.867.3514

Tri County Vet Service
Graham 910.376.6838

Burlington Road Anml Hosp
Greensboro 910.375.3939

Cobb Anml Clnc
Greensboro 910.288.8550

Frndly Anml Clnc Guilford
Cllg
Greensboro 910.299.6011

Greensboro Vet Hosp
Greensboro 910.299.5431

Sedgefield Anml Hosp
Greensboro 910.294.1944

Havelock Anml Hosp
Havelock 919.447.7119

Haywood Anml Hosp
Hendersonvlle 704.697.0446

Westchester Vet Hosp
High Point 910.885.0067

Piedmont Vet Clnc
Hillsborough 919.732.2569

Mills River Anml Clnc
Horse Shoe 704.891.9685

Huntersville Anml Care Hosp
Huntersville 704.875.0974

Hopkins Road Anml Hosp
Kernersville 910.996.2190

Caldwell Anml Hosp
Lenoir 704.728.6100

Lolnton Anml Hosp
Lolnton 704.732.0728

Lewis Vet Clnc
Lumberton 910.738.9368

All Pet Care Clnc
Matthews 704.847.7001

Matthews Anml Clnc
Matthews 704.847.9856

Mint Hill Anml Clnc
Mint Hill 704.545.3422

Monroe Anml Hosp
Monroe 704.289.5242

Healthy Petz Vet Clnc
Morganton 704.437.4524

Craven Anml Hosp
New Bern 919.637.4541

Ridgeway Anml Clnc
New Bern 919.633.1204

Barton Hayes Anml Hosp
Raleigh 919.833.2666

Boulevard Anml Hosp
Raleigh 919.828.7468

Brookwood Vet Clnc
Raleigh 919.779.2940

Falls Village Vet Hosp
Raleigh 919.847.0141

Hidden Valley Anml Hosp
Raleigh 919.847.9396

Litchford Village Anml Hosp
Raleigh 919.850.9600

Quail Corners Anml Hosp
Raleigh 919.876.0739

Swift Creek Anml Hosp
Raleigh 919.851.8387

Eastern Randolph Vet Clnc
Ramseur 910.824.4005

Reidsville Vet Hosp
Reidsville 910.349.3194

Dr Claudia Berryhill
Roxboro 910.599.0611

T L James Dr Anml Hosp
Salisbury 704 636.1100

Myres Anml Hosp
Sanford 919.775.2258

Crossroads Eqn & Lvstck
Clnc
Stokesdale 910.643.7447

N Wake Anml Hosp
Wake Forest 919.556.1121

Anml Hosp Of Waynesville
Waynesville 704.456.9755

College Road Anml Hosp
Wilmington 910.395.6555

Dineen Anml Hosp
Wilmington 910.799.3400

Needham Anml Hosp
Wilmington 910.799.2970

NORTH DAKOTA
Midway Vet Clnc
Mandan 701.663.9841°

Minot Vet Clnc
Minot 701.852.4831

Park River Vet Clnc
Park River 701.284.6514

Towner Vet Service
Towner 701.537.5175

Stockmens Supply
W Fargo 701.282.3255

NEBRASKA
Two Town Vet Clnc
Battle Creek 402.675.5300

A & M Vet Clnc
Columbus 402.564.7456

Dodge Vet Clnc
Dodge 402.693.2234

Anml Hosp
Gothenburg 308.537.3771

Anml Med Clnc
Grand Island 308.382.6330

Gretna Anml Clnc
Gretna 402.332.4632

Anml Clnc
Hastings 402.463.9805

Forney Anml Cntr
Loln 402.423.9100

Pitts Vet Hosp
Loln 402.423.4120

Candlewood Anml Hosp
Omaha 402.493.9650

Mapleview Anml Clnc
Omaha 402.397.4344

Omaha Anml Med Group
Omaha 402.496.6075

Ralston Vet Clnc
Omaha 402.331.6322

Rohrig Anml Hosp
Omaha 402.399.8100

The Pet Clnc
Omaha 402.330.3096

Nebraska Equine Clnc
Papillion 402.331.6322

S Sioux Anml Hosp Pc
S Sioux City 402.494.3844

Pioneer Anml Clnc
Scottsbluff 308.635.3188

NEW HAMPSHIRE
Hillsborough Cnty Vet Hosp
Amherst 603.672.2300

Riverside Vet Hosp
Boscawen 603.224.5615

Concord Anml Hosp Pro
Assn
Concord 603.228.0107

Anml Clnc Of Enfield
Enfield 603.632.4100

Hudson Anml Hosp
Hudson 603.883.5481

Kingston Anml Hosp
Kingston 603.642.5241

Londonderry Anml Clnc
Londonderry 603.434.2428

Lockridge Anml Hosp
Manchester 603.624.4378

State Line Vet Hosp
Nashua 603.888.2751

Fritz Tenney & Combs Anml
Hosp
Peterborough 603.924.3881

Rochester Equine Clnc
Rochester 603.332.6482

NEW JERSEY
Anml General
Augusta 201.579.1224

Countryside Vet Hosp
Flemington 908.788.1800

Hackettstown Anml Hosp
Hackettstown 908.852.3166

Springmills Vet Hosp
Milford 908.995.4959

The Highlands Vet Hosp
Sparta 201.726.8080

Whitehouse Vet Hosp
White Hse Sta 908.534.4121

NEW MEXICO
Leslie Anml Clnc
Alamogordo 505.437.4190

Albuquerque Anml Emer
Clnc
Albuquerque 505.884.3443

Albuquerque Equine Clnc
Albuquerque 505.344.1131

NorthW Anml Clnc & Hosp
Albuquerque 505.898.1491

Petroglyph Pet Clnc
Albuquerque 505.897.1810

Petsmart Vet Services
Albuquerque 505.271.6990

Sandia Anml Clnc
Albuquerque 505.299.9533

St Francis Anml Clnc
Albuquerque 505.881.3030

VCA Vet Care Anml Hosp
Albuquerque 505.292.5353

Vet-Co
Albuquerque 505.344.0780

Angel Peak Vet Hosp
Farmington 505.632.8081

Hobbs Anml Clnc
Hobbs 505.392.5563

Johnson Vet Clnc
Las Cruces 505.524.2973

White Rock Vet Hosp
Los Alamos 505.672.3881

College Garden Anml Hosp
Roswell 505.624.2424

Cedarwood Vet Clnc
Santa Fe 505.982.4469

Sangre De Cristo Anml Hosp
Santa Fe 505.471.6594

Arenas Valley Anml Clnc
Silver City 505.388.1993

Canyon Crssrds An Hosp
Tijeras 505.281.1515

NEVADA
Parkway Springs Anml Hosp
Henderson 702.433.9111

All Pets Mobile Clnc
Las Vegas 702.382.4292

American Pet Hosp
Las Vegas 702.454.7740

Decatur Anml Clnc
Las Vegas 702.646.3777

Mauer Anml Clnc
Las Vegas 702.870.1011

Nellis Anml Hosp
Las Vegas 702.453.1220

Sandy Hill Anml Clnc
Las Vegas 702.451.8808

S Shores Anml Hosp
Las Vegas 702.255.8050

SouthW Anml Hosp
Las Vegas 702.367.6700

Spring Mountain Anml Hosp
Las Vegas 702.876.9228

Sunset Eastern Anml Hosp
Las Vegas 702.361.2566

Carson Valley Vet Hosp
Minden 702.782.3693

Carey Anml Clnc
N Las Vegas 702.649.4291

Fairgrounds Anml Hosp
Reno 702.329.4106

Petsmart Vet Clnc
Reno 702.826.6880

Truckee Meadows Hosp
Reno 702.825.0400

Yerington Vet Hosp
Yerington 702.463.3521

NEW YORK
Thousand Island Anml Hosp
Alex Bay 315.686.5080

Village Anml Clnc
Ardsley 914.693.2626

Avon Anml Hosptl
Avon 716.226.6144

Baldwin Harbor Anml Hosp
Baldwin 516.379.5010

N Shore Anml Hosp
Bayside 718.423.9600

Bellmore Anml Hosp
Bellmore 516.221.2966

Allen Vet
Binghamton 607.648.5246

Lancaster Small Anml Hosp
Bowmansville 716.681.3033

Brentwood Islip Hosp
Brentwood 516.231.7755

Brewerton Vet Clnc
Brewerton 315.676.2860

AAAa Anml Medcn & Surg
Clnc
Brooklyn 718.444.5151

Anml Kind Vet Hosp
Brooklyn 718.832.3899

VETERINARIANS

Brooklyn Vet Emer Hosp
Brooklyn 718.748.5180

Mobile Vet Anml Clnc
Brooklyn 718.373.0240

Buffalo Sm Anml Vet Svces
Buffalo 716.852.1112

Summer Street Cat Clnc
Buffalo 716.883.3324

Canandaigua Vet Hosptl
Canandaigua 716.394.3340

Countryside Vet Clnc
Carthage 315.493.7387

Cheektowaga Vet Hosp
Cheektowaga 716.634.8736

The Anml Kngdm Vet Hosp
Clay 315.699.0375

Anml Emer Svce
Commack 516.462.6044

Towne & Country Vet Hosp
Corning 607.937.8222

Croton Anml Hosp
Croton Hdsn 914.271.6222

Deer Hills Anml Hosp
Deer Park 516.667.0870

Commack Anml Hosp
E Northport 516.499.6622

Vet Clnc Of E Hampton
E Hampton 516.324.7900

Anml Hosp
Elmira 607.734.5261

Fairview Vet Hosptl
Fairport 716.223.0940

Fayetteville Vet Hosp
Fayetteville 315.637.9801

Vines Anml Clnc
Forest Hills 516.897.6773

Fort Plain Anml Hosp
Fort Plain 518.993.3332

Fredonia Anml Hosp
Fredonia 716.679.1561

Orange County Vet Hosp
Goshen 914.294.5044

Great Neck Anml Hosp
Great Neck 516.482.0588

Roslyn Greenvale Vet Grp
Greenvale 516.621.4010

Hauppauge Anml Hosp
Hauppauge 516.265.5551

Sachem Anml Hosp
Holbrook 516.467.2121

Cold Spring Hills Anml Hosp
Huntington 516.692.6458

Housecall Vet Care
Huntington 516.367.8030

Estates Anml Hosp
Jamaica 718.297.5400

Katonah Vet Group
Katonah 914.232.1800

Kingston Anml Hosp
Kingston 914.331.0240

Capitaland Anml Hosp
Latham 518.785.5531

Island Trees Vet Hosp
Levittown 516.735.0090

Sunnyside Anml Clnc
Long Is City 718.472.4600

Crawford Anml Hosp
Lynbrook
Lynbrook 516.599.0256

Lyons Vet Clnc
Lyons 315.946.4875

Miller-Clark Anml Hosp
Mamaroneck 914.698.1756

Park Anml Hosp
Massapequa Pk
516.798.1294

Goosepond Anml Hosp
Monroe 914.783.2333

Anml Med Of New City
New City 914.638.3600

Andrea Russo
New Paltz 914.255.5055

Anml General
New York 212.501.9600

Feline Health
New York 212.879.0700

Lenox Hill Veterinarians
New York 212.879.1320

Manhattan Vet Group Ltd
New York 212.988.1000

St Marks Vet Hosp
New York 212.477.2688

The Humane Society Of N Y
New York 212.752.4840

Abbott Road Anml Hosp
Orchard Park 716.648.1340

Oyster Bay Anml Hosp
Oyster Bay 516.624.7387

Peekskill Anml Hosp
Peekskill 914.737.2620

Clark Anml Care Ctr
Penfield 716.377.1160

Plainview Anml Hosp
Plainview 516.694.5050

Champlain Valley Vet Svc
Plattsburgh 518.563.5551

Community Anml Hosp
Poughkeepsie 914.471.7459

Caring For Cats
Rochester 716.865.5220

Stoneridge Vet Hosptl
Rochester 716.227.4990

Vet Specialists Rochstr
Rochester 716.271.7700

Anml Hosp Of Rockaways
Rockaway Park
718.474.0500

Sunrise Anml Hosp
Rockville Ctr 516.766.4350

Rye Harrison Vet Hosp
Rye 914.967.1293

Sayville Anml Clnc
Sayville 516.563.1411

Central Anml Hosp
Scarsdale 914.723.1250

Aqueduct Anml Hosp
Schenectady 518.346.3467

Sodus Vet Clnc
Sodus 315.483.8900

S Salem Anml Hosp
S Salem 914.763.3123

Springville Anml Hosp
Springville 716.592.2879

Dongan Hills Vet Prac
Staten Island 718.987.7777

Northside Anml Hosp
Staten Island 718.981.4445

Staten Island Vet Group
Staten Island 718.370.0390

Vet Emer Cntr
Staten Island 718.720.4211

Suffern Anml Hosp
Suffern 914.357.0317

Central Vet Assoc
Valley Stream 718.525.5454

Valley Anml Hosp
Vestal 607.754.7164

W Hempstead Anml Hosp
W Hempstead 516.483.9720

Bide-A-Wee Home Assn
Wantagh 516.785.4687

Wantagh Anml Hosp
Wantagh 516.221.2020

Warwick Valley Vet Hosp
Warwick 914.986.5678

Westbury Anml Hosp
Westbury 516.333.1123

Knollwood Anml Hosp
White Plains 914.949.5696

Meadow Vet Hosp
White Plains 914.949.1115

Harris Hill Anml Hosp
Williamsville 716.634.1000

Yorktown Anml Hosp
Yorktown Hts 914.962.3111

Burrstone Anml Hosp
Yorkville 315.736.0863

OHIO
Countryside Clnc
Ada 419.634.2802

Valley Anml Hosp
Akron 330.836.1971

Amherst Anml Hosp
Amherst 216.282.5220

Tri County Vet Svc
Anna 937.693.2131

Country Road Vet Svc
Apple Creek 330.698.3701

Ashland Vet Clnc
Ashland 419.281.8611

Spring Meadow Vet Clnc
Ashland 419.289.2466

Landings Anml Hosp
Avon Lake 216.933.2148

Creekside Anml Clnc
Barberton 330.334.5891

Vet Referral Clnc
Bedford 216.831.6789

Northside Anml Clnc
Bellefontaine 937.593.6951

Bryan Area Anml Hosp
Bryan 419.636.3848

Anml Emer Clnc W
Cleveland 216.362.6000

Anml Hosp Of Fairview
Cleveland 216.777.2700

Drs Sayle&Sayle
Cleveland 216.461.2226

Euclid Vet Hosp
Cleveland 216.731.4345

Paw Patch Vet Services
Clyde 419.547.9403

Gahanna Anml Hosp
Columbus 614.471.2201

Swenson Vet Hosp
Columbus 614.451.1204

The Vet Clnc E
Columbus 614.837.3008

Miami Valley Anml Hosp
Dayton 937.293.6962

NorthW Vet Hosp
Delta 419.822.5030

Town & Country Vet Clnc
Eaton 937.456.7147

Broad Street Anml Clnc
Elyria 216.322.3220

Dr S Scott Harmon
Fredericktown 614.694.5926

Horizon Anml Hosp
Galion 419.468.2169

Hkley Anml Hosp
Hkley 216.278.4700

Stow-Kent Anml Hosp
Kent 330.673.0049

Kingston Vet Clnc
Kingston 614.642.3031

The Pet Practice
Lakewood 216.521.7060

Lebanon Equine Clnc
Lebanon 513.932.4181

Sheffield Vet Clnc
London 614.852.9151

N Ridge Vet Hosp
Madison 216.428.5166

The Pet Practice
Marietta 614.374.7419

Nova Vet Service
Medina 330.723.3200

Feeder Creek Vet Svc
Millersport 614.467.2949

Anml Clnc Northview
N Ridgeville 216.327.8282

Royalton Road Anml Hosp
N Royalton 216.237.5662

Bretton Ridge Vet Hosp
N Olmsted 216.777.7575

Douds Vet Hosp
Oberlin 216.774.4542

Snow-Ridge Vet Hosp
Parma 216.845.7744

Rocky River Anml Hosp
Rocky River 216.331.7711

Sidney Vet Hosp
Sidney 937.492.6536

Solon Vet Clnc
Solon 216.232.8383

Crossroads Anml Hosp
Strongsville 216.238.5900

Sugarcreek Vet Clnc
Sugarcreek 330.852.2321

Tiffin Anml Hosp
Tiffin 419.447.8073

Airport Anml Hosp
Toledo 419.385.5680

Alexis Anml Hosp
Toledo 419.472.1104

Christopher Vet Clnc
Toledo 419.385.0325

Twinsburg Vet Hosp
Twinsburg 216.425.4226

Town & Country Vet Hosp
Warren 330.856.1862

Countryside Anml Clnc
Wauseon 419.335.3006

Waynesville Vet Hosp
Waynesville 513.897.6691

Wellington Vet Clnc
Wellington 216.647.4100

Annehurst Vet Hosp
Westerville 614.882.4728

Anml Hosp
Willoughby 216.946.2800

New Pittsburg Vet Clnc
Wooster 330.264.7799

Vet Assocs Hosp
Xenia 937.864.1895

Anml Charity
Youngstown 330.788.1064

OKLAHOMA
Arlingon Anml Clnc
Ada 405.436.1030

Town & Country An Hosp
Ardmore 405.223.0472

Manley Anml Hosp
Bartlesville 918.333.7286

Broken Arrow Vet Group
Broken Arr 918.455.4648

Equine Med Associates
Edmond 405.348.3130

Stockmans Vet Hosp
Elk City 405.225.0200

Jenks Vet Hosp
Jenks 918.299.9483

Meadow Wood Anml Hosp
Lawton 405.353.0344

Village W Vet Clnc
Lawton 405.536.1667

Renegar Anml Hosp
McAlester 918.423.1960

Newcastle Anml Hosp
Newcastle 405.387.5684

Westwood Vet Hosp
Norman 405.364.1100

Anml Medl Ctr Windsor Hills
Oklahoma City 405.943.7733

Azlin Vet Clnc
Oklahoma City 405.732.0043

Family Pet Hosp
Oklahoma City 405.751.9228

Penn S Pet Clnc
Oklahoma City 405.691.5245

Warwick Anml Hosp
Oklahoma City 405.722.7717

Woodlake Anml Hosp
Oklahoma City 405.721.6604

Leflore County Vet Clnc
Poteau 918.647.8253

All About Anmls
Stillwater 405.372.3333

Cat Clnc Of Tulsa
Tulsa 918.492.9292

N Harvard Anml Hosp
Tulsa 918.835.9593

Petsmart Vet Services
Tulsa 918.627.8865

Woodland Pet Care Cntrs
Tulsa 918.252.3595

OREGON
George F Reid Vet Hosp
Albany 541.928.8341

Companion Pet Clncs
Aloha 503.690.1939

Columbia Vet Hosp
Astoria 503.325.2250

Anml Clnc
Baker City 541.523.3611

Anml Health Services
Beaverton 503.641.6393

Vetsmart Pet Hosp & Hlth Ctr
Beaverton 503.644.1100

Bend Vet Clnc
Bend 541.382.0741

Companion Pet Clnc
Bend 541.389.6612

Dollarhide Vet Clnc
Cave Junction 541.592.3222

The Village Vet
Clackamas 503.658.4200

Hanson Anml Hosp
Coos Bay 541.269.2415

Willamette Vet Clnc
Corvallis 541.753.2223

Cottage Grove Vet Clnc
Cottage Grove 541.942.9181

Double Arrow Vet Clnc
Enterprise 541.426.4470

Amazon Park Anml Clnc
Eugene 541.485.0161

Del Oeste Vet Hosp
Eugene 541.689.0205

Dr Richard H Pitcairn
Eugene 541.342.7665

Eugene Anml Hosp
Eugene 541.342.1178

Westmoreland Anml Hosp
Eugene 541.485.4595

Forest Grove Vet Clnc
Forest Grove 503.357.6106

Allen Creek Vet Hosp
Grants Pass 541.476.2233

Anml Health Services
Gresham 503.667.6963

Companion Pet Clncs
Gresham 503.666.4942

Gresham Anml Hosp
Gresham 503.666.1600

Brookings Harbor Vet Hosp
Harbor 541.469.7788

Hood River Alpine VHosp
Hood River 541.386.6658

Companion Pet Clnc
Klamath Fls 541.882.7674

Klamath Anml Clnc
Klamath Fls 541.882.8854

Lapine Anml Hosp
La Pine 541.536.2001

Groves Anml Clnc
Lake Oswego 503.635.3573

Anml Clnc
Lebanon 541.451.1319

Madras Vet Clnc
Madras 541.475.7226

Third Street Vet Hosp
McMinnville 503.472.9418

Rogue Anml Hosp
Medford 541.779.4414

Linwood Anml Clnc
Milwaukie 503.774.3363

Southgate Anml Clnc
Milwaukie 503.771.0857

S Clackamas Vet Svc
Molalla 503.829.4428

Treasure Valley Anml Clnc
Nyssa 541.372.2251

Anml Cancer Clnc
Portland 503.629.5580

Anml Med Clnc
Portland 503.222.1254

Barbur Blvd Vet Hosp
Portland 503.246.4226

Capitol Hill Vet Hosp
Portland 503.244.7565

Companion Pet Clncs
Portland 503.285.4908

Fremont Vet Clnc
Portland 503.282.0991

Gladstone Vet Clnc
Portland 503.653.6621

Halsey-E Anml Clnc
Portland 503.255.0261

Hayden Meadows Pet Clnc
Portland 503.286.9155

Lewis Dove Emer Anml Hosp
Portland 503.228.7281

Raleigh Hills Vet
Portland 503.292.9227

Sandy Blvd Vet Clnc
Portland 503.234.9229

Town & Country Anml Hosp
Portland 503.761.2330

Valley Vet Clnc
Rainier 503.728.2129

Highland Vet Hosp
Redmond 541.548.6114

Anml Clnc Of Salem
Salem 503.581.1438

E Salem Vet Clnc
Salem 503.585.6701

Salem Vet Emer Clnc
Salem 503.588.8082

Sandy Anml Clnc W
Sandy 503.668.4139

Honahlee Pc
Sherwood 503.682.3898

Abiqua Anml Clnc
Silverton 503.873.3691

Sorrento Anml Hosp
Tigard 503.524.5029

Evergreen Vet Clnc
Tualatin 503.692.4840

Anml Clnc Associates
Wilsonville 503.682.1794

PENNSYLVANIA
Abe Vet Hosp
Allentown 610.820.9224

Lehigh Valley Anml Hosp
Allentown 610.395.0328

Dr E J Straley
Bellefonte 814.355.3243

Bernville Vet Clnc
Bernville 610.488.0166

Lehigh Valley Anml Hosp
Bethlehem 610.865.9072

Wright Vet Med Ctr
Bethlehem 610.865.2611

Dr Lillian Giuliani
Bryn Mawr 610.525.5041

Camp Hill Anml Hosp
Camp Hill 717.737.8669

Canon Hill Vet Clnc
Canonsburg 412.746.4220

Northside Vet Clnc
Carlisle 717.249.3313

Chambersburg Anml Hosp
Chambersburg 717.264.4712

Anml Health Clnc Of Eagle
Chester Sprgs 610.458.8789

Susquehanna Vet Clnc
Clearfield 814.765.6541

Columbia Anml Hosp
Columbia 717.684.2285

Moon Vet Hosp
Coraopolis 412.262.2100

Leighow Vet Hosp
Danville 717.275.0202

Doylestown Anml Med Clnc
Doylestown 215.345.7782

Camboro Vet Hosp
Edinboro 814.734.1628

Elizabethville Vet Hosp
Elizabethvle 717.362.3003

E Penn Vet Assocs
Emmaus 610.967.2156

Conestoga Anml Hosp
Ephrata 717.733.2155

Erie Anml Hosp
Erie 814.838.7638

Twinbrook Vet Hosp
Erie 814.899.0694

Vet Med Cntr
Everett 814.652.5108

Exeter Anml Hosp
Exeter 717.655.4536

Montgomery Anml Hosp
Flourtown 215.233.3958

Frazer Anml Hosp
Frazer 610.644.6996

Neshaminy Anml Med Ctr
Fstrvl Trvose 215.355.1116

Franklin Vet Associates
Greencastle 717.597.7711

Hanover Vet Hosp
Hanover 717.632.6711

Harleysville Vet Hosp
Harleysville 215.256.4664

Derry Anml Hosp
Harrisburg 717.564.4470

Noahs Place Anml Hosp
Harrisburg 717.652.5923

Delaware County Anml Medl
Ctr
Havertown 610.449.5100

Hermitage Vet Hosp & Clnc
Hermitage 412.962.5725

Horsham Vet Hosp
Horsham 215.674.1738

Bethayres Vet Hosp
Huntingdon Vy 215.947.5110

Prothero Anml Hosp
Johnstown 814.536.5105

Anml Med Pavilion
Kittanning 412.543.2814

Northern Tier Vet Clnc
Knoxville 814.326.4145

Manor Anml Hosp
Lancaster 717.393.5084

Neffsville Vet Clnc
Lancaster 717.569.5381

Gwynedd Vet Hosp
Lansdale 215.699.9294

Lakeview Anml Hosp
Latrobe 412.537.5881

Anml Clnc Of Avon
Lebanon 717.273.0171

Lewisburg Vet Hosp
Lewisburg 717.523.3640

Lititz Vet Clnc
Lititz 717.627.2750

Valley Vet Hosp
Lower Burrell 412.339.1525

Hope Good Anml Clnc
Mechanicsburg
717.766.5535

Morrisville Vet Hosp
Morrisville 215.295.5009

W Shore Vet Hosp
New Cumberlnd
717.774.0685

Patricia S Farrell Vmd
Newville 717.776.6311

Garber Vet Hosp
Norristown 610.272.1766

Valley Anml Hosp Ltd
Palmyra 717.533.6645

Anml Clnc Of Phila
Philadelphia 215.336.7727

Cat Doctor
Philadelphia 215.561.7668

Cntr City Anml Clnc
Philadelphia 215.928.9289

Knightswood Anml Hosp
Philadelphia 215.632.2525

Main Street Anml Clnc
Philadelphia 215.487.1037

Mt Airy Anml Hosp
Philadelphia 215.248.1886

Simmons Anml Hosp
Philadelphia 215.468.2814

W Park Anml Med Ctr
Philadelphia 215.473.0210

N Boros Vet Hosp
Pittsburgh 412.821.5600

Penn Anml Hosp
Pittsburgh 412.471.9855

Pittsburgh Anml Hosp
Pittsburgh 412.661.9817

VCA Fox Chapel Anml Hosp
Pittsburgh 412.781.6446

Hickory Vet Hosp
Plymouth Mtng 610.828.3054

Prospect Park Vet Clnc
Prospect Park 610.461.7887

Pleasant Valley Anml Hosp
Quakertown 610.346.7854

Antietam Valley Anml Hosp
Reading 610.779.4796

VCA Detwiler Anml Hosp
Reading 610.777.6546

Patton Vet Hosp
Red Lion 717.246.3611

Richboro Vet Hosp
Richboro 215.322.6776

Scranton Anml Hosp
Scranton 717.347.8612

Highland Anml Hosp
Slatington 610.767.1100

Old Marple Vet Hosp
Springfield 610.328.1300

Metzger Anml Hosp
State College 814.237.5333

Sunbury Anml Hosp
Sunbury 717.286.5131

Warminster Vet Hosp
Warminster 215.675.4319

Waynesboro Vet Clnc
Waynesboro 717.762.0221

W Chester Anml Hosp
W Chester 610.696.3476

W Chester Vet Medl Clnc
W Chester 610.696.8712

Loyalsock Anml Hosp
Williamsport 717.326.1709

Wyomissing Anml Hosp
Wyomissing 610.372.2121

Leader Heights Anml Hosp
York 717.741.4618

RHODE ISLAND
Oaklawn Anml Hosp
Cranston 401.943.0500

E Greenwich Anml Hosp
E Greenwich 401.885.2221

Loln Anml Hosp
Loln 401.725.7387

N Kingstown Anml
N Kingstown 401.295.9777

Gansett Anml Hosp
Rumford 401.434.2751

Warren Anml Hosp
Warren 401.245.8313

Warwick Anml Hosp
Warwick 401.785.2222

SOUTH CAROLINA
The Anml Hosp Ladys Isle
Beaufort 803.524.0198

Charles Towne Vet Clnc
Charleston 803.571.4291

Ohlandt Vet Clnc
Charleston 803.795.7574

Cheatham Anml Clnc
Columbia 803.776.4554

Elam Anml Hosp & Emer Ctr
Columbia 803.738.1515

Seven Oaks Anml Hosp
Columbia 803.731.9200

Shandon-Wood Anml Hosp
Columbia 803.254.9257

Spring Valley Anml Hosp
Columbia 803.788.8481

Palmetto Anml Hosp-501
Conway 803.347.1144

Hoffmeyer Anml Hosp
Florence 803.669.5231

Anml Med Clnc Goose Crk
Goose Creek 803.569.3647

Poinsett Anml Hosp
Greenville 864.233.6903

W Spartan County Anml
Hosp
Greer 864.877.3489

Cold Stream Anml Hosp
Irmo 803.781.5050

College Park Rd Vet Clnc
Ladson 803.797.1493

Holmes Vet Clnc
Laurens 864.984.2365

Anml Med Cntr
Mt Pleasant 803.881.5858

Northwoods Vet Clnc
N Charleston 803.553.0441

Thompson Anml Hosp
Orangeburg 803.536.1284

Oakbrook Vet Clnc
Summerville 803.871.2900

Ark Anml Hosp
Surfside Bch 803.238.1414

Triangle Vet Clnc
Union 864.427.3177

Pet-Vac Anml Hosp
W Columbia 803.796.8241

Walhalla Vet Clnc
W Union 864.638.5436

SOUTH DAKOTA
Dakota Large Anml Clnc
Harrisburg 605.338.5558

Huron Vet Hosp
Huron 605.352.6063

NorthW Vet Supply
Parkston 605.928.3025

All W Anml Clnc
Rapid City 605.787.4822

Black Hills Anml Hosp
Rapid City 605.343.6066

Anml Med Clnc
Sioux Falls 605.338.3223

Lake Area Vet Clnc
Watertown 605.886.5002

TENNESEE
Airport Anml Clnc
Alcoa 423.984.5620

Petmed
Antioch 615.731.8074

Bryan Anml Clnc
Ardmore 615.427.2084

Jones Anml Hosp
Bristol 423.968.7011

Camden Anml Clnc
Camden 901.584.6475

Emer Anml Clnc
Chattanooga
Chattanooga 423.698.4612

All Gods Creatures Vet
Clarksville 615.551.9997

Anml Hosp
Clarksville 615.648.1696

Anml House Vet Clnc
Clarksville 615.645.7757

Anml Med Cntr
Cleveland 423.479.4744

Taylor Anml Hosp
Cleveland 423.476.6551

Collierville Anml Clnc
Collierville 901.853.8519

Eastside Anml Hosp
Columbia 615.381.1888

Medicine Man Vet Clnc
Dickson 615.446.5044

Anml Care Clnc
Dyersburg 901.285.6270

Farrar Anml Clnc
Fayetteville 615.433.8368

Companion Anml Hosp
Goodlettsvlle 615.851.0833

Mountain Empire Anml Hosp
Gray 423.282.3771

Anmls W Vet Hosp
Greeneville 423.639.9677

Greene County Vet Medl Ctr
Greeneville 423.639.1621

Robinson Anml Hosp
Johnson City 423.928.1616

Johnson City Small Anml
Hosp
Jonesborough 423.926.2232

Indian Ridge Anml Hosp
Kingsport 423.378.4753

Kingston Springs Anml Hosp
Kingston Spgs 615.952.4556

Concord Vet Hosp
Knoxville 423.966.4135

Knoxville Anml Clnc
Knoxville 423.584.1588

Lafollette Hosp For Anmls
La Follette 423.562.4911

Anml Health Clnc
Manchester 615.728.6633

Anml Health Cntr
Maryville 423.982.2270

Village Vet Hosp
Maryville 423.984.6660

Airport Anml Hosp
Memphis 901.345.0510

Anml Emer Cntr
Memphis 901.323.4563

Anml Hosp Raleigh Bartlett
Memphis 901.388.9550

Central Anml Hosp
Memphis 901.274.1444

Fox Meadows Anml Hosp
Memphis 901.365.9690

Parkway Village Anml Hosp
Memphis 901.363.4077

Pet Health Cntr
Memphis 901 382.0330

Millington Anml Hosp
Millington 901.872.0157

Anml Care Cntr
Mount Juliet 615.754.7387

Brogli Miller Lane Weaver &
W
Murfreesboro 615.893.1728

Memorial Anml Clnc
Murfreesboro 615.893.9513

Berry Hill Anml Hosp
Nashville 615.292.3332

Denney Anml Hosp
Nashville 615.833.4423

Hillsboro Anml Hosp
Nashville 615.298.2663

Murphy Road Anml Hosp
Nashville 615.383.4241

Southside Anml Hosp
Nashville 615.831.0834

Coley Vet Services
New Market 423.475.5121

Portland Anml Hosp
Portland 615.325.6453

Mountain Home Vet Clnc
Sevierville 423.453.9346

Town&Country Vet Clnc
Trenton 901.855.3822

TEXAS
Abilene Anml Hosp
Abilene 915.672.4744

Companion Vet Care
Abilene 915.676.1414

Dearing Vet Clnc
Abilene 915.698.3090.

Amarillo Vet Clnc
Amarillo 806.373.7454

Angleton Vet Clnc
Angleton 409.849.8524

Arlington S Vet Hosp
Arlington 817.465.1401

Cooper Street Anml Hosp
Arlington 817.277.1127

Creature Comfort Anml Clnc
Arlington 817.472.0404

Green Oaks Arkansas Anml
Hosp
Arlington 817.451.1640

Park Plaza Anml Clnc
Arlington 817.277.1195

Morton Small Anml Clnc
Athens 903.675.5708

Anderson Mill Anml Clnc
Austin 512.258.4163

Anml Med Cntr
Austin 512.832.1088

Austin Hills Anml Hosp
Austin 512.263.2288

Austin Vet Hosp
Austin 512.476.9191

Century Anml Hosp
Austin 512.459.4336

Griffith Small Anml Hosp Pc
Austin 512.453.5828

Manchaca Road Anml Hosp
Austin 512.442.6744

N Austin Anml Hosp
Austin 512.459.7676

North W Austin Vet Ctr
Austin 512.250.8048

Oak Hill Vet Clnc
Austin 512.288.1016

S Lamar Anml Hosp
Austin 512.441.3192

Westlake Anml Hosp &
Brdng Knl
Austin 512.327.1703

Baytown Anml Hosp
Baytown 281.424.5575

Beaumont Vet Associates
Beaumont 409.842.3681

Boerne Vet Hosp
Boerne 210.249.2141

Stone Oak Vet Clnc
Boerne 210.249.2147

Bridge City Anml Hosp
Bridge City 409.735.8107

Brown County Anml Clnc
Brownwd 915.643.1523

Bryan Anml Clnc
Bryan 409.822.5953

El Cerrito Anml Clnc
Bryan 409.846.7771

Agri Research Cntr
Canyon 806.499.3392

Trinity Pet Hosp
Carrollton 972.245.3596

Cedar Park Anml Clnc
Cedar Park 512.258.2221

Cleveland Anml Hosp
Cleveland 281.592.5224

Lovan Care Anml Hosp
College Sta 409.846.8716

Columbus Anml Clnc
Columbus 409.732.5758

Conroe Vet Clnc
Conroe 409.756.5233

The Pets Paw Anml Hosp
Conroe 409.756.0304

Crossroads Vet Hosp
Copperas Cove
817.542.8700

Annaville Anml Hosp
Crp Christi 512.241.2034

Everhart Anml Hosp
Crp Christi 512.854.1439

Padre Anml Hosp
Crp Christi 512.937.2631

Santa Fe Anml Hosp
Crp Christi 512.854.5911

Dalhart Anml Hosp
Dalhart 806.249.5589

Anml Foundation
Dallas 214.372.9999

Central Expy Vet Clnc
Dallas 972.235.6861

Cornerstone Anml Clnc
Dallas 972.385.3555

E Dallas Vet Clnc
Dallas 214.328.9935

E Lake Vet Hosp
Dallas 214.321.8773

Highland Park Anml Clnc
Dallas 214.528.3360

Lakewood Anml Clnc
Dallas 214.826.6601

Love Field Pet Hosp
Dallas 214.357.0348

Oak Lawn Vet Clnc
Dallas 214.528.9100

Petsmart Vet Services
Dallas 972.458.7387

Prestonwood Pet Clnc
Dallas 972.233.7343

S Oak Cliff Anml Hosp
Dallas 214.372.4646

Summertree Anml Clnc
Dallas 972.387.4168

University Anml Hosp
Dallas 214.357.5501

Valwood Anml Hosp
Dallas 972.241.2311

White Rock Anml Hosp
Dallas 214.328.3255

Deer Park Anml Hosp
Deer Park 281.479.0405

Best Friends Anml Hosp
Denison 903.463.6980

Dickinson Anml Hosp
Dickinson 281.337.4535

Cedar Ridge Anml Clnc
Duncanville 972.298.4993

Coronado Anml Clnc
El Paso 915.581.3327

Crossroads Anml Hosp
El Paso 915.584.3459

Harwood Rd Anml Hosp
Euless 817.283.4411

Equiplex Vet Hosp
Flower Mound 817.430.8145

Anml Clnc Of Watauga
Fort Worth 817.581.1277

Berry Street Anml Hosp
Fort Worth 817.926.0921

Central Anml Hosp
Fort Worth 817.332.3518

Lakeside Vet Clnc
Fort Worth 817.237.1267

Mont Del Vet Clnc
Fort Worth 817.732.5636

Ridglea Anml Hosp
Fort Worth 817.738.2186

Ridgmar 24 Hr Anml Hosp
Fort Worth 817.246.2431

Town & Country Vet Clnc
Fort Worth 817.626.3981

Friendswood Anml Clnc
Friendswood 281.482.1258

Frisco Vet Clnc
Frisco 972.335.9825

Refinery Road Vet Clnc
Gainesville 817.665.4478

Campeche Cove Anml Hosp
Galveston 409.740.0808

Country Brook Anml Hosp
Garland 972.530.3951

Dallas Pet Assoc-Petmobile
Garland 972.423.7387

Forest Lane Anml Clnc
Garland 972.494.1341

Kindness Small Anml Hosp
Garland 972.530.5463

Guadalupe Valley Vet Clnc
Gonzales 210.672.8676

Granbury Anml Clnc
Granbury 817.573.5553

Pet Care Vet Clnc
Harlingen 210.428.6775

Aldine Anml Hosp
Houston 281.448.3256

Alief Anml Hosp
Houston 281.498.6702

Anml Hosp
Houston 281.440.4441

Bear Creek Anml Clnc
Houston 281.463.8091

Beechnut Highway 6 Clnc
Houston 281.568.9792

Bellaire Boulevard Anml Clnc
Houston 713.772.5574

Brittmoore Anml Hosp
Houston 713.468.8253

Brookdale Anml Hosp
Houston 281.484.4733

Central Houston Anml Hosp
Houston 713.526.1306

Fairbanks Anml Clnc
Houston 713.937.7274

Gulf Coast Vet Spec
Houston 713.666.4414

Houston Vet Dental Clnc
Houston 281.879.7387

Kirkwood Memorial Anml
Clnc
Houston 281.497.6222

Memorial 610 Hosp For
Anmls
Houston 713.688.0387

Mt Houston Anml Clnc
Houston 281.931.6237

Neartown Anml Clnc
Houston 713.526.1502

Petsmart Vet Svc Tx
Houston 281.597.9696

San Felipe Anml Clnc
Houston 713.977.8600

Space Cntr Pet Clnc
Houston 281.480.7387

Vet Pets Anml Clnc
Houston 281.550.6980

Village Vet Clnc
Houston 713.468.7955

Westbury Anml Hosp
Houston 713.723.3666

Westheirner Anml Clnc
Houston 713.622.1270

Wilcrest Anml Hosp
Houston 713.781.3770

Howe Anml Clnc
Howe 903.532.5539

Petsmart
Humble 281.540.3227

Huntsville Pet Clnc
Huntsville 409.295.8106

Hurst Anml Clnc
Hurst 817.282.1463

183 Anml Hosp
Irving 972.579.0115

Irving Anml Hosp
Irving 972.259.5731

Anml Hosp
Jacksonville 903.586.4229

Kerrville Vet Clnc
Kerrville 210.895.5533

E Lake Vet Clnc
Killeen 817.690.4000

Town & Country Vet Hosp
Killeen 817.634.0391

Underwood Anml Clnc
La Porte 281.471.4864

Lake Dallas Vet Clnc
Lake Dallas 817.497.4044

Brock Vet Clnc
Lamesa 806.872.3183

Anml Care Clnc
Laredo 210.722.3333

Lago Vista Anml Clnc
Leander 512.267.7387

W Loop Anml Hosp
Longview 903.759.6604

Anml Hosp Of Lubbock
Lubbock 806.794.4543

Walnut Creek Anml Clnc
Mansfield 817.473.1168

N 23Rd St Vet
McAllen 210.686.5871

Dallas County Vet Hosp
Mesquite 972.222.2101

Greens Anml Clnc
Midland 915.684.4475

Lake Olympia Anml Hosp
Missouri City 281.499.7242

N Street Vet Clnc
Nacogdoches 409.569.9516

Loop 337 Vet Clnc
New Braunfels 210.625.6200

Anml Hosp Of New Caney
New Caney 281.399.9977

Eighth Street Anml Hosp
Odessa 915.332.5782

University Sm Anml Clnc &
Hosp
Odessa 915.362.0341

Palestine Vet Hosp
Palestine 903.729.0141

Anml Hosp Of Paris
Paris 903.785.7606

Red Bluff Anml Hosp
Pasadena 281.487.1101

Westside Vet Hosp
Pearland 281.485.9840

Valley Anml Hosp
Pharr 210.787.2709

Pittsburg Vet Clnc
Pittsburg 903.856.6518

Humane Spay & Neuter Clnc
Plano 972.578.2553

Legacy Drive Anml Hosp
Plano 972.517.2828

Park Mall Anml Clnc
Plano 972.423.1804

Rutty Anml Clnc
Port Arthur 409.727.2626

Arapaho Road Anml Clnc
Richardson 972.235.5215

Canyon Creek Anml Clnc
Richardson 972.234.1181

Plano Arapaho Vet Clnc
Richardson 972.690.8741

Rose-Rich Vet Clnc
Richmond 281.342.3727

San Angelo Vet Hosp
San Angelo 915.653.3301

Affordable Pet Care
San Antonio 210.684.2273

Anml Emer Clnc
San Antonio 210.680.1800

Anml Hlth Assocs Vet Clnc
San Antonio 210.655.1373

Austin Highway Vet Hosp
San Antonio 210.826.6383

Castle-W Anml Hosp
San Antonio 210.344.8259

Churchill Vet Hosp & Dntl
San Antonio 210.344.8961

Fredericksburg Road Anml
Hosp
San Antonio 210.732.1981

Heritage Anml Hosp
San Antonio 210.673.1632

Loln Heights Anml Hosp
San Antonio 210.826.6100

Perrin-410 Anml Hosp
San Antonio 210.650.3141

Pet Care Cntr & Vet Hosp
San Antonio 210.490.0036

Rigsby Vet Clnc
San Antonio 210.648.3183

Town & Country Vet Hosp
San Antonio 210.684.1448

Westover Hills Anml Clnc
San Antonio 210.520.5514

Wiseman Anml Hosp
San Antonio 210.344.9741

Woodlawn Hills Anml Hosp
San Antonio 210.433.3293

San Marcos Vet Clnc
San Marcos 512.392.7107

Seagoville Vet Hosp
Seagoville 972.287.4521

Seguin Anml Hosp
Seguin 210.379.3821

Texoma Vet Hosp
Sherman 903.868.9434

Panther Creek Pet Clnc
Spring 281.367.7733

Pineland Anml Hosp
Spring 281.298.6000

Spring Anml Hosp
Spring 281.353.5167

Stuebner Arln Champions
Spring 281.376.2505

River N Small Anml Hosp
Stephenville 817.968.7387

Anml Hosp Hwy 6
Sugar Land 281.980.7387

Lexington Boulevard Anml
Hosp
Sugar Land 281.980.3737

Sugar Land Pet Hosp
Sugar Land 281.491.5533

Vet Svc Sulphur Spr
Sulphur Spgs 903.885.6551

Anml Med Care
Temple 817.778.5246

Austin & Assocs Vet Hosp
Texas City 409.948.8401

Glenwood Anml Hosp
Tyler 903.592.3877

S Tyler Anml Clnc
Tyler 903.561.1717

Universal City Anml Hosp
Univll Cty 210.658.6326

Anml Clnc
Waco 817.772.7611

Anml Health Cntr
Waco 817.776.3588

Anml Hosp Of Waco
Waco 817.753.0101

Nasa Vet Clnc
Webster 281.332.3418

Alamont Vet Clnc
Wharton 409.532.5569

Parker Road Vet Hosp
Wylie 972.442.6523

UTAH
Anml Med Clnc Bountiful
Bountiful 801.292.7219

Bear River Anml Hosp
Brigham City 801.734.9652

A Anml Hosp
Clearfield 801.776.4507

Dr Jodi Way
Draper 801.572.5403

Layton Vet Hosp
Layton 801.773.2570

Petsmart Vet Cntr
Layton 801.547.5090

Petsmart Vet Cntr
Midvale 801.569.3088

Johnston Anml Hosp
Ogden 801.393.7387

White Pine Vet Clnc
Park City 801.649.7182

American Fork Pet Clnc
Pleasant Grv 801.785.3583

Sevier Valley Anml Clnc
Richfield 801.896.4421

Valley Vet Services
Richmond 801.258.2484

Dr David R Pearson
Roy 801.825.9701

Central Valley Vet Hosp
S Salt Lake 801.487.1321

Brickyard Anml Hosp
Salt Lake Cty 801.486.0123

Cottonwood Anml Hosp
Salt Lake Cty 801.278.0505

Millcreek Vet Clnc
Salt Lake Cty 801.487.7791

Redwood Vet Hosp
Salt Lake Cty 801.487.9981

Sandy Anml Clnc
Sandy 801.566.2410

VCA All Pet Anml Hosps
Sandy 801.572.4600

Intermountain Vet Care
S Jordan 801.254.3661

Hunter Anml Hosp
W Valley City 801.968.0123

VIRGINIA
Abingdon Anml Med Cntr
Abingdon 540.628.9655

Lee Highway Anml Hosp
Abingdon 540.466.6494

Del Ray Anml Hosp
Alexandria 703.739.0000

Fort Hunt Anml Hosp
Alexandria 703.360.6100

Hayfield Anml Hosp
Alexandria 703.971.2127

Annandale Anml Hosp
Annandale 703.941.3100

Columbia Pike Anml Hosp
Annandale 703.256.8414

Ballston Anml Hosp
Arlington 703.528.2776

Battletown Anml Clnc
Berryville 540.955.2171

Georgetown Vet Hosp
Charlottesvle 804.977.4600

Brentwood Vet Clnc Ltd
Chesapeake 757.487.2531

Chester Anml Clnc
Chester 804.748.2244

Anml Care Associates
Colonial Hgts 804.520.2273

Roanoke Valley Equine Clnc
Daleville 540.992.3507

Mount Hermon Anml Clnc
Danville 804.836.2499

Dumfries Anml Hosp
Dumfries 703.221.1880

Earlysville Anml Hosp
Earlysville 804.973.9699

Blue Cross Anml Hosp
Fairfax 703.560.1881

Pender Vet Clnc
Fairfax 703.591.3304

Ferry Farm Anml Clnc Ltd
Fredericksbrg 540.371.5090

Headling Springs Anml Hosp
Galax 540.236.5103

York Vet Hosp
Grafton 757.898.3700

Great Falls Anml Hosp
Great Falls 703.759.2330

Freed Vet Hosp
Hampton 757.723.6049

SouthW Virginia Vet Svc
Lebanon 540.628.4023

Leesburg Vet Hosp Ltd
Leesburg 703.777.3313

Peakland Vet Hosp
Lynchburg 804.384.1009

The Anml Hosp
Lynchburg 804.845.7021

Battlefield Anml Clnc
Manassas 703.361.0271

Independent Hill Vet Clnc
Manassas 703.791.2083

Henry County Anml Clnc
Martinsville 540.632.5262

Old Dominion Anml Health
Ctr
Mc Lean 703.356.5582

Hanover Green Vet Clnc
Mechanicsvlle 804.730.2565

Midlothian Anml Clnc
Midlothian 804.794.2099

Boulevard Vet Hosp
Newport News 757.874.3200

Carpenter Pope Vet Hosp
Norfolk 757.588.8755

Friendship Vet Hosp
Norfolk 757.489.4083

Tidewater Anml Hosp
Norfolk 757.588.0608

Crater Rd Vet Hosp
Petersburg 804.733.8202

Churchland Anml Hosp
Portsmouth 757.484.2733

Allied Anml Hosp & Pet Htl
Richmond 804.672.7200

Anml Hosp
Richmond 804.321.7171

Boulevard Anml Hosp
Richmond 804.232.8951

Broad Street Vet Hosp
Richmond 804.353.4491

Colonial Vet Hosp
Richmond 804.741.1763

Hilliard Road Vet Hosp
Richmond 804.266.5534

Patterson Vet Hosp
Richmond 804.784.5758

Three Chopt Anml Clnc
Richmond 804.270.1080

Vet Emer Ctr
Richmond 804.353.9000

Brandon Anml Hosp
Roanoke 540.345.8486

Harris Anml Hosp
Roanoke 540.362.3753

Valley Anml Hosp
Roanoke 540.366.3433

Colonial Anml Hosp
Springfield 703.451.5400

Saratoga Anml Hosp
Springfield 703.455.1188

Aquia Garrisonville Anml
Hosp
Stafford 540.659.8140

Countryside Anml Clnc
Sterling 703.444.1666

Nansemond Vet Clnc
Suffolk 757.539.6371

Acredale Anml Hosp
Virginia Bch 757.523.6100

Anml Med Cntr Va Bch
Virginia Bch 757.481.5213

Kempsville Vet Hosp
Virginia Bch 757.474.0507

Sajo Farm Vet Hosp
Virginia Bch 757.464.6009

Strawbridge Anml Hosp
Virginia Bch 757.427.6120

Timberlake Vet Hosp
Virginia Bch 757.467.5090

Anml Care Cntr Warrenton
Warrenton 540.347.7788

New Baltimore Anml Hosp
Warrenton 540.347.0964

Agape Avian & Exotic Care
Williamsburg 757.253.0656

Colonial Vet Clnc
Williamsburg 757.220.5589

Whester Anml Hosp
Whester 540.667.0260

Lake•Dale-Wood Anml Hosp
Woodbridge 703.491.1600

Occoquan Anml Hosp
Woodbridge 703.491.1400

Ridge Lake Anml Hosp
Woodbridge 703.491.1111

Community Anml Clnc
Wytheville 540.223.1234

Magruder Tabb Anml Clnc
Yorktown 757.865.6510

VERMONT
Cats Vt Vet Clnc For Cats
Burlington 802.863.2470

Onion River Anml Hosp
Montpelier 802.223.7765

Poultney Vet Services
Poultney 802.287.9292

Green Mountain Anml Hosp
Ltd
S Burlington 802.862.7021

WASHINGTON
Aberdeen Anml Hosp
Aberdeen 360.532.9390

Smokey Point Anml Hosp
Arlington 360.653.4519

Green River Vet Clnc
Auburn 206.854.4414

Day Road Anml Hosp Ps
Bainbridge Is 206.842.1200

Battle Ground Vet Hosp
Battle Ground 360.687.7151

Cat & Dog Clnc Of Bellevue
Bellevue 206.641.1170

Cat Care Clnc
Bellevue 206.455.2273

Companion Anml Hosp
Bellevue 206.882.0770

Bellingham Whatcom Cnty
Humane
Bellingham 360.738.7619

Fountain Vet Hosp
Bellingham 360.733.2660

Anml Clnc Of Bothell
Bothell 206.486.3251

Canyon Park Vet Hosp
Bothell 206.481.1444

Wheaton Way Vet Clnc
Bremerton 360.377.0078

Highline Vet Hosp
Burien 206.243.2900

Chuckanut Valley Vet Clnc
Burlington 360.757.3722

Macomber & Wesselius Vet
Centralia 360.736.3361

Cascade E Anml Clnc
Cle Elum 509.674.4367

Deer Park Vet Clnc
Deer Park 509.276.5091

Des Moines Vet Hosp
Des Moines 206.878.4111

Robert Thompson
E Wenatchee 509.884.3122

Plateau Vet Services
EnumcLaw 360.825.1919

Diamond Vet Associates
Everett 206.252.1106

Dr Mark Bloxham
Ferndale 360.384.0892

Gig Harbor Vet Hosp
Gig Harbor 206.858.9111

All Critters Anml Hosp Ps
Issaquah 206.392.7387

Alpine Anml Hosp
Issaquah 206.392.8888

Dr Lillian Moen Sigle
Kelso 360.577.1093

Riverside Anml Hosp
Kelso 360.577.1093

Spg Lk Eqn Vet Assocs
Kent 206.639.2909

Evergreen Vet Hosp
Kirkland 206.821.9040

Puget Sound Anml Hosp
Kirkland 206.827.5686

Vetsmart Pet Hosp & Hlth Ctr
Lacey 360.459.8242

Tacoma Vet Assocs Psi
Lakewood 206.584.2114

Ocean Beach Vet Clnc
Longview 360.425.0850

Kulshan Vet Hosp Ps
Lynden 360.354.5095

Mt Bkr Vet & Embryo Trnsfr
Lynden 360.354.5699

Alderwood Companion Hosp
Lynnwood 206.775.7655

Kindness Anml Clnc
Monroe 360.794.8813

N Whidbey Vet Hosp
Oak Harbor 360.679.3772

Anml Hosp Of Pasco
Pasco 509.545.9949

Dr David H Reed
Port Orchard 360.871.3336

Prosser Anml Hosp
Prosser 509.786.1393

Firgrove Vet Clnc
Puyallup 206.848.1563

Blue Spruce Anml Hosp
Redmond 206.885.1554

Redmond Anml Clnc & Hosp
Redmond 206.885.1476

Highlands Pet Clnc
Renton 206.235.7387

Spay&Neuter Hosp
Renton 206.643.1170

Scatter Creek Anml Clnc
Rochester 360.273.5908

Burien Vet Hosp
Seattle 206.242.1290

Cat Clnc Of Seattle
Seattle 206.633.1133

Crown Hill Vet Hosp
Seattle 206.782.6363

Elliott Bay Anml Hosp
Seattle 206.285.7387

NorthE Vet Hosp
Seattle 206.523.1900

Northgate Vet Clnc
Seattle 206.363.8421

Rainier Vet Hosp
Seattle 206.324.4144

Richmond Highlands Vet
Seattle 206.546.2426

Olympic Anml Hosp
Silverdale 360.692.0919

Pet Chec Vet Clnc & Pet
Snohomish 206.485.7173

Pilchuck Vet Hosp
Snohomish 360.568.3111

AAA Evening Pet Clnc
Spokane 509.327.9354

Country Homes Vet Ctr
Spokane 509.467.5130

E Wind Vet
Spokane 509.535.3642

Garland Anml Clnc
Spokane 509.326.3151

L L H Wood
Spokane 509.328.7120

Southcare Anml Clnc Ps
Spokane 509.448.4480

NorthW Vet Clnc
Stanwood 360.629.4571

Sumner Vet Hosp
Sumner 206.863.2258

Jones Anml Hosp Ps
Tacoma 206.383.2616

Parkway Vet Clnc
Tacoma 206.531.0454

SouthE Vet Clnc
Tacoma 206.473.4484

Deschutes Anml Clnc
Tumwater 360.943.8144

Cascade Park Anml Hosp
Vancouver 360.892.2122

Feline Med Clnc
Vancouver 360.892.0224

Salmon Crk Vet Clnc Ps
Vancouver 360.574.0833

Vetsmart Pet Hosp & Hlth Ctr
Vancouver 360.253.7732

Heart Arrow Vet
Veradale 509.924.4558

Associated Vet Clnc Ps
Walla Walla 509.525.2502

Cottage Lake Vet Hosp
Woodinville 206.788.0693

Woodinville Anml Hosp
Woodinville 206.483.5005

S First St Vet Cl
Yakima 509.248.0084

WISCONSIN
Amherst Vet Hosp
Amherst 715.824.2545

All Creatures Anml Hosp Ltd
Appleton 414.739.4122

Apple Valley Vet Clnc Sc
Appleton 414.735.1656

Arcadia Vet Clnc Sc
Arcadia 608.323.3361

St Croix Vly Vet Clnc Sc
Baldwin 715.684.4900

Prairie Anml Hosp
Beloit 608.365.7400

Clinton Darien Vet Svc
Clinton 608.676.5200

Clintonville Vet Svc
Clintonville 715.823.4747

Coleman Vet Clnc Sc
Coleman 414.897.3121

Edgerton Vet Clnc
Edgerton 608.884.3311

Grassland Vet Service
Granton 715.238.7686

Grantsburg Anml Hosp
Grantsburg 715.463.2536

Allouez Anml Hosp
Green Bay 414.494.2221

Bay E Anml Hosp Sc
Green Bay 414.468.5800

Brown County Vet Hosp
Green Bay 414.435.5000

Anml Clnc
Howards Grove
414.565.2125

Blackhawk Vet Hosp
Janesville 608.752.5000

Janesville Vet Clnc
Janesville 608.752.8127

Jefferson Vet Clnc
Jefferson 414.674.2383

La Crosse Vet Clnc
La Crosse 608.781.3466

Loyal Vet Service Sc
Loyal 715.255.8888

Petcare-Cat Clnc Of Madison
Madison 608.829.2999

Port Cities Anml Hosp
Manitowoc 414.682.6801

Marshfield Vet Svc Sc
Marshfield 715.387.1119

Appanasha Pet Clncs
Menasha 414.725.8307

Milton Vet Clnc
Milton 608.752.6580

Kronenwetter Vet Care
Mosinee 715.693.4560

Country View Anml Hosp Sc
Neenah 414.722.1518

Countryside Vet Clnc Sc
New Richmond
715.246.5606

Anml Med Cntr Oshkosh
Oshkosh 414.233.8409

Valley Vet Hosp
Oshkosh 414.233.8081

River Valley Vet Clnc Sc
Plain 608.546.4911

Corriente Anml Hosp Sc
Plover 715.342.1212

Harris Pet Hosp Sc
Salem 414.843.4251

Valley Vet Clnc
Seymour 414.833.6833

Shawano Vet Clnc
Shawano 715.524.4190

Castlerock Vet Hosp
Spencer 715.659.5599

Stevens Point Anml Hosp
Stevens Point 715.341.6409

Rivers Two Vet Hosp
Two Rivers 414.793.1187

Anml Hosp Of Verona
Verona 608.845.6700

Viroqua Vet Cntr S C
Viroqua 608.637.2001

Waupaca Vet Service Sc
Waupaca 715.258.3343

Companion Care Pet Hosp
Sc
Wausau 715.848.5326

Pet-Vet Webster
Webster 715.866.4275

Whitewater Vet Hosp Sc
Whitewater 414.473.2930

Mona Hodkiewicz
Wisc Dells 608.253.7361

WEST VIRGINIA
Beckley Vet Hosp
Beckley 304.255.4159

Vet Associates
Bluefield 304.327.8554

Anml House Small Anml
Clnc
Parkersburg 304.422.3352

Jackson Anml Clnc
Ripley 304.372.3802

WYOMING
Anml Health Cntr
Casper 307.235.4889

Anml Hosp Of Casper
Casper 307.266.1660

Avenues Pet Clnc
Cheyenne 307.778.3007

Tri State Large Anml Hosp
Cheyenne 307.634.3080

Bear River Vet Clnc
Evanston 307.789.5230

Lovell Vet Service
Lovell 307.548.2452

Moxey Vet Hosp
Sheridan 307.672.5533

Frontier Vet Clnc
Wheatland 307.322.5533

TOLL FREE NUMBERS FOR MAJOR ACCOMMODATIONS

These toll free numbers can help you make reservations faster and less costly. Don't forget to declare your pet when you call!

AUBERGES WANDLYN 800.561.0000	FAIRFIELD INNS 800.228.2800	MARRIOTT 800.228.2800	RODEWAY INNS 800.424.6243
BEST WESTERN 800.528.1234	FRIENDSHIP INNS 800.424.4777	MARRIOTT 800.228.9290	SANDMAN INNS 800.726.3626
BUDGET HOST 800.283.4678	HAMPTON INNS 800.426.7866	MASTER HOSTS INNS 800.251.1962	SCOTTISH INNS 800.251.1962
CLARION 800.424.6423	HAWTHORN SUITES 800.527.1133	MOTEL 6 800.440.6000	SHERATON 800.325.3535
COMFORT INNS 800.424.6423	HEARTLAND INNS 800.334.3277	OMNI HOTELS 800.843.6664	SHILO INNS 800.222.2244
COUNTRY INNS 800.456.4000	HILTON 800.445.8667	PARK INN 800.437.7275	SIGNATURE INNS 800.822.5252
COURTYARD 800.321.2211	HO JO INNS 800.654.2000	PARK PLAZA 800.437.7275	SLEEP INNS 800.424.6423
CROWN STERLING 800.362.2779	HOLIDAY INN 800.465.4329	PASSPORT INN 800.251.1962	SUPER 8 800.800.8000
CROWNE PLAZA 800.465.4329	HOMEWOOD SUITES 800.225.5466	QUALITY INNS 800.424.6423	THE FOUR SEASONS 800.332.3442
DAYS INN 800.329.7466	HOWARD JOHNSON 800.446.4656	RADISSON 800.333.3333	THRIFTLODGE 800.578.7878
DOUBLETREE 800.222.8733	HYATT 800.223.1234	RAMADA 800.228.2828	TOWNE PLACE SUITES 800.257.3000
DOWNTOWNER INNS 800.251.1962	IMA HOTELS 800.341.8000	RED CARPET INNS 800.251.1962	TRAVELODGE 800.578.7878
DRURY INNS 800.325.8300	INNS OF AMERICA 800.826.0778	RED LION 800.547.8010	VAGABOND INNS 800.522.1555
ECONO LODGE 800.424.6423	KNIGHTS INN 800.843.5644	RED ROOF INNS 800.843.7663	WESTIN 800.228.3000
ECONOMY INNS 800.826.0778	KNIGHTS STOP 800.843.5644	RENAISSANCE HOTELS 800.468.3571	WOODFIN SUITES 800.237.8811
EMBASSY SUITES 800.362.2779	LA QUINTA 800.531.5900	RESIDENCE INNS 800.331.3131	WYNDHAM HOTELS 800.922.9222
EXEL INN 800.356.8013	MAIN STAY SUITES 800.666.6214	RITZ CARLTON 800.241.3333	

TOLL FREE NUMBERS FOR TOURIST BUREAUS

The following resources can help you with information about areas, activities, and pet-specific state rules and laws.

Alabama 800.252.2262	Iowa 800.345.4692	New Jersey 800.537.7397	Vermont 802.828.3236
Alaska 800.280.2267	Kansas 800.252.6727	New Mexico 800.545.2040	Virginia 800.847.4882
Arizona 888.520.3434	Kentucky 800.225.8747	New York 800.225.5692	Washington 206.461.5840
Arkansas 800.862.2543	Louisiana 800.334.8626	North Carolina 800.847.4862	West Virginia 800.225.5982
California 800.862.2543	Maine 207.623.0363	North Dakota 800.345.5663	Wisconsin 800.432.8747
Colorado 303.866.3437	Maryland 800.543.1036	Ohio 800.282.5393	Wyoming 800.225.5996
Connecticut 800.282.6863	Massachusetts 800.447.6277	Oklahoma 800.652.6552	
Delaware 800.441.8846	Michigan 800.543.2937	Oregon 800.547.7842	
District of Columbia 202.724.4091	Minnesota 800.657.3700	Pennsylvania 800.847.4872	
Florida 904.487.1462	Mississippi 800.927.6378	Rhode Island 800.556.2484	
Georgia 800.847.4842	Missouri 800.877.1234	South Carolina 803.743.0122	
Hawaii 808.587.0300	Montana 800.847.4868	South Dakota 800.732.5682	
Idaho 800.635.7820	Nebraska 800.228.4307	Tennessee 800.836.6200	
Illinois 800.233.0121	Nevada 800.638.2328	Texas 800.452.9292	
Indiana 800.289.6646	New Hampshire 800.258.3608	Utah 801.538.1030	

NEED ANOTHER COPY?

If you have trouble finding this directory at your local bookstore, or if you want to send it as a gift, your can order it directly from the publisher for $13.95 plus $3.00 shipping (California residents add 8.25% sales tax).

To order, simply complete the order form on the reverse side, send payment, and mail off today!

And if your organization wants to buy copies for a number of its members, just write us on your letterhead, and we'll see what we can do for you!

NEW LISTINGS FORM

Have you found an accommodation, kennel or petsitter to add to this directory? If so, we need to hear from you!!!

Simply send us the name, address and phone of the person or place you are referring. Also send rate information if you have it. Fill out the form on the back or and attach your information on a separate piece of paper.

We also accept submissions of travel stories and photos. Sorry, we can't return any photos, so send us a copy!

THANKS IN ADVANCE FOR YOUR HELP!

PLEASE SEND ME _____ COPIES OF
TRAVEL WITH OR WITHOUT PETS

I am enclosing $16.95 per copy plus 8.25% CA sales tax if I am a CA resident.

Name_____

Address_____

City_____ State_____ Zip_____

Mail to: ACI, 8th Edition, PO Box 3930, Torrance, CA 90510-3930

HERE'S A RECOMMENDATION!

Please attach a separate sheet of paper with your recommended hotels, motels, kennels, petsitters, or emergency vet clinic. We are also intersted in beaches, campgrounds, resorts, and other pet-friendly places. And if you want to send photos or stories about your trip, we'll keep them for our next edition. Sorry, we cannot return your photos, so make sure that you send us a copy.

Name_____

Address_____

City_____ State_____ Zip_____

Mail to: ACI, Recommendations, PO Box 11374, Torrance, CA 90510-1374

WANT TO GIVE A GIFT TO A FRIEND?

If you want to send the directory as a gift, your can order it directly from the publisher for $13.95 plus $3.00 shipping (California residents add 8.25% sales tax).

To order, simply complete the order form on the reverse side, send payment, and mail off today!

Just be sure to tell us the gift-giver's name and the recipient's name, and we'll do the rest.

NEW LISTINGS FORM

Have you found an accommodation, kennel or petsitter to add to this directory? If so, we need to hear from you!!!

Simply send us the name, address and phone of the person or place you are referring. Also send rate information if you have it. Fill out the form on the back or and attach your information on a separate piece of paper.

We also accept submissions of travel stories and photos. Sorry, we can't return any photos, so send us a copy!

THANKS IN ADVANCE FOR YOUR HELP!

PLEASE SEND A GIFT OF _____ COPIES OF TRAVEL WITH OR WITHOUT PETS

I am enclosing $16.95 per copy plus 8.25% CA sales tax if I am a CA resident.

Name_____

Address_____

City_____ State_____ Zip_____

Mail to: ACI, 8th Edition, PO Box 3930, Torrance, CA 90510-3930

HERE'S A RECOMMENDATION!

Please attach a separate sheet of paper with your recommended hotels, motels, kennels, petsitters, or emergency vet clinic. We are also intersted in beaches, campgrounds, resorts, and other pet-friendly places. And if you want to send photos or stories about your trip, we'll keep them for our next edition. Sorry, we cannot return your photos, so make sure that you send us a copy.

Name_____

Address_____

City_____ State_____ Zip_____

Mail to: ACI, Recommendations, PO Box 11374, Torrance, CA 90510-1374

!!!!WARNING!!!!

THIS BOOK IS
SELF DESTRUCTING!!!

According to studies by the American Hotel & Motel Association, as many as 1 in 3 accommodations will be sold, change names, phone numbers or replace management. When management changes, so can PET POLICIES! To receive information on updates you must complete and send in the registration form on the back of this page.

YOU MUST SEND IN THIS FORM TO REGISTER TO KEEP UPDATED

- - - - - - - - - - - - - - - - - -

FREE $200 VALUE PET SAVINGS PACK
WHILE QUANTITY LASTS

We have arranged with a number of pet products and services to provide special offers for our readers. There's only a limited quantity of Pet Savings Packs available, so act soon!

The free $200 value PET SAVINGS PACK is available by sending a business size SASE "self addressed stamped envelope" with 2oz. postage (currently $0.55)

I WANT TO REGISTER FOR UPDATES

Name_____

Address_____

City_____State_____Zip_____

Type of pet(s), breed(s) & name(s)_____

_____

where purchased_____

Mail to: ACI, Purchase Registration, PO Box 11374, Torrance, CA 90510-1374

****FREE $200 VALUE PET SAVINGS PACK****
WHILE QUANTITY LASTS

I am enclosing a business sized SASE "self addressed stamped envelope" with 2oz. postage (currently $0.55)

Name_____

Address_____

City_____State_____Zip_____

Mail to: ACI, Pet Savings Pack, PO Box 11374, Torrance, CA 90510-1374

THE "MUST HAVE" RESOURCE FOR *EVERY* PET OWNER

Whether you "take 'em" or "leave 'em". Since 1990, it's the longest running pet travel resource of its kind. You get the answers you need to prepare for, and feel good about, whatever type of petcare you choose. It includes advice from pet experts:

- Avoid faux paws with "Pet-Etiquette" tips from Mathew Margolis NBC Today Show pet expert

- Make tracks with travel training tips from Hollywood animal behaviorist Maureen Hall

- Dr. Carin Smith, DVM & Petcare Author "de-tails" health considerations, feeding, and first-aid preparedness

- Avoid lodging industry Pet Peeves with the 10 Commandments of good guest & pet behavior

- Learn the Plane Truth about taking your pet along on airplanes - Crucial DOs & DON'Ts

- Point yourself and your pet in the right direction with pointers for smooth moves

- Pack for pet travel and first-aid needs using our comprehensive, time-tested checklists

EVERY PET OWNER NEEDS THIS BOOK!
because
Every day *ANY* pet owner may need to decide what to do with pets when travel (planned or *EMERGENCY*) disrupts normal routines.

This is the only sourcebook with ALL the answers: from pet sitting, to taking them with you, to day-kenneling along the way, to extended kennel stays, to pet motels, veterinarians and more!

THE ONLY COMPREHENSIVE SOURCEBOOK OF TRAVELTIME PETCARE OPTIONS

Over 25,000 Resources for Pets and their Owners:

- Tens of thousands of accommodations from posh to primitive where PETS-R-PERMITTED

- Kenneling and petcare information for theme parks and tourist attractions

- ABKA kennels for day-boarding along the way or extended kennel stays

- Arrange in-home care with a listed petsitter or through a listed referral service

- Find a veterinarian in a new city or on-the-road through listings or AAHA referral